P9-BZU-626

ANNOTATED INSTRUCTOR'S EDITION

SECOND EDITION

Simon & Schuster

HANDBOOK
for WRITERS

Lynn Quitman Troyka

with

Emily R. Gordon

and

Ann B. Dobie

PRENTICE HALL

Englewood Cliffs, New Jersey 07632

Library of Congress Cataloging-in-Publication Data

Troyka, Lynn Quitman
    Simon & Schuster handbook for writers / Lynn Quitman Troyka. —
2nd ed.
       p.   cm.
      ISBN 0-13-809476-4
   1. English language—Rhetoric—Handbooks, manuals, etc.
   2. English language—Grammar—1950—Handbooks, manuals, etc.
   I. Title. II. Title: Simon and Schuster handbook for writers.
PE1408.T696   1990
808'.042—dc20   89-23132
                                    CIP

for David,
<u>*who makes it all worthwhile*</u>

Editorial/production supervision: **Virginia Rubens**
Interior and cover design: **Lorraine Mullaney**
Manufacturing buyer: **Mary Ann Gloriande**
Associate Art Director: **Florence D. Silverman**

© 1990, 1987 by Lynn Quitman Troyka

Printed in the United States of America
10 9 8 7 6 5 4 3 2 1

ISBN 0-13-809518-3   01

Prentice-Hall International (UK) Limited, *London*
Prentice-Hall of Australia Pty. Limited, *Sydney*
Prentice-Hall Canada Inc., *Toronto*
Prentice-Hall Hispanoamericana, S.A., *Mexico*
Prentice-Hall of India Private Limited, *New Delhi*
Prentice-Hall of Japan, Inc., *Tokyo*
Simon & Schuster Asia Pte. Ltd., *Singapore*
Editora Prentice-Hall do Brasil, Ltda., *Rio de Janeiro*

CONTENTS

The complete student edition appears next. Annotations, which do not appear in the student edition, include exercise answers, teaching tips, biographies of quoted writers, and a rich variety of other resources.

Brief Contents of Student Edition

PREFACE TO
THE ANNOTATED INSTRUCTOR'S EDITION

This *Annotated Instructor's Edition (AIE)* of the *Simon & Schuster Handbook for Writers,* Second Edition, seeks to enhance instructors' enjoyment of the teaching of writing. The two major sections of the *AIE* correspond to my two major purposes in composing this volume.

One purpose of the *AIE* is to set forth the intellectual grounding of the *Simon & Schuster Handbook for Writers.* To achieve this, the volume's front section is the collection of five bibliographic essays that summarize current scholarship in rhetoric and composition. Commissioned exclusively for the *AIE,* the essays are intended as catalysts for study and discussion among faculty, including teaching assistants and part-time instructors. New for the Second Edition are essays on writing across the curriculum and on testing; updated for the Second Edition are essays on the writing process, the history of rhetoric, and linguistics. These essays help me meet the challenge that I set for myself with the *Handbook:* to demonstrate that effective teaching of composition relies upon theory and research outcomes translated into practice honed by experience.

The second purpose of the *AIE* is to give instructors multiple resources to draw upon while teaching. The *AIE* consists of an exact duplicate of the student edition of the *Handbook* along with a potpourri of teaching tips, background information on material in the text, quotations about writing, brief biographies of some of the writers quoted, alternate examples, alternate exercises, and answers to the exercises. These materials celebrate the pleasures of teaching freshman composition as well as advanced academic writing.

A new feature that appears throughout the *AIE,* Second Edition, is called "Coverage." Designed to complement exercise answers, each Coverage listing shows exactly what each item in an exercise treats. Because the exercises in the *Handbook* were crafted with great care so that all major concepts would receive balanced attention, teachers can use the Coverage listings to pinpoint student misunderstandings and to design further instruction.

Now more convenient in hardback, the *AIE,* Second Edition, is designed for multiple uses. Faculty can turn to it to for information about scholarship and the teaching of writing. Teachers can consult it as they plan their classes and check student work. And, of course, instructors can carry it to their classrooms confident that it includes everything the students have in their edition—and much more.

I also intend this volume for growth. I cordially invite instructors to collaborate on the next edition of the *Annotated Instructor's Edition.* If you have material for the marginals, or comments, please send them to me c/o College English Editor, Prentice Hall, Englewood Cliffs, NJ 07632. Any item published will carry the byline of its contributor.

I am grateful to many people for helping make the *AIE,* Second Edition, a reality. Most particularly, I want to thank Emily R. Gordon and Ann B. Dobie for their considerable, lively contributions to the "marginals" that accompany the student text. Both are gifted instructors whose students are fortunate indeed. I also want to acknowledge the authors of the specially commissioned essays, who generously shared their important knowledge in this unusual forum (listed here in the order in which their essays appear): Josephine Koster Tarvers, Rutgers University at New Brunswick; William F. Woods, Wichita State University; Alice M. Roy, California State University at Los Angeles; Barbara E. Walvoord, Loyola College in Baltimore; and Emily R. Gordon, Hofstra University. At Prentice Hall three people were indispensable. Phil Miller, Editor in Chief for Humanities, and Nancy Perry, Executive Editor for English, served as invaluable sounding boards and facilitators. Virginia Rubens, Production Editor, handled the myriad details of the project with impressive skill and enormous goodwill.

Lynn Quitman Troyka
Beechhurst, New York

The Composing Process: An Overview

Josephine Koster Tarvers

On the surface, rhetoricians used to suppose, the composing process looked easy to explain. All we had to do was explain how ideas got into a writer's head, and from there onto paper. But nearly three decades of research into the composing process have convinced us that this process is far more complex than we initially thought. In this essay I will discuss briefly some of the major theories about the composing process, to show you not only where these theories intersect but also where they differ, and I will conclude with suggestions about applying these theories to your teaching.

First of all, when we speak of the "composing process," we are amalgamating a number of processes, both psychological and physical, both for discovering ideas and for actually committing them to writing. Research suggests that each person's writing process is different and that it changes with the writer's age, experience, level of knowledge about the subject, and particular writing situation. However, most theories acknowledge some shared stages of the process: a period of gathering information and noting down ideas, one of "roughing out" those ideas, and one in which the information is reshaped and adjusted according to the writer's intentions and certain conventions of lin-

JOSEPHINE KOSTER TARVERS *is Assistant Professor of English at Rutgers University, where she teaches writing, grammar theory, history of the language, and other courses in language, gender, and medieval literature. Her recent publications include* Teaching Writing: Theories and Practices *(1987). She is currently at work on a book examining the relationship of rhetorical theory and Anglo-Saxon narrative, and she continues to study the development of women's literacy in the Middle Ages.*

guistic etiquette. Among the labels for the first stage are *prewriting, planning,* and *hypothesizing;* among those for the second stage are *writing, drafting,* and *sentence construction;* among those for the final stage are *revising and editing, rewriting and correcting,* and *polishing and producing.* Our knowledge of these stages is drawn from the research summarized below.

It is important to note at the outset that the composing process is heavily influenced by the writer's purpose nd audience. Richard Gebhardt [item 15 in the Annotated Bibliography at the end of this essay] has suggested, in fact, that there are two large classes of composing processes, one in which the writer is relatively certain about audience, purpose, and the information these require, and one in which the writer discovers the relationship among these three elements. More recently, Maxine Hairston has proposed a three-category continuum [16] between these elements, calling the categories *message writing,* needed to conduct well-understood business between writer and reader; *self-limiting writing,* where the writer knows audience and purpose and has the necessary information at hand; and *extended reflective writing,* where the writer discovers information, purpose, and sometimes even the audience through the composing process. James Reither [30] has recently argued that we must broaden our perspective on composing even further, seeing it as a way of participating in the many discourse and knowledge communities to which we belong.

Most theories of the writing process, however, attempt to narrow rather than broaden the focus of composing. Usually such theories fall into one of two broadly defined "camps." The first, and historically older, camp, to which Lester Faigley has given the label *romantic* [13], holds that composing occurs through writing, as an intuitive, organic process which can be facilitated and stimulated but not really taught. The second, newer camp, which has been called the *classical* or *cognitive* school, has been heavily influenced both by classical rhetoric and modern social sciences. The proponents of this camp see composing as a problem-solving exercise, which can be analyzed and diagrammed and which can be taught to students through a series of strategies. Let us consider each school separately.

One of the first *romantic* studies was conducted by D. Gordon Rohman and Albert O. Wlecke. In *Pre-Writing* [32], they argue that a pre-assimilation of ideas occurs in the mind before writing, and that writers must learn to "picture the process" in order to imitate it consciously. They suggest techniques such as keeping journals, writing meditations, and developing analogies as ways for students to discover their messages. They also insist on the separation from and primacy of prewriting over other stages of the composing process, a view that has been assailed by later theorists.

One of the most recognized names in the romantic school is that of Peter Elbow. In *Writing Without Teachers* [10] he promotes the technique of *freewriting,* which encourages writers to record ideas quickly and continuously, without the premature editing for spelling, punctuation, and word choice which so often interrupts or destroys the writer's train of thought. In twenty years many variations of freewriting have been developed. Two of the most notable are *looping,* described by Elizabeth Cowan Neeld [28] as a recursive process in which the original freewriting is ransacked for ideas and words which become the centers of new pieces of freewriting; and *clustering,* described by Gabriele Lusser Rico [31] as a process in which the writer starts from a central idea, clusters related ideas around that, and draws lines and circles to establish patterns of words and images which may lead to a first draft. The result of clustering is a picture which is sometimes called a *subject chart.*

Donald Murray, one of the most notable "romantics," describes the composing process as "the cultivation of surprise," that is, the discovery of new ideas and new combinations of ideas by writing, learning from one's own errors and experiments [27]. As might be expected, Murray encourages writers to use a number of prewriting techniques such as freewriting and clustering to explore their intuitions, and to use open-ended plans which lead to further discoveries. Murray recommends a preliminary or "discovery" draft to help writers learn what other kinds of plans and explorations they might make before beginning the formal writing process. Like Elbow, Murray privileges prewriting; revision in his scheme is the repetition of the prewriting stages of collecting, planning, and developing as many times as is needed until the text is ready for editing.

Another member of the romantic school is William Coles. In two books, *Composing* [4] and *The Plural I* [5], Coles describes two writing courses which force students to look beyond their preconceptions and redefine their personae as writers. (In questioning the relationship of persona, audience, information, and purpose, Coles foreshadows the work of Gebhardt and Hairston described above.) Another theory of challenge, examination, and intuition is proposed by Ken Macrorie [23, 24]. He views the composing process as one in which writers attempt to discover and tell the truth about their subjects; he challenges them to explore their material until they discover "something amazing" (his equivalent of Murray's "surprise") which will lead them to better, more honest writing and less "Engfish" (his term for pompous, superficial student prose). Macrorie also encourages writers to defy or ignore conventions that obscure the truth and to trust and follow their own intuitions.

The *classical* or *cognitive* school, on the other hand, advocates a logical, systematic approach to composing. Kenneth Burke [3, 6] establishes a heuristic (list of questions) based on the old journalistic recipe for a lead story: *what* was done? (act); *where* or *when* was it done? (scene); *who* did it? (agent); *how* was it done? (agency); *why* was it done? (purpose). Burke's "dramatistic" line of questioning is adjusted according to the writer's purpose and audience.

If the aim is reporting, then *what* predominates; if the aim is description, then *where* and *when* predominate; and so forth. An expansion of this paradigm, with examples and writing suggestions, can be found in William Irmscher's *Holt Guide to English* [19].

Another paradigmatic theory, this one drawing more heavily on classical rhetoric, has been proposed by Frank D'Angelo [8]. He divides the typical patterns of organization into two classes, *static* (fixed in time and space) and *dynamic* (changing over time or through space). Static patterns include the well-recognized modes of description, definition, analysis, division, classification, exemplification, and comparison; dynamic patterns include the modes of narration, process, and cause–effect. D'Angelo provides a skeleton of expected development for each pattern; writers then arrange previously generated material and develop new material to fill in the flesh of the essay.

Richard Young, Alton Becker, and Kenneth Pike apply the paradigms of modern physics to encourage writers to see their work as part of many processes simultaneously [38]. Their "tagmemic" theory (from the Greek word for *arrangement*) asks writers to view their subject (whether it be an idea, event, or object) from three perspectives: as an isolated entity, as a dynamic process, and as a fully developed system. Doing this enables writers to discover how the subject is unique, how much it can change without losing its essential identity, and how it fits into larger systems. This multifaceted perspective of a subject leads writers to new discoveries through systematic exploration. Kneupper [21] explores these ideas and applies them to instruction.

Some of the most significant avenues to exploring composing have come from psychology. James Moffett, for instance, bases his work on the theories of Jean Piaget [1], who divided all childhood learning experiences into four stages, based on the behaviors children can learn in each stage (assimilation) and the changes they can make in those behaviors (adaptation). In Moffett's curriculum [25, 26], students begin by recording experiences (drama) for various audiences, then sequentially learn to report experiences (narrative) and to generalize from them (exposition) until they can theorize about them (argumentation).

At each stage students are encouraged to return to the previous ones for help in planning and developing, so that their writing processes are not separate and linear but recursive, hierarchic, and spiraling, drawing on earlier knowledge to produce new kinds of writing for new audiences.

The construction of cognitive plans is central to the research in composing conducted by Linda Flower, John Hayes, and their many associates [17]. They base their conclusions on the study of *writing protocols,* chronological descriptions of all the activities a writer uses in composing a text and transcripts of the writer narrating her decisions and choices in those activities. Flower and Hayes postulate a three-stage model of the composing process: planning, sentence generation, and revising. *Planning* involves probing one's own memory, organizing that information, and making an initial plan for producing a text. In *sentence generation* the writer puts sentences on paper, leading to a draft; in *revision* the writer improves problem areas in the draft. This process is recursive: students might plan, generate, and revise one paragraph before moving onto another, or might plan the whole essay, generate a draft, and revise globally, or might use some combination of these processes. Composing is goal-directed, and students use different kinds of strategic knowledge in setting these goals and evaluating how effectively they have been realized.

Flower and Hayes use their model to explain how writers solve the problems of moving from the planning to generating stages by juggling, discarding, or subdividing the constraints on their writing; by drawing on routines or familiar procedures (such as the five-paragraph theme); and by readjusting their goals and hypotheses. This latter stage, revision, has recently been investigated in more detail. Nancy Sommers [34, 35] has found that student writers frequently confuse revising with correcting, focusing only on "mistakes," whereas more experienced writers reconsider audience and purpose, paying attention to global issues. Sommers suggests that learning to distinguish between revising and editing in the composing process produces better student writing. Many other researchers are following her lead.

Flower and Hayes' protocol analysis has a respected history in composition research. Two of the most significant early research projects in composition laid the groundwork for such later studies. Janet Emig, in *The Composing Process of Twelfth Graders* [11], conducted case studies of eight average to above-average high school writers. She discovered through examining their composing processes that they wrote extensively, in response to school assignments, and reflexively, for themselves. In extensive writing, the students spent or were permitted to spend little time on prewriting, did not revise their work voluntarily, and seemed most concerned with meeting teacher-imposed standards for spelling, punctuation, and the like. In reflexive writing, students spent more time discovering material, pausing to reflect and contemplate what they found. They were more willing to revise and less obsessed with correctness. Much of Emig's later work, recently collected in *The Web of Meaning* [12], has drawn out the implications of this early study.

James Britton and his colleagues at the University of London Institute of Education conducted what remains one of the largest studies of writing to date, involving about 2,000 student texts. In *The Development of Writing Abilities (11–18)* [2] they reported that most writing in school was aimed at teacher audiences, students having little chance to write for different or larger readerships. Students at all ages seemed most comfortable with expressive (personal) writing but were most often required to produce transactional (expository) writing and got only sporadic exposure to poetic (creative) writing. These factors seem to have inhibited the students' abilities to write and think speculatively, to produce written reflections of independent thought. Emig's and Britton's techniques have been adapted by ethnographic researchers including Kenneth Kantor [20] and Lee Odell and Dixie Goswami [29], among others, to study variance in the composing process in a number of situations and for a number of audiences.

Although no two theories completely agree on a description of or labels for the composing process, most theorists agree in many respects about what is important in the process:

- Writing takes many forms, depending in each case on the writer's purpose and audience. Although writers may develop certain writing habits, their composing processes will vary with every writing occasion.

- The composing process contains several distinct stages. Each is important, and, depending on the kind of writing, the purpose, the writer's available fund of information, and the audience, each will require different amounts of attention for any particular writing task. No one stage is intrinsically "more important" than any other.

- Before writers actually begin *writing,* they need to find subjects and gather ideas and information to write about. The time this takes will be determined by the writer's purpose, audience, and existing fund of knowledge.

- Many techniques can stimulate the composing process; none is inherently "better" than others. Writers need to find the strategy or strategies that work best for them in each kind of writing situation they face.

- The need to put ideas on paper "correctly" may inhibit writers. By drafting quickly and suspending editing until a text is nearly complete, many writers can compose more successful early drafts.

- Many inexperienced writers do not distinguish between revising and editing. Revision allows writers to test drafts against their intentions and to add, delete, and rearrange what they have produced until it suits their purpose and audience.

- Editing is an act of social etiquette in which writers decide how closely they wish their texts to conform to the audience's accepted conventions of language and then adjust their texts accordingly. Writers who choose to violate these conventions take their audience and purpose into account and accept the consequences.

- Composing processes are recursive, not linear; only in the ideal world of textbooks do writers blithely choose an idea, make a neat outline, develop it, write about it, and make final cosmetic changes before presenting it to an audience. In reality, writers struggle, chew their pencils, cross out, go back, pause, reconsider, find other information, rack their brains, juggle ideas, fling curses, and even start over from scratch in the process of composing a text.

Knowing what we do, then, about the composing process, how can we incorporate this knowledge in our teaching? We can encourage students to write frequently—and not always for grades—to make their own discoveries about the composing process. We can allow regular time in class for writing to help students develop the habit of writing. Students need to learn many different strategies to facilitate their composing. By introducing them to freewriting, brainstorming, looping, paradigms, tagmemics, and revision (not all at once!), we can help them become more productive writers. Questions of grammar, spelling, punctuation, and "where to start the next paragraph" often hinder students' attempts to produce texts; we can encourage them to postpone those worries and decisions until the editing stage, where they can be productively addressed. Students also need to learn to revise their papers to suit their purposes and audiences; by scheduling draft review sessions; encouraging peer editing, and holding conferences, we can direct students' attention away from "error-hunting" to questions of arrangement, tone, voice, and so on.

Since students must also learn to write for audiences outside the classroom and in forms other than essays, we can provide them with practice by varying the design of our assignments. We can include other possibilities and other audiences, give students time in class not only to write, but to plan, discuss, reflect on, and generate ideas that prompt writing. We can encourage students to practice these activities by collecting their prewritings and drafts along with the finished products. (Of course, the preliminary materials shouldn't be marked or graded, but we can examine them to help our students. If the student's papers rely heavily on generalities, we can encourage more or different kinds of prewriting to generate concrete information. If the drafts show only cosmetic editing, we can teach more about revision, and so on.) Above all, we can make our students more conscious of their composing processes, help them work more effectively as writers, and help them realize that their texts are not merely products, but journeys—journeys of discovery, of growth, and sometimes of liberation.

Annotated Bibliography of Suggested Readings

Below I list a number of works that deal, in part or totally, with the views of the writing process discussed above. This is by no means a complete bibliography, but it will provide plenty of information and leads to follow. Abbreviations used are *CCC, College Composition and Communication; CE, College English;* NCTE, National Council of Teachers of English; *RTE, Research in the Teaching of English.*

1. Beard, Ruth M. *An Outline of Piaget's Developmental Psychology for Students and Teachers.* New York: NAL, 1969.

    Contains sections on the development of intelligence, on each of Piaget's four stages of cognitive growth, and on the implications of these theories for teachers.

2. Britton, James, et al. *The Development of Writing Abilities (11–18).* London: Macmillan, 1975.

    A study of about 2,000 pieces of student writing focusing on the relationships between writer and audience and the functions of the writing produced.

3. Burke, Kenneth. *A Grammar of Motives.* Englewood Cliffs: Prentice, 1945.

    Thought and language are symbolic forms of action and can be regarded as dramatic. A "dramatistic pentad" of questions enables us to analyze motives by subdividing action in act, scene, agent, agency, and purpose.

4. Coles, William E., Jr. *Composing: Writing as a Self-Creating Process*. Rochelle Park: Hayden, 1974.

A 30-assignment sequence of writing assignments centers around teaching and learning, encouraging students to explore these topics as ways of discovering new information about themselves.

5. ———. *The Plural I: The Teaching of Writing*. New York: Holt, 1978.

A semester of writing assignments focusing on self-discovery through the consideration of amateurism and professionalism.

6. Comprone, Joseph. "Kenneth Burke and the Teaching of Writing." *CCC* 29 (1978): 336–40.

A consideration of how Burke's dramatistic method can be adapted for the classroom.

7. Cooper, Charles R., and Lee Odell, eds. *Research on Composing: Points of Departure*. Urbana: NCTE, 1978.

Ten essays on the composing process by well-known specialists.

8. D'Angelo, Frank J. *A Conceptual Theory of Rhetoric*. Cambridge, MA: Winthrop, 1975.

Rhetorical forms are derived from linguistic concepts which reflect human cognitive processes. These can be described through heuristics which parallel rhetorical strategies.

9. Elbow, Peter. *Writing with Power*. New York: Oxford UP, 1981.

Emphasizes writing as a way of controlling one's world; discusses freewriting, revision, and peer editing, with many teaching suggestions.

10. ———. *Writing Without Teachers*. New York: Oxford UP, 1973.

Encourages writers to break away from traditional practices (such as outlining) and to use other prewriting methods (especially freewriting) to discover new information.

11. Emig, Janet. *The Composing Process of Twelfth Graders*. Urbana: NCTE, 1971.

A case study of eight student writers, considering their habits when writing for themselves and for teachers. Her methodology and approach have been much imitated.

12. ———. *The Web of Meaning*. Upper Montclair, NJ: Boynton, 1983.

A collection of her work on the composing process, accompanied by interviews in which she discusses the concerns each essay raises.

13. Faigley, Lester, et al. *Assessing Writers' Knowledge and Processes of Composing*. Norwood, NJ: Ablex, 1985.

Surveys the cognitive backgrounds of composing and the applications of this knowledge in pedagogy and theory.

14. Faigley, Lester, and Stephen Witte. "Analyzing Revision." *CE* 32 (1981): 400–14.

There are two kinds of revision: surface (correcting minor flaws) and text-based (addressing larger concerns). The latter must be taught to students as an integral part of composing.

15. Gebhardt, Richard C. "Initial Plans and Spontaneous Composition: Toward a Comprehensive Theory of the Writing Process." *CE* 44 (1982): 620–27.

Identifies two relatively large groups of composing processes, one in which writers handle information they already possess, and another in which they discover the information they need.

16. Hairston, Maxine. "Different Products, Different Processes." *CCC* 37 (1986): 442–52.

Identifies and gives examples of the three kinds of composing, based on purpose, audience, and writer's information.

17. Hayes, John R., and Linda Flower. "Writing Research and the Writer." *American Psychologist* 41 (1986): 1106–113.

The fullest articulation of Hayes' and Flower's theories, with full bibliography.

18. Hume, Ann. "Research on the Composing Process." In *Writing: Policies, Problems, and Possibilities*.

Eds. Bruce Cronnell and Joan Michael. Los Alamitos, CA: Southwest Regional Laboratory of Educational Research and Development, 1982.

A comprehensive, detailed account of research on composing to about 1981.

19. Irmscher, William. *The Holt Guide to English.* 3rd ed. New York: Holt, 1981.

A student text containing a number of prewriting strategies, including an expanded version of Burke's pentad.

20. Kantor, Kenneth. "Classroom Contexts and the Development of Writing Intuitions: An Ethnographic Case Study." *RTE* 17 (1983): 72–94.

Case study of seven high school students in a creative writing class, focusing on the revision stage of composing.

21. Kneupper, Charles W. "Revising the Tagmemic Heuristic: Theoretical and Pedagogical Considerations." *CCC* 31 (1980): 160–68

An adaptation of tagmemics for the classroom.

22. Lindemann, Erika. *A Rhetoric for Writing Teachers.* 2nd ed. New York: Oxford UP, 1987.

An overview of theories and research in the teaching of writing, with suggestions for classroom applications. A comprehensive and accessible summary for beginners and experts alike, with an extensive bibliography.

23. Macrorie, Ken. *Searching Writing.* Rochelle Park, NJ: Hayden, 1980.

Encourages students to seek truth, not clichés, and to confront the questions and problems posed by their own lives.

24. ———. *Writing to Be Read.* 2nd ed. Rochelle Park: Hayden, 1976.

Emphasizes a variety of prewriting techniques as ways of exploring and developing ideas; encourages the cultivation of surprise in discovery.

25. Moffett, James. *Teaching the Universe of Discourse.* Boston: Houghton, 1968.

A theory of discourse drawing on students' cognitive development in producing increasingly more abstract texts. Emphasizes the relations between speaker and audience and speaker and subject.

26. Moffett, James, and Betty Jane Wagner. *Student-Centered Language Arts and Reading K-13.* 3rd ed. Boston: Houghton, 1983.

A complete language arts text based on Moffett's discourse theory.

27. Murray, Donald M. *A Writer Teaches Writing.* 2nd ed. Boston: Houghton, 1985.

A book of advice for writers who are teachers, teachers who are writers, and nearly everyone else involved in composing. Sections on each of the stages of composing, with many teaching strategies and a full bibliography.

28. Neeld, Elizabeth Cowan, et al. *Writing.* 3rd ed. Glenview: Scott, 1990.

A text containing numerous prewriting strategies.

29. Odell, Lee, and Dixie Goswami, Eds. *Writing in Nonacademic Settings.* New York: Guilford, 1985.

Fourteen essays on composing outside of the composition classroom.

30. Reither, James A. "Writing and Knowing: Toward Redefining the Writing Process." *CE* 47 (1985): 620–28.

31. Rico, Gabriele Lusser. *Writing the Natural Way: Using Right-Brain Techniques to Release Your Expressive Powers.* New York: Tarcher (St. Martin's), 1983.

Uses right-brain cognitive strategies such as clustering to help writers generate and find patterns in material.

32. Rohman, D. Gordon, and Albert O. Wlecke. *Pre-Writing: The Construction and Application of Models for Concept-Formation in Writing.* USOE Cooperative Research Project No. 2174. East Lansing: Michigan State University, 1964.

The writing process has three distinct stages: prewriting, writing, and revising. Prewriting has primacy; students can improve prewriting by keeping journals, writing meditations, and constructing analogies.

33. Scardamalia, Marlene, and Carl Bereiter. "Written Composition." In *Handbook of Research on Teaching*. 3rd ed. Ed. Merlin C. Wittrock. New York: Macmillan, 1985.

> A thorough survey of all areas of research on writing, including the composing process.

34. Sommers, Nancy. "Responding to Student Writing." *CCC* 33 (1982): 148–56.

> Students confuse revision with correction because teacher comments usually focus on errors in editing. When teachers comment on matters of revision, students learn to pay more attention to this stage of composing.

35. ———. "Revision Strategies of Student Writers and Experienced Adult Writers." *CCC* 31 (1980): 378–88.

> Suggests that major differences between student and experienced writers are the manner and amounts of their revisions; students make few revisions and focus on correctness, while adults are more willing to address global issues and to address the needs of their readers.

36. Tate, Gary, ed. *Teaching Composition: Twelve Bibliographic Essays*. rev. and enlarged ed. Fort Worth: Texas Christian UP, 1987.

> Experts in twelve areas of composition studies survey the field; excellent bibliographical essays.

37. Warnock, John. "The Writing Process." In *Research in Composition and Rhetoric*. Ed. Michael G. Moran and Ronald Lunsford. Westport: Greenwood, 1984.

> A review of recent research and theory of composing.

38. Young, Richard E., Alton L. Becker, and Kenneth L. Pike. *Rhetoric: Discovery and Change*. San Diego: Harcourt, 1970.

> A student text which introduces and explains the "tagmemic" method of composing.

The History of Rhetoric: An Overview

William F. Woods

From its beginnings in Sicily around 450 B.C., rhetoric has been known as the art or "science" of persuasive discourse, the theory and practice of how to use available means of persuasion to affect the opinions of an audience. The earliest known treatise on rhetoric, by Corax of Syracuse, was a response to the citizens' need to speak well in litigations over land rights. A little more than a century later, Aristotle wrote his famous *Rhetoric* [item 7 in the Annotated Bibliography at the end of this essay] a work based on a systematic description of persuasive oratory as it was practiced in the law courts and the assembly of Athens. The key to Aristotle's approach to persuasion is *probability.* Logic can demonstrate a truth, but rhetoric can show that a position is worthy of belief—that it has a high probability of being true. Thus, while logical proofs are to be preferred in philosophical or scientific works, the persuasiveness of rhetoric is more effective in speaking or writing about practical affairs, and for a general audience.

Aristotle's *Rhetoric* assumes that there are three modes of appeal that can be used to reach an audience: the appeal to logic or reason (*logos,* in the Greek), the appeal to emotion (*pathos*), and the appeal to the moral or ethical sense (*ethos*). In them-

WILLIAM F. WOODS is Associate Professor of English at Wichita State University, where he teaches medieval literature and the history of rhetoric. Some of his recent published articles are "The Reform Tradition in Nineteenth-Century Composition Teaching," Written Communication 2 (October 1985): 377–90; "The Cultural Tradition of Nineteenth-Century 'Traditional' Grammar Teaching," Rhetoric Society Quarterly 15 (nos. 1–2, 1985): 3–12; and "Chivalry and Nature in The Knight's Tale, Philological Quarterly *66(1987): 287–301.*

selves, these modes are only guidelines—ways of orienting the speaker to the task. However, each of the modes was also associated with certain kinds of discourse, as well as with the rhetorical devices proper to that sort of appeal. Perhaps the easiest way to give the flavor of Aristotle's rhetoric is to describe some of the devices he suggests for appealing to the mind, heart, and moral character of an audience.

As Aristotle saw it, the appeal to reason (*logos*) involved the use of certain basic concepts—fundamental, universally recognized formulas for thinking and expressing thought. Aristotle calls them the "common topics," because they are the commonplaces of thought. *Definition,* for example, is the classification of a subject, which in practice means identifying it by placing it in a class with other similar things (e.g., Man is an animal) and then further defining it by pointing out characteristics (*differentiae*) that distinguish it from the other things in that class (Man is a rational animal—"an animal that thinks"). The other topics that belong to the appeal to reason are as familiar and essential to us as definition. *Comparison* brings out the similarity, the difference, and the degree of difference between two subjects. *Relationship* refers to patterns such as cause and effect, antecedent and consequence, contraries, and contradictions. *Circumstance* refers to the process we go through in deciding whether something is or was possible or impossible, given the particular circumstances; here we are defining the subject in relation to its occasion, or context.

These common topics were not originated by Aristotle, of course. He merely gave them names, grouped them, and showed how they function in persuasive discourse. In the history of rhetoric since Aristotle, however, the topics have been one of the most useful and enduring parts of classical rhetorical theory. In the Middle Ages and the Renaissance they were adapted to theories of logical proof. In the nineteenth and twentieth centuries they have been used mainly as patterns for the development and organization of paragraphs and essays. All of these uses are valid, for the topics are simply a formalized reflection of the ways in which we think, and so they enter into every intellectual task. Indeed, we need to keep in mind that the topics are both fundamental and versatile, hard to pigeonhole. They are handy for organizing one's thoughts, for shaping a paragraph, for arranging an essay—but they can also lend incisive clarity to efforts to revise a piece of writing; they can be a productive guide to the solving of a problem; and they can help writers to think about a subject in ways that will extend the material, unfolding its implications. That is why Aristotle also identified the topics as aids to *invention,* or the *discovery* of arguments for or against a position.

The second kind of appeal Aristotle talks about (*pathos*) is the appeal to the emotions—to the heart. Aristotle recognized that the most powerful appeals are those that harness the primal human emotions, our tendencies to feel protectiveness, anger, envy, pride, fear, desire. Aristotle and the rhetoricians who came after him devoted considerable thought to what we would call "audience psychology"—the types of emotions, and the types of people who experience them—but they also tried to identify the kinds of subjects that would evoke such an emotional response. What are the types of description, they asked, that powerfully involve an audience by helping them to place themselves within an imagined experience? What are the phrases and the words associated with deeply felt issues? And then there were the stylistic effects associated with emotional states. The periodic or suspended sentence, for instance, was thought to create tension and a feeling of building to climax. The "rhetorical" question had its place here, as did the use of exaggeration (hyperbole), metaphor, and various other figures of speech. The study of style has always

been closely connected with the appeal to the emotions. That is why the Sophists, professional orators who flourished about the second century A.D., were both praised and condemned for their panegyrics (elaborate eulogies and other ceremonial speeches) which appealed to the emotions but were not always calculated to inspire careful thought.

The third mode of appeal (*ethos*) is best described as a perceived relationship between the character of the speaker or writer, and the social and ethical beliefs of the audience. It is an appeal to ethical values, perhaps, but it also has much to do with the ability of the audience to *identify* with the speaker, to accept him or her as someone who speaks for *them.* This appeal often derives as much from the personal qualities of a speaker or writer as it does from the overt content of the discourse. "Is this a person like us, who shares our values, and whose opinion can be trusted?" These are the sorts of questions addressed by the ethical appeal, which has a great deal to do with the *tone* of a piece of writing, and therefore with its syntax and choice of words. Tone also depends on the purpose of the discourse (to explain, persuade, entertain, etc.), and on the level of style adopted by the writer or speaker. Classical rhetoricians after Aristotle liked to identify three levels of style: (1) the high, or grand style (appropriate for epics and for the sublime, high-flown passages of persuasive oratory); (2) the middle ("pleasing," ornate) style associated with literary works and with ceremonial oratory; and (3) the low or plain style associated with the language of instruction and everyday affairs. More recently, linguists have tended to identify levels of style by their social function. For instance, Martin Joos [21] identifies five levels of usage: frozen (genteel), formal, consultative, casual, and intimate.

It is worth noting that Aristotle's three modes of appeal—*logos, pathos,* and *ethos*—reflect a basic way in which western culture has conceived or "pictured" the mind ever since the days of Plato. We say *mind, body,* and *spirit,*—or *reason, memory, imagination*—as if thought and substance were somehow united by a perceptive consciousness: our bond with the world outside us and the source of our state of being. Indeed, there is a basic "threeness" that runs through classical discussions of art and psychology like a magic thread. For example, beginning, middle, and end stood for the parts of a narrative or dramatic plot (Aristotle again). Invention, arrangement (organization), and style were the three essential phases of composition as classical rhetoricians described it. That is, writers first *discover* and gather together their materials, then they *arrange* them, and finally they *express* them in language that is appropriate to the aim, audience, and circumstances of the discourse. Memory and the techniques of delivery were also included as parts of rhetoric, but they were not directly involved in what we in our industrial age call the "process" of writing. The actual teaching of rhetoric in classical times again took the form of a sequential, three-stage program: *precept,* the learning of principles; *practice,* under the supervision of a grammar or rhetoric teacher; and *imitation* of the style and structure of various model passages.

As oratory gave way to written rhetoric in the seventeenth and eighteenth centuries (a recurrent trend in history of rhetoric), it became easier to characterize discourse by its literary form rather than by its appeal to an audience. Whereas ancient oratory had been divided into deliberative (persuasive), epideictic (ceremonial), and judicial (courtroom) oratory, the rhetorical spectrum by the 1700s had broadened to admit formal letters (epistles), history, argument, narration, description, persuasion, and poetry. Since spoken and written discourse were both represented, it was now customary to describe them as the art of "rhetoric and *belles lettres*" (borrowing a term from French literary criticism, which was then enjoying a period of authority). The theory of rhetoric was also changing. Rhetoricians had followed the empiricist philosophers (e.g., Locke) in assuming that language and thought reflected sense impressions, especially those received through sight. They further assumed that the forms of discourse must derive from the different patterns of language we use to record our perceptions, to form a "point of view," and to influence the opinions (views) of others. For example, we record our perceptions of things (thus, *descriptive* writing); we record our perceptions of events, or "things in action" (*narrative* writing); we interpret the pattern, or "logic" of relationships in the things and events perceived (*expository,* or explanatory writing); finally, we arrange our perceptions as proof, in support of our point of view (*argumentative* writing; "persuasion" generally meant spoken persuasive discourse). Authors of nineteenth-century textbooks on written rhetoric ("composition") found in these four terms, and in the kinds of writing they implied, a comprehensive schema for describing the teaching of writing.

These four "modes of discourse" [24] (which had little or nothing to do with Aristotle's three modes of appeal) were a typical feature of composition textbooks after 1850; they continued to shape teachers' approaches to English composition for at least the next hundred years. Rightly or wrongly, the four modes are now associated with the more conservative side of nineteenth-century composition teaching, which borrowed much from traditional methods of teaching English (and before that, Latin) grammar. There were other emphases, other theories at work in nineteenth-century composition teaching, but that period is remembered mainly for its drills, for the practice of having students memorize principles of grammar and style, for its increasing tendency to stress exposition (essay writing), and for giving first priority to the structuring of sentences, paragraphs, and essays. This was also a pedagogy associated with the rigorous methods and the sometimes endearing eccentricities of writing masters and textbooks writers like Alexander Bain, George Quackenbos, and A. S. (Adams Sherman) Hill.

But while the main thrust of nineteenth-century rhetoric and composition teaching was on style and structure, the *character* of the speaker or writer was beginning to receive a new emphasis. In a time when political, religious, and artistic individualism was much respected, the mental nature of the individual thinker, writer, and student became a serious subject of inquiry. The ultimate results of this spirit of romantic individualism, and the studies of child nature that accompanied it, can be seen today in the contemporary work of James Britton [18], a British educator specializing in research on student writing.

Britton's central insight was that written discourse can be described in terms of "function categories" (see Figure 1) which represent what the writer is doing, in each case, in the act of writing. Writing is no longer seen as reflecting three aspects of the mind; rather, writing is assumed to represent three basic types of observed language behavior (which may, of course, reflect three types of mental activity).

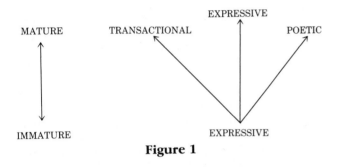

Figure 1

In Britton's first function category, the *transactional,* students are participating in a problem, discussion, or other event: they are getting things done with words. The language relates closely to the needs of the audience and to the features of the task at hand. Language here is seen as a means to an end. In the second category, the *expressive,* the students express their responses to an outside situation in language that relates closely to their own points of view or inner experiences of the situation. Here the language is less a way of getting things done than it is a way of putting feelings into an intelligible form; thus, expressive discourse probably serves the writer's needs more than it does the needs of the audience or the demands of the task at hand. In the third category, the *poetic,* the writer is a spectator to the problem or situation at hand and uses language that relates closely to the overall concept, or "global context," of what is being done, created, or argued. Here the writer is more a disinterested analyst than a partici-

pator in an interactive task or someone trying to verbalize an inner experience.

The striking difference between Britton's system and the classical rhetorics is the centrality of the expressive, or personal, aspect of writing. Britton assumes that child language *begins* as expressive discourse and diversifies as the child grows older; the transactional and poetic modes are gradually acquired, and the resources of the expressive mode are further developed. So while Aristotle's three modes of appeal were intended as ways of describing the impact of discourse on an audience, Britton's function categories are ways of identifying the kinds of discourse that emerge from three kinds of writing behavior. To put it another way, while Aristotle's modes are reader-oriented, Britton's categories are writer-oriented, since they describe discourse as the reflection of mental processes associated with certain adaptive social behaviors. Because of this emphasis on behavior, Britton's discussions are helpful to teachers trying to figure out "where students are coming from" in each of the various assignments that they write. Also, Britton's work may be a corrective influence on those who think of expressive discourse as a sloppy aberration from expository writing, or believe it should surface only in creative writing courses. Despite some real differences in theoretical orientation, however, Aristotle and Britton are not mutually exclusive. Teachers who have studied Aristotle's account of the appeals to the reason and the emotions will probably arrive at a better appreciation of Britton's transactional and poetic functions than those who come to Britton with no preparation in rhetoric.

In fact, even though social and historical conditions are vastly different now than they were in ancient Greece, Aristotle's *Rhetoric* continues to stand us in good stead, for the truth is that there have been no modern Aristotles, and no modern rhetoric has made the impact on rhetorical tradition that Aristotle's work did. James Kinneavy [22] has come as close to that goal as anyone, perhaps, in his attempt to write a comprehensive modern theory of rhetoric, or "discourse," as he calls it, to allow for the enlarged role of writing in modern communication.

Kinneavy's achievement is to distinguish the basic kinds of discourse and describe the forms and characteristics that are essential to each of them. He derives four kinds of discourse from a theory of communication which he expresses by the familiar "communication triangle" (see Figure 2). The three points of the triangle refer to (1) the *writer,* (2) the *audience,* and (3) the *subject* of discourse, while the body of the triangle refers to (4) the *signal,* which is, in this case, the written language that conveys the message.

SUBJECT
[REFERENCE]

SIGNAL
[LITERARY]

WRITER
[EXPRESSIVE]

AUDIENCE
[PERSUASIVE]

Figure 2 (Adapted from Kinneavy)

Each of these four terms is the point of origin for one of the four *aims,* the purposes for which we produce discourse: (1) Discourse that derives from the point of view or "inner experience" of the wrier is *expressive* (as in Britton's function theory). (2) Discourse that is oriented more toward the audience's concerns, ideas, and feelings is called *persuasive* (as in Aristotle's theory of rhetoric). (3) Discourse that is meant to represent accurately a subject of investigation is called *reference* discourse—this aim includes the nonpersuasive aspects of most academic and scientific writing, as well as what we call *expository* prose. (4) Discourse that is self-referential or mimetic in purpose and that is meant to be used or enjoyed for its own sake is called *literary* discourse or literature (similar to Britton's *poetic* function category but not synonymous with it).

Unlike Britton, Kinneavy is not concerned mainly with the development of students' discourse toward maturity. His emphasis is on the description of the kinds of writing and on their use, rather than on the way they evolve in childhood or the ways they have evolved in history. We can generalize by calling Kinneavy's work a comprehensive, painstaking description of the ways prose writing is used or understood in the twentieth century. In this sense his work is reminiscent of Aristotle's systematic, analytical description of persuasive oratory in fourth-century Athens. A basic understanding of Kinneavy's four aims lends a perspective on written communication; moreover, it gives us a way of thinking about the entire profession of teaching writing. For example, it makes sense of the differences between the kinds of writing we find in personal experience papers and term papers. It also helps in defining the intellectual tasks we expect students to carry out when they write a particular assignment; for instance, a term paper is predominantly a piece of reference discourse and requires the skills of observation, distinction, comparison, and so forth. In general, teachers who know the four aims, and the features associated with them, can shape their students' writing with more confidence because they will have a better sense of the goals of each assignment. And for those who wish to backtrack Kinneavy's research and pursue their own investigations in one direction or another, full bibliographies are appended to each chapter of his book [22].

If there is a moral to be drawn from this lightning sketch of a few important works on rhetoric and composition, it is that a little knowledge is not a dangerous thing, but our only salvation. Not one of us has the time or dedication to absorb over two thousand years of rhetorical treatises, debates, and biases; even to desire such a thing is to miss the point badly. Our goal as teachers of writing is rather, by knowing something of the needs, ideas, and practices of former times, to understand more deeply and truly what we are engaged in doing and where we are tending. Neither Aristotle nor Kinneavy should be adopted as teachers' manuals. These two books, as well as the others that we have examined or that are listed in the bibliography, are parts of the history of our profession and should be sampled, experimented with, and pondered as we proceed with our own teaching, in our own times, in our own ways. To do so is to use history well; in so doing, we become rhetoricians—and enter history.

Annotated Bibliography of Suggested Readings

I. HISTORIES OF RHETORIC

1. Horner, Winifred, et al. *Historical Rhetoric: An Annotated Bibliography of Selected Sources in English.* Boston: Hall, 1980.

2. Howell, Wilbur Samuel. *Eighteenth-Century British Logic and Rhetoric.* Princeton: Princeton UP, 1988.

3. ———. *Logic and Rhetoric in England, 1500–1700.* Princeton: Princeton UP, 1956.

> This classic study and its sequel catalog the changes rhetoric went through in response to the birth of empirical science and the resurgence of classical learning in the period between the early English Renaissance and the end of the seventeenth century.

4. Kennedy, George A. *Classical Rhetoric and Its Christian and Secular Tradition from Ancient to Modern Times.* Berkeley: California UP, 1980.

> A reliable overview of rhetoric in its cultural tradition, but weaker in the periods following the Middle Ages. For those interested in Greek, Roman, or early Christian rhetoric, Kennedy's specialized works in those areas are standard sources.

5. Murphy, James J. *Rhetoric in the Middle Ages.* Berkeley: California UP, 1974.

> The best survey of medieval rhetoric now available.

6. Vickers, Brian. *Classical Rhetoric and English Poetry.* New York: St. Martin's, 1970.

> Contains an excellent chapter-length history of rhetoric.

II. CLASSICAL AND MEDIEVAL THEORIES OF RHETORIC

7. Aristotle. *Rhetoric and Poetics.* Trans. Rhys Carpenter and Ingram Bywater. New York: Modern Library, 1984.

> This edition has the added benefit of a new preface by Edward P. J. Corbett, who edited the volume and contributed some useful bibliographies and notes to the text.

8. Augustine of Hippo. *De Doctrina Christiana,* trans. D. W. Robertson, Jr. Indianapolis: Bobbs-Merrill, 1958.

> Books I–III of this treatise are a guide to the reading and interpretation of the scriptures. Book IV (on preaching) is probably the most important statement of rhetorical theory in the Middle Ages.

9. Cicero. *De Oratore.* Trans. E. W. Sutton and H. Rackham. 2 vols. Loeb Classical Library. Cambridge, MA: Harvard UP, 1942.

> The comprehensive treatise that represents Cicero's mature rhetorical theory.

10. Corbett, Edward J. P. *Classical Rhetoric for the Modern Student.* 2nd ed. New York: Oxford UP, 1971.

> The best of the modern textbooks that make classical rhetorical theory and pedagogy available to teachers and students of English composition.

11. Quintilian. *Institutio Oratoria.* Trans. H. E. Butler. 4 vols. Loeb Classical Library. New York: Putnam's, 1921–922.

> Quintilian was a teacher of rhetoric in Rome, under the Empire. His "Institute" of rhetoric is a thoroughgoing description of the art as it was practiced and taught during his times.

12. Anon. *Rhetorica Ad Herennium.* Trans. Harry Caplan. 2 vols. Loeb Classical Library. Cambridge, MA: Harvard UP, 1954.

> This relatively brief manual, and Cicero's early work *De Inventione* (*On Rhetorical Invention*), were the classical treatises which most influenced medieval rhetoric.

III. RENAISSANCE AND NEOCLASSICAL THEORIES OF RHETORIC

13. Erasmus, Desiderius. *On Copia of Words and Ideas* (*De Utraque Verborem ac Rerum Copia*).

Trans. Donald B. King and H. David Rix. Milwaukee: Marquette UP, 1963.

> A much imitated treatise on the art of writing an "amplified," or richly developed style, which reflects a major emphasis in Renaissance rhetoric.

14. Fenelon. *Fenelon's Dialogues on Eloquence.* Trans. W. S. Howell. Princeton: Princeton UP, 1951.

> "The greatest work on classical rhetoric written in French and the finest statement of the philosophical strand of the tradition since antiquity" (Kennedy).

15. Blair, Hugh. *Lectures on Rhetoric and Belles Lettres.* Ed. Harold F. Harding. 2 vols. Carbondale: Southern Illinois UP, 1965.

16. Campbell, George. *The Philosophy of Rhetoric.* Ed. Lloyd F. Bitzer. Carbondale: Southern Illinois UP, 1963.

17. Whately, Richard. *Elements of Rhetoric.* Ed. Douglas Ehninger. Carbondale: Southern Illinois UP, 1963.

> Blair, Campbell, and Whately—sometimes called the "Scottish rhetoricians"—reflect the influence of empirical philosophy (e.g., Hume, Locke) on rhetorical theory; they also illustrate the nineteenth-century shift in emphasis from spoken to written rhetoric (or "composition").

IV. MODERN THEORIES OF DISCOURSE

18. Britton, James, et al. *The Development of Writing Abilities (11–18).* London: Macmillan Education, 1975.

> Considered one of the best studies of how writing skills develop in young students. Britton offers a theory of composition based on extensive surveys of children's writing.

19. Gibson, Walker. *Tough, Sweet, and Stuffy: An Essay on Modern American Prose Styles.* Bloomington: Indiana UP, 1966.

> A readable yet relatively sophisticated attempt to characterize prose styles by classifying their choice of words, syntax, and other features.

20. Hirsch, E. D., Jr. *The Philosophy of Composition.* Chicago: Chicago UP, 1977.

> Known as a conservative approach to the theory of composition, Hirsch's book was nevertheless based on a careful study of discourse production, and it deserves a close reading.

21. Joos, Martin. *The Five Clocks.* Bloomington: Indiana UP, 1962.

> A modern classification of the levels of style by reference to their use in a social context.

22. Kinneavy, James. *A Theory of Discourse.* 1971. New York: Norton, 1980.

> Classifies the kinds of discourse according to purpose and describes the features associated with each of these purposes, or "aims." Grounded in the scholarship of linguistics, literature, communications, and philosophy, Kinneavy's is perhaps the reigning modern theory of discourse.

23. Moffett, James. *Teaching the Universe of Discourse.* Boston: Houghton, 1956.

> Helpful in understanding the neo-progressive or student-centered attitudes toward teaching writing that dominated the Dartmouth Conference (1966) and later produced the "open classroom."

V. SECONDARY SOURCES

24. Connors, Robert J. "The Rise and Fall of the Modes of Discourse." *CCC* 32 (1981): 444–55.

> A brief history of the growth and subsequent decline of the four "modes" of discourse (description, narration, exposition, and argumentation) in composition teaching.

25. Ong, Walter J. "The Writer's Audience Is Always a Fiction." *PMLA* 90 (1975): 9–21.

> In this milestone essay, Ong argues that writers project their own sense of an audience—an assumption that parallels current reader-response theory.

26. Reid, Ronald F. "The Boyleston Professorship of Rhetoric at Harvard." *QJS* 45 (1959): 239–57.

Probably the best account of the nineteenth-century transition from spoken to written rhetoric.

27. Tate, Gary, ed. *Teaching Composition: Twelve Bibliographical Essays.* Rev. and enlarged ed. Fort Worth: Texas Christian UP, 1987.

Comprehensive overview of research in major areas related to rhetoric and composition.

28. Tate, Gary, and Edward P. J. Corbett, eds. *The Writing Teacher's Sourcebook.* New York: Oxford UP, 1982.

A standard aid to research.

29. Woods, William F. "Nineteenth-Century Psychology and the Teaching of Writing." *CCC* 36 (1985): 20–41.

Describes the three major theories of nineteenth-century psychology which parallel, and therefore illuminate, similar developments in the teaching of writing.

Linguistics for Composition Teachers: An Overview

Alice M. Roy

We write in a language. This means that we need to use words, phrases, and sentences that are similar to but not always the same as those we use in speaking a language. Speaking is primary, writing secondary, in that we learn speaking first and also in that it is quite possible to go through life without writing but not "natural" to go through life without speaking. In college, however, writing becomes primary. Our own dialect affects our writing. Further, our communal history of attitudes toward grammar and usage affects readers' perceptions of our writing, and ours of theirs. Still further, how we learn a language, whether a first or second language, affects how we may learn to write or teach others to write. We can get a window on written language by looking at some features of spoken language.

HOW DO SPEAKING AND WRITING DIFFER?

Many years ago Roman Jakobson [item 8 in the Annotated Bibliography at the end of this essay] de-

ALICE M. ROY is Assistant Professor of Linguistics and English at California State University, Los Angeles, and directs the Freshman Writing Program there. She has Master's Degrees in English and in Linguistics with a concentration in Teaching English as a Second Language, and she holds a Ph. D. in Linguistics from the University of Michigan. She has published articles on discourse analysis, and her article "Alliance for Literacy" appeared in Col-lege Composition and Communication in 1984. She is co-chair of the Committee on Engish as a Second Language for the Confer-ence on College Composition and Communication and gives workshops on writing and second-language acquisition at the national meetings of the Conference. She serves on the editorial boards of College Composition and Communication and the Jour-nal of Basic Writing.

scribed six basic functions of verbal communication. His list of functions is instructive as we consider the amazingly complex task we undertake, trying to do in writing what we achieve so unconsciously in speaking. Jakobson pointed out, first (though these are not in any sense an ordered list), an *emotive* function, through which we transmit an attitude toward what we are speaking about; second, a *connative* function, through which we send a request to the hearer about how to respond, such as "Act!" or "Believe" or "Know"; third, a *referential* function in that we talk to each other *about* something.

Our speaking also serves to check whether our hearer is listening, understanding, and attending to our communication: Jakobson called this the *phatic* function. We can ask actual questions, such as "Do you agree?" but usually we check our listener's state with raised intonation, or with fillers like "Y'know," or with facial expressions and body language such as raised eyebrows, smiles, and hand gestures. The two remaining functions in the communicative act are the *metalingual* and the *poetic*. We use the former when we talk about how we are talking, giving cues such as "What I really meant to say was . . . ." We display the latter when we use language in special ways, playing with the language itself, making puns, and manipulating linguistic resources creatively.

What a richness there is in the shared act of speaking and hearing. How can all this be accomplished in writing? It is clear that speaking and writing are integrally linked, and equally clear that they are not identical. The writer must do in words and structures what the speaker can do with intonation, facial expressions, and body gestures. Further, the speaker can rely on conversational conventions such as those described by conversational analysts. These researchers show that feedback either is immediately forthcoming or can be asked for, a luxury the writer does not have. There is also in the speaking situation a community of shared assumptions: usually we're talking to people who already understand who we are, how we feel about things, and how we're likely to respond to what *they* say when they respond to us—more luxuries the writer doesn't have. Often, particularly in college writing, we're sending something out in an amorphous arena, the "paper" for the college course to the professor who stands for the generalized educated reading public.

When a writer succeeds in communicating phatic, referential, and metalinguistic messages, we say the writer has achieved "reader-based" prose [5]. If a writer relies too much on the shared assumptions of close friends or people in a fairly close cultural community, however, then the writer risks producing "writer-based" prose. In this case, readers who do not know the writer well, or who perhaps are not part of the immediate cultural community, are left out of the communicative interaction. The writer does not succeed in transmitting the message, whether the source of stimulation is the writer's own wish to communicate or an outside assignment, as is normally the case in college writing.

Although there are some difficulties inherent in the differences between speaking and writing, writing offers the tremendous advantage that it can be changed and even erased before it is offered to the world. When thoughts are spoken, they are irrevocable—there's no taking back even when we say "I take it back." The fluidity involved in writing, the flexibility of expression, is especially apparent as we move into the era of writing with word processors.

HOW DOES DIALECT AFFECT WRITING?

Another way that speaking can differ from writing is in the area of dialect. In popular usage, "dialect" is something *other people* speak. Someone else's dialect differs from our own mainly in pronunciation, but we may also notice differences in vocabulary (is it a "hoagie" or a "submarine"? or a "seesaw" or a "teeter-totter"?), and we are very aware of differences in grammar. When someone's grammar differs greatly from what we are used to calling "correct" English, we might just say that person doesn't use "good English." Linguists, however, would refer to that person's speech as dialect.

Each of us speaks a dialect—it is impossible not to. Our dialect is a result of many factors: where we lived as a child; where we have lived since childhood; where our parents lived when they were young; our parents' education, occupation, and income; our own age, sex, and ethnicity. Most of us are not surprised to learn that where we live and even where our parents lived contribute a great deal to our way of speaking. These are regional factors and we are familiar with them. The role of socioeconomic factors in our speech—education, occupation, and income—is harder to realize and perhaps to accept. We are taught from early grade school that our country was founded on the principle of a "classless" society. However, the work of sociolinguists such as William Labov [10] has shown clearly that these social and economic factors have much to do with how we speak—with our pronunciation and especially with our grammar. In fact, dialect studies have shown that while pronunciation may differ more from region to region, grammar differs more across classes. That is, while someone from Boston may *sound* very different to us compared with someone from Dallas or Philadelphia or Chicago, the *grammar* of middle-class speakers of any one of those cities will be much more like that of middle-class speakers from the other cities than it will be like the grammar of lower-class speakers in that same city. Grammar, of course, shows up more in writing than pronunciation does. In some instances, however, pronunciation affects grammar. For example, for many speakers of the dialect known as Black English, the second consonant in a "consonant cluster" may not be pronounced. A consonant cluster occurs when two or more consonants appear together, as they do at the end of words such as *cold* or *left*. When we consider that adding the regular past tense to any verb that ends in a consonant is automatically going to create such a cluster—*name* plus *d* gives us a cluster of *m* plus *d* (since the *e* is not pronounced)—we can see that pronunciation and grammar are in many ways interconnected.

Dialect and writing are related also because written standard English, or what some writers call Edited American English (EAE), is a dialect itself, a special form of English. Probably no one actually *speaks* EAE—it exists only in writing. Thus everyone to some extent has to acquire a new dialect in learning to write EAE. For those writers whose spoken dialect is closer at the outset to the grammar, vocabulary, and level of formality that characterize EAE, the learning task may not be so great as it is for those whose spoken dialect is quite different grammatically and stylistically. More than the dialect forms affect the ease with which a learner apprehends EAE, however, since we know that our dialect is dependent upon our parents' education, occupation, and income, among other factors. While it may seem that dialect depends on education (a good education helps a person learn to speak "better"), in fact it is more likely that education depends to a large extent on dialect and the social ramifications of dialect: what kind of schools are available, what kind of reading and writing activities go on there, and so on. Thus a speaker of a dialect that differs greatly from EAE may struggle more because of lack of familiarity with literature—with reading and writing as part of a tradition of communication—than merely because of dialect differences.

HOW DO USAGE AND DIALECT AND GRAMMAR INTERACT?

Closely linked to the issue of the relationship of dialect to writing is that of usage. For some people, usage means grammatical features such as the third-person singular *-s* required for subject–verb agreement in standard spoken English; for others, usage includes stylistic options such as whether to use an adverb between the *to* and the verb of an infinitive. For example, on the *Star Trek* television show, and later the *Star Trek* movies, the mission of the space voyagers was "to boldly go . . ." where none had gone before. Under the traditional Latinate rule for English

usage, such a construction as "to boldly go" would not be acceptable, because a Latin infinitive was all one word and thus could not possibly have an adverb in the middle. As long as Latin was held as the model for English, such usages, though entirely common in normal English speech over many hundreds of years, could not be condoned. How much attention to give "usage" has been a problem for grammarians for many centuries. As far back as Greek and Roman times, we find disagreement among grammarians as to whether usage should be taken into account in describing or defining a language.

In the eighteenth century, because of the high prestige of Latin, which was viewed as an elegant and logical and unchanging language, because of the new middle class wish for how-to books on speaking and writing, and because writers like Jonathan Swift worried that they would not be understood in a hundred years if the language were not protected against change, scholars and grammarians like Samuel Johnson codified many of the grammatical "rules" that have led to the usage problems we struggle with today. For example, Chaucer used the form "It am me," whereas we are now taught (and have been for a couple of hundred years) that we must say "it is *I*." Because Latin required the same ending on the noun or adjective after any form of *be* as that which was attached to the subject (that is, the nominative ending), eighteenth-century grammarians felt that English should also behave that way. Similarly, in earlier periods of our history the use of *they* for the indefinite personal pronoun was quite all right; however, Johnson and other scholars of the time felt that it was illogical to use the plural pronoun referring to a singular antecedent, so they endorsed "Does everyone have *his* ticket?" rather than "*their* ticket." For most of us, "their ticket" remains the most likely choice in speaking, unless we are in a situation that calls for more careful speech, in which case we may be able to think ahead and produce "his," or we may avoid it altogether, or we may correct ourselves part way through. Today especially we feel that the illogic of having the masculine pronoun stand for the female half of the population is at least as serious as the singular–plural disjunction that led to this rule in the

ALICE M. ROY

first place, and so writers and speakers try to say "his or her," "her or his," and sometimes just "her."

Up to approximately the beginning of the twentieth century, "ain't I," as well as dropped *g*'s (e.g., *goin'* and *comin'*) were quite acceptable in upper-class British English. Now those forms are evaluated differently: *ain't* is always nonstandard, and while speakers of standard English drop *g*'s regularly in normal speech and never notice it, they consider it inappropriate in formal speaking situations. Similarly, at the time of the colonization of North America, the use of *loan* and *progress* as verbs was common in British English; that use was transported to the colonies, but then the British (unconsciously, of course) stopped using those words as verbs. We find in the literature of the eighteenth century derogatory comments about American English usage because it allowed such barbarisms as "I will loan you some money," even though such usage was quite appropriate in British English of an earlier period. Now we find these items presented as right-or-wrong options in workbooks for students.

These examples let us see that language is always changing and that what people accept at one period may differ from what is seen as appropriate usage, for whatever reasons, at another period. In the United States we have tended to look to our dictionaries for guidance in such issues, assuming that the purpose of a dictionary is to evaluate and prescribe usage. Children used to say in school, enjoying the irony of the form of the utterance, " 'Ain't' ain't in the dictionary." Then, in the 1960s, Webster's *Third International* shocked users by withdrawing its traditional evaluative labels and merely listing what occurred. *Ain't* was now in the dictionary, and so were many other forms, some of which middle-class speakers of standard English *knew* were not acceptable, some of which were genuine issues because people's regular spoken usage didn't match the schoolroom rules and workbook exercises that were remembered imperfectly—they existed, but what was the rule?

The editors of the *American Heritage Dictionary,* published in 1969, thought to redress this problem by empaneling a group of "experts" on English usage. They were writers, editors, educators, business people, and professionals, though later review showed that they were largely of an avowed conservative bent, unsympathetic to accepting change in English usage or allowing common spoken English to affect our legacy of rules from eighteenth-century grammarians. Yet even with the conservative nature of the experts selected, there was much disagreement among the panel members. Was it all right to split an infinitive? Some said yes, some said no. In 1944 Leonard Bloomfield [1] had described what he called "tertiary responses" about language. A primary response involves the automatic usage of unconscious rules by native speakers. A secondary response is an utterance about language. Such an utterance may be accurate ("start a sentence with a capital letter"), stylistic ("don't end a sentence with a preposition"), or quite mistaken ("the languages of some primitive tribes have only a few hundred words"). Tertiary responses, Bloomfield said, are heated reactions of English speakers either when someone produces a form they have been taught is improper, or when someone questions a form they consider to be proper. Certainly, a good deal of tertiary response arose during the compilation of the *American Heritage Dictionary,* showing that there remain areas of our language usage not set in cement—they are changing, or have changed, or never quite fit the rules laid out long ago.

The problem remains: even if we decide to include usage in our description of our language, whose usage shall it be? The only way to answer that question is to add, "in what circumstances?" Some usage is appropriate on the playground, some in religious settings, some in the barrio, some in college writing. Linguists sometimes call these different contextually determined types of language "style"; the more common label is "register." Generally, standard English is defined as the usage of educated people in government, business, education itself, and the professions—a middle- and upper-middle-class group. In 1974 the Conference on College Composition and Communication (CCCC) published its statement on "Students' Right to Their Own Language." A main feature of this document was that students have a right to use and maintain "the dialect that expresses their family and community identity." Many teachers and parents feared that this represented an abdication of teachers' responsibility. A few years later the National Council of Teachers of English passed a resolution supporting and clarifying the CCCC statement, affirming "the responsibility of all teachers of English to assist all students in the development of their abilities" in speaking and writing, and "to provide opportunities for all students to learn the conventions of . . . written Edited American English." Today we teachers generally hold that it is inhumane of us to insist that students give up their language or dialect just because that language or dialect does not match standard English. We also agree that we are irresponsible if we do not make available to our students the options of Edited American English. But how is this to be accomplished?

HOW DO WE LEARN LANGUAGE?

Dialect, usage, and edited written English all connect with principles of language learning, and language learning connects with principles of learning in general. We can clearly see the difference between the rote oral memorization used in the one-room schoolhouse of old and our current classroom activities. Recognizing more recent changes in learning theory and methodology is a little harder. Many of us studied a second language in school under the "grammar–translation" method: each chapter of our book had a short reading selection, a vocabulary list, a grammatical rule or two, and some exercises to be written out. We took vocabulary tests, had dictations, and translated aloud. Under this method, if we didn't "learn" as evidenced by the tests, we simply had not studied enough—with "study" being defined as book study, written exercises, and memorization. Though perhaps not the most efficient method, some of us did learn to read a foreign language under the grammar–translation method.

As the goals for learning a language shifted, however, so did theories of learning. People decided they wanted to be able to speak the new language, an achievement which the grammar–translation method certainly didn't ensure (it was never designed to). At the same time, behavioral psychology was becoming the most powerful theory of how people learned, particularly how they learned language. Anyone who has studied a language since the 1950s may well have experienced the "audiolingual" or "direct" method of language teaching. In this system, a learner memorizes dialogues; spends many hours in language labs, practicing to sound as much like a native speaker as possible; and repeats pattern practices and substitution drills under the leadership of the tutor or teacher. Errors are signs of bad habits developing, and the instructor's job is to protect the student against error by controlling the student's "output." Not learning—as evidenced by being unable to repeat the dialogues, for example— is seen in that model as the result of insufficient drill. "Free" conversation is rarely permitted in such a system, because that's when errors are most likely to occur.

In both these models—grammar–translation and audiolingual—the teacher was in control and was responsible for the progress of the learner. The teacher took the learner through a syllabus of grammar, whether written or spoken, and monitored the learner's performance by identifying and counting errors. Today, however, our model of learning has changed to focus on the process the learner goes through, to focus on the learners themselves. In fact, the model of how we learn *all* things has shifted: rather than being derived from behavioral psychology, it is now based on cognitive psychology. Research on language learning in the past decade and a half has been learner-centered, asking: What do people *do* when they learn language?

This research has led to some important principles. One is the distinction between language *learning* and language *acquisition,* a concept developed in particular by Stephen Krashen [9]. Although these two categories are not truly discrete, *learning* is applied to formal classroom work, with articulated rules, and *acquisition* is applied to the unconscious development of language, often in a "natural" setting. One of the sources of error in this model—for some linguists perhaps the main source—is "hypothesis testing," sometimes called "creative construction." That is, given sufficient interaction with speakers of the target language (thus "input" to the learner's mental grammar), the learner unconsciously tests out various explanations of forms and uses in the new language. Thus, when a nonnative speaker writes, "I could worked," we do not consider it an unreasonable production. Instead we think that the speaker still has to learn that tense is marked only once in a verb phrase. Linguists see the overgeneralization of the past tense as a constructive stage in the acquisition process. No amount of correction, of control of output, or of pre-practice will protect against such errors. In this model, error is seen as the result of not enough interaction between the learner and the speakers and writers of the target language. Acquisition comes from interaction with speakers of the target language over meaningful issues, in situations that meet psychological and social needs.

Thus the principal distinction maintained in the theory of language learning today is that some things can be learned through formal rule and formal practice and some things cannot. A corollary holds that given enough time and interaction with native speakers of the target language, all of language can be acquired unconsciously, or "naturally." Pushed to its logical extent, this tenet might suggest that the teacher is therefore superfluous. Lev Vygotsky [12] and Margaret Donaldson [3], however, have shown us that the learner can move forward sooner and more securely with the help of a teacher. Thus, while we *could* learn everything in language unconsciously, given enough time and interaction with native speakers, we can also learn *some* things consciously with the guidance of a teacher in the role of facilitator. For example, we know that the use of articles in English is an area of language learning that is highly resistant to change, highly unsusceptible to application of rules or practice. On the other hand, past-tense endings are fairly easy to "key on" for advanced speakers in the editing stage of writing. Krashen's term for this sort of "keying" is "monitoring." That is, some rules of language use are easy enough to articulate and keep track of, especially in writing, where there is time to edit what we have written. We need therefore to leave time for students to write without worrying about correctness, whether they come to the writing of Edited American English as speakers of standard English, as speakers of another dialect of English, or

as speakers of another language. When we choose exercises and practices for a student, we need to know that mainly we are raising the learner's consciousness about the existence of, or the need for attention to, a particular form; we don't really teach the form with the drill because we cannot affect the unconscious acquisition of language so directly.

Researchers in second-language acquisition have found a "natural order" of acquisition of the basic morphemes (for example, endings on nouns and verbs, and function words such as articles, prepositions, and auxiliaries). Roger Brown, in his research on child first-language acquisition [2], found this natural order. When linguists investigated the progress of second-language learners in spoken English, they also found a fairly regular order: *ing* (progressive), plural, forms of *be* as main verb, forms of *be* as auxiliary with progressive, article, irregular past, regular past, third-person singular, possessive. Not only is there a fairly predictable order, but perhaps the most surprising finding is that the order of acquisition does not depend on the learner's first language. That is, even though we are used to thinking of certain problems in English as connected with speakers of certain languages, researchers found that this same order held for speakers of languages as disparate as Spanish, Arabic, and Chinese.

We teachers need to know about principles of language learning because we have to invoke them as we work with students on grammar and usage. Many of us learned "grammar" at school (I walk, you walk, he-she-it walks, we walk, you walk, they walk); we did usage exercises (is it *will* or *shall? lie* or *lay?*); and we learned to rely on the dictionary as a source of firm information about pronunciation, meaning, and correctness. We—or our classmates—were often told and perhaps shown with liberal applications of red ink that our writing wasn't good. Yet it fit the way we—or our classmates—spoke. Many students were left with a feeling of much wrongdoing and a sense of writing as a vast dangerous field, full of traps, pitfalls, and quicksand—how could there be so many possible errors? No wonder now when we tell people we teach English, their frequent response is, "Oh, oh, I'd better watch my grammar!"

When we understand that variety across dialects is legitimate and that change across time is normal, we can have a healthy attitude toward our students' developing competence at any level of writing skill. As we apply principles of language acquisition to helping our students develop their writing skills, defining our role as facilitators of the process, we can guide students to a healthier sense of language and writing and can thus offer our students access to writing as a liberating experience.

Annotated Bibliography of Suggested Readings

1. Bloomfield, Leonard. "Secondary and Tertiary Responses to Language." *Language* 20 (1944): 45–55.

> Bloomfield describes metalinguistic responses to language use, looking at how distressed we become when someone questions or disagrees with what we think is "correct" usage.

2. Brown, Roger. *A First Language: The Early Stages.* Cambridge, MA: Harvard UP, 1972.

> Brown examines the linguistic development of very young children, finding that language forms are acquired in very similar, regular order.

3. Donaldson, Margaret. *Children's Minds.* New York: Norton, 1978.

> Donaldson, a former student and colleague of Piaget, examines some of Piaget's findings about the relationship of children's maturation and their cognitive abilities. Donaldson shows that with reasonable help from adults, children can do tasks otherwise thought beyond them.

4. Finegan, Edward. *Attitudes Toward English Usage: The History of a War of Words.* New York: Teachers College P, 1980.

> Finegan shows how we have arrived at many of our beliefs and prescriptions about our language.

5. Flower, Linda. "Writer Based Prose: A Cognitive Basis for Problems in Writing." *College English* 41 (1979): 19–37.

> Flower shows how some writing successfully contextualizes the message for the reader while other writing is too dependent on the writer's local knowledge and experience.

6. Goelman, Hillel, Antoinette Oberg, and Frank Smith, Eds. *Awakening to Literacy.* London: Exeter, 1984.

> Goelman et al. have edited and contributed to this collection of studies of how children acquire literacy. Important information for those who work with young adults and mature writers.

7. Halliday, M. A. K. *Language as Social Semiotic.* Baltimore: Arnold, 1978.

> Halliday's work provides an explanation of the concept of "register" and the types and functions of language use.

8. Jakobson, Roman. "Linguistics and Poetics." *Essays on the Language of Literature.* Eds. Seymour Chatman and Samuel R. Levin. Boston: Houghton, 1967.

> Jakobson examines linguistic features of poetry and poetics by providing an important schema of the factors, or components, of discourse and their functions.

9. Krashen, Stephen D. *Second Language Acquisition and Second Language Learning.* Oxford: Pergamon, 1981.

> Krashen compiles recent theory and research in second-language acquisition, explains the difference between *learning* and *acquisitions,* and sets out the rationale for a natural approach to language acquisition.

10. Labov, William. *Sociolinguistic Patterns.* Philadelphia: Pennsylvania UP, 1972.

> Labov's work on speech features and patterns of Black Vernacular English is a classic in sociolinguistics.

ALICE M. ROY

11. Marckwardt, Albert. *American English*. New York: Oxford UP, 1958.

> In this interesting and very readable book, Marckwardt traces the development of English in America: a must for teachers, and enjoyable as well.

12. Vygotsky, Lev. *Mind in Society: The Development of Higher Psychological Processes*. Eds. Michael Cole et al. Cambridge, MA: Harvard UP, 1978.

> Vygotsky outlines his concept of the "zone of proximal development," which helps us to see the role of teacher or facilitating adult in a child's learning. This book is also notable for the foreword and afterword by researchers in literacy Schribner and Cole, and John-Steiner and Soberman, which provide readable explanations of Vygotsky's place in current learning theory.

13. Wolfram, Walt, and Ralph W. Fasold. *The Study of Social Dialects in American English*. Englewood Cliffs: Prentice, 1974.

> Wolfram and Fasold present the history, phonology, grammar, and sociology of black English and some other nonstandard dialects such as Appalachian English.

Writing Across the Curriculum: An Overview

Barbara E. Walvoord

Halfway through a three-day workshop on writing across the curriculum that I was leading, a college chemistry instructor suddenly exclaimed, "This is really a workshop about thinking!" The "writing" in writing across the curriculum refers to the entire process of planning, gathering information, shaping, drafting, and revising.

WHY USE WRITING IN THE DISCIPLINES?

Why and how should instructors in the disciplines integrate this "writing" into their courses? One explanation lies in theories about the close relationship between thought and language. We experience this bond when we find ourselves thinking and discovering *as* we write. Philosopher Susanne Langer proposes that sense data are translated into symbols, which themselves are our ideas [item 11 in the Annotated Bibliography at the end of this essay]. In order to think and learn, we manipulate symbols by talking to ourselves in what psychologist Lev Vygotsky calls "inner speech"—the mediator between thought and language [20, p. 149]. "Thought is born through words," he says [20, p. 153].

A body of research in psychology [summarized in Walvoord, 21, pp. 3–5] indicates that when people verbalize an idea, they can remember it longer, understand it more thoroughly, and manipulate it in more sophisticated ways. Writing is one of the most effective modes for learning. "When I think back on my own student days, I realize I learned and retained more when I wrote" recalls Laurence Shute [17], an instructor at California Polytechnic Institute. "I'm going to give my students the same opportunity." He describes how, after a workshop on writing across the curriculum, he is "now rethinking every course I offer from the perspective of how to assign some kind of writing in each class." Because writing and thinking develop in complex ways across a student's years of schooling, every instructor needs to support their development.

Another reason for integrating writing across the disciplines is that a biologist and a literature teacher think, write, explore, use evidence, and pose questions in different ways. Walvoord and McCarthy [22] demonstrate how differently questions of evaluation and problem-solving are handled in classrooms in biology, history, psychology, and business. Faigley and Hansen [4] show how differently an English instructor and a sociology instructor may react to a student's writing in sociology. Bartholomae [1] and Bizzell [3] have described some characteristics of writing and thinking common to the academic community as a whole and have explored how different these modes are from students' customary ways of thinking and writing outside the academy.

BARBARA E. WALVOORD is Associate Professor of Writing at Loyola College in Baltimore, Maryland. She was co-founder and co-director of the Maryland Writing Project and the Baltimore Consortium for Writing Across the Curriculum. She conducts workshops on writing across the curriculum for interdisciplinary faculty groups at colleges and community colleges. Her guide for teachers, Helping Students Write Well, *now in its second edition, is published by the Modern Language Association. In addition, she has authored two textbooks as well as a number of articles on writing. She is currently working on a book that will report the results of a five-year study of students' thinking and writing processes in college classes in four disciplines.*

Elaine Maimon [12] characterizes students as "strangers" to the academic conversation. She recalls her own experience as a "stranger" when she was a new faculty member at a small college, joining a group of her new colleagues at lunch the first day, and understanding little of their talk, filled as it was with references to people, events, and ongoing debates unknown to her. As she gradually became part of the conversation of those lunchtime tables, so we, as college instructors, seek to help our students become participants in the conversations by which our disciplines advance and transmit knowledge. A discipline, as Bazerman [2] has noted, is heavily dependent upon written conversation. Each instructor, by helping students develop their ability to use language within a discipline, can contribute to students' ability to join the conversation of the discipline, and, more broadly, of educated people

For further explication of the theories that undergird writing across the curriculum, see Fulwiler [5, 6] and Parker and Goodkin [15].

WHAT MIGHT FACULTY IN THE DISCIPLINES DO?

The following discussion of how faculty in the disciplines might implement writing across the curriculum relies on the example of a history instructor, John R. Breihan of Loyola College in Maryland, and a biology instructor, Virginia Johnson Gazzam of Towson State University in Maryland. I have worked closely with both of them over the past six years and am currently coauthoring, with them, chapters in a book on how students write and think in the disciplines (Walvoord and McCarthy).

In any discipline, planning a college course that effectively integrates writing and thinking begins with clarification of course goals. For example, the biology instructor wanted her students to master a body of information and to be able to use the scientific method. The history instructor's goal was to help his students understand and write historical arguments.

The next step in course planning is to examine whether present practices are meeting the course goals. The biologist, who lectured to classes of more than 100 students, had been testing content by short-answer tests that often called for comparison/contrast, definition, or the explanation of a process. Tests sometimes showed her, too late, where students had not mastered lecture or laboratory material. Also, students were not skilled at handling comparison/contrast or shaping definitions and explanations in the ways that she wanted. She wondered whether, even in such a large class, there were ways to use writing to facilitate learning rather than just testing it.

The historian had been assigning essay tests, a term paper, and quizzes, but was very unhappy with the quality of student thinking and writing. He realized that he himself wrote arguments about material he knew well, he redrafted and revised many times, and he sought response to drafts from colleagues. His essay tests, in contrast, were eliciting hasty, loosely connected "fact dumping" from students, and students' term papers were often thinly veiled paraphrases of library sources. Quizzes encouraged students to concentrate on the individual facts of their readings rather than on the arguments and lines of inquiry. At the end of the semester, he found himself writing, often in despair or frustration, red-ink comments on students' papers, telling them what they had done wrong and justifying the grades he was giving them. But his comments, he suspected, were neither carefully read nor fully used by his students. His traditional writing assignments, he concluded, were neither based on his own experience as a writer, nor were they furthering his course goals as effectively as he wished.

To discover how they might better help students to learn, the biologist and the historian next took two steps: they examined their students and they explored what other teachers were doing. For example, the biologist recognized that students were passive (sometimes sound asleep) in lecture, and that in lab they went through the instructions cookbook style, sometimes without knowing the broader implications of what they were doing. The historian carefully examined his students' writing to identify specific competencies that his students needed for argument but did not always possess when they entered his class. He saw, for example, that they did not always know how to identify, in their reading, material that could be used as pros and cons for an argument, or how to categorize primary source material into factors such as social, economic, and religious, or how to defend a position on a debatable historical issue. As one of his history students said, "In high school we took the answers out of the book. I am not accustomed to writing arguments" [Walvoord and McCarthy, 21, p. 22].

The instructors also explored the options other teachers had used to integrate writing and learning in their courses. Such options are discussed, for example, in Fulwiler [5], Fulwiler and Young [7], Griffin [8], Stanford et al. [18], Thaiss [19], and Walvoord [21]. Other suggestions about using writing in disciplines outside English appear in journals, conference presentations, and documents that can be accessed through the computerized data base ERIC, using the search terms listed as item 24 in the bibliography at the end of this essay. A review of the literature on teaching strategies shows that instructors are:

- Using a wide variety of types of writing rather than relying only on essay tests and term papers.
- Using not just formal polished writing but also informal writing such as journals, dialogues, responses to readings, and exploratory essays to help their students apply, challenge, and muse about what they read and learn.
- Varying their responses to student writing according to the type of writing, the goal, and the instructor's available time. For example, the instructor will respond to journals differently than to a formal, polished research paper.
- Guiding the writing process: helping students to select topics, generate ideas, and plan, shape, and revise their writings, rather than merely giving the assignment and then collecting the finished product, with little attention to students' writing and thinking processes.

This last teaching approach is based on a body of literature that shows major differences between the writing processes of experienced writers and the processes of novice writers. The research is summarized in Hayes and Flower [9]. In brief, experienced writers

appear to draw upon a broader base of knowledge, generate more comprehensive plans and goals for the writing task, and plan and revise with greater attention to the structure and purpose of the entire paper rather than merely to local issues.

Most writing-across-the-curriculum programs in colleges and universities across the country have begun with workshops for faculty to explore the theories and options we have just discussed. One description of such a workshop appears in Raimes [16]. Others, including descriptions of the larger programs of which workshops are a part, appear in McLeod [14] and Fulwiler and Young [7]. More can be located through ERIC, using the search terms listed as item 23 in the bibliography at the end of this essay.

Building on such a workshop and also on their careful observation of their students, the biologist and historian revised their courses to integrate writing more effectively than before, but not to bury themselves under an insupportable avalanche of student papers which they had to "correct." To do this, they used four strategies: (1) they substituted a more effective type of writing assignment for a less effective one, (2) they shifted their own times from a less effective activity to a more effective one, (3) they sometimes moved a former in-class activity into out-of-class time so as to make more time for in-class writing or writing-based activities, and (4) they varied their responses to student writing depending on its purpose.

For example, the historian abandoned the essay tests and the long, final term paper in favor of three short but carefully crafted historical essays. Now his students were able to shape and reshape their arguments in the same way that he and other historians did. To help them further, the historian shifted his time investment from the end of the writing process to the middle—that is, instead of spending most of his time writing extensive comments on finished writings where students, faced with an unchangeable grade, were not motivated to read and apply his suggestions, he shifted his time to respond to students' *drafts.* When the final papers came in, he made much shorter and more general comments, trying to give students the one or two broad pieces of advice they could

BARBARA E. WALVOORD

carry with them into the next paper or the next course. On the basis of his comments to their drafts, students were often able to see where their arguments were weak and then to apply their new understanding immediately by revising their arguments. The instructor was gratified by the improvement in his students' ability to shape historical arguments, and now, eight years later, he is still doing draft response, despite the time it takes, because he shifted his time to make his load manageable.

The historian also instituted a series of informal writings, done outside of class, all designed to help students master the skills necessary to the historical arguments. For example, for one writing, students were asked to discuss, in a paragraph, how the material from that day's reading could be used as evidence in an argument over whether Louis XIV was a good king. On another day, students had to list the "economic," "social," "political," and "religious" factors from a series of first-hand accounts of seventeenth-century riots. The instructor was teaching students to read for arguments, not just for disconnected facts or mere summary, and he was teaching them to categorize data as historians do. The results of these exercises began to show in the essays. Because these short writings fed into the essays and because their primary purpose was to help students with reading and thinking, the instructor did not mark the writings extensively for grammar and punctuation, nor did he even try to comment on every point of content and structure. Rather, he read the short writings very quickly and concentrated on making one or two suggestions. For each short writing that met a minimum standard, the student accumulated points toward the final course grade. Further discussion of this historian (John R. Breihan) and his methods appears in Walvoord [21, 22] and in Mallonee and Breihan [13].

Other instructors may use informal writings in different ways. The historian arranged for all writing to be completed by students outside of class; however, the biologist used class time during her lectures for writing, because she felt it was better to help students become active learners than to "cover" more material they would not learn. She would stop the lecture and ask students to write for five minutes on questions such as "Summarize the most important ideas of last Friday's lecture" or "Compare the phylum we've covered today to the phylum we covered last time." To help her students understand the implications of their lab work, she asked them, before they began the lab, to write, for example, "Why are we using *E. coli* in the lab today?" Sometimes she asked students to share their writings with a peer in the next seat, or used them to encourage questions. Students kept all these short writings in their own folders, and at the end of the semester each student would choose three of his or her best short writings, polish them, and turn them in for a grade.

WHAT MIGHT ENGLISH FACULTY DO?

The role of the writing teacher in writing across the curriculum may encompass three areas: (1) articulation of the freshman composition course with other courses students take, (2) exemplification of strategies for integrating writing and learning, and (3) coordination of campus writing-across-the-curriculum activities.

Chapters 35–40 on "Writing Across the Curriculum" in the *Simon & Schuster Handbook for Writers*, Second Edition attempt to prepare composition students to understand the kinds of thinking and writing they will meet in other disciplines. In some schools, teachers of composition and teachers in the disciplines have agreed on basic terms or texts that will be required in the composition courses and used later by other teachers as well. Some instructors ask students to analyze the characteristics of writing in various disciplines or professions.

Instructors who teach writing often also teach literature. The literature class can be a model for the effective integration of writing and learning.

On most campuses it is the writing instructors who initiate and coordinate writing-across-the-curriculum programs. However, instructors in other disciplines must quickly become spokespeople and leaders in the effort, and the writing instructors must coordinate rather than dominate the program.

The task of integrating writing and learning within courses across the disciplines, including composition, is complex and difficult. Some of our best attempts so far, however, have come when instructors in composition and other disciplines identify their goals, examine their students' needs and their own practices, and then institute teaching strategies that seem best calculated to help students learn to participate in the ongoing conversation of the discipline and of the academy.

Annotated Bibliography of Suggested Readings

1. Bartholomae, David. "Inventing the University." *When a Writer Can't Write: Studies in Writer's Block and Other Composing-Process Problems.* Ed. Mike Rose. New York: Guilford, 1985.

> Characterizes various levels of students' ability to "invent" the university—that is, to adopt the specialized language and persona of someone who is a member of the discipline's community.

2. Bazerman, Charles. "What Written Knowledge Does: Three Examples of Academic Discourse." *Philosophy of the Social Sciences* 11 (1981): 361–87.

> Points out that academic disciplines are primarily bound by their exchange of written communication, and analyzes the features of that writing.

3. Bizzell, Patricia L. "What Happens When Basic Writers Come to College?" *College Composition and Communication* 37 (1986): 294–301.

> "Basic writers" (i.e., those least well prepared for college) face a conflict of world view, which may force them to give up old world views.

4. Faigley, Lester, and Kristin Hansen. "Learning to Write in the Social Sciences." *College Composition and Communication* 36 (1985): 140–49.

> Explores the learning and writing process of students in college social science classes and shows the differing reactions of social science and English teachers to the same piece of student writing.

5. Fulwiler, Toby. *Teaching with Writing.* Portsmouth, NH: Boynton, 1987.

> A guide for teachers in all disciplines who want to integrate writing with learning. Includes theoretical background on the interconnection of writing and learning, as well as practical suggestions for activities such as using journals or helping students revise.

6. ———. "Writing as an Act of Cognition." *Teaching Writing in All Disciplines.* Ed. C. Williams Griffin. San Francisco: Jossey, 1982.

> Explains how students learn through writing, particularly relying on James Britton. Discusses implications for classroom teachers in all disciplines.

7. Fulwiler, Toby, and Art Young, eds. *Writing Across the Curriculum: Programs, Practices, and Problems.* Portsmouth, NH: Boynton, in press.

> Describes a number of outstanding writing-across-the-curriculum programs across the country.

8. Griffin, C. Williams, ed. *Teaching Writing in All Disciplines.* San Francisco: Jossey, 1981.

> A collection of essays about the practical and theoretical issues in writing across the curriculum.

9. Hayes, John R., and Linda S. Flower. "Writing Research and the Writer." *American Psychologist* 41 (1986): 1106–113.

> Summarizes research on the organization of cognitive processes underlying the act of writing, specifically the processes of planning, sentence generating, and revising.

10. Kolln, Martha. "Closing the Books on Alchemy." *College Composition and Communication* 32 (1981): 139–51.

> Explores the often misinterpreted research results on students' errors in punctuation and usage. Concludes that instruction in "grammar" should be integrated with writing experiences for students.

11. Langer, Susanne. *Philosophy in a New Key.* 3rd ed. Cambridge, MA: Harvard UP, 1957.

> Describes human ability to perform "symbolic transformation" as the key to both scientific and humanistic problems.

12. Maimon, Elaine P. "Talking to Strangers." *College Composition and Communication* 30 (1979): 364–69.

> Instructors are guides who help their students become part of the conversation of the academy. Explores implications of this concept for classroom teachers in all disciplines.

13. Mallonee, Barbara, and John R. Breihan. "Responding to Students' Drafts: Interdisciplinary Consensus." *College Composition and Communication* 36 (1985): 213–31.

> Reports the team teaching experience of a history instructor and a writing instructor, exploring the points of difference with which they struggled and the areas of consensus they believe appropriate for teachers of writing and other disciplines.

14. McLeod, Susan, ed. *Strengthening Programs for Writing Across the Curriculum.* San Francisco: Jossey, 1988.

> A collection of essays about supporting established writing-across-the-curriculum programs. Discusses issues such as developing programs beyond the initial workshops, finding continuing funding, assessing the program, and developing research projects.

15. Parker, Robert, and Vera Goodkin. *The Consequences of Writing: Enhancing Learning in the Disciplines.* Upper Montclair, NJ: Boynton, 1987.

> Describes the origins of the writing-across-the-curriculum movement and its theoretical background. Shows how writing is used in five courses in different disciplines.

16. Raimes, Ann. "Writing and Learning Across the Curriculum: The Experience of a Faculty Seminar." *College English* 41 (1980): 797–801.

> Describes a series of writing-across-the-curriculum seminars held during the academic year at Hunter College.

17. Shute, Laurence. "Getting Them to Write." Letter to the Editor. *New York Times* 5 Nov. 1988: 26.

> A letter to the editor from a faculty member at California State Polytechnic University, urging teachers in the disciplines to integrate writing into their classrooms.

18. Stanford, Gene, and the Committee on Classroom Practices. *How to Handle the Paper Load.* Classroom Practices in Teaching English, 1979–1980. Urbana: National Council of Teachers of English, 1979.

> Practical suggestions for teachers at all levels and in all disciplines, about how to use writing for learning.

19. Thaiss, Christopher, ed. *Writing to Learn: Essays and Reflections on Writing Across the Curriculum.* Dubuque: Kendall, 1983.

> Essays about the writing-across-the-curriculum experiences and teaching strategies of faculty from a variety of disciplines at George Mason University.

20. Vygotsky, Lev S. *Thought and Language.* Cambridge, MA: MIT Press, 1962.

> Shows how children and adults use language as a mediator between humans and the world of physical stimulation so that humans can react in terms of their own symbolic conception of reality.

21. Walvoord, Barbara E. Fassler. *Helping Students Write Well: A Guide for Teachers in All Disciplines.* 2nd ed. New York: MLA, 1986.

> Guides college teachers in all disciplines through the process of planning a course that integrates writing and learning, guiding students' writing processes, and responding to student writers.

22. Walvoord, Barbara E. Fassler, and Lucille McCarthy. *Thinking and Writing in College* (working title). In process.

> The results of a five-year naturalistic study of students' thinking and writing processes as they fulfilled their normal assignments in college classes in four disciplines.

23. *ERIC descriptors:* For articles on the content and structure of writing across-the-curriculum workshops: "Higher-Education," "Writing-Across-the-Curriculum," "Workshops," and inclusive dates.

24. *ERIC descriptors:* For articles on using writing in a particular discipline: "Higher-Education," "Writing," "Interdisciplinary-Approach," the name of the discipline, and inclusive dates.

Large-Scale Essay Tests: An Overview

Emily R. Gordon

The pressure on composition programs to "measure up" continues to increase. Our colleagues in colleges and universities complain about students' inability to write intelligibly, and even we composition instructors occasionally question the standards being applied in some writing classes. The pressure from the larger community is even more intense: parents, facing increasing tuition bills, demand that their children obtain salable skills; periodic tax revolts call into question the success of open admissions and compensatory programs, while demand increases in class size; personnel officers throughout industry complain that college graduates lack the writing skills needed for even entry-level positions. In response to all these pressures, more and more colleges have turned to uniform examinations to generate statistics that will support existing programs or argue for desired programs. These schools also increasingly are using such tests to determine student placement and to assess achievement against criteria for graduation.

EMILY R. GORDON is Adjunct Instructor of English at Hofstra University, where she teaches composition and business communication. She is co-author of the Simon & Schuster Workbook for Writers *(with Lynn Quitman Troyka) and author of the* Diagnostic and Competency Tests to Accompany the Simon & Schuster Handbook for Writers, *and she is a member of the editorial board of the* Journal of Basic Writing. *She holds an M.A. in English Literature from Queens College of the City University of New York and is currently pursuing a Ph.D. in Composition at New York University. She serves as a reader for the Educational Testing Service, for Queensborough Community College of the City University of New York, and for Hofstra University; she also acts as Chief Reader and consultant to private institutions implementing holistically scored essay tests.*

Sometimes administrators see short-answer, objective tests as the most efficient way of making placement and graduation determinations. Yet, because essay tests are an important indicator of proficiency in composition, experts urge that essay tests be administered in place of, or in concert with, objective tests whenever possible.

This discussion first addresses the philosophical and pedagogical rationale for essay testing, then presents a plan for administering the examination, and finally explains the two most commonly used scoring procedures.

USES OF AN ESSAY TEST

Perhaps one of the most obvious characteristics of essay testing is that it is time-consuming. However, when essay testing is compared with objective testing, it becomes obvious that the time is well spent. Objective testing is simple to administer and grade and, when properly normed, it is highly predictive of students' composition skills. (For those who wish to complement essay tests with objective tests, Prentice Hall offers *Diagnostic and Competency Tests to Accompany the Simon & Schuster Handbook for Writers* [item 6 in the Annotated Bibliography at the end of this essay], a series of matching test forms useful for pre- and post-testing.)

Objective testing is only an indirect measure. It tests students' ability to manipulate the language of others rather than the ability to compose, a process that requires attention to multiple, overlapping concerns of audience, purpose, message, organization, grammar, diction, and mechanics.

EMILY R. GORDON

Certainly, essay testing presents a few difficulties. Departmental consensus must be reached regarding the reason for testing, the skills to be evaluated, the test's wording, and scoring standards. Costly clerical and administrative support is essential to the reproduction of examinations, scheduling of testing and scoring facilities, notification of students, and recording and interpretation of scores.

Is this investment of time, energy, and resources worthwhile? The experts think so. According to Marie Jean Lederman [10], past University Dean for Academic Affairs of the City University of New York, essay tests serve as rites of passage to the world in which our students will eventually function: "drawing material together into a coherent written whole is vital to membership in a group of educated adults" (p. 45).

Essay testing also has other, more immediate, benefits. Preparing the prompt and scoring guidelines brings an English department together. Faculty share in the process of determining the purpose of the examination and deciding what constitutes acceptable and unacceptable writing for a particular situation. Participation in scoring contributes to a sense of unity among instructors and gives them a rare opportunity to share their responses and their underlying philosophy, a discussion that does not end with the last test paper.

Additional benefits of essay testing appear in the classroom. Where objective tests reign, institutions teach objective-test-taking. Conversely, where essay tests are given, instructors teach essay-test-taking strategies: brainstorming, outlining, thesis statements and topics sentences, relevant detail, supporting anecdotes and examples, editing, and proofreading. Finally, when students are required to take essay tests, they (and their parents and the community) realize that writing is important.

The benefits of giving essay tests may be summarized as follows:

- Instructors of English focus on the essay rather than on isolated grammatical errors.
- By sharing a uniform set of standards, instructors are less likely to use idiosyncratic standards in their own classrooms.
- More attention is placed on the teaching of writing as a process. Editing and proofreading skills are placed in perspective, as final steps rather than as ends in themselves.
- Faculty and administrators unite in the pursuit of a common goal.
- Assessment results can be used to revise curricula.
- Faculty in other disciplines see that writing is being stressed and so may be more willing to incorporate it into their own courses.
- Students take writing more seriously, realizing it can and will be evaluated.

ESSAY TEST TOPICS

Selecting a test topic (a prompt) depends upon two factors: the purpose of the examination and the amount of time available for testing. The two most commonly used time limits are 20 minutes and 50 minutes. Untimed essays also are a possibility, but the procedure is usually too cumbersome when large numbers of students are involved.

Purposes for testing can be divided into two broad categories: placement within a sequence of courses (including exemption from a required course) and exit from a program (for example, a departmental final for Freshman Composition or a graduation requirement). An exit examination seeks to ascertain whether certain minimum standards have been met. In this situation, a 20-minute test can provide enough information for readers to distinguish competent from incompetent writing.

A placement examination, in contrast, is given to a much more heterogeneous population. Far subtler distinctions must be made. It is not uncommon for one examination to be used to place students in one of as many as seven courses within a sequence. When such fine distinctions are being made, a 50-minute test is a necessity.

Students need to be prepared for whatever time limit has been set, by being given practice essays in class. If this is not possible, letters sent to students notifying them that they will be writing an essay test should specify the time limit.

The Qualities of a Good Topic

What makes a good essay topic? The Educational Testing Service offers some solid advice in their pamphlet for new readers of the English Composition Test [2]:

> [A good essay topic] must be self-explanatory; it must be defined and limited. It must be a topic that every student . . . can be expected to have some information about. It must be a topic so stimulating that every candidate will have something to say immediately. It must be a topic that young and inexperienced candidates can write about intelligently. (1)

Research by Gordon Brossell has done much to clarify what makes an effective topic. Brossell [1] shows how an overly elaborate prompt inhibits composition. Teachers have known for years that students need prompts that guide their thinking, that one-word prompts ("excellence" or "freedom") elicit fuzzy essays. In an effort to stimulate thought, some test-makers go too far in the other direction and offer students elaborate scenarios. The results are startlingly poor, with many students doing little more than parroting the prompts. Brossell's work shows that prompts of a few sentences work better than longer ones; students receive enough information to stimulate thought, but not so much as to intimidate them.

More recently, Brossell has joined with James Hoetker to make specific suggestions for generating useful topics [9]. In 1983 Hoetker and Brossell agreed to write a set of topics for Florida's College-Level Academic Skills Test (CLAST). Working with the underlying assumption that "wording and content of a topic may affect what and how well a student writes" (p. 328), they wrote short, simple topics, all having the same form. Their goal was to eliminate any factors that might misdirect students. To compensate for the varying intellectual backgrounds of students, Hoetker

and Brossell engineered topics that let students write about the subjects they knew best. The resulting formula is modeled on the parts of the traditional definition: a category, a linking verb, a class specification, and differentiating criteria. The student is given the class specification and differentiating criteria. He or she then must supply an example of that category. By changing the class specification or the criteria, testers can produce similar topics.

> "A book/ that many students read/ that may affect them harmfully."
>
> "A book/ that many students read/ that may affect them beneficially."
>
> "A course/ that many students take/ that may affect them in important ways."

Topics such as these have produced positive results. Essays tend to have strong thesis statements rather than the rambling openings typical of essays written in response to earlier CLAST topics.

Despite the burgeoning interest in essay assessment over the last twenty years, the sharing of findings has been a haphazard affair. Leo Ruth and Sandra Murphy [11] have gone a long way toward correcting this situation. Drawing upon the work of ten leading practitioners ("'exemplars' of wise practice"), formal research in diverse areas (psychometrics, writing topics, and discourse theory), and their own experiences with the Bay Area Writing Project (1980–82), Ruth and Murphy suggest guidelines for designing topics for writing assessment. The scope of this review is impressive, and its tone is even-handed. The various studies are not always in agreement about the best way to reduce misinterpretation of text; test writers, students, and test readers do not all interpret directions and prompts in the same way, nor do student-writers and teacher-readers see the same essay in the same way. Ruth and Murphy point future research in the direction of reducing these "misfirings." Their book is presented not as the endpoint of research, but as a compilation of findings to date. They call emphatically for further exploration of the best way to create assessment situations in which writers can produce their best work.

EMILY R. GORDON

Suggested Topics

You might want to create topics using the Hoetker/Brossell model above, or you may wish to use topics of the types illustrated below.

1. The following prompts guide students toward informative writing without imposing particular structures. Students are thus able to demonstrate their ability to organize an essay by choosing appropriate rhetorical strategies.

- Describe a visit to the dentist. Use specific details and anecdotes to convince the reader that your dental visits are as pleasant or unpleasant as you believe they are.

- What is your favorite color? Explain what this color represents that makes it special for you. Use specifics, such as details and anecdotes, to support your generalizations.

- Describe a formal social gathering that you have attended, such as a wedding or funeral. Compare the appearance and behavior of people on such an occasion with the way they usually look and behave.

- What career do you plan to pursue? Explain the reasons why you chose this field and tell what you hope to accomplish.

- Pick something you know how to do well, and teach someone how to do it. Be sure to include all the necessary steps and define any unusual terms.

2. Persuasive essays can be given focus if students are asked to agree or disagree with a brief statement. Often writers adapt this part of the prompt into a clear thesis statement. Background, such as that given here, stimulates thinking and suggests sources of evidence.

Follow each of the suggested prompts below with these directions: *Agree or disagree with this statement. Support your position with evidence based on your own experience, observation of others, and reading.*

- Overall, Americans feel the elderly are useless. We tear our older people away from their friends and send them off to live in nursing homes. Television and movies routinely portray the elderly as helpless, easily confused, and having little interest in life.

  In the United States, we have mistaken ideas about older people. [Insert above directions here.]

- Anyone who has ever tried to drive through the center of a large city must realize that something is wrong. Too many cars enter the central business districts, creating massive traffic jams that prevent emergency vehicles from passing, pollute the air, and waste gasoline.

  Private cars should be banned in the center of large cities. [Insert above directions here.]

- People have been arguing for years about whether boys and girls who return from school to an empty house are at a disadvantage. Some studies indicate that because these latchkey children do not have the supervision of an adult during the afternoon, they spend too much time alone watching television or getting into trouble. Other studies show, however, that latchkey children grow up to be responsible, self-confident adults.

  Children who return from school to a home without adult supervision suffer. [Insert above directions here.]

- In recent years, students from the United States have scored lower than students from Europe and Asia on tests of basic academic skills and reasoning ability. Seeking an explanation, some people have suggested that American schools are too easy. They say students are not made to think through problems nor are they given enough homework to help them practice new skills.

  American high schools are too easy. [Insert above directions here.]

- The world seems to get noisier every day. Garbage trucks and the people who pick up the trash make a terrible noise. The sound of machinery coming from construction sites can make it impossible to concentrate. Also some people play their stereos at top volume in the middle of the night.

Local governments should enact laws to control noise pollution. [Insert above directions here.]

3. Some prompts enable students to choose whether they wish to inform or persuade their readers. With these prompts, students must make their own decisions about purpose, audience, and organization.

Follow each of the suggested prompts below with these directions: *Relate this statement to your personal experiences and your observation of others. You may also want to draw on your reading in your response.*

■ Worries can be very distracting.
■ Every person is a mirror of his or her parents.
■ The only thing permanent in life is change.
■ The person who speaks in anger will probably regret it.
■ Every right brings with it an equal obligation.

4. More experienced writers can be asked to respond to brief quotations. However, the literary cadence of even the shortest quotations makes such prompts challenging. Again, students need to make independent decisions about audience, purpose, and organization.

Follow each of the suggested prompts below with these directions: *Relate this statement to your personal experiences and your observation of others. You may also want to draw on your reading in your response.*

■ We must make the best of those ills which cannot be avoided. —ALEXANDER HAMILTON
■ In a dream you are never eighty. —ANNE SEXTON
■ Common sense is the knack of seeing things as they are, and doing things as they ought to be done. —JOSH BILLINGS
■ Understanding is a two-way street. —ELEANOR ROOSEVELT

■ Difficulties strengthen the mind, as labor does the body. —SENECA

ADMINISTERING AN ESSAY TEST

Administration of an essay test may be seen as having five stages: organization, on-site preparation, proctoring, scoring, and reporting. The first three stages are discussed below; scoring procedures are discussed in the next section. Reporting methods depend upon the facilities available at each institution; however, students should receive prompt written notice of their test scores, along with an explanation of what further steps they should take.

Organizing an Essay Test

Before the actual test day, certain essential preparations must be made.

1. After the department or a committee has decided what skills are being tested, a suitable topic must be chosen and directions written.
2. The examination must be reproduced and stored in a secure area.
3. The day (or days) for administering the test must be chosen and announced.
4. Unless the test will be administered during regular classes, a test location must be selected.
5. Time for scoring must be scheduled, and a location must be reserved.
6. Supplies must be ordered: blue books, pencils, perhaps microphones.
7. If any students who will take the test are not currently in English classes, letters must be written and mailed to their homes, telling them of the nature, time, place, and *significance* of the examination.
8. Student aides must be hired to help with paperwork and distribution and collection of materials.

On-Site Preparation for an Essay Test

If the test is to be given in individual English classes, someone must see that each teacher receives sufficient question sheets, blue books, and pencils a day in advance. Scrap paper is not necessary, since question sheets or the back of the blue book may be used.

If the test is to be given outside regular classes, each proctor should pick up supplies an hour before the test is scheduled to begin. This will give the proctor time to prepare the test room and greet early arrivals.

Since posting the time distracts some students seriously, try to have a working clock in each room, if possible. If no clock is available, then posting the time at 10- or 15-minute intervals is essential.

Proctoring an Essay Test

Proctors should not spend all their time at the desk reading, but neither should they be constantly pacing. The recommended procedure is to stay in the front of the room making occasional supportive eye contact with students.

To ensure uniform administration of the examination, the test committee should prepare a script—or at least a detailed set of directions—for all proctors. In this way, students are guaranteed a fair policy on such matters as time limit and use of dictionaries, and no students will receive more guidance than others.

SCORING AN ESSAY TEST

The two most widely used procedures for assessing essay examinations are holistic and analytical scoring. Studies indicate that holistic scoring is more efficient and reliable than analytical, but both systems are discussed here so that departments may select the one most in keeping with their needs.

Holistic Scoring

The underlying assumptions of holistic scoring are well stated in the Educational Testing Service pamphlet on scoring the English Composition Test [2]:

> The basic assumptions of holistic scoring are that each of the factors involved in writing skill is related to all the others and that no one factor can be separated from the others. Readers must judge each essay as a whole; they must read each paper for the impression its totality makes. A misspelled word, a comma splice, a sentence fragment, a misplaced modifier should carry no great weight in scoring an otherwise well-written paper. The candidate is entitled to make some mistakes: he or she is writing hurriedly in a tense situation. (2)

Holistic scoring has several advantages. First, by considering each essay as a whole, readers are encouraged to focus on writing as a process leading to a unified product, rather than as a series of minimally connected errors. Second, training enables readers to discover their implicit priorities and the rationales behind them. Third, because readers see a wider range of writing skill than is found in any single course, their perspective is enlarged and therefore their ability to grade their own students fairly increases. Fourth, having two readers per paper reduces the chances of any idiosyncratic judgments and increases reliability in assessment.

Admittedly, holistic scoring also has a few disadvantages. First, scoring sessions take time, especially when training is properly conducted. Second, scoring sessions can be expensive. Release time or stipends need to be provided to participating faculty, and additional clerical help must be hired and trained. Someone at the institution must have extensive experience with holistic scoring in order to organize a reading and conduct training. If no such person is available, a consultant must be hired to act as chief reader and to train an on-campus successor. Finally, holistic scoring neither diagnoses specific weaknesses nor prescribes appropriate action.

However, despite these drawbacks, holistic scoring is preferred by most experts in the field. A brief overview of holistic scoring follows; anyone interested in a more thorough presentation is referred to Edward M. White's *Teaching and Assessing Writing* [13].

A great deal of work occurs behind the scenes before the reading begins. The chief reader, assistant chief reader(s), and table leaders read a large sampling of the essays. From these, they select papers representing various levels of skill, and they assign scores that, in their experienced judgment, reflect the quality of these essays *in relation to the other essays written in response to this particular prompt*. These essays, reflecting the entire range of scores, will be used to train the readers.

The scoring procedures are designed to promote uniform standards. The session begins with the chief reader presenting the topic to the readers and explaining the purpose behind that topic. He or she then discusses key aspects of evaluating the papers, such as the amount of emphasis to be placed on surface features and what constitutes an off-topic response.

The chief reader next explains the process of scoring: Two readers independently grade each essay, and their scores are either recorded in code or covered with removable tape, so that the second reader is not influenced by the first. After a paper has been read twice, clerks decode the scores. If the scores match or are within one point of each other, they are totaled to give the paper's final score. If scores are more than one point apart, a third, highly experienced, reader independently scores the essay, and the two most closely matching scores are added together.

Then the chief reader explains the scoring scale. The number of scores on a scale vary depending upon the purpose of the examination. Common scoring systems include a four-point scale (recommended for uncomplicated situations, such as exiting a course or program) and a six-point scale (useful for making the finer discriminations needed to place students within a course sequence). Sample four- and six-point scales are given in Appendices A and B. Studies indicate that even-numbered scales are preferable, because tired readers are likely to fall toward a neutral middle score, if one is available, rather than making the sometimes difficult distinction between passing and failing essays. Whatever the number of scoring options on a scale, 1 represents the lowest score and the highest number represents the top score. The following discussion assumes a six-point scale.

Readers, initially working with the sample essays selected by the chief reader and his or her associates, are urged to decide on scores using a two-stage process. First, they must decide if an essay is above average (4 to 6) or below average (1 to 3). The second step is to decide if a passing paper is just above average (4), clearly above average (5), or well above average (6), and if a

failing paper is just below average (3), clearly below average (2), or well below average (1).

Since no score exists to label a paper as exactly average, each reader must decide if such a piece is ever-so-slightly above or below average. In fact, one reader may give a score of 3 and another a 4. Some scoring systems treat this split grade as a pass; others treat it as a disagreement and refer the paper to a third reader. Each institution needs to agree on a policy for such scores.

During training, participants read and score up to twenty sample essays. Scores are tabulated, and in cases where readers disagree among themselves or with the scores given by the chief reader and his or her assistants, discussions are held to clarify criteria. Sample essays are read until readers have absorbed appropriate standards and are scoring consistently and accurately. Only then does actual reading of "live" essays begin.

To ensure that standards remain consistent, the reading is interrupted periodically for ongoing training. Even highly experienced readers need to participate in these sessions because they, as much as any beginner, tend to score more harshly when tired. As before, sample essays are read, scored, and discussed in an effort to maintain consensus. As a safeguard between training sessions, table leaders randomly select for review several of each reader's scored essays. If the two rate an essay differently, they discuss the reasons behind the scores. The table leader does not force a reader to change a score, but instead seeks to clarify how that score was determined and whether appropriate criteria are being applied.

The reading continues until all papers have been read twice (or three times, if necessary). Compilation of scores and reporting are left to clerical support personnel.

Analytical Scoring

The assumption behind analytical scoring is that the evaluation of discrete writing skills can be used to rate a whole piece of writing and simultaneously provide a prescription for further work.

Analytical scoring has a few advantages. First, the

EMILY R. GORDON

scoring of a limited number of preselected criteria makes reader training minimal. Second, students and teachers receive specific diagnoses; as a result, student objections to placement decisions are easily handled and teachers know immediately in what areas their students need work. Third, papers are read just once, reducing the clerical workload.

However, the disadvantages of analytical scoring are significant. First, measuring separate skills is incompatible with the philosophy that writing is a process leading to a single, complex product. Second, counting errors encourages readers (teachers who will carry the lesson of the reading back to their students) to focus on weaknesses rather than strengths. Finally, although each essay is read only once, that reading can take far longer than two readings done holistically.

If your department feels, nevertheless, that analytical scoring best suits its needs, two key decisions need to be made. First, decide what categories will be scored. Limit the number of characteristics to be rated, or readers will have to spend far too much time on each essay. Second, since points are awarded for high, middle, and low skill in each area, define what merits a high, middle, or low score. For some qualities, counting the number of errors will do. However, some important features of essay writing (among them ideas, organization, and tone) do not easily lend themselves to quantification.

Anyone desiring more information about analytical scoring should see Paul B. Diederich's *Measuring Growth in English* [4], which features an analytical scale and an explanation of the criteria for high, middle, and low scores in each of eight areas.

APPENDIX A

A Four-Point Scale

4 This essay is *among the best* written on the topic. It is organized around a clear thesis that is relevant to the prompt. The essay contains numerous appropriate details and examples in support of generalizations. Paragraphs follow a logical order and exhibit unity and coherence. Sentences are grammatically correct and demonstrate the writer's mastery of subordination and coordination. Diction is lively, showing the writer's understanding of levels of diction, denotation and connotation, and metaphor. Errors in punctuation, mechanics, and usage are rare.

3 This essay is a *slightly better than average response* to the prompt. A thesis clearly states the author's purpose, although some sentences may not relate to that purpose. The essay contains appropriate details and examples in support of generalizations. Paragraphs generally follow a logical order; they exhibit unity and coherence most of the time. Sentences are usually grammatically correct and reflect some grasp of subordination and coordination. Diction is adequate, but not especially lively. Some errors in punctuation, mechanics, and usage occur, but they do not seriously interfere with meaning.

2 The essay is a *somewhat below average response* to the prompt. It may lack a thesis statement altogether; if one is present, little is done to provide support. The essay contains some details and examples, but they may not be relevant to the generalizations which they follow. Paragraphs may relate to the thesis, but they are usually underdeveloped, vague, or lacking in unity and coherence. Sentences may be ungrammatical, illogical, or unsophisticated; they show little understanding of subordination or coordination. Diction is lackluster and sometimes inappropriate. Errors in punctuation, mechanics, and usage sometimes interfere with meaning.

1 This essay is a *well-below-average response* to the prompt. It may lack a thesis; if one is present, it is very weak. Details and examples are lacking or inappropriate. Most generalizations are completely unsupported or supported with other, often re-

dundant, generalizations. Paragraphs are undeveloped and incoherent, and they have little connection to any thesis or to one another. Sentences may be illogical or badly constructed; most consist of simple subject-verb-object combinations, with little or no use of subordination and coordination. Diction is immature and often nonidiomatic. Errors in punctuation, mechanics, and usage seriously interfere with meaning.

APPENDIX B

A Six-Point Scale

6 This essay is *among the very best* written on the topic. It contains a clear thesis and is well organized throughout. Generalizations are supported with relevant details and explanations. Sentences demonstrate a mastery of basic grammar, as well as subordination, coordination, and parallel structure. Diction is highly appropriate. Punctuation, mechanics, and usage are almost always correct.

5 This essay is *clearly an upper-half response* to the topic. It contains a thesis and is generally well organized, including transitions between and within most paragraphs. Most generalizations are supported with appropriate details and examples. Sentence structure is generally correct, indicating some control of subordination, coordination, and parallel structure, although some errors may occur in especially complicated sentences. Diction is appropriate. Punctuation, mechanics, and usage are usually correct; whatever errors do occur are not particularly confusing to the reader.

4 This essay is a *slightly above-average response* to the topic. It contains a thesis and is fairly well organized, although digressions or omissions may occur. An attempt is made to support generalizations with appropriate details and examples. While sentence structure is correct enough to be clear, it is often unsophisticated, with little use of

subordination, coordination, or parallel structure. Diction is usually appropriate, but some slang and regionalisms may be present and vocabulary may be limited. Agreement, tense, and possession are usually, although perhaps not always, correct. Punctuation shows an understanding of sentence boundaries, but other punctuation may sometimes be nonstandard. Spelling, including homonyms, is generally correct.

3 This essay is a *slightly below-average response* to the topic. Although the connection to the prompt is apparent, the thesis is either missing or vague. Most, but not all, paragraphs are underdeveloped and lacking in unity and coherence. Transitions within and between paragraphs are also missing. Sentence structure is monotonous and unsophisticated; few errors may occur because sentences are kept very simple, or there may be frequent errors in sentence punctuation. Diction is often inappropriately informal, and vocabulary is often inexact. Indirect and direct discourse are confused. Common words are sometimes misspelled.

2 This essay is *clearly a lower-half response* to the topic. Some attempt has been made to discuss the prompt, but ideas generally remain undeveloped. Supporting details and examples are rare; repetition and irrelevancies are common. Paragraph development is minimal. Sentence structure is elementary and often unclear. Diction is highly informal, more appropriate to conversation than to academic writing. Sound-alike words are frequently confused, and vocabulary is juvenile. Errors in punctuation, mechanics, and usage are common.

1 This essay is *among the weakest* written on the topic. It has no thesis or pattern of organization, and its connection to the prompt may not be apparent. Errors in grammar, punctuation, mechanics, usage, and spelling are so frequent as to seriously distract the reader. This grade is also given to any essay that is too brief to judge.

Annotated Bibliography of Suggested Readings

1. Brossell, Gordon. "Rhetorical Specification in Essay Examination Topics." *College English* 45 (1983): 165–73.

    Based upon experimental evidence, Brossell calls into question the assumed superiority of essay test prompts that provide detailed scenarios and that specify fictional speakers, purposes, and audiences. His findings suggest that the prompts most likely to elicit good impromptu responses are those that make only a brief statement about a subject before asking for a personal response.

2. Conlan, Gertrude. *How the Essay in the College Board English Composition Test Is Scored: An Introduction to the Reading for Readers.* Princeton: Educational Testing Service, 1985.

    This pamphlet is given to new readers of the English Composition Test, the essay portion of the College Board's English Achievement Test. The discussion, outlining how holistic scoring procedures operate for this particular test, is noteworthy for its emphasis on the respect due student writers.

3. Cooper, Charles R., and Lee Odell, eds. *Evaluating Writing: Describing, Measuring, Judging.* Urbana: National Council of Teachers of English, 1977.

    The editors present six essays, each discussing a different method of assessing writing. See especially "Holistic Evaluation of Writing" by Charles R. Cooper and "Primary Trait Scoring" by Richard Lloyd-Jones.

4. Diederich, Paul B. *Measuring Growth in English.* Urbana: National Council of Teachers of English, 1974.

    Diederich suggests ways of improving the reliability of essay scoring and argues that a properly graded final essay examination (supported by a short-answer test) can accurately assess each student's writing ability.

5. Fishman, Judith. "Do You Agree or Disagree: The Epistemology of the CUNY Writing Assessment Test." *WPA: Writing Program Administration* 8 (1984): 17–25.

    Fishman takes issue with the agree/disagree format of the much imitated Writing Assessment Test of the City University of New York, saying that it does not elicit each student's best writing. This critique is responded to by Greenberg [7] and by Troyka [12].

6. Gordon, Emily R. *Diagnostic and Competency Tests to Accompany the Simon & Schuster Handbook for Writers.* 2nd ed. Englewood Cliffs, NJ: Prentice, 1990.

    This testing package offers two matching forms of diagnostic tests for use on IBM and Apple II computers (Form CX and Form CY); two different matching forms of printed diagnostic tests (Form A and Form B); and two matching forms of printed competency tests (Form AA and Form BB), along with guidelines for administration and scoring.

7. Greenberg, Karen L. "Writing Assessment Test Design: Response to Two *WPA* Essays." *WPA: Writing Program Administration* 9 (1985): 31–40.

    Greenberg responds to Fishman's charges (see item 5 above), noting that a competence test need not measure each student's best work, but must evoke thoughtful essays from members of a heterogeneous population while remaining valid and reliable.

8. Greenberg, Karen L., Harvey S. Wiener, and Richard A. Donovan, eds. *Writing Assessment: Issues and Strategies.* New York: Longman, 1986.

    Three leading founders of the National Testing Network in Writing have gathered essays by major figures in writing assessment. The volume presents an overview of the issues facing the testing community, and several of the essays indicate fruitful directions for additional work.

9. Hoetker, James, and Gordon Brossell. "A Procedure for Writing Content-Fair Essay Examination Topics for Large-Scale Writing Assessment." *College Composition and Communication* 37 (1986): 328–35.

    Based on their work for Florida's College-Level Academic Skills Test, Hoetker and Brossell suggest that essay prompts based on the structure of formal definition reduce the chances of student misinterpretation and help students focus on subjects about which they are knowledgeable.

10. Lederman, Marie Jean. "Why Test?" *Journal of Basic Writing* 7 (1988): 38–46; rpt. Greenberg, Wiener, and Donovan [see item 8 above].

Lederman places testing in an historical perspective in order to demonstrate that testing is a rite of passage. Hence the values and essential skills of a society must be determined and acknowledged by those developing tests.

11. Ruth, Leo, and Sandra Murphy. *Designing Writing Tasks for the Assessment of Writing.* Norwood: Ablex, 1988.

Ruth and Murphy analyze a large body of studies conducted on variables in writing-topic design and on the potential for misinterpretation of topics and directions among test writers, students, and readers.

12. Troyka, Lynn Quitman. "The Phenomenon of Impact: The CUNY Writing Assessment Test." *WPA: Writing Program Administration* 8 (1984): 27–35.

Writing in response to Fishman's attack on the CUNY WAT (see item 5 above), Troyka recounts the successes of the examination and provides guidelines for the development of unbiased assessment topics.

13. White, Edward M. *Teaching and Assessing Writing.* San Francisco: Jossey, 1986.

White draws together previously hard-to-find information as he makes a case for schools using essay tests to evaluate writing ability. He shows how such tests can be fair, reliable, and economical and how they foster a variety of changes beneficial to students and teachers.

SECOND EDITION

Simon & Schuster

HANDBOOK
for WRITERS

Lynn Quitman Troyka

PRENTICE HALL
Englewood Cliffs, New Jersey 07632

Library of Congress Cataloging-in-Publication Data

Troyka, Lynn Quitman
    Simon & Schuster handbook for writers / Lynn Quitman Troyka. —
2nd ed.
      p.   cm.
      ISBN 0-13-809476-4
       1. English language—Rhetoric—Handbooks, manuals, etc.
  2. English language—Grammar—1950—Handbooks, manuals, etc.
I. Title. II. Title: Simon and Schuster handbook for writers.
PE1408.T696 1990
808′.042—dc20
                                     89-23132
                                        CIP

for David,
who makes it all worthwhile

Development Editor: Stephen Deitmer
Production Editor: Virginia Rubens
Interior and cover design: Lorraine Mullaney
Manufacturing Buyer: Mary Ann Gloriande
Associate Art Director: Florence Silverman
Page layout: Meg Van Arsdale

Printed in the United States of America
10 9 8 7 6 5 4 3 2 1

ISBN 0-13-809476-4 01

Prentice-Hall International (UK) Limited, *London*
Prentice-Hall of Australia Pty. Limited, *Sydney*
Prentice-Hall Canada Inc., *Toronto*
Prentice Hall Hispanoamericana, S.A., *Mexico*
Prentice-Hall of India Private Limited, *New Delhi*
Prentice-Hall of Japan, Inc., *Tokyo*
Simon & Schuster Asia Pte. Ltd., *Singapore*
Editora Prentice-Hall do Brasil, Ltda., *Rio de Janeiro*

CONTENTS

1

Thinking about Purposes and Audiences   2

2

Planning and Shaping   14

THE WRITING PROCESS

Part One offers a student-oriented introduction to the process of writing an essay. Chapter 1, adapted from the rhetorical theory of James L. Kinneavy, presents the *why* of writing before the *how*. Chapters 2 and 3 show the writing process in action, with student examples of each strategy. Two complete student essays, one with an informative purpose and one with a persuasive purpose, illustrate the writing process. New to Chapter 3 are specific guidelines for being a peer critic.

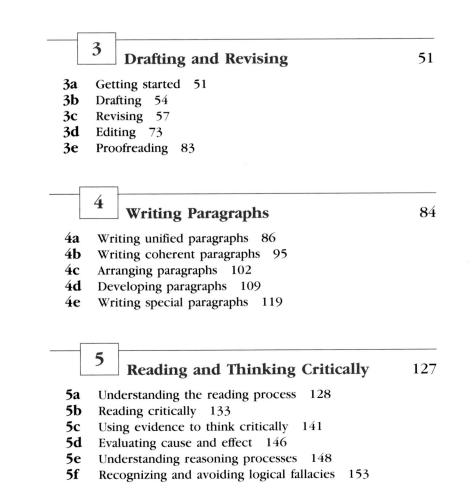

ARGUMENTATIVE WRITING

Chapter 6, entirely new to this edition, deals with the special demands of written argument. It complements Chapter 5, which covers critical thinking and, with added emphasis in this edition, critical reading skills. Chapter 6 includes two student papers taking different positions on the same topic.

Part Two

"FOCUS ON REVISING" FEATURE

Integrated throughout the book, the entirely new "Focus on Revising" sections tie revision concepts in Part One to material presented in later chapters. The "Focus on Revising" sections show case studies of students revising, the first for observation, the second for participation. See Chapters 8, 10, 11, 13, 14, 15, 16, 19, 21, 24, and 30.

Part Three
WRITING CORRECT SENTENCES 303

Part Four

FEATURES TO FACILITATE USE AS A REFERENCE

The book has been carefully designed to facilitate its use as a reference source. Inside the front cover is an organization chart providing a convenient overview of the book's structure. Inside the back cover is a list of symbols used in responding to student writing—now including some for positive responses. An unusually thorough index lists hundreds of terms, including common synonyms as well as the terms employed in the book itself. Throughout the book, colors are used to reinforce cognitive aspects of the material. All revised examples are shown in blue. Buff is used for the 161 charts (listed alphabetically inside the back cover) providing summaries, guidelines, and checklists for quick reference. Headings and tabs are printed in burgundy.

Part Six

RESEARCH WRITING

Part Seven, expanded in this edition to four chapters, shows the interplay of two processes: the research process and the writing process. Chapter 31, on working with sources, offers specific strategies for avoiding plagiarism. Chapter 33, on MLA and APA documentation styles, is new to this edition. It features a mini-handbook (with red-bordered pages for ease of reference) showing how to cite over forty types of sources. Also new to this edition are the "Process Notes" in Chapter 34, which narrate a student writer's decision-making process.

Part Eight

WRITING ACROSS THE CURRICULUM

Part Eight of the new edition offers five full chapters on writing in a wide range of academic disciplines. Chapter 35 includes a new discussion of collaborative writing. Chapter 36, which offers expanded treatment of writing about literature, now includes three student papers: literary analysis of a primary source; literary analysis using secondary sources; and analysis of a poem and a painting for a humanities course. Chapter 38 provides expanded coverage of research writing in the sciences, including a complete student paper using secondary sources—in addition to a student's report of empirical research.

WORD PROCESSING

The new edition includes an entirely new appendix on using a computer at each stage of the writing process.

PREFACE

TO THE INSTRUCTOR

In its Second Edition, the *Simon & Schuster Handbook for Writers* once again reflects my belief that students are empowered by knowledge. Access to information about writing processes and writing products greatly increases students' chances to fulfill their potential and to function effectively in academic, business, and personal settings. I have written this handbook to reach out to all college freshmen, students like those I have been teaching for over twenty years. Designed as a classroom text and as a comprehensive reference source for college and beyond, the *Handbook* offers uncomplicated but complete discussions, a supportive tone, and an easy-to-use format.

Scholarship and practice in the teaching of writing are quite sophisticated today, especially compared to fifty years ago, when handbooks for writers began to be widely used. The *Simon & Schuster Handbook for Writers,* Second Edition, combines the best of traditional and contemporary theory, and it draws on practices confirmed by research and experience. Taking my cue from the very gratifying enthusiasm of faculty across the nation who have used the First Edition of this handbook, I have retained all the innovations that set this book apart, and I have added some to make the book even more useful to faculty and to students.

- The *Handbook* starts with six chapters about the whole essay, thereby giving students a context for studying writing.
- It sets the scene with a short opening chapter about purposes and audiences for writing, thereby explaining the *why* of writing before turning to the writing process and to written products.
- It explains the entire writing process, emphasizing that the steps of the process are rarely linear and that the process varies with the writer, the topic, and the writing situation.

- It illustrates variations of writing purposes and processes with two student papers, one with an informative purpose and one with a persuasive purpose. The former is shown in three drafts with student and instructor comments.
- **New for this edition,** an expanded discussion of the reading process adds to the already thorough chapter on critical thinking.
- **New for this edition,** a separate chapter on writing argument offers many helpful charts and two new student essays, each taking a different position on the same topic.
- It provides a complete chapter on avoiding plagiarism, including detailed guidance for paraphrasing, summarizing, and quoting.
- **New for this edition,** coverage of research writing is expanded to four chapters to give students added resources. These chapters treat the research process from two related perspectives: the research process *and* the writing process. A new, separate chapter on documenting sources provides a free-standing "mini-handbook" about using MLA style and APA style. Its pivotal section, with red-tinted edges for instant identification, features a directory for easy location of examples.
- **New for this edition,** innovative Process Notes accompany the student research paper. They narrate the student's composing and decision-making processes, thus demonstrating that research writing calls for using critical thinking.
- **New for this edition,** coverage of writing across the curriculum is expanded to five chapters to give students additional information about the demands of writing in the different disciplines. Writing about literature receives more attention, including an added student paper of literary analysis using secondary sources.
- **New for this edition,** an appendix on writing with a computer explains the relation between word processing and the writing process.

To unify these necessarily varied materials and to establish a context in which students can make connections among elements, I am repeating and adding to the pedagogic innovations that characterized the First Edition of this handbook. My favorite addition is **Focus on Revising,** a unique feature that I created especially for the Second Edition. It applies concepts of revision covered early in the handbook to later chapters on grammar, language, and style. Focus on Revising directs students to reexamine their own writing, and then shows case studies of students revising. The case studies offer reinforcing opportunities to observe and participate in the revision process.

To enhance visual impact and to reinforce the conceptual framework of this handbook, a **four-color design** is new for the Second Edition. Burgundy remains the color for the main sections throughout the book and for the alphanumeric tabs on each page. Buff sets off all charts for easy location. Most important, blue is the color of revision (and also for occasional design elements). Blue is the color of all revised examples in explanations, and blue is the background shade for the Focus on Revising feature.

Charts in tinted boxes number over 160, a fifty percent increase from the First Edition. These charts present checklists, guidelines, sentence patterns, flow charts, and summaries. In this edition, an alphabetized list at the back of the book serves as a handy reference to the charts. Many faculty have confirmed my own happy experiences with my charts: Students often work their way into new information by first looking at a chart and then reading the section's explanation and examples; students use the charts as quick references when they want to refresh their memories; and faculty mark papers by directing students to consult particular charts.

Once again, 95 percent of the **exercises are in connected discourse** so that they replicate for students the processes of revising and editing. To keep the material fresh, almost half the exercises have new content. Rather than offering random examples in the explanations of grammar and style, I have composed **clusters of examples with related content** so that students can focus on the instruction and not be distracted by a new topic with each example. As before, I have drawn on **all subjects in the curriculum for the exercises and examples.**

Because student writers may sometimes feel overwhelmed by having to remember smaller matters in larger contexts, I introduced an ♣ ALERT ♣ system in the First Edition and have fine-tuned it in the Second Edition. In a discussion of coordination, for example, students find a brief Punctuation Alert that puts in context a particular function of a comma; similarly, students find a brief Capitalization Alert in a discussion of quotation marks. This system helps students see the interplay of elements, yet it does not take the place of the full chapters devoted to each element.

Also, I use a **degree symbol** (°) to signal that a technical term is defined in the *Handbook*'s Glossary of Terms. Inaugurated in the First Edition, this system proved very popular because it allows students to concentrate on the material at hand, with the assurance that they can easily locate a definition they might need. For the Second Edition, I have created a new type of **response symbols for instructors.** Complimentary Symbols, designed to facilitate praise of student writing, now coexist with the correction symbols on the inside back cover.

As in the First Edition, the Second Edition purposely seeks to be inclusive rather than exclusive of all people. Explanations, examples, and exercises do not use sexist language. Role stereotyping is avoided, and *man* is not used generically for the entire human race. An approximately equal number of male and female writers are represented in the examples by professional writers and by student writers. Also, the number of student examples of writing is up by fifty percent. Model papers now number twelve instead of eight. Many more model paragraphs and sentences are by students. And the two case studies in each of the new Focus on Revising sections are by students.

The **supplementary materials** for the First Edition of this handbook set a new standard. Prentice Hall has added even more for the Second Edition. New supplements include *Strategies for Teaching Writing* (by Linda Julian), filled with information about practical matters such as course design, syllabi, evaluation, conferencing, and more; *Rough Drafts* (by Kathleen Shine Cain), an innovative book containing many first drafts so that students can practice planning, revising, and editing; *Teaching Writing Across the Curriculum: A Guide for Instructors in All Disciplines* (by Ann O. Gebhard); specially prepared study guides for the CLAST and TASP exams, in Florida and Texas, respectively; the *Prentice Hall/Simon & Schuster Transparencies for Writers* (by Duncan Carter), a boxed set of one-, two-, and four-color acetates to coordinate with and supplement the *Handbook*; and a specially produced videotape on the writing process and research writing, called *Writing: A Video Guide*.

The package of materials updated for the Second Edition includes the groundbreaking *Annotated Instructor's Edition* (with Emily R. Gordon and Ann B. Dobie), which is now available in hardback and includes the pages of the student text accompanied by a wealth of resources in the extended margins. The volume starts with five specially commissioned bibliographic essays (two new and three updated for this edition), written by experts in their fields, that discuss the scholarly underpinnings I drew upon in writing this handbook. Also revised are the *Simon & Schuster Workbook for Writers,* Second Edition (co-authored by Emily R. Gordon and me), which is closely coordinated with the *Handbook;* the very popular, acclaimed software program *Blue Pencil,* available for IBM and Macintosh computers, that offers uniquely interactive editing exercises in many skills areas; a collection of diagnostic and competency tests available in print and software versions; and a book of 100 transparency masters that includes the major tinted charts from the Second Edition of the *Handbook*. For more information, contact your Prentice Hall representative or write the Marketing Manager for Humanities, Prentice Hall College Book Division, Englewood Cliffs, NJ 07632.

When I was a college student, handbooks for writers were not mentioned by my instructors, nor were they stocked by the campus bookstore. Questions about writing and written products nagged at me; so when I discovered handbooks in graduate school, I took to them instantly. I greatly enjoyed browsing through them, looking up what I wanted to know as well as happening upon new material. I dove enthusiastically into handbook-based class discussions concerning written conventions and writers' choices. I have written this *Simon & Schuster Handbook for Writers,* Second Edition, for this more enlightened time, when college faculty encourage their students to become active, independent learners who are empowered by knowledge.

Acknowledgments

Writing is an intensely private yet social activity, and I am deeply grateful to students, colleagues, friends, and family who sustained me with their valuable reactions and suggestions. Responsibility for whatever flaws remain in this book rests with me, not with the many people I thank here.

Emily R. Gordon, Hofstra University and Queensborough Community College, once again enriched my work with her intelligence and invaluable friendship; and she contributed importantly to the *Handbook* as co-author with me of the *Workbook*, as a contributing author with me to the *Annotated Instructor's Edition,* and as author of the testing package. Judith Stanford, Merrimack College, is a special friend and was an indispensable advisor from planning through early drafting. Linda Julian, Furman University, proved an astute researcher; and she wrote the excellent supplement *Strategies for Teaching.* Kathleen Shine Cain, Merrimack College, was a talented researcher and advisor during planning and early drafting; and she wrote the innovative supplement *Rough Drafts.* Pat Morgan, Louisiana State University, shared fully her especially clear vision of students and their writing. Rebecca Innocent, Southern Methodist University, provided fine creative direction in my development of the discussion on writing with computers.

I also want to acknowledge three groups of colleagues. For keeping detailed logs of their work with the first edition of my handbook, I thank these dedicated instructors: Mary Alice Hawkins, Columbia Basic College; Robert L. Jones, University of Southwestern Louisiana; Linda C. Pelzer, Ball State University; and Monte H. Prater, Tulsa Junior College. For participating in a thorough Reviewer Conference, I am very grateful to Judith Burnham, Tulsa Junior College; Russ

Meyer, University of Missouri; Careta Rose Russell, Florida Junior College; and Sandy Stephan, Youngstown State University. For their reviews and "conversations on paper" for the Second Edition, I warmly thank Margaret Berdine, Parkersburg Community College; Wendy Bishop, Florida State University; Alexandra d'Aste-Surcouf, Clark County Community College; Thomas Copeland, Youngstown State College; Kitty Chen Dean, Nassau Community College; Ralph G. Dille, University of Southern Colorado; Betty Engleberg, Stern College; Michael Flanigan, University of Oklahoma; Elizabeth Griffey, Florida Community College; Gloria John, Catonsville Community College; Larry Kelly, Widener University; Eo D. Luttrell, Youngstown State College; Lisa J. McClure, Southern Illinois University; Anne C. Meyers, DeVry Institute of Technology, Phoenix; Kenneth T. Rainey, Memphis State University; and Annie Stevens, Trevecca Nazarene College. For their reviews of the First Edition, I thank Gary Acton, Eastern Montana College; Bruce C. Appleby, Southern Illinois University; Dorothy Bankston, Louisiana State University; Vivian Brown, Laredo Junior College; Lennet Daigle, Georgia Southwestern College; Sally Geil, Brevard Community College; G. Dale Gleason, Hutchinson Community College; Mary Ellen Grasso, Broward Community College; Dorothy M. Guinn, Florida Atlantic University; Virginia C. Hinton, Kennesaw College; Albert M. Katz, University of Wisconsin; George E. Kennedy, Washington State University; Mark L. Knapp, University of Texas at Austin; Rosemary Lanshe, Broward Community College; Joyce M. Pair, DeKalb Community College; Edgar V. Roberts, Lehman College, CUNY; Barbara Saigo, University of Northern Iowa; Roy Saigo, University of Northern Iowa; Louise Z. Smith, University of Massachusetts at Boston; Barbara R. Stout, Montgomery College; Carolyn West, Daytona Beach Community College; and Stephen Worchel, Texas A&M University.

Other valued colleagues contributed importantly to the First Edition. I want to renew my thanks to Alan Adelson, City College, CUNY; Anne Agee, Anne Arundel Community College; Duncan Carter, Boston University; Karen Anderson, Midway College; Mary Kay Mahoney, University of Massachusetts at Boston; and Laura Zaidman, University of South Carolina at Sumter. Michael Goodman, Fairleigh Dickinson University, gave me skilled guidance as I prepared the chapter on business writing, a subject I have rarely taught. For their participation in the "Student Writing Project," whose purpose was to gather a national sample of student writing from which to select the student work in this book, I thank Vivian Brown, Laredo Community College; Jean M. English, Tallahassee Community College; Rodney F. Farnsworth, Indiana University-Purdue University; Christine Hult,

Utah State University; Joan Karbach, Indiana University-Purdue University; James E. Porter, Indiana University-Purdue University; John Reedy, State University of New York College at Buffalo; Elizabeth Wahlquist, Brigham Young University; Carolyn West, Daytona Beach Community College; and the entire English Department at Dean Junior College. Bonnie Sunstein, Rivier College, also contributed student writing to the pool. For their attending a Reviewer Conference while the manuscript of the First Edition was evolving, I owe a special debt to Kenneth Davis, University of Kentucky; Louis Emond, Dean Junior College; Jean M. English, Tallahassee Community College; Elizabeth Penfield, University of New Orleans; and Josephine Koster Tarvers, Rutgers University at New Brunswick.

The outstanding team at Prentice Hall understood my purpose and lent me vital support. Stephen K. Deitmer, Managing Editor of College Book Editorial Development, a man of uncommon grace and superb skill as a close reader, magically transformed my revision process for the Second Edition into an intellectually stimulating endeavor. Phil Miller, Humanities Editor in Chief, once again gave of his energy, optimism, and keen judgment. Virginia Rubens is every author's dream of a production editor: steady, skilled, wise, and gently tolerant of the foibles of writers. Jennifer Plane, Marketing Manager for Humanities, gave generously of her insight and enthusiasm. Others at Prentice Hall who mattered much: Ed Stanford, President of the College Division, inspired me to accept the invitation to write this handbook; Bud Therien, former Executive Editor for Humanities, helped me begin; Joyce Perkins, Senior Development Editor, encouraged me and strengthened the First Edition immeasurably; Nancy Perry, Executive Editor for English, helped me think and stay on track; Carol Carter, Director of College Marketing, kept me invigorated; and Jane Baumann, former Assistant to Phil Miller, agilely solved knotty problems.

Closer to home, friends and family surrounded me with the special moral support and patience that help a writer thrive: Irving Bieber, Kristen and Dan Black, Michael and Jayne Brookes, Rita and Hy Cohen, Ruth Davis of the *Journal of Basic Writing*, Elliott Goldhush, Myra Kogen, Jo Ann Lavery, Marilyn Maiz of the *Journal of Basic Writing*, Jerrold Nudelman, Claire Perlmutter, Betty Renshaw, Magdalena Rogalskaja, Avery and Jimmy Ryan, Shirley and Don Stearns, Marilyn Sternglass, Muriel Wolfe, and Gideon Zwas. My parents, Belle and Sidney Quitman, and my sister, Edith Klausner, gave fully of their love and enthusiasm. Above all, I am grateful to my husband, David Troyka, for his discerning reader's eye, for his unflagging belief in my work, and for the joy of each new day with him.

TO THE STUDENT

I hope that you find this handbook a companion and trusted friend. You, the student, were always on my mind as I wrote this book. I have asked students in my classes and in classes of colleagues to help me plan the Second Edition. My purpose is to give you full, direct, accessible answers to your questions; to offer you the chance to think about aspects of writing that might be new to you; and to provide you with a helpful, stimulating resource for your college years and afterwards.

This handbook offers you information about the *conventions* of written English so that you have a complete collection of rules and standard practices concerning grammar, punctuation, spelling, and mechanics. You will also find an honest presentation of the *choices* that all writers have when drafting essays and paragraphs, crafting sentences, and selecting words.

To gain access easily to the information in this handbook, you can use any of a number of systems. When you first have this book in hand, take an hour or so to get to know its format so that you can make it work for you.

- The **inside front cover** (sometimes called *front endpapers* or *chart of organization*) gives you an overview of the book's contents. A number/letter code next to each entry lists the location of the material in the book.

- The **table of contents** gives you more detail about the book's contents. The corresponding number/letter codes on the inside front covers and the tabs also appear here.

- The red **tabs** at the top corner of each page give the number/letter code of that section of the *Handbook*. Thumb through the corners of this handbook to locate material according to the number/letter code you want to find.

- The **index** provides a detailed listing of every topic covered in the book. It has been extensively class-tested to make sure that all terms and concepts in this book, along with alternate ways of naming them, are included. Each entry shows the number/letter code as well as the page number for the material.

- The list of **charts in tinted boxes,** starting on the page that faces the inside back cover of the book, alphabetically presents the topics in the 160 charts that include guidelines, checklists, summaries, sentence patterns, and other convenient capsules of information.

You might want to read the section in the Preface called "To The Instructor" to understand the rationale of this handbook. One feature discussed there that you might want to note in particular is my special use of the **degree symbol** (°). I hope it helps you feel more comfortable with the technical terms about grammar and writing that are necessary in a handbook. **A term is defined when it is introduced for the first time, and when it is used subsequently it is marked with a degree symbol to signal that its definition can be found in the Glossary of Grammatical and Selected Composition Terms toward the back of the book.** Whenever you encounter an unfamiliar term, you can feel confident that you can locate its meaning easily.

While you are gaining experience as a student writer, you are often likely to want to ask new questions. Sometimes an instructor will be available to answer them, but often the questions will occur to you when you are writing with no one around. I have, therefore, designed this handbook so that you can learn from it with your class as well as on your own. Throughout your college career and beyond, keep this handbook close by so that you can always look up what you need to know. It belongs in your permanent library, alongside your dictionary and other reference books. I welcome your reactions. Please feel free to write me about a small detail or a large issue. Use this address: Lynn Quitman Troyka, c/o English Editor, Prentice Hall, Englewood Cliffs, NJ 07632. I promise to answer.

LYNN QUITMAN TROYKA
Beechhurst, New York

CREDITS

One

WRITING
AN ESSAY

When you write an essay, you engage in a process. The parts of that process vary with the writer and the demands of the subject. Part One explains all aspects of the act of writing, and of thinking and reading in relation to writing, so that you can evolve your personal style of composing and thereby become an effective writer.

Thinking about Purposes and Audiences

TEACHING TIP

To start a course in composition, you might ask students to think of personal experiences that support the four claims about writing that open this chapter. To get things started, you might talk about a few of your experiences that support the claims. Do you recall a college paper you wrote? What do you remember about its contents and the experience of writing it? Have you found that writing about something makes you better able to teach it? Have you ever discovered what you wanted to say—or a connection among the ideas you already had in mind—as the words were formed "at the point of utterance"?

To encourage students to share their experiences, you might ask them first to jot down some notes and then participate in a discussion. If the group is large, you might divide it into small groups and give each group specific directions (written are more effective than oral) about what to discuss. The directions can have students discuss in turn each question listed in the paragraph above. You can appoint one person to serve as informal chair and another as secretary of the group. After a suitable amount of time, you might ask each group to report to the whole class.

Why write? In this age of telephones and tape recorders, television and film, computers and communication satellites, why should you bother with writing? The answer has overlapping parts, starting with the inner life of a writer and moving outward.

Writing is a way of thinking and learning. Writing gives you unique opportunities to explore ideas and acquire information. By writing, you come to know subjects well and make them your own. Even thirty years later, many people can recall details about the topics and content of essays they wrote in college, but far fewer people can recall specifics of a classroom lecture or a textbook chapter. Writing helps you learn and gain authority over knowledge. As you communicate your learning, you are also teaching. When you write for a reader, you play the role of a teacher, someone who knows the material sufficiently well to organize and present it clearly. Little is as hospitable to learning as the act of teaching.

Writing is a way of discovering. The act of writing allows you to make unexpected connections among ideas and language. As you write, thoughts emerge and interconnect in ways unavailable until the physical act of writing began. An authority on writing, James Britton, describes discovery in writing as "shaping at the point of utterance." Similarly, a well-known writer, E. M. Forster, talked about discovery during writing by asking, "How can I know what I mean until I've seen what I said?" You can expect many surprises of insight that come only when you write and rewrite, each time trying to get closer to what you want to say.

Writing creates reading. Writing creates a permanent, visible record of your ideas for others to read and ponder. Writing is a powerful means of communication, for reading informs and shapes human thought. In an open society, everyone is free to write and thereby to create reading for other people. For that freedom to be exercised, however, the ability to write cannot be concentrated in a few people. All of us need access to the power of the written word.

Writing ability is needed by educated people. Your skill with writing is often considered to reflect your level of education. College work demands that you write many different types of assignments. Most jobs in today's technological society require writing skill for preparing documents ranging from letters and memos to formal reports. Indeed, throughout your life, your writing will reveal your ability to think clearly and to use language effectively.

1a Understanding the elements of writing

What does writing do? Writing can be explained by its elements: *Writing is a way of communicating a message to a reader for a purpose.* Each word in this definition carries important meaning.

Communicating in writing means sending a message that has a destination. The historian Barbara Tuchman says that it takes two to complete the function of the written word.

The **message** of writing is its content. Whether the subject you write about is your choice or is assigned, you must transform it into a message worthy of communication. You can present your message in a variety of ways. Traditionally, forms for writing are divided into *narration, description, exposition,* and *argumentation.* In this handbook, narration and description are two among many strategies for developing ideas, explained in section 4c. Exposition and argumentation are the major **purposes** for academic writing, explained in section 1b. The final element of writing is the **reader,** or audience, explained in section 1c.

1b Understanding purposes for writing

Writing is often defined by its **purpose.** Writing purposes have to do with goals, sometimes referred to as *aims of writing* or *writing intentions.* Thinking about purposes for writing means thinking about the motivating forces that move people to write. As a student, you might assume that your only purpose for writing is to fulfill a class assignment. More is involved, however. Fulfilling an assignment is external to the content of the writing. As a writer, you need to think about writing purpose in the context of what you are writing and how you are writing it. The concept of purpose in writing refers to what the writing seeks to achieve. Major purposes for writing are shown in the chart on the next page.

BACKGROUND

A Theory of Discourse by James L. Kinneavy explores the fundamental purposes for which people use language. Kinneavy explains the centrality of the concept of *purpose* in writing:

> Purpose in discourse is all important. The aim of a discourse determines everything else in the process of discourse. "What" is talked about, the oral or written medium which is chosen, the words and grammatical patterns used—all of these are largely determined by the purpose of the discourse (48).

Kinneavy is enthusiastic about the potential for composition as a field of scholarship:

> It is the thesis of this work that the field of composition—or discourse as it will presently be termed—is a rich and fertile discipline with a worthy past which should be consulted before being consigned to oblivion, an exciting present, and a future that seems as limitless as either linguistics or literature (2).

Kinneavy's theories, and those of similar bent that focus on purposes for writing, are widely accepted today among scholars and teachers. Other modern influential theorists who concentrate on writers' purposes include the highly respected James Britton, who classifies purposes as *poetic, expressive,* and *transactional.*

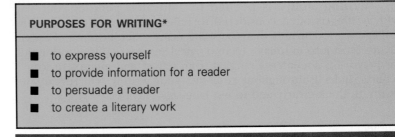

PURPOSES FOR WRITING*

- to express yourself
- to provide information for a reader
- to persuade a reader
- to create a literary work

The purposes of writing *to express yourself* and *to create a literary work* contribute importantly to human thought and culture. This handbook, however, concentrates on the two purposes most prominent and practical in your academic life: *to inform a reader* and *to persuade a reader.*

1 Writing to inform a reader

Informative writing seeks to give information and, frequently, to explain it. This writing is known also as **expository writing** because it expounds on, or sets forth, ideas and facts. *Informative writing focuses on the subject being discussed.* (In contrast, persuasive writing focuses on the reader, whom the writer wants to influence.) Informative writing includes reports of observations, ideas, scientific data, facts, statistics. It can be found in textbooks, encyclopedias, technical and business reports, books of nonfiction, newspapers, and magazines.

When you write exposition, you present information. You are expected to offer that information with a minimum of bias, for you are aiming to educate, not persuade. Like all effective teachers, you need to present the information completely and clearly. The material has to be accurate. The material should be verifiable by additional reading, talking with others, or personal experience. For example, consider this passage that aims to inform the reader.

> In 1914 in what is now Addo Park in South Africa, a hunter by the name of Pretorius was asked to exterminate a herd of 140 elephants. He killed all but 20, and those survivors became so cunning at evading him that he was forced to abandon the hunt. The area became a preserve in 1930, and the elephants have been

---

*Adapted from the ideas of James L. Kinneavy, a modern rhetorician, discussed in *A Theory of Discourse.* 1971; New York: Norton, 1980.

protected ever since. Nevertheless, elephants now four generations removed from those Pretorius hunted remain shy and strangely nocturnal. Young elephants evidently learn from the adults' trumpeting alarm calls to avoid humans.

—CAROL GRANT GOULD, "Out of the Mouths of Beasts"

This passage is successful because it *communicates* (transmits) a *message* (about young elephants learning to avoid humans) to a *reader* (the general reading public who might be interested in the subject) for a *purpose* (to inform). In this passage, the writer's last sentence states the main idea. Each sentence before the last offers information that builds support for the main idea.

CHECKLIST FOR INFORMATIVE WRITING

1. Is its major focus the subject being discussed?
2. Is its primary purpose to inform rather than persuade?
3. Is its information complete and accurate?
4. Can its information be verified?
5. Is its information arranged for clarity?
6. Is it interesting to read?

---

2 | **Writing to persuade a reader**

Persuasive writing seeks to convince the reader about a matter of opinion. This writing is sometimes called **argumentative** because it argues a position.

As a writer of persuasion, you deal with the debatable, that which has other sides to it. *Persuasive writing focuses on the reader, whom the writer wants to influence.* (In contrast, informative writing focuses on the subject being discussed.) Persuasive writing seeks to change the reader's mind, to bring the reader's point of view closer to the writer's. Examples of persuasive writing include editorials, letters to the editor, reviews, sermons, business or research proposals, opinion essays in magazines, and books that argue a point of view.

To be persuasive, you cannot merely state an opinion. You must offer convincing support for your point of view. To argue well, your reasoning must be logical and sensible (see Chapter 6) and

BACKGROUND

Writing is sometimes classified according to four modes of discourse: *narration, description, exposition,* and *argumentation.* These modes describe the *what* of writing. They describe characteristics that written products seem to feature, although much overlap exists. A writer can narrate an incident in the service of arguing an opinion; a writer can describe a scene in the service of offering information.

This handbook starts with the *why* of writing. Thus it begins with *purposes* for writing. Purposes are familiar territory for instructors used to modes, because two of the modes are purposes: people write for the purpose of informing (expositing) and for the purpose of persuading (arguing). Purposes are based on the notion that people write for a reason; most college writing is done either to inform or to persuade. Research shows that few writers sit down and say to themselves, "I am going to write a comparison and contrast"; instead they say to themselves, "I want to give my readers some information" or "I want to convince my readers to change their minds." In the service of those purposes, writers compare and contrast, narrate, describe, draw analogy, and so forth.

Narration and description are discussed fully in Chapter 4, "Writing Paragraphs," along with many other writing strategies for idea development, including process, definition, comparison and contrast, cause-and-effect relationship, and analogy.

5

clearly arranged. For example, consider this passage of persuasive writing.

> The search for some biological basis for math ability or disability is fraught with logical and experimental difficulties. Since not all math under-achievers are women, and not all women are mathematics-avoidant, poor performance in math is unlikely to be due to some genetic or hormonal difference between the sexes. Moreover, no amount of research so far has unearthed a "mathematical competency" in some tangible, measurable substance in the body. Since "masculinity" cannot be injected into women to test whether or not it improves their mathematics, the theories that attribute such ability to genes or hormones must depend for their proof on circumstantial evidence. So long as about 7 percent of the Ph.D.'s in mathematics are earned by women, we have to conclude either that these women have genes, hormones, and brain organization different from those of the rest of us, or that certain positive experiences in their lives have largely undone the negative fact that they are female, or both.
>
> —SHEILA TOBIAS, *Overcoming Math Anxiety*

This passage is successful because it sends a *message* (about math ability and disability) to a *reader* (to a person who thinks that math ability or disability has a biological basis) for a *purpose* (to persuade a reader that math ability or disability is not related to gender). The writer's first sentence summarizes the point of view that she argues in the rest of the paragraph. Each sentence after the first sentence offers a logical argument in support of the writer's assertion. The aim of each sentence is to convince the reader to agree with the writer's point of view. Not all readers might agree with the writer's assertion, but the writer has given a sufficient number of logical reasons to support her point of view adequately.

CHECKLIST FOR PERSUASIVE WRITING

1. Is its major focus the reader?
2. Is its primary purpose to convince rather than inform?
3. Does it offer information or reasons to support its point of view?
4. Is its point of view based on sound reasoning and logic?
5. Are the points of its argument arranged for clarity?
6. Does it motivate the reader to action or otherwise evoke the intended response?

QUOTATION ABOUT WRITING

[Writing is] the sense of being in contact with people who are part of a particular audience that really makes a difference to me in writing.

—Sherley Anne Williams

QUOTATION ABOUT WRITING

Writing is making sense of life.

—Nadine Gordimer

QUOTATION ABOUT WRITING

Writing is a dog's life, but the only life worth living.

—Gustave Flaubert

QUOTATION ABOUT WRITING

The desire to write grows with writing.

—Erasmus

QUOTATION ABOUT WRITING

I write books to find out about things.

—Rebecca West

1b

EXERCISE 1

For each paragraph, decide if the dominant purpose is *informative* or *persuasive*. Then, answer the questions in the appropriate checklist in relation to the paragraph, and explain your answers.

A.   Trees are living archives, carrying within their structure a record not only of their age but also of precipitation and temperature for each year in which a ring was formed. The record might also include the marks of forest fires, early frosts and, incorporated into the wood itself, chemical elements the tree removed from its environment. Thus, if we only knew how to unlock its secrets, a tree could tell us a great deal about what was happening in its neighborhood from the time of its beginning. Trees can tell us what was happening before written records became available. They also have a great deal to tell us about our future. The records of past climate that they contain can help us to understand the natural forces that produce our weather, and this, in turn, can help us plan.

—JAMES S. TREFIL, "Concentric Clues From Growth Rings Unlock the Past"

B.   Come forward and turn off your set. When the die-out dot appears, get up and take a walk to the library and get a book. Or turn to your husband and wife and surprise them with a conversation. Or call a neighbor you haven't spoken with in months. Write a letter to a friend who has lost track of you. Turn off your set now. When we devise some worthwhile programing, we'll be back on the air. Meanwhile, you'll be missing almost nothing.

—COLMAN McCARTHY, "Ousting the Stranger from the House"

C.   The PLOMS attitude, better known as the "Poor Little Old Me Syndrome," reflects selfishness and a need for pity. This blasé state haunts many students, and it often hinders their academic and social productivity. A new day does not bring joy to their lives; on the contrary, it brings only disappointments. Opportunities for interaction with peers do not inspire these gloomy individuals because they pretend that they do not care about anyone's acceptance. They isolate themselves from others, and they have low commitment to, or interest in, group activities. Seclusion becomes their best friend. Unfortunately, they never give anyone else a chance to bring happiness into their lives.

—DEBORAH LAMB, student

D.   During the past generation, the amount of time devoted to historical studies in American public schools has steadily decreased. About twenty-five years ago, most public high-school youths studied

ANSWERS: EXERCISE 1

A. Dominant purpose is informative. It meets the criteria.

B. Dominant purpose is persuasive. It meets the criteria.

C. Dominant purpose is persuasive. It meets the criteria.

D. Dominant purpose is informative. It meets the criteria.

E. Dominant purpose is persuasive. It meets the criteria.

one year of world history and one of American history, but today, most study only one year of ours. In contrast, the state schools of many other Western nations require the subject to be studied almost every year. In France, for example, all students, not just the college-bound, follow a carefully sequenced program of history, civics and geography every year from the seventh grade through the twelfth grade.

—DIANE RAVITCH, "Decline and Fall of Teaching History"

E.   For the past few years, our city has been in a downward slump, especially in terms of its recreational facilities and economy. Our parks and buildings have been the target of considerable vandalism. The lake, which has been sorrowfully neglected, could be improved with more trees, better roads, and additional security. Our unemployment is the highest in the state and our economy the worst. Both situations could be improved by attracting new industries to our city. Reclaiming our land by planting orange trees, onions, and melons would help the farm economy. Our city could be one of the best places to live if it would employ its available work force to effect these kinds of improvements.

—GERARDO ANTONIO GARZA, student

ANSWERS: EXERCISE 2

A. Answers will vary. Samples have to come from a single issue of a newspaper. Editorials, essays, letters to the editor, and reviews can serve as examples of writing with the dominant purpose of being persuasive. News reports can serve as examples of informative writing.

B. Answers will vary, as for above.

EXERCISE 2

A.   In a single issue of a newspaper, find one informative article and one persuasive article. Explain why you identify them as you do. Next, for each article, go back to the checklist above that corresponds to the purpose you have identified, and answer the questions on the checklist. Explain each answer.

B.   Repeat this process with a magazine.

ANSWERS: EXERCISE 3

For each topic the student should write one paragraph (or more, according to how you have assigned the exercise) with an informative purpose and one paragraph with a persuasive purpose. The student should also be prepared to discuss (orally or in writing, according to your assignment) the differences in the two treatments of the same topic.

EXERCISE 3

Assume that you have to write on each of these topics twice, once to inform your reader and once to persuade your reader. Be prepared to discuss how your two treatments of each topic would differ.

1.   Diets
2.   Canada
3.   Garbage
4.   Résumés
5.   Emily Dickinson

7.   Automobile insurance
7.   Forest fires
8.   Video cassette recorders (VCR's)
9.   Beach erosion
10. Weight-training

1c Understanding audiences for writing

Good writing is often judged by its ability to reach its intended **audience.** To be effective, informative and persuasive writing (1b) need to be geared to the fact that someone is "out there" to receive the communication. If you write without considering your readers, you risk communicating only with yourself.

Experienced writers think about the background of their audience as they write to inform or to persuade their readers. For example, a sales report filled with technical language assumes that its readers know the specialized vocabulary. The general reading public would, of course, have trouble understanding such a report. But if the material were rewritten without technical terms, general readers could understand it.

As a writer for an audience, you need to be sensitive to your readers' beliefs and concerns. For example, in writing meant to persuade people to vote for a particular candidate, if you imply disrespect for people who stay home and raise children, you risk losing votes of many homemakers and their spouses. Or, if you want to persuade lawmakers that homemakers should be allowed to draw

---

CHECKLIST OF AUDIENCE CHARACTERISTICS

WHO ARE THEY?

age/sex/education?

ethnic background/political philosophy/religious beliefs?

role(s): student/veteran/parent/wage earner/voter/other?

employment/economic status?

interests/hobbies?

WHAT INFORMATION DO THEY HAVE?

level of education?

experience with reading academic or business writing?

amount of general knowledge about the subject?

amount of specialized knowledge about the subject?

preconceptions brought to the material?

TEACHING TIP

You might find that some students feel inhibited in their writing when they have to think about an audience for their writing. Studies show that some students misunderstand the concept of audience. They think it means that writers should act as if someone is constantly looking over their shoulders. Other students have trouble with the concept of audience because they think that they can never say something that would be unpopular with their audience. Some students might not want to admit these or other misunderstandings of the concept, so you might want to clear up the matter without asking anyone to give you their negative impressions. Once you start talking about the subject, you will often find that the students start chiming in to help you get at their concerns.

The concept of audience is meant to help writers get their message across. The concept is supposed to facilitate, not block. A writer is not expected to tell readers what they want to hear even if the writer disagrees with the readers. A writer is, however, expected to choose words the readers know and to use a tone suitable to the occasion. As writer Gary Provost says in "How to Make the Reader Like You" published in *Writer's Digest* in September 1986:

> You need some sense of your reader's knowledge. If you're writing a report for oceanographers, mention the *dorsal carapace* and the *chelipeds* if you must, but if you're writing a brochure for visitors to a public aquarium, please write *shell* and *claws*. Remember that any time, you don't have your entire vocabulary to work with. You have only that portion of your vocabulary that you share with the readers (37–38).

from the Social Security system, you would need to address some of the lawmakers' practical concerns, such as the impact of your proposal on the federal budget.

The more explicit information that you have about your audience, the better you can think about how to reach it. Often, of course, you can only guess at the details. The checklist on the previous page can help you think about possible characteristics of your audience. If you know about or can reasonably assume even a few characteristics, your chances of reaching your audience improve.

1   Understanding the general reading public

The **general reading public** is educated, sometimes less and sometimes more than you. Its members are experienced readers, people who frequently read newspapers, magazines, and books. These readers often have some general information about the subject you are dealing with, but they enjoy a chance to learn something new or see something from a different perspective.

The general reading public expects you to know how to reach them. For example, the general reader expects material to be clear and to be free of advanced technical information. Equally important, the general reading public expects to be treated respectfully. As experienced readers, they are sensitive to your **tone**—the way what you say reflects your attitude toward the subject and the audience. If the tone implies you feel superior to your audience, your material will be condescending and distasteful. Similarly, if your tone hints that you are uninformed or unsure, readers will lose confidence in your material. Tone is created largely by word choice (see Chapter 21). Although the general reading public enjoys lively language, it is jarred by an overly informal tone in the middle of a serious presentation of informative or persuasive writing. For example, in a newspaper report about the results of an election, you would not refer to the loser or winner as *guy* or *gal,* no matter how relaxed the candidate's demeanor. Likewise, in the middle of a serious critique, using *pretty* as a synonym for *very* or *fairly* would be out of place (as in "The weak script was helped by some pretty good acting"). An artificial tone also can drive away your readers (see 21d). Do not, for example, use pretentious phrases such as "the aforementioned occurrence that transpired" when you mean "the event." Also, if your language is biased or slanted (see 21a), your tone will seem underhanded, and your readers will distrust what you say. For more about the writer's role and tone, see 2e-3.

1c

2 Understanding your instructor as a reader

When you write for a class assignment, your audience will almost certainly be your **instructor.** Sometimes, especially when you are planning or revising your work, your instructor might want other students in your class to collaborate as an audience. In most cases, your final audience remains your instructor.

Your instructor is a member of the general reading public and also someone who recognizes that you are an apprentice. Your instructor knows that few students are experienced writers or complete experts on their subjects. Still, your instructor always expects your writing to reflect that you took time to learn the material thoroughly and to write about it well. In part, therefore, an instructor is a *judge,* someone to whom you must demonstrate that you are doing your best. Instructors are very experienced readers who can quickly recognize a minimal effort or a negative attitude (as when a paper carries a tone that suggests "Tell me what you want and I'll give it to you").

Inexperienced writers sometimes wrongly assume that instructors will fill in mentally what is missing on the page. Instructors expect what they read to include everything that the writer wants to say or imply. Do not leave out material. Even if you write immediately after your instructor has heard you give an oral report on the same subject, write as if no one is aware of what you know.

Your instructor is also an *academic,* a member of a group whose professional lives center on intellectual endeavors. You must, therefore, write within the constraints of academic writing. For example, if you are told to write on a topic of your choice, you definitely do not have total freedom to choose. Your topic must have some intrinsic intellectual interest. For example, an essay should not merely give directions on how to cut a wedding cake or use an eraser.

3 Understanding specialists as readers

Specialists are members of the general reading public who have expert knowledge on specific subjects. In writing for specialists, you are expected to know the specialty and also to realize that your readers have advanced expertise.

Specialized readers often share not only knowledge but also assumptions, interests, and beliefs. For example, they may be mem-

---

QUOTATION ABOUT WRITING

First and foremost I write for myself. Writing has been for a long time my major tool for self-instruction and self-development.

—Toni Cade Bambara

QUOTATION ABOUT WRITING

I shall live badly if I do not write, and I shall write badly if I do not live.

—Françoise Sagan

QUOTATION ABOUT WRITING

Many people who want to be writers don't really want to be writers. They want to *have been* writers. They wish they had a book in print.

—James Michener

QUOTATION ABOUT WRITING

The role of writers is not to say what we can all say, but what we are unable to say.

—Anaïs Nin

QUOTATION ABOUT WRITING

Writing is the hardest work in the world not involving heavy lifting.

—Pete Hamill

QUOTATION ABOUT WRITING

I started writing because of a terrible feeling of powerlessness: I felt I was drifting and obscure, and I rebelled against that. I didn't see what I could do to change my condition. I wanted to control rather than be controlled, to ordain rather than be ordained, and to relegate rather than be relegated.

—Anita Brookner

bers of a club that concentrates on a hobby, such as amateur astronomy or orchid raising. They may have similar backgrounds, such as having immigrated from another country or having fought in a particular war. They may have similar views on matters related to religion and politics. When you write for readers who share specialized knowledge, you have to balance the necessity to be thorough with the demand not to go into too much detail about technical terms and special references.

ALTERNATE EXERCISE

Ask students to write three letters: one to a close friend, a second to their parents, and the third to the class. In each they are to recount an experience they had at an imaginary party when someone they knew (perhaps the person they went to the party with) embarrassed them in some way. In writing groups they can read the letters, discussing the differences in them that result from the different readers to whom they were written.

EXERCISE 4

Each of these passages was written for a general reading audience. Read each paragraph and decide (a) if it has the right tone for academic writing and (b) if it assumes knowledge that only a specialist would have.

A.   Before one can begin to solve the problem of poor intonation, the inability to stay on pitch while singing, one must understand the probable causes of poor intonation. Excessive heat in the rehearsal room can distract the singers since drowsiness drains the body of its energy. A more likely cause is poor posture. The body must be erect, yet comfortable for one to sing with an accurate tone. A related problem, and the most common cause of poor intonation, is a lack of good breath support.

—CHRISTOPHER BROWN, student

B.   Biology may not be destiny, but genes apparently have a far greater influence on human behavior than is commonly thought. Similarities ranging from phobias to hobbies to bodily gestures are being found in pairs of twins separated at birth. Many of these behaviors are "things you would never think of looking at if you were going to study the genetics of behavior," says psychologist Thomas J. Bouchard, Jr., director of the Minnesota Center for Twin and Adoption Research at the University of Minnesota. Bouchard reports that so far, exhaustive psychological tests and questionnaires have been completed with approximately 50 pairs of identical twins reared apart, 25 pairs of fraternal twins reared apart and comparison groups of twins reared together. "We were amazed at the similarity in posture and expressive style," says Bouchard. "It's probably the feature of the study that's grabbed us the most." Twins tend to have similar mannerisms, gestures, speed and tempo in talking, habits, and jokes.

—CONSTANCE HOLDEN, "Genes and Behavior: A Twin Legacy"

C.   Without mucus, a slug would quickly be invaded by a host of microbial denizens and die. It would also be immobile, for slugs require mucus underfoot on which to crawl. Secreted from the pedal gland, located just beneath the head, the mucus flows down to the slug's single muscular foot. Like a miniature asphalt machine, the slug first lays its road and then, with wavelike motions of its foot, moves over it. As the mucous "road" dries, it becomes a silvery map of a slug's travels.

SCOTT MCCREDIE, "They're Still Slimy, But Naked Snails Are Finding New Friends"

D.   The consumer of electricity usually accepts the fact that power outages frequently occur during wind and thunderstorms. However, when outages occur during calm and dry weather, the consumer becomes upset and blames the power company. In reality, most non-weather-related outages occur either because of circumstances beyond the control of the power company or in order to insure the safety of its workers. Squirrels and other animals with the ability to reach the top of power poles cause outages by unknowingly completing a circuit between a hot wire and a ground wire, an act which can knock out power to many houses. Occasionally, rehabilitating old lines to decrease future outages forces the power company to kill the lines temporarily to insure safety. And, a power company that purchases its power from larger companies often loses power because of trouble on the other company's line.

—BURL CARRAWAY, student

E.   There is for many young girls another less tangible factor in the sequence of events leading to parenthood. It is a sense of fatalism, passivity, even pleasure at the prospect of motherhood—especially among the poor. For young girls trapped in poverty, pregnancy becomes a means of fulfillment. In the largely white community of North Adams, Massachusetts, an old mill town where unemployment has been high, or in the mostly white, down-at-the-heels southern counties of Illinois, underlying reasons for the high rate of unwed teenage pregnancies are no different from those in urban ghettos: lack of opportunity, absence of interesting alternatives to childbearing.

—CLAUDIA WALLIS, "The Tragic Costs of Teenage Pregnancy"

ANSWERS: EXERCISE 4

A. **(a)** The tone is right for academic writing.
   (b) The material does not assume a specialized reader.

B. **(a)** The tone is right for academic writing.
   (b) The material does not assume a specialized reader.

C. **(a)** The tone is right for academic writing.
   (b) The material assumes a specialized reader who would be familiar with words such as *microbial, mucus, pedal,* and *gland.*

D. **(a)** The tone is right for academic writing.
   (b) The material assumes a small amount of specialized knowledge, though the gist of the message can be understood from the context. Specialized words include *outrage, hot wire,* and *ground wire.*

E. **(a)** The tone is right for academic writing.
   (b) The material does not assume a specialized reader.

2 Planning and Shaping

Many people assume that a real writer can pick up a pen (or sit at a typewriter or word processor) and magically write a finished product, word by perfect word. Experienced writers know better. They know that **writing is a process,** a series of activities that start the moment they begin thinking about a subject and end when they complete a final draft. Experienced writers know, also, that good writing is rewriting. Their drafts are filled with additions, deletions, rearrangements, and rewordings.

For example, on the next page you can see how the paragraph you just read was reworked into final form. Notice that two sentences were dropped, two sentences were combined, one sentence was added, and various words were dropped, changed, or added. Such activities are typical of writing.

2a Understanding the writing process

Writing is an ongoing process of considering alternatives and making choices. The better you understand the writing process, the better you will write and the more you can enjoy writing. For the sake of explanation, the parts of the writing process are discussed separately in this chapter. In real life, you will find that the steps overlap, looping back and forth as each piece of writing evolves.

Understanding writing as a multistage process allows you to work efficiently, concentrating on one activity at a time rather than trying to juggle all of the facets of a writing project simultaneously. An overview of the steps in the writing process is given in the chart on the opposite page.

Writers who like to visualize their work might prefer to see the writing process represented pictorially (see diagram on page 16). A simple straight line would not be adequate because it would exclude the recursive nature of writing. The arrows on the diagram imply movement. Planning is not over when drafting begins, drafting is not *plan* 2a

~~Chapter One discusses what writing is.~~ ~~This chapter~~

~~explains how writing happens.~~ Many people assume that a real

      pick up a pen

writer can ˄ ~~put pen to paper~~ (or sit at ~~the keyboard of~~ a

         magically—a

typewriter or word processor) and ˄ write finished product, *word*

by perfect word.

˄ Experienced writers ~~all~~ know better. They know that writing

is a process, ~~Writing is~~ a series of activities that start

    they begin

the moment ˄ thinking about a subject ~~begins~~ and end when they

complete ~~the~~ a

˄ final draft. ~~is complete.~~ Experienced writers know, also,

that good writing is rewriting. *Their drafts are filled with*

additions, deletions, rearrangements, and rewordings.

Draft and Revision of Opening Paragraph in Chapter 2 by Lynn Troyka

AN OVERVIEW OF THE WRITING PROCESS

Planning calls for you to gather ideas and think about a focus.

Shaping calls for you to consider ways to organize your material.

Drafting calls for you to write your ideas in sentences and paragraphs.

Revising calls for you to evaluate your draft and, based on your decisions, rewrite it by adding, cutting, replacing, moving—and often totally recasting material.

Editing calls for you to check the technical correctness of your grammar, spelling, punctuation, and mechanics.

Proofreading calls for you to read your final copy for typing errors or handwriting legibility.

BACKGROUND

On several occasions (e.g., "Understanding Composing," *CCC* 31 [December 1980], 363–69), Sondra Perl has described the writing process as recursive, the several stages of planning, drafting, and revising occurring not in a straight, linear fashion, but doubling back on each other as the work takes shape. In the *New York University Education Quarterly* (1979), p. 18, she refers to the process as "retrospective structuring." "Composing," she writes, "does not occur in a straightforward, linear fashion. The process is one of accumulating discrete words or phrases down on the paper and then working from these bits to reflect upon, structure, and then further develop what one means to say." The reaching back and sensing forward have what she describes as "a clarifying effect," the written form serving, as it does, as a window on the intended meaning.

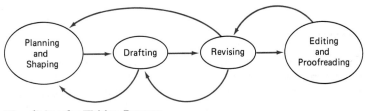

Visualizing the Writing Process

necessarily over merely because the major activity shifts to revision, and editing sometimes inspires writers to see the need for additional revising—and perhaps some new planning.

As you work with the writing process, rest assured that there is no *one* way to write. When you start, allow yourself to move through each stage of the writing process and see what is involved. Then as you gain experience, begin to observe what works best for you. After you master the differences that separate planning from shaping, drafting from revising, and editing from proofreading, you might want to experiment a little. For example, some people write a "discovery" draft to see what emerges before they begin shaping. Some writers outline immediately and use planning techniques to flesh out points on the outline. Many writers find during revising that they need more ideas, so they use planning techniques once again. Still other writers edit during revision because a grammar or spelling error keeps getting in the way.

Most writers struggle some of the time with ideas that are difficult to express, sentences that will not take shape, and words that are not precise. Do not be impatient with yourself and do not get discouraged. Writing takes time. The more you write, the easier it will be, but remember that experienced writers know that writing never happens magically.

An aside about the words used to discuss writing: Instructors refer to written products in different ways. Often the words are used interchangeably, but sometimes they have specific meanings for specific instructors. Listen closely and ask if you are unsure of what you hear. For example, the words *essay, theme,* and *composition* usually—but not always—refer to writing that runs from about 500 to 1,000 words. This handbook uses *essay.* The words *report* and *project* usually mean writing that draws on outside sources. The word *paper* can mean anything from a few paragraphs to a long and detailed report of a complex research project. This handbook uses *paper* to refer to research writing.

QUOTATION ABOUT WRITING

I don't know anything about inspiration because I don't know what inspiration is; I've heard about it, but I never saw it.

—William Faulkner

plan **2b**

2b Thinking about writing

Writing begins with thinking. When you are given a writing assignment, you are immediately cast into a **writing situation.** The decisions you make as you write an essay depend on the particulars of each writing situation: topic, purpose, audience, and special requirements.

AN OVERVIEW OF THE WRITING SITUATION

1. The topic
2. The purpose
3. The audience
4. The special requirements

Underlying all aspects of the writing situation is the **topic.** If you are supposed to choose your own topic or narrow an assigned general topic, you need to keep in mind the constraints of academic writing. If the topic is assigned, you have to write without going off the track. No matter what the topic, *you* are the starting place for your writing. You must draw upon yourself as a source. All writers depend on their accumulated experience and education as they write. Whatever they have seen, heard, read, and even dreamed contributes to their fund of ideas and knowledge. No matter how much you have learned from your reading, going to plays and movies, and watching television, the starting point for your writing is always you, the writer. As you think through and gather ideas (2d) for your topic, your task is to establish a *focus,* or a point of view, about the topic and *support* for that focus.

The writing situation includes the **purpose** for your writing. In college, the major purposes for writing are *to inform* and *to persuade,* as explained fully in 1b. Effective informative and persuasive writing succeed in part because they reflect a clear sense of purpose. Some writing assignments include or clearly imply a statement of purpose. For example, your purpose is informative if you are asked to write about the dangers of smoking. On the other hand, your purpose is persuasive if your assignment calls for an argument against smoking. Many assignments, however, do not stipulate the writing purpose. In such cases, one of your tasks is to choose either an

BACKGROUND

Writers, both amateurs and professionals, tend to devise rituals that help them begin and carry out a piece of writing. Some of them are elaborate, some of them relatively simple. They are identifiable by the fact that they are repeated actions that seem to be irrelevant to the task at hand but that are in some way helpful to the writer looking for ideas and ways to express them. Some are silly, such as using the same coffee mug each time one writes, or illogical, such as sweeping the front walk before getting started, but the fact is that they are effective in helping a writer make the transition from some other activity to that of composition.

Writers who are in the process of devising writing rituals can make their individual habits more productive by being aware of which steps are helpful and which are not. They can begin by asking themselves questions about where, when, and with what they write. Where do they get the most work done? Does it afford them access to materials they need? Is it free from interruptions? Does it make them comfortable but not too relaxed? Can they see well? Do they have room to spread out notes and books? What time of day or night do they usually do their writing? Are they alert and energetic at that time? Does it give them a block of time in which to work? Do they use typewriter? A legal pad? A word processor? A spiral notebook? What objects, environments, or activities that are not directly connected with writing provide a sense of well-being during the process? The answers will vary from one writer to another, but for best results the process should remain fairly constant with the individual.

Rituals are habits that provide structure—reassurance that the writer has done a task this way once before. With each repetition they become more comfortable, making the writer feel more competent, more at home with the act of writing.

BACKGROUND

In his article "To Be Read" (*English Journal,* 57 [May 1968], 686–92); rpt. *Rhetoric and Composition: A Sourcebook for Teachers,* ed. Richard L. Graves, pp. 51–59), Ken Macrorie discusses, among other issues, ways to help students arrive at a topic worth their effort. He begins by asking them for free writing that strives to be honest (in contrast to phony), followed by discussion of strong passages that seem to speak the truth, a slowly developing focus on one subject, an effort to tighten the expression, and then an extension of the discussion to a full-length writing. By acting as editor instead of "grader" or "corrector," the teacher establishes a situation closer to that in which "real" writing takes place. Macrorie describes traditional "themes," papers assigned by teachers on topics that have no context, as papers that are "not meant to be *read,* but *corrected.*"

informative or persuasive purpose based on the topic, what you want to say about it (often referred to as the *focus*), and how you develop what you want to say.

The **audience** for your writing is also part of the writing situation. For college writing, your audience is primarily—though not necessarily exclusively—your instructor. Your instructor is both a member of the general reading public and an academic. Your writing needs to be sensitive to such backgrounds, as explained fully in 1c. Sometimes a writing assignment names a very specific audience, such as the head of a major corporation or veterans who have served in Vietnam. These audiences are specialists, people who have more technical knowledge than does the general reading public. You have to write to their level. Sometimes an assignment stipulates that the writing will be read by other students in the class. Students in such situations serve as surrogate instructors, so you are expected to write with the same tone and level of information as you would for your instructor alone.

Special requirements influence every writing situation. These include the time allotted for the assignment, the expected length of the writing, and other practical constraints. If an assignment includes a word count, you have to take it into consideration when you make decisions about topic, purpose, and audience. If an assignment is due in one week, you have to expect that your instructor wants writing that shows more than one day's work. If research is required, you have to build time for it into your schedule.

Your assignment is a key resource as you write. Reread it as you work to make sure you have not lost track of what you are expected to do. Throughout this chapter and the next, you will see the work of two students, Tara Foster and Gary Lee Houseman.

Tara Foster was given this assignment: Write an essay of 500 to 700 words that discusses any important problem facing adult men and women today. Your first and second drafts are due in one week. I will read your second draft as an "essay in progress" and will make comments to help you toward a third draft. Your third draft is due one week after I hand back your second draft.

Gary Lee Houseman was given this assignment: Write a 1,000-word essay in which you argue against some aspect of the destruction of our environment. Your final draft is due in two weeks, but bring your earlier drafts to class for possible discussion.

---

plan **2c**

In analyzing her writing situation, Foster saw that the assignment specified the special requirements of length and time. She decided that her audience would be her instructor. She tentatively chose an informative purpose, knowing that as she got further into planning she might change her mind. Her decision process about the topic is also discussed in 2c.

In analyzing his writing situation, Houseman saw that the assignment told him about length, time, and purpose. He realized that the due date of two weeks might imply that research was required, so he asked his instructor. He was told not to use outside sources but to draw on his own fund of knowledge and his personal focus—point of view—about the subject. Once Houseman knew that, he decided that his audience would be his instructor. His decision process about his topic is also discussed in 2c.

EXERCISE 1

For each assignment listed below, answer these questions: (a) Is its purpose to inform or to persuade? (b) Is the audience the general reading public or specialists? (c) What special requirements of length and time are stated or implied?

1. *Biology:* You have twenty minutes to list and explain three ways that the circulatory system contributes to homeostasis in the human body.
2. *English:* Write a 500- to 700-word essay arguing for or against tougher academic requirements for student athletes. This assignment is due in one week.
3. *Political Science:* Write a 1,000-word essay about television's impact on elections.
4. *English:* Write a 300-word editorial for the student newspaper praising or criticizing the college's library. Draw on your personal experience. Also, interview at least one member of the library staff for his or her reaction to your point of view.
5. *Art:* Write a one-paragraph summary of the difference between a wide-angle lens and a telephoto lens.

2c Choosing a topic for writing

Choosing a topic calls for using good judgment and making sound decisions. Experienced writers know that the quality of their writing depends on how they handle a topic. You should, therefore, think through a topic before you rush in and get too deeply involved to pull out within the time allotted. You will write more effectively

---

ANSWERS: EXERCISE 1

1. The purpose is to inform. Because the assignment is for a biology class, the audience will likely be the instructor and perhaps other students in the class; these people are specialists. The assumption about an audience of specialists is further confirmed by the time limit of twenty minutes, which means that the student has to pack in many technical terms and processes in a short period of time. The special requirements include the twenty-minute time limit and, implied by the wording of the assignment, in-class writing.

2. The purpose is to persuade. The audience is the general reading public (such as the course instructor and students in the class). The special requirements include a 500- to 700-word limit and a due date of one week.

3. A student receiving this assignment has many decisions to make. The purpose can be either informative or persuasive, depending on the student's focus on the topic. The audience can be the general reading public or specialists, according to the student's judgment; if the political science course is advanced, chances are that the instructor expects the writing to be addressed to specialists. The only stated special requirement is a length of 1,000 words. The student should ask the instructor when the assignment is due and if the assignment calls for research. The student might also want to set a purpose and audience and check them with the instructor before proceeding, if time permits.

4. The purpose is to persuade. The audience is readers of the college's student newspaper; they could be considered specialists in that they share the experience of attending the same college, but they are not specialists in technicalities concerning the functioning of college libraries. The special requirements include a 300-word limit, the need to draw on personal experience, and

(continued next page)

QUOTATION ABOUT WRITING

Writing is just having a sheet of paper, a pen and not a shadow of an idea of what you're going to say.

—Françoise Sagan

QUOTATION ABOUT WRITING

I am a camera with its shutter open, quite passive, recording, not thinking.

—Christopher Isherwood

if your topic is suitable for college writing and if it is one that can be presented and developed well.

Of course, some assignments leave no room for making choices about the topic. You may be given very specific instructions such as "Explain how oxygen is absorbed from the lungs." You may be asked to describe the view from your classroom window or to compare and contrast the personalities of two major characters in a short story. Your job with such assignments is to do precisely what is asked and not go off the topic.

 Selecting a topic on your own

Some instructors will ask you to write on whatever topic you wish. In such situations, do not assume that all subjects are suitable for informative or persuasive writing in college. Academic settings call for topics that can reflect your ability to think ideas through. For example, the old reliable essay about a summer vacation is probably not safe territory for a college essay if you have nothing extraordinary to report. Your essays need to dive into issues and concepts, and they should demonstrate that you can use specific, concrete details to support what you want to say. The need for specifics should not, however, tempt you to go to extremes by writing very technical information, especially when an audience is unfamiliar with the particular specialized vocabulary.

When you choose a topic on your own, be careful not to use a very narrow one. You will have little success with topics that give you little to say. For example, for a course in informative and persuasive writing, you might reach a dead end if you tried to write a 500-word essay about what your cat looks like while sleeping, unless you were asked to write an elaborate description of a common sight. Similarly, for the same course, you might find yourself out of ideas if you tried to write 500 words about a single apple. You need to take purpose, audience, and special requirements into account when you make decisions about topics. A cat sleeping might be a fine topic for a zoology course, and an apple might be a suitable topic for a nutrition class.

 Narrowing an assigned topic

The real challenge in dealing with topics comes when you choose or are assigned a subject that is very broad. You have to *narrow the subject*. This means thinking of subdivisions of the subject, of different areas within the subject. Most very broad subjects can be broken down in hundreds of ways, but you need to think of only a few until you come to one that seems possible for an essay. Think it through before rushing in, however. Think about whether the topic as narrowed can be developed well in writing. **What separates most good writing from bad is the writer's ability to move back and forth between general statements and specific details.** A suitably narrowed topic permits such movement.

For example, if the subject is marriage, you might decide to talk about what makes marriages successful. But you cannot depend merely on generalizations such as "In successful marriages husbands and wives learn to accept each other's faults." You need to explain why accepting faults is important, and you need to give concrete illustrations of what you are talking about.

Whenever you narrow a broad subject to obtain a writing topic, keep in mind the writing situation of each assignment: purpose, audience, and special requirements. Think about what you can handle well according to the conditions of each assignment.

SUBJECT	*Music*
WRITING SITUATION	Freshman composition class
	Informative purpose
	Instructor as audience
	500 words, one week
POSSIBLE TOPICS	the moods music creates
	classical music
	country-western music

SUBJECT	*Cities*
WRITING SITUATION	Sociology course
	Persuasive purpose
	Students and then instructor as audience
	500 to 700 words, one week
POSSIBLE TOPICS	comforts of city living
	discomforts of city living
	how cities develop

SUBJECT	*Mythology*
WRITING SITUATION	Humanities course
	Informative purpose
	Instructor as audience—a specialist in mythology
	1,000 words, two weeks
POSSIBLE TOPICS	the purpose of myths
	mythical views of gods and goddesses
	myths about the origins of the world

TEACHING TIP (see chart page 17)

The concept of a "writing situation" might be new to many students. It is an inclusive term for the combination of topic, purpose, audience, and special requirements such as word or time limits. Each of these four variables influences every decision a writer makes. You might want to ask your students to memorize that short list of key variables: TOPAS (with the two letters "to" for "topic") can be an easy memory device for students. These variables are especially important in narrowing a topic, as demonstrated by the inclusion of "writing situation" in the examples for narrowing a topic.

QUOTATION ABOUT WRITING

Since long before the invention of universities, not to mention university programs in creative writing, authors have acquired their authority in four main ways—first, by paying a certain sort of attention to the experience of life as well as merely undergoing it; second, by paying a certain sort of attention to the works of their great and less great predecessors in the medium of written language, as well as merely reading them; third, by practicing that medium themselves, usually a *lot* (Charles Newman, the writer and critic, declares that the first prerequisite for aspiring writers is sufficient motor control to keep their pens moving left to right, line after line, hour after or, day after day, and I would add year after year, decade after decade); and fourth, by offering their apprentice work for discussion and criticism by one or several of their impassioned peers, or by some more experienced hand, or by both.

—John Barth

Both Tara Foster and Gary Lee Houseman faced the task of narrowing their topics. Foster's assignment asked for a discussion of "an important problem facing adult men and women today." She knew immediately that "an important problem" was too vague and general, and she realized the assignment implied that she was expected to make it specific, and suitably narrow. Being one of today's "adult men and women," she thought of many problems: war, the dangers of nuclear energy, unemployment, divorce. She saw a danger in these topics, however. She knew that she had to avoid what her instructor called *canned rhetoric,* the use of standard statements made commonly by everyone. She wanted to test out what she might say on various topics, so she did some "freewriting" (2d-2). This helped her realize that what interested her most was the problem of divorce. Still, she felt that she did not have enough information to write a 500- to 700-word essay on the subject. She used divorce as a springboard for "brainstorming" (2d-3). She knew people who had gone through divorce, and she was aware that learning to live alone was a major problem for some. This led her to think about many types of people who have to face living alone at one time or another in their lives. She began to think about what they needed to know to be able to live alone. She felt that she had found a good topic, but she confirmed this by asking the "journalist's questions" (2d-4) to see if she would have enough to write about.

Houseman's assignment asked for an argument about "some aspect of the destruction of our environment." Houseman's process of narrowing the subject was very different from Foster's. For a number of years, he had been very interested in conservation issues, and so he had a solid fund of knowledge from having read many newspaper and magazine articles. He thought of choosing the topics of acid rain or toxic wastes or pollution. But the topic he cared about most was the destruction of rain forests. To check whether he could remember many details from his reading, he tried "mapping" (2d-5), and he decided that he had made a good choice for himself.

ANSWERS: EXERCISE 2

Answers will vary, but each topic should have an explanation of why it would be suitable for the writing situation described in the exercise.

EXERCISE 2

For five of these general topics, think of three narrowed topics that would be suitable for a 500- to 700-word essay in a writing course. Assume that each essay is due in one week and that the audience is the general reading public, as represented by the course's instructor. List your three narrowed topics and explain briefly why each is suitable for the writing situation.

1. Computers
2. Movies
3. Political campaigns
4. Health
5. Literature
6. Popular music
7. Vocational education
8. Driver training
9. Imagination
10. Slang

EXERCISE 3

Think of three subjects that interest you. List them. Then pick one and narrow it to three topics suitable for an essay. Assume that the essay is for a writing class, that it should run from 500 to 700 words, that it is due in one week, and that it will be read by other students in the class as well as by the course's instructor. After you finish listing three topics, explain briefly why each is suitable for the writing situation.

2d Gathering ideas for writing

Techniques for gathering ideas, sometimes called *prewriting strategies* or *invention techniques*, can help you while you are narrowing your topic. They help you discover what you know and, often, how much you know about a topic before you decide to write on it. As such, techniques for gathering ideas are important aids for thinking of the ideas and of details to use in essays.

Many techniques for gathering ideas have been developed and used by experienced writers. The ones discussed and illustrated in this chapter are listed in the following chart.

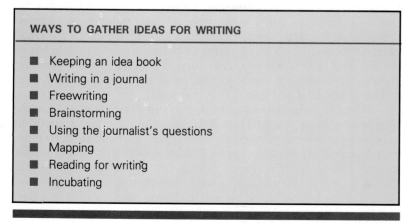

WAYS TO GATHER IDEAS FOR WRITING

- Keeping an idea book
- Writing in a journal
- Freewriting
- Brainstorming
- Using the journalist's questions
- Mapping
- Reading for writing
- Incubating

TEACHING TIP: JOURNALS

Students often have trouble thinking of journal topics. Frequently the result is journals that read like parodies of diaries, shopping lists, descriptions of meals or clothes, transcripts of routine conversations. You can avoid this problem if you give students suggested topics. In addition to offering students something to write about, such topics act as models for the creation of original topics. You might distribute this list in groups of five or ten so that they can last for most of a semester.

1. How do you feel about having to keep a journal? How do you feel about writing? Explain.

2. Why are you in college? If there is something else you would rather be doing, what is it? Why are you in school instead?

3. What is your definition of success? Do your friends tend to share your definition or to have a different one? Discuss.

4. Do you think information about sex should be taught at home, in school, or both? Why?

5. How does your religion affect your daily life? Have you ever had to defend or explain your religious beliefs to someone? Do you think you were effective? Why or why not?

6. Do you plan to marry someday? Why? What do you expect married life to be like? (If you are married, were your expectations fulfilled? Why or why not?)

(continued next page)

7. What do you want as a career? How are you preparing for it? How did you choose this career? Have you ever had to defend or explain your choice to parents or friends? Do you think you were effective? Why or why not?

8. Is the United States really a melting pot? Should immigrant children be educated in English or in their native languages? Should there be non-English radio and television stations in the United States? For each question, why or why not?

9. If you could give advice to your friend(s), what would you say?

10. Where do you go when you feel like being alone? Why?

11. Where do you go when you feel sociable? Why?

12. Does anything make you depressed? What? What do you do when you feel this way? What advice can you give others who feel this way?

13. What is your favorite place? What makes it so special?

14. What do you think your life will be like in the year 2000? What will your family life be like? What work will you be doing? Where will you be living? How will technology have influenced your life?

15. Who is your favorite relative? Why?

16. If you could change one thing about your personality, what would it be? Why?

17. If you could change one aspect of the way you look, what would it be? Why?

18. In what ways is college *not* what you expected? In what ways *is* it what you expected?

19. If you could be given a talent you do not already have, what would it be?

20. What is the most expensive thing you ever bought? Why did you buy it? How did you get the money? Was it worth the money?

21. How would you feel if you were told

Students sometimes worry that they have nothing to write about. Often, however, students know far more than they give themselves credit for. The challenge is to uncover what is there but seems not to be. Start with the assumption that you know more than you think, and try some of these techniques for discovering what is not coming easily to mind.

No one technique of generating ideas always works for all writers in all situations. Experiment with all these methods. If one does not provide enough useful material, try an alternative. Also, even if one strategy produces some good material, you may still want to try another technique to see what additional possibilities it may turn up.

1 **Keeping an idea book and writing in a journal**

Your ease with writing will grow as you develop the habits of mind that typify writers. Professional writers are always on the lookout for ideas to write about and for details to develop their ideas. They listen, watch, talk with people, and generally keep their minds open. For this reason, many writers carry an **idea book**—a pocket-size notebook—with them at all times so that they can jot down ideas that spring to mind. They do not trust their memories because they know that good ideas can melt away like snowflakes. If you keep an idea book handy throughout your college years, you will find that a ready source of ideas is at hand—and that your powers of observation become increasingly strong.

Like an idea book, a **journal** is a record of your ideas, but the entries are written daily. Many writers, both amateur and professional, write journals. Any size notebook can serve well for a journal. Fifteen minutes a day can be enough—before going to bed, between classes, on a bus. When you write in your journal, *you* are your audience. The writing is not for publication, so the content and tone can be as personal and informal as you wish.

When writing in your journal, you can draw on your reading, your observations, your dreams. You can write down and respond to quotations that seem particularly meaningful. You can react to movies, plays, and television programs that are memorable. You can think on paper about your opinions, beliefs, family, friends. Writing in a journal gives you the chance to write about whatever you wish. Unlike a diary, a journal is not merely for listing what you did that day. In a journal you put down your thoughts. Writing is a way of thinking, a way of working through ideas that need time to develop, a way *plan*

2d

of wrestling with problems not given to easy solution. Equally important, writing is a way of discovering, of allowing thoughts to emerge as the physical act of writing moves along.

Keeping a journal can help you in three ways. First, writing every day gives you the habit of productivity. The more you write, the more you get used to the feeling of words pouring out of you onto paper, the easier it will become for you to write in all situations. Second, a journal instills the habit of close observation and thinking. Third, a journal serves as an excellent source of ideas when you need to write in response to an assignment.

Having served overseas in the armed forces before going to college, Gary Lee Houseman was attuned to other places and perspectives. He sometimes wrote in his journal about world issues. When he got the assignment to argue against the destruction of the environment, he looked in his journal for possible starting points. Here is a brief excerpt from Houseman's journal.

> October 15
> Conservation issues always seem to pop up at me when I am reading or watching TV. I get steamed up. What are they doing to our world? I saw a program on TV last night about rain forests. It confirmed what I've been reading about for the last few years. They are destroying the rain forests in the name of progress. They are robbing *me* of a factory that manufactures oxygen and helps clean the air. One species of plant or animal a day, many of which have potential to give us cures for diseases. I read a year ago that a drug from a plant in a South American rain forest is being used to treat Parkinson's disease.

When Gary Lee Houseman saw this journal entry, he realized that he had found a starting point: rain forests.

EXERCISE 4

Write a journal entry about one of these subjects. Write to discover what you have to say or to think through what is already on your mind.

1. Learning self-discipline
2. Coping with stress
3. Budgets
4. Halloween
5. Classical music
6. Short stories
7. Heroes
8. Self-respect
9. The Vietnam War
10. Mechanization

that you had to cook a healthy dinner for six people, including yourself? Who would you go to for advice or help? What would you serve? How successful do you think the dinner would be?

22. Who are some of the most important people in your life? Why? How do you let these people know how much they mean to you?

23. If you could travel anywhere on this planet, where would you like to go? Why? Where would you least like to go? Why?

24. If you could live in any earlier time period, what would you choose? Why?

25. What is your favorite kind of movie? Why? What are its characteristics? What is the best movie of the kind that you have ever seen?

26. How does the weather affect your mood?

27. Do you enjoy playing a sport? Why or why not? What sport do you enjoy the most? Why?

28. If you were fated to be a public figure, what would you want to be: politician, rock star, movie star, environmental activist, news reporter? Why? What would your life be like? How would you treat people less famous than you?

29. If you were to be reincarnated as an animal that reflected your behavior in this life, what would you be? Why? If you could choose what animal to be, what would you be? Why?

30. What teacher has had a great deal of influence on you? Describe the teacher and his or her effect on you.

ANSWERS: EXERCISE 4

The student should write a paragraph or two (or a longer entry, if you prefer) that would reflect the nature of journal entries: informal language, conversational tone and rhythms, sincerity, subjectivity, and detail.

TEACHING TIP

Journal writing and freewriting are often unpopular with students at first, but on their end-of-the-semester evaluations of my classes, students consistently mention these activities as being among the most helpful in my course. Perhaps one of the reasons students resist at first is that they don't believe that journal writing and freewriting will not be corrected or graded.

BACKGROUND

In *Writing with Power* (Oxford UP, 1981), Peter Elbow suggests that keeping a freewriting diary can be helpful to the aspiring writer. Writing for only ten minutes a day can provide "a brief mind sample" of that day. He also discusses loop writing, a variation of free writing, which allows the reader a degree of control over the material the mind produces.

TEACHING TIP

Students may be surprised to learn that all writers find the blank sheet of paper (or empty computer screen) a source of anxiety. The experienced writer knows that the most effective way to move past that feeling is to write *something,* regardless of its value. Once the clean surface has words on it, other words follow more easily. Unrelated ideas, notes, questions, examples—all help to relieve the writer's discomfort with getting started. A good habit to cultivate is to jot down responses and reactions to writing tasks as soon as they are given.

2   **Knowing how to use freewriting**

Freewriting is writing nonstop. Freewriting means writing down whatever comes into your mind without stopping to worry about whether the ideas are good or the spelling is correct. When you freewrite, you do nothing to interrupt the flow. Let your mind make all kinds of associations. Do not censor any thoughts or flashes of insight. Do not go back and review. Do not cross out. Some days your freewriting might seem mindless, but other days it can reveal interesting ideas to you.

Freewriting gives you the "feel" of pen moving across paper or of fingers in constant motion on the keyboard of a typewriter or computer. This feeling that comes with the physical act of writing serves you well when you draft and revise your writing.

Freewriting works best if you set a goal, such as writing for fifteen minutes or until you have filled one page. Keep going until you reach that goal, even if you must repeat a word over and over until a new word comes to mind.

If you use a word processor, you can avoid the temptation to stop and criticize your writing by doing "invisible writing." Dim the monitor screen so you cannot see your writing. The computer's memory will still be recording your ideas, but you will not be able to see them until you brighten the screen again. The same effect is possible for writing by hand if you use a worn-out ballpoint pen and a piece of carbon paper between the paper you are writing on and another piece of paper.

Focused freewriting means starting with a set topic. You may focus your freewriting in any way you like—perhaps with a phrase from your journal or a quotation you like. Use the focus as a starting point for writing down as many of your thoughts as you can until you meet the time or page limit you set. Again, do not censor what you say. Keep moving forward.

As with journals, freewriting can be a source for ideas and details to write about. Here is an excerpt from Tara Foster's focused freewriting. She was thinking about narrowing her topic from the subject "an important problem facing today's adult men and women."

Well, the assignment says a problem. Let's see if I'm going to write a lot of old junk about things. War. War. War is stupid. Unemployment lines and trying to find a job on this campus. Nuclear energy is too frightening to think about. Anyway, I don't know enough to write about it. I really want to think about divorce. The big D. Why bother getting married if I only have a 50–50 chance of making it?

I think I'll be in the 50% that makes it. But many of my friends are not making it. Lives ripped apart. Writing like this gets tiring for my hand. Keep moving, keep moving. Sounds like a movie theater usher. My parents had a great marriage. Since my dad died my mother has had a hard time. She has to live alone now that I am out of the house. It isn't easy for her to get used to a new lifestyle.

EXERCISE 5

Freewrite for five minutes on one of these topics.

1. Worrying
2. Procrastinating
3. A famous person, alive or dead
4. Taking tests
5. Playing a sport
6. Mark Twain
7. Libraries
8. Spelling
9. Falling in love
10. World peace

3 Knowing how to use brainstorming

Brainstorming means making a list of all the ideas that come to mind associated with a topic. The ideas can be listed as words or phrases. Listmaking, like freewriting, produces its best results when you let your mind range freely, generating quantities of ideas before analyzing them.

You may find that brainstorming allows you to generate many ideas quickly because the format does not call for sentences or paragraphs. You can brainstorm in one concentrated session or over several days, depending on how much time is available for the assignment. In courses that use collaborative learning procedures, brainstorming in groups can work especially well. One person's ideas bounce off the next person's, and collectively more ideas get listed.

Brainstorming is done in two steps. First, you make a list. Then you go back and try to find patterns in the list and ways to group the ideas into categories. The items do not have to be in any particular order within the groups. Set aside any items that do not fit into groups. The areas that have the most items in their lists are likely to be ones you can write about most successfully. If an area interests you but its list is thin, brainstorm on that area alone. If you run out of ideas, ask yourself questions to stimulate your thinking. You might try exploratory questions about the topic, such as: What is it? What is it the same as? How is it different? Why or how does it happen? How is it done? What caused it or results from it? What does it look, smell, sound, feel, or taste like?

Tara Foster used brainstorming while she was narrowing her

ANSWERS: EXERCISE 5

Answers will vary. What surprising ideas and details did the writer discover?

topic about a problem facing today's adult men and women. She decided to see what she could brainstorm about divorce. The result is shown in her random list. Then she grouped her ideas and discovered that she had more to say about living alone than any other aspect of the topic. She used an asterisk (*) to mark off the items that referred to being alone. A few items did not fit into her grouped list, so she dropped them. She then decided to try writing on the topic of living alone, but first she expanded her ideas by asking the "journalist's questions" (2d-4).

Divorce (random list)

financial problems	arguments
many causes of divorce	being on your own again
personality conflicts	sexual problems
shopping alone	impact of divorce
pressure from parents	buying a car alone
children's reactions	incompatibility
religious laws	splitting up the money
hurt and disappointment	living alone
having to start over	fears of loneliness
finding a lawyer	different tastes

Divorce (grouped list)

causes of divorce

—financial problems	—pressure from parents
—personality conflicts	—incompatibility
—arguments	—different tastes
—sexual problems	

results of divorce

—living alone*	—splitting up the money
—being on your own again*	—buying a car alone*
—shopping alone*	—hurt and disappointment
—children's reactions	—having to start over
	—fears of loneliness*

If you do not like to make lists, you can brainstorm by writing down random sentences that come to mind as you think about your topic. You can jot them down in whatever order they occur to you. You can list the sentences or put them into what looks like a paragraph. Once you have the sentences on paper, you can move them around until they fall logically into an order that makes sense for your purpose.

plan 2d

EXERCISE 6

Here is a brainstormed list for an assignment in marketing class on advertising strategies in magazines. Look over the list and group ideas. Some ideas may not fit into any group.

intentional misuse of English
status symbols
suitability for readership
grabs readers' attention
product identification
placement of objects
sex appeal
slogans
self-esteem of reader
celebrities
layout
size of advertisement

black and white vs. color
level of sophistication
imagination
stimulates senses
witty language
facts
focal point
amount of writing
clarity of design
connotations of words
suitability for audience
creativity

EXERCISE 7

Brainstorm on a subject that interests you. First make a random list. Then group ideas within the list. If you cannot think of a subject, use one from Exercise 4 or 5.

 4 **Using the journalist's questions**

Another common means for generating ideas is using the **journalist's questions:** *Who? What? When? Why? Where? How?* Asking these questions forces you to approach a topic from several different perspectives.

To expand her ideas about living alone, Tara Foster used the journalist's questions. She looked over the answers and decided that she had enough details to write an essay.

WHO lives alone?
—students going off to college
—students finish school and move to get a job
—singles leaving the military
—divorced people (1 out of 2 marriages end in divorce)
—widowed people (8 out of 10 married women will be widows)

WHAT does living alone entail?
—handling practical things
—balancing a checkbook
—opening a checking or savings account

ANSWERS: EXERCISE 6

Class discussion will likely reveal disagreement about the main categories and the distribution of items. You can emphasize the role of the individual writer as decision maker. The list might be arranged in this way:

A. *Appeals of advertisement:* Celebrities (as salespeople), self-esteem (appeal to), sex appeal, suitability for readership, status symbols, level of sophistication

B. *Use of color:* black and white vs. color, stimulates senses

C. *Language:* amount of writing, connotations of words, intentional misuse of English, witty language, facts, slogans

D. *Layout:* size of advertisement, placement of objects, product identification, grabs readers' attention, focal point, clarity of design

Note: Imagination and *creativity* do not fit because they are part of all of these and thus too general.

ANSWERS: EXERCISE 7

Answers to this exercise will vary. The writer should be able to explain the principle that underlies each grouping.

QUOTATION ABOUT WRITING

Had I known the answer to any of these questions, I would never have needed to write.

—Joan Didion

TEACHING TIP

To teach the journalist's questions effectively, you might ask students to bring in some newspaper articles that cover the *w*'s in the first paragraph or two. Consider, for example, this brief opening paragraph (a single sentence) from an article in the *New York Times* (April 16, 1989) about a tragic incident at an English soccer game.

> London, April 15—At least 93 people were killed and more than 180 others were injured today when soccer fans surged forward in severely overcrowded stands at a match in the northern English city of Sheffield, according to police and hospital officials.

Who: Ninety-three people attending a soccer match
What: Were killed
When: April 15, 1989
Why: The fans surged forward
Where: Sheffield, England

ANSWERS: EXERCISE 8

Each student will come up with a different response, but each one should be encouraged to write as detailed an answer as possible. Here is a sample response for item 2, *watching soap operas:*

who?—housewives, college students of both sexes, an increasing number of males of all ages, unsupervised young children; *what?*—watching soap operas regularly; *where?*—everywhere from office lounges in companies to college dorm rooms and nursing homes; *how?*—some for whole afternoons, some for selective viewing of only one or two shows, some openly, some secretly; *why?*—to escape reality, perhaps, or possibly simply to relax regularly or to keep up with peers' interests

—locating important papers (will, birth certificate, insurance)
—making necessary major purchases
—making new friends
—getting along socially
—dealing with loneliness
—dealing with depression

WHEN do people have problems living alone?
—when they are used to being taken care of
—when they do not know what to expect
—when they try to hide from the statistics

WHY do people live alone?
—want to (May Sarton's essay on the solitary life)
—have no choice
—prefer to live alone than to be unhappily married or to live with a roommate they dislike

WHERE do people live alone?
—apartments
—houses
—motel rooms
—cities
—suburbs
—rural areas

HOW do people cope with living alone?
—they learn how to take care of themselves
—self-reliance
—they get out and meet new people
—they fight loneliness by staying busy

EXERCISE 8

Ask the journalist's questions about one of these subjects.

1. Day-care centers
2. Watching soap operas
3. Contemporary art
4. Collecting stamps
5. Street vendors
6. Wind surfing
7. Snobs
8. Eating junk food
9. Shoplifting
10. Writing personal letters

plan

5   Knowing how to use mapping

Mapping, also called *clustering* or *webbing,* is much like brainstorming, but it is more visual and less linear. A "map" looks quite different from sentences, paragraphs, or lists. Many writers find that mapping frees them to think more creatively, to associate ideas more easily.

When you map, start with your subject circled in the middle of a sheet of unlined paper. Next draw a line radiating out from the center and label it with the name of a major division of your subject. Circle it and from that circle move out further to subdivisions. Keep associating to further ideas and to details related to them. When you finish with one major division of your subject, go back to the center and start again with another major division. As you go along, add anything that occurs to you for any section of the map. Continue the process until you run out of ideas.

Gary Lee Houseman used mapping (page 32) to check what he knew about rain forests, the topic he wanted to write about for his assignment about the destruction of the environment. After mapping, he felt confident that he could begin shaping and drafting his essay.

EXERCISE 9

Think of a topic about which you have some information. Use mapping to chart what you know. Start with the topic in the middle of a blank page. Work out from there.

6   Using reading for writing

Reading can inspire you to think about a topic *before* you write. For example, in her Freshman English class a few weeks before she wrote her essay on living alone (shown in Chapter 3), Tara Foster had read "The Rewards of Living a Solitary Life," by May Sarton. When Tara wanted to improve the introductory paragraph in the second draft of her essay, she thought of Sarton's essay and decided to select a quote from it to open the paragraph.

Reading can also help you plan *after* you receive an assignment. Reading is a way to get new information and to confirm what you already know. Be aware, however, that reading is not always part of an assignment. Unless an assignment specifically calls for the use of outside sources, ask your instructor if you can use them. Some instructors want students to use what they know rather than what they learn from new reading at the time of the assignment. Gary Lee

TEACHING TIP

Mapping is a relatively new concept. It is likely that many of your students—and perhaps even you—have not heard of it before now. Mapping can be a refreshing change of pace in place of or in addition to other more traditional idea-gathering techniques. Because mapping is highly visual, it holds a special appeal for some students. Those who hate to do anything formal (such as an outline or even a list) find the apparent anarchy of a map enticing. Students are often engaged by the bunch of balloons developing on the board. Because entire branches of a map can be omitted from an actual essay, dead ends and short roads are not "errors."

Some students take to mapping readily. Others, especially in the beginning, may prefer to have some guidance, at least in the selection of subtopics. For example, an assignment calling for a persuasive essay about air pollution might benefit from a map based on the senses. Ask students to write an example of air pollution in a circle in the center of the page. Then have them draw a line for each sense and circle the name of that sense (smell, taste, sight, hearing, touch). The students can then draw additional lines and circles for each branch of the map.

ANSWERS: EXERCISE 9

Answers will vary, but they should look somewhat like the model on the following page.

Houseman, as explained in 2b, was not sure if research was part of his assignment, so he asked and found out that it was not.

On the other hand, some assignments ask you to read a specific work, such as an essay or short story, and write in reaction to it. Other assignments ask for research writing (see Chapter 32). When you read to write, be sure to *read critically.* Critical reading, a key part of critical thinking, is expected of college students. Critical thinking and its application to reading are discussed fully in Chapter 5.

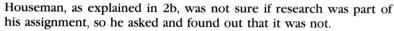

7 Using incubation

When you allow your ideas to **incubate,** you give them time to grow and develop. Time is a key element for successful incubation. You need time to think, to allow your mind to wander, and then to come back and focus on the writing. Incubation works especially well when you need to solve a problem in your writing (for example, if material is too thin and needs expansion, if material covers too much and needs pruning, or if connections among your ideas are not clear for your reader).

To use incubation effectively, arrange your time to ensure that you will not be interrupted. Focus your attention on the problem you have encountered. Try to define what the problem is, as best you can. Incubation rarely works if you skip this step. Next, use one of two strategies that experienced writers report they find most successful.

Using one strategy, turn your attention to something entirely different from your writing problem. (Many writers avoid all writing and reading at this point.) Concentrate *very hard* on your new focus of attention so that your conscious mind is totally distracted from the writing problem. After a while, relax and guide your mind back to the writing problem you want to solve. Now try to think it through.

Using a second strategy, you can allow your mind to relax completely and wander rather aimlessly, without concentrating deeply on anything special. Let yourself daydream, recall a pleasant memory, or think about something you are looking forward to. Open your mind to random thoughts, but do not dwell on any one thought very long. After a while, force your mind back to the writing problem you are trying to solve.

When you come back to the writing problem, you might see solutions that did not occur to you before. If not, try the incubation process again. Experiment with the amount of time you need before

BACKGROUND

Donald Graves was the first to use the term *rehearsing* to describe the activities that precede a completed draft. In *Balance the Basics: Let them Write* (Ford Foundation Papers on Research About Learning, 1978), he discusses the stage of the writing process in which the writer (mentally and on paper) prepares to write, without yet knowing what that writing will be. Drawing conclusions from his observations of children writing, Graves points out the importance of experimenting with meaning, form, and voices, an attitude of play that is important in making meaning. It allows the writer to make unexpected relationships from surprising inner voices.

QUOTATION ABOUT WRITING

The ideal view for daily writing, hour on hour, is the blank brick wall of a cold-storage warehouse. Failing this, a stretch of sky will do, cloudless if possible.

—Edna Ferber

QUOTATION ABOUT WRITING

I like a room with a view, preferably a long view. I dislike looking out on gardens. I prefer looking at the sea, or ships, or anything which has a vista to it.

—Norman Mailer

BACKGROUND

In "Writing as Process: How Writing Finds Its Own Meaning" (*Eight Approaches to Teaching Composition,* ed. Timothy Donovan and Ben McClelland [NCTE, 1980], pp. 3–20), Donald Murray discusses four forces that interact as the writer goes through the stages of rehearsing, drafting, and revising, moving in a recursive manner from exploration to clarification. They are the forces of collecting and connecting, writing and reading. Although writing may be ignited by any one of these forces in conjunction with any other, says Murray, once writing has begun, all of them begin to interact with each other. The writer is often unaware of this interaction, as innate curiosity leads naturally to the act of collecting information, which at some point calls for control and order that make the act of connecting necessary. Connections, in turn, make the writer see information in a new way, hence generating more collected data. The acts of writing and reading act in a similar fashion. The writer sets down what is heard mentally, then reads the product, checking it against what was heard, then rewrites it. Murray asserts that although each writing act is a complex, instantaneous interaction, the scale tips rapidly from one force to the other in response to the various needs of the writer dealing with rehearsing, drafting, or revising.

you return to solve the writing problem. Even if the technique of incubation does not seem to work for you, you might later find that a solution suddenly "pops" into your head when you least expect it. Of course, in such cases you are not in control of when the solution will come to mind, so you cannot depend on reaching a solution at a specific time. Still, having a sudden insight is a delightful experience, and perhaps the next time you try using incubation, it will produce results for you more quickly.

If you find that incubation does not work for you at first, practice it a few times before you reject it as a possible tool. Be patient with yourself; allow your mind the chance to adjust to this thinking technique.

2e Shaping ideas for writing

Shaping is an important step in making the transition from gathering ideas to drafting an essay. Shaping activities are related to the idea that writing is often called *composing,* the putting together of ideas to create a *composition,* one of the synonyms for *essay.* To shape the ideas that you have gathered, you need to group them, decide on your role and tone, draft a thesis statement, and know how to outline.

As you shape ideas, keep in mind that the form of an essay is related to the ancient notion of a story's having a beginning, a middle, and an end. An essay always has an introduction, a body, and a conclusion. The body consists of a number of paragraphs while the introduction and conclusion are usually one paragraph each. The length of each paragraph is in proportion to the overall length of the essay. Introductory and concluding paragraphs are generally shorter than body paragraphs, and no body paragraph should overpower the others by its length. Chapter 4 discusses and illustrates many types of paragraphs for informative and persuasive writing.

1 Grouping ideas

When you group ideas, your task is to make connections and find patterns. You put related ideas into separate groups. If you used brainstorming (2d-3) or mapping (2d-5) when you were gathering ideas for writing, you have had some experience with the underlying principle of grouping.

When you group material for writing, the concept of *levels of generality* helps you make decisions. One idea is more general than another if it is a larger category—less specific—than the next. For example, "cures for diseases" is more general than "Parkinson's treatment." Also "bank account" is more general than "checking account." In turn, "checking account" is more general than "business checking account" or "regular checking account." And those terms are more general than "account 221222 at the E–Z Come, E–Z Go Bank." Thus, generality is a relative term. Each idea exists in the context of a whole relationship of ideas. An idea may be general in relationship to one set of ideas, but specific in relation to another set.

Thinking about levels of generality can help you remember that effective writing includes both general statements and specific details. In informative and persuasive writing, general statements must be developed with facts, reasons, examples, and illustrations.

To group ideas, review the material you accumulated while gathering ideas. Then look for general ideas. Next group less general ideas under them. If you find that your notes contain only general

BACKGROUND

In his essay "Invention: A Topographical Survey" (*Teaching Composition: 10 Bibliographical Essays,* ed. Gary Tate [Fort Worth: Texas Christian University Press, 1976], pp. 1–43), Richard Young classifies the theoretical bases for teaching invention in four main categories: Neo-Classical Invention, Pre-Writing, Tagmemic Invention, and the Dramatistic Method. Neo-Classical Invention refers to those systems based on the theories of Aristotle, Cicero, and Quintilian. Pre-Writing is a more recent technique, dating from the 1960s. Related to Jerome Bruner's writing on crativity, it emphasizes the self-actualization of the writer. Tagmemic Invention is derived from Kenneth Pike's tagmemic linguistic theory, but it has its fullest realization in Richard Young, Alton Becker, and Kenneth Pike's *Rhetoric: Discovery and Change* (1970). Kenneth Burke's Dramatistic Method of invention is explored in his *Grammar of Motives* (1945) and *Rhetoric of Motives* (1950), but other theorists have used it in various forms since that time.

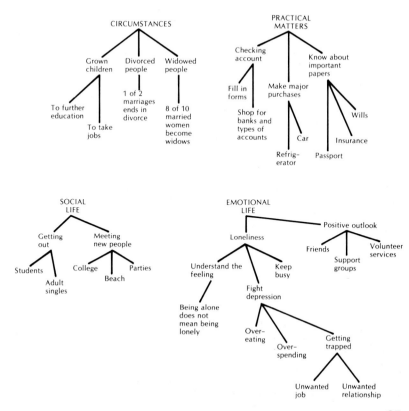

ideas, or only very specific details, return again to gathering techniques to supply what you need. One of the standard tools for ordering ideas is making a "subject tree." It shows ideas and details in order from most general at the top to most specific at the bottom. The tree Tara Foster made for her essay on living alone is illustrated on page 35. As happens with most writers, Foster did not use every item on the tree when she wrote her essay (she dropped the positive outlook section under "Emotional Life," for example). The material did, however, give her a good start for her drafting.

EXERCISE 10

Prepare a subject tree on food, on crime, on family life, or on another subject of your choice.

2   Ordering ideas

When you order ideas for writing, you put them into a logical sequence. You decide what you want your audience to encounter first, second, and on until the last. When readers can follow your line of reasoning, they are more likely to understand the message that you want your material to deliver.

You have a number of choices about how to order your ideas. Within paragraphs, you can arrange your ideas in any of the ways explained and illustrated in section 4c. For essays, effective and commonly used sequences include *climactic, chronological, and spatial.*

WAYS TO ORDER IDEAS WITHIN ESSAYS

Climactic order: from least to most important
Chronological order: according to a time sequence
Spatial order: according to physical location

Climactic order, also called *emphatic order,* moves from least to most important. Ideas are arranged according to degree of impact on your reader or importance to your subject. The order builds to a climax. You can see examples of such arrangements in Chapter 3: Tara Foster's third draft on living alone and Gary Lee Houseman's essay on rain forests.

Climactic order also refers to structures that move from the simplest to most complex idea or from the most familiar to least familiar idea. For example, you might start an essay about softball by explaining how to grip the bat. You could then proceed to talk about achieving a good swing and finish by discussing how to hit a pitched softball. The strategy of climactic order is useful not only for ordering major groups of ideas within a large framework, but also for ordering supporting details within each major group.

Chronological order presents ideas according to a time sequence. Chronological order is frequently used in narrating a series of events and in showing a process where steps are normally given in the order in which they occur. For example, you might use chronological order to discuss the career of Martin Luther King or to describe the discovery of the sunken *Titanic.*

Spatial order presents ideas arranged according to their physical locations in relation to one another. This can include top to bottom, near to far, left to right. Spatial order is useful for such topics as describing a stage set or a street scene. Similarly, it would work well for moving from the East Coast to the West Coast when comparing historic preservation programs in New York, Chicago, and San Francisco.

3 Determining your role and tone

In all writing situations, you have to play a **role.** Some assignments specify a role, such as being a high school teacher writing to students who have graduated and gone to college. In such cases, you have to imagine what that person would say and would sound like when saying it. Most assignments, however, do not specify a role. You are expected to be yourself.

How you define yourself is important. As an adult writing to an adult audience, you are expected to sound reasonable and moderate. This stance is reflected in your **tone**—*what you say* and *how you say it.* Tone can be broadly described as informal or formal. The tone is informal in the journal entry on page 25 and the freewriting on page 26. As you move from writing for the private you to writing for an audience, you are expected to move toward a more formal tone. This does not mean that you should use overblown language or put on airs that make you sound artificial (see 21e). Most audiences for whom you write expect a tone midway between informal and highly formal. For examples of student writing using a tone appropriate for a general audience, see the third drafts of the essays in Chapter 3;

the paragraphs by students in Chapter 4; the research paper in Chapter 34; and various other papers and essays in Chapters 36–39.

Your tone also has to take into account the writing situation—especially topic, purpose, and audience. For example, if you are supposed to write a humorous piece about current politics, you should inject humor and use a tone that fits what you are saying. On the other hand, if you are asked to discuss how local officials are handling a serious drought or an increase in violent crimes, you should assume that you are supposed to be serious. *Serious* does not mean without spirit, however.

4

Drafting a thesis statement

A **thesis statement** is the central message of an essay. It is evidence that you have something definite to say about the topic. An effective thesis statement prepares your reader for the essence of what you discuss in an essay. As the writer, therefore, you want to compose a thesis statement with care so that it accurately reflects the content of your essay. You want to avoid misleading your reader into an inaccurate prediction. If you find a mismatch between your thesis statement and the rest of your essay, revise to coordinate them better. A list of the basic requirements for a thesis statement appears below.

Often, instructors ask for more than the basic requirements. For example, you might be required to put your thesis statement at the end of your introductory paragraph. The third draft of the essay on living alone and the essay on rain forests (Chapter 3) are examples. In addition, many instructors require that the thesis statement be contained in one sentence. Other instructors permit two sentences

TEACHING TIP

You may want to ask your students to test their thesis statements by exchanging them with each other. By asking the readers to answer questions about the thesis statements, the writers may discover weaknesses (and strengths) that were not apparent to them. Some questions they can ask are the following:

1. Is the main idea, the central point, clearly stated?

2. Is the purpose of the essay clear?

3. What is the purpose: to inform or persuade?

4. What is the focus of the essay?

5. Does the thesis statement identify the major subdivisions of the essay's topic?

6. Does it make the topic seem interesting?

7. Can this thesis be developed in the time available?

8. Can this thesis be developed in an essay of the length planned?

9. Is the thesis limited enough for development, but general enough to be worth the effort?

10. Is the thesis stated in specific terms? Does it avoid overly general, vague ones?

BASIC REQUIREMENTS FOR A THESIS STATEMENT

1. It states the essay's **subject**—the topic that you are discussing.
2. It reflects the essay's **purpose**—either to give your readers information or to persuade your readers to agree with you.
3. It includes a **focus**—your assertion that conveys your point of view.
4. It uses **specific language**—vague words are avoided.
5. It *may* briefly state the major subdivisions of the essay's topic.

---

plan 2e

if the material to be covered warrants such length. All requirements, basic and additional, are designed to help you learn to think in structured patterns that communicate clearly with readers.

In most writing situations, you will not be certain that all parts of a thesis statement accurately reflect what you say in the essay until you have written one or more drafts. To start shaping your essay, however, you need a **preliminary thesis statement.** Often a preliminary thesis statement is too broad ("Rain forests must not be destroyed") or too vague ("Rain forests are important to the human race"). Expect to revise a preliminary thesis statement as you write successive drafts of your essay, but an early version helps you find direction in your writing. When you revise into a **final thesis statement,** make sure that it clearly applies to the content of the essay as it has evolved through its drafts.

Consider the final thesis statement in Tara Foster's essay on living alone (in Chapter 3).

> Chances are high that most adult men and women will have to know how to live alone, briefly or longer, at some time in their lives.

Foster's thesis statement reveals that the *topic* is living alone, the *purpose* is to give information, and the *focus* is that chances are high that most people will have to know how to live alone at some time in their lives. The language avoids vague words and uses specific terms such as "adult men and women," "how to live alone," and "briefly or longer."

Here are thesis statements written for 500- to 700-word essays with an **informative purpose.** The ineffective versions resemble some types of preliminary thesis statements. The effective versions are final thesis statements written by students after they had gathered and grouped ideas. The material here on music is built on one of the "possible topics" evolved on page 21. Note that the good versions contain the five characteristics listed in the Basic Requirements chart.

TOPIC	*classical music*
No	Classical music combines many different sounds.
Yes	Classical music can be played by groups of various sizes, ranging from chamber ensembles to full symphony orchestras.
TOPIC	*malpractice suits*
No	There are many kinds of malpractice suits.
Yes	Most people are familiar with malpractice suits against medical doctors, but an increasing number of suits are being filed against lawyers, teachers, and even parents.

TEACHING TIP

The notion of *focus* in a thesis statement might be new to some students. A useful analogy can be that the topic is the subject, but the focus is the predicate. Without predication, sentences make no assertion. As Josephine Miles, Professor of English at the University of California at Berkeley, said in her important monograph "Working Out Ideas: Predication and Other Uses of Language": "Sentence making is predication, and to predicate is to assert an idea, selecting and treating facts from a point of view."

TOPIC	*women artists*
No	The paintings of women are getting more attention.
Yes	During the past ten years the works of artists such as Mary Cassatt and Rosa Bonheur have finally gained widespread critical acclaim.

For a persuasive purpose, Gary Lee Houseman wrote this thesis statement for his essay about rain forests (Chapter 3):

Rain forests must be preserved because they offer the human race many irreplaceable resources.

Houseman's thesis statement reveals that the *topic* is rain forests, the *purpose* is to persuade, and the *focus* is that rain forests must be preserved because they are irreplaceable. The language avoids vague words and uses specific terms such as "the human race" and "irreplaceable resources."

Here are ineffective and effective thesis statements written for 500- to 700-word essays with a **persuasive purpose.** The ineffective versions resemble some types of preliminary thesis statements. The effective versions are final thesis statements written by students after they had gathered and grouped ideas. The material here on city living is built on one of the "possible topics" evolved on page 21. Note that the good versions contain the first four characteristics listed in the Basic Requirements chart. Two of the good versions also include the major subdivisions of the topic.

TOPIC	*discomforts of city living*
No	The discomforts of living in a modern city are many.
Yes	Rising crime rates, increasingly overcrowded conditions, and growing expenses make living comfortably in a modern city difficult.
TOPIC	*defense spending*
No	Many problems exist in the way federal defense spending is controlled.
Yes	Congress should enact laws requiring specific checks and balances for the process of defense spending.
TOPIC	*deceptive advertising*
No	Deceptive advertising can cause many problems for consumers.
Yes	Deceptive advertising can cost consumers not only money but also their health.

The *No* examples of thesis statements shown above suffer from being too broad. They are so general that they offer no focus, and readers

---

ALTERNATE EXERCISE

Write thesis statements for persuasive papers on the following topics, making sure that they have the five characteristics of a good thesis statement listed in the Basic Requirements chart.

1. Topic: rock music
2. Topic: athletic scholarships
3. Topic: ethnic foods
4. Topic: a holiday ritual
5. Topic: mothers and daughters

plan 2e

cannot predict the essay's thrust. Another type of ineffective thesis statement results from an overly narrow focus. In such cases, the thesis statement is closer in scope to a topic sentence that begins a paragraph. Here are two examples of overly narrow thesis statements, one for an informative purpose and one for a persuasive purpose.

No   The classical composer Béla Bartók was Hungarian.

No   Car thefts on Silver Avenue between First and Second Streets are intolerable.

EXERCISE 11

Identify the topic, purpose, and focus of each thesis statement.

1. Although recent tax reforms have helped stimulate the economy, additional reforms would benefit the government, business, and consumers.
2. To learn to use a word processor, a student needs plenty of time for practice and access to a clearly written, well-indexed manual.
3. Reading poetry can help students improve their analytical skills.
4. Emphasizing foreign languages in U.S. schools would benefit U.S. culture, business, and politics.
5. Although programs to eliminate drunk driving have been somewhat effective, additional programs are sorely needed.
6. The earth's surface can be divided into four major landforms: plains, plateaus, hills, and mountains.
7. To be successful, marriages have to adjust to unexpected problems that come along.
8. In the first year of life, babies acquire increasingly sophisticated motor skills as they move from reflexive to nonreflexive activities.
9. Opera combines acting, singing, music, dancing, costumes, and scene design.
10. Journalists should have an extensive liberal arts education.

EXERCISE 12

Each of the following sets of sentences offers several versions of a thesis statement. Within each set, the thesis statements progress from weak to strong. The fourth thesis statement in each set is the best. Based on the Basic Requirements chart on page 38, identify the characteristics of the fourth thesis statement in each set. Then explain why the other choices in

---

ANSWERS: EXERCISE 11

1. *Topic:* tax reforms. *Purpose:* to persuade. *Focus:* more reforms would benefit the government, business, and consumers.

2. *Topic:* learning to use a word processor. *Purpose:* to inform, though perhaps to persuade. *Topic:* students need time for practice and a clearly written, well-indexed manual.

3. *Topic:* reading poetry. *Purpose:* to persuade, though it could also inform. *Focus:* it can help students improve their analytical skills.

4. *Topic:* emphasizing foreign languages in U.S. schools. *Purpose:* to persuade. *Focus:* such knowledge would benefit U.S. culture, business, and politics.

5. *Topic:* programs to eliminate drunk driving. *Purpose:* to persuade. *Focus:* have been somewhat effective but more are needed.

6. *Topic:* the earth's surface. *Purpose:* to inform. *Focus:* four major landforms: plains, plateaus, hills, and mountains.

7. *Topic:* successful marriages. *Purpose:* to persuade. *Focus:* have to adjust to the unexpected problems that come along.

8. *Topic:* babies in their first year of life. *Purpose:* to inform. *Focus:* acquire increasingly sophisticated motor skills as they move from reflexive to nonreflexive activities.

9. *Topic:* opera. *Purpose:* to inform. *Focus:* it includes the components of acting, singing, music, dancing, costumes, and scene design.

10. *Topic:* journalists. *Purpose:* to persuade. *Focus:* they need an extensive liberal arts education.

ANSWERS: EXERCISE 12

A. The fourth thesis statement succeeds because it states a main idea (about magazine advertisements' appeal to readers); it reflects a purpose (to persuade); it has a focus (that magazine advertisements must be skill-

(continued next page)

ANSWERS: EXERCISE 12 (continued)

fully done); and it briefly presents subdivisions (language, color, and design). The first and second thesis statements are too general, showing neither a purpose nor a focus. The third thesis statement shows a persuasive purpose but is still too general and has no focus ("must" is not explained).

B. The fourth thesis statement succeeds because it states a main idea (about playing tennis for fun and exercise); it reflects a purpose (to inform); it has a focus (what is required for playing tennis for fun and exercise); and it briefly presents subdivisions (agility, stamina, and strategy). The first statement is too general ("excellent" is a very broad term) and shows no purpose or focus. The second statement is also too vague ("fun" is a very broad term when used without a context) and shows no purpose or focus. The third statement reflects an informative purpose but lacks a focus ("various skills" is too vague).

C. The fourth statement succeeds because it states a main idea (characters in *Hamlet* seek revenge); it reflects a purpose (to inform); it has a focus (all three characters seek revenge); and it briefly states the major subdivisions (Hamlet, Fortinbras, and Laertes). The first statement is much too general, and though it suggests an informative intent, the statement lacks a focus. The second and third statements reflect an informative purpose but lack a focus ("must" and "want" are vague words here).

D. The fourth statement succeeds because it states a main idea (strong friendships); it reflects a purpose (to persuade); it has a focus (what builds strong friendships); and it briefly states the major subdivisions (sensitivity and communication). The first statement uses vague language ("maintaining" and "work"), and it suggests neither a persuasive nor informative intent. The second statement reflects a persuasive purpose but depends on "good" used in a vague sense. The third statement reflects a persuasive

each set are weak. (The first set relates to the material in Exercise 6 in this chapter.)

A. 1. Advertising is complex.
    2. Magazine advertisements appeal to readers.
    3. Magazine advertisements must be creative.
    4. To appeal to readers, magazine advertisements must skillfully use language, color, and design.
B. 1. Tennis is excellent exercise.
    2. Playing tennis is fun.
    3. Tennis requires various skills.
    4. Playing tennis for fun and exercise requires agility, stamina, and strategy.
C. 1. *Hamlet* is a play about revenge.
    2. Hamlet must avenge his father's murder.
    3. Some characters in *Hamlet* want revenge.
    4. In *Hamlet,* Hamlet, Fortinbras, and Laertes all seek revenge.
D. 1. Maintaining friendships requires work.
    2. To have good friends, a person must learn how to be a good friend.
    3. To be a good friend, a person must value the meaning of friendship.
    4. Unless a person is sensitive to others and communicates with them honestly, that person will not be able to build strong friendships.
E. 1. Many people are uninterested in politics.
    2. Adults have become increasingly dissatisfied with the political process.
    3. Fewer adults than ever vote in local elections.
    4. Fewer college students participated in state primaries and voted in state elections this year than in either of the last two elections.

EXERCISE 13

Here are writing assignments, narrowed topics, and tentative thesis statements. Evaluate each thesis statement according to the Basic Requirements chart on page 38.

1. **Marketing assignment:** 700- to 800-word persuasive report on the college's cafeteria. *Audience:* the instructor and the cafeteria's manager. *Topic:* cafeteria conditions. *Thesis:* the college cafeteria could attract more students if it improved the quality of its food, its appearance, and the friendliness of its staff.

2. **Music assignment:** 300- to 500-word review of a performance. *Audience:* the instructor and other students in the class. *Topic:* the local

symphony's final spring concert. *Thesis:* The "Basically Beethoven" program that ended the local symphony's spring season was pleasing.

3. **Chemistry assignment:** 800- to 1,000-word informative report about the ozone layer. *Audience:* the instructor and visiting students and instructors attending a seminar at State College. *Topic:* recent research on the ozone layer. *Thesis:* The United States should increase efforts to slow the destruction of the ozone layer.

4. **Journalism assignment:** 200- to 300-word article about campus crime. *Audience:* the instructor, the student body, and the college administration. *Topic:* recent robberies. *Thesis:* During the fall term, campus robberies at State College equaled the number of robberies that took place in the prior five years combined.

5. **Business writing assignment:** 400- to 500-word persuasive report about the career-counseling services of State College. *Audience:* college seniors, career counselors, and the instructor. *Topic:* job placement for seniors. *Thesis:* State College's liberal arts graduates are hired mainly by business and industry.

5 Knowing how to outline

Many writers find outlining a useful planning strategy. An outline helps pull together the results of gathering and ordering ideas and preparing a thesis statement. It also provides a visual guide and checklist. Some writers always use outlines; others prefer not to outline. Writers who outline do so at various points in the writing process: for example, before drafting, to arrange and organize material; or while revising, to check the logic of an early draft's arrangement and organization. Especially for informative and persuasive writing, outlines can clearly reveal flaws—missing information, undesirable repetitions, digressions from the thesis.

As a college writer, you will likely find that some instructors require outlines. Understandably, they want you to practice the discipline of planning the arrangement and organization of your writing. The more clearly and sensibly your material is presented, the better chance it has of reaching your audience.

Before the final draft of an essay is complete, an outline is only a projection, an estimate of what the essay will say. Once you start writing, the act of writing might lead you to change your plans somewhat. If you are working from an outline and you make changes, be sure to revise your outline at the end. Then check to make sure that your changes have not upset the logic and arrangement of your essay.

purpose but "value" is too vague to provide a focus.

E. The fourth statement succeeds because it states a main idea (college students voting); it reflects a purpose (to inform); and it has a focus (how these students voted in state primaries and state elections this year compared with the last two years). The first statement relies on too much vague language ("many," "people," "uninterested") and it lacks a purpose or focus. The second statement suggests an informative purpose, but it relies on vague language ("dissatisfied" and "political process") and it lacks a focus. The third statement suggests an informative purpose but lacks a focus.

ANSWERS: EXERCISE 13

1. The thesis is good because it reflects the purpose (to persuade), states a main idea, and focuses specifically on logical subdivisions of the topic.

2. The thesis suggests that the concert review will do what such reviews should do: evaluate in an attempt to persuade a reader. The words "was pleasing," however, are too vague; they need to be revised to be more specific. A brief indication of subdivisions might help the thesis communicate its message.

3. The thesis, though specific and focused, does not reflect a careful response to the assignment: the assignment requires an informative report, but this thesis reflects a persuasive purpose.

4. This thesis is good because it states a main idea, reflects a purpose (to inform), and includes a focus.

5. This thesis does not address the assignment adequately because it deals only with liberal arts majors (not all of the seniors) and reflects an informative rather than a persuasive purpose, as was required by the assignment.

TEACHING TIPS

Writers use outlines in a variety of ways. They turn to them, for example, at different stages of the composing process. Whereas some find it productive to move from mapping or freewriting directly into a listing of ideas in a particular order, using the outline to plan the drafting process, others use outlines to check the organization of a draft after it is written, testing to see if the paper has order and balance. Some writers find topic outlines helpful; some prefer a sentence outline. Each writer has to find the shaping strategies that prove to be most effective in his or her case.

BACKGROUND

In the chapter on "Shaping Discourse" in *A Rhetoric for Writing Teachers* (Oxford UP, 2nd ed., 1987, pp. 158–70), Erika Lindemann warns teachers and students against making inflexible writing plans that cause them to force ideas into a prescribed form. In particular, she points out that slavishly following an outline can limit a writer's options. It can, for example, prevent a writer from discovering the material's organic unity or from making choices that might improve the piece. Rigid adherence to an outline, says Lindemann, can create an inadequate and incomplete understanding of the paper, since an outline may offer little help in determining proportions or deciding on rhetorical strategies. In addition, it may also divert a writer from considering audience and purpose.

An **informal outline** does not have to follow all the formal conventions of outlining. It lists the main ideas of an essay—the major subdivisions of the thesis statement. It also lists subordinate ideas and details, but without attention to levels of generality (see 2e-2). An informal outline is particularly useful for planning when the order within main ideas is still evolving or when topics imply their own arrangement, such as spatial arrangement for describing a room or chronological order for describing an event.

An informal outline can also be a *working plan,* a layout of the major parts of the material intended for an essay. It can be the next logical step after a brainstormed list (2d-3), a map (2d-5), or a subject tree (2e-2). An informal outline can also serve as an early draft of a formal outline. Here is part of an informal outline that served as a working plan for Gary Lee Houseman when he was writing his essay on rain forests. This excerpt includes the thesis and three of the five body paragraphs.

Thesis statement: Rain forests must be preserved because they offer the human race many irreplaceable resources.

Definition of rain forest
   80 inches rainfall a year
   Tropical regions (warm temperatures)
   Lush, dense vegetation
   Canopy
      Branches overlap
      As high as the trees (I think about 98 feet)
      Evergreens
      Plant and insect life thrive

Biomedical uses
   Over 1,400 plants and animals
   Compounds for medicines
      Parkinson's
      Mental illnesses
      Anticancer

Natural balances
   Level forests $\longrightarrow$ birds leave $\longrightarrow$ insects are no longer eaten
      by birds $\longrightarrow$ insects overgrow and eat crops $\longrightarrow$ hunger
   Level forests $\longrightarrow$ natives displaced $\longrightarrow$ become dependent on
      government $\longrightarrow$ more pressure on national debt

A **formal outline** follows conventions concerning content and format. The conventions are designed to display material so that relationships among ideas are clear and so that the content is orderly. A formal outline can be a *topic outline* or a *sentence outline.* Each item in a topic outline is a word or phrase; each item in a sentence

plan 2e

PATTERN FOR FORMAL OUTLINE OF AN ESSAY

Thesis Statement: ....

I. First main idea..

   A. First subordinate idea...

      1. First reason or example ....

      2. Second reason or example ....

         a. First supporting detail ....

         b. Second supporting detail ....

   B. Second subordinate idea..

II. Second main idea...

TEACHING TIP

If your students have trouble organizing an outline, you might suggest that they write each item on a 3×5 index card. The ability to move the cards around, make piles, and easily eliminate items often facilitates students' work.

TEACHING TIP

Computers are increasingly helpful in organizing material and preparing outlines. Several software programs are commercially available for use in creating short outlines that can be expanded into more complex ones. They encourage experimentation with ideas and arrangements because they are flexible. Outlines can be quickly and easily expanded by the addition of subheadings or tightened by the removal of subheadings from the screen, though the writer can keep them available for possible inclusion.

---

outline is a complete sentence. Formal outlines never mix the two. Many experienced writers who use formal outlines find that a sentence outline brings them closer to drafting than does a topic outline. For example, "compounds for medicines" on a topic outline would carry more information on a sentence outline: "Compounds for medicines come from many plants and animals in the rain forests."

When writing a formal outline, you are expected to observe the following conventions.

1. **Numbers, letters, and indentations.** All parts of a formal outline are systematically indented and numbered or lettered. Capital roman numerals (I, II, III) signal major subdivisions of the topic. Indented capital letters (A, B) signal the next level of generality. Further indented arabic numbers (1, 2, 3) show the third level of generality. Indented lowercase letters (a, b) show the fourth level, if there is one. The principle here is that within each major

subdivision, each succeeding level of the outline shows more specific detail than the one before it. If an outline entry is longer than one line, the second line is indented as far as the first word of the preceding line.

2. **More than one entry at each level.** At all points on an outline, there is no I without a II, no A without a B, and so on. Unless a category has at least two parts, it cannot be divided. If a category has only one subdivision, you need to either eliminate that subdivision or expand the material to at least two subdivisions.

No   A.   Grown children leaving home
           1.   Moving to other cities
        B.   Married people not being together forever

Yes   A.   Grown children moving to other cities
        B.   Married people not being together forever

Yes   A.   Grown children moving to other cities
           1.   Going away to school
           2.   Taking jobs
        B.   Married people not being together forever

3. **Levels of generality.** All subdivisions are at the same level of generality. A main idea cannot be paired with a supporting detail.

No   A.   Opening a checking account
        B.   Comparing bank service

Yes   A.   Opening a checking account
        B.   Making major purchases

4. **Overlap.** Headings do not overlap. What is covered in 1, for example, must be quite distinct from what is covered in 2.

No   A.   Grown children moving to other cities
           1.   Going away to school
           2.   Continuing an education

Yes   A.   Grown children moving to other cities
           1.   Going away to school
           2.   Taking jobs

5. **Parallelism.** All entries are grammatically parallel. For example, all items start with *-ing* forms of verbs, all items begin with verbs not in the *-ing* form, or all items are adjectives and nouns. For more about parallelism in outlines, see 18e.

No A. Understanding the feeling
     B. Avoid depression

Yes A. Understanding the feeling
      B. Avoiding depression

Yes A. Understand the feeling
      B. Avoid depression

6. **Capitalization and punctuation.** Except for proper nouns°*, only the first word of each entry is capitalized. In a sentence outline, end each sentence with a period. Do not punctuate the ends of entries in a topic outline.

7. **Introductory and concluding paragraphs.** The content of the introductory and concluding paragraphs is not part of a formal outline. The thesis statement comes before (above) the roman numeral I entry.

BUILDING A FORMAL OUTLINE

1. Numbers, letters, and indentations signal groupings and levels of importance.
2. Each level has more than one entry.
3. All subdivisions are at the same level of generality.
4. Headings do not overlap.
5. Entries are grammatically parallel.
6. Only the first word of each entry is capitalized. (All proper nouns are also capitalized.)
7. Periods end each sentence in a *sentence outline* but not in a *topic outline*.
8. The introductory and concluding paragraphs are omitted, but the thesis statement is usually given before the outline itself.

---

*Throughout this book a degree mark (°) indicates a term that is defined in the book's Glossary.

Here is a topic outline of the final draft of Tara Foster's essay on living alone (shown in 3c). A sentence outline appears on the opposite page so that you can compare the two types of outlines.

Thesis Statement: Chances are high that adult men and women will have to know how to live alone, briefly or longer, at some time in their lives.

I. Living alone because of circumstances
   A. Grown children moving to other cities
      1. Going away to school
      2. Taking jobs
   B. Married people not being married forever
      1. One out of two marriages ending in divorce
      2. Eight out of ten married women becoming widowed, usually late in life

II. Taking care of practical matters
   A. Opening a checking account
      1. Comparing bank services
      2. Comparing advantages of different kinds of checking accounts
   B. Making major purchases
      1. Replacing a refrigerator
      2. Buying a car

III. Establishing new friendships
   A. Students getting used to going to classes without old friends
      1. Being able to concentrate better
      2. Being able to meet new friends
   B. Single adults going to the beach or parties

IV. Dealing with loneliness
   A. Understanding the feeling
   B. Avoiding depression
      1. Not overeating
      2. Not overspending
      3. Not getting into unwanted situations
         a. Taking the wrong job
         b. Going into the wrong relationship
   C. Keeping busy

Compare the topic outline on the opposite page with the following sentence outline of the same material. Notice that each item is a complete sentence (and therefore that each item ends with a period).

Thesis Statement: Chances are high that adult men and women will have to know how to live alone, briefly or longer, at some time in their lives.

I. Circumstances sometimes force people to live alone.
   A. Grown children leave home.
      1. They go to college or graduate school.
      2. They go to other cities to get jobs.
   B. Many married people do not stay married forever.
      1. One out of two marriages ends in divorce.
      2. Eight out of ten married women become widowed, usually late in life.

II. People living alone have to take care of practical matters.
   A. Students might have to open a checking account.
      1. They can compare bank services.
      2. They can compare advantages of different kinds of checking accounts.
   B. Divorced or widowed people might have to make major purchases.
      1. A refrigerator might have to be replaced.
      2. A car might not be worth fixing.

III. People living alone can establish new friendships.
   A. Students get used to going to classes without old friends.
      1. One advantage is students might concentrate better.
      2. A second advantage is students can meet new friends.
   B. Single adults get used to going to the beach or parties alone.

IV. People living alone sometimes have to deal with loneliness.
   A. First comes the importance of understanding the feeling.
   B. Second comes the importance of avoiding depression.
      1. Overeating can result.
      2. Overspending can result.
      3. Getting into unwanted situations can result.
         a. People might take the wrong job.
         b. People might go into the wrong relationship.
   C. Third comes the importance of keeping busy.

ANSWER: EXERCISE 14

Answer may vary from the following.

I. Sources of noise pollution
   A. Large cities
      1. Traffic
      2. Construction work
      3. Airplanes
   B. Workplace
      1. Factory machines
      2. Outdoor construction machines
   C. Leisure-time activities
      1. Stereo headphones
      2. Film soundtracks
      3. Disco music
II. Problems from noise pollution
   A. Damages hearing
   B. Alters moods
   C. Limits learning ability
III. How to reduce noise pollution
   A. Pressure from community groups
   B. Traffic regulations
   C. Pressure on management by workers
   D. Earplugs
   E. Reasonable sound levels

EXERCISE 14

Here is a sentence outline. Revise it into a topic outline. Decide which form you would prefer as a guide to writing. Explain your decision.

Thesis Statement: Common noise pollution, although it causes many problems in our society, can be reduced.

I. Noise pollution comes from many sources.
   A. Noise pollution occurs in many large cities.
      1. Traffic rumbles and screeches.
      2. Construction work blasts.
      3. Airplanes roar overhead.
   B. Noise pollution occurs in the workplace.
      1. Machines in factories boom.
      2. Machines used for outdoor construction thunder.
   C. Noise pollution occurs during leisure-time activities.
      1. Stereo headphones blare directly into eardrums.
      2. Film soundtracks bombard the ears.
      3. Music in discos assaults the ears.
II. Noise pollution causes many problems.
   A. Excessive noise damages hearing.
   B. Excessive noise alters moods.
   C. Constant exposure to noise limits learning ability.
III. Reduction in noise pollution is possible.
   A. Pressure from community groups can support efforts to control excessive noise.
   B. Traffic regulations can help alleviate congestion and noise.
   C. Pressure from workers can force management to reduce noise.
   D. People can wear earplugs to avoid excessive noise.
   E. Reasonable sound levels for headphones, soundtracks, and discos can be required.

3 Drafting and Revising

In the writing process, drafting and revising follow from planning and shaping, discussed in Chapter 2. **Drafting** means getting ideas onto paper in sentences and paragraphs. In everyday conversation, people usually use the word *writing* when they talk about the activities involved in drafting. In discussing the writing process, however, the word *drafting* is more descriptive. It conveys the idea that the final product of the writing process is the result of a number of versions, each successively closer to what the writer intends and to what will communicate clearly to readers. **Revising** means taking a draft from its preliminary to its final version by evaluating, adding, cutting, moving material, editing, and proofreading.

3a Getting started

If ever you have trouble getting started when the time arrives for drafting (or for any other part of the writing process), you are not alone. When experienced writers get temporarily stalled, they recognize what is happening and deal with it.

If you run into a writing block, make sure that you are not being influenced by any of these common myths about writing.

MYTH	Writers are born, not made.
TRUTH	Everyone can write. Writers do not expect to "get it right" the first time. Being a good writer means being a patient rewriter.
MYTH	Writers have to be "in the mood" to write.
TRUTH	If writers always waited for "the mood" to descend, few would write at all. After all, news reporters have to write to meet deadlines for stories, and professional writers often have to meet deadlines set by their contracts.

MYTH Writers have to know how to spell every word and to recite the rules of grammar perfectly.

TRUTH Writers do not let spelling and grammar block their way. They write, and then they check themselves. A good speller can be defined as someone who does not ignore the quiet inner voice that says a word's spelling should be checked in a dictionary. Similarly, writers use a handbook to check grammar rules.

MYTH Writers do not have to revise.

TRUTH Writers expect to revise. Once words are on paper, writers can see what readers see. This "re-vision" helps writers revise so that the writing delivers its intended message.

MYTH Writing can be done at the last minute.

TRUTH Writing takes time. Ideas do not leap onto paper in final, polished form. Not only do writers need to go through the various activities of the writing process, but they also need time to get distance from a draft so that they can revise with fresh eyes.

Once you realize the truths behind myths about writing, you are ready to try the time-proven ways experienced writers get started when they are blocked. The key to getting these suggestions to work is to suspend judgment; do not criticize yourself when you are trying to get underway. The time for evaluation comes during revision, but revising too soon can stall some writers. The writing that results from these ideas is most certainly not a final draft, but having something on paper to work with is a comfort—and can serve as a springboard to drafting.

1. **Avoid staring at a blank page.** Fill up the paper. Relax your mind and allow your hand to move across the page or keyboard. Write words, scribble, or draw while you think about your topic. The movement of filling the paper while thinking can help stimulate your mind to turn to actual drafting.

2. **Use "focused freewriting"** (see 2d-2). Think about your topic, and write sentences about it nonstop for ten or fifteen minutes or until you fill a few pages. Some of the sentences you write can help you begin actual drafting.

3. **Picture yourself writing.** Before you get up in the morning, when you are waiting for a bus, or as you are walking to classes, get a full visual image of yourself writing. Imag-

ine yourself in the place where you usually write, with the materials you need, busy at work. Many professional writers say that they write more easily if they first picture themselves doing it.

4. **Picture an image or scene, or imagine a sound or taste, that relates to your topic.** For example, to argue against the destruction of the rain forest, call to mind a visual contrast between a lush area and a destroyed area. To report on a concert, recall the sound of your favorite part. Start writing by describing and discussing what you see or hear.

5. **Write your material in a letter to a friend.** This gives you a chance to relax and chat on paper to someone you like and feel comfortable with. The letter can be a good beginning for a less informal draft.

6. **Write your material as if you are someone else.** Take your pick: you can be a friend writing to you, an instructor writing to you or a whole class, your parent writing to you, a person in history writing to you or to someone else. Once you take on a role, you often will feel less inhibited about writing.

7. **Switch your method of writing.** If you usually typewrite or use a word processor, try writing by hand. If you usually use a pen, switch to a pencil. Whenever you write by hand, especially when you are having trouble getting started, try to treat yourself to good quality paper. The pleasure of writing on smooth, strong paper is considerable and helps many experienced writers want to keep going.

8. **Start in the middle.** If you do not know what you want to write in your introductory paragraph, start with a body paragraph. Write from the center of your essay out, instead of from beginning to end.

As you use these springboards to drafting, seek out places and times of the day that encourage you to write. You might write best in a quiet corner of the library; at 4:30 a.m. at the kitchen table, before anyone else is awake; or outside when the sun is shining and people are walking by. Most experienced writers find that they concentrate best when they are alone, working without the risk of interruption. But occasionally background noise—in a crowded cafeteria, for example—might be comforting. Be sure, however, not to mislead yourself: you will not write well or efficiently while you are talking to other people, stopping now and then to jot down a sentence or

BACKGROUND

In an article published in *U.S. News and World Report* (November 9, 1987, p. 106), Erica E. Goode cites tips for people who tend to procrastinate. They include the following helpful suggestions.

1. Break your work into small, clearly defined steps. Instead of vowing vaguely to "catch up on paper work," resolve to spend one hour sorting out the papers on your desk.

2. Reward yourself for progress toward your goal. Ice cream is nice, as is a walk in the park.

3. The hardest step to take is the first, so pick something easy. A task that can be polished off in fifteen minutes is a good one for a starter.

4. Set a series of small but realistic deadlines rather than a final date.

5. Enlist support. Other people may be able to tell you if you're setting up expectations that are impossible to meet.

TEACHING TIP

Your students may find it helpful to keep a writing log. At the top of each piece of writing they can note where, when, and how they are working. The more detailed the notations, the more they will help students to draw conclusions about the manner in which their best writing takes place. After making a number of such notations, the students can write a paragraph evaluating the approaches used, trying to assess their effectiveness.

two. Also, writers can sometimes mistake delaying tactics for preparation. You do need pencil and paper (or their equivalent) to write, but you do not need fifteen perfectly sharpened pencils sitting in a neat row.

3b Knowing how to draft

Once you have your ideas planned and shaped for an essay, you are ready to **compose** them on paper. When you compose, you put together sentences and paragraphs into a unified whole. A *first draft* is a preliminary draft. First drafts are not meant to be perfect; they are meant to give you something to revise. According to your personal preferences and each writing situation, you can use any of these ways (or your own ways) of writing a first draft.

1. **Put aside all your notes from planning and shaping.** Write a "discovery draft." As you write, be open to discovering ideas and making connections that spring to mind during the physical act of writing. When you finish a discovery draft, you can decide to use it either as a first draft or as part of your notes when you write a structured first draft.

2. **Keep your notes from planning and shaping in front of you and use them as you write.** Write a structured first draft. Work through all of your material. Depending on the expected length of your essay, draft either the entire essay or blocks of one or two paragraphs at one time.

3. **Use a combination of approaches.** When you know the shape of your material, write according to that structure. When you feel "stuck" about what to say next, switch to writing as you would for a discovery draft.

The direction of drafting is forward: *keep pressing ahead.* If you are worried about the spelling of a word or a point in grammar, underline the material so that you can come back later and check it—and keep moving ahead. If you cannot think of a word that says precisely what you want, write an easy synonym and circle it so that you will remember to change it later—and move on. If you are worried about your sentence style or the order in which you present the supporting details within a paragraph, write *Style?* or *Order?* in the margin so that you can return to that spot later to revise—and press forward. If you feel that you are running dry, reread what you have *draft*

3b

written—but only to propel yourself to further writing, not to distract you into rewriting.

As you move into drafting an essay, use the essay's thesis statement as your springboard. A thesis statement has great organizing power. It expresses the central theme that controls and limits what the essay will cover. A thesis statement contains (1) the *topic,* narrowed appropriately for the writing situation; (2) a *focus,* which presents what you are saying about the topic; and (3) a *purpose,* which is either informative or persuasive, as explained in 1b. For more about thesis statements, see 2e-4.

As you use your thesis statement, remember that its role is to serve as a connecting thread that unifies the essay. **Unity** is important for communicating clearly to an audience. You achieve unity when all parts of the essay relate to the thesis statement and to each other. Also, an essay is unified when it meets two criteria: (1) the thesis statement clearly ties into all topic sentences (for a full discussion of topic sentences, see 4a); (2) the support for each topic sentence—the paragraph development—contains examples, reasons, facts, and details directly related to the topic and, in turn, to the thesis statement.

Equally important, your essay must be **coherent** to communicate clearly to an audience. An essay is coherent when it supplies guideposts that communicate the relations among ideas. Coherence is achieved through the use of transitional expressions, pronouns, repetition, and parallel structures. These techniques operate within paragraphs and to connect paragraphs; they are discussed and illustrated fully in 4b.

When you write, plan your practical arrangements. For example, try to work in a place where you are comfortable and will not be disturbed. If someone comes along and interrupts, you might lose a train of thought or an idea that has flashed into your mind. Also, have enough paper on hand so that you need to use only one side of each sheet of paper. When you revise, you should be able to spread your full draft in front of you so that you can physically see how the parts relate to one another. As you write, leave large margins and plenty of room between lines so that you have space to enter changes when you revise.

This chapter (and Chapter 2) refers to the writing processes of two students, Tara Foster and Gary Lee Houseman, for illustration. Their writing assignments are shown on page 18. Their work in gathering ideas and shaping their material is shown in Chapter 2. In this chapter, you will see three drafts of Foster's essay and the final draft of Houseman's essay.

QUOTATION ABOUT WRITING

Writing is a deliberate act; one has to make up one's mind to do it.

—James Britton

QUOTATION ABOUT WRITING

To write is to write is to write is to write is to write is to write is to write.

—Gertrude Stein

The dominant purpose of Foster's essay is *informative*. Here is the thesis statement that serves as Foster's central theme:

> Chances are high that most adult men and women will have to know how to live alone, briefly or longer, at some time in their lives.

Here is how Foster used her thesis statement to help her write the first draft of her essay.

BACKGROUND

To gather examples of student writing for the *S & S Handbook,* Prentice Hall sponsored a project that enlisted the help of faculty across the United States. Dubbed the "Student Writing Project," this search resulted in my being able to draw on a bank of student essays (all in three drafts) and student paragraphs. The names of the participating faculty appear in the handbook's "Preface to the Instructor."

FIRST DRAFT

Lots of people are scared of living alone.
They like to live with others. When the statistics
catch up with you, therefore, you are never prepared.
Chances are high that most adult men and women will
have to know how to live alone, briefly or longer,
at some time in their lives.

Many grown children move away from their
hometowns to get an education or take jobs. Also,
married people think they'll always be together, but
many marriages end in divorce. The divorce rate is
frightening. People are not making the right choices,
or they are too immature to work out their differences.
Fighting over money, parents, or religion although
the underlying reason is lack of compatibility.
Divorce brings the couple and their children a great
deal of pain.

I read recently in the newspaper where estimates
are that in the next twety years, 8 out of 10
married women end up widows. This will happen to
most of them late in life. This statistic is even
sadder than divorce. I feel sorry for any happily
married person whose spouse dies.

```
        People living alone need to establish new
    friendships.  When single people feel self-reliant.
    It's easier for them to start getting out and meeting
    new people.  Some students are in the habit of always
    going to classes with a friend, and they can be find
    that they can concentrate better on the course.  And
    also have a chance to make some new friends.
    Friends can help people take care of practical
    by keeping them company and going with them.

        One good way to prepare for living alone is to
    learn how to take care of practical matters.  Many
    people don't know how to do something as simple as
    opening a checking account.  Making major purchases
    is something people have to handle.  Such as a
    refrigerator that can't be repaired or a useless car.
    Shop around and make price comparisons.  All decisions
    are much easier than at first.

        Feelings of lonliness are the hardest to take.
    I think this is what people fear the most.  First,
    people have to understand what is going on.  Being
    alone does not mean being lonely.  Second, singles have
    to fight depression.  Third, they have to keep busy.

        People living alone have to handle practical,
    social, and emotional problems.
```

3c   Knowing how to revise

To **revise** you must evaluate. You assess your first (or subsequent) draft and decide where improvements are needed. Then you make the improvements and evaluate them alone and in the context of the surrounding material. This process continues until you are satisfied that the essay is in final draft.

QUOTATION ABOUT WRITING

I can't write five words but that I change seven.

—Dorothy Parker

BACKGROUND

In "Revision Strategies of Student Writers and Experienced Writers" *(CCC* 31 [December 1980], 46–49) Nancy Sommers makes distinctions between revising and editing. The former, she points out, encompasses the entire composition and often takes several times to complete; the latter, which has the purpose of polishing the text, deals with grammatical and usage problems. During the process of revision, the writer not only focuses on stylistic concerns, but also continues to mold the text to its purpose and audience. Sommers points out that student writers, in contrast to experienced writers, are more likely to edit than to rewrite. They approach rewriting primarily as a matter of rewording: eliminating repetition, finding synonyms, deleting words. Less frequently do they deal with rearrangement or addition of material. Experienced writers, on the other hand, continue to search for the shape of their discussion as they revise, making changes primarily in sentences, by addition and deletion. Sommers suggests the appropriate uses of revision in a question she raised a year earlier in "The Need for Theory in Composition Research," *(CCC* 30 [February 1979], 48). She asks: "Instead of thinking of revision as an activity at the end of the process, what if we thought of revision as a process of making a work congruent with what a writer intends—a process that occurs throughout the writing of a work?"

QUOTATION ABOUT WRITING

Let your literary compositions be kept from the public eye for nine years at least.

—Horace

To revise successfully you need first to expect to revise. Some people think that anyone who revises is not a good writer. Only the opposite is true. Writing is largely revising. Experienced writers know that the final draft of any writing project shows on paper only a fraction of the decisions made from draft to successive draft. Revision means "to see again," to look with fresh eyes. Good writers are rewriters, people who can truly *see* their drafts and rework them into better form.

To revise successfully you need also to distance yourself from each draft. You need to read your writing with objective eyes. A natural reaction of many writers is to want to hold onto their every word, especially if they had trouble getting started with a draft. If you ever have such feelings, resist them and work on distancing yourself from the material. Before revising, give yourself some time for that rosy glow of authorial pride to dim a bit. The classical writer Horace recommended waiting nine years. Given the hectic pace of modern life, you do not have that much time. But wait a few hours, if at all possible, before going back to look anew at your work.

If time does not help you develop an objective perspective, try reading your draft aloud; hearing the material can give you a fresh new sense of an essay's content and organization. Another useful method is to read the paragraphs in your essay in reverse order, starting with the conclusion; eventually, of course, you must read your essay from beginning to end, but to achieve distance you can temporarily depart from that sequence.

1 Knowing the steps and activities of revision

Once you understand the attitudes that underlie the revision process, you are ready to move into actual revising.

As you revise, you are working to improve your draft at all levels: whole essay, paragraph, sentence, and word. A revised draft usually looks quite different from its preceding draft. To revise you need to engage in all the activities in the charts on p. 59. As you engage in each activity, keep the whole picture in mind. Changes affect more than the place revised. Check that your separate changes operate well in the context of the whole essay or a particular paragraph. Here again, getting distance from your material allows you the chance to be more objective.

Revising is usually separate from editing (3d). During editing you concentrate on important surface features such as correct spelling and punctuation. During revising, you pay attention to the meaning you want your material to deliver effectively.

STEPS FOR REVISING

1. Shift mentally from suspending judgment (during idea gathering and drafting) to making judgments.

2. Read your draft critically to evaluate it. Be guided by the questions on the Revision Checklist in this chapter or by material supplied by your instructor.

3. Decide whether to write an entirely new draft or to revise the one you have. Do not be overly harsh. While some early drafts serve best as "discovery drafts" rather than first drafts, many early drafts provide sufficient raw material for the revision process to get underway.

4. Be systematic. Do not evaluate at random. You need to pay attention to many different elements of a draft, from overall organization to choice of words. Some writers prefer to consider all elements concurrently, but most writers work better when they concentrate on different elements during separate rounds of revision.

MAJOR ACTIVITIES DURING REVISION

Add. Insert needed words, sentences, and paragraphs. If your additions require new content, return to idea-gathering techniques (see 2d).

Cut. Get rid of whatever goes off the topic or repeats what has already been said.

Replace. As needed, substitute new words, sentences, and paragraphs for what you have cut.

Move material around. Change the sequence of paragraphs if the material is not presented in logical order (see 2e-2). Move sentences within paragraphs or to other paragraphs if arrangements seem illogical (see 4c).

TEACHING TIP

You might want to emphasize to your students that the change in attitude is fairly sharp when writers switch from generating prose to revising it. Making students aware of this fact often helps them understand and feel comfortable with the notion of writing as a process.

TEACHING TIP

Many students think that revisers are poor writers. Indeed, I have been scolded more than once by people who have seen me writing in waiting rooms, on the bus, or on a park bench. "Don't you know not to make a mess when you write?" The tone is always well meaning, as if the person is trying to help me out of a deep difficulty I seem to be having. I have always been amazed at how forward strangers can get after watching me write while they supposedly stare straight ahead. Some people start to squirm, and the wise ones simply move away. But a few hardy folks want to let me know that I could suddenly become A WRITER if only I would stop crossing out and drawing arrows on my paper. For a while the confrontations inhibited me about writing outside my home, but I soon became so interested in the reactions that I got caught up in the "research" of the situations. (Try it sometime— a doctor's office or a barber or beauty shop are prime territory.) Students are always similarly surprised when they see how messy real writing can be.

Diana Hacker and Betty Renshaw *(Writing with a Voice* [Boston: Little, Brown, 1985], p. 26) have compiled a list of reasons students are reluctant to revise their writing. They include the following:

1. I wait until the last minute, so there's no time to rewrite.

2. My first draft is the best I can do. I can't improve it.

3. I don't know whether my first draft is any good or not, so how can I improve it?

4. I don't know where to begin, and I wouldn't know when to stop.

5. Well, frankly, I'm lazy.

6. When I tinker with my sentences, they just turn out worse.

7. I don't really care about what I'm writing, so I just want to get it over with.

8. Rewriting is too messy. I like to work with clean-looking pages.

9. I'm such a bad writer I hate to read my own writing.

10. Rewriting is my instructor's responsibility.

11. Rewriting is painful. I can't stand the agony.

12. If I can't get it right the first time, I must be stupid.

QUOTATION ABOUT WRITING

Titles distinguish the mediocre, embarrass the superior, and are disgraced by the inferior.

—George Bernard Shaw

2 | Using the organizing power of your thesis statement and essay title

When you revise, you need to pay special attention to your essay's thesis statement and title. Both of these features help you stay on the track, and they orient your reader to what to expect.

If your **thesis statement** does not match what you say in your essay, you need to revise either the thesis statement or the essay— and sometimes both. A thesis statement, as explained in 2e-4, must present the topic of the essay, the writer's particular focus on that topic, and the writer's purpose for writing the essay. The first draft of a thesis statement often is merely an estimate of what will be covered in the essay. Early in the revision process, you may want to check the accuracy of your estimate. You can then use the thesis statement's controlling role to bring it and the essay in line with each other.

Each writer's experience with revising a thesis statement varies from essay to essay. Tara Foster wrote a number of versions of her thesis statement before she started drafting. When she checked her thesis statement after she wrote her first draft, Foster decided that her thesis statement communicated what she wanted to say. But she did decide to change parts of her essay to conform more closely to her thesis statement. (For an example of a thesis statement being revised for a research paper, from the first through the final draft, see 32k.)

The **title** of an essay also plays an important organizing role. A good title can set you on your course and tell your reader what to expect. A *direct title* tells exactly what the essay will be about. A direct title contains key words under which the essay would be cataloged in a library or a computerized database system. As a result, a direct title is very efficient. The titles of the two essays in this chapter are direct: Tara Foster's "Knowing How to Live Alone" and Gary Lee Houseman's "Rain Forests Must Not Be Destroyed." Each title is specific and prepares the reader for the topic of the essay.

A direct title should not be too broad. An overly broad title implies that the writer has not thought through the essay's content. For example, an unsatisfactory title for Foster's essay would be "Living Alone." On the other hand, a direct title should not be too narrow. An equally unsatisfactory title for Foster's essay would be "Knowing How to Live Alone Is Important for Practical, Social, and Emotional Reasons." Such a title is closer to a thesis statement.

An *indirect title* is also acceptable in some situations, according to the writer's taste and instructor's requirements. An indirect title hints at the essay's topic. It presents a puzzle that can be solved when the essay is read. This approach can be intriguing for the reader, but the writer has to be sure that the title is not too obscure. "Solitary Strength," for example, would be a satisfactory indirect title for Tara Foster's essay, but "The Test" would be too indirect.

As you write, plan your essay's title carefully. Do not wait until the last minute to tack on a title. You might write a title before you start to draft or after a first draft while you are revising, but always check as you review your essay and make sure that the title clearly relates to the content of the evolving essay.

Whether direct or indirect, a title stands alone. The opening of an essay should never refer to the essay's title as if it were part of a preceding sentence. For example, after the title "Knowing How to Live Alone," a writer should not begin the essay with the words "This skill is very important" or "Everyone should know how to do this." The title sets the stage, but it is not the first sentence of the essay.

3 Using revision checklists

A revision checklist can help you focus your attention as you evaluate your writing. Use a checklist provided by your instructor, or compile your own based on the revision checklists here. These checklists are comprehensive and detailed; do not let them overwhelm you. Feel free to adapt them to the emphases in each course and writing assignment. Also, tailor them to your personal needs. If you know that you are weak in certain areas, spend more time on those areas.

These checklists move from the whole essay to paragraphs to sentences to words. This progression from larger to smaller elements works well for many writers.

Revision Checklists

The answer to each question on these checklists should be "yes." If it is not, you need to revise. If you are unsure of the meaning of any question, look up the material in this handbook. The reference numbers in parentheses tell you what chapter or section to consult.

The list of questions on the next page guides you to evaluate **the larger elements** of your essay. The more you work with this list, the more you can tailor it to your needs.

PROCESS/PRODUCT DEBATE

Writers are judged in the outside world by their products, not their processes. Teaching students to view writing as process is extremely useful as an instructional technique and as a guide to what real writers do. But telling students that product does not mater is to mislead them about what they will face in other courses and in the workplace.

The call for balance has been made particularly well by one of the editors of the journal *Research in the Teaching of English* in the "Musings" column in May 1984, excerpted here.

Yet that separation has been replaced by another that is likely to be equally unproductive. In the enthusiasm provoked by a focus on process, we have sometimes lost sight of the enterprise in which the process is engaged. Though our best philosophers have always warned us against false dualisms, our best research has often defined itself in reaction to the limitations of previous work. Thus the initial enthusiasm for the study of process was conditioned by a rejection of the earlier preoccupation with product. The research that has followed has been extraordinarily productive, extending both our theoretical understanding and our practical approaches. Yet one characteristic of any new idea is that, in the course of exploring its implications most fully, we learn not only its strengths but also its limitations. The strengths of the process studies of the last decade have been many, and the weaknesses minor relative to the insights we have gained. But as happens with most paradigms, we seem now to be

---

REVISION CHECKLIST: THE WHOLE ESSAY

1. Is the topic of your essay suitable for college writing and sufficiently narrow? (2c)
2. Does your thesis statement clearly communicate the topic and focus of the essay (2e-4) and the purpose of the essay (1b)?
3. Does your essay reflect an awareness of its audience? (1c)
4. Does your essay take into account the special requirements—the assignment's time limit, word limit, and other practical constraints? (2b)
5. Does your essay have a logical organization pattern? (2e-2)
6. Is the tone of your essay appropriate and consistent throughout? (2e-3)
7. Is your thesis supported well by the main ideas of the paragraphs (2e-4), and do the paragraphs cover separate but related main ideas (2e-1 and 2e-5)?
8. Have you covered all the material promised by your thesis statement? (2e-4)
9. Does your introduction lead into the thesis statement and the rest of the essay (4e), and are the connections among your paragraphs clear (4b-6)?
10. Does your conclusion provide a sense of completion? (4e)
11. Have you cut all material that goes off the topic?
12. Is the length of each paragraph in proportion to the whole essay and the length of the other paragraphs? (Remember that an introduction and a conclusion are usually shorter than any of the body paragraphs in an essay.)
13. Does your essay have a title? Does it reflect the content of the essay, directly or indirectly? (3c-2)
14. Do you use sound reasoning (5c-5e) and avoid logical fallacies (5f)?

The next list of questions guides you to evaluate the effectiveness of your **paragraphs.** When you review a paragraph within an essay, keep in mind how each paragraph functions as a separate unit *and* as a part of the whole essay. As you practice using this list, adapt it to emphasize your personal strengths and weaknesses.

REVISION CHECKLIST: PARAGRAPHS

1. Does your introduction help your audience make the transition to the body of your essay? (4e)
2. Does each body paragraph express its main idea in a topic sentence as needed? (4a-1)
3. Are your main ideas—and topic sentences (4a-1) clearly related to the thesis statement (2e-4) of the essay?
4. Are your body paragraphs *developed?* Is the development sufficient? (4a-2)
5. Does each body paragraph contain specific and concrete support for its main idea? Do the details provide reasons, examples, facts? (4a-2 and 4d)
6. Is each body paragraph arranged logically? (4c)
7. Does the conclusion give your reader a sense of completion? (4e)
8. Have you cut all material that goes off the topic?
9. Have you used necessary transitions? (4b-1, 4b-6)
10. Do your paragraphs maintain coherence with pronouns (4b-2), selective repetition (4b-3), parallel structures (4b-4 and Chapter 18)?
11. Do you show relationships between paragraphs? (4b-6)

---

approaching a point where the limitations as well as the advantages of process-oriented research are beginning to be clear.

In particular, the separation of process and product is beginning to reemerge as the unnatural dualism that our past might suggest it would inevitably become. Indeed, when reading, writing, or spoken language processes are separated from the ends they serve, we lose the essence of the process itself. Process does not consist of isolated behaviors that operate willy-nilly, but of purposeful activities that lead toward some end for the person who has chosen to engage in them.

Everyone seems to agree that process is good. So do we. The issue we raise is whether any process can ever be looking at alone. This comes from our belief that just as top-down and bottom-up approaches are interactive, so too do all processing behaviors need to be looked at interactively, as they interrelate with their outcomes. For us, process only has meaning as it works toward some end. Examination of *only* the means keeps us from understanding the most interesting complications of the human mind as it works in different ways toward different destinations.

—Judith A. Langer

The next list of questions guides you to evaluate the quality of your **sentences.** As you look at your sentences, make judgments about correctness *and* about effective style. As you gain experience using this list, delete questions you do not need and add questions that suit your individual needs.

REVISION CHECKLIST: SENTENCES

1. Are your sentences concise? (Chapter 16)
2. Have you eliminated sentence fragments? (Chapter 13)
3. Have you eliminated comma splices and fused sentences? (Chapter 14)

(continued on next page)

TEACHING TIP

Students may find it helpful to know that the strengths and weaknesses in a piece of writing are often easier for the writer to recognize if a "cooling off" period intervenes between the time of writing and the time of revision. If there is an opportunity to put the piece away for a day or so, the writer returns to it not as the composer, but as a reader, thus finding it easier to spot confusing passages or awkward statements. Since students are not famous for working far ahead of schedule, they should be encouraged to provide at least a few hours to distance themselves from the writing before trying to revise it. On the other hand, if too much time elapses between the draft and the rereading, a writer is likely to lose the sense of purpose and meaning that accompanied the original effort.

REVISION CHECKLIST: SENTENCES *(continued)*

4. Have you eliminated confusing shifts? (15a)
5. Have you eliminated misplaced modifiers (15b) and dangling modifiers (15c)?
6. Have you eliminated mixed sentences (15d) and incomplete sentences (15e)?
7. Do your sentences express clear relationships among ideas? (Chapter 17)
8. Do you correctly use coordination (17a–17c) and subordination (17d–17g)?
9. Do your sentences avoid faulty parallelism? (Chapter 18)
10. Do you use parallelism as needed to help your sentences deliver their meaning? (Chapter 18)
11. Does your writing style reflect variety and emphasis? (Chapter 19)

The final list of questions guides you to evaluate the effectiveness of your **word choice.** Use what helps you, and modify the list to make it your own.

REVISION CHECKLIST: WORDS

1. Have you used exact words? (20b) Is your usage correct? (Usage Glossary)
2. Does your word choice reflect your intentions in denotation and connotation? (20b-1)
3. Have you used specific and concrete language to bring life to general and abstract language? (20b-2)
4. Does your word choice reflect a level of formality appropriate for your purpose and audience? (21a-1)
5. Do you avoid sexist language (21b-3), slang and colloquial language (21a-3), slanted language (21a-4), clichés (21d), and artificial language (21e)?

When Tara Foster revised her first draft, she concentrated first on the overall essay and then on the paragraphs, the sentences, and the words. As many writers do, sometimes she changed words as she looked at the whole essay, and sometimes she made changes in paragraphs as she looked at her word choice. Nevertheless, she proceeded systematically through the elements so that she was sure she had covered everything.

In working with the larger elements, Foster decided that her thesis statement was working well. But she realized that she needed a title and a better topic sentence in her next-to-last paragraph. She decided that the conclusion sounded "tacked on." She also saw that the sequence of her paragraphs was not logical. She felt that taking care of practical matters should come before establishing new friendships, so she rearranged the sequence in her presentation.

In working at the paragraph level, Foster cut some material that went off the topic. She then decided to integrate what remained into the next paragraph. She also saw that she had insufficiently developed two paragraphs, so she added examples and details to them; she used the advice in 4a-2 to help her think of specifics. To help her readers understand the relations among her ideas, Foster saw that some transitional expressions were called for. She felt that the introduction and conclusion were flat, worked on new ones, and then worked to tie her conclusion more closely to the rest of her essay.

At the sentence and word level, Foster combined sentences to be more concise in discussing a statistic. She also worked for sentence variety by using an occasional short sentence and by transforming one statement into a question. She then changed some words to be more exact. For example, she replaced "what is going on" with "the feeling." As often happens with writers, she did some editing as she was revising: she changed two numerals to spelled-out numbers and she got rid of contractions.

FIRST DRAFT REVISED BY STUDENT

(I need a title)

~~Lots of~~ People are ~~scared~~ terrified of living alone.

are used to living

They ~~like to live~~ with others. When the statistics

catch up with you, therefore, you are never prepared.

I need a better introduction. Check Chapter 4

Chances are high that most adult men and women will

have to know how to live alone, briefly or longer,

QUOTATION ABOUT WRITING

I do a lot of revising. Certain chapters six or seven times. Occasionally you can hit it right the first time. More often, you don't.

—John Dos Passos

QUOTATION ABOUT WRITING

I don't write easily or rapidly. My first draft usually has only a few elements worth keeping. I have to find out what those are and build from them and throw out what doesn't work, or what simply is not alive.

—Susan Sontag

QUOTATION ABOUT WRITING

I am strongly in favor of intelligent, even fastidious revision, which is, or certainly should be, an art in itself.

—Joyce Carol Oates

---

at some time in their lives.

Many grown children move away from their hometowns to ~~get an education~~ *continue their educations* or take jobs. ~~Also,~~ *M*arried people ~~think they'll~~ *might feel they will* always be together, but *currently one out of two* ~~many~~ marriages end in divorce. [The divorce rate ~~is~~ frightening. People are not making the right choices, or they are too immature to work out their differences. Fighting over money, parents, or religion although the underlying reason is lack of compatibility. Divorce brings the couple and their children a great deal of pain.] *(Cut. I'm off the topic here)*

~~I read recently in the newspaper where~~ *E*stimates are that in the next twenty years, ~~8~~ *eight* out of ~~10~~ *ten* married women end up widows, ~~This will happen to~~ *usually* ~~most of them~~ late in life. ~~This~~ *An* (statistic) ~~is~~ even sadder ~~than divorce. I feel sorry for any happily~~ *concerns the death of a spouse.* ~~married person whose spouse dies.~~ *(Change order of these two sentences)*

People living alone need to establish new friendships. When single people feel self-reliant, *they can have an* ~~It's~~ easier ~~for them to start~~ *time* getting out and meeting new people. *For instance,* ~~S~~ome students are in the habit of always going to classes with a friend, ~~and~~ *but* they can be *pleasantly surprised to* find that they can concentrate better on the course, *and* also have a chance to make some new friends. *(Move this ¶ to come after next ¶)*

The idea of going places alone can paralyze some ~~Friends can help people take care of practical~~ people. *Once you make the attempt, however, you find* ~~by keeping them company and going with them.~~ *that everyone welcomes a new friendly face.*

One good way to prepare for living alone is to learn how to take care of practical matters. ~~Many~~ *For example, they might not* ~~people don't~~ know how to do something as simple as opening a checking account. *Similarly,* ~~m~~*M*aking major purchases *(Move this paragraph up)*

is something people have to handle. *How long can a person manage with* ~~Such as a~~
refrigerator that ~~can't~~ *cannot* be repaired or a useless car*?*
After some *ping* Shop around and mak*ing* price comparisons. ~~All~~ *Most* decisions
are much ~~easier~~ *less complicated* than *they seem* at first.
Probably the most difficult problem for people living alone is dealing with feelings of lonliness ~~are the hardest to take.~~

~~I think this is what people fear the most.~~ First,
the feeling, they confuse
people have to understand ~~what is going on.~~ Being *people living alone*
with
alone ~~does not mean~~ being lonely. Second, ~~singles~~ have
everyone needs to get involved
to fight depression. Third, ~~they have to keep busy.~~
with activities such as volunteering their services to help others.
People living alone have to handle practical,

social, and emotional problems.

Last paragraph is boring. I need a more interesting concluding device. Check Chapter 4

Foster then typed her second draft neatly and, as required by the assignment, submitted it with the first draft on which she had handwritten her revisions.

SECOND DRAFT

Tara Foster

Professor Rittenhouse

English 101, Section G

25 October 19XX

Knowing How to Live Alone

"Alone one is never lonely," says May Sarton.

Most people, however, are terrified of living alone.

They are used to living with others. When the

statistics catch up with you, therefore, you are

BACKGROUND

How to keep going with a piece of writing when spirits sag and ideas seem to be few and far between is a problem that writers deal with in a variety of ways. In the August 3, 1987, issue of *New York* Magazine, Frederick Kaufman reports the answers several writers gave him in answer to his questions about moving forward in their work. Kaufman says Gay Talese commented that "he writes best in the morning, and so creates two mornings each day: He rises at nine, writes for three hours, works out, takes a nap, then writes some more." Using a sharply different work habit, Tama Janowitz reported that she "used to write on the bus, working until the end of the line. Now she gets creative by thinking about last night's dinner: 'I'll start by describing a hot-fudge sundae or a pizza. I never have trouble writing about food.' " Kaufman reports that according to Norman Mailer, "The *only* trick is to go in each morning and write, even if your spirit has the taste of aspirin in it." Mailer warns, however, "—this does not apply to poets." Kaufman himself agrees with Mailer, reporting that he took Mailer's advice: "went in, sat down, and wrote. When I got stuck, I did some dishes, then wrote some more."

BACKGROUND

In "Revision With a Computer: Seven Strategies" *(The English Record* 39 [1988], 18–21), James Strickland outlines revision techniques that can be taught to writers who have used word processing to enter text into a text file. He suggests the following helpful strategies. (They can be used in conjunction with Appendix A in this handbook.)

1. Students create cumulative sentences through the addition of noun phrases, verb phrases, and absolutes, as suggested by Christensen's generative rhetoric, which adds right-branch modifiers to sentences, elaborates on the basic premise, explains a term, or completes a thought. Students can return at any point in the text to add information, which may generate more ideas. Strickland comments that word processing "encourages cumulative sentence revision because it moves the text over to make room for the new modifiers, and with 'word-wrap' and 'paragraph reformatting' features, it adjusts everything so that the text looks untouched."

2. To check the coherence of a text, students select the MVS, the "most valuable sentence" of each paragraph. Working with a renamed copy of their text file to protect the original, they delete all but the MVS from each paragraph, producing a compressed version of the writing. As Strickland points out, it is "a map of the forward motion of the essay, a top-level view of its structure."

3. Using the compressed text as an outline, the writer returns to the original text to create the "stairway of elaboration," sentences and paragraphs added to improve coherence. It is a process of expansion. Using the metaphor of the stairway to explain the process, Strickland says the writer is like a builder who can increase the number of stairs but can also elaborate on each step, making it wider and deeper.

never prepared. Chances are high that most adult men and women will have to know how to live alone, briefly or longer, at some time in their lives.

Many grown children move away from their hometowns to continue their educations or take jobs. Married people might feel they will always be together, but recent news reports say that one out of two marriages end in divorce. An even sadder statisitic concerns the death of a spouse. Estimates are that in the next twenty years eight out of ten married women will end up widows, usually late in life.

One good way to prepare for living alone is to learn how to take care of practical matters. For example, they might not know how to do something as simple as opening a checking account. Similarly, making major purchases is something people might have to handle. How long can a person manage with a refrigerator that cannot be repaired or a useless car? After some shopping around and making price comparisons. Most decisions are much less complicated than they seem at first.

People living alone need to establish new friendships. When, single people feel self-reliant they can have an easier time getting out and meeting new people. For instance, some students are in the habit of always going to classes with a friend, but they can be pleasantly surprised to find that they can concentrate better on the course and also have a

chance to make some new friends. The idea of going
places alone can paralyze some people. Once you
make the attempt, however, you find that everyone
welcomes a new friendly face.

   Probably the most difficult problem for people
living alone is dealing with feelings of lonliness.
First, people have to understand the feeling, they
confuse being alone with being lonely. Second,
people living alone have to fight depression.
Third, everyone needs to get involved with activities,
such as volunteering their services to help others.

   People need to ask themselves, "If I had to
live alone starting tomorrow morning, would I know
how?" This is an important question.

4 Knowing how to use criticism

When criticism is constructive, you can learn a great deal about your writing through the eyes of others. Still, you have much company among writers if your initial reaction to criticism is defensive. Someone else's reactions to your writing can feel like an intrusion at first. Writing is a personal act, even when a writer is trying to communicate with a reader. The more you write, however, the more you will come to welcome constructive criticism.

The eyes of another person, someone who cares to help you improve, can give you an objective view of your material. Useful criticism helps you move your writing closer to what a reader needs to complete the act of communication. In working with comments, look at each one separately. First, make sure that you understand what the comment says. If you are unsure, ask. Next, be open-minded about the comment. If you resist every comment, you will miss many opportunities to improve. Finally, use the comments to revise according to what you think will improve your draft.

4. To teach the copy/move function of the software, which can rearrange and reorganize parts of a text, an instructor can ask students to move their concluding paragraph to the opening of the essay, and the introductory one to the end. Reading the rearranged work can lead to a new understanding of the purposes of beginnings and endings, specifically that writers' discoveries are often made at the end of a writing attempt, after they find what they wanted to say, and that readers usually need to know about that discovery at the beginning.

5. Stylistic revision can be carried out with the search-and-replace function of the software to find what Strickland calls "fuzzy" words—such as *very, really, quite, rather,* excessive *which* phrases, *th* words, and nominalizations. After they have been identified, the writer can decide if and how they are to be revised.

6. A spell checker helps students edit their orthography. By pointing out questionable spellings and offering alternative ones, the computer repeats, according to Strickland, the time-honored injunction to "look it up in the dictionary."

7. The final strategy is a computer conversation, which Strickland calls collaborative revision. Writers respond to each other's writing by way of on-line conversations: a new version of writers talking to each other about their work.

The value of revision with a computer, says Strickland, is that students see their work as a fluid text that can be easily added to, subtracted from, rearranged, and manipulated.

Certainly, all of us sometimes feel that we are drowning in student writing. The battle rages constantly: Do I spend twenty minutes on each short essay or do I spend five minutes and get to respond to more of what my students write?

Given the few minutes that we have for each essay, decisions about what and how to write are important. Codes (abbreviations such as *sp* and *agr*; references to the text, such as *15a*) are a clear, fast way to refer to unambiguous matters in grammar, punctuation, and mechanics. Make sure students know what the symbols mean: you might review the symbols you ordinarily use as part of the follow-up to their receiving their first piece of writing back from you. Along with citing errors, many symbols send a secondary message: "This matter is important but relatively uninspiring. Fix it quickly (and learn the information) and move on to the more interesting aspects of your essay."

Many issues of substance are difficult to discuss exclusively by code. Besides, students like to feel that a real human being is reading their work—and real people ask questions when they are puzzled. Therefore, whenever possible, phrase your reactions as questions. Instead of writing *"unclear"*, ask "How does this relate to your thesis?" If you do not have time to write many questions, try to get at least one in per paper. Psychologically, people can't help but answer questions—at least in their own minds. So, to ask a question is to guarantee an answer. And with the answer in mind a student can revise.

Whenever time permits, a good description deserves more than "nice" scribbled in the margin; you might say "You really made me see the lake at sundown." If a student tells you about a cooking disaster, you might say "You had me laughing in sympathy. The

Tara Foster's assignment, shown on page 18, called for Foster to hand in both a first and second draft. Foster's instructor explained that the second draft would be considered an "essay in progress" and all comments would be geared toward helping students write a final draft. When her second draft was returned, Foster saw two types of comments from her instructor: questions to stimulate further writing and codes referring to places in this handbook for Foster to consult. Here is Foster's second draft with comments from her instructor.

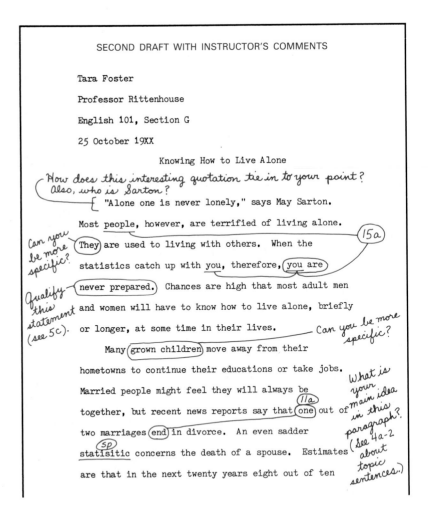

SECOND DRAFT WITH INSTRUCTOR'S COMMENTS

Tara Foster

Professor Rittenhouse

English 101, Section G

25 October 19XX

Knowing How to Live Alone

How does this interesting quotation tie in to your point? Also, who is Sarton?

"Alone one is never lonely," says May Sarton.

Most people, however, are terrified of living alone. *Can you be more specific?* They are used to living with others. When the statistics catch up with you, therefore, you are never prepared. *Qualify this statement (see 5c).* Chances are high that most adult men and women will have to know how to live alone, briefly or longer, at some time in their lives. *Can you be more specific?*

Many grown children move away from their hometowns to continue their educations or take jobs. *What is your main idea in this paragraph? (see 4a-2 about topic sentences.)* Married people might feel they will always be together, but recent news reports say that one out of two marriages end in divorce. An even sadder statisitic concerns the death of a spouse. Estimates are that in the next twenty years eight out of ten

15a *11a* *sp*

married women will (end up) widows, usually late in
life.

informal (see 21a-1)

10b *Unclear pronoun ref.*

One good way to prepare for living alone is to
learn how to take care of practical matters. For
example, <u>they</u> might not know how to do something as
simple as opening a (checking account.) Similarly,
making (major purchases) is something people might
have to handle. How long can a person manage with a
refrigerator <u>that cannot be repaired or a useless</u>

Can you help your readers tie this information in to your thesis?

18 *parallelism*

<u>car?</u> [After some shopping around and making price
comparisons.] Most decisions are much less
complicated than they seem at first.

13b *fragment*

How does this idea relate to the previous one?

People living alone need to establish new
friendships. When, single people feel self-reliant,
they can have an easier time getting out and meeting
new people. [For instance, some students are in the
habit of always going to classes with a friend, but
they can be pleasantly surprised to find that they
can concentrate better on the course and also have a
chance to make some new friends.] The idea of going

24b-1 *comma error*

What is the relationship among these ideas? See Chap. 17 about subordination.

Can you be more specific?

(places) alone can paralyze some <u>people</u>. Once <u>you</u>
make the attempt, however, <u>you</u> find that (everyone)
welcomes a new friendly face.

15a

Are there no exceptions?

Probably the most difficult problem for people
living alone is dealing with feelings of <u>lonliness</u>.
First, people have to understand the feelings, they
confuse being alone with being lonely. Second,

SP

14a *comma splice*

same thing happened to me." Such comments validate students' experiences and
also demonstrate compassionate reading.

In many cases, reaction comments are
most useful in the final response to an essay.
Many students turn to the end of their essays before reading marginal comments. After the grade, this is the part of our response
that is most crucial to students. The final
comment is our total impression, while the
margins represent a kind of running commentary. To be useful, a closing comment
needs to clarify our response, not duplicate
the grade: a student whose grade has
jumped from D to B knows his or her work
is "better," so try to be specific.

A useful end comment consists of at least
several sentences. A serviceable pattern consists of a personal response, a sentence
about the content and organization of the
piece (positive as well as negative observations—see the end comment to Foster), and
where pertinent a few sentences about a recurring mechanical or grammatical issue
(e.g., "Try to hear and pronounce the ends
of words, You frequently omit -*s* and -*ed*
endings, resulting in tense and number
errors that can confuse a reader").

TEACHING TIP

Many of us have had the experience of reading what is supposedly a student's revision of an essay we have already read and responded to, only to find that most of our comments have been ignored; the revision turns out to be the original essay with a few spelling errors corrected. Sometimes students do not know how to respond fully to an instructor's comments.

One step in demystifying comments is to have the class collectively respond to the instructor's comments on Tara Foster's second draft. Ask the students to read the instructor's comments on Tara Foster's essay and decide what Foster might do in response to each one. You might lead a discussion of the options for fixing each problem. As you come to each comment, allow sufficient time for students to think about and draft revisions or to look up the needed information in their *S & S Handbook for Writers*. Invite students to offer their revisions at each comment, and keep students alert to the many good alternatives that can emerge in response to the instructor's questions. You might also point out that responses are more likely to be identical to the coded comments of the instructor because most of them call for corrections of grammar or punctuation.

An alternative to the class discussion comment-by-comment is to assign the entire revision as a home or class exercise. Then students can discuss their thought-through answers and compare their results.

As much as possible, try to use dittoed material or overhead transparencies for the discussion of alternate complete third drafts. Students often cannot follow the discussion if too much relies on memory of various similar versions.

number and shift agreement problem ~~people~~ living alone have to fight depression.

Third, ~~everyone~~ needs to get involved with activities, *Develop your paragraph as explained in 4a-2.* such as volunteering ~~their~~ services to help others.

How does this question tie in to your thesis? People need to ask themselves, "If I had to live alone starting tomorrow morning, would I know how?" This is an important question.

You revised your first draft well, so this second draft shows good progress. Your thesis statement clearly reflects your purpose and focus. Now you are ready to develop your paragraphs more fully. When you revise, think through the questions I ask, and refer to the handbook material I point out. I'm looking forward to reading your final draft. You are writing on a fresh and interesting topic.

---

5 | Knowing how to be a peer critic

Being a **peer critic** means using structured procedures to react to and make suggestions about another student's writing. Peer critiquing is an interactive communication process. It involves reading and thinking together, asking and explaining, talking and listening. As a student writer, be sure that your instructor wants you to use peer critiquing before you do so. There can be a fine line between giving opinions and doing others' work for them.

When you are a peer critic, you are part of a respected tradition of colleagues helping colleagues. Professional writers often seek to improve their rough drafts by asking other writers for comments. When you give comments as a student writer, know that you are not expected to be an expert. What you do offer can be quite valuable: opinions from the point of view of a writer who understands what his or her peer is going through. Try always to base your comments on an understanding of the writing process and of the features that characterize effective writing. The more concrete and specific your comments, the more helpful. The comment "this is good" might seem pleasant, but it says little. What makes the writing "good": ideas, patterns of organization, sentences, words?

When you receive comments from a peer critic, remain open-minded about what is said. Constructive criticism can help you read your writing in a fresh way that results in better revision. Encourage your peer to be honest. You, however, are the person who decides which comments to use, and which to ignore, when revising.

If your instructor distributes a list to guide peer discussion, follow it carefully. If you are expected to decide what to discuss with peers, you can use or adapt the revision checklists in this handbook section. Guidelines for being an effective peer critic appear in the chart.

GUIDELINES FOR BEING AN EFFECTIVE PEER CRITIC

1. Think of the writing as "work in progress."
2. Think of yourself in the role of a coach, not a judge.
3. After reading your peer's writing, give a brief summary of what you have read. This provides a check to determine that what you understand is what the writer intended.
4. Be sure to compliment. Being specific, point out what you think is well done.
5. Be sure to offer honest, constructive suggestions for improvement. Being specific, point out what you think needs revision.
6. As you work through the material, invite the writer to ask questions and say how you might be most helpful.
7. When possible, write down your comments to give to your peer (or provide for your peer to take notes while you are commenting).

3d   Knowing how to edit

To **edit,** you focus on surface features. When you edit, you check the technical correctness of your writing. You pay attention to correct grammar, spelling, and punctuation, and to correct use of capitals, numbers, italics, and abbreviations.

Editing is sometimes referred to as revising (3c). Editing is discussed separately here because it focuses more on presentation than on meaning. If you edit too soon in the writing process, you might distract yourself from checking to see if your material delivers its

BACKGROUND

Many instructors are strongly attracted to the use of peer revision and editing groups, since they provide immediate feedback from an audience other than the teacher plus the increased opportunity for one-on-one consultations between teacher and student. Some even build entire courses around the workshop model. A concise statement of how to use the classoom as a writing workshop appears in Chapter 12 of Erika Lindemann's *A Rhetoric for Writing Teachers* (2nd ed., New York: Oxford UP, 1987, pp. 184–6). Her suggestions include the following guidelines for teachers:

1. Use groups of no more than three students. Let students work with whomever they choose, as long as they do the work.

2. Assign specific work and define it concretely. Begin with brief tasks of 10 to 20 minutes, expanding the work period to a maximum of 30 or 35 minutes as students become comfortable working with each other.

3. Suggest specific questions, especially in the beginning, that writers and readers can ask each other. The session should begin with a writer's explanation of some strategy in the paper. Readers should begin by noting strengths of the writing. When readers or writers identify a problem, they should explain why it is a problem and suggest a solution.

4. Stay involved with what is going on, but avoid taking control. Initially make sure that each group is underway, then listen, from a distance, to each group, intervening only when one is not making progress. Refrain from giving "the answer" to groups that ask for help. Instead, pose questions that will help them discover a solution to their problems.

The result, according to Lindemann, is a classroom that realizes the primary objective of a writing course: "students and teachers writing and discussing each other's work."

QUOTATION ABOUT WRITING

Purpose and craftsmanship—ends and means—these are the keys to your judgment.

—Marya Mannes

QUOTATION ABOUT WRITING

I love spending an hour or two with a dictionary and a thesaurus looking for a more nearly perfect word. Or taking my pen and ruthlessly pruning all the unnecessary adjectives, or fooling around with the rhythm of a sentence or a paragraph by changing a verb into a participle or making any number of little changes that a magazine editor I work with calls "mouse milking."

—Marie Winn

TEACHING TIP

A personal editing checklist, a list of problems that recur from one piece of writing to the next, can help any writer spot potential trouble spots. You may want to suggest that students go through returned papers, listing each marked error and grouping those that are similar, such as spelling errors, subject–verb agreement errors, and comma splices. After becoming aware of the kinds of problems that are most likely to occur, the writer can devise ways of checking new manuscripts to make sure they are not present. For example, if the s is left off most third-person singular verbs, the writer should go through a new paper checking each such construction for agreement.

meaning effectively. You are ready to edit when you have a final draft that contains suitable content, organization, development, and sentence structure. Your job during editing is not to generate a new draft but to fine-tune the surface features of the draft you have. Once you have polished your work, you are ready to transcribe it into a final copy.

Editing is crucial in writing. No matter how much attention you have paid to planning, shaping, drafting, and revising, you need to edit carefully. Slapdash editing will distract your readers and, in writing for assignments, lower your grade.

Editing takes patience. Inexperienced writers sometimes rush editing, especially if they have revised well and feel that they have prepared a good essay. When you edit, resist any impulses to hurry. Matters of grammar and punctuation take concentration—and frequently the time to check yourself by looking up rules and conventions in this handbook. As you edit, be systematic. Use a checklist supplied by your instructor or one you compile from the following editing checklist.

Editing Checklist

The answer to each question on this checklist should be "yes." If it is not, you need to edit. If you are unsure of the meaning of any question, look up the material in this handbook. The reference numbers in parentheses tell you what chapter or section to consult.

EDITING CHECKLIST

1. Is the grammar correct? That is, have you used correct verb forms (Chapter 8); have you used the correct case of nouns and pronouns (Chapter 9); do pronouns refer to clear antecedents (Chapter 10); do subjects and verbs agree (Chapter 11); do pronouns and antecedents agree (Chapter 11); have you distinguished between adjectives and adverbs (Chapter 12)?

2. Is the spelling correct? (Chapter 22)

3. Have you used hyphens correctly both for compound words and for dividing words at the end of a line? (Chapter 22)

4. Have you correctly used commas? (Chapter 24)

3d

EDITING CHECKLIST *(continued)*

5. Have you correctly used semicolons (Chapter 25), colons (Chapter 26), apostrophes (Chapter 27), quotation marks (Chapter 28)?

6. Have you correctly used other marks of punctuation? (Chapter 29)

7. Have you correctly used capital letters, italics, numbers, and abbreviations? (Chapter 30)

8. Have you followed the format requirements of the assignment? (Manuscript Form Appendix)

QUOTATION ABOUT WRITING

What makes me happy is rewriting. . . . It's like cleaning house, getting rid of all the junk, getting things in the right order, tightening things up.

—Ellen Goodman

Tara Foster revised her work into a final draft based on her instructor's comments and her own sense of what she needed. She then edited it into final form. Here is Foster's final draft.

FINAL DRAFT: ESSAY WITH INFORMATIVE PURPOSE*

Tara Foster

Professor Rittenhouse

English 101, Section G2

31 October 19XX

Knowing How to Live Alone

Introduction: Identification of situation

"Alone one is never lonely," quotes May Sarton in her essay "The Rewards of Living A Solitary Life." Most people, however, are terrified of living alone. They are used to

---

TEACHING TIP

Revising is a process just as composing is a process. Students may find it helpful to examine the steps they go through when revising, editing, and proofreading. Here are some questions they can use to look carefully at how they approach these final stages of writing a paper.

1. How did you make the mental shift from suspending judgment to making judgment?

2. Did you use the questions on the Revision Checklist in this chapter or material supplied by your instructor?

3. How did you decide whether to write an entirely new draft or to revise the one you had?

4. If you had readers other than the teacher, how did you use their suggestions? Did you use all of them? None of them?

5. Did you reconsider your original purpose and audience?

6. Did you need to make any changes in your introduction or conclusion because of other changes in your text?

7. Was your original title still appropriate?

(continued on next page)

*First draft on pages 56–57; first draft with student's comments on pages 65–67; second draft on pages 67–69; second draft with instructor's comments on pages 70–72.

TEACHING TIP *(continued)*

8. Did you consider different elements of your writing during separate rounds of revision?

9. How much new material did you add? In how many places did you add new words, sentences, or paragraphs?

10. How much material did you delete? In how many places did you cut out words, sentences, or paragraphs?

11. How many changes in the sequence of paragraphs did you make?

12. Did you use a checklist, either the one in this chapter, your own, or one supplied by your instructor, to examine your writing for grammar, spelling, punctuation, or capitalization problems?

13. Did you edit your paper in a single reading or look for possible errors in a series of readings?

14. Did you read your paper aloud to find errors? Did you start at the end? Did you read it line by line?

15. Did you reconsider the format of your paper?

living with others--children with parents, roommates with roommates, friends with friends, husbands with wives. When the statistics catch up with them, therefore, they are rarely prepared.

Thesis statement

Chances are high that most adult men and women will need to know how to live alone, briefly or longer, at some time in their lives.

Background: facts that relate to the thesis

In the United States, circumstances often force people to live alone. For example, many high school and college graduates move away from their hometowns to continue their educations or take jobs. Most schools assign roommates, but employers usually expect people to take care of their own living arrangements. Also, married people might feel they will always be together, but recent news reports say that one out of two marriages ends in divorce. An even sadder statistic concerns the death of a spouse. Estimates are that in the next twenty years eight out of ten married women will become widows, usually late in life. These facts show that most people have to live by themselves at least once in their lives whether they want to or not.

Support: first area

One good way to prepare for living alone is to learn how to take care of practical matters. For example, some students and newly single people might not know how to do something as simple as opening a checking account. When making arrangements alone, they might be too tense to find out that they can

compare banks as well as the benefits of various
types of accounts. Similarly, making major purchases
is something people living alone might have to
handle. When divorced or widowed people were
married, perhaps the other spouse did the choosing
or the couple made the decisions together. But how
long can a person manage with a refrigerator that
cannot be repaired or a car that will not run? After
shopping around and making price comparisons, most
people find that these decisions are much less
complicated than they seem at first.

Support:
second area

The confidence that single people get from
learning to deal with practical matters can boost
their chances for establishing new friendships. When
singles feel self-reliant, they can have an easier
time getting out and meeting new people. For
instance, some students are in the habit of always
going to classes with a friend. When they break this
dependency, they can be pleasantly surprised to find
that they can concentrate better on the course and
also have a chance to make some new friends.
Likewise, the idea of going alone to the beach or to
parties can paralyze some singles. Once they make
the attempt, however, people alone usually find that
almost everyone welcomes a new, friendly face.

Support:
third area

Probably the most difficult problem for people
living alone is dealing with feelings of loneliness.
First, they have to understand the feeling. Some

people confuse being alone with feeling lonely. They need to remember that unhappily married people can feel very lonely with spouses, and anyone can suffer from loneliness in a room crowded with friends. Second, people living alone have to fight any tendencies to get depressed. Depression can lead to much unhappiness, including compulsive behavior like overeating or spending too much money. Depression can also drive people to fill the feeling of emptiness by getting into relationships or jobs that they do not truly want. Third, people living alone need to get involved in useful and pleasurable activities, such as volunteering their services to help others.

Conclusion: call for awareness

    People need to ask themselves, "If I had to live alone starting tomorrow morning, would I know how?" If the answer is "No," they need to become conscious of what living alone calls for. People who face up to life usually do not have to hide from it later on.

Gary Lee Houseman went through all steps in the writing process as he wrote his essay on rain forests. (See page 18 for the assignment.) His work in gathering ideas is shown in 2d-1 and 2d-5, and his informal outline is shown in 2e-5. The dominant purpose of Houseman's essay is *persuasive*. He used a reliable format for presenting an argument or an opinion. He put his thesis statement at the beginning of the introductory paragraph. Next, he sequenced the body paragraphs by first giving background (along with a definition) of the topic, then supporting his thesis with several main ideas, and then refuting major objections to his position. Finally, he wrote a conclusion that points to the future and calls for awareness. Here is Houseman's final draft.

FINAL DRAFT: ESSAY WITH PERSUASIVE PURPOSE

Gary Lee Houseman

Professor Anchor

English 101, Section S4

15 November 19xx

Rain Forests Must Not Be Destroyed

Introduction: Identification of the problem

Developers' bulldozers have been leveling thousands of acres of rain forests every day in recent years. The rain forests of Central and South America, Africa, and the Orient are being destroyed to make way for civilization. As a result, one plant or animal a day is added to the list of extinct species on this planet. By 1990 the number will rise to one life form per hour. Early in the next century, rain forests will disappear forever. This destruction must stop.

Thesis statement

Rain forests must be preserved because they offer the human race many irreplaceable resources.

Background: definition and description

Rain forests are a special category of forests. They are found only in tropical regions of the world, usually close to the equator. Rainfall averages 80 inches a year, which explains why the forests are identified as rain forests. The rain combined with the warm tropical temperatures creates dense, lush vegetation. The huge evergreen trees are so close together their branches overlap and form an enormous, towering "canopy." Little light gets through to the ground, but on the canopy and immediately below on

BACKGROUND: RAIN FORESTS

According to Dr. Terry Erwin, entomologist at the National Museum of Natural History, samplings of the insect life of rain forests indicate that there are probably from 15 or 30 million species of insects on Earth (the previous estimate was from .75 to 1.5 million). This radical shift in our knowledge of insect populations is due to new technology that now enables scientists to study the canopy of a rain forest. (Certainly, analogous findings about new plant life are possible.)

Before Erwin's work, scientists estimated that insects made up 75.9% of the species on Earth (all invertebrates, including insects, 96.7%). Revised figures as of 1986 indicate that invertebrates make up 99.1% of all species. Humans and other vertebrates (all fish, birds, and mammals) make up less than 1% of species. For all the crowding in our cities, people are a tiny minority on this planet.

the trees, plant and insect life are abundant and
rich with benefits for humanity.

Support:
first reason

One major value of rain forests is biomedical.
The plants and animals of rain forests are the source
of many compounds used in today's medicines. A drug
that helps treat Parkinson's disease is manufactured
from a plant that grows only in South American rain
forests. Some plants and insects found in rain
forests contain rare chemicals that relieve certain
mental disorders. Discoveries, however, have only
begun. Scientists say that rain forests contain over
a thousand plants that have great anticancer
potential. To destroy life forms in these forests is
to deprive the human race of further medical advances.

Support:
second reason

Not only for their medical riches but also for
their role in maintaining global natural balances,
rain forests must be saved. Living organisms exist
in check with each other, so when one is destroyed,
another can overgrow and cause terrible problems.
For example, when developers level rain forests,
birds lose their nesting areas and no longer feed
on the insects there. The insects flourish and attack
farm crops. Then the devastation of agriculture
causes an increase in food prices and a resulting
increase in human hunger world wide. Similarly,
when thousands of acres of rain forest are bought up
by developers and stripped of their vegetation, the
natives who support themselves on the land have no

means of subsistence. Deprived of their livelihood, as well as their dignity, the natives who used to be self-sufficient often become dependent on their already debt-ridden governments.

Support: third reason

Most important, rain forests must be protected because their trees regulate the planet's oxygen supply and climate. Rain forests help to balance conditions in the atmosphere by manufacturing oxygen and absorbing carbon dioxide. As the number of trees decreases, the world has less oxygen. Furthermore, deforestation leads to reduced ability to absorb carbon dioxide. Excess carbon dioxide creates what is called a "greenhouse effect," a process that is gradually warming the planet. By the middle of the next century, the warming of Earth's atmosphere could cause some melting of the polar ice caps. The sea levels would then rise and put some coastal areas and islands under water. Although the melting would be gradual enough to give people a chance to relocate, the rising ocean would cover such landmarks as the Statue of Liberty and such cities as New Orleans. Also, the greenhouse effect would change rainfall patterns. Areas formerly good for agriculture could become deserts.

Major likely objections and responses to them

Some people see no problem in the destruction of rain forests. These people say that developing the land provides needed raw materials. They point to the hungry demand for firewood for natives and people in third-world countries. In most cases, however, synthetic fuels could be used and the trees spared. The extra cost of such measures would be repaid many times in the benefits from rain forests. Another justification for destroying rain forests is the need for land to farm. This plan is extremely shortsighted because the topsoil in leveled rain forests erodes quickly in the rain and becomes useless for crops of any kind. Land cleared of rain forests usually looks like moonscapes within a few years. An equal lack of foresight is shown by greedy investors who argue for modernizing by building roads and cities at the expense of the forests. They fail to recognize that the economy of the entire world is tied to the balanced natural setting which they want to uproot.

Conclusion: point to the future and call for action

The demands on rain forests will get worse, not better, in the future. The pessimist says that nothing can be done. The optimist says that people can work together to slow and even reverse the pace of destruction. Anyone who wants to take part can begin by sending a contribution to an organization like Friends of the Earth, an environmental group based in London. They buy seedlings to reforest stripped areas and publicize the dangers of leveling rain forests. No one can afford any longer to be apathetic about the devastating destruction of the world's precious rain forests.

3e   Knowing how to proofread

When you **proofread,** you check a final version carefully before handing it in. To make sure that your work is an accurate and clean transcription of your final draft, proofread after you revise and edit. If you try to proofread while you edit, one process might distract from the other.

DISTINCTIONS AMONG THE LATER PARTS OF THE WRITING PROCESS	
Revising ———————→	Adding, cutting, replacing, and moving around material to lead to unedited final draft
Editing ———————→	Correcting surface features for technical correctness in final draft
Proofreading ———→	Repairing typed or handwritten errors in final draft

Proofreading involves a careful, line-by-line reading of your writing. You may want to proofread with a ruler so that you can focus on one line at a time. Starting at the end also helps you avoid becoming distracted by the content of your paper. Another effective proofreading technique is to read your final draft aloud, to yourself or to a friend. This can help you hear and see errors that might have slipped past your notice.

In proofreading, look for letters inadvertently left out. If you handwrite your material, be legible. If you type, neatly correct any typing errors. If a page has numerous errors, retype the page. Do not expect your instructor to make allowances for crude typing; if you cannot type well, arrange to have your paper typed properly. No matter how hard you have worked on other parts of the writing process, if your final copy is inaccurate or messy, you will not reach your audience successfully.

For information on properly presenting your final manuscript, see Appendix B.

4 Writing Paragraphs

TEACHING TIP

Essay paragraphing differs considerably from newspaper-article paragraphing. Anyone can see at a glance that newspapers frequently have paragraphs of a sentence or two. Such paragraphs are rare in essays, except perhaps as transitions. The reason for the difference in the look of essays and articles is the rationale behind each. Essays attempt to present material in a simultaneously logical and dramatic way. They begin with a hook to grab the reader's interest, and then most proceed from point to point until the end (of the narrative or of the list of causes, etc.) is reached. Rarely is the first paragraph used to reveal key information. Essays are written on the assumption that they will be read from beginning to end.

In contrast, newspaper articles (not to be confused with essays in newspapers) use few such dramatic devices as suspense. Usually, the only hook is the headline. Then in paragraph 1 the reader gets the *Who, What, Where, When, Why,* and *How.* Subsequent paragraphs reveal additional details, but all the key facts are given in paragraph 1—the opposite of the procedure in the essay's first paragraph. The further one gets into most newspaper articles, the less important the contents. In some cases, a reader can get the idea that the piece doesn't conclude so much as trail off. This is because newspaper articles are written on the assumption that they will *not* be read from beginning to end. Editors may cut off the last few inches of a story to make it fit on a page; readers may go only as far as the first paragraph.

A **paragraph** is a group of sentences that work in concert to develop a unit of thought. Without paragraphs, even a brief essay could be unwieldy for you and your reader. Paragraphing permits you to subdivide material into manageable parts and, at the same time, to arrange those parts into a unified whole that effectively communicates its message.

Paragraphing is signaled by indentation. The first line is indented five spaces in a typewritten paper and one inch in a handwritten paper. (Business letters are sometimes typed in a "block" format, with paragraphs separated by a skipped line between them but no paragraph indentations. The "block" format is generally not appropriate for essays.)

A paragraph's purpose determines its structure. In college, the most common purposes for writing are *to inform* and *to persuade,* as discussed in 1b. Some paragraphs in informative and persuasive essays serve special roles: they introduce, conclude, or provide transitions. Most paragraphs, however, are **topical paragraphs,** which are also called *developmental paragraphs* or *body paragraphs.* They consist of (1) a statement of a main idea and (2) specific, logical support for that main idea. Here is an example of a topical paragraph that seeks to inform.

1   The cockroach lore that has been daunting us for years is mostly true. Roaches can live for twenty days without food, fourteen days without water; they can flatten their bodies and crawl through a crack thinner than a dime; they can eat huge doses of carcinogens and still die of old age. They can even survive "as much radiation as an oak tree can," says William Bell, the University of Kansas entomologist whose cockroaches appeared in the movie *The Day After.* They'll eat almost anything—regular food, leather, glue, hair, paper, even the starch in book bindings. (The New York Public Library has quite a cockroach problem.) They sense the slightest breeze, and they can react and start running in .05 seconds; they can also remain motionless for days. And if all this isn't creepy enough, they can fly too.

—JANE GOLDMAN, "What's Bugging You"

ence. She then gives
here is much truth to
ates to the thesis° of
from the world, but
artments."

that seeks to per-

hat we don't know
of illiteracy in the
rance about pain—
n it without panic.
east a dozen drugs
ause—all the way
knowledge about
limiting, that it is
most frequently,
frustration, sup-
balanced diet,
stale air, or any
ody in modern

my of an Illness

Cou   The second
sent   tage for the
supp   of a chapter
whos   Is Not the
Enem

major   the three
the ch   shown in

MAJO
1. **U** a pa (4a).
2. **Co** nex
3. **De** the 4c and 4d).

support for the main idea of

These differences have several implications in the writing classroom. First, most newspaper articles make poor models for paragraphing (unless you are teaching journalism). Second, encouraging students to read a newspaper regularly may make them better informed and expose them to new vocabulary used in complete sentences, but such reading alone is not likely to help them form subconscious ideas about paragraph structure that can be usefully applied to academic writing. To learn to write essays, the students must—at least part of the time—read essays.

One way to show your students the difference between essay paragraphing and newspaper paragraphing is to give them copies of pieces dealing with the same experience: a newspaper account of a fire and an essay (such as an editorial) written in response to the event; a newspaper account of a trial and a magazine essay discussing the case. Ask students to list the differences. At the least, they will mention differences in length, number of paragraphs, and the presence of personal opinion. They may also notice the lack of a thesis statement and of a conclusion in the newspaper article and the presence of both in the essay.

You might also ask students how satisfied they would be if they were given only the first paragraph of the newspaper article and of the essay. The article's introduction will probably be far more satisfying in terms of information, less satisfying in terms of graceful presentation, background, pacing, and the like.

Another way to underscore the difference between the genres is to give students (or assign them to find) a meaty newspaper article—the kind that runs for two pages, usually about a scandal or a major crime. Have them rewrite the article as an essay. Before the students write, you might discuss with them the kinds of changes they anticipate making.

BACKGROUND

In *Errors and Expectations* Mina Shaughnessy (Oxford UP, 1977, p. 250) points out that just as novice writers must learn the structure of sentences and words by viewing them in unfamiliar, more abstract ways, they must similarly develop a new way of thinking if they are to learn paragraph and essay structure. She names two types of instruction that have merit: practice in "seeing" structure in a wide range of written materials, and practice in recognizing thought patterns that frequently appear in conventional writing tasks for college.

BACKGROUND

u-ni-ty (yoó nə tē) n. *pl* -ties (1) The state, property, or product of being united physically, socially, or morally; oneness; opposed to *division, plurality.*

—*Britannica World Language Dictionary,*
Edition of Funk and Wagnalls Standard,
p. 1373.

To raise your awareness of the features described in the chart on the previous page, read and analyze effective paragraphs such as those in this chapter. Then, as you write, you will find that your understanding of paragraph structure can help you at various points during your writing process. Before you start drafting, you might decide to subdivide your material into paragraphs and to develop each in an effective way. If you prefer to plan less at first and instead write a "discovery" or a rough draft that gets all your ideas down on paper, you can later sort out your material and arrange it into manageable paragraphs. When you are revising, you might find that a particular paragraph is weak because it does not clearly state its main idea or it does not develop that idea well. Also, you might notice that although each paragraph is well structured on its own, the paragraphs do not work together very well. This chapter offers you paragraphing options to consider as you plan, draft, and revise your writing.

4a Writing unified paragraphs

A paragraph is **unified** when all its sentences relate to the main idea. Unity is lost if a paragraph goes off the topic by including sentences unrelated to the main idea. Here is a paragraph about data bases, which lacks unity because two deliberately added sentences go off the topic.

No   We have all used physical data bases since our grammar school days. Grammar school was fun, but high school was more challenging. Our class yearbooks, the telephone book, the shoebox full of receipts documenting our deductions for the IRS—these are all data bases in one form or another, for a data base is nothing more than an assemblage of information organized to allow the retrieval of that information in certain ways. The IRS requires that taxpayers have documentation to support all but standard deductions.

In the preceding paragraph, the first sentence states the main idea, and the third sentence expands upon it. But the second and last sentences wander away from the topic of data bases. As a result, unity is lost. A reader quickly loses patience with material that rambles and therefore fails to communicate a clear message. Here is an improved version. All its sentences, including the ones adding interesting details, bear on the subject of data bases.

YES

3   We have all used physical data bases since our grammar school days. Our class yearbooks, the telephone book, the shoebox full of receipts documenting our deductions for the IRS—these are all data bases in one form or another, for a data base is nothing more than an assemblage of information organized to allow the retrieval of that information in certain ways. A telephone book, for example, assuming that you have the right one for the right city, will enable you to find the telephone number for, say, Alan Smith. Coincidentally it will also give you his address, provided there is only one Alan Smith listed. Where there are several Alan Smiths, you would have to know the address or at least part of it, to find the number of the particular Alan Smith you had in mind. Even without the address, however, you would still save considerable time by the telephone database. The book might list 50,000 names but only 12 Alan Smiths, so at the outset you could eliminate 49,988 telephone calls when trying to contact the elusive Mr. Smith.

—ERIK SANBERG-DIMENT, "Personal Computers"

1   Knowing how to use a topic sentence

The sentence that contains the main idea of a paragraph is called the **topic sentence.** Some paragraphs use two sentences to present a main idea. In such cases, the topic sentence is followed by a **limiting** or **clarifying sentence,** which serves to narrow the paragraph's focus. In paragraph 3 the second sentence is its topic sentence, and the third sentence is its limiting sentence. The rest of the sentences support the main idea.

Because it contains the main idea of a paragraph, a topic sentence focuses and controls what can be written in the paragraph. The words that create the focus and control usually appear in the sentence's predicate°. To check this, look at the example paragraphs in this chapter.

Some professional essay writers do not always use topic sentences because these writers have the skill to carry the reader along without explicit signposts. Student writers are usually required to use topic sentences so that their essays will be clearly organized and their paragraphs will not stray from the controlling power of each main idea.

BACKGROUND

Many of the conventions followed by contemporary writers did not exist in the ancient world. For example, words were not divided from each other until sometime in the seventh century A.D., and the system was not systematically followed until the eleventh. Some marks of punctuation, such as the question mark and the exclamation mark, evolved during the Middle Ages. Paragraphs had been indicated since pre-Christian days, first by short horizontal strokes or wedge-shaped signs. Later they were noted in Latin manuscripts by a new line. At the same time, it became the practice to indicate the beginning of a new paragraph with enlarged letters, sometimes extending the length of the page. Such elaborate figures became the ancestors of our capital letters. The paragraph as it is known today took shape late in the seventeenth century but was not systematically described until the nineteenth century, when Alexander Bain published his *English Composition and Rhetoric* (1866).

A school that devotes itself totally and une-quivocally to salable skills, especially in a time of high unemployment, sending young men and women into the world armed with only a narrow range of skills, is also sending lambs into the lion's den. If those people gain nothing more from their studies than supposedly salable skills, and can't make the sale because of changes in the job market, they have been cheated. But if those skills were more than salable, if study made them better citizens and made them happier to be human beings, they have not been cheated. They will find some kind of job soon enough. It might even turn out that those humanizing and liberating skills are salable. Flexibility, an ability to change and learn new things, is a valuable skill. People who have learned how to learn can learn outside of school. That is where most of us have learned to do what we do, not in school. Learning to learn is one of the highest liberal skills.

—Robert A. Goldwin, "Is It Enough to Roll with the Times?"

TEACHING TIP

To help students to make connections be-tween what happens in the classroom and what goes on in their lives in other situ-ations, you may want to encourage them to look for topic sentences in the newspapers and magazines that they read. They may be surprised to discover that in materials pub-lished for a nonacademic setting, topic sen-tences occur at beginnings and endings of paragraphs, just as they do in textbook ex-amples. In some cases they will probably find that paragraphs manage to make a uni-fied statement without the presence of a stated topic sentence. The examples they find can provide a basis for class discussion.

Topic sentence at the beginning of a paragraph

Most informative and persuasive paragraphs place the topic sentence first so that a reader knows immediately what to expect.

> 4   *Everyone must have had at least one personal experience with a computer error by this time.* Bank balances are suddenly reported to have jumped from $379 into the millions, appeals for charitable contributions are mailed over and over to people with crazy-sounding names at your address, department stores send the wrong bills, utility companies write that they're turning everything off, that sort of thing. If you manage to get in touch with someone and complain, you then get instantaneously typed, guilty letters from the same computer, saying, "Our computer was in error, and an adjustment is being made in your account."
>
> —Lewis Thomas, "To Err Is Human"

When the main idea of a paragraph comes first, deductive reasoning is being used. Deductive reasoning, as is explained in 5e-2, is a nat-ural thought pattern that starts with a general statement and moves to specific details supporting that general statement (see also 4c).

Sometimes the main idea in the topic sentence starts a para-graph and is then restated at the end of the paragraph.

> 5   *Every dream is a portrait of the dreamer.* You may think of your dream as a mirror that reflects your inner character—the aspects of your personality of which you are not fully aware. Once we understand this, we can also see that every trait portrayed in our dreams has to exist in us, somewhere, regardless of whether we are aware of it or admit it. *Whatever characteristics the dream figures have, whatever behavior they engage in, is also true of the dreamer in some way.*
>
> —Robert A. Johnson, *Inner Work*

Topic sentence at the end of a paragraph

Some informative and persuasive paragraphs reveal the sup-porting details before the main idea. The topic sentence, therefore, comes at the end of a paragraph. This arrangement reflects inductive reasoning, another natural thought pattern, discussed in 5e-1. It starts with specifics and finishes with the generalization (see also 4c). This approach is particularly effective for building suspense and for dra-matic effect. This arrangement forces readers to move through all the details before encountering the organizing effect of a main idea.

The next two paragraphs end with a topic sentence. In the first example, the main idea is fairly easy to predict as the concrete details build upon themselves. The main idea in the second example is less predictable—thus more satisfying for some readers but more challenging for others.

6   A combination of cries from exotic animals and laughter and gasps from children fills the air along with the aroma of popcorn and peanuts. A hungry lion bellows for dinner, his roar breaking through the confusing chatter of other animals. Birds of all kinds chirp endlessly at curious children. Monkeys swing from limb to limb performing gymnastics for gawking onlookers. A comedy routine by orangutans employing old shoes and garments incites squeals of amusement. Reptiles sleep peacefully behind glass windows, yet they send shivers down the spines of those who remember the quick death many of these reptiles can induce. *The sights and sounds and smells of the zoo inform and entertain children of all ages.*

—DEBORAH HARRIS, student

7   One of the most common observations anyone can make about honeybees is that they are extraordinarily good at finding honey. Furthermore, not long after one bee finds a source of honey, the whole hive seems to show up to carry it off. A young biologist named Karl von Frisch noted this fact and then asked what seemed to be a very simple question: How does the whole hive find out about a source of honey so quickly? To answer this question completely took him the rest of his life and changed the science of biology in ways still not fully appreciated. Without complicated equipment and with very little laboratory work, von Frisch and his co-workers discovered a whole universe of previously unsuspected senses and behaviors in honeybees. For more than five decades they painstakingly explored the perceptual world of the honeybee, and in recognition of his discoveries and his contribution to the founding of the modern science of animal behavior, Karl von Frisch was awarded the Nobel prize in physiology and medicine in 1973. *It all began with an observation, a question, and application of the scientific method.*

—ALLEN D. MACNEILL AND LORRIE PENFIELD,
"The Scientific Method in Biology"

Topic sentence implied

Some paragraphs make a unified statement without the use of a topic sentence. Writers must carefully construct such paragraphs, so that a reader can easily discern the main idea.

BACKGROUND

The use of topic sentences by published writers has been the subject of a great deal of research and study over the past two decades. Richard Braddock's "The Frequency and Placement of Topic Sentences in Expository Prose" (*Research in the Teaching of English* 8 [1974], pp. 287–302) reports the surprising information that in the paragraphs he examined, he found topic sentences only 13 percent of the time. Admitting that it is difficult to know exactly what a topic sentence is, he also points out that "percentages vary greatly among individual writers." Several years later, in 1979, William Irmscher reported in *Teaching Expository Writing* (Holt, Rinehart and Winston, p. 98) that his graduate students found topic sentences in 40 to 50 percent of the paragraphs they analyzed, a significantly higher percentage than Braddock discovered. Clearly we still have much to learn about how writers arrive at effective methods of paragraph development.

QUOTATION ABOUT WRITING

Within time and type, then, the individual writer makes his [or her] own unique combinations of choice. What it seems to me important for the young writer to know is what these choices are, how they have been made in the past, and how he [or she] may make them in the present. They are not infinitely various, for example, but limited and significant for certain tones and attitudes. . . .

—Josephine Miles, "The Paragraph and Beyond," *CCC,* October 1963, pp. 146–154.

8   Already, in the nation's heartland—Des Moines or Omaha—you'll find widespread use of Oriental and Mexican vegetables. Houston has some of the best Vietnamese restaurants in the world. The Los Angeles area has more than two hundred Thai restaurants. Mexican fast food has become a $1.6 billion industry covering the whole country—even Barrow, Alaska, north of the Arctic Circle, has a Mexican restaurant. And springing up throughout the land are Ethiopian, Afghan, Brazilian and other exotic ethnic eating places. Indeed, it is no longer enough for a restaurant to be just Chinese; it may be Szechuan, Hunan or Shanghai, but also Suzhou, Hangzhou or some other ethnic specialty within an ethnic specialty.

—NOEL VIETMEYER,

"Exotic Edibles Are Altering America's Diet and Agriculture"

Vietmeyer uses many details to communicate the main idea that exotic foods and restaurants are appearing all across the country. A reader does not expect to puzzle over material, so implied topic sentences must be very clear, even though they are silent.

EXERCISE 1

Identify all topic sentences, limiting sentences, and topic sentences repeated at the ends of paragraphs. If there is no topic sentence, compose an implied one.

A.   9   A good college program should stress the development of high-level reading, writing, and mathematical skills and should provide you with a broad historical, social, and cultural perspective, no matter what subject you choose as your major. The program should teach you not only the most current knowledge in your field but also—just as important—prepare you to keep learning throughout your life. After all, you will probably change jobs, and possibly even careers, at least six times, and you'll have other responsibilities, too—perhaps as a spouse and as a parent and certainly as a member of a community whose bounds extend beyond the workplace.

—FRANK T. RHODES, "Let the Student Decide"

B.   10   The once majestic oak tree crashes to the ground amid the destructive flames, as its panic-stricken inhabitants attempt to flee the fiery tomb. Undergrowth that formerly flourished smolders in ashes. A family of deer darts furiously from one wall of flame to the other, without an emergency exit. On the outskirts of the inferno, fire fighters try desperately to stop the destruction. Somewhere at the source of this chaos lies a former campsite containing the cause of this destruction—an untended campfire. This scene is one of many which illustrate how human apathy and carelessness destroy nature.

—ANNE BRYSON, student

ANSWERS: EXERCISE 1

A. The topic sentence is the first sentence.

B. The topic sentence is the last sentence.

C. The topic sentence is the first sentence, and the second sentence is a limiting sentence.

D. The topic sentence is implied: The main idea is that because interns are new on July 1, people should avoid being in a hospital in July.

E. The topic sentence is the first sentence.

BACKGROUND

In "A Generative Rhetoric of the Paragraph" (originally published in *CCC*, October 1965, and reprinted in *Notes Toward a New Rhetoric*, Harper and Row, 1967) Francis Christensen notes the similarities between the structure of the sentence and that of the paragraph. He points out that the topic sentence is parallel to the base clause of a sentence, and the supporting sentences are parallel to the added sentence modifiers. Given such a structure, the paragraph, like the sentence, develops with *addition* that has *direction of modification* or *direction of movement*. When sentences are added to develop a topic, they are usually at a lower *level of generality,* and the more sentences the writer adds, the denser the *texture*. To use this structural analysis of the paragraph to generate paragraphs, Christensen

C.   Education which involves only the gathering of knowledge for its own sake ignores the need of all people to learn to ask larger questions. People may possess a wealth of individual facts, a pile of unrelated names, dates, formulas, structures, and equations, and yet be unable to apply their knowledge to issues such as justice and dignity. For example, it is a fact that more than half the U.S. population is female. Why has the American woman always played a subordinate role in a society where she is the majority? Also, it is a fact that the rate of infant death in the United States is thirteen in every thousand births, a rate higher than that in twelve other countries. How is it possible in a country as wealthy and as technologically advanced as the United States such a cruel problem can exist?

11

—AMY DUNBAR, student

D.   This July 1, more than 13,000 doctors will invade over 600 hospitals across the country. Within minutes they will be overwhelmed. Last July 1, Dr. John Baumann, then twenty-five, walked into Washington, DC's Walter Reed Army Medical Center, where he was immediately faced with caring for "eighteen of the sickest people I have ever seen."

12

—MARILYN MACHLOWITZ, "Never Get Sick in July"

E.   There are at least two important reasons for the surplus of women in urban areas. First, cities are the best places for women to find jobs. Men account for 79 percent of the nation's farmers, 85 percent of miners, and 95 percent of loggers. But the service economy is urban and dominated by women. The second reason is the high death rate for young men in inner cities. The Bronx, for example, has only about 47 men for every 53 women in the target age group—the highest disparity of any county in New York State. Higher male mortality also explains the female skew in some rural counties, such as many of those that include Indian reservations.

13

—BRAD EDMONDSON and BLAYNE CUTLER, "Where the Boys Are"

2   Developing a paragraph

As a writer, when you know how to achieve effective **paragraph development,** your material is far more likely to deliver its message to your reader. Most successful topical paragraphs that seek to inform or persuade (see 1b) contain a generalization, which is communicated in the topic sentence of the paragraph (see 4a-1). But more is needed. In writing most topical paragraphs, you must be sure to *develop the paragraph.* Development is provided by specific,

proposes nine principles that can be applied and taught:

1. The paragraph may be defined as a sequence of structurally related sentences. They are related by coordination and subordination.

2. The top sentence of the sequence is the topic sentence. It is the sentence on which the others depend.

3. The topic sentence is nearly always the first sentence of the sequence. Topics may be established explicitly, or sometimes only be suggested; they may be presented in the shortest sentence of the paragraph, in a fragment, or in a question. They usually appear at the beginning, however.

4. Simple sequences are of two sorts—coordinate and subordinate. At this point Christensen draws the closest parallel between the structures of the sentence and paragraph. In a coordinate sequence, repetition of structure is necessary; in a subordinate sequence, repetition must be avoided, each added sentence taking a different form.

5. The two sorts of sequence combine to produce the commonest sort—the mixed sequence. The opportunity to generate the paragraph lies here with the addition of subordinate sentences to clarify and of coordinate sentences to emphasize or to enumerate.

6. Some paragraphs have no top, no topic, sentence. Where there is no top, the topic can usually be inferred from the preceding paragraph, where it may be implied or placed.

7. Some paragraphs have sentences at the beginning or at the end that do not belong to the sequence. They furnish a transition either to the new paragraph (at the beginning) or from the current paragraph at the (end), or, at the end they may provide a conclusion or coda.

8. Some paragraphing is illogical.

9. Punctuation should be by the paragraph, not by the sentence. Paragraph punctuation involves choosing whether to make compound sentences or not.

BACKGROUND

In *The Elements of Style* (2nd ed., The Macmillan Company, 1972, p. 12), William Strunk and E. B. White discuss paragraph length under their rubric that states: "Make the paragraph the unit of composition." They advise the following:

> In general, remember that paragraphing calls for a good eye as well as a logical mind. Enormous blocks of print look formidable to a reader. He [or she] has a certain reluctance to tackle them. . . . Therefore, breaking long paragraphs in two, even if it is not necessary to do so for sense, meaning, or logical development, is often a visual help. But remember, too, that firing off many short paragraphs in quick succession can be distracting. Paragraph breaks used only for show read like the writing of commerce or of display advertising. Moderation and a sense of order should be the main considerations in paragraphing.

concrete details that support the generalization. Without development, a topical paragraph contains only the broad claim of the generalization. It goes around in circles because it merely repeats the generalization over and over. It therefore does little to inform or persuade the reader.

Here is a paragraph that is unsuccessful because it contains one generalization restated four times in different words. Compare it to Paragraph 1, a successful paragraph.

No   The cockroach lore that has been daunting us for years is mostly true. Almost every tale we have heard about cockroaches is true. These tales have been disheartening people for generations. No one seems to believe that it is possible to control roaches.

This *No* paragraph is stalled. It goes nowhere. Such material does not hold the reader's interest because it neither informs nor persuades.

When you write a topical paragraph, remember that **what separates most good writing from bad is the writer's ability to move back and forth between generalizations and specific details.** A successful topical paragraph, as the sample paragraphs in this chapter illustrate, includes a generalization and specific, concrete supporting details.

Using detail is the key to effective, successful development in topical paragraphs. Details bring generalizations to life by providing concrete, specific illustrations. "RENNS" is a memory device that many writers use when they want to check whether or not they have included sufficient detail in the development of their topical paragraphs.

USING "RENNS" TO CHECK FOR SPECIFIC, CONCRETE DETAILS

- **R**easons
- **E**xamples
- **N**ames
- **N**umbers
- **S**enses (sight, sound, smell, taste, touch)

A well-developed paragraph usually has only a selection of RENNS, so do not expect your paragraphs to have all categories in the list. Also, RENNS does not mean that the details of development must occur in the order of the letters in RENNS. To see RENNS in action,

¶ *unity*

4a

read the many sample paragraphs in this chapter with an eye for the details. Also, consider the examples shown below.

Here is a paragraph that has three of the five types of RENNS. Locate as many RENNS as you can before you read the analysis of RENNS that follows the paragraph.

> Whether bad or good, in tune or not, whistling has its practical side. Clifford Pratt is working with a group of speech therapists to develop whistling techniques to help children overcome speech problems through improved breath control and tongue flexibility. People who have a piercing whistle have a clear advantage when it comes to hailing cabs, calling the dog or the children, or indicating approval during a sporting event. And if you want to leave the house and can't remember where you put your keys, there's a key chain on the market now with a beep that can be activated by a whistle: You whistle and the key chain tells you where it is.
>
> —CASSANDRA TATE, "Whistlers Blow New Life Into a Forgotten Art"

14

Paragraph 14 succeeds because it does more than merely repeat its topic sentence, which is its first sentence. It develops the topic sentence by offering concrete, specific illustrations to support the generalization that whistling has its practical side. It has Examples, including treatment for children with speech difficulties; convenience for hailing cabs, dogs, and children, and for sounding off at sporting events; and a signaling key chain. It has Names, such as Clifford Pratt, speech therapists, and children (not the general term *people*), and dogs (not the general term *animals*). It appeals to the Senses by including the feeling of tongue flexibility, the piercing sound of a whistle, the roar at a sporting event, and the sound of a key chain beeping for its owner.

Here is a paragraph that has four of the five types of RENNS. Locate as many RENNS as you can before you read the analysis of RENNS that follows the paragraph.

> We live in a changed world from that of 1888, and we are a changed nation. Our founders knew an America with rising expectations, while we see a superpower riddled with self-doubt. Tropical rain forests were a mysterious challenge in 1888. The challenge in 1988 is saving them from disappearance. Automobiles had just been invented, and airplanes were unknown. Would our founders be impressed by rush-hour traffic, a brown cloud over Denver, or aerial gridlock at Chicago's O'Hare Airport? Could they have conceived of a Mexico City with 20 million people in an atmosphere so murky that the sun is obscured, so poisonous that school is sometimes delayed until late morning, when the air clears?
>
> —GILBERT M. GROSVENOR, "Will We Mend Our Earth?"

15

QUOTATION ABOUT WRITING

I don't know why I am so helplessly led to condensation in both my fiction and my essays. Some people find it hard to follow my meaning because I don't spell it out, not entirely. My writing is simple but I like to be sort of emphatic and let it go. I remember when I was writing exams in school I'd be the first one finished. All these people writing away. As I look back on it I think I didn't want to tell the teacher what he already knew, but to try to get at things from an angle—nothing very grand, just a little twist.

—Elizabeth Hardwick, *Writers at Work*

ANSWERS: EXERCISE 2

A (paragraph 9). Reasons include learning current knowledge, keeping you learning through life, having a job, being a spouse, a parent, and a member of the community. Examples include job, spouse, parent, and member of the community. Number named is six.

B (paragraph 10). Names include oak, deer, fire fighters. Senses are invoked by sound of crashing oak, sight of flames, "fiery tomb," smoldering in ashes, deer family darting furiously, and the smell (implied) of burning trees.

C (paragraph 11). Examples include the questions about the proportion of the population that is female and the questions about the rate of infant deaths. Numbers include "majority" and a death rate of thirteen in a thousand births, which is higher than in twelve other countries.

D (paragraph 12). Reasons include the fact that all interns are new (and therefore inexperienced) as of July 1. Names include Dr. John Baumann and Walter Reed Army Medical Center. Numbers include July 1, 600 hospitals, twenty-five years of age, and eighteen sick people.

E (paragraph 13). Reasons include cities are the best places for women to find jobs, and the death rate is higher for young men in cities. Example named is the Bronx. Names used are the Bronx, New York State. Numbers include 79 percent, 85 percent, 95 percent, and 47 men for every 53 women.

ANSWERS: EXERCISE 3

Obviously answers will vary considerably, but the main goal is to help students distinguish between generalities and good detail. Perhaps having each student share with the class what he or she considers the best detail in his or her paragraph would help make this point.

Paragraph 15 succeeds because it does more than repeat its topic sentence, which is the first sentence. The paragraph develops its topic sentence with specific, concrete illustrations of the changed world that makes the United States a changed nation. It has Examples, including rain forests disappearing, automobiles and the rush hour traffic they cause, airplanes and the aerial gridlock they cause, and air pollution that cars and plane cause. It has Names: America, Denver, Chicago's O'Hare Airport, and Mexico City. It has Numbers: the years 1888 and 1988, and 20 million people. And it elicits one of the five senses: the *sight* of a "brown cloud" over Denver and the *sight* of a murky atmosphere that obscures the sun.

Some well-developed paragraphs have a single extended example to support the topic sentence.

> He was one of the greatest scientists the world has ever known, yet if I had to convey the essence of Albert Einstein in a single word, I would choose *simplicity*. Perhaps an anecdote will help. Once, caught in a downpour, he took off his hat and held it
> 16   under his coat. Asked why, he explained, with admirable logic, that the rain would damage the hat, but his hair would be none the worse for its wetting. This knack of going instinctively to the heart of the matter was the secret of his major scientific discoveries—this and his extraordinary feeling for beauty.
>
> —BANESH HOFFMAN, "My Friend, Albert Einstein"

EXERCISE 2

Reread the paragraphs in Exercise 1 and identify the RENNS in each paragraph.

EXERCISE 3

Using your own words to complete the thought, fill in the blanks with a word or phrase that is specific. Then choose one of the five as a topic sentence and write a well-developed paragraph. Use as many RENNS as you need to give the topic sentence concrete, specific support.

1. The place where I feel most comfortable is _____.
2. _____ can cause major problems for students.
3. The development of _____ is intriguing.
4. _____ is the United States's greatest asset.
5. Getting a good job depends largely on _____.

4b **Writing coherent paragraphs**

A paragraph is **coherent** when its sentences are related to each other, not only in content but also in grammatical structures and choice of words. Decisions about coherence are often made during revising, after you have written a first draft and can begin to see how your sentences might more effectively relate to one another. Here are the major ways of achieving coherence in writing.

TECHNIQUES OF COHERENCE

1. Use **transitional expressions** effectively (4b–1).
2. Use **pronouns** effectively (4b–2).
3. Use **deliberate repetition** effectively (4b–3).
4. Use **parallel structures** effectively (4b–4).
5. Use a **combination of techniques** effectively (4b–5).

---

1   Using transitional expressions

Transitional expressions—words and phrases that signal connections among ideas—can help you achieve coherence in your writing. Each expression is a signal to the reader that explains how one idea is connected to the next. The most commonly used transitional expressions are shown in the chart on the next page. ❖ COMMA ALERT: Transitional expressions are usually set off with commas. ❖

Notice how the transitional expressions (shown in boldface) help to make this paragraph coherent.

> Jaguars, **for example,** were once found in the United States from southern Louisiana to California. Today they are rare north of the Mexican border, with no confirmed sighting since 1971. They
17   are rare, **too,** in Mexico, where biologist Carl Koford estimated their population at fewer than a thousand in a 1972 survey. Some biologists think the number is even smaller today. **Similarly,** jaguars have disappeared from southern Argentina and Paraguay.
>
> —JEFFREY P. COHN, "Kings of the Wild"

EXTRA EXERCISE A

Mark all of the transitional expressions used in the following paragraph.

Edith Newbold Jones was the descendant of wealthy, socially prominent New York families. As a result, she made her formal debut before she married Edward Wharton of Boston in 1885. Soon after her marriage she began writing as a therapeutic measure. She also used her writing as a means of occupying her free time when her husband was suffering from a mental illness. Naturally, much of her writing was concerned with the closed, wealthy new York society which she had known as a child. In the 1890's, as a result of her "hobby," she published her first short stories in *Scribner's* magazine, leading, subsequently, to her recognition as one of America's best popular writers. For example, in 1924 she became the first woman ever to receive an honorary degree from Yale University. Equally important, she was awarded the Pulitzer Prize in 1921 for *The Age of Innocence*, a novel about the unbreakable moral code of Victorian society. Her most famous work, however, is *Ethan Frome*, a tragic love story. Although she continued to write about American subjects and characters, she spent much of her later life in France, where she had a home. She died there in 1937.

TRANSITIONAL EXPRESSIONS	
SIGNAL	**WORDS**
ADDITION	also, in addition, too, moreover, and, besides, further, furthermore, equally important, next, then, finally,
EXAMPLE	for example, for instance, thus, as an illustration, namely, specifically,
CONTRAST	but, yet, however, on the other hand, nevertheless, nonetheless, conversely, in contrast, on the contrary, still, at the same time,
COMPARISON	similarly, likewise, in like manner, in the same way, in comparison,
CONCESSION	of course, to be sure, certainly, naturally, granted,
RESULT	therefore, thus, consequently, so, accordingly, due to this,
SUMMARY	as a result, hence, in short, in brief, in summary, in conclusion, finally, on the whole,
TIME SEQUENCE	first, firstly, second, secondly, third, fourth, next, then, finally, afterwards, before, soon, later, during, meanwhile, subsequently, immediately, at length, eventually, in the future, currently,
PLACE	in the front, in the foreground, in the back, in the background, at the side, adjacent, nearby, in the distance, here, there,

2 | Using pronouns

When you use pronouns that clearly refer to nouns or other pronouns, you help your reader follow the bridges you build from one sentence to the next. (For advice on maintaining clear pronoun reference, see Chapter 10.) Notice how the pronouns, shown in boldface, help make this paragraph coherent.

In the morning, before the sun has broken through, the sandpiper begins to look for food. A tiny thing with gray feathers and a white underbelly, the "peep" looks, front to back, like awl and ball and cotton ball. **He** darts along the wave front, probing the sand for buried flecks of nourishment. Each feeding lasts but seconds and is sneaked in between a departing wave and the one soon to follow. With **his** head poked down into the sand, it seems impossible for the sandpiper to notice the water about to overtake **him.** Yet, at the last possible instant—later than the last possible instant, it sometimes seems—**he** turns, body suddenly erect, and races to higher ground. Rejecting flight, **he** races overland, body perfectly still, feet pounding a noiseless rat-tat-tat-tat-tat into the wet sand. The water is never more than a stride behind **him.**

—RICK HOROWITZ, "The Sandpiper's Politics"

3 Using deliberate, selective repetition

You can achieve coherence by repeating key words in a paragraph. A key word is usually one related to the main idea in the topic sentence or to a major detail in one of the supporting sentences. Repeating a key word now and then helps your reader follow your material. This technique must be used sparingly, however, because you risk being monotonous. The shorter a paragraph, the less likely that repeated words will be effective.

Notice how the careful reuse of the key words *sounds, words, hear,* and *hearing* (shown in boldface) helps make this paragraph coherent.

I was then a listening child, careful to **hear** the very different **sounds** of Spanish and English. Wide-eyed with **hearing,** I'd listen to **sounds** more than to **words.** First, there were English (gringo) **sounds.** So many **words** still were unknown to me that when the butcher or the lady at the drugstore said something, exotic polysyllabic **sounds** would bloom in the midst of their sentences. Often the speech of people in public seemed to me very loud, booming with confidence. The man behind the counter would literally ask, "What can I do for you?" But by being so firm and clear, the **sound** of his voice said that he was a gringo; he belonged in public society. There were also the high, nasal notes of middle-class American speech—which I rarely am conscious of **hearing** today because I **hear** them so often, but could not stop **hearing** when I was a boy. Crowds at Safeway or at bus stops were noisy with birdlike **sounds** of *los gringos.* I'd move away from them all—all the chipping chatter above me.

—RICHARD RODRIGUEZ, "Aria: A Memoir of a Bilingual Childhood"

18

19

EXTRA EXERCISE B

Rewrite the following paragraph using transitional words and phrases to make it more coherent. Combine and rearrange the sentences where necessary.

Americans are beginning to recognize the importance of regular exercise. Jogging gives the heart a good workout. It can damage the runner's ankles and calves. Jogging by itself does little to exercise the upper body. Some people prefer to walk. Bicycling is popular. In a pleasant setting it provides visual pleasures as well as a way to burn up calories. Some people ride a stationary bicycle at home. They can watch television while they rotate the pedals. Swimming involves the upper body as well as the legs. It allows a person to exert as much energy as possible without straining muscles. On a hot summer day swimming seems more like fun than exercise.

BIOGRAPHY

Richard Rodriquez (1944–) was born in San Francisco of Mexican parents. He received his Ph.D. from the University of California at Berkeley. In his essay "Aria: A Memoir of a Bilingual Childhood," published in 1981 in *The American Scholar,* he argues against bilingual education and what he considers to be other types of reverse discrimination. Drawing on his experience as a Spanish-speaking child in America, he extends his discussion in his widely acclaimed autobiographical book *Hunger of Memory: The Education of Richard Rodriquez,* published in 1982.

I am not complaining that the brewing and
baking were taken over by the men. If they
can brew and bake as well as women or better, then by all means let them do it. But
they cannot have it both ways. If they are
going to adopt the very sound principle that
the job should be done by the person who
does it best, then that rule must be applied
universally. If the women make better office-
workers than men, then they must have the
office work. If any individual woman is able
to make a first-class lawyer, doctor, architect
or engineer, then she must be allowed to try
her hand at it. Once lay down the rule that
the job comes first and you throw that job
open to every individual, man or woman, fat
or thin, tall or short, ugly or beautiful, who
is able to do that job better than the rest of
the world.

—Dorothy L. Sayers, "Are Women Human?"

In every structure we may distinguish the
relation or *relations,* and the items related.

—Suzanne Langer

---

4 Using parallel structures

Parallel structures are grammatically equivalent forms. They
create **parallelism,** in one sentence or among sentences in a paragraph. You can achieve coherence by using parallelism in a paragraph. Parallelism, a refinement of the deliberate, selective repetition
discussed in 4b-3, is created when the same form is used several
times, thus creating a rhythm that unifies the paragraph. The repeated tempos and sounds of parallel structures reinforce connections among ideas and create a dramatic effect. Be aware, however,
that a thin line exists between effective parallelism (explained in full
in Chapter 18) and lack of conciseness (explained in full in Chapter
16). In paragraph 20, the author uses parallel structures (shown in
boldface) for key words in his paragraph. Other parallel structures
are more subtle but highly effective: *sight and sound; under blazing
suns, in rainstorms, in pitch black nights; walking to or walking
from.* Read the paragraph aloud to hear as well as see the effect of
parallelism.

20   **The world of work** into which Jacinto and the other seven-
year-olds were apprenticed was within sight and sound of the
pueblo. **It was work** under blazing suns, in rainstorms, in pitch-
black nights. **It was work** that you were always walking to or walking from, **work without wages** and **work without end. It was
work** that gave you a bone-tired feeling at the end of the day, so
you learned **to swing a machete, to tighten a cinch, and to
walk without lost motion.** Between seven and twelve you
learned all this, each lesson driven home when your *jefe* said with
a scowl: "Así no, hombre; así." And he showed you how.

—Ernesto Galarza, *Barrio Boy*

5 Combining techniques of coherence

Often techniques of coherence work in unison, though they are
shown separately in this chapter for the sake of clear illustration.
Indeed, in most of the sample paragraphs in this chapter, many techniques of unity and coherence work together. Notice in the following paragraph by Loren Eiseley how pronouns and deliberate repetition, in particular, combine. The key words, *flower* and *pollen* and
their derivatives, are boxed. The repeated pronouns *it* and *its* are
circled, and arrows point to the antecedent. A transitional word is
underlined.

¶ *coh*

4b

When the first simple flower bloomed on some raw upland late in the Dinosaur Age, it was wind pollinated, just like its early pine-cone relatives. It was a very inconspicuous flower because it had not yet evolved the idea of using the surer attraction of birds and insects to achieve the transportation of pollen. It sowed its own pollen and received the pollen of other flowers by the simple vagaries of the wind. Many plants in regions where insect life is scant still follow this principle today. Nevertheless, the true flower—and the seed that it produced— was a profound innovation in the world of life.

—LOREN EISELEY, "How Flowers Changed the World"

21

6 — Showing relationships among paragraphs

Paragraphs in an essay do not stand in isolation. You can use the techniques of coherence discussed in this chapter to communicate relationships among paragraphs in an essay. Transitional expressions, pronouns, deliberate repetition, and parallel structures help you link ideas from paragraph to paragraph throughout an essay.

One excellent way to connect paragraphs is to start a new paragraph with a reference to the previous paragraph. The two student essays discussed in Chapter 3 use this technique. In the final draft of "Knowing How to Live Alone" (pages 75–78), Tara Foster has a paragraph about taking care of practical matters. She suggests that learning to make important practical decisions has positive benefits. Foster then knits the next paragraph, about making new friends, into the essay by referring to the idea of gaining confidence from handling practical matters:

> The confidence that single people get from learning to deal with practical matters can boost their chances for establishing new friendships.

Gary Lee Houseman uses a similar bridging technique in his essay "Rain Forests Must Not Be Destroyed" (pages 79–82). Houseman follows a paragraph about the biomedical benefits of rain forests with one about the role of rain forests in maintaining the balance of nature. He starts the paragraph about maintaining natural balances this way:

> Not only for their medical riches but also for their role in maintaining global balances, rain forests must be saved.

Houseman also links the center of the essay—the reasons why rain forests must be preserved—with words that set up a climactic order. The three paragraphs in which Houseman discusses the importance of rain forests begin this way:

PARAGRAPH PRESENTING FIRST REASON

> One major value of rain forests is biomedical.

PARAGRAPH PRESENTING SECOND REASON

> Not only for their medical riches but also for their role in maintaining global natural balances, rain forests must be saved.

PARAGRAPH PRESENTING LAST REASON

> Most important, rain forests must be protected because their trees control the planet's oxygen supply and climate.

With "Most important," Houseman links three paragraphs and establishes the order he wants readers to use as they evaluate his reasons.

EXERCISE 4

Identify the techniques of coherence—words of transition, pronouns, deliberate repetition, and parallel structures—in each paragraph.

A.   Writing is one of the ways I participate in struggle—one of the ways I help to keep vibrant and resilient that vision that has kept the Family going on. Through writing I attempt to celebrate the tradition of resistance, attempt to tap Black potential, and try to join the chorus of voices that argues that exploitation and misery are neither inevitable nor necessary. Writing is one of the ways I participate in the

22 transformation—one of the ways I practice the commitment to explore bodies of knowledge for the usable wisdoms they yield. In writing, I hope to encourage the fusion of those disciplines whose split (material science versus metaphysics versus aesthetics versus politics versus . . .) predisposes us to accept fragmented truth and distortions as the whole. Writing is one of the ways I do my work in the world.

—TONI CADE BAMBARA, "What Is It I Think I'm Doing Anyhow"

¶ *cob* 4b

B. However, we must try even harder to prevent cancer before it starts, since so far it has been difficult to find many biochemical differences between cancer cells and normal cells that can be exploited in therapy. For prevention, we must devise better methods of testing for factors in the environment, including chemicals from industrial processes and possibly food additives, that can cause cancer, and

23 after we find all these factors we must try to remove them. In addition, we must try to understand more of the mechanisms by which chemicals and radiation cause cancer in the hope that such knowledge will make it easier for us to recognize these carcinogens and perhaps to devise means to prevent their action. However, when, as in the case of smoking, we find that a carcinogen exists, we must act to prevent it from entering the environment.

—HOWARD TEMIN, "Editor's Notebook" of the *Wisconsin State Journal*

C. The factory mode of production, the beginnings of urbanization, and the rise of an urban middle class provoked profound changes. First, it transferred the production of goods out of the home, greatly altering the relationship between husband and wife. While his workplace moved to the factory, store, or office, she remained isolated within the home. As he acquired a circle of male acquaintances at

24 work, she developed a circle of women friends in the neighborhood. As he ceased to share in training his sons in a craft or as farmer, she shouldered increasing responsibility for mothering the children. As the husband's economic role was greatly augmented, the wife's was diminished. As he assumed the support of the family, she became his dependent.

—ROBERT L. DANIEL, *American Women in the 20th Century*

D. Kathy sat with her legs dangling over the edge of the side of the hood. The band of her earphones held back strands of straight copper hair which had come loose from two thick braids that hung down her back. She swayed with the music that only she could hear.

25 Her shoulders raised, making circles in the warm air. Her arms reached out to her side; her opened hands reached for the air; her closed hands brought the air back to her. Her arms reached over her head; her opened hands reached for a cloud; her closed hands brought the cloud back to her. Her head moved from side to side; her eyes opened and closed to the tempo of the tunes. Kathy was motion.

—CLAIRE BURKE, student

ANSWERS: EXERCISE 4

The following answers form a basic list. You and your students might find more.

A (paragraph 22). *Pronoun:* I. *Deliberate repetition:* writing, writing is one, one of the ways, attempt, versus. *Parallel structures:* I participate, I help, I participate, I practice.

B (paragraph 23). *Transitional expressions:* however, in addition, however. *Pronouns:* we, it [cancer], them [factors], us, it [carcinogen that exists]. *Deliberate repetition:* we, we must.

C (paragraph 24). *Transitional expression:* first. *Pronouns:* his, she, he. *Parallel structures:* As he . . . , she . . . moved/remained, acquired/developed, ceased/shouldered, augmented/diminished.

D (paragraph 25). *Pronouns:* her, she. *Deliberate repetition:* Kathy, arms, hands opened, closed. *Parallel structures:* Many parallel clauses starting with "Her shoulders raised"; open hands reaching out and closed hands bringing back.

E (paragraph 26). *Transitional expressions:* however, also. *Deliberate repetition:* brown bear, grizzlies. *Parallel structures:* Brownies tend to be, grizzlies tend to be.

E.   A full-grown brown bear can weigh more than 1,000 pounds, stand 12 feet tall on its hind legs and outrun a horse for short distances. Technically, brown bears are the same species as the grizzly bear—the one known as *Ursus arctos.* There are some differences, however. Brown bears occupy the coastal rim of southern Alaska and parts of the Yukon and British Columbia. Grizzlies are found farther inland, for the most part; their range also includes much of western Canada and some of Montana, Idaho, and Wyoming. Brownies tend to be larger; grizzlies tend to have a more dish-shaped face and a more pronounced hump. The main difference, however, is that brown bears have access to migrating salmon and grizzlies don't.

—BOYD NORTON,
''It's a Good Thing McNeil's Big Bears Get Plenty to Eat''

26

EXERCISE 5

Reread the paragraphs in Exercise 1 and identify all techniques of coherence—words of transition, pronouns, deliberate repetition, and parallel structures.

EXERCISE 6

Develop three of the following topic sentences into unified paragraphs, with RENNS and techniques of coherence. On separate paper, list the RENNS and the techniques of coherence you built into each paragraph.

1. Current newspaper comic strips reflect the problems of today's culture.
2. The United States's garbage says a great deal about American culture.
3. Children begin to compete at too early an age.
4. Learning to do laundry can be perilous to one's clothes.
5. College athletics is big business.

ANSWERS: EXERCISE 5

Students are likely to find more examples than the answers given here.

A (paragraph 9). *Transitional expressions:* after all, too. *Pronoun:* you. *Parallel structure:* historical, social, cultural; as a parent, as a member of the community.

B (paragraph 10). *Deliberate repetition:* destructive, destruction, destroy. *Parallel structure:* crashes, smolders, darts, lies.

C (paragraph 11). *Transitional expressions:* for example, also. *Pronouns:* its, their, she. *Deliberate repetition:* people, U.S. and United States. *Parallel structures:* a wealth of individual facts, a pile of unrelated names; dates, formulas, structures, and equations; it is a fact, it is a fact.

D (paragraph 12). *Pronouns:* they, he. *Deliberate repetition:* July 1. *Parallel structures:* this July 1, last July 1.

E (paragraph 13). *Transitional expressions:* first, but, second, for example. *Deliberate repetition:* men, women.

ANSWERS: EXERCISE 6

Each paragraph will obviously differ in content, but this exercise should help students see that they need to support general statements with graphic details (developed through RENNS) that are smoothly linked by the techniques of coherence discussed in 4b: transitional expressions, pronouns, repetition, and parallelism.

 Arranging a paragraph

Arranging a paragraph means putting its sentences into an order logical for communicating that paragraph's message clearly and effectively. The choices for arrangement for topical paragraphs are discussed in this section. Introductions, conclusions, and transitions are discussed in 4e. Decisions about arrangement often come during the revising process, after you have written a first draft and can begin to see how your sentences might be arranged for greatest impact.

In informative and persuasive writing, writers have a variety of options for arranging sentences in topical paragraphs. Choices include moving from general to specific, from specific to general, and from least to most important; progressing from problem to solution; and sequencing according to location and to time.

From general to specific

An arrangement of sentences from the general to the specific is the most common organization for a paragraph. Seen in many of the examples earlier in this chapter, a general-to-specific arrangement begins with a topic sentence (and perhaps is followed by a limiting or clarifying sentence) and ends with specific details. This arrangement is a reflection of deductive thinking, a natural thought pattern discussed in 5e-2.

27   Unwanted music is privacy's constant enemy. There is hardly an American restaurant, store, railroad station or bus terminal that doesn't gurgle with melody from morning to night, nor is it possible any longer to flee by boarding the train or bus itself, or even by taking a walk in the park. Transistor radios have changed all that. Men, women and children carry them everywhere, hugging them with the desperate attachment that a baby has for its blanket, fearful that they might have to generate an idea of their own or contemplate a blade of grass. Thoughtless themselves, they have no thought for the sufferers within earshot of their portentous news broadcasts and raucous jazz. It is hardly surprising that RCA announced a plan that would pipe canned music and pharmaceutical commercials to 25,000 doctors' offices in eighteen big cities— one place where a decent quietude might be expected. This raises a whole new criterion for choosing a family physician. Better to have a second-rate healer content with the sounds of his stethoscope than an eminent specialist poking to the rhythms of Gershwin.

—WILLIAM ZINSSER, *The Haircurl Papers*

From specific to general

A less common arrangement than general to specific moves from the specific to the general. Like paragraphs 6 and 7, the paragraph ends with a topic sentence and begins with the details that support the topic sentence. This arrangement reflects inductive reasoning, a natural thought pattern discussed in 5e-1.

BIOGRAPHY

William Zinsser (1922–   ) served as a writer, editor, and critic for the *New York Herald Tribune* from 1946 to 1959. Zinsser has been a free-lance writer since 1959 and has written regular columns for *Look* (1967) and *Life* (1968–1972). His civic work includes membership on the Board of Governors of the Brooklyn Museum and on the Board of Directors of the Municipal Art Society of New York. He is now head of the Book of the Month Club. His books include *Any Old Place with You, Seen Any Good Movies Lately?, Search and Research, The City Dwellers, The Hair-curl Papers, Pop Goes America, The Paradise Bit* (a novel), *The Lunacy Boom,* and *On Writing Well.*

28   Replacing the spark plugs probably ranks number one on the troubleshooting list of most home auto mechanics. Too often this effort produces little or no improvement, as the problem lies elsewhere. Within the ignition system the plug wires, distributor unit, coil, and ignition control unit play just as vital a role as the spark plugs. However, performance problems are by no means limited to the ignition system. The fuel system and emissions control system also help determine engine performance, and each of these systems contains several components which equal the spark plug in importance. The do-it-yourself mechanic who wants to provide basic care for a car should be able to do more than change the spark plugs.

—DANNY WITT, student

From least to most important

A sentence arrangement that moves from the least to the most important is known as *climactic order* because it saves the climax for the end. This arrangement can be effective in holding the reader's interest because the best part comes at the end. In informative and persuasive writing, this type of arrangement usually calls for the topic sentence at the beginning of the paragraph, although sometimes the topic sentence works well at the end. Here is a climactic paragraph that begins with a topic sentence.

29   But probably the most dumbfounding of nature's extraordinary creations is the horned toad of our Southwest. A herpetologist once invited me to observe one of these lizards right after it had molted. In a sand-filled glass cage I saw a large male. Beside him lay his old skin. The herpetologist began to annoy the beast with mock attacks, and the old man of the desert with his vulnerable new suit became frightened. Suddenly his eyeballs reddened. A final fast lunge from my friend at the beast and I froze in astonishment—a fine spray of blood shot from the lizard's eye, like fire from a dragon! The beast struck back with a weapon so shocking that it terrifies even the fiercest enemy.

—JEAN GEORGE, "That Astonishing Creature—Nature"

From problem to solution

An effective arrangement can be to present a problem and move quickly to a suggested solution. The topic sentence presents the problem and the next sentence—the limiting or clarifying sentence—presents the main idea of the solution. The rest of the sentences give the specifics of the solution.

¶ 4c

Burnout is a potential problem for any hard working and persevering student. A preliminary step for preventing student burnout is for students to work in moderation. Students can concentrate on school every day, provided that they do not overtax themselves. One method students can use is to avoid concentrating on a single project for an extended period of time. For example, if students have to read two books for a midterm history test, they should do other assignments at intervals so that the two books will not get boring. Another means to moderate a workload is to regulate how many extracurricular projects to take on. When a workload is manageable, a student's immunity to burnout is strengthened.

30

—BRADLEY HOWARD, student

According to location

A paragraph arranged according to location is put into a *spatial sequence.* It describes the position of objects relative to one another, often from a central point of reference. The topic sentence usually establishes a location that serves as the orientation for all other places mentioned. The other sentences in the paragraph often use transitional expressions (see the chart on page 84) that indicate *place.*

31

About two-hundred feet from where I had waded ashore, the coral rose to a high promontory and I decided to start my exploration there. I climbed carefully to the top of the ledge and looked around. Only a narrow strait, about the length of a football field, separated me from the nearest island, which I assumed was one of the bird sanctuaries. A submerged reef seemed to join the two islands together. On the other side of the rock ledge was more coral and no sign of sand. As far as I could see, which was no more than a few hundred feet because the island curved sharply, there was nothing but a forest of coconut palms, coral, and the sea. I turned and went back to my arrival point. My government friend had told me there was a sand beach on the island; I decided the best way to find it would be to go inland and come out on the other side.

—CASKIE STINNETT, *Grand and Private Pleasures*

According to time

A paragraph arranged according to time is put into a *chronological sequence.* It tells what happened or what is happening during a period of time.

ALTERNATE EXAMPLE:
SPATIAL SEQUENCE

The wash [low land that is sometimes flooded, at other times nearly dry] looked perfectly dry in my headlights. I drove down, across, up the other side and on into the night. Glimpses of weird humps of pale rock on either side, like petrified elephants, dinosaurs, stone-age hobgoblins. Now and then something alive scurried across the road: kangaroo mice, a jackrabbit, an animal that looked like a cross between a raccoon and a squirrel—the ringtail cat. Farther on a pair of mule deer started from the brush and bounded obliquely through the beams of my lights, raising puffs of dust which the wind, moving faster than my pickup truck, caught and carried ahead of me out of sight into the dark. The road, narrow and rocky, twisted sharply left and right, dipped in and out of tight ravines, climbing by degrees toward a summit which I would see only in the light of the coming day.

—Edward Abbey,
"The Most Beautiful Place on Earth"

BIOGRAPHY

N(avarre) Scott Momaday (1934–   ) is a major figure in the American Indian cultural awareness movement. He received his Ph.D. from Stanford in 1963. Momaday has taught at the University of California, Stanford University, and the University of Arizona. His awards include a Guggenheim fellowship (1966–1967) and the 1969 Pulitzer Prize for fiction for the novel *House Made of Dawn.* His other works include *The Complete Poems of Frederick Goddard Tuckerman* (editor); *The Journey of Tai-me* (a collection of Kiowa Indian folktales, an enlarged edition of which is the famous *The Way to Rainy Mountain*); *Angle of Geese and Other Poems; The Ground Dancer;* and *The Names.* Momaday is also a frequent reviewer for the *New York Times Book Review,* specializing in Indian subjects.

Writing of *The Way to Rainy Mountain,* critic John R. Milton is quoted in *Contemporary Authors* as saying it "evokes the spirit of his people and their land, and does so in prose that is often close to poetry."

32 Her name was Aho, and she belonged to the last culture to evolve in North America. Her forebears came down from the high country in western Montana nearly three centuries ago. They were a mountain people, a mysterious tribe of hunters whose language has never been positively classified in any major group. In the late seventeenth century they began a long migration to the south and east. It was a journey toward the dawn, and it led to a golden age. Along the way the Kiowas were befriended by the Crows, who gave them the culture and religion of the Plains. They acquired horses, and their ancient nomadic spirit was suddenly free of the ground. They acquired Tai-me, the sacred Sun Dance doll, from that moment the object and symbol of their worship, and so shared in the divinity of the sun. Not least, they acquired the sense of destiny, therefore courage and pride. When they entered upon the southern Plains, they had been transformed. No longer were they slaves to the simple necessity of survival; they were a lordly and dangerous society of fighters and thieves, hunters and priests of the sun. According to their origin myth, they entered the world through a hollow log. From one point of view, their migration was the fruit of an old prophecy, for indeed they emerged from a sunless world.

—N. Scott Momaday, *The Way to Rainy Mountain*

EXERCISE 7

For each paragraph, arrange the sentences into a logical sequence. Begin by locating the topic sentence and placing it at the beginning of the paragraph.

Paragraph A

1. Handel, through his use of a major key and a dynamic and melismatic melody in the Hallelujah Chorus of his *Messiah,* gives us a sense of hopeful elation.

2. Although defined as "the art of arranging sounds with reference to rhythm, pitch and tone quality" by Funk and Wagnall, music is, in reality, much, much more.

3. Chopin, on the other hand, through his use of the minor mode, bass register and slow tempo, conveys to us the feeling of sullen despair in the third movement of his Second Piano Sonata.

4. There is no doubt that we experience certain feelings when we fall under its hypnotic influence.

5. For example, music is surely the art of creating emotional responses through the skillful manipulation of sounds.

6. Examples of this power can be found among the works of any of the great composers.

—Kevin Kerwood, student

¶ **4c**

PARAGRAPH B

1. After a busy day, lens wearers often do not feel like taking time out to clean and disinfect their lenses, and many wearers skip the chore.
2. When buying a pair of glasses, a person deals with just the expense of the glasses themselves.
3. Although contact lenses make the wearer more attractive, glasses are easier and less expensive to care for.
4. However, in addition to the cost of the lenses themselves, contact lens wearers must shoulder the extra expense of cleaning supplies.
5. This inattention creates a danger of infection.
6. In contrast, contact lenses require daily cleaning and weekly enzyming that inconvenience lens wearers.
7. Glasses can be cleaned quickly with water and tissue at the wearer's convenience.

—HEATHER MARTIN, student

PARAGRAPH C

1. Indeed, there are moments today—amid outlaw litter, tax cheating, illicit noise and motorized anarchy—when it seems as though the scofflaw represents the wave of the future.
2. Already, Riesman says, the ethic of U.S. society is in danger of becoming this: "You're a fool if you obey the rules."
3. Yet it is painfully apparent that millions of Americans who would never think of themselves as lawbreakers, let alone criminals, are taking increasing liberties with the legal codes that are designed to protect and nourish their society.
4. Harvard sociologist David Riesman suspects that a majority of Americans have blithely taken to committing supposedly minor derelictions as a matter of course.
5. Law-and-order is the longest-running and probably the best-loved political issue in U.S. history.

—FRANK TIPPETT, "A Red Light for Scofflaws"

EXERCISE 8

For paragraphs 33-37, first identify the topic sentence. Then identify the arrangement or arrangements that organize the sentences in each paragraph. Choose from general to specific, specific to general, least to most important, problem to solution, location, and time.

ANSWERS: EXERCISE 7

Answers to this exercise may vary; alternate versions that can be defended are acceptable.

A. In the original paragraph, the sentences appeared in this order: 2, 5, 4, 6, 1, 3.

B. In the original paragraph, the sentences appeared in this order: 3, 7, 6, 1, 5, 2, 4.

C. In the original paragraph, the sentences appeared in this order: 5, 3, 1, 4, 2.

ANSWERS: EXERCISE 8

Students will likely see more than one arrangement in some of these paragraphs. *Note:* You might also ask students to analyze these paragraphs in light of what was previously discussed in this chapter: topic sentence, words in topic sentences that create focus and control (4a–1), development with RENNS (4a–2), and techniques of coherence (4b).

A (paragraph 33). general to specific and least to most important

B (paragraph 34). problem to solution (and perhaps time)

C (paragraph 35). time (and perhaps least to most important)

D (paragraph 36). least to most important

E (paragraph 37). time (and perhaps general to specific)

A.

33   The dampness clings to the land and everything on the land. In cities like Durham and Richmond and Winston-Salem, it weaves itself into the rich aroma of processed tobacco rising from the cigarette factories. The invisible shroud thus formed drops over the cities, testing the olfactory sense of the natives and reassuring their sense of economic security. In the fields, the dampness engulfs the machinery and fertilizes the germ of rust. It bathes and swells the doors of the barn and the privies and the little tenant houses so that the doors will not shut tight, allowing the dampness into the houses. It creeps in on the wind, through cracks in the doors and windows and walls. It rises on air currents through the floor. It seeps in with the rain that spatters onto the tin roof and trickles into the nail holes and seam cracks, permeating the tenant houses; and then it attacks the tenants.

—DWAYNE E. WALLS, "The Golden Token"

B.

34   No one even agrees anymore on what "old" is. Not long ago, 30 was middle-aged and 60 was old. Now, more and more people are living into their 70's, 80's and beyond—and many of them are living *well,* without any incapacitating mental or physical decline. Today, old age is defined not simply by chronological years, but by degree of health and well being.

—CAROL TAVRIS, "Old Age Is Not What It Used to Be"

C.

35   We walked down the path to the well-house, attracted by the fragrance of the honeysuckle with which it was covered. Someone was drawing water and my teacher placed my hand under the spout. As the cool stream gushed over one hand she spelled into the other the word *water,* first slowly, then rapidly. I stood still, my whole attention fixed upon the motions of her fingers. Suddenly I felt a misty consciousness as of something forgotten—a thrill of returning thought; and somehow the mystery of language was revealed to me. I knew then that "w-a-t-e-r" meant the wonderful cool something that was flowing over my hand. That living word awakened my soul, gave it light, hope, joy, set it free! There were barriers still, it is true, but barriers that could in time be swept away.

—HELEN KELLER, *The Story of My Life*

D.

36   Lately, bee researchers have been distracted by a new challenge from abroad. It is, of course, the so-called "killer bee" that was imported into Brazil from Africa in the mid-1950s and has been heading our way ever since. The Africanized bee looks like the Italian bee but is more defensive and more inclined to attack in force. It consumes much of the honey that it produces, leaving relatively little for anyone who attempts to work with it. It travels fast, competes with

BIOGRAPHY

Helen Keller, born in Tuscumbia, Alabama, in 1880, contracted a severe illness, diagnosed as brain fever, that deprived her of her sight and hearing when she was nineteen months old. Her education did not begin until she was seven, when Miss Anna Sullivan of the Perkins Institute of the Blind came to live with her and her family. Miss Sullivan introduced Helen Keller to language by touch. She then taught her to read by the braille system and to write using a special typewriter. In 1890 Helen Keller also learned to speak under the instruction of Miss Sarah Fuller of the Horace Mann School for the Deaf in Boston. She was graduated from Radcliffe College, with honors, in 1904. Throughout her life she traveled to bring her message of courage and hope to handicapped people everywhere. Her achievements have been recounted many times, perhaps most movingly in her own words in *The Story of My Life.*

local bees and, worse, mates with them. It has ruined the honey industry in Venezuela and now the big question is: Will the same thing happen here?

—JIM DOHERTY,
"The Hobby That Challenges You to Think Like a Bee"

E.   When children begin to play with other children and when they finally go to school, their names take on a public dimension. The child with a "funny" name is usually in for trouble, but most kids are proud of their names and want to write them on their books and pads and homework. There was a time when older children carved their names or initials on trees. Now that there are so many people and so few trees, the spray can has taken over from the jackknife, but the impulse to put one's identifying mark where all the world can see it is as strong as ever. The popularity of commercially produced name-on objects of every kind, from teeshirts to miniature license plates, also attests to the importance youngsters (and a lot of grown-ups too) place on claiming and proclaiming their names.

37

—CASEY MILLER AND KATE SWIFT, "Women and Names"

EXERCISE 9

What arrangement (one or more) would be effective for discussing each of the listed subjects? Choose from general to specific, specific to general, least to most important, problem to solution, location, and time. Explain your choice.

1. ways to make friends
2. automobile accidents
3. how to combine work and college
4. role of the U.S. Supreme Court
5. what parents of teenagers can learn from *Romeo and Juliet,* by William Shakespeare
6. the role of computers at home
7. traveling by bus
8. how to survive an earthquake
9. the problems with junk food
10. music favorites today

4d Knowing patterns for developing a paragraph

Patterns for **paragraph development** in informative and persuasive writing have evolved as writers have sought methods to express their ideas most effectively. By knowing a variety of patterns for paragraph development, you have more choices when you are

BIOGRAPHY

Casey Miller (1919–   ) began her career in publishing but left in 1964 to become a free-lance writer and editor. She served in the U.S. Naval Reserve on active duty from 1943 to 1946. She is a member of the Women's Institute for Freedom of the Press.

Kate Swift (1923–   ) worked in journalism and public relations until 1953, when she became a science writer for the American Museum of Natural History. She also has served as director of the news bureau at Yale's School of Medicine (1965–1970). She has been a free-lance writer and editor since 1970. Swift served in the U.S. Army, Women's Army Corps from 1945 to 1946. She also is a member of the Women's Institute for Freedom of the Press.

Miller and Swift have contributed to magazines, including *New York, Ms.,* and *New York Times Magazine,* and they have co-authored *Words and Women* (1976). In *Contemporary Authors,* they speak about how they came to write on women and language.

We have an editorial partnership known as Miller/Swift, and it was out of our work as free-lance editors that we became interested in the effect of language on women. After writing two articles on the subject ('Desexing the English Language' and 'One Small Step for Genkind'), we found we had barely scratched the surface of this topic, which until recently was ignored. *Words and Women* is an expansion of the evidence presented in the articles and is primarily drawn from contemporary sources with historical material as backup. We document many changes occurring in English today as a result of women's changing perceptions of themselves.

ANSWERS: EXERCISE 9

Answers will vary according to how each student conceives of each subject. Comparisons of the methods of arrangement can reveal the multiplicity of available choices.

BIOGRAPHY

June Jordan (1936–   ), poet, essayist, and story writer, was born in Harlem in New York City. After attending Barnard College and the University of Chicago and working for two years as a research writer for New York's Mobilization for Youth, Inc., Jordan began teaching. She has been on the faculty of the City College of New York, Connecticut College (SEEK Program), Sarah Lawrence College, the State University of New York at Stony Brook, and Yale. She is a member of the board of directors of Teachers and Writers Collaborative, Inc. Her books include *Some Changes* (poems), *Biography of Fannie Lou Hamer, New Days: Poems of Exile and Return, New Room: New Life, Selected Poems of June Jordan: Things That I Do in the Dark, Okay Now.*

As a teacher, Jordan has strong views on student poetry (quoted in *Contemporary Authors*):

> A great variety of black people are writing poetry today—it is not any elitist preoccupation but an activity involving everybody. Black youths are finding they don't have to worry about putting together someone else's idea. Frequently, in their own poetic way, they express themselves in classrooms and a teacher will ask, 'What are you trying to say?' Actually, he has already said it—communicated it very well and poetically—but the teacher, who is not tuned in, did not understand it.

seeking ways to help your paragraphs deliver their meanings most effectively.

For the purpose of illustration, the patterns shown here are discussed in isolation. In essay writing, however, paragraph patterns often overlap. For example, narrative writing often contains descriptions; explanations of processes often include comparisons and contrasts; and so on. As you write paragraphs of various patterns, you will likely find that many patterns share characteristics. Your goal is to use paragraph patterns in the service of communicating meaning, not for their own sakes.

Narration

Narrative writing tells about what is happening or what has happened. In informative and persuasive writing, narration is usually written in chronological sequence. Narrative paragraphs that illustrate other aspects of informative and persuasive writing include paragraphs 16, 19, 20, 29, 31, and 32.

Here is another example of a narrative paragraph. Its main idea appears in the third-from-last sentence when the author asks a question that reveals the focus of her story.

38   When I visited the birthplace of my mother twelve years ago, I was embarrassed by the shiny rented car that took me there. Even in 1974, there were no paved roads in Clonmel, a delicate dot of a mountain village in Jamaica. And despite the breathtaking altitude, you could not get yourself into a decent position for "a view": The vegetation was that dense, that lush, and that chaotic. On or close to the site of my mother's childhood home, I found a neat wood cabin, still without windowpanes or screens, a dirt floor, and a barefoot family of seven, quietly bustling about. I was stunned. There was neither electricity nor running water. How did my parents even hear about America, more than half a century ago? In the middle of the "Roaring Twenties," these eager black immigrants came, by boat. Did they have to borrow shoes for the journey?

—JUNE JORDAN, "Thank You, America!"

Description

Descriptive writing appeals to a reader's senses—sight, sound, smell, taste, and touch. Descriptive writing permits you to share your sensual impressions of a person, a place, or an object. Descriptive paragraphs that illustrate other aspects of informative and persuasive writing include paragraphs 6, 18, 28, and 31. Here is another example of a descriptive paragraph.

To a fugitive from the surface world, an underground construction site seems like a cave filled with unidentifiable structures angling off in various directions. Two rust-coated electrical conduits are suspended from the street-level planks that form the cavern's roof. A vertical slab of masonry on one side of the 150-foot-long corridor turns out to be one wall of an abandoned coal chute. A large pipe perpendicular to the rest, which crosses the corridor, is a sewerline connector. The place has a strange bluish light at the end open to the outside, where a large blue curtain has been hung to keep out the weather. A little swirl of dust and gas collects near the roof of the tunnel, and there is an occasional whiff of sewage. Ladders, tools, and plank walkways clutter the narrow workspace. At the point where the corridor ends, a dozen pipes and conduits of varying sizes disappear into a solid 12-foot-high wall of New York dirt.

39

—DONALD DALE JACKSON,
"It Takes a 'Sixth Sense' to Operate
Underneath the Streets of New York"

Process

Process is a term used for writing that describes a sequence of actions by which something is done or made. Usually a process description is developed in chronological order. For examples, see paragraphs 18, 21, and 30. To be effective, process writing must include all steps. The amount of detail depends on whether you want to instruct the reader about how to do something or you want to offer a general overview of the process. Here is a process description written to give the reader a general picture. A process description that gives directions appears on the next page, in paragraph 41.

40

The new earth, freshly torn from its parent sun, was a ball of whirling gases, intensely hot, rushing through the black spaces of the universe on a path and at a speed controlled by immense forces. Gradually the ball of flaming gases cooled. The gases began to liquefy, and Earth became a molten mass. The materials of this mass eventually became sorted out in a definite pattern: the heaviest in the center, the less heavy surrounding them, and the least heavy forming the outer rim. This is a pattern which persists today—a central sphere of molten iron, very nearly as hot as it was two billion years ago, an intermediate sphere of semiplastic basalt, and a hard outer shell, relatively quite thin and composed of solid basalt and granite.

—RACHEL CARSON, *The Sea Around Us*

BIOGRAPHY

Rachel Carson (1907–1964), the woman who alerted America to the time bomb of pollution, received her A.M. degree from Johns Hopkins University in 1932. She did further graduate work at the Marine Biological Laboratory in Woods Hole, Massachusetts.

The Sea Around Us, Carson's second book, was based on extensive research. It took two years to write, but the book's reception indicated that the time had been well spent. Typical is this comment from the *Saturday Review of Literature,* quoted in *Contemporary Authors.*

> Rare indeed is the individual who can present a comprehensive and well-balanced picture of such a complex entity as the sea in an easy and fluent style and in terms anyone can understand. Rachel Carson is such an individual. Many books have been written on the sea, most of them by scholars with a very detailed knowledge of some aspect of oceanography but with a limited knowledge of popular presentation. Miss Carson's book is different.

Silent Spring is, no doubt, Carson's most famous work—in large part because of its highly controversial stand against the misuse of chemical fertilizers and pesticides. Public pressure in response to *Silent Spring* led President John F. Kennedy to initiate a federal investigation into agricultural chemical abuse. The report of the President's Science Advisory Committee (May 1963) agreed with Carson and called for better control of pesticides and more research into their effects. Shortly after the Committee's report verifying her conclusions, Rachel Carson died of cancer.

BACKGROUND

In 1970 Richard A. Meade and W. Geiger El-lis published "Paragraph Development in the Modern Age of Rhetoric" (*English Journal*, 59, February 1970, 219–226), reporting the findings of a study carried out to discover whether published writers regularly use the methods of paragraph development that are taught in composition texts and classrooms. They found that in 600 paragraphs taken from such publications as the *English Journal, Saturday Review,* and the *Richmond Times-Dispatch,* 56 percent of the paragraphs followed no textbook method. The textbook method most often employed was that of examples, with reasons the second. The methods of development found in the paragraphs but not in textbooks included combinations of methods, additional comment, two themes, one-sentence paragraphs, opposition, and questions.

EXTRA EXERCISE C

Write a paragraph defining one of the terms listed below. You may find it helpful to begin by determining the class (genus) of the term and the characteristics that distinguish it from other members of the class. Means for developing paragraphs that have been discussed earlier in this chapter, such as examples and illustrations, can be used to develop the definition. In a paragraph of definition, synonyms, etymological information, and contrasting examples are also helpful.

1. chemistry
2. extrasensory perception
3. movies
4. weather
5. physical fitness

Here is a process description that gives the reader specific, step-by-step instructions.

> 41   Stand or tread water, until you see the right wave far out, gathering momentum. Then position yourself—swim farther out or farther in if necessary—so that you are ready to plunge toward shore in the trough created in front of the cresting wave. Once you are in the trough, swim as hard as you can. Ideally, you will be sucked down into the trough. Suddenly the cresting water above you lifts you, holds you, and shoots you forward. At the moment, arch, point your body with your arms like tensed wings down at your sides, flat and bulletlike. You become a missile projected by the churning, breaking wave. If it works, you are *in,* if you *catch* the wave, you become part of it, the forward part of the cresting wave, like the prow of a boat made somehow of churning foam, and you can ride all the way home to the sand, and come home *into* the sand like a wedge, grinding into the shore like the wave itself.
>
> —RUTH RUDNER, *Forgotten Pleasures*

Example

A paragraph developed by example uses illustrations to provide evidence in support of the main idea. Examples are highly effective for developing topical paragraphs. They supply a reader with concrete, specific information. Many of the sample paragraphs in this chapter are developed with examples, among them paragraphs 1, 3, 5, 6, 14, and 27. Here is another paragraph with examples used to develop the topic sentence.

> 42   In fact, mistranslation accounts for a good share of verbal errors. The slogan "Come Alive with Pepsi" failed understandably in German when it was translated: "Come Alive out of the Grave with Pepsi." Elsewhere it was translated with more precision: "Pepsi Brings Your Ancestors Back from the Grave." In 1965, prior to a reception for Queen Elizabeth II outside Bonn, Germany's President Heinrich Lübke, attempting an English translation of *Gleich geht es los* ("It will soon begin"), told the Queen: "Equal goes it loose." The Queen took the news well, but no better than the President of India, who was greeted at the airport in 1962 by Lübke, who, intending to ask "How are you?" instead said: "Who are you?" To which his guest answered responsibly: "I am the President of India."
>
> —ROGER ROSENBLATT, "Oops! How's That Again?"

Definition

A paragraph of definition develops a topic by explaining the meaning of a word or a concept. A paragraph of definition is an *extended definition*—it is more extensive than a dictionary denotation (although the paragraph may include a dictionary definition). An effective paragraph of definition does not use abstractions to explain abstractions. Here is a paragraph that offers an extended definition of the concept of democracy.

43   Surely the Board knows what democracy is. It is the line that forms on the right. It is the don't in Don't Shove. It is the hole in the stuffed shirt through which the sawdust slowly trickles; it is the dent in the high hat. Democracy is the recurrent suspicion that more than half of the people are right more than half of the time. It is the feeling of privacy in the voting booths, the feeling of communion in the libraries, the feeling of vitality everywhere. Democracy is the score at the beginning of the ninth. It is an idea which hasn't been disproved yet, a song the words of which have not gone bad. It's the mustard on the hot dog and the cream in the rationed coffee. Democracy is a request from a War Board, in the middle of the morning in the middle of a war, wanting to know what democracy is.

                        —E. B. WHITE, "Democracy"

Analysis and Classification

Analysis (sometimes called *division*) divides things up. Classification groups things together. A paragraph developed by analysis divides one subject into its component parts. Paragraphs of analysis written in this pattern usually start by identifying the one subject and continue by explaining that subject's distinct parts. For example, here is a paragraph that identifies the problem of families living long distances apart and then analyzes new roles that families and friends play in our mobile society.

44   The trouble with the clans and tribes many of us were born into is not that they consist of meddlesome ogres but that they are too far away. In emergencies we rush across continents, and if need be, oceans to their sides, as they do to ours. Maybe we even make a habit of seeing them, once or twice a year, for the sheer pleasure of it. But blood ties seldom dictate our addresses. Our blood kin are often too remote to ease us from our Tuesdays to our Wednesdays. For this we must rely on our families of friends. If our relatives are not, do not wish to be, or for whatever reasons cannot be our friends, then by some complex alchemy we must try to transform our friends into our relatives. If blood and roots don't do the job, then we must look to water and branches, and sort ourselves into new constellations, new families.

                        —JANE HOWARD, "A Peck of Salt"

EXTRA EXERCISE D

The sentences in the following paragraph of definition have been jumbled. Indicate which is the topic sentence, then record the order of the remaining sentences by numbering them.

_____1. It is the sum total of substantive things called economics goods.

_____2. In other words, wealth is a stock, while income is a flow of economic goods.

_____3. The wealth of a nation is the stock of economic goods owned by its inhabitants as individuals or as members of the national group.

_____4. Most economists use the term "economic goods" to refer to those sources of satisfaction which are scarce enough to be able to command a price.

_____5. Wealth differs from income because it is the sum of the goods owned at a particular time as opposed to the goods consumed during a specific period.

ANSWERS: EXTRA EXERCISE D

The order of sentences in the paragraph of definition above should be 3, 1, 4, 5, 2.

EXTRA EXERCISE E

To practice the principles of classification, arrange the following terms into three groups based on their similarities. Give each group a heading.

1. violin	9. blossom
2. helmet	10. baton
3. bulb	11. Mozart
4. conductor	12. quarterback
5. perennial	13. leaves and stems
6. referee	14. spectators
7. concerto	15. nursery
8. Barry Switzer	

A paragraph developed by classification groups information according to some scheme. The separate groups must be *from the same class*—they must have some underlying characteristics in common. For example, different types of sports—football, Rugby, and soccer—can be classified together according to their handling of the ball, their playing fields, the placement of their goals, and the like. Here is a paragraph that discusses three classes of sports signals.

45   Many different kinds of signals are used by the coaches. There are flash signs, which are just what the name implies: the coach may flash a hand across his face or chest to indicate a bunt or hit-and-run. There are holding signals, which are held in one position for several seconds. These might be the clenched fist, bent elbow, or both hands on knees. Then there are the block signals. These divide the coach's body into different sections, or blocks. Touching a part of his body, rubbing his shirt, or touching his cap, indicates a sign. Different players can be keyed to various parts of the block so the coach is actually giving several signals with the same sign.

—ROCKWELL STENSRUD, "Who's on Third?"

Comparison and Contrast

Comparison deals with similarities, while contrast deals with differences. Paragraphs using comparison and contrast can be structured in two ways. A *point-by-point structure* allows you to move back and forth between the two items being compared. A *block structure* allows you to discuss one item completely before discussing the other.

PATTERNS FOR COMPARISON AND CONTRAST

POINT-BY-POINT STRUCTURE

Student body: college A, college B
Curriculum: college A, college B
Location: college A, college B

BLOCK STRUCTURE

College A: student body, curriculum, location
College B: student body, curriculum, location

Here is a paragraph structured point-by-point for comparison and contrast.

> My husband and I constantly marvel at the fact that our two sons, born of the same parents and only two years apart in age, are such completely opposite human beings. The most obvious differences became apparent at their births. Our first born, Mark, was big and bold—his intense, already wise eyes, broad shoulders, huge and heavy hands, and powerful, chunky legs gave us the impression that he could have walked out of the delivery room on his own. Our second son, Wayne, was delightfully different. Rather than have the football physique that Mark was born with, Wayne came into the world with a long, slim, wiry body more suited to running, jumping, and contorting. Wayne's eyes, rather than being intense like Mark's, were impish and innocent. When Mark was delivered, he cried only momentarily, then seemed to settle into a state of intense concentration, as if trying to absorb everything he could about the strange, new environment he found himself in. Conversely, Wayne screamed from the moment he first appeared until the nurse took him to the nursery. There was nothing helpless or pathetic about his cry either—he was damned angry!
>
> —ROSEANNE LABONTE, student

46

Here is a block-form comparison of the impact of building construction a thousand years ago and now. Notice how the word *today* signals the transition between the two parts of the paragraph.

> A thousand years ago in Europe, acres of houses and shops were demolished and their inhabitants forced elsewhere so that great cathedrals could be built. For decades, the building process soaked up all available skilled labor; for decades the townspeople stepped around pits in the streets, clambered over ropes and piles of timber, breathed mortar dust, and slept and worked to the crashing noise of construction. The cathedrals, when finished, stood half-empty six days a week, but most of them at least had beauty. Today, the ugly skyscrapers go up, shops and graceful homes are obliterated, their inhabitants forced away, and year after year New Yorkers step around the pits, stumble through wooden catwalks, breathe the fine mist of dust, absorb the hammering noise night and day, and telephone in vain for carpenter or plumber. And the skyscrapers stand empty two days and seven nights a week. This is progress.
>
> —ERIC SEVAREID, *This Is Eric Sevareid*

47

ANSWERS: EXTRA EXERCISE E

Symphony Orchestra
violin
conductor
concerto
baton
Mozart

Football
helmet
referee
Barry Switzer
quarterback
spectators

Flowers
bulb
perennial
blossom
leaves and stems
nursery

EXTRA EXERCISE F

To practice the skills of comparing and contrasting, make a list of the most important aspects of the following pairs of words. Using that information, write a topic sentence about their relative value or about their similarities and differences.

1. Baseball and football
2. Halloween and the Fourth of July
3. Small towns and cities
4. Apartments and houses
5. Books and television

ANSWERS: EXTRA EXERCISE F

Answers to this exercise will vary, but in each case the information listed should lead to a topic sentence.

ALTERNATE EXAMPLE: ANALOGY

Consider the analogies developed by George Herbert in this short poem.

The Coming of Good Luck

So Good Luck came, and on my roof did
   light,
Like noiseless snow, or as the dew of night:
Not all at once, but gently, as the trees
Are, by the sun beams, tickled by degrees.

BIOGRAPHY

Alison Lurie (1926–   ) has been a member of the English Department at Cornell University since 1968. She has been the recipient of a Rockefeller Foundation grant, a New York State Cultural Council Foundation grant, and the American Academy of Arts and Letters award in literature. Her works include *Love and Friendship, The Nowhere City, Imaginary Friends, Real People, The War Between the Tates,* and *Only Children.*

About her best-known work, *The War Between the Tates,* Julian Jebb writes (quoted in *Contemporary Authors*): "No other writer tells the truth with the sophisticated directness of Alison Lurie; an obsessive hatred of deceit and a minutely exact response to the surface and inner substance of ordinary life go to produce her art."

Analogy

Analogy is a type of comparison. It compares objects or ideas from different classes—things not normally associated. For example, a fatal disease has certain points in common with war. Analogy is particularly effective when you want to explain the unfamiliar in terms of the familiar. Often a paragraph developed with analogy starts with a simile or metaphor (see 21c) to introduce the comparison. Here is a paragraph developed by analogy that starts with a simile and then explains the effect of casual speech by comparing it to casual dress.

48

Casual dress, like casual speech, tends to be loose, relaxed and colorful. It often contains what might be called "slang words": blue jeans, sneakers, baseball caps, aprons, flowered cotton housedresses, and the like. These garments could not be worn on a formal occasion without causing disapproval, but in ordinary circumstances they pass without remark. "Vulgar words" in dress, on the other hand, give emphasis and get immediate attention in almost any circumstances, just as they do in speech. Only the skillful can employ them without some loss of face, and even then they must be used in the right way. A torn, unbuttoned shirt, or wildly uncombed hair can signify strong emotions: passion, grief, rage, despair. They are most effective if people already think of you as being neatly dressed, just as the curses of well-spoken persons count for more than those of the customarily foul-mouthed.

—ALISON LURIE, *The Language of Clothes*

Cause-and-effect analysis

Cause-and-effect analysis involves examining outcomes and reasons for those outcomes. Causes lead to an event or an effect; and effects result from causes. Section 5d describes making reasonable connections between causes and effects. Here is a paragraph developed through a discussion of how television (the cause) becomes indispensable (the effect) to parents of young children.

49

Because television is so wonderfully available as child amuser and child defuser, capable of rendering a volatile three-year-old harmless at the flick of a switch, parents grow to depend upon it in the course of their daily lives. And as they continue to utilize television day after day, its importance in their children's lives increases. From a simple source of entertainment provided by parents when they need a break from child care, television gradually changes into a powerful and disruptive presence in family life. But despite their increasing resentment of television's intrusions into their family life, and despite their considerable guilt at not being able to control their children's viewing, parents do not take steps to extricate themselves from television's domination. They can no longer cope without it.

—MARIE WINN, *The Plug-In Drug*

EXERCISE 10

Identify the pattern or patterns each paragraph illustrates. Choose from narration, description, process, example, definition, analysis, classification, comparison and contrast, analogy, and cause and effect.

A.   What was South Vietnam still seems like a different country from the North—more commercial, more casual, seemingly less wrapped up in political correctness. The main market in Hanoi had little to offer except local vegetables, a few plastic tools, and the incongruously colonial-looking green pith helmets that most northern men wear. (Hanoi's market also featured several tubs of live bullfrogs while we were there. Two market ladies chatted with each other while lopping the frogs' legs off with strokes of their cleavers.) In
50   Saigon, there are rows of "shop-houses," the tan-colored buildings with red-tile roofs and open storefronts that are found throughout Southeast Asia, and stores selling paintings, lacquerware, and a few cheap imported calculators and digital watches. In Hanoi, there are virtually no private cars—the streets look the way China's must have looked fifteen or twenty years ago, dense with bicycle traffic but very quiet. In Saigon, there are lots of motorcycles and a few private cars, including original Mustangs and other veteran American models. Still, no place in Vietnam has anything like the bustle of a typical Southeast Asian trading center.

—JAMES FALLOWS, "No Hard Feelings?"

B.   I retain only one confused impression from my earliest years: it is all red, and black, and warm. Our apartment was red: the upholstery was of red moquette, the Renaissance dining-room was red, the figured silk hangings over the stained-glass doors were red, and
51   the velvet curtains in Papa's study were red too. The furniture in this awful sanctum was made of black pear wood; I used to creep into the knee-hole under the desk and envelop myself in its dusty glooms; it was dark and warm, and the red of the carpet rejoiced my eyes. That is how I seem to have passed the early days of infancy. Safely ensconced, I watched, I touched, I took stock of the world.

—SIMONE DE BEAUVOIR, *Memoirs of a Dutiful Daughter*

BIOGRAPHY

Marie Winn (1937–   ) was born in Czechoslovakia. After she moved to America she received her B.A. from Radcliffe College. In addition to having written many books for children, she has published two well-received and critical studies: *Children Without Childhood* (1983) and *The Plug-In Drug: Television, Children, and the Family* (1977, updated edition 1985).

ANSWERS: EXERCISE 10

Some paragraphs can be interpreted to illustrate more than one pattern. This is a basic list only. *Note:* Exercise 13 asks students to analyze these paragraphs for many other features.

A (paragraph 50). comparison and contrast—point by point, example

B (paragraph 51). description, narration, analysis, example

C (paragraph 52). definition, example, analogy

D (paragraph 53). analysis, definition, example

E (paragraph 54). narration

F (paragraph 55). analogy

G (paragraph 56). comparison and contrast—point by point, example

BACKGROUND

In *A Conceptual Theory of Rhetoric* (Little, Brown, 1975) Frank D'Angelo points out that the act of thinking involves relating objects and events to each other and to one's own past experiences. In other words, by thinking, we organize perceptions into patterns that are ultimately expressed in paragraphs. The process inevitably causes the categories to which we assign paragraphs to overlap. D'Angelo explains:

> Description, for example, is related to definition. Describing something provides a means of analyzing and identifying it. Defining is a kind of abstract description. Definition, division into parts, and classification share fundamental relationships: to define is to limit or set boundaries to a thing by separating it from other things (division); to define is to put the thing to be defined into a class (classification): to classify is to divide into categories, so classification and division are related categories. Exemplification is related to definition (giving examples is one way of defining), to division in parts (examples are parts of wholes), and to classification (each example is a member of a group or class of persons and things) (p. 44).

BIOGRAPHY

Maya Angelou (1928–   ) was born in St. Louis, Missouri, and was raised by her grandmother in Stamps, Arkansas. Before receiving wide recognition as a major novelist, she was highly respected as an actress, singer, poet, and playwright. She served as coordinator of the Southern Christian Leadership Conference under Martin Luther King, Jr. Her autobiographical novels have been received well by critics and the public. The books include *I Know Why the Caged Bird Sings* (1970), *Gather Together in My Name* (1974), *Singin' and Swingin' and Gettin' Merry Like Christmas (1976),* and *The Heart of a Woman* (1981).

C.

52

It is Rimsky-Korsakov's bumblebee in its helter-skelter flight, buzzing its way through a summer breeze. It is Greig's "Morning," with the sun peeking over the horizon, its golden rays projecting like spears which prod a world to life, accompanied by sweet birdsong. It is the tumultuous thunder and growling wind of a Beethoven tempest breaking the great solitude of a pastoral scene, and it is the gallant fierceness and the ethereal mystique of Wagner's Valkyries, riding their powerful steeds to Valhalla. It is Rodrigo's Madrid, at times bustling, at times serene, and it is Gershwin's Paris, always brilliant and boisterous. It is music.

—KEVIN KERWOOD, student

D.

53

Hard, in terms of wood, really means *harder* to cut, but most hardwoods are also fine and even-grained. They are not apt to split, and they take polish well. For these reasons, they are generally better for small wood carving than the softwoods; most sculptors prefer to use hardwoods for large pieces, too. All the fruitwoods, like cherry, apple, pear, and orange, are hard, and so are oak, mahogany, walnut, birch, holly, and maple. Hardwoods range in color from the almost white of holly to the almost black of walnut. Oak and mahogany are the most open-grained, and therefore more apt to split. They are probably less good for small carvings than the other kinds.

—FLORENCE H. PETTIT, *How to Make Whirligigs and Whimmy Doodles*

E.

54

They were flat round wafers, slightly browned on the edges and butter-yellow in the center. With the cold lemonade they were sufficient for childhood's lifelong diet. Remembering my manners, I took nice little lady-like bites off the edges. She said she had made them expressly for me and that she had a few in the kitchen that I could take home to my brother. So I jammed one whole cake in my mouth and the rough crumbs scratched the insides of my jaws, and if I hadn't had to swallow, it would have been a dream come true.

—MAYA ANGELOU, *I Know Why the Caged Bird Sings*

F.

55

Consider cancer cells and non-cancer cells in the human body. The normal cells are aimed at reproducing and functioning in a way that is beneficial to the body. Cancer cells, on the other hand, spread in a way that threatens and ultimately destroys the whole body. Normal cells work harmoniously, because they "know," in a sense, that their preservation depends upon the health of the body they inhabit. While they are organisms in themselves, they also act as part of the whole body. We might say, metaphorically, that cancer cells do not know enough about self-preservation; they are, biologically, more ignorant than normal cells. The aim of cancer cells is to spread throughout the body, to conquer all the normal cells—and when they reach their aim, the body is dead. *And so are the cancer cells.*

SYDNEY J. HARRIS, "War Is Cancer of Mankind"

G.   Although Littleman, my eleven-year-old poodle, has never been separated from his thirteen-year-old mother, Simone, they are remarkably different. Simone weighs in at about ten pounds with very delicate, sophisticated features and coarse, curly hair. Slightly shorter, Littleman tops the scale at no more than seven pounds and is quite handsome with his teddy-bear features and soft wavy hair. **56** Simone was the first dog in the family and is a pedigreed poodle. In many ways she is the picture of a thoroughbred, with her snobby attitude and nonchalant manners. On the other hand, Littleman came into the family a year later with four other puppies of pure breeding, but they were never registered. Unlike his mother, Littleman is very friendly, almost to the point of being pesty at times.

—LINDA NEAL, student

EXERCISE 11

Write three of the following paragraphs.

1. A classification of drivers.
2. A personal definition of *political freedom*.
3. A narrative of your first experience as an authority figure.
4. A cause-and-effect analysis of the increase in crime in the United States.
5. An analogy about learning to use a college library.

ANSWERS: EXERCISE 11

Each student's paragraph will differ, but they all should have in common a clear use of RENNS and techniques of coherence.

4e Writing special paragraphs

    Special paragraphs—**introductory paragraphs, concluding paragraphs,** and **transitional paragraphs**—have special roles in an essay. Introductions prepare a reader for the topical paragraphs that follow. Conclusions bring the topical paragraphs to a close for a reader. Transitional paragraphs—usually reserved for longer pieces of writing—help the reader move through complex material. Generally, special paragraphs are proportionately shorter than the topical paragraphs with which they appear.

QUOTATION ABOUT WRITING

If I didn't know the ending of a story, I wouldn't begin. I always write my last line, my last paragraph, my last page first.

—Katherine Anne Porter

Effective beginnings and endings are indispensable for successful essays. Introductions and conclusions are not merely "ceremonial." Experienced writers expect to plan, draft, and revise introductory and concluding paragraphs as carefully as topical paragraphs.

Introductory paragraphs

In informative and persuasive writing, an introductory paragraph sets the stage and prepares a reader for what lies ahead. Introductions provide a bridge from the reader's mind to yours. For this reason, its introduction must clearly relate to the rest of your essay. If it points in one direction and your essay goes off in another, your reader will be confused—and will likely stop reading.

As you write successive drafts of an essay, you might change your mind about what to say in the introductory paragraph. An early draft might contain an idea that does not belong once your topical paragraphs are written. Indeed, when a subject is new to you, you might decide to write your introduction *after* having written a "discovery" draft (see 3a) or first draft (see 3b) of your topical paragraphs.

In college writing, many instructors require that an introductory paragraph include a statement of the essay's thesis—the central idea of an essay. Many instructors want students to demonstrate from the start that all parts of any essay are related. Professional writers do not necessarily include a thesis statement in their introductory paragraphs; with experience comes skill at maintaining a line of thought without overtly stating a central idea. Student writers, however, often need to practice explicitly and demonstrate openly external clues to essay organization.

When instructors require a thesis statement, they often want it to be in the last sentence or two of the introductory paragraph. Here is an example of an introductory paragraph with a thesis statement (shown in italics).

> 57 Most sprinters live in a narrow corridor of space and time. Life rushes at them quickly, and success and failure are measured by frustrating, tiny increments. Florence Griffith Joyner paints her running world in bold, colorful strokes. *For her, there's a lot of romance to running fast.*
>
> CRAIG A. MASBACK, "Siren of Speed"

You can see additional examples of introductory paragraphs with a thesis statement in the last sentence, in the student essays in sections 3c and 6h.

An introductory paragraph often includes an **introductory device** to lead into the thesis. Introductory devices serve to stimulate a reader's interest in the subject of the essay. Some of the most com-

¶ 4e

SELECTED DEVICES FOR INTRODUCTORY PARAGRAPHS

- Provide relevant background information
- Tell an interesting brief story or anecdote
- Give a pertinent statistic or statistics
- Ask a provocative question or questions
- Use an appropriate quotation
- Make a useful analogy
- Define a term used throughout the essay
- Identify the situation

TEACHING TIP

To make students more aware of the wide variety of introductory strategies available to them, you may find it helpful to ask them to bring to class articles from the campus and city newspapers. Discussion can center on identifying the device, the type of introduction, and the appropriateness of both for the subject, audience, and purposes of the writer.

mon introductory devices are listed in the chart. Usually the introductory device precedes the thesis statement.

Here is an introduction that uses an anecdote before its two-sentence thesis statement (shown in italics).

> 58 Bridget and Dorothy are 39-year-old British housewives, identical twins raised apart who first met each other a little over a year ago. When they met, to take part in Thomas Bouchard's twin study at the University of Minnesota, the manicured hands of each bore seven rings. Each also wore two bracelets on one wrist and a watch and bracelet on the other. *Investigators in Bouchard's study, the most extensive investigation ever made of identical twins reared apart, are still bewitched by the seven rings. Was it coincidence, the result of similar influences, or is this small sign of affinity a true, even inevitable, manifestation of the mysterious and infinitely complex interaction of the genes the two women have in common?*
>
> —CONSTANCE HOLDEN, "Identical Twins Reared Apart"

The key to the effectiveness of an introductory device is how well it relates to the essay's thesis and to the material in the topical paragraphs. An introductory device must be well integrated into the paragraph, not mechanically slotted in for its own sake. Note how smoothly the message of the quotation in the following introduction becomes a dramatic contrast that leads into thesis (shown in italics).

> 59 In 1895 Sir William Harcourt said to him: "My dear Winston, the experiences of a long life have convinced me that nothing ever happens." *But some things did happen in the stimulating next five decades, in which Winston Churchill was the largest figure.*
>
> —GEORGE F. WILL, "Winston Churchill: In the Region of Mass Effects"

121

In the following paragraph, the author uses unusual questions to arouse interest and to set the stage for his thesis statement (shown in italics).

> 60   Today, what respectable person would call a candidate for the highest office in the land a carbuncle-faced old drunkard? A pot-bellied, mutton-headed cucumber? A pickpocket, thief, traitor, lecher, drunkard, syphilitic, a gorilla, crook, anarchist, murderer? *Such charges were commonplace in Presidential contests in the nineteenth century.*
>
> —PAUL F. BOLLER, JR., "Election Fizzle-Gigery"

In the following paragraph, statistics and numbers help the author lead into his thesis statement.

> 61   In a Milwaukee suburb, a teenage gang awarded points to members for vandalizing streetlights and lawns. A 16-year-old in Santa Clara County, California, took 12 classmates to look at the body of his ex-girlfriend. None of them told police. Later, the boy was charged with her murder. In Chicago's affluent North Shore suburbs, more than 40 teenagers have taken their own lives in the past two years. *These episodes point up what many social scientists regard as one of the most significant—and disturbing—trends of recent years: A new generation of American teenagers is deeply troubled, unable to cope with the pressures of growing up in what they perceive as a world that is hostile or indifferent to them.*
>
> —STANLEY N. WELLBORN, *Troubled Teenagers*

An effective introduction has no room for self-conscious statements or overused expressions. Guidelines on what to avoid in introductory paragraphs are given in the chart below.

WHAT TO AVOID IN INTRODUCTORY PARAGRAPHS

1. Do not be too obvious. Avoid bald statements such as "In this paper I will discuss the causes of falling oil prices" or "My assignment asks me to discuss Hamlet's inability to take action."

2. Do not apologize. Avoid self-critical statements such as "I do not have much background in this subject," "Of course, other people are more expert in this subject than I am," or "I am not sure if I am right, but here is my opinion."

3. Do not use overworn expressions. Avoid statements such as "Haste makes waste," "A penny saved is a penny earned," "Love is what makes the world go around," and "War is hell."

¶

Concluding paragraphs

In informative and persuasive writing, a conclusion serves to bring your discussion to a logical end. Too abrupt an ending leaves your reader suddenly cut off. A conclusion that is merely tacked onto an essay does not give the reader a sense of completion. An ending that flows gracefully and sensibly from what has come before it reinforces the writer's ideas and enhances an essay. A concluding paragraph often takes one of several forms. The most common ways of concluding an essay are given in the chart.

SELECTED DEVICES FOR CONCLUDING PARAGRAPHS

- Use the devices for introductory paragraphs (see chart on page 121) but avoid using the same device in the introduction and conclusion of an essay
- Summarize the main points of the essay
- Call for awareness and/or action
- Point to the future

Here is a concluding paragraph that summarizes a persuasive essay about the problem of teenagers getting married for the wrong reasons.

> 62 Teenagers may contemplate marriage for a variety of reasons—most of them misguided. Before they pledge their lifelong devotion to their "one and only," however, teenagers should secure the counsel of an impartial party, and they should seriously consider their options.
>
> —ADRIAN GONZALEZ, student

You can see additional examples of concluding paragraphs by students in sections 3c and 6h.

The essay for which the following conclusion was written is a condemnation of racism as demonstrated by the existence of urban ghettos. This concluding paragraph reinforces the message of the essay by calling for awareness and, by extension, action.

> 63 It is a terrible, an inexorable, law that one cannot deny the humanity of another without diminishing one's own: in the face of one's victim, one sees oneself. Walk through Harlem and see what we, this nation, have become.
>
> —JAMES BALDWIN, "Fifth Avenue, Uptown: A Letter from Harlem"

QUOTATION ABOUT WRITING

The perfect ending should take the reader slightly by surprise and yet seem exactly right to him. He didn't expect the article to end so soon, or so abruptly, or to say what it said. But he knows it when he sees it. Like a good lead, it works. It is like the curtain line in a theatrical comedy. We are in the middle of a scene (we think) when suddenly one of the actors says something funny, or outrageous, or epigrammatic, and the lights go out. We are momentarily startled to find the scene over, and then delighted by the aptness of how it ended. What delights us, subconsciously, is the playwright's perfect control.

—William Zinsser, *On Writing Well*

ANSWERS: EXERCISE 13
(on page 126)

1. **Topic sentences**
    A **(paragraph 50).** first sentence
    B **(paragraph 51).** first sentence
    C **(paragraph 52).** last sentence
    D **(paragraph 53).** first sentence
    E **(paragraph 54).** implied (Cookies were a special treat when I was a child.)
    F **(paragraph 55).** first sentence
    G **(Paragraph 56).** first sentence

2. **RENNS**
    A **(paragraph 50).** *Reasons:* Hanoi's main market has little to offer. Saigon has rows of "shop-houses." Hanoi has bicycles, while Saigon has motorcycles and a few private cars. *Examples:* The specific products in each market. *Names:* South Vietnam, Hanoi, Saigon, China, Mustangs, *Senses:* The sight of the frogs' legs being chopped off, the sight of dense bicycle traffic.
    B **(paragraph 51).** *Examples:* upholstery, Renaissance dining room, figured silk hangings over stained-glass doors, velvet curtains, black pear wood. *Names:* Renaissance dining room, Papa's study, black pear wood. *Senses:* sight of red and black, sight of "dusty glooms," darkness, watching, touching.
    C **(paragraph 52).** *Examples:* all sentences but the last. *Names:* Rimsky-Korsakov's bumblebee, Grieg's "Morning," Beethoven, Wagner's Valkyries, Valhalla, Rodrigo's Madrid, Gershwin's Paris. *Senses:* buzzing, breeze, golden rays projecting like spears, bird song, tumultuous thunder, growling wind, tempest breaking solitude of pastoral scene, riding powerful steeds, boisterous.

The following conclusion ends an essay that discusses the failure of public schools to educate students well. The author points to the future and calls for action.

64   Our schools provide a key to the future of society. We must take control of them, watch over them, and nurture them if they are to be set right again. To do less is to invite disaster upon ourselves, our children, and our nation.

—JOHN C. SAWHILL, "The Collapse of Public Schools"

An effective conclusion does not detract from the central message of an essay. Refer to the chart for a list of what to avoid when writing concluding paragraphs.

WHAT TO AVOID IN CONCLUDING PARAGRAPHS

1. Do not go off the track. Avoid introducing an entirely new idea or adding a fact that belongs in the body of the essay. Your conclusion should flow from the rest of your essay.

2. Do not reword your introduction. Avoid simply listing the main idea in each topic sentence or restating the thesis. While a summary can refer to those points, it must tie them into what was covered in the essay. A good test is to check if the introduction and conclusion are interchangeable. If they are, you need to revise.

3. Do not announce what you have done. Avoid statements such as "In this paper I have tried to show the main causes for the drop in oil prices."

4. Do not make absolute claims. Avoid statements such as "This proves that . . ." and "If we take this action, the problem will be solved." Always qualify your message with expressions such as "This seems to prove . . ." and "If we take this action, we will begin working toward a solution of the problem."

5. Avoid logical fallacies. Concluding paragraphs are particularly vulnerable to errors in reasoning. Logical fallacies are explained and illustrated in 5f.

6. Do not apologize. Avoid casting doubt on your material by making statements such as "I may not have thought of all the arguments, but . . ." and "Even though I am not an expert, I feel that what I have said is correct."

¶ 4e

Transitional paragraphs

A transitional paragraph provides one or two sentences to help a reader move from one major point to another. Transitional paragraphs often restate a main idea briefly. Transitional paragraphs are uncommon in short essays. In most writing for college, short transitional paragraphs are not appropriate. They can be mistaken for undeveloped topical paragraphs and can confuse readers.

Here is a two-sentence transitional paragraph written as a bridge between a discussion of people's gestures and people's eating habits. This paragraph is followed by a number of paragraphs each of which discusses a different type of eater.

65   Like gestures, eating habits are personality indicators, and even food preferences and attitudes toward food reveal the inner self. Food plays an important role in the lives of most people beyond its obvious one as a necessity.

—JEAN ROSENBAUM, M.D., *Is Your Volkswagon a Sex Symbol?*

EXERCISE 12

Write an introduction and conclusion for each essay informally outlined below.

A. Humor in current movies
   Thesis: Today's movies illustrate several types of humor.
   Topical paragraph 1: slapstick
   Topical paragraph 2: understatement and overstatement
   Topical paragraph 3: wit

B. Uses of computers
   Thesis: Many new applications for computers are emerging in the worlds of business, finance, and the arts.
   Topical paragraph 1: business
   Topical paragraph 2: finance
   Topical paragraph 3: the arts

C. Starting a new job
   Thesis: Starting a new job demands much concentration.
   Topical paragraph 1: learning or adapting skills
   Topical paragraph 2: fitting in with co-workers
   Topical paragraph 3: adjusting to the surroundings

ANSWERS: EXERCISE 13
(on page 126) *(continued)*

  D (paragraph 53). *Reasons:* not even grained, not apt to split, take polish well. *Examples:* fruitwoods, cherry, apple, pear, orange, oak, mahogany, walnut, birch, holly, maple. *Senses:* white of holly, almost black of walnut.

  E (paragraph 54). *Senses:* slightly browned on the edges, butter-yellow in the center, cold lemonade, lady-like bites, rough crumbs scratched the insides of my jaws.

  F (paragraph 55). *Examples:* normal cells, cancer cells—and the aim of normal cells to reproduce and of cancer cells to destroy.

  G (paragraph 56). *Examples:* Littleman and Simone, their features, hair, and personalities. *Numbers:* eleven-year-old, thirteen-year-old, ten pounds, seven pounds, four other puppies.

(continued next page)

ANSWERS: EXERCISE 12

One way to help students succeed with this exercise is to talk them through these imaginary essays before they think about the beginnings and endings. A class discussion about what details might support the topics of each paragraph will strengthen students' understanding of the importance of evidence. At the same time, it will give students a fuller concept of the essay on which to base their introductory and concluding paragraphs. When the students write the introductions and conclusions, alert them to the lists of useful devices and of "what to avoid," explained in this section of Chapter 4.

ANSWERS: EXERCISE 13 *(continued)*

3. **Techniques of coherence.** In this order, if they appear: transitional expressions *(te)*, pronouns *(p)*, deliberate repetition *(dr)*, and parallel structures *(ps)*.

  A (paragraph 50). *te:* still; *dr:* Hanoi, Saigon; *ps:* In Saigon there are/in Hanoi, there are.

  B (paragraph 51). *p:* I; *dr:* red, black; *ps:* red, and black, and warm / I watched, I touched, I took stock.

  C (paragraph 52). *dr:* it is; *ps:* buzzing / peeking / growling / breaking / riding / bustling.

  D (paragraph 53). *te:* too, therefore; *p:* they, other kinds; *dr:* hardwoods, apt; *ps:* all verbs in simple present, they are.

  E (paragraph 54). *p:* they, I, my, she, them, me.

  F (paragraph 55). *te:* on the other hand; *p:* they, their, we; *dr:* cancer, cells, body, normal; *ps:* all verbs in simple present, to spread / to conquer.

  G (paragraph 56). *te:* on the other hand; *p:* my, his, she, her; *dr:* Littleman, mother, Simone; *ps:* Simone weighs / Littleman tops, Simone was / Littleman came.

4. **Paragraph arrangement**

  A (paragraph 50). general to specific

  B (paragraph 51). least to most important

  C (paragraph 52). specific to general

  D (paragraph 53). general to specific

  E (paragraph 54). time

  F (paragraph 55). general to specific and least to most important

  G (paragraph 56). general to specific

D. Violence on television

  Thesis: Violence on television is harmful to children.

  Topical paragraph 1: cartoons

  Topical paragraph 2: series

  Topical paragraph 3: made-for-television movies

E. Adjusting to college

  Thesis: Many challenges face students as they adjust to college.

  Topical paragraph 1: financial

  Topical paragraph 2: emotional

  Topical paragraph 3: academic

EXERCISE 13

Reread the paragraphs in Exercise 10 and do the following.

1. Referring to Section 4a-1, identify all topic sentences, limiting sentences, and implied topic sentences.

2. Referring to Section 4a-2, identify all RENNS.

3. Referring to Section 4b, identify all techniques of coherence.

4. Referring to Section 4c, identify paragraph arrangements.

5 Reading and Thinking Critically

Thinking is not something you choose to do, any more than a fish "chooses" to live in water. To be human *is* to think. But while thinking may come naturally, awareness of *how* you think does not. Thinking about thinking is the key to thinking critically. When you think critically, you take control of your conscious thought processes. Without such control, you risk being controlled by the ideas of others. Indeed, critical thinking is at the heart of a liberal (from the Latin word for *free*) education.

The word **critical** here has a neutral meaning. It does not mean taking a negative view or finding fault, as when someone criticizes another person for doing something wrong. The essence of critical thinking is thinking beyond the obvious—beyond the flash of visual images on a television screen, the alluring promises of glossy advertisements, the evasive statements by some people in the news, the half-truths of some propaganda, the manipulations of slanted language and faulty reasoning.

Critical thinking is an attitude as much as an activity. If you face life with curiosity and a desire to dig beneath the surface, you are a critical thinker. If you do not believe everything you read or hear, you are a critical thinker. If you find pleasure in contemplating the puzzle of conflicting ideologies, theories, personalities, and facts, you are a critical thinker.

Activities of the mind and higher-order reasoning—the core of a college education—are processes of contemplation and deliberation. These processes take time. They contrast with the glorification of speed in today's culture: fast foods, instant mixes, self-developing film, short-spurt images in movies and videos. If you are among the people who assume that speed is a measure of intelligence, consider this true anecdote about Albert Einstein. The first time that Banesh Hoffman, a scientist, was expected to talk about his work to Albert Einstein, Hoffman was speechless and overawed. Einstein instantly put Hoffman at ease when he said: "Please go slowly. I don't understand things quickly."

QUOTATION ABOUT THINKING

Most people would sooner die than think; in fact, they do so.

—Bertrand Russell

QUOTATION ABOUT THINKING

Cogito, ergo sum. (I think, therefore I am.)

—René Descartes, *Principles of Philosophy*

QUOTATION ABOUT THINKING

Man is but a reed, the weakest in nature, but he is a thinking reed.

—Blaise Pascal, *Pensées, VI*

QUOTATION ABOUT READING

Literature is no one's private ground, literature is common ground; let us trespass freely and fearlessly and find our own way for ourselves.

—Virginia Woolf

QUOTATION ABOUT READING

My education was the liberty I had to read indiscriminately and all the time, with my eyes hanging out.

—Dylan Thomas

Some features of critical thinking differ slightly from academic discipline to academic discipline, but all critical thinking is rooted in the activities of analysis, synthesis, and evaluation. These activities apply when you think about lectures and discussions in your college classes, when you read your textbooks and other assignments for your college courses, and also when you conduct your daily life.

ACTIVITIES FOR CRITICAL READING AND THINKING

1. **Analysis.** You take ideas apart so that you can consider components of ideas separately.
2. **Synthesis.** You make connections among different ideas or components of ideas, seeking relationships and interactions with which to tie them together.
3. **Evaluation.** You assess the quality of ideas to see if they hold up to an examination that focuses on quality of reasoning (see 5c-5d) and soundness of logic (see 5f).

5a Understanding the reading process

Reading, like writing, helps you to come to "know," to compose meaning. In college you get many reading assignments that assume you have the ability to read critically. A critical reader reads with a questioning mind, open to new ideas but careful to recognize when material is distorted because it is incomplete. A critical reader also recognizes when material is slanted to manipulate the reader improperly, or is based on incorrect information. If you understand **the reading process,** you can effectively meet the demands of critical reading.

Reading is not a passive activity. It involves more than looking at words. Reading is an active process—a dynamic, meaning-making encounter involving the interaction of the page, eye, and brain. When you read, your brain actively makes connections between what you know already and what is new to you. You comprehend and learn new material by associating it with material you already know.

Experts who have researched the reading process report that the key activity in reading is *making predictions.* As you read, your brain is always involved in guessing what is coming next. Once it discovers what comes next, it either confirms or revises its prediction and moves on. For example, if you encountered a chapter title "The Heartbeat," your predictions could be diverse, ranging from romance to how the heart pumps blood. As you read on, you would confirm or revise your prediction according to what you found— you would be in the realm of romance if you encountered a paragraph about lovers and roses, and you would be in the realm of biology if you encountered material that included diagrams of the physiology of the heart. Predicting during reading happens at split-second speed without the reader's being aware of it. Without predictions, the brain would have to consider infinite possibilities for assimilating every new piece of information; with predictions, the brain can narrow its expectations to reasonable proportions. Predicting keeps the reader sane.

1 Knowing your purpose in reading

Purposes for reading vary. Most reading in college is for the purpose of learning new information, appreciating literary works, or reviewing notes on classes or readings. These types of reading involve much *rereading;* one encounter with the material rarely suffices. Vladimir Nabokov, a respected novelist and lecturer on literature, observed: "Curiously enough, one cannot *read* a book: one can only *reread* it. A good reader, a major reader, an active and creative reader, is a rereader."

Your purpose in reading determines the speed at which you can expect to read. When you are hunting for a particular fact in an almanac, you can skim the material until you come to what you want. When you read about a subject that you know well, your brain is familiar with the material, so you can move somewhat rapidly through most of it, slowing down when you come to new material. When you are unfamiliar with the subject, your brain needs time to absorb the new material, so you have to slow down.

2 Using a system for reading to learn

Three universals about reading to learn hold for all material. These universals have parallels in the writing process, with slightly different labels, as explained in the chart on the next page. These

QUOTATION ABOUT READING

Like writing, reading requires the creation of meaning, this time in collaboration with an author. Like writing, reading becomes meaningful only when it involves the particular response of an individual—one's own ways of perceiving reality through the prism of written language.

—Nancie Atwell, *In the Middle*

BACKGROUND

In *Illiterate America* (1985) Jonathan Kozol cites figures from a 1979 Ford Foundation study that places the number of illiterate Americans at about 60 million. Supporting those assertions are United Nations statistics that rank the United States forty-ninth in literacy among 158 U.N. countries.

QUOTATION ABOUT READING

The one thing I regret is that I will never have time to read all the books I want to read.

—Françoise Sagan

QUOTATION ABOUT READING

Some books are to be tasted, others to be swallowed, and some few to be chewed and digested. . . .

—Francis Bacon, *Essays: of Studies*

UNIVERSALS IN READING TO LEARN	
SKIM	Like *planning* (see Chapter 2) in the writing process, **skimming** means getting ready to read.
READ	Like *drafting* (see 3a-3b) in the writing process, **reading** means moving through the material, according to your purpose for reading.
REINFORCE	Like *revising* (see 3c) and *editing* (3d) in the writing process, **reinforcing** means rereading, clarifying, fine tuning, and getting into final form.

universals help you use what you know about the reading process to study and think critically. Various structured systems for applying these universals have been suggested by experts in reading. Here is one widely endorsed system, popularly known as SQ3R.*

S = *Survey.* Surveying is part of *skimming.* You survey to get an overview of the material before you start reading closely. As you survey, your brain begins unconsciously to make predictions about the material.

If you are surveying a textbook, first quickly survey the entire text, and then as you read each chapter, survey it more slowly. If the material has headings, subheadings, words in italics or boldface, or visuals, use them as a road map during your surveying. If you are reading a book that has no headings, (1) read the title; (2) establish a general sense of the length of the material you need to read; (3) read the opening and closing paragraphs—unless you do not want to know the ending—and, if the material is long, glance over some intervening paragraphs.

Q = *Question.* Questioning is part of *skimming.* Asking questions stimulates your brain to prepare for learning. Experiments have shown that college students who actively use structured questioning before reading improve dramatically in comprehension and in recall over both short and long periods of time. Question in small chunks, in contrast to covering large amounts of material during surveying. If you are reading a textbook, it is best to question when you encounter each new subsection. Working in small chunks allows your

---

*Originated by Francis P. Robinson in 1946, the system has been adapted by many others since. The version here is adapted for college students.

5a

brain to narrow its focus and to make more accurate predictions about what is coming next.

Ask questions deliberately and consciously. Base your questions on titles, key words, headings, and any other material that seems to be central. Here are some examples, based on the first three pages of this chapter.

TITLE	Thinking Critically
QUESTION	What is thinking critically?
KEY WORD	critically
QUESTION	What does "critically" mean here?
HEADING	Understanding the reading process
QUESTIONS	What is the reading process? What should I understand about it?

Answers during questioning do not necessarily have to be precise. The goal is to get your thinking started so that your brain will be alerted to focus on key matters as you read.

R = *Read.* Reading is the core activity in SQ3R. The speed at which you read depends on your purpose. Surveying and questioning before you start reading will allow you to get more meaning out of the written word. The full meaning will emerge on the literal level, the inferential level, and the evaluative level (these three levels are explained in 5b).

Comprehension can break down for a number of reasons: (1) If you are reading about a totally unfamiliar subject, your brain might not be able to associate so much new material to what you already know. In such a situation, take the time to build up your store of information by reading easier material in other sources on the subject; of course, for academic work you must return as quickly as possible to the more difficult material you are required to read. (2) Comprehension can elude you if your mind wanders, thus taking up some of your brain's activity with extraneous material. If this happens, you must be fiercely determined to concentrate and resist the appeal of other thoughts. Do whatever it takes. Arrange for silence or music, for being alone or in a crowded library's reading room, for studying at your best time of day—some people concentrate better in the morning, others in the evening. (3) You cannot comprehend new material if you have not allotted sufficient time to work with it. College students are pulled in many different directions and have to discipline themselves to balance their class, study, social, and

---

QUOTATION ABOUT READING

Whenever I feel uneasy about my writing, I think: What would be the response of the people in the book if they read the book? That's my way of staying on track. Those are the people for whom I write.

—Toni Morrison

BACKGROUND

According to Larry Mikulecky of Indiana University, the level of the literacy skills needed for a person to function in American society is rising. Surveying 107 workers in this country, he discovered that 99 did "some reading" on the job. The average time spent reading was 113 minutes per day. He also notes that the readability level of news articles has risen since the end of World War II from about a sixth-grade level to an eleventh-grade level today. (E. B. Fiske, *New York Times,* September 8, 1983, p. 1.)

BACKGROUND

In *Society and Solitude,* Emerson suggests three practical rules for reading.

1. Never read any book that is not a year old.

2. Never read any but the famed books.

3. Never read any but what you like.

QUOTATION ABOUT READING

When I am not walking, I am reading; I cannot sit and think. Books think for me.

—Charles Lamb, *Last Essay of Elia*

job—if any—schedules with the unavoidable and time-consuming demands of a reading and studying schedule. Nothing prevents learning so much as lack of time.

R = *Recite.* Reciting is part of *reinforcing.* Reciting calls for you to look away from the page and repeat the main points, aloud or to yourself. For best success, recite in chunks—subsections of textbook chapters, for example. Do not try to cover too much material at once. Knowing ahead of time that when you finish a section you will have to recite stimulates your concentration during reading. If you cannot recite the main points of the material, reread it and try again. If you still have trouble, go back to surveying and questioning and then reread.

R = *Review.* Reviewing is part of *reinforcing.* When you finish reading, survey again. This process refreshes your memory about the initial overview you got during surveying. It also gives you a larger framework into which to fit new material you have just learned. Be honest with yourself about what you cannot recall and need to re-read. The next day, and again about a week later, repeat your review—always adding whatever new material you have learned since the previous review. As much as your time permits, review again at set intervals during a course. The more reinforcement, the better.

Collaborative learning can help you reinforce what you learn from reading. Ask a friend or classmate who knows the material well to discuss it with you, even test you. Conversely, offer to teach the material to someone, and you will know quickly whether or not you have mastered it sufficiently to communicate it.

Writing can help you reinforce your learning. There is little that promotes authority over knowledge as does writing about it. Keep a learning log: draw a line down the center of your notebook page; on one side take notes on the reading material, and on the other side list key words, ask questions, make connections among ideas, and have a "conversation on paper" with the material. Also, you can master difficult sections by writing paraphrases, the techniques of which are described in 31b.

EXERCISE 1

(1) List the steps you usually go through when you read a textbook. (2) Next, apply SQ3R to reading a chapter in a textbook. (3) Observe your SQ3R reading process and list the steps you go through. (4) Compare the two lists—what you usually go through and what you did when you used the SQ3R system. Note how your lists are alike and how they are different. (5) Write a brief discussion that compares your two lists and that explains which steps in either or both lists helped you learn most successfully from your reading.

ANSWERS: EXERCISE 1

The answers will vary somewhat, depending on the material each student selects.

5b Reading critically

During the reading process, the full meaning of a passage emerges on three levels: the **literal,** the **inferential,** and the **evaluative.** If you are like most readers, you stop reading at the literal level. Unless you move to the next two levels, however, your critical reading and thinking skills will suffer.

STEPS FOR READING CRITICALLY

1. **Read for literal meaning.** You read "on" the lines to see what is stated.
2. **Read to make inferences.** You read "between" the lines to see what is not stated but implied.
3. **Read to evaluate.** You read "beyond" the lines to assess the soundness of the writer's reasoning, the accuracy of the writer's choice of words, and the fairness of the writer's treatment of the reader.

A reflection on having once read 800 pages of *War and Peace* in one day:

> It took me a long time to forget the way I read that book. For a long time it seemed to me I had betrayed reading itself. Coming back to it now, I still find it disturbing. Something had been sacrificed in my quick dash through the book—another reading altogether. I had limited myself to the story at the expense of a deep, receptive, non-narrative reading of Tolstoy's writing itself. It was as though I had realized that day, once and for all, that a book consists of two layers: on top, the readable layer I had read that day on the train, and underneath, a layer that was inaccessible. You only sense its existence in a moment of distraction from the literal reading, the way you see childhood through a child. It would take forever to tell what you see, and it would be pointless.

—Marguerite Duras, "On Tolstoy, Racine, and Reading by the Light of the Book"

---

1 Reading for literal meaning

Reading for literal meaning, sometimes called *reading "on" the line,* calls for you to understand what is said. It does not include impressions or opinions about the material. Depending on the discipline in which you are reading, the literal level has to do with (1) the key facts, the central points in a line or argument, or the central details of plot and character; and (2) the minor details that lend texture to the picture. You need to understand the literal meaning of a passage, before you move beyond it to the next two levels crucial for critical thinking.

The more vocabulary you know, the more likely you are to understand the literal meaning of your reading. When you encounter unfamiliar words while reading, try to figure them out by using clues from the context of the material (for advice on using context clues, see 20c-2). If you cannot figure out a word's meaning, underline or highlight it to remind yourself to look it up after your first reading and before you begin your second.

When you encounter a complex writing style, take time to "unpack" the sentences. Try to break them down into shorter units or reword them into a simpler style. Do not assume that all writing is clear merely because it is in print. Authors write with a rich variety of styles, not all equally accessible on a first reading.

When you find a concept that you need to think through, take the time needed to come to know the new idea. Although no student has unlimited time for reading and thinking, rushing through material to "cover" it rather than understand it ends up costing more time in the long run.

2 Reading to make inferences

Reading to make inferences, sometimes called *reading "between" the lines,* means understanding what is implied but not stated. Often you have to infer information, or background, or the author's purpose. Consider this passage:

> How to tell the difference between modern art and junk puzzles many people although few are willing to admit it. The owner of an art gallery in Chicago had a prospective buyer for two sculptures made of discarded metal and put them outside his warehouse to clean them up. Unfortunately, some junk dealers, who apparently didn't recognize abstract expressionism when they saw it, hauled the two 300-pound pieces away.
>
> —ORA GYGI, "Things Are Seldom What They Seem"

The literal meaning is that many people cannot tell the difference between art and junk. Two abstract metal sculptures were carted away as junk when an art dealer left them outside a warehouse to clean them.

Now read the material inferentially. You can begin with the unexplained statement "few are willing to admit" they do not know the difference between art and junk. Reading between the lines, you realize that people feel embarrassed *not* to know; they feel uneducated, or without good taste, or perhaps left out. With this inference in mind, you can move to the last two sentences, in which the author offers not only the literal irony (see 21c) of the art's being carted away as junk, but also the implied irony that the people who carted it away are not among those who might feel embarrassed. This implied irony suggests that the people either do not care if they know the difference between art and junk (after all, they assumed it was junk and went on their way) or they "apparently" (a good word for inference making) want to give the impression that they do not know the difference. Thus, it is the art dealer who ends up being embarrassed, for it is he who created the problem by leaving the sculptures outdoors unattended.

The process of inferring is a critical thinking skill that adds not only texture but also invaluable background for the interpretation of any passage.

QUOTATION ABOUT READING

Books: The most effective weapon against intolerance and ignorance.

—Lyndon Baines Johnson

CHECKLIST FOR MAKING INFERENCES DURING READING

1. What is being said beyond the literal level?

2. What is implied rather than stated?

3. What words need to be read for their implied meanings (connotations) as well as for their stated meanings (denotations) (see 20b-1)?

4. What information does the author expect me to have before I start to read the material?

5. What does the author seem to assume are my biases?

6. What information does the author expect me to have about his or her background, philosophy, and the like?

7. What do I need to be aware of concerning author bias?

---

3 | **Reading to evaluate**

Evaluative reading, sometimes called *reading "beyond" the lines,* is essential for critical thinking. Once you know an author's literal meaning, and once you have drawn as many inferences as possible from the material, you must evaluate.

Evaluative reading calls for many skills, including knowing how to recognize faulty reasoning (5c-5e), logical fallacies (5f), slanted language (21a-4), and artificial language (21e). Evaluative reading also demands the ability to recognize the impact of an author's tone, to detect prejudice, and to differentiate fact from opinion.

EVALUATIVE READING

- ■ Recognize whether an author's tone is appropriate
- ■ Detect prejudice
- ■ Differentiate fact from opinion

TEACHING TIP

Your students may enjoy analyzing the tone of the following two passages. How can they be compared and contrasted?

A. I can't eat or drink anything. I can't go anywhere. I have become a victim of the consumer reporter. Every since Ralph Nader and his pals started investigating, I have gradually become an anorexia nervosa hermit. My friends warn me that I've been taking the news too seriously. But if you read the paper and watch television every night, you begin to get the feeling that if the mugger doesn't kill you—BOTULISM will!

—Joanna Wolper, "A Victim of the Consumer Crusaders"

B. Too much of anything—too much music, entertainment, happy snacks, or time spent with one's friends, creates a kind of impotence of living by which one can no longer hear, or taste, or see, or love, or remember. Life is short and precious, and appetite is one of its guardians, and loss of appetite is a sort of death. So if we are to enjoy this short life we should respect the divinity of appetite, and keep it eager and not too much blunted.

It is a long time now since I knew that acute moment of bliss that comes from putting parched lips to a cup of cold water. The springs are still there to be enjoyed—all one needs is the original thirst.

—Laurie Lee, "Appetite,"
from *I Can't Stay Long*

Recognizing whether an author's tone is appropriate

Tone is communicated by all aspects of a piece of writing, from its choice of words to the content of the message. An author's tone should be appropriate to the author's purpose (see 1b) and audience (see 1c). For example, most academic writing should not use language that is either informal or overly stiff and formal (see 21a-1).

Most authors use a serious tone, but sometimes they use humor to get their point across; if you read such material exclusively for its literal meaning, you will miss the point. Here is a passage from an argument against the destruction of buildings that house small, friendly neighborhood stores and their replacement by large, impersonal buildings.

> Every time an old building is torn down in this country, and a new building goes up, the ground floor becomes a bank. The reason for this is that banks are the only ones who can afford the rent for the ground floor of the new buildings going up. . . . Most people don't think there is anything wrong with this, and they accept it as part of the American free-enterprise system. But there is a small group of people in this country who are fighting for Bank Birth Control.
>
> ART BUCHWALD, "Birth Control for Banks"

Buchwald clearly respects his readers, for he expects that they will realize that (1) although he is talking only of banks, the banks stand for many aspects of urban renewal; (2) the first sentence is an exaggeration intended to elicit a smile—Buchwald is being slightly ridiculous to get across his point; and (3) the group "Bank Birth Control" does not exist—it is Buchwald's creation to advance his argument.

Most readers are wary of a highly emotional tone whose purpose is not to give information but to incite the reader.

> Urban renewal must be stopped! Urban redevelopment is ruining this country. Money-hungry capitalists are robbing treasures from law-abiding citizens! Corrupt politicians are murderers, caring nothing about people being thrown out of their homes into the streets.

Writers of such material do not respect their readers, for such writers assume that readers do not recognize screaming in print when they see it. Discerning readers instantly know the tone here is emotional and unreasonable. The exaggerations (robbing treasures, politicians as murderers) hint at the truth of some cases, but they are generalizations too extreme to be taken seriously.

On the other hand, if a writer's tone sounds reasonable and moderate, readers are more likely to pay attention.

> Urban renewal is revitalizing our cities, but it has caused some serious problems. While investors are trying to replace slums with decent housing, they must also remember that they are displacing people who do not want to leave their familiar neighborhoods. Surely a cooperative effort between government and the private sector can lead to creative solutions.

Detecting prejudice

Writers often express opinions, which readers should expect to be based on sound reasoning (see 5c-5f). **Prejudice** is revealed in negative opinions based on beliefs rather than on facts or evidence. Negative opinions might be expressed in positive language, but the underlying assumptions are negative. Prejudicial statements are like these: *Poor people like living in crowded conditions because they are used to the surroundings, Women are not aggressive enough to succeed in business, Men make good soldiers because they enjoy killing.* Often writers imply their prejudices rather than state them outright. Detecting underlying negative opinions that distort information is important for critical reading, because discerning readers must call into question any argument that rests upon a weak foundation. (See also Hasty Generalization in 5f.)

Differentiating fact from opinion

Facts are statements that can be verified. A person may use experiment, research, and/or observation to verify facts. Opinions are statements of personal beliefs that are open to debate. *Opinions* often contain information that cannot be verified, such as abstract ideas.

An author sometimes intentionally blurs the difference between fact and opinion, and a discerning reader must be able to tell the difference. Sometimes that difference is quite obvious.

EXTRA EXERCISE A

Determine which of the following sentences state facts and which state opinions.

1. Nuclear fusion releases energy.

2. Nuclear fusion is a possible solution of our energy problems.

3. Solar energy has attracted a great deal of public attention over the past decade.

4. Many people hope that it will produce a clean, nonpolluting means of heating our homes and offices.

5. Oil and gas production in the United States has been falling for over a decade.

6. The petroleum industry is shrinking yearly.

7. In the interest of national security, the petroleum industry should be encouraged by government legislation.

8. The early pioneers generated energy from the wind on the frontier.

9. Such nonpolluting means of creating energy should replace those produced by fossil fuels immediately.

10. Because natural gas, methane, is a clean fuel, the government should encourage its use.

ANSWERS: EXTRA EXERCISE A

1. fact
2. opinion
3. fact
4. fact
5. fact
6. fact
7. opinion
8. fact
9. opinion
10. opinion

A. A woman can never make a good mathematician.

B. Although fear of math is not purely a female phenomenon, girls tend to drop out of math sooner than boys, and adult women experience an aversion to math and math-related activity that is akin to anxiety.

Because of the word *never,* statement A is clearly an opinion. Statement B seems to be factual. Knowing who made these statements can sometimes help a reader distinguish between fact and opinion. Statement A is by a male Soviet mathematician living in Russia, as reported by David K. Shipler, a well-respected veteran reporter on Russian affairs for the *New York Times;* statement B is in a book called *Overcoming Math Anxiety* by Sheila Tobias, a university professor who has undertaken research studies to find out why many people dislike math. Thus, statement B can be confirmed to be fact.

One aid in differentiating between fact and opinion is to *think beyond the obvious.* For example, is "Strenuous exercise is good for your health" a fact? Although the statement has the ring of truth, it is not a fact. People with severe arthritis or heart trouble could be harmed by some forms of exercise. Also, what does "strenuous" mean—a dozen pushups, jogging, aerobics, or playing tennis?

A second aid in differentiating between fact and opinion is to *remember that facts sometimes masquerade as opinions, and opinions sometimes try to pass for facts.* Evaluative reading demands concentration and a willingness to deal with matters that are relative and sometimes ambiguous. For example, in an essay for or against capital punishment, you would likely evaluate the argument differently if you knew that the author is currently on death row, or a victim of a crime committed by someone on death row, or a disinterested party with a philosophy to discuss.

At times, however, the stance of the author is less clear. Consider these statements:

C. The common wart usually occurs on the hands, especially on the backs of the fingers, but they may occur on any part of the skin. These dry, elevated lesions have numerous projections on the surface.

D. Warts are wonderful structures. They can appear overnight on any part of the skin, like mushrooms on a damp lawn, full grown and splendid in the complexity of their architecture.

Both statements are about warts. Judging only from the words—often all the evidence available—and without knowing who the authors are, we might say that C is fact and D is opinion.

Information about the authors can make your judgments more subtle and therefore more reliable. Statement C is from a respected medical encyclopedia; thus it can be confirmed as fact. Statement *D* is by Lewis Thomas, a distinguished physician, hospital administrator, researcher, and writer who won the National Book Award for his popular essays revealing the intricacies of biology to laypeople. Given this information and the comparatively benign nature of the material, the words in *D* move into the realm of fact—fact drawing on metaphor (see 21c) to illustrate its point. The author is trying to bring the facts to life by looking at them in a new way and explaining them inventively.

EXERCISE 2

Decide if each statement is a fact or an opinion. When the author and source are provided, explain how that information influences your judgment.

1. Jogging promotes good mental health.
2. Cotton clothing is more comfortable than polyester clothing.
3. "Every journey into the past is complicated by delusions, false memories, false namings of real events." (Adrienne Rich, poet, *Of Woman Born*)
4. Edmund Hillary performed two major feats: he not only led the first successful climb to the top of Mount Everest but also he led the first group to cross the Antarctic continent from sea to sea.
5. "History is the branch of knowledge that deals systematically with the past." (*Webster's New World Dictionary,* Third College Edition)
6. "Rock music encourages passions and provides models that have no relation to any life the young people who go to universities can possibly lead, or to the kinds of admiration encouraged by liberal studies." (Allan Bloom, a professor at the University of Chicago, *The Closing of the American Mind*)
7. The earth's temperature is gradually rising.
8. Slaves in ancient Egypt were often killed when they finished building a pyramid so that they could not reveal the entrances to thieves who would loot the tombs.
9. "You change laws by changing lawmakers." (Sissy Farenthold, political activist, interview reported in *The Bakersfield Californian*)
10. "But since it opened to the public in 1982, Elvis's place in suburban Whitehaven, a 30-minute drive from downtown Memphis, has attracted more than 3 million visitors. That figure makes it one of the top house attractions in the U.S. This year alone, some 640,000 people will visit Graceland, and in the process they will spend more than $10 million on tickets, food, and souvenirs." (J. D. Reed, "The Mansion Music Made," *Time*)

ANSWERS: EXERCISE 2

1. opinion
2. opinion
3. opinion
4. fact
5. fact (It's a dictionary definition.)
6. opinion
7. fact
8. fact
9. opinion
10. fact

ANSWERS: EXERCISE 3

Answers may vary somewhat, but here is a fairly complete list of possibilities:

A. Literal information
1. It is the first of February.
2. "Everyone" (see implied information, below) is talking about starlings.
3. Starlings came to this country on a passenger liner from Europe.
4. "This country" is the United States. (Central Park and New York are mentioned.)
5. One hundred starlings were deliberately released in Central Park.
6. From these 100 are descended the countless millions of starlings today.
7. Edwin Way Teale said, "Their . . . Shakespeare."
8. Eugene Schieffelin was a wealthy New York drug manufacturer.
9. Schieffelin's hobby was introducing into America all the birds mentioned in Shakespeare.
10. The starlings adapted to their new country.

A. Implied information
1. "Everyone" is used for effect; the author does not mean each and every person.
2. By saying that the birds came "on a passenger liner" (rather than, for example, "in the cargo hold of a ship") the author begins to alert the reader to expect the unexpected (in this case, that someone wanted to introduce to America all the birds in Shakespeare).
3. Central Park is in New York City. (This is information the author assumes the reader has.)
4. "One man's fancy" are words that suggest that the man had somewhat unusual tastes.
5. The drugs that Schieffelin manufactured were legitimate, not illegal.
6. See item 2 in "Opinions" below.

EXERCISE 3

After you read this passage, (1) list all literal information, (2) list all implied information, and (3) list the opinions stated.

EXAMPLE   The study found many complaints against the lawyers were not investigated, seemingly out of a "desire to avoid difficult cases."

—Norman F. Dacey

Literal information: Few complaints against lawyers are investigated.

Implied information: The words "difficult case" imply a coverup: lawyers, or others in power, hesitate to criticize lawyers for fear of being sued, or for fear of a public outcry if the truth about abuses and errors were revealed.

Opinions: None—all is factual because it refers to, and contains a quote from, a study.

A.   It is the first of February, and everyone is talking about starlings. Starlings came to this country on a passenger liner from Europe. One hundred of them were deliberately released in Central Park, and from those hundred descended all of our countless millions of starlings today. According to Edwin Way Teale, "Their coming was the result of one man's fancy. That man was Eugene Schieffelin, a wealthy New York drug manufacturer. His curious hobby was the introduction into America of all the birds mentioned in William Shakespeare." The birds adapted to their new country splendidly.

—ANNIE DILLARD, *Terror at Tinker Creek*

B.   In recent years, the Soviet Union has been taking increasing interest in its Russian roots. As a result Soviet archeologists and restorers are in the enviable position of having more government funds than they can spend. What they lack, they say, are experts to do the job. Only 2.5 percent of Novgorod has been explored; Yanin estimates that at least 20,000 more manuscripts are buried beneath the city. At the current rate of excavation, it will take a thousand years to exhaust the dig.

—RUTH DANILOFF, "Letters from Medieval Russia"

C.   The kind of constitution and government Gandhi envisaged for an independent India was spelled out at the forty-fifth convention of the All-India Congress, which began at Karachi on March 27, 1931. It was a party political convention the like of which I had not seen before—nor seen since—with its ringing revolutionary proclamations acclaimed by some 350 leaders, men and women, just out of jail, squatting in the heat under a tent in a semicircle at Gandhi's feet, all of them, like Gandhi, spinning away like children playing with toys as

they talked. They made up the so-called Subjects Committee, selected from the five thousand delegates to do the real work of the
convention, though in reality, it was Gandhi alone who dominated the
proceedings, writing most of the resolutions and moving their adoption with his customary eloquence and surprising firmness.

—WILLIAM L. SHIRER, *Gandhi: A Memoir*

5c Using evidence to think critically

The cornerstone of all reasoning is evidence. Readers expect
writers to provide solid evidence for any assertion made or conclusion reached. Writers who successfully communicate their messages
use evidence well to support their assertions or conclusions. Evidence consists of facts, statistical information, examples, and opinions of experts.

1 Using evidence effectively

Keep these guidelines in mind as you gather, evaluate, and use
evidence.

GUIDELINES FOR USING EVIDENCE EFFECTIVELY

1. Use sufficient evidence.
2. Use representative evidence.
3. Use relevant evidence.
4. Qualify the claims you make based on the evidence.
5. Use accurate evidence, whether from primary or secondary
   sources.

---

1. **Evidence should be sufficient.** In general, the more evidence, the better. A survey that draws upon a hundred respondents is likely to be more reliable than a survey involving only ten. As a writer, you may convince your reader
   that violence is a serious problem in the high schools on
   the basis of two specific examples, but you will be more
   convincing if you can give five examples—or, better still,
   statistics for a school district, a city, or the nation.

ANSWERS: EXERCISE 3 *(continued)*

A. Opinions
   1. (In Teale's opinion) Schieffelin's
      hobby was somewhat strange ("curi-
      ous").
   2. (In Dillard's opinion) the starlings
      adapted too well ("splendidly"); here
      Dillard assumes that the reader knows
      that flocks of starlings can be a nui-
      sance and even a danger (e.g., getting
      into airplane engines).

B. Literal information
   1. In recent years, the Soviet Union has
      been taking increasing interest in its
      Russian roots.
   2. Soviet archaeologists and restorers
      have more government funds than
      they can spend.
   3. They say that they do not have
      enough experts to do the job.
   4. Only 2.5 percent of Novgorod has
      been explored.
   5. Yanin estimates that at least 20,000
      more manuscripts are buried beneath
      the city. (See also "Opinions," item 3,
      below.)
   6. At the current rate of excavation, it
      will take a thousand years to exhaust
      the dig. (See also "Opinions," item 4,
      below.)

B. Implied information
   1. The Soviets had not taken an interest
      in their roots until recent years.
   2. It is because of this recent interest
      that more government money has be-
      come available for archaeologists and
      restorers.
   3. The Soviets cannot do the job with-
      out more experts.
   4. Novgorod is worth exploring.

B. Opinions
   1. It is enviable to have so much gov-
      ernment money that it cannot be
      spent.

(continued next page)

ANSWERS: EXERCISE 3 *(continued)*

2. Although "they say" they lack experts, they might not.
3. Yanin's estimates are his opinion (based on his expertise).
4. "A thousand years" is an opinion (based on estimating the current rate).

C. Literal information

1. Gandhi envisaged a constitution and government for an independent India.
2. The constitution was spelled out at the forty-fifth convention of the All-India Congress.
3. The Congress began at Karachi on March 27, 1931.
4. The Congress was a political convention.
5. The Congress was attended by some 350 leaders.
6. The leaders were both men and women.
7. The leaders were just out of jail.
8. The leaders squatted in the heat under a tent in a semicircle at Gandhi's feet.
9. They all worked at spinning wheels.
10. They made up the so-called Subjects Committee, which was selected from the 5,000 delegates.
11. Gandhi wrote most of the resolutions and moved their adoption.

C. Implied information

1. India was not independent before March 27, 1931.
2. Even though the Congress had met 45 times, India was still not independent.
3. The Congress took more than one day—it only "began" on March 27, 1931.
4. Most of the leaders likely were revolutionaries who had been political prisoners—because all were "just out of jail."

2. **Evidence should be representative.** Readers expect as much objectivity and fairness as possible. People should not trust an assertion or conclusion if it is based on only some members of a group being discussed. An assertion or conclusion must be based on a truly *representative,* or typical, sample of the group. A political pollster would not get representative evidence by asking questions of the first 1,500 people to walk by a street corner in Austin, Texas, because no such group would truly represent the various regional, racial, political, and ethnic subgroups of the American electorate. Leading political and media pollsters, like those who do the Gallup polls and the Nielsen ratings, use sophisticated sampling techniques to try to ensure that their evidence is representative.

3. **Evidence should be relevant.** Evidence should relate directly to the assertion made. Determining relevance can demand subtle thinking. If you heard evidence that one hundred students who had watched television for more than two hours a day throughout their high school years earned significantly lower scores on the Scholastic Aptitude Test than one hundred students who had not, you might conclude that students who watch less television perform better on achievement tests. Yet closer examination of the evidence might reveal other, more important differences between the two groups—differences in geographical region, family background, socioeconomic group, even quality of schools attended. Your evidence would be both ample and representative but your conclusion would not be *relevant to* the evidence.

4. **Evidence should be qualified.** Rarely does evidence allow claims that use words such as *all, certainly, always,* or *never.* Conclusions are more reasonable if they are qualified with words such as *some, many, a few, probably, possibly, perhaps, may, usually,* and *often.*

5. **Evidence must be accurate.** Without accuracy, evidence is useless. Evidence must therefore come from reliable sources. For reliable evidence, you can refer to either *primary sources* or *secondary sources* (explained and illustrated in the next few pages). Equally important, once you have reliable evidence, you need to present it carefully so that you do not misrepresent or distort it when you communicate it to others.

2 Using primary and secondary evidence

Primary evidence is first-hand evidence provided by your own (or someone else's) direct observation. Primary evidence has the greatest impact on a reader. Consider this eyewitness account:

> Poverty is dirt. . . . Let me explain about housekeeping with no money. For breakfast I give my children grits with no oleo or cornbread without eggs and oleo. This does not use up many dishes. What dishes there are, I wash in cold water and with no soap. Even the cheapest soap has to be saved for the baby's diapers. Look at my hands, so cracked and red. Once I saved for two months to buy a jar of Vaseline for my hands and the baby's diaper rash. When I had saved enough, I went to buy it and the price had gone up two cents. The baby and I suffered on. I have to decide every day if I can bear to put my cracked sore hands into the cold water and strong soap. But you ask, why not hot water? Fuel costs money. If you have a wood fire it costs money. If you burn electricity, it costs money. Hot water is a luxury. I do not have luxuries. . . .
>
> —JO GOODWIN PARKER, in *America's Other Children*

As a reader and as a writer, remember that not all eyewitness accounts are equally reliable. What is it about Parker's account that makes you trust what she says? She is specific. She is also authoritative. It is doubtful that anyone would have invented the story about being two cents short of the price of a jar of Vaseline. As a writer of personal observations, you need to be as specific as possible—to prove that you truly saw what you say you saw. Use language that appeals to all five senses: describe sights, sounds, and experiences that could have been seen, heard, or experienced only by someone who was there. Show your readers *your* cracked, red hands.

Primary evidence can also come from a reported observation. Few will ever see the surface of the moon or the top of Mt. Everest. People rely, therefore, upon the reports of the astronauts and mountain climbers who have been there. History depends heavily on letters, diaries, and journals—the reports of eyewitnesses. Consider the impact of this reported observation:

> The immediate causes of death from nuclear attack are the blast wave, which can flatten heavily reinforced buildings many kilometers away, the firestorm, the gamma rays and the neutrons, which effectively fry the insides of passersby. A school girl who survived the American nuclear attack on Hiroshima, the event that ended the Second World War, wrote this first-hand account:
>
> Through a darkness like the bottom of hell, I could hear the voices of the other students calling for their mothers. And at

ANSWERS: EXERCISE 3 (continued)

5. The leaders were very dedicated—they were willing to squat in the heat under a tent.
6. The ruling government did not provide the basic amenities for a convention: room in a building, decent ventilation, chairs, tables, and so forth.
7. The leaders' sitting at Gandhi's feet implies how they respected him.
8. Gandhi often worked at a spinning wheel as he spoke.
9. Everyone's spinning implies that they wanted to imitate Gandhi.
10. Five thousand people is too large a group to get policy matters decided.
11. Gandhi dominated the proceedings because everyone respected him so much.

C. Opinions
1. The author had not seen before—or since—a political convention like this one in achievement and tone.
2. The revolutionary proclamations were "ringing."
3. The leaders were spinning away like children playing with toys as they talked.
4. Gandhi dominated the proceedings.
5. Gandhi wrote and spoke with his customary eloquence and surprising firmness.

the base of the bridge, inside a big cistern that had been dug out there, was a mother weeping, holding above her head a naked baby that was burned bright red all over its body . . . . But every single person who passed was wounded, all of them, and there was no one, there was no one to turn to for help. And the singed hair on the heads of the people was frizzled and whitish and covered with dust. They did not appear to be human, not creatures of this world.

—CARL SAGAN, *Cosmos*

As with the eyewitness account, the strength or value of reported observation hinges on the reliability of the observer. That reliability is a function of how specific, accurate, and authoritative the observations are.

Surveys, polls, and experiments are some of the means by which people extend their powers of observation beyond what can be "seen" in the everyday sense of the word. These surveys, polls, and experiments must be carefully controlled—through weighing, measuring, or quantifying information that would otherwise not be available. Jo Parker could look at her hands, as the Japanese schoolgirl could see the singed hair of passersby. Who can see, however, the attitude of the American public toward marriage, toward a presidential candidate, toward inflation? For evidence on these matters, polls or surveys are necessary.

Secondary evidence is provided by the opinions of experts. Here the standard maxim "consider the source" becomes crucial. Expertise comes from long familiarity with primary evidence. An expert's reputation must stem from some special experience (as the parents of many children could be "experts" on child rearing) or training (as an accountant could be an expert on taxes). To discover who is a reliable source, notice what names keep coming up when you read about your subject. Here are guidelines for evaluating a secondary source.

CHECKLIST FOR EVALUATING A SECONDARY SOURCE

1. Is the source written by an expert on the subject?
2. Does the material appear in a reputable publication—in a book published by an established publisher or a respected journal or magazine?
3. Do you find the source cited elsewhere as you read about the subject (which would indicate fairly wide acceptance of the authority of the source)?

(continued on next page)

CHECKLIST FOR EVALUATING A SECONDARY SOURCE *(continued)*
4. Is the source's material based on primary evidence, such as experience or observation?
5. Is the source's language relatively objective (therefore more reliable) or slanted (therefore likely not reliable)?
6. Is the material current (therefore more reliable) or outdated (therefore likely not reliable)?

EXERCISE 4

(a) Is each passage based on primary or secondary evidence? (b) Is the evidence acceptable? Why or why not?

1.   I went one morning to a place along the banks of the Madeira River where the railroad ran, alongside rapids impassable to river traffic, and I searched for any marks it may have left on the land. But there was nothing except a clearing where swarms of insects hovered over the dead black hen and other items spread out on a red cloth as an offering to the gods of macumba, or black magic. This strain of African origins in Brazil's ethnic character is strong in the Northwest Region.

—WILLIAM S. ELLIS, "Brazil's Imperiled Rain Forest"

2.   In the fall of 1982, only 4.7 percent of first-year college students indicated an interest in elementary or secondary teaching as a career. In 1970 that percentage was more than 19 percent. And there are other equally disturbing statistical measures. More than a third of the nation's teachers have told pollsters that if they had to start their own careers over again, they would not select teaching. Thirteen out of every 100 teachers say they *certainly* would not become teachers again, and 30 more maintain they *probably* would not do so.

—MARY HATWOOD FUTRELL, "Towards Excellence"

3.   Most climatologists believe that the world will eventually slip back into an ice age in 10,000 to 20,000 years. The Earth has been unusually cold for the last two to three million years, and we are just lucky to be living during one of the warm spells. But the concern of most weather watchers looking at the next century is with fire rather than ice. By burning fossil fuels and chopping down forests, humans have measurably increased the amount of carbon dioxide in the atmosphere. From somewhere around 300 parts per million at the turn of the century, this level has risen to 340 parts per million today. If the use of fossil fuels continues to increase, carbon dioxide could reach 600 parts per million during the next century.

—STEVE OLSON, "Computing Climate"

ANSWERS: EXERCISE 4

1. *Primary evidence:* The author is describing his own experiences in a first-person narrative. It can be assumed to be reliable since a reliable journal, *National Geographic,* published the account.

2. *Primary evidence:* The paragraph describes the results of a poll. This information seems reliable because of the facts, although if Futrell later includes information about the design of the poll—the size, the representativeness of the sample, and other questions that might have influenced these answers—the argument will be even more reliable.

3. *Secondary evidence:* The assertions in this paragraph are carefully qualified and seem well substantiated by evidence. The material was published in a reliable science magazine.

4. *Primary evidence:* This is an eyewitness account. This argument is based on some assumptions that the reader might not share. For example, are all of today's children "struggling with feelings of worthlessness"? On the other hand, Smith is a suitable expert to discuss the effects of a large family on her children's needing to pitch in and help. Additional specific examples about Smith's family and testimony from people in other big families would strengthen this argument.

5. *Both secondary and primary evidence:* The opening paragraph presents secondary evidence, but the quoted material that follows this paragraph serves to make Schlissel's observations reliable. The second paragraph presents primary evidence—an eyewitness account by Mrs. John Kirkwood, which is reliable evidence because it is firsthand from a diary.

4.   Back in the days when large families were desired for their labor, at least children knew they were really needed. Today's child,
overwhelmed with possessions and catered to endlessly by parents,
is struggling with feelings of worthlessness. Even with labor-saving
devices, big families are a lot of work. My children know they have to
pitch in, and they know we appreciate their help. Maybe I don't have
time to read to the three-year-old, but the eight-year-old does—to the
benefit of them both.

—SARA L. SMITH, "Big Families Can Be Happy, Too"

5.   Marriages on the frontier were often made before a girl was half
through her adolescent years, and some diaries record a casualness
in the manner in which such decisions were reached. [As] Mrs. John
Kirkwood recounts:

> The night before Christmas, John Kirkwood . . . the path finder,
> stayed at our house over night. I had met him before and when
> he heard the discussion about my brother Jasper's wedding, he
> suggested that he and I also get married. I was nearly fifteen
> years old and I thought it was high time that I got married so I
> consented.

—LILLIAN SCHLISSEL, *Women's Diaries of the Westward Journey*

5d   Evaluating cause and effect to think critically

Cause and effect is a type of thinking that seeks to establish
some relationship, or link, between two or more specific pieces of
evidence. Regardless of whether you begin your thinking with a
cause or an effect, you are working with this basic pattern:

BASIC PATTERN FOR CAUSE AND EFFECT

Cause A ⟶ produces ⟶ effect B

You may seek to understand the effects of a known cause (for
example, studying two more hours each night):

More studying ⟶ produces ⟶ ?

Or you may attempt to determine the cause or causes of a known
effect (for example, recurrent headaches):

? ⟶ produces ⟶ recurrent headaches

If you want to use reasoning based on a relationship of cause
and effect, evaluate the connections carefully. As you evaluate cause-
and-effect relationships, keep the following guidelines in mind.

TEACHING TIP

You may want to ask your students to think
about their own experiences, analyzing
them for their causes and effects. The questions that follow can help to stimulate their
thinking.

1. How did you get your first job?

2. What did you learn from that job?

3. Whose advice is particularly important
to you?

4. How do you reach a decision?

5. What difference do you expect college
to make in your life?

6. Why do you have a particular way of
doing something?

7. How do you make friends?

8. Who is the most important person in
your life? Why?

9. When did you learn to drive a car?

10. What will you be doing in ten years?

GUIDELINES FOR EVALUATING CAUSE-AND-EFFECT RELATIONSHIPS

1. Establish a clear relationship between events.
2. Determine whether the events can be repeated.
3. Avoid oversimplifying: Look for multiple causes and/or effects.

1. **Is there a clear relationship?** When you read or write about causes and effects, carefully think through the reasoning. Causes and effects normally occur in chronological order: *first* a door slams, *then* a pie that is cooling on a shelf falls. But suppose you are walking down the sidewalk when, first, a car backfires, and then the person walking in front of you falls to the ground. Does this mean that the backfire is related to the fall? A cause-and-effect relationship must be linked by more than chronological sequence. The fact that *B* happens after *A* does not prove that it was caused by *A*.

2. **Is there a pattern of repetition?** To establish the relationship of *A* to *B*, there must be proof that every time *A* was present, *B* occurred—or that *B* never occurred unless *A* was present. The need for a pattern of repetition explains why the Food and Drug Administration performs thousands of tests before declaring a new food or medicine safe for human consumption.

3. **Has oversimplification been avoided?** The basic pattern of cause and effect—single cause, single effect—rarely gives the full picture. Most complex social or political problems have **multiple causes,** not a single cause and a single effect.

It is oversimplifying to assume that high schools were the only cause of the nationwide decline in scores on the Scholastic Aptitude Test between 1964 and 1984. Not only would it be unfair to high schools, it would also be ignoring a variety of other possible important causes, such as

EXTRA EXERCISE B

Supply answers for the blanks in the sentences that follow, checking each choice by the guidelines for evaluating cause and effect to be sure that it is accurate.

1. Eating food with high sodium content causes ____.

2. ____ will lead to a traffic citation.

3. Regular exercise produces ____.

4. ____ is leading cause of ____.

5. Because she ____, she is expected to be named Gourmet of the Year.

6. Her mother refuses to intervene because ____.

7. If you don't quit ____, you are likely to end up in a lawsuit.

8. She decided to stay in college when she learned that ____.

9. Additional funding for preschool education is needed in order to ____.

10. ____ has resulted in increased numbers of homeless people in our major cities.

television viewing habits, family life, level of textbooks, and so on. Similarly, one cause can produce **multiple effects:**

Some people are guilty of oversimplification of effects in how they present diets. A certain diet, for example, may bring about weight reduction and may lower salt intake, but the dieter may also suffer from the loss of valuable nutrients not included in the diet.

5e Understanding reasoning processes to think critically

To think critically you need to be able to understand reasoning processes. When you understand reasoning processes, you can recognize and evaluate them in your reading and use them correctly in your writing. **Induction** and **deduction** are reasoning processes. Inductive reasoning and deductive reasoning are natural thought patterns that people use every day to think through ideas and to make decisions.

COMPARISON OF INDUCTIVE AND DEDUCTIVE REASONING		
	INDUCTIVE REASONING	**DEDUCTIVE REASONING**
ARGUMENT BEGINS	with specific evidence	with a general claim
ARGUMENT CONCLUDES	with a general claim	with a specific statement
CONCLUSION IS	reliable or unreliable	true or false
REASONING IS USED	to discover something new	to apply what is known

1 Recognizing and using inductive reasoning

Induction is the process of arriving at general principles from particular facts or instances. Suppose that you go to the Registry of Motor Vehicles to renew your driver's license, and you have to stand in line for two hours until you get the document. Then a few months later, when you return to the Registry for new license plates, a clerk gives you the wrong advice, and you have to stand in two different lines for three hours. Another time you go there in response to a letter asking for information, and you discover that you should have brought your car registration form, although the letter failed to mention that fact. You conclude that the Registry is inefficient and seems not to care about the convenience of its patrons. You have arrived at this conclusion by means of induction.

SUMMARY OF INDUCTIVE REASONING

1. Inductive reasoning moves from the specific to the general. It begins with the evidence of specific facts, observations, or experiences and moves to a general conclusion.

2. Inductive conclusions are considered *reliable* or *unreliable,* not true or false. An inductive conclusion indicates probability, the degree to which the conclusion is likely to be true. Frustrating though it may be for those who seek certainty, inductive thinking is, of necessity, based only on a sampling of the facts.

3. An inductive conclusion is held to be reliable or unreliable in relation to the quantity and quality of the evidence (see 5c) supporting it.

4. Induction leads to new "truths." Induction can support statements about the unknown on the basis of what is known.

---

2 Recognizing and using deductive reasoning

If several unproductive visits to the Registry of Motor Vehicles have convinced you that the Registry cares little about the convenience of its patrons (as the experiences described in 5e-1 suggest), you will not be happy the next time you must return. Your reasoning might go something like this:

Using analogy is a way to think inductively. An analogy compares two dissimilar objects, ideas, or experiences by focusing on what they have in common. For example, some people make an analogy between the role of a teacher and that of a coach. Like coaches, teachers train people in fundamentals through repetition and practice, recommend changes in technique, and try to inspire excellence. However, despite points of similarity, two dissimilar items remain dissimilar.

First, coaches work primarily with the body rather than the mind, developing physical rather than mental skills. Second, team coaches praise the team player while good teachers reward independence and originality. Thus the analogy between teachers and coaches breaks down at some point.

In the absence of other evidence, an analogy will not *prove* anything. Nevertheless, although an analogy can always be shown as flawed under close scrutiny, it can still help explain a point and thus help persuade an audience.

> The Registry wastes people's time.
>
> I have to go to the Registry tomorrow.
>
> Therefore, tomorrow my time will be wasted.

You reached the conclusion—"therefore, tomorrow my time will be wasted"—by means of deduction.

Deductive arguments have three parts: two **premises** and a **conclusion.** This three-part structure is known as a **syllogism.** The first premise of a deductive argument may be a fact or an assumption. The second premise may also be a fact or an assumption.

Whether or not an argument is **valid** has to do with the argument's form or structure. Here the word *valid* is not the general term people use in conversation to mean "acceptable" or "well grounded." In the context of reading and writing logical arguments, the word *valid* has a very specific meaning. A deductive argument is *valid* when the conclusion logically follows from the premises. The following argument is valid.

VALID

PREMISE 1	When it snows, the streets get wet. [fact]
PREMISE 2	It is snowing. [fact]
CONCLUSION	Therefore, the streets are wet.

The following argument is invalid.

INVALID

PREMISE 1	When it snows, the streets get wet. [fact]
PREMISE 2	The streets are wet. [fact]
CONCLUSION	Therefore, it is snowing.

The invalid argument has acceptable premises because the premises are facts. The argument's conclusion, however, is wrong. It ignores other reasons for why the streets may be wet. The street could be wet from rain, from street-cleaning trucks that spray water, or from people using hoses to cool off the pavement or to wash their cars. Because the conclusion does not follow logically from the premises, the argument is invalid.

The following argument is also invalid. The conclusion does not flow from the premises (the car may not start for many reasons other than a dead battery).

INVALID

PREMISE 1	When the battery is dead, a car will not start. [fact]
PREMISE 2	My car will not start. [fact]
CONCLUSION	My battery is dead.

150

log

Invalid:
> Some circular things are bubbles.
> Some human heads are circular things.
> Some human heads are bubbles.

Valid:
> All mammals are animals.
> All whales are mammals.
> Therefore, all whales are animals.

When a premise is an assumption, the premise must be able to be defended with evidence. The following argument is valid. Its conclusion flows logically from the premises. An argument's validity, however, is independent of its truth. Is premise 1 true? Different economists will offer different opinions. *Only if both premises are true is an argument true.* This argument may be true or false depending on whether the first premise is true or false. The writer must support the claim that is the first premise.

VALID

PREMISE 1	When the unemployment rate rises, an economic recession occurs. [assumption: the writer must present evidence in support of this statement]
PREMISE 2	The unemployment rate has risen. [fact]
CONCLUSION	An economic recession will occur.

The following argument is valid. Its conclusion follows from its premises. Is the argument, however, true? Because the argument contains an assumption in its first premise, the argument can be true only if the premise is proved true. Such proof is not possible. Therefore, although the argument is valid, it is not true.

VALID

PREMISE 1	If you buy a Supermacho 357 sports car, you will achieve instant popularity. [assumption]
PREMISE 2	Kim just bought a Supermacho 357 sports car. [fact]
CONCLUSION	Kim will achieve instant popularity.

In any deductive argument, beware of premises that are implied but not stated—called **unstated assumptions.** Remember that an argument can be logically valid even though it is based on wrong assumptions. The response to such an argument is to attack the assumptions, not the conclusion. Often the assumptions are wrong. For example, suppose a corporation argued that it should not be required to install pollution control devices because the cost would cut into their profits. This argument rests on the unstated assumption that no corporation should be asked to do something that would lower its profits. That assumption is wrong, and so is the argument. But it can be shown to be wrong only when the assumptions are challenged. Similarly, if someone says that certain information has to be correct because it was printed in a newspaper, the person's deductive reasoning is flawed. Here the unstated assumption is that everything in a newspaper is correct—which is not true. Whenever there is an unstated assumption, supply it and then check to make sure it is true.

ANSWERS: EXERCISE 5

1. Invalid. The shirt's being expensive does not mean that it shares other characteristics of faddish clothing.

2. Valid. The conclusion follows logically from the premises.

3. Invalid. Some outstanding literary works have not received a Pulitzer Prize.

4. Invalid. All states do send representatives, but that does not mean that all representatives come from a state.

5. Valid. The argument is valid, although some people may not agree that all risks are frightening.

6. Valid. The conclusion flows logically from the premises.

7. Invalid. The premises do not contain the conclusion. It is impossible to know whether this magazine is part of "most."

8. Invalid. The qualifying word "usually" in the first premise leaves open the possibility that there are science fiction novels that are not violent.

9. Valid. The conclusion is contained in the premises.

10. Invalid. The first premise does not stipulate that all great college basketball teams come from the Midwest (and Georgetown is among universities not in the Midwest that produce great basketball teams).

EXERCISE 5

Ignoring for the moment whether the premises seem to you to be true, determine if each conclusion is valid. Explain your answer.

1. Faddish clothes are expensive.
    This shirt is expensive.
    This shirt must be part of a fad.

2. When a storm is threatening, small-craft warnings are issued.
    A storm is threatening.
    Small-craft warnings will be issued.

3. The Pulitzer Prize is awarded to outstanding literary works.
    The Great Gatsby never won a Pulitzer Prize.
    The Great Gatsby is not an outstanding literary work.

4. All states send representatives to the United States Congress.
    Puerto Rico sends a representative to the United States Congress.
    Puerto Rico is a state.

5. All risks are frightening.
    Changing to a new job is a risk.
    The change to a new job is frightening.

6. Before an occupancy permit can be issued, a new home must be inspected.
    Our new home has been issued an occupancy permit.
    Our new home has been inspected.

log 5f

7. Most weekly news magazines give only superficial coverage of world affairs.
   This is a weekly news magazine.
   This will give only superficial coverage of world affairs.
8. Science fiction novels are usually violent.
   This is a science fiction novel.
   This novel is obviously violent.
9. All veterans are entitled to education benefits.
   Elaine is a veteran.
   Elaine is entitled to education benefits.
10. Midwestern universities produce great college basketball teams.
    Georgetown has a great college basketball team.
    Georgetown is a midwestern university.

5f Recognizing and avoiding logical fallacies

Logical fallacies are flaws in reasoning that lead to illogical statements. They tend to occur most often when ideas are being argued, although they can be found in all types of writing. Most logical fallacies masquerade as reasonable statements, but they are in fact attempts to manipulate readers by reaching their emotions instead of their intellects, their hearts rather than their heads. Most logical fallacies are known by labels; each indicates a way that thinking has gone wrong during the reasoning process.

Hasty generalization

A **hasty generalization** occurs when someone generalizes from inadequate evidence. If the statement "My hometown is the best place in the state to live" is supported with only two examples of why it is pleasant, the generalization is hasty. **Stereotyping** is a type of hasty generalization that occurs when someone makes prejudiced, sweeping claims about all of the members of a particular religious, ethnic, racial, or political group: "Everyone from country X is dishonest." **Sexism** occurs when someone discriminates against people on the basis of sex. (See 11n and 21b for advice on how to avoid sexism in your writing.)

erage, workers in the oil fields of Texas are paid more than are loggers in the timber industries of Idaho." *To correct:* Drop the phrase and substitute evidence that supports your claim.

A *complex question* (also known as a *loaded question*) contains one or more unproven assumptions: "Are you still spending time with known drug addicts?" Notice what happens when you try to answer such a question. If you say "yes," you are guilty. If you say "no," you are still guilty, because you are admitting that you used to spend time with drug addicts. *To correct:* Split the question into its parts ("Are you still spending time with those people?" "Are those people drug addicts?") and deal with each separately.

Appeal to fear uses scare tactics instead of legitimate evidence. Such an argument implies danger: "Anyone who stages a protest against the government is a communist, so we must outlaw all protests."

Appeal to the people (also known as *ad populum*) draws on whatever the people hold dear—for example, country, religion, or family. This approach tries to sway people by using a favorable label instead of providing reasons: "A vote for Joe Smith is a vote for the flag."

Name-calling attaches an unpleasant label to something or someone. Consider how a label can stop people from thinking: "Jane Jones was once an alcoholic, so she cannot possibly say anything of value about politics."

Appeal to pity attempts to arouse sympathy: "He embezzled $1,500 of company money, but after all, his wife recently died and his child needs surgery."

The genetic fallacy, a special form of *hasty generalization,* predicts something about a person based on that person's origins: "Joe Smith is from New York City, so he knows how to deal with street crime." Often this fallacy involves a person's religion, sex, race, or economic status.

False analogy

A **false analogy** is a comparison in which the differences outweigh the similarities, or the similarities are irrelevant to the claim the analogy is intended to support. "Old Joe Smith would never make a good President because an old dog cannot learn new tricks." Homespun analogies like this often seem to have an air of wisdom about them, but just as often they fall apart when examined closely. Learning the role of the President is hardly comparable to a dog's learning new tricks.

Circular argument

A **circular argument,** sometimes called a **circular definition,** is an assertion merely restated in slightly different terms: "Boxing is a dangerous sport because it is unsafe." Here, "unsafe" conveys the same idea as "dangerous" rather than adding something new. This "begs the question" because the conclusion is the same as the premise.

Non sequitur

Non sequitur in Latin translates as "does not follow," meaning a conclusion does not follow from the premises: "Jane Jones is a forceful speaker, so she will make a good mayor." It does not follow that someone's ability to be a forceful speaker means that person would be a good mayor.

Post hoc, ergo propter hoc

Post hoc, ergo propter hoc—which means "after this, therefore because of this"—results when someone assumes that sequence alone proves something. This cause-and-effect fallacy is very common: "Because a new weather satellite was launched last week, it has not stopped raining."

Self-contradiction

Self-contradiction occurs when two premises are used that cannot simultaneously be true: "Only when nuclear weapons have finally destroyed us will we be convinced of the need to control them." This statement is self-contradictory in that no one will be around to be convinced after everyone has been destroyed.

log **5f**

Red herring

A **red herring,** sometimes referred to as **ignoring the question,** sidetracks an issue by bringing up a totally unrelated issue: "Why worry about pandas becoming extinct when we should be concerned about the plight of the homeless?" Someone who introduces an irrelevant issue hopes to distract the audience as a red herring might distract bloodhounds from a scent.

Appeal to the person

An **appeal to the person,** also known as **ad hominem,** attacks the appearance, personal habits, or character of the person involved instead of dealing with the merits of the issue at hand: "We could take her plea for money for the homeless seriously if she were not so nasty to the children who live next door to her."

Bandwagon

Bandwagon, also known as **going along with the crowd,** implies that something is right because everyone is doing it, that truth is determined by majority vote: "Smoking must not be bad for people because millions of people smoke."

False or irrelevant authority

Using **false or irrelevant authority,** sometimes called **ad verecundiam,** means citing the opinion of an "expert" who has no claim to expertise about the subject at hand. This fallacy attempts to transfer prestige from one area to another. Many television commercials rely on this tactic—a famous tennis player praising a brand of motor oil or a popular movie star lauding a brand of cheese.

Card-stacking

Card-stacking, also known as **special pleading,** ignores evidence on the other side of a question. From all the available facts, the person arguing selects only those that will build the best (or worst) possible case. Many television commercials use this strategy. When three slim, happy consumers rave about a new diet plan, they do not mention (a) the plan does not work for everyone and (b) other plans work better for some people. The makers of the commercial selected evidence that helped their cause, ignoring any that did not.

The either–or fallacy

The either–or fallacy, also known as **false dilemma,** offers only two alternatives when more exist. Such fallacies often touch on emotional issues and can therefore seem accurate at first. When people reflect, however, they quickly come to realize that more alternatives are available. Here is a typical example of an either–or fallacy: "Either go to college or forget about getting a job." This statement implies that a college education is a prerequisite for all jobs, which is not true.

Taking something out of context

Taking something out of context separates an idea or fact from the material surrounding it, thus distorting it for special purposes. Suppose a critic writes about a movie saying, "The plot was predictable and boring but the music was sparkling." Then an advertisement for the movie says, "Critic calls this movie 'sparkling.'" The critic's words have been taken out of context—and distorted.

Appeal to ignorance

Appeal to ignorance assumes that an argument is valid simply because there is no evidence on the other side of the issue. Something is not true merely because it cannot be shown to be false. Conversely, something is not false simply because it cannot be shown to be true. Appeals to ignorance can be very persuasive because they prey on people's superstitions or lack of knowledge. Here is a typical example of such flawed reasoning: "Since no one has proven that depression does not cause cancer, we can assume that it does." The absence of opposing evidence proves nothing.

Ambiguity and equivocation

Ambiguity and **equivocation** describe expressions that are not clear because they have more than one meaning. An ambiguous expression may be taken either way by the reader. A statement such as "They were entertaining guests" is ambiguous. Were the guests amusing to be with or were people giving hospitality to guests? An equivocal expression, by contrast, is one used in two or more ways within a single argument. If someone argued that the President *played an important role* in arms control negotiations and then, two sentences later, accused him of *merely playing a role,* the person would be equivocating.

log 5f

SUMMARY OF LOGICAL FALLACIES

Hasty generalization: generalizing from inadequate evidence. Stereotyping is hasty generalization using prejudiced claims about a group of people.

False analogy: using a comparison in which the differences outweigh the similarities, or in which the similarities are irrelevant to the claim the analogy is intended to support

Circular argument: asserting the same point merely in slightly different terms

Non sequitur: reaching a conclusion that does not follow from the premises

Post hoc, ergo propter hoc: assuming that the sequence alone proves the conclusion

Self-contradiction: using two premises that cannot both be true

Red herring: sidetracking the issue by raising a second, unrelated issue

Appeal to the person: attacking the person making the argument rather than the argument itself

Bandwagon: implying that something is right because of its popularity

False or irrelevant authority: citing the opinion of a person who has no expertise about the subject

Card-stacking: ignoring evidence on the other side of a question

The either-or fallacy: offering only two alternatives when more exist

Taking something out of context: distorting an idea or fact by separating it from the material surrounding it

Appeal to ignorance: assuming that an argument is valid simply because there is no evidence on the other side of the issue

Ambiguity and equivocation: using expressions that are not clear because they have more than one meaning

QUOTATION ABOUT WRITING

Logic is in the eye of the logician.

—Gloria Steinem

QUOTATION ABOUT WRITING

I've always disliked words like *inspiration*. Writing is probably like a scientist thinking about some scientific problem, or an engineer about an engineering problem.

—Doris Lessing

ANSWERS: EXERCISE 6

1. *False authority.* A movie star is not an authority on the CIA.

2. *Red herring.* The social issue is introduced to divert attention from the real issue—whether or not money should have been spent to rescue the whales.

3. *Non sequitur.* A person can be nervous about something and still be very good at it.

4. *Circular argument.* "Dishonest" is merely a slightly different term for "deceitful."

5. *Ad hominem.* These people are being attacked for their materialism, but they are perhaps excellent environmentalists.

6. *Appeal to ignorance.* Just because no evidence exists for one side of the argument does not mean that the other side of the argument is valid.

7. *Post hoc ergo propter hoc.* The sequence of events does not prove any connection between them.

8. *False analogy.* Analogies are dangerous in argument because they equate things that are not the same. Riding a bicycle is much different from learning to run a company, and although the skills for riding a bicycle remain the same, those of running a company may change with the economy and other pressures so that one could "fall" if he or she did not adopt those skills.

9. *Self-contradiction.* Medicare cannot be free if it is paid for.

10. *Either–or.* Reading good literature is not the only way to appreciate culture.

EXERCISE 6

Identify and explain the fallacy in each item. If the item is correct, circle its number.

EXAMPLE   Seat belts are the only hope for reducing the death rate from automobile accidents. [This is an *either-or fallacy* because it assumes that nothing but seat belts can reduce the number of fatalities from car accidents.]

1. Joanna Hayes should write a book about the Central Intelligence Agency (CIA). She has starred in three films that show the inner workings of the CIA.

2. It is ridiculous to have spent thousands of dollars to rescue those two whales from being trapped in the Arctic ice. Why, look at all of the people trapped in jobs that they don't like.

3. Every time my roommate has a math test, she becomes extremely nervous. Clearly, she is not good at math.

4. Plagiarism is deceitful because it is dishonest.

5. The local political coalition to protect the environment would get my support and that of many other people if its leaders did not drive cars that get poor gasoline mileage.

6. UFO's must exist because no reputable studies have proven conclusively that they do not.

7. Water fluoridation affects the brain. Citywide, students' test scores began to drop five months after fluoridation began.

8. Learning to manage a corporation is exactly like learning to ride a bicycle: once you learn the skills, you never forget how, and you never fall.

9. Medicare is free; the government pays for it from taxes.

10. Reading good literature is the one way to appreciate culture.

6 Writing Argument

When writing **argument** for your college courses, you seek to convince a reader to agree with you concerning a topic open to debate. A written argument states and supports one position about the debatable topic. Support for that position depends on evidence, reasons, and examples chosen for their direct relation to the point being argued. One section of the written argument might present and attempt to refute other positions on the topic, but the central thrust of the essay is to argue for one point of view.

Taking and defending a position in a written argument is an engaging intellectual process, especially when it involves a topic of substance about which universal agreement is unlikely. The ability to think critically by analyzing, synthesizing, and evaluating (see page 128) is challenged by the activity of examining all sides of a topic, choosing one side to defend, and marshaling convincing support for that one side.

If you are among the people who find any type of arguing distasteful, you are not alone. But rest assured that written argument differs drastically from everyday, informal arguing. Informal arguing sometimes originates in anger and might involve bursts of temper or unpleasant emotional confrontations. Written argument, in contrast, can always be a constructive activity. When you write an argument, you can disagree without being disagreeable. An effective written argument sets forth its position calmly, respectfully, and logically. Any passion that underlies a writer's position is evident not from angry words but from the force of a balanced, well-developed, clearly written discussion.

Much of the material in the earlier chapters of this handbook can help you compose a written argument. A list of useful sections is given in the box on the next page. This chapter concentrates on the special demands of writing argument. At the end of this chapter are two student essays that argue opposite sides of the same subject.

QUOTATION ABOUT WRITING

Rhetoric may be defined as the faculty of observing in any given case the available means of persuasion.

—Aristotle

QUOTATION ABOUT WRITING

The art of writing has for backbone some fierce attachment to an idea.

—Virginia Woolf

QUOTATION ABOUT WRITING

. . . In order to persuade, there are two things which must be carefully studied by the orator. The first is to excite some desire or passion in the hearers; the second is to satisfy their judgment that there is a connexion between the action to which he would persuade them and the gratification of the desire or passion he excites.

—George Campbell

BACKGROUND

Although rhetoric, as defined by Aristotle, appears in the speeches and debates of the epics and plays of ancient Greece, its principles were not systematically formulated until the fifth century B.C. Corax of Syracuse, recognizing the need for a system by which citizens of Sicily could argue in the courts to recover property that they had lost during the reign of Thrasybulus, began to set down the principles of argumentation. Lacking documents to prove their claims, ordinary citizens had to argue their cases by relying on inferential reasoning and probability. Tisias, the student of Corax, extended the study of rhetoric from the courtroom and wrote speeches for other people to deliver. Others who quickly followed to develop the art of rhetoric, or persuasion, include Gorgias of Leotini (fl. 420 B.C.), known principally for his ornate style characterized by extensive use of figures of speech, and Isocrates (436–338 B.C.), one of the leading Athenian teachers of rhetoric and an author of influential books on rhetorical theory.

MATERIAL FROM EARLIER CHAPTERS IN THIS HANDBOOK TO USE WHEN WRITING AN ARGUMENT

- Checklist for persuasive writing (1b–1)
- Audiences for writing (1c)
- Choosing a topic (2c)
- The writing process: planning and shaping (Chapter 2)
- The writing process: drafting and revising (Chapter 3)
- Writing paragraphs (Chapter 4)
- Reading and thinking critically (Chapter 5)
- Using evidence to think critically (5c)
- Analyzing cause and effect (5d)
- Using inductive and deductive reasoning (5e)
- Avoiding logical fallacies (5f)

The terms *persuasive writing* and *argumentative writing* often are used interchangeably. When a distinction is made between them, persuasive writing is the broader term. It includes advertisements, letters to editors, emotional pleas in speeches or writing, and formal written arguments. The focus of this chapter is formal written argument as usually assigned in college courses.

6a   Choosing a topic for a written argument

When you choose a topic for written argument, be sure that it is open to debate. Be careful not to confuse matters of information with matters of debate. Facts are matters of information, not debate. An essay becomes an argument when it takes a position concerning the fact or other piece of information.

FACT	Students at Deitmer College **are required** to take physical education.
POSITION OPEN TO DEBATE	Students at Deitmer College **should not be** required to take physical education.
OPPOSITE POSITION OPEN TO DEBATE	Students at Deitmer College **should be** required to take physical education.

A written argument could take one of these opposing positions and defend it. The essay could not argue for two or more sides, though it might mention other points of view and attempt to refute them.

When you are assigned a written argument, be sure to read and think through the assignment carefully. Instructors construct assignments for written argument in a number of ways. You might be given both the topic and the position to take on that topic. In such cases, you are expected to fulfill the assignment whether or not you agree personally with the given point of view. You are judged on your ability to marshal a defense of the assigned position and to reason logically about it. Another type of assignment is unstructured, requiring you to choose the debatable topic and the position to defend. In such cases, the topic that you choose should be **suitable for college writing** (see 2c–1). The topic should not be trivial (for example, the best color for a kitchen wall). The topic should be **narrowed sufficiently** (see 2c–2) to fit the writing situation. You are judged on your ability to think of a debatable topic of substance, to narrow the topic so that your essay can include general statements and specific details, to choose a defensible position about that topic, and to present and support your position convincingly. If you cannot decide what position you agree with personally because all sides of a debatable topic have merit, do not get blocked. You need not make a lifetime commitment to your position. Rather, concentrate on the merits of one position, and present that position as effectively as possible.

The two sample essays at the end of this chapter were written in response to the assignment shown in the box below. This assignment states the topic but asks students to choose a position to take about the topic.

Daniel Casey and Lindsey Black were given this assignment: Write an essay of 500 to 700 words that argues about whether holidays have become too commercialized in the United States. Your final draft is due in one week. Bring your earlier drafts to class for possible discussion.

Black and Casey analyzed the four aspects of the **writing situation** (see 2b) reflected in the assignment. The essay *topic* is stated (whether holidays have become too commercialized in the United States). The essay's *purpose* is to argue, but students are free to choose the position to argue for (the student can choose to argue that the holidays have become too commercialized *or* that they have not become too commercialized). The *audience* for the essay is not specified and is therefore assumed to be the instructor and, perhaps, other members of the class. The *special requirements* include the essay's length (between 500 and 700 words) and the time for getting the essay into final draft (one week).

EXTRA EXERCISE A

Which of the following topics are concerned with fact and which state a position open to debate?

1. The term *journalism* refers to the business of publishing a regularly recurring text.

2. Television news programs are more influential than they should be.

3. Journalists in the United States operate under the protection of the First Amendment to the Constitution.

4. Most reporters are biased in their descriptions of political figures.

5. The government should not let journalists have access to information dealing with national security.

6. Journalism involves both reporting the news and forming public opinion.

7. Reporters should verify a controversial story with two sources before running it.

8. Weekly newspapers are becoming increasingly popular in large cities.

9. Cartoons furnish one of the more entertaining features of newspapers.

10. Television commentators should not give their own opinions about political and social matters.

ANSWERS: EXTRA EXERCISE A

1. fact	**6.** fact
2. opinion	**7.** opinion
3. fact	**8.** fact
4. opinion	**9.** opinion
5. opinion	**10.** opinion

BACKGROUND

Chapter Two of this book, Planning and Shaping, lists four aspects of writing situations that affect the decisions that the writer makes. They are (1) the topic, (2) the purpose, (3) the audience that will read or hear it, and (4) the special requirements that influence every writing situation, such as deadlines and length. For explanations of each aspect, see Section 2b.

6b

BACKGROUND

Many techniques for discovering means of developing a subject have been devised over the past decade. It is helpful to be reminded, however, that the ancient Greeks long ago devised a set of topics—*topoi,* meaning "places or regions"—that can be used to generate "arguments" to persuade an audience. They suggest material for the writer who does not have a ready opinion on a subject or an effective way to present it. They include the topics of definition (including genus and division), comparison (similarity, difference, and degree), relationship (cause and effect, antecedent and consequence, contraries, and contradictions), circumstance (the possible and impossible, past and future fact), and testimony (authority, testimonial, statistics, maxims, law, and examples). They remain the basis for many arguments of a general nature presented today. Particular kinds of argument were (and are) drawn from special topics devised to suit the type of discourse chosen by the writer. For example, the writer, or speaker, engaged in judicial discourse is concerned with justice and injustice, making it necessary to establish whether something happened, (evidence), what it is (definition), and what kind of thing it is (cause and effect).

6b Developing an assertion and a thesis statement for written argument

An **assertion** is a statement that gives a position about a debatable topic and that can be supported by evidence, reasons, and examples (including facts, statistics, names, experiences, and experts). The thinking process that moves you from a topic to a defensible position calls, first, for you to make an assertion about the topic. The wording of the assertion often does not find its way into the essay itself, but the assertion serves as a focus for your thinking and your writing.

TOPIC	*The commercialization of holidays*
ASSERTION	Holidays have become too commercialized.
ASSERTION	Holidays have not become too commercialized.

Next, using your assertion as a base, you compose a **thesis statement** (see 2e-4) to use in the essay. It states the position that you present and support in the essay.

THESIS STATEMENT	The spirit of the holidays is being destroyed by commercialism.
THESIS STATEMENT	Commercial uses of holidays benefit the nation's economy and lift people's spirits.

Before you decide on an assertion—the position that you want to argue—you need to explore the topic. Do not rush into deciding on your assertion. Try to wait until you have as full a picture as possible. Consider all sides. Remember that **what separates most good writing from bad is the writer's ability to move back and forth between general statements and specific details.** Try to avoid a position that limits you to *only* general statements or to *only* specific details.

Even if you know immediately what assertion you want to argue for, do not stop there. The more that you think through all sides of the topic, the broader will be the perspective that you bring to your writing. Also, as you think through the position that you have taken and consider alternative points of view, be open to changing your mind and taking an opposite position. Before too long, however, do settle on a position; switching positions at the last minute lessens your chances of writing an effective essay.

To stimulate your thinking about the topic and your assertion about the topic, use the techniques for gathering ideas explained and illustrated in 2d. Jot down your thoughts as they develop. Do not lose the unique opportunity that the act of writing gives you for discovering new ideas and fresh insights. Many writers of argument make a list of the points that come to mind. Use two columns to visually represent two contrasting points of view. Head the columns with labels that emphasize contrast: for example, *agree* and *disagree* or *for* and *against.*

Whenever possible, use outside resources for developing an assertion. These include talking with other people and conducting research. Getting points of view from other people helps you explore a debatable topic. As you talk with people, interview them rather than argue with them. Your goal is to come to know opposing points of view, so resist any temptation to "win" a verbal argument; people sometimes hesitate to offer their ideas fully and openly when their listener is hostile. If your assignment permits you to use the library, do so. Written argument can be particularly enhanced when your position is supported with facts and by reference to experts. (For complete information about the process and techniques of research, consult Chapter 32.)

EXERCISE 1

Develop an assertion and a thesis statement for a written argument on each of the following topics. You may choose any defensible position.

EXAMPLE **Topic:** *Book censorship in high school*

Assertion: *Books should not be censored in high school.*

Thesis statement: *When book are taken off high school library shelves and are dropped from high school curricula, students are denied exposure to an open exchange of ideas.*

1. Television
2. Prisons
3. Drugs and athletics
4. Diets for weight loss
5. Grades

6c Structuring written argument

No one structure fits all written argument. For college courses, most written arguments include certain elements. Lindsey Black's essay in this chapter (and Gary Lee Houseman's essay in Chapter 3) uses a structure based on the **classical pattern of argument** developed by the ancient Greeks and Romans and still highly respected today. Daniel Casey's essay in this chapter uses a modified form of that structure. Here is a chart to help you recognize the elements in a written argument.

ANSWERS: EXERCISE 1

Assertions and thesis statements will vary for this exercise.

EXTRA EXERCISE B

Practice devising assertions and thesis statements by working with some of the following topics.

1. Safety on interstate highways
2. The importance of knowing a second language
3. U. S. Savings Bonds as investments
4. The use of television with commercials in elementary school classrooms
5. Diminishing access to clean water
6. The future of motion pictures
7. Violence on television
8. The need for greater airport security
9. Computer literacy as a requirement for high school graduation
10. Sex education in public schools

BACKGROUND

Classical persuasion consisted of six parts that represented six basic functions. Although the writer or orator was granted some flexibility in how and in what order the parts were presented, they provided effective guidelines for presenting an argument. Often used today, the six parts of an argument, according to the classical precept, are:

1. *Exordium,* meaning "beginning a web." As an introduction, the purpose of the exordium is to attract the attention of the audience, indicate the subject, and favorably dispose the audience to what will follow.

2. *Narratio.* In this section, now usually referred to as "statement of fact," the issue is defined by stating pertinent facts about the subject. It is, therefore, basically expository.

3. *Partitio.* If the thesis has not yet been identified, it will be presented here, along with an indication of how the rest of the argument will be organized. The purpose of partition is to prepare the reader or listener for what will follow.

4. *Confirmatio.* Arguments to support the thesis, forming the bulk of the piece, are developed at this point. The question of the order of presentation of arguments is critical to the effectiveness of the confirmation.

5. *Refutatio.* Opposing arguments are considered and rendered ineffective in the refutation section. To ignore them is to risk letting them appear to be more attractive than one's own thesis. The refutation may be placed at various points in the piece, depending on where it will be most effective.

6. *Peroratio.* While the classical rhetoricians used a number of different terms to indicate the conclusion of a piece, it usually furnished a summary of proofs and refutations, a restatement of the major points, and a recreation of emotional and ethical appeals.

ELEMENTS IN A WRITTEN ARGUMENT

1. **Introductory paragraph:** sets the context for the position that is argued in the essay. (For a full discussion of introductory paragraphs, see 4e.)

2. **Thesis statement:** states the position being argued. In a short essay, the thesis statement often appears at the end of the introductory paragraph. (For a full discussion of thesis statements, see 2e–4.)

3. **Background information:** gives the reader basic information needed for understanding the position being argued. This information can be part of the introductory paragraph (as in Daniel Casey's essay) or can appear in its own paragraph (as in Lindsey Black's essay).

4. **Reasons or evidence:** supports the position being argued. This material is the core of the essay. Support must be sufficient; only one reason or one type of evidence is *not* enough to make a case. Each reason or type of evidence usually consists of a general statement backed up with specific details or specific examples. Each generalization and its related specifics can be discussed using inductive reasoning (see 5e-1), deductive reasoning (see 5e-2), or a combination of the two. Depending on the length of the essay, one or two paragraphs are devoted to each reason or type of evidence.

   The best sequence for presenting the complete set of reasons and types of evidence depends on the impact you want to achieve. Moving from evidence most familiar to the reader to evidence least familiar helps the reader move from the known to the unknown. This order might catch the reader's interest early on. Moving from evidence least important to evidence most important might build the reader's suspense. (For a full discussion of arrangement, see 4c.)

5. **Anticipation of likely objections and responses to them:** mentions positions in opposition to the one being argued and responds to them briefly. In classical argument, this "refutation" appears in its own paragraph, immediately before the concluding paragraph (as in Lindsey Black's essay). An alternative placement for this discussion is immediately after the introductory paragraph, as a bridge to the rest of the essay; in such arrangements the essay's thesis statement falls either at the end of the introductory paragraph or at the end of the "refutation" paragraph (as in Daniel Casey's essay). In another

(continued on next page)

ELEMENTS IN A WRITTEN ARGUMENT *(continued)*

arrangement each paragraph that presents a type of evidence or reason (item 4 on this list) also mentions and responds to the opposing position.

6. **Concluding paragraph:** brings the essay to a logical end. It does not cut off the reader abruptly. (For a full discussion of concluding paragraphs, see 4e.)

6d Considering the audience for written argument

The purpose of written argument is to convince a reader—the audience—about a matter of opinion. Key factors in considering audience are discussed in 1c. When you write argument, consider one additional factor about audience: the degree of agreement expected from the reader.

When a topic is emotionally charged, chances are high that any position being argued will elicit either strong agreement or strong disagreement. For example, topics such as abortion, capital punishment, and gun control arouse very strong emotions in many people. Such topics are emotionally loaded because they touch on matters of personal beliefs, including religion and individual rights. Topics such as the commercialization of holidays (see the two essays at the end of this chapter) and the destruction of rain forests (see Gary Lee Houseman's essay in Chapter 3) are somewhat less emotionally loaded. Even less emotionally loaded, yet still open to debate, are topics such as whether everyone needs a college education or whether Computer X is better than Computer Y.

The degree to which a reader might be friendly or hostile can influence what strategies you use to try to convince that reader. For example, when you anticipate that many readers will not agree with you, consider using techniques of **Rogerian argument.** Rogerian argument has been adapted from the principles of communication developed by psychologist Carl Rogers. Communication, according to Rogers, is eased when people find common ground in their points of view. The common ground in a debate over capital punishment might be that both sides find crime to be a growing problem today. Once both sides agree about the problem, they might have more tolerance for the divergence of opinion concerning whether capital punishment is a deterrent to crime.

BACKGROUND

The ideal format of a Rogerian argument, according to Richard Coe (*Form and Substance*, John Wiley and Sons, 1981, pp. 342–343) follows this pattern:

Introduction. State the subject as a problem rather than as an issue to interest your audience in reading about something with which they disagree.

Fair statement of the opposing position. In this section the writer states the reader's position in a manner that seems fair and accurate to the reader.

Statement of contexts in which that position may be valid. Here the writer is trying to show readers that he or she understands their position by asserting that it is valid in some contexts.

Fair statement of the writer's position. The goal of this section is to get readers to understand the writer's position as fairly and thoroughly as the writer has understood theirs.

Statement of contexts in which the writer's position is valid. The writer tries to get readers to look at the problem from new perspectives and in new contexts.

Statement of how readers would benefit by adopting at least elements of the writer's position. The writer appeals to readers' self-interests. In this section the writer's position turns from a threat to a promise.

EXTRA EXERCISE C

The following persuasive paragraph is not as effective as it could be because it uses undefined abstract words and words that vary in meaning with the context in which they appear. Rewrite the paragraph, improving its persuasiveness by defining key words that may be vague to the reader.

Some Americans react strongly to actions that show disrespect for our flag. They revere it as a symbol of the values for which the United States is known around the world. They are quick to rise up against those who would use their freedom to desecrate Old Glory, calling them traitors to the Constitution and all it upholds: our rights and our democratic form of government. Calling for a Constitutional Amendment, they even want to restrict our freedoms by making it illegal to misuse the flag. Wouldn't such an amendment show disrepect for the freedom the flag represents?

QUOTATION ABOUT WRITING

Mere knowledge of the truth will not give you the art of persuasion.

—Plato

6e Defining terms in written argument

When you **define terms,** you explain what you mean by key words that you use. Words are key words when they are central to the message that you want to communicate. The meaning of some key words is readily evident. Key words open to interpretation, however, should be made more specific to be clear.

No	Commercialism at holiday time is **bad.**
Yes	Commercialism at holiday time is **ruining the spirit of the holidays.**
Yes	Commercialism at holiday time **tempts too many people to spend more money than they can afford.**

Some key words might vary with the context of a discussion and should be explained in an essay. Abstract words such as *love, freedom,* and *democracy* have to be explained because they have different meanings in different contexts. Daniel Casey uses *economy,* a word with many meanings, in the topic sentence of the third paragraph of his essay. He explains *economy* as the *ongoing circulation of money,* and he uses the rest of the paragraph to explain how that circulation operates. In this way, Casey makes clear that he is not referring to any of the other meanings of *economy:* the management of finances, the avoidance of waste, or the efficient use of resources.

Other key terms might be unfamiliar to the reader even though they are known words. For example, Daniel Casey opens his essay with the words *signs of commercialism.* Although each word by itself is familiar, the term is not. Casey therefore gives examples to illustrate the concept. In so doing, he creates an effective introduction to his essay by bringing the reader to a quick understanding of his topic.

Many students ask whether they should use actual dictionary definitions in an essay. Looking words up in a dictionary to understand precise meanings is a very important activity for writers. Quoting a dictionary definition, however, is not always wise. Dictionary definitions tend to be overused in student writing, and they are often seen as the "easy way out." Using an **extended definition** is usually a more effective approach, which is what Casey did for *economy* in the third paragraph of his essay. (For another example of extended definition, see 4d for a paragraph by E. B. White that defines the concept of democracy.) If you do use a dictionary definition in your writing, be sure to work it into your material gracefully. Do not simply tack it on abruptly to what you are saying. In general, do not rely on it for your opening sentence. Also, be aware that references to a dictionary must be complete. Do not simply refer to "Webster's," which is far too general. Each dictionary has its own name, such as *Webster's New World Dictionary.*

6f Reasoning effectively in written argument

When you reason effectively, you increase your chances of convincing your reader to agree with you. In many instances, of course, you cannot literally expect to change your reader's mind. The basis for a debatable position is often personal opinion or belief, neither of which can be expected to change as the result of one written argument. Nevertheless, you still have an important goal: to convince your reader that your point of view has merit. People often "agree to disagree," in the best spirit of intellectual exchange. Round-table discussions among various experts heard on National Public Radio (NPR) or television's Public Broadcast System (PBS) are conducted in such a spirit.

The opposite positions taken by Lindsey Black and Daniel Casey concerning commercialism at holiday time stem from their personal beliefs and perceptions of the world. Black feels that commercialism is ruining the holidays. Casey recognizes the existence of commercialism, but he sees it as beneficial. The chance of either person convincing the other is slight. What can happen, however, is that each person can respect the quality of the other's argument.

An argument of good quality relies on three types of appeals to reason: the logical, the emotional, and the ethical. Here is a summary of how to use the three appeals.

GUIDELINES FOR REASONING EFFECTIVELY IN WRITTEN ARGUMENT

1. **Be logical:** use sound reasoning.
2. **Enlist the emotions of the reader:** enlist the values and beliefs of the reader, usually by arousing "the better self" of the reader.
3. **Establish credibility:** show that you as the writer can be relied upon as a knowledgeable person with good sense.

ALTERNATE EXAMPLES
Logical Appeal

According to a recent publication of the Equal Employment Opportunity Commission, at the present rate of "progress" it will take forty-three years to end job discrimination—hardly a reasonable timetable.

If our goal is educational and economic equity and parity—and it is—then we need affirmative action to catch up. We are behind as a result of discrimination and denial of opportunity. There is one white attorney for every 680 whites, but only one black attorney for every 4,000 blacks; one white physician for every 659 whites, but only one black physician for every 5,000 blacks; and one white dentist for every 1,900 whites, but only one black dentist for every 8,400 blacks. Less than 1 percent of all engineers—or of all practicing chemists—is black. Cruel and uncompassionate injustice created gaps like these. We need creative justice and compassion to help us close them.

—Jesse Jackson, "Why Blacks Need Affirmative Action"

Emotional Appeal

Apart from our children, who gave and still give rise to an additional set of family activities—but they are after all grown up now and can take care of themselves—apart from them, since my husband and I have reached that particular time of life, I wonder how either of us would get on without the other. I know this problem has to be faced every hour of the day by somebody. The survivor picks up the pieces and there are kind young people to help and life goes on. But it must be different; it must be very different. Fortunately, like everything about the future, it is unknowable and therefore unimaginable.

What may be learned after long association in friendship or marriage is that each partner in the relationship finds something of himself in the other. A man is not a Man

(continued next page)

in a box with a wall around him. His humanness partakes of the humanness of the person or persons closest to him. He is neither
a man nor woman but a human being. If he
is lucky, he has learned something about another human being. If he is especially lucky,
he has learned something about himself.

—Dorothy Van Doren,
"Men, Women, and Cats"

Ethical Appeal

Our tragedy today is a general and universal physical fear so long sustained by now
that we can even bear it. There are no
longer problems of the spirit. There is only
the question: When will I be blown up? Because of this, the young man or woman writing today has forgotten the problems of the
human heart in conflict with itself which
alone can make good writing because only
this is worth writing about, worth the agony
and the sweat.

He must learn them again. He must teach
himself that the basest of all things is to be
afraid; and, teaching himself that, forget it
forever, leaving no room in his workshop for
anything but the old verities and truths of
the heart, the old universal truths lacking
which any story is ephemeral and doomed—
love and honor and pity and pride and compassion and sacrifice. Until he does so, he
labors under a curse. He writes not of love
but of lust, of defeats in which nobody loses
anything of value, of victories without hope
and, worst of all, without pity or compassion. His griefs grieve on no universal bones,
leaving no scars. He writes not of the heart
but of the glands.

—William Faulkner,
Nobel Prize Acceptance Speech

The most widely used appeal in written argument is the **logical appeal,** called *logos* by the ancient Greeks. Logical reasoning is sound reasoning. Logical reasoning is important in all thinking and writing. Chapter 5 of this handbook, therefore, is a close companion to this chapter. Logical reasoning calls for using evidence well, as explained in 5c. Logical reasoning also means analyzing cause and effect correctly, as explained in 5d. A sound argument uses patterns of inductive reasoning and deductive reasoning, as explained in 5e. A sound argument also clearly distinguishes between fact and opin-ion, as explained in 5b–3. And, finally, sound reasoning means avoid-ing logical fallacies, as explained in 5f.

Written argument for college courses relies heavily on logic. Both Lindsey Black and Daniel Casey used logical reasoning through-out their essays. While the reader might not agree with the reasons or types of evidence presented, the reader can respect the logic of their arguments.

The **emotional appeal,** called *pathos* by the ancient Greeks, can be effective when used in conjunction with logical appeals. The word *emotional* has a specific meaning in this context. It means arousing and enlisting the emotions of the reader. Often it arouses the "better self" of the reader by eliciting sympathy, civic pride, and other feelings based on values and beliefs. Effective emotional ap-peals use description and examples to stir emotions. But they leave the actual stirring to the reader. Restraint is more effective than ex-cessive sentimentality.

Both Casey and Black use emotional appeals in their essays, but always in conjunction with a logical presentation of material. Casey appeals to the emotions when in his fifth paragraph he mentions stores giving toys to children in hospitals. But he does not overdo it. He does not say that anyone who disagrees with him hates children and feels no pity for their suffering from dreadful illnesses that ravage their tiny bodies. If he had indulged in such excesses, the reader would resent being manipulated and therefore would probably reject his argument. Black appeals to the emotions when she writes in her second paragraph about the origins of the holiday spirit. With re-straint, she mentions the meaning of each holiday. She does not at-tempt to tell the reader how to feel; she simply points out facts that support the logic of her argument and that might also stir the read-er's pride in country and heritage.

The **ethical appeal,** called *ethos* by the ancient Greeks, means establishing the credibility of the writer. Credibility is gained if the writer uses correct facts, undistorted evidence, and accurate inter-pretations of events. Readers do not trust a writer who states opin-ions as fact or who makes a claim that cannot possibly be supported.

6g

The statement "A child who does not get gifts for Christmas suffers a trauma from which recovery is impossible" is an opinion as well as an exaggeration. It has no place in written argument.

Ethical appeals cannot take the place of logical appeals, but the two types of appeals work well together. One effective way to make an ethical appeal is to draw on personal experience. (Some college instructors do not want students to write in the first person, so ask your instructor before you use it.) If you use personal experience, always be sure that it relates directly to a generalization that you are supporting. Also, be aware that a personal experience can say as much about the writer as the experience. For example, if Casey had been a volunteer at a hospital when gifts from a local business were distributed, the story of the experience not only would have supported his claim in his fifth paragraph, but also would have illustrated his good character.

6g Establishing a reasonable tone in written argument

To be reasonable, you have to be fair. By anticipating opposing positions and responding to them (see 6c) you have a particularly good chance to show that you are fair. When you alert your reader to other ways of thinking about the issue, you demonstrate that you have not ignored other positions. This implies respect for the other side, which in turn makes the tone of the essay more reasonable.

To achieve a reasonable tone, choose your words carefully. Avoid words that exaggerate. Use figurative language, such as similes and metaphors (see 21c), to enhance your point rather than distort it. Avoid slanted language (see 21a–4). No matter how strongly you disagree with opposing arguments, never insult the other side. Name-calling is impolite, shows poor self-control, and demonstrates poor judgment. The more emotionally loaded a topic (for example, abortion, capital punishment, and gun control), the more might be the temptation to use angry words. Words such as *stupid* or *pigheaded,* however, say more about the writer than about the issue.

Artificial language (see 21e) also ruins a reasonable tone.

No   Emblems of commercial enterprise are ubiquitously visible as the populace prepares for the celebration of festivals and commemorations throughout the venerable United States of America.

Yes   Signs of commercialism at holiday time are easy to see in the United States.

EXTRA EXERCISE D

Analyze the following paragraphs to discover the dominant appeal of each.

(1) We observe today not a victory of party but a celebration of freedom—symbolizing an end as well as a beginning—signifying renewal as well as change. For I have sworn before you and Almighty God the same solemn oath our forebears prescribed nearly a century and three quarters ago.

The world is very different now. For man holds in his mortal hands the power to abolish all forms of human poverty and all forms of human life. And yet the same revolutionary beliefs for which our forebears fought are still at issue around the globe—the belief that the rights of man come not from the generosity of the state but from the hand of God.

We dare not forget today that we are the heirs of that first revolution. Let the word go forth from this time and place, to friend and foe alike, that the torch has been passed to a new generation of Americans—born in this century, tempered by war, disciplined by a hard and bitter peace, proud of our ancient heritage—and unwilling to witness or permit the slow undoing of those human rights to which this nation has always been committed, and to which we are committed today at home and around the world.

—John F. Kennedy, "Inaugural Address"

(2) Harlem got its first private project, Riverton—which is now, naturally, a slum—about twelve years ago because at that time Negroes were not allowed to live in Stuyvesant Town. Harlem watched Riverton go up, therefore, in the most violent bitterness of spirit, and hated it long before the builders arrived. They began hating it at about the time people began moving out of their condemned houses to make room for this additional proof of how thoroughly the white world despised them. And they had scarcely moved in, naturally, before they began smashing windows, defacing walls, urinating

(continued next page)

in the elevators, and fornicating in the play-
grounds. Liberals, both white and black,
were appalled at the spectacle. I was appalled by the liberal innocence—or cyn-
icism, which comes out in practice as much
the same thing. Other people were delighted to be able to point to proof positive
that nothing could be done to better the lot
of the colored people. They were, and are,
right in one respect: that nothing can be
done as long as they are treated like colored
people. The people in Harlem know they are
living there because white people do not
think they are good enough to live anywhere else. No amount of "improvement"
can sweeten this fact. Whatever money is
now being earmarked to improve this, or
any other ghetto, might as well be burnt. A
ghetto can be improved in one way only:
out of existence.

—James Baldwin, "Fifth Avenue Uptown:
A Letter from Harlem"

6h Writing and revising a written argument

Lindsey Black chose the position that holidays have become
too commercialized. Daniel Casey, on the other hand, chose the position that the commercialization of holidays has advantages. The
final draft of each essay appears at the end of this chapter. The labels
identify the structural elements of written argument discussed in 6c.

In an early draft of her essay, Black wrote an introduction that
included the background information on the holidays, now in her
second paragraph. When she revised, she moved the information to
a separate paragraph because she saw that the draft introductory paragraph was too long and the thesis statement was being overshad-
owed. Also, she felt that a separate paragraph giving background information had the additional advantage of giving her the space to use
an emotional appeal (see 6f). An early draft of Black's third paragraph consisted only of the topic sentence and the last three sentences of the final draft. When she revised, Black saw that she needed
more examples to support the generalization in her topic sentence. She
added the material about greeting cards and about time and stress.

Daniel Casey wrote a discovery draft (see 3b) to find and explore his ideas. He discovered, for example, that he needed to define
the term *signs of commercialism* by giving specific examples. He
also found that he had two reasons he could develop in support of
his thesis: an enriched economy and an enhanced spirit. He wanted
a third reason, so he interviewed some friends who worked in a
shopping mall, and they mentioned what some of the stores do for
the community at holiday time. The second paragraph of Casey's essay was the next-to-last paragraph in an early draft. He moved it
when he revised because he decided that it built an effective bridge
to his thesis statement.

As both Black and Casey revised, they consulted the Revision
Checklists in 3c to remind them of general principles of writing, and
they looked over the checklist on the opposite page.

EXERCISE 2

Write an argument defending a position on a topic chosen from the following list. Apply all the principles you have learned in this chapter.

1.	Animal experimentation	6.	Surrogate mothers
2.	Nuclear power	7.	Gun control
3.	Value of the space program	8.	School prayer
4.	Celebrity endorsements	9.	Drug testing
5.	Day-care centers	10.	Highway speed limits

6h

REVISION CHECKLIST FOR WRITTEN ARGUMENT

1. Does the thesis statement concern a debatable topic (see 6b)?
2. Is the material structured well for a written argument (see 6c)?
3. Do the reasons or evidence support the thesis statement? Are the generalizations supported by specific details? (See 6c.)
4. Are opposing positions mentioned and responded to (see 6c)?
5. Are terms defined (see 6e)?
6. Are the appeals to reason used correctly and well (see 6f)?
7. Is the tone reasonable (see 6g)?

Lindsey Black

Professor Gregory

English 101

April 10, 19XX

Commercialism is Ruining the Holidays

Introduction: identification of the situation

Holidays should be special occasions that have religious, historical, and cultural significance. Increasingly, however, holidays in the United States are turning into little more than business opportunities. From coast to coast, the jingles and beeps of cash registers drown out the traditional sounds of holiday observance. The spirit of the holidays is being destroyed by commercialism.

Thesis statement

Background: origins and significance

The origins of the holiday spirit are varied in the United States. Thanksgiving reminds Americans to be grateful for their blessings, and the Fourth of July stimulates pride in the founding of the nation. Labor Day is a tribute to workers. Memorial Day honors soldiers who died in defense of the country, and Veterans Day honors all veterans of the armed

---

TEACHING TIP

Most newspapers, including campus newspapers, carry numerous pieces of persuasive discourse in the letters to the editor, daily columns, and editorials. You may want to ask students to bring examples to class that can be analyzed in terms of assertions and thesis, as well as the order and means of development.

A different kind of experience, but an equally interesting one, can come from analysis of a longer, more sustained argument, such as Thoreau's essay "Civil Disobedience" or Martin Luther King, Jr.'s "Letter from Birmingham Jail."

QUOTATION ABOUT WRITING

What makes me happy is rewriting. . . . It's like cleaning house, getting rid of all the junk, getting things in the right order, tightening things up.

—Ellen Goodman

EXTRA EXERCISE E

Make a list of audiences that will be favorable to the following thesis statements and audiences that will be hostile to them. Consider the effect each will have on how the topic is approached.

1. Gun control legislation should be passed at the next meeting of the state legislature.

2. Eighteen-year-olds are too young to vote responsibly.

3. Motorcycle drivers should not be allowed on interstate highways.

4. Water from the Mississippi River should be diverted to irrigate the deserts of the American Southwest.

5. College football players should not be required to take college courses that lead to a degree.

6. Companies should provide free, on-site day care for children of employees.

7. Fathers should be granted paternity leave of six weeks after the birth of a child.

8. Reading knowledge of a foreign language should be a requirement for high school graduation.

9. Smoking should not be permitted in public restaurants.

10. College students should spend one semester working off-campus in the professional field they hope to enter.

forces. Christmas and Easter have great religious significance to Christians. Holidays used to be occasions for people to come together and celebrate their heritages. Today, however, the overriding message of the holidays is "spend money."

Evidence: one type

The most visible evidence that commercialism now dominates holidays is the unfortunate emphasis on spending money in preparation for religious holidays. For example, buying and mailing Christmas cards has become standard practice for individuals, families, and industry. How many people can ignore the social and the business pressures to mail cards? The commitment of money and time for this activity is not small. The gift situation is equally stressful. Although exchanging gifts on Christmas or Hanukah was always part of the celebration, the thought behind the present used to be the point. Today, however, advertising—particularly on television—sets a high standard of expectations. Can home-baked cookies compare to a microwave oven? Can hand-drawn, handwritten cards be as impressive as elaborate greeting cards that play music?

Evidence: another type

Other evidence that commercialism is ruining holidays is the emphasis on shopping for bargains rather than on activities related to cultural history. Huge sales held before holidays, and often on the holiday itself, are advertised heavily in newspapers, on television, and on radio. Veterans Day has become the day to buy fall and winter clothing at reduced prices, and Memorial Day means specially lowered prices on products for the coming summer. Parades and ceremonies on Labor Day honoring the workers of America get less attention than back-to-school sales. The image of the family gathering on Thanksgiving Day is being replaced with the image of the family shopping the day after Thanksgiving, when stores are more crowded than any other day except the day before Christmas.

Major likely objections and responses to them

In spite of all this, not all people are troubled by the spirit of commercialism on holidays. Many people enjoy the festivity of exchanging cards and gifts. Some people feel that the chance to buy at sales helps them stay within their budgets and therefore enjoy life more. What these people do not realize is that the festive spirit of giving can quickly turn sour when large amounts of money are suddenly not available for necessities. Also, these people do not realize that holiday sales tend to lure shoppers into spending more money than they had planned, often for things that they did not think they needed until they saw them "on sale."

Conclusion: call for awareness

Holiday celebrations in the United States today have more to do with the wallet than the spirit. Some people refuse to participate in the frenzy of a commercial interpretation of holidays, of course. But for too many people, holidays are becoming stressful rather than joyful, and upsetting rather than uplifting.

Daniel Casey

Professor Gregory

English 101

April 10, 19XX

Commercialism at Holiday Time Benefits the Nation

Introduction: gives background

Signs of commercialism at holiday time are easy to see in the United States. Christmas decorations begin their call to consumers in October. Memorial Day and Labor Day remind shoppers to prepare for the seasonal change in clothing fashions. Halloween and Easter mean children can make toll calls to the Great Pumpkin or the Easter Bunny.

6h

Presentation and refutation of opposite view

Some people disapprove of these commercial uses of holidays in the United States. These people feel that the meaning of a holiday gets lost when television is blaring news of the latest holiday sale or expensive gift item. Many people also feel that the proliferation of gifts and greeting cards creates stressful pressure on budgets and ruins any pleasure derived from giving and receiving. No one, however, has to forget the meaning of a holiday simply because commerce is involved. In fact, commercialism can increase people's enjoyment of the holidays. After all, commercial uses of holidays benefit the nation's

Thesis statement

economy and lift people's spirits.

Reason: one effect

Commerce at holiday time in the United States enriches the economy. Prosperity in the United States is based on the ongoing circulation of money, which holidays encourage. When people spend money on gifts and holiday products, jobs are created. The jobs are in many sectors of the economy: manufacturing, distribution, advertising, and retailing. Jobs help people support their families. Profits help business and industry grow. Salaries and profits bring about tax revenues that support schools, police, hospitals, and other government services.

Reason: second effect

In addition to economic benefits, commercial activity enhances the spirit of holidays. Most people feel more cheerful at holiday time. Everyone takes part in one big party. Advertising related to holidays, along with stores filled with holiday products, creates an atmosphere of festivity across the nation. Being able to say "Happy Thanksgiving" or "Merry Christmas" to strangers while shopping breaks down barriers and helps everyone feel part of one big family. The festivity on the streets, in malls, and in stores is infectious. Giving and getting gifts and greeting cards helps people stay in touch with each other and express their feelings. Children look forward all year to wearing a store-bought costume for Halloween, sitting on Santa's lap in a department store, and talking to the Easter Bunny at the local shopping mall.

Reason: third effect

The holiday activities that help businesses prosper also inspire many businesses to improve everyone's quality of life. Many companies, for example, organize collections of clothing and preparation of hot meals for needy people at holiday time. Toy stores often give away toys for Christmas and Hanukah to children in hospitals and in caretaking homes. Macy's department store annually delights people of all ages with its Thanksgiving Day Parade in New York City. The entire nation is invited to enjoy the parade in person or on television. In small towns and large cities, many businesses sponsor fireworks, mounted and displayed safely by professionals, to celebrate the Fourth of July. Good will and good business go together to everyone's benefit at holiday time.

Conclusion: summary of main points

The United States is a nation blessed with economic strength and resourceful people. While commercialism can detract from the true meaning of a holiday, it does not have to. People can discipline themselves to balance the spiritual with the commercial. Americans recognize that the advantages of a stimulated economy and a collective festive spirit are worth the effort of such self-discipline.

Two

UNDERSTANDING GRAMMAR

When you understand grammar, you have one tool to help you think about and discuss the ways that your sentences deliver their meaning to your readers. Part Two describes the elements of language and explains the standard rules for using those elements. As you use Chapters 7 through 12, remember that grammar is only a tool. Other parts of this handbook offer you additional perspectives on writing and the choices that writers make.

7 Parts of Speech and Structures of the Sentence

BACKGROUND

The English language has many grammars, some of them based on opposing theories and spawning contrasting pedagogies. For example, prescriptive grammarians hold that some forms are inherently correct and incorrect, but descriptive grammarians argue that no form is any more correct than another. As concern grew during the latter part of the nineteenth century over the writing competence of college freshmen, prescriptivists called for increased efforts to improve the correctness of students' prose. Their concern was apparent not only in college curricula, but also in the popularity of magazines for the general public that promised the uncertain writer and speaker a guide to correctness. Christopher Gould describes one such publication ("Josephine Baker's *Correct English*," *Righting Words*, November/December 1988.) Josephine Baker's *Correct English* was issued continuously between 1899 and 1950. The journal as well as her sixteen books (which went through 53 editions in 38 years) were published with the purpose of preserving the English language from the mistakes of careless speakers. The post-World War II shift of influence from the prescriptive to the descriptive grammarians is evident in the 1949 NCTE call for a "completely revised method of teaching the English language." The two new fundamentals were to be "the ability to read intelligently" and "the ability to express ideas and thoughts to others clearly."

When you recognize **parts of speech** and **structures of the sentence,** you have one way to describe how words are put together to create meaning.

PARTS OF SPEECH

When you know the **parts of speech,** you have a basic vocabulary for identifying words and understanding how language works. Sections 7a through 7i explain the **noun, pronoun, verb, adjective, adverb, preposition, conjunction,** and **interjection.** As you use this material, be aware that no part of speech exists in a vacuum. To correctly identify a word's part of speech, see how the word functions in the sentence you are analyzing. Often, the same word functions differently in different sentences.

We ate **fish.** [*Fish* is a noun. It names a thing.]
We **fish** on weekends. [*Fish* is a verb. It names an action.]

7a Recognizing nouns

A **noun** names a person, place, thing, or idea. A chart showing the types of nouns appears at the top of the next page. Most nouns change form to show number°: *pilot* (singular) and *pilots* (plural); *mouse* (singular) and *mice* (plural). Nouns also change form for the possessive case°: the *pilot's* hometown. Nouns function as subjects°, objects°, and complements°.

Articles often appear with nouns. These little words—*a, an, the*—are also called **limiting adjectives, noun markers,** or **noun determiners.** *A* and *an* "limit" a noun less than *the* does: *a plan, the plan.* When you choose between *a* and *an,* remember that *a* is

178

NOUNS		
PROPER	Names specific people, places, or things (first letter is always capitalized)	**John Lennon** **Paris** **Buick**
COMMON	Names general groups, places, people, or things	**singer** **city** **automobile**
CONCRETE	Names things experienced through the senses: sight, hearing, taste, smell, and touch	**landscape** **pizza** **thunder**
ABSTRACT	Names things *not* knowable through the senses	**freedom** **shyness**
COLLECTIVE	Names groups	**family** **team** **committee**
MASS	Names "uncountable" things	**water** **time**

the right word to use when the word following it starts with a consonant sound: *a carrot, a broken egg, a hip. An* is the right word to use when the word following it starts with a vowel sound: *an egg, an old carrot, an honor.*

WHERE TO FIND INFORMATION RELATED TO NOUNS

BACKGROUND

The effectiveness of teaching grammar in composition courses has long been a controversial subject. In 1963 Richard Braddock, Richard Lloyd-Jones, and Lowell Schoer declared: "In view of the widespread agreement of research studies based upon many types of students and teachers, the conclusion can be stated in strong and unqualified terms: the teaching of formal grammar has a negligible or, because it usually displaces some instruction and practice in composition, even a harmful effect on improvement in writing" (*Research in Written Composition,* NCTE, 1963, 37–38). Sara D'Eloia restated the case several years later in "The Uses—and Limits—of Grammar": "If there is one conclusion to be drawn which cuts across all the studies, it is this: the more time spent analyzing grammar as grammar, the less time spent writing; the less time spent writing, the less the improvement in the written product" (*Journal of Basic Writing* I [Sp/Su 1977]: 1–20. Rpt. in *A Sourcebook for Writing Teachers,* ed. Gary Tate and Edward P. J. Corbett. New York: Oxford UP, 1981, 225–43). Despite such negative assessments, most composition teachers, faced with student writing that fails to adhere to basic principles of standard English grammar, recognize an obligation to deal with students' lack of understanding. As Mina Shaughnessy points out in *Errors and Expectations,* one inevitably comes to the question of "how to help students reduce their errors to a level that is tolerable to their readers" (Oxford UP, 1977, 128). In answer to that question, Janice Neubleib, in "The Relation of Formal Grammar to Composition," would place grammar instruction firmly in the center of composition study (*College Composition and Communication* 23 [1977], 247–50.). Others who argue for the teaching of grammar are Patrick F. Basset, "Grammar—Can We Afford Not to Teach It?" (*NASSP Bulletin,* 64, no. 10 [1980], 55–63), and Sydney Greenbaum, "What Is Grammar and Why Teach It?" (ERIC 222 917).

QUOTATION ABOUT WRITING

People who don't understand linguistic principles generally confuse the terms *grammar* and *usage*. . . . *Grammar* has several meanings. First, it denotes that intuitive knowledge of language human beings gain by about age five. In this sense, *grammar 1* means "a capacity for language," a native ability to create and comprehend English utterances. The term also refers to various formal systems *(grammar 2)* scholars developed to explain our capacity for language. Traditional grammar, for example, represents an accumulation of terms, rules, and methods for analyzing what we do when we use language. *Grammar 2,* the field of study, generates theories about *grammar 1,* an unconscious process or behavior. *Usage,* on the other hand, refers to linguistic etiquette, to socially sanctioned styles of language appropriate to given situations and audiences.

—Erika Lindemann, *A Rhetoric for Writing Teachers,* 2nd ed.

QUOTATION ABOUT WRITING

The grammar is an attempt to make explicit and conscious what the speaker of English does intuitively and unconsciously.

—Mark Lester

7b   Recognizing pronouns

A **pronoun** takes the place of a noun. The word (or words) a pronoun replaces is called its **antecedent.** Here is a chart showing types of pronouns.

PRONOUNS		
PERSONAL *I, you, they, we, her, its, ours,* and others	Refers to people or things	I saw **her** take your book to **them.**
RELATIVE *who, which, that, what, whoever,* and others	Introduces certain noun clauses° and adjective clauses°	**Whoever** took the book **that** I left must return it.
INTERROGATIVE *who, whose, what, which,* and others	Introduces a question	**Who** called?
DEMONSTRATIVE *this, these, that, those*	Points out the antecedent°	Is **this** a mistake?
REFLEXIVE; INTENSIVE *myself, yourself, herself, themselves,* and all *-self* or *-selves* words	Reflects back to the antecedent°; intensifies the antecedent°	They claim to support **themselves.** I **myself** doubt it.
RECIPROCAL *each other, one another*	Refers to individual parts of a plural antecedent°	We respect **each other.**
INDEFINITE *all, anyone, each,* and others	Refers to nonspecific persons or things	**Everyone** is welcome here.

gr 7c

David is an accountant. [noun]

He is an accountant. [pronoun]

David gave **his** report to the finance committee. [The pronoun *his* replaces the antecedent *David.*]

Some pronouns change form to show number°. Singular pronouns include *I, her, himself.* Plural pronouns include *we, them, themselves.* Some pronouns change form to show case° changes: *I, me, mine,* for example.

WHERE TO FIND INFORMATION RELATED TO PRONOUNS

Using correct case forms: for example, *we* or *us, who* or *whom*	9b–9h
Using pronouns and antecedents clearly	10
Making pronouns and antecedents agree	11l–11o
Understanding the difference between *its* and *it's*	27b

EXERCISE 1

Underline and label all nouns (N) and pronouns (P). Circle all articles.

EXAMPLE   <u>Queen Elizabeth II</u>^N served as ⓐ <u>driver</u>^N and <u>mechanic</u>^N in <u>World War II</u>^N.

1. She joined the Auxiliary Territorial Service in 1944.
2. At the time, she was still a princess.
3. She was treated like all the others, though.
4. When she started, she did not know how to drive.
5. The princess quickly learned to strip and repair many kinds of engines.

7c   Recognizing verbs

Main verbs express action, occurrence, or state of being.

I dance. [action]

The audience **became** silent. What **happened?** [occurrence]

You **were** wonderful, but the show **seemed** too long. [state of being]

Main verbs may act as linking verbs, and main verbs may combine with auxiliary verbs to form verb phrases.

BACKGROUND

Grammar, as one of the subjects that composed the ancient Greek *trivium* (grammar, logic, and rhetoric), is one of the oldest fields of study, as well as one of the most durable. Even Plato can be labeled an early grammarian, because he was responsible for dividing the sentence into subject and verb (*onoma* and *rheme*), a division it has retained. In the Middle Ages study of the *trivium* was expanded, but not replaced, by the addition of the *quadrivium,* four additional "liberal arts." Despite attacks from modern researchers, grammar has remained firmly in place to this day as basic to the studies of the educated person.

ANSWERS: EXERCISE 1

1. She^P joined (the) <u>Auxiliary Territorial Service</u>^N in 1944.

2. At (the) <u>time</u>^N, she^P was still (a) princess^N.

3. She^P was treated like all (the) <u>others</u>^P, though.

4. When she^P started, she^P did not know how to drive.

5. (The) <u>princess</u>^N quickly learned to strip and repair many <u>kinds</u>^N of <u>engines</u>^N.

QUOTATION ABOUT WRITING

Grammar, logic, and rhetoric are the three arts of language.

—Edward P. J. Corbett

BACKGROUND

Most people think of the English they speak as being the standard version. People who use other forms, they assume, have dialects. The fact is that most of us speak a dialect, a language reflective of a particular region, class, or group of persons. The written version of the language that our society has generally agreed upon, called Edited American English (EAE), is used in most printed materials and in public utterances. EAE is discussed for students in Section 21a–2.

TEACHING TIP

As students explore their own dialects, you might ask them how they might say the following in a conversation with a close friend.

1. They have a blind date for a party next weekend.

2. They need to spend extra time studying for the next history test because they did not do well on the last one.

3. They have been given a homework assignment in math, but they do not understand the directions.

4. They play basketball every day.

5. Their talent is very impressive.

TEACHING TIP

Using the most appropriate verb can make the difference between writing a vague sentence and a meaningful one. You might stimulate a lively discussion if you ask students to explain the differences in meanings (and to compose a sentence for each meaning) of these verbs that deal with the same subjects.

- stride   march   glide   strut
- gobble   nibble   devour   eat
- giggle   guffaw   chuckle   snicker

LINKING VERBS

Linking verbs are main verbs that indicate a state of being or a condition. They link a subject° with a subject complement—a word (or words) that renames or describes the subject. Think of a linking verb as an equal sign between a subject and its complement.

Linking verbs may be forms of the verb *to be* (*am, is, was, were;* see 8c for a complete list).

George Washington   **was**   president.

SUBJECT   LINKING VERB   COMPLEMENT = DESCRIBES SUBJECT

Linking verbs may deal with the senses (*look, smell, taste, sound,* and *feel*).

George Washington   **sounded**   confident.

SUBJECT   LINKING VERB   COMPLEMENT = DESCRIBES SUBJECT

Certain other verbs—*appear, seem, become, grow, turn, remain,* and *prove,* for example—may be linking verbs.

George Washington   **grew**   old.

SUBJECT   LINKING VERB   COMPLEMENT = DESCRIBES SUBJECT

WHERE TO FIND INFORMATION RELATED TO VERBS

Verb forms and principal parts	8a
Learning irregular verbs	8b-2
Forms of *be, do, have*	8d
Using *be, do, have* as auxiliaries	8d
Using *can, may, will* (modal auxiliaries)	8d
Using *lie, lay; sit, set; rise, raise*	8e
Showing time with verbs	8f-8j
Making subjects and verbs agree	11a-11k

EXERCISE 2

Underline all verbs.

EXAMPLE   Albert Einstein <u>was offered</u> the presidency of Israel.

1. Israel's first president died in office.

AUXILIARY VERBS

Auxiliary verbs, also called **helping verbs,** are forms of *be, do, have, can, may, might, will,* and others. Auxiliary verbs combine with main verbs to make **verb phrases.**

I   **am**   **shopping** for new shoes.

       AUXILIARY VERB   MAIN VERB

            VERB PHRASE

Clothing prices   **have**   **soared** recently.

       AUXILIARY VERB   MAIN VERB

            VERB PHRASE

Leather shoes   **might**   **cost**   hundreds of dollars.

       AUXILIARY VERB   MAIN VERB

            VERB PHRASE

---

2. An Israeli newspaper suggested Einstein for the presidency.
3. Many people wanted him for that position.
4. Nevertheless, he refused the nomination.
5. He was not interested in politics.

7d   Recognizing verbals

Verbals are verb parts functioning as nouns°, adjectives°, or adverbs°. A chart showing the types of verbals appears on the next page.

WHERE TO FIND INFORMATION RELATED TO VERBALS

TEACHING TIP

In the chapter on "Common Errors" in *Errors and Expectations,* Mina Shaughnessy recommends approaching the study of grammar inductively by encouraging students not only to have the right answers but to know why they do what they do. "Grammar," she states, "is more a way of thinking, a style of inquiry, than a way of being right." Students who have been introduced to key concepts in grammar have a frame within which to recognize, analyze, and address their own problems. They can develop their editorial skills by looking closely at their own work to mine those concepts. They can practice and improve them by carrying out appropriate exercises and drills (Oxford UP, 1977, 90–159).

ANSWERS: EXERCISE 2

1. Israel's first president <u>died</u> in office.

2. An Israeli newspaper <u>suggested</u> Einstein for the presidency.

3. Many people <u>wanted</u> him for that position.

4. Nevertheless, he <u>refused</u> the nomination.

5. He <u>was</u> not interested in politics.

QUOTATION ABOUT WRITING

It is not the business of grammar to give law to the fashions which regulate our speech. On the contrary, from its conformity to these, and from that alone, it derives all its authority and value.

—George Campbell

TEACHING TIP

To give students a sense of the range of uses for *-ing* words, you might hand out a list of *-ing* words and ask your students to use each in three different sentences: in one as a noun, in another as an adjective, and in a third as part of a verb phrase. You can start with the chart of verbals and/or with Section 7m. Then you can collect the sentences and select 25 to 30 to reproduce and distribute. As an exercise or quiz, you can ask the students to identify each *-ing* word as a noun, an adjective, or part of a verb phrase. Often the author of a sentence is eager for others to get the identification correct and is therefore quite willing to explain the answer. You might use these *-ing* words or any others: (1) swimming, (2) painting, (3) flying, (4) reading, (5) cooking.

Here are some possible responses (the words appear first as nouns, then as adjectives, and finally as parts of verb phrases):

1. *Swimming* is fun. The *swimming* pool is crowded. She is *swimming* laps.

2. Oil *painting* requires an eye for detail. The *painting* equipment is in the shed. We will be *painting* the bedroom this weekend.

3. He likes *flying*. The *flying* squirrel leaped out of sight. Are you *flying* to Vancouver?

4. *Reading* is the basis of many other skills. The *reading* room at the library has comfortable chairs. What are you *reading?*

5. *Cooking* is a creative experience. The *cooking* class meets on Wednesday evenings. I am *cooking* something special for your birthday.

VERBALS

INFINITIVE *to* + simple form° of verb	1. Noun°: names an action, state, or condition 2. Adjective° or adverb°: describes or modifies	**To eat** now is inconvenient. Still, we have far **to go.**
PAST PARTICIPLE *-ed* form of regular verb° or equivalent in irregular verb°	Adjective°: describes or modifies	**Boiled, filtered** water is usually safe to drink.
PRESENT PARTICIPLE *-ing* form of verb	1. Adjective°: describes or modifies 2. Noun°: see *Gerund,* below	**Running** water may not be safe.
GERUND *-ing* form of verb	Noun°: names an action, state, or condition	**Eating** in turnpike restaurants can be an adventure.

7e   Recognizing adjectives

Adjectives modify—they describe or limit—nouns°, pronouns°, and word groups that function as nouns.

> I saw a **green** tree. [*Green* modifies the noun *tree.*]
> It was **leafy.** [*Leafy* modifies the pronoun *it.*]
> The flowering trees were **beautiful.** [*Beautiful* modifies the noun phrase *the flowering trees.*]

Descriptive adjectives, like *leafy* and *green,* can show levels of intensity: *green, greener, greenest; beautiful, more beautiful, most beautiful.*

Proper adjectives are formed from proper nouns: *American, Victorian.*

Some words quite different from descriptive adjectives still function to limit nouns, so they are classified as adjectives. Articles, one type of these **limiting adjectives,** are discussed in 7a. The chart on the next page lists other types.

gr **7f**

LIMITING ADJECTIVES	
DEMONSTRATIVE *this, these, that, those*	**Those** students rent **that** house.
INDEFINITE *any, each, other, some,* and others	**Few** films today have complex plots.
INTERROGATIVE *what, which, whose*	**What** answer did you give?
NUMERICAL *one, first, two, second,* and others	The **fifth** question was tricky.
POSSESSIVE *my, your, their,* and others	**My** violin is older than **your** cello.
RELATIVE *what, which, whose, whatever, whichever, whosever*	We don't know **which** road to take.

Most of these words also function as pronouns. To identify its part of speech, see how each word functions in a sentence.

That car belongs to Harold. [*that* = demonstrative adjective]
That is Harold's car. [*that* = demonstrative pronoun]

WHERE TO FIND INFORMATION RELATED TO ADJECTIVES

Avoiding double negatives	12b
Good and *well*	12c
Bad and *badly*	12c
Forming comparatives and superlatives: *-er, more; -est, most*	12d
Using adjectives, instead of nouns, as modifiers	12e
Spelling compound words: e.g., *well-known* or *well known*	22e-3
Using commas with two or more adjectives	24c, 24d
Capitalizing proper adjectives	30e

7f Recognizing adverbs

An **adverb** modifies—that is, describes or limits—verbs°, adjectives°, other adverbs, and entire sentences.

TEACHING TIP
The following passage from "The Mark on the Wall" by Virginia Woolf provides important sensory details through the use of well-chosen adjectives. To heighten student awareness of strong adjectives, you may want to read the excerpt aloud, asking students afterwards how many of those details they can recall.

Perhaps it was the middle of January in the present year that I first looked up and saw the mark on the wall. In order to fix a date it is necessary to remember what one saw. So now I think of the fire; the steady film of yellow light upon the page of my book; the three chrysanthemums in the round glass bowl on the mantelpiece. Yes, it must have been the wintertime, and we had just finished our tea, for I remember that I was smoking a cigarette when I looked up and saw the mark on the wall for the first time. I looked up through the smoke of my cigarette and my eye lodged for a moment upon the burning coals, and that old fancy of the crimson flag flapping from the castle tower came into my mind, and I thought of the cavalcade of red knights riding up the side of the black rock. Rather to my relief the sight of the mark interrupted the fancy, for it is an old fancy, an automatic fancy, made as a child perhaps. The mark was a small round mark, black upon the white wall, about six or seven inches above the mantelpiece.

Chefs plan meals **carefully.** [*Carefully* modifies the verb *plan.*]

Vegetables provide **very** important vitamins. [*Very* modifies the adjective *important.*]

Those potato chips are **too** highly salted. [*Too* modifies the adverb *highly.*]

Fortunately, people are learning that salt can be harmful. [*Fortunately* modifies the entire sentence.]

Many adverbs are easy to recognize because they are formed by adding *-ly* to adjectives: *sadly, loudly, normally.* Some adjectives, however, end in *-ly: brotherly, lovely.* Also, many adverbs do not end in *-ly: very, much, always, not, yesterday, so,* and *well* are a few that do not. For a complete explanation of how to distinguish between adverbs and adjectives, see Chapter 12.

Conjunctive adverbs modify by creating logical connections in meaning. The chart below contains a list of conjunctive adverbs. Conjunctive adverbs can appear in the first position of a sentence, in the middle of a sentence, or in the last position of a sentence.

Therefore, we consider Isaac Newton an important scientist.

We consider Isaac Newton, **therefore,** an important scientist.

We consider Isaac Newton an important scientist, **therefore.**

Be careful to use a period or a semicolon to separate the sentence (or the independent clause°) that contains the conjunctive

CONJUNCTIVE ADVERBS AND THE RELATIONSHIPS THEY EXPRESS	
SHOWING ADDITION	*also, furthermore, moreover, besides*
SHOWING CONTRAST	*however, still, nevertheless, conversely, nonetheless, instead, otherwise*
SHOWING COMPARISON	*similarly, likewise*
SHOWING RESULT OR SUMMARY	*therefore, thus, consequently, accordingly, hence, then*
SHOWING TIME	*next, then, meanwhile, finally, subsequently*
SHOWING EMPHASIS	*indeed, certainly*

adverb from the sentence (or independent clause) that precedes it or follows it. If you use only a comma, you will create the error known as a comma splice° (see 14e).

Descriptive adverbs can show levels of intensity, usually by adding *more* (or *less*) and *most* (or *least*): *more happily, least clearly.*

WHERE TO FIND INFORMATION RELATED TO ADVERBS

Using adverbs as modifiers	7l-2, 12a
Well and *good*	12c
Badly and *bad*	12c
Forming comparatives and superlatives	12d
Punctuation with conjunctive adverbs	14e, 24f, 25c
Splitting infinitives with adverbs	15b-3

EXERCISE 3

Underline and label all adjectives (ADJ) and all adverbs (ADV).

               ADJ   ADV
EXAMPLE   <u>Beautiful</u> Niagara Falls is eroding <u>rapidly.</u>

1. The famous falls are already 12,000 years old.
2. Erosion has steadily destroyed seven miles of precious land.
3. Not less than one foot of that land disappears annually.
4. In about 35,000 years, the world-famous falls likely will merge with Lake Erie, which is now twenty miles away.
5. Recently, the relentless rate of erosion has diminished very slightly, as the powerful water has been diverted to hydroelectric plants.

7g   Recognizing prepositions

Prepositions function with other words, in **prepositional phrases.** A list of prepositions appears on the next page. A prepositional phrase includes a preposition and a noun or pronoun object. It may contain modifying words too. Prepositional phrases often set out relationships in time or space: *in April, under the orange umbrella.*

> **In the fall,** we will hear a concert **by our favorite tenor.**
> **After the concert,** he will fly **to Paris.**

WHERE TO FIND INFORMATION RELATED TO PREPOSITIONS

Objects of prepositions	9a
Unintentional omission of prepositions	15e-3
Repetition of prepositions, in parallel forms	18c-3

ANSWERS: EXERCISE 3

1. famous (adj); already (adv)

2. steadily (adv); precious (adj)

3. Not less than (adv); that (adj); annually (adv)

4. about (adv); world-famous (adj); likely (adv); now (adv); away (adv)

5. Recently (adv); relentless (adj); very slightly (adv); powerful (adj); hydroelectric (adj)

A HUMOROUS NOTE

Misplaced prepositions and prepositional phrases can sometimes turn the serious into the comical, as Richard Lederer demonstrates in sentences he has collected from various publications.

- The patient was referred to a psychiatrist with a severe emotional problem.
- The judge sentenced the killer to die in the electric chair for the second time.
- Two cars were reported stolen by the Groveton police yesterday.
- Please take time to look over the brochure that is enclosed with your family.
- Berra had driven over with his wife, Carmen, from their home in a Mercedes for the softball game.

From Richard Lederer, *Anguished English* (Wyrick and Company, 1987)

BACKGROUND

In Middle English the relationships between words were indicated by inflectional endings. By the beginning of the fourteenth century, however, prepositions had replaced the endings, and only the possessive and plural endings were still in use.

COMMON PREPOSITIONS		
about	concerning	onto
above	despite	on top of
according to	down	out
across	during	out of
after	except	outside
against	except for	over
along	excepting	past
along with	for	regarding
among	from	round
apart from	in	since
around	in addition to	through
as	in back of	throughout
as for	in case of	till
at	in front of	to
because of	in place of	toward
before	inside	under
behind	in spite of	underneath
below	instead of	unlike
beneath	into	until
beside	like	up
between	near	upon
beyond	next	up to
but	of	with
by	off	within
by means of	on	without

Some words that function as prepositions also function as other parts of speech. To check whether a word is a preposition, see how it functions in its sentence.

The mountain climbers have not radioed in **since** yesterday. [preposition]

Since they left base camp yesterday, the mountain climbers have not radioed in. [subordinating conjunction: see 7h]

At first I was not worried, but I have **since** changed my mind. [adverb: see 7f]

gr 7h

7h Recognizing conjunctions

A **conjunction** connects words, phrases°, or clauses°. **Coordinating conjunctions** join two or more grammatically equivalent structures.

COORDINATING CONJUNCTIONS		
and	nor	so
but	or	yet
for		

And, but, and *or* can join structures of any kind: two or more nouns°, pronouns°, verbs°, adjectives°, adverbs°, phrases°, or clauses°. As a coordinating conjunction, *yet* can do the same.

Oregon *and* Washington are north of California. [nouns]

We **hike *and* camp** there every summer. [verbs]

The air is **fresh *and* clean.** [adjectives]

I love the outdoors, *and* my family does too. [independent clauses]

As coordinating conjunctions, *for* and *so* can connect only independent clauses°.

My vacation is in May, *so* we will go camping then. [independent clauses]

We will take warm clothing, *for* the outdoors will be cold. [independent clauses]

Correlative conjunctions function in pairs, joining equivalent grammatical structures.

CORRELATIVE CONJUNCTIONS
both . . . and
either . . . or
neither . . . nor
not only . . . but (also)
whether . . . or

TEACHING TIP

To help students become aware of what conjunctions do, you might want to distribute the following passage from "Salvation" by Langston Hughes. Omit all conjunctions and ask students to supply them. When the passage is complete, ask students to discuss the function and the effect of each word they supplied. Then distribute the original, complete passage.

I was saved from sin *when* I was going on thirteen. But not really saved. It happened like this. There was a big revival at my Auntie Reed's church. Every night for weeks there had been much preaching, singing, praying *and* shouting, *and* some very hardened sinners had been brought to Christ, *and* the membership of the church had grown by leaps *and* bounds. Then just *before* the revival ended, they held a special meeting for children, "to bring the young lambs to the fold." My aunt spoke of it for days ahead. That night I was escorted to the front *and* placed on the mourners' bench with the other young sinners, who had not yet been brought to Jesus. . . . Then I was left all alone on the mourners' bench. My aunt came *and* knelt at my knees *and* cried, *while* prayers *and* songs swirled all around me in the little church. The whole congregation prayed for me alone, in a mighty wail of moans *and* vices. *And* I kept waiting serenely for Jesus, waiting, waiting—*but* he didn't come. I wanted to see him, *but* nothing happened to me. Nothing! I wanted something to happen to me, *but* nothing happened.

189

Both English **and** Spanish are spoken in many homes in the United States.

Anyone who knows two or more languages **not only** can understand multiple cultures **but also** can communicate with a wider range of people.

Subordinating conjunctions begin one type of dependent clause, known as the adverb clause° (see 7n-2).

Because the hotel was overbooked, many people with reservations had to be turned away.
Many people were furious **after** they heard the news.

SUBORDINATING CONJUNCTIONS AND THE RELATIONSHIPS THEY EXPRESS	
TIME	after, before, once, since, until, when, whenever, while
REASON OR CAUSE	as, because
RESULT OR EFFECT	in order that, so, so that, that
CONDITION	if, even if, provided that, unless
CONTRAST	although, even though, though
LOCATION	where, wherever
CHOICE	rather than, than, whether

WHERE TO FIND INFORMATION RELATED TO CONJUNCTIONS

7i   Recognizing interjections

An **interjection** is a word or expression that conveys surprise or another strong emotion. Alone, an interjection is usually punctuated with an exclamation point. As part of a sentence, an interjection is set off with a comma (or commas). In academic writing, use interjections sparingly, if at all.

Alas!

Hooray! I got the promotion.

Oh, they are late.

EXERCISE 4

Identify the part of speech of each word in italics. Choose from noun, pronoun, verb, adjective, adverb, preposition, coordinating conjunction, and subordinating conjunction.

One[1] of the most devastating *natural*[2] *disasters*[3] *of*[4] recorded history *began*[5] on April 5, 1815, *when*[6] Mount Tambora, located *in*[7] present-day Indonesia, erupted. The *volcano*[8] blew off the top 4,000 feet of the mountain, creating a seven-mile-wide crater. Twelve thousand people *were killed*[9] *immediately,*[10] *and*[11] 80,000 died *later*[12] of starvation because the ash *from*[13] the volcano *destroyed*[14] farmland. The *blast,*[15] eighty times stronger than that of Mount St. Helens, was heard over 900 miles away. The cloud of *volcanic*[16] ash *circled*[17] the globe, reaching North America the following summer. The cloud *was*[18] *so*[19] thick that even the sun's rays could not penetrate *it.*[20] *Freezing*[21] temperatures and snow continued through the *entire*[22] summer, resulting in crop failures and death.

STRUCTURES OF THE SENTENCE

When you know how sentences are formed, you have one tool for understanding the art of writing.

The sentence has several definitions, each of which views it from a different perspective. On its most mechanical level, a sentence starts with a capital letter and finishes with a period, question mark, or exclamation point. A sentence can be defined according to its purpose. Most sentences are **declarative;** they make a statement: *Sky diving is dangerous.* Some sentences are **interrogative;** they ask a question: *Is sky diving dangerous?* Some sentences are

---

ANSWERS: EXERCISE 4

Instructors can require students to identify the part of speech of any word in this paragraph, in addition to those with superscript numbers.

1. pronoun	12. adverb
2. adjective	13. preposition
3. noun	14. verb
4. preposition	15. noun
5. verb	16. adjective
6. subordinating conj.	17. verb
7. preposition	18. verb
8. noun	19. adverb
9. verb	20. pronoun
10. adverb	21. adjective
11. coordinating conj.	22. adjective

QUOTATION ABOUT WRITING

Many language difficulties can be lumped together as "grammar problems," but they are problems of quite different sorts and they are not all equally important.

—Ruth V. Elcan, *Elements of College Writing*

imperative; they give a command: *Be careful.* Some sentences are **exclamatory:** *How I love sky diving!* Grammatically, a sentence contains an independent clause, a group of words that can stand alone as an independent unit: *Sky diving is dangerous.* Sometimes a sentence is described as a "complete thought," but the concept of "complete" is too subjective to be reliable.

An infinite variety of sentences can be composed, but all sentences share a common foundation. Sections 7j through 7o present the basic structures of sentences.

7j Recognizing subjects and predicates

A sentence consists of two basic parts: a subject and a predicate.

1 Recognizing subjects

The **simple subject** is the word or group of words that acts, is described, or is acted upon.

The **telephone** rang. [Simple subject, *telephone*, acts.]
The **telephone** is red. [Simple subject, *telephone*, is described.]
The **telephone** was being connected. [Simple subject, *telephone*, is acted upon.]

The **complete subject** is the simple subject and its modifiers—all the words that describe or limit it.

SENTENCE I		
	THE SENTENCE	
COMPLETE SUBJECT	**+**	**COMPLETE PREDICATE**
The red telephone		rang.

SIMPLE SUBJECT

The **lawyer** listened. [simple subject = *lawyer*]
The wise lawyer listened. [complete subject = *the wise lawyer*]

A subject can be **compound,** consisting of two or more nouns or pronouns and their modifiers.

SENTENCE II

THE SENTENCE

COMPLETE SUBJECT	+	COMPLETE PREDICATE
The telephone and the doorbell		rang.

COMPOUND SUBJECT

The lawyer and her client met. [compound subject = the lawyer, her client]

2 Recognizing predicates

The **predicate** is the part of the sentence that contains the verb. The predicate tells what the subject is doing or experiencing or what is being done to the subject.

The telephone **rang.** [*Rang* tells us what the subject, *telephone,* did.]

The telephone **is** red. [*Is* tells what the subject, *telephone,* experiences.]

The telephone **was** being connected. [*Was being connected* tells what was being done to the subject, *telephone.*]

The **simple predicate** contains only the verb. The **complete predicate** contains the verb and its modifiers° as well as any objects° or complements° and their modifiers.

SENTENCE III

THE SENTENCE

COMPLETE SUBJECT	+	COMPLETE PREDICATE
The red telephone		rang loudly.

SIMPLE SUBJECT   SIMPLE PREDICATE (VERB)

TEACHING TIP

Erasmus, in his *De Copia,* demonstrated 150 ways of phrasing the Latin sentence *Tuae literae me magnopere delectarunt* (Your letter has delighted me very much). Given so many possibilities for stating a simple fact, how does a writer decide which is "better" or "best"? Some of the criteria for judgment include economy, grace, emphasis, rhythm, as well as appropriateness to subject, occasion, audience, and authorial voice.

To help students develop critical judgment about syntax, you may want to ask them to explore how many ways they can restate a single sentence, and then to evaluate which is the most effective. For example, how many ways can they state the following? Of the statements they compose, which is best?

1. Your suggestion has pleased me a great deal.

2. Photographs of our family bring back many pleasant memories.

3. When I look at my birth certificate, I often wonder what was going on when I was born.

The lawyer listened. [simple predicate = *listened*]

The lawyer listened carefully. [complete predicate = *listened carefully*]

A predicate can be **compound,** consisting of two or more verbs and any objects° or modifiers°.

SENTENCE IV

THE SENTENCE

COMPLETE SUBJECT	+	COMPLETE PREDICATE
The red telephone		rang loudly and startled everyone.

COMPOUND PREDICATE

EXERCISE 5

Use a slash to separate the complete subject from the complete predicate.

EXAMPLE   Ordinary water / is essential for all life.

1. Water evaporates constantly.
2. Evaporation alternates with condensation in the water cycle.
3. Water vapor enters the air by evaporation from water surfaces, such as the oceans.
4. Oceans and other bodies of water cover more than seventy percent of our planet.
5. Molecules of water in the air condense and fall as rain or snow.

7k   **Recognizing direct and indirect objects**

Direct and indirect objects occur in the predicate° of a sentence.

1   **Recognizing direct objects**

A **direct object** receives the action—it completes the meaning—of a transitive verb° (see 8e).

SENTENCE V

THE SENTENCE		
COMPLETE SUBJECT +	**COMPLETE PREDICATE**	
The caller	offered money.	
	↑ ↑	
	VERB DIRECT OBJECT	

To find a direct object, make up a *whom?* or *what?* question about the verb. The caller offered what? *Money.*

2   Recognizing indirect objects

An **indirect object** answers a *to whom? for whom? to what?* or *for what?* question about the verb.

SENTENCE VI

THE SENTENCE		
COMPLETE SUBJECT +	**COMPLETE PREDICATE**	
The caller	offered the lawyer money.	
	↑ ↑ ↑	
	VERB INDIRECT DIRECT	
	OBJECT OBJECT	

EXERCISE 6

Draw a single line under all direct objects and a double line under all indirect objects.

EXAMPLE   President Woodrow Wilson bought <u>the White House garden</u><u>ers</u> <u>sheep</u> to serve as lawnmowers during World War I.

1. The government needed the gardeners to serve as soldiers.
2. The sheep attracted tourists to the White House.

ANSWERS: EXERCISE 6

1. The government needed the <u>gardeners</u> to serve as soldiers.

2. The sheep attracted <u>tourists</u> to the White House.

3. Mrs. Wilson gave <u>the Red Cross</u> <u>money</u> from the sale of their wool.

4. More recently, the U.S., Army gave <u>goats</u> the <u>task</u> of trimming the <u>lawns</u> at ammunition dumps.

5. If you tell <u>people</u> <u>this fact</u>, they may not believe <u>you</u>.

3. Mrs. Wilson gave the Red Cross money from the sale of their wool.

4. More recently, the U.S. Army gave goats the task of trimming the lawns at ammunition dumps.

5. If you tell people this fact, they may not believe you.

71 Recognizing complements, modifiers, and appositives

1 Recognizing complements

A **complement** occurs in the predicate° of a sentence. It renames or describes a subject or an object°.

A **subject complement** is a noun°, pronoun°, or adjective° that follows a **linking verb.** (Linking verbs—such as *was* and *seemed*—operate like an equal sign, signaling that the subject is being renamed or described; see 7c.)

SENTENCE VII

THE SENTENCE		
COMPLETE SUBJECT	**+**	**PREDICATE**
The caller		was a student.

LINKING VERB SUBJECT COMPLEMENT

The caller was **a sophomore.** [noun *sophomore* = subject complement]

The student seemed **nervous.** [adjective *nervous* = subject complement]

Some systems of grammar use the term **predicate nominative** for a noun used as a subject complement and the term **predicate adjective** for an adjective used as a subject complement.

196

An **object complement** is a noun° or an adjective° that immediately follows a direct object and either describes or renames it.

SENTENCE VIII		

THE SENTENCE

COMPLETE SUBJECT	+	COMPLETE PREDICATE
The student		called himself a victim.

VERB · DIRECT OBJECT · OBJECT COMPLEMENT

The student called himself **a pawn.** [noun *pawn* = object complement renaming *himself,* which refers to *student*]

The student considered the situation **hopeless.** [adjective *hopeless* = object complement describing *situation*]

EXERCISE 7

Underline all complements and identify each as a subject complement or an object complement.

EXAMPLE   The dodo is <u>extinct</u>. (subject complement)

1. The dodo was a native of Mauritius, an island in the Indian Ocean.
2. Explorers found the dodo fat and clumsy.
3. The dodo was incapable of flight or fight.
4. By 1681, all the dodos were gone.
5. In the eighteenth century, many people thought the dodo a myth.

2	**Recognizing modifiers**

Modifiers are words or groups of words that describe other words. There are two basic kinds of modifiers: adjectives and adverbs.

Adjectives modify only nouns° or words acting as nouns, such as pronouns°, noun phrases°, or relative clauses°. Adjectives can appear in the subject or the predicate of a sentence.

BACKGROUND

For an early, landmark work on expanding sentences by adding and directing modifiers, see Francis Christensen's "A Generative Rhetoric of the Sentence," in *Notes Toward a New Rhetoric,* 2nd ed., ed. Bonniejean Christensen (New York: Harper and Row, 1978, 23–44). Christensen maintains that instructional time is most effectively spent in dealing with the cumulative sentence. This type of sentence presents the main clause first, then adds details that "move backward . . . to modify the statement of the main clause or more often to explicate or exemplify it, so that the sentence has a flowing and ebbing movement, advancing to a new position and then pausing to consolidate it, leaping and lingering as the popular ballad does." The additions are usually at a lower level of generality, going back over the main point in a more concrete and specific manner. Christensen argues that a writer generates ideas while composing multilevel sentences rich with details that expand the opening clause.

TEACHING TIP

Edward Corbett, in *Classical Rhetoric for the Modern Student,* 2nd ed. (New York: Oxford UP, 1971), suggests having students analyze their own writing by counting the number of words in the sentences of a paper they have written, then identifying the longest sentence (in number of words), the shortest sentence, and the average sentence. The student can go on to compute the number of sentences and the percentage of sentences that contain more than ten words over the average and five below the average. The whole can be compared with a passage from an essay by a professional writer.

SENTENCE IX

THE SENTENCE

COMPLETE SUBJECT	+	COMPLETE PREDICATE
The red telephone		rang.

ADJECTIVE (↑ pointing to *red*)

The **large red** telephone rang. [adjectives *large* and *red* modifying the noun *telephone*]

The **worried** student needed a **good** lawyer. [adjective *worried* modifying the noun *student;* adjective *good* modifying the noun *lawyer*]

Adverbs modify verbs°, adjectives°, other adverbs, and independent clauses°. Adverbs can appear in the subject or the predicate of a sentence.

SENTENCE X

THE SENTENCE

COMPLETE SUBJECT	+	COMPLETE PREDICATE
The telephone		rang very loudly.

ADVERBS (↑ ↑ pointing to *very loudly*)

The lawyer answered **quickly.** [adverb *quickly* modifying the verb *answered*]

The student was **extremely** upset. [adverb *extremely* modifying adjective *upset*]

The student spoke **very quickly.** [adverb *very* modifying the adverb *quickly;* adverb *quickly* modifying the verb *spoke*]

Therefore, the lawyer spoke quietly. [adverb *therefore* modifying the independent clause *the lawyer spoke quietly*]

3   Recognizing appositives

An **appositive** is a word or group of words that renames the noun° or noun group preceding it. Most appositives are nonrestrictive, which means they are not necessary for identifying the noun being renamed. ❖ PUNCTUATION ALERT: Use a comma or commas to separate a nonrestrictive appositive° from what it renames. ❖

SENTENCE XI

THE SENTENCE

COMPLETE SUBJECT	**+**	**COMPLETE PREDICATE**
The victim, Joe Jones,		asked to speak to his lawyer.

↑
APPOSITIVE

The victim's story, **a tale of broken promises,** was complicated. [*A tale of broken promises* renames the noun *story.*]

SENTENCE XII

THE SENTENCE

COMPLETE SUBJECT	**+**	**COMPLETE PREDICATE**
The victim		asked to speak to his lawyer, Ms. Smythe.

↑
APPOSITIVE

The lawyer consulted an expert, **her law professor.** [*Her law professor* renames the noun *expert.*]

7m   Recognizing phrases

A **phrase** is a group of related words that does not contain a subject° or a predicate°. A phrase cannot stand alone as an indepen-

TEACHING TIP

Combining sentences by using modifiers and appositives can not only reduce repetition but also create more graceful statements. Students are sometimes surprised by what they produce when they are asked to combine several choppy sentences into a single effective one. For example, the following separate sentences, repetitious and boring, can be turned into a fluent one by combining them through the use of modifiers and appositives.

1. The president of the company resigned.

2. The president's name is Karen McCrae.

3. She resigned in protest against company policies.

4. She objected to the governing board's refusal to grant maternity leave to women employees.

5. She had been president of the company for seven years.

6. The company's name is General Services, Inc.

TEACHING TIP

Students sometimes feel that phrases are peculiar constructions invented by the writers of grammar books. As an antidote to this misconception, you might find it useful to reproduce and distribute copies of a newspaper article on a popular subject (e.g., Dear Abby or a sports column). Ask the students to identify noun phrases, verb phrases, and prepositional phrases. As absolute phrases rarely occur in informal writing, it is perhaps best to omit them from this assignment. Students will be amazed at how often phrases appear in "real" writing. Class discussion might next cover the functions of the noun phrases and prepositional phrases (subject, object, complement, adjective, adverb).

TEACHING TIP

Imitation can be an effective means of expanding students' sentence-writing strategies. You can provide some samples, asking students to write a sentence on another topic, following the pattern of clauses and phrases in the model. Here are some varied possibilities for imitation, though you may want to choose your own.

- For three thousand years, poets have been enchanted and moved and perplexed by the power of their own imagination.

  —Jacob Bronowski,
  "The Reach of Imagination"

- The sea, which looks so near and so tempting, is often difficult to reach.

  —Henry Miller, "The Big Sur"

- Hearing the rising tide, I think how it is pressing also against other shores I know—rising on a southern beach where there is no fog, but a moon edging all the waves with silver and touching the wet sands with lambent sheen, and on a still more distant shore sending its streaming currents against the moonlit pinnacles and the dark caves of the coral rock.

  —Rachel Carson, "The Enduring Sea"

A HUMOROUS NOTE

Dangling participial phrases can produce some unintended meanings, such as these:

- Plunging 1000 feet into the gorge, we saw Yosemite Falls.
- He rode his horse across Highway 12 and up and down the sidewalk in front of the saloon a good half hour before deputies arrived, shouting obscenities and being obnoxious.
- Locked in a vault for 50 years, the owner of the jewels has decided to sell them.

  Richard Lederer, *Anguished English*
  (Wyrick and Company, 1987)

dent unit. Phrases function as parts of speech. A **noun phrase** functions as a noun in a sentence.

> The **modern population census** dates back to the **seventeenth century.**

A **verb phrase** functions as a verb in a sentence.

> Two military censuses **are mentioned** in the Bible.
> The Romans **had been conducting** censuses every five years to establish tax liabilities.

A **prepositional phrase,** which always starts with a preposition°, functions as an adjective or an adverb.

> After the collapse **of Rome,** the practice was discontinued **until modern times.**
> William the Conqueror conducted a census **of landowners in newly conquered England in 1086.** [three prepositional phrases in a row]

An **absolute phrase** consists of a subject° and a participle°. It functions as a modifier° of the entire sentence to which it is attached.

> **Census-taking being the fashion,** Quebec and Nova Scotia took sixteen counts between 1665 and 1754.
> Eighteenth-century Sweden and Denmark had complete records of their populations, **each adult and child having been accounted for.**

A **verbal phrase** is a word group that contains a verbal. Verbals are infinitives°, present participles°, and past participles°. **Infinitive phrases** function as nouns or modifiers. An infinitive is the simple form° of a verb, usually preceded by the word *to,* but not always. (For more about the infinitive, see 8a-2.)

> In 1624, Virginia began **to count its citizens** in a census. [infinitive phrase = direct object]

Participial phrases function as adjectives°. Participial phrases can be formed from a verb's present participles (its *-ing* form) and from its past participle (the *-ed* form of a regular verb).

> **Going from door to door,** census takers interview millions of people. [participial phrase = adjective modifying *census takers*]
> **Amazed by some people's answers,** the census takers always listen carefully. [participial phrase = adjective modifying *census takers*]

Gerund phrases function as nouns. A gerund is the *-ing* form of a verb—its present participle.

200

The first U.S. census was conducted without **asking anyone's occupation, birthplace, marital status, or exact age.** [gerund phrase = object (noun) of preposition *without*]

Understanding the questions on a census is important. [gerund phrase = subject (noun)]

Telling the difference between a gerund phrase and a participial phrase using a present participle can be tricky because both use the *-ing* verb form. The key is to determine how the verbal phrase is functioning: a gerund phrase functions only as a noun, and a participial phrase functions only as a modifier.

Wanting to win the trivia contest was an obsession. [gerund phrase = noun used as the subject]

Wanting to win the trivia contest, Abby studied the faces of her opponents. [participial phrase = modifier used as adjective describing *Abby*]

EXERCISE 8

Combine each set of sentences into a single sentence, converting one sentence in each set into a phrase. Choose from among noun phrases, verb phrases, prepositional phrases, absolute phrases, infinitive phrases, participial phrases, and gerund phrases. You can omit, add, or change words. Most sets can be combined in several equally correct ways, but be sure to check that your combined sentence makes sense.

EXAMPLE   The word *chauvinism* comes from the name of Nicholas Chauvin, a retired French soldier. Chauvin was obsessed with Napoleon's greatness.

             The word *chauvinism* comes from the name of Nicholas Chauvin, a retired French soldier obsessed with Napoleon's greatness.

1. Chauvin was wounded in battle at least seventeen times. When he retired he received a medal, a ceremonial sword, and a pension of about $40.

2. Chauvin turned away from bitterness. He became a champion of Napoleon and France.

3. Napoleon was defeated. Chauvin became even more fanatical in his support.

4. Word of his hero worship spread beyond his village. Chauvin was used as a character in a comedy.

5. Other playwrights also used Chauvin as a character. That made his name synonymous with excessive dedication to one's country.

6. Many other words started out as someone's name. These include *sandwich* and *bloomer*.

BACKGROUND

Marilyn Sternglass, in "Sentence-Combining and the Reading of Sentences" (*College Composition and Communication,* 31 [1980], 325–28), maintains that sentence combining shows students how to cluster groups of words into phrases and clauses. This activity improves students' ability to recognize word groups as meaning-bearing units. She finds strong justification for including sentence-combining activities in writing classes, not only for their positive effect on writing skills, but also because they improve a student's ability to read sentences.

ANSWERS: EXERCISE 8

Answers may vary. For the instructor's information, each type of clause is identified. The example sentence is a participial phrase.

1. Wounded in battle at least seventeen times, Chauvin received a medal, a ceremonial sword, and a pension of about $40 when he retired. (participial phrase)

2. Chauvin turned away from bitterness *to champion Napoleon and France.* (infinitive phrase)

3. Napoleon having been defeated, Chauvin became even more fanatical in his support. (absolute phrase)

4. Word of his hero worship having spread beyond his village, Chauvin was used as a character in a comedy. (participial phrase)

5. Other playwrights' using Chauvin as a character soon made his name synonymous with excessive dedication to one's country. (gerund phrase)

6. Many other words, *including sandwich and bloomer,* started out as someone's name. (noun phrase)

(continued on next page)

QUOTATION ABOUT WRITING

A *dependent clause* is like a dependent child: incapable of standing on its own but able to cause a lot of trouble.

—William Safire, "About Language"

A HUMOROUS NOTE

Each year the number of children coming to the mall to see Santa Claus grew larger, so the store owners decided to hire additional Santas and station them around the mall. The most experienced Santa was in charge. He referred to the trainees as his "Subordinate Clauses."

7. Other words enter the language in other ways. Some words were originally slang. Some words have actually been voted into existence.

8. The number *googol* is a one followed by a hundred zeroes. Milton Sirotta made up the word when he was nine years old.

9. His mathematician uncle used the word in a book in 1940. It caught on.

10. The uncle was named Edward Kasner. He lived from 1878 to 1955.

7n Recognizing clauses

A **clause** is a group of words that contains a subject and a predicate. Clauses are divided into two categories: **independent clauses** (also known as **main clauses**) and **dependent clauses** (including **subordinate clauses** and **relative clauses**).

1 Recognizing independent clauses

An **independent** (or **main**) **clause** contains a subject° and a predicate°. It can stand alone as a sentence because it is an independent grammatical unit.

SENTENCE XIII		
THE SENTENCE		
INDEPENDENT CLAUSE		
COMPLETE SUBJECT	+	**COMPLETE PREDICATE**
The telephone		rang.

2 Recognizing dependent clauses

A **dependent clause** contains a subject° and a predicate° and usually starts with a word that makes the clause unable to stand alone as a sentence. A dependent clause must be joined to an independent clause°.

Some dependent clauses start with **subordinating conjunctions.** Each subordinating conjunction expresses a relationship between the meaning in the dependent clause and the meaning in the independent clause. See the chart in 7h for a complete list.

SENTENCE XIV				
THE SENTENCE				
DEPENDENT (ADVERB) CLAUSE		+	**INDEPENDENT CLAUSE**	
Although	the hour	was quite late,	the telephone	rang.
↑	↑	↑	↑	↑
SUBORDINATING CONJUNCTION	COMPLETE SUBJECT	COMPLETE PREDICATE	COMPLETE SUBJECT	COMPLETE PREDICATE

Most clauses that start with subordinating conjunctions function as adverbs. **Adverb clauses** modify verbs, adjectives, other adverbs, and entire independent clauses. Adverb clauses may appear in different parts of sentences, but they always begin with subordinating conjunctions. They usually answer some question about the independent clause: *how? why? when?* or *under what conditions?* ❖ PUNCTUATION ALERT: When an adverb clause comes before its independent clause, the clauses are usually separated by a comma. ❖

> **If the bond issue passes,** the city will install sewers. [The adverb clause modifies the verb *install;* it explains "under what conditions."]

> They are drawing up plans as quickly **as they can.** [The adverb clause modifies the adverb *quickly;* it explains "how."]

> The homeowners feel happier **because they know the flooding will soon be better controlled.** [The adverb clause modifies the adjective *happier;* it explains "why."]

Adjective clauses modify nouns and pronouns. Most adjective clauses start with relative pronouns or *when, where,* or *why.* Relative pronouns include *who, that, which, whom, whose, whoever, whomever, whichever, what,* and *whatever.* Adjective clauses beginning with a relative pronoun may also be called **relative clauses.**

The word starting an adjective clause refers to something—a specific antecedent°—in the independent clause.

> The car **that Jack bought** is practical. [The adjective clause describes the noun *car; that* refers to *car.*]

> The day **when I can buy my own car** is getting closer. [The adjective clause modifies the noun *day; when* refers to *day.*]

TEACHING TIP

According to Forrest Burt, who teaches writing at Texas A & M, sentence-combining "in reverse" can improve the syntactical fluency of students. He suggests giving them sentences to break into "kernels." Take, for instance, this sentence:

Appearing before the dour, skeptical judge, Henry Winston, a carpenter who had not worked for over three months, said that he hijacked the bakery truck because he wanted to feed his family.

Here is the sentence broken into its kernels:

- Henry Winston appeared before the judge.
- The judge was dour and skeptical.
- Henry Winston said SOMETHING.
- Henry Winston was a carpenter.
- Henry Winston had not worked for over three months.
- Henry Winston hijacked the bakery truck.
- Henry Winston wanted SOMETHING.
- Henry Winston feeds his family.

Here are sentences that Burt suggests using:

1. They intended to buy groceries when they came home from work, but when they saw the heavy, cold rain falling, they decided to take a taxi, which was standing on the corner.

2. The consequences of pedantic, cryptic, sometimes deceptive language are funny, unless efficient communication is the purpose for which we resort to language.

SENTENCE XV

THE SENTENCE

FIRST PART OF INDEPENDENT CLAUSE	DEPENDENT (ADJECTIVE) CLAUSE	SECOND PART OF INDEPENDENT CLAUSE
The red telephone,	**which** belonged to Ms. Smythe,	rang loudly.
COMPLETE SUBJECT	RELATIVE PRONOUN	COMPLETE PREDICATE

When you write adjective clauses, use *who, whom, whoever, whomever,* and *whose* when the antecedent° is a person or an animal with a name or a special talent.

> The Smythes, **who collect cars,** are wealthy.

> Their dog Bowser, **who is quite large,** likes to lean out the car window.

When you write adjective clauses, use *which* or *that* if the antecedent° is a thing or an animal. Either *which* or *that* begins restrictive° adjective clauses, and *which* begins nonrestrictive° ones.
❖ PUNCTUATION ALERT: When an adjective clause is nonrestrictive, use commas to separate it from the independent clause°. (A restrictive clause is essential to limit meaning; a nonrestrictive clause is nonessential. See 24e for more information.) ❖

> The car **that I want to buy** has a cassette player.

> The car **which I want to buy** has a cassette player. [The adjective clause is restrictive, and so either *that* or *which* may be used.]

> My current car, **which I bought used,** needs major repairs. [The adjective clause is nonrestrictive, so it begins with *which* and is set off with commas.]

Sometimes, *that* can be omitted from a sentence. For purposes of grammatical analysis, however, the omitted *that* is considered to be implied and therefore present.

> The car [that] **I buy** will have to get good mileage.

Often the word *that* makes a sentence easier to understand. Be sure to use *that* when it makes your writing clearer.

> Pat Smythe saw **that** Dale Smythe, along with her dog, was not in the car.

EXERCISE 9

Underline the dependent clauses. Write (ADJ) at the end of adjective clauses and (ADV) at the end of adverb clauses.

EXAMPLE   The scientists who discovered disease-carrying bacteria (ADJ) did so in the second half of the nineteenth century (ADV).

1. The bacteria that led to typhoid fever and cholera were spread when water was contaminated by solid human waste.
2. Sewers were built so that water supplies could be protected.
3. Waste water pipes from the sewers were connected to storm drainage systems, which took the waste to distant rivers.
4. The people who constructed these systems believed this practice to be safe because a river can purify itself.
5. They were wrong because the rivers cannot renew themselves as quickly as we can pollute them.

Noun clauses function as subjects°, objects°, or complements°. Noun clauses begin with many of the same words as adjective clauses: *that, who, which,* and their derivatives, as well as *when, where, whether, why,* or *how.* Noun clauses do not *modify.* They replace a noun with a clause.

> **Promises** are not always dependable. [noun]
> **What politicians promise** is not alway dependable. [noun clause]
> The electorate often cannot figure out the **truth.** [noun]
> The electorate often cannot know **what the truth is.** [noun clause]

Because they start with similar words, it is easy to confuse noun clauses and adjective clauses. A noun clause *is* a subject°, object°, or complement°. An adjective clause *modifies* a subject°, object°, or complement°. The word starting an adjective clause has an antecedent° in the sentence. The word that starts a noun clause does not.

> Politicians understand **whom they must please.** [noun clause = direct object; *whom* does not need an antecedent here]
> Politicians **who make promises** sometimes fail to keep them. [adjective clause modifying *politicians; politicians* is the antecedent of *who*]

Elliptical clauses are grammatically incomplete for the deliberate purpose of concise prose. The elliptical clause gets its name from the word *ellipsis,* meaning "omission." An elliptical clause delivers its meaning only if the missing elements can be filled in from context. Commonly omitted in an elliptical clause are the relative pronouns *that, which,* or *whom* in adjective clauses, the subject and verb in adverb clauses, and the second half of a comparison.

ANSWERS: EXERCISE 9

1. The bacteria *that led to typhoid fever and cholera*[ADJ] were spread *when water was contaminated by solid human waste*[ADV].

2. Sewers were built *so that water supplies could be protected*[ADV].

3. Waste water pipes from the sewers were connected to storm drainage systems *which took the waste to distant rivers*[ADJ].

4. The people *who constructed these systems*[ADJ] believed this practice to be safe *because a river can purify itself*[ADV].

5. They were wrong *because the rivers cannot renew themselves*[ADV] as quickly *as we can pollute them*[ADV].

TEACHING TIP

Elliptical clauses: To enhance students' appreciation of their options, you might ask them whether they prefer the elliptical or full forms of the text's sentences—and why. Here are alternate examples to use also.

- Living in Spain was one of the best experiences [that] Carol had during college. When [she was] living with a family in Spain, Carol started to feel like a native. Air travel is faster than sea [travel].

- James Naismith, [who was] a Presbyterian minister, believed that through athletics he could teach lessons in Christian ideals. After [he had graduated from] divinity school, Naismith enrolled in the School for Christian Workers, [which] later [became] known as the International YMCA Training School. Naismith, [who was] a young man full of ideas, was given the job of devising a game that had less running and tackling than other ball games [had]. Limited indoor space and the hard surface of a wooden floor were two of the biggest problems [that] he faced. The game [that] he devised is known today as basketball.

Engineering is one of the majors **[that] she considered.** [relative pronoun omitted]

After **[he was granted]** a retrial, he was released. [subject and verb omitted]

Broiled fish tastes better **than boiled fish [tastes].** [second half of the comparison omitted]

EXERCISE 10

Combine each of the following pairs of sentences using some of the subordinating conjunctions and relative pronouns from this list. Some pairs may be combined in a variety of ways. Create at least one elliptical clause. Subordinators may be used more than once, but try to use as many different ones as possible.

which	because	of which	since	if
while	as	how	that	although

EXAMPLE Famine occurs. Insects or rodents destroy crops or stored food.

When insects or rodents destroy crops or stored food, famine occurs.

1. Destruction of crops has been a problem for ages. The human race has an equally long history of trying to eliminate pests.
2. The earliest pesticides were not very effective. The earliest pesticides included sulfur, lead, mercury, and arsenic.
3. We now realize something. These original pesticides are poisonous.
4. They accumulate in the soil. They can limit or stop plant growth.
5. Some pests develop immunity to the chemicals. The pests are never completely destroyed.
6. The surviving pests reproduce quickly, passing on resistant genes. A new generation of resistant pests takes the place of those killed.
7. New pesticides are manufactured organic chemicals. The most famous is DDT, dichlorodiphenyltrichloroethane.
8. No one thought about something. DDT would contaminate and threaten the entire planet.
9. Some birds have trouble forming eggs. DDT accumulates in them.
10. In 1971 a special committee began reviewing pollutants. DDT was one.

---

70 Recognizing sentence types

Sentences can be **simple, compound, complex,** and **compound-complex.**

ANSWERS: EXERCISE 10

Answers to this exercise will vary somewhat. Below is one set of possibilities. Note that the directions require students to write at least one elliptical clause.

1. While destruction of crops has been a problem for ages, the human race has an equally long history of trying to eliminate pests.

2. The earliest pesticides, which included sulfur, lead, mercury, and arsenic, were not very effective. (An elliptical alternative is: Not very effective, the earliest pesticides included sulfur, lead, mercury, and arsenic.)

3. We now realize that these original pesticides are poisonous. (An elliptical alternative is to drop *that.*)

4. If they accumulate in the soil, they can limit or stop plant growth.

5. Because some pests develop immunity to the chemicals, the pests are never completely destroyed.

6. Since the surviving pests reproduce quickly, passing on resistant genes, a new generation of resistant pests takes the place of those killed.

7. New pesticides are manufactured organic chemicals of which the most famous is DDT, dichlorodiphenyltrichloroethane.

8. No one thought about how DDT would contaminate and threaten the entire planet. (An elliptical alternative is to drop *about how.*)

9. Some birds have trouble forming eggs because DDT accumulates in them.

10. In 1971 a special committee began reviewing pollutants, of which DDT was one.

gr **70**

1 Recognizing simple sentences

A **simple sentence** is composed of a single independent clause° with no dependent clauses°. It has one subject° and one predicate° (either or both may be compound). It can contain modifying words or phrases.

> Charlie Chaplin was born in London on April 16, 1889.
>
> He specialized in pantomime and became famous for his character "The Tramp."

2 Recognizing compound sentences

A **compound sentence** is composed of two or more independent clauses°. These clauses may be connected by a coordinating conjunction (*and, but, for, or, nor, yet,* or *so*). Use a comma before a coordinating conjunction connecting two independent clauses.

> His father died early, **and** his mother often had to spend time in mental hospitals.

Use a semicolon in compound sentences without a coordinating conjunction or with a conjunctive adverb.

> Chaplin lived in orphanages or boarding schools; sometimes he left them to perform in theaters.
>
> Many people enjoy Chaplin films; **however,** some critics dislike his work.

3 Recognizing complex sentences

A **complex sentence** is composed of one independent clause° and one or more dependent clauses°. When a dependent clause comes before its independent clause, the clauses are usually separated by a comma.

> **When times were bad,** Chaplin lived in the streets. [dependent clause starting *when;* independent clause starting *Chaplin*]
>
> **When Chaplin was performing with a troupe which was touring the United States,** he was hired by Mack Sennett, **who owned the Keystone Comedies.** [dependent clause starting *when;* dependent clause starting *which;* independent clause starting *he;* dependent clause starting *who*]

TEACHING TIP

The class discussion of compound sentences may be a good time to review compounding of all sorts. A series of examples to show compound subjects, objects, verbs, adjectives, adverbs, phrases, and clauses may help your students see the compound sentence as the final step in a logical progression.

John F. Kennedy and Richard M. Nixon were the candidates in the 1960 presidential election. [compound subject] Kennedy won the election because of his popularity in *the South and the East.* [compound object of preposition] Many people admired *his energy and his wholesomeness.* [compound object] He *made* respected cabinet appointments *and sponsored* far-sighted legislation. [compound verb] The first months of his administration were *smooth-running and successful.* [compound adjectives] However, the period *quickly and unexpectedly* came to an end. [compound adverbs] There were many successes: *establishment of the Alliance for Progress to aid Latin America, increased foreign aid to underdeveloped nations, the development of the Peace Crops, and reduced tariffs to encourage foreign trade.* [compound noun phrases] *Yet within a few months, an attempt by Cuban exiles to invade Cuba failed, Communist forces expanded their operations in Laos and Vietnam, and the East Germans built the Berlin Wall.* [compound independent clauses, which comprise a compound sentence]

This is probably also a good time to point out the difference between sentences such as these:

John F. Kennedy was President of the United States and a hero to many young people. [compound subject complement] John F. Kennedy was President of the United States, *and he was* a hero to many young people. [compound sentence]

BACKGROUND

Professor Joe R. Christopher, Tarleton State University, responded to my invitation in the first edition of this text to send in material for the second edition. He writes:

> In addition to the simple, compound, complex, and compound-complex sentences usually listed in handbooks, there is one idiomatic pattern which is acceptable as an English sentence but which does not fit any of these patterns very comfortably; it may be considered a variation of the compound sentence, but the comparative forms it uses and the appearance of a comma without a conjunction make it an oddity.

Thus, this less common construction used to create balanced sentences joins independent clauses with a comma but without a conjunction. It yields an interdependent, comparative structure. Here are a few examples based on what Professor Christopher sent in:

- The higher he climbed, the thinner the air became.
- The closer the coyote approached, the more Louisa and Frank were mesmerized by its eyes.
- The more miles the trip [takes], the more exhausted you feel.

ANSWERS: EXERCISE 11

1. complex	6. simple
2. compound	7. simple
3. compound	8. complex
4. complex	9. compound-complex
5. compound	10. simple

---

4   **Recognizing compound-complex sentences**

A **compound-complex sentence** joins a compound sentence (70-2) and a complex sentence (70-3). It contains two or more independent clauses° and one or more dependent clauses°.

Chaplin's comedies were immediately successful, **and** his salaries were huge **because of the enormous popularity of his tramp character, who was famous for his tiny mustache, baggy trousers, big shoes, and trick derby.** [independent clause starting *Chaplin's*; independent clause starting *his salaries*; dependent clause starting *because*; dependent clause starting *who*]

Once studios could no longer afford him, Chaplin co-founded United Artists, **and** then he was able to produce and distribute his own films. [dependent clause starting *Once*; independent clause starting *Chaplin*; independent clause starting *then he was able*]

EXERCISE 11

Identify each sentence as simple, compound, complex, or compound-complex.

EXAMPLE   The teachings of Voltaire, Montesquieu, and Rousseau contributed to the French Revolution. (simple)

1. Each helped to convince middle-class French intellectuals that the monarchy was corrupt and that they could create a better government.
2. Voltaire considered many social institutions insensitive; his favorite target was the Catholic Church.
3. Voltaire saw the Church as narrow-minded and unsympathetic to the people, so he sought its elimination from politics.
4. The Baron de Montesquieu was a political theorist who traveled all over Europe studying various governments.
5. Montesquieu popularized the English system of checks and balances among the branches of governement, and this ideal was adopted as a model by the writers of the American constitution.
6. He also argued that people should select their form of government, an idea of appeal to the French as well as the Americans.
7. Jean Jacques Rousseau saw humanity as pure and good.
8. Rousseau, who was born in Switzerland but lived in France, believed that children are born in a natural and unspoiled state but that civilization corrupts people.

9. Because of private ownership of property, people become selfish, and they must be taught to act for the common good.

10. Rousseau's ideas have had a strong impact on modern socialist and communist thought.

EXERCISE 12

Combine each set of sentences into a sentence of the type given in parentheses.

EXAMPLE Nine people were killed in London on October 17, 1814. A vat in a brewery burst, releasing 3,500 barrels of beer. (complex)

Nine people were killed in London on October 17, 1814, *when* a vat in a brewery burst, releasing 3,500 barrels of beer.

1. The neighborhood was flat. Runoff accumulated in the basements of local buildings. (complex)

2. Rescuers had to wade through waist-high beer. No one got drunk. (compound)

3. A flood of molasses killed 21 people in Boston. This happened in 1919. (simple)

4. The Food and Drug Administration (FDA) allows cola makers to keep "essential ingredients" secret. Rival companies have to rely on chemists to try to duplicate secret formulas. (complex)

5. The original secret ingredient of Coca-Cola was known to fewer than ten people. That ingredient made up less than one percent of the drink. (complex)

6. The original secret ingredient in Seven Up was lithium carbonate. Lithium carbonate is now used to treat severe manic depressive behavior. (complex).

7. Seven Up was a big success during the Depression. Some people suggest something. The suggestion is that Seven Up was popular during the Depression because lithium had a calming effect that people very much needed during those hard times. (compound-complex)

8. In the 1940s lithium was taken out of Seven Up. Lithium was restricted by the FDA. The drink remains a favorite today. (compound-complex)

9. Coffee is popular throughout the world today. It was unknown in most countries just a few hundred years ago. (compound)

10. Venetian traders introduced coffee to Europe. It became popular there in the sixteenth and seventeenth centuries. (complex)

ANSWERS: EXERCISE 12

Answers will vary somewhat. Here is one set of possibilities.

1. Because the neighborhood was flat, runoff accumulated in the basements of local buildings.

2. Rescuers had to wade through waist-high beer, but no one got drunk.

3. A flood of molasses killed 21 people in Boston in 1919.

4. Because the Food and Drug Administration (FDA) allows cola makers to keep "essential ingredients" secret, rival companies have to rely on chemists to try to duplicate secret formulas.

5. The original secret ingredient of Coca-Cola, which was known to fewer than ten people, made up less than one percent of the drink.

6. The original secret ingredient in Seven Up was lithium carbonate, which is now used to treat severe manic depressive behavior.

7. Seven Up was a big success during the Depression, and some people suggest that this was so because lithium had a calming effect that people very much needed during those hard times.

8. In the 1940s lithium was taken out of Seven Up because it was restricted by the FDA, but the drink remains a favorite today.

9. Coffee is popular throughout the world today, but it was unknown in most countries just a few hundred years ago.

10. Venetian traders introduced coffee to Europe, where it became popular in the sixteenth and seventeenth centuries.

8 Verbs

Verbs convey information about what is happening, what has happened, and what will happen. In English, a verb tells of an action *(eat, wrestle, argue),* an occurrence *(become, change, happen),* or a state of being *(be, seem, feel, exist).*

> The earth **rotates** on its axis approximately every twenty-four hours. [action]
> Mother's Day **falls** on the second Sunday in May. [occurrence]
> The cockroach still **exists** after hundreds of millions of years. [state of being]

Verbs do more work than this, however. Verbs convey information through their changes in form.

INFORMATION VERBS CONVEY	
PERSON	who or what acts or who or what experiences an action—the **first person** (the one speaking), the **second person** (the one being spoken to), or the **third person** (the person or thing being spoken about)
NUMBER	how many subjects act or experience an action—**one** (singular) or **more than one** (plural)
TENSE	when an action occurs—in the **past, present,** or **future;** see 8f-8j
MOOD	what attitude is expressed toward the action—**indicative, imperative,** or **subjunctive;** see 8k-8l
VOICE	whether the subject acts or is acted upon—the **active voice** or the **passive voice;** see 8m-8n

VERB FORMS

8a   Recognizing the forms of main verbs

A verb usually changes form by adding an ending *(change, changes, changing, changed)*. Some verbs change forms more extensively *(eat, ate, be, is)*. A **main verb** names an action, an occurrence, or a state of being: *earth **rotates**, Mother's Day **fell**, the cockroach **existed**.* Main and **auxiliary verbs** (see 8d) together form **verb phrases.**

> The earth **is rotating** on its axis. [*is* = auxiliary verb; *rotating* = main verb; *is rotating* = verb phrase]

1   Identifying a main verb's three principal parts

Every main verb has three principal parts: a **simple form,** a **past tense,** and a **past participle.** The simple form is also called the **dictionary form** (because it is the form given first in the dictionary entry for a verb) and the **base form.** The simple form shows action, occurrence, or state of being that is taking place in the present. The simple form is also the basis for the future tense (I will *learn,* they will *go*).

The **past-tense** form indicates an action or occurrence or state of being completed in the past. The past tense of all regular verbs adds final *-ed* or *-d* to the simple form. Many verbs, however, are irregular, which means that their past-tense forms either change in spelling or make use of different words (instead of adding *-ed* or *-d*): *sing, **sang, sung;** go, **went, gone.*** For the principal parts of common irregular verbs, see the chart in 8c-2.

The **past participle** in regular verbs uses the same form as the past tense. In many irregular verbs, these forms differ. For ease in handling the language, writers need to memorize the principal parts of irregular verbs (see the chart in 8c-2.). To function as a verb, a past participle must combine with an auxiliary verb (see 8d) in a **verb phrase.**

> They were startled. [*were* = auxiliary verb; *startled* = past participle; *were startled* = verb phrase]

Used alone, past participles function as adjectives, modifying nouns or pronouns: *crumbled* cookies, *fallen* trees. Alone, a past participle can never function as a verb.

separate issue, and so is *voice*. A verb can show all four qualities, but you might want to focus on the interplay of tense and aspect first.

It may be useful to go over a chart, such as the one below, with your students, discussing the possible uses of each tense.

TO LOVE

Time	Form	Tense
present	love	simple present
	am, is, are loving	present progressive
	loved	simple past
past	was, were loving	past progressive
	has, have loved	present perfect
	had loved	past (or pluperfect)
	has, have been loving	present perfect prog.
	had been loving	past (or pluperfect) prog.

Time	Form	Tense
future	will love	future
	will be loving	future progressive
	will have loved	future perfect
	will have been loving	future perfect prog.

WORD HISTORY

Infinitive comes from the Latin *infinitivus,* meaning *unlimited* or *indefinite.* This is appropriate, since the infinitive shows no person or number. Coming from the same Latin verb, *finire (to limit),* the term *finite verb* refers to a verb that is limited by person and number. In contrast, a *nonfinite verb* (also known as a *verbal*) is not limited in these ways.

TEACHING TIP

Leaving the *-s* off verbs is a common error, even among students who can quote the rule for its use. Many of these students speak or have studied second languages that have much more complex systems of verb endings. A discussion of the English *-s* in the context of other languages the students know may reduce the number of carelessly omitted *-s*'s. You can let students know, jokingly, that anyone who accurately writes and speaks French, Spanish, or Italian and still

---

2 Recognizing present participles and infinitives

Verbs also have a **present participle.** It is formed by adding *-ing* to the simple form: *eating, falling, learning.* Like the past participle, the present participle needs an auxiliary verb to function as a verb.

> The sun **was setting.** [*was* = auxiliary verb; *setting* = present participle]

Used alone, a present participle functions as an adjective (a *diving* board, the *boiling* broth, a *thinking* person) or a noun (*swimming* is fun; *leaving* can be painful). When it functions as a noun, a present participle is called a **gerund.** Alone, a present participle can never function as a verb.

The **infinitive** is another verb form that functions as a noun or an adjective but not as a verb. Infinitives use the simple form and usually, but not always, *to.*

> **To dance** is my dream. [*to dance* = infinitive functioning as noun subject°]
>
> We expected you **to leave.** [*to leave* = infinitive as noun object°]
>
> We heard you **leave.** [*leave* = infinitive, without *to,* as noun object°]

Participles and infinitives functioning as nouns or modifiers are called **verbals.** They are also called **nonfinite verbs,** in contrast to **finite verbs. Finite verbs** are the verb forms that convey information about tense, mood, voice, person, and number (see chart in opening section of this chapter) while they deliver meaning about an action, occurrence, or state of being.

8b Using the *-s* form of verbs

The *-s* (and *-es*) form of verbs deserves special attention because of its central role in subject–verb agreement (see Chapter 11). The *-s* form of a verb occurs in the third-person singular in the present tense. The *-s* ending is added to a verb's simple form: *love, loves; kiss, kisses.*

> The **rabbit travels** faster than the tortoise.
>
> **She chooses** a rapid pace.
>
> The slow **one,** however, often **wins** the race.

Be and *have* do not use their simple forms in the third-person singular of the present tense. Instead, *be* uses *is* and *have* uses *has*.

The **rabbit is** unarguably quick.

The **tortoise has** more stamina.

Some dialects of spoken English use forms such as *he be, the rabbit have* for third-person singular in the present tense. Academic writing requires *is* and *has*. Also, if you tend to drop the *-s* or *-es* ending when you speak, you may forget to use it when you write. Be sure to proofread your writing to make sure you have used the *-s* form correctly (see 11a).

EXERCISE 1

Rewrite each sentence, changing the subject to the word given in parentheses. Change the form of the verb to match this new subject. Keep all sentences in the present tense.

EXAMPLE   In many cultures, shamans heal the sick. (a shaman)

In many cultures, *a shaman heals* the sick.

1. They also protect the community from danger. (he)
2. They cure patients by calling on supernatural powers. (he)
3. Some shamans are extremely rich. (The shaman)
4. Some shamans have great political power. (The shaman)
5. Shamanism still exists in societies of the far north, such as those in Siberia, Alaska, and Canada. (Shamans)

8c Recognizing regular and irregular verbs

A **regular verb** forms its past tense and past participle by adding *-ed* or *-d* to the simple form (8a-1). Most verbs in English are regular.

SIMPLE FORM	PAST TENSE	PAST PARTICIPLE
enter	entered	entered
smile	smiled	smiled

Some English verbs are **irregular.** They form the past tense and past participle in a number of different ways.

SIMPLE FORM	PAST TENSE	PAST PARTICIPLE
bring	brought	brought
swim	swam	swum

doesn't bother to keep track of "one little *-s*" is too strange to be believed.

Here is a comparison of the verb *speak* (present tense) in four languages, with endings shown in boldface. When no pronouns are given, the pronoun is communicated by the verb's ending.

ENGLISH

Singular	*Plural*
I speak	we speak
you speak	you speak
he, she, it speaks	they speak

SPANISH

hablo	hablamos
hablas	habláis
habla	hablan

ITALIAN

parlo	parliamo
parli	parlate
parla	parlano

FRENCH

je parle	nous parlons
tu parles	vous parlez
il, elle, on parle	ills, elles parlent

ANSWERS: EXERCISE 1

1. He also protects
2. He cures
3. The shaman is
4. The shaman has
5. Shamans still exist

COVERAGE: EXERCISE 1

1. change from plural subject to singular;
2. change from plural subject to singular;
3. change from plural subject to singular;
4. change from plural subject to singular;
5. change from singular subject to plural.

1 | **Forming the past tense and past participle of a regular verb by adding *-ed* or *-d***

Adding *-ed* or *-d* to the simple form makes the past tense and past participle of any regular verb. Some verbs that end in a vowel followed by a consonant double the consonant before adding *-ed*: *occur, occurred; transfer, transferred.* Others do not: *label, labeled; focus, focused.* Many are spelled either way: *travel, traveled, travelled; program, programed, programmed.* You can confidently follow the preferred spelling shown in an up-to-date college dictionary.

Regular verbs ending in *-y* are more consistent. If the final two letters of the simple form are a vowel followed by *y*, simply add *-ed*: *obey, obeyed; display, displayed.* If the final two letters are a consonant followed by *y*, change the *y* to *i* before you add *-ed*: *spy, spied; reply, replied.* For more about spelling verbs, see Chapter 22.

Speakers sometimes skip over the *-ed* sound in the past tense, hitting it lightly or not at all. If you are unused to hearing or pronouncing this sound, you may forget to add it when you write the past tense and past participles. Be sure to proofread your writing for *-ed* endings.

No	He **promise** to pay me by Tuesday.
Yes	He **promised** to pay me by Tuesday.
No	We were **suppose** to study for class today.
Yes	We were **supposed** to study for class today.

EXERCISE 2

Rewrite each sentence, changing the italicized verb to the past tense.

EXAMPLE   The religious beliefs of many agricultural societies *include* the worship of family and tribal ancestors.

The religious beliefs of many agricultural societies *included* the worship of family and tribal ancestors.

1. In these societies, extended family groups often *own* the land.
2. Ancestor worship *stabilizes* social and economic relationships.
3. It *provides* continuity from generation to generation.
4. It *strengthens* family structures.
5. The belief that long-dead family members *participate* in daily life *creates* a bond between generations.

2 | **Memorizing the principal parts of irregular verbs**

About two hundred of the most common verbs in English are **irregular:** They do not add *-ed* or *-d* to form the past tense and past participle. Some irregular verbs change an internal vowel to make past tense and past participle: *sing, sang, sung.* Some change an internal vowel and add an ending other than *-ed* or *-d; grow, grew, grown.* Some use the simple form throughout: *read, read, read.*

Unfortunately, a verb's simple form provides no clue about whether the verb is irregular or regular. If you do not know the principal parts of a verb you are using, you can find them in a college dictionary. Most college dictionaries use the simple form for the dictionary entry, listing after it the past-tense form and the past participle only if the verb is irregular. If only the simple form is given, you will know the verb is regular and adds *-ed* or *-d.*

Although you can always look up the principal parts of any verb, memorizing them is much more convenient in the long run. The following chart lists most of the common irregular verbs.

BACKGROUND

Old English, ancestor of our language as we know it today, used only two tenses, present and past. All other information, such as number, person, mood, and voice, was indicated by inflectional endings. All that remains of the personal endings is the *-es* or *-s* of the third person singular, which comes from an earlier *-eth* used by Chaucer, translators of the King James Bible, and Shakespeare. English verbs, like all their Germanic cognates, are distinguished by their division into weak and strong classes. In Old English the strong classes indicated tense by changing the medial vowels; the weak ones did so by their endings. After the Norman Invasion, when French and Latin became the languages of power (the court and the church), many strong English verbs became weak, adopting the *-ed* ending to indicate tense changes. New verbs admitted to the language were all placed in the weak category. Today the mixture of strong and weak forms makes it necessary for English speakers to memorize the principal parts of irregular verbs.

COMMON IRREGULAR VERBS

SIMPLE FORM	PAST TENSE	PAST PARTICIPLE
arise	arose	arisen
awake	awoke *or* awaked	awaked *or* awoken
be (is, am, are)	was, were	been
bear	bore	borne *or* born
beat	beat	beaten
become	became	become
begin	began	begun
bend	bent	bent
bet	bet	bet
bid (offer)	bid	bid
bid (command)	bade	bidden
bind	bound	bound
bite	bit	bitten *or* bit
blow	blew	blown
break	broke	broken
bring	brought	brought
build	built	built
burst	burst	burst
buy	bought	bought
cast	cast	cast
catch	caught	caught
choose	chose	chosen
cling	clung	clung

(continued on next page)

EXAMPLE: VERBS IN CONTEXT

Despite the popular idea that the human brain *is* a very delicate organ, scientific evidence *indicates* that the brain *can continue* functioning even after much of it *has been damaged* or even when as much as half of it *has been removed* by surgery. It *seems* that although brain functions *are* localized, sometimes other parts of the brain *take* over the work of damaged or removed areas. Even in cases where half the brain *was removed* in order to control life-threatening seizures, people *were* able to live normal lives. In fact, in one case removal of the right half of the brain *led* to an increase of over twenty points in a patient's IQ (as reported when he *was tested* fifteen years later). Apparently loss of the right half of the brain *did* not *interfere* with his ability to think and learn, and removal of the diseased area *allowed* him to live free from distracting seizures. We *do* not *know* how the brain *compensates* for such losses, but researchers *hope* they *will find* an answer soon.

COMMON IRREGULAR VERBS *(continued)*

SIMPLE FORM	PAST TENSE	PAST PARTICIPLE
come	came	come
cost	cost	cost
creep	crept	crept
cut	cut	cut
deal	dealt	dealt
dig	dug	dug
dive	dived *or* dove	dived
do	did	done
draw	drew	drawn
drink	drank	drunk
drive	drove	driven
eat	ate	eaten
fall	fell	fallen
feed	fed	fed
feel	felt	felt
fight	fought	fought
find	found	found
flee	fled	fled
fling	flung	flung
fly	flew	flown
forbid	forbade *or* forbad	forbidden
forget	forgot	forgotten *or* forgot
forgive	forgave	forgiven
forsake	forsook	forsaken
freeze	froze	frozen
get	got	got *or* gotten
give	gave	given
go	went	gone
grow	grew	grown
hang (suspend)*	hung	hung
have	had	had
hear	heard	heard
hide	hid	hidden
hit	hit	hit
hurt	hurt	hurt

*When it means to execute by hanging, *hang* is a regular verb: "In wartime, armies routinely **hanged** deserters."

COMMON IRREGULAR VERBS *(continued)*

SIMPLE FORM	PAST TENSE	PAST PARTICIPLE
keep	kept	kept
know	knew	known
lay	laid	laid
lead	led	led
leave	left	left
lend	lent	lent
let	let	let
lie	lay	lain
light	lighted *or* lit	lighted *or* lit
lose	lost	lost
make	made	made
mean	meant	meant
pay	paid	paid
prove	proved	proved *or* proven
quit	quit	quit
read	read	read
rid	rid	rid
ride	rode	ridden
ring	rang	rung
rise	rose	risen
run	ran	run
say	said	said
see	saw	seen
seek	sought	sought
send	sent	sent
set	set	set
shake	shook	shaken
shine (glow)*	shone	shone
shoot	shot	shot
show	showed	shown *or* showed
shrink	shrank	shrunk
sing	sang	sung
sink	sank	sunk
sit	sat	sat
slay	slew	slain
sleep	slept	slept

*When it means to polish, *shine* is a regular verb: "We **shined** our shoes."

(continued on next page)

ALTERNATE EXAMPLE: VERBS IN CONTEXT

Cities, like people, *have* personalities. Some of them *have acquired* their character through a long, gradual period of growth. Other *are* still *developing* their "image." London, for example, *has* for centuries *been* a center of banking and power. After its period of empire, Rome *developed* as a religious center, and Florence *had been known* for its artists and craftsmen long before the settlement of the New World. American cities, on the other hand, *have* less history but no less distinctive personalities. Even the first-time visitor *will* easily *distinguish* between New York and Los Angeles. The climatic differences alone *have resulted* in contrasting cultures. One aspect that all cities *share,* however, *is* the need for urban planning for the twenty-first century. By that time problems of transportation, air quality, and housing *will require* solutions not yet devised. By that time it *will have become* necessary to protect the environment so that humanity itself *will be surviving.*

COMMON IRREGULAR VERBS *(continued)*

Simple Form	Past Tense	Past Participle
sling	slung	slung
speak	spoke	spoken
spend	spent	spent
spin	spun	spun
spring	sprang *or* sprung	sprung
stand	stood	stood
steal	stole	stolen
sting	stung	stung
stink	stank *or* stunk	stunk
stride	strode	stridden
strike	struck	struck
strive	strove	striven
swear	swore	sworn
sweep	swept	swept
swim	swam	swum
swing	swung	swung
take	took	taken
teach	taught	taught
tear	tore	torn
tell	told	told
think	thought	thought
throw	threw	thrown
understand	understood	understood
wake	woke *or* waked	waked *or* woken
wear	wore	worn
wring	wrung	wrung
write	wrote	written

EXERCISE 3

In each blank, write the correct past-tense form of the verb in parentheses. Use the list of irregular verbs on pages 000–000.

EXAMPLE   The colorful butterflies (begin) _____ to arrive a few at a time in November.

The colorful butterflies *began* to arrive a few at a time in November.

1. As the month of November (wear) _____ on, millions of black, white, and orange flocks of monarch butterflies (fly) _____ through the sky.

2. Scientists (know) _____ that the monarch butterfly (have) _____ been migrating between Canada and Mexico for more than ten thousand years.

3. Zoologists visiting from the University of Florida (rise) _____ early to observe the migration of these butterflies.

4. In 1975, the scientists (find) _____ evidence suggesting that monarch butterflies might be threatened by the destruction of the Mexican forests for farmland.

5. A group concerned about the monarchs (seek) _____ help from the Mexican government, which in 1980 (take) _____ legal steps to protect the butterflies.

6. Laws were passed that (make) _____ it illegal to establish agricultural development in or around the monarch retreats.

7. The laws also (forbid) _____ logging, an industry essential to many local residents.

8. Conservation groups (understand) _____ the peasants' concerns and (begin) _____ looking for ways to help these people.

9. For example, scientists (seek) _____ ways to improve production of crops that (grow) _____ on existing farmland.

10. Also, residents of the area (lead) _____ tours of sightseers through the regions.

ANSWERS: EXERCISE 3

1. wore, flew
2. knew, had
3. rose
4. found
5. sought, took
6. made
7. forbade
8. understood, began
9. sought, grew
10. led

8d   Recognizing *be, do, have,* and other auxiliary verbs

The verbs *be, do,* and *have* deserve special attention because their different forms are quite irregular in form. The forms are shown in the boxes on the opposite page. For an explanation of the name of each form (simple form, etc.), see 8a and 8c.

Auxiliary verbs, also called **helping verbs,** are forms of *be, do, have* and others. Auxiliary verbs combine with main verbs to make **verb phrases.**

The sun **is shining** today. [*is* = auxiliary verb; *shining* = main verb; *is shining* = verb phrase]

The verb *be,* along with its various forms, is also a **linking verb.** It joins a subject to its subject complement (a word or group

WORD HISTORY

An *auxiliary verb* is also called a *helping verb,* and, not surprisingly, *auxiliary* comes from *auxiliarius,* a Latin word for *help.* Linking verbs were, until recently, often called *copulative verbs.* This usage dates back to the seventeenth century and comes from the Latin *copulativus,* meaning *connective.*

TEACHING TIP

Although *to be* is always a linking verb, others verbs may or may not be, depending upon how they are used in a given sentence. When in doubt, try substituting a form of *to be:* If the sentence makes sense, it contains a linking verb; if it no longer makes sense, it does not contain a linking verb.

He *seems* ill./He *is* ill.[The *to be* verb makes sense, so *seems* is a linking verb.]

Daisies *grow* in the park./Daisies *are* in the park.[The *to be* verb makes sense, so *grow* is a linking verb.]

Joyce *grows* orchids./Joyce *is* orchids. [The *to be* verb does not make sense, so *grows* is not a linking verb.]

WORD HISTORY

The word *conjugation* has been used since the early sixteenth century to refer to all the forms of a particular verb. *Conjugation* and *conjugate* both come from the Latin *conjugāre,* basically meaning *to join together.* In Latin, a list of the forms of a verb was called a *conjugatio,* and *conjugata verba* (literally *joined words*) referred to words that were etymologically related.

THE FORMS OF *BE*

SIMPLE FORM	be
PAST TENSE	was, were
PAST PARTICIPLE	been
-s FORM	is
PRESENT PARTICIPLE	being

PERSON	PRESENT TENSE	PAST TENSE
I	am	was
you (singular)	are	were
he, she, it	is	was
we	are	were
you (plural)	are	were
they	are	were

THE FORMS OF *DO* AND *HAVE*

SIMPLE FORM	do	SIMPLE FORM	have
PAST TENSE	did	PAST TENSE	had
PAST PARTICIPLE	done	PAST PARTICIPLE	had
-s FORM	does	-s FORM	has
PRESENT PARTICIPLE	doing	PRESENT PARTICIPLE	having

of words that renames the subject). When *be* functions as a linking verb, it takes on the role of a **main verb** (see 8a), rather than being an auxiliary verb.

The sun **is** a source of light. [*sun* = subject; *is* = linking verb; *source of light* = subject complement]

❖ USAGE ALERT: **Academic writing requires standard forms and uses of *be*.** ❖

No	He driving his car to work. [missing *be* form]
No	He **be** driving his car to work. [nonstandard *be* form]
Yes	He **is** driving his car to work. [standard form of *be* supplied]

The verbs *can, could, may, might, should, would, must,* and *ought to* are called **modal auxiliary verbs.** Modal auxiliary verbs have only one form; they do not change, no matter what constructions they appear in.

I, you, he, she, it, we, you, they
- can
- could
- may
- might
- should
- would
- must
- ought to

Modal auxiliaries add to the main verb a sense of needing, wanting, or having to do something, a sense of possibility, likelihood, obligation, permission, or ability.

Exercise **can lengthen** lives. [possibility]

The exercise **must occur** regularly. [requirement]

Most of us **should take** better care of our bodies. [obligation]

May I exercise? [permission]

She **can** jog for five miles. [ability]

EXERCISE 4

Using auxiliary verbs from the list below, fill in the blanks. For some sentences, more than one correct answer is possible, but use each auxiliary verb only once.

      are   can   may   must   should   will

EXAMPLE   When firefighters search the scene of a fire, they _____ first find where the fire originated.

            When firefighters search the scene of a fire, they *must* first find where the fire originated.

1. In searching for the point of origin, a keen investigator _____ look for the telltale signs of arson.

2. For example, there _____ be evidence that the fire had multiple points of origin, or *streamers,* trails of gasoline that were used to spread the fire from area to area.

3. The discovery of containers that _____ hold an accelerant is another clue.

Identify all modal auxiliaries in the following passage. (Answers are in italics.)

Most professionals in the field of medicine agree that the public *ought to* be better informed about recent developments in medical science. One of the tools that patients frequently experience but *may* know little about is the X-ray. Its discoverer, Professor Wilhelm Roentgen, thought he *might* have a powerful new means of examining the body when, in 1895, he saw the glimmer of a fluorescent screen. His discovery meant that mankind *could* peer into the innermost recesses of the body without surgery. For example, Dr. William B. Cannon realized that fluoroscopy *could* be used to examine the alimentary canal or digestive system. Today X-ray means that doctors *can* carry diagnostic methods to previously inaccessible areas of the human body by painless techniques. To enumerate all of the diagnostic uses of X-ray films *would* be too lengthy to include here, but it is safe to say that they *can* be used on all parts of the body. Of course, because improper use of X-rays *may* be harmful, technologists *should* have adequate training. They *must* complete a rigorous course of study before being allowed to operate X-ray machines.

ANSWERS: EXERCISE 4

Answers may vary slightly. A possible set is:

1. will
2. may
3. can
4. are
5. should

4. Ignition devices, from a simple candle to complex electronic mecha-nisms, _____ convincing evidence of arson.

5. Investigators _____ also look for signs of breaking and entering or theft.

ANSWERS: EXERCISE 5

Answers may vary slightly. A possible set is:

1. were
2. can
3. do
4. may
5. have

EXERCISE 5

Using each of the auxiliary verbs listed below just once, fill in the blanks. For some sentences, more than one correct answer is possible. Use up all the words by the end of the exercise.

do   may   will   can   have   were

EXAMPLE   Maintaining an aquarium may seem complicated, but if you follow a few simple steps, you _____ find it rather easy.

Maintaining an aquarium may seem complicated, but if you follow a few simple steps, you *will* find it rather easy.

1. The first pet fish were probably goldfish, which _____ kept captive in China over a thousand years ago.

2. You _____ forget the stresses and strains of everyday life as you watch your fish swim about.

3. Fish are unlike any other pets because they _____ not make noise, eat much, or scratch the furniture.

4. Landlords who prohibit other pets _____ permit people to have aquar-iums.

5. Fish thrive when they _____ been placed in a relatively roomy tank.

A HUMOROUS NOTE

The English major was working for the sum-mer as morning shift manager at a fast-food restaurant. One day her least reliable worker was missing again. She called over a friend of the boy and asked, "Where's Bill?"

"He decided to lay on the beach," replied the friend.

Not wishing to embarrass the worker but unable to overcome the urge to correct him the manager whispered, "Lie."

"All right," he said with a shrug, "Bill had to take his cat to the vet for an emergency appendectomy."

8e **Using intransitive and transitive verbs correctly, especially *sit* and *set*, *lie* and *lay*, *rise* and *raise***

Many verbs are both **intransitive** and **transitive**; other verbs are only one or the other. A verb is intransitive when it does not need an object (see 7k) to complete its meaning: *I **sing** loudly.* A verb is transitive when it needs an object to complete its meaning: *I **sing** a song.*

Three important pairs of verbs, which happen to look and sound very much alike, are not so flexible. In these pairs—*sit* and *set*, *lie* and *lay*, *rise* and *raise*—one verb is intransitive, the other transitive. If you do not already know the forms of these verbs, memorize them.

COMPARISON OF INTRANSITIVE AND TRANSITIVE VERBS

INTRANSITIVE (NO OBJECT)	TRANSITIVE (WITH AN OBJECT)
The cat **sees** in the dark. [*In the dark* is not a direct object; it is a modifier°.]	The cat **sees** the dog. [*dog* = direct object]
I can **hear** well. [*Well* is not a direct object; it is a modifier°.]	I can **hear** you. [*you* = direct object]
We **teach** tomorrow. [*Tomorrow* is not a direct object; it is a modifier°.]	We **teach** French. [*French* = direct object]

SUMMARY OF FORMS FOR *SIT, LIE, RISE,* AND *SET, LAY, RAISE*

INTRANSITIVE (NO OBJECT)

SIMPLE FORM	PAST TENSE	PAST PARTICIPLE	-*s* FORM	PRESENT PARTICIPLE
sit	sat	sat	sits	sitting
lie	lay	lain	lies	lying
rise	rose	risen	rises	rising

TRANSITIVE (WITH AN OBJECT)

SIMPLE FORM	PAST TENSE	PAST PARTICIPLE	-*s* FORM	PRESENT PARTICIPLE
set	set	set	sets	setting
lay	laid	laid	lays	laying
raise	raised	raised	raises	raising

To *sit* means to seat oneself; to *set* means to place something else down. The word *straight* is a modifier°, not a direct object.

INTRANSITIVE

PRESENT TENSE	I **sit** straight.
PAST TENSE	I **sat** straight.

QUOTATION ABOUT WRITING

You lie down, you lay down, and you've lain down; whenever you die, you'll be laid to rest.

—Mary Ellen Thornton

QUOTATIONS ABOUT WRITING

Here lies a man who was killed by lightning;
He died when his prospects seemed to be brightening.

—Anonymous

Here lies the body of Ann Mann,
Who lived to be an old woman
And died an Old Mann.

—Anonymous

QUOTATION ABOUT WRITING

True ease in writing comes from art, not chance,
As those move easiest who have learned to dance.
'Tis not enough no harshness gives offense,
The sound must seem an echo to the sense.

—Alexander Pope

EXTRA EXERCISE B

Circle all transitive verbs and underline all intransitive verbs in the following paragraph.

1. Yellowstone National Park is the oldest and largest park in the national system.

2. It lies in the northwestern corner of Wyoming, slightly overlapping the boundaries of Montana on the north and Idaho on the west and south.

3. The planners originally designed the park to run 62 miles east-west and 54 miles north-south.

4. Yellowstone has several lofty plateaus, and the Continental Divide crosses it.

5. The Yellowstone River flows north into Yellowstone Lake, then through its canyon across Montana to joint the Missouri.

6. The most famous sights in Yellowstone Park are the geysers.

7. The park has more than 3,000 springs, pools and geysers.

8. Old Faithful is the most famous of the geysers, but in the same basin with it are a number of other impressive water jets.

9. Wildlife in the park, which includes bear, deer, elk, antelope, and mountain sheep, is protected.

10. The magnificent evergreen forests, severely damaged by fire in the summer of 1988, are beginning to sprout again.

ANSWERS: EXTRA EXERCISE B

1. is (intransitive)
2. lies (intransitive)
3. designed (transitive)
4. has (transitive); crosses (transitive)
5. flows (intransitive)
6. are (intransitive)
7. has (transitive)
8. is (intransitive); are (intransitive)
9. includes (transitive); is (intransitive)
10. are (intransitive)

TRANSITIVE	
PRESENT TENSE	I **set** the books down every day.
PAST TENSE	I **set** the books down yesterday.

The word *books* is a direct object. *Set* also has one specialized intransitive meaning—the passing of a celestial body below the horizon: *The sun set.*

To *lie* means to recline or place oneself down or to remain; to *lay* means to place something down. The word *down* is a modifier°, not a direct object. The word *tiles* is a direct object.

INTRANSITIVE	
PRESENT TENSE	Vern **lies** down for a nap.
PAST TENSE	Vern **lay** down for a nap.

TRANSITIVE	
PRESENT TENSE	Vern **lays** tiles in the kitchen.
PAST TENSE	Vern **laid** tiles in the kitchen.

Note that the word *lay* is both the past tense of *lie* (intransitive) and the present tense simple form of *lay* (transitive).

> The hikers **lay** down to rest. [Here *lay* is present tense and intransitive.]
> The hikers **lay** their backpacks against the rocks. [Here *lay* is past tense and transitive.]

To *rise* means to stand up, get up out of bed, or elevate oneself in some other way or to ascend; to *raise* is to lift up or elevate someone or something else. The phrase *at six o'clock* is a modifier°, not a direct object.

INTRANSITIVE	
PRESENT TENSE	Lee **rises** every morning at six o'clock.
PAST TENSE	Lee **rose** every morning at six o'clock.

The word *cup* is a direct object.

TRANSITIVE	
PRESENT TENSE	Lee **raises** the cup high.
PAST TENSE	Lee **raised** the cup high.

EXERCISE 6

Select the appropriate verb from each pair in parentheses.

EXAMPLE   One day I was (laying, lying) on my towel at the beach.

            One day I was *lying* on my towel at the beach.

1. When I woke up after a nap, I (raised, rose) my head and saw the sun (sitting, setting) in the east.
2. I was about to (lay, lie) down again when it occurred to me that the sun (rises, raises) in the east and (sets, sits) in the west.
3. So I (lay, laid) my book down and (rose, raised) myself into a (sitting, setting) position.
4. As I (set, sat) there surrounded by sand and the (raising, rising) surf, I thought about this puzzling situation.
5. I had (lain, laid) down for a nap in the late afternoon as the humidity was (raising, rising), but something was now wrong.
6. Then an idea (rose, raised) out of my subconscious.
7. I now (sat, set) with the water in front of me, while before my nap it had (laid, lain) at my back. The sun had not changed positions during my nap: I had.

ANSWERS: EXERCISE 6

1. raised; setting
2. lie; rises; sets
3. laid; raised; sitting
4. sat; rising
5. lain; rising
6. rose
7. sat; lain

COVERAGE: EXERCISE 6

1. transitive; intransitive
2. intransitive; intransitive; intransitive
3. transitive; transitive; participle
4. intransitive; participle
5. intransitive; participle
6. intransitive
7. intransitive; intransitive

VERB TENSE

8f   Understanding verb tense

Tense conveys when the action, occurrence, or state of being expressed by a verb takes place. Verbs express time. They do this by changing form. Time changes are indicated by the addition of final *-ed* or *-d* to the simple form° of the verb; by the use of auxiliary verbs°; and by other form changes.

English has six verb tenses, divided into simple and perfect groups. The three **simple tenses** divide time into present, past, and future. The **present tense** describes what is happening, what is true at the moment, and what is consistently true: *Rick **wants** to speak Spanish fluently.* The **past tense** tells of an action completed or a condition ended: *He **wanted** to improve rapidly.* The **future tense** indicates action yet to be taken or a condition not yet experienced: *Next year Rick **will want** to progress even further.*

The three **perfect tenses** also divide time into present, past, and future. They show more complex time relationships than do the simple tenses (see 8h).

225

SUMMARY OF TENSES—INCLUDING PROGRESSIVE FORMS

SIMPLE TENSES

	REGULAR VERB	IRREGULAR VERB	PROGRESSIVE FORM
PRESENT	I talk	I eat	I am talking; I am eating
PAST	I talked	I ate	I was talking; I was eating
FUTURE	I will talk	I will eat	I will be talking; I will be eating

PERFECT TENSES

	REGULAR VERB	IRREGULAR VERB	PROGRESSIVE FORM
PRESENT PERFECT	I have talked	I have eaten	I have been talking; I have been eating
PAST PERFECT	I had talked	I had eaten	I had been talking; I had been eating
FUTURE PERFECT	I will have talked	I will have eaten	I will have been talking; I will have been eating

All six verb tenses also have **progressive forms.** These forms show an ongoing or continuing dimension to whatever the verb describes (see 8i).

8g Using the simple present tense correctly

The **simple present tense** uses the simple form of the verb (see 8a-1). It describes what is happening, what is true at the moment, and what is consistently true. It also has special functions, summarized in the chart below.

8h Using the perfect tenses correctly

The **perfect tenses** use the past participle (see 8c) together with auxiliary verbs. The **perfect tenses** generally describe actions

SUMMARY OF USES FOR THE SIMPLE PRESENT TENSE

■ **DESCRIBING WHAT IS HAPPENING NOW, IN THE PRESENT**

They **work** efficiently.
The gale **rattles** the windows.

■ **DESCRIBING A HABITUAL OR REGULARLY OCCURRING ACTION**

The accounting class **meets** at 10:00 on Tuesdays.
Horror movies **give** him nightmares.

■ **EXPRESSING A GENERAL TRUTH OR WIDELY HELD OPINION**

A kilogram **is** roughly 2.2 pounds.
Good fences **make** good neighbors.

■ **DESCRIBING A FIXED-TIME FUTURE EVENT**

The semester **ends** on May 30.
The ship **leaves** port at midnight.
His birthday **falls** on a Sunday this year.

■ **DISCUSSING "TIMELESS" EVENTS AND ACTIVITIES**

Jay Gatsby **wants** it all.
Laurel and Hardy repeatedly **get** into trouble.
Einstein **speaks** of matter as something that **is** interchangeable with energy.

---

or occurrences that have already been completed or that will be completed before a more recent point in time.

The **present perfect tense** shows that action begun and completed in the past also continues—or its effects continue—into the present.

Our government **has offered** to help. [action completed but condition still in effect]

Severe drought **has created** terrible hardship for the people of Africa. [condition completed and still prevailing]

I **have** always **believed** in freedom of speech. [condition true once and still true]

The **past perfect tense** indicates that an action was completed before another one took place. When two actions both started and stopped in the past, the earlier action uses *had* as a helper.

EXTRA EXERCISE D

What meanings are expressed by use of the present tense in the following statements?

EXAMPLE
One yard is equal to thirty-six inches. (It is a fact, true in the past, present, and future.)

1. December 21 is the shortest day of the year.

2. My employer works every weekend.

3. We are going to my grandmother's house for Christmas.

4. She is to assume her duties as college president the first of the month.

5. The rain is beating against the windows.

6. Hamlet postpones his revenge throughout the five acts of the play.

7. A stitch in time saves nine.

8. Passover comes in three weeks.

9. Shakespeare's plays entertain audiences of all ages and cultures.

10. College students learn that they must be serious about their studies.

ANSWERS: EXTRA EXERCISE D

1. stating a general truth
2. describing habitual action
3. describing a fixed-time future event
4. describing a fixed-time future event
5. describing what is happening now
6. discussing "timeless" events
7. stating a general truth
8. describing a fixed-time future event
9. describing a "timeless" activity
10. describing a regularly occurring action

EXTRA EXERCISE E

Identify each verb that takes the past tense or a perfect tense in the following paragraph. (Answers are in italics.)

Embroidery *has been* a popular form of needlework since earliest history. The earliest pieces of embroidery still extant *were produced* in Egypt during the sixteenth century B.C. Fragments of Greek origin from the fourth century B.C. *have been found* in the Crimea. The oldest known Chinese embroideries *were done* in chain stitch, but Turkish pieces from the same period (200 B.C.–220 A.D.) show several complex stitches as well as applique and patchwork. Clearly, ancient peoples all over the world *produced* elaborate embroidery of great richness and elaboration.

In the early medieval period in Europe the finest embroideries *must have been* those made at Constantinople. Some other pieces from that time *have been found* in the tomb of St. Cuthbert at Durham, England. One of the most famous works of the Middle Ages is the Bayeux tapestry, which *was produced* around the end of the eleventh century. Since the Renaissance, European embroidery *has been* of three main types: peasant embroidery (colorful and produced to be used), amateur embroidery (complicated but not useful), and professional embroidery (works of art).

Embroidery *had* always *been employed* for the decoration of garments, but from the sixteenth to the nineteenth century it *was used* far more extensively than it *has been* in the present century. Whereas it *had been used* to decorate ecclesiastical garments, with the Renaissance it *became* a means of ornamenting carpets, bookbindings, gloves, and shoes as well. Upholstered furniture is still sometimes embroidered, though not as often as it once *was*.

The first embroidery machine *was invented* in 1829. With its appearance, embroidered products that *had been* exclusively handmade *became* industrial products.

The tornado **had** barely passed when the town **was hit** by heavy rain.

The **future perfect tense** indicates that an action will be complete before some specified or predictable time.

World population **will have reached** 8 billion by the year 2000.

8i Using the progressive form of each tense correctly

The **progressive form** uses the present participle (the *-ing* form) of the verb together with auxiliary verbs. The progressive form shows that an action or condition is ongoing. This continuing action or state is not infinite, however. Sometimes the sentence itself states an explicit time.

The **present progressive** indicates something taking place at the time it is written or spoken about.

The damp weather **is making** her knee ache.

Many doctors **are studying** why damp weather leads to pains in joints.

The **past progressive** shows the continuing nature of past action, sometimes within stated or implied limits.

Computers **were selling** well this Christmas season.

The demand for software programs **was growing** fast until last week.

The **future progressive** shows that a future action will continue for some time. Often, this future action depends on another action or condition stated in the sentence.

Because more people **are starting** families, we will be expecting more buyers to shop for larger houses.

The **present perfect progressive** describes something ongoing in the past that is likely to continue in the future.

The baby **has been crying** ever since his parents brought him home.

The child's fears **have been growing** steadily.

The **past perfect progressive** describes an ongoing condition in the past that has been ended by something stated in the sentence.

The musicians **had been practicing** long hours before the performance.

The **future perfect progressive** describes an action or condition ongoing until some specific future time.

> In May, our college's radio station **will have been operating** for twenty years.

EXERCISE 7

Select the verb in parentheses that best suits the meaning. If there is more than one possible answer, be prepared to explain the differences in meaning among them.

EXAMPLE   Most people (caught, will catch) a cold sometime during the next year.

Most people *will catch* a cold sometime during the next year.

1. A recent poll (reveals, has been revealing) that 82 percent of people (believe, will be believing) kissing spreads colds.
2. Fortunately, this belief (proves, has been proven) false.
3. Doctors at a large New York medical center recently (conduct, conducted) research concerning the common cold.
4. They interviewed hundreds of people who (had been catching, had caught) a cold during the previous year.
5. The researchers concluded that cold viruses are most likely to be communicated when a person (has, will have had) hand contact with someone who is sick.
6. People who conscientiously (wash, are washing) their hands significantly (reduce, are reducing) the danger of catching a cold.
7. Through various tests and observations, doctors (discover, have discovered) that exposure to cold weather (does, did) not make a person (catch, have been catching) a cold.
8. During the past decade, the American economy (loses, has lost) more than five million dollars per year from lost wages and medical expenses due to the common cold.
9. Unfortunately, no cure (has been discovered, will have been discovered) for this persistent illness.
10. By the time a miracle drug (has been found, was being found), millions of Americans (are spending, will have spent) millions of dollars in trying to relieve their miseries.

8j   Using verbs in accurate tense sequences

Sequences often include more than one verb, and these verbs often refer to actions taking place at different times. Showing the right time relationship—that is, using **accurate tense sequences**—

EXTRA EXERCISE F

Supply the progressive form of an appropriate verb in the blanks in the following sentences. (Answers will vary.)

1. Don't bother me now; I am _____.
2. My brother is _____ to apply for a job in France.
3. The committee is _____ at 5 P.M.
4. The professor was _____ on the topic of the European Common Market.
5. The doctor was _____ in the hospital.
6. My dog was _____ in the yard.
7. I can't go swimming because I am _____.
8. The garden is _____ more beautifully every day.
9. Whose car is _____ in the driveway?
10. The telephone has been _____ all day.

ANSWERS: EXERCISE 7

1. reveals; believe
2. has been proven
3. conducted
4. had caught
5. has
6. wash; reduce
7. have discovered; does; catch
8. has lost
9. has been discovered
10. has been found; will have spent

COVERAGE: EXERCISE 7

1. present; present
2. present perfect
3. past
4. past perfect
5. present
6. present; present
7. present perfect; present; present
8. present perfect
9. present perfect
10. present perfect; future perfect

EXTRA EXERCISE G

Circle the verbs in the following sentences, then name their tenses and explain what meaning is expressed by them.

1. Dolphins, porpoises, and whales belong to the order Cetacea, which are not fish, but mammals.

2. They give birth to their young, nourish them with milk, and have warm blood.

3. Once whales probably lived on the land and walked on four legs, but now they are completely aquatic.

4. Once they had left the land and moved to the water, their body structure changed radically.

5. Because they are land mammals that have become adapted to an aquatic existence, if water enters their lungs, they will die.

6. Consequently, when a whale is diving beneath the surface, it literally holds its breath by closing its nostrils.

7. Whales dive for different periods of time to various depths.

8. The humpback whale has been known to remain submerged for twenty minutes and the blue whale for fifty, though both could probably remain longer if necessary.

9. For years scientists have been researching the depths to which the various types of whale can dive.

10. The sperm whale has been known to dive to a depth of over 3000 feet, subjecting it to a pressure of around 1,400 pounds per square inch.

SUMMARY OF SEQUENCE OF TENSES

WHEN INDEPENDENT-CLAUSE VERB IS IN THE SIMPLE PRESENT TENSE, FOR THE DEPENDENT-CLAUSE VERB:

■ Use the present tense to show same-time action.

> The director **says** that the movie **is** a tribute to Chaplin.
> I **avoid** shellfish because I **am** allergic to them.

■ Use the past tense to show earlier action.

> I **am** sure that I **deposited** the check.

■ Use the present perfect tense to show a period of time extending from some point in the past to the present.

> They **claim** that they **have visited** the planet Venus.

■ Use the future tense for action to come.

> The book **is** open because I **will be reading** it later.

WHEN INDEPENDENT-CLAUSE VERB IS IN THE PAST TENSE, FOR THE DEPENDENT-CLAUSE VERB:

■ Use the past tense to show earlier action.

> I **ate** dinner before you **offered** to take me out for pizza.

■ Use the past perfect tense to show earlier action.

> The sprinter **knew** she **had broken** the record.

■ Use the present tense to state a general truth.

> Christopher Columbus discovered that the world **is** round.

WHEN INDEPENDENT-CLAUSE VERB IS IN THE PRESENT PERFECT OR PAST PERFECT TENSE, FOR THE DEPENDENT-CLAUSE VERB:

■ Use the past tense.

> The agar plate **has become** moldy since I **poured** it last week.
> Sugar prices **had** already **declined** when artificial sweeteners first **appeared.**

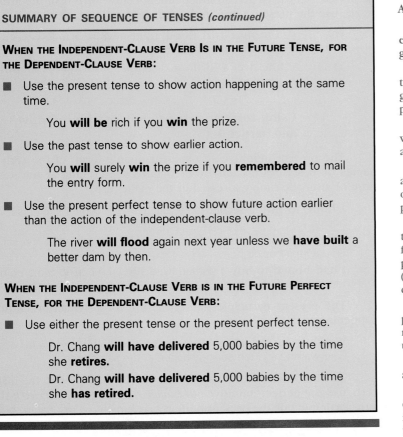

SUMMARY OF SEQUENCE OF TENSES *(continued)*

WHEN THE INDEPENDENT-CLAUSE VERB IS IN THE FUTURE TENSE, FOR THE DEPENDENT-CLAUSE VERB:

■ Use the present tense to show action happening at the same time.

> You **will be** rich if you **win** the prize.

■ Use the past tense to show earlier action.

> You **will** surely **win** the prize if you **remembered** to mail the entry form.

■ Use the present perfect tense to show future action earlier than the action of the independent-clause verb.

> The river **will flood** again next year unless we **have built** a better dam by then.

WHEN THE INDEPENDENT-CLAUSE VERB IS IN THE FUTURE PERFECT TENSE, FOR THE DEPENDENT-CLAUSE VERB:

■ Use either the present tense or the present perfect tense.

> Dr. Chang **will have delivered** 5,000 babies by the time she **retires.**
> Dr. Chang **will have delivered** 5,000 babies by the time she **has retired.**

ANSWERS: EXTRA EXERCISE G

1. belong (present tense, expresses a general truth); are (present tense, expresses a general truth)

2. give (present tense, expresses a general truth); nourish (present tense, expresses a general truth); have (present tense, expresses a general truth)

3. lived (past tense, expresses past event); walked (past tense, expresses past event); are (present tense, expresses current fact)

4. had left (past perfect tense, expresses an act completed in the past before another one took place); changed (past tense, expresses an act completed in the past)

5. are (present tense, expresses current truth); have become adapted (present perfect tense, act begun and completed in the past but continuing into the present); enters (present tense, expresses general truth); will die (future tense, expresses future action)

6. is diving (present progressive tense, expresses an action taking place at the moment); holds (present tense, expresses regularly occurring action)

7. dive (present tense, expresses habitual action)

8. has been known (present perfect tense, expresses action in the past which continues into the present); could remain (present tense with modal auxiliary, expresses possible action)

9. have been researching (present perfect progressive, expresses action ongoing in the past and likely to continue in the future); can dive (present tense with modal auxiliary, expresses possible action)

10. has been known (present perfect tense, expresses action in the past which continues into the present)

is important. Always check tense sequences carefully in your writing to be sure that your sentences are delivering accurate meaning about the actions, occurrences, and states you intend those verbs to express.

1   Using accurate tense sequences in complex sentences

Complex sentences use dependent clauses° as well as independent clauses°. The tense of the verb in an independent clause determines the possibilities for verb tense in that sentence's dependent clauses. See the chart opposite and above for a summary of sequences of tenses.

EXTRA EXERCISE H

Select the verb in parentheses that best suits the meaning. If there is more than one possible answer, be prepared to explain the differences in meaning.

EXAMPLE

In the United States in 1964, only 64.4 percent of the eligible voters (turned, had turned, were turning, had been turning) out to vote. In the United States in 1964, only 64.4 percent of the eligible voters *turned* out to vote.

1. By the 1970 congressional elections, this figure (fell, had fallen, was falling, had been falling) to about 50 percent.

2. The figure (remained, has remained, will have remained) at about 50 percent through the mid-1980s.

3. These low turnouts (compare, are comparing, have been comparing) poorly to the voting records of many other countries.

4. The USSR (leads, has led, has been leading) the world, with an impressive 99.6 percent reported voter turnout.

5. Many other countries (had, have had, were having) voter turnouts of over 95 percent, including Czechoslovakia, East Germany, and Hungary.

6. Many other countries (require, are requiring, have been requiring) their citizens to vote.

7. Of the countries that require their citizens to vote, however, only the Netherlands (ranks, is ranking, has been ranking) in the top twenty countries, at 92.1 percent.

8. In Argentina, despite mandatory voting, fewer people (vote, have been voting, are voting) than in the United States.

9. Some authorities say that Americans cannot vote because they are at work, and these authorities (have suggested, had suggested, had been suggesting) that voting take place on Sundays.

(continued page 241)

❧ USAGE ALERT: **When an independent-clause verb is in the future tense, use the present tense in the dependent clause.** ❧

No   The river **will flood** again next year unless we **will build** a better dam.

YES   The river **will flood** again next year unless we **build** a better dam.

2	Using correct tense sequences with infinitives and participles

The present infinitive—*to* and the simple form° of the verb—names or describes an activity or occurrence coming at the same time or after the time expressed in the main verb.

> I **hope to buy** a second-hand car. [*To buy* comes later than the hoping.]
>
> I **hoped to buy** a second-hand car. [*To buy* comes at the same time as the hoping.]
>
> I **had hoped to buy** a second-hand car. [The hoping came before the attempt to buy.]

The present participle—a verb's *-ing* form—describes action happening at the same time.

> **Walking** into his office, the detective **saw** his car keys on his desk. [The walking and the seeing happen at the same time.]

To describe an action that occurs before the action in the main verb, use the perfect infinitive *(to have eaten, to have worried)*; the past participle°; or the present perfect participle *(having eaten, having worried)*.

> Candida **is said to have written** fifty short stories in college. [The perfect infinitive *to have written* comes earlier in time than the saying.]
>
> **Pleased** with the short story, Candida **sent** it off to several magazines. [The past participle *pleased* comes earlier in time than the mailing.]
>
> **Having sold** one short story, Candida **invested** in a word processor. [The perfect participle *having sold* comes earlier in time than the investing.]

EXERCISE 8

Select the verb form in parentheses that best suits the sequence of tenses. Be prepared to explain your choices.

EXAMPLE   Over seventy-five years ago, after Albert Schweitzer left Europe, he (traveled, had traveled) up the Ogooue River in Africa.

Over seventy-five years ago, after Albert Schweitzer left Europe, he *traveled* up the Ogooue River in Africa.

1. The Ogooue is a vast, brown waterway that (stretched, stretches) across the central African wilderness.
2. Schweitzer had been traveling for many days when he (had come, came) to a small village.
3. He (had been seeing, saw) that the natives (have not been receiving, had not been receiving) proper health care.
4. Even though Schweitzer anticipated difficulties, he (establishes, established) a jungle clinic.
5. When Schweitzer died at age ninety, he (was providing, had been providing) medical treatment to the native population for over fifty years.
6. Today visitors to the clinic (learned, learn) that many changes (had been made, have been made) over the years.
7. For example, a few years ago an electrical link with the nearest city (has allowed, allowed) the staff to shut down the noisy generators that (have been providing, had been providing) all the clinic's power.
8. Impressed by Schweitzer's work, European and American donors (gave, had given) money for five new buildings, which were completed in the late 1970s.
9. Although nearly everyone admires Schweitzer, he (has been criticized, had been criticized) for ignoring preventive medicine.
10. Doctors presently at the clinic (planned, plan) to address this issue by giving workshops on nutrition and hygiene.

EXERCISE 9

The verbs in each of the following sentences are in correct sequence. For each sentence, change the main verb as directed in the parentheses. Then adjust dependent verbs, infinitives, or participles if necessary to maintain correct verb sequence. Some sentences may have several correct answers.

EXAMPLE   The resemblance of electric sparks and lightning flashes led some people to believe they were the same. (Change *led* to *leads*.)

The resemblance of electric sparks and lightning flashes *leads* some people to believe they *are* the same.

ANSWERS: EXERCISE 8

1. stretches
2. came
3. saw; had not been receiving
4. established
5. had been providing
6. learn; have been made
7. allowed; had been providing
8. gave
9. has been criticized
10. plan

COVERAGE: EXERCISE 8

Independent Clause

1. present
2. past perfect progressive
3. past
4. past
5. past perfect progressive
6. present
7. past
8. past
9. present perfect
10. present (followed by infinitive)

Dependent Clause

1. present
2. past
3. past perfect progressive
4. past
5. past
6. present perfect
7. past perfect progressive
8. past
9. present
10. (none)

ANSWERS: EXERCISE 9

1. For lightning to have occurred, there must have been a great electrical pressure caused by large opposite charges on the clouds and the earth.

2. In most storms, the earth will have a positive charge and the low-lying clouds will have a negative charge.

3. The electrical charges involved can be so tremendous that lightning flashes of five miles from cloud to earth, or of ten miles from cloud to cloud, can occur frequently.

4. The thunderclap that follows the flash is caused by inrushing air, creating a partial vacuum that sucks in the surrounding air.

5. Ben Franklin's lightning rod works by providing an easy way for the lightning's charge to reach the ground, bypassing the building itself.

1. For lightning to occur, there must be a great electrical pressure caused by large opposite charges on the clouds and the earth. (Change *to occur* to *to have occurred.*)

2. In most storms, the earth has a positive charge and the low-lying clouds have a negative charge. (Change *has* to *will have.*)

3. The electrical charges involved are so tremendous that lightning flashes of five miles from cloud to earth, or of ten miles from cloud to cloud, occur frequently. (Change *are* to *can be.*)

4. The thunderclap that followed the flash was caused by inrushing air, creating a partial vacuum that sucked in the surrounding air. (Change *followed* to *follows.*)

5. Ben Franklin's lightning rod worked by providing an easy way for the lightning's charge to reach the ground, bypassing the building itself. (Change *worked* to *works.*)

MOOD

8k Understanding mood

Mood refers to the ability of verbs to convey a writer's attitude toward a statement. The most common mood in English is the **indicative mood.** It is used for statements about real things, or highly likely ones, and for questions about fact.

> **INDICATIVE**   The door opened.
>
>   In walked the student.
>
>   Do you need a tutor?

The **imperative mood** expresses commands and direct requests. It always uses the simple form° of the verb. When the subject is omitted in an imperative sentence—and it often is—the subject is assumed to be either *you* or the indefinite pronouns *anybody, somebody,* or *everybody.* ❖ PUNCTUATION ALERT: A strong command is followed by an exclamation point; a mild command is followed by a period (see 23a). ❖

> **IMPERATIVE**   Please shut the door.
>
>   Fasten your seatbelts.
>
>   Watch out!

The **subjunctive mood** expresses conditions including wishes, recommendations, indirect requests, and speculations. The subjunctive mood is used less often in English than it once was.

SUBJUNCTIVE   Whether it be now or later, he must eventually pay his tax bill.

But many people now use the indicative to express the same idea:

INDICATIVE   Whether he does it now or later, he must eventually pay his tax bill.

Sooner or later, he must pay his tax bill.

81   Using correct subjunctive forms

For the **present subjunctive,** use the simple form of the verb (see 8a-1) for all persons° and numbers°.

The prosecutor asks that **she testify** [not *testifies*] again.
It is important that **she be** [not *is*] prepared.

For the **past subjunctive,** use the same form as the simple past tense: *I wish that I had* a car. The one exception is that the past subjunctive of *be* is *were* for all persons and numbers.

I wish that **I were** [not *was*] leaving on vacation today.
They asked if **she were** [not *was*] leaving on vacation today.

1   Using the subjunctive in *if* clauses and some *unless* clauses for speculations or conditions contrary to fact

In dependent clauses introduced by *if* and sometimes by *unless,* use the subjunctive to describe speculations or conditions contrary to fact.

If **my party were** [not *was*] in power, we would run the city well.
If **it were** [not *was*] to rain, voter turnout would be low.

In an *unless* clause, the subjunctive signals that what the clause says is very unlikely.

Unless *war were* [not *was*] to break out, the elections will be held on Tuesday.

Not every clause introduced by *if* requires the subjunctive. Use the subjunctive only when an *if* clause describes a speculation or condition contrary to fact.

INDICATIVE   If she is going to leave late, I **will** drive her to the train station.

SUBJUNCTIVE   If she were going to leave late, I **would** drive her to the train station.

BACKGROUND

William Safire recently quoted Robert Burchfield, overseer of the new four-volume *Oxford English Dictionary,* on the supposed death of the subjunctive mood: " 'This very useful verbal distinction is not at all tottering toward extinction.' " Safire adds:

> If it were not for the subjunctive, we would be less able to express desire, supposition, doubt; more important, we would find it hard to set up a situation contrary to fact—a shocker, something ridiculous—to see how we would deal with it.

Then he gives a complex but thought-provoking example:

> A law professor testified at a recent Congressional hearing that Senator John C. Danforth's product-liability bill "reads as though it were written by James Joyce." Obviously, the bill was not written by the long-dead author of the punctuation-disdaining novel "Ulysses," which meant that the witness's don't-you-believe-it subjunctive *were* was necessary; if the indicative, here-comes-a-fact *was* had been used, hordes of illiterate legislators would have been led to assume that James Joyce was a Danforth staffer.

ALTERNATE EXAMPLES

People find it interesting to speculate about how the future *could be* affected if a single aspect of our world *were* different today. For example, if the average yearly temperature *were* only a few degrees higher, the oceans *would* rise due to the melting of the polar ice caps. If serious worldwide droughts *were* to occur in several successive summers, the food supply *would* dwindle. Unless science *were* able to divert the swelling oceans or grow crops without the use of water, civilization as we know it *would be* radically changed. It is, consequently, important that mankind *recognize* the importance of environmental decisions. The world *should* not act as though the future *were* inevitably bad. If, in the early part of this century, the industrialized world *had considered* the effects of water and air pollution, our world *would be* a healthier one today.

2 Using the subjunctive for conjectures introduced by *as if* or *as though*

Use the subjunctive to express conditions that are possible but cannot be confirmed.

This refrigerator sounded as if it **were** [not *was*] broken.

The air smelled as though a fire **were** [not *was*] burning nearby.

3 Using the subjunctive in *that* clauses for wishes, indirect requests, recommendations, and demands

Things that people wish for, ask for, or demand have not yet become reality. Use the subjunctive to express these unrealized goals.

I wish that this week **were** [not *was*] over.

It is important that the doctor **finish** [*finishes*] the examination because someone is demanding that **she go** [not *goes*] to the clinic.

4 Using the subjunctive with modal auxiliary verbs

The modal auxiliary verbs *would, could,* and *should* are often used with the subjunctive. These modal auxiliaries convey the notion of speculations and conditions contrary to fact.

If the runner **were** [not *was*] faster, I **would** expect stiffer competition.

When an independent clause uses *would have,* be sure to use *had* in any related *if* clause.

No	If I **would have** trained, I **would have** won the race.
Yes	If I **had** trained, I **would have** won the race.

Sometimes the word *should* appears in the *if* clause to convey speculation.

Should the runners jump the starting gun, the official **would have** [not *will have*] to restart the race.

Should the race be cancelled because of rain, it **could** [not *can*] be held tomorrow.

| 5 | Using the subjunctive in certain standard expressions that appear in everyday language |

If I **were** you . . .   Please let me **be**.
If only I **were** there . . .   Be that as it **may** . . .
Come what **may** . . .   Far **be** it from me . . .

EXERCISE 10

Fill in the blanks with the appropriate subjunctive form of the verb in parentheses.

EXAMPLE   To improve a patient's general health, a doctor may ask that the person (diet) _____.

To improve a patient's general health, a doctor may ask that the person *diet.*

1. Suppose that George thought he (to be) _____ in good physical shape.
2. George's doctor, however, believed it important he (lose) _____ at least twenty pounds.
3. Medical experts urge that dieters (to be) _____ aware that the family may be uncooperative.
4. A jealous family member may even wish that the overweight person (gain) _____ weight.
5. For example, an insecure spouse may demand that the dieter (eat) _____ a food forbidden for that diet.

ANSWERS: EXERCISE 10

1. were
2. lose
3. be
4. gain
5. eat

COVERAGE: EXERCISE 10

1. Subjunctive for conjecture—irregular verb "to be"
2. Subjunctive for recommendation—regular verb
3. Subjunctive for recommendation—irregular verb "to be"
4. Subjunctive for wish—regular verb (in subjunctive form)
5. Subjunctive for demand—regular verb (in subjunctive form)

VOICE

| 8m | Understanding voice |

Voice refers to verbs' ability to show whether a subject° acts or receives the action named by the verb. English has two voices: active and passive. In the **active voice,** the subject performs the action.

> **Most clams live in salt water.** [The subject *clams* does the acting; they *live.*]
> **They burrow into the sandy bottoms of shallow waters.** [The subject *they* does the acting; they *burrow.*]

237

In the **passive voice,** the subject is acted upon, and the person or thing doing the acting often appears as the object° of the preposition *by.*

> Clams have long been considered a delicacy by many people. [The subject *clams* are acted upon by *people,* the object of the preposition *by*]

> They are also admired by crabs and starfish. [The subject *they* are acted upon by *crabs and starfish,* the objects of the preposition *by.*]

Misusing voice usually creates problems of writing style rather than problems of incorrect grammar. To make your writing clear, use voice consistently in sentences on the same topic. (See 15a-2 for ways to identify and correct confusing shifts in voice.)

 ## 8n Writing in the active voice, not the passive voice, except to convey special types of emphasis

Because the active voice emphasizes the doer of an action, active constructions are more direct and dramatic. Active constructions also use fewer words than passive constructions. Most sentences in the passive voice can easily be converted to the active voice.

PASSIVE	African tribal masks are often imitated by Western sculptors.
ACTIVE	Western sculptors often imitate African tribal masks.

The passive voice, however, does have some uses. If you learn what they are, you can use the passive to advantage.

1 Using the passive voice when the doer of the action is unknown or unimportant

When no one knows who or what did something, the passive voice is often used.

> The lock **was broken** sometime after four o'clock. [Who broke the lock is unknown.]

When the doer of an action is unimportant, writers often use the passive voice.

> In 1899, the year I was born, **a peace conference was held** at The Hague. [The doers of the action—holders of the conference—are unimportant to White's point.]
>
> —E. B. White, "Unity"

2 Using the passive voice to focus attention on the action rather than on the doer of the action

The passive voice emphasizes the action, while the active voice focuses on the doer of the action. In a passage about important contributions to the history of science, you might want to emphasize a doer by using the active voice.

Active   **Joseph Priestley discovered** oxygen in 1774.

But in a passage summarizing what is known about oxygen, you may want to emphasize what was done.

Passive   **Oxygen was discovered** in 1774 by Joseph Priestley.

The passive voice is an important feature of some writing in the sciences. (For more about writing in the sciences, see Chapter 39).

> Most of the oxygen in the blood **is carried** by the red blood cells.
>
> —Malinda Murray, *Fundamentals of Nursing*

Your choices about audience and purpose for your writing greatly influence the voice you should choose for a sentence.

Passive   The news that the dictator had fled **was received** before the order to attack the palace **could be given.** [Here the emphasis is on events, not on the doers of the action.]

Active   Before he could give the order to attack, the commander received the news that the dictator had fled the palace. [Here the emphasis is on the people rather than the actions.]

EXTRA EXERCISE I *(continued)*

5. Additions were made by later kings of England.

6. Sir Christopher Wren was asked by Charles II to design several important additions.

7. The state apartments are open to the public when the royal family is not in residence.

8. The state apartments include the grand staircase, state bedrooms, and reception rooms.

9. Many rulers were buried at Windsor Castle, including Henry VIII.

10. St. George's Chapel, one of the most beautiful parts of the castle, was built in the fifteenth century and redecorated throughout the following centuries.

ANSWERS: EXTRA EXERCISE I

1. is, active voice

2. built, active voice; occupies, active voice

3. was improved, passive voice

4. demolished, active voice; built, active voice

5. were made, passive voice

6. was asked, passive voice

7. are, active voice; is, active voice

8. include, active voice

9. were buried, passive voice

10. was built, passive voice; [was] redecorated, passive voice

ANSWERS: EXERCISE 11

Rewrites may vary somewhat from the possibilities shown here.

1. Active; rewrite in passive: Around the turn of the century, a story about a clever horse was carried by Berlin newspapers.

2. Passive; rewrite in active: The horse's owner named him Clever Hans.

3. Passive; rewrite in active: The horse gave answers to math problems by tapping his hoofs.

4. Active; rewrite in passive: Fraud was suspected by many people.

5. Passive; rewrite in active: People who doubted Hans's talents called in two zoologists and a horse trainer to investigate.

6. Active; rewrite in passive: Even with Hans's master out of the horse's sight, perfect answers to every question were still provided by Hans.

7. Active; rewrite in passive: Doubts were still entertained by a young psychologist.

8. Passive; rewrite in active: The psychologist used people who did not know the answers to the problems to ask Hans questions.

9. Passive; rewrite in active: Clever Hans failed the math test.

10. Active; rewrite in passive: Apparently small, subconscious human gestures that indicated the correct answers had been read by Clever Hans.

COVERAGE: EXERCISE 11

Five passive to active sentences; five active to passive sentences.

EXERCISE 11

First, determine whether each of these sentences is in the active or the passive voice. Second, rewrite the sentence in the other voice. Then decide which voice best suits the meaning.

EXAMPLE   Scientists were fooled by a horse and its owner about one hundred years ago. [passive voice]

A horse and its owner fooled scientists about one hundred years ago. [active voice]

1. Around the turn of the century, Berlin newspapers carried a story about a clever horse.

2. The horse was named Clever Hans by his owner.

3. Answers to math problems were given by taps from the horse's hoofs.

4. Many people suspected some kind of fraud.

5. Two zoologists and a horse trainer were called in to investigate by the people who doubted Hans's talents.

6. Even with Hans's master out of the horse's sight, Hans still provided perfect answers to every question.

7. A young psychologist still entertained doubts.

8. People who did not know the answers to the problems were used by the psychologist to ask Hans questions.

9. The math test was failed by Clever Hans.

10. Apparently Clever Hans had been reading small, subconscious human gestures that indicated the correct answers.

Focus on Revising

REVISING YOUR WRITING

If you have trouble with your verbs (including unnecessary use of the passive voice) when you write, go back to your writing and locate the problems. Using this chapter as a resource, revise your writing to correct the problems.

Error	Section
-s ending	8b
-ed ending	8c-1
auxiliary verbs	8d
lie/lay, set/sit, rise/raise	8e
tenses	8f–8i
tense sequences	8j
the subjunctive	8l
passive voice	8n

CASE STUDY: REVISING TO ELIMINATE VERB ERRORS

First, this case study lets you observe a student writer revising. Second, it gives you the opportunity to revise some student writing on your own.

Observation

A student wrote the following draft for a course called Popular Culture. The assignment called for reading a section in the course's textbook and then writing about a year in which important contributions were made to popular culture in the United States. While this paragraph is well organized and offers good examples to support its topic, the draft's effectiveness is diminished by the presence of errors in verb forms and verb tense, and by the unnecessary use of the passive.

Read through the draft. The verb errors are highlighted and explained. Before you look at how the student revised to eliminate the verb errors, revise the material yourself. Then compare what you and the student did.

EXTRA EXERCISE H (continued from page 232)

10. Other authorities (had been saying, have said, have been saying) that complicated residency laws are the problem.

11. In 1855, despite only 2,000 registered voters in Kansas, 6,000 ballots were cast in an election when people from neighboring Missouri (crossed, were crossing, had been crossing) the state line to vote for candidates in sympathy with Missouri's policies.

12. Episodes like this (led, have led, were leading, have been leading) to the enactment of strict residency laws for voters.

ANSWERS: EXTRA EXERCISE H

Other answers than these may be possible.

1. fell	**7.** ranks
2. remained	**8.** vote
3. compare	**9.** have suggested
4. leads	**10.** have said
5. have had	**11.** crossed
6. require	**12.** have led

COVERAGE: EXTRA EXERCISE H

1. past	**7.** present
2. past	**8.** present
3. present	**9.** present perfect
4. present	**10.** present perfect
5. present perfect	**11.** past
6. present	**12.** present perfect

COVERAGE: PARTICIPATION ESSAY (opposite page)

At election time, government leaders and the media always *encouraged* [8g: simple present needed] citizens to exercise one of their most basic rights: the right to vote. How many young women today realize that until the Nineteenth Amendment to the United States Constitution *was approve* [8c: -ed needed] in 1920, women in the United States *were deny* [8c: -[i]ed needed] the right to vote?

In the 1830s, almost a century before the Nineteenth Amendment was approved, *the battle for women's rights was being waged by Elizabeth Cady Stanton and other leading women.* [8n: unneeded passive voice] In 1848, the first women's rights convention *take* [8g: present tense used; need simple past of irregular verb] place in Seneca Falls, New York. Stanton *rises* [8e: present tense of intransitive verb used; simple past needed] to the occasion and produced what was *call* [8c: -ed needed] "A Declaration of Sentiments." Its inspiration *lays* [8e: -s form of transitive verb used; past tense of intransitive verb needed] in the Declaration of Independence, but it revealed one shortcoming in Thomas Jefferson's language. Instead of the words "all men are created equal," Stanton's document *proclaim* [8c: -ed needed] that "all men and women are created equal."

Later, Stanton *was working* [8i: past progressive form used; simple present needed] to convince California Senator Aaron Sargeant to propose a constitutional amendment that would give women the vote. *It was introduced to the U.S. Congress by him in 1878.* [unneeded passive voice] Forty years later the amendment was approved, but Stanton never *seen* [8c: past participle of irregular verb used; simple past needed] the victory because she died eighteen years before the amendment be-

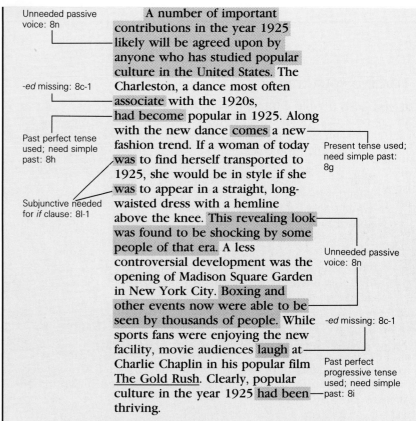

Here is how the student revised the material to eliminate the verb errors. In revising from the unneeded passive voice to the active voice, the student had alternatives in word choice. Your revisions into the active voice might differ in wording from the student's.

Anyone who has studied popular culture in the United States likely will agree upon a number of important contributions in the year 1925. The Charleston, a dance most often associated with the 1920s, became popular in 1925. Along with the new dance came a new fashion trend. If a woman of today were to find herself transported to 1925, she would be in style if she were to appear in a straight, long-waisted dress with a hemline above the knee. Some people of that era found this revealing look shocking. A less controversial development was the opening of Madison Square

Garden in New York City. Thousands of people could now see boxing and other events. While sports fans were enjoying this new facility, movie audiences laughed at Charlie Chaplin in his popular film <u>The Gold Rush</u>. Clearly, popular culture in the year 1925 was thriving.

Participation

A student wrote the following draft for a course called Introduction to Women's Studies. The assignment was to write a brief report about a significant contribution to society in the United States. The material is concise and logical, but the draft's effectiveness is diminished by errors in verb forms and verb tense and by the unnecessary use of the passive voice.

Read through the draft. Then revise it to eliminate the errors. Also, make any additional revisions you think would improve the content, organization, and style of the material.

At election time, government leaders and the media always encouraged citizens to exercise one of their most basic rights: the right to vote. How many young women today realize that until the Nineteenth Amendment to the United States Constitution was approve in 1920, women in the United States were deny the right to vote?

In the 1830s, almost a century before the Nineteenth Amendment was approved, the battle for women's rights was being waged by Elizabeth Cady Stanton and other leading women. In 1848, the first women's rights convention take place in Seneca Falls, New York. Stanton rises to the occasion and produced what was call "A Declaration of Sentiments." Its inspiration lays in the Declaration of Independence, but it revealed one shortcoming in Thomas Jefferson's language. Instead of the words "all men are created equal," Stanton's document proclaim that "all men and women are created equal."

Later, Stanton was working to convince California Senator Aaron Sargeant to propose a constitutional amendment that would give women the vote. It was introduced to the U.S. Congress by him in 1878. Forty years later the amendment was approved, but Stanton never seen the victory because she died eighteen years before the amendment became law. Her legacy lives and should be remembered by all women when the time come to vote.

COVERAGE: PARTICIPATION ESSAY *(continued)*

came law. Her legacy lives and should be remembered by all women when the time *come* to vote. [8b: simple present used; *-s* form needed]

ANSWER: PARTICIPATION ESSAY

This version revises the errors in verb forms and verb tense and the unnecessary use of the passive voice. Answers might vary slightly, especially in the revisions of the passives. Also, answers will vary if students have revised for content, organization, or style.

At election time, government leaders and the media always encourage citizens to exercise one of their most basic rights: the right to vote. How many young women today realize that until the Nineteenth Amendment to the United States Constitution was approved in 1920, women in the United States were denied the right to vote?

In the 1830s, almost a century before the Nineteenth Amendment was approved, Elizabeth Cady Stanton and other leading women waged the battle for women's rights. In 1848, the first women's rights convention took place in Seneca Falls, New York. Stanton rose to the occasion and produced what was called "A Declaration of Sentiments." Its inspiration lay in the Declaration of Independence, but it revealed one shortcoming in Thomas Jefferson's language. Instead of the words "all men are created equal," Stanton's document proclaimed that "all men and women are created equal."

Later, Stanton convinced California Senator Aaron Sargeant to propose a constitutional amendment that would give women the vote. He introduced it to the U.S. Congress in 1878. Forty years later the amendment was approved, but Stanton never saw the victory because she died eighteen years before the amendment became law. Her legacy lives and should be remembered by all women when the time comes to vote.

9 Case of Nouns and Pronouns

LANGUAGE FACTS

Many languages have noun and/or pronoun case systems. The smallest number of cases is two, as in the Masai language of East Africa. In contrast, Sanskrit has eight cases. Latin has six; Greek has five. The prize, however, goes to Finnish, with fifteen noun cases.

BACKGROUND ON LANGUAGE

The pronoun *you* indicates little more than that the second person is being used. Unlike the first- and third-person personal pronouns, it tells the reader nothing about gender or number. Until the thirteenth century, however, *th-* forms, such as *thee, thy,* and *thou,* indicated use of the singular, and *y-* forms, such as *ye, you,* and *your* indicated the plural. Later, the *th-* forms came to suggest a close relationship between the speaker and listener, the *y-* forms to suggest a formal one. Today the pronouns *thou* and *three* linger only among some religious sects.

Case refers to the different forms that nouns° and pronouns° take to deliver information. The case of a noun or a pronoun communicates how that word relates to other words in a sentence. For example, *I, me,* and *mine* are three different cases of the singular first-person pronoun. (*I wanted a small wedding, but my parents asked **me** to invite all their friends. Unlike my sister's wedding, **mine** was quite large.*)

This chapter presents the cases of pronouns and nouns and explains how case operates, with special emphasis on the pronouns that writers sometimes find troublesome. English has three cases: *subjective, objective,* and *possessive.*

Personal pronouns are the most common type of pronouns. They have a full range of cases that show changes in **person** (first, second, and third person) and **number** (singular and plural). For more about how person and number work, see the review chart in the opening section of Chapter 11.

CASES OF PERSONAL PRONOUNS						
	SUBJECTIVE		**OBJECTIVE**		**POSSESSIVE**	
PERSON	SING.	PLUR.	SING.	PLUR.	SING.	PLUR.
FIRST	I	we	me	us	my/mine	our/ours
SECOND	you	you	you	you	your/yours	your/yours
THIRD	he she it	they	him her it	them	his her/hers its	their/theirs

A pronoun in the **subjective case** functions as a subject°.

We were going to get married. [*We* is the subject.]

John and **I** wanted an inexpensive band to play at our wedding. [*I* is part of the compound subject *John and I*.]

He and **I** found a one-person band we could afford. [*He* and *I* are compound subjects.]

A pronoun in the **objective case** functions as a direct object°, an indirect object°, or the object of a preposition°.

We saw **him** perform in a public park. [*Him* is the direct object.]

We showed **him** our budget. [*Him* is the indirect object.]

He understood and shook hands with **me**. [*Me* is the object of the preposition *with*.]

A pronoun in the **possessive case** indicates possession or ownership. ❖ PUNCTUATION ALERT: Do not use an apostrophe for a personal pronoun in the possessive case (see 27b). ❖

The **musician's** contract was in the mail the next day. [*Musician's*, a noun in the possessive case, indicates ownership.]

Our signatures quickly went on the contract. [*Our*, a pronoun in the possessive case, indicates possession.]

His was entered soon after. [*His*, a pronoun in the possessive case, indicates ownership and also implies the inclusion of the noun *signature*.]

The pronouns **who** and **whoever** also change form for case changes, as explained in 9d.

9a Using the same cases for pronouns in compound constructions as in single constructions

A compound construction contains more than one subject° or object°.

He saw the eclipse of the sun. [single subject]

He and **I** saw the eclipse of the sun. [compound subject]

That eclipse astonished **us**. [single object]

That eclipse astonished **him** and **me**. [compound object]

A compound construction has no effect on the choice of pronoun case. A compound subject uses the subjective case, and a compound object uses the objective case. Sometimes, however, people make the

---

TEACHING TIP

If you have students who know other languages, they may enjoy explaining the noun and pronoun case systems of those other tongues to the native English speakers in the class. Their examples will demonstrate that case is not nearly as important an aspect of English as it is of other languages.

TEACHING TIP

Just as English once distinguished between the personal and impersonal relationships in the second-person pronoun *you*, some modern languages continue to do so. French, for example, makes a distinction between *tu* and *vous*; Spanish does so between *tu* (singular) *vosotros* (plural) informally and *Usted* (singular) *Ustedes* (plural) formally. You might wish to have your bilingual students explain the difference in such forms.

QUOTATION ON LANGUAGE

Words are like leaves, and where they most abound, / Much fruit of sense beneath is rarely found.

—Alexander Pope

QUOTATION ON LANGUAGE

High thoughts must have high language.

—Aristophanes

Joseph M. Williams explains in *Origins of the English Language* (New York: Free Press, 1975; 248–49) that changes in the second-person singular pronouns (subjective and objective cases) are rooted in the Roman Empire of the fourth century A.D. At that time there were two emperors, one in Rome and one in Constantinople. People speaking to either emperor were required to use the plural form of address. The practice of using the plural as a sign of respect slowly spread to France, where *tu* is the second-person singular pronoun and *vous* the plural. During the thirteenth century, in imitation of the *tu/vous* of the French nobles who occupied their country, the English began using *thee* (objective), *thou* (subjective), and *you* the same way. *You* became a mark of mutual respect in conversations among the elite and a sign of deference when a person spoke to a social superior. In contrast, *thee/thou* became a sign of intimacy among members of the same family or among those who believed in the same things.

The "drop test" can be more effective if students are given both oral and written activities in which they are asked not only to select correct pronouns from prepared sentences but also to generate their own sentences using pronouns as parts of compounds.

mistake of switching cases for compounds. If you sometimes are unsure which case to use, try the "drop test."

Here is a three-step drop test for compound constructions to help you stay in the appropriate case: Temporarily drop *all of the compound elements except the pronoun in question,* and then you will be able to tell which pronoun case is needed. Here is how the method works for compound subjects.

TEST FOR COMPOUND SUBJECTS	
EXAMPLE	**Janet and (me, I)** read that the moon has one-eightieth the mass of the earth.
STEP 1	Drop "Janet and."
STEP 2	Which reads correctly: "**Me** read that the moon has one-eightieth the mass of the earth" or "**I** read that the moon has one-eightieth the mass of the earth"?
STEP 3	Answer: Janet and **I** read that the moon has one-eightieth the mass of the earth.

This "drop test" works also when both parts of the compound subject are pronouns: *She and I* [not *Her and me*] *read that the moon has one-eightieth the mass of the earth.* The same "drop test" works for compound objects.

TEST FOR COMPOUND OBJECTS	
EXAMPLE	The instructor told **Janet and (I, me)** that the moon has one-fiftieth the volume of the earth.
STEP 1	Drop "Janet and."
STEP 2	Which reads correctly: "The instructor told **I** that the moon has one-fiftieth the volume of the earth" or "The instructor told **me** that the moon has one-fiftieth the volume of the earth"?
STEP 3	Answer: The instructor told Janet and **me** that the moon has one-fiftieth the volume of the earth.

This "drop test" works also when both parts of the compound object are pronouns: *The instructor told **her** and **me*** [not *she and I*] *that the moon has one-fiftieth the volume of the earth.*

When pronouns in a prepositional phrase° occur in compound constructions, inexperienced writers sometimes allow pronouns to slip into the wrong case. A prepositional phrase always has an object°, so any pronouns that follow words such as *with, to, from, for, after,* and *between* must be in the objective case.

No   The instructor gave an assignment **to Sam and I.** [*To* is a preposition; *I* is in the subjective case and cannot follow a preposition.]

Yes   The instructor gave an assignment **to Sam and me.** [*To* is a preposition; *Me* is in the objective case, so it is correct.]

No   The instructor spoke **with he and I.** [*With* is a preposition; both *he* and *I* are in the subjective case and cannot follow a preposition.]

No   The instructor spoke **with him and I.** [*With* is a preposition; *him* is in the objective case, so it is correct. *I* is in the subjective case and cannot follow a preposition.]

Yes   The instructor spoke **with him and me.** [*With* is a preposition; *him* and *me* are both in the objective case, so this construction is correct.]

Between is a preposition that frequently leads people to pronoun error. A pronoun after *between*, like other prepositions, must always be in the objective case.

No   The instructor divided the work **between Sam and I.** [*Between* is a preposition; *I* is in the subjective case and cannot follow a preposition.]

Yes   The instructor divided the work **between Sam and me.** [*Between* is a preposition; *me* is in the objective case, so it is correct.]

If you are in doubt when you use pronouns in prepositional phrases use the test for compound objects on the opposite page.

EXERCISE 1

From each pair of pronouns in parentheses, select the correct one and circle it.

EXAMPLE   A friend who works with (I, (me)) decided to have her eyes examined.

     Both (her, she)[1] and her supervisor agreed that she should make an appointment to see an eye doctor. She asked (me, I)[2] to help her find a

ANSWERS: EXERCISE 1

1. she	**8.** him and me
2. me	**9.** we
3. We	**10.** me
4. she and I	**11.** us
5. him	**12.** her
6. whoever	**13.** him
7. I	

COVERAGE: EXERCISE 1

(1) subjective case; (2) objective case; (3) subjective case; (4) subjective case; (5) objective case; (6) subjective case; (7) subjective case; (8) objective case; (9) subjective case; (10) objective case; (11) objective case; (12) objective case; (13) objective case

good optometrist. (We, Us)[3] two together searched through the telephone yellow pages. The name "Dr. John Bright" looked promising, so (she and me, her and me, she and I, her and I)[4] called (he, him)[5]. When the time for her appointment came, my friend had to leave work early, and she asked (whoever, whomever)[6] was free to answer her telephone. Another of our sales representatives and (I, me)[7] were able to cover all her calls. When my friend returned, she asked (him and me, him and I, he and I)[8] for her messages. Curious, (we, us)[9] asked how her doctor visit went. She laughed and said, "Between you and (I, me)[10], Dr. Bright needs to change his approach." Then she explained to (us, we)[11] that the doctor had asked (her, she)[13] whether she had trouble threading needles or reading recipes. "No," she had told (he, him)[13], "but I do have difficulty reading the fine print in *The Wall Street Journal.*"

9b ## Matching noun and pronoun cases

When *we* (subjective case) occurs with a noun, the noun must be functioning as a subject°; when *us* (objective case) occurs with a noun, the noun must be functioning as an object°. The drop test shown in Section 9a can be adapted here. Temporarily drop the noun following the pronoun and see which pronoun reads correctly.

EXAMPLE	*(We, Us) tennis players practice hard.*
No	**Us** practice hard.
Yes	**We** practice hard.
Yes	**We** tennis players practice hard. [*Tennis players* is the subject, so the pronoun must be in the subjective case.]
EXAMPLE	*Our coach tells (we, us) tennis players to practice hard.*
No	Our coach tells **we** to practice hard.
Yes	Our coach tells **us** to practice hard.
Yes	Our coach tells **us** tennis players to practice hard. [*Tennis players* is the object, so the pronoun must be in the objective case.]

The same principles hold when pronouns occur in an **appositive**—a word or group of words that renames the noun or noun phrase° preceding it. The drop test shown in Section 9a can be adapted here. Drop the noun and test each pronoun separately to see if it is correct.

EXAMPLE *The winners, (she, her) and (I, me) advanced to the finals.*

No The winners, **her** and **me,** advanced to the finals. [*Her* and *me* rename the subject, *the winners,* so objective pronouns are incorrect.]

YES The winners, **she** and **I,** advanced to the finals. [*She* and *I* rename the subject, *the winners,* so subjective pronouns are correct.]

EXAMPLE *The crowd cheered the winners, (she, her) and (I, me).*

No The crowd cheered the winners, **she** and **I.** [*She* and *I* rename the object, *the winners,* so subjective pronouns are incorrect.]

YES The crowd cheered the winners, **her** and **me.** [*Her* and *me* rename the object, *the winners,* so objective pronouns are correct.]

9c Using the subjective case after linking verbs

A **linking verb** connects a subject° to a word that renames it. Linking verbs indicate a state of being (*am, is, are, was, were,* etc.), relate to the senses *(look, smell, taste, sound, feel),* or indicate a condition *(appear, seem, become, grow, turn, remain,* and *prove).*

Because a pronoun coming after any linking verb renames the subject, the pronoun must be in the subjective case.

> The contest winner was **I.** [*I* renames *the contest winner,* the subject, so the subjective case is required.]

> The ones who will benefit are **they** and **I.** [*They* and *I* rename *the ones who will benefit,* the subject, so the subjective case is required.]

> May I please speak to Guy? This is **he.** [*He* renames *this,* the subject, so the subjective case is required.]

> Who is there? It is **I.** [*I* renames *it,* the subject, so the subjective case is required.]

In speech and informal writing, the objective case is sometimes substituted in the constructions shown in the last two examples above. Be sure to use the subjective case for these usages in academic writing.

EXERCISE 2

Circle the correct pronoun in each pair in parentheses.

EXAMPLES Bob Soak, Jr.: Sally and (I, me) lent a friend five hundred dollars, but we have no proof.

Bob Soak, Sr.: Between you and (I, me), son, you are in an awkward situation.

Jr.: The two of us, Sally and (I, me),[1] know. To make matters worse, another friend told Sally and (I, me)[2] today that our friend has moved to another city.

Sr.: Don't you know better, you and (she, her)[3], not to give someone cash and forget to ask for a receipt?

Jr.: It was (we, us)[4] who did exactly that.

Sr.: (Us, We)[5] Soaks are usually more careful, but I think that together you and (I, me)[6] can work out a solution.

Jr.: Sally and (I, me)[7] would truly appreciate your help, and I will not forget that one of the people who created this problem is (I, me).[8]

Sr.: Here is what to do. You and Sally write your friend a letter saying that you and (she, her)[9] have an emergency and need the one thousand dollars back right away.

Jr.: Between you and (I, me),[10] Dad, he will think I am crazy because Sally and (I, me)[11] lent him only five hundred dollars.

Sr.: Give (we, us)[12] experienced folks a little credit. When your friend reads that you expect one thousand dollars from (he, him),[13] he will write quickly to say that (he, him)[14] is the person who owes you five hundred dollars. Then you will have your proof in writing.

9d Using *who* and *whoever* when the subjective case is needed; using *whom* and *whomever* when the objective case is needed

The pronouns *who* and *whoever* are in the subjective case, and *whom* and *whomever* are in the objective case. Within each case, the pronouns do not change form for singular or plural, and they do not change form for first, second, or third person.

1 Knowing how to use *who, whoever, whom,* and *whomever* in dependent clauses

A **dependent clause** contains a subject° and predicate° and starts with a word that makes the clause unable to stand alone as a sentence. (For a complete discussion of dependent clauses, see

CASES OF RELATIVE AND INTERROGATIVE PRONOUNS		
SUBJECTIVE	**OBJECTIVE**	**POSSESSIVE**
who whoever	whom whomever	whose -------

7n-2.) Pronouns such as *who, whoever, whom,* or *whomever* start many dependent clauses.

To determine what pronoun case is correct in a dependent clause, it is not necessary to determine whether the entire clause is functioning as a subject or an object in the sentence. All that matters is how the pronoun functions in its own clause. Because informal, spoken English tends to blur distinctions between *who* and *whom*, some writers cannot rely entirely on what sounds right.

If you want to check your use of *who* and *whom*, try this variation of the drop test shown in Section 9a. Temporarily drop everything in the sentence up to the pronoun in question, and then make substitutions. Remember that *he, she, they, who,* and *whoever* are subjects, and *him, her, them, whom,* and *whomever* (the *-m* forms and *her*) are objects. Here is how the method works for the subjective case.

TEST FOR WHO/WHOM IN SUBJECTIVE CASE	
EXAMPLE	I wondered **(who, whom)** would vote.
STEP 1	Omit "I wondered."
STEP 2	Test the sentence with *he* and *him* (or *she* and *her*): "**He** would vote" or "**Him** would vote."
STEP 3	Answer: "**He** would vote."
STEP 4	Therefore, because *he* is subjective, *who* which is also the subjective is correct: "I wondered **who** would vote."

This four-step drop test works also for *whoever.*

Voter registration drives attempt to enroll **whoever** is eligible to vote. ["*He* (not *him*) is eligible to vote" proves that the subjective case of *whoever* is needed.]

The subjective case is called for even when expressions such as *I think* or *he says* come between the subject and verb. Ignore these expressions when you are trying to determine the correct pronoun: *She is the candidate who [I think] will get my vote.*

The same method works for the objective case.

TEST FOR WHO/WHOM IN OBJECTIVE CASE

EXAMPLE	**Volunteers go to senior citizen centers hoping to enroll people (who, whom)** others have ignored.
STEP 1	Omit "Volunteers . . . people."
STEP 2	Test the sentence with *they* and *them:* "Others have ignored **they**" or "Others have ignored **them.**"
STEP 3	Answer: "Others have ignored **them.**"
STEP 4	Therefore, because *them* is objective, *whom,* which is also objective, is correct: "Volunteers go to senior citizen centers hoping to enroll people **whom** others have ignored."

This four-step drop test works also for *whomever:*

The senior citizens can vote for **whomever** they wish. ["The senior citizens can vote for *him*" proves that the objective case of *whomever* is needed.]

2 | Knowing how to use *who* and *whom* in questions

At the beginning of questions, use *who* if the question is about the subject° and *whom* if the question is about the object°. To determine whether the case if subjective or objective, recast the question into a statement.

Who watched the space shuttle lift-off? ["*I* watched the space shuttle lift-off" uses the subjective pronoun *I*. *Who* is correct.]

Ann admires **whom?** ["Ann admires *her*" uses the objective pronoun *her*. *Whom* is correct.]

Whom does Ann admire? ["Ann admires her" uses the objective pronoun *her*. *Whom* is correct.]

EXTRA EXERCISE

If your students have trouble choosing the appropriate pronoun in questions, you might offer them practice with these questions:

1. (Who, whom) was initially responsible for the making of silk? [*Who*]

2. (Who, whom) developed the first method of weaving silk? [*Who*]

3. In the nineteenth century, (who, whom) claimed to produce the best silk? [*who*]

4. Theories about early fabrics come from (who, whom)? [*whom*]

5. Silkworm eggs were carried out of China by (who, whom)? [*whom*]

6. The French silk industry was developed for (whom, whom)? [*whom*]

To **whom** does Ann speak about becoming an astronaut? ["Ann speaks to *them* about becoming an astronaut" uses the objective pronoun *them*. *Whom* is correct.]

EXERCISE 3

Circle the correct pronoun in each pair in parentheses.

EXAMPLE   Experts say that our personal philosophies depend largely upon ((who) , whom) or what has been important in our lives.

1. For example, many people vote for (whoever, whomever) their parents prefer.

2. Parents transmit to us their ideas about politics and (who, whom) to respect in government.

3. Research shows that children (who, whom) have been overprotected often become adults for (who, whom) life is difficult beyond the protective family circle.

4. Adults (who, whom) were consulted as children about some family decisions, such as (who, whom) to invite to dinner or what to name the dog, usually are more active politically than people (who, whom) had no voice in family matters.

5. In totalitarian countries, schools indoctrinate youngsters (who, whom) have learned never to question authority, so adults believe that trouble waits for (whoever, whomever) challenges the system.

9e Using the pronoun case that reflects intended meaning after *than* or *as*

A sentence of comparison often can be clear even though some of the words following *than* or *as* are implied but not directly stated. For example, the word *are* does not have to be expressed at the end of this sentence: *My two-month-old Saint Bernard is larger **than** most full-grown dogs* [*are*]*.*

When a pronoun follows *than* or *as*, the pronoun case carries essential information about what is being said. For example, these two sentences convey two very different messages, simply because of the choice between the words *me* and *I* after *than*.

1. My sister loved that dog more **than me.**
2. My sister loved that dog more **than I.**

Sentence 1 means "My sister loved that dog more *than she loved me*." On the other hand, sentence 2 means "My sister loved that dog more *than I loved it*." To make sure that any sentence of comparison delivers its message clearly, either include all words in the second half of a comparison or mentally fill in the words to check that you have chosen the correct pronoun case.

9f   Using the objective case when a pronoun is the subject or the object of an infinitive

An **infinitive** is the simple form° of a verb usually, but not always, following *to: to laugh, to dance.* Objective pronouns occur as both subjects and objects of infinitives.

> Our tennis coach expects **me to serve.** [The word *me* is the subject of the infinitive *to serve,* and so it is in the objective case.]

> Our tennis coach expects **him to beat me.** [The word *him* is the subject of the infinitive *to beat,* and *me* is the object of the infinitive; both are in the objective case.]

9g   Using the possessive case before gerunds

A **gerund** is a verb's *-ing* form functioning as a noun. (***Brisk walking** is excellent exercise.*) When a noun or pronoun precedes a gerund, the possessive case is called for. (***Kim's brisk walking** built up her stamina. **Her brisk walking** built up her stamina.*) In contrast, a present participle—a form that also ends in *-ing*—functions as a modifier. It does not take the possessive case. (*Kim, **walking briskly,** caught up to me.*)

The possessive case, therefore, communicates important information. Consider these two sentences, which convey two different messages, entirely as a result of the possessive:

1. The detective noticed the **man staggering.**
2. The detective noticed the **man's staggering.**

Sentence 1 means that the detective noticed the man; sentence 2 means that the detective noticed the staggering. The same distinction applies to pronouns:

1. The detective noticed **him** staggering.
2. The detective noticed **his** staggering.

In conversation, the distinction is often ignored, but readers of academic writing expect that information will be precise. Consider the difference in the following two examples:

GERUND (AS A SUBJECT)	The **governor's calling for a tax increase** surprised her supporters.

PARTICIPLE (MODIFIER)	The governor, **calling for a tax increase,** surprised her supporters.

EXERCISE 4

Circle the correct pronoun in each pair in parentheses.

EXAMPLE   Sam Houston, leader of the drive for Texas's independence, is less well-known for ((his), him) championing of the rights of the Cherokees.

1. Houston's concern grew out of (him, his) living with the Cherokees for three years in his late teens.
2. From 1817 to 1818 he served as a government subagent helping to settle some Cherokees on a reservation, but a reprimand from Secretary of War John C. Calhoun persuaded (he, him) to resign.
3. Calhoun was angry about (Houston, Houston's) wearing Indian clothing to meet (he, him).
4. Not only as tall and energetic as Andrew Jackson, Houston was also as popular as (he, him).
5. He lived with the Cherokees, who decided to adopt (he, him) as a member of their nation, and later he went to Washington on behalf of the Cherokees to help (them, they) protest the fraud of some government agents.

9h Reserving -*self* forms of pronouns for reflexive or intensive use

Reflexive pronouns reflect back on the subject° or object°.

The detective disguised **himself.**

He had to rely on **himself** to solve the mystery.

Reflexive pronouns should not be used as substitutes for subjects or objects.

The detective and **I** (not *myself*) had a long talk.

He wanted my partner and **me** (not *myself*) to help him.

Intensive pronouns provide emphasis by making another word more intense in meaning.

The detective felt that his career **itself** was at stake.

Avoid the following nonstandard forms of reflexive and intensive pronouns in academic writing: *hisself,* nonstandard for *himself; theirself, theirselves, themself,* and *themselfs,* nonstandard for *themselves.*

Focus on Revising

REVISING YOUR WRITING

If you make errors with the case of nouns and pronouns when you write, go back to your writing and locate the errors. Using this chapter as a resource, revise your writing to correct the problems.

CASE STUDY

The case study at the end of Chapter 10 offers you the chance to observe and participate in a revision that eliminates errors in pronoun case (this chapter) and pronoun reference (Chapter 10).

10 Pronoun Reference

The term **pronoun reference** refers to the fact that the meaning of a pronoun comes from its **antecedent,** the noun or pronoun to which the pronoun refers. (Nouns are explained in 7a, and pronouns are explained in 7b.) For your writing to communicate its message clearly, each pronoun must relate directly to an antecedent. This chapter describes clear pronoun reference and alerts you to ways in which unclear pronoun reference can occur.

Consider these sentences in which each pronoun has a clear referent.

Facts do not cease to exist just because **they** are ignored.

—ALDOUS HUXLEY

Martyrdom does not end something; **it** is only the beginning.

—INDIRA GANDHI

I have found that the best way to give advice to children is to find out what **they** want and then advise **them** to do **it.**

—HARRY S TRUMAN

When pronoun reference is unclear, meaning gets muddled. Unless each pronoun refers clearly to a noun or pronoun, the reader will become confused about the meaning that the sentences are trying to deliver. For example, consider this passage, which contains unclear pronoun reference.

In 1911, **Roald Amundsen** reached the South Pole just thirty-five days before **Robert F. Scott** arrived. **He** [who? Amundsen or Scott?] had told people that **he** was going to sail for the Arctic, but **he** turned south for the Antarctic. Then on the journey home, **he** [who? Amundsen or Scott?] and **his** party froze to death just a few miles from safety.

WORD HISTORY

Antecedent comes from the Latin *ante,* meaning *before,* and *cedere,* meaning *to go.* Thus the *antecedent* is the word that "goes before" the pronoun.

BIOGRAPHY

Indira Gandhi was born in Allahabad, India, the only child of Jawaharlal Nehru, the first prime minister of an independent India. Her parents were fiercely nationalistic, and their periodic imprisonments during her childhood served as a model for her own dedication to an autonomous India. She first served as prime minister from 1966 to 1977. During this time, she implemented several unpopular social and political policies (including large-scale birth control by sterilization and declaring a state of emergency, which entailed the arrest of opposition leaders and complete press censorship). As a result of such policies, she was badly defeated in the 1977 elections. However, the Janata party, which succeeded her, collapsed, and Gandhi was restored to power in 1980.

The most serious problem of her second administration was agitation by the Sikhs (a religious minority) for an independent state

(continued on next page)

BIOGRAPHY (*continued*)

in the Punjab, a major agricultural region of India. When the Sikhs threatened to withhold badly needed food crops from the rest of the country, Gandhi ordered troops to take the Sikh's headquarters and holiest shrine, the Golden Temple at Amritsar. Hundreds were killed. Soon after, Gandhi was assassinated on October 31, 1984, by Sikh members of her own bodyguard.

HOW TO CORRECT FAULTY PRONOUN REFERENCE

REVISION STRATEGY	SEE SECTION
Make a pronoun refer clearly to a single nearby antecedent.	10a
Place pronouns close to their antecedents.	10b
Make a pronoun refer to a definite antecedent.	10c

A HUMOROUS NOTE

Carelessly placed pronouns can result in some unintentionally funny statements, as Richard Lederer demonstrates in *Anguished English* (Wyrick and Company, 1987). Consider the difference between what the writers of the following sentences meant to say and what they really said.

1. Anti-nuclear protestors released live cockroaches inside the White House Friday, and these were arrested when they left and blocked a security gate.

2. My mother wants to have the dog's tail operated on again, and if it doesn't heal this time, she'll have to be put away.

3. About two years ago, a wart appeared on my left hand, which I wanted removed.

4. Guilt, vengeance, and bitterness can be emotionally destructive to you and your children. You must get rid of them.

10a **Making a pronoun refer clearly to a single antecedent**

To be understood, a pronoun must refer clearly to a single nearby antecedent. Often the same pronoun is used to serve as a referent to more than one antecedent. For example, in the paragraph above, *he* in different places refers to two different men, thus creating confusion for the reader. You can clarify such a passage by replacing some pronouns with nouns so that all the remaining pronouns clearly refer to a single antecedent.

In 1911, **Roald Amundsen** discovered the South Pole just thirty-five days before **Robert F. Scott** arrived. **Amundsen** had told people that **he** was going to sail for the Arctic but then **he** turned south for the Antarctic. On the journey home, **Scott** and **his** party froze to death just a few miles from safety.

You can use more than one pronoun in a sentence, but be sure that each has a clear antecedent. Here is an example:

Robert F. Scott used **horses** for **his** trip to the Pole, but **they** perished quickly because **they** were not suited for travel over ice and snow.

Said and *told,* when used with pronouns that refer to more than one person, are particularly likely to create confusion for readers. Quotation marks and slight rewording can clarify meaning.

NO	Her mother told her she was going to visit Alaska.
YES	Her mother told her, "You are going to visit Alaska."
YES	Her mother told her, "I am going to visit Alaska."

10b Placing pronouns close to their antecedents for clarity

If too much material comes between a pronoun and its antecedent, even though they may be logically related, unclear pronoun reference results. Readers lose track of the meaning of a passage if they have to trace back too far to find the antecedent of a pronoun.

No   **Alfred Wegener,** a highly trained German meteorologist and professor of geophysics and meteorology at the University of Graz in Austria, was the first person to suggest that all the continents on earth were originally part of one large land mass. According to this theory, the supercontinent broke up long ago and the fragments drifted apart. **He** named this supercontinent **Pangaea.** [Although *he* can refer only to *Wegener,* too much material intervenes between the pronoun and its antecedent.]

Yes   **Alfred Wegener,** a highly trained German meteorologist and professor of geophysics and meteorology at the University of Graz in Austria, was the first person to suggest that all the continents on earth were originally part of one large land mass. According to this theory, the supercontinent broke up long ago and the fragments drifted apart. **Wegener** named this supercontinent Pangaea.

At the beginning of a new paragraph within an essay, many writers avoid using a pronoun that refers to a name in a prior paragraph. They prefer to repeat the name instead of using a pronoun, particularly when the prior paragraph is long or when the material in the writing is complex. Repeating the name can help your reader follow more easily the message you want your material to deliver.

EXERCISE 1

Revise so that each pronoun has a single, nearby antecedent. Either replace pronouns with nouns or restructure the material to clarify pronoun reference.

EXAMPLE   Georgia O'Keeffe's art has amazed and enlightened Americans for nearly three generations. She was born in 1887 and died in 1985, having lived ninety-eight years. She grew up on a farm near Sun Prairie, Wisconsin, and she was the second

TEACHING TIP

To help students become more aware of the connections between pronouns and their antecedents, you might want to use this excerpt from Jim Bouton's essay "A Few World Series Sinkers." You might ask students to draw connecting lines between each pair. (The pronouns are italicized here.) Do they find any misleading or vague references?

> Another thing to watch during one of the little delays *that* make up such a big part of the [baseball] game is *what* the pitcher is up to. *I* don't mean when *he's* looking in to get the sign, winding up, throwing the ball. *I* mean during the time *he* steps off the mound and seems to be looking out at *his* outfielders or into the stands at girls. What *he's* really doing is rubbing up the ball and under the latest rules *he* has to walk off the mound to do so.
>
> *This* gives him some marvelous opportunities. *He* can, for one thing, stick a finger between *his* belt and trousers and come up with a gob of previously concealed vaseline. *This* while *he* has *his* back to the plate umpire. And what good is vaseline? Well, *it's* slippery like spit. *This* means *you* can throw the ball exactly as hard as *you* would a fastball and have *it* come off *your* hand behaving like a curve. *This* is very confusing for the hitter.
>
> Sometimes the sharp observer will see the batter shouting out at the pitcher. *He* will wonder what the batter is saying, and well *he* might. Because chances are *he's* not saying anything to the pitcher at all; *he's* shouting at the umpire, probably because *he* didn't like the last called strike.

259

ANSWERS: EXERCISE 1

Answers may vary somewhat. Some students may think that some of the pronouns replaced here with nouns are acceptable, but clarity is the issue—avoiding intervening information that distracts the reader, ambiguous references, and so on. Possible answers follow.

By the time Georgia O'Keeffe was twelve, she told a friend that she had made up her mind about her future. O'Keeffe was determined to become an artist. When she grew up, she attended art school in Chicago and then in New York City. Later, she spent two years as a commercial artist and then held a teaching job in Texas. The landscape of Texas impressed her deeply.

In 1916 O'Keeffe sent some charcoal drawings to a woman friend in New York. The friend took them to the renowned art dealer Alfred Stieglitz, who was astounded by O'Keeffe's talent. Stieglitz fell in love first with O'Keeffe's drawings, then with her letters, and finally with her. In 1924 Stieglitz and O'Keeffe were married, although she never wore a wedding ring or used the name "Mrs. Stieglitz."

Because O'Keeffe wanted to return to the landscapes of the Southwest, she began spending her summers alone at a ranch in New Mexico. She spent her winters in New York with her husband. In New Mexico, her work flourished. She was inspired by the spectacular cliffs, bleached animal bones, and constantly changing skies of that region of the United States. After Stieglitz died, O'Keeffe moved permanently to the area of Santa Fe, New Mexico.

of seven children. Her mother believed in the importance of her children's education. Realizing she had artistic talent, she took her at a young age to a nearby town for art lessons.

(To revise, replace the second *she* with *O'Keeffe*. Also, change the last sentence to read: *Realizing that her second-born daughter had artistic talent, O'Keeffe's mother took the youngster to a nearby town for art lessons.*)

By the time Georgia O'Keeffe was twelve, she told a friend that she had made up her mind about her future. She was determined to become an artist. When she grew up, she attended art school in Chicago and then in New York City. Later, she spent two years as a commercial artist and then held a teaching job in Texas. The landscape of Texas impressed her deeply.

In 1916 she sent some charcoal drawings to a woman friend in New York. She took them to the renowned art dealer Alfred Stieglitz, who was astounded by her talent. He fell in love first with her drawings, then with her letters, and finally with her. In 1924 he and she were married, although she never wore a wedding ring or used the name "Mrs. Stieglitz."

Because she wanted to return to the landscapes of the Southwest, she began spending her summers alone at a ranch in New Mexico. She spent her winters in New York with him. In New Mexico, her work flourished. She was inspired by the spectacular cliffs, bleached animal bones, and constantly changing skies of that region of the United States. After he died, she moved permanently to the area of Santa Fe, New Mexico.

10c   Making a pronoun refer to a definite antecedent

The antecedent of a pronoun must be clear, or your writing will not succeed in delivering its intended message.

1   Not using a pronoun to refer to a noun's possessive form

A noun's possessive form cannot be the antecedent to a pronoun, unless the pronoun is also in the possessive case.

No   The **geologist's** discovery brought **her** fame. [The pronoun *her* is not possessive and therefore cannot refer to the possessive *geologist's*.]

Yes   The **geologist** became famous because of **her** discovery.

Yes   The **geologist's** discovery was **hers** alone.

2   **Not using a pronoun to refer to an adjective**

An adjective cannot serve double duty as both a modifier and a noun to which a pronoun° refers.

No   Avery likes to study **geological** records. **That** will be her major. [*That* cannot refer to the adjective *geological*.]

Yes   Avery likes to study **geological** records. **Geology** will be her major.

3   **Making *it, that, this,* and *which* refer to only one antecedent**

Pronouns such as *it, that, this,* and *which* are particularly prone to creating unclear pronoun reference. As you write and revise, check carefully to see that the referent of these pronouns can be determined easily by your readers.

No   Comets usually fly by the earth at 100,000 m.p.h., whereas asteroids sometimes collide with the earth. **This** interests scientists. [What does *this* refer to? . . . the speed of the comets? . . . comets flying by the earth? . . . asteroids colliding with the earth?]

Yes   Comets usually fly by the earth at 100,000 m.p.h., whereas asteroids sometimes collide with the earth. **This difference** interests scientists.

No   A fireball, caused by the impact of either a comet or an asteroid, rose twelve miles above central Siberia in 1908, but **it** is still unknown. [What does *it* refer to?]

Yes   A fireball, caused by the impact of either a comet or an asteroid, rose twelve miles above central Siberia in 1908, but **the source of the explosion** is still unknown.

No   According to some scientists, a rain of comets lasting hundreds of centuries hits the earth every 26 million years. Maybe **that** is how the dinosaurs perished in a mass extinction 65 million years ago. [What does *that* refer to?]

Yes   According to some scientists, a rain of comets lasting hundreds of centuries hits the earth every 26 million years. Maybe **such a bombardment of comets killed the dinosaurs** in a mass extinction 65 million years ago.

BACKGROUND

Many people are aware that the dinosaurs became extinct, apparently suddenly, about 65 million years ago. Fewer people realize that more than half of all the other kinds of animals and plants on earth also became extinct at that time. The theory that a gigantic comet or asteroid was responsible for this mass extinction was first proposed in 1980 by Nobel Prize-winning physicist Dr. Luis Alvarez and his geologist son, Dr. Walter Alvarez. They claimed that the collision of a comet or asteroid with the Earth sent up clouds of dust that hid the sun for months or even years, causing vegetation, and the animals dependent on it for food, to die.

Their theory remains controversial, but evidence is accumulating in its support. For example, in an effort to determine the nature of the object that might have hit the earth, scientists collected from sites around the world carbon particles deposited at the time of the supposed impact. Surprisingly, all the samples contained more than 10,000 times the amount of carbon expected. The pattern of the carbon was peculiar too—of the kind made only by burning vegetation.

Some scientists say the Alvarez hypothesis must be modified. They state that the impact probably occurred in the Bering Sea, gouging out a crater 100 miles across. A 3000 F fireball, moving at the speed of sound, ignited the forests of Europe, Asia, and North America. Hundreds of billions of tons of plants and animals were burned, creating huge clouds of smoke that joined the original impact dust in the atmosphere. This dark mixture encircled the earth, blocking the sun. Many plants and large animals were killed by the impact blast, the fire, and clouds of carbon monoxide; and many others could not withstand the climatic changes caused by the lack of sunlight.

No   I told my friends that I was going to major in geology, **which** annoyed my parents. [What does *which* refer to?]

Yes   My parents were annoyed because I discussed my major with my friends.

Yes   My parents were annoyed because I chose to major in geology.

 4   Using *it* and *they* precisely

In speech, common statements are *It said on the radio* or *In Washington they say*. Because such expressions are inexact and wordy, they should be avoided in academic writing.

The newspaper reports [not *It said in the newspaper*] that minor earthquakes occur almost daily in California.

Californians say [not *In California they say*] that no one feels a minor earthquake.

5   Not using a pronoun in the first sentence of a work to refer to the work's title

When referring to a title, repeat or reword whatever part of the title you want to use.

TITLE   Geophysics as a Major

FIRST SENTENCE

No   This subject unites the sciences of physics, biology, and ancient life.

Yes   Geophysics unites the sciences of physics, biology, and ancient life.

10d   Not overusing *it*

It has three different uses in English.

1. *It* is a personal pronoun: *Doug wants to visit the 18-inch Schmidt telescope, but* ***it*** *is on Mount Palomar.*

2. *It* is an expletive, a word that postpones the subject: ***It is interesting to observe the stars.***

3. *It* is part of idiomatic expressions of weather, time, or distance: ***It is sunny. It is midnight. It is not far to the hotel.***

All of these uses are acceptable, but combining them in the same sentence can create confusion.

No   Because our car was overheating, **it** came as no surprise that **it** broke down just as **it** began to rain. [*It* is overused here even though all three uses—2, 1, and 3 above, respectively—are acceptable.]

Yes   **It** came as no surprise that our overheating car broke down just as the rain began to fall.

10e   Using *you* only for direct address

In academic writing, *you* is not a suitable substitute for specific words that refer to people, situations, and occurrences. Exact language is always preferable. Also, *you* used for other than direct address tends to lead to wordiness. This handbook uses *you* to address you directly as the reader; it never uses *you* to refer to people in general.

No   Uprisings in prison often occur when **you allow** overcrowded conditions to continue. [Are you, the reader, allowing the conditions to continue?]

Yes   Uprisings in prison often occur when **the authorities allow** overcrowded conditions to occur.

No   In many states, **you have prisons** with few rehabilitation programs. [Do you, the reader, have few programs?]

Yes   In many states, **prisons have** few rehabilitation programs.

No   In the Soviet Union **you** usually have to stand in long lines to buy groceries. [Are you, the reader, planning to do your grocery shopping in the Soviet Union?]

Yes   **Soviet consumers** usually have to stand in long lines to buy groceries.

EXERCISE 2

Rewrite each sentence so that all pronoun references are clear. If you consider a passage correct as written, circle its number.

EXAMPLE   It is claimed that slips of the tongue happen to everyone.

Experts claim that slips of the tongue happen to everyone. (Revision avoids imprecise use of *it.*)

1.   It is interesting to note that it is thought that slips of the tongue might be the result of more than merely momentary mental lapses.

BACKGROUND

The usefulness of pronouns is clearly demonstrated by W. Nelson Francis and Henry Kucera in their *Frequency Analysis of English Usage* (Boston: Houghton, 1982). After analyzing a substantial body of publications in Edited American English, Francis and Kucera determined the frequency with which specific words are used. They report that when compared with other words, the following pronouns were ranked as follows in frequency of usage.

Word	*Rank*
he	10
it	12
his	15
I	20
they	30
you	33
she	37
we	41
him	42

ANSWERS: EXERCISE 2

Answers will vary somewhat. Here is one set of possibilities.

1. Interestingly, slips of the tongue might be the result of more than merely momentary mental lapses. (Revision eliminates overuse of *it.*)

(continued on next page)

ANSWERS: EXERCISE 2 (*continued*)

2. Sigmund Freud developed theories about the connection between slips of the tongue and unconscious thoughts. (Revision eliminates the pronoun *he* referring to a noun in the possessive case.)

3. Most psychologists agree, however, that simple slips do not indicate that a person is covering up deeply hidden secrets. (Revision drops *you* because it was not used for direct address.)

4. Research reports by psychologists and language experts say that ordinary slips of the tongue provide important clues about how the brain learns information. (Revision eliminates the imprecise *It says.*)

5. Correct

6. Information about slips can also be very interesting. (Revision eliminates having *it* refer to more than one antecedent.)

7. When people are suffering from anxiety, and when people have a great deal on their minds, they tend to make more slips because they are distracted. (Revision eliminates *this* referring to more than one antecedent.)

8. Correct

9. The first person to have written about slips of the tongue was the linguist Meringer, who published a book on the subject in 1895 and whose ideas helped Sigmund Freud develop a theory of the unconscious mind. (Revision clarifies who *he* refers to.)

10. People are less likely to make slips of the tongue if they do not make other kinds of slips, as forgetting people's names or bumping into things. (Revision replaces *you* not used for direct address.)

2. Sigmund Freud's theories include what he thought about the connection between slips of the tongue and unconscious thoughts.

3. Most psychologists agree, however, that a simple slip does not indicate that you are covering up deeply hidden secrets.

4. It says in research reports by psychologists and language experts that ordinary slips of the tongue provide important clues about how the brain learns information.

5. Understanding the slips and why they occur has scientific value.

6. It can also be very interesting.

7. When people are suffering from anxiety, and when people have a great deal on their minds, they tend to make more slips. This is the result of being distracted.

8. A slip, for example, can occur when a person uses a familiar expression of speech, but those words are incorrect at that time.

9. The first person to have written about slips of the tongue was the linguist Meringer, who published a book on the subject in 1895. Sigmund Freud was helped by Meringer's ideas. He developed a theory of the unconscious mind.

10. You are less likely to make slips of the tongue if you do not make other kinds of slips, such as forgetting people's names or bumping into things.

10f   Using *who*, *which*, and *that* correctly

Who refers to people or to animals with names or special talents.

Theodore Roosevelt, who served from 1901 to 1909 as the twenty-sixth President of the United States, inspired the creation of the stuffed animal called the "teddy bear."

Lassie, the famous movie and TV collie, **who** was known for her intelligence and courage, was actually played by a series of male collies.

Which and *that* refer to animals, things, and sometimes anonymous or collective groups of people. The choice between *which* and *that* depends on whether the clause introduced by the pronoun is restrictive or nonrestrictive. (A restrictive clause is essential to limit meaning; a nonrestrictive clause is nonessential; see 24e.) Use *that* or *which* with restrictive clauses and *which* with nonrestrictive clauses. Use *who,* for people, in both kinds of clauses.   ♣ COMMA CAUTION: Set off nonrestrictive clauses with commas. ♣

In modern zoos, **animals that** are dangerous are exhibited so that the public can observe them from monorails or other types of moving cages for humans.

Modern **zoos that** are being built or renovated today provide natural habitats for their animals.

Giant pandas, which are native to China, are in danger of extinction.

Bamboo, which is their primary food source, recently has become scarce in many areas of China.

Children, who nearly all like zoos, especially enjoy zoos where they can touch animals safely.

Children who like animals usually grow up to be affectionate adults.

EXERCISE 3

Fill in the blanks with *who, which,* or *that.*

EXAMPLE   Sometimes words <u>that</u> [or <u>which</u>] look alike may have several different meanings.

1. One such word is *hydra,* _____ refers to a monster, an island, and a group of animals.

2. In Greek legend, Hydra was a gigantic monster _____ had nine heads, each of _____ grew back two new heads as soon as one was cut off.

3. Hercules, _____ was a Greek hero, was given twelve supposedly impossible tasks, one of _____ was to destroy the monster.

4. Hydra was also the old name of the Greek island now called Idhra, _____ is located in the Aegean Sea.

5. In zoology, hydras are small, tentacled polyps _____ are found in fresh water throughout the world.

ANSWERS: EXERCISE 3

Note: As the text mentions, distinctions between *that* and *which* are becoming less rigid, although many writers reserve *that* for restrictive clauses and *which* for nonrestrictive clauses. Because of common practice in academic writing today, in this exercise both words are shown as acceptable for the example and for item 5. However, if you prefer to reserve *that* for restrictive clauses and *which* for nonrestrictive clauses, the answer to the example and to item 5 is *that.*

1. which
2. who, that, *or* which; which
3. who, which
4. which
5. that *or* which

COVERAGE: EXERCISE 3

1. reference to a thing, nonrestrictive clause
2. ambiguous identification as human or animal, restrictive; reference to a thing, nonrestrictive clause
3. reference to a person, nonrestrictive clause; reference to a thing, nonrestrictive clause
4. reference to a thing, nonrestrictive clause
5. reference to a thing, restrictive clause

Focus on Revising

REVISING YOUR WRITING

If you make errors in pronoun reference when you write, go back to your writing and locate the errors. Using this chapter as a resource, revise your writing to correct the problems.

CASE STUDY: REVISING TO CORRECT NOUN AND PRONOUN CASE AS WELL AS PRONOUN REFERENCE

This case study lets you observe a student writer revising. It also gives you the opportunity to revise some student writing on your own.

Observation

A student wrote the following draft for a course called Twentieth-Century American History. The assignment was to write about an influential woman in American politics. This material is well organized as a narrative and offers good examples to support its topic, but the draft's effectiveness is diminished by errors in noun and pronoun case as well as in pronoun reference.

Read through the draft. The errors are highlighted. Before you look at how the student revised to eliminate the errors, revise the material yourself. Refer to this chapter and also to Chapter 9. Then compare what you and the student did.

Few people who have grown up in the United States are unaware of Franklin Delano Roosevelt many accomplishments. Not everyone, however, knows much about one of his most valued aides and advisors: his wife Eleanor. In fact, it was her who was his strongest supporter in his decision to seek the governorship of New York as well as the presidency of the United States.

After he was stricken with polio in 1921, his legs were paralyzed. His mother, who Eleanor did not always agree with,

Marginal annotations:

Possessive case of noun needed: opening Chapter 9

Objective case used; need subjective case after linking verb: 9c

Antecedent too far away; repeat noun: 10b

Repeat noun at start of new paragraph: 10b

Subjective case used; need objective case: 9d

urged her son to retire from politics. But Eleanor, with the approval of physicians and friends, urged him to continue with his career. Franklin listened to her, and he was elected governor of New York in 1928 and president of the United States in 1932.

> Should refer to a single antecedent: 10a

> Objective case used; calls for subjective case for correct comparison: 9e

As the new president's wife, she quickly showed that she cared as much about the nation as him. No sooner had her and her husband settled into the White House than she began touring the country and speaking to sharecroppers, slum dwellers, and unemployed workers. A first lady taking it upon herself to spread political messages created quite a stir across the nation. Even more unusual was her support of what were then unpopular causes, such as civil rights. This did not represent Franklin Roosevelt policy.

Through lecture tours, radio broadcasts, newspaper columns, and press conferences for women reporters, she changed forever the world perception of the role of first lady of the United States.

> Repeat noun at start of new paragraph: 10b

> Objective case used; need subjective case in the compound: 9a

> Objective case used; need possessive case before gerund: 9g

> *This* should refer to one antecedent: 10c-3

> Possessive case of noun needed: opening Chapter 9.

> Possessive case of noun needed: opening Chapter 9.

> Antecedent too far away; repeat noun: 10b

Here is how the student revised the draft to correct errors in noun and pronoun case as well as in pronoun reference. In a few places, the student had alternatives for correcting the errors. Your revision, therefore, might not be exactly like this one, but it should deal with each error highlighted on the draft.

Few people who have grown up in the United States are unaware of Franklin Delano Roosevelt's many accomplishments. Not everyone, however, knows much about one of his most valued aides and advisors: his wife Eleanor. In fact, it was she who was Franklin's strongest supporter in his decision to seek the governorship of New York as well as the presidency of the United States.

COVERAGE:
PARTICIPATION ESSAY (next page)

Television programming mirrors the society that watches it. In the 1950's, *you saw* [10e: not a direct address] situation comedies with a traditional family with a father who was the breadwinner, a mother who enjoyed housekeeping, and children who were always adorable. Later, *they* [10c: pronoun should refer to a definite antecedent] replaced the traditional families seen on *Father Knows Best* and *Leave It to Beaver* with people which [10f: *who* needed] fit a broader definition of "family."

Reflecting an updated concept of family life in the 1970's, situation comedies like *All in the Family* portrayed nontraditional situations. A young couple lived with the *wife* [intro material for Chapter 9: possessive case needed for noun] parents. One spinoff from that series involved the father, his business, and *him* [9g: a gerund, so possessive case needed] raising a foster child alone. The long-running *Mary Tyler Moore Show* featured single women *whom* [9d: subjective case, *who* needed] were supporting themselves, raising children, and enjoying good friendships.

As working women have become the norm in society, situation comedies have changed to portray women who juggle home and career. Lead roles on situation comedies portary women as lawyers, architects, and factory workers. Some shows include unemployed husbands and husbands whose wives make more money than *them* [9e: after *than* subjective case needed for this meaning].

In many ways today, however, *they* [10c: pronoun should refer to a definite antecedent] still differ from reality. In contrast to

(continued next page)

COVERAGE:
PARTICIPATION ESSAY (*continued*)

real life, most comedies show no child who is ever inconvenienced by parents or upset about *them* [9g: a gerund, so possessive case needed] working at demanding jobs. And parents are never too busy or too tired for the children. The kitchen is still primarily the domain of the woman, and it is *her* [9c: subjective case needed after a linking verb] *who* [9d: objective case, *whom* needed] the children usually turn to for personal advice.

As traditional patterns in family life are changing, so are the situations shown on television comedy series. It seems clear that it [10d: overuse of it] will not be long before *us* [9b: wrong case, *we* needed] viewers will see more comedies that come closer to reality.

ANSWER: PARTICIPATION ESSAY

This version revises the errors in noun and pronoun case and in pronoun reference. Answers might vary slightly. Also, answers will vary if students have revised for content, organization, or style.

Television programming mirrors the society that watches it. In the 1950's, situation comedies showed a traditional family with a father who was the breadwinner, a mother who enjoyed housekeeping, and children who were always adorable. Later, the writers of situation comedies replaced the traditional families seen on *Father Knows Best* and *Leave It to Beaver* with people who fit a broader definition of "family."

Reflecting an updated concept of family life in the 1970's, situation comedies like *All in the Family* portrayed nontraditional situations. A young couple lived with the wife's parents. One spinoff from that series involved the father, his business, and his raising a foster child alone. The long-running *Mary Tyler Moore Show* featured single women who were supporting themselves,

After Franklin was stricken with polio in 1921, his legs were paralyzed. His mother, whom Eleanor did not always agree with, urged Franklin to retire from politics. But Eleanor, with the approval of physicians and friends, urged him to continue with his career. Franklin listened to his wife, and he was elected governor of New York in 1928 and president of the United States in 1932.

As the new president's wife, Eleanor Roosevelt quickly showed that she cared as much about the nation as he did. No sooner had she and her husband settled into the White House than she began touring the country and speaking to sharecroppers, slum dwellers, and unemployed workers. A first lady's taking it upon herself to spread political messages created quite a stir across the nation. Even more unusual was Eleanor's support of what were then unpopular causes, such as civil rights. Eleanor's making public statements in support of such causes was not part of Franklin Roosevelt's policy.

Through lecture tours, radio broadcasts, newspaper columns, and press conferences for women reporters, Eleanor Roosevelt changed forever the world's perception of the role of first lady of the United States.

Participation

A student wrote the following draft for a sociology course called Faces of America. The assignment was to discuss the changing culture in the United States as reflected on television. The material is well organized and uses specific details, but the draft's effectiveness is diminished by errors in noun and pronoun case and in pronoun references.

Read through the draft. Then revise it to eliminate the errors. Also, make any additional revisions you think would improve the content, organization, and style of the material.

Television programming mirrors the society that watches it. In the 1950s, you saw situation comedies with a traditional family with a father who was the breadwinner, a mother who enjoyed housekeeping, and children who were always adorable. Later, they replaced the traditional families seen on <u>Father Knows Best</u> and <u>Leave It to Beaver</u> with people which fit a broader definition of "family."

Reflecting an updated concept of family life in the 1970s, situation comedies like All in the Family portrayed nontraditional situations. A young couple lived with the wife parents. One spinoff from that series involved the father, his business, and him raising a foster child alone. The long-running Mary Tyler Moore Show featured single women whom were supporting themselves, raising children, and enjoying good friendships.

As working women have become the norm in society, situation comedies have changed to portray women who juggle home and career. Lead roles on situation comedies portray women as lawyers, architects, and factory workers. Some shows include unemployed husbands and husbands whose wives make more money than them.

In many ways today, however, they still differ from reality. In contrast to real life, most comedies show no child who is ever inconvenienced by parents or upset about them working at demanding jobs. And parents are never are too busy or too tired for the children. The kitchen is still priimarily the domain of the woman, and it is her who the children usually turn to for personal advice.

As traditional patterns in family life are changing, so are the situations shown on television comedies series. It seems clear that it will not be long before us viewers will see more comedies that come closer to reality.

raising children, and enjoying good friendships.

As working women have become the norm in society, situation comedies have changed to portray women who juggle home and career. Lead roles on situation comedies portray women as lawyers, architects, and factory workers. Some shows include unemployed husbands and husbands whose wives make more money than they do.

In many ways today, however, situation comedies still differ from reality. In contrast to real life, most comedies show no child who is ever inconvenienced by parents or upset about their working at demanding jobs. And parents are never are too busy or too tired for the children. The kitchen is still primarily the domain of the woman, and it is she to whom the children usually turn for personal advice.

As traditional patterns in family life are changing, so are the situations shown on television comedy series. It seems clear that before long we viewers will see more comedies that come closer to reality.

ALTERNATE EXAMPLE

Notice how many subject-verb pairs are in the following passage from *Our Space Environment* by Phillip D. Stern:

> *It is* common to refer to the sky as blue. Actually, the *sky is* black and our *atmosphere is* blue. *That is* because the tiny particles of *dust* and little moisture *droplets* in the air *are* small enough to interfere with and scatter the shorter wavelengths of the sun's light, the blue and violet colors, to produce an illusion of a blue sky. *Astronauts,* circling our planet at heights of hundreds of miles, *report* the *sky is* black and that the *sun, moon, stars,* and *planets can be seen* in the daytime hours.

The concept of *agreement* in human affairs rests on matching knowledge and opinions. Grammatical agreement is also based on matching. Before language can work properly, certain parts of speech that change number (singular or plural), person (first, second, or third), and, less often, gender (male or female) must match each other in form when they work together. Although the rules governing agreement are not difficult, their applications can seem tricky. Indeed, almost everyone has to consult a handbook once in a while to be reminded of one or another of the rules for agreement. This chapter discusses the only two combinations in which questions of matching forms arise: agreement between (1) subjects and verbs and (2) pronouns and antecedents.

SUBJECT–VERB AGREEMENT

Subject–verb agreement occurs at least once per sentence. To be grammatically correct, subjects and verbs must match in number (singular or plural) and in person (first, second, or third).

The **firefly glows** with luminescent light. [*firefly* = singular subject in the third person; *glows* = singular verb in the third person]

Fireflies glow with luminescent light. [*fireflies* = plural subject in the third person; *glow* = plural verb in the third person]

This **insect is** nocturnal.

These **insects are** nocturnal.

REVIEW OF "NUMBER" AND "PERSON" FOR AGREEMENT

Number refers to *singular* and *plural*.

The **first person** is the speaker or writer. *I* (singular) and *we* (plural) are the only subjects that occur in the first person.

SINGULAR	**I** see a field of fireflies.
PLURAL	**We** see a field of fireflies.

The **second person** is the person spoken or written to. *You* (both singular and plural) is the only subject that occurs in the second person.

SINGULAR	**You** see a shower of sparks.
PLURAL	**You** see a shower of sparks.

The **third person** is the person or thing being spoken or written of. Most rules for subject–verb agreement involve the third person. A subject in the third person can vary widely—for example, *student* and *students* (singular and plural people), *table* and *tables* (singular and plural things), and *it* and *they* (singular and plural pronouns).

SINGULAR	The **scientist sees** a cloud of cosmic dust.
	She (he, it) sees a cloud of cosmic dust.
PLURAL	The **scientists see** a cloud of cosmic dust.
	They see a cloud of cosmic dust.

11a Using the final *-s* or *-es* either for plural subjects or for singular verbs

Subject–verb agreement often involves one letter: *s.* The key is the distinction between the *-s* added to subjects and the *-s* added to verbs. These uses of *s* have very different functions.

Most **plural subjects** are formed by adding an *-s* or *-es: lip* becomes *lips; princess* becomes *princesses.* Exceptions include most pronouns *(they, who);* a few nouns that do not change form *(deer, deer);* and a few nouns that change in other ways *(mouse, mice; child, children).* **Singular verbs** in the present tense of the third person are formed by adding *-s* or *-es* to the simple form of the verb:

BACKGROUND

Although English requires agreement between subject and verb, it is unlike some other modern languages in that it does not extend agreement to the gender and number of adjectives. Mario Pei, in *The Story of English* (Fawcett Publications, 1952), says that although the diminished number of endings used to indicate number and gender is thought to represent a great economy of time, space, and thought, it is probably as natural for a Spanish speaker to indicate that information by the article, adjective, and noun—e.g., *las muchachas bonitas*—as it is for the English speaker not to do so. Another situation is found in the Chinese languages, which use word order instead of agreement to establish proper relationships among words.

EXTRA EXERCISE A

Fill in the blank with the correct present-tense form of the verb in parentheses.

EXAMPLE

Psychologists often (to use) _____ projective tests to investigate clients' unconscious memories and drives. [*use*]

1. Psychologists sometimes (to present) _____ their clients with questions to which there are no correct answers.

2. The client then (to tell) _____ what he (to see) _____, thus showing the psychologist some of his inner self.

3. The popular *Rorschach Psychodiagnostic Inkblot Test* (to require) _____ the client to examine ten cards containing symmetrical inkblots and say what he (to think) _____ each means.

4. Next, the client (to point) _____ out where in the blot he (to find) _____ each image or idea.

5. Several scoring systems (to exist) _____ to help psychologists interpret clients' responses.

ANSWERS: EXTRA EXERCISE A

1. present
2. tells; sees
3. requires; thinks
4. points; finds
5. exist

laugh becomes *laughs; kiss* becomes *kisses.* Exceptions include the verb *be (is)* and *have (has).* Even though *is* and *has* end in -*s,* they are not formed from the simple form of the verb.

SUBJECT–VERB AGREEMENT PATTERN I

BASIC SUBJECT–VERB AGREEMENT

The **student works** long hours.

↑   ↑
SINGULAR   SINGULAR
SUBJECT   VERB

The **students work** long hours.

↑   ↑
PLURAL   PLURAL
SUBJECT   VERB

Here is a memory device to help you to visualize how, in most cases, the *s* works in agreement. The -*s* (or -*es*) can take only one path at a time, going either to the top or to the bottom.

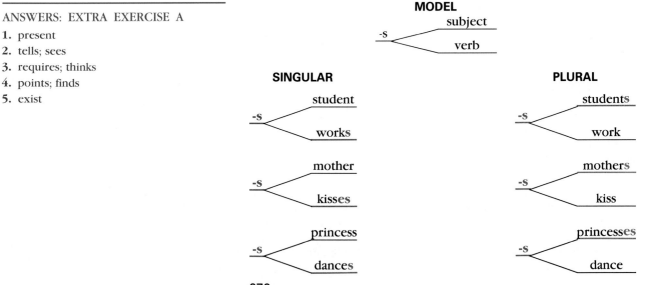

MODEL

-s   subject / verb

SINGULAR

-s   student / work**s**

-s   mother / kiss**es**

-s   princess / dance**s**

PLURAL

-s   student**s** / work

-s   mother**s** / kiss

-s   princess**es** / dance

The principle of the memory device holds, even though some plural subjects do not have a final *s*. For example, the final *s* does not appear in some plural nouns (such as *people, children*), in plural personal pronouns *(we, you, they)*, in the plural demonstrative pronouns *(these* and *those)*, or in certain indefinite pronouns when they are used as plurals *(few, some, more, many, most,* and *all)*.

> The **child enjoys** watching cartoons.
> **Children enjoy** watching cartoons.
> **We watch** cartoons every Saturday morning.
> **They reflect** rudimentary human impulses.
> **Most involve** a startling amount of violence.

❖ USAGE ALERT: Do not add *-s* to a singular main verb in the third person after a modal auxiliary verb (a helping verb like *can, might, must, would;* see 8c). ❖

> **No**   The coach **can walks** to campus.
> **Yes** The coach **can walk** to campus.

EXERCISE 1

Using the subject and verb in each set shown, write two complete sentences—one with the subject as a singular and one with the subject as a plural. Keep all verbs in the present tense.

1. boat race	2. flag fly	3. critic applaud	4. woman cheer
5. chorus sing	6. baby burp	7. judge might decide	8. winner kiss

11b For the purposes of agreement, ignoring words that come between a subject and verb

Words that separate the subject from the verb can cause confusion about what a verb should agree with. This intervening material often appears as a prepositional phrase°. To locate the subject of a sentence, eliminate all prepositional phrases from consideration. The object of a preposition can never be a subject.

> **No**   The **winners** in the state competition **goes** to the national finals. [*Winners* is the subject with which the verb must agree; *in the state competition* is a prepositional phrase.]
>
> **Yes** The **winners** in the state competition **go** to the national finals.

EXTRA EXERCISE B

Fill in the blank with the correct present-tense form of the verb in parentheses.

EXAMPLE

In the eyes of many people, the Rorschach Inkblots (to be) _____ the psychologists' standard tool for getting at clients' hidden thoughts and feelings. [*are*]

1. Yet either the Holtzman Inkblot Technique or the Thematic Apperception Test (TAT) (to be) _____ given by psychologists who feel the Rorschach is unreliable.

2. Not only does the Holtzman series have more inkblots (45) than the Rorschach (10), but it also (to have) _____ a more standardized system of administration.

3. The TAT (to use) _____ a series of pictures showing people engaged in a wide range of activities.

4. Although the pictures show people in realistic situations, there (to be) _____ many possible acceptable answers.

5. It (to be) _____ the task of the person interpreting the picture to make up a story, deciding what has occurred and what the characters are thinking and feeling.

ANSWERS: EXTRA EXERCISE B

1. is
2. has
3. uses
4. are
5. is

273

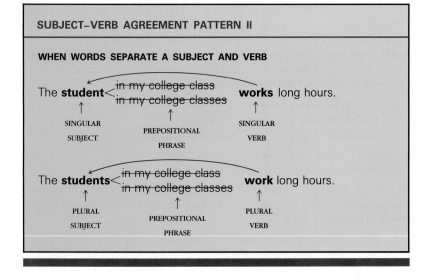

SUBJECT–VERB AGREEMENT PATTERN II

WHEN WORDS SEPARATE A SUBJECT AND VERB

No	The **sponsor** of the concerts **pay** all expenses. [*Sponsor* is the subject with which the verb must agree; *of the concerts* is a prepositional phrase.]
YES	The **sponsor** of the concerts **pays** all expenses.

Also, to locate the subject of a sentence, eliminate any phrases that start with *including, together with, along with, accompanied by, in addition to, except,* and *as well as.*

No	The **moon,** as well as Venus, **are** visible in the night sky. [*The moon* is the subject with which the verb must agree; ignore *as well as Venus.*]
YES	The **moon,** as well as Venus, **is** visible in the night sky.
No	The **Big Dipper,** along with many other constellations, **are** easy to learn to find. [*The Big Dipper* is the subject with which the verb must agree; ignore *along with many other constellations.*]
YES	The **Big Dipper,** along with many other constellations, **is** easy to learn to find.

Be especially careful when you use a construction that starts with the words *one of the.* This construction takes a singular verb, to agree with the word *one.* Do not be distracted by a plural noun in the prepositional phrase.

No	**One** of the problems **are** broken equipment.
YES	**One** of the problems **is** broken equipment.

274

11c Using a plural verb for subjects connected by *and*

SUBJECT–VERB AGREEMENT PATTERN III

WHEN TWO SUBJECTS ARE JOINED BY *and*

The student and the instructor work long hours.

⟍ ⟍
COMPOUND   PLURAL

SUBJECT   VERB

(uses *and*)

When two or more subjects are joined by *and,* they become plural as a group; therefore, they need a plural verb.

> **The moon and Venus are** visible in the night sky.
> **Herb and Phyllis like** to gaze at the stars.

However, if the word *each* or *every* precedes a singular subject, use a singular verb.

> **Each human hand and foot leaves** a distinctive print.
> **Every police chief, sheriff, and federal marshal in the country has used** these prints to identify people.

But when *each* or *every* follows subjects joined by *and,* they do not affect the basic rule: use a plural verb for subjects joined by *and.*

> **The Splitting Devil and the Masked Marvel each claim** to be the meanest wrestler alive.
> **Memphis and St. Louis each claim** to be the birthplace of the blues.

The one exception to the *and* rule occurs when the parts combine to form a single thing or person.

> **Ham and cheese is** our best-selling sandwich.
> **My best friend and neighbor feeds** my cat when I go away.

275

EXERCISE 2

Supply the correct present-tense form of the verb in parentheses.

EXAMPLE   Increased heartbeat, rapid breathing, muscular tension, and
sweaty palms (to be) _____ physical signs of anxiety.

Increased heartbeat, rapid breathing, muscular tension, and
sweaty palms *are* physical signs of anxiety.

1. Every adult, as well as most children, (to experience) _____ some
anxiety.
2. Each man, woman, and child (to have) _____ a different reaction to
feelings of anxiety.
3. When a person (to suffer) _____ from anxiety, the person might (to
feel) _____ a need to escape from some imagined danger.
4. Anxiety, as expressed in behavior disorders, (to take) _____ several
forms.
5. Sigmund Freud, one of the founders of modern psychoanalysis, (to
be) _____ said to have been the first to call severe anxieties *neuroses*.

ANSWERS: EXERCISE 2

1. experiences
2. has
3. suffers; feel
4. takes
5. is

COVERAGE: EXERCISE 2

1. 11b: words between subject and verb;
11c: *every*
2. 11c: *each*
3. 11a: singular subject; 11a: modal auxiliary verb
4. 11b: words between subject and verb
5. 11a: singular subject and words between subject and verb

11d Making the verb agree with the subject closest to it

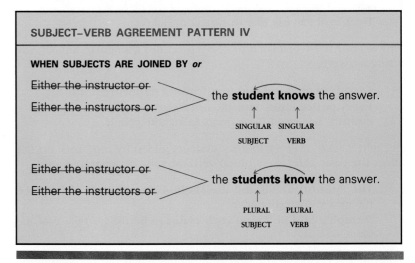

SUBJECT–VERB AGREEMENT PATTERN IV

WHEN SUBJECTS ARE JOINED BY *or*

Either the instructor or
Either the instructors or   the **student knows** the answer.

SINGULAR   SINGULAR
SUBJECT   VERB

Either the instructor or
Either the instructors or   the **students know** the answer.

PLURAL   PLURAL
SUBJECT   VERB

When you join subjects with *or, nor, either . . . or, neither
. . . nor,* or *not only . . . but (also),* make the verb agree with the
subject closest to it. These conjunctions do not create plurals. For
subject-verb agreement, ignore everything before the final subject.

~~Not only the spider but also all other~~ **arachnids have** four pairs of legs.

~~Neither spiders nor~~ **flies tempt** my appetite.

~~Six clam fritters, four blue crabs, or one steamed~~ **lobster tempts** my appetite.

If the final example sounds awkward, rearrange the items so that the plural subject is next to the verb: *One steamed lobster, four blue crabs, or six clam fritters tempt my appetite.*

11e With inverted word order, making sure the verb agrees with its subject

---

SUBJECT–VERB AGREEMENT PATTERN V

WHEN WORD ORDER IS INVERTED

Is the **student** voting?

SINGULAR   SINGULAR
VERB   SUBJECT

Are the **students** voting?

PLURAL   PLURAL
VERB   SUBJECT

In English, the subject of a sentence normally precedes its verb: *Astronomy is interesting.* Inverted word order occurs primarily in two situations: in questions, and in sentences using *there* or *it* in expletive° constructions.

In questions, the auxiliary verb that has to agree with the subject often comes before the subject. Be sure to look ahead to check that the subject and verb agree.

Is astronomy interesting?

What **are** the **requirements** for the major?

Do John and Mary study astronomy?

Expletive constructions postpone the subject. Expletives using *there* or *it* plus a form of the verb *be* can be tricky because the form of *be* must agree with the sentence subject. Check ahead in such sentences to identify the subject, and make the form of *be*—*is, are, was, were,* for example—agree with the subject.

> **There are** nine **planets** in our solar system. [The verb *are* agrees with the subject, *planets.*]
>
> **There is** probably no **life** on eight of them. [*Is* agrees with *life.*]

The introductory *it* plus a form of the verb *be* can be an expletive construction as well, but one that always takes a singular verb.

> **It is** astronomers who want to talk about the possibility of life in other galaxies.
>
> **It was** the Viking mission to Mars ten years ago that ruled out any possibility of life on Mars.

For advice on making sentences more direct and concise by eliminating expletives, see 16a-1.

You may occasionally want to write a statement in inverted word order for special effect (see 19e). Be sure to locate the subject and make the verb agree with it.

> Into deep space **shoot** probing **satellites.** [*Shoot* agrees with the inverted subject, *satellites.*]
>
> On the television screen **appears** an **image** of Saturn. [*Appears* agrees with the inverted subject, *image.*]

EXERCISE 3

Supply the correct present-tense form of the verb in parentheses.

EXAMPLE   Either sales and marketing or finance (to provide) _____ the basic training for most top corporate executives.

Either sales and marketing or finance *provides* the basic training for most top corporate executives.

1. To an outsider, the chief executive officer (CEO) of a company or conglomerate of companies (to seem) _____ to be an independent decision-maker.

2. Neither the economic climate nor a business's social responsibilities (to permit) _____ independence today, however.

3. There (to be) _____ many conflicting demands to reconcile from both stockholders and consumers.

4. Not only daily operations but also the public image of the corporation (to set) _____ the environment for a CEO.

5. It (to be) _____ up to the finance people to set the corporation's short-term goals.

ANSWERS: EXERCISE 3

1. seems
2. permit
3. are
4. sets
5. is

COVERAGE: EXERCISE 3

1. 11d: *or*
2. 11d: *neither . . . nor*
3. 11e: expletive
4. 11d: *not only . . . but also*
5. 11e: expletive

BACKGROUND ON LANGUAGE

Most of us spend a fair proportion of our time reminding students that indefinite pronouns (with the exception of *all, any, some,* and *none*) are always singular. Yet widespread informal usage does not adhere to this rule, and we hardly seem to make a dent in our students' habit of following *everyone, anybody,* and the like with *their.*

According to Martha Kolln of Pennsylvania State University, we shouldn't be too

11f   Using singular verbs for most indefinite pronouns

Indefinite pronouns do not refer to any particular person, thing, or idea. In context, however, they take on very clear meanings. Most indefinite pronouns are singular and therefore take singular verbs. (See 11n for a discussion of masculine pronouns with indefinite pronouns as antecedents.)

INDEFINITE PRONOUNS			
another	either	neither	somebody
anybody	every	nobody	someone
anyone	everybody	no one	something
anything	everyone	nothing	
each	everything	one	

Everything about that intersection **is** dangerous.

But whenever **anyone says** anything, **nothing is** done.

Everyone knows that **something** terrible **is** likely to happen.

A few indefinite pronouns—*none, some, more, most, any,* and *all*—may be either singular or plural, depending on the meaning of the sentence.

Some of our streams **are** polluted. [*Some* refers to more than one stream.]

Pollution is always a threat, but **some is** easy to reverse. [*Some* refers to a portion of *pollution,* so it is singular and the verb *is* is used.]

All he asks **is** a chance. [*Chance* is singular; therefore, *all* is singular, and *is* is a singular verb.]

All are gone. [*All* here refers to more than one, so the verb *are* is correct.]

11g   With collective nouns, using singular or plural verbs according to context

A **collective noun** names a group of people or things: *family, group, audience, class, number, committee, team,* and the like.

concerned about this usage. In "Everyone's Right to Their Own Language" (*College Composition and Communication,* Feb. 1986, 100–102), she looks at the issue. Most handbooks treat this usage as, at best, informal, while some continue to label it an outright error. Yet, Kolln points out, studies of usage patterns indicate that *everybody* has been treated as a plural for over four hundred years and *everyone* for over two hundred, appearing this way in the works of Cardinal Newman, Shakespeare, and Swift. Despite this evidence (available since 1957), the rule stands—at least on the record.

Kolln argues for treating indefinite pronouns as we treat collective nouns. A collective noun such as *crowd* takes a singular verb but takes a plural pronoun when it clearly refers to more than one person. She gives as an example:

> At first *the crowd* was singing; then *they* began to laugh.

Kolln gives this example for indefinite pronouns:

> At first *everyone* in the room was singing; then *they* began to laugh.

In fact, a singular pronoun would be out of place in the second clause. She demonstrates that the same applies when the indefinite pronoun appears as the direct object or as the subject of a tag question.

Kolln ends by calling for the acceptance of the plural possessive pronoun *(their)* after collective indefinite pronouns:

> These dicta that designate all indefinite pronouns as singular have no basis either in actual usage or in the rules of logic. Yet the current handbooks apply the same rule to all of the indefinite pronouns, whether they are collective or not, whether singular or not. (102)

Whether you agree or disagree with Kolln, the issue is certainly worth discussion.

When the group acts as one unit, use a singular verb. When the members of the group act individually, thus creating more than one action, use a plural verb.

> **The senior class** nervously **awaits** final exams. [*Class* is acting as a single unit, so the verb is singular.]
>
> **The senior class were fitted** for their graduation robes today. [Each member was fitted individually, but because there was more than one fitting the verb is plural.]
>
> **The couple** in blue **is** engaged. [*Couple* refers to a single unit, so the verb is singular.]
>
> **The couple say** their vows tomorrow. [Each of the two people will take a separate action, so because there is more than one action, the verb is plural.]

11h Making a linking verb agree with the subject—not the subject complement

Linking verbs indicate a state of being or a condition. They include *be (am, is, are, was, were);* verbs related to the senses, including *look, smell, taste, sound,* and *feel;* and verbs such as *appear, seem, become, grow, turn, remain,* and *prove.* Linking verbs connect the subject° to a complement—a word that renames or describes the subject. You can think of a linking verb as an equal sign between a subject and its complement called the **subject complement.**

> You **seem** angry. [*You = angry; you* is the subject, and *angry* is the subject complement.]

When you write a sentence that contains a subject complement, remember that the verb always agrees with the subject, no matter what the number° of the subject complement.

> **No**   **The worst part** of owning a car **are** the bills. [The subject is *the worst part,* with which the verb *are* does not agree; the subject complement is *the bills.*]
>
> **Yes**   The worst part of owning a car **is** the bills.

When the wording of a sentence is revised so that the word or words that were the subject complement become the subject, the same rule applies: the verb always agrees with the subject. For the purposes of agreement, ignore the subject complement.

> **No**   **Bills is** the worst part of owning a car.
>
> **Yes**   **Bills are** the worst part of owning a car.

11i With *who, which,* and *that* as subjects, using verbs that agree with the antecedents of these pronouns

Who, which, and *that* have the same form in singular and plural. Find their antecedents—words to which the pronouns refer—before deciding whether the verb is singular or plural.

> The scientist will share the income from her new patent with the graduate **students who work** with her. [*Who* refers to *students,* so the verb *work* is plural.]

> George Jones is **the student who works** in the science lab. [*Who* refers to *student,* so the verb *works* is singular.]

Be especially careful to identify the antecedent of *who, which,* or *that* when you see *one of the* or *the only one of the* in a sentence. When you write a sentence with *one . . . who, one . . . which,* or *one . . . that,* decide whether the relative pronoun° refers to *one* or to the group named after *one of the.* If the pronoun refers to *one,* use a singular verb. If the pronoun refers to what comes after *one of the,* use a plural verb.

> George Jones is one of the lab assistants **who deserve** recognition. [*Who* refers to *lab assistants,* so *deserve* is plural.]

> George Jones is the only one of the lab assistants **who deserves** recognition. [*Who* refers to *one,* so *deserve* is singular.]

EXERCISE 4

Supply the correct present-tense form of the verb in parentheses.

EXAMPLE   Everyone (to know) _____ that a good laugh (to make) _____ most people feel better.

            Everyone *knows* that a good laugh *makes* most people feel better.

1. Now a group of humor consultants (to work) _____ to introduce laughter to American businesses.
2. They believe the best introduction for a speech (to be) _____ jokes and humorous observations.
3. C. W. Metcalf has developed one of the programs that (to encourage) _____ people to laugh at their own problems.
4. A large number of personnel officers (to say) _____ they prefer to hire workers who (to have) _____ a sense of humor.
5. Sales representatives find that almost anyone (to listen) _____ more attentively to a person who (to make) _____ an amusing comment.

ANSWERS: EXERCISE 4

1. works
2. is
3. encourage
4. say; have
5. listens; makes

COVERAGE: EXERCISE 4

1. collective noun
2. verb agrees with subject, not subject complement
3. use of *that*
4. collective noun; use of *who*
5. indefinite pronoun; use of *who*

EXTRA EXERCISE C

In writing groups students can work together to edit the following sentences for subject–verb agreement.

1. When a couple move into a new apartment, they face many decisions.

2. One of the biggest choices have to do with how to decorate it.

3. Probably the most important decision of all are the color choices.

4. Green is one of the colors that looks good in any room.

5. Two hours are about all the time a person can spend looking at color samples without becoming confused.

ANSWERS: EXTRA EXERCISE C

1. When a couple *moves* into a new apartment, they face many decisions.

2. One of the biggest choices *has* to do with how to decorate it.

3. Probably the most important decision of all *is* the color choices.

4. Green is one of the colors that *look* good in any room

5. Two hours *is* about all the time a person can spend looking at color samples without becoming confused.

11j Using singular verbs with subjects that specify amounts and with singular subjects that are in plural form

Subjects that refer to sums of money, distance, or measurement are considered singular and take singular verbs.

> **Ninety cents is** the current bus fare.
> **Three hundred dollars is** the price.
> **Three-quarters of an inch is** all we need.
> **Two miles is** a short sprint for a serious jogger.

Many words that end in *-s* or *-ics* are singular in meaning and so need singular verbs, despite their plural appearance. These words include *news, ethics, and measles.* They also include *economics, mathematics, physics,* and *statistics* when these words refer to courses of study.

> The **news gets** better each day. [*News* agrees with the singular verb *gets.*]
> **Statistics is** required of science majors. [*Statistics* is a course of study, so it agrees with the singular verb *is.*]
> **Statistics show** that a teacher shortage is coming. [*Statistics* refers to separate pieces of information, so it agrees with the plural verb *show.*]

Some nouns are singular in some contexts but not in others. They include *politics* and *sports.* Such words agree with singular or plural verbs, depending on the meaning of the sentence.

> Some people think that **politics is** a noble profession.
> Corrupt **politics are** behind the ruling.
> **Sports is** a good way to build physical stamina.
> Three **sports are** offered at the recreation center.

Some words are treated as plural, even though they refer to one thing: *jeans, pants, scissors, clippers, tweezers, eyeglasses, thanks,* and *riches.* If, however, the word *pair* is used in conjunction with *jeans, pants, scissors, clippers, tweezers,* or *eyeglasses,* the verb agrees with *pair,* so the verb is singular.

> **My eyeglasses fog up** in damp weather, so **my thanks go** to the inventor of contact lenses.
> **My slacks need** pressing.
> **My pair of slacks needs** pressing.

Series and *means* have the same form in singular and plural, so the meaning determines whether the verb is singular or plural.

> **The new television series is** beginning on Sunday night.
> **A series of disasters are** plaguing our production.

11k   Using singular verbs for titles of written works, companies, and words as terms

Even though plural and compound nouns occur in a title, the title itself signifies one work or entity. Therefore, these subjects are singular and always take singular verbs.

> ***Breathing Lessons*** by Ann Tyler **is** a Pulitzer-prize-winning novel.
> ***Dreamgirls*** **was** a major Broadway hit.

Even if a word is plural, when you refer to it as a term, it takes a singular verb.

> ***Our*** implies that I am included.
> During the Vietnam War, ***protective reaction strikes*** **was** a euphemism used by the United States government to mean *bombing*.

EXERCISE 5

Supply the correct present-tense form of the verb in parentheses.

EXAMPLE   In the United States, most business cards (to show) _____ a person's name, address, and telephone number.

            In the United States, most business cards *show* a person's name, address, and telephone number.

1. In some parts of the world, business cards (to make) _____ an important first impression.
2. One of the countries that almost (to require) _____ people to carry business cards is Japan.
3. In Japan, every business person, as well as most people in professions, (to need) _____ to carry a carefully designed card.
4. Everyone who (to use) _____ business cards must (to observe) _____ certain rules of etiquette and tradition.
5. The *Tokyo Times* (to publish) _____ articles on international business customs.
6. One of the most important parts of offering someone a business card (to be) _____ to exchange slight bows.

EXTRA EXERCISE D

Complete the following sentences by supplying an appropriate verb.

1. Physics _____ a demanding subject.

2. Do you think physics or economics _____ harder?

3. Sports _____ the popular favorite.

4. Three-quarters of an hour of exercise several times a week _____ enough to keep a person in reasonably good shape.

5. Statistics _____ that exercise of the body as well as the mind _____ important for good health.

ANSWERS: EXTRA EXERCISE D

1. is
2. is
3. is
4. is
5. show (indicate); is

QUOTATION ON WRITING

When used as a grammatical term *antecedent* means the word or group of words referred to by a pronoun. It does not necessarily come before the pronoun and it may not be mentioned at all.

—Cornelia Evans and Bergen Evans,
*A Dictionary of Contemporary
American Usage*

7. People also (to explain) _____ that a male visiting Japan should not (to use) _____ business cards with rounded corners, which (to be) _____ reserved for females.

8. Malaysian business people, however, (to believe) _____ that anyone, male or female, (to be) _____ free to carry a round-cornered card.

9. The European community of countries (to be) _____ less strict in business card etiquette.

10. Throughout the world, the most important part of handling business cards (to be) _____ the customs of the country the person is visiting.

PRONOUN–ANTECEDENT AGREEMENT

The form of most pronouns depends on **antecedents**—nouns, noun phrases, or other pronouns to which the pronouns refer. The connection between a pronoun and its antecedent must be clear if writing is to be clear and coherent; see Chapter 10 for advice on pronoun reference. These connections are achieved by agreement in number (singular or plural), person (first, second, or third), and gender (male or female).

Pronouns must match their antecedents in number (singular pronouns refer to singular antecedents, and plural pronouns to plural antecedents).

PRONOUN–ANTECEDENT AGREEMENT PATTERN I

BASIC PRONOUN–ANTECEDENT AGREEMENT

Loud music has **its** harmful side effects.

SINGULAR ANTECEDENT   SINGULAR PRONOUN

The **musicians** damaged **their** auditory nerves.

PLURAL ANTECEDENT   PLURAL PRONOUN

111   Using a plural pronoun when its antecedents are joined by *and*

Two or more antecedents joined by *and* require a plural pronoun, even if the antecedents are singular.

> **The United States and Canada** maintain **their** border as the longest open frontier in the world.
>
> Although **France and Spain** are friendly nations, **they** control access across **their** common border.

When *each* or *every* precedes singular nouns joined by *and*, use a singular pronoun.

> **Every American and Canadian** may cross the border without showing **his or her** passport.
>
> **Each car and truck** that comes through the border station has **its** contents inspected.

When the singular nouns joined by *and* refer to a single person or thing, use a singular pronoun.

> **Our guide and translator** told us to watch out for scorpions as **she** took us into the ancient tomb. [The guide is the same person as the translator. If the guide and translator were two people, *our* would appear before *translator* and *she* would be *they*.]

11m   Making the pronoun agree with the antecedent closest to it

Antecedents joined by *or, nor,* or correlative conjunctions (such as *either . . . or, neither . . . nor),* often mix the masculine and feminine or singular and plural. For the purposes of agreement, ignore everything before the final antecedent.

> ~~Neither Chef Jacques nor~~ **the waiters** eat **their** dinners early.
>
> ~~Neither the waiters nor~~ **Chef Jacques** eats **his** dinner early.

> Each night after the restaurant closes, ~~either the resident mice or~~ **the owner's cat** manages to get **itself** a good meal of leftovers.
>
> Each night after the restaurant closes, ~~either the owner's cat or~~ **the resident mice** manage to get **themselves** a good meal of leftovers.

(continued next page)

EXTRA EXERCISE E *(continued)*

fell over the left shoulder so that they left the right arm free. Early in the eighteenth century, the "belted plaid" disappeared. They were replaced by the kilt. The particular pattern of tartans which distinguish each clan must have been fixed before 1645, probably before 1600. Later, in 1746, trying to end the clan system, the British Parliament prohibited the Scots from wearing tartans. The action against it was taken following the Battle of Culloden where Prince Charles, Edward Stuart, grandson of James II, was defeated by the Duke of Cumberland. To be caught wearing them carried a penalty of six months' imprisonment. The kilt is worn today so that when the wearer is standing erect, their edges should reach the center of the kneecap. They should be made of a tartan associated with the name of the wearer. In the absence of a family claim to wear them, the Scots allow the wearing of the Royal Stuart tartan.

ANSWERS: EXTRA EXERCISE E

Plaids have been favorite fabric *designs* for many centuries. *They* consist of bars of color crossing each other at right angles. Scotland is the home of the plaid, where *it* is called a tartan, or, in song, story, and legend, a *plaidie*. The tartan, *which distinguishes* the clan of *its wearer,* is ancient, but *its* origin is unknown. In its earliest form, *it* was *a piece* of cloth about two yards broad and four yards long, which was drawn round the waist in folds that *were* tightly buckled with a belt. The lower part came down to the knees, and the upper part fell over the left shoulder so that *it* left the right arm free. Early in the eighteenth century, the "belted plaid" disappeared. *It* was replaced by the kilt. The particular pattern of *tartan which distinguishes* each clan must have been fixed before 1645, probably before 1600. Later, in 1746, trying to end the clan system, the British Parliament prohibited the Scots

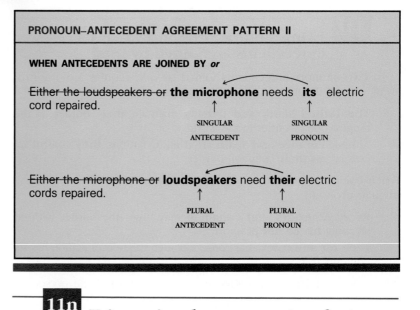

PRONOUN–ANTECEDENT AGREEMENT PATTERN II

WHEN ANTECEDENTS ARE JOINED BY *or*

~~Either the loudspeakers or~~ **the microphone** needs **its** electric cord repaired.

SINGULAR ANTECEDENT   SINGULAR PRONOUN

~~Either the microphone or~~ **loudspeakers** need **their** electric cords repaired.

PLURAL ANTECEDENT   PLURAL PRONOUN

11n Using a singular pronoun to refer to most indefinite-pronoun antecedents

Indefinite pronouns (see 11f for a list) do not refer to any particular person, thing, or idea. In context, however, they take on very clear meanings. Indefinite pronouns are usually singular, so the pronouns that refer to them should also be singular.

> **Anyone** who knows the answer should raise **his or her** hand.
> **Everybody** hopes **he or she** will find it.

1 Using a plural pronoun when an indefinite-pronoun antecedent is plural

Some indefinite pronouns can be singular or plural *(none, some, more, most, any, all),* depending on the meaning of the sentence. When an indefinite pronoun is plural, the pronouns that refer to it should be plural.

> **None** are confident that **they** will pass. [The entire group does not expect to pass.]
> **None** is confident that **he or she** will pass. [No one individual expects to pass.]

Be especially careful when you use the words *this* (singular) and *these* (plural). Make sure that they agree with their antecedent, and make sure that they agree with any other pronoun used in the same sentence.

This kind of hard work has **its** advantages.
These kinds of difficult jobs have **their** advantages.

2   Using masculine pronouns appropriately

Until the 1960s, grammatical convention specified using masculine pronouns to refer to indefinite pronouns and nouns and pronouns naming general categories to which any person might belong: "*Everyone* should admit *his* mistakes." Today people are more conscious that the pronouns *he, his, him,* and *himself* exclude women, who make up over half the population. Experienced writers try to avoid using masculine pronouns to refer to the entire population. The chart shows three ways to avoid using masculine pronouns to refer to males and females together. For advice on how to avoid other types of sexist language, see 21a-3.

HOW TO AVOID USING ONLY THE MASCULINE PRONOUN TO REFER TO MALES AND FEMALES TOGETHER

Solution 1: Use a pair—but try to avoid a pair more than once in a sentence or in many sentences in a row. When you use a *he or she* construction, remember that it acts as a singular pronoun.

> **Everyone** hopes that **he or she** will win the scholarship.
> **A successful doctor** knows that **he or she** has to work long hours.
> With the explosion of knowledge, no **doctor** can read much outside **his or her** specialty.

Solution 2: Revise into the plural.

> **Many people** hope that **they** will win the scholarship.
> **Successful doctors** know that **they** have to work long hours.
> With the explosion of knowledge, few **doctors** can read much outside **their** specialties.

Solution 3: Recast the sentence.

> Everyone hopes to win the scholarship.
> Successful doctors should expect to work long hours.

---

from wearing *the tartan.* The action against it was taken following the Battle of Culloden where Prince Charles, Edward Stuart, grandson of James II, was defeated by the Duke of Cumberland. To be caught wearing *it* carried a penalty of six months' imprisonment. The kilt is worn today to that when the wearer is standing erect, *its* edges should reach the center of the kneecap. *It* should be made of a tartan associated with the name of the wearer. In the absence of a family claim to wear *one,* the Scots allow the wearing of the Royal Stuart tartan.

EXTRA EXERCISE F

Rewrite this paragraph so that pronoun–antecedent agreement in person and number is maintained. It may also be necessary to change verbs or other words.

Buying stock involves many steps. Once a stockbroker receives an order, they call their firm's telephone clerk, who is located near the edge of the trading area. The telephone clerk summons his firm's floor broker by flashing their code number on a large electronic board posted in the trading area. Seeing their number, the floor broker goes to the telephone clerk and picks up the buy order. You then go to the small area set aside for trading in that company's stock. An employee of the Stock Exchange keeps track of all bids to buy and sell that particular stock. The floor broker makes an offer. If they are accepted by the selling broker, the stock is his. If you have bid too low, he must make another bid before someone else gets the stock. Then a reporter enters the deal into the Exchange computer, and they become part of the official record in seconds. After all this, the floor broker returns to the telephone clerk, who reports the deal to the original stockbroker, who bills the client.

(answers on next page)

11o

ANSWERS: EXTRA EXERCISE F
(previous page)

Buying stock involves many steps. Once a stockbroker receives an order, *he* calls *his* firm's telephone clerk, who is located near the edge of the trading area. The telephone clerk summons his firm's floor broker by flashing *his* code number on a large electronic board posted in the trading area. Seeing *his* number, the floor broker goes to the telephone clerk and picks up the buy order. *He* then *goes* to the small area set aside for trading in that company's stock. An employee of the Stock Exchange keeps track of all bids to buy and sell that particular stock. The floor broker makes an offer. If *it is* accepted by the selling broker, the stock is his. If *he has* bid too low, he must make another bid before someone else gets the stock. Then a reporter enters the deal into the Exchange computer, and *it* becomes part of the official record in seconds. After all this, the floor broker returns to the telephone clerk, who reports the deal to the original stockbroker, who bills the client.

11o With collective-noun antecedents, using singular or plural pronouns according to context

A **collective noun** names a group of people or things: *family, group, audience, class, number, committee, team,* and the like. When the group acts as one unit, use a singular pronoun to refer to it. When the members of the group act individually, thus creating more than one action, use a plural pronoun.

The audience is cheering as **it** stands to applaud the performers. [The audience is acting as one unit, so the pronoun is singular.]

The audience put on **their** coats and walk out. [Here the audience is acting as individuals, so all the actions collect to become plural. The verbs *put* and *walk* must be plural as well as the pronoun *their*.]

The family is spending **its** vacation in Maine. [All the family members went to one place together.]

The family are spending **their** vacations in Maine, Hawaii, and Rome. [Each family member went to a different place.]

EXERCISE 6

Revise each sentence so that all pronouns agree with their antecedents. When necessary, change verbs and other words to maintain subject-verb agreement. Some sentences have more than one solution.

EXAMPLE   Many people wonder what gives rainbows its colors.
          Many people wonder what gives rainbows *their* colors.

1. A raindrop acts as a prism when sunlight enters them.
2. For people to see a rainbow, he must have their back to the sun and the raindrops in front of him.
3. Rays of light come over the observer's head, and it then enters into the raindrops.
4. A rainbow looks like an arch, but actually they are part of a circle.
5. If two people are looking at a rainbow, each sees their own version.
6. Because their angles of viewing are different, both observers see a rainbow that is unique to his or her eyes.
7. When people see one rainbow inside another, the outside rainbow has their colors in reverse order.
8. A third and even a fourth rainbow may form, but it is usually too faint to be seen.
9. A garden hose or lawn sprinklers create its own small rainbows.
10. To view a homemade rainbow, people must stand with his or her back to the sun and the spray in front.

ANSWERS; EXERCISE 6

1. enters *it*
2. *they* must have . . . in front of *them*
3. *they* then *enter*
4. *it is* part
5. *his or her* own version
6. *their* eyes
7. *its* colors
8. *they are* usually
9. *their* own
10. with *their* back

Focus on Revising

REVISING YOUR WRITING

If you make errors in agreement when you write, go back to your writing and locate the errors. Using this chapter as a resource, revise your writing to correct the problems. Sections 11a through 11k discuss subject-verb agreement. Sections 11l through 11o look at pronoun-antecedent agreement.

CASE STUDY: REVISING FOR AGREEMENT

This case study lets you observe a student writer revising. It also gives you the opportunity to revise some student writing on your own.

Observation

A student wrote the following draft for a course for students training as rehabilitation therapists. The assignment was to discuss the main idea of a film about handicapped athletes. The material offers a good summary of the film, but the draft's effectiveness is diminished by errors in subject–verb agreement and in pronoun–antecedent agreement.

Read through the draft. The errors are highlighted and explained. Before you look at how the student revised to eliminate the errors, revise the material yourself. Then compare what you and the student did.

Singular verb needed for this collective noun: 11g

Singular pronoun needed: 11n

Verb should be plural for subjects joined by *and*: 11c

The linking verb should agree with the subject: 11h

Last week students training as physical therapists saw a film about severely handicapped people participating actively in sports. The class know now that doing the impossible is becoming normal for many handicapped people.

General fitness and eagerness to compete is among the reasons that a handicapped person might want to develop their skill in sports. All that is needed is a minimum of mobility and the will to train very hard. Either artificial

COVERAGE: PARTICIPATION ESSAY
(opposite page)

Without kidney function, the body's ability to regulate fluids, blood pressure, red-cell production, protein levels, and blood chemistry *are* [11b: intervening words, singular verb needed] destroyed. If the kidneys no longer function, the standard prescription *are* [11h: linking verb, singular verb needed] dialysis treatments. Two or three times a week *are* [11j: amounts, singular verb needed] the norm for the treatments, which sometimes *continues* [11i: plural verb needed to agree with *treatments*] for months or even years. Dialysis, though, does not do everything that healthy kidneys *does* [11i: relative pronoun use here calls for plural verb].

Reregulating the amount of water in the blood and tissues *are* [11b: intervening words, singular verb needed] the best-known function of the kidney. Therefore, someone without functioning kidneys must be careful to keep *their* [11n: indefinite pronoun as antecedent, *his or her* needed] fluid intake within limits set by the doctor. Dialysis *help* [11a: singular subject calls for singular verb] to remove excess fluid. Reducing salt and controlling fluid intake also *helps.* [compound subject, plural verb needed] Neither medical procedures nor diet *are* [11d: closest subject calls for singular verb] effective, however, without cooperation from the patient.

The whole family *are* [11g: collective noun calls for singular verb] affected, so it is important that the medical team *discuss* [collective noun calls for singular verb] the functions of a healthy kidney with the patient and the family so that *he* [11l: compound antecedent calls for plural pronoun *they*] better understand the problems involved. Once the team makes *their* [11o: collective noun calls for singular pronoun *its*] treatment recommendations known, everyone can work together with greater patience and understanding.

limbs—called *prostheses*—or a wheelchair allow many severely handicapped people to become athletes. Advances in design and material have led to better athletic equipment for the handicapped.

> Verb should agree with subject closest to it: 11d

Barriers are broken daily. Rafting, rock climbing, and basketball have found enthusiasts among the handicapped. Marathon racing, along with skiing and cycling, also have great appeal. Many has tried their skill at these sports. One competitive event for the handicapped was the eighth Paralympic Games, which was held in Seoul, South Korea, the site of the 1988 Olympics.

> Verb should agree with subject, not with words between subject and verb: 11b

> Singular verb needed to agree with indefinite pronoun *many*: 11f

> Plural verb needed to agree with this use of *which*: 11i

Every disabled athlete needs to train somewhat differently to accommodate their particular handicap. One of the most versatile athletes known today compete in a triathlon event by wearing one kind of prosthesis for cycling, another for running, and none for swimming.

> Singular pronoun needed: 11n

> Singular verb needed to agree with *one*: 11b

Here is how the student revised the paragraph to correct the agreement errors. In a few places, the student had alternatives for the revision, so your revision might not match this one exactly. Your revision should, however, deal with each error highlighted on the draft.

Last week students training as physical therapists saw a film about severely handicapped people participating actively in sports. The class knows now that doing the impossible is becoming normal for many handicapped people.

General fitness and eagerness to compete are among the reasons that a handicapped person might want to develop his or her skill in sports. All that is needed are a minimum of mobility and the will to train very hard. Either artificial limbs—called *prostheses*—or a wheelchair allows many severely handicapped people to become athletes. Advances in design and material have led to better athletic equipment for the handicapped.

Barriers are broken daily. Rafting, rock climbing, and basketball have found enthusiasts among the handicapped. Marathon racing, along with skiing and cycling, also has great appeal. Many have tried their skill at these sports. One competitive event for the handicapped was the eighth Paralympic Games, which were held in Seoul, South Korea, the site of the 1988 Olympics.

Every disabled athlete needs to train somewhat differently to accommodate his or her particular handicap. One of the most versatile athletes known today competes in a triathlon event by wearing one kind of prosthesis for cycling, another for running, and none for swimming.

Participation

A student wrote the following draft for a course called Introduction to Health Sciences. The assignment was to write about a function of the body. The material is concisely written and explains the material clearly, but the draft's effectiveness is diminished by pronoun-antecedent agreement errors and by subject-verb agreement errors.

Read through the draft. Then revise it to eliminate the errors. Also, make any additional revisions you think would improve the content, organization, and style of the material.

Without kidney function, the body's ability to regulate fluids, blood pressure, red-cell production, protein levels, and blood chemistry are destroyed. If the kidneys no longer function, the standard prescription are dialysis treatments. Two or three times a week are the norm for the treatments, which sometimes continues for months or even years. Dialysis, though, does not do everything that healthy kidneys does.

Regulating the amount of water in the blood and tissues are the best-known function of the kidney. Therefore, someone without functioning kidneys must be careful to keep their fluid intake within limits set by the doctor. Dialysis help to remove excess fluid. Reducing salt and controlling fluid intake also helps. Neither medical procedures nor diet are effective, however, without cooperation from the patient.

(continued on next page)

ANSWER: PARTICIPATION ESSAY

This version revises the agreement errors. Answers will vary if students have revised for content, organization, or style.

Without kidney function, the body's ability to regulate fluids, blood pressure, red-cell production, protein levels, and blood chemistry is destroyed. If the kidneys no longer function, the standard prescription is dialysis treatments. Two or three times a week is the norm for the treatments, which sometimes continue for months or even years. Dialysis, though, does not do everything that healthy kidneys do.

Regulating the amount of water in the blood and tissues is the best-known function of the kidney. Therefore, someone without functioning kidneys must be careful to keep his or her fluid intake within limits set by the doctor. Dialysis helps to remove excess fluid. Reducing salt and controlling fluid intake also help. Neither medical procedures nor diet is effective, however, without cooperation from the patient.

The whole family is affected, so it is important that the medical team discusses the functions of a healthy kidney with the patient and the family so that they better understand the problems involved. Once the team makes its treatment recommendations known, everyone can work together with greater patience and understanding.

The whole family are affected, so it is important that the medical team discuss the functions of a healthy kidney with the patient and the family so that he better understand the problems involved. Once the team makes their treatment recommendations known, everyone can work together with greater patience and understanding.

12 Using Adjectives and Adverbs

Both adjectives and adverbs are **modifiers**—words or groups of words that describe other words.

ADJECTIVE	The ***brisk** wind* blew.
ADVERB	The wind *blew **briskly**.*

The key to distinguishing between adjectives and adverbs is understanding that they modify different words or groups of words. The chart below explains these distinctions.

Inexperienced writers sometimes interchange adjectives and adverbs because of the *-ly* ending. Even though many adverbs° do end in *-ly* (eat, *swiftly,* eat *frequently,* eat *hungrily*), some do not (eat *fast,* eat *often,* eat *little*). To complicate matters further, some adjectives end in *-ly* (*lovely* flower, *friendly* dog). The *-ly* ending, therefore, is not a reliable way to identify adverbs.

SUMMARY OF DIFFERENCES BETWEEN ADJECTIVES AND ADVERBS

WHAT ADJECTIVES MODIFY	EXAMPLE
nouns°	The **busy** *lawyer* rested.
pronouns°	*She* felt **triumphant.**
WHAT ADVERBS MODIFY	**EXAMPLE**
verbs°	The lawyer *spoke* **quickly.**
adverbs°	The lawyer spoke **very** *quickly.*
adjectives°	The lawyer was **extremely** *busy.*
independent clauses°	**Therefore,** *the lawyer rested.*

WORD DERIVATION

Adjective comes from the Latin *adjectus,* meaning *that is added,* and *adverb* comes from the Latin *adverbus,* meaning *to a word.* Both etymologies reflect the use of adjectives and adverbs as enhancers of other words' meanings.

LANGUAGE HISTORY

Adverbs in Old English and Middle English were formed differently than they are today: to make an adverb, an *-e* was simply added to an adjective. The modern *-ly* ending for adverbs comes from an adjective ending, *-lice* (meaning *like*), which became softened to *-ly* and was somehow reinterpreted as an adverb signal. Some modern adjectives ending in *-ly* (such as *friendly* and *heavenly*) are descendants of those old *-lice* adjectives.

ANSWERS: EXERCISE 1 (next page)

    ADV   ADJ

1. Many American teenagers

ADV   ADV ADV

always worked very hard

   ADJ   ADJ

part-time jobs high school

  ADJ   ADJ

greater percentage teenage students

ADV

ever before

293

ANSWERS: EXERCISE 1 *(continued)*

ADJ
2. Reliable statistics

ADV ADJ ADV
almost one third of all

ADJ ADJ
ninth and tenth graders and

ADV ADJ
almost one half of

ADJ ADJ
all eleventh and twelfth graders

ADV
3. Interestingly, they are

[whole clause] ⟶

ADJ
working longer hours than the

ADJ
high school students of

ADJ ADJ
twenty-five years ago

ADV ADV
4. Not surprisingly, the number of

[whole clause] ⟶

ADV
hours worked greatly influences

ADJ
school performance.

ADJ ADV
5. important study conducted recently

ADV ADJ ADJ
most eleventh and twelfth graders

ADJ
weekly work schedule

ADJ
twenty hours

ADJ
their grades

You can determine whether a specific occasion calls for an adjective or an adverb by seeing how the word functions in its sentence. If a noun or pronoun is being modified, use an adjective; if a verb, adjective, or other adverb is being modified, use an adverb.

EXERCISE 1

First underline and label all adjectives (ADJ) and adverbs (ADV). Then go back and draw an arrow from each adjective and adverb to the word or words it modifies.

ADJ ADV
EXAMPLE Do American teenagers frequently take jobs while attending

ADJ
high school?

1. Many American teenagers have always worked very hard at part-time jobs while going to high school, but a greater percentage of teenage students work today than ever before.

2. Reliable statistics reveal that almost one-third of all ninth and tenth graders and almost one-half of all eleventh and twelfth graders are employed.

3. Interestingly, they are working longer hours than the high school students of twenty-five years ago.

4. Not surprisingly, the number of hours worked greatly influences school performance.

5. An important study conducted recently at the University of California disclosed that most eleventh and twelfth graders can manage a weekly work schedule of twenty hours without damaging their grades.

12a Using adverbs—not adjectives—to modify verbs, adjectives, and other adverbs

Using adjectives as adverbs creates nonstandard structures.

No The chauffeur drove **careless.** [Adjective *careless* cannot modify verb *drove*.]

YES The chauffeur drove **carelessly.** [Adverb *carelessly* modifies verb *drove*.]

No The candidate felt **unusual** energetic today. [Adjective *unusual* cannot modify adjective *energetic*.]

YES The candidate felt **unusually energetic** today. [Adverb *unusually* modifies adjective *energetic*.]

No	The candidate spoke **exceptional forcefully** today. [Adjective *exceptional* cannot modify adverb *forcefully*.]
Yes	The candidate spoke **exceptionally forcefully** today. [Adverb *exceptionally* modifies adverb *forcefully*.]

12b Not using double negatives

A **double negative** is a statement that contains two negative modifiers, the second of which repeats the message of the first. (This form, nonstandard today, was standard in the days of Chaucer and Shakespeare.) Negative modifiers include *no, never, not, none, nothing, hardly, scarcely,* and *barely.*

No	The factory workers will **never** vote for **no** strike.
Yes	The factory workers will **never** vote for a strike.

The words *not, no,* and *nothing* are particularly common in double negatives.

No	The union members did **not** have **no** money in reserve.
Yes	The union members did **not** have **any** money in reserve.
Yes	The union members have **no** money in reserve.
No	The supervisor did **not** hear **nothing.**
Yes	The supervisor did **not** hear **anything.**

If you use contractions, which many writers prefer to avoid in their academic writing, be especially careful not to use double negatives. When the word *not* is used in a contraction—such as *isn't, don't,* or *haven't*—the negative message carried by *not* tends to slip by some inexperienced writers. They add a second—incorrect—negative.

No	He did**n't** hear **nothing.**
Yes	He did**n't** hear **anything.**
No	She **couldn't hardly** hear the music.
Yes	She **could hardly** hear the music.

12c Using adjectives—not adverbs—as complements after linking verbs

Linking verbs indicate a state of being or a condition. They include *be (am, is, are, was, were)*; verbs related to the senses, including *look, smell, taste, sound,* and *feel*; and verbs such as *appear,*

BACKGROUND

In the chapter on vocabulary in *Errors and Expectations,* Mina Shaughnessy describes the use of modifiers by three groups of freshman writers. The few adverbs used by *basic* writers, she notes, usually come from the most overworked ones in the language, such as *too, very, quite,* and *hardly.* Similarly, basic writers modify their nouns and verbs with what she calls "the common adjectives": *a lot, many, good, easy, big, certain,* familiar words that slip into place without mental effort, thereby making it impossible for the writer to achieve the precision needed for complex consideration of the topic. *Intermediate* writers, moving closer to precise diction, use *-ly* adverbs and more specific adjectives. Although they are likely to use multiple adjectives, doing so does not usually increase the precision of the statement. *Advanced* freshman writers, working with more confidence, lean on adverbial conjunctions for paragraph cohesion—e.g., *furthermore, however, consequently*—and even include figurative language in an effort to be descriptive.

BACKGROUND

William Safire makes the point that understanding grammar helps us to perceive emphasis and meaning. For example, if at a wine tasting someone says, "They taste *good,*" we know that the reference is to the wines, but if we hear "They taste *well,*" we know that someone has made a comment about the tasters.

—William Safire,
"Going Gentle on My Mind"

seem, become, grow, turn, remain, and *prove.* Linking verbs connect the subject° to a complement—a word that renames or describes the subject. You can think of a linking verb as an equal sign between a subject and its complement.

> The guests looked **happy.** [subject *guests* = adjective *happy*]
> The party was **successful.** [subject *party* = adjective *successful*]

Problems can arise with verbs that are sometimes linking verbs and sometimes action verbs, depending on the sentence. As linking verbs, these verbs use adjectives in complements. As action verbs, these verbs use adverbs.

> Anne **looks happy.** [*looks* = linking verb; *happy* = adjective]
> Anne **looks happily** at the sunset. [*looks* = action verb; *happily* = adverb]

Bad—Badly

The words *bad* (adjective) and *badly* (adverb) are particularly prone to misuse with linking verbs such as *feel, grow, smell, sound, taste.* Only the adjective *bad* is correct when a verb is functioning as a linking verb.

FOR DESCRIBING A FEELING

No   The student felt **badly.**
YES   The student felt **bad.**

FOR DESCRIBING A SMELL

No   The food smelled **badly.**
YES   The food smelled **bad.**

Good—Well

Well functions both as an adverb and as an adjective. *Good* is always an adjective. *Well* is an adjective referring to good health. When it is describing anything other than good health, *well* is an adverb.

> You look **well** = You look in good health. [*well* = adjective]
> You write **well** = You write skillfully. [*well* = adverb]

Except when *well* is an adjective referring to health, use *good* only as an adjective and *well* only as an adverb.

No   She sings **good.** [*sings* = action verb; adverb, not adjective, required]
YES   She sings **well.** [*well* = adverb]

296

EXERCISE 2

Revise these sentences to eliminate double negatives and to make the use of all adjectives and adverbs suitable for academic writing.

EXAMPLE   Does love come natural?

Does love come *naturally?*

1. If sales of Valentine's Day cards are a good indicator, many people in the United States do not never want to forget to say "I love you" on February 14.

2. Every year the cards sell good; from 900 million to 1.1 billion Valentine's Day cards sell yearly, suggesting that many people would feel badly if they did not remember the occasion.

3. Interesting, adults exchange only 20 percent of all the cards; children seem awful eager to express affection, for they buy enormous numbers of the cards for good friends and for teachers they consider unusual nice.

4. Many sweethearts and spouses feel strong about their mutual love, but card shops do especially good in sales of Valentine's Day cards for mothers.

5. Some people, however, do not have no feelings for Valentine's Day because they do not feel well about its having become so commercial.

12d   Using correct comparative and superlative forms of adjectives and adverbs

When comparisons are made, descriptive adjectives and adverbs often carry the message. Adjectives and adverbs, therefore, have forms that communicate relative degrees of intensity.

1   Using correct forms of comparison for regular adjectives and adverbs

Most adjectives and adverbs show degrees of intensity by adding *-er* and *-est* endings or by combining with the words *more* and *most.* (All adjectives and adverbs show diminishing or negative comparison by combining with the words *less* and *least: less jumpy, least jumpy; less surely, least surely.*) A few adjectives and adverbs are irregular, as explained in 12d-2.

ANSWERS: EXERCISE 2

1. If sales of Valentine's Day cards are a good indicator, many people in the United States do not ever want to forget to say "I love you" on February 14.

2. Every year the cards sell well; from 900 million to 1.1 billion Valentine's Day cards sell yearly, suggesting that many people would feel bad if they did not remember the occasion.

3. Interestingly, adults exchange only 20 percent of all the cards; children seem awfully eager to express affection, for they buy enormous numbers of the cards for good friends and for teachers they consider unusually nice.

4. Many sweethearts and spouses feel strongly about their mutual love, but card shops do especially well in sales of Valentine's Day cards for mothers.

5. Some people, however, do not have feelings for Valentine's Day because they do not feel good about its having become so commercial.

COVERAGE: EXERCISE 2

(1) *good* as adjective is correct; double negative error; (2) *well*, not *good*, needed as adverb; *bad*, not *badly*, needed as adjective after linking verb *feel*; negative form is correct; (3) adverb, not adjective, should modify independent clause; adverb, not adjective, should modify adjective *eager*; *good* as adjective is correct; adverb, not adjective, should modify adjective *nice*; (4) adverb, not adjective, should modify verb *feel*; *well*, not *good*, needed as adverb; (5) double negative error; *good*, not *well*, needed as adjective after linking verb *feel*

QUOTATION ABOUT LANGUAGE

Adjectives are used so freely these days that we feel almost naked, robbed, if we don't get at least a couple.

—Paul Stevens

WORD HISTORIES

Common irregular adjectives (and adverbs) can be confusing to students because the comparative and superlative forms seem unconnected to the positive form. The realization that these irregularities are only accidents of history rather than the product of difficult rules can make them less intimidating.

For example, *good* comes from the Old English *god,* related to the German *gut,* both of which come from the Indo-European word meaning *to be suitable. Better* and *best* come from Old English *betera* and *betst* respectively, based on the Indo-European word meaning *good.*

Another example is *worse* and *worst,* which come from their Old English synonyms: *wiersa* and *wyrsta.* However, *bad* does not come from *yfel,* the Old English word for *bad* or *evil,* but from Old English *baeddel,* meaning *hermaphrodite.* Perhaps your students would like to theorize about why this happened.

BACKGROUND

Adjectives can be made from nouns by adding different endings that sometimes color the meaning of the word. For example, an *-ish* ending can give a word a derogatory slant, as in *high-schoolish* or *childish.* On other occasions the *-ish* ending, and the *-y* ending, mean "similar to" or "becoming." For example, a *yellowish substance* or a *flowery paragraph* suggest a substance and paragraph that are not entirely yellow or flowered, but close. Materials often take an *-en* ending when they turn from nouns into adjectives (as in *wooden* and *silken*), and adjectives that suggest a Latin origin frequently end in *-al, or,* or *-ory* (as in *beneficial, oracular,* and *promissory*).

FORMS OF COMPARISON FOR REGULAR ADJECTIVES AND ADVERBS	
FORM	**FUNCTION**
Positive	Used for a statement when nothing is being compared
Comparative	Used when only two things are being compared—with *-er* ending or *more* (or *less*)
Superlative	Used when three or more things are being compared—with *-est* ending or *most* (or *least*)

POSITIVE	COMPARATIVE	SUPERLATIVE
green	greener	greenest
happy	happier	happiest
selfish	less selfish	least selfish
beautiful	more beautiful	most beautiful

Her tree is **green.**

Her tree is **greener** than his tree.

Her tree is the **greenest** tree on the block.

His flower garden is **beautiful.**

His flower garden is **more beautiful** than her flower garden.

His flower garden is the **most beautiful** on the block.

The choice of whether to use *-er, -est* or *more, most* depends largely on the number of syllables in the adjective or adverb. With **one-syllable words,** the *-er, -est* endings are most common: *large, larger, largest* (adjective); *far, farther, farthest* (adverb). With **three-syllable words,** *more, most* are used. With **adverbs of two or more syllables,** *more, most* are used: *easily, more easily, most easily.* With **adjectives of two syllables,** practice varies: some take the *-er, -est* endings; others combine with *more* and *most.* One general rule covers two-syllable adjectives ending in *-y:* use the *-er, -est* endings after changing the *-y* to *i.* For other two-syllable adjectives, often you will form comparatives and superlatives intuitively, based on what you have heard or read for a particular adjective.

Be careful not to use a **double comparative** or **double superlative.** The words *more* or *most* cannot be used if the *-er* or *-est* ending has been used.

ad 12d

He was **younger** [not *more younger*] than his brother.
Her music was the **snappiest** [not *more snappiest*] on the radio.
People danced **more easily** [not *more easier*] to her music.

 2 | **Using correct forms of comparison for irregular adjectives and adverbs**

Some comparative and superlative forms are irregular. The list, in the chart below, is short, so you can memorize it easily.

The Perkinses saw a **good** movie.
The Perkinses saw a **better** movie than the Smiths did.
The Perkinses saw **the best** movie that they had ever seen.

The Millers had **little** trouble finding jobs.
The Millers had **less** trouble finding jobs than the Smiths did.
The Millers had **the least** trouble finding jobs of everyone.

IRREGULAR COMPARATIVES AND SUPERLATIVES

POSITIVE [1]	COMPARATIVE [2]	SUPERLATIVE [3+]
good (adjective	better	best
well (adjective and adverb)	better	best
bad (adjective)	worse	worst
badly (adverb)	worse	worst
many	more	most
much	more	most
some	more	most
little	less	least

EXTRA EXERCISE

Underline the adjectives and adverbs. If any adjective or adverb is in an incorrect form, write the correct form above it.

EXAMPLE

The music played <u>loud</u> *more loudly* in the disco than in the restaurant.

1. The Joneses have the bigger tree on the block.

2. Colorado has some of the most prettiest scenery in the country.

3. Which of the sick twins has the highest fever?

4. Juan is friendlier than his cousin.

5. The more faster runner of the two received a ribbon.

6. The red blouse is the most attractive in the store.

7. Leontyne Price sings good.

8. That is the worse coffee shop in town.

9. Spain is near to Africa than most people realize.

10. Marc Chagall is the more famous modern artist from Russia.

ANSWERS: EXTRA EXERCISE

1. biggest	6. Correct
2. prettiest (drop *most*)	7. well
	8. worst
3. higher	9. nearer
4. Correct	10. most famous
5. faster (drop *more*)	

❖ USAGE ALERT: Do not use *less* and *fewer* interchangeably. *Less* refers to amounts or values that form one whole. *Fewer* refers to numbers or anything that can be counted. *They consumed fewer calories; the sugar substitute had less aftertaste.* ❖

Answers will vary, but each sentence should set a context for the use of each word. (For example, *He is big* is less satisfactory than *Weighing 270 pounds and standing seven feet tall, he is big, even for a football player.*)

big	bigger	biggest
hungry	hungrier	hungriest
hungry	more hungry	most hungry
quickly	more quickly	most quickly
important	more important	most important
thick	thicker	thickest
thirsty	more thirsty	most thirsty

EXERCISE 3

First complete this chart. Next, write sentences that set a context for each word in the completed chart.

EXAMPLE   *big:* Weighing 270 pounds and standing seven feet tall, he is big, even for a football player.

POSITIVE [1]	COMPARATIVE [2]	SUPERLATIVE [3+]
big	_____	_____
_____	_____	hungriest
	more hungry	_____
quickly	_____	_____
important	_____	_____
_____	thicker	_____
_____	_____	most thirsty

EXERCISE 4

Revise these sentences so that all comparative and superlative forms are suitable for academic writing.

EXAMPLE   Most people say that airlines serve the worse food they have ever tasted.

Most people say that airlines serve the *worst* food they have ever tasted.

1. Passengers say that often the chicken sauce is more thick than glue, and the pasta is more soggier than a wet sponge.

2. Of the more than a dozen caterers who supply airline food, the larger prepares 90 million meals a year.

3. Controlling quality might be more easiest if less people had to be served.

4. Still, some airlines are trying hardest: One large airline offers the choice of a low-cholesterol meal with less calories.

5. A recent survey revealed, however, that frequent flyers consider food least important compared with on-time records.

1. Passengers say that often the chicken sauce is *thicker* than glue and the pasta is *soggier* than a wet sponge.

2. Of the more than a dozen caterers who supply airline food, the *largest* prepares 90 million meals a year.

3. Controlling quality might be *easier* if *fewer* people had to be served.

4. Still, some airlines are trying *harder:* One airline offers the choice of a low-cholesterol meal with *fewer* calories.

5. A recent survey revealed, however, that frequent flyers consider food *less* important compared with on-time records.

QUOTATION ABOUT WRITING

Writers have two main problems. One is writer's block, when the words won't come at all, and the other is "logorrhea," when the words come so fast that they can hardly get to the wastebasket in time.

—Cecilia Bartholomew

12e   Avoiding too many nouns as modifiers

Sometimes nouns—words that name a person, place, thing, or idea—can modify other nouns: *truck driver, train track, security system.* These very familiar terms create no problems. However, when nouns pile up in a sequence of modifiers, it can be difficult to know which nouns are being modified and which nouns are doing the modifying. As a result, the reader finds it hard to understand the writer's message. Depending on the particular sentence, writers have several routes to revision.

SENTENCE REWRITTEN

No   I asked my advisor to write **two college recommendation** letters for me.

YES   I asked my advisor to write **letters of recommendation** to **two colleges** for me.

**ONE NOUN CHANGED TO POSSESSIVE CASE
AND ANOTHER TO ITS ADJECTIVE FORM**

No   Some students might take the **United States Navy examination** for **navy engineer training**.

YES   Some students might take the **United States Navy's examination** for **naval engineer training**.

NOUN CHANGED TO PREPOSITIONAL PHRASE

No   Our **student advisement program** has won awards for excellence.

YES   Our **program in student advisement** has won awards for excellence.

EXERCISE 5

Revise the following sentences so that they are suitable for academic writing. Apply all the material covered in this chapter.

EXAMPLE   Increasing in recent years, bankrupt businesses are being rescued by their employees who think creative.

Increasingly in recent years, bankrupt businesses are being rescued by their employees who think *creatively*.

1. Workers who want bad to keep their jobs pool their money careful and become worker-owners who buy shares in the business and participate democratic in its operations.
2. The resulting "cooperative" often has unusual enthusiastic workers and the most happiest customers.
3. The worker-owners have to work more harder because they have to do their original jobs good and at the same time not do nothing wrong as managers.
4. Collective decision making does not never work good unless the worker-owners number less than four hundred, so in large cooperatives the worker-owners elect managers about whom they feel well.
5. Cooperative managed businesses are considered by some experts as the better hope for the future of small, local owned businesses.

ANSWERS: EXERCISE 5

Answers may vary slightly. Here is one set of possibilities.

1. Workers who want *badly* to keep their jobs pool their money *carefully* and become worker-owners who buy shares in the business and participate *democratically* in its operations.

2. The resulting "cooperative" often has *unusually* enthusiastic workers and the *happiest* customers.

3. The worker-owners have to work *harder* because they have to do their original jobs *well* and at the same time *not do anything* wrong as managers.

4. Collective decision making *never works well* unless the worker-owners number *fewer* than four hundred, so in large cooperatives the worker-owners elect managers about whom they feel *good*.

5. *Cooperatively* managed businesses are considered by some experts as the *best* hope for the future of small, *locally* owned businesses.

COVERAGE: EXERCISE 5

(1) *badly,* not *bad,* as adverb; adverb, not adjective, should modify verb *pool;* adverb, not adjective, should modify verb *participate;* (2) adverb *unusually,* not adjective, should modify adjective *enthusiastic;* double superlative error; (3) double comparative error; *well,* not *good,* needed as adverb; double negative error; (4) double negative error; *well,* not *good,* needed as adverb; *fewer,* not *less,* needed for comparison; *good,* not *well,* needed as adjective after linking verb *feel;* (5) adverb *cooperatively,* not adjective, should modify adjective *managed;* superlative *best* needed instead of comparative *better;* adverb *locally,* not adjective, should modify verb *owned*

Three

WRITING CORRECT SENTENCES

When you write correct sentences, you have a better chance of communicating clearly with your readers. Part Three offers you practical advice about how to avoid the most common sentence errors that interfere with the delivery of meaning. As you use Chapters 13 through 15, keep in mind that correct sentences give you a foundation. On it you can build an effective, graceful, and memorable writing style.

13 Sentence Fragments

One useful way to introduce discussion of sentence fragments is to speak to the class in fragments. For example, you might enter the class one morning and make the following, unembellished announcement: "Before we discuss the midterm." Students will, of course, be confused. Feign ignorance when they ask what you mean: "Wasn't my announcement clear?"

Finally, someone might tell you that your announcement was not clear because the thought was incomplete. Tell that student that he or she has just given one definition of a sentence fragment. If no one can tell what is wrong, you can write your original announcement on the board, and have students identify the problem. Then you can ask students to supply (at the board or orally) whatever they feel is needed to complete the statement. Most will add independent clauses. Use these revisions to explain (or review) the Three-Step Test for Sentence Completeness.

A **sentence fragment** is a portion of a sentence that is punctuated as though it were a complete sentence. Most sentence fragments are phrases° or dependent clauses°. You can avoid writing sentence fragments if you recognize the difference between a fragment and a complete sentence.

FRAGMENT	The telephone with two outside lines. [no verb°]
REVISED	The telephone has two outside lines.
FRAGMENT	Rang loudly for ten minutes. [no subject°]
REVISED	The telephone rang loudly for ten minutes.
FRAGMENT	At midnight. [no verb° or subject°]
REVISED	The telephone rang at midnight.
FRAGMENT	**Because** the telephone rang loudly. [dependent clause° with subordinating conjunction°]
REVISED	Because the telephone rang loudly, the family was awakened.
FRAGMENT	The telephone call **that** woke the family. [dependent clause° with relative pronoun°]
REVISED	The telephone call that woke the family was a wrong number.

Sentence fragments distract readers by intruding on the clarity of the message you want your material to deliver.

No	The lawyer was angry. When she returned from court. She found the key witness waiting in her office. [Was the lawyer angry when she returned from court or when she found the witness in her office?]
YES	The lawyer was angry when she returned from court. She found the key witness waiting in her office.
YES	The lawyer was angry. When she returned from court, she found the key witness waiting in her office.

13a Testing for sentence completeness

If you write sentence fragments frequently, you need a system to check that your sentences are complete. Here is a test to use if you suspect that you have written a sentence fragment.

TEST FOR SENTENCE COMPLETENESS

1. **Is there a verb?** If no, there is a sentence fragment.
2. **Is there a subject?** If no, there is a sentence fragment.
3. **Do the subject and verb start with a subordinating word— and lack an independent clause to complete the thought?** If yes, there is a sentence fragment.

QUESTION 1: Is there a verb?

If there is no verb, you are looking at a sentence fragment. Verbs convey information about what is happening, what has happened, or what will happen. In testing for sentence completeness, find a verb that can change form to communicate a change in time.

> Yesterday, the telephone **rang.**
> Now the telephone **rings.**

Verbals° do not function as verbs. Do not, therefore, mistake a verbal for a verb. Verbals are gerunds° (*-ing* forms as nouns), present participles° (*-ing* forms as modifiers), past participles° (*-ed* or irregular past forms), and infinitives° (*to* forms).

FRAGMENT	Yesterday, taking special night classes.
REVISED	Yesterday, the student **began** taking special night classes.
FRAGMENT	Now taking special night classes.
REVISED	Now the students **begin** taking special night classes.
FRAGMENT	Yesterday, the students registering for classes.
REVISED	Yesterday, the students **were** registering for classes.
REVISED	Yesterday, the students **registered** for classes.
FRAGMENT	Now the students registering for classes.
REVISED	Now the students **are** registering for classes.

FRAGMENT	Yesterday, the students to register for classes.
REVISED	Yesterday, the students **wanted** to register for classes.
FRAGMENT	Yesterday, told about an excellent teacher.
REVISED	Yesterday, I **was** told about an excellent teacher.
FRAGMENT	Now the students to register for classes.
REVISED	Now the students **want** to register for classes.

In the sentences above, *registered, were, are, was, wanted,* and *want* are verbs that change form to indicate time. As they appear in the sentences above, they are examples of complete-sentence verbs.

QUESTION 2: Is there a subject?

If there is no subject, you are looking at a sentence fragment. To find a subject, ask the verb "who?" or "what?"

FRAGMENT	Studied hard for class. [Who studied? unknown]
REVISED	The students studied hard for class. [Who studied? students]
FRAGMENT	Contained some difficult questions. [What contained? unknown]
REVISED	The test contained some difficult questions. [What contained? the test]

Every sentence must have its own subject. A sentence fragment without a subject often occurs when the missing subject is the same as the subject in the preceding sentence.

NO	World War II ended in 1945 for most people. **Continued for others, however, until the end of their lives.**
YES	World War II ended in 1945 for most people. **It continued for others, however, until the end of their lives.**

Imperative statements—commands and some requests—are an exception. They are not sentence fragments. Imperative statements imply the word "you" as the subject.

Run! = (You) run!

Think fast. = (You) think fast.

Please return my books. = (You) please return my books.

QUESTION 3: Do the subject and verb start with a subordinating word—and lack an independent clause to complete the thought?

If the answer to Question 3 is "yes," you are looking at a sentence fragment. Clauses that begin with subordinating words are called **dependent clauses.** They cannot stand alone as independent units. A dependent clause must be joined to an independent clause in order to be part of a complete sentence. One type of subordinating word is a **subordinating conjunction.** A complete list of subordinating conjunctions and the relationships they imply appears in 7h-2. Here are the most frequently used subordinating conjunctions:

after	even though	until
although	if	when
as	since	whenever
because	though	where
before	unless	wherever

FRAGMENT	**Because** she returned my books.
REVISED	**Because** she returned my books, I can study.
FRAGMENT	**When** I study.
REVISED	I have to concentrate **when** I study.

❧ PUNCTUATION ALERT: **When a dependent clause starting with a subordinating conjunction comes before an independent clause, a comma often separates the clauses.** ❧

Another type of subordinating word is a **relative pronoun.** Here are the most frequently used relative pronouns.

that	which	who
what	whichever	whoever
whatever		

FRAGMENT	The test **that** we studied for.
REVISED	The test **that** we studied for was cancelled.
FRAGMENT	The professor **who** taught the course.
REVISED	The professor **who** taught the course was ill.
FRAGMENT	**Whoever** registered early.
REVISED	**Whoever** registered early got a good schedule.

Questions are an exception—they can begin with words such as *when, where, who,* and *which* without being sentence fragments: *When do you want to study? Where is the library? Who is your professor? Which class are you taking?*

ANSWERS: EXERCISE 1

Two pieces of information are given for each item: the reason for the sentence fragment and the number of the question in the "Test for Sentence Completeness" that explains what has caused each sentence fragment. (Exercise 3 asks students to correct the sentence fragments in this exercise.)

1. No verb; question 1

2. No verb; question 1

3. No verb; question 1

4. No subject; question 2

5. Complete sentence

6. Starts with a subordinating word—without an independent clause to complete the thought; question 3

7. Starts with a subordinating word—without an independent clause to complete the thought; question 3

8. Has a subordinating word—without an independent clause to complete the thought; question 3

9. Has a subordinating word—without an independent clause to complete the thought; question 3

10. Complete sentence

ALTERNATE EXAMPLE

To generate discussion about effective use of sentence fragments, you might want to read the opening of Mark Strand's essay "Wooley," which originally appeared in *The New Yorker,* analyzing the effect of each of the fragments he uses. (They are indicated here by italics.)

> I speak of George Wooley, my friend. *Wooley the watchful. Wooley the wily. Wooley the warm.* I speak of him because he is dead. The world never knew him, never gave him a chance, and he passed unacknowledged into his grave.

HOW TO CORRECT SENTENCE FRAGMENTS

REVISION STRATEGY	SEE SECTION
If the sentence fragment is a dependent clause, join it to an adjacent independent clause.	13b
If the sentence fragment is a dependent clause, revise it into an independent clause.	13b
If the sentence fragment is a phrase, join it to an adjacent independent clause.	13c
If the sentence fragment is a phrase, revise it into an independent clause.	13c

EXERCISE 1

Check each word group according to the Test for Sentence Completeness on page 305. If a word group is a sentence fragment, explain what makes it incomplete. If a word group is a complete sentence, circle its number.

EXAMPLE   The rescue of thousands of whales. [no verb; Question 1 on the Test]

1. A Soviet icebreaker trying to rescue the whales.
2. Thousands of ten-foot-long whales struggling for air in the thick ice.
3. In the Arctic Ocean in the winter.
4. Raced to reach the whales.
5. The icebreaker arrived in time.
6. Because the whales were afraid of the ship.
7. Although the ship wanted to cut a path through the ice.
8. A crew member who found a solution.
9. Classical music which he played over the ship's loudspeaker.
10. The whales then followed the ship to the open sea.

13b Revising dependent clauses punctuated as sentences

A **dependent clause** contains both a subject and verb but starts with a subordinating word and is thus unable to stand on its own as a sentence. Subordinating words include subordinating conjunctions and relative pronouns (listed on page 307).

To correct a dependent clause punctuated as a sentence, you can do one of two things. (1) You can join the dependent clause to an independent clause that comes directly before or after; sometimes you will need to add words so that the combined sentence makes sense. (2) You can drop the subordinating word and, if necessary, add words to create an independent clause.

FRAGMENT	Many people over twenty-five years of age are deciding to get college degrees. **Because they want the benefits of an advanced education.**
REVISED	Many people over twenty-five years of age are deciding to get college degrees because they want the benefits of an advanced education. [joined into one sentence]
REVISED	Many people over twenty-five years of age are deciding to get college degrees. They want the benefits of an advanced education. [subordinating conjunction dropped to create an independent clause]
FRAGMENT	College is an attraction for many older people. **Who could not attend upon graduation from high school.**
REVISED	College is an attraction for many older people who could not attend upon graduation from high school. [joined into one sentence]
REVISED	College is an attraction for many older people. They could not attend upon graduation from high school. [relative pronoun dropped and *they* added to create an independent clause]

When trying to identify dependent clauses, be especially careful with words that indicate time—such as *after, before, since,* and *until.* In some sentences they function as subordinating conjunctions°, but in other sentences they function as adverbs° and prepositions°. Do not automatically assume when you see these words that you are looking at a dependent clause.

Before, the class was never full. Now it is overfilled. [These are two complete sentences. In the first sentence, *before* is an adverb° modifying the independent clause° *the class was never full.*]

Before this semester, the class was never full. [This is a complete sentence. *Before* is the preposition° in the prepositional phrase° *before this semester.*]

ANSWERS: EXERCISE 2

Answers will vary. Here is one set of possible responses.

1. Some people are depressed in July and August because high summer temperatures trigger a strong negative reaction.

2. Researchers who have studied the disorder are not sure whether sufferers need to be in the dark longer or whether they need colder temperatures.

3. Although depression in summer affects some people, far more people experience mood disorders during the cold months.

4. Researchers at the National Institute of Mental Health who began studying and defining the problem in the early 1980s called the syndrome SAD, short for seasonal affective disorder.

5. The disorder gained formal acceptance when it was included in 1987 in the American Psychiatric Association's *Diagnostic and Statistical Manual of Mental Disorders.*

6. SAD is more than winter doldrums. Because it can be a severe problem, it is a condition that must be treated.

7. People who refuse to get help when they have been diagnosed with SAD should realize that they are risking their jobs, their relationships, and perhaps even their lives.

8. After researchers tested many possible therapies, they concluded that the best treatment comes from what is called a "sunbox," an invention that uses several fluorescent bulbs to provide light at far greater intensities than regular indoor lighting.

9. Whoever wants to use the device to relieve SAD has to be willing to spend from thirty minutes to five hours daily basking in the artificial sun rays.

10. Although SAD affects mainly people in their twenties, it has been observed in children as young as nine as well as in high school students who are often misdiagnosed as being depressed about school-related issues or personal problems.

Before the professor arrived. [This is a sentence fragment. *Before* is a subordinating conjunction°.]

Before the professor arrived, the room was empty. [This is a complete sentence. The dependent clause precedes an independent clause.]

EXERCISE 2

Find and correct any sentence fragments in each numbered item.

EXAMPLE   Many people suffer from mood disorders that are related to the weather. And particularly to the change of seasons.

Many people suffer from mood disorders that are related to the weather and particularly to the change of seasons.

1. Some people are depressed in July and August. Because high summer temperatures trigger a strong negative reaction.

2. Researchers who have studied the disorder. These scientists are not sure whether sufferers need to be in the dark longer. Or whether they need colder temperatures.

3. Although depression in summer affects some people. Far more people experience mood disorders during the cold months.

4. Researchers at the National Institute of Mental Health who began studying and defining the problem in the early 1980s. The Institute called the syndrome SAD, a short form for "seasonal affective disorder."

5. The disorder gained formal acceptance. When it was included in 1987 in the American Psychiatric Association's *Diagnostic and Statistical Manual of Mental Disorders.*

6. SAD is more than winter doldrums. Because it can be a severe problem. It is a condition that must be treated.

7. People who refuse to get help when they have been diagnosed with SAD. They should realize that they are risking their jobs, their relationships, and perhaps even their lives.

8. After researchers tested many possible therapies. They concluded that the best treatment comes from what is called a "sun-box." An invention that uses several fluorescent bulbs to provide light at far greater intensities than regular indoor lighting.

9. Whoever wants to use the device to relieve SAD. The person has to be willing to spend from thirty minutes to five hours daily basking in the artificial sun rays.

10. Although SAD affects mainly people in their twenties. It has been observed in children as young as nine as well as in high school students. Who are often misdiagnosed as being depressed about school-related issues or personal problems.

13c   Revising phrases punctuated as sentences

A **phrase** is a group of words that lacks a subject, a verb, or both. A phrase, therefore, is not a sentence. To revise a phrase into a complete sentence, either you can rewrite it to become an independent clause, or you can join it to an independent clause that comes directly before or after.

A **verbal phrase** contains a verbal. Verbals are infinitives°, past participles°, present participles°, and gerunds° (see 7d).

FRAGMENT	The mayor called a news conference last week. **To announce new programs for crime prevention and care for the homeless.**
REVISED	The mayor called a news conference last week to announce new programs for crime prevention and care for the homeless. [joined into one sentence]
REVISED	The mayor called a news conference last week. She wanted to announce new programs for crime prevention and care for the homeless. [rewritten]
FRAGMENT	**Introduced by her assistant.** The mayor began with an opening statement.
REVISED	Introduced by her assistant, the mayor began with an opening statement. [joined into one sentence]
REVISED	The mayor **was** introduced by her assistant. She then began with an opening statement. [rewritten]
FRAGMENT	**Hoping for strong public support.** She gave many examples of problems everywhere in the city.
REVISED	Hoping for strong public support, she gave many examples of problems everywhere in the city. [joined into one sentence]
REVISED	She hoped for strong public support. She gave many examples of problems everywhere in the city. [rewritten]

COVERAGE: EXERCISE 2 (page 310)

1. Dependent clause introduced by subordinating conjunction without an independent clause

2. Relative clause without an independent clause; dependent clause introduced by subordinating conjunction without an independent clause

3. Dependent clause introduced by subordinating conjunction without an independent clause

4. Relative clause without an independent clause

5. Dependent clause introduced by subordinating conjunction without an independent clause

6. Dependent clause introduced by subordinating conjunction without an independent clause

7. Relative clause without an independent clause

8. Dependent clause introduced by subordinating conjunction without an independent clause; relative clause without an independent clause

9. Relative clause without an independent clause

10. Dependent clause introduced by subordinating conjunction without an independent clause; relative clause without an independent clause.

QUOTATION ABOUT WRITING

Anyone who can improve a sentence of mine by the omission or placing of a comma is looked upon as my dearest friend.

—George Moore

A **prepositional phrase** contains a preposition° (for a complete list, see 7g), its object°, and any modifiers°.

FRAGMENT	Cigarette smoke made the conference room seem airless. **During the long news conference.**
REVISED	Cigarette smoke made the conference room seem airless during the long news conference. [joined into one sentence]
REVISED	Cigarette smoke made the conference room seem airless. It was hard to breathe during the long news conference. [rewritten]

An **appositive** is a word or word group that renames a noun° or a group of words functioning as a noun.

FRAGMENT	Most people respected the mayor. **A politician with fresh ideas and practical solutions.**
REVISED	Most people respected the mayor, a politician with fresh ideas and practical solutions. [joined into one sentence]
REVISED	Most people respected the mayor. She seemed to be a politician with fresh ideas and practical solutions.

Compound predicates contain two or more verbs° along with any objects° and modifiers°. To be part of a complete sentence, a predicate must have a subject. If the second half of a compound predicate is punctuated as a separate sentence, it is a sentence fragment.

FRAGMENT	The reporters asked the mayor many questions about the details of her program. **And then discussed her answers thoroughly among themselves.**
REVISED	The reporters asked the mayor many questions about the details of her program and discussed her answers thoroughly among themselves. [joined into one sentence]
REVISED	The reporters asked the mayor many questions about the details of her program. Then the reporters discussed her answers thoroughly among themselves. [rewritten]

EXERCISE 3

Go back to Exercise 1 and revise any sentence fragments into complete sentences.

EXERCISE 4

Correct all sentence fragments.

(1) The reign of Czar Nicholas II of Russia beginning with misfortune. (2) And ended in disaster. (3) For the coronation ceremony in Moscow. (4) The czar had promised gifts to all who attended. (5) The huge number of guests who got to the ceremony waited patiently. (6) To get their presents, which were displayed on stands in a nearby field. (7) A rumor then spread that there were not enough gifts for all. (8) Hundreds of greedy guests stampeding to the stands. (9) Many were killed. (10) Or seriously injured. (11) The czar's reign ended with the Russian Revolution. (12) Brought on by the Bolshevik uprising. (13) A mass protest against the excesses of the czar.

13d Recognizing intentional fragments

Professional writers sometimes intentionally use fragments, sparingly, for emphasis and effect.

> The cars were jammed for 30 miles along the Karagatch road. Water buffalo and cattle were hauling carts through the mud. **No end and no beginning. Just carts loaded with everything they owned.** The old men and women, soaked through, walked along keeping the cattle moving.
>
> —ERNEST HEMINGWAY, *In Our Time*

> What is right at one stage may be restricting at another or too soft. During the passage from one stage to another, we will be between two chairs. **Wobbling no doubt, but developing.**
>
> —GAIL SHEEHY, *Passages*

The ability to judge the difference between an acceptable and unacceptable sentence fragment comes from much exposure to reading the work of skilled writers. Many instructors, therefore, often do not accept sentence fragments in student writing until a student can demonstrate the firm ability to write well-constructed complete sentences.

ANSWERS: EXERCISE 4

Answers will vary. Here is one possible revision.

The reign of Czar Nicholas II began with misfortune and ended in disaster. For the coronation ceremony in Moscow, the Czar had promised gifts to all who attended. The huge number of guests who got to the ceremony waited patiently to get their presents, which were displayed on stands in a nearby field. A rumor then spread that there were not enough gifts for all. Hundreds of greedy guests stampeded to the stands. Many were killed or seriously injured. The czar's reign ended with the Russian Revolution, brought on by the Bolshevik uprising, a mass protest against the excesses of the czar.

COVERAGE: EXERCISE 4

(1) no verb; (2) no subject; (3) no subject and no verb; (4) complete sentence; (5) complete sentence; (6) no independent clause; (7) complete sentence; (8) no verb; (9) complete sentence; (10) no subject or verb; (11) complete sentence; (12) no subject or verb; (13) no verb

ANSWERS: EXERCISE 5 (next page)

Answers will vary. Here is one set of possible answers.

Telemarketing is the selling of goods and services over the phone. This business practice is growing at a very fast rate. United States companies generated $56 billion through telephone sales in 1983. According to current estimates by a major telemarketing company, by the late 1980s the figure skyrocketed and reached over $163 billion. In the early 1980s, only 1,650 telemarketing companies employed approximately 4,500 people, while today more than 142,000 companies employ over 2,000,000 telesales workers. Telemarketing is highly effective,

(continued next page)

ANSWERS: EXERCISE 5 (continued)

but ethical questions arise. For instance, it intrudes on the privacy of prospective buyers. In addition, cases of fraud are increasing. A 1982 U.S. Senate subcommittee estimated that phone fraud cost unwary buyers of financial investments more than $200 million.

COVERAGE: EXERCISE 5

(1) has a subordinating word without an independent clause; (2) no verb; (3) correct; (4) no subject, no verb; (5) correct; (6) no subject; (7) no verb; (8) begins with subordinating word without an independent clause; (9) correct; (10) no subject, no verb; (11) correct; (12) no verb

ANSWERS: EXERCISE 6

Answers will vary. Here is one set of possible answers.

Students looking for jobs need more than the "Help Wanted" section of a newspaper. One major tool is a carefully written resumé. A resumé should be written in a standard form (see Chapter 35) and proofread carefully to eliminate errors in spelling, punctuation, or grammar. For the content of the resumé students should analyze all types of experiences. A resumé can include not only paid jobs but also volunteer positions and extracurricular activities. Students have a better chance of getting a job if they have supervised other people, handled money, or taken on highly responsible tasks such as participating in political campaigns or chairing major committees at school. Many employers will consider student resumés, especially when the resumés include names of the students' supervisors.

EXERCISE 5

Revise this paragraph to eliminate any sentence fragments. In some cases you can join word groups to create complete sentences; in other cases, you have to revise the word groups into complete sentences. In the final version, check not only the individual sentences but also the clarity of the whole paragraph.

(1) Telemarketing, which is the selling of goods and services over the phone. (2) A business practice growing at a very fast rate. (3) United States companies generated $56 billion through telephone sales in 1983. (4) According to current estimates by a major telemarketing company. (5) By the late 1980s, the figure skyrocketed. (6) And reached over $163 billion. (7) In the early 1980s, only 1,650 telemarketing companies employing approximately 4,500 people. (8) While today more than 142,000 companies employ over 2,000,000 telesales workers. (9) Telemarketing is highly effective, but ethical questions arise. (10) For instance, intruding on the privacy of prospective buyers. (11) In addition, cases of fraud are increasing. (12) A 1982 U.S. Senate subcommittee estimating that phone fraud cost unwary buyers of financial investments more than $200 million.

EXERCISE 6

Revise this paragraph to eliminate any sentence fragments. In some cases, you can join word groups to create complete sentences; in other cases, you have to revise the word groups into complete sentences. In the final version, check not only the individual sentences but also the clarity of the whole paragraph.

(1) Students looking for jobs need more than the "Help Wanted" section of a newspaper. (2) One major tool, a carefully written résumé. (3) A résumé should be written in a standard form. (4) And proofread carefully to eliminate errors in spelling, punctuation, or grammar. (5) For the content of the résumé. (6) Students should analyze all types of experiences. (7) A résumé including not only paid jobs but also volunteer positions and extracurricular activities. (8) Students have a better chance of getting a job. (9) If they have supervised other people, handled money, or taken on highly responsible tasks. (10) Such as participating in political campaigns or chairing major committees at school. (11) Many employers will consider student résumés. (12) Especially when the résumés include names of the students' supervisors.

Focus on Revising

REVISING YOUR WRITING

If you write sentence fragments, go back to your writing and locate them. Then figure out why each is a sentence fragment by using the Test for Sentence Completeness, explained in 13a. Next, revise each sentence fragment into a complete sentence. For help, use what you learned from analyzing the cause of each sentence fragment (13a) and from studying sections 13b and 13c.

CASE STUDY: REVISING TO AVOID SENTENCE FRAGMENTS

This case study lets you observe a student writer revising. It also gives you the opportunity to revise some student writing on your own.

Observation

A student wrote the following draft for a course called Introduction to the Novel. The assignment was to compose a paragraph about the childhood of a major novelist. This material is well organized as a narrative and tells an interesting story, but the draft's effectiveness is diminished by the presence of sentence fragments.

Read through the draft. The sentence fragments are highlighted. Before you look at how the student revised to eliminate the sentence fragments, revise the material yourself. Then compare what you and the student did.

Dependent clause punctuated as a sentence: 13b

The creative imagination of Victorian novelist Charlotte Brontë got an early start. When she was a child. Her father brought her brother, Branford, a set of wooden soldiers. Her father who was a clergyman and who wrote poetry and a novel as well as sermons. After he gave Branford the set. He told Charlotte and her sisters, Emily and Anne, to each pick one of the toy soldiers. And give it a name. Each sister than made up a

Phrase—part of compound predicate—punctuated as a sentence: 13c

COVERAGE: PARTICIPATION ESSAY (page 317)

In seventeenth-century England, from the death of Elizabeth I in 1603 to William of Orange's ascension to the throne in 1689 [13c: prepositional phrase punctuated as sentence]. The monarchy in England was the cause of unrest and uncertainty.

Queen Elizabeth I died single and childless in 1603. *Because she did not have a direct descendent* [13b: dependent clause punctuated as sentence]. The throne passed to the Queen's cousin. *Who was crowned James I* [13b: dependent clauses punctuated as sentence]. Discord over the relative power of Parliament and the crown emerged under James I. *And erupted during the reign of James' son, Charles I* [13c; second half of compound predicate punctuated as sentence]. Incapable of resolving the conflicts, Charles I lost both the crown and his head to Oliver Cromwell's Puritan Revolution in 1649.

Holding fast to his anti-monarchy sentiments and refusing a crown [13c: participial phrase punctuated as sentence]. Oliver Cromwell did not establish a new line of English monarchs. Instead, he became Lord Protector of England. When Cromwell died, his son Richard lacked the charisma and political astuteness to hold on to power. As a result, the son of Charles I was recalled from France. *Where he had fled to live in safety* [13b: dependent clause punctuated as sentence]. He was crowned Charles II in 1660. *And had very limited power, according to new laws passed by Parliament* [13c: second half of compound predicate punctuated as sentence]. Charles II sired no legitimate heirs, so the succession passed to his brother, James. *An apparently able man with one serious political handicap in seventeenth-century England* [13c: phrase punctuated as sentence]. He was Catholic, at a time when England feared that the Pope was plotting to reclaim England and rule it from Rome. *When the second wife of James*

(continued next page)

baptized her newborn son Catholic [13b: dependent clause punctuated as sentence]. Unease over James's rule escalated rapidly. *To ensure the safety of his wife and new son* [13c: phrase punctuated as sentence]. James sent them to France and followed soon after. James's Protestant daughter Mary took the throne. *With her husband William of Orange* [13c: phrase punctuated as sentence]. *A Dutchman who was a staunch supporter of Protestantism* [13b: dependent clause punctuated as sentence]. Their union was so popular with the English that William continued to rule after Mary's death in 1694. Thus, the century that saw much upheaval and instability in England ended in relative calm.

ANSWER: PARTICIPATION ESSAY

This version is revised to correct the sentence fragments. Because of the many options available for corrections, answers will vary somewhat. Also, answers will vary if students have revised for content, organization, or style.

In seventeenth-century England, from the death of Elizabeth I in 1603 to William of Orange's ascension to the throne in 1689, the monarchy in England was the cause of unrest and uncertainty.

Queen Elizabeth I died single and childless in 1603. Because she did not have a direct descendent, the throne passed to the Queen's cousin who was crowned James I. Discord over the relative power of Parliament and the crown emerged under James I and erupted during the reign of James' son, Charles I. Incapable of resolving the conflicts, Charles I lost both the crown and his head to Oliver Cromwell's Puritan Revolution in 1649.

Holding fast to his anti-monarchy sentiments and refusing a crown, Oliver Cromwell did not establish a new line of English

---

history of her soldier. Soon creating tales of heroism. Inspired by the pleasure of telling stories. Charlotte, together with her brother, invented an imaginary kingdom. With Angria as its name. Because she treasured her fantasies and wanted to remember them. Charlotte began to write them in notebooks. Wanting them to look like miniature editions of books. She printed in a tiny, almost microscopically small handwriting. Those notebooks stand as a reminder of how early in life Charlotte Brontë expressed her creativity.

Phrase—with *-ing* form of verb—punctuated as a sentence: 13c

Dependent clause punctuated as a sentence: 13b

Phrase—with past participle of verb—punctuated as a sentence: 13c

Prepositional phrase punctuated as a sentence: 13c

Phrase—using *-ing* form of verb—punctuated as a sentence: 13c

Here is how the student revised the paragraph to eliminate the sentence fragments. In many cases, the student had alternatives for correcting the errors. Your revision, therefore, might not be exactly like this one, but it should not contain any sentence fragments.

The creative imagination of Victorian novelist Charlotte Brontë got an early start. When she was a child, her father brought her brother, Branford, a set of wooden soldiers. Her father was a clergyman who wrote poetry and a novel as well as sermons. After he gave Branford the set, he told Charlotte and her sisters, Emily and Anne, to each pick one of the toy soldiers and give it a name. Each sister then made up a history of her soldier, and each soon was creating tales of heroism. Inspired by the pleasure of telling stories, Charlotte, together with her brother, invented an imaginary kingdom with Angria as its name. Because she treasured her fantasies and wanted to remember them, Charlotte began to write them in notebooks. Wanting her notebooks to look like miniature editions of books, she printed in a tiny, almost microscopically small handwriting. Those notebooks stand as a reminder of how early in life Charlotte Brontë expressed her creativity.

Participation

A student wrote the following draft for a course called European History. The assignment was to discuss the political atmosphere of a European nation during the seventeenth century. This material is effectively organized for chronological presentation of information, and it uses specific details well. The draft's effectiveness, however, is diminished by the presence of sentence fragments.

Read through the draft. Then revise it to eliminate the sentence fragments. Also, make any additional revisions that you think would improve the content, organization, and style of the material.

In seventeenth-century England, from the death of Elizabeth I in 1603 to William of Orange's ascension to the throne in 1689. The monarchy of England was the cause of unrest and uncertainty.

Queen Elizabeth I died single and childless in 1603. Because she did not have a direct descendant. The throne passed to the Queen's cousin. Who was crowned James I. Discord over the relative power of Parliament and the crown emerged under James I. And erupted during the reign of James' son, Charles I. Incapable of resolving the conflicts, Charles I lost both the throne and his head to Oliver Cromwell's Puritan Revolution in 1649.

Holding fast to his anti-monarchy sentiments and refusing a crown. Oliver Cromwell did not establish a new line of English monarchs. Instead, he became Lord Protector of England. When Cromwell died, his son Richard lacked the charisma and political astuteness to hold on to power. As a result, the son of Charles I was recalled from France. Where he had fled to live in safety. He was crowned Charles II in 1660. And had very limited power, according to new laws passed by Parliament. Charles II sired no legitimate heirs, so the succession passed to his brother, James. An apparently able man with one serious political handicap in seventeenth-century England. He was Catholic, at a time when the English feared that the Pope was plotting to reclaim England and rule it from Rome. When the second wife of James baptized her newborn son Catholic. Unease over James' rule escalated rapidly. To ensure the safety of his wife and new son. James sent them to France and followed soon after. James's Protestant daughter Mary took the throne. With her husband William of Orange. A Dutchman who was a staunch supporter of Protestantism. Their union was so popular with the English that William continued to rule after Mary's death in 1694. Thus, the century that saw much upheaval and instability in England ended in relative calm.

monarchs. Instead, he became Lord Protector of England. When Cromwell died, his son Richard lacked the charisma and political astuteness to hold on to power. As a result, the son of Charles I was recalled from France where he had fled to live in safety. He was crowned Charles II in 1660 and had very limited power, according to new laws passed by Parliament. Charles II sired no legitimate heirs, so the succession passed to his brother, James, an apparently able man with one serious political handicap in seventeenth-century England. He was Catholic, at a time when England feared that the Pope was plotting to reclaim England and rule it from Rome. When the second wife of James baptized her newborn son Catholic, unease over James's rule escalated rapidly. To ensure the safety of his wife and new son, James sent them to France and followed soon after. James's Protestant daughter Mary took the throne with her husband William of Orange, a Dutchman who was a staunch supporter of Protestantism. Their union was so popular with the English that William continued to rule after Mary's death in 1694. Thus, the century that saw much upheaval and instability in England ended in relative calm.

14 Comma Splices and Fused Sentences

QUOTATION ABOUT WRITING

A writer is not someone who expresses his thoughts, his passion or his imagination in sentences but someone who thinks sentences. A Sentence-Thinker.

—Roland Barthes

QUOTATION ABOUT WRITING

Word-carpentry is like any other kind of carpentry: you must join your sentences smoothly.

—Anatole France

A **comma splice** (or **comma fault**) occurs when a comma by itself joins independent clauses°. The only time that a comma is correct between two independent clauses is when the comma is followed by a coordinating conjunction *(and, but, for, or, nor, yet,* and *so)*. The word *splice* means "to fasten ends together." The end of one independent clause and the beginning of another cannot be fastened together with a comma alone.

> **COMMA SPLICE**   The hurricane intensified, it turned toward land.

A **fused sentence** occurs when two independent clauses° are not separated by punctuation or joined by a comma with a coordinating conjunction *(and, but, for, or, nor, yet,* and *so)*. The word *fused* means "to unite as if by melting together." Two independent clauses cannot be united as if melted together. A fused sentence is also known as a **run-on sentence** or a **run-together sentence.**

> **FUSED SENTENCE**   The hurricane intensified it turned toward land.

Comma splices and fused sentences are two versions of the same problem: incorrect joining of two independent clauses°. A fused sentence, however, reveals less awareness of the need for a separation between the independent clauses.

Comma splices and fused sentences distract readers from understanding the meaning you want your material to deliver.

The chart that follows shows you how to correct these errors and refers you to sections in this chapter for fuller explanations and illustrations.

HOW TO CORRECT COMMA SPLICES AND FUSED SENTENCES

- ■ Use a period (14b and 14e).

  The hurricane intensified. It turned toward land.

- ■ Use a semicolon (14b and 14e).

  The hurricane intensified; it turned toward land.

- ■ Use a semicolon and a conjunctive adverb (14e).

  The hurricane intensified; then it turned toward land.

- ■ Use a comma and a coordinating conjunction (14c).

  The hurricane intensified, and it turned toward land.

- ■ Revise one of two independent clauses into a dependent clause (14d).

  As the hurricane intensified, it turned toward land.

  The hurricane intensified as it turned toward land.

14a   Recognizing comma splices and fused sentences

To recognize comma splices and fused sentences, you need to be able to recognize an independent clause. As explained in 7j, an independent clause contains a subject° and predicate°. Also, an independent clause can stand alone as a sentence because it is an independent grammatical unit.

SUBJECT	PREDICATE
Thomas Edison	was an American inventor.

If you tend to write comma splices, here is a useful technique for proofreading your work. Cover all the words on one side of the comma and see if the words remaining constitute an independent clause. If they do, cover that clause and uncover all the words on the other side of the comma. If the second side of the comma is also an independent clause, you have written a comma splice. To further help yourself avoid writing comma splices, become familiar with cor-

TEACHING TIP

You might want to liven up a class by running a "revision contest." Divide the class into an even number of teams, each composed of four students. Tell the students that in preparation for the competition, everyone is to bring to class two paragraphs containing comma splices and fused sentences: (1) a published paragraph that the student has intentionally edited to have three such errors; and (2) an original paragraph written for the competition, containing three intentional comma splices or fused sentences. Ask each student to supply two copies of each paragraph: one for the contest and one filled in as an answer key.

On the day of the competition, pair up teams and have them exchange paragraphs. Collect the answer keys. Give the teams thirty minutes to revise the paragraphs they have received. When they finish, compare their revisions with the answer keys. Here is one way to score.

+ 5 points	for each correct revision
+ 2 points	for each minute by which a team beats the time limit
− 5 points	for each incorrect revision, missed comma splice, or missed fused sentence
+ 5 points	added to the *finder's* team score for each unintentional error in end punctuation found in a contest paragraph (fragments, missing questions marks, etc.)
− 10 points	deducted from the *writer's* team score for each unintentional error in end punctuation in a contest paragraph
+ 10 points	bonus for a perfect response

Team scores can be adjusted along a curve, if you wish, for group grades.

TEACHING TIP

Students who write comma splices and/or fused sentences have a better chance of finding and correcting their errors if they can find a pattern in them. To help students detect patterns, set aside one class or conference session to have students review all the paragraphs and essays they have written for the course. First, if they have not already done so, they should correct all comma splices and fused sentences. Then they should tally the *types* of sentences involved, using for reference the chart, Leading Causes of Comma Splices and Fused Sentences. Encourage students to create additional categories, if needed, for their errors that do not fit the three basic patterns. Make yourself available to answer questions, and encourage students to ask advice of their peers. At the end of the exercise have students submit a review statement. Here is one student's response:

> Of the twelve comma splices and fused sentences I have written this semester, seven involved a second independent clause starting with a pronoun, four involved conjunctive adverbs, and one involved an explanation. I need to be careful, when I use a pronoun as the subject of an independent clause, to punctuate that clause as a sentence.

An explicit statement of results will force students to do the analysis, and the "I need to be careful . . ." sentence will force them to verbalize a plan of attack. Both steps work to overcome students' perceptions of punctuation errors as being random and uncontrollable.

You can then keep the statements on file (1) to help you determine who needs to work on a particular kind of comma splice or fused sentence, and (2) as a contract between you and each student acknowledging that he or she knows what to do—and will do it.

LEADING CAUSES OF COMMA SPLICES AND FUSED SENTENCES

1. **Pronouns.** A comma splice or fused sentence often occurs when the second independent clause° starts with a pronoun°

No	Thomas Edison was a productive inventor, **he** held over 1,300 U.S. and foreign patents.
Yes	Thomas Edison was a productive inventor. **He** held over 1,300 U.S. and foreign patents.

2. **Conjunctive adverbs and other transitional expressions.** A comma splice or fused sentence often occurs when the second independent clause° starts with a conjunctive adverb (see page 186 for a list) or other transitional expression (see page 96 for a list). Remember that these words are *not* coordinating conjunctions *(and, but, or, nor, for, so,* and *yet)* so they cannot work in concert with a comma to join two independent clauses.

No	Thomas Edison was a brilliant scientist, **however,** his schooling was limited to only three months of his life.
Yes	Thomas Edison was a brilliant scientist. **However,** his schooling was limited to only three months of his life.

3. **Explanations or examples.** A comma splice or fused sentence often occurs when the second independent clause° explains or gives an example of the information in the first independent clause°.

No	Thomas Edison was the genius behind many inventions, the phonograph and the incandescent lamp are among the best known.
Yes	Thomas Edison was the genius behind many inventions. The phonograph and the incandescent lamp are among the best known.

---

rect uses for commas, explained in Chapter 24. Experienced writers sometimes use a comma to join very brief parallel° independent clauses: *Mosquitos do not bite, they stab.* Many readers, including many instructors, consider this form an error in student writing; therefore, use a semicolon or period instead of the comma unless otherwise instructed.

If you tend to write fused sentences, you are ignoring the need to signal the end of one sentence before another one starts. If you are making this error because you are unsure about how to identify a complete sentence, use the Test for Sentence Completeness given in 13a.

You will also avoid writing comma splices and fused sentences if you are aware that the majority of such errors occur for the three reasons listed in the chart on the opposite page.

14b Using a period or semicolon to correct comma splices and fused sentences

You can use a period or semicolon to correct comma splices and fused sentences. For the sake of sentence variety and emphasis, however, do not always choose punctuation to correct this type of error. (Other methods are discussed in 14c and 14d.) Strings of too many short sentences rarely establish relationships and levels of importance among ideas.

A **period** can separate the independent clauses° in a comma splice or fused sentence.

COMMA SPLICE	The Muir Woods National Monument is located in northern California, its dominant tree is the coast redwood.
FUSED SENTENCE	The Muir Woods National Monument is located in northern California its dominant tree is the coast redwood.
CORRECTED	The Muir Woods National Monument is located in northern California. Its dominant tree is the coast redwood.

A **semicolon** can separate independent clauses° that are closely related in meaning. See also 25a.

COMMA SPLICE	The coast redwood is named "Sequoia" after a Cherokee Indian, he developed the first alphabet used by that tribe.
FUSED SENTENCE	The coast redwood is named "Sequoia" after a Cherokee Indian he developed the first alphabet used by that tribe.
CORRECTED	The coast redwood is named "Sequoia" after a Cherokee Indian; he developed the first alphabet used by that tribe.

The question mark and exclamation point also signal the ends of independent clauses°.

BACKGROUND

In the second chapter of *Errors and Expectations*, "Handwriting and Punctuation," Mina Shaughnessy observes that the urge to string sentences together reflects a need on the part of the writer for other ways of making links between sentences. Comma splices, for example, reflect a writer's effort to control a sentence, to simplify it by breaking it up into smaller segments by the use of a comma as a conjunction. She argues that punctuation should not be studied apart from other aspects of writing; instead, it should be integrated with work in composition, for "the process whereby writers *mark* sentences is related to the process whereby they *make* them." She suggests that punctuation skills will improve as novice writers study first to recognize and create simple subject and predicate phrases; second, to embed sentences in sentences (using *who, which, that, when,* and *if*); third, to embed appositional forms; and fourth, to embed *-ing* phrases.

BACKGROUND

Noting that writers who have trouble producing good sentences do not necessarily compose simple linguistics structures, Richard Graves concludes that slow learners are insensitive to the simple sentence. He recommends that their understanding of "the limits of the sentence" be improved through observation of examples of sentences and nonsentences (the way most people learn the distinction between them), by study of English sentence patterns (the finite number of basic patterns available to writers), and by experimentation with the plasticity of the English sentence (the use of various structures to express the same idea) ("A Strategy for Teaching Sentence Sense," rpt. in *Rhetoric and Composition,* ed. Richard L. Graves. Rochelle Park, NJ: Hayden, 1976).

14c Using coordinating conjunctions to correct comma splices and fused sentences

When ideas in independent clauses° are closely related and grammatically equivalent, you might decide to connect them with a coordinating conjunction *(and, but, or, nor, for, so,* and *yet).* If you are correcting a comma splice, you can insert a coordinating conjunction and retain the comma. If you are correcting a fused sentence, you can insert a coordinating conjunction along with a comma.

When using a coordinating conjunction, be sure that it fits the meaning of the material. *And* signals addition; *but* and *yet* signal contrast; *for* and *so* signal cause; and *or* and *nor* signal alternatives. A sentence consisting of two independent clauses° joined by a coordinating conjunction and a comma is called a **compound sentence** (7o-2). ❖ PUNCTUATION ALERT: Use a comma before a coordinating conjunction that links independent clauses° (see 24a). ❖

COMMA SPLICE	Redwood trees can grow to over 300 feet in height and up to 16 feet in diameter, their seeds are only a sixteenth of an inch long.
FUSED SENTENCE	Redwood trees can grow to over 300 feet in height and up to 16 feet in diameter their seeds are only a sixteenth of an inch long.
CORRECTED	Redwood trees can grow to over 300 feet in height and up to 16 feet in diameter, **but** their seeds are only a sixteenth of an inch long.
COMMA SPLICE	The foot-thick bark of the redwood tree is a barrier to destructive insects, the bitter chemicals and tannins in the bark further discourage insects and fungi.
FUSED SENTENCE	The foot-thick bark of the redwood tree is a barrier to destructive insects the bitter chemicals and tannins in the bark further discourage insects and fungi.
CORRECTED	The foot-thick bark of the redwood tree is a barrier to destructive insects, **and** the bitter chemicals and tannins in the bark further discourage insects and fungi.

EXERCISE 1

Revise any comma splices or fused sentences by using a period, a semicolon, or a coordinating conjunction (and a comma, if the sentence is fused). If an item is correct, circle its number.

EXAMPLE   Huge numbers of people have become used to the speed of air travel, they do not like to take trains.

Huge numbers of people have become used to the speed of air travel. They do not like to take trains.

1. In the twenty-first century, a new type of transportation may be available, we may be riding superfast trains that connect major cities.
2. These trains, which are called maglevs, are moved along by magnets they provide a magnetic field that keeps the train just inches off the ground.
3. The French T.G.V. is the fastest rail train in use today it can travel 170 miles per hour, but an experimental maglev has traveled 260 miles per hour.
4. A group of transportation officials in Florida plans a train system connecting major cities, Tampa, Miami, and Orlando may be serviced by maglevs as early as 1995.
5. According to some experts, maglevs may someday replace railroad trains, they would use less energy and have fewer moving parts to service.

14d   Revising one of two independent clauses into a dependent clause to correct a comma splice and fused sentence

You can revise a comma splice or fused sentence by changing one of two independent clauses° into a dependent clause°. This method is suitable when one idea can be logically subordinated to the other.

One way to create a dependent clause is to insert a subordinating conjunction (see page 190 for a complete list) in front of the subject and verb. When using a subordinating conjunction, be sure that it fits the meaning of the material. For example, *as* and *because* signal reason, *although* signals contrast, *if* signals condition, and *when* signals time. ❧ PUNCTUATION ALERT: (1) If you put a period after a dependent clause that is not attached to an independent clause, you will create the error called a sentence fragment; see Chapter 13. (2) Generally, use a comma after an introductory dependent clause that starts with a subordinating conjunction; see 24b-1. ❧

ANSWERS: EXERCISE 1

Answers may vary. Here is one set of possible revisions.

1. In the twenty-first century, a new type of transportation may be available. We may be riding superfast trains that connect major cities.

2. These trains, which are called maglevs, are moved along by magnets; they provide a magnetic field that keeps the train just inches off the ground.

3. The French T.G.V. is the fastest rail train in use today. It can travel 170 miles per hour, but an experimental maglev has traveled 260 miles per hour.

4. A group of transportation officials in Florida plans a train system connecting major cities; Tampa, Miami, and Orlando may be serviced by maglevs as early as 1995.

5. According to some experts, maglevs may someday replace railroad trains, and they would use less energy and have fewer moving parts to service.

COVERAGE: EXERCISE 1

(1) comma splice corrected by using a period; (2) fused sentence corrected by using a semicolon; (3) fused sentence corrected by using a period; (4) comma splice corrected by using a semicolon; (5) comma splice corrected by using a comma and a coordinating conjunction

BIOGRAPHY

Although Gertrude Stein was born in Allegheny, Pennsylvania, in 1874, she spent little time in the United States once she had completed her education. She attended Radcliffe from 1893 to 1897, and Johns Hopkins Medical School from 1897 to 1902. In 1903 she went to Paris, where she stayed. Her writing was considered unusual: repetitious and sometimes nonsensical. According to Edmund Wilson, "Widely ridiculed and seldom enjoyed, she has yet played an important role in connection with other writers who have become popular." For forty years her home was a gathering place for famous and not-yet-famous artists and writers: Henri Matisse, Pablo Picasso, Juan Gris, Wyndham Lewis, Sherwood Anderson, Ezra Pound, Ernest Hemingway, Andre Gide, Paul Robeson.

QUOTATION ABOUT WRITING

Wearing down seven number two pencils is a good day's work.

—Ernest Hemingway

COMMA SPLICE	Gertrude Stein wanted to support struggling artists in the 1920s, she bought many paintings by Picasso and others.
FUSED SENTENCE	Gertrude Stein wanted to support struggling artists in the 1920s she bought many paintings by Picasso and others.
CORRECTED	**Because Gertrude Stein wanted to support struggling artists in the 1920s,** she bought many paintings by Picasso and others.
COMMA SPLICE	Gertrude Stein wrote many novels, short stories, essays, poems, plays, and one opera, she is better known for her art collection.
FUSED SENTENCE	Gertrude Stein wrote many novels, short stories, essays, poems, plays, and one opera she is better known for her art collection.
CORRECTED	Gertrude Stein wrote many novels, short stories, essays, poems, plays, and one opera **although she is better known for her art collection.**

A relative pronoun can also create a dependent clause. Commonly used relative pronouns are *who, which,* and *that*. ❖ PUNCTUATION ALERT: When an adjective clause is nonrestrictive, use commas to separate it from the independent clause. (A restrictive clause is essential to limit meaning; a nonrestrictive clause is nonessential. See 24e for more information.) ❖

COMMA SPLICE	Gertrude Stein moved from America to Paris in 1902, she quickly became fascinated by impressionist painting.
FUSED SENTENCE	Gertrude Stein moved from America to Paris in 1902 she quickly became fascinated by impressionist painting.
CORRECTED	Gertrude Stein, **who moved from America to Paris in 1902,** quickly became fascinated by impressionist painting.

EXERCISE 2

Revise any comma splices or fused sentences.

(1) Most sporting events have a positive effect on the economy. (2) They attract sports fans, they provide income for those who run the concessions, for example. (3) The longest sporting event in the world might be assumed to bring in correspondingly large profits, however, that

is not the case. (4) The *Tour de France,* a cycling race that originated in 1903, covers over three thousand miles and lasts twenty-three days. (5) At least one-third of the workers in France take time off to watch the race they stay away from work for two-thirds of the time the race is in progress. (6) Because of the lost work hours, the total damage to the French economy is astronomical, it can add up to three-quarters of one percent of the nation's gross national product. (7) That figure may not seem very large, nevertheless, it adds up to many millions of dollars annually. (8) Although French economists are very worried about the problem, they do not want the race discontinued they also take time off to enjoy the festivities.

14e   Using a semicolon or a period before a conjunctive adverb or other transitional expression between two independent clauses

Conjunctive adverbs and other transitional expressions link ideas between sentences. Remember, however, that these words are *not* coordinating conjunctions, which work in concert with commas to join independent clauses (see 14c). Conjunctive adverbs and other transitional expressions that fall between sentences must be immediately preceded by a period or semicolon.

Conjunctive adverbs include such words as *however, therefore, also, next, then, thus, furthermore,* and *nevertheless* (see page 186 for a complete list). ✤ PUNCTUATION ALERT: Usually, use a comma after a conjunctive adverb at the beginning of a sentence (see 24b-3). ✤

COMMA SPLICE	Car theft has increased alarmingly in most major cities, **however,** one city has decided to fight back.
FUSED SENTENCE	Car theft has increased alarmingly in most major cities **however,** one city has decided to fight back.
CORRECTED	Car theft has increased alarmingly in most cities; **however,** one city has decided to fight back.
CORRECTED	Car theft has increased alarmingly in most major cities. **However,** one city has decided to fight back.

ANSWERS: EXERCISE 2

(1) Most sporting events have a positive effect on the economy. (2) They attract sports fans, who provide income for those who run the concessions, for example. (3) The longest sporting event in the world might be assumed to bring in correspondingly large profits; however, that is not the case. (4) The *Tour de France,* a cycling race that originated in 1903, covers over three thousand miles and lasts twenty-three days. (5) At least one-third of the workers in France take time off to watch the race. They stay away from work for two-thirds of the time the race is in progress. (6) Because of the lost work hours, the total damage to the French economy is astronomical, adding up to three-quarters of one percent of the nation's gross national product. (7) That figure may not seem very large; nevertheless, it adds up to many millions of dollars annually. (8) Although French economists are very worried about the problem, they do not want the race discontinued because they also take time off to enjoy the festivities.

COVERAGE: EXERCISE 2

(1) correct; (2) comma splice corrected with relative pronoun *who* to subordinate second independent clause; (3) comma splice corrected with semicolon before conjunctive adverb *however*; (4) correct; (5) fused sentence corrected by division of sentences by a period; (6) comma splice corrected by use of participle *adding* to turn independent clause into a modifier; (7) comma splice corrected by semicolon before conjunctive adverb *nevertheless*; (8) fused sentence corrected by subordinating conjunction *because* to make final clause dependent

Transitional expressions include *for example, for instance, in addition, in fact, of course,* and *on the other hand* (see page 96 for a complete list). ❖ PUNCTUATION ALERT: Usually, use a comma after transitional words at the beginning of a sentence (see 24b-3). ❖

COMMA SPLICE
In Boston stolen car reports are broadcast over the radio, **in fact,** a police officer "deputizes" about 500,000 listeners to be on the alert for stolen vehicles.

FUSED SENTENCE
In Boston stolen car reports are broadcast over the radio **in fact,** a police officer "deputizes" about 500,000 listeners to be on the alert for stolen vehicles.

CORRECTED
In Boston stolen car reports are broadcast over the radio; **in fact,** a police officer "deputizes" about 500,000 listeners to be on the alert for stolen vehicles.

CORRECTED
In Boston stolen car reports are broadcast over the radio. **In fact,** a police officer "deputizes" about 500,000 listeners to be on the alert for stolen vehicles.

A conjunctive adverb or other transitional expression can appear in more than one location within an independent clause. In contrast, a coordinating conjunction *(and, but, or, nor, for, so,* and *yet)* can appear only between the independent clauses it joins.

Car theft has increased alarmingly in most major cities. One city, **however,** has decided to fight back.

Car theft has increased alarmingly in most major cities. One city has decided, **however,** to fight back.

Car theft has increased alarmingly in most major cities. One city has decided to fight back, **however.**

Car theft has increased alarmingly in most major cities, **but** one city has decided to fight back.

EXERCISE 3

Revise any comma splices or fused sentences caused by a conjunctive adverb or other transitional expression. If an item is correct, circle its number.

ANSWERS: EXERCISE 3

1. Sir Arthur Conan Doyle created the famous detective; however, the stories are told through the voice of Sherlock Holmes's assistant, Dr. Watson.

2. Many people know Holmes through reading Doyle's stories; in addition, the character of Sherlock Holmes has appeared on stage, screen, radio, and television.

3. Correct.

4. Learning the complex details of these stories is not easy; in fact, many Holmes fans take great pride in being experts about the detective's life.

5. Much has been written about the character of Sherlock Holmes; indeed, Sir Arthur Conan Doyle's detective has received considerable literary attention.

COVERAGE: EXERCISE 3

(1) comma splice: conjunctive adverb; (2) fused sentence: transitional expression; (3) correct; (4) fused sentence: transitional expression; (5) comma splice: conjunctive adverb

326

EXAMPLE   Sherlock Holmes is a most popular fictional detective, in fact, his exploits have been translated into fifty-seven languages.

Sherlock Holmes is a most popular fictional detective. In fact, his exploits have been translated into fifty-seven languages.

1. Sir Arthur Conan Doyle created the famous detective, however, the stories are told through the voice of Sherlock Holmes's assistant, Dr. Watson.

2. Many people know Holmes through reading Doyle's stories in addition, the character of Sherlock Holmes has appeared on stage, screen, radio, and television.

3. The sixty original Holmes stories are important to Holmes's admirers; consequently, they study these stories intently.

4. Learning the complex details of these stories is not easy in fact, many Holmes fans take great pride in being experts about the detective's life.

5. Much has been written about the character of Sherlock Holmes, indeed, Sir Arthur Conan Doyle's detective has received considerable literary attention.

EXERCISE 4

Revise all comma splices or fused sentences, using a different method of correction for each one. If an item is correct, circle its number.

EXAMPLE   Cro-Magnon people lived between 35,000 and 12,000 years ago, these ancient humans cared about status symbols.

Cro-Magnon people lived between 35,000 and 12,000 years ago. These ancient humans cared about status symbols.

1. Some Cro-Magnon people were buried with many valuable possessions, we can assume, therefore, that Cro-Magnons had a society based on class distinctions, also they probably believed in an afterlife.

2. In one 24,000-year-old grave that was found in Russia, for example, a man was buried in clothing decorated with over 3,000 ivory beads.

3. A young boy and girl were buried together with many rings, ivory spears, and 8,000 ivory beads, these possessions indicated their high rank.

4. The living Cro-Magnons also wore jewelry, this practice indicates that they were not simply struggling to survive.

5. People who were worried about mere subsistence would not have had the time and energy to spend hundreds of hours stringing beads they would have had to devote every waking minute to securing food and shelter.

ANSWERS: EXERCISE 4

Answers will vary. Here is one set of possible revisions.

1. Some Cro-Magnon people were buried with many valuable possessions. We can assume, therefore, that Cro-Magnons had a society based on class distinctions. Also, they probably believed in an afterlife.

2. Correct

3. A young boy and girl were buried together with many rings, ivory spears, and 8,000 ivory beads, which indicated their high rank.

4. The living Cro-Magnons also wore jewelry; this practice indicates that they were not simply struggling to survive.

5. People who were worried about mere subsistence would not have had the time and energy to spend hundreds of hours stringing beads, for they would have had to devote every waking minute to securing food and shelter.

COVERAGE: EXERCISE 4

(1) Two comma splices corrected with periods; (2) correct; (3) comma splice corrected with independent clause changed to dependent clause with relative pronoun *which*; (4) comma splice corrected with semicolon; (5) fused sentence corrected with comma and coordinating conjunction

ANSWERS: EXERCISE 5

Answers will vary. Here is one possible revision.

(1) During the nineteenth century, a number of fearless women traveled long distances from their homes. They visited places far more exotic than their native France or England. (2) Isabella Bird, for example, a British clergyman's daughter, began traveling and writing when she was in her forties; she often wrote by the light of a portable oil lamp and with a gun in her pocket. (3) In 1896, she celebrated her sixty-fourth birthday, and that same year she crossed northwest China hoping to reach Tibet. (4) While she was traveling, her guides collapsed with fever. Then her rice supply grew dangerously low. (5) Only when tribal warfare broke out, however, and the bridges were torn down did she turn around. (6) Like Isabella Bird, Flora Tristan, a native of France, proved her adventurous spirit when she sailed from France to Peru, a trip that inspired her to write a book. (7) The book was published in 1838; however, its title, *Peregrinations of a Pariah,* meaning "travels of an outcast," suggests that not everyone admired its courageous author.

COVERAGE: EXERCISE 5

(1) comma splice with pronoun; (2) comma splice with pronoun; (3) fused sentence with pronoun; comma splice with pronoun; (4) comma splice with conjunctive adverb; (5) correct; (6) comma splice with pronoun; (7) comma splice with conjunctive adverb

EXERCISE 5

Revise any comma splices and fused sentences, using as many different methods explained in this chapter as you can.

(1) During the nineteenth century, a number of fearless women traveled long distances from their homes, they visited places far more exotic than their native France or England. (2) Isabella Bird, for example, a British clergyman's daughter, began traveling and writing when she was in her forties, she often wrote by the light of a portable oil lamp and with a gun in her pocket. (3) In 1896, she celebrated her sixty-fourth birthday that same year she crossed northwest China, she hoped to reach Tibet. (4) While she was traveling, her guides collapsed with fever, then her rice supply grew dangerously low. (5) Only when tribal warfare broke out, however, and the bridges were torn down did she turn around. (6) Like Isabella Bird, Flora Tristan, a native of France, proved her adventurous spirit, she sailed from France to Peru, a trip that inspired her to write a book. (7) The book was published in 1838, however, its title, *Peregrinations of a Pariah,* meaning "travels of an outcast," suggests that not everyone admired its courageous author.

EXERCISE 6

Revise any comma splices and fused sentences, using as many different methods explained in this chapter as you can.

(1) Most baseball fans know many amusing stories and wild tales about Casey Stengel, he could be a clown on the ball field but a great strategist behind the scenes. (2) Stengel was born in Kansas City, Missouri, in 1890 he died in Glendale, California, in 1975, he had eighty-five years in between to devote to baseball. (3) He claimed that he did not play golf or go to the movies, baseball was all that was left. (4) In 1929 he was managing a last-place team called the Toledo Mud Hens, he was not, of course, very happy with their performance. (5) He told the players that they should all get interested in the stock market; in fact, he told them to invest in Pennsylvania Railroad stock. (6) He told the team that they had to improve, otherwise they would be riding trains out of town. (7) The railroad would get many new customers, therefore, Stengel reasoned, the stock would go up. (8) Baseball history does not reveal whether the players bought the stock, they did start playing better.

Focus on Revising

REVISING YOUR WRITING

If you write comma splices or fused sentences, go back to your writing and locate them. Then figure out why each is an error by using the chart on Leading Causes of Comma Splices and Fused Sentences, explained in 14a. Then revise your writing to eliminate the errors. For help, use what you learned from analyzing the cause of each comma splice or fused sentence (14a) and from studying sections 14b through 14e.

CASE STUDY: REVISING TO AVOID COMMA SPLICES AND FUSED SENTENCES

This case study lets you observe a student writer revising. It also gives you the opportunity to revise some student writing on your own.

Observation

A student wrote the following draft for a course called Introduction to Criminal Justice. The assignment was to discuss a current controversy in trial law. This material is well organized and presents its information clearly and fully. However, the draft's effectiveness is diminished by comma splices and fused sentences.

Read through the draft. The errors are highlighted and explained. Before you look at how the student revised to eliminate the errors, revise the material yourself. Then compare what you and the student did.

When fingerprinting was first introduced in the late nineteenth century, many judges hesitated to accept fingerprints as legal evidence. Recently, a similar controversy has arisen, it involves hypnosis. During this century, various state and federal courts have issued contradictory rulings on the admissibility of testimony obtained under hypnosis, however, in 1987 the United States Supreme

> Comma splice with pronoun *it:* 14a, Cause 1

> Comma splice with conjunctive adverb *however:* 14a, Cause 2

ANSWERS: EXERCISE 6 (on opposite page)

Answers will vary. Here is one possible revision.

Most baseball fans know many amusing stories and wild tales about Casey Stengel. He could be a clown on the ball field but a great strategist behind the scenes. Stengel was born in Kansas City, Missouri, in 1890, and he died in Glendale, California, in 1975. He had eighty-five years in between to devote to baseball. He claimed that he did not play golf or go to the movies, so baseball was all that was left. In 1929, he was managing a last-place team called the Toledo Mud Hens. He was not, of course, very happy with their performance. He told the players that they should all get interested in the stock market; in fact, he told them to invest in Pennsylvania Railroad stock. He told the team that they had to improve, or otherwise they would be riding trains out of town. The railroad would get many new customers. Therefore, Stengel reasoned, the stock would go up. Baseball history does not reveal whether the players bought the stock, but they did start playing better.

COVERAGE: EXERCISE 6

(1) comma splice with pronoun; (2) fused sentence with pronoun; comma splice with pronoun; (3) comma splice with explanation in second independent clause; (4) comma splice with pronoun; (5) correct; (6) comma splice with pronoun; (7) comma splice with pronoun; (8) comma splice with pronoun

COVERAGE: PARTICIPATION ESSAY (opposite page)

As consumers, when we buy clothes, we often make choices on the basis of the *fabric of an article of clothing, therefore,* [14a, Cause 2: comma splice with conjunctive adverb] fashion designers always pay attention to matters of composition and design in fabrics.

Fabric is composed of natural fibers, synthetic fibers, and blends of the two. Natural fibers include cotton, linen, and *wool, they* [14a: comma splice with pronoun] offer the advantages of durability and absorbency. Synthetic fibers include rayon, polyester, acrylic, or combinations of them and other synthetic *fibers they* [14a, Cause 1: fused sentence with pronoun] resist wrinkling and retain their color well. Fiber blends combine natural and synthetic fibers to create combinations such as cotton and polyester, which offer the advantages of each but have their own problems, such as retaining stains.

The design of fabric is affected by the way that the fabric is *produced, for example,* [14a, Cause 2: comma splice with transitional expression] a fabric can be produced on a loom to create woven fabrics such as crepe and *denim, conversely,* [14a, Cause 2: fused sentence with transitional expression] a fabric can be produced on a knitting machine to create fabrics such as jersey and velour. Once the basic fabric is being produced, special patterns can be woven or knit into it, for instance, diagonal patterns can be woven into cotton fabrics for a geometric effect, and vertical patterns can be woven into a cable-stitched fabric for a thicker look and feel. Various finishes can further alter a fabric's *appearance stone* [14a, Cause 3: fused sentence with example] washing gives denim a worn look, and brushing gives flannel a softer look. Puckers or wrinkles can be set into a *fabric, these* [14a, Cause 1: comma splice with pronoun] features characterize fabrics such as seersucker and crinkle gauze.

These many options, and others, in fabrics permit fashion designers to satisfy the needs

Court ruled that such evidence is admissible. This ruling is a major new development, but the public should not look to hypnosis as a miracle technique, because testimony obtained under hypnosis is no more reliable than that obtained when witnesses search their memories.

There is one major advantage of hypnosis it usually allows witnesses to recall incidents in far greater detail than they would otherwise. Hypnotized people will still recall what they think they saw or what they wished they had seen. In fact, it is possible for people to lie when hypnotized furthermore, a hypnotist can unintentionally lead witnesses to give certain responses.

One thing is certain, lively legal debates lie ahead. Hypnotists are not licensed professionals, they can be circus entertainers or serious practitioners. It would be up to a jury to decide on the competence of a hypnotist most people who sit on juries have no idea of what standards to apply.

Fused sentence with pronoun it; 14a, Cause 1

Comma splice with conjunctive adverb furthermore; 14a, Cause 2

Explanation in second independent clause: 14a, Cause 3

Comma splice with pronoun they: 14a, Cause 1

Fused sentence with explanation in second independent clause: 14a, Cause 3

Here is how the student revised the paragraph to correct comma splices and fused sentences. The student had alternatives for correcting the errors. Your revision, therefore, might not be exactly like this one, but it should deal with each error highlighted on the draft.

When fingerprinting was first introduced in the late nineteenth century, many judges hesitated to accept fingerprints as legal evidence. Recently, a similar controversy has arisen. It involves hypnosis. During this century, various state and federal courts have issued contradictory rulings on the admissibility of testimony obtained under hypnosis. However, in 1987 the United States

Supreme Court ruled that such evidence is admissible. This ruling is a major new development, but the public should not look to hypnosis as a miracle technique, because testimony obtained under hypnosis is no more reliable than that obtained when witnesses search their memories.

There is one major advantage of hypnosis; it usually allows witnesses to recall incidents in far greater detail than they would otherwise. Hypnotized people will still recall what they think they saw or what they wished they had seen. In fact, it is possible for people to lie when hypnotized; furthermore, a hypnotist can unintentionally lead witnesses to give certain responses.

One thing is certain. Lively legal debates lie ahead. Hypnotists are not licensed professionals. They can be circus entertainers or serious practitioners. It would be up to a jury to decide on the competence of a hypnotist, but most people who sit on juries have no idea of what standards to apply.

Participation

A student wrote the following draft for a course called Introduction to Fashion Design. The assignment was to describe characteristics of fabric. This material is well organized and uses specific examples well, but the draft's effectiveness is diminished by comma splices and fused sentences.

Read through the draft. Then revise it to eliminate the comma splices and fused sentences. Also, make any additional revisions that you think would improve the content, organization, and style of the material.

As consumers, when we buy clothes, we often make choices on the basis of the fabric of an article of clothing, therefore, fashion designers always pay attention to matters of composition and design in fabrics.

Fabric is composed of natural fibers, synthetic fibers, and blends of the two. Natural fibers include cotton, linen, and wool, they offer the advantages of durability and absorbency. Synthetic fibers include rayon, polyester, acrylic, or combinations of them and other synthetic fibers they resist wrinkling and retain their color well. Fiber blends combine natural and synthetic fibers to create

of many different types of *people, some* [14a, Cause 3: Fused sentence with example] consumers care more about being in style than building a long-lasting wardrobe, while others place high priority on ease of care or on comfortable fit.

ANSWER: PARTICIPATION ESSAY

This version revises the common splices and fused sentences. Answers might vary because of the options in correcting the errors. Also, answers will vary if a student revised the content, organization, or style.

As consumers, when we buy clothes, we often make choices on the basis of the fabric of an article of clothing. Therefore, fashion designers always pay attention to matters of composition and design in fabrics.

Fabric is composed of natural fibers, synthetic fibers, and blends of the two. Natural fibers include cotton, linen, and wool. They offer the advantages of durability and absorbency. Synthetic fibers include rayon, polyester, acrylic, or combinations of them and other synthetic fibers; they resist wrinkling and retain their color well. Fiber blends combine natural and synthetic fibers to create combinations such as cotton and polyester, which offer the advantages of each but have their own problems, such as retaining stains.

The design of fabric is affected by the way that the fabric is produced. For example, a fabric can be produced on a loom to create woven fabrics such as crepe and denim; conversely, a fabric can be produced on a knitting machine to create fabrics such as jersey and velour. Once the basic fabric is being produced, special patterns can be woven or knit into it. For instance, diagonal patterns can be woven into cotton fabrics for a geometric effect, and vertical patterns can be woven into a cable-stitched fabric for

(continued next page)

ANSWER: PARTICIPATION ESSAY
(continued)

a thicker look and feel. Various finishes can further alter a fabric's appearance. Stone washing gives denim a worn look, and brushing gives flannel a softer look. Puckers or wrinkles can be set into a fabric; these features characterize fabrics such as seersucker and crinkle gauze.

These many options, and others, in fabrics permit fashion designers to satisfy the needs of many different types of people. Some consumers care more about being in style than building a long-lasting wardrobe, while others place a high priority on ease of care or on comfortable fit.

combinations such as cotton and polyester, which offer the advantages of each but have their own problems, such as retaining stains.

The design of fabric is affected by the way that the fabric is produced, for example, a fabric can be produced on a loom to create woven fabrics such as crepe and denim, conversely, a fabric can be produced on a knitting machine to create fabrics such as jersey and velour. Once the basic fabric is being produced, special patterns can be woven or knit into it, for instance, diagonal patterns can be woven into cotton fabrics for a geometric effect, and vertical patterns can be woven into a cable-stitched fabric for a thicker look and feel. Various finishes can further alter a fabric's appearance stone washing, for example, gives denim a worn look, and brushing gives flannel a softer look. Puckers or wrinkles can be set into a fabric, these features characterize fabrics such as seersucker and crinkle gauze.

These many options, and others, in fabrics permit fashion designers to satisfy the needs of many different types of people, some consumers care more about being in style than building a long-lasting wardrobe, while others place a high priority on ease of care or on comfortable fit.

15 Sentences That Send Unclear Messages

A sentence can seem structurally correct at first glance—as if no grammatical principles of English have been violated—but still have internal flaws that keep it from delivering a sensible message. To help you sort through the various ways that sentences can send unclear messages, use this chart.

WAYS THAT SENTENCES SEND UNCLEAR MESSAGES	
PROBLEM	**SEE SECTION**
Unnecessary shifts	
Person and number	15a-1
Subject and voice	15a-2
Tense and mood	15a-3
Direct and indirect discourse	15a-4
Misplaced modifiers	15b
Dangling modifiers	15c
Mixed sentences	
Mixed constructions	15d-1
Faulty predication	15d-2
Incomplete sentences	15e

Most sentence flaws can be hard to spot because of the way the human brain works. When writers know what they mean to say, they sometimes misread what is on the paper for what they intend. The brain unconsciously "adjusts" an error or "fills in" missing material. Readers, on the other hand, see only what is on paper.

QUOTATION ABOUT WRITING

You write with ease to show your breeding,
But easy writing's curst hard reading.
—Richard Brinsley Sheridan

QUOTATION ABOUT WRITING

Proper words in proper places, make the true definition of a style.
—Jonathan Swift

QUOTATION ABOUT WRITING

The creative potential of human language is miraculous. Consider this: The number of possible different ways of expressing any given idea or emotion is infinite.
—Ann Martin Scott

No   Heated for 30 seconds, you get bubbles on the surface of the mixture. [This sentence says *you* are heated for 30 seconds.]

YES   After the mixture is heated for 30 seconds, bubbles form on the surface.

No   After you boil the mixture for two minutes, it is cooled in a test tube. [This sentence shifts from *you* to *it* and from the active voice to the passive voice.]

YES   After you boil the mixture for two minutes, you cool it in a test tube.

YES   After the mixture is boiled for two minutes, it is cooled in a test tube.

No   The chemical reaction taking place rapidly creates a salt. [Does *rapidly* refer to the pace of the reaction or to the speed at which the salt is created?]

YES   The chemical reaction takes place rapidly and creates a salt.

YES   The chemical reaction rapidly creates a salt.

If you make such errors and have trouble noticing them, what can you do to get yourself to "see" the flaws? Here are some suggestions.

PROOFREADING TO FIND SENTENCE FLAWS

1. Finish your revision well before its deadline so that you can put it aside and go back to it with fresh eyes that will pick up flaws more easily as you proofread.

2. Proofread by working backwards, from your last sentence to your first; this can help you see each sentence as a separate unit free of context that might trick your brain into overlooking flaws.

3. Ask your instructor or other experienced readers to check you. Then look over their findings and try to raise your consciousness about what went wrong. If you make any of the errors discussed in this chapter, the chances are that you make that error repeatedly in your writing. Once you become aware of the pattern of your errors, you will have made a major step toward eliminating your errors.

4. Proofread an extra time exclusively for any error that you tend to make more than any other.

15a Avoiding unnecessary shifts

Shifts within sentences blur meaning quickly. Readers expect to stay on the track you started them on. If you switch to another track, your readers become confused. Few readers have the patience to read material that seems garbled.

Unless the meaning or grammatical structure of a sentence requires it, always avoid shifting between person and number, subject and voice, and tense and mood. Also do not shift from indirect to direct discourse within a sentence without using punctuation and grammar to make the changes clear.

1 Staying consistent in person and number

Person in English consists of the *first person* (I, we), who is the speaker; the *second person* (you), who is the person spoken to; and the *third person* (he, she, it, they), who is the person or thing being spoken about. See page 271 for a chart that explains "person" fully. Do not shift person within a sentence or a longer passage unless the meaning calls for a shift.

No	**They** enjoy feeling productive, but when a job is unsatisfying **you** usually become depressed. [*They* switches to *you.*]
Yes	**They** enjoy feeling productive, but when a job is unsatisfying **they** usually become depressed.

Number refers to one (singular) and more than one (plural). Do not start to write in one number and then shift suddenly to the other. Such shifting gives your sentences an unstable quality and your message becomes fuzzy.

No	By the year 2000, most **people** will live longer, and **an employed person** will retire later. [The plural *people* shifts to the singular *person.*]
Yes	By the year 2000, most **people** will live longer, and **employed people** will retire later.

A common cause of inconsistency in person and number is shifts to the second-person *you* from the first-person *I* or a third-person noun such as *person, the public,* or *people.* You will avoid this error in academic writing if you remember to reserve *you* for sentences that directly address the reader and to use third-person pronouns for general statements.

335

BACKGROUND

English emphasizes the number of every noun or pronoun in a sentence. In fact, it is impossible to talk or write about anything in English without signaling its number. English speakers take such information for granted, but the system is not universal. In Chinese, for example, the speaker decides if it is necessary to mention whether an item is singular or plural. Usually, number is considered irrelevant, and few sentences make any reference to it.

ANSWERS: EXERCISE 1

Answers may vary somewhat because of the alternate ways to eliminate shifts in person and number.

(1) Hyperactivity in children is a problem that affects up to 6 percent of young boys and girls, although *boys are* more likely to be affected than *girls.* (2) Teachers can find teaching hyperactive children difficult, especially if *the teachers* do not know how to recognize the characteristics of such *children.* (3) In one study, teachers called as many as 30 percent of their students hyperactive. (4) In school, these children may daydream excessively, fidget a great deal, or talk. (5) *They show* other traits including tactlessly blurting out whatever is on their minds or racing around charging into people. (6) *Hyperactive children are* often impatient, cannot wait *their turns,* and are unable to follow directions. (7) New studies recently have been published. (8) *They indicate* that a key element in hyperactivity is a short attention span, possibly because *these children* eat too much sugar.

COVERAGE: EXERCISE 1

(1) shift in number, shift in number; (2) shift in person, shift in number; (3) no shift; (4) no shift; (5) shift in number; (6) shift in number, shift in person; (7) no shift; (8) shift in number, shift in person

No	I enjoy reading forecasts of the future, but **you** wonder which will turn out to be correct. [*I,* which is first person, shifts to *you,* which is second person.]
Yes	I enjoy reading forecasts of the future, but **I** wonder which will turn out to be correct.
No	By the year 2000, **Americans** will pay twice today's price for a car, and **you** will get twice the gas mileage. [*Americans,* which is third person, shifts to *you,* which is second person.]
Yes	In 2000, **Americans** will pay twice today's price for a car, and **they** will get twice the gas mileage.

Another common cause of inconsistency in person and number is shifts from singular to plural in the third person. When a singular noun (for example, *person*) or a singular pronoun (for example, *someone*) has to be referred to by a pronoun, the pronoun should not be plural (for example, *they*). Use *he, she,* or the construction *he or she,* which acts as a singular pronoun. When you use words such as *person* or *someone,* you may not have any specific "person" or "someone" in mind. Thus, the "person" does not seem to be a "he" or "she." Still, you have to choose a singular pronoun. You can also choose to change to the plural *people* so that the plural pronoun *they* would be correct.

No	When a **person** is treated with respect at work, **they** usually feel more fulfilled. [The singular *person* shifts to the plural *they.*]
Yes	When **a person** is treated with respect at work, **he or she** usually feels more fulfilled.
Yes	When **people** are treated with respect at work, **they** usually feel more fulfilled.

Indefinite pronouns (for example, *someone* and *everyone;* see 11f for a complete list) can be particularly troublesome for writers who want to avoid using sexist language. For advice on handling pronouns in such situations, see 11n-2 and especially 21b.

EXERCISE 1

Eliminate shifts in person and number. Be alert to shifts between, as well as within, sentences.

(1) Hyperactivity in children is a problem that affects up to 6 percent of young boys and girls, although a boy is more likely to be affected than a girl. (2) Teachers can find teaching hyperactive children difficult, especially if you do not know how to recognize the characteristics of such a

child. (3) In one study, teachers called as many as 30 percent of their students hyperactive. (4) In school, these children may daydream excessively, fidget a great deal, or talk. (5) He shows other traits including tactlessly blurting out whatever is on their minds or racing around charging into people. (6) A hyperactive child is often impatient, cannot wait your turn, and are unable to follow directions. (7) New studies recently have been published. (8) It indicates that a key element in hyperactivity is a short attention span, possibly because we eat too much sugar.

2 | Staying consistent in subject and voice

The **subject** of a sentence is the word or group of words that acts, is acted upon, or is described: ***People** laugh, **people** were entertained, **people** are nice.* Do not shift subjects within a sentence unless the meaning justifies the shift.

YES   **People** look forward to the future, but **the future** holds many secrets.

Shifts in subjects are rarely justified when they are accompanied by a shift in voice. The **voice** of a sentence is either **active** *(People expect changes)* or **passive** *(Changes are expected).* The active voice emphasizes the doer of an action, and the passive voice does not. (For a complete discussion of active and passive voice, see 8m and 8n.) Unnecessary shifts in subject and voice reflect a lack of planning that causes a sentence or longer stretch of writing to drift out of focus.

No   Most of **the people polled expect** major improvements by the year 2000, but some **hardships are anticipated.** [The subject shifts from *people* to *hardships,* and the voice shifts from active to passive.]

YES   Most of **the people polled expect** major improvements by the year 2000, but **they anticipate** some hardships.

No   When some **respondents consider** the year 2000, very optimistic **predictions are made.** [The subject shifts from *respondents* to *predictions,* and the voice shifts from active to passive.]

YES   When some **respondents consider** the year 2000, **they make** very optimistic predictions.

YES   Some **respondents consider** the year 2000 very optimistically.

3 Staying consistent in tense and mood

Tense refers to the ability of verbs to show time. Tense changes are required when time movement is described: *We will go to the movies after we finish dinner.* If tense shifts are illogical, sentence clarity suffers. (See 8j for guidance about correct sequences of tenses.)

No	The campaign in the United States to clean up the movies **began** in the 1920s as civic and religious groups **try** to ban sex and violence from the screen. [The tense shifts from the past *began* to the present *try*.]
Yes	The campaign in the United States to clean up the movies **began** in the 1920s as civic and religious groups **tried** to ban sex and violence from the screen.
No	Producers and distributors **created** a film Production Code in the 1930s. At first, violating its guidelines **carried** no penalty. Eventually, however, films that **fail** to get the board's Seal of Approval **are not distributed** widely. [This shift occurs between sentences: the past tense *created* and *carried* shift to the present tense *fail* and *are not distributed*.]
Yes	Producers and distributors **created** a film Production Code in the 1930s. At first, violating its guidelines **carried** no penalty. Eventually, however, films that **failed** to get the board's Seal of Approval **were not distributed** widely.

Mood refers to whether a sentence is a statement or question (indicative mood), a command or request (imperative mood), or a conditional or other-than-real statement (subjunctive mood). For more about mood, see 8k. Shifts among moods blur your message. The most common error in shifts is between the imperative and indicative, though other types sometimes occur.

No	The Production code included two guidelines about violence. **Do not show** the details of brutal killings, and **movies should not be** explicit about how to commit crimes. [The verbs shift from the imperative mood *do not show* to the indicative mood *movies should not be.*]
Yes	The Production code included two guidelines about violence. **Do not show** the details of brutal killings, and **do not be** explicit about how to commit crimes.
Yes	The Production code included two guidelines about violence. **Movies should not show** the details of brutal killings, and **should not be** explicit about how to commit crimes.

WORD HISTORY

According to the *Oxford English Dictionary* (OED), the term *mood* has been used since the sixteenth century to refer to verb forms that indicate commands or wishes. The earliest recorded use of the word in this way dates back to 1573, when a scholar named Golding asked a question that still concerns our students: "How shall men directly fynde the Coniugation, Nomber, Person, Tence, and Moode of Verbes togither in their Kynde?"

When we speak of the *mood* of a verb, we are not discussing its emotional state. *Mood* when it refers to a mental state is related to Latin *mos,* meaning *custom.* In contrast, *mood* used to discuss verbs is an alteration of *mode,* which comes from the Latin *modus,* meaning *measure, moderation,* or (most relevant here) *manner.* The earliest use of *mode* to refer to verbs dates back to 1520: "Sometyme of the infinytyve mode folowynge." Other early references make it clear that *mood/mode* was originally used for discussions of Greek and Latin rather than of English.

shift 15a

No	**If a movie were going to be shown** outside the United States, the **guidelines are** less strict. [The verbs shift from the subjunctive mood *if a movie were going to be shown* to the indicative mood *guidelines are.*]
YES	**If a movie were going to be shown** outside the United States, the **guidelines would be** less strict.

4 | **Avoiding unmarked shifts between indirect and direct discourse within the same sentence**

Indirect discourse reports speech or conversation and is not enclosed in quotation marks. **Direct discourse** repeats speech or conversation exactly and encloses the spoken words in quotation marks (see 24g). Sentences that merge indirect and direct discourse without quotation marks and other markers confuse readers and distort the message you want to deliver.

No	Professor Anderson attributed acid rain specifically to carbon fuels but **are we ready to give them up?** [The first clause is indirect discourse; the second clause shifts to unmarked direct discourse.]
YES	Professor Anderson attributed acid rain specifically to carbon fuels but **asked whether we are ready to give them up.** [This revision consistently uses indirect discourse.]
YES	Professor Anderson attributed acid rain specifically to carbon fuels but **asked, "Do we really want to give them up?"** [This revision uses direct and indirect discourse correctly because the quotation marks and grammatical structures clearly signal which is which.]

EXERCISE 2

Revise these sentences to eliminate all incorrect shifts discussed so far in this chapter. Some sentences have several possible revisions.

EXAMPLE   British women began their fight for the right to vote later than their counterparts in the United States, but the British suffragist was far more militant.

British women began their fight for the right to vote later than their counterparts in the United States, *but the British suffragists were far more militant.*

1. Emmeline Pankhurst urged her two daughters to join the fight, but were they prepared to commit civil disobedience?

ALTERNATE EXAMPLE

To improve your students' skill in identifying direct and indirect discourse, you might ask them to work in groups to identify the types of discourse found in the following passage from Russell Baker's "Country Living."

In the country, I am told, the trick is to let the weather roam free through the house. [indirect] "You're spoofing me, aren't you?" [direct] I asked the real-estate man. He wasn't.

In the country, he explained, you're supposed to wear long underwear all winter. [indirect] "It can get itchy if you don't have freezing wind coming between the logs," [direct] he said.

In the summer, you're expected to hang flypaper in the kitchen. "If your logs are chinked tightly they'll keep out the varmints that give your flypaper a businesslike appearance," [direct] he explained.

ANSWERS: EXERCISE 2

Here are some possible revisions. Your students may come up with other effective ones.

1. Emmeline Pankhurst urged her two daughters to join the fight, but she asked whether they were prepared to commit civil disobedience.

2. Both Cristabel and Sylvia Pankhurst willingly adopted their mother's views and chained themselves to the gates of public buildings as they gave speeches urging that women be given the vote.

3. Some suffragists urged the Pankhursts to use "gentle persuasion," but most of their followers favored more radical action.

4. Suffragists once watched the Pankhursts climb into the rafters above the British Parliament and shout pro-vote slogans at important moments in the debate.

5. When British suffragists were arrested, they were often treated brutally, and they were noted for their brave persistence in spite of forced feedings aimed at breaking their hunger strikes.

COVERAGE: EXERCISE 2

(1) direct-indirect discourse shift; (2) two tense shifts; (3) subject and voice shift; (4) shift in person; (5) tense shift

ANSWERS: EXERCISE 3

(1) The robots of today can perform many more tasks than their earlier counterparts. (2) Twenty years ago, robots remained stationary and welded car bodies or lifted heavy steel bars. (3) Today's robots, on the other hand, perform work that includes cleaning offices, guarding hotel rooms, and inspecting automobiles. (4) At

2. Both Cristabel and Sylvia Pankhurst willingly adopted their mother's views and chain themselves to the gates of public buildings as they give speeches urging that women be given the vote.

3. Some suffragists urged the Pankhursts to use "gentle persuasion," but more radical action was favored by most of their followers.

4. Suffragists once watched the Pankhursts climb into the rafters above the British Parliament, and you could hear them shout pro-vote slogans at important moments in the debate.

5. When British suffragists were arrested, they were often treated brutally, and they are noted for their brave persistence in spite of forced feedings aimed at breaking their hunger strikes.

EXERCISE 3

Revise this paragraph to eliminate incorrect shifts. Be alert to shifts between, as well as within, sentences.

(1) The robots of today can perform many more tasks than its earlier counterpart. (2) Twenty years ago, a robot remained stationary and welded a car body or lifted heavy steel bars. (3) Today's robot, on the other hand, performs work that included cleaning offices, guarding a hotel room, and inspecting automobiles. (4) At California's Memorial Medical Center of Long Beach, a doctor has performed brain surgery using a robot arm that allows them to drill into a person's skull and reach your brain more accurately. (5) A robot recently joined the police force in Dallas, and a suspect was forced into surrendering by the robot. (6) When the robot broke a window, the suspect shouted "Help," and asked what is that? (7) Many people do not realize that service robots often prepare your fast food or sort the packages you brought to the post office. (8) In the near future, robots selling for about $20,000 will work without human assistance, and you will be able to buy a robot costing $50,000 that will do household chores.

15b   Avoiding misplaced modifiers

A **modifier** is a word, phrase°, or clause° that describes other words, phrases, or clauses. A **misplaced modifier** is a description that is incorrectly positioned in a sentence, thus distorting meaning. As you write and revise, always check to see that your modifiers are placed as close as possible to what they describe so that your reader will attach the meaning where you intend it to be.

1   Avoiding ambiguous placements

With **ambiguous placement,** a modifier can refer to two or more words in a sentence.

Little limiting words (such as *only, just, almost, hardly, nearly, even, exactly, merely, scarcely, simply*) can change meaning according to where they are placed. When you use such words, position them precisely. Consider how different placements of *only* change the meaning of this sentence: *Professional coaches say that high salaries motivate players.*

Only professional coaches say that high salaries motivate players. [No one else says this.]

Professional coaches **only** say that high salaries motivate players. [The coaches probably do not mean what they say.]

Professional coaches say **only** that high salaries motivate players. [The coaches say nothing else.]

Professional coaches say that **only** high salaries motivate players. [Nothing except high salaries motivates players.]

Professional coaches say that high salaries **only** motivate players. [High salaries do nothing other than motivate players.]

Professional coaches say that high salaries motivate **only** players. [No others on the team, such as coaches and managers, are motivated by high salaries.]

Squinting modifiers also cause ambiguity. A squinting modifier can describe both what precedes and what follows it. Since a modifier cannot do double duty, either move the modifier to a position where its meaning will be precise or revise the sentence.

No   The high school's football star being recruited **actively** believed each successive offer would be better. [What was active—the recruitment or the star's belief?]

Yes   The high school's football star being recruited believed **actively** that each successive offer would be better.

Yes   The **actively** recruited high school's football star believed each successive offer would be better.

California's Memorial Medical Center of Long Beach, a doctor has performed brain surgery using a robot arm that allows her [or him] to drill into a person's skull and reach the brain more accurately. (5) A robot recently joined the police force in Dallas, and it forced a suspect into surrendering. (6) When the robot broke a window, the suspect shouted, "Help," and asked, "What is that?" (7) Many people do not realize that service robots often prepare their fast food or sort the packages they bring to the post office. (8) In the near future, robots selling for about $20,000 will work without human assistance, and robots costing $50,000 will do household chores.

COVERAGE: EXERCISE 3

(1) number; (2) number between sentences 1 and 2; number within the sentence; (3) number between sentences 1 and 3; tense; number within the sentence; (4) number within the sentence; person; (5) voice; (6) indirect/direct discourse; (7) person; tense; (8) voice; number

---

TEACHING TIP

If your students feel that modifier placement is a slapdash business, you might ask them to look at some ludicrous sentences and have them try to draw what is written. Here are a few.

1. When people first saw whales, they were still wearing animal skins and had stone axes.

2. The man kissed the baby with a beard.

3. Walking down the street, the Eiffel Tower came into view.

4. The wildlife specialist said that most bears are dangerous on television.

5. Poison ivy is common in the forest which gives many people an itchy rash.

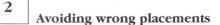

TEACHING TIP

Working in groups, your students might enjoy experimenting with the following passage from Colin Fletcher's *The Winds of Mara* to see how movement of the italicized modifiers will change the meaning. The groups can compare their completed versions to see how many different readings have been created from the same original one simply by the change of location of modifiers.

> The lions continued their *slow and lazy* passage, directly toward us. Once a lioness stopped and turned her head to look *briefly* at the zebras, then walked on. A trio of cubs began to romp and tumble; an adult cuffed them into order. The gap between us narrowed. Soon we could see *magnificently self-assured* expressions on *golden* faces; then rib cages showing *faintly, sculpturally;* then muscles rippling beneath *powerful* haunches. Eventually it seemed as if we could see each hair adjusting to the animal's *slow and lazy* movements.

BACKGROUND

Pointing out that the rule against splitting an infinitive contradicts the principles of English grammar and the practice of our best writers, Cornelia and Bergen Evans demonstrate that meaning is sometimes distorted by adhering to it. They conclude that frequently the only way to avoid a split infinitive and still write good English is to avoid the infinitive. However, with the increasing use of the infinitive, in place of the *-ing* form or clause that was previously preferred, avoiding the infinitive may lead to wordy paraphrases that are not good English (*A Dictionary of Contemporary American Usage,* New York: Random House, 1957).

2 Avoiding wrong placements

With **wrong placement,** modifying words are misplaced in a sentence, thus garbling the meaning.

No   The history of college athletics sheds light on current policies and practices of college football **beginning in the nineteenth century.** [This sentence says that current policies and practices, not the history, started in the nineteenth century.]

Yes   The history of college athletics, **beginning in the nineteenth century,** sheds light on current policies and practices of college football.

No   Most college athletic departments in the 1920s evolved from academic divisions, **especially those with large football programs.** [This sentence says that academic divisions, not athletic departments, had football programs.]

Yes   Most college athletic departments in the 1920s, **especially those with large football programs,** evolved from academic divisions.

3 Avoiding awkward placements

Awkward placements are interruptions that seriously break the flow of a message and thereby distract your reader from understanding your material.

A **split infinitive** is one type of awkward placement. An **infinitive** is a verb form that starts with *to: to convince, to create.* When material comes between the *to* and its verb, it can interrupt meaning. This happens particularly when the intervening material could easily go before or after the infinitive.

No   Orson Welles's radio drama "War of the Worlds" managed **to,** on October 30, 1938, **convince** listeners that they were hearing an invasion by Martians.

Yes   On October 30, 1938, Orson Welles's radio drama "War of the Worlds" managed **to convince** listeners that they were hearing an invasion by Martians.

Often the intervening word that splits an infinitive is an adverb ending in *-ly.* Many such adverbs sound awkward unless they are placed either before or after the infinitive.

No	People feared they would no longer be able **to happily live** in peace.
Yes	People feared they would no longer be able **to live happily** in peace.

Nevertheless, sometimes an adverb seems awkward in any position except between *to* and the verb. Many readers, therefore, are not distracted by split infinitives like these:

The starship Enterprise on "Star Trek" was charged **"to boldly go. . . ."**

Welles wanted **to realistically portray** a Martian invasion for the radio audience.

If you think your readers prefer that infinitives never be split, you can usually revise the sentence to avoid the split:

Welles wanted his "Martian invasion" to sound realistic to the radio audience.

Interruptions of subjects and verbs by highly complex phrases or clauses disturb the smooth flow of a sentence.

No	**The announcer,** because the script, which Welles himself wrote, called for perfect imitations of emergency announcements, **opened** with a warning that included a description of the "invasion."
Yes	Because the script, which Welles himself wrote, called for perfect imitations of emergency announcements, **the announcer opened** with a warning that included a description of the "invasion."

When a **verb phrase** (a group of words that functions as a verb in a sentence: *was kissed, had been kissed*) is interrupted by words unrelated to the time sequence of the verb, the sentence lurches instead of flows. Your reader has to work too hard to understand the message you want your sentence to deliver.

No	People who tuned in late to "The War of the Worlds" believed that New Jersey **had,** by Martians bent on destruction, **been invaded.**
Yes	People who tuned in late to "The War of the Worlds" believed that New Jersey **had been invaded** by Martians bent on destruction.
No	Police switchboards **were,** not surprisingly, **jammed** with frantic phone calls.
Yes	Not surprisingly, police switchboards **were jammed** with frantic phone calls.

QUOTATION ABOUT WRITING

A good style should show no sign of effort. What is written should seem a happy accident.

—W. Somerset Maugham

ANSWERS: EXERCISE 4

Answers might vary somewhat. The final result must avoid all shifts. Here is one possible set.

1. If we look back in history, the origins of the automobile can be found in 1769 in France.

2. Because of his determination to travel without the assistance of animals, the Frenchman Nicholas Cugnot built the first self-propelled vehicle.

3. Only steam powered Cugnot's invention.

4. The vehicle was run by a huge steam boiler that hung in front of its single front wheel. It was difficult to steer and hard to stop, and during a trial drive it knocked over a rock wall.

5. Beginning in 1860, the invention of various types of gas-combustion engines provided an alternative to clumsy steam power.

6. In Germany, two other inventors, Karl Benz and Gottlieb Daimler, were trying to invent a gas-driven vehicle.

7. They lived only sixty miles apart, but they did not know each other.

8. Benz is the man who finally produced the first car and was given credit for the invention of the automobile.

9. After the finishing touches had been added, the first car rolled out of a workshop in a small German town.

10. It rattled and banged down the street to announce loudly and dramatically a revolution in transportation.

COVERAGE: EXERCISE 4

(1) interruption of verb phrase; (2) separation of subject and verb; (3) squinting modifier; (4) separation of subject and verb; (5) wrong placement; (6) wrong placement; (7) ambiguous placement; (8) ambiguous placement; (9) interruption of verb phrase; (10) split infinitive

When a verb and its object are interrupted by words that should modify both those elements, clarity often suffers.

No   Many churches **held** for their frightened communities **"end of the world" prayer services.**

YES   Many churches **held "end of the world" prayer services** for their frightened communities.

EXERCISE 4

Revise these sentences to correct any ambiguous, wrong, or awkward placements. If a sentence is correct, circle its number.

EXAMPLE   One of the greatest accomplishments in history took place in 1885, the invention of the first car.

One of the greatest accomplishments in history, *the invention of the first car, took place in 1885.*

1. The origins of the automobile can, if we look back in history, be found in 1769 in France.

2. The Frenchman Nicholas Cugnot, because of his determination to travel without the assistance of animals, built the first self-propelled vehicle.

3. Cugnot's invention only was powered by steam.

4. During a trial drive, the vehicle, which was run by a huge steam boiler that hung in front of its single front wheel and which was difficult to steer and hard to stop, knocked over a rock wall.

5. The invention, beginning in 1860, of various types of gas-combustion engines provided an alternative to clumsy steam power.

6. Two other inventors, Karl Benz and Gottlieb Daimler, were, in Germany, trying to invent a gas-driven vehicle.

7. Only they lived sixty miles apart, but they did not know each other.

8. Benz is finally the man who produced the first car and was given credit for the invention of the automobile.

9. The first car rolled, after the finishing touches had been added, out of a workshop in a small German town.

10. It rattled and banged down the street to loudly and dramatically announce a revolution in transportation.

EXERCISE 5

Combine each list of words or word groups to create all the possible logical sentences. Each list offers more than one possibility. Explain any differences in meaning among the alternatives you create.

dm **15c**

EXAMPLE   college graduates
on the average
than do high school graduates
earn more money

a. On the average, college graduates earn more money than do high school graduates.

b. College graduates earn more money, on the average, than do high school graduates.

c. College graduates, on the average, earn more money than do high school graduates.

d. College graduates earn more money than do high school graduates, on the average.

1. the microbiologist
frequently
new
to explore
old
used
problems
methods

2. to become
engineering
medicine
the student
a biomedical engineer
studied
successfully
and

3. eagerly
the computer specialists
to solve problems
worked
artificial intelligence
in
only

4. know
scientists
that
smoking
lung
not
causes
only
cancer

5. air travel
than travel by rail
has become less expensive
in many cases

1a. Frequently, the microbiologist used old methods to explore new problems.

1b. The microbiologist used old methods to explore new problems frequently.

1c. To explore new problems, the microbiologist used old methods frequently.

1d. To explore new problems frequently, the microbiologist used old methods.

2a. To become a biomedical engineer, the student studied engineering and medicine successfully.

2b. The student studied engineering and medicine successfully to become a biomedical engineer.

3a. Eagerly, the computer specialists worked only to solve problems in artificial intelligence.

3b. The computer specialists worked eagerly only in artificial intelligence to solve problems.

3c. Only the computer specialists worked eagerly in artificial intelligence to solve problems.

3d. The computer specialists worked eagerly in artificial intelligence only to solve problems.

4a. Not only scientists know that smoking causes lung cancer.

4b. Scientists know that smoking causes not only lung cancer.

4c. Scientists know that not only smoking causes lung cancer.

5a. In many cases, air travel has become less expensive than travel by rail.

5b. Air travel has become less expensive in many cases than travel by rail.

5c. Air travel has become less expensive than travel by rail, in many cases.

15c   Avoiding dangling modifiers

A **dangling modifier** modifies—describes or limits—what is implied but not stated in a sentence. Dangling modifiers can be hard for a writer to spot. Because the writer knows the intended meaning, the writer's brain tends to supply the missing material. While the

A HUMOROUS NOTE

Dangling modifiers can sometimes create statements that are unintentionally humorous. Consider the following examples collected and published by Richard Lederer in *Anguished English* (Wyrick and Company, 1988).

1. Locked in a vault for fifty years, the owner of the jewels has decided to sell them.

2. Do not sit in a chair without being fully assembled.

3. Washed from a layer of mudstone estimated to be more than three million years old, a young American paleoanthropologist has found several leg bones and a skull fragment.

writer therefore does not notice the error, the reader usually does and realizes that the meaning is unclear.

> **No**   **Reading Faulkner's short story "A Rose for Emily,"** the ending surprised us.

This sentence says that the story's ending is doing the reading. The implied subject of the modifier is *we*, but nowhere is that subject stated—thus the modifier dangles. You can correct a dangling modifier by revising the sentence so that the intended subject is stated.

> **YES**   **Having read Faulkner's short story "A Rose for Emily," we** were surprised by the ending.
>
> **YES**   We read Faulkner's short story "A Rose for Emily" and were surprised by the ending.
>
> **No**   **Shocked by her father's death, the family home** became a refuge for Emily. [*The family home* cannot be shocked.]
>
> **YES**   **Shocked by her father's death, Emily** took refuge in the family home.
>
> **No**   **When courting Emily, the townspeople** gossiped about her. [*The townspeople* were not courting Emily.]
>
> **YES**   **When Emily was being courted by Homer Barron, the townspeople** gossiped about her.

Dangling modifiers sometimes result from unnecessary use of the passive voice. (For a complete discussion of passive voice, see 8m and 8n.)

> **No**   **To earn money, china-painting lessons** were offered by Emily to wealthy young women. [*China-painting lessons* cannot earn money.]
>
> **YES**   **To earn money, Emily** offered china-painting lessons to wealthy young women.

EXERCISE 6

Identify and correct any dangling modifiers in these sentences. If a sentence is correct, circle its number.

EXAMPLE   Assigned to interview an unfriendly person, the experience can be instructive to a student journalist.

Assigned to interview an unfriendly person, *a student journalist can find the experience instructive.*

1. To be successful, careful plans must be made by the student journalist.

2. Being tense, the interview might begin on the wrong note for an inexperienced journalist.

3. Until relaxed, questions should mention only neutral topics.
4. After the journalist is more at ease, the person being interviewed might also relax.
5. With a list of questions, the interview process goes more smoothly for everyone involved.
6. Although easy to answer, mistakes are sometimes made on factual questions by a hostile interviewee.
7. By being analytic and evaluative, those mistakes can reveal a great deal to an experienced journalist.
8. Knowing how to pace an interview, the hard questions are more likely to be answered honestly after the interviewee has been caught off guard.
9. Until an interview is complete, the seasoned journalist always remains alert.
10. Essential information might be revealed when leaving.

 ## 15d Avoiding mixed sentences

A **mixed sentence** has two or more parts that do not make sense together. It often occurs when the writer loses track of the beginning of a sentence while writing the end of the sentence. Careful proofreading, including reading aloud, can help a writer avoid this error.

1 Revising mixed constructions

A **mixed construction** starts out taking one grammatical form and then changes, derailing the meaning of the sentence.

No   Because television's first transmissions in the 1920s included news programs became popular with the public. [The opening subordinate clause° starts off on one track, but the independent clause° goes off in another direction. What does the writer want to emphasize—the first transmissions or the popularity of news programs?]

Yes   Television's first transmissions in the 1920s included news programs, which quickly became popular with the public. [The idea of the first transmissions is now emphasized. *Because* has been dropped, making the first clause independent; and *which* has been added, making the second clause subordinate and logically related to the first.]

Answers may vary somewhat. Here is one set of possibilities.

1. To be successful, the student journalist must plan carefully.

2. Being tense, an inexperienced journalist might begin on the wrong note.

3. Until relaxed, the student journalist should mention only neutral topics.

4. Correct

5. With a list of questions, the interviewer can make the process go more smoothly for everyone involved.

6. A hostile interviewee sometimes answers factual questions incorrectly, although they are easy to answer.

7. By being analytic and evaluative, an experienced journalist can learn a great deal from those mistakes.

8. Knowing how to pace an interview, a journalist will more likely get honest answers to hard questions after he or she has caught the interviewee off guard.

9. Correct

10. Essential information might be revealed when the journalist is leaving.

(1) dangling infinitive; (2) dangling participle; (3) unexpressed subject; (4) correct; (5) unexpressed subject; (6) unnecessary passive voice; (7) dangling participle; (8) unexpressed subject; (9) correct; (10) unexpressed subject

ALTERNATE EXAMPLES

What is inconsistent in the following mixed constructions? You might want to ask students to work in groups to revise these five sentences so that the parts make sense together.

1. Because you want to visit the great art museums of the world is why you should go to the Louvre in Paris.

2. Paris, the capital of France, one of the great museums of the world is located there.

3. Tourists from all over the world, the Louvre draws them.

4. The collection is composed of arts works from many cultures is what distinguishes the Louvre.

5. By being the site of many important historical events makes it especially interesting.

BACKGROUND

In Chapter Three, "Syntax," of *Errors and Expectations,* Mina Shaughnessy presents an analysis of the causes of syntactic problems in the sentences produced by beginning students. She concludes that many such problems are linked to the manual process of writing, but others to the difficulty that non-writers have learning the "dialect" of written formal English. Writing calls for specificity and coherence that are likely to seem "unnatural" because they are provided by other means in daily speech: gestures, tone of voice, tolerance for loose coordination, for example. In short, "the inexperienced writer is indeed not likely to have command of the language he needs to bring off the consolidations that are called for in writing." Another source of mismanaged syntax that has pedagogical implications is the beginning writer's lack of familiarity with how writers work. Unlike the speaker, the writer must have skills of encoding (handwriting, spelling, punctuation) and of experimenting with sentences (by additions, subtractions,

No   By doubling the time allotment for network news to thirty minutes increased the prestige of network news programs. [A prepositional phrase°, such as *by doubling,* cannot be the subject of a sentence.]

Yes   Doubling the time allotment for network news to thirty minutes increased the prestige of network news programs. [Dropping the preposition *by* clears up the problem.]

Yes   By doubling the time allotment for network news to thirty minutes, the network executives increased the prestige of network news programs. [Inserting a logical subject, *the network executives,* clears up the problem; an independent clause° is now preceded by a modifying prepositional phrase°.]

The phrase *the fact that* is sometimes the cause of a mixed sentence.

No   The fact that quiz show scandals in the 1950s prompted the networks to produce even more news shows.

Yes   The fact is that quiz show scandals in the 1950s prompted the networks to produce even more news shows. [The added *is* clarifies the meaning.]

Yes   Quiz show scandals in the 1950s prompted the networks to produce even more news shows. [Dropping *the fact that* clarifies the meaning.]

---

2   **Revising faulty predication**

Faulty predication, sometimes called **illogical predication,** occurs when a subject and its predicate (the part of the sentence that says something about the subject) do not make sense together.

No   The **purpose** of television **was invented** to entertain people.

Yes   The **purpose** of television **was** to entertain people.

Yes   **Television was invented** to entertain people.

One key cause of illogical predication is a breakdown in the connection between a subject° and its complement°. (For information about complements, see 7c-1.)

No   Walter Cronkite's outstanding characteristic as a newscaster was credible.

The subject of this sentence is *characteristic.* While *credible* can re-name (and would complement) a person, it cannot rename (or com-plement) a characteristic. A suitable renaming of a characteristic is *credibility.*

YES Walter Cronkite's outstanding characteristic as a news-caster was credibility.

Illogical predication is the problem in most constructions that begin *is when* or *is where.* Avoid these constructions in academic writing.

No A disaster *is when* television news shows get some of their highest ratings.

YES Television news shows get some of their highest rat-ings during a disaster.

Similarly, avoid *reason . . . is because* in academic writing.

No **One reason** television news captured national atten-tion **is because** it covered the Vietnam War thor-oughly.

YES **One reason** television news captured national atten-tion **is that** it covered the Vietnam War thoroughly.

YES Television news captured national attention **because** it covered the Vietnam War thoroughly.

substitutions, and inversions) to make mean-ing and statement fit as closely as possible. The third cause of syntactic problems, ac-cording to Shaughnessy, is the lack of confi-dence felt by novice writers in academic sit-uations. She notes that self-doubt may be a memorable lesson they have learned in school. The solutions she suggests to help writers gain syntactic maturity are varied, including "direct intervention in the form of drills or grammatical explanations," pattern practice, and sentence-combining exercises. Shaughnessy attributes the greatest gains, however, to those times when the writer has to claim his or her meaning "within the con-straints of a specific situation." It is "only as a writer," she asserts, "rather than as an ex-erciser" that a student can "develop the ver-bal responsiveness to his own thoughts and to the demands of his reader that produces genuinely mature syntax" (New York: Ox-ford UP, 1977).

EXERCISE 7

Revise the mixed sentences below so that the beginning of each sentence fits logically with its end. If a sentence is correct, circle its number.

EXAMPLE As a result of the increasing amount of sewage in the United States is a crisis in disposing of these wastes.

The increasing amount of sewage in the United States is cre-ating a crisis in waste disposal.

1. The fact that millions of gallons of raw sewage are being dumped into the nation's waters are becoming unfit for use.
2. The reason that ecologists are extremely concerned is because waste disposal problems will get worse in the future.
3. Because of multiple sewage spills in San Diego transformed a wildlife refuge into a public health hazard.
4. Also, when hospital waste and other sewage created a fifty-mile-long slick closed beaches in New Jersey and New York.
5. This situation is similar to what happened in the nineteenth century, when sewage in overexpanded cities led to outbreaks of typhoid and cholera.

ANSWERS: EXERCISE 7

Answers will vary. Here is one set of possi-bilities.

1. Millions of gallons of raw sewage are being dumped into the nation's waters, which are becoming unfit for use.
2. Ecologists are extremely concerned be-cause waste disposal problems will get worse in the future.
3. Multiple sewage spills in San Diego transformed a wildlife refuge into a public health hazard.
4. Also, hospital waste and other sewage created a fifty-mile-long slick that closed beaches in New Jersey and New York.
5. Correct

(continued next page)

ANSWERS: EXERCISE 7 *(continued)*

6. Sewage treatment plants were constructed that no longer are sufficient to handle today's volume of water.

7. One modern solution is the "greening" of sewage systems that occurs when trees are planted and then fertilized with sewage partially treated to retain soil nutrients.

8. In Lubbock, Texas, recycled wastes keep a six-mile-long strip of community area green and lush.

9. The source of pollution in some cities is the fact that storm runoffs from farmlands and urban streets are too huge and sudden to be handled without detention basins.

10. The problem is still enormous, because by the year 2005 the present 27 billion gallons of sewage a day will increase to 43 billion gallons, which means we have to take immediate, drastic action.

COVERAGE: EXERCISE 7

(1) mixed construction with *the fact that*; (2) faulty predication with the *reason . . . is because*; (3) mixed construction; (4) faulty predication; (5) correct; (6) mixed construction; (7) faulty predication with *is when*; (8) faulty predication with *is where*; (9) mixed construction; (10) mixed construction wtih *the fact that* and faulty predication with *reason . . . is because* and then mixed construction.

6. Back then sewage treatment plants were constructed no longer are sufficient to handle today's volume of waste.

7. One modern solution is "greening" of sewage systems is when trees are planted and then fertilized with sewage partially treated to retain soil nutrients.

8. In Lubbock, Texas, is· where recycled wastes keep a six-mile-long strip of community area green and lush.

9. Because the source of pollution in some cities is storm runoffs from farmlands and urban streets are too huge and sudden to be handled without detention basins.

10. The fact is that the problem is still enormous, and the reason is because by the year 2005 the present 27 billion gallons of sewage a day will increase to 43 billion gallons means we have to take immediate, drastic action.

15e Avoiding incomplete sentences

An **incomplete sentence** has missing words, phrases, or clauses necessary for grammatical correctness or sensible meaning. Such omissions blur your meaning, and your reader has to work too hard to understand your message.

1 Using elliptical constructions carefully

An **elliptical construction** deliberately leaves out words that have already appeared in the sentence: *I have my book and Joan's [book].* For an elliptical construction to be correct, the words that are left out must be exactly the same as the words that do appear in the sentence.

No   The first important jazz **period belongs** to Dixieland, and the later **periods** to diverse styles ranging from ragtime to classical. [The word *belongs* cannot take the place of *belong*, needed in the second independent clause°.]

Yes   The first important jazz **period belongs** to Dixieland, and the later **periods belong** to diverse styles ranging from ragtime to classical.

No   During the 1920s in Chicago, the cornetist Manuel Perez **was leading** one outstanding jazz group, Tommy and Jimmy Dorsey another. [The words *was leading* cannot take the place of *were leading*, needed in the second independent clause°.]

YES   During the 1920s in Chicago, the cornetist Manuel Perez **was leading** one outstanding jazz group; Tommy and Jimmy Dorsey **were leading** another.

YES   During the 1920s in Chicago, the cornetist Manuel Perez **led** one outstanding jazz group; Tommy and Jimmy Dorsey another. [The verb *led* works in both clauses, so it can be omitted from the second clause.]

No   The period of the big jazz dance bands **began** and **lasted through** World War II. [This construction implies *began through* in the first independent clause°, but *began* requires *in,* not *through.*]

YES   The period of the big jazz dance bands **began in** and **lasted through** World War II.

| 2 |

Making comparisons complete, unambiguous, and logical

In writing a comparison, be sure to include all words needed to make clear the relationship between the items or ideas being compared.

No   **Individuals with high concern for achievement make better business executives.** [*Better* indicates a comparison, but none is stated.]

YES   Individuals with high concern for personal achievement make better business executives than do people with little interest in getting ahead.

No   **Most personnel officers value high achievers more than risk takers.** [Not clear: more than risk takers value high achievers, or more than personnel officers value high achievers?]

YES   Most personnel officers value high achievers more than they value risk takers.

YES   Most personnel officers value high achievers more than risk takers do.

No   **An achiever's chance of success in business is greater than a gambler.** [*Chance* is compared with *a gambler;* a thing cannot be compared logically to a person.]

YES   An achiever's chance of success in business is greater than a gambler's. [A correct elliptical construction, with the word *chance* omitted]

No   **Achievers value success as much, if not more than, a high salary.** [Comparisons using *as . . . as* require the second *as.*]

YES   Achievers value success as much as, if not more than, a high salary.

BACKGROUND

Using "words which the hearer easily supplies" as a brief definition of *ellipsis,* Cornelia and Bergen Evans comment that speech, which is highly elliptical, would "scarcely be endurable otherwise." It is also "indispensable to the writer or speaker who wants to be brief and pithy, but it can easily cause confusion and obscurity and must be used with skill" (*A Dictionary of Contemporary American Usage,* New York: Random House, 1957).

TEACHING TIP

Because conversation frequently includes incomplete comparisons, you might want to ask students to turn the following spoken dialogue into a paragraph written in the third person.

Speaker A: I'm so glad we came here. This restaurant is so much better.

Speaker B: You're right. A place that has fresh flowers on the tables is more appealing.

Speaker A: I always think linen napkins are nicer.

Speaker B: This place has a fine reputation for good service, but it's a shame that it's so much more expensive.

351

No	Achievers have such a reputation for success. [In academic writing, intensifiers such as *such, so,* and *too* must be completed.]
YES	Achievers have such a reputation for success that often they are offered jobs before they complete their formal educations.

---

3   Proofreading carefully to catch inadvertently omitted articles, pronouns, conjunctions, and prepositions

Small words—articles°, pronouns°, conjunctions°, and prepositions°—that are needed to make sentences complete sometimes slip into the cracks. If you tend to omit words needed to complete your intended meaning, proofread your work an extra time exclusively to discover where you have left out words.

No	On May 2, 1808, citizens Madrid rioted against French soldiers.
YES	On May 2, 1808, **the** citizens **of** Madrid rioted against French soldiers.
No	On following day, captured rioters were taken into country and shot.
YES	On **the** following day, captured rioters were taken into **the** country and shot.
No	The Spanish painter Francisco Goya recorded both the riot the execution in a pair of pictures painted 1814.
YES	The Spanish painter Francisco Goya recorded both the riot **and** the execution in a pair of pictures painted in 1814.

EXERCISE 8

Revise this paragraph to create correct elliptical constructions and to complete comparisons. Also, insert any missing words.

(1) Engineering students use practical thinking to solve difficult problems as much as academic training. (2) One group students at the University California Berkeley received challenging assignment. (3) These students had to create a package that would allow an egg to be dropped as much, but not more than eighty feet onto cement without breaking. (4) This complex problem was considered and possible solutions analyzed by fourth-year chemical engineering student, Carla St. Laurent. (5) She gave so much thought to professor's challenge. (6) She created a mother hen made papier-maché that kept safe egg she dropped from fourth-floor window.

ANSWERS: EXERCISE 8

Answers may vary somewhat. One set of possibilities is the following.

(1) Engineering students use innovative thinking to solve difficult problems as much as *they use* theoretical knowledge. (2) One group *of* students at the University *of* California *at* Berkeley received *a* challenging assignment. (3) They had to create a package that would allow an egg to be dropped as much *as,* but not more than, eighty feet on *to* cement without breaking. (4) This complex problem was considered and possible solutions *were* analyzed by fourth-year chemical engineering student Carla St. Laurent. (5) She gave so much thought to *her* professor's challenge *that she came up with the winning solution.* (6) She created a mother hen made *of* papier-maché that kept safe *the* egg dropped from *a* fourth-floor window.

COVERAGE: EXERCISE 8

(1) ambiguous comparison; (2) small words omitted; (3) incomplete comparison; (4) incorrect elliptical; (5) incomplete comparison/small words omitted; (6) small words omitted

15

Here is how the student revised the draft to correct the errors. In a few places, the student had alternatives for correcting the errors. Your revision, therefore, might not be exactly like this one, but it should deal with each error highlighted on the draft.

> Moving to a different part of the United States was one of the most difficult experiences of my life. At the time that I was looking forward to my senior year in high school, my father's company informed him that he had been transferred to Colorado Springs, and we would need to be ready to move in a month. I liked Boston much better than my father did, so I was less than thrilled about having to leave. But after days of arguing with and talking to my parents, I knew that the decision was final.
>
> When our family arrived in Colorado Springs, I was depressed. Our house was comfortable, about twice the size of our Boston apartment, but I had the feeling that it was in the middle of nowhere. Living in the outskirts of the city, I couldn't go anywhere without a car. In Boston, all I had to do was hop on the "T" to go anywhere in the city.
>
> Also, when I discovered that the expressions for some everyday things were different, Boston was the place that I wanted to be. When I asked for submarine, a thick sandwich on a long roll, the convenience store clerk looked confused and said she didn't have kits for making model ships. When I would buy something in Colorado, salespeople offered me "a sack" instead of a bag. As far as I knew, a sack means that the quarterback has been tackled in a football game.
>
> Slowly, however, I began to realize that even in Colorado there are movies, fast-food restaurants, and shopping malls. Mostly, the people made the big difference for me. Happily, it didn't take long for me get to know some students in my high school, and to find, much to my surprise, that most were eager to make me feel at home. By now, I can't imagine a better place to live than Colorado Springs.

Participation

A student working in the college peer counseling program for job hunters wrote the following draft for an article in the campus newspaper. This material shows a very good awareness of audience, and it contains well-organized, useful information. The draft's effectiveness is diminished, however, by the presence of sentences that send

COVERAGE: PARTICIPATION ESSAY (continued)

what is likely to be a fifteen-minute interview?

By understanding the objectives of the interview will help an applicant prepare [15d-1: mixed construction]. *An applicant who knows the company's needs is better equipped* [15e-2: incomplete comparison]. Most businesses with a position to fill interview with three basic questions in mind: Is this applicant qualified to do the job? Will this applicant perform if hired? Will *you* [15a-1: shift in person] fit into the work environment?

A job applicant can use a well-prepared résumé to present information about experience and training. At the interview, *applicants* [15a-1: shift in number] should be prepared to talk about courses taken, jobs held, and capabilities demonstrated. *Probing for specific details* [15c: dangling modifier], the applicant's abilities will be judged by the employer. *Job applicants should be aware that personal questions about marital status or plans to have children are illegal; however, such matters might be raised by some interviewers anyway* [15a-2: shift from passive to active voice]. *By preparing an answer like "Those areas of my life are personal," or "I make it a rule never to let my personal life interfere with business" will help an applicant's confidence* [15d-1: mixed construction].

A major concern of an interviewer is focused on whether the applicant would fit into the company [15d-2: faulty construction]. An applicant who plays *merely* [15b-1: ambiguous placement of modifier] a role to impress an interviewer is making a mistake, particularly if *you* [15a-1: shift in person used in rest of essay] are offered a job that *you* [15a-1: shift in person used in rest of essay] are not suited for. *Present a natural image. Use the interview to find out how the company's work environment will fit your* [15a-1: shift in person used in rest of essay] *personal style* [15a-3: shift in mood, with two imperative sentences].

ANSWER: PARTICIPATION ESSAY

This version is revised to eliminate errors that cause sentences to send unclear messages. Because options are available for handling corrections, answers will vary somewhat. Also, answers will vary if students have revised for content, organization, or style.

Most job hunters enter the business world through a door labelled "Job Interviews." Regardless of training and experience, the job candidate makes an impression on an employer during an interview. What can a person do so that he or she can perform successfully at what is likely to be a fifteen-minute interview?

Understanding the objectives of the interview will help an applicant prepare. An applicant who knows the company's needs is better equipped than someone who does not have such information. Most businesses with a position to fill interview with three basic questions in mind: Is this applicant qualified to do the job? Will this applicant perform if hired? Will this applicant fit into the work environment?

A job applicant can use a well-prepared résumé to present information about experience and training. At the interview, an applicant should be prepared to talk about courses taken, jobs held, and capabilities demonstrated. Probing for specific details, the employer will judge the applicant's abilities. Job applicants should be aware that personal questions about marital status or plans to have children are illegal; however, some interviewers might raise such matters anyway. Preparing an answer like "Those areas of my life are personal" or "I make it a rule never to let my personal life interfere with business" will help an applicant's confidence.

A major concern of an interviewer is whether the applicant would fit into the company. An applicant who merely plays a role to impress an interviewer is making a mistake, particularly if the person is offered a job that he or she is not suited for. A wise job candidate presents a natural image and finds out whether the company's work environment fits his or her personal style.

unclear messages because of unnecessary shifts, misplaced modifiers, dangling modifiers, mixed sentences, and incomplete sentences.

Read through the draft. Then revise it to eliminate the errors. Also, make any additional revisions that you think would improve the content, organization, and style of the material.

Most job hunters enter business world through a door labeled "Job Interviews." Regardless of training and experience the interview is the occasion when an employer gets an impression of the candidate. What can a person do so that you perform successfully at what is likely to be a fifteen-minute interview?

By understanding the objectives of the interview will help an applicant prepare. An applicant who knows the company's needs is better equipped. Most businesses with a position to fill interview with three basic questions in mind: Is this applicant qualified to do the job? Will this applicant perform if hired? Will you fit into the work environment?

A job applicant can use a well-prepared résumé to present information about experience and training. At the interview, applicants should be prepared to talk about courses taken, jobs held, and capabilities demonstrated. Probing for specific details, the applicant's abilities will be judged by the employer. Job applicants should be aware that personal questions about marital status or plans to have children are illegal; however, such matters might be raised by some interviewers anyway. By preparing an answer like "Those areas of my life are personal," or "I make it a rule never to let my personal life interfere with business" will help an applicant's confidence.

A major concern of an interviewer is focused on whether the applicant would fit into the company. An applicant who plays merely a role to impress an interviewer is making a mistake, particularly if you are offered a job that you are not suited for. Present a natural image. Use the interview to find out how well the company's work environment will fit your personal style.

Four

Writing Effective Sentences

 When you write effective sentences, you move beyond correctness to writing characterized by style and grace. Part Four shows you how to employ various techniques of writing style that enhance the delivery of your message to your readers. As you use Chapters 16 through 19, remember that writers have many choices for making form and content work in concert to create memorable prose.

16 Conciseness

Conciseness describes writing that is direct and to the point. Wordy writing is not concise. It forces readers to clear away excess words before sentences can deliver their messages.

WORDY VERSION

Computers are good at some things, and people are good at some things, but as a matter of fact, the things people and computers are good at tend to be rather different. It is clear that computers have good memories. It is also true that computers are fast, consistent, and reliable. However, as of yet, it appears that computers are not creative, and they are also not able to adapt readily to novel and unusual situations. It can be seen that people have memories that are poor. People are also slow, seldom do something in the same manner twice, and are unreliable in nature, but they can also be viewed as adaptable and full of creativity. Computers seem on the whole to belong to a totally different race when considered in comparison with people. It would be a wonderful ideal to consider the possibility of designing and creating systems wherein these two groups can complement and wed together the talents which each one of them has.

Wordy, indirect writing irritates readers. In contrast, concise writing appeals to readers because it is direct and uses words economically.

CONCISE ORIGINAL VERSION

What computers are good at and what people are good at tend to be different. Computers have good memories and are fast, consistent, and reliable but as yet are not creative or readily able to adapt to novel situations. People have poor memories, are slow, seldom do things the same way twice, and are unreliable, but they are adaptable and creative. Computers are a different race from people. It is a wonderful ideal to design systems wherein these two can complement and wed their talents.

—THOMAS B. SHERIDAN, "Computer Control and Human Alienation"

HOW TO MAKE YOUR WRITING MORE CONCISE	
REVISION STRATEGY	**SEE SECTION**
Eliminate wordy sentence structures.	16a
Drop unneeded words.	16b
Omit redundancies.	16c

Good writers avoid wordiness. Some professional writers publicly endorse the principle of conciseness, though they differ in their illustrations of it.

If it is possible to cut out a word, then always cut it out.

—GEORGE ORWELL, "Politics and the English Language"

Omit unnecessary words.

—WILLIAM STRUNK JR. AND E. B. WHITE, *The Elements of Style*

16a   Eliminating wordy sentence structures

Wordy sentence structures, including expletive and passive constructions, can make writing seem abstract and uninteresting.

1   Revising unnecessary expletive constructions

An **expletive** postpones the subject and diminishes its effect by putting *it* or *there* plus a form of the verb *be* before the subject. If you remove the expletive and revise slightly, you give the subject—and the entire sentence—greater power.

No	It is necessary for students to fill out both registration forms.
YES	Students must fill out both registration forms.
No	There are three majors offered by the computer science department.
YES	Three majors are offered by the computer science department.
YES	The computer science department offers three majors.

2 Revising unnecessary passive constructions

In the **active voice,** the subject of a sentence *does* the action named by the verb.

> **ACTIVE**   **Professor Higgins teaches** public speaking. [*Professor Higgins* is the subject, and he does the action: he *teaches.*]

In the **passive voice,** the subject of a sentence *receives* the action named by the verb.

> **PASSIVE**   **We are taught** public speaking by Professor Higgins. [*We* is the subject, and we receive the action: we are *taught.*]

For most writing, the active voice adds liveliness as well as conciseness. One way to revise from the passive to the active voice is to make the doer of the action the subject of the sentence. For example, when a passive construction names the doer of an action, it does so in a phrase starting with *by.* Therefore, when you want to switch from passive voice to active voice, make the noun or pronoun in the *by* phrase the sentence subject.

> **No**   Volunteer work **was done by the students** for credit in sociology. [The students are doers of the action, but they are not the subject of the sentence.]
>
> **YES**   The **students did** volunteer work for credit in sociology.
>
> **No**   The new spending bill **was vetoed by the governor.** [The governor is the doer of the action, but he is not the subject of the sentence.]
>
> **YES**   The **governor vetoed** the new spending bill.

Sometimes you can revise a sentence from passive voice to active voice by using a new verb. This works especially well when you want to keep the same subject.

> **PASSIVE**   Britain **was defeated** by the United States in the war of 1812.
>
> **ACTIVE**   Britain **lost** the war of 1812 to the United States.
>
> **PASSIVE**   Hundreds of soldiers **were stricken** with yellow fever.
>
> **ACTIVE**   Hundreds of soldiers **caught** yellow fever.

Writers use the passive voice when the doer of an action is unknown or when naming the doer would disrupt the focus they want a sentence to have. Such situations are discussed in detail in 8n. Also, science writing, which often calls for the passive voice, is discussed in Chapter 38. In situations that do not call for the passive voice, writers sometimes deliberately use it for sentence after sentence in the mistaken belief that it sounds "mature" or "academic." When the doers of the action are important, as in the following example, you should use the active voice.

No	One very important quality developed by an individual during a first job is self-reliance. This strength was gained by me when I was allowed by my supervisor to set up and conduct my own survey project.
Yes	During their first job, many individuals develop the very important quality of self-reliance. I gained this strength when my supervisor allowed me to set up and conduct my own survey project.
Yes	During a first job, many people develop self-reliance, as I did when my supervisor let me set up and conduct my own survey project.

One important caution about the passive voice: Do not use it to hide information about who acts. For example, a report might say this:

> Cracks in the foundation of the structure had been found in 1984, but these problems were not considered serious.

Left out of this sentence is possibly important information about who found cracks and who decided the cracks were not serious. Such omissions may be intentional; writers may choose the passive voice to sound impersonal or objective. In most cases, however, use of the passive voice creates distorting omissions of information. For more advice on acceptable uses of the passive voice, see 8m and 8n.

3	**Combining sentences, reducing clauses to phrases, and reducing phrases to words**

Clarity is among your main concerns during revision. When you see the need for conciseness, often you can combine sentences or reduce a clause to a phrase or reduce a phrase to a single word. When you aim for conciseness, often you also achieve better clarity.

Combining sentences

When you revise, look carefully at sets of sentences in your draft. You may be able to reduce the information in one sentence to a group of words that you can include in another sentence.

EXTRA EXERCISE

Rewrite each of the following groups of sentences as a single statement by reducing the information in one of them to a group of words that you can include in the other.

1. William Shakespeare had seven brothers and sisters. He was the third child.

2. He attended Stratford's free grammar school until he was about thirteen. Later he was apprenticed to a local tradesperson.

3. Anne Hathaway was eight years older than Shakespeare. He married her in 1582.

4. Their first child was born the next year. They named her Susanna.

5. In 1585 Anne bore twins. They were named Hamnet and Judith.

6. In 1597 Shakespeare moved from London back to Stratford. He bought a large house called New Place.

ANSWERS: EXTRA EXERCISE

Answers will vary, but here are some possibilities.

1. William Shakespeare was the third of eight children.

2. He attended Stratford's free grammar school until he was about thirteen, when he was apprenticed to a local tradesperson.

3. Shakespeare married Anne Hathaway, who was eight years his senior, in 1582.

4. Susanna, their first child, was born the next year.

5. In 1585 Anne bore the twins Hamnet and Judith.

6. In 1597 Shakespeare moved back from London to New Place, a large house in Stratford.

TWO SENTENCES

The *Titanic* was discovered seventy-three years after being sunk by an iceberg. The wreck was located in the Atlantic by a team of French and American scientists.

COMBINED SENTENCE

Seventy-three years after being sunk by an iceberg, the *Titanic* was located in the Atlantic by a team of French and American scientists.

TWO SENTENCES

These scientists used several million dollars worth of equipment to locate the wreck. This electronic equipment included sonar devices.

COMBINED SENTENCE

These scientists used several million dollars worth of electronic equipment, including sonar devices, to locate the wreck.

TWO SENTENCES

The stern of the ship was missing and there was some external damage to the hull. Otherwise, the Titanic seemed to be in excellent condition.

COMBINED SENTENCE

Aside from its missing stern and external damage to its hull, the *Titanic* seemed to be in excellent condition.

You will find more advice about reducing sentence structures and about combining and subordinating information in Chapter 17.

Reducing clauses

You can often reduce adjective clauses° to phrases°, sometimes just by dropping the opening relative pronoun° and its verb.

The *Titanic,* **which was a huge ocean liner,** sank in 1912.
The *Titanic,* **a huge ocean liner,** sank in 1912.

Sometimes you can reduce the clause to a single word.

The scientists held a memorial service for the passengers and crew members **who had died.**
The scientists held a memorial service for the **dead** passengers and crew members.

Creating elliptical constructions° is another way you can reduce clauses. Be sure to omit only words that are clearly implied.

When they were confronted with disaster, some passengers behaved heroically, **while others behaved selfishly.**

Confronted with disaster, some passengers behaved heroically, **others selfishly.**

Keep your meaning clear when you reduce clauses. Making your writing concise should never get in the way of clarity.

Reducing phrases

Sometimes you will be able to reduce phrases to shorter phrases or to single words.

Although loaded with luxuries, the liner was thought to be unsinkable.
The **luxury** liner was thought to be unsinkable.
Over fifteen hundred **travelers on that voyage** died in the shipwreck.
Over fifteen hundred **passengers** died in the shipwreck.
Objects found inside the ship **included unbroken** bottles of wine and expensive **undamaged** china.
Found undamaged inside the ship were bottles of wine and expensive china.

4   Using strong verbs and avoiding nouns formed from verbs

Your writing will have more impact when you choose strong verbs—verbs that directly convey an action. *Be* and *have* are not strong verbs, and they tend to create wordy structures. When you revise weak verbs to strong ones, you will often reduce the number of words in your sentences.

WEAK VERB

The proposal before the city council **has to do with** locating the sewage treatment plant outside city limits.

STRONGER VERB

The proposal before the city council **suggests** locating the sewage treatment plant outside city limits.

WEAK VERBS

The board members **were of the opinion** that the revisions in the code **were not** changes they could accept.

STRONGER VERBS

The board members **said** that they **could not accept** the revisions in the code.

QUOTATION

I don't wait to be struck by lightning and don't need certain slants of light in order to write.

— Toni Morrison

When you look for weak verbs to revise, look also for nominals—nouns derived from verbs, often by adding suffixes such as *-ance*, *-ment*, or *-tion*. To achieve conciseness, turn a nominal back into a verb, thus reducing words and gaining impact.

No   We **oversaw the establishment of** a student advisory committee.

Yes   We **established** a student advisory committee.

No   The building **had the appearance of** being renovated.

Yes   The building **appeared** to be renovated.

EXERCISE 1

Combine each set of sentences. Eliminate wordy constructions, such as expletives and unnecessary passives, and condense clauses and phrases.

EXAMPLE   An event in the history of Scotland occurred in 1542 when Mary Stuart became queen of Scotland when she was only six days old. The death of James V, who was king of Scotland and also her father, followed Mary Stuart's birth.

Mary Stuart became queen of Scotland in 1542, when she was only six days old, after her father, King James V of Scotland, died.

1. Mary Stuart was too young to lift the crown. Mary Stuart could not hold the scepter. Mary Stuart was unable to repeat her solemn vows.

2. Her formal crowning, nevertheless, took place when she had reached the age of only nine months. The service was held in the chapel of Stirling Castle.

3. It is known that Mary was not the first monarch to ascend the throne as an infant. It was in 1422 in England that Henry VI, who was king of England, was crowned at the same age, which was nine months.

4. There was a decision made by her guardians when Mary was six years old, in 1548. The decision was to send the young queen to France, where she was supposed to prepare herself for marriage with Francis, who was the heir to the French throne.

5. Some famous and well-educated men and women were to be found living at the court of the French king. Mary was given the opportunity to observe and talk with these famous and well-educated people.

6. Young Mary Stuart learned the lessons that were taught to her quickly. The reputation that she gained at court was for being witty and clever, and, in addition, she became known as being diplomatic.

7. When the time had arrived for Mary's marriage to take place, a French custom was broken by her. Her favorite color, which was

ANSWERS: EXERCISE 1

1. Mary Stuart was too young to lift the crown, hold the scepter, or repeat her solemn vows.

2. She was formally crowned, nevertheless, in Stirling Castle chapel when she was only nine months old.

3. Mary was not the first infant monarch, for Henry VI was also only nine months old when he was crowned king of England in 1422.

4. In 1548, when Mary was six years old, her guardians decided to send her to France to prepare to marry Francis, the heir to the French throne.

5. Mary observed and talked with the famous and well-educated people who lived at the French king's court.

6. Young Mary Stuart learned quickly and gained the reputation of being witty, clever, and diplomatic.

white, was what she insisted on wearing. The royal seamstresses who sewed the gown warned her that in France white was not considered a color of good luck for a wedding.

8. What Mary was told by the seamstresses was that white was the traditional color of mourning for French queens who had lost a loved one. When Francis, who was Mary's young husband, died two years after the wedding, many people said the gown had been an omen that had predicted disaster.

9. It is known that in 1565 Mary married Lord Darnley, who was her cousin. The color of her gown for that wedding is not recorded by history.

10. Less than two years after the wedding, Lord Darnley was to fall victim to death. It was in 1567 that Lord Darnley died as a result of the fact that the house he was visiting was blown up because of political sabotage.

7. When Mary married, she broke a French custom by wearing white, her favorite color, even though the royal seamstresses warned her that white was bad luck for a wedding.

8. The seamstresses told Mary that white was the traditional color of mourning for French queens, so when Mary's young husband Francis died two years after the wedding, many people said the gown had been a disastrous omen.

9. In 1565, Mary married her cousin Lord Darnley, but history does not record the color of her wedding gown.

10. Lord Darnley died in 1567, less than two years after the wedding, when political saboteurs blew up the house he was visiting.

16b   Eliminating unneeded words

Unneeded words clutter your writing. Always eliminate them to achieve conciseness. Also, imprecise language creates wordiness. A writer should not use six inexact words when one precise word works better.

When a writer tries to write very formally or tries to reach an assigned word limit, **padding** usually results. Sentences are loaded down with **deadwood**—empty words and phrases that increase the word count but lack meaning. Deadwood never substitutes for a new idea or additional evidence. If you find deadwood, clear it away.

PADDED	In fact, the television station ~~which was situated in the local area~~ had won ~~a great~~ many awards as ~~a result of its having been involved in the~~ coverage of ~~all kinds of~~ controversial issues.
CONCISE	The local television station had won many awards for its coverage of controversial issues.
PADDED	~~In a manner of speaking,~~ the PTA ~~could be seen as having~~ cancelled the play ~~due to the pressure~~ of financial problems.
CONCISE	The PTA cancelled the play because of financial problems.
PADDED	The bookstore ~~entered the order for~~ the books ~~that the instructor has said will be utilized in~~ the course ~~sequence.~~
CONCISE	The bookstore ordered the books for the course.

TEACHING TIP

Since empty words and phrases occur with some frequency in documents people receive every day, you might want to ask students to bring a memo from work, an advertising brochure from the mail, or a quotation from a newspaper that demonstrates useless verbal padding. The examples can be used for group discussion and revision, then presented to the class in the original as well as their revised forms.

Clearing out deadwood may require a few structural changes in sentences, such as the addition of *because* in the example about the PTA. Still, the final version is shorter than the original.

Here is a list of empty words that are the worst offenders. The chart includes wordy examples and their revisions.

GUIDE FOR ELIMINATING EMPTY WORDS AND PHRASES

EMPTY WORD OR PHRASE	WORDY EXAMPLE	REVISION
as a matter of fact	*As a matter of fact,* statistics show that many marriages end in divorce.	Statistics show that many marriages end in divorce.
because of the fact that	*Because of the fact that* a special exhibit is scheduled, the museum will be open until ten P.M.	Because of a special exhibit, the museum will be open until ten P.M.
exist	The crime rate that *exists* is unacceptable.	The crime rate is unacceptable.
factor	The project's final cost was an essential *factor* to consider.	The project's final cost was essential to consider.
for the purpose of	Work crews were dispatched *for the purpose of* fixing the potholes.	Work crews were dispatched to fix the potholes.
in a very real sense	*In a very real sense,* the drainage problems caused the house to collapse.	The drainage problems caused the house to collapse.
in light of the fact that	*In light of the fact that* the rainfall was so heavy, we had flooding.	Because the rainfall was so heavy, we had flooding.

w **16b**

GUIDE FOR ELIMINATING EMPTY WORDS AND PHRASES *(continued)*

Empty Word or Phrase	Wordy Example	Revision
in the case of	*In the case of* the proposed water tax, residents were very angry.	Residents were very angry about the proposed water tax.
manner	The child touched the snake in a reluctant *manner*.	The child touched the snake reluctantly.
nature	His comment was of an offensive *nature*.	His comment was offensive.
seems	It *seems* that the union called a strike over health benefits.	The union called a strike over health benefits.
tendency	The team had a *tendency* to lose home games.	The team often lost home games.
that is to say	*That is to say* that we cannot afford a strike.	We cannot afford a strike.
the point I am trying to make	*The point I am trying to make* is that news reporters should not invade people's privacy.	News reporters should not invade people's privacy.
to get to the point	*To get to the point,* the crime rate is going up.	The crime rate is going up.
type of	Gordon took a relaxing *type of* vacation.	Gordon took a relaxing vacation.
what I mean to say	*What I mean to say* is that I expect a bonus.	I expect a bonus.

BACKGROUND

In "What Means? Who Says? Teaching College Freshmen to Write Clearly" (rpt. in *Rhetoric and Composition: A Sourcebook for Teachers,* ed. Richard L. Graves, Rochelle Park, NJ: Hayden, 1976), Elizabeth Christman discusses ways to deal with two literary "diseases" that often afflict college freshmen writers: pretentiousness and verbosity. Reviewing the advice of professional writers and editors, she demonstrates how detailed classroom discussion of student writing can encourage students to support generalizations with specific details, cut out unnecessary words, examine the logic of their statements, and discover awkward syntax. Some of the teaching strategies are unusual, such as the practice of one newspaper editor who, in an effort to teach students to be sure of their facts, asked a class to write a few sentences about a package of Life Savers he had placed on the desk. After reading their sentences aloud, he revealed that the package was empty, a fact that rendered most of their statements inaccurate.

ANSWERS: EXERCISE 2

Answers will vary somewhat, but at the least students should revise the italicized words.

(1) *It is a fact for* many people that when they are anesthetized for surgery, *that is to say so that they may have an operation performed,* they feel no pain but still maintain some degree of consciousness. (2) Many fully anesthetized patients *have a sense of being able to* recognize sounds when they hear doctors and nurses *alike* talking in the operating room, *the place where the surgery is performed.* (3) In an experiment at the University of California at Davis Medical Center, eleven patients were given commands *that were of a nonthreatening nature* while *they were* under anesthesia. (4) *It seems that* while under anesthesia they were told to do a simple *type of* thing like pulling their ears during a postoperative interview. (5) Patients who had been given the instruction *had a tendency to* pull on their ears six times more *often* than did patients *who were* given no orders. (6) *It is interesting to note that it seems likely that the reason* people can hear while they are anesthetized *is* because the highly specialized endings of the auditory nerve cells are hard for anesthetics to block. (7) Because *of the fact that* anesthesiologists are now aware of this phenomenon, many of them counsel surgeons to make *positive,* encouraging *types of* comments to patients under anesthesia. (8) *As a matter of fact,* some surgeons ask their patients to listen through earphones to music or *to* tapes with suggestions *of a* positive *nature, which in a very real sense* can speed *and hasten* recovery.

EXERCISE 2

Eliminate unnecessary words or phrases. Be especially alert for empty words that add nothing to meaning.

EXAMPLE   In view of the fact that most people at some time or other in their lives face surgery, the effects of anesthesia are factors of great interest to the general public.

Because most people at some time face surgery, the effects of anesthesia are of great interest to the general public.

(1) It is a fact for many people that when they are anesthetized for surgery, that is to say so that they may have an operation performed, they feel no pain but still maintain some degree of consciousness. (2) Many fully anesthetized patients have a sense of being able to recognize sounds when they hear doctors and nurses alike talking in the operating room, the place where the surgery is performed. (3) In an experiment at the University of California at Davis Medical Center, eleven patients were given commands that were of a nonthreatening nature while they were under anesthesia. (4) It seems that while under anesthesia they were told to do a simple type of thing like pulling their ears during a postoperative interview. (5) Patients who had been given the instruction had a tendency to pull on their ears six times more often than did patients who were given no orders. (6) It is interesting to note that it seems likely that the reason people can hear while they are anesthetized is because the highly specialized endings of the auditory nerve cells are hard for anesthetics to block. (7) Because of the fact that anesthesiologists are now aware of this phenomenon, many of them counsel surgeons to make positive, encouraging types of comments to patients under anesthesia. (8) As a matter of fact, some surgeons ask their patients to listen through earphones to music or to tapes with suggestions of a positive nature, which in a very real sense can speed and hasten recovery.

16c   Revising redundancies

Planned repetition can create a powerful rhythmic effect (see 19f). The dull drone of unplanned repetition, however, can bore a reader and prevent the delivery of your message. Unplanned repetition is called **redundancy.** A redundant phrase gives the same message more than once.

No   Bringing the project to **final completion** three weeks early, the new manager earned our **respectful regard.**

Yes   **Completing** the project three weeks early, the new manager earned our **respect.**

No	**Astonished,** the architect **circled around** the building in **amazement.**
Yes	**Astonished,** the architect **circled** the building.
Yes	The architect **walked around** the building in **amazement.**

Notice how redundancies deaden a sentence's impact.

No	The council members **proposed a discussion** of the amendment, but that **proposal for a discussion** was voted down after they had **discussed** it for a while.
Yes	The council members' proposal to discuss the amendment was eventually voted down.
No	The package, **rectangular in shape,** lay on the counter.
Yes	The rectangular package lay on the counter.

EXERCISE 3

Eliminate redundant words and phrases. Then revise the paragraph so that it is concise.

EXAMPLE   Many people will be surprised to learn that, amazingly enough, labor-saving household devices that are intended to save people from working hard as a matter of fact often do not accomplish their aim or goal.

Many people will be surprised to learn that labor-saving household devices often fail to accomplish their goal.

(1) Why would people pay good money and spend hard-earned dollars to buy labor-saving household appliances unless the devices really and truly lived up to their promise and saved work hours? (2) Think of the fact that time is saved in light of the fact that clothes are now washed in a washing machine instead of being washed on a washboard. (3) Today the vacuum cleaner now cleans floors in place of the broom doing all the sweeping and cleaning. (4) Instead of the manual egg beater people have the electric mixer. (5) Nevertheless, regardless of these inventions, homemakers in the United States spend about the same number of hours doing housework, laundry, and cleaning as people did in the year of 1910. (6) How could this situation and state of affairs come to be? (7) The reasons are because labor-saving household devices, in a very real sense, have not saved much labor nor have they lessened the time devoted to housework. (8) Surprisingly, it is amazing to note that people's wealth today is one essential factor to consider as a reason. (9) It seems that more people in this day and age compared with the year of 1910 can afford the expense of larger apartments or houses. (10) In addition, the level of cleanliness people expect of themselves has increased at about the same rate of speed as the advances in inventions.

ANSWERS: EXERCISE 3

Answers will vary somewhat, but at the least students should revise the underlined words and recast sentences as needed.

(1) Why would people <u>pay good money and spend hard-earned dollars</u> to buy labor-saving household appliances unless the devices <u>really and truly</u> lived up to their promise <u>and saved work hours?</u> (2) Think of the <u>fact that</u> time <u>is</u> saved <u>in light of the fact that</u> clothes are now <u>washed in a washing machine</u> instead of <u>being washed</u> on a washboard. (3) Today the vacuum cleaner <u>now cleans</u> floors in place of the broom <u>doing all the sweeping and cleaning.</u> (4) Instead of the manual egg beater, people have the electric mixer. (5) Nevertheless, <u>regardless of these inventions,</u> homemakers in the United States spend about the same number of hours doing housework, <u>laundry, and cleaning</u> as people did in <u>the year of</u> 1910. (6) How could this situation <u>and state of affairs come to</u> be? (7) <u>The reasons are because</u> labor-saving household devices, <u>in a very real sense,</u> have not saved <u>much</u> labor nor <u>have they lessened the time devoted to housework.</u> (8) Surprisingly, <u>it is amazing to note that</u> people's wealth today is one essential <u>factor to consider</u> as a reason. (9) <u>It seems that</u> more people <u>in this day and age</u> compared with <u>the year of</u> 1910 can afford <u>the expense of</u> larger apartments or houses. (10) In addition, <u>the level of</u> cleanliness people expect of themselves has increased at <u>about</u> the same rate <u>of speed</u> as <u>the</u> advances in inventions.

COVERAGE: PARTICIPATION ESSAY (page 372)

College students seeking alternatives to dormitories, young adults moving out on their own, and newcomers to an area often rent apartments or houses. All of these potential renters should keep in mind that *renting or leasing* [16c: redundancy] involves a legal agreement between landlord and tenant. *It is recommended* [16a-1: expletive construction; also 16a-2: unnecessary passive] that anyone preparing to rent conduct *thorough and extensive* [16c: redundancy] evaluations [16a-4: noun from a verb] of the *entire situation* [16b: unneeded word] before making any decisions. *One major area to investigate is the evaluation of the type of landlord* [16b: unneeded words]. *It is also recommended* [16a-1: expletive construction; also 16a-2: unnecessary passive] that renters carefully examine the *condition and nature* [16c: redundancy] of the premises before any lease is signed by them [16a-2: unnecessary passive].

An initial step in the rent process is the investigation of the landlord [16b: unneeded words]. Renters can determine the nature of [16b: unneeded words] the landlord's management style by several strategies. A list of current and former tenants *of the facility* [16b: unneeded words] can *be requested* [16a-2: unnecessary passive] from the landlord. *Renters should not hesitate to contact a reasonable number of parties on the list. Renters should ask all of those with whom they come in contact whether the management of the property, in particular the landlord, is easy to contact if problems should arise and whether the landlord is willing to handle such problems without delay* [16a-3: combine sentences]. If anyone is of the opinion [16b: unneeded words] that the landlord has a poor reputation for handling problems properly, *it is better* [16a-1: expletive construction; also 16a-2: unnecessary passive] to find out before signing a lease or deposit check.

Focus on Revising

REVISING YOUR WRITING

If you need to write more concisely, go back to your writing and locate wordy material. Using this chapter as a resource, revise your writing to eliminate wordiness in sentences (16a) and to avoid unneeded words (16b) and redundancy (16c).

CASE STUDY: REVISING FOR CONCISENESS

This case study lets you observe a student writer revising. It also gives you the opportunity to revise some student writing on your own.

Observation

A student wrote the following draft for a course called Business Management. The assignment was to write a summary of a research study related to the course. This material summarizes the source material thoroughly, but the draft's effectiveness is diminished by a lack of conciseness.

Read through the draft. The wordy material is highlighted and explained. Before you look at how the student revised to eliminate the wordiness, revise the material yourself. Then compare what you and the student did.

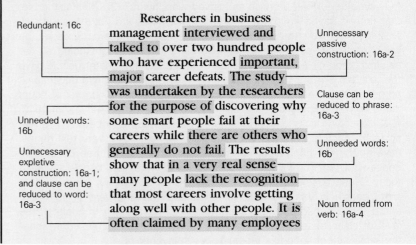

Weak verb: 16a-4 — who fail that "office politics" was the cause of the problems. In point—Unneeded words: 16b of fact, however, those employees often have no ability to listen to others sensitively and to give and take criticism constructively. The —Redundant: 16c researchers also found that some people fail to have success because— they have an absence of

Sentences can be combined: 16a-3

commitment to their work. Sometimes the underlying reason is —Noun formed from verb: 16a-4 a fear. That fear is the fear of

Weak verb: 16a-4

failure, which has the manifestation —Noun formed from verb: 16a-4 of being a lack of motivation. When people do not attempt to try to succeed, they do not expose —Redundant: 16c

Unnecessary passive construction: 16a-2

themselves to the risk of failure. Finally, it was discovered by the researchers that the fact of the

Unneeded words: 16b

matter is that luck sometimes has a— role, as when a change in management means that the new —Weak verb: 16a-4 people bring in their own team.

Also, *for the purpose of being* [16b: unneeded words] protected *in the event of* [16b: empty phrase] future disagreements, *it is recommended* [16a-1: expletive construction; also 16a-2: unnecessary passive] that renters inspect the premises carefully. If there is any *type of* [16b: emtpy words] damage in the apartment, the details should be *written down in a written inventory* [16c: redundancy] by the renters, and *it should be signed and dated by the renters and the landlord* [16a-2: unnecessary passive]. If any damages are to be repaired by the landlord, those promises should also be put in writing. *In the event that* [16b: empty words] any damage is present when renters leave the property, *it is* [16a-1: expletive construction] the renters who will probably be held legally liable for repairs since the landlord would be able to claim that the damage was done during the term of the renters' lease.

In short, only after careful *consideration of the landlord and the premises should the renter even consider* [16c: redundancy] *signing a lease or leaving a deposit or signing anything that might be legally binding* [16c: redundancy].

Here is how the student revised the paragraph to achieve conciseness. In a few places, the student had alternatives for correcting the errors. Your revision, therefore, might not be exactly like this one, but it should eliminate the wordy material highlighted on the draft.

Researchers in business management interviewed over two hundred people who have experienced major career defeats. The researchers wanted to discover why some smart people fail at their careers while others do not. The results show that many people do not recognize that most careers involve getting along well with other people. Many employees who fail claim that "office politics" caused the problem. However, those employees often do not listen to others sensitively and do not give and take criticism constructively. The researchers also found that some people fail because they are not committed to their work. Sometimes the underlying reason is a fear of failure, which manifests itself as a lack of motivation. When people do not try to succeed, they do not risk failure. Finally, the researchers discovered that luck sometimes plays a role, as when a change in management means that the new people bring in their own team.

ANSWER: PARTICIPATION ESSAY

This version is revised for conciseness. Answers will vary but here is one possible revision. Also, answers will vary if students have revised content, organization, or style.

College students seeking alternatives to dormitories, young adults moving out on their own, and newcomers to an area often rent apartments or houses. All of these potential renters should keep in mind that renting involves a legal agreement between landlord and tenant. Anyone preparing to rent should thoroughly evaluate the situation before making any decisions. One factor to investigate is the landlord. Renters should also examine the condition of the premises carefully before they sign a lease.

First, renters should investigate the landlord. Renters can determine the landlord's management style by several strategies. They can ask the landlord for a list of current and former tenants. Renters should not hesitate to contact a reasonable number of parties on the list to ask them whether the landlord is easy to contact and prompt about handling problems. If anyone thinks that the landlord has a poor reputation, renters are better off knowing before they sign a lease or deposit check.

Also, to be protected against future disagreements, renters should inspect the premises carefully. If there is any damage in the apartment, the renters should make a written inventory, and they and the landlord should sign and date it. Also, renters should get in writing all promises of repairs. If any damage is present when renters leave the property, they will probably be held legally liable for repairs since the landlord would be able to claim that they caused the damage.

In short, only after carefully considering the situation should renters sign a lease or leave a deposit.

Participation

A student wrote the following draft for a journalism class called Feature Writing. The material is logically presented and informative, but the draft's effectiveness is diminished by wordy constructions, padding, and redundancies.

Read through the draft. Then revise it to eliminate the errors. Also, make any additional revisions you think would improve the content, organization, and style of the material.

College students seeking alternatives to dormitories, young adults moving out on their own, and newcomers to an area often rent apartments or houses. All of these potential renters should keep in mind that renting or leasing involves a legal agreement between landlord and tenant. It is recommended that anyone preparing to rent conduct careful and extensive evaluations of the entire situation before making any decisions. One major area to investigate is the evaluation of the type of landlord. It is also recommended that renters carefully examine the condition and nature of the premises before any lease is signed by them.

An initial step in the rent process is the investigation of the landlord. A list of current and former tenants of the facility can be requested from the landlord. Renters should not hesitate to contact a reasonable number of parties on the list. Renters should ask all of those with whom they come in contact whether the management of the property, in particular the landlord, is easy to contact if problems should arise and whether the landlord is willing to handle such problems without delay. If anyone is of the opinion that the landlord has a poor reputation for handling problems properly, it is better to find out before signing a lease or deposit check.

Also, for the purpose of being protected in the event of future disagreements, it is recommended that renters inspect the premises carefully. If there is any type of damage in the apartment, the details should be written down in a written inventory by the renters, and it should be signed and dated by the renters and the landlord. If any damages are to be repaired by the landlord, those promises should also be put in writing. In the event that any damage is present when renters leave the property, it is the renters who will probably be held legally liable for repairs since the landlord would be able to claim that the damage was done during the term of the renters' lease.

In short, only after careful consideration should the renter even consider signing a lease or leaving a deposit or signing anything that might be legally binding.

17 Coordination and Subordination

The techniques of coordination and subordination help writers communicate relationships between two or more ideas. These techniques can help you make your writing style work in concert with the meaning that you want your sentences to deliver.

Coordination uses grammatical equivalency to communicate a balance or sequence in ideas. **Subordination** puts an idea to which the writer wants to give less importance in a dependent clause° and puts the more important idea in an independent clause°.

TWO IDEAS	The sky became dark gray. The air stilled ominously.
COORDINATED VERSION	The sky turned dark gray, and the air stilled ominously.
SUBORDINATED VERSION	As the sky turned dark gray, the air stilled ominously. [The *air* is the focus.]
SUBORDINATED VERSION	As the air stilled ominously, the sky turned dark gray. [The *sky* is the focus.]

COORDINATION

Coordination can produce harmony by bringing together related but separate elements to function smoothly in unison. A **coordinate sentence** is also known as a **compound sentence.** It consists of grammatically equivalent independent clauses° joined by a semicolon or a coordinating conjunction *(and, but, for, or, nor, yet, or so).* The compounding of a sentence must be justified by its meaning, for coordinate sentences communicate balance or sequence in ideas they contain.

EXTRA EXERCISE

Combine the following simple sentences into compound sentences by using the appropriate coordinating conjunction or by using the semicolon. Add conjunctive adverbs where appropriate. In some cases you may find it helpful to create independent clauses with a compound subject or verb or complement, or to use correlative conjunctions.

1. The telephone has made the instantaneous exchange of information possible. It has also reduced individual privacy.

2. Some people worry that television has a negative influence on society. Others think it is an effective means of education.

3. The computer is changing the way we write. It is hard to know whether we are writing better because of it.

4. The automobile has influenced the way

COORDINATE (COMPOUND) SENTENCE

Independent clause	, and , but , for , nor , or , so , yet ;	independent clause.

MEANING OF THE COORDINATING CONJUNCTIONS

CONJUNCTION	MEANING	FUNCTION
and	also, in addition to	to join
but	however	to contrast
for	because	to show cause
nor	an additional negative	to make the second element negative
or	an alternative	to show more than one possibility
so	therefore	to show result
yet	nevertheless	to contrast

Each coordinating conjunction has a specific meaning that establishes the relationship between the ideas in a coordinate sentence.

❖ PUNCTUATION ALERT: **Always use a comma before a coordinating conjunction that joins two independent clauses.** ❖

The sky became dark gray, **and** the air stilled ominously.
The November morning had just begun, **but** it looked like dusk.

Correlative conjunctions (*either . . . or, not only . . . but also* and others; see 7h for a complete list) also coordinate ideas.

People chose **either** to ignore the signs **or** to prepare for a storm.
[correlative conjunctions joining phrases]

The blizzard brought **not only** gale-force winds that ripped off roofs **but also** twelve feet of snow that crippled the area for days. [correlative conjunctions joining dependent clauses]

Conjunctive adverbs (*however, therefore,* and others; see 7f for a complete list) also coordinate ideas. They can connect only independent clauses°. ❖ PUNCTUATION ALERT: Use a semicolon, not a comma, before the conjunctive adverb that connects independent clauses. If you use a comma, you will create the error known as a comma splice (see Chapter 14). ❖

The monster storm destroyed millions of dollars in property; **however,** it took no lives.

17a Using coordinate sentences to show relationships

Some writers like to use a string of short sentences for the impact of the style, as discussed in 19a. In most cases, however, a series of short sentences does not communicate well the relationships among the ideas. Coordination can help you avoid writing a series of short sentences that have unclear relationships.

UNCLEAR RELATIONSHIPS

We decided not to go to class. We planned to get the notes. Everyone else had the same plan. Most of us ended up failing the quiz.

CLEAR RELATIONSHIPS

We decided not to go to class, **but** we planned to get the notes. Everyone else had the same plan, **so** most of us ended up failing the quiz.

Overuse of coordination, however, can bore a reader with its unbroken rhythm (see 17c-2). For another technique to help you avoid an unwanted series of short sentences, see the discussion of subordination later in this chapter.

17b Using coordinate sentences for effect

Coordinate sentences can help you communicate an unfolding of events.

The first semester of my junior year at Princeton University is a disaster, **and** my grades show it. D's and F's predominate, **and** a note from the dean puts me on academic probation. Flunk one more course, **and** I'm out.

—JOHN A. PHILLIPS AND DAVID MICHAELS, "Mushroom: The Story of an A-Bomb Kid"

modern cities have grown. It has created problems of air pollution.

5. Air travel is frightening to many people. Statistics show that it is safer than travel in the family car.

BIOGRAPHY

Francis Scott Key Fitzgerald, an American novelist famous for his portraits of life in the Roaring Twenties, was born in St. Paul, Minnesota, in 1896. He came from a middle-class family but was sent to private schools catering to the wealthy. He must have felt a perennial outsider—near money, but never having it—and this dilemma turned into a recurring theme in his work.

He left Princeton to join the army in 1917. Hoping to see action, he was disappointed, for he was never sent overseas. Instead, he used his free time, while stationed in Alabama, to write his first (semi-autobiographical) novel. The book was originally rejected by publishers, but Fitzgerald revised it, and *This Side of Paradise* became a huge success in 1920. He married Zelda Sayre, whom he had met while in the Army, and spent his time writing a second novel and short stories for magazines. However, Fitzgerald did not reach his full power until 1925 with *The Great Gatsby.* It combined the Jazz Age portraits of the magazine stories with an examination of the American soul and mind—and its protagonist was, like Fitzgerald, an outsider trying desperately to get into the golden circle.

The next eight years were difficult ones for Fitzgerald: He traveled abroad, drank heavily, and tried to cope with the deepening insanity of his wife. He wrote and destroyed thousands of pages while writing *Tender Is the Night* (1934), considered by some his best work. The novel was poorly received—and Fitzgerald turned to more lucrative projects, such as writing for the movies. He described his agony in *Esquire,* in a series of essays called "The Crack-Up" (1936). He died on December 21, 1940. His incomplete novel about Hollywood was published, together with his notes, as *The Last Tycoon* (1941).

F. Scott Fitzgerald (as well as Ernest Hemingway) often used coordination in his fiction to achieve dramatic effect. In this passage, coordination underlines the contrasts in the scene.

> It was a hidden Broadway restaurant in the dead of night, **and** a brilliant and mysterious group of society people, diplomats, and members of the underworld were there. A few minutes ago the sparkling wine had been flowing, **and** a girl had been dancing gaily upon a table, **but** now the whole crowd were hushed and breathless.

—F. SCOTT FITZGERALD, "The Freshest Boy"

17c Avoiding the misuse of coordination

1 Avoiding illogically coordinated sentences

Coordination is illogical when ideas in the compounded independent clauses are not related. Your reader expects one part of a coordinate construction to lead logically to the other.

No   Computers came into common use in the 1970s, and they sometimes make costly errors.

The statement in each independent clause is true, but the ideas are not closely enough related. The date computers became commonly used is unrelated to their making errors. The two ideas should not be coordinated. Here are two ideas that do coordinate well.

YES   Computers came into common use in the 1970s, but they have not been improved sufficiently to prevent occasional costly errors.

2 Avoiding the overuse of coordination

Like all good techniques, coordination can be used too often. Overused coordination creates "babble"—the writing that results from putting down whatever comes into a writer's head, without later revision to ensure that the meaning justifies the compounding. Readers become impatient with "babble" and quickly lose interest.

No   Dinosaurs could have disappeared for many reasons, and one theory holds that the climate suddenly became cold, and another theory suggests that a sudden shower of meteors and asteroids hit the earth, so the impact created a huge dust cloud that caused a false winter. The winter lasted for years, and the dinosaurs died, for most of the vegetation they lived on died out.

YES   Dinosaurs could have disappeared for many reasons. One theory holds that the climate suddenly became cold, and another suggests that a sudden shower of meteors and asteroids hit the earth. The impact created a huge dust cloud that caused a false winter. The winter lasted for years, killing most of the vegetation that dinosaurs used for food.

In the corrected version, the sentences deliver their meanings clearly.

Writers also overuse coordination if they fail to feature some ideas more prominently than others. Such writing tends to drone on monotonously.

No   Laughter seems to help healing, so many doctors are prescribing humor for their patients, and some hospitals are doing the same. Comedians have donated their time to several California hospitals, and the nurses in one large hospital in Texas have been trained to tell each patient a joke a day.

YES   Laughter seems to help healing. Many doctors and hospitals are prescribing humor for their patients. Comedians have donated their time to several California hospitals, and the nurses in one large hospital in Texas have been asked to tell each patient a joke a day.

In the corrected version, some ideas are kept separate and some are put into a coordinate sentence.

EXERCISE 1

Revise these sentences to eliminate illogical or overused coordination. If you think a sentence needs no revision, circle its number.

EXAMPLE   Anthropologists can tell the age of a skeleton by analyzing its structure and chemical makeup, and most people know this, but many do not know that skeletons can tell us much more.

Most people know that anthropologists can tell the age of a skeleton by analyzing its structure and chemical makeup, but many do not know that skeletons can tell us much more.

1. The life that a person leads often leaves marks on the bones, so anthropologists study stress marks on bones, and they often can figure out the life habits of a person, and they often can guess a person's occupation.

QUOTATION ABOUT WRITING

In stating as fully as I could how things really were, it was often very difficult and I wrote awkwardly and the awkwardness is what they called my style. All mistakes and awkwardness are easy to see, and they called it style.

—Ernest Hemingway

ALTERNATE EXAMPLE: EXCESSIVE COORDINATION

Soap operas have earned a bad name, and they don't always deserve it. Some people may watch too many programs, or some people may take the plots too seriously, but that does not make the programs themselves unworthy. Years ago the soap opera viewer was regarded as unintelligent, but today studies show that many professionals take time each day to relax with their favorite continuing story. Some hospitals tell patients to watch soap operas to pass the time, or therapists sometimes urge their emotionally disturbed patients to watch certain programs. Later the patients discuss the characters' problems, and therapists encourage the patients to relate those problems to their own, and often the patients are helped by this process.

ANSWERS: EXERCISE 1

Answers will vary somewhat. Here is one set of possibilities.

1. The life that a person leads often leaves marks on the bones. Anthropologists who study stress markers on bones often can figure out the life habits and occupation of a person.

(continued next page)

ANSWERS: EXERCISE 1 *(continued)*

2. Correct

3. Also, women who always carry their babies on their backs have stress marks at the base of the spine. In addition, a professional clarinet player usually has an irregular lower jaw.

4. Professor Kenneth A. R. Kennedy, who teaches at Cornell University, has compiled a list of over 140 skeletal markers that indicate occupation.

5. Professor Kennedy's work has great legal and practical value, for it is another tool to help investigators identify accident and murder victims, missing people, and war casualties.

COVERAGE: EXERCISE 1

(1) overused; (2) correct; (3) illogical; (4) illogical; (5) overused

ANSWERS: EXERCISE 2

Answers will vary somewhat. Students have to choose ideas best given to effective compounding. They are to choose which ideas seem to have equal weight and could therefore be contained in compound sentences. Their final version should have no more than two compound sentences—all other sentences should be left as they are.

Many modern couples choose traditional weddings, *and* some do not. Some couples are very sentimental about how they met, *so* they decide to have unique marriage ceremonies. For example, a firefighter and his fiancée exchanged vows in a burning building. Two marathon runners got married while participating in a race. An adventurous couple said "I do" as they parachuted from an airplane. One modern wedding reportedly took place in a California hot tub. The guest and the Justice of the Peace got into the water with the bride and groom. Perhaps the next unusual wedding will be in outer space.

2. For example, the forearm bone is usually enlarged in baseball pitchers, and a similar enlargement appears in the skeletons of spear-throwing hunters from prehistoric times.

3. Also, women who always carry their babies on their backs have stress marks at the base of the spine, but a professional clarinet player usually has an irregular lower jaw.

4. Professor Kenneth A. R. Kennedy has compiled a list of over 140 skeletal marks that indicate occupation, and he teaches anthropology at Cornell University.

5. Professor Kennedy's work has great legal value, and it is also very practical, for it is another tool to help investigators identify accident and murder victims, and the information can provide clues about the identities of missing people, and it can help with identifying war casualties.

EXERCISE 2

Revise this paragraph. Choose which ideas seem to have equal weight and could therefore be contained in compound sentences. Your final version should have no more than two compound sentences—all other sentences should be left as they are.

Many modern couples choose traditional weddings. Some do not. Some couples are very sentimental about how they met. They decide to have unique marriage ceremonies. For example, a firefighter and his fiancée exchanged vows in a burning building. Two marathon runners got married while participating in a race. An adventurous couple said "I do" as they parachuted from an airplane. One modern wedding reportedly took place in a California hot tub. The guests and the Justice of the Peace got into the water with the bride and groom. Perhaps the next unusual wedding will be in outer space.

SUBORDINATION

Use **subordination** when you want to give one idea more importance than another idea within a sentence. The more important idea appears in the independent clause—a group of words that can stand alone as a grammatical unit. The subordinated idea or ideas appear in the dependent clause—a group of words that cannot stand alone as a grammatical unit. (See 7e for a full discussion.) What information you choose to subordinate depends on the meaning you want a sentence to deliver.

The major patterns of subordination with dependent clauses are shown in the chart, with examples immediately following.

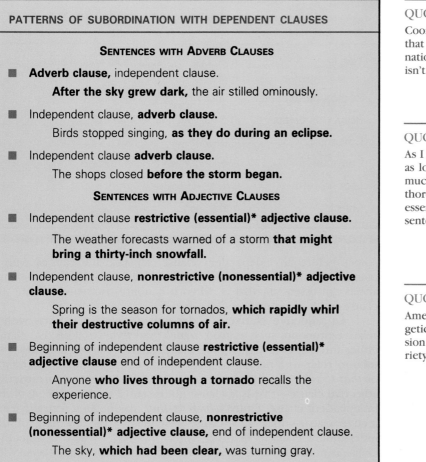

PATTERNS OF SUBORDINATION WITH DEPENDENT CLAUSES

SENTENCES WITH ADVERB CLAUSES

■ **Adverb clause,** independent clause.

    After the sky grew dark, the air stilled ominously.

■ Independent clause, **adverb clause.**

    Birds stopped singing, **as they do during an eclipse.**

■ Independent clause **adverb clause.**

    The shops closed **before the storm began.**

SENTENCES WITH ADJECTIVE CLAUSES

■ Independent clause **restrictive (essential)* adjective clause.**

    The weather forecasts warned of a storm **that might bring a thirty-inch snowfall.**

■ Independent clause, **nonrestrictive (nonessential)* adjective clause.**

    Spring is the season for tornados, **which rapidly whirl their destructive columns of air.**

■ Beginning of independent clause **restrictive (essential)* adjective clause** end of independent clause.

    Anyone **who lives through a tornado** recalls the experience.

■ Beginning of independent clause, **nonrestrictive (nonessential)* adjective clause,** end of independent clause.

    The sky, **which had been clear,** was turning gray.

QUOTATION ABOUT WRITING

Coordination is simply a way to show ideas that are equal in importance, but subordination indicates what's powerful and what isn't.

—Betty Jean Goodwin

QUOTATION ABOUT LANGUAGE

As I remained in the Third Form three times as long as anyone else, I had three times as much of it [sentence analysis]. I learned it thoroughly. Thus I got into my bones the essential structure of the ordinary British sentence—which is a noble thing.

—Winston Churchill, *A Roving Commission*

QUOTATION ABOUT LANGUAGE

American speech is conceded to be energetic and picturesque, possibly as an expression or reflection of national activity and variety.

—William Eben Schultz

You can use subordination by writing sentences that contain an adverb clause or an adjective clause, which are dependent clauses. An **adverb clause** is a dependent clause that starts with a subordinating conjunction, such as *after, if,* and *although.* Each subordinating conjunction has a specific meaning that establishes a relationship between the dependent clause and the independent clause, as shown in the list of subordinating conjunctions on the next page. An adverb clause usually occurs before or after the independent clause.
❖ PUNCTUATION ALERTS: (1) Generally, when an adverb clause

---

*For an explanation of restrictive and nonrestrictive elements, see 24e.

SUBORDINATING CONJUNCTIONS AND THE RELATIONSHIPS THEY EXPRESS	
TIME	*after, before, once, since, until, when, whenever, while*
REASON OR CAUSE	*as, because*
RESULT OR EFFECT	*in order that, so, so that, that*
CONDITION	*if, even if, provided that, unless*
CONTRAST	*although, even though, though*
LOCATION	*where, wherever*
CHOICE	*rather than, than, whether*

BIOGRAPHY

Eric Arthur Blair (better known by his pseudonym, George Orwell) was born at Motihari, Bengal, in 1903. He was educated in England and came back to Asia in 1922. From then until 1927 he served as a police officer in Burma. Upon his return to Europe, he lived in poverty while writing his first two books, including *Down and Out in Paris and London* (1903).

He had no patience with writers whose politics struck him as insincere. Although he was a leftist, he detested the Communists. He had seen their methods while he was fighting in the Spanish Civil War, and he abhorred them (*Homage to Catalonia,* 1938). When he returned from Spain, he moved to Hertfordshire, where he raised hens and grew vegetables while writing his best-known works. These also reflected his war experiences. *Animal Farm* (1945) shows his opinion of Stalinism, and *Nineteen Eighty-Four* (1949) shows his hatred of powerful political parties.

Orwell volunteered to fight in World War II, but he was rejected, so he joined the British Broadcasting Company and worked in India.

TEACHING TIP

You might want to ask your students to consider these two versions of the same passage from the opening of the twenty-second chapter of Genesis, marking the instances of coordination and subordination, then considering the differences in style and meaning that result. The first, from the King James

comes before an independent clause, separate the clauses with a comma. (2) When an adverb clause follows an independent clause and is not essential—that is, when it is nonrestrictive—separate the clauses with a comma. See 24e. ❖

An **adjective clause** is a dependent clause that starts with a relative pronoun, such as *who, which,* and *that.* An adjective clause either interrupts or follows the independent clause it modifies. Use *who* to refer to a person or a special, intelligent animal. Use *which* or *that* to refer to a thing or an animal. *Which* begins a nonrestrictive adjective clause—that is, a clause not essential to the meaning of the independent clause. Either *which* or *that* may begin a restrictive adjective clause—that is, a clause essential to the meaning of the independent clause. ❖ PUNCTUATION ALERT: When an adjective clause is nonrestrictive, separate it from the independent clause with a comma or commas. See 24e. ❖

17d Using subordination to show relationships

Subordination directs your reader's attention to the idea in the independent clause while at the same time using the idea in the dependent clause to provide context and support. Consider these examples (the dependent clauses are in boldface).

As soon as I saw the elephant, I knew with perfect certainty that I ought not to shoot it.

—GEORGE ORWELL, "Shooting an Elephant"

If they are very lucky, the passengers may catch a glimpse of dolphins playfully breaking water near the ship.

—ELIZABETH GRAY, student

Subordination usually communicates relationships among ideas more effectively than does a group of separate sentences. (You may want to use an occasional string of short sentences for impact. See 19a.)

UNCLEAR RELATIONSHIPS

In 1888, two cowboys had to fight a dangerous Colorado snowstorm. They were looking for cattle. They came to a canyon. They saw outlines of buildings through the snow. Survival then seemed certain.

CLEAR RELATIONSHIPS

In 1888, two cowboys had to fight a dangerous Colorado snowstorm **while they were looking for cattle. When they came to a canyon,** they saw outlines of buildings through the snow. Survival then seemed certain.

In the clearer version the first four short sentences have been combined into two subordinate sentences. The last sentence is left short for dramatic impact.

17e Choosing the subordinate conjunction appropriate to your meaning

Subordinating conjunctions are your allies in communicating the relationship between major and minor ideas in sentences. Consider the influence of the subordinating conjunction in each of the following sentences.

After you have handed it in, you cannot make any changes in your report. [time limit]

Because you have handed it in, you cannot make any changes in your report. [reason]

Unless you have handed it in, you cannot make any changes in your report. [condition]

Although you have handed it in, you can make changes in your report. [contrast]

I want to read your report **so that I can evaluate it.** [purpose]

Since you handed in your report, three more people have handed in theirs. [time]

Since I have seen the report, I can comment on it. [condition]

translation of 1611, uses coordination heavily; the second, from the Revised Standard Version of 1971, uses much less.

King James Version

And it came to pass after these things, that God did tempt Abraham, and said unto him, Abraham: and he said, Behold, here I am. And he said, Take now thy son, thine only son Isaac, whom thou lovest, and get thee into the land of Moriah; and offer him there for a burnt offering upon one of the mountains which I will tell thee of. And Abraham rose up early in the morning, and saddled his ass, and took two of his young men with him, and Isaac his son, and clave the wood for the burnt offering, and rose up, and went unto the place of which God had told him. Then on the third day Abraham lifted up his eyes, and saw the place afar off. And Abraham said unto his young men, Abide ye here with the ass; and I and the lad will go yonder and worship, and come again to you. And Abraham took the wood for the burnt offering, and laid it upon Isaac his son; and he took the fire in his hand, and a knife; and they went both of them together.

Revised Standard Version

After these things God tested Abraham, and said to him, "Abraham!" And he said, "Here am I." He said, "Take your son, your only son Isaac, whom you love, and go to the land of Moriah, and offer him there as a burnt offering upon one of the mountains of which I shall tell you." So Abraham rose early in the morning, saddled his ass, and took two of his young men with him, and his son Isaac; and he cut the wood for the burnt offering, and arose and went to the place of which God had told him. On the third day Abraham lifted up his eyes, and saw the place afar off. Then Abraham said to his young men, "Stay here with the ass; I and the lad will go yonder and worship, and come again to you." And Abraham took the wood of the burnt offering, and laid it on Isaac his son; and he took in his hand the fire and the knife. So they went both of them together.

ANSWERS: EXERCISE 3

Ask students to discuss the differences in emphasis between *a* and *b* in each item.

1a. Although Blackbeard has been dead for over a hundred years, his modern counterparts tyrannize today's shipping companies.

1b. Blackbeard has been dead for over a hundred years, although his modern counterparts tyrannize today's shipping companies.

2a. Because no ship is safe from modern pirates, these buccaneers feel free to use commando tactics.

2b. Because modern pirates feel free to use commando tactics, no ship is safe from these buccaneers.

3a. While pirates of yesteryear looked for gold, modern buccaneers often look for drugs as their treasure.

3b. While modern buccaneers often look for drugs as their treasure, pirates of yesteryear looked for gold.

4a. People thought that government ships were safe from pirate raids until a Navy cargo ship was robbed of nearly $20,000.

4b. A Navy cargo ship was robbed of nearly $20,000, although people thought that government ships were safe from pirate raids.

5a. Because the raiders were silent and stealthy, none of the crew ever saw them.

5b. The raiders were silent and stealthy so that none of the crew ever saw them.

ANSWERS: EXERCISE 4

You might find that having students compare and discuss the differences in emphasis between the *a* and *b* answers to each item helps them clarify their understanding of the differences.

1a. Pablo Picasso, who had mastered all the traditional art techniques at a young age, quickly became interested in experimenting with different styles.

EXERCISE 3

Combine each pair of sentences, using an adverb clause to subordinate one idea. Then revise each sentence so that the adverb clause becomes the independent clause. Refer to the list of subordinating conjunctions on page 380.

EXAMPLE   The days of Captain Hook are gone forever. Pirates still sail the oceans.

    a: *Although the days of Captain Hook are gone forever, pirates still sail the oceans.*

    b: *Although pirates still sail the oceans, the days of Captain Hook are gone forever.*

1.   Blackbeard has been dead for over a hundred years. His modern counterparts tyrannize today's shipping companies.

2.   Modern pirates feel free to use commando tactics. No ship is safe from these buccaneers.

3.   Pirates of yesteryear looked for gold. Modern buccaneers often look for drugs as their treasure.

4.   People thought that government ships were safe from pirate raids. A Navy cargo ship was robbed of nearly $20,000.

5.   The raiders were silent and stealthy. None of the crew ever saw them.

EXERCISE 4

Combine each pair of sentences, using an adjective clause to make one idea subordinate to the other. Then revise each sentence so that the adjective clause becomes the independent clause. Use the relative pronoun given in parentheses.

EXAMPLE   The artist Pablo Picasso died in 1973 at the age of 92. He is best known for creating the Cubist style in art. (who)

    a: *Pablo Picasso, who died in 1973 at the age of 92, is best known for creating the Cubist style in art.*

    b: *Pablo Picasso, who is best known for creating the Cubist style in art, died in 1973 at the age of 92.*

1.   Pablo Picasso had mastered all the traditional art techniques at a young age. He quickly became interested in experimenting with different styles. (who)

2.   Picasso's style is characterized by designs that depart from strict reality. It is heavily influenced by the primitive art of Africa. (which)

3.   Picasso created shapes. The shapes seemed to some people to be grotesque distortions of reality. (that)

4. An art critic enjoyed Picasso's use of geometric shapes to present multiple viewpoints of an object on one canvas. The art was nicknamed "Cubism" by the art critic. (who)

5. Experts agree that the entire body of Picasso's art is not solely in any one style. The entire body of Picasso's art is amazingly varied. (which)

17f Avoiding the misuse of subordination

1 Avoiding illogical subordination

Subordination is illogical when the subordinating conjunction does not make clear the relationship between the independent and dependent clause.

No   Because he was deaf when he wrote them, Beethoven's final symphonies were masterpieces.

The above sentence is illogical because it was not Beethoven's deafness that led to his writing symphonic masterpieces.

YES   Although Beethoven was deaf when he wrote his final symphonies, they are musical masterpieces.

2 Avoiding the overuse of subordination

Like all good writing techniques, subordination can be overused. Too many images or ideas may crowd together, confusing readers and making them lose track of the message. If you have used more than two subordinating conjunctions or relative pronouns in a sentence, check carefully to see if your meaning is clear.

No   A new technique for eye surgery, which is supposed to correct nearsightedness, which previously could be corrected only by glasses, has been developed, although many doctors do not approve of it because it can create unstable eyesight.

YES   A new technique for eye surgery, which is supposed to correct nearsightedness, has been developed. Previously, nearsightedness could be corrected only by glasses. Because it can create unstable eyesight, many doctors do not approve of it, however.

1b. Pablo Picasso, who quickly became interested in experimenting with different styles, had mastered all the traditional art techniques at a young age.

2a. Picasso's style, which is characterized by designs that depart from strict reality, is heavily influenced by the primitive art of Africa.

2b. Picasso's style, which is heavily influenced by the primitive art of Africa, is characterized by designs that depart from strict reality.

3a. Picasso created shapes that seemed to some people to be grotesque distortions of reality.

3b. The shapes that Picasso created seemed to some people to be grotesque distortions of reality.

4a. The art critic who enjoyed Picasso's use of geometric shapes to present multiple viewpoints of an object on one canvas nicknamed the art "Cubism."

4b. The art critic, who nicknamed the art "Cubism," enjoyed Picasso's use of geometric shapes to present multiple viewpoints of an object on one canvas.

5a. Experts agree that the entire body of Picasso's art, which is amazingly varied, is not solely in any one style.

5b. The entire body of Picasso's art, which experts agree is not solely in any one style, is amazingly varied.

QUOTATION ABOUT WRITING

I revise the manuscript till I can't read it any longer, then I get somebody to type it. Then I revise the typing. Then it's retyped again. Then there's a third typing, which is the final one. Nothing should then remain that offends the eye.

—Robert Graves

ANSWERS: EXERCISE 5

Answers will vary considerably. Here is one possibility.

Although most parents continue to read their old favorites to their children, some experts question the value of traditional fairy tales. For instance, some experts think that fairy tales are too scary because they have characters like witches and dragons. These characters often frighten little children who are not yet mature enough to understand the difference between fantasy and reality. Other experts object to the theme of the "handsome prince and beautiful princess" which many fairy tales feature. The princess is always shown as weak, and the prince is always depicted as infallibly strong. Thus, children get a distorted impression of what they should expect of themselves and the opposite sex.

ANSWERS: EXERCISE 6 (next page)

Answers may vary somewhat. One set of possibilities is the following.

1. Five-figure prices, which are shocking to buyers of new cars, may keep you away from the showrooms.

2. Perhaps you should lease your next car because you may pay less as a down payment, and you may pay less each month.

3. If you are a potential customer, you should shop carefully, because you may find a particularly good arrangement that might save you money.

4. Although ten years ago only one in every ten private cars was leased, in 1984 one of every six private cars was leased, and by now many more drivers favor car leasing.

5. Leasing has become popular with many drivers, but it is particularly popular with young professionals who want to save their money for necessities or other luxuries.

In the revised version the first sentence has a relative clause, the second is a simple sentence°, and the third has a dependent clause starting *Because*. Some words have been moved to new positions. The revision communicates its message more clearly because it provides a variety of sentence structures (see 19a) while avoiding the clutter of overused subordination.

EXERCISE 5

Correct illogical or excessive subordination in this paragraph. As you revise, use not only some short sentences but also some correctly constructed adverb clauses. Also, you can apply the principles of coordination discussed in 17a–17c.

Although some experts question the value of traditional fairy tales, most parents continue to read old favorites to their children. For instance, some experts think that fairy tales are too scary because they have characters like witches and dragons which often frighten little children who are not yet mature enough to understand the difference between fantasy and reality, while other experts object to the theme of the "handsome prince and beautiful princess" which many fairy tales feature because the princess is always shown as weak while the prince is always depicted as infallibly strong so that children get a distorted impression about what they should expect of themselves and the opposite sex.

17g Achieving a balance between subordination and coordination

Coordination and subordination are not always used in separate sentences. Compound-complex sentences°, for example, combine coordination with subordination.

> **When two Americans look searchingly into each other's eyes,** emotions are heightened, **and** the relationship is tipped toward greater intimacy.

> —FLORA DAVIS, "How to Read Body Language"

Varying sentence types improves your ability to emphasize key points in your writing. Consider the following paragraph, which demonstrates a good balance in the use of coordination and subordination. It contains compound sentences, sentences that combine dependent and independent clauses, and simple sentences.

> **When I was growing up,** I lived on a farm just across the field from my grandmother. My parents were busy trying to raise six children and to establish their struggling dairy farm. It was nice

to have Grandma so close. **While my parents were providing the necessities of life,** my patient grandmother gave her time to her shy, young granddaughter. I always enjoyed going with Grandma and collecting the eggs that her chickens had just laid. Usually she knew which chickens would peck, **and** she was careful to let me gather the eggs from the less hostile ones.

—PATRICIA MAPES, student

EXERCISE 6

Using subordination and coordination, combine these sets of short, choppy sentences.

EXAMPLE   Some people love their cars. Some people give their cars pet names.

Because some people love their cars, they like to give them pet names.

1. Five-figure prices are for new cars. The prices are shocking. The prices may keep you away from the showrooms.
2. Perhaps you should lease your next car. You may pay less as a down payment. You may pay less each month.
3. You are a potential customer. Potential customers should shop carefully. You may find a particularly good arrangement. The arrangement might save you money.
4. Ten years ago only one in every ten private cars was leased. In 1984, one of every six private cars was leased. By now many more drivers favor car leasing.
5. Leasing has become popular with many drivers. It is particularly popular with young professionals. They want to save their money for necessities or luxuries.

EXERCISE 7

Using topics of your choosing, imitate the style of three different examples shown in this chapter. Choose from Fitzgerald, Orwell, Gray, Davis, and Mapes.

EXERCISE 8

Revise this passage by using coordination and subordination.

The Anasazi Indians built cities in Colorado. These Indians disappeared in the thirteenth century. They left behind an advanced culture. Archaeologists have been able to study them carefully. Their beautiful buildings gleam in the afternoon sun. Historians believe these structures may have started the legend of golden cities. In 1540 Francisco de Coronado tried to find the fabled cities of gold. He found no treasure.

COVERAGE: EXERCISE 6

(1) subordination by *which*; (2) subordination by *because*; coordination by *and*; (3) subordination by *if*; subordination by *because*; subordination by *that*; (4) subordination by *although*; coordination by *and*; (5) coordination by *but*; subordination by *who*

ANSWERS: EXERCISE 7

Students use a topic of their own to imitate the styles of three different examples shown in this chapter. Imitation has a proud tradition as a learning tool. The classic rhetoricians said that versatility in style came from (1) a study of principles, (2) practice in writing, and (3) imitation of the practice of others. For a modern interpretation of classical rhetoric, see Edward P. J. Corbett, *Classical Rhetoric for the Modern Student* (New York: Oxford UP, 1971), especially pp. 416 and 496–538.

ANSWERS: EXERCISE 8

Answers may vary. Here are two possibilities that students might enjoy comparing with their own.

1. Although the Anasazi Indians built cities in Colorado, these Indians disappeared in the thirteenth century. They left behind an advanced culture, and archaeologists have been able to study them carefully. Because their beautiful buildings gleam in the afternoon sun, historians believe these structures may have started the legend of golden cities. Although in 1540 Francisco de Coronado tried to find the fabled cities of gold, he found no treasure.

2. The Anasazi Indians, who disappeared in the thirteenth century, built cities in Colorado. Because they left behind an advanced culture, archaeologists have been able to study them carefully. Historians believe their beautiful buildings that gleam in the afternoon sun may have started the legend of golden cities. In 1540 Francisco de Coronado tried to find the fabled cities of gold, but he found no treasure.

EXTRA EXERCISE

Evaluate these paragraphs to see if they have excessive subordination or coordination. If they do, revise to achieve a balance.

1. Many people are amazed when they learn that there are women in the United States who control estates and businesses which are worth hundreds of millions of dollars. For example, Iphigene Ochs Sulzberger, whose wealth is estimated at $400 million, is particularly noteworthy because she has served on the board of the *New York Times* while at the same time she has presided over the *Times'* other publications and stations. Mary Kay Ash left her sales career in order to start her own cosmetic company, which is now highly successful and which is said to be worth $100 million. In comparison with these two women, Jackie Kennedy Onassis, who now works as an editor for Doubleday Publishers, can be considered poor because she has a fortune estimated at only $25 million.

2. We hear many complaints about rising costs, and statistics show those complaints are justified. Food costs have gone up, and house costs have increased, but hospital costs have skyrocketed. In 1974 one-half gallon of milk cost $.78, and in 1984 one-half gallon of milk cost $1.13. An average house cost $35,800 in 1974, but in 1984 the same house cost $86,400. The real shock comes from hospital costs, for they have increased 229 percent. In 1974 one day in the hospital cost an average of $113.49, but in 1984 an average day cost $373.62.

Focus on Revising

REVISING YOUR WRITING

If you would like to use coordination and subordination effectively when you write, go back to your writing and locate sentences that need improvement in style. Also, if you realize that you misuse coordination and subordination, go back to your writing and locate the problems. Using this chapter as a resource, revise your writing.

Your Goal	See Section
Use coordination effectively	17a and 17b
Correct coordination errors	17c
Use subordination effectively	17d and 17e
Correct subordination errors	17f
Balance coordination and subordination	17g

CASE STUDY

The case study at the end of Chapter 19 offers you the chance to observe and participate in a revision that achieves a balance in coordination and subordination (this chapter), uses parallelism (Chapter 18), and employs the techniques of variety and emphasis (Chapter 19).

18 Parallelism

This chapter shows you how to use the grace and power of **parallelism** to strengthen your writing. This chapter also helps you avoid **faulty parallelism.** Parallelism in writing, related to the concept of parallel lines in geometry, calls for the use of equivalent grammatical forms to express equivalent ideas.

PARALLEL STRUCTURES

PARALLEL WORDS

Recommended exercise includes
> **running,**
> **swimming,**
> and
> **cycling.**

The *-ing* words are parallel in structure and equal in importance.

PARALLEL PHRASES

Exercise helps people
to maintain healthy bodies
and
to handle mental pressures.

The phrases are parallel in structure and equal in importance.

PARALLEL CLAUSES

Many people begin to exercise
because they want to look healthy,
because they need to have stamina,
and
because they hope to live longer.

The clauses starting with *because they* are parallel in structure and equal in importance.

WORD HISTORY

The Complete Oxford English Dictionary (OED) has seven columns on *parallel* and related words. The OED reports the first use of *parallel* in 1549, in relation to geometry. *Parallelism* was used to describe biblical poetry in 1800, when Paley wrote of "correspondences between the Gospel of Mark and of Luke in sentences, words, and order of words."

TEACHING TIP

Classical rhetoric teaches that successful speaking or writing comes, in part, from the imitation of good examples. This imitation can take the form of copying passages verbatim or of imitating particular sentence patterns. Classical rhetoricians are not the only ones who have written abut the benefits of imitation. Benjamin Franklin writes in his *Autobiography* (1771) of using essays in *The Spectator* as models for organization, sentence structure, and vocabulary. Malcolm X writes in his *Autobiography* of the benefits he gained from simply copying the dictionary in longhand. Winston Churchill and Somerset Maugham also write of the lessons they learned by imitating written models.

A possible first step in imitation is copying verbatim passages from favorite writers. This is not as brainless as it seems, for done prop-

(continued next page)

TEACHING TIP *(continued)*

erly it enables students to observe the details of an author's style. For this exercise to succeed, students should follow these guidelines adapted from Corbett, *Classical Rhetoric for the Modern Student* (New York: Oxford UP, 1971):

1. Students should read a piece through before beginning to copy it, in order to see the purpose and style of the whole. While working, they should read each sentence before beginning to write it. Once the passage has been completed, students should read their transcriptions in order again to "get a sense of the passage as a whole."

2. Students should copy for fifteen minutes per session. If they copy much longer, their minds will no longer focus on the work and the copying will become mechanical.

3. Students should copy by hand. Typing is too fast to allow students to see the qualities of a writer's style. Writing lets students work slowly enough to see the selection and placement of words, and the lengths and types of sentences.

4. Students should copy from a variety of authors. If they concentrate on one author to the exclusion of others, they may end up aping a single style rather than getting the feel of a variety of styles.

5. Students should copy patiently and with care. Too much speed can make the exercise meaningless. One way of controlling speed is to require that work be legible.

A second kind of imitation exercise uses sentences as patterns. The students duplicate the *kind, number,* and *order* of clauses and phrases in the model. The aim of this exercise is not to achieve a word-for-word correspondence with the model but rather to achieve an awareness of the variety of sentence structures of which the English language is capable. (Corbett 533)

To line up a putt correctly, **examine** the grain of the grass, **observe** the contours of the green, and **gauge** the slope between the ball and the cup. [The same part of speech—all verbs in the present tense—introduces each parallel word group.]

An **equivalent grammatical form** is a word or group of words that matches—is parallel to—the structure of a corresponding word or group of words. When you are expressing similar information or ideas in your writing, parallel sentence structures echo that fact.

18a Using words in parallel form

Words in parallel structures must occur in the same grammatical form. Be sure to use matching forms for parallel items.

No	The strikers had tried **pleading, threats,** and **shouting.**
Yes	The strikers had tried **pleading, threatening,** and **shouting.**
Yes	The strikers had tried **pleas, threats,** and **shouts.**

Parallelism offers you a writing style that uses balance and rhythm to help deliver the meaning of a sentence.

> **Briefly, solemnly,** and **sternly,** they delivered their awful message.
>
> —JAMES ANTHONY FROUDE, "The Execution of Queen Mary"

If Froude had expressed the same idea without using parallelism, his message would have been weaker. He could have used an ordinary sentence such as "They were stern and solemn as they delivered their awful message," but his words would have lost their opportunity for drama. Froude's words unfold ominously to the reader—just as surely as did the "awful message" to Queen Mary. Froude's placing the three parallel words first in his sentence also contributed to their impact.

18b Using phrases and clauses in parallel form

Phrases and clauses in parallel structures must occur in the same grammatical form. Be sure to use matching forms for parallel items.

No The committee members **read the petition, were discussing its arguments,** and **the unanimous decision was to ignore it.**

Yes The committee members **read the petition, discussed its arguments,** and unanimously **decided to ignore it.**

1 Using the rhythm of parallel phrases and clauses for impact

Deliberate repetition of word forms, word groups, and sounds creates a rhythm that underlines the message your sentence delivers. This technique can be highly effective if not overused.

> Go back to Mississippi, go back to Alabama, go back to South Carolina, go back to Georgia, go back to Louisiana, go back to the slums and ghettos of our northern cities, knowing that somehow this situation can and will be changed.
>
> —Martin Luther King, Jr., "I Have a Dream"

If King had expressed the same idea without parallelism, his message would have been weaker. His words reinforce the power of his message. An ordinary sentence would have been less effective: "Return to your homes in Mississippi, Alabama, South Carolina, Georgia, Louisiana, or the cities, and know that the situation will be changed."

2 Arranging parallel elements from least to most important

Elements arranged from least to most important are arranged in **climactic order,** in which the material builds to a climax. Parallel structures in climactic order are particularly effective.

> You can fool some of the people all of the time, and all of the people some of the time, but you cannot fool all of the people all of the time.
>
> —Abraham Lincoln

3 Using parallel forms in balanced sentences

Balanced sentences use parallel structures to enhance the message of compared or contrasted ideas.

> Ask not what your country can do for you, ask what you can do for your country.
>
> —John F. Kennedy

BIOGRAPHY

Martin Luther King, Jr. (1929–1968) is best known for having been a Baptist minister, powerful speaker, and civil rights leader who won the 1964 Nobel Peace Prize for his efforts to achieve racial equality in the United States. His influence helped shape the Civil Rights Act passed by the U.S. Congress in 1964.

In his attempts to spread the word about his mission, King also became a writer of considerable impact. His works include *Stride Toward Freedom* (1958), *Strength to Love* (1963), *Why We Can't Wait* (1964), and *Where Do We Go from Here: Chaos or Community* (1967).

Among King's best-known speeches is "I Have a Dream," delivered in 1963 at the Lincoln Memorial to a crowd of over 250,000 people who had marched to Washington, D.C., to demonstrate their support for civil rights. Among King's best-known writings is his *Letter from Birmingham Jail,* which he wrote while imprisoned in 1963. He wrote the essay in response to a published statement from eight Alabama clergymen who called his activities "unwise and untimely." King was not allowed to have paper in jail, so he wrote his letter in the margins of the newspaper in which the statement was printed and on scraps of paper given him by a sympathetic black "trusty." He finished his letter on a pad his lawyer fought to get him. The letter is both a defense of his crusade and a reproof to those who, like the eight clergymen, wanted King to stop demonstrating and settle for slower progress in civil rights.

QUOTATION ABOUT WRITING

I see no reason to keep silent about my enjoyment of the sound of my own voice as I work.

—Muriel Spark

TEACHING TIP

You may want to ask your students to identify the various techniques by which parallelism is set up in the following sentences.

1. Standing on a concrete jetty at seven-thirty of a drizzly morning, looking across the gray Hudson at the shore softened by fog, one can just make out an endless miniature procession of Manhattan-bound cars going down the ramp to the Lincoln Tunnel.

        "Gray Manhattan," *The New Yorker*

2. There is a crazy restaurant in the south of France where you are expected to eat well and copiously, to drink to excess, to listen to music and perhaps to spin to it—and also to break up the joint before you leave.

        —Richard Atcheson, "Le Pirate"

3. On one side of this line are They: the bribers, the cheaters the chiselers, the swindlers, the extortioners. On the other side are We . . . .

        —Marya Mannes, "The Thin Grey Line"

BACKGROUND

Although parallelism is the best known of the balanced sentence patterns, some others are also available. *Antithesis,* for one, juxtaposes contrasting ideas, often in parallel structure. Neil Armstrong was using antithesis when he made his famous comment as he stepped on the moon in 1969: "That's one small step for a man, one giant leap for mankind." *Chiasmus,* sometimes called "the criss-cross," reverses grammatical structures in successive phrases or clauses. One of John Kennedy's well-known statements in his inaugural address, for example, uses chiasmus: "Ask not what your country can do for you, ask what you can do for your country."

By night the litter and desperation disappeared as the city's glittering lights came on, and by day the filth and despair reappeared as the sun rose.

        —JENNIFER KIRK, student

Being aware that certain words call for parallel structures

1   Using parallel forms with coordinating conjunctions

Whenever you join words, phrases, or clauses with coordinating conjunctions *(and, but, for, or, nor, yet, so),* be sure that they occur in parallel form.

You come to understand what to expect when you **tease a cat, or toss a pebble** in a pool, **or touch a hot stove.**

        ANN E. BERTHOFF, *Forming, Thinking, and Writing*

2   Using parallel forms with paired words (correlative conjunctions)

Be sure to use parallel form when you link elements of a sentence with pairs of words known as **correlative conjunctions,** such as *both . . . and, not only . . . but also, either . . . or, neither . . . nor.*

Differences between classical and modern style in ballet affect **both** dance **and** dancer.

        —LISA LANG, student

Writing permits us to understand **not only** the world **but also** the self.

        —ERIKA LINDEMANN, *A Rhetoric for Writing Teachers*

3   Repeating certain words to begin parallel elements

To enhance the effect of parallelism, you can intentionally repeat certain words that begin parallel phrases or clauses. Such words include prepositions (see list in 7g), articles *(a, an, the),* and the *to* of the infinitive°. Consider how Didion uses the infinitive form to reinforce her message with the impact and grace of parallelism.

To assign unanswered letters their proper weight, **to free us** from the expectations of others, **to give us** back to ourselves—here lies **the great, the singular** power of self-respect.

—JOAN DIDION, "On Self-Respect"

Because repetition can create dull prose, the technique has to be used carefully. The Didion passage avoids monotony by mixing parallel repetition with much variety in her other word choices. Consider the rich combination of parallel elements in this famous passage:

It was the best of times, it was the worst of times, it was the age of wisdom, it was the age of foolishness, it was the epoch of belief, it was the epoch of incredulity, it was the season of Light, it was the season of Darkness, it was the spring of hope, it was the winter of despair, we had everything before us, we had nothing before us, we were all going direct to Heaven, we were all going direct the other way.

—CHARLES DICKENS, *A Tale of Two Cities*

Dickens mixes repetition *(it was the)* with variety *(times, age, epoch, season)* and with contrasts *(best* and *worst, wisdom* and *foolishness, belief* and *incredulity, Light* and *Darkness, spring* and *winter, hope* and *despair, everything* and *nothing, Heaven* and *the other way)*.

4	Using parallel clauses beginning with *and who, and whom, and which,* or *and that* when they follow clauses beginning with *who, whom, which,* or *that*

I have in my own life a precious friend, a woman of 65 **who has** lived very hard, **who is** wise, **who listens** well, **who has** been where I am and can help me understand it; **and who represents** not only an ultimate ideal mother to me but also the person I'd like to be when I grow up.

JUDITH VIORST, "Friends, Good Friends—and Such Good Friends"

18d Using parallel sentences in longer passages for impact

Parallel sentences in longer passages create a dramatic unity through carefully controlled repetition of words and word forms. Consider this rich passage of repeated words, concepts, and rhythms.

You ask me what is **poverty? Listen** to me. Here I am, dirty, **smelly,** and with no "proper" underwear on and with the **stench** of my rotting teeth near you. I will tell you. **Listen** to me. **Listen** without pity. I cannot use your pity. **Listen** with understanding. Put yourself in my dirty, worn-out, ill-fitting shoes, and hear me.

Poverty is getting up every morning from a dirt- and illness-stained mattress. The sheets have long since been used for diapers. **Poverty** is living in a **smell** that never leaves. **This is a smell** of urine, sour milk, and spoiling food sometimes joined with the strong **smell** of long-cooked onions. Onions are cheap. If you have **smelled** this **smell,** you did not know how it came. **It is the smell** of the out-door privy. **It is the smell** of young children who cannot walk the long dark way in the night. **It is the smell** of the mattresses where years of "accidents" have happened. **It is the smell** of the milk which has gone sour because the refrigerator long has not worked, and it costs money to get it fixed. **It is the smell** of rotting garbage. I could bury it, but where is the shovel? Shovels cost money.

—Jo Goodwin Parker, "What Is Poverty?"

EXERCISE 1

Reread the Jo Goodwin Parker passage above. Discover all parallel elements in addition to those shown in boldface.

EXERCISE 2

Using topics of your choosing, imitate the writing style of three different passages shown in this chapter. Choose from King, Lincoln, Didion, Dickens, Viorst, or Parker.

EXERCISE 3

Revise these sentences to eliminate any errors in parallel structure.

EXAMPLE   Widely known as the sick-building syndrome, indoor air pollution causes office workers to suffer from burning eyes, from breathing that has become difficult, rashes that cause severe pain, and from throbbing headaches.

Widely known as the sick-building syndrome, indoor air pollution causes office workers to suffer *from burning eyes, difficult breathing, severely painful rashes, and throbbing headaches.*

1. In many new office buildings today not only are the windows sealed shut but also the problem is that internal ventilation systems are inadequate and filthy.

ANSWERS: EXERCISE 1

Elements of parallelism in Parker's passage not shown in boldface are: *Repetitions:* you, me, I, dirty (dirt), pity, onions, mattress(es), urine (privy, "accidents"), long, it, shovels. *Paired words:* with / with. *Imperatives (mild commands):* Listen, Put, hear. *Contrasts:* pity and understanding, with / without. *Words in a series:* my dirty, worn-out, ill-fitting shoes; smell of urine, sour milk, and spoiling food.

ANSWERS: EXERCISE 2

Students use topics of their own to imitate the parallel style of three of the passages shown in this chapter: by King, Lincoln, Didion, Dickens, Viorst, or Parker. Style imitation has a proud tradition as a learning tool. The classical rhetoricians said that versatility in style came from (1) a study of principles, (2) practice in writing, and (3) imitation of the practice of others. For a modern interpretation of classical rhetoric see Edward P. J. Corbett, *Classical Rhetoric for the Modern Student* (New York: Oxford UP, 1971), especially pp. 416 and 496–538.

ANSWERS: EXERCISE 3

Answers will vary. Here is one set of possibilities.

1. In many new office buildings today *not only are the windows sealed shut but also the internal ventilation systems are inadequate and filthy.*

2. Indoor pollutants include tobacco smoke, *copy-machine fumes, carbonless-paper gases, cleaning chemicals, and even fibers from rugs and draperies.*

2. Indoor pollutants include tobacco smoke, the fumes that come from copy machines, the gas that is released from carbonless paper when it is written on, cleaning chemicals, and even fibers from rugs and draperies.

3. Other pollutants come from outdoors when the intake ducts for air into a ventilation system are located right over loading docks where trucks spew out exhaust fumes, or streets and highways filled with truck and car traffic are located right next to air-intake ducts of buildings.

4. Environmental experts have studied sick buildings and made recommendations that are easy to implement, and that do not cost very much, and they would be able to solve most of the problems that contribute to the indoor air pollution.

5. Some of the simpler remedies range from frequently cleaning air ducts and the replacement of air filters to the rearrangement of office partitions so that the air can flow more freely.

EXERCISE 4

For each numbered item, combine the sentences using techniques of parallelism.

EXAMPLE   Philippine rain forests provide shelter for plants. They also protect animals. A Stone Age tribe called the Tasaday lives in a Philippine rain forest.

Philippine rain forests shelter plants, protect animals, and provide a home for a Stone Age tribe called the Tasaday.

1. The Tasaday had not developed even the most primitive forms of agriculture. They did not know how to weave. Making pottery was unknown to them.

2. Animals and plants provided their food. They used leaves as clothes. They lived in caves.

3. The Tasaday were unaware of modern conveniences. Also, they showed no evidence of modern anxieties either.

4. The Philippine government decided to protect the tribe's Stone Age culture. Also, the Tasaday's safety was ensured when the government declared the forest a national preserve.

5. Throughout the ages, the Tasaday have never had a war. This fact amazes anthropologists. The lack of war also inspires peace-loving people everywhere.

3. Other pollutants come from outdoors when the intake ducts for air into a ventilation system are located *right over loading docks where trucks spew out exhaust fumes or right next to streets and highways filled with truck and car traffic.*

4. Environmental experts have studied sick buildings and made recommendations *that are easy to implement, that are not very costly, and that would solve most of the problems of indoor pollution.*

5. Some of the simpler remedies range from frequently *cleaning air ducts and replacing air filters to rearranging office partitions* so that the air can flow more freely.

COVERAGE: EXERCISE 3
(1) correlative conjunctions (18c-2); (2) words (18a); (3) clauses (18b); (4) beginning with *which* (18b-4); (5) phrases (18b)

ANSWERS: EXERCISE 4
Answers may vary. Here is one set of possibilities.

1. The Tasaday had not developed even the most primitive forms of *agriculture, weaving,* **or** *pottery making.*

2. Animals and plants *provided their food,* leaves *provided their clothing,* **and** caves *provided their shelter.*

3. The Tasaday were unaware of ***not only*** *modern conveniences* **but also** *modern anxieties.*

4. The Philippine government decided *to protect* the tribe's Stone Age culture **and** *to ensure* the Tasaday's safety by declaring the forest a national preserve.

5. Throughout the ages, the Tasaday have never had a war, a fact ***that*** *amazes* anthropologists **and** ***that*** *inspires* peace-loving people everywhere.

18e

TEACHING TIP

To teach *faulty parallelism,* you might show students nonparallel examples in contrast to the ones given. For demonstrating the problem of faulty parallelism, you might find nonparallel examples useful. Contrasting the parallel examples that start this chapter, you might show these or other nonparallel versions:

Words: Recommended exercises include running, swimming, and some people like to go cycling.

Phrases: Exercise helps people maintain healthy bodies and with coping with mental pressures.

Clauses: Many people begin to exercise because they want to look healthy, hoping they can build up their stamina, and to live longer.

ALTERNATE EXAMPLES

Because parallelism gives statements a stately, dignified sound, it appears often in official declarations, as in the following.

1. . . . for the support of this declaration, with a firm reliance on the protection of Divine Protection, we mutually pledge to each other our Lives, our Fortunes, and our sacred Honor.

—The Declaration of Independence

2. It is rather for us to be here dedicated to the great task remaining before us—that from these honored dead we take increased devotion to that cause for which they gave the last full measure of devotion; that we here highly resolve that these dead shall not have died in vain; that this nation, under God, shall have a new birth of freedom; and that government of the people, by the people, for the people, shall not perish from the earth.

—Abraham Lincoln

3. We are saddened; we are stunned; we are perplexed.

—Earl Warren, on the death of John Kennedy

18e Using parallel structure for formal outlines and lists

Items in formal outlines and lists must be parallel in structure. If the parallelism is faulty, the information fails to be clear to the reader and fails to communicate that the items are equally important. (For information about developing outlines, see 2e-5.)

OUTLINE NOT IN PARALLEL FORM

Reducing Traffic Fatalities

I. Stricter laws
   A. Top speed on any highway should be 50 m.p.h.
   B. Higher fines
   C. Repeat offenders sentenced to jail
II. Legislating installation of safety devices
   A. All automobiles should be required to have safety belts in both front and back seats
   B. Making seat belt use mandatory for all drivers
   C. We should force auto manufacturers to offer airbags as an option in all cars

OUTLINE IN PARALLEL FORM

Reducing Traffic Fatalities

I. **Passing** stricter speed laws
   A. **Making** 50 m.p.h. top speed on any highway
   B. **Raising** fine for first-time speeding offenders
   C. **Requiring** jail sentences for repeat offenders
II. **Legislating** installation and use of safety devices
   A. **Requiring** all automobiles to have safety belts in front and back seats
   B. **Making** seat belt use mandatory for all drivers
   C. **Forcing** auto manufacturers to offer airbags as an option in all cars

Although the faulty outline might be useful as a scratch outline for a writer's private purposes in the early stages of the writing process, only the parallel outline communicates clearly to a reader. The parallel outline fills in the gaps of information and communicates equivalencies. The same principles apply to lists.

LIST NOT IN PARALLEL FORM

Workaholics share the following characteristics:

1. They are intense, energetic, competitive, and driven.
2. Strong self-doubters.
3. Labor is preferred to leisure by workaholics.
4. Workaholics: work any time and anywhere.
5. Making the most of their time.
6. Workaholics will blur the distinction between business and pleasure.

LIST IN PARALLEL FORM

Workaholics share the following characteristics:

1. **They are** intense, energetic, competitive, and driven.
2. **They have** strong self-doubts.
3. **They prefer** labor to leisure.
4. **They can—and do—work** any time and anywhere.
5. **They make** the most of their time.
6. **They blur** the distinction between business and pleasure.

The list not in parallel format appears disorganized and is more difficult and unpleasant to read. The list in parallel format carries the unspoken message that all these items are equivalent and contribute equally to the definition of a workaholic.

EXERCISE 5

Revise this outline into parallel form.

Problems in Weather Forecasting

I. Information unavailable from some areas
  A. Politics leads some countries not to cooperate.
  B. If war breaks out, no one communicates about the weather.
  C. Cost
II. Computer problems
  A. Computer repairs not easily available in remote areas.
  B. Unreliable computers send garbled messages.
III. Unstable atmosphere
  A. The weather is harsh.
    1. South Pole
    2. The North Pole is extremely cold and windy.
  B. Conditions shift suddenly.
  C. There is a lack of reliability over time.

BACKGROUND

In "The Common Writer: A Case for Parallel Structure" (*College Composition and Communication* 21 [December 1970], 373–79), Robert L. Walker reports on a study in which he started out to test Francis Christensen's conclusion that the cumulative sentence is the "typical sentence of modern English" and ended with the conviction that teaching parallelism is of fundamental importance in composition classes. His statistical study of approximately one hundred consecutive sentences from ten representative twentieth-century writers indicates not only that the cumulative sentence is a minority sentence, but that parallelism "is the most common and fundamental of the rhetorical schemes." He ends by asserting that college students should be drilled in the use of parallel structures if they are to develop a prose style that is polished and mature.

ANSWERS: EXERCISE 5

I. Information unavailable from some areas
  A. Politics
  B. Wars
  C. Cost
II. Computer problems
  A. Computer repairs not easily available in remote areas
  B. Garbled messages from unreliable computers
III. Unstable atmosphere
  A. Weather harsh
    1. South Pole
    2. North Pole
  B. Sudden shifts
  C. Lack of reliability over time

QUOTATION ABOUT WRITING

It doesn't matter how you write the first draft or even the second draft, but it makes all the difference in the world how you write the *final* draft.

—Elizabeth White

QUOTATION ABOUT WRITING

Writers should be read—but neither seen nor heard.

—Daphne du Maurier

QUOTATION ABOUT WRITING

There is such an animal as a nonstylist, only they're not writers—they're typists.

—Truman Capote

EXERCISE 6

Find the parallel elements in the following examples. Next, using your own topics, imitate the style of two of the examples.

1. I think I learned more from the town dump than I learned from school: more about people, more about how life is lived, not elsewhere but here, not in other times but now.

   —WALLACE STEGNER, "The Town Dump"

2. I have never been lonely in a cemetery. They are perfect places to observe the slow changing of the seasons, and to absorb human history—the tragedies and anguishes, the violences and treacheries, and always the guilts and sorrows of vanished people.

   —WILLIE MORRIS, "A Love That Transcends Sadness"

3. I am lonely only when I am overtired, when I have worked too long without a break, when for the time being I feel empty and need filling up. And I am lonely sometimes when I come back home after a lecture trip, when I have seen a lot of people and talked a lot, and am full to the brim with experience that needs to be sorted out.

   —MAY SARTON, "The Rewards of a Solitary Life"

4. The more you live and the more you look, the more aware you are of a consistent pattern—as universal as the stars, as the tides, as breathing, as night and day—underlying everything.

   —MARYA MANNES, "How Do You Know It's Good?"

5. Each afternoon around three-thirty, as some of the workers were about to go home to prepare their early dinners, Uncle Kwok slowly and deliberately ambled in through the Wong front door, dragging his feet heavily, and gripping in one hand the small black satchel from which he was never separated.

   —JADE SNOW WONG, "Fifth Chinese Daughter"

Focus on Revising

REVISING YOUR WRITING

If you would like to use parallel structures effectively when you write, go back to your writing and locate sentences that need improvement in style. Also, if you realize that you do not use parallelism when it is needed, go back to your writing and locate the problems. Using this chapter as a resource, revise your writing.

Your Goal	See Section
Parallel form with words	18a
Parallel form with phrases and clauses	18b
Parallel structures	18c
Parallel form for long passages	18d
Parallel form for formal outlines and lists	18e

CASE STUDY

The case study at the end of Chapter 19 offers you the chance to observe and participate in a revision that uses parallelism (this chapter), achieves a balance in coordination and subordination (Chapter 17), and employs the techniques of variety and emphasis (Chapter 19).

TEACHING TIP

To introduce students to creating parallel structures, you might want to begin with lists. For example, they can list the steps they go through when carrying out some ordinary task, such as changing a tire or baking cookies. Then students can incorporate those items in sentences that explain an activity. You might help get students started by offering sentences that need completion. Here are two examples:

> Moving into one's first apartment can be expensive; you need to buy _____, _____, and _____. Settling into a new apartment can be tiring: *hanging curtains*, _____, _____, and _____.

TEACHING TIP

Parallelism is easily found in advertising, public speeches, and promotional letters. You might ask students to bring to class examples that they see on television, or find in advertisements in magazines, newspapers, or their mail. You can then analyze the parallelism and discuss the effectiveness of the examples, including any instances of faulty parallelism (which appear in published material with surprising frequency).

QUOTATION ABOUT WRITING

Every competent writer has to know how to write a concise sentence and how to edit a long one down to comprehensible length. But a writer has also to know how to manage a long sentence gracefully, how to make it as clear and as vigorous as a series of short ones.

—Joseph M. Williams, *Ten Lessons in Clarity and Grace.*

19 Variety and Emphasis

Your writing style has **variety** when your sentence lengths and patterns vary. Your writing style is characterized by **emphasis** when your sentences are constructed to communicate the relative importance of their ideas. This chapter shows you how variety and emphasis work in concert to create graceful, memorable writing.

Consider the following passage, which successfully employs key techniques of variety and emphasis. The authors vary their sentence length (19a), include a variety of structures (19b), and use different kinds of modifiers in various positions (19d).

> Henri Poincaré, a famous mathematician who lived in the nineteenth century, devised an exercise in imagination to help people understand the relativity of measures. Imagine that one night while you were asleep everything in the universe became a thousand times larger than before. Remember this would include electrons, planets, all living creatures, your own body, and all the rulers and other measuring devices in the world. When you awoke, could you tell that anything had changed? Is there any experiment you could make to prove that some change had occurred? According to Poincaré there is no such experiment.
>
> —JUDITH AND HERBERT KOHL, *The View from the Oak*

The techniques of variety and emphasis can help your writing move beyond being correct to having style and grace. Rarely do variety and emphasis emerge in an early draft. Expect to apply the principles in this chapter during your revision process.

HOW TO ACHIEVE VARIETY AND EMPHASIS IN YOUR WRITING

STRATEGY	SEE SECTION
Vary your sentence length to make your writing lively.	19a
Call on four basic sentence types. Use an occasional question, mild command, or exclamation in addition to declarative sentences.	19b
Choose the subject of a sentence according to your intended meaning.	19c
Add modifiers to basic sentences.	19d
Invert standard word order.	19e
Repeat important words or ideas.	19f

ALTERNATE EXAMPLE

This sentence has five words. This is five words, too. Five-word sentences are fine. But several together become monotonous. Listen to what is happening. The writing is getting boring. The sound of it drones. It's like a stuck record. The ear demands some variety. Now listen. I vary the sentence length and I create music. Music. The writing sings. It has a pleasant rhythm, a lilt, a harmony. I use short sentences. And I use sentences of medium length. And sometimes when I am certain the reader is rested I will engage him with a sentence of considerable length, a sentence that burns with energy and builds with all the impetus of a crescendo, the roll of the drums, the crash of the cymbals, sounds that say, "Listen to this; it is important."

—Gary Provost, "Sound Advice"

19a Varying sentence length

If you vary your sentence length, your writing will be lively. Also, when you use a variety of sentence lengths, you communicate clear distinctions among ideas so that your readers can understand the focus of your material. The unbroken rhythm of monotonous sentence length can eventually lull a reader into losing attention.

1 Revising strings of too many short sentences

Strings of too many short sentences rarely establish relationships and levels of importance among ideas. Readers cannot easily make distinctions between major and minor points. Such strings, unless deliberately planned in a longer piece of writing for occasional impact, suggest that the writer has not thought through the material and decided what to emphasize. The style tends to read like that of young children.

No   There is a legend. This legend is about a seventeenth-century Algonquin Indian. It says that he was inspired. He had an idea about popcorn. He transformed it into a gift. It was the first gift to a hostess in American history. He was invited to the Pilgrims' harvest meal. He brought along a bag of popcorn. This was a demonstration of good will. The occasion is honored to this day with Thanksgiving dinner.

The ten short sentences in the No version range from four to eleven words. The sentence structures do not feature significant ideas over unimportant ones.

Yes   According to legend, in the seventeenth century an inspired Algonquin transformed popcorn into the first hostess gift in history. Invited to the Pilgrims' harvest meal, the Indian brought along a bag of popcorn as a demonstration of good will. The occasion is honored today with Thanksgiving dinner.

—Patricia Linden, "Popcorn"

In the revised version, the sentence structures permit the key ideas to be featured. The two versions use almost the same short last sentence, but because the improved version leads up to it with longer sentences, the message in the last sentence is emphasized. (Also, this version employs techniques of conciseness discussed in Chapter 16: ten sentences reduce to three and 73 words reduce to 47.)

2	Revising a string of too many compound sentences

A **compound sentence** consists of two or more independent clauses° that present closely related and equally important ideas (see 7o-2). The compounding of a sentence must be justified by its meaning. Too often, compound sentences are short sentences only strung together with *and* or *but,* without consideration of the relationships among the ideas.

No   Science fiction writers are often thinkers, and they are often dreamers, so they let their imaginations wander. Jules Verne was such a writer, and he predicted space ships and atomic submarines, but most people did not believe airplanes were possible.

Yes   Science fiction writers are often thinkers and dreamers who let their imaginations wander. Jules Verne was one such writer. He predicted space ships and atomic submarines before most people believed airplanes were possible.

In the revised version the relationships among the ideas are clear and key ideas are featured. In the last sentence a particularly obscure connection is clarified. (In addition, this version employs techniques of conciseness discussed in Chapter 16: one independent clause is reduced to a word, *dreamers;* another is reduced to a relative clause, *who let their imaginations wander;* another starts a new sentence, *He predicted . . .;* and another is reduced to a subordinate clause, *before most people . . . possible.*)

3 | Revising for a suitable mix of sentence lengths

To emphasize one idea among many others, you can express it in a sentence noticeably different in length or structure from the sentences surrounding it. Consider this passage, which carries its emphasis in one short sentence among longer ones:

> Today is one of those excellent January partly cloudies in which light chooses an unexpected landscape to trick out in gilt, and then shadow sweeps it away. **You know you are alive.** You take huge steps, trying to feel the planet's roundness arc between your feet. Kazantzakis says that when he was young he had a canary and a globe. When he freed the canary, it would perch on the globe and sing. All his life, wandering the earth, he felt as though he had a canary on top of his mind, singing.
>
> —ANNIE DILLARD, *Pilgrim at Tinker Creek*

A long sentence among shorter ones is equally effective.

> Mistakes are not believed to be part of the normal behavior of a good machine. **If things go wrong, it must be a personal, human error, the result of fingering, tampering, a button getting stuck, someone hitting the wrong key.** The computer, at its normal best, is infallible. I wonder whether this can be true.
>
> —LEWIS THOMAS, "To Err Is Human"

EXERCISE 1

Revise these sets of sentences to vary the sentence lengths effectively.

1. Horror tales are not new. *Frankenstein* was written in the nineteenth century. It was written by Mary Shelley. She was the wife of the poet Percy Bysshe Shelly. *Frankenstein* tells the story of a scientist. He makes a monster. He makes it from a human corpse.

2. Another famous horror tale of the nineteenth century is "The Monkey's Paw," by W. W. Jacobs, and it tells about an old English couple with a teenage son, and they get a monkey's paw. It has the power

ANSWERS: EXERCISE 1

In this exercise, the first item has too many short sentences, the second too many compounds, the third long and complicated sentences. Students will revise in various ways. Here is one set of possiblities:

1. Horror tales are not new. *Frankenstein* was written in the nineteenth century by Mary Shelley, the wife of the poet Percy Bysshe Shelley. *Frankenstien* tells the story of a scientist who makes a monster from a human corpse.

(continued next page)

ANSWERS: EXERCISE 1 *(continued)*

2. Another famous horror tale of the nine-teenth century is "The Monkey's Paw," by W. W. Jacobs. It tells about an old English couple, parents of a teenage son, who get a monkey's paw. The paw has the power to grant three wishes. The father wishes for 200 pounds, but the money comes because their son is killed in an accident at work. The mother uses the second wish to bring her son back. Soon there is a knocking at their door. The mother rushes to unbolt it, but terrified of seeing a walking, rotting corpse, the father uses the last wish. The knocking stops.

3. After radios became common, horror programs broadcast their tales of terror into the living rooms of America. Many families, including children of all ages, grouped around the radio while they listened for the latest story of monsters and strange events. The many programs included *The Inner Sanctum,* which featured a creaking door, and *The Fat Man,* who had a madman's laugh. The scared, delighted audience came from different parts of the country, different occupations, and different economic and social groups.

BIOGRAPHY

Isaac Asimov is probably best known as a science fiction writer, but he is much more than that. Born in the U.S.S.R. in 1920, he came to the United States in 1923 and was naturalized in 1928. Writing throughout his school years, he had published over a dozen pieces of science fiction by the time he was 21. Since then he has written and edited hundreds of books, both fiction and nonfiction. He states, "I'm on fire to explain, and happiest when it's something reasonably intricate which I can make clear step by step. It's the easiest way I can clarify things in my own mind."

to grant three wishes, so the father wishes for 200 pounds, but the money comes because their son is killed in an accident at work. The mother uses the second wish to bring her son back, and soon there is a knocking at their door, and the mother rushes to unbolt it, but the father is terrified of seeing a walking, rotting corpse, so he uses the last wish, and the knocking stops.

3. After radios became common, horror programs broadcast their tales of terror into the living rooms of America which were filled with families that included children of all ages who were grouped around the radio while they listened for the latest story of monsters and strange events. The many programs, which included *The Inner Sanctum,* which featured a creaking door, and *The Fat Man* who had a madman's laugh, scared and delighted the audience who came from different parts of the country, from different occupations, and from different economic and social groups.

19b Using an occasional question, mild command, or exclamation

To vary your sentence structure and to emphasize material, you can call on four basic sentence types. The most typical English sentence is **declarative.** A declarative sentence makes a statement—it declares something. Declarative sentences offer an almost infinite variety of structures and patterns.

A sentence that asks a question is called **interrogative.** Occasional questions can help you involve your reader.

A sentence that issues a mild or strong command is called **imperative.** Occasional mild commands are particularly helpful for gently urging your reader to think along with you. A sentence that makes an exclamation is called **exclamatory.** ❖ PUNCTUATION ALERT: A mild command ends with a period. A strong command or an exclamation ends with an exclamation mark. ❖

Consider the following examples from *Change!* by Isaac Asimov, a writer who often uses different sentence types to keep his material lively and to focus attention on what he wants to emphasize.

QUESTION   The colonization of space may introduce some unexpected changes into human society. **For instance, what effect will it have on the way we keep time?** Our present system of time-keeping is a complicated mess that depends on accidents of astronomy and on 5,000 years of primitive habit.

MILD COMMAND	**Consider the bacteria.** These are tiny living things made up of single cells far smaller than the cells in plants and animals.
EXCLAMATION	**The amazing thing about the netting of the coelacanth was that till then zoologists had been convinced the fish had been extinct for 60 million years!** Finding a living dinosaur would not have been more surprising.

EXERCISE 2

In each passage, change one sentence to a question, a command, or an exclamation. Choose the sentence to change according to what you would like to emphasize. Be prepared to explain your choice.

EXAMPLE   You can think about race horses. They are among the most valuable animals in the world.

Think about race horses. They are among the most valuable animals in the world.

1. Easy Jet, a multi-race winner, was sold for 30 million dollars. That is more than the average combined yearly income of a town of 2,000 people.

2. We may wonder what the popularity of horse racing suggests about the American national character. We may be a nation of gamblers. On the other hand, we simply may want financial independence.

3. Tradition holds that no race horse can have a name that contains more than eighteen letters. Apostrophes, hyphens, and spaces count in the total. Longer names would take up too much room on written records.

4. Lotteries have become as popular as horse racing. Many states run lotteries to raise money for services earlier provided from taxes. You may not know that in many states school books are purchased with funds gambled on lottery tickets.

5. Some television commercials for lotteries show winners riding in limousines. Most lottery ticket holders lose, though. That tempting chance to win a million dollars has odds worse than a million to one.

ANSWERS: EXERCISE 2

Answers may vary. Ask students to explain their choices. Here is one set of possibilities.

1. Easy Jet, a multi-race winner, was sold for 30 million dollars. That is more than the average combined yearly income of a town of 2,000 people!

2. What might the popularity of horse racing suggest about the American national character? We may be a nation of gamblers. On the other hand, we simply may want financial independence.

3. Tradition holds that no race horse can have a name that contains more than eighteen letters. Apostrophes, hyphens, and spaces count in the total! Longer names would take up too much room on written records.

4. Lotteries have become as popular as horse racing. Many states run lotteries to raise money for basic services earlier provided from taxes. Did you know that in many states school books are purchased with funds gambled on lottery tickets?

5. Some television commercials for lotteries show winners riding in limousines. Most lottery ticket holders lose, though. That tempting chance to win a million dollars has odds worse than a million to one!

19c Choosing the subject of a sentence according to your intended emphasis

The subject° of a sentence establishes the focus for that sentence. The subject you choose should correspond to the emphasis you want to communicate to your reader.

The following sentences, each of which is correct grammatically, contain the same information. Consider, however, how changes of the subject (and its verb) influence meaning and impact.

1. **Our study showed** that 25 percent of college students' time is spent eating or sleeping.

2. **College students eat or sleep** 25 percent of the time, according to our study.

3. **Eating or sleeping occupies** 25 percent of college students' time, according to our study.

4. **Twenty-five percent** of college students' time **is spent** eating or sleeping, according to our study.

Sentence 1 focuses on the study, 2 on the students, 3 on eating and sleeping, and 4 on percentage of time. Each sentence provides a different emphasis. You would use whichever version most effectively delivers your message in relation to your purpose. For example, sentence 4 seems more suitable for a statistical report while sentence 2 might work well in an article for a college newspaper.

19d   Adding modifiers to basic sentences for variety and emphasis

A **modifier** is a word, phrase°, or clause° that describes other words, phrases, or clauses. Adding modifiers to basic sentences permits you to expand a simple subject and verb into a rich variety of sentence patterns.

Expanding basic sentences with modifiers

Sentences that consist only of a subject and verb usually seem very thin. You might use a very short sentence for its dramatic effect in emphasizing an idea. When you want to avoid a very short sentence, you can expand the basic sentence with modifying words, phrases, and clauses (as shown in boldface in the chart at the top of the next page). Your decision to expand a basic sentence will depend on the focus of each sentence and how it works in concert with its surrounding sentences.

WAYS TO EXPAND A BASIC SENTENCE

BASIC SENTENCE	The river rose.
ADJECTIVE	The **swollen** river rose.
ADVERB	The river rose **dangerously.**
PREPOSITIONAL PHRASE	**In April,** the river rose **above its banks.**
PARTICIPIAL PHRASES	**Swollen by melting snow,** the river rose, **flooding the farmland.**
ABSOLUTE PHRASE	**Trees swirling away in the current,** the river rose.
ADVERB CLAUSE	**Because the snows had been heavy that winter,** the river rose.
ADJECTIVE CLAUSE	The river, **which runs through vital farmland,** rose.

ALTERNATE EXAMPLES

1. The guests arrived. (Basic sentence)
2. The hungry guests arrived. (Adjective)
3. The hungry guests arrived late. (Adverb)
4. After the concert, the hungry guests arrived late in a thunderstorm. (Prepositional phrases)
5. Delayed by the weather, the hungry guests, running and laughing, arrived late. (Participles)
6. Shoes soaked from the rain, the hungry guests arrived. (Absolute phrase)
7. Because they were hungry, the guests hurried to the restaurant. (Adverb clause)
8. The guests, who were hungry, hurried to the restaurant. (Adjective clause)

EXERCISE 3

Expand each sentence by adding (a) an adjective, (b) an adverb, (c) a prepositional phrase, (d) a participial phrase, (e) an absolute phrase, (f) an adverb clause, and (g) an adjective clause. For guidance, look at how the basic sentence is expanded in the preceding box.

1. We went to register for classes.
2. The lines were long.
3. The students seemed edgy.
4. The staff remained calm.
5. Both of us got the schedules we wanted.

2 Positioning modifiers to create variety and emphasis

Learning research suggests that readers are more likely to retain the message at the very beginning or the very end of a sentence. Although you do not have unlimited choices about where to place modifiers, you do have some. Try to place them according to the emphasis you want to achieve. At the same time, be sure to place your modifiers precisely within sentences so that you avoid the error of misplaced modifiers° (see 15b).

ANSWERS: EXERCISE 3

Students are to expand each sentence by adding (a) an adjective, (b) an adverb, (c) a prepositional phrase, (d) a participial phrase, (e) an absolute phrase, (f) a subordinate clause, and (g) a relative clause. They can refer for guidance to the expansion example shown in 19d-1. The answers will vary considerably. Here is a possible set of answers for item 1:

a. We went to register for *our college* classes.

b. We went *eagerly* to register for classes.

c. We went to register for classes *at the college.*

d. *Forced to wait until the storm passed,* we went to register for classes, *hoping we were not too late.*

e. *Clothing still unpacked in our dormitory,* we went to register for classes.

f. *As soon as we got to the college,* we went to register for classes.

g. We, *who had never attended college before,* went to register for classes.

BACKGROUND

In *Classical Rhetoric for the Modern Student,* Edward P. J. Corbett discusses how using different sentence openers can provide sentence variety. He lists several specific beginnings that are in common use. (2nd ed., New York: Oxford UP, 1971. 457.)

A. Subject (e.g., *John* broke the window.)

B. Expletive (e.g., *It* is plain that . . . .)

C. Coordinating conjunction *(and, but, or, nor, for, yet, so)*

D. Adverb word (e.g., *first, thus, moreover, nevertheless, namely*)

E. Conjunctive phrase (e.g., *on the other hand, as a consequence*)

F. Prepositional phrase (e.g., *after the game, in the morning*)

G. Verbal phrase (e.g., participial, gerundive, or infinitive)

H. Adjective phrase (e.g., *Tired but happy,* we . . .)

I. Absolute phrase (e.g., *The ship having arrived safely,* we . . .)

J. Adverb clause (e.g., *When the ship arrived safely,* we . . .)

K. Front-shift (e.g., inverted word order: *Gone was the wind. Happy were they to be alive.*)

BACKGROUND

Periodic and cumulative sentences work by placing the weight of a sentence's message at one end. On the other hand, the balanced sentence, using the concept of parallel structure, presents two equally weighted pieces of meaning. Usually a punctuation mark and/or a coordinating conjunction acts as a centerpoint upon which the meaning balances, much like a see-saw on its base.

Freedom is the right to be wrong, not the right to do wrong.

—John Diefenbaker

A sentence that starts with a subject and verb is called a **cumulative sentence.** You add information by placing modifiers after the subject and verb. This is the most common sentence structure. It is called "cumulative" because information accumulates. Sometimes it is referred to as a **loose sentence** because it lacks the tightly planned structure of other sentence varieties. Such sentences are easy to read because they reflect how humans receive and pass on information. Cumulative sentences, however, often do not provide impact.

In contrast, a **periodic sentence** (sometimes called a **climactic sentence**) is highly emphatic. It builds up to the period of the sentence, reserving the main idea for the end. It draws the reader in as it builds to its climax.

PERIODIC	At midnight last night, on the road from Las Vegas to Death Valley Junction, **a car hit a shoulder and turned over.**
	—JOAN DIDION, "On Morality"
CUMULATIVE	**A car hit a shoulder and turned over** at midnight last night on the road from Las Vegas to Death Valley Junction.
PERIODIC	**The driver,** very young and apparently drunk, **was killed instantly.**
	—JOAN DIDION, "On Morality"
CUMULATIVE	**The driver, killed instantly,** was very young and apparently drunk.

Periodic sentences can be very effective, but if you overuse them they lose their punch. For this reason, Joan Didion follows her two periodic sentences shown above with a cumulative sentence: *His girl was found alive but bleeding internally, deep in shock.*

Another way to vary your sentence structures is to start sentences with introductory words, phrases, or clauses.

WORD	**Fortunately,** I taught myself to read before I had to face boring reading drills in school.
	—ANDREW FURMAN, student
PHRASE	**Along with cereal boxes and ketchup labels,** comic books were the primers that taught me how to read.
	—GLORIA STEINEM
CLAUSE	**Long before I wrote stories,** I listened for stories.
	—EUDORA WELTY, *One Writer's Beginnings*

Often, modifiers may appear in several different positions within a sentence. Positioning modifiers offers you a chance to lend your writing style both variety and emphasis. Be careful, however, to avoid placing modifiers in positions that create ambiguous meaning; see 15b–1.

Angrily the physician slammed down the chart, **sternly** speaking to the patient.

The physician slammed down her chart **angrily,** speaking **sternly** to the patient.

The physician **angrily** slammed down her chart, speaking to the patient **sternly.**

EXERCISE 4

Combine each set of sentences by changing one sentence to a clause, phrase, or word that will modify the other sentence.

EXAMPLE   According to a story about the Tower of Babel, all people once spoke the same language. The story appears in the Old Testament.

According to a story in the Old Testament about the Tower of Babel, all people once spoke the same language. [sentence changed to phrase]

1. The people of Babel tried to build a tower that would reach to heaven. They wanted to become famous.
2. God punished them for their arrogance. God made them all speak different languages.
3. Different languages create barriers between people. This is certainly true.
4. Some linguists have tried to develop universal languages. These linguists were ambitious.
5. The British linguist John Wilkins created an artificial language. This happened in 1668.
6. Wilkins wanted to promote universal communication. He made the rules of his invented language consistent and easy to learn.
7. The language had a written form that looked like Arabic. The form was difficult.
8. Another international language was created by L. L. Zamenhof, a Russian physician. This happened two hundred years later.
9. Zamenhof's language is based on European languages and is still used by some people today. It is called Esperanto.
10. The name of the language comes from a verb. The verb means *hope* in Spanish and French.

ANSWERS: EXERCISE 4

Answers will vary. Here is one set of possibilities.

1. The people of Babel tried to build a tower that would reach to heaven because they wanted to become famous.
2. God punished them for their arrogance by making them all speak different languages.
3. Different languages certainly create barriers between people.
4. Some ambitious linguists have tried to develop universal languages.
5. In 1668, the British linguist John Wilkins created an artificial language.
6. Because Wilkins wanted to encourage universal communication, he made the rules of his invented language consistent and easy to learn.
7. The language had a difficult written form that looked like Arabic.
8. Two hundred years later, another international language was created by L. L. Zamenhof, a Russian physician.
9. Zamenhof's language, called Esperanto, is based on European languages and is still used by some people today.
10. The name of the language comes from a verb that means *hope* in Spanish and French.

COVERAGE: EXERCISE 4

(1) clause; (2) phrase; (3) word; (4) word; (5) phrase; (6) clause; (7) word; (8) phrase; (9) phrase; (10) phrase

ANSWERS: EXERCISE 5

Answers will vary. Here is one set of possibilities.

(1) Molly Brown, a tough settler of the American Frontier, is remembered for bravery because she saved some of the *Titanic* passengers. (2) A hero who lived on a hacienda in Southern California, Don Diego opposed a cruel governor. (3) Wearing a mask and assuming the name *Zorro*, Diego would take unfairly gained riches from the governor's friends and would return the goods to the poor. (4) John Henry, a man who worked building the railroads, could drive steel spikes faster than anybody in the world. (5) Sacajawea, a Native American, was chosen to guide an important expedition led by Lewis and Clark because she knew how to find mountain passages that no one else could find.

TEACHING TIP

Self-analysis of a writer's style can be an effective beginning to composing better sentences. You might encourage students to find out what kind of sentences they usually write (simple, compound, complex); the average length of the sentences and how often the sentences exceed or fall short of that length; and the rhetorical forms most often used (cumulative, periodic, balanced). This process can help students see how much variety (or lack of it) exists in a their prose style. It will also reveal underused strategies of sentence composition. You may want to ask your students to gather such information about their sentences in a passage from one of their recent papers, and then to write a brief analysis that reviews the data and proposes specific changes that will enhance the passage's variety and emphasis.

EXERCISE 5

Revise each set of sentences—a new set starts at each number in parentheses—by combining them. Choose one sentence in each set to be the main focus, and reduce the other(s) to modifying clauses, phrases, or words.

EXAMPLE   Characters in folklore are usually strong. Many of them perform daring acts. They are often described as bigger than people in real life.

Characters in folklore are usually described as strong, daring, and bigger than people in real life.

(1) Molly Brown was a tough settler of the American Frontier. She is remembered for bravery because she saved some of the *Titanic* passengers. (2) Don Diego was a hero who lived on a hacienda in Southern California. He opposed a cruel governor. (3) He wore a mask and assumed the name *Zorro*. He would take unfairly gained riches from the governor's friends. Then he would return the goods to the poor. (4) Then there was John Henry. He was a man. He worked building the railroads. He could drive steel spikes very fast. He could drive them faster than anybody else. (5) Sacajawea was a Native American. She knew how to find mountain passages. No one else could find these passages. Because of this skill, she was chosen to guide an expedition. The expedition was important. The expedition was led by Lewis and Clark.

19e Inverting standard word order

Standard word order in the English sentence places the subject before the verb: *The mayor walked into the room.* Because this pattern is so common, it is set in people's minds. Any variation automatically creates emphasis. Inverted word order places the verb before the subject. Used too often, inverted word order can be distracting, but used sparingly, it can be very effective.

STANDARD	**The mayor walked** in. **The governor walked** out.
INVERTED	In **walked the mayor.** Out **walked the governor.**
STANDARD	**The house** that shelters a friend **is happy.**
INVERTED	**Happy is the house** that shelters a friend.

—RALPH WALDO EMERSON

19f   Repeating important words or ideas to achieve emphasis

The repetition of carefully chosen words helps emphasize meaning. Choose for repetition only words that contain a main idea or that use rhythm to focus attention on a main idea. Consider this passage, which uses deliberate repetition along with a variety of sentence lengths to deliver its meaning.

> Coal is **black** and it warms your house and cooks your food. The night is **black,** which has a moon, and a million stars, and is beautiful. Sleep is **black** which gives you rest, so you wake up **feeling good.** I am **black. I feel** very **good** this evening.
>
> —LANGSTON HUGHES, "That Word *Black*"

Hughes repeats the word *black,* each time linking it to something related to joy and beauty. The rhythm that results from the deliberate repetition of *black* and *good* emphasizes Hughes's message and helps the reader remember it.

While deliberate repetition is a good ally when you use it occasionally to achieve variety and emphasize selected ideas, it can be misused. Be sure to use deliberate repetition sparingly, with central words, and only when your meaning justifies such a technique. Consider this passage, which misuses repetition:

No   **An insurance agent** can be an excellent adviser when you want to buy a **car. An insurance agent** has records on most **cars. An insurance agent** knows which **models** tend to have most accidents. **An insurance agent** can tell you which **models** are the most expensive to repair if they are in a collision. **An insurance agent can** tell you which **models** are most likely to be stolen.

The misused repetition in the No passage seems the result of a limited vocabulary and a dull, unvaried style. Although few synonyms exist for the words *an insurance agent, car,* and *model,* some do. Also, the writer provides no variety in sentence structure. The passage's content does seem to call for the rhythmic effect of deliberate repetition. Consider this improved revision.

YES   If you are thinking of buying a new car, an insurance agent can be an excellent adviser. An insurance broker has complete records on most automobiles. For example, he or she knows which models are accident prone.

ANSWERS: EXERCISE 6 (next page)

Answers will vary. In the version below, the word *dreams* is deliberately repeated, many short sentences are combined, the second half of the compound sentence becomes a single sentence for particular emphasis, and the word order is rearranged in the last sentence.

Dreams come in many forms, some pleasing and others distressing. Dreams can be about the future or past successes or joys. Sometimes they are bizzare. According to researchers, some dreams recur over and over again, such as those about flying or falling. Many people dream they are failing tests or unable to make an important telephone call. Experts have suggested various explanations for some dreams, which makes a person's dreams seem objective and impersonal. They are not. Special is the dream, no matter how common, to its dreamer.

ANSWERS: EXERCISE 6 (on previous page)

ANSWERS: EXERCISE 7

Answers will vary One possible revision is shown here. In this version, *pigeons* and *scientists* are deliberately repeated. Many short sentences are combined (in two places, three sentences are combined into one) into a variety of sentence types, and unneeded words are dropped in that process. The first compound sentence is revised to a simple sentence containing compound phrases. The second compound sentence is revised to a contain a relative clause. Word order is inverted in one sentence, to which an exclamation point is added. One complex sentence is unpacked for greater clarity. The last sentence is revised into a question. Some sentences are not revised.

Pigeons adjust to many environments. Pigeons adjust to farm life, and they adjust to city streets where they peck their livelihoods from garbage heaps or from crumbs tossed to them. They even thrive well in science laboratories. Recently, scientists at the University of Iowa wanted to find out about the conceptual abilities of pigeons. The scientists worked with ordinary pigeons. The pigeons, trapped on an Iowa farm, were treated well by the scientists. The pigeons were given tests that required thinking ability. The pigeons had to assign pictures of objects to categories. The pigeons learned easily to tell apart photographs of different objects. The pictures were of separate items such as cats, flowers, people, and even manufactured items such as automobiles and furniture. Then came a big surprise! The scientists discovered that the pigeons did not learn by rote. When photographs varied only slightly in different features or degrees of light, the pigeons could tell them apart. Can humans doubt any longer that pigeons are far smarter than they look?

Did you know that some car designs suffer more damage than others in a collision? If you want to know which automobiles crumple more than others and which are least expensive to repair, ask an insurance agent. Similarly, some models are more likely to be stolen, so find out from the person who specializes in dealing with claims.

EXERCISE 6

Revise this paragraph to achieve emphasis through varied sentence length and deliberate repetition. You can reduce or increase the number of sentences.

Dreams come in many forms. Some are pleasing. They also can be distressing. They can be about the future. They can be about past successes or joys. Sometimes, they are bizarre. According to researchers, some visions during sleep recur over and over again. Typical ones are about flying or falling. Many people see themselves failing tests. Being unable to make an important telephone call is also common. Experts have suggested various explanations for some dreams. This makes a person's dreams seem objective and impersonal, but they are not. No matter how common, a dream is special to the dreamer.

EXERCISE 7

Revise this paragraph to achieve emphasis through varied sentence length and deliberate repetition. You can reduce or increase the number of sentences. You can drop words to reduce unneeded repetition. Each writer's revision will vary somewhat, but try to include at least one revision to a question or exclamation (19b) and one revision to an inverted word order (19e).

Pigeons adjust to many environments. Pigeons adjust to farm life. They adjust to city streets. In an urban setting they peck their livelihoods from garbage heaps, and they sometimes survive on crumbs tossed to them. They even thrive well in science labs. Recently, scientists wanted to find out something. The scientists wanted to know about the conceptual abilities of pigeons. The scientists were at the University of Iowa. The scientists worked with ordinary pigeons. The pigeons had been trapped on an Iowa farm. The pigeons were treated well by the scientists. The pigeons were given tests, and the tests required thinking ability. The pigeons had to assign pictures of objects to categories. The pigeons learn easily. The pigeons could tell apart photographs of different objects. The pictures were of separate items such as cats, flowers, people. The pictures even included manufactured items such as automobiles and furniture. Then a big surprise came. The scientists discovered that the pigeons did not learn by rote in that when photographs varied only slightly in different features or degrees of light, the pigeons could tell them apart. Humans can no longer doubt that pigeons are far smarter than they look.

EXERCISE 8

Using the techniques of variety and emphasis discussed in this chapter, revise the following paragraph.

Many amazing events in bathtubs have taken place. Three different women died by drowning in the bathtub while they were married to George Joseph Smith of England. There was great surprise at Mr. Smith's trial when the fact that he now had a fourth wife, Edith, was revealed. Edith testified at the trial that she remembered George's taking only one bath during the whole time they were married. Other things besides gory murders, however, happen in the bathtub. For example, French author Edmond Rostand took baths while he was writing plays like *Cyrano de Bergerac* to escape interruptions from friends. Also, many people know that the discovery of the scientific theory of displacement by Archimedes took place in the bathtub. Archimedes shouted "Eureka!" jumped out of his bath, and ran through the streets in the nude because he was so excited by his discovery. A modern example of the importance of the bathtub is illustrated by what happened to astronaut John Glenn. There was going to be an election for senator in Ohio, but Glenn had to withdraw from the race because he hurt himself when he fell in a bathtub.

EXERCISE 9

Using topics of your choosing, imitate the variety and emphasis of two different passages shown in this chapter: choose from the Kohls, Dillard, Thomas, or Hughes.

ANSWERS: EXERCISE 8

Answers will vary. This is a summary exercise, and so it should reflect many of the techniques of variety and emphasis discussed in the chapter. Here is one possible answer.

Did you know that bathtubs have been the setting for many amazing events? While married to George Joseph Smith of England, three different women died by drowning in the bathtub. Mr. Smith's trial revealed that he now had a fourth wife, Edith. During the whole time they were married, Edith testified at the trial, she remembered George's taking only one bath. More than gory murders happen in the bathtub, however. For example, to escape interruptions from friends, French author Edmond Rostand took baths while he was writing plays like *Cyrano de Bergerac*. Also Archimedes discovered the scientific theory of displacement in the bathtub. Jumping out of his tub, Archimedes shouted "Eureka!" and ran through the streets in the nude because he was so excited by his discovery. Astronaut John Glenn provides a modern example of the importance of the bathtub. Glenn was planning to run for senator in Ohio, but he hurt himself when he fell in the bathtub. He had to withdraw from the race!

ANSWERS: EXERCISE 9

Using their own topics, students imitate the variety and emphasis of two different passages shown in this chapter. They can choose from the Kohls, Dillard, Thomas, or Hughes. For a discussion of the technique of imitation, see the answer to Exercise 2 in Chapter 18.

Focus on Revising

REVISING YOUR WRITING

If you would like to use variety and emphasis effectively when you write, go back to your writing and locate sentences that need improvement in style. Also, if you realize that you do not use parallelism when it is needed, go back to your writing and locate the problems. Using this chapter as a resource, revise your writing.

Your Goal	See Section
Vary sentence lengths effectively	19a
Use questions, mild commands, or exclamations effectively	19b
Choose sentence subjects for effective emphasis	19c
Add modifiers effectively	19d
Invert word order effectively	19e
Use repetition effectively	19f

CASE STUDY: REVISING FOR EFFECTIVE USE OF SUBORDINATION, PARALLELISM, AND VARIETY AND EMPHASIS

This case study lets you observe a student writer revising. It also gives you the chance to revise some student writing on your own.

Observation

A student wrote the following draft for her campus newspaper. The newspaper editor asked the student to compose a brief article about Soviet teenagers' interest in products made in the United States. The draft opens with an attention-getting reference and offers engaging information. The draft's effectiveness is diminished, however, by problems with subordination (Chapter 17), parallelism (Chapter 18), and variety and emphasis (this chapter).

Read through the draft. The sections that could be written in a more effective style are highlighted and explained. Before you look at how the student revised the problems, revise the material yourself. Then compare what you and the student did.

Does not show relationships among ideas: 17d

Parallel form needed: 18a and 18b

Coordination overused: 17c-2

Not a suitable mix of sentence lengths: 19a-3

Subordination illogical: 17f-1

Parallel form needed: 18a and 18b

In 1987, singer Billy Joel toured the Soviet Union. He played to capacity crowds throughout the Soviet Union. A television special about the concert tour provided viewers in the United States with a startling picture of Soviet youth. The concertgoers were wearing bluejeans, running shoes, and they had let their hair grow long and wore T-shirts. Simply put, they looked startlingly similar to American teenagers. The sight of a teenager in American-style clothing was nothing new in Russia, but most Americans did not realize this, for western products have been "hot items" over a decade in the Soviet Union, and popular items range from stereos to chewing gum. Detente started during the 1970s. This refers to the lessening of tension between the United States and the Soviet Union. Detente led to a number of American businesses opening in Moscow. At the same time, the country played host to hordes of American tourists and professionals. Soviet teenagers seemed intrigued by whatever the visitors brought with them, although tourists returned home with stories of Russian teenagers offering to buy the very jackets and shoes the Americans were wearing. Journalists talked about and were publishing stories about a thriving black market in American cigarettes, records, and electronic gear.

COVERAGE: PARTICIPATION ESSAY

Many people enjoy playing sports in high school and college. *Sports like football and basketball are team sports, and they can be fun to play, and they can keep players in excellent physical condition.* [17c-2: coordination overused] These sports have one major shortcoming, however. *They are hard to play after college. Finding enough people to make up two teams is usually difficult outside of school.* [17d: does not show relationship among ideas]

People plan to play sports over a lifetime. A wise choice is golf. This sport is not particularly popular in school. [17d: does not show relationship among ideas] Swinging a golf club promotes flexibility and agility. Also, golf players can maintain their physical conditioning if they *walk* the golf course briskly and *are carrying* [18a: not parallel form for words] their golf clubs. Golf courses often measure between three-and-a-half and five miles, which is a good distance for a workout. *Golfers begin to age. They can use a pull cart. The pull cart is for the bags. The pull cart helps prevent strain. The strain can be on muscles and joints. Then, golfers age further. The golfers have a new solution. They can use electric carts. Electric carts allow golfers to ride part or all of the course.* [19a-3: not a suitable mix of sentence lengths; and 17d: does not show relationship among ideas]

In addition to being physically demanding, golf offers a mental challenge. Most long-time, nonprofessional golfers know that they are playing against the golf course. They are not playing against someone who is *younger* and *has more strength*. [18a: not parallel form for words] In golf, the lower the score, the better. Professional golfers hope for scores in the high sixties or low seventies. My grandfather is a lifetime golf player. *Because he is 82, he still plays golf almost every day.* [17f-1: illogical subordination] He says that his goal is to get a golf score that matches his age. Therefore, with each added year, he has a better chance to reach his goal. That is mental health!

Soviet teenagers have developed a big appetite for a wide range of U.S. styles and items. This will help break down barriers between the two countries.

Here is how the student revised for effective use of subordination, parallelism, and variety and emphasis. The student had alternatives for correcting the problems. Your revision, therefore, might not be exactly like this one, but it should eliminate all the problems highlighted in the draft.

In 1987, singer Billy Joel toured the Soviet Union and played to capacity crowds. A television special about the concert tour provided viewers in the United States with a startling picture of Soviet youth.

The concertgoers wore bluejeans, running shoes, long hair, and T-shirts. Simply put, they looked startlingly similar to American teenagers. Most Americans did not realize, however, that the sight of a teenager in American-style clothing was nothing new in Russia, for western products, from stereos to chewing gum, have been "hot items" for over a decade in the Soviet Union.

Detente, the lessening of tension between the United States and the Soviet Union that started during the 1970s, led to a number of American businesses opening in Moscow. At the same time, the country played host to hordes of American tourists and professionals. Soviet teenagers seemed intrigued by whatever the visitors brought with them; and tourists returned home with stories of Russian teenagers offering to buy the very jackets and shoes the Americans were wearing. Journalists talked about and published stories about a thriving black market in American cigarettes, records, and electronic gear.

Soviet teenagers have developed a big appetite for a wide range of U.S. styles and items. This will help break down barriers between the two countries.

Participation

A student wrote the following draft for a course called Health and The Aging Process. The assignment was to write about sports that people can play all their lives. The material contains useful information logically presented, but the draft's effectiveness is diminished by problems with subordination (Chapter 17), parallelism (Chapter 18), and variety and emphasis (this chapter).

Read through the draft. Then revise it to eliminate the problems. Also, make any additional revisions you think would improve the content, organization, and style of the material.

> Many people enjoy playing sports in high school and college. Sports like football and basketball are team sports, and they can be fun to play, and they can keep players in excellent physical condition. These sports have one major shortcoming, however. They are hard to play after college. Finding enough people to make up two teams is usually difficult outside of school.
>
> People plan to play sports over a lifetime. A wise choice is golf. This sport is not particularly popular in school. Swinging a golf club promotes flexibility and agility. Also, golf players can maintain their physical conditioning if they walk the golf course briskly and are carrying their golf clubs. Golf courses often measure between three-and-a-half and five miles, which is a good distance for a workout. Golfers begin to age. They can use a pull cart. The pull cart is for the bags. The pull cart helps prevent strain. The strain can be on muscles and joints. Then, golfers age further. The golfers have a new solution. They can use electric carts. Electric carts allow golfers to ride part or all of the course.
>
> In addition to being physically demanding, golf offers a mental challenge. Most long-time, nonprofessional golfers know that they are playing against the golf course. They are not playing against someone who is younger and has more strength. In golf, the lower the score, the better. Professional golfers hope for scores in the high sixties or low seventies. My grandfather is a lifetime golf player. Because he is 82, he still plays golf almost every day. He says that his goal is to get a golf score that matches his age. Therefore, with each added year, he has a better chance to reach his goal. That is mental health!

ANSWER: PARTICIPATION ESSAY

This version revises the problems with coordination and subordination (Chapter 17), parallelism (Chapter 18), and variety and emphasis (this chapter). Answers will likely vary somewhat from this version because so many options are available. Also, answers will vary if students have revised for content, organization, or style.

Many people enjoy playing sports in high school and college. Team sports like football and basketball are fun to play and can keep players in excellent physical condition. These sports have one major shortcoming, however. They are hard to play after college, because finding enough people to make up two teams is usually difficult outside of school.

People who plan to play sports over a lifetime would be wise to choose golf, even though this sport is not particularly popular in school. Swinging a golf club promotes flexibility and agility. Also, golf players can maintain their physical conditioning if they walk the golf course briskly and carry their golf clubs. Golf courses often measure between three-and-a-half and five miles, which is a good distance for a workout. As golfers age, they can use a pull cart for the bags so that they do not strain their muscles and joints. Even later in life, golfers can use electric carts to ride the course.

In addition to being physically demanding, golf offers a mental challenge. Most long-time, nonprofessional golfers know that they are playing against the golf course. They are not playing against someone who is younger and stronger. In golf, the lower the score, the better. Professional golfers hope for scores in the high sixties or low seventies. My grandfather is a lifetime golf player. Although he is 82, he still plays golf almost every day. He says that his goal is to get a golf score that matches his age. Therefore, with each added year, he has a better chance to reach his goal. That is mental health!

Five

U SING
E FFECTIVE
W ORDS

When you use words effectively, you choose words that communicate your message precisely. Part Five alerts you to the meanings that reside in words and the effect that words have on your reader.

20 Understanding the Meaning of Words

Note: See the annotations of Chapter 22 for a series of "Language History" items related to spelling and to the origins of American English.

WORD DERIVATION

The Greeks felt all foreigners were savages, speaking crude, primitive languages. *Barbarous* and *barbaric* come from the nonsense syllables the Greeks used in imitation of foreign speech: *barbar*.

WORD DERIVATION

Arkansas comes from the French adaptation of a Siouan tribal name believed to have meant "downstream people."

WORD DERIVATION

The name *California* originally referred to an imaginary island in a Spanish romance written by Montalvo in 1510.

WORD DERIVATION

Florida was named by explorer Ponce de León. The name is Spanish for "abounding in flowers."

American English, evolving over centuries into a rich language, reflects the many cultures that have merged in our melting-pot society. The earliest varieties of American English can be traced from sixteenth-century Elizabethan English—the language of Shakespeare. As the United States expanded, so did American English. Changes from Elizabethan forms occurred in vocabulary, spelling, and syntactic patterns. Distinctly American words originated colloquially—in spoken language—and words from all the cultures settling the United States became part of the language. Food names, for example, show how other languages and cultures loaned words to English. Africans brought the words *okra, gumbo,* and *goober* (peanut). Spanish and Latin American peoples contributed *tortilla, taco, burrito,* and *enchilada.* From German we got *hamburger, wiener,* and *pretzel;* Italian supplied *spaghetti, pasta, pizza,* and *antipasto;* and Yiddish is responsible for *gefilte fish, tsimmes,* and *bagel.* American English creates a truly international *smorgasbord,* a Scandinavian word meaning "a wide variety of appetizers and other tasty foods."

Etymology is the study of a word's origins and historical development, including its changes in form and meaning. For example, *alphabet* originates from the names of the first two letters in Greek: *a = alpha, b = beta.* The word *nice* shows how a word's meaning can change with time. As W. Nelson Francis points out in *The English Language, nice* "has been used at one time or another in its 700-year history to mean . . . foolish, wanton, strange, lazy, coy, modest, fastidious, refined, precise, subtle, slender, critical, attentive, minutely accurate, dainty, appetizing, agreeable."

American English is a growing, changing language. As a writer, you want to stay informed about the language so that you can use it effectively. To use American English well, you need to be familiar with the kinds of information that dictionaries offer (20a), to know how to choose exact words (20b), and to employ strategies that actively build your vocabulary (20c).

Using dictionaries

Good dictionaries show how language has been used and is currently being used. Such dictionaries give at each entry not only the word's meaning but also much additional important information. Many dictionaries also include essays on the history and use of language.

 1 **Understanding the information in a dictionary entry**

A dictionary entry usually includes items 1 through 11 discussed below, and sometimes items 12 and 13. As you use the list, consult the entry shown below for *celebrate,* taken from *Webster's New World Dictionary,* Third College Edition.

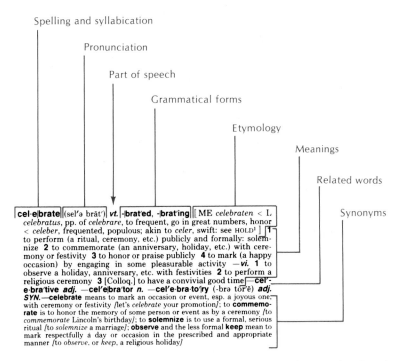

Spelling and syllabication

Pronunciation

Part of speech

Grammatical forms

Etymology

Meanings

Related words

Synonyms

cel·e·brate (sel′ə brāt′) *vt.* -brat′ed, -brat′ing [ME *celebraten* < L *celebratus,* pp. of *celebrare,* to frequent, go in great numbers, honor < *celeber,* frequented, populous; akin to *celer,* swift: see HOLD¹] **1** to perform (a ritual, ceremony, etc.) publicly and formally: solemnize **2** to commemorate (an anniversary, holiday, etc.) with ceremony or festivity **3** to honor or praise publicly **4** to mark (a happy occasion) by engaging in some pleasurable activity —*vi.* **1** to observe a holiday, anniversary, etc. with festivities **2** to perform a religious ceremony **3** [Colloq.] to have a convivial good time —**cel′e·bra′tive** *adj.* —**cel′e·bra·tor** *n.* —**cel′e·bra·to′ry** (-brə tôr′ē) *adj.* **SYN.**—**celebrate** means to mark an occasion or event, esp. a joyous one, with ceremony or festivity /let's *celebrate* your promotion/; to **commemorate** is to honor the memory of some person or event as by a ceremony /to *commemorate* Lincoln's birthday/; to **solemnize** is to use a formal, serious ritual /to *solemnize* a marriage/; **observe** and the less formal **keep** mean to mark respectfully a day or occasion in the prescribed and appropriate manner /to *observe,* or *keep,* a religious holiday/

1. **Spelling.** If more than one spelling is shown, the first is the most commonly used, and the others are acceptable.

   Celebrate has only one spelling.

The earliest dictionary, really a combination grammar and dictionary, was a tablet from Sumerian Nippur that attempted to enunciate the rules of language use. Not until the early seventeenth century was the first English dictionary produced by Henry Cockeram. The earliest attempt to list all the words in the English language was Nathaniel Bailey's *Universal Etymological English Dictionary* of 1721. Mulcaster had urged such a compilation as far back as 1582, but the only result was Robert Cawdrey's *Table Alphabeticall of Hard Words* (about 3,000 of them) published in 1604. Following Bailey's effort, dictionary makers dutifully tried to include all words, not just the difficult ones. Consequently, the seventeenth and eighteenth centuries saw the size of dictionaries grow substantially. Further innovations included Samuel Johnson's use of quotations to exemplify usage in his *Dictionary of the English Language* (1755) and Noah Webster's inclusion of quotations from the Founding Fathers in his *An American Dictionary of the English Language* (1828). Webster's nationalistic feelings were also evident in his insistence on American spellings. Contemporary dictionaries, such as *The American Heritage Dictionary of the English Language* and *Random House Dictionary,* will include photographs, illustrations, and maps. Today's unabridged dictionaries include well over one million words, although the average adult is said to have a use-and-recognition vocabulary of between 30,000 and 60,000 words. A highly literate adult may know 100,000. Since it is estimated that only 20,000 to 30,000 words are in full use today, average adults can get along well, although they may not know nine out of ten words in the official language because these are terms from special fields with which they have no contact.

2. **Word Division.** The dots (or bars, in some dictionaries) show a word's syllables. In *Webster's New World Dictionary,* Third College Edition, a hairline (a thin vertical line) indicates a syllable where the break should not be used for hyphenating.

> *Celebrate* has three syllables: *cel, e,* and *brate.* A hyphen is acceptable after *cel* but not after the second *e.*

3. **Pronunciation.** The symbols in parentheses show pronunciation. If more than one pronunciation is given, the first is the most common, and others are acceptable. A guide to the pronunciation of the symbols appears in the front of most dictionaries, and some dictionaries provide a brief guide to the most common symbols at the bottom of pages.

> *Celebrate* is pronounced *sel′ ə brāt.* The accent mark after the *l* means that the stressed syllable is *sel.* The unusual looking symbol /ə/, called a *schwa,* is pronounced "uh," as in *ago.* The line over the *a* indicates the long *a* sound, as in *ate.*

4. **Part of Speech Labels.** Abbreviations, explained in the front of the dictionary, indicate parts of speech. Many words can function as more than one part of speech.

> *Celebrate* is a transitive verb° (**vt.**), for which four definitions are given; also, it is an intransitive verb° (**vi.**), for which three definitions are given.

5. **Grammatical Forms.** This information tells of variations in grammar: for a verb, its principal parts and form variations; for a noun, its plural when the spelling demands other than the addition of *s*; for an adjective or adverb, its comparative form° and superlative form°.

> The principal parts of the verb *celebrate* are *celebrated* and *celebrating.*

6. **Etymology.** A word's history that tells how the word evolved through different languages to the definition in current use.

> *Celebrate* comes from a Middle English (ME) word that is derived from the Latin (L). The meaning evolved from the idea of "going in great numbers, honoring." This is related to the first definition listed in the entry.

7. **Definitions.** If a word has more than one meaning, the definitions are numbered in most dictionaries from the oldest to the newest meaning. A few dictionaries start with the most common use.

> The oldest meaning of *celebrate* is given first, and its most recent use is given last (item 4 in the **vt.** list and item 3 in the **vi.** list).

8. **Usage Labels.** Usage labels indicate how a word is used. The tinted box that follows explains the most common usage labels in dictionaries.

> The most recent meaning of *celebrate* as a **vi** is *colloquial,* which means that meaning is informal (and probably should be avoided in academic writing).

9. **Field Labels.** A field label identifies a specialized area of study, such as chemistry or law. Abbreviations signal that a word has a specialized meaning within a field of study. For example, along with its everyday meanings, the word *center* has specialized meanings in these fields: sports, mechanics, the military, and politics.

10. **Related Words.** Words based on the defined word appear, with their part of speech, at the end of the definitions.

> Words related to *celebrate* are *celebrative* (adjective), *celebrator* (noun), and *celebratory* (adjective).

11. **Synonyms and Antonyms.** Synonyms—words close in meaning—are listed, and their subtle differences explained. Also, for each word in the list of synonyms, a cross-reference appears at that word's entry so that the reader can tell where to find the complete list. For example, at the entry *commemorate,* this information appears: —*SYN.* CELEBRATE. This tells the reader that synonyms for *commemorate* are given at the entry for *celebrate.* Antonyms—words opposite in meaning to the word defined—are given, if any, after the synonyms.

> *Celebrate* and four of its synonyms are listed and explained; it has no antonyms.

12. **Idioms.** Common expressions that use the defined word in slightly different ways are idioms. For example, the slang expression *hit the ceiling* is an idiom defined under

WORD DERIVATION

Louisiana comes from *La Louisianne.* The French, who had controlled the Mississippi Valley before selling the area to the United States in 1803, had named the area after their king, Louis XIV.

WORD DERIVATION

Nevada is a shortening of the Spanish *Sierra Nevada* ("snowy range"), a mountain range in eastern California.

WORD DERIVATION

New Mexico is a literal translation of the Spanish *Nuevo Méjico. Méjico* is the Spanish rendering of *Mexitli,* the name of an Aztec war god.

WORD DERIVATION

The state of *Pennsylvania* is named after a man and the local geography. *Sylvania* means "wooded land" in Latin. The *Penn* part is less clear. Some say that the *Penn* is William Penn, the colonist to whom King Charles II of England gave the land. Others say that under orders from King Charles, Penn named the land after his own late father, an English admiral. In either case, the admiral had died before the king could repay a debt of 16,000 pounds. The king gave the land to William Penn in settlement of the debt—and to keep the religious activist out of England.

WORD DERIVATION

Rhode Island's etymology is a mystery. There are two theories. According to one, Italian explorer Giovanni da Verrazano saw a resemblance between the island on which the city of Newport is now located and the Greek island of Rhodes. According to the second, Dutch explorers named the area *Roode Eylandt* ("red island") because of its red clay soil.

EXTRA EXERCISE A

Find the answers to the following questions in the dictionary you commonly use. Name the sections consulted for any answers you are unable to find.

1. When was the University of the South (in Tennessee) founded?

2. What is the population of Midland, Texas?

3. What was George Eliot's real name?

4. Who took the Elgin marbles to England?

5. When did Mary Cassatt live?

6. What is the highest peak in the Elk Mountains?

7. Where is the Bonneville Dam?

8. What large city is near Evanston?

9. What is the meaning of the abbreviation *e.g.?*

10. Where does a cockney live?

11. What is the zip code for Auburn University?

12. What is the mathematical symbol for infinity?

13. To what genus does the mandrill belong?

14. What is the size (in square miles) of Manitoba?

15. What is the etymology of *helicopter?*

ceiling. Idioms are shown with usage labels (see 8 above), so that a writer can decide when their use is appropriate.

13. **Examples.** Some definitions provide an example sentence that illustrates the defined word in use.

Usage refers to the customary manner of using particular words or phrases. As a writer, you can refer to the **usage labels** in a dictionary to help you decide when a word is appropriate for use. For example, a word labelled *slang* usually is not suitable for academic writing, unless you are writing about the word itself. A word labelled *poetic* is common in poetry, though perhaps not modern poetry, but usually not in prose.

USAGE LABELS

LABEL	DEFINITION	EXAMPLE
COLLOQUIAL	Characteristic of conversation and informal writing	**pa** [father] **ma** [mother]
SLANG	Not considered part of standard language, but sometimes used in informal conversation	**whirlybird** [helicopter]
OBSOLETE	No longer used; occurred in earlier writing	**betimes** [promptly, quickly]
POETIC	Found in poetry or poetic prose	**o'er** [for *over*]
DIALECT	Used only in some geographical areas	**poke** [Southern: a bag or sack]

ANSWERS: EXERCISE 1

Answers will vary.

EXERCISE 1

Use a dictionary that has entries which include a list of synonyms and some labels, as in the entry for *celebrate* on page 419. Then, assuming as your audience a student unfamiliar with such entries, write an explanation of each part.

EXERCISE 2

Consult a dictionary that gives usage labels. First, for each word below, give the usage label or labels: colloquial, slang, obsolete, poetic (called "old poetic" in *Webster's New World Dictionary,* Third College Edition), or dialect. Then use the word in a sentence to show the meaning clearly.

1. *mutt*
2. *yore*
3. *a wrap-up*
4. *darkling*
5. *yon*

6. *flunk*
7. *jive* (verb)
8. *lea* (noun) not referring to yarn
9. *fixings*
10. *nerd*

EXERCISE 3

Consult a college dictionary for the etymology of the following words.

1. *current*
2. *pasteurize*
3. *mausoleum*
4. *nicotine*
5. *boycott*

6. *Taoism*
7. *erotic*
8. *humble*
9. *popular*
10. *company*

2 Knowing about unabridged dictionaries

Unabridged means "not shortened." Unabridged dictionaries have the most in-depth, accurate, complete, and scholarly entries of the various kinds of dictionaries. They give many examples of a word's current uses and changes in meanings over time. They include infrequently used words that abridged dictionaries (see 20a-3) may omit.

The most important and comprehensive unabridged dictionary of English is the *Oxford English Dictionary (OED).* The OED, second edition, has twenty volumes defining more than 616,500 words and terms. These volumes comprise the definitive dictionary of the English language. The *OED* traces the history of each word and gives updated quotations to illustrate changes in meaning and spelling. The *OED2* is made up of three parts: (1) the first-edition *OED,* largely unchanged; (2) the contents of the four supplements that accompanied the first-edition *OED;* and (3) the approximately 5,000 words or terms new in this edition. The *OED,* first edition or second edition, is particularly useful for people with an intense or scholarly interest in language.

ANSWERS: EXERCISE 2

Usage labels here are from *Webster's New World Dictionary,* Third College Edition.

1. slang for "a mongrel dog" or "a stupid person"

2. obsolete for "long ago"

3. colloquial for "a concluding or summarizing statement"

4. (old) poetic for "in darkness"

5. dialect for "yonder"

6. colloquial for "to fail"

7. slang for "speak in a way that is exaggerated, insincere, trying to mislead"

8. (old) poetic for "meadow or grassy field"

9. colloquial for "accessories or trimming"

10. slang for someone who is "dull, unsophisticated"

COVERAGE: EXERCISE 2

1. slang	**6.** colloquial
2. obsolete	**7.** slang
3. colloquial	**8.** (old) poetic
4. (old) poetic	**9.** colloquial
5. dialect	**10.** slang

ANSWERS: EXERCISE 3

Answers may vary a little. These are based on *Webster's New World Dictionary,* Third College Edition.

1. From the Latin *currere,* meaning "to run"

2. After Louis Pasteur, a French bacteriologist

3. After the tomb of King Mausolus in ancient history

4. After Jean Nicot, a French diplomat who introduced tobacco to France in 1560

(continued next page)

ANSWERS: EXERCISE 3 *(continued)*

5. After Captain Boycott of Ireland, ostracized by his neighbors during the Land League agitation

6. From the Chinese *tao,* meaning "the way"

7. From the Greek *eros,* meaning "love"

8. From Latin *humilis,* meaning "low, small, slight, akin to *humus,* soil, earth"

9. From the Latin *populus,* meaning "people"

10. From Vulgar Latin *compania,* literally, "group sharing bread"

BACKGROUND

In 1989 Oxford University published a second edition of the *Oxford English Dictionary,* commonly known as the *OED.* The idea for the first edition came from a paper delivered in 1857 to Britain's Philological Society by Richard Trench, Dean of Westminster; it was entitled "On Some Deficiencies in Our English Dictionaries." His concerns led the Society to make plans for compiling a completely new dictionary that would include "every word occurring in the literature of the language." In 1859 Herbert Coleridge, a grandson of the poet, became editor of the new work, expecting to publish it in two years. After his untimely death, he was succeeded by Frederick J. Furnivall, who agreed to devote four or five years to producing the first part of the dictionary. Overburdened by work, Furnivall in 1876 turned over his duties to James Murray, who agreed to produce a dictionary of between 6,000 and 7,000 pages within ten years. Beginning with one and three-quarters tons of materials collected by Furnivall, he made a public appeal for a thousand readers of English to assist with finding quotations for unusual as well as ordinary words. Working

The following entry for *celebrate* is taken from the *OED,* second edition. It is a small excerpt from the entire entry, but it serves to illustrate the kinds of information you can get from the *OED.* Compare this material and format with the entry for *celebrate* taken from *Webster's New World Dictionary,* Third College Edition, which appears on page 419. In addition to the elements already familiar to you, the *OED* offers a complete history of the word. Note the historical definition from 1656. Also note the historical examples of *celebrate* following its third meaning.

celebrate ('sɛlɪbreɪt), *v.* [f. prec., or on analogy of vbs. so formed. See -ATE³.]
(**1656** BLOUNT *Glossogr., Celebrate,* to frequent, to solemnize with an Assembly of men, to make famous, also to keep a festival day or other time with great solemnity.)

3. To observe with solemn rites (a day, festival, season); to honour with religious ceremonies, festivities, or other observances (an event, occasion). Also *absol.* (see quot. 1937).
1560 BIBLE (Genev.) *Lev.* xxiii. 32 From euen to euen shall ye celebrate [WYCL. halowe, COVERD. kepe] your Sabbath. **1591** SHAKS. *1 Hen. VI.* I. vi. 14 Feast and banquet in the open streets, To celebrate the ioy that God hath giuen vs. **1672** DRYDEN *Conq. Granada* I. i, With Pomp and Sports my Love I celebrate. **1697** —— *Virg. Georg.* I. 466 Celebrate the mighty Mother's Day. **1737** L. CLARKE *Hist. Bible* IX. (1840) I. 376 The Feast of Tabernacles being then celebrating. **1841** LANE *Arab. Nts.* I. 71 The Minor Festival ..is celebrated with more rejoicing than the other. **1929** *Randolph Enterprise* (Elkins, W. Va.) 26 Sept. 3/2 [He] came over..Sunday night to celebrate a little. **1937** PARTRIDGE *Dict. Slang* 136/1 *Celebrate,* v.i., to drink in honour of an event or a person; hence, to drink joyously. **1963** J. T. STORY *Something for Nothing* i. 40 It's Treasure's wedding day. Somebody's got to celebrate.

For most college students *Webster's Third New International Dictionary of the English Language* will provide any needed information. This highly respected, one-volume work has more than 470,000 entries and is especially strong in new scientific and technical terms. It uses quotations to show various meanings, and its definitions are given in order of their appearance in the language.

Random House Dictionary of the English Language, second edition, is another one-volume work. It has more than 315,000 entries. It is the least detailed of the three unabridged dictionaries, but it has an atlas with color maps as well as appendixes that list reference books.

3 | Knowing about abridged dictionaries

Abridged means "shortened." Abridged dictionaries contain the most commonly used words. They are convenient in size and economical to buy. They serve as practical reference books for writers and readers. Many good abridged dictionaries are referred to as "college" editions because they serve the needs of most college students.

Webster's New World Dictionary of American English, Third College Edition, has more than 170,000 entries and gives detailed etymologies. Names of people, places, abbreviations, and foreign expressions appear in the main body of the work (rather than in appendixes). Definitions appear in chronological order of their acceptance into the language. *Webster's New World Dictionary* has a contemporary American emphasis. It uses a star symbol (☆) for Americanisms—words that first became part of the language in the United States. It gives the origins of American place names (cities, states, rivers, and so on). It supplies usage labels for many words and gives synonyms, often in lists that explain distinctions among closely related words. An appendix covers punctuation, italics, numbers, capitalization, abbreviations, and source documentation. Its introductory material includes essays on the English language and etymology.

Webster's New World Compact School and Office Dictionary is based on *Webster's New World Dictionary,* Third College Edition. Far more complete than "pocket" dictionaries, this compact version of *Webster's New World Dictionary* has 56,000 entries, clearly and precisely defined. Its coverage of frequently encountered terms from the sciences, arts, business, technical, and professional fields is thorough and up-to-date. It contains pronunciation and spelling guidance, common abbreviations, foreign words and phrases often used in English writing, and etymologies. It gives tables of weights and measures, a dictionary of geography, a list of Presidents and Vice-Presidents of the United States, and lists of principal cities in the United States and in the rest of the world.

The American Heritage Dictionary of the English Language has more than 200,000 entries and 3,000 photographs, illustrations, and maps. This dictionary lists a word's most common meaning first, departing from the traditional practice of listing the oldest meaning first. *The American Heritage Dictionary* has thorough guidance on usage and extensive notes on synonyms. It lists biographical and geographical names in a separate section. Its introductory material contains essays on language, culture, and usage, as well as sections on grammar, spelling, and pronunciation.

Random House College Dictionary, revised edition, has more than 173,000 entries. It gives a word's most common definition first and has full synonymies. It includes recent technical words and is generously illustrated. Its introductory section presents essays on usage, dialects, and functional varieties of English; its appendixes include a style manual.

twelve to fifteen hours a day, with the help of his eleven children, Murray had, by 1894, completed sections A, B, C, and D, whereupon the work was first called *The Oxford English Dictionary.* Murray died in 1915 with a sixth of the work unfinished. The completed dictionary emerged in 1928 after 70 years of work by a series of devoted researchers. Since that time four supplements to the original work have been published.

The new edition combines the original *OED* and the supplements, which add 5,000 new words as well as revised, corrected, and updated information. Revision will continue, and new supplements will appear as time goes on. Meanwhile, the first edition is now available in a CD-ROM (Compact Disk—Read Only Memory) version that presents not only the full text of the *OED,* but also eight indexes that cover such matters as etymology and quotations. Work on a CD-ROM for the second edition is underway.

EXTRA EXERCISE B

List two synonyms for each of the following words. On the basis of information that you can find about them in a dictionary, explain the differences between the pairs of synonyms.

1. indulge
2. egotism
3. lazy
4. fame
5. friendly
6. frugal
7. red
8. good
9. govern
10. industry

EXTRA EXERCISE C

Write an explanation of the organization of your dictionary for someone who has never used it. Be sure to include all the different types of information it presents, a description of the order in which that information appears, and an evaluation of the relative ease or difficulty with which one can find that information.

4 | Knowing about specialized dictionaries of English

A specialized dictionary focuses on a single area, such as slang, word origins, synonyms, antonyms, usage, or almost any other aspect of language.

SPECIALIZED DICTIONARIES

SYNONYMS	*New Roget's Thesaurus of the English Language in Dictionary Form*
SLANG	*Dictionary of Slang and Unconventional English,* ed. Eric Partridge
	Dictionary of American Slang, ed. Harold Wentworth and Stuart Berg Flexner [out of print, but available in many libraries]
	The Thesaurus of Slang, by Esther Lewin and Albert E. Lewin.
ETYMOLOGIES	*Dictionary of Word and Phrase Origins,* ed. William Morris and Mary Morris
	Origins: A Short Etymological Dictionary of Modern English, ed. Eric Partridge [out of print, but available in many libraries]
USAGE	*Modern American Usage,* ed. Jacques Barzun
REGIONALISMS	*Dictionary of American Regional English,* ed. Frederic Cassidy

20b | Choosing exact words

The English language offers you a wealth of words to choose among as a writer. **Diction**—choice of words—affects the clarity and impact of the message you want your sentences to deliver. To be successful at choosing exact words for each particular context in your writing, you need to understand the denotation and connotation of words (20b-1) and to understand the relation between specific, concrete language and general, abstract language (20b-2).

1   Understanding denotation and connotation

Denotation is the explicit dictionary meaning of a word—its definition. When you look up a new word in the dictionary to find out what it means, you are looking for its denotation. For example, the denotation of the word *semester* is "a period of time of about eighteen weeks that makes up part of a school or college year."

Readers expect words to be used according to their established meanings for their established functions. Exactness is essential. Thus dangers, as well as benefits and pleasures, arise when you use a thesaurus or dictionary of synonyms. Be aware that subtle shades of meaning differentiate words with the same general definitions. These small differences in meaning allow you to be very precise in choosing just the right word, but they also oblige you to make sure you know what meanings your words convey. For instance, describing a person famous for praiseworthy achievements in public life as *notorious* would be wrong. Although *notorious* means "well-known" and "publicly discussed"—which famous people are likely to be—*notorious* also carries the meaning "unfavorably known or talked about." George Washington is *famous,* not *notorious.* Al Capone, on the other hand, is *notorious.*

Here is another example. *Obdurate* means "not easily moved to pity or sympathy," and its synonyms include "inflexible, obstinate, stubborn, hardened." You could correctly use *obdurate* in sentences like the following:

YES   The supervisor remained *obdurate* in refusing to accept excuses.

YES   My roommates, *obdurate* people who are unwilling to compromise, want me to get rid of my pet boa constrictor.

The synonym *hardened* for *obdurate,* however, might prompt someone unfamiliar with *obdurate* to use the word incorrectly.

No   Footprints showed in the *obdurate* concrete.

Here is a final example of the importance of explicit meaning. Suppose a writer who is describing a mine shaft has used the word *deep* several times. Searching for a synonym, the writer consults a thesaurus and finds, among other alternatives for *deep*, the word *profound.* The writer then states: "Shaft 4, outside Woodville, is the most profound in the state." *Profound* means "deep" in reference to thoughts or ideas; it cannot be used in reference to a mine shaft.

lore journals, regional publications, diaries and other materials in library archives, records of folk speech, historical dictionaries, and linguistic atlases.

Astonishingly, Cassidy chose to go beyond the written word, and the *DARE* benefits from five years of original fieldwork aimed at finding out how people speak in their daily lives. Eighty-two trained fieldworkers, most of them graduate students in linguistics or the history of English, went across the United States conducting personal interviews.

The 2,777 informants represented 1,002 communities across the United States. The informants were chosen to create a balance of male and female, city and country, black and white, North and South. However, in order to preserve vanishing words, about two-thirds of the informants were 60 years old or older. Each questionnaire contained 1,847 questions. One questionnaire was filled in for each community. In some cases, one informant answered all the questions; in others, the questions were divided among a number of informants. The fieldworkers also brought back 1,843 tape recordings of conversations: a total of 2 million oral responses and 900 hours of tape recordings.

EXTRA EXERCISE D

Be prepared to discuss differences in the connotations of the following pairs of words.

1. passive–shy
2. giggle–snicker
3. buddy–cohort
4. brave–foolhardy
5. wise–intelligent
6. economical–miserly
7. aggressive–assertive
8. cook–chef
9. hairdresser–beautician
10. violinist–fiddler

Connotation refers to the ideas implied, but not directly indicated, by a word. Connotations convey associations as emotional overtones beyond a word's direct, explicit definition. For example, the word *home* probably evokes more emotion than does its denotation, "a dwelling place," and its synonym *house*. *Home* may have very pleasant connotations of warmth, security, the love of family. Or *home* may have unpleasant connotations of an institution for elderly or disabled people. Experienced writers understand the additional layer of meaning connotations deliver. Connotations are never completely fixed, for the associations to a word often are individual. Still, people can communicate effectively because most words have relatively stable connotations and denotations in most contexts.

Being sensitive to the differences between a word's denotation and connotation is essential for critical thinking. Critical thinkers must first consider material at its literal level (5b-1). Doing so calls for dealing with the denotation of words. Next, critical thinkers must move to the inferential level (5b-2)—to what is implied, although not explicitly stated. Here the connotations of words often carry the message.

COMPARING DENOTATION AND CONNOTATION		
SAMPLE WORD	**DENOTATION**	**CONNOTATION**
ADDITIVE	an added substance	in food, a preservative, but perhaps also harmful to health
CHEAP	inexpensive	of products, low quality; of people, stingy
NUCLEAR ACCIDENT	unintentional meltdown of fuel rods in nuclear reactor	release of dangerous radiation; possibility of imminent death or eventual cancer; poisoning of food chain

EXERCISE 4

Separate the words in each set of words into one of three groups: *Neutral* if you think the word has no connotations; *Positive* if you think it has good connotations; *Negative* if you think it has bad connotations.

428

ww, wc **20b**

EXAMPLE   alibi, excuse, pretext, reason, explanation

>   *Positive:* explanation; *Neutral:* reason; *Negative:* alibi, pretext, excuse

1. fat, fleshy, stout, portly, rotund, chubby, plump, obese, corpulent, heavy, paunchy, overweight, rolypoly, large-sized.
2. thin, lean, lanky, skinny, gaunt, scrawny, rawboned, slender, slim, slight, skin and bones.
3. teacher, lecturer, instructor, professor, pedant, pedagogue, mentor, scholar, educator.
4. politician, lawmaker, senator, representative, leader, demagogue, rabble-rouser.
5. loyal, dedicated, devoted, determined, stubborn, firm, unyielding.

 2   **Using specific and concrete language to bring life to general and abstract language**

Specific words identify individual items in a group *(Oldsmobile, Honda, Ford)*. **General** words relate to an overall group *(car)*. **Concrete** words identify persons and things that can be perceived by the senses—seen, heard, tasted, felt, smelled (the *black padded vinyl dashboard* of my car). **Abstract** words denote qualities, concepts, relationships, acts, conditions, ideas *(transportation)*.

As a writer, you need to choose words suitable for your writing purpose (1b) and your audience (1c). Usually, specific and concrete words bring life to general and abstract words. Whenever you choose general and abstract words, be sure to supply enough specific, concrete details and examples to illustrate effectively your generalizations and abstractions. Consider how sentences with general words come to life when they are revised with words that refer to specifics.

GENERAL	My car has a great deal of power, and it is very quick.
SPECIFIC	My Trans Am with 220 horsepower can go from zero to fifty in six seconds.
GENERAL	The car gets good gas mileage.
SPECIFIC	The Dodge Lancer gets about 35 mpg on the highway and 30 mpg in the city.
GENERAL	Her car is comfortable and easy to drive.
SPECIFIC	When she drives her new Buick Regal on a five-hour trip, she arrives refreshed and does not need a long nap to recover, as she did when she drove her ten-year-old Upusho.

ANSWERS: EXERCISE 4

The response to this exercise is likely to elicit much debate, given that shades of connotative meaning are often fairly personal. The list below is the result of a poll of the students in a half dozen classes; some votes were very close.

1. *Positive:* portly; *Neutral:* rotund, large-sized, overweight; *Negative:* fat, fleshy, stout, chubby, plump, obese, corpulent, heavy, paunchy, roly-poly

2. *Positive:* lean, lanky, slender, slim; *Neutral:* thin, slight; *Negative:* skinny, gaunt, scrawny, rawboned, skin and bones

3. *Positive:* mentor, scholar, educator; *Neutral:* teacher, lecturer, instructor, professor; *Negative:* pedant, pedagogue

4. *Positive:* senator, representative, leader; *Neutral:* politician, lawmaker; *Negative:* demagogue, rabble-rouser

5. *Positive:* loyal, dedicated, devoted, determined; *Neutral:* firm; *Negative:* stubborn, unyielding

Specific language is not always preferable to general language, and concrete language is not always preferable to abstract language. Effective writing usually combines them. In the following sentences from an essay comparing cars, the combination works effectively.

GENERAL AND SPECIFIC COMBINED

GENERAL   SPECIFIC   SPECIFIC   ABSTRACT
My car, a **220-horsepower Trans Am,** is **quick.** It accelerates

     SPECIFIC   SPECIFIC
from **0 to 50** miles per hour in **6 seconds**—but it gets only

     SPECIFIC   SPECIFIC
18 miles per gallon. The **Dodge Lancer,** on the other hand, gets

ABSTRACT   GENERAL   SPECIFIC   GENERAL
very good gas **mileage:** about **35 mpg** in **highway driving** and

SPECIFIC   SPECIFIC   GENERAL
30 mpg in **stop-and-go driving conditions.**

In being specific and concrete, do not overdo it. If you want to inform a nonspecialist reader about possible automobile fuels other than gasoline, *do* name the fuels and be very specific about their advantages and drawbacks. *Do not,* however, go into a detailed, highly technical discussion of the chemical profiles of the fuels. Always base your choices on an awareness of your purpose and audience.

EXERCISE 5

Revise the following paragraph by providing specific and concrete words to explain and enliven the general and abstract words.

I enjoy good food. I do not like to eat greasy foods or foods made with more artificial ingredients than real ones. To me, good food starts with sweet, delicious desserts. I am also fond of many ethnic dishes. Bread is one of my other favorites. As long as I watch my weight, I can look forward to years of pleasure from good food.

20c   Increasing your vocabulary

The benefits of increasing your vocabulary are many. The more words you know, the more easily and the faster you can read. A large, rich vocabulary also helps you understand ideas and communicate them clearly and effectively in your writing. Knowing prefixes and suffixes (20c-1) and using context clues (20c-2) are two ways you can build your vocabulary.

ANSWERS: EXERCISE 5

Because of the many possibilities for re-wording posed by this exercise, the answers are likely to vary widely. Students may enjoy comparing the different choices they have made. The important principle for revision is that the new versions should have a high degree of specificity and concreteness.

TECHNIQUES FOR BUILDING YOUR VOCABULARY

1. Using a highlighter pen, mark all unfamiliar words in your textbooks and other reading material you own. Then define the words in the margin so you can study the meaning in context. Use context clues (20c-2) to figure out definitions, or look up the words in a dictionary. Write each word and its definitions on an index card or in a special notebook.

2. Listen carefully to learn how speakers use the language. Jot down new words. Later look them up, and write each word and its definitions on an index card or in a special notebook.

3. Select words to study each week. Put the date next to the word on your cards or in your notebook so that you have a record of your goals. If you have too many words to study in a week, choose first the ones you see or hear most frequently. Whenever you look up a word, put a small checkmark next to the definition—if you are using your own dictionary. When you accumulate three or more checkmarks next to a word, it is time to learn that word.

4. Set aside time each day to study the new words. You can carry your cards or notebook in your pocket to study in spare moments during the day.

5. Use mnemonics to help you memorize words (see 22b-2). Set a goal of learning eight to ten new words a week. *Use the words in your writing and, when possible, in conversation.*

6. Every few weeks go back to the words from the previous weeks. Make a list of any words you still have not learned well. Study them again, and *use* them.

---

1   Knowing prefixes and suffixes

Prefixes are syllables in front of a **root** word that modify its meaning. *Ante-* (before) placed before the root *bellum* (war) gives *antebellum,* which means "before the war." *Antebellum* refers to the time before the Civil War. **Suffixes** are syllables added to the end of a root word that modify its meaning. For example, *excite* (formed by adding the prefix *ex-,* "out," to the past participle of *cierce,* "to summon") has the various forms of adjective, adverb, and noun when suffixes are added: *excited, exciting, excitedly, excitement.* A word's part of speech is often signaled by the suffix.

TEACHING TIP

Knowledge of prefixes and suffixes can help students figure out the meaning of many words. If this skill is coupled with the ability to recognize root words, however, many students' power to decipher new words can increase dramatically. Fundamentally, a root word is a base to which prefixes and suffixes can be added. For example, *-graph* (from the Greek *-graphos,* "to write") refers to something that writes or records, such as a *telegraph* or *graphite,* or something written, such as a *paragraph* or the *graphic arts; graphology* is the study of handwriting.

Here are a few of the most common Greek and Latin roots, their meanings, and a sample word built from each root.

LATIN

aequs	equal (equivalent)
amare, amatum	to love (amiable)
dicere, dictum	to say, to speak (diction)
manus	hand (manuscript)
omnis	all (omnipotent)
portare, portatum	to carry (porter)
scribere, scriptum	to write (scribble)
sentire, sensum	to feel (sense)
spirare, spiratum	to breathe (inspiration)
verbum	word (verb)

GREEK

bios	life (biology)
chronos	time (chronology)
gamos	marriage (bigamy)
geo-	earth (geology)
krates (-crat)	member of a group (democrat)
metron	to measure (thermometer)
pathos	suffering, feeling (sympathy)
phobos	fear (agoraphobia)
photos	light (photograph)
podos	foot (tripod)

Roots are the central parts of words, to which prefixes and suffixes are added. Once you know, for example, the Latin root *bene* ("well, good"), you can decipher various forms: **bene**factor, **bene**diction, **bene**ficial, **bene**ficiary, **bene**volent, **bene**fit, **ben**ign.

Knowing common prefixes and suffixes is an excellent way to learn to decode unfamiliar words and increase your vocabulary.

PREFIXES		
PREFIX	**MEANING**	**EXAMPLE**
ante-	before	*antebellum*
anti-	against	*antiballistic*
auto-	self	*autobiography*
contra-	against	*contradict*
dis-	not	*disagree*
extra-	more	*extraordinary*
hyper-	more	*hyperactive*
il-	not	*illegal*
im-	not	*immoral*
in-	not	*inadequate*
inter-	between	*interpersonal*
intra-	inside	*intravenous*
ir-	not	*irresponsible*
mal-	poor	*malnutrition*
mis-	not	*misunderstood*
mono-	one	*monopoly*
non-	not	*noninvolvement*
poly-	many	*polygamy*
post-	after	*postscript*
pre-	before	*prehistoric*
re-	back	*return*
retro-	back	*retroactive*
semi-	half	*semicircle*
sub-	under	*submissive*
super	more	*supernatural*
trans-	across	*transportation*
ultra-	more	*ultraconservative*
un-	not	*unhappy*
uni-	one	*uniform*

SUFFIXES		
NOUNS		
Suffix	**Meaning**	**Example**
-dom	state of	*freedom*
-hood	state of	*childhood*
-ness	state of	*kindness*
-ship	state of	*friendship*
-tion	act of	*integration*
-tude	state of	*solitude*
VERBS		
Suffix	**Meaning**	**Example**
-ate	to make	*integrate*
-ify	to make	*unify*
-ize	to make	*computerize*
ADJECTIVES		
Suffix	**Meaning**	**Example**
-able	able to be	*comfortable*
-ate	full of	*fortunate*
-ible	able to be	*compatible*
-ful	full of	*tactful*
-less	without	*penniless*
-ous	full of	*pompous*
-y	full of	*gloomy*

EXERCISE 6

Add a prefix to each italicized word to match the definition given. Consult a dictionary if necessary.

EXAMPLE   not *happy* = *unhappy*

1. not *logical*
2. excessively *sensitive*
3. against the *freeze*
4. *existing* before
5. *consider* again

ANSWERS: EXERCISE 7

1. happiness
2. flirtation
3. roomy
4. agreeable
5. beautify

COVERAGE: EXERCISE 7

1. -ness (noun)
2. -tion (noun)
3. -y (adjective)
4. -able (adjective)
5. -ify (verb)

EXTRA EXERCISE G

Working in groups and without a dictionary, compile a list of as many words as you can think of that end with the suffixes in the accompanying chart. What does the suffix tell you about the meaning of each word?

EXERCISE 7

Add a suffix to each italicized word to match the definition given. Notice that you will be changing the form of the word to match the exact definition.

EXAMPLE   state of being *lazy* = laziness

1. state of being *happy*
2. act of *flirting*
3. full of *room*
4. able to *agree*
5. to make *beautiful*

2 **Using context clues to figure out word meanings**

The familiar words that surround an unknown word can give you hints about the new word's meaning. Such **context clues** include four main types.

1. **Restatement context clue:** You can figure out an unknown word when a word you know repeats the meaning: *He jumped into the* fray *and enjoyed every minute of the fight. Fray* means "fight." The restatement may be set off with punctuation, such as commas, dashes, or parentheses: Et al. *("and others") is used in a bibliography to indicate other authors of a work.* But often a restatement is not set off: Et al. *indicates that other authors' names have been omitted.*

2. **Contrast context clue:** You can figure out an unknown word when an opposite or contrast is presented: *We feared that the new prime minister would be a* menace *to society, but she turned out to be a great peacemaker. Menace* means "threat." The explanatory contrast is *but she turned out to be a great peacemaker.*

3. **Example context clue:** You can figure out an unfamiliar word when an example or illustration relating to the word is given: *They were* conscientious *workers, making sure that everything was done correctly and precisely. Conscientious* means "motivated by a desire to do what is right." You can get close to that definition with "done correctly and precisely."

4. **General sense context clue:** An entire passage can convey a general sense of particular difficult words. For example, in *Nearly forty million Americans are overweight; obesity has become an epidemic,* you can deduce that *epidemic* refers to something happening to many people.

Sometimes a "general sense context clue" will not make clear a word's exact denotation. In the example in clue 4 above, for instance, you might guess that *epidemic* indicates a widespread threat, but you might miss the connection of the word *epidemic* with the concept of disease. Interpreting a word's meaning from the general sense of a passage can allow subtle variations that distinguish one word from another to slip by. When you believe, therefore, that you have deciphered a meaning by using context clues, check the exact definition in a dictionary. Then add the word to your vocabulary.

QUOTATION ABOUT WRITING

For your born writer, nothing is so healing as the realization that he [or she] has come upon the right word.

—Catherine Drinker Bowen

21 Understanding the Effect of Words

QUOTATION ABOUT WRITING

Appropriate words are like appropriate clothes. Satin and silk don't work at a barbecue, and denim looks strange at the annual arts ball.

—Jane F. Bonin

EXTRA EXERCISE A

After analyzing the sentences that follow, decide if they are in formal, medium, or informal language. Which words are particularly effective in establishing the level of usage in the sentence?

1. Weather forecasting is a pretty good field to be in.

2. My old man watches the TV weather news every morning.

3. It takes a lot of work to put a forecast together.

4. The Weather Bureau collects data from reporting stations that, after analysis, are reported to the public as forecasts, weather maps, and storm warnings.

5. The Bureau conducts research on a variety of topics from solar radiation and the ozone layer to snowfall patterns.

6. My father just wants to know if it's going to rain.

Words do not exist in a vacuum. They communicate meaning and so have an effect on the people reading or hearing them. As a writer, you want to use words carefully for their correct meaning (Chapter 20) and for their effect.

Using words well for their effect depends on making good choices. Sometimes the choices are either right or wrong, but often the choices are subtler. Your awareness of your purpose in writing, your audience, and the situation in which you are writing should influence your choice of words. Your choice of words affects the **tone** of your writing. A casual tone is fine for a letter to a friend but inappropriate for an essay written for a college course. A humorous tone might be fine for an essay about the time you wore an unmatched pair of shoes to an interview, but a serious tone would be needed in your letter of application for a job.

GUIDELINES FOR EFFECTIVE USE OF LANGUAGE

1. Use proper level of formality (21a-1).
2. Use edited American English (21a-2).
3. Avoid slang or inappropriate colloquial words or regional words (21a-3).
4. Avoid slanted language (21a-4).
5. Avoid sexist language (21b).
6. Use figurative language appropriately (21c).
7. Avoid clichés (21d).
8. Avoid artificial language (21e).

21a Using appropriate language

As a writer, you need to pay special attention to **diction**—choice of words. You need to make certain that the words you use will communicate your meaning as clearly and effectively as possible. As you choose your words, be aware of their connotations and denotations (see 20b). Also, your word choice should be appropriate for your purpose (see 1b) and audience (see 1c).

1 Using appropriate levels of formality

Informal and highly formal levels of writing differ clearly in **tone.** They use different vocabulary and sentence structures. Tone in writing indicates the attitude of the writer toward the subject and toward the audience. Tone may be highly formal, informal, or somewhere in between. Different tones are appropriate for different audiences, different subjects, and different purposes. An informal tone occurs in casual conversation or letters to friends. A highly formal tone, in contrast, occurs in sermons and proclamations, treatises, and treaties.

Informal language, which creates an informal tone, may include slang, colloquialisms, and regionalisms (see 21a-3). In addition, informal writing often includes sentence fragments, contractions, and other forms that approximate casual speech. **Medium** language level uses general English—not too casual, not too scholarly. Unlike informal language, medium-level language is acceptable for academic writing. This level uses standard vocabulary (for example, *learn* instead of *wise-up*), conventional sentence structure, and few or no contractions. A **highly formal** language level uses a multisyllabic Latinate vocabulary *(edify* instead of *learn)* and often stylistic flourishes such as extended or complex figures of speech. Academic writing, along with most writing for general audiences, should range from medium to somewhat formal levels of language.

INFORMAL	Ya know stars? They're a gas!
MEDIUM	Gas clouds slowly changed into stars.
FORMAL	The condensations of gas spun their slow gravitational pirouettes, slowly transmogrifying gas cloud into star.

—Carl Sagan, "Starfolk: A Fable"

7. I can't get into all that stuff either.

8. You gotta admit that the Bureau has done plenty of good things.

9. In 1942 Dr. F. W. Reichelderfer was the recipient of a prestigious award for his pioneering work in advancing the practice of meteorology as applied to aeronautics.

10. Back in the 1940s the Bureau started a humongous project to study thunderstorms.

EXTRA EXERCISE B

Rewrite the following advertisements so that they conform to edited American English.

1. Quite simply, Hartmann is dedicated to building the best case. With the best leathers. The best tweed. The best vinyl. And the best locks. Hartmann. No one builds a better a case.

—Hartmann Luggage
The New Yorker, May 29, 1989

2. Selling off the work of a lifetime to pay estate taxes is unnecessary. But planning is key. Planning and creativity. Our agents may go by the book when setting up an estate plan. But chances are they wrote a few of the chapters, too. That's blue chip advice.

—Connecticut Mutual Life Insurance
Company, An Alliance of Blue Chip
Companies
The New Yorker, May 29, 1989

3. Drive somebody else's sports car. Any sports car. We don't think you'll find one that gives you what the RX-7 Turbo does. Not even one that costs thousands more. That's because Mazda engineers do more than make the RX-7 look and perform like a world-class sports car. They engineer the RX-7 so it feels as if it's an extension of you; almost as if you and the car are one, sweeping through turns, leveling hills, devouring miles. And that's a difference you'll be able to feel the first time you drive one. Go feel it for yourself. This afternoon.

—Mazda
The New Yorker, May 29, 1989

4. When you're travelling it's reassuring to know you can rely on a perfectly coordinated flight schedule. Carefully devised to allow for time differences at each destination, with no-wait connections, at convenient times. Ensuring you can make the most of your day.

Iberia, Airlines of Spain
The New Yorker, June 19, 1989

5. There's only one thing we can be absolutely sure the future will bring. Change.

INFORMAL	Basically, we're ex-chimps.
MEDIUM	The human race's genes evolved like those of other reproducing things on earth.
FORMAL	And then one day there came to be a creature whose genetic material was in no major way different from the self-replicating molecular collectives of any of the other organisms on his planet, which he called Earth.

—CARL SAGAN, "Starfolk: A Fable"

The informal examples would be appropriate in a letter to a close friend or in a journal; the writer's attitude toward the subject is playful and humorous. Word choice and sentence structure assume great familiarity between writer and audience. The medium examples would be appropriate in most academic and professional situations. It is easy to imagine an instructor as the audience for these sentences; the writer's attitude toward the subject is serious and straightforward. The formal examples are addressed to an audience with considerable interest in and knowledge of scientific phenomena—perhaps readers of a science journal or magazine.

2 Using edited American English for academic writing

The language standards you are expected to use in academic writing are those of **edited American English**—the accepted written language of a book like this handbook or a magazine like *Newsweek* or *The Atlantic.* Such language conforms to widely established rules of grammar, sentence structure, punctuation, and spelling. Because advertising language and other language intended to reach and sway a large audience often ignores conventional usage, you do encounter English that varies from the standard. Do not let these published departures from edited American English influence you into believing they are acceptable in academic writing.

Edited English is not a fancy dialect for the elite; it is a practical form of the language that most educated people use. As a student writer, you might find that early drafts of your essays contain language that departs from edited American English. Do not worry about this too early in the writing process. Get your ideas down on paper. Then revise your writing (see 3c–3e) so that your final drafts are in edited American English. When you use edited American English in your academic writing, you will not risk distracting your readers from the message you want to communicate.

_ww, wc_ 21a

<table>
<tr><td>3</td><td>

Avoiding slang and colloquial or regional language for most academic writing

</td></tr>
</table>

Slang consists of coined words and new or extended meanings attached to established terms. Slang words and phrases usually pass out of use quickly. Occasionally slang terms become accepted into standard usage. **Colloquial** language is characteristic of casual conversation and informal writing: *The student flunked chemistry* instead of *the student failed chemistry.* **Regional (dialectal) language** is specific to some geographic areas: *They have nary a cent.*

Although slang and colloquial words and regional language are neither substandard nor illiterate, they are not appropriate for academic writing. Replacing slang, colloquial, and regional language with general English in your college writing allows you to communicate clearly with the large number of people who speak and write in medium or somewhat formal levels of language. Slang, colloquial, and regional expressions can have a place in narratives in which you describe the exact speech of individuals, however.

Slang words are used only in very informal situations. Sometimes slang terms are inventions: *hippie* from the 1960s and its 1980s counterpart *yuppie* are examples. Sometimes slang terms are redefinitions of existing words. For example, *awesome* has been used informally for "excellent" or "wonderful" as has *wired* for "nervous." Slang varies according to time and place. For example, slang in New York City in the mid-1980s included *chill out* for "relax, be cool," *say what?* for "excuse me?" *box* for "radio," and *gear* for "stylish clothing." These expressions might not have communicated the same meanings to teenagers in California in the mid-1980s or to teenagers anywhere by 1990. And they certainly would not communicate accurate meanings in an academic paper or business report at any time or place. Slang is fun, informal, and personal; it rarely has a place in writing for college.

Dialects are different from slang because dialectical differences reflect geographical regions and socioeconomic status. Although no regional or social dialect can be designated as the one "correct" form of a language, dialects spoken by educated people usually hold the attention of educated people more than do the speech patterns of others. Using a dialect when writing for the general reading public tends to shut some people out of the communication. One way to assess the appropriateness of dialect is to remember that the best form of language is that which clearly communicates to a given audience for a specific purpose. Except when dialect is the topic of the writing, academic writing rarely accommodates dialect well.

The ups, downs, twists and turns that stand in the way of achieving your financial goals. At Merrill Lynch, we know change. We've understood it, managed it and turned it to our clients' advantage for over 70 years. And they've come to trust our ability to deal with it.

—Merrill Lynch
The New Yorker, June 12, 1989

ANSWERS: EXTRA EXERCISE B

Answers to this exercise will vary, but in all cases sentences should be complete and slang should be recast.

QUOTATION ABOUT WRITING

Slang helps define a student's identity, distinguishing him or her from the faculty and community at large, while making school life feel less forbidding and more familiar.

—Nicolai Duroussoff, "If It's 'Rad,'
It's Campus Slang"
New York Times, April 12, 1987

TEACHING TIP

Because language varies from one geographic area to another, students who have lived in several different parts of the country often know expressions that are used in one region but not in another. Other members of a class may find it interesting to hear some of those regionalisms, afterwards compiling a list of words and phrases peculiar to their own area.

TEACHING TIP

Discussions about slanted language make students more aware of biased writing. A logical follow-up assignment is to ask them to be alert to loaded diction in news articles and television broadcasts. Examples are particularly abundant during an election year. The words and phrases students collect can be the basis of another lesson, this one specific and close to home.

TEACHING TIP

If you have any doubts about whether encouraging nonsexist language is worth the effort, consider this passage from the introduction to "Guidelines for Nonsexist Use of Language in NCTE [National Council of Teachers of English] Publications":

> "Sexism" may be defined as words or actions that arbitrarily assign roles or characteristics to people on the basis of sex. Originally used to refer to practices that discriminated against women, the term now includes any usage that unfairly delimits the aspirations or attributes of either sex. Neither men nor women can reach their full potential when men are conditioned to be only aggressive, analytical, and active and women are conditioned to be only submissive, emotional, and passive. The man who cannot cry and the woman who cannot command are equally victims of their socialization.
>
> Language plays a central role in socialization, for it helps teach children the roles that are expected of them. Through language, children conceptualize their ideas and feelings about themselves and their world. Thought and action are reflected in words, and words in turn condition how a person thinks and acts. Eliminating sexist language will not eliminate sexist conduct, but as the language is liberated from sexist usages and assumptions, women and men will begin to share more equal, active, caring roles.

4   Avoiding slanted language

To communicate clearly, you need to choose words that convince your audience of your fairness as a writer. When you are writing about a subject on which you hold strong opinions, it is easy to slip into biased or emotionally loaded language. Such **slanted language** usually does not convince a careful reader to agree with your point. Instead, it makes the reader wary or hostile. For example, suppose you are arguing against the practice of scientific experimentation on animals. If you use language such as "laboratory Frankensteins" who "routinely and viciously maim helpless kittens and puppies," you are using slanted language. A neutral audience will doubt your ability to write fairly about the subject. Especially in writing argument (see Chapter 6), you want to use words that make your side of an issue the more convincing one. Once you start using slanted, biased language, readers feel manipulated rather than reasoned with. Only those who already agree with you will be convinced. Those who disagree will be annoyed. And those who might have been persuaded will easily think of rebuttals to your unfair, slanted choice of words.

21b   Avoiding sexist language

Sexist language assigns roles or characteristics to people on the basis of sex. Such practices unfairly limit or discriminate against both sexes. Sexist language inaccurately assumes all nurses and homemakers are female (and therefore refers to them as "she") and all physicians and wage earners are male (and therefore refers to them as "he"). One of the most widespread occurrences of sexist language is the use of the pronoun *he* to refer to someone of unidentified sex. Although tradition holds that *he* is correct in such situations, using only masculine pronouns to represent the human species excludes females—a distortion of reality.

If you want to avoid sexist language in your writing, follow the guidelines in the chart on the next page. Also, you can avoid sexism by not lapsing into demeaning, outdated stereotypes, such as *women are bad drivers* or *men are bad cooks*. Do not describe a woman by her looks, clothes, or age (unless you do the same for men). Do not use the first name of a wife when you use only the last name of the husband (*Mr. Miller* [should be *Phil Miller*] *and his wife Jeannette were interviewed by the press.*). Do not use *girls* to refer to adult females (*The girls* [should be *women*] *went to Paris*).

HOW TO AVOID SEXIST LANGUAGE

1. Avoid using only the masculine pronoun to refer to males and females together. Use a pair of pronouns.

   No A doctor cannot read much outside **his** specialty.

   Yes A doctor cannot read much outside **his or her** specialty.

   The "he or she" construction acts as a singular pronoun, and it therefore calls for a singular verb when it serves as the subject of a sentence. Try to avoid using the "he or she" construction in several consecutive sentences. Revising into the plural may be a better solution.

   No A successful doctor knows that **he** has to work long hours.

   Yes Successful doctors know that **they** have to work long hours.

   You may also recast a sentence to omit the gender-specific pronoun.

   No Everyone hopes that **he** will win the scholarship.

   Yes Everyone hopes to win the scholarship.

2. Avoid the use of *man* when men and women are clearly intended in the meaning.

   No **Man** is a social animal.

   Yes **People** are social animals.

   No A **man's** best friend is a dog.

   Yes A **person's** best friend is a dog.

3. Avoid stereotyping jobs and roles by gender when men and women are included.

No	**Yes**
chairman	chair, chairperson
policeman	police officer
businessman	businessperson, business executive
statesman	diplomat, prime minister, statesperson

   No teacher . . . **she;** principal . . . **he**

   Yes teachers . . . **they;** principals . . . **they**

   (continued on next page)

TEACHING TIP

In addition to the techniques given in the chart How to Avoid Sexist Language, here are a few additional tactics.

1. When appropriate, use the first person or the second person.

   NO A person should always keep an eye on his luggage in airports.

   YES I should always keep my eye on my luggage in airports.

   YES We should always keep an eye on our luggage in airports.

   YES Keep an eye on your luggage in airports.

2. Repeat a noun or use a synonym in place of the troublesome pronoun.

   NO A preoccupied traveler is an easy target for thieves, who can pick his pocket in a second.

   YES A preoccupied traveler is an easy target for thieves, who pick a traveler's pocket in a second.

   YES A preoccupied traveler is an easy target for thieves, who can pick a tourist's pocket in a second.

3. Use *who.*

   NO A traveler has little to worry about, if he stays alert.

   YES A traveler who stays alert has little to worry about.

How does a violinist get to Carnegie Hall? Practice, practice, practice. How does a writer get a publication? Revise, revise, revise.

—Kathy Rugoff

ANSWERS: EXERCISE 1

Answers to this exercise will vary. Some acceptable responses follow.

1. Everyone enrolled in the program expects that he or she will enter a good college or university.

2. The doctor had to perform an emergency operation.

3. Effective businesspersons understand the needs of their staff members.

4. Almost all lawyers say that they enjoy selecting jury members.

5. People are their own worst enemies.

6. All the secretaries said they would work overtime if the boss needed them.

7. The glorification of war has led to many of humanity's greatest disasters.

8. The department chairperson promised that the assistant would schedule an appointment for later that week.

9. The teacher has to prepare the lessons, and the principal has to submit the teacher evaluations to the board of education.

10. By nature and temperament, people like to learn and to master new skills.

HOW TO AVOID SEXIST LANGUAGE *(continued)*

4.   Avoid expressions that exclude one sex.

No	Yes
mankind	humanity
the common man	the average person
man-sized sandwich	huge sandwich
old wives' tale	superstition

5.   Avoid using demeaning and patronizing labels.

No	Yes
lady lawyer	lawyer
male nurse	nurse
gal Friday	assistant
career girl	professional woman
coed	student

No   My **girl** will help you.

Yes   My ~~secretary~~ will help you.

   Jane Baumann will help you.

EXERCISE 1

Revise the following sentences, changing sexist language to nonsexist language.

1.   Everyone enrolled in the program expects that he will enter a good college or university.

2.   The lady doctor had to perform an emergency operation.

3.   An effective businessman understands the needs of his staff members.

4.   Almost every lawyer says that he enjoys selecting jury members.

5.   Man is his own worst enemy.

6.   Every secretary said she would work overtime if the boss said that he needed her to.

7.   The glorification of war has led to many of mankind's greatest disasters.

8.   The department chairman promised that his girl would schedule an appointment for later that week.

9.   The teacher has to prepare her lessons, and the principal has to submit his teacher evaluations to the board of education.

10.   By nature and temperament, man likes to learn and to master new skills.

21c Using figurative language

Figures of speech use words for more than their literal meanings. Figurative language creates comparisons and connections that use one idea or image to enhance or explain another.

TYPES OF FIGURATIVE LANGUAGE

Analogy: a comparison of similar traits between dissimilar things (An analogy may extend for several sentences.)

> A cheetah sprinting across the dry plains after its prey, the base runner dashed for home plate, his cleats kicking up dust.

Irony: the use of words to suggest the opposite of their usual sense

> Told that the car repair would cost $2,000 and take at least two weeks, she said, "Oh, that would be wonderful!"

Metaphor: a comparison between otherwise dissimilar things without using the word *like* or *as* (Be alert to avoid the error of a mixed metaphor, explained following this chart.)

> The rush-hour traffic bled out of all the city's major arteries.

Overstatement (also called *hyperbole*): deliberate exaggeration for emphasis

> If I don't get this paper in on time, the professor is going to kill me.

Personification: the assignment of a human trait to a nonhuman thing

> The book begged to be read.

Simile: a direct comparison between otherwise dissimilar things, using the word *like* or *as*

> Langston Hughes says that a deferred dream dries up like a raisin in the sun.

Understatement: deliberate restraint for emphasis

> It gets a little warm when the temperature reaches 105 degrees.

WORD DERIVATIONS

Metaphor comes from *metapherein* (Greek for "to transfer"), a combination of *pherein* ("to carry") and *meta* ("over"). A metaphor carries over the meaning. The first recorded use of the word in English was by Henry VIII in 1533: "And rather than men would note a lye when they know what is meant, they will sooner by allegory or metaphor draw the word to the truth."

Simile comes from *similis* (Latin for "like"). Similes always contain *like* or *as,* making the comparison explicit. *Simile* was first used in 1393 in William Langland's "Piers Plowman."

ANSWERS: EXERCISE 2

1. metaphor
2. mixed metaphor (change "like a clam snapping shut its shell" to "firmly" or another appropriate word or image)

A mixed metaphor combines images that do not work well together. Consider this sentence, for example: *Milking the migrant workers for all they were worth, the supervisors barked orders at them.* Here the initial image is of taking milk from a cow, but the final image has supervisors barking, an action suggesting dogs. Avoid confusing your reader by combining two or more images that do not work well together.

EXERCISE 2

Identify each figure of speech. Revise any mixed metaphors.

1. The challenger, another Goliath, fell with the first blow.
2. She went inside the house, shutting the door like a clam snapping shut its shell.
3. The ocean screamed its fury.
4. Triple bypass heart surgery is no tea party.
5. The champion was like a cobra ready to strike.
6. The individual bees worked together in the hive, the separate parts of a single, purposeful animal.
7. The world ended when his parents divorced.
8. The inventor's ideas took root and grew, seeds becoming flowers.
9. At night, the lights along the bridge's suspension cables looked like a giant diamond necklace mounted on black velvet in a celestial jewelry showcase.
10. Changing a flat tire is exactly how I love to spend my time.

21d Avoiding clichés

A **cliché** is an overused, worn-out expression that has lost its capacity to communicate effectively. Some comparisons, once clever, have grown trite: *dead as a doornail, gentle as a lamb, straight as an arrow.* If you have heard words over and over again, so has your reader. If you cannot think of a way to rephrase a cliché, delete the phrase entirely.

The word *cliché* is often used to describe both overused expressions and overused words. But a single word cannot really be a cliché, although it can become tiresome and trite. Such words are called **vogue words** by linguists. For a while you hear and see them everywhere; their use is a kind of fad. Like fads, vogue words soon lose their popularity, and then they once again take their place as useful, but not overused, terms. An example of a vogue word is *relevant,* which in the early 1970s was used to describe everything from school curricula to political party platforms. Occasionally a perfectly useful phrase will also enjoy a span of overpopularity and become a vogue phrase. For example, during the period following World War II "in our time"—perhaps echoing Chamberlain's ringing conviction that there would be "peace in our time"—became popular and was overused by the journalists and newscasters of that period. Now the phrase has receded to its former status, and a writer can use it without fear of being thought unoriginal.

The difference between a vogue phrase and a cliché is that although a vogue phrase can return to being a useful part of the language, a cliché cannot. The language loses its punch *(happily ever after, face the music, ripe old age),* and new ways of expressing the ideas are needed. Nevertheless, clichés are not created simply by being repeated or by becoming overly familiar. English is full of word groups that are very common and are frequently used, yet they do not become clichés: We can always say "up and down" and "in and out." Adjectives also fall into certain patterns. We usually say "a tiny blue book" rather than "a blue, tiny book." Common patterns are not clichés and so do not need to be avoided.

Proverbs are also often confused with clichés. Although both proverbs and clichés are used frequently, they are very different. Proverbs are lean and economical phrases that express a great deal with a few words. A true proverb cannot be shortened or edited. For example, "Don't count your chickens before they hatch" or "a stitch in time saves nine" communicates its message economically. A cliché, on the other hand, can easily be turned into a more direct expression. For instance, the cliché "keep your nose to the grindstone" is better expressed as "work hard." Proverbs rarely work well in academic writing, for they often take on the tone of a cliché. If you do decide to use a proverb, put it in quotation marks.

EXERCISE 3

Revise these clichés. Use the idea in each cliché for a sentence of your own in plain English.

1. If you want a sale, you have to take the bull by the horns.
2. You can't be shrinking violets when it comes to getting a sale.
3. Being aggressive means knocking the socks off prospective buyers with an impressive sales pitch.
4. To make customers as happy as a lark, give them a good product and good service.
5. Slowly but surely they realize that you are there to help them.

3. personification
4. understatement
5. simile
6. analogy
7. overstatement
8. metaphor
9. simile
10. irony

COVERAGE: EXERCISE 2

The exercise has examples of two metaphors, one mixed metaphor, one personification, one understatement, two similes, one analogy, one overstatement, and one irony.

ANSWERS: EXERCISE 3

Answers to this exercise will vary. Here is one set of possibilities.

1. If you want a sale, you have to take control of the situation.

2. You can't be shy when it comes to getting a sale.

3. Being aggressive means getting the attention of prospective buyers with an impressive sales presentation.

4. To make customers happy, give them a good product and good service.

5. Eventually they realize that you are there to help them.

21e   Avoiding artificial language

Sometimes a beginning writer thinks that using ornate words and complicated sentence structures makes writing impressive. Experienced writers work hard to communicate as clearly and directly as they can. As a student writer, avoid spending time looking for long, fancy words to explain a point. Instead, try to make what you write as accessible as possible to your readers. Extremely complex ideas or subject areas may require complex terms or phrases to explain them, but in general the simpler the language, the more likely it is to be understood.

1   Avoiding pretentious language

Pretentious language is too showy, calling undue attention to itself with complex sentences and polysyllabic words. Academic writing does not call for big words used for their own sake. Plain English that communicates clearly is far better than embellished English that makes the reader aware that you are trying to be "fancy" for no reason. Overblown words are likely to obscure your message. "The clearer, the better" is good advice.

> I hate it when he tries ostentatiously to flaunt his accoutrements recently acquired in the haberdashery shop. [*Translation:* I hate it when he tries to show off his new clothes.]
>
> The raison d'être for my matriculation in this institution of higher learning is the acquisition of a better education. [*Translation:* The reason I am in college is to get a better education.]

2   Avoiding unnecessary jargon

Jargon is specialized vocabulary of a particular group—words that an outsider unfamiliar with this field might not understand. As you write, consider your purpose (1b) and audience (1c) to decide whether a word is jargon in the context of your material. For example, a football fan easily understands a sportswriter's use of words such as *gridiron, sacked, TD,* and *safety,* but these words are jargon and would not be understood by people who are not familiar with football. Specialized language evolves in every field: professions, academic disciplines (see Chapters 35–38), commerce, and even hob-

---

bies. However, using jargon unnecessarily is inappropriate. Also, jargon may shut readers out. Therefore, when you need to use jargon for a general audience, be sure to explain the specialized meanings.

ACCEPTABLE SPECIALIZED LANGUAGE

As the lake eutrophicates, it gradually fills until the entire lake will be converted into a terrestrial community. Eutrophic changes (or eutrophication) is the nutritional enrichment of the water, promoting the growth of aquatic plants.

—DAVIS AND SOLOMON, *The World of Biology*

Remote job entry is a batch-processing application. The job is entered into the system at a remote terminal or card reader, and the output is returned to a remote printer at some later time. Routing instructions that specify the output destination are submitted along with the job. Remote job entry usually involves medium-sized volumes of data and a response time of one to two hours. This application tends to be vulnerable to error because the input is difficult to check and errors show up only in the output.

—MARY SUMNER, *Computers: Concepts and Uses*

These examples show acceptable specialized language. They are from college textbooks that expect that students either know or can decipher the meaning of *eutrophicates, eutrophic, remote job entry, batch-processing,* and *output.*

3   Avoiding euphemisms

Euphemisms attempt to avoid the harsh reality of truth by using more pleasant-sounding, "tactful" words. The word *euphemism* comes from the Greek meaning "words of good omen" (*eu-,* "good" + *pheme,* "voice"). Euphemisms are sometimes necessary for tact in social situations (using *passed away* instead of *died* when offering condolences, for example). Most of the time, euphemisms drain meaning from truthful writing. Some people use unnecessary euphemisms to describe socially unacceptable behavior: "Johnny has a wonderfully vivid imagination" instead of "Johnny lies." Some people use unnecessary euphemisms to hide unpleasant facts: "She is between assignments" instead of "She lost her job." Euphemisms like these fool no one, and they are unlikely to spare feelings.

BACKGROUND

P. T. Barnum, the great showman, wanted people to move through his sideshow more quickly than they were doing on their own. The exhibits were too successful, causing people to stay too long and prevent the entry of new paying customers. To solve his problem, Barnum hung a sign in front of a doorway: "This way to the Egress." Eager to see what kind of monster an egress might be, people passed through the door—to find themselves in an alley on the other side of the exit.

ANSWERS: EXERCISE 4

Answers to this exercise will vary. Here is one set of possibilities.

1. Students who want to do well in school must budget their time.

2. She was arrested.

3. I am worried about teaching myself to become a computer programmer.

4. She is a homemaker.

5. He was a witty conversationalist.

6. She wanted to fire the sales representative.

7. The administrative assistant typed a letter for his boss.

8. They are expecting a baby.

9. I remember when my school burned.

10. When their cat died, they buried it at Slumber Haven Pet Cemetery.

ALTERNATE EXAMPLES: DOUBLESPEAK

The following verbal machinations have been reported in the *Quarterly Review of Doublespeak,* published by the National Council of Teachers of English.

- Pacific Bell has a "variance elimination program," which is designed to "help employees avoid variances on initial service orders" and which has resulted in a 20 percent drop in "service order variances." In other words, the company is working to reduce the number of mistakes made by employees.

- A Colorado educational consulting firm issued a report on higher education which contains the following sentence: "Current decennial review processes required by the board should include a more explicit outcomes component."

EXERCISE 4

Revise each example of pretentious language, jargon, or euphemism.

1. It is of utmost importance that students prioritize their hours in the day in a type of apportionment to fulfill all their academic obligations.

2. She came within the venue of the law enforcement establishment.

3. It is with grave misgivings that I undertake this endeavor to instruct myself in the intricacies of computer programming.

4. Her occupation is domestic engineering.

5. His conversation was full of amusing thoughts concisely expressed with humor.

6. She announced herself to be in favor of terminating the employment of the sales representative.

7. The administrative assistant typed an epistle for his superior.

8. They are awaiting a little bundle of joy from heaven.

9. I recall the time in my past when the school I matriculated at was razed by an incendiary event.

10. Their cat passed away and is now reposing in the Slumber Haven Pet Cemetery.

4   Avoiding "doublespeak"

Doublespeak is artificial, evasive language. It aims to distort, deceive, and confuse. For example, many automobile dealerships today have renamed "used cars" as "pre-owned cars" or "previously distinguished cars." A major corporation has described its notice that laid off 5,000 workers as a "career alternative enhancement package." A government official was quoted as calling an atomic warhead on a missile "a physics package." Such distortions try to make the bad and unpleasant seem good.

To use doublespeak is to try to hide the truth, a highly unethical practice that seeks to control people's thoughts. So severe has the doublespeak problem become in our society that the National Council of Teachers of English yearly announces a Doublespeak Award to the "best" example of language that purposely misleads. A recent nominee for the award went to a government advisor who said that withholding information is a long way from telling a lie. An award went to the U.S. State Department for a report on violations of human rights in other countries that substituted "unlawful or arbitrary deprivation of life" for "killing." Such misuses of language have devastating social and political consequences in a free society. As a writer, always avoid using doublespeak; use language truthfully.

5   Avoiding bureaucratic language

Like doublespeak, **bureaucratic language** is distorting. Unlike doublespeak, it is not intended to mislead. Rather, it is carelessly written, stuffy, overblown language.

> You can include a page that also contains an Include instruction. The page including the Include instruction is included when you paginate the document but the included text referred to in its Include instruction is not included.

The irony here is that the writer seems to be trying to communicate very precisely. Bureaucratic language (or *bureaucratese,* the coined word to describe the style) is marked by jargon, euphemism, and unnecessary complexity. Such writing becomes meaningless because it is evasive, ambiguous, and wordy.

EXERCISE 5

Rewrite into plain English these examples of doublespeak and bureaucratic language.

1. The government will add a "user fee" to the cost of gasoline.
2. The memorandum previously circulated should be ignored and replaced by the memorandum sent before the previous one. The memorandum presently being held by the reader should be attached to the previous one to call attention to the fact that the previous one should be ignored.
3. For fire safety, all homes must have a "combustion enunciator" to warn people of smoke.
4. At a commercial postal delivery service, the "least-best" drivers are the ones who have poor driving and/or delivery records.
5. Our airline is experiencing "schedule irregularities"; they are not called "delays."

■ This is how one college catalogue describes its Master of Science in Nursing degree: "The focus of graduate education is the family unit comprised of individuals viewed as enfamilied selves. In undergraduate education health is viewed on a continuum of health/ diminished health and as a purposeful interaction with ecological variables which seeks to maintain a state of well-being. In graduate education health is viewed as an evolving process which occurs throughout the life span of enfamilied selves in interrelationship with the ecosystem. Family health is perceived as expansion of consciousness of enfamilied selves."

■ When several women's groups protested the Pakistani law that accords the legal testimony of women half the weight of the testimony of men, Qazi Hussain Ahmed, leader of the Islamic Party, said, "These laws do not affect women adversely. Our system wants to protect women from unnecessary worry and save them the trouble of appearing in court."

—*The New York Times,* June 14, 1988, p. A1

ANSWERS: EXERCISE 5

Answers to this exercise will vary. Here is one set of possible answers.

1. The government is raising gasoline taxes. (doublespeak)

2. The first memorandum you received should replace the one that followed it. Please attach this notice to the cancelled version. (bureaucratic)

3. For fire safety, all homes should have a smoke detector. (doublespeak)

4. At a commercial postal delivery service, some employees have poor driving and/or delivery records. (doublespeak)

5. Our airline is experiencing delays. (doublespeak)

REVISING YOUR WRITING

If you need to write using more effective words, go back to your writing and locate the ineffective words. Using this chapter as a resource, revise your writing to communicate effectively through using appropriate language (21a), avoiding sexist language (21b), correctly using figurative language (21c), and eliminating clichés (21d) and artificial language (21e).

CASE STUDY: REVISING FOR EFFECTIVE LANGUAGE

This case study lets you observe a student writer revising. It also gives you the opportunity to revise some student writing on your own.

Observation

A student wrote the following draft for a course called American Government. The assignment was to present a situation in which legislation designed to protect the rights of one group necessarily infringes on the rights of another. The material focuses on the essential features of the controversy, but the draft's effectiveness is diminished by errors in the use of language.

Read through the draft. The errors are highlighted and explained. Before you look at how the student revised to eliminate the errors, revise the material yourself. Then compare what you and the student did.

Slang: 21a-3

Bureaucratic language: 21e-5

In 1961, Great Britain's Royal College of Physicians issued a report that served as a major downer for the tobacco industry worldwide. The report said that medical researchers had found that smoking was directly related to health problems. The Report of the U.S. Surgeon General confirmed those findings nine years later, and the U.S. Congress embarked on a policy of disallowing cigarette advertising on television. Then, in the late 1980s, a whole lot was widely known about the bad effects of smoking on smokers and nonsmokers alike. Advocates of a smoke-free environment began to get their feet wet and rushed into battle. Individual communities passed "clean air" ordinances, industries established "smoke free" work zones, and the U.S. Congress passed legislation banning smoking on some airplane flights.

Overly informal: 21a-1

Mixed metaphor: 21c

These antismoking regulations have upset many smokers, a vocal minority. Many smokers say that bans constitute "unfair discrimination." Sometimes actions speak louder than words. Before fines were legislated by the federal government, stewardesses and stewards on one airline found themselves physically grappling with selfish, unreasonable passengers who acted like pigs by insisting on lighting up during a nonsmoking flight. Before nonsmoking regulations went into effect at most restaurants across the nation, some dining establishments experienced an exodus of patrons to restaurants in nearby communities that had no smoking prohibitions. The days of being able to grab a smoke at any place and time seem to be over for smokers. Still, exchanging gripes is likely to continue between smokers and nonsmokers.

Cliché: 21d

Sexist language: 21b

Slanted language: 21a-4

Pretentious language: 21e-1

Slang: 21a-3

Slang: 21a-3

Inappropriate colloquial language: 21a-3

Here is how the student revised the paragraph to correct errors in language use. In a few places, the student had alternatives for correcting the errors. Your revision, therefore, might not be exactly like this one, but it should deal with each error highlighted on the draft.

COVERAGE: PARTICIPATION ESSAY (pages 452–453)

The average person needs to sleep seven and a half to eight hours every twenty-four hours. What happens to a person when he loses *his* [21b: sexist language] needed *shut eye* [21a-3: slang]?

When a person does not sleep one night, *his* [21 b: sexist language] divergent thinking suffers. Divergent thinking calls for originality and flexibility. Convergent thinking, on the other hand, is possible. *Notwithstanding the deprivation of a sole night's lapse into a sleep modality* [21e-1: pretentious language], a person can perform routine, familiar tasks. Even those tasks, however, become almost impossible to do when a person loses *forty winks* [21a-3: colloquial] for two nights.

This information comes as a result of a study at Loughborough University in England. The researchers used a group of twenty-four healthy students. First, all the students took an *array of assessments that measure the duration of time it usually takes people to perform certain tasks of cognitive activity* [21e-1: pretentious lan-

(continued next page)

COVERAGE: PARTICIPATION ESSAY (*continued*)

guage]. The tests had no right answers. Instead, the tests called for originality and the ability to elaborate on thoughts. Students had to be *quick on the uptake* [21d: cliché] to respond to the questions. One question required the students to think of as many uses as possible for a cardboard box. Another question asked students to imagine the consequences if clouds had strings attached to them that hung down to earth.

After the tests, the students were divided into two subgroups that were evenly matched on their scores on the thinking tests. One subgroup slept as usual. The other subgroup stayed up all night, fighting off any *somnolent* [21a: overly formal] feelings. The next day, all the students were retested. During the second night, the subgroup that had slept was once again allowed to sleep. The other subgroup again stayed up all night, even though the members felt *dead as dogs* [21d: cliché]. All the students retook the tests the next day. On the average, the students who had spent two nights without sleep did far worse than did the students in the other subgroup. After one night, divergent thinking suffered; after two nights, convergent thinking *went into a nose dive* [21d: cliché].

This research has important implications for students. *Hitting the books* [21a-3: slang] all night before a test is *really a pretty* [21a-1: overly informal] bad mistake. Abilities to analyze information or answer an essay question are severely reduced after the loss of one night's sleep.

ANSWER: PARTICIPATION ESSAY

This version revises the errors in language use, though answers will likely vary somewhat from those shown here. Also, answers will vary if students have revised content, organization, or style.

The average person needs to sleep seven and a half to eight hours every twenty-four hours. What happens to a person who loses needed sleep?

In 1961, Great Britain's Royal College of Physicians issued a report that hurt the tobacco industry worldwide. The report said that medical researchers had found that smoking was directly related to health problems. The Report of the U.S. Surgeon General confirmed those findings nine years later, and the U.S. Congress passed a law prohibiting cigarette advertising on television. Then, in the late 1980s, much was widely known about the bad effects of smoking on smokers and nonsmokers alike. Advocates of a smoke-free environment began to work actively for their cause. Individual communities passed "clean air" ordinances, industries established "smoke free" work zones, and the U.S. Congress passed legislation banning smoking on some airplane flights.

These antismoking regulations have upset many smokers, a vocal minority. Many smokers say that bans constitute "unfair discrimination." Sometimes the smokers have taken action. Before fines were legislated by the federal government, flight attendants on one airline found themselves physically grappling with passengers who insisted on smoking during a nonsmoking flight. Before nonsmoking regulations went into effect at most restaurants across the nation, some dining establishments lost customers to restaurants in nearby communities that had no smoking prohibitions. The days of being able to smoke at any place and time seem to be over for smokers. Still, friction is likely to continue between smokers and nonsmokers.

Participation

A student wrote the following draft for a course called Introduction to Psychology. The assignment was to explain the effects of sleep on thinking processes. The material is well organized and uses specific details, but the draft's effectiveness is diminished by errors in use of language.

Read through the draft. Then revise it to eliminate the errors. Also, make any additional revisions you think would improve the content, organization, and style of the material.

The average person needs to sleep seven and a half to eight hours every twenty-four hours. What happens to a person when he loses his needed shut-eye?

When a person does not sleep one night, his divergent thinking suffers. Divergent thinking calls for originality and flexibility. Convergent thinking, on the other hand, is possible. Notwithstanding the deprivation of a sole night's lapse into a sleep modality, a person can perform routine, familiar tasks. Even those tasks, however, become almost impossible to do when a person loses forty winks for two nights.

This information comes as a result of a study at Loughborough University in England. The researchers used a group of twenty-four healthy students. First, all the students took an array of assessments that measure the duration of time it usually takes people to perform certain tasks of cognitive activity. The tests had no right answers. Instead, the tests called for originality and the ability to elaborate on thoughts. Students had to be quick on the uptake to respond to the questions. One question required the students to think of as many uses as possible for a cardboard box. Another question asked students to imagine the consequences if clouds had strings attached to them that hung down to earth.

After the tests, the students were divided into two subgroups that were evenly matched on their scores on the thinking tests. One subgroup slept as usual. The other subgroup stayed up all night, fighting off any somnolent feelings. The next day, all the students were retested. During the second night, the subgroup that had slept was once again allowed to sleep. The other subgroup again stayed up all night, even though the members felt dead as dogs. All the students retook the tests the next day. On the average, the students who had spent two nights without sleep did far worse than did the students in the other subgroup. After one night, divergent thinking suffered; after two nights, convergent thinking went into a nose dive.

This research has important implications for students. Hitting the books all night before a test is really a pretty bad mistake. Abilities to analyze information or answer an essay question are severely reduced after the loss of one night's sleep.

When a person does not sleep one night, divergent thinking suffers. Divergent thinking calls for originality and flexibility. Convergent thinking, on the other hand, is possible. In spite of losing one night's sleep, a person can perform routine, familiar tasks. Even those tasks, however, become almost impossible to do when a person loses needed sleep for two nights.

This information comes as a result of a study at Loughborough University in England. The researchers used a group of twenty-four healthy students. First, all the students took a set of tests that measure how long certain thinking tasks usually take. The tests had no right answers. Instead, the tests called for originality and the ability to elaborate on thoughts. Students had to be clever and quick to respond to the questions. One question required the students think of as many uses as possible for a cardboard box. Another question asked students to imagine the consequences if clouds had strings attached to them that hung down to earth.

After the tests, the students were divided into two subgroups that were evenly matched on their scores on the thinking tests. One subgroup slept as usual. The other subgroup stayed up all night, fighting off any drowsy feelings. The next day, all the students were retested. During the second night, the subgroup that had slept was once again allowed to sleep. The other subgroup again stayed up all night, even though the members were exhausted. All the students retook the tests the next day. On the average, the students who had spent two nights without sleep did far worse than did the students in the other subgroup. After one night, divergent thinking suffered; after two nights, convergent thinking declined sharply.

This research has important implications for students. Studying all night before a test is surely a bad mistake. Abilities to analyze information or answer an essay question are severely reduced after the loss of one night's sleep.

22 Spelling and Hyphenation

One reason English spelling can be difficult is that English words originate from several sources. Some come from Latin, some from Greek, some from French (the French invaded Britain in the eleventh century). Many words have come into the language recently from technical jargon; nobody spoke of *lasers* or *bytes* thirty years ago. These various origins and the various ways English-speaking people pronounce words make it almost impossible to rely on pronunciation in spelling a word. What you *can* rely on, however, is a system of proofreading, studying, and learning spelling rules.

22a Eliminating careless errors

Many spelling errors are not *spelling* errors at all. They are the result of illegible handwriting, slips of the pen, or typographical errors. Although you may not be able to change your handwriting, you can make it legible enough so that readers know what words you are writing. Catching "typos" requires careful proofreading. Try these techniques:

TECHNIQUES FOR PROOFREADING FOR SPELLING

1. Slow down your reading speed so that you can concentrate on individual letters of words rather than on the meaning of the words.
2. Stay within your "visual span," the number of letters you can identify with a single glance. Most people have a visual span of about six letters.
3. Put a ruler or large index card under each line as you proofread, to focus your concentration and vision.
4. Read each paragraph *backwards,* from the last sentence to the first. This method helps to prevent your being distracted by the meaning of the material.

For information on how to correct typos by using proofreaders' marks, see Appendix B, Using Correct Manuscript Format.

EXERCISE 1

Proofread this paragraph, using one or more of the methods described above. Find and correct eight typos.

I'll never forget the day I thought my car had been stollen. I had finished an hour-long ordeal in the super market after haveing spent three hours studying. As I stepped out of the 68° air-conditioned store into the 97° Kansas sunshine, I headed for the car quickly. Not only was I about to mealt, but the two bowls of low-calorie non-dairy whipped topping and the four cans of frozen lemonad were already dripping in the bag. When I reached the spot where I knew I had parked the car, all I saw were three cricles of motor oil, a popsicle stick oozing green goo, and a crumpled ticket from the prevous week's lottery. Not an orange Vega in sight! Do you know what my first thought was? "Who could be fool enogh to steal a '76 Vega?"

22b Training yourself to improve your spelling

1   **Using the dictionary and keeping alert for new words**

Not all good spellers remember how to spell every word, but most good spellers know when to consult the dictionary for help. If you are unsure of how to spell a word but you know how it starts, look it up in the dictionary. The first spelling listed in most college dictionaries is the *preferred* spelling; use it. If you have no idea of how a word is spelled or if you do not know how to spell the beginning of a word, think of a synonym you can spell and look that word up in a thesaurus. Chances are you will find the original word listed.

To increase your spelling ability, watch for words that are new to you. For example, when you come across key terms in a textbook, highlight or underline them as you read. (Do not underline *all* unfamiliar words; stick to the terms that are essential to the subject.) Then, *after you have finished reading*, memorize the spelling of those words. Writing each new word on a 3 × 5″ card can be especially helpful; an isolated word on a card stands out far more clearly than does one word in a long list. You will benefit even more if you write the word twice on the card, once regularly and once dividing it into parts. For example, you may find it easier to spell *environment* if you isolate the *iron: env iron ment.*

LANGUAGE HISTORY

Soon after the Romans left Britain, three Germanic tribes—the Jutes, the Angles, and the Saxons—began crossing the English Channel. Over a period of about 200 years they drove the Celts into hiding in the mountains of Wales and Scotland. The common language of these Germanic warriors is called Anglo-Saxon or Old English. It was the first native ancestor of modern English. Although Anglo-Saxon does not look or sound much like the language we know, many of our words for basic concepts are descended from it: *faeder (father), sittan (sit), hring (ring), hund (hound), hūs (house),* and *Englaland (England, "land of the Angles")*.

At this point, English contained few foreign words. The Anglo-Saxons had picked up a small number of Latin words before migrating to Britain: *wine, cup.* Other Latin words entered Old English through the works of Christian missionaries: *paegel (pail), pott (pot), munuc (monk), catt (cat), leahtric (lettuce), purs (purse), discipul (disciple), son* (musical *sound*), *schol (school), cometa (comet).*

LANGUAGE HISTORY

During the ninth century the Danes (Vikings) attacked Britain in such numbers that by A.D. 878 the English had to give them the eastern half of the country to get peace. These Vikings had a similar language and culture to those of the Anglo-Saxons, so there was easy transference between the two.

The Danes contributed a number of words to English, many of them containing the *sk* sound: *skull, sky, skill, skin, scrape,* and *skirt; band, bull, dirt, down* (feathers), *egg, sister, slaughter, gift, want, awkward, low.* The personal pronouns *they, their,* and *them* also came from the Danes, replacing Anglo-Saxon words. By the year 1000, the Danes had been completely assimilated, but not before they had contributed almost 1,000 words to English.

BACKGROUND

In his article "Improving Spelling and Vocabulary in the Secondary School" (NCTE, 1982), Richard Hodges points out that individuals make few, if any, random spelling errors. Each incorrect spelling has a cause. Students who want to improve their spelling can save themselves a fair amount of energy and time if they discover the causes behind the misspellings, then write the rules that would, if followed, have averted the errors. A related activity is described by Anne Dodd ("Demons, Dictionaries, and Spelling Strategies," *English Journal* 77 [Dec. 1988]: 52–53) who suggests that students can set up personal spelling dictionaries with problem words recorded in alphabetical order, each one used in a sentence and accompanied by notes deemed to be helpful (such as the category of error the word exemplifies). At least such a personalized dictionary simplifies the process of looking up words for the speller who has trouble finding them in an unabridged version because they are not spelled as expected.

2 **Using visuals and mnemonic devices to help you spell**

As you become aware of words that you frequently misspell, print each carefully on a 3 × 5 " card, highlighting the problem area by using larger print, a different color ink, or a highlighter pen.

neCESSary   sepARATe

Mnemonic devices—techniques to improve memory—can also help you to remember the spelling of difficult words. Remember "the principal is your pal" line from high school? That mnemonic has helped many students distinguish between *principle* and *principal* by associating the latter word with a simple, familiar word. Memory techniques allow your brain to do more than simply memorize letters. For example, if you have trouble with the homonyms *stationary* and *stationery* try this: "*Stationary* means standing still while *stationery* is used to write on." The *a* and the *e* are the problem letters here, so by associating the *a* in *stationary* with the *a* in the word *stand,* you can remember more easily. The same principle holds for the *e* in *stationery.* Try to make up similar mnemonics for words you misspell.

3 **Looking for patterns in your misspelled words and keeping a spelling chart**

Misspellings usually occur in patterns. Many people, for example, are confused by words containing *ei* or *ie.* You might find it easier to learn the rule for these vowels than to try to memorize each word separately.

Patterns of misspellings often relate to memory, not to stated rules in this handbook. Many people have their own particular misspelling patterns, unlike those of any other writer. Whatever your misspelling patterns, remember that your brain can handle five different *patterns* more easily than fifty-five different *words.* Not only is the number more manageable, but the concept of a pattern makes it easier for your brain to recognize possible misspelled words.

To group your spelling errors into patterns, keep a spelling chart. List on the chart all of the words you misspell, their correct spelling, the problem area, and the corresponding handbook section or pattern. Set up your chart like this:

INCORRECT	CORRECT	PROBLEM AREA	RULE OR PATTERN
recieve	receive	ie/ei	22d-2
writting	writing	tt/t	22d-1
labratory	laboratory	ra/ora	deleted syllable: 22c-4
Febuary	February	ua/rua	missing letter: 22c-4

TYPICAL PATTERNS OF MISSPELLINGS

DOUBLING CONSONANTS	**coming** not *comming* (22d-1)
ADDING SYLLABLES	**athletic** not *atheletic*
DELETING SYLLABLES	**mathematics** not *mathmatics*
USING APOSTROPHES FOR PLURALS	ten **boys** not ten *boy's*
DROPPING FINAL *e*	**management** not *managment* (22d-1)
RETAINING FINAL *e*	**debatable** not *debateable* (22d-1)
RETAINING FINAL *y*	**merriment** not *merryment* (22d-1)
BLENDING SOUNDS	**length** not *lenth*
OMITTING SILENT LETTERS	**wealthy** not *welthy*
TRANSPOSING LETTERS	**relevant** not *revelant*
COMBINING SEPARATE WORDS	**a lot** not *alot* (22c-3)
USING IMPROPER FORMS	they **used to,** not *use to,* laugh (22d-1)

LANGUAGE HISTORY

In 1066 England was invaded yet again. This time the invaders were the Normans. The Normans' ancestors were Vikings, who had settled in France in the eighth and ninth centuries and adopted the local customs and language. Led by William the Conqueror, the Normans overran England in just one year. They killed many of the Saxon nobles and divided up the land among themselves. Norman French was declared the official language: businesses, schools, law courts, and the government used French for the next 200 years. Literature was written in French or Latin; English was considered too barbaric to be used for such an elevated purpose. The Normans never bothered to control what the masses spoke, however, so although French was the official language, English remained the language of daily activity among most people.

Eventually, the Normans were cut off from France. They remained bilingual, but speaking pure French became less important. English began to reappear in schools as well as in business and legal papers. By 1400 Chaucer's *The Canterbury Tales* showed that English was suitable for literature after all.

LANGUAGE HISTORY

During the period of colonization, English continued to expand. From the American Indians, we learned *tomahawk, wigwam, squaw,* and place names, such as *Nebraska, Allegheny, Kentucky, Seattle,* and *Dakota.* From the Spanish in the New World: *mustang, ranch, patio, bonanza, rodeo, vigilante, sombrero.* From India: *thug, loot, pajamas, bandana.* From Germany: *kindergarten, semester, delicatessen, frankfurter, hamburger.*

Borrowing continues unabated. Recent borrowings have come from Italian (*casino, malaria, studio*); Spanish (*cigar, canyon, cafeteria*); German (*pumpernickel, iceberg,*

(continued next page)

LANGUAGE HISTORY (continued)

protein); Slavic *(pogrom, soviet, robot)*; Arabic *(genie, candy, safari)*; Hebrew *(hallelujah, kosher)*; Persian *(spinach, lilac, bazaar)*; Tibeto-Chinese *(tea, ketchup)*; and Japanese *(zen, karate)*.

Over the centuries, the Anglo-Saxons' vocabulary of 50,000 words has expanded to more than 600,000 words. Irregular spellings is the price we pay for this acquired richness and flexibility.

TEACHING TIP

A sophisticated relative of the spelling test is the dictation exercise. Passages can be created to test student ability to spell, punctuate, or capitalize. Here is a sample dictation passage aimed at testing whether students can distinguish among homonyms and commonly confused words. The context gives students clues to which word is intended (much as the sentences normally given as part of a spelling test do); at the same time, the paragraph format is more interesting than random illustrative sentences. (Homonyms and commonly confused words are in italics.)

Many people *are* under the *illusion* that ostriches stick *their* heads in the sand when they *are* scared. This is a myth that began among the ancient Arabs and *then* was *passed* on *by* Roman *writers*. *Maybe* the *sight* of an ostrich sleeping with *its* head stretched out along the ground *led to* the error. Ostriches also have been *seen* placing *their* heads *to* the ground *to hear* if an enemy is still on *their* trail. Instead *of* hiding, ostriches rely on sharp senses of *sight* and *hearing*. They *are* the first animals on the *plains to* spot danger; they serve as unofficial guard, warning *herds of deer*. They run *quite* fast, attaining top speeds of thirty-five miles per *hour*, so they can usually *elude* capture. When cornered, they *are* not *altogether* helpless; they can kick hard enough *to break* the bones of *their* attackers.

22c Solving spelling problems that arise from difficult words and word groups

1 Recognizing homonyms and commonly confused words

Homonyms are words that sound exactly like others *(its/it's, morning/mourning)*. Many other words sound so much alike that they are often confused with each other. The best way to distinguish between homonyms or between other commonly confused words is to use mnemonic devices and/or to identify patterns, as explained in 22b.

HOMONYMS AND COMMONLY CONFUSED WORDS

accept	to receive
except	with the exclusion of
advice	recommendation
advise	to recommend
affect	to produce an influence on *(verb)*; an emotional response *(noun)*
effect	result *(noun)*; to bring about or cause *(verb)*
aisle	space between rows
isle	island
allude	to make indirect reference to
elude	to avoid
allusion	indirect reference
illusion	false idea, misleading appearance
already	by this time
all ready	fully prepared
altar	sacred platform or place
alter	to change
altogether	thoroughly
all together	everyone or everything in one place
angel	supernatural being, good person
angle	the shape made by joining two straight lines at one end
are	plural form of *to be*
hour	sixty minutes
our	plural form of *my*
ascent	the act of rising or climbing
assent	consent
assistance	help
assistants	helpers
bare	nude, unadorned
bear	to carry; an animal

HOMONYMS AND COMMONLY CONFUSED WORDS *(continued)*

board	piece of wood
bored	uninterested
breath	air taken in
breathe	to take in air
brake	device for stopping
break	destroy, make into pieces
buy	to purchase
by	next to, through the agency of
canvas	heavy cloth
canvass	to poll
capital	major city
capitol	government building
choose	to pick
chose	past tense of *to choose*
cite	to point out
sight	vision
site	a place
clothes	garments
cloths	pieces of fabric
coarse	rough
course	path; series of lectures
complement	something that completes
compliment	praise, flattery
conscience	sense of morality
conscious	awake, aware
corps	regulated group
corpse	dead body
council	governing body
counsel	advice
dairy	place where milk products are collected, manufactured, and/or sold
diary	personal journal
descent	downward movement
dissent	disagreement
dessert	final, sweet course in a meal
desert	to abandon; dry, sandy area
device	a plan; an implement
devise	to create
die	to lose life; one of a pair of dice
dye	to change the color of something
dominant	commanding, controlling
dominate	to control

A HUMOROUS NOTE

In *Anguished English* (Wyrick and Company, 1988), Richard Lederer reprints some misspellings that convey unintended, and comical, meanings. Here are a few of those he has collected.

1. They gave William IV a lovely funeral. It took six men to carry the beer.

2. On Thanksgiving morning we could smell the foul cooking.

3. I am in the mists of choosing colleges.

4. During peek season the beach is covered with hundreds of bikini-clad beauties.

5. In Pittsburgh they manufacture iron and steal.

6. Dickens spent his youth in prison because his father's celery was cut off.

7. Due to repairs to the air-conditioning system, offices will be very humid for the next three days. Please bare with us.

8. Mr. and Mrs. Garth Robinson request the honor of your presents at the marriage of their daughter Holly to Mr. James Stockman.

BACKGROUND

A powerful but seldom used method of spelling study is suggested by Edward Tolman's theory of latent learning. Tolman describes a process of information acquisition that takes place immediately below the level at which it can be observed or demonstrated. The learner is not aware that he or she is learning. This process accounts, for example, for the sudden flash of insight that sometimes seems to occur from nowhere.

In terms of spelling study, latent learning can be utilized by keeping the correctly spelled problem words in the speller's line of sight for a week: on the desk, on bookmarks, on the bathroom mirror. The words need not be directly "studied." In a week, according to the theory of latent learning, the correct spellings will have been internalized by the student.

BACKGROUND

The earliest writing systems were developed not much more than 6,000 years ago to meet the needs of increasingly complex cultures. In particular, the Egyptians and Babylonians contrived ways of recording their sacred records, commercial transactions, and royal decrees by pictographs, drawings that attempted to convey a general idea by visually reproducing the major elements in it. Writing can be said to have begun when a method for making a linguistic statement of the facts was devised. The earliest of such systems did not make use of the phonology, or sounds of language. Instead, they used signs to represent morphemes (roots and affixes). Chinese is the only language that continues to use this system. The Egyptians and other Middle East cultures based their writing systems on the sounds of the syllables that made up words. Alphabetic writing was discovered by the peoples of the Eastern Mediterranean. At first they used only consonants, depending on readers to fill in the vowels as well as to supply such missing information as intonation and stress. When the Greeks took over a Semitic alphabet, they used the unneeded consonants to represent vowels. That tradition is the basis of all modern alphabets used in the West today. The principle of a one-to-one relationship between letters and sounds has been named *acrophony* by the Czech linguist Vachek.

QUOTATION ABOUT WRITING

English orthography satisfies all the requirements of the canons of reputability under the law of conspicuous waste. It is archaic, cumbrous, and ineffective; its acquisition consumes much time and effort; failure to acquire it is easy of detection.

—Thorstein Veblen,
Theory of the Leisure Class

HOMONYMS AND COMMONLY CONFUSED WORDS *(continued)*

dyeing	changing the color of something
dying	losing life
elicit	to draw out
illicit	illegal
eminent	prominent
immanent	living within; inherent
imminent	about to happen
envelop	to surround
envelope	container for a letter or other papers
fair	light-skinned; just, honest
fare	money for transportation; food
formally	conventionally, with ceremony
formerly	previously
forth	forward
fourth	number four
gorilla	animal in ape family
guerilla	soldier specializing in unconventional, surprise attacks
hear	to sense sound by ear
here	in this place
heard	past tense of *to hear*
herd	group of animals
hole	opening
whole	complete; an entire thing
human	relating to the species *homo sapiens*
humane	compassionate
its	possessive form of *it*
it's	contraction for *it is*
know	to comprehend
no	negative
later	after a time
latter	second one of two things
lead	heavy metal substance; to guide
led	past tense of *to lead*
lessen	to decrease
lesson	something learned and/or taught
lightning	storm-related electricity
lightening	making lighter
loose	unbound, not tightly fastened
lose	to misplace
maybe	perhaps
may be	might be
meat	animal flesh
meet	to encounter

HOMONYMS AND COMMONLY CONFUSED WORDS *(continued)*

miner	a person who works in a mine
minor	under age
moral	distinguishing right from wrong; the lesson of a fable, story, or event
morale	attitude or outlook, usually of a group
of	preposition indicating origin
off	away from
passed	past tense of *to pass*
past	at a previous time
patience	forbearance
patients	people under medical care
peace	absence of fighting
piece	segment or part of a whole; musical arrangement
personal	intimate
personnel	employees
plain	simple, unadorned
plane	to shave wood; aircraft
precede	to come before
proceed	to continue
presence	being at hand; attendance at a place or in something
presents	gifts
principal	foremost *(adjective);* administrator of a school *(noun)*
principle	moral conviction, basic truth
quiet	silent, calm
quite	very
rain	water drops falling to earth; to fall like rain
reign	to rule
rein	strap to guide or control an animal *(noun);* to guide or control *(verb)*
raise	to lift up
raze	to tear down
respectfully	with respect
respectively	in that order
reverend	title given to clergy; deserving reverence or respect
reverent	worshipful
right	correct; opposite of *left*
rite	ritual
write	to put words on paper

BACKGROUND

A notion commonly but mistakenly held is that English orthography differs radically from the oral code. A 1963 study at Stanford University, sponsored by the Bureau of Cooperative Research of the United States Office of Education, disproved that idea by using computer techniques to analyze 17,310 words from the "common core" vocabulary. The results indicated that the spelling of English phonemes is much more consistent than was heretofore believed, suggesting that students can be encouraged to depend on their ears—at least some of the time (Thomas D. Horn, "Research on Handwriting and Spelling," National Conference on Research in English, 1966, ERIC ED 036 507).

Listening is not very helpful in the case of homonyms, however, which Thomas Pollock found, after an extensive study of about 50,000 misspelled words in high school English papers, to be the third largest group of spelling errors ("Misspelling in Grades 9–12," *English Record* 22 [1971], ERIC ED 059 190). When sound alone cannot help the student distinguish between two words, Virginia Irwin's advice in "Reds, Greens, Yellows Ease the Spelling Blues" is helpful. She says to select the easier of the two words to remember, learn how to spell it and when to use it, then use the second one on all other occasions (*Missouri English Bulletin* 28 [1971], pp. 1–8).

QUOTATION ABOUT WRITING

Bad spellers of the world, untie!

—Graffito

QUOTATION ABOUT WRITING

Two common beliefs undermine the teaching of spelling—the belief that spelling cannot be taught, perhaps not at all but certainly not by the time people are young adults, and the belief that spelling can be taught only one way. The first belief keeps both teachers and students from trying at all and the second keeps the teacher from trying something else when The Method doesn't work. To teach spelling, a teacher must be prepared to move, with the student, straight into the tangle, systematically scrutinizing and classifying misspellings until patterns of difficulty begin to emerge.

—Mina Shaughnessy,
Errors and Expectations

BACKGROUND

One of the persons most responsible for the differences between British and American spellings was Noah Webster. Not only did he produce the dictionary for which he is well remembered, but he also published a speller (as well as a grammar and a reader). In his efforts to standardize the language, he gave us "Americanized" spellings by making such changes as dropping the *u* from words that carried an *-our* ending, such as *glamour* and *labour.* He also dropped the final *k* in words ending in *-ick*—e.g., *musick,*—and substituted *-er* endings for *-re* endings—*theater* for *theatre.*

HOMONYMS AND COMMONLY CONFUSED WORDS *(continued)*

road	path
rode	past tense of *to ride*
scene	place of an action; segment of a play
seen	viewed
sense	perception, understanding
since	measurement of past time; because
stationary	standing still
stationery	writing paper
straight	unbending
strait	narrow waterway
taught	past tense of *to teach*
taut	tight
than	besides
then	at that time; next; therefore
their	possessive form of *they*
there	in that place
they're	contraction for *they are*
through	finished; into and out of
threw	past tense of *to throw*
thorough	complete
to	toward
too	also
two	number following one
track	course, road
tract	pamphlet
waist	midsection of the body
waste	discarded material; to squander, to fail to use up
waive	forgo, renounce
wave	flutter, move back and forth
weak	not strong
week	seven days
weather	climatic condition
whether	if
where	in which place
were	past tense of *to be*
which	one of a group
witch	female sorcerer
whose	possessive form of *who*
who's	contraction for *who is*
your	possessive form of *you*
you're	contraction for *you are*
yore	long past

EXERCISE 2

From each group in parentheses, select the appropriate homonym.

Last week (are, our) county's governing (council, counsel) (passed, past) a new ordinance. As of July 1, no hazardous (waist, waste) dumping (cites, sights, sites) may be built within three miles of any populated area. Local factories will now have to ship (their, there, they're) refuse to another county or (choose, chose) to dispose of it in another way. We will (know, no) longer (accept, except) living in fear of poisons we might (breath, breathe). We are (know, no) longer willing (to, too, two) allow our water to be polluted. The owners might try (to, too, two) have the regulations (waived, waved) for businesses (all ready, already) in existence, but the issue is (to, too, two) serious (to, too, two) permit any exceptions. Would you want a creek mixing red, blue, and green (all together, altogether) running (threw, through) (your, you're) backyard?

2   Learning to tell apart words with multiple forms

Some expressions may be written either as one word or two, depending on meaning. Memorize the two expressions that are always written as two words: *all right* (not *alright*), and *a lot* (not *alot*).

An **everyday** occurrence is something that happens **every day.**

The guests were there **already** by the time I was **all ready.**

When we were **all together,** there were five of us **altogether.**

We were there **a while** when the host said dinner would be **awhile** longer.

Maybe the main course will be sushi, but it **may be** tofuburgers.

When we went **in to** dinner, he walked **into** the table.

3   Avoiding spelling problems based on faulty pronunciation

Pronunciation can cause spelling problems. Sometimes people have trouble hearing the differences between two forms of the same word. For example, *prejudice* can be a noun, *prejudiced* an adjective ("I am guilty of *prejudice* [noun] if I am a *prejudiced* [adjective] person"). *Advice* is a noun, *advise* a verb ("If I *advise* [verb] you, I hope you will take my *advice* [noun]").

Some expressions are often mispronounced. Here are the three most common: **used to,** not *use to;* **supposed to,** not *suppose to;* **should have,** not *should of.*

TEACHING TIP

Much of the recent research on spelling improvement stresses the importance of using as many of the senses as possible during word study. You may want to suggest to students that they try to improve their visual memory by writing a word in the air, using a finger to make the troublesome letters especially large. Ask them to try to imagine a word as if it were on an outdoor movie screen. Then they can try to write the word mentally in "longhand." The auditory sense can be invoked by making exaggerated pronunciations. That is, the speaker emphasizes the problem portion of a word when saying it. For example, the person who habitually leaves off the final *-d* of *used* should practice pronouncing the word as "you said." The kinesthetic and tactile senses are combined when a writer records a problem word on paper using a different kind of medium to write the difficult spots, changing from a ball-point pen, for instance, to a crayon. This technique can include a visual element if the student puts the problem letters in red or some other bright color.

WORDS OFTEN MISSPELLED

Here is a collection of commonly misspelled words. To help you locate the words your students have difficulty with, the lists are organized in these categories: Word Endings (Suffixes), Double Consonants, Unstressed Syllables, Silent Letters and Blended Sounds, *ei/ie,* and Other Commonly Misspelled Words. It's a good idea to assign words for study in groups of 25 at a time.

Word Endings (Suffixes)

acceptable	barbarous
accessible	basically
accidentally	beautiful
accuracy	beginning
acreage	beneficial
actually	biggest
admission	bureaucracy
affectionately	business
aggression	
announcement	calculator
apparent	carrying
appearance	changeable
approximately	changing
arguing	characteristic
argument	Christianity
assassination	commitment
attendance	competent

Imprecise pronunciation often leads to misspelling familiar words. Some people, for example, add an extra syllable to the word *athletic,* spelling it with an extra *e.* On the other hand, some people delete a syllable from the word *privilege,* spelling it without the second *i.* When you are unsure of a spelling, check your dictionary.

4   Distinguishing between pronoun forms

When spelling pronouns, always consider the meaning of the pronoun. In general, the form containing an apostrophe is a contraction. See the chart in 27c for a complete list of contractions and their full forms. The forms of pronouns without contractions are possessive forms of the pronouns. Note carefully, for example, that *its'* and *the'ir* are not words.

it's	*= it is*	*its*	is the possessive form of *it*
they're	*= they are*	*their*	is the possessive form of *they*
who's	*= who is*	*whose*	is the possessive form of *who*
you're	*= you are*	*your*	is the possessive form of *you*

22d   **Solving spelling problems within words**

1   Spelling suffixes (word endings) carefully

A **suffix** is an ending added to the basic (root) form of a word. Suffixes can change a present-tense verb to past tense *(talk, talked),* an adjective to an adverb *(quick, quickly),* a verb to a noun *(govern, government),* and a noun to an adjective *(courage, courageous).* Spelling problems can arise when different suffixes sound alike or when changes must be made in the base word before the suffix is added.

The -d and -ed suffixes change many verb forms in the present tense into the past tense or into past-participle forms: *change, changed; work, worked.* Do not rely on how words sound in conversation to guide your spelling. The *-d* sound at the end of verbs is not always clearly pronounced; for example, although you may hear "use to," write *used to.*

The -ble suffixes *(-able* and *-ible)* have no consistent rules for their use. More words end in *-able: advisable, comfortable.* Still, some common words end in *-ible: audible, forcible.* The best rule to follow with these two endings is "When in doubt, look it up."

The *-ally* and *-ly* suffixes turn words into adverbs. The suffix *-ally* is added to words ending in *-ic: logic + ally = logically; tragic + ally = tragically*. The suffix *-ly* is added to adjectives not ending in *-ic: quick + ly = quickly; slow + ly = slowly*.

The *-nce* and *-nt* suffixes have no rules for their use. Some words end in *-ance: compliance, defiance*. Other words end in *-ence: confidence, convenience*.

If a noun ends in *-ance*, its adjective form ends in *-ant: compliance, compliant; defiance, defiant*. Similarly, if a noun ends in *-ence*, the adjective form ends in *-ent: confidence, confident; convenience, convenient*.

Two words, *confident* and *confidant*, can be troublesome. Their spellings differ only in the third-to-last letter, but each word is pronounced differently and has a different meaning. *Confident* means "self-assured" and *confidant* means "a person confided in."

The *-cede*, *-ceed*, and *-sede* suffixes have very dependable rules. Only one word ends in *-sede: supersede*. Three words end in *-ceed: exceed, proceed*, and *succeed*. All other words whose endings sound like these suffixes end in *-cede:* for example, *accede, concede, intercede, precede*. A common misspelling involves *proceed:* its noun form drops an *e* from *-ceed* and is spelled *procedure*.

Suffixes added to words that end in *e* occur according to a basic rule, in most cases. The general rule is to drop the final *e* before a suffix that begins with a vowel (*-ing*, for example) and keep the final *e* before a suffix that begins with a consonant (*-ment*, for example). Examples include *require, requiring, requirement; like, likely; tribe, tribal*.

Some words retain the final *e* to prevent confusing them with other words. For example, *dye + ing* is *dyeing* to avoid confusion with *dying (die + ing)*.

The most common exceptions are few and can be memorized: *argument, awful, judgment, truly*, and *wisdom*. Other exceptions are less frequently used words (*acknowledgment*, for example), so when in doubt, check your dictionary.

Suffixes added to words that end in *y* are influenced by the letter that comes immediately before the final *y*. When a consonant comes before a final *y*, the *y* changes to an *i* (unless the suffix itself begins with an *i*, such as *-ing*). Examples include *fry, fried, frying; write, writer, writing; supply, supplier, supplying*.

When a vowel comes before the final *y*, always keep the final *y: employ, employed, employer, employing; joy, joyous; stay, staying*.

competition, completely, confident, consistent, continuous, convenient, coolly, criticism, criticize, cruelty, curiosity, decision, definitely, description, desirable, desperate, despicable

disastrous, discussion, dormitory, easily, elaborately, entirely, environment, equipment, especially, evidently, existence, experiment, explanation, extremely, finally, financially, generally, government, governor, guidance, happily, hindrance, hoping, humorous, hungry

hurriedly, hypocrisy, ideally, idiosyncrasy

ignorant, illogical, imaginary, immediately, immensely, incalculable, incidentally, incredible, independent, indispensable, individually, influential, innocuous, insurance, intelligent, interference, irrelevant, irresistible, irritated, likelihood, listening

liveliest, livelihood, lying, magnificent, maintenance, manageable, management, marriage, meanness, mischievous, mysterious, narrative, naturally, necessary, noticeable, noticing, nuisance, numerous, occasionally, occurrence, occurring, official, omission, omitting, opponent

(continued on page 467)

ANSWERS: EXERCISE 3

A. 1. contemptible
   2. resistible
   3. believable
   4. reversible
   5. dispensable

B. 1. relevant
   2. prominent
   3. variant
   4. resistant
   5. convenient

C. 1. managing
   2. management
   3. completely
   4. completion
   5. creating

D. 1. studying
   2. studied
   3. supplied
   4. merriment
   5. various

E. 1. writing
   2. beginning
   3. stopped
   4. occurred
   5. questioning

F. 1. relief
   2. conceive
   3. niece
   4. deceive
   5. freight

COVERAGE: EXERCISE 3

A. (1), (2), and (4) are *-ible*; (3) and (5) are *-able*.

B. (1), (3), and (4) are *-ant*; (2) and (5) are *-ent*.

C. (1), (4), and (5) drop the final *e*; (2) and (3) retain it.

D. (1) retains the final *y*; (2), (3), (4), and (5) drop it and change to *i*.

E. (1) and (5) do not double the final consonant; (2), (3), and (4) double it.

F. (1) and (3) are *i* before *e*; (2), (4), and (5) are *e* before *i*.

Suffixes that lead to the doubling of final consonants require special attention. If a one-syllable word ends in a consonant preceded by a single vowel, then double the final consonant before adding a suffix. For example, if you add *-ing* to the word *flip*, double the *p*: *flipping*. Here are more examples: *blot, blotted; cram, cramming; pit, pitted; quit, quitting.*

With two-syllable words, an additional rule applies: double the final consonant only if the last syllable is stressed. If you add *-ing* to *refer*, you should double the final consonant: *referring*. However, if you add *-ence*, do not double the final consonant: *reference*. The difference here is in pronunciation. In *referring*, the accent is on the last syllable of *refer*, while in *reference* the accent is on the first syllable. Here are more examples: *control, controlled; omit, omitting; prefer, preferring, preference.*

2 Knowing the *ie*, *ei* rule and exceptions

The old rhyme for *ie* and *ei* is usually true: "*I* before *e*, except after *c*, or when sounded like *ay*, as in *neighbor* and *weigh*."

IE	believe, field, grief
EI	ceiling, conceit, eight, neigh, receive, vein

Because there are so few exceptions, they are worth memorizing.

IE	conscience, financier, science, species
EI	counterfeit, either, foreign, forfeit, height, leisure, neither, seize, sleight, weird

EXERCISE 3

Follow the directions for each section.

A. Add *-able* or *-ible:* 1. contempt; 2. resist; 3. believe; 4. reverse; 5. dispense.

B. Add *-ant* or *-ent:* 1. relev_____; 2. promin_____; 3. vari_____; 4. resist_____; 5. conveni_____.

C. Drop the final *e* as needed: 1. manage + ing; 2. manage + ment; 3. complete + ly; 4. complete + ion; 5. create + ing.

D. Change the final *y* to *i* as needed: 1. study + ing; 2. study + ed; 3. supply + ed; 4. merry + ment; 5. vary + ous.

E. Double the final consonant as needed: 1. write + ing; 2. begin + ing; 3. stop + ed; 4. occur + ed; 5. question + ing.

F. Insert *ie* or *ei* correctly: 1. rel_____f; 2. conc_____ve; 3. n_____ce; 4. dec_____ve; 5. fr_____ght.

3   Knowing how to use prefixes

Prefixes are syllables placed in front of words, either changing or adding to the word's meaning. For example, the prefixes *un-* and *in-* turn a word into its opposite (***un**cooperative,* ***in**admissible*); *re-* adds the meaning "again" to a word (***re**create,* ***re**incarnation*); and *pre-* adds the meaning "before" to a word (***pre**cook,* ***pre**destination*). A prefix does not alter the spelling of the word to which it is added: for example, *un + reliable = unreliable; re + locate = relocate.* Some prefixes, however, do require hyphens (see 22e). For a complete list of prefixes, see 20c.

4   Knowing how to form plurals

Plurals in English are formed in a number of different ways, but they are relatively easy to learn because the rules are fairly consistent.

Regular plurals use an added *-s,* in most cases: *leg, legs; desk, desks; elephant, elephants; shoe, shoes.*

When a word ends in *-ch, -s, -sh, -x, or -z,* pronunciation demands that *-es* be added: *beach, beaches; iris, irises; ash, ashes; tax, taxes; topaz, topazes.*

Most words ending in *o* become plural with the addition of *-s: alto, altos; radio, radios; cameo, cameos; tobacco, tobaccos.* A few words ending in *o* become plural with the addition of *-es* (those that do so have a consonant before the final *o*): *hero, heroes; tomato, tomatoes; potato, potatoes; veto, vetoes.* A few words ending in *o* preceded by a consonant take either *-s* or *-es* (always be consistent in the form you use): *cargo, cargoes, cargos; volcano, volcanoes, volcanos; tornado, tornadoes, tornados; zero, zeroes, zeros.*

Plurals of words ending in *f* **or** *fe* use a *v* in place of the *f,* in most cases: *leaf, leaves; loaf, loaves; life, lives; wife, wives.*

Three exceptions to this rule come up often: *belief, beliefs; motif, motifs; safe, safes.* These exceptions avoid confusion with the singular verbs *believes* and *saves* and with the plural noun *motives.*

When a word ends in *ff* or *ffe,* simple add *-s: giraffe, giraffes; staff, staffs.*

BACKGROUND

Some grammarians point out that context usually clarifies whether a writer means *research* or *re-search, re-creation* or *recreation,* and other words beginning with the *re-* prefix. Carl Kane, writing in *The Cedar Rapids Gazette* (August 20, 1986), contends that hyphens should not be neglected. "Anything that might even temporarily mislead a reader should be eliminated. Throw in a hyphen. It can't hurt." He leaves the reader with a short quiz. He asks, "Are hyphens needed in this list: *resummon, reform, retape, resound, restock, retreat?*"

WORDS OFTEN MISSPELLED

Word Endings (Suffixes) *(continued)*

opportunity	questionnaire
opposite	rarity
oppression	reality
optimism	realize
ordinarily	really
originally	recession
particularly	recommend
peaceable	referring
peculiar	regulate
performance	rehearsal
permanence	religious
permissible	remembrance
politician	repetition
possession	representative
practicality	resemblance
predominant	ridiculous
preparation	scarcity
prevalent	scenery
prisoner	secretary
probably	senseless
professor	shining
prominent	shrubbery
pronunciation	significant
publicly	simply
pursuing	sincerely

(continued next page)

467

WORDS OFTEN MISSPELLED

Word Endings (Suffixes) *(continued)*

skiing	tragedy
strenuous	tremendous
stubbornness	truce
studying	unanimous
suburban	unconscious
succession	undoubtedly
sufficient	usage
summary	
superintendent	using
supersede	usually
suppress	valuable
surely	various
susceptible	vegetable
suspicious	vengeance
swimming	violence
technical	visible
temporary	writing
tendency	written

ANSWERS: EXERCISE 4

1. vetoes	8. selves
2. brothers-in-law	9. bacteria
3. marches	10. spoonfuls
4. stresses	11. tomatoes
5. deer	12. shelves
6. teeth	13. lives
7. children	

COVERAGE: EXERCISE 4

(1) consonant before the final -*o*; (2) major word is the first word; (3) word ends in -*ch*; (4) word ends in -*s*; (5) name of animal; (6) internal change; (7) internal change; (8) word ends in -*f*; (9) foreign word; (10) compound word; (11) word ends in -*o* preceded by a consonant; (12) word ends in -*f*; (13) word ends in -*fe*.

Plurals of compound words use an -*s* or -*es* at the end of the whole compound word: *checkbook, checkbooks; player-coach, player-coaches; nurse-midwife, nurse-midwives.* When, however, the major word in the compound is the first word, add the -*s* or -*es* to the first word: *mile per hour, miles per hour; professor emeritus, professors emeritus; sister-in-law, sisters-in-law.*

Plurals formed by internal changes do not use the added -*s* or -*es*: *child, children; foot, feet; man, men; mouse, mice; ox, oxen.* Fortunately, these plurals sound so different that they do not cause spelling problems, except in the case of *woman* and *women.* Remember that these words add *wo-* to *man* and *men.*

Plurals of foreign words are formed according to the rules of each language. Latin words ending in -*um* usually form their plurals by changing the -*um* to *a: curriculum, curricula; datum, data; medium, media; stratum, strata.*

For Latin words ending in -*us*, the plural is -*i: alumnus, alumni; syllabus, syllabi.* Less common Latin forms and words borrowed from other languages usually form their plurals according to the rules of the language: *alumna, alumnae; criterion, criteria; axis, axes; thesis, theses.*

Plurals that retain their singular form are spelled the same whether they are being used in a singular or plural sense. Usually they are the names of animals or grains: *deer, elk, fish, quail, rice, wheat.*

EXERCISE 4

Form the plurals of these words.

1. veto	8. self
2. brother-in-law	9. bacterium
3. march	10. spoonful
4. stress	11. tomato
5. deer	12. shelf
6. tooth	13. life
7. child	

22e Using hyphens correctly

1 Learning when and how to divide a word at the end of a line

Unless the last word on a line would use up most of the right margin of your paper, do not divide it. If you absolutely must divide a word, remember not to divide the last word on the first line of a paper, the last word in a paragraph, or the last word on a page. When you must divide a word, follow these guidelines:

Never divide single-syllable words or very short words. No matter how long a word is, if it has only one syllable or is pronounced as one syllable, do not divide it—for example, *cleansed, drought, screamed, wealth.* Do not divide short words, even ones that have two or more syllables—for example, *area, every, envy.*

Always divide words between syllables. The dictionary listing of a word shows its syllables. The dictionary shows *distinction,* for example, as *dis-tinc-tion,* so you should divide it after the *s* or after the *c,* but nowhere else.

Never leave or carry over only one or two letters. This guideline means that words like *alive* and *ocean* are not divided at all. It also means that a word like *he-li-cop-ter* can be divided after the *i* or the *p,* but not after the *e.*

Follow rules for double consonants. Suffixes (word endings; see 22d-1) usually add syllables. If a base word ends in a double consonant, usually divide the word after the double consonant: *full-ness,* not *ful-lness; success-ful,* not *succes-sful.* On the other hand, when you double a consonant only to add a suffix, divide the word between the double consonants: *omit-ting,* not *omitt-ing; regrettable,* not *regrett-able; swim-ming,* not *swimm-ing.*

Never violate pronunciation when you divide words. Not all word endings add new syllables that can be pronounced. The *-ed* ending, for example, often simply adds a *d* sound to the end of a word. If you divide such a word at the *ed,* a reader will read a syllable that the word's pronunciation does not reflect. For example, *cleared* should not be divided, and *compelled* should be divided *com-pelled,* not *compel-led.* Also, do not divide a word like *issue,* because both its syllables are pronounced differently when they are separated than when they are together: *is-sue.*

WORDS OFTEN MISSPELLED
Double Consonants

accommodate	committee	missile
accompanied	controlled	occasion
accomplish	different	occurred
accordion	disappear	parallel
accustomed	disappoint	processes
address	disapprove	quizzes
annihilate	efficient	satellite
appoint	equipped	stepped
appreciate	fulfill	succeed
appropriate	happened	suppose
arrest	harass	surround
bulletin	interrupt	tyranny
commercial	mirror	villain

WORDS OFTEN MISSPELLED

Unstressed Syllables (including syllables frequently not pronounced)

adolescent	category
alcohol	cemetery
amateur	census
analysis	certain
angel	challenge
apology	channel
article	children
aspirin	chocolate
average	chosen
bargain	coarsely
boundary	concentrate
cafeteria	controversial
calendar	

(continued next page)

WORDS OFTEN MISSPELLED

Unstressed Syllables (including syllables frequently not pronounced) *(continued)*

curious	poison
decorate	practical
delicate	prepare
despair	privilege
destroy	propaganda
develop	pumpkin
disease	purpose
dispel	pursue
divide	
divine	pursuit
ecstasy	quandary
embarrass	rebel
enemy	recognize
escape	regular
everything	remember
exercise	reproduce
family	resources
favorite	restaurant
grammar	sacrifice
heroes	saxophone
holiday	sentence
hundred	separate
imagine	several
imitate	sheriff
integrate	similar
	sophomore
interest	specimen
introduce	sponsor
laboratory	statistics
liable	strategy
luxury	surprise
magazine	temperature
manual	therefore
mathematics	thorough
medicine	
miniature	tobacco
particle	together
perhaps	tomorrow
persuade	typical
physical	vitamins
pigeon	Wednesday
pitiful	woman
pleasant	women

---

2 | Dividing words with prefixes and suffixes correctly

Most prefixes form **closed words,** or words written as one *(semi + sweet = semisweet)*. When you divide a word that has a prefix of three or more letters, divide after the prefix rather than between other syllables: *mis-understand,* not *misunder-stand; non-conformist,* not *noncon-formist; super-impose,* not *superim-pose.*

Some prefixes must be separated from the base word with a hyphen. Here are some guidelines.

When using the prefixes *all-, ex-, quasi-,* and *self-,* usually add a hyphen: *all-inclusive, all-knowing, ex-husband, ex-president, quasi-judicial, quasi-psychological, self-assured, self-confidence.*

Selfish and *selfless* do not have hyphens because in each case *self* is a base word followed by a suffix, *-ish* and *-less,* respectively. Only when *self* is a prefix is it followed by a hyphen. It is never hyphenated when it is a suffix *(herself).*

When a proper name or a number is the main word, the prefix is followed by a hyphen: *all-American, anti-Communist, pro-Republican, pre-1950.*

When the main word is a compound, the prefix is followed by a hyphen: *anti-gun control, mini-baby boom, post-middle age.* Because such compounds often are not very clear, you should revise, not so much to solve a hyphen problem as to make your meaning unambiguous for readers.

When confusion in meaning or pronunciation can occur without a hyphen after a prefix, the hyphen is needed. If a prefix added to a word causes it to look exactly like another word, a hyphen after the prefix should help a reader understand which word you mean. For example, the hyphen in *re-dress* signals a reader that you mean "dress again" rather than "set right" *(redress).*

If the last letter of a prefix is the same as the first letter of the main word, or if adding a prefix results in three vowels in a row, you may use a hyphen after the prefix: *anti-intellectual, re-ionize.* Some words are commonly spelled without this hyphen: *cooperation, preeminent,* and *reexamine,* for example.

When two prefixes occur with one base word, writers can choose to write the base word only after the second prefix. In such cases, each of the two prefixes must be followed by a hyphen: *pre- or post-test, pre- and post-war eras, two- and four-year colleges.* Note that the first hyphen is separated from the next word by a space.

QUOTED WORDS *"O Romeo! Romeo!"*

No   "O Romeo! Romeo!," called Juliet as she stood at her window.

No   "O Romeo! Romeo," called Juliet as she stood at her window.

YES   "O Romeo! Romeo!" called Juliet as she stood at her window.

QUOTED WORDS *"Wherefore art thou Romeo?"*

No   "Wherefore art thou Romeo?," continued Juliet as she yearned for her new-found love.

No   "Wherefore art thou Romeo," continued Juliet as she yearned for her new-found love.

YES   "Wherefore art thou Romeo?" continued Juliet as she yearned for her new-found love.

EXERCISE 9

Punctuate the following dialogue correctly. If a sentence is correct, circle its number.

EXAMPLE   "Was anyone with the injured boy?," asked the admissions clerk.

"Was anyone with the injured boy?" asked the admissions clerk.

1. "His father" replied the ambulance driver "but he's unconscious."
2. "This boy looks like he needs surgery, but he is the son of the surgeon now on duty" said the clerk.
3. She explained in an agitated voice "Surgeons do not operate on their own family members."
4. "How can he be the surgeon's son when his father is still in the ambulance?" asked the driver.
5. With a disgusted look, the clerk told the driver "The surgeon is the boy's mother."

24h

Using commas in dates, names, addresses, and numbers according to accepted practice

When you write dates, names, and numbers, be sure to use commas according to accepted practice.

ALTERNATE EXAMPLE

This excerpt from Ernest Hemingway's story "The Short Happy Life of Francis Macomber" exemplifies the importance of commas in dialogue when it occurs in fiction.

"Here's to the lion," he [Francis Macomber] said. "I can't ever thank you for what you did."

Margaret, his wife, looked away from him and back to Wilson.

"Let's not talk about the lion," she said.

Wilson looked over at her without smiling and now she smiled at him.

"It's been a very strange day," she said. "Hadn't you ought to put your hat on even under the canvas at noon? You told me that, you know."

"Might put it on," said Wilson.

"You know you have a very red face, Mr. Wilson," she told him and smiled again.

"Drink," said Wilson.

"I don't think so," she said. "Francis drinks a great deal, but his face is never red."

"It's red today," Macomber tried a joke.

"No," said Margaret. "It's mine that's red today. But Mr. Wilson's is always red."

"Must be racial," said Wilson. "I say, you wouldn't like to drop my beauty as a topic, would you?"

"I've just started on it."

"Let's chuck it," said Wilson.

"Conversation is going to be so difficult," Margaret said.

ANSWERS: EXERCISE 9

1. "His father," replied the ambulance driver, "but he's unconscious."

2. "This boy looks like he needs surgery, but he is the son of the surgeon now on duty," said the clerk.

3. She explained in an agitated voice, "Surgeons do not operate on their own family members."

4. Correct

5. With a disgusted look, the clerk told the driver, "The surgeon is the boy's mother."

(Coverage: see next page)

COVERAGE: EXERCISE 9
(on previous page)

1. explanatory words in the middle of a quotation

2. explanatory words at the end of a quotation

3. explanatory words at the beginning of a quotation

4. Correct (no comma should follow the question mark)

5. explanatory words at the beginning of a quotation.

QUOTATION ABOUT WRITING

Any one who finds himself putting down several commas close to one another should reflect that he is making himself disagreeable, and question his conscience, as severely as we ought to do about disagreeable conduct in real life, whether it is necessary.

—H. W. Fowler

RULES FOR COMMAS WITH DATES

1. Use a comma between the date and the year: **July 20, 1969.**
2. Use a comma between the day and the date: **Sunday, July 20, 1969.**
3. Within a sentence, use commas after the day *and* the year in a full date.

   > Everyone wanted to be near a television set on **July 20, 1969,** to watch Armstrong emerge from the lunar landing module.

4. Do not use a comma in a date that contains the month with only a day or the month with only a year. Also, do not use a comma in a date that contains only the season and year.

   > The major news story during **July 1969** was the moon landing; news coverage was especially heavy on **July 21.**

5. An inverted date takes no commas: **20 July 1969.**

   > People stayed near their television sets on **20 July 1969** to watch the moon landing.

RULES FOR COMMAS WITH NAMES, PLACES, AND ADDRESSES

1. When an abbreviated title (Jr., M.D., Ph.D.) comes after a person's name, use a comma between the name and the title—**Rosa Gonzales, M.D.**—and also after the title if it is followed by the rest of the sentence:

   > The jury listened closely to the expert testimony of **Rosa Gonzales, M.D.,** last week.

2. When you invert a person's name, use a comma to separate the last name from the first: **Troyka, David.**
3. Use a comma between a city and state: **Philadelphia, Pennsylvania.** In a sentence, use a comma after the state, as well:

   > The Liberty Bell has been on display in **Philadelphia, Pennsylvania,** for many years.

(continued on next page)

RULES FOR COMMAS WITH NAMES, PLACES, AND ADDRESSES *(cont.)*

4. When you write a complete address as part of a sentence, use a comma to separate all the items, with the exception of the zip code. The zip code follows the state after a space without a comma. A comma does not follow the zip code.

   > I wrote to **Mr. U. Lern, 10-01 Rule Road, Englewood Cliffs, New Jersey 07632** for the instruction manual.

RULES FOR COMMAS WITH NUMBERS *(continued)*

1. For the opening of an informal letter, use a comma:
   Dear Betty,
   (The opening of a business or formal letter takes a colon.)

2. For the close of a letter, use a comma:
   Sincerely yours,
   Love,
   Best regards,
   Very truly yours,

RULES FOR COMMAS WITH NUMBERS

1. Counting from the right, put a comma after every three digits in numbers over four digits: **72,867   156,567,066**

2. In a number of four digits, a comma is optional for money, distance, and most other measurements. A comma is optional for amounts, as long as you use a consistent style within a given piece of writing.

$1776	**$1,776**
1776 miles	**1,776 miles**
1776 potatoes	**1,776 potatoes**

3. Do not use a comma for a four-digit year: **1990** (a year of five digits or more gets a comma: **25,000 B.C.**); in an address of four digits or more—**12161 Dean Drive;** or in a page number of four digits or more: **see page 1338**

(continued on next page)

(continued on next page)

QUOTATION ABOUT WRITING

The commas are the most useful and usable of all the stops. It is highly important to put them in place as you go along. If you try to come back after doing a paragraph and stick them in the various spots that tempt you you will discover that they tend to swarm like minnows into all sorts of crevices whose existence you hadn't realized and before you know it the whole long sentence becomes immobilized and lashed up squirming in commas. Better to use them sparingly, and with affection, precisely when the need for each one arises, nicely, by itself.

—Lewis Thomas

ANSWERS: EXERCISE 10

1. Eden, Texas, lies 165 miles north of San Antonio, Texas, and has a population of 1,400 [or 1400].

2. Correct

3. Eden Prairie, Minnesota, must be an attractive spot, for its population soared between January 1, 1970, and January 1, 1980, from 6,938 [or 6938] to 16,263.

4. The citizens of Edenton, North Carolina, publish a brochure saying their town is the "South's Prettiest Town."

5. The brochure reports that the town is 135 miles from Raleigh, North Carolina, and has a population of 5,264 [or 5264].

COVERAGE: EXERCISE 10

1. comma after city and state; commas with numbers

2. correct

3. comma after city and state; commas with dates; comma with numbers

4. comma after city and state

5. comma after city and state; comma with numbers

QUOTATION ABOUT WRITING

Anyone who undervalues the use of the commas in creating meaning should compare the statement "God rest you, merry gentlemen" with its older form, "God rest you merry, gentlemen."

—Carolyn Good

> **RULES FOR COMMAS WITH NUMBERS** *(continued)*
>
> 4. Use a comma to separate related measurements written as words: **five feet, four inches**
>
> 5. Use a comma to separate a scene from an act in a play: **Act II, scene iv**
>
> 6. Use a comma to separate a reference to a page from a reference to a line: **page 10, line 6**

EXERCISE 10

Insert commas where they are needed. If a sentence is correct, circle its number.

EXAMPLE   Perhaps Eden Texas offers people an earthly paradise.
Perhaps Eden, Texas, offers people an earthly paradise.

1. Eden Texas lies 165 miles north of San Antonio Texas and has a population of 1400.

2. A researcher reported in the summer of 1983 that there are 16 Edens listed in the zip code book.

3. Eden Prairie Minnesota must be an attractive spot, for its population soared between January 1 1970 and January 1 1980 from 6938 to 16263.

4. The citizens of Edenton North Carolina publish a brochure saying their town is the "South's Prettiest Town."

5. The brochure reports that the town is 135 miles from Raleigh North Carolina and has a population of 5264.

24i Using commas to clarify meaning

Sometimes you will need to use a comma to clarify the meaning of a sentence, even though no other rule calls for one.

No	Of the gymnastic team's twenty five were injured.
Yes	Of the gymnastic team's twenty, five were injured.
No	Those who can practice many hours a day.
Yes	Those who can, practice many hours a day.
No	George dressed and performed for the sellout crowd.
Yes	George dressed, and performed for the sellout crowd.

EXERCISE 11

Insert commas to prevent misreading. If a sentence is correct, circle its number.

EXAMPLE   Though controversial subliminal learning appeals to many people.

Though controversial, subliminal learning appeals to many people.

1. Using specially prepared tape recorders communicate hidden messages to listeners.

2. Some people who want to learn supposedly without effort by listening to the tape.

3. To prevent shoplifting, twenty major department stores started using subliminal tapes.

4. Of the twenty nine reported pilferage had decreased by about 37 percent.

5. Many people worry that governments or businesses might use subliminal learning to control people against their wills.

ANSWERS: EXERCISE 11

1. Using specially prepared tape, recorders communicate hidden messages to listeners.

2. Some people who want to, learn supposedly without effort by listening to the tape.

3. Correct

4. Of the twenty, nine reported pilferage had decreased by about 37 percent.

5. Correct

24j Avoiding misuse of the comma

Using commas correctly helps you deliver your meaning to your reader. As a writer, you frequently have to make decisions about whether a comma is needed. Try to avoid checking for the correct use of commas while you are drafting (3b) and concentrating on ideas. Check for your commas later, when you are revising (3d) and editing (3e). If as you are drafting you are in doubt about a comma, insert and circle it clearly so that you can go back to it later and think through whether it is correct. Throughout this chapter, most sections that discuss a correct use of the comma include a COMMA CAUTION to alert you to a related misuse of the comma. This section summarizes common misuses of the comma.

1   Avoiding misuse of a comma with coordinating conjunctions

Section 24a discusses the correct use of commas with sentences joined by coordinating conjunctions. Do not put a comma *after* a coordinating conjunction that joins two independent clauses°.

No   The sky was dark gray **and,** it looked like dusk.

YES   The sky was dark gray, **and** it looked like dusk.

BACKGROUND

Erika Lindemann, in *A Rhetoric for Writing Teachers* (2nd ed., Oxford UP, 1987, p. 135) discusses how sentence combining can improve comma usage in student writing.

Students who have learned to be careful about commas understandably "write around" the problem. Sentence-combining exercises not only illustrate how punctuation organizes sentence elements for a reader but also how to solve punctuation problems which for years have limited a student's range of syntactic options. Furthermore, the exercises sometimes expose misunderstood punctuation rules discussed in previous English classes . . . [and] grammatical labels [that] sometimes create punctuation problems. Sentence combining allows teachers to dispense with terminology altogether or, if they wish, to name constructions *after* students have practiced them.

TEACHING TIP

You may want to give your students this excerpt from the conclusion of William Faulkner's short story "Barn Burning," asking them to analyze the grammatical and stylistic uses of the commas—and their absence. Students may be interested in experimenting with changes of punctuation that result in different effects.

Behind him the white man was shouting, "My horse! Fetch my horse!" and he thought for an instant of cutting across the park and climbing the fence into the road, but he did not know the park nor how high the vine-massed fence might be and he dared not risk it. So he ran on down the drive, blood and breath roaring; presently he was in the road again though he could not see it. He could not hear either: the galloping mare was almost upon him before he heard her, and even then he held his course, as if the very urgency of his wild grief and need must in a moment more find him wings, waiting until the ultimate instant to hurl himself aside and into the weed-choked roadside ditch as the horse thundered past and on, for an instant in furious silhouette against the stars, the tranquil early summer night sky which, even before the shape of the horse and rider vanished, strained abruptly and violently upward: a long, swirling roar incredible and soundless, blotting the stars, and he springing up and into the road again, running again, knowing it was too late yet still running even after he heard the shot an instant later, two shots, pausing now without knowing he had ceased to run, crying "Pap! Pap!," running again before he knew he had begun to run, stumbling, tripping over something and scrabbling up again without ceasing to run, looking backward over his shoulder at the glare as he got up, running on among the invisible trees, panting, sobbing, "Father! Father!"

---

2 Avoiding misuse of commas to separate items

Section 24c discusses the correct use of commas with items in a series. Do not use a comma *before* the first or *after* the last item in a series, unless another rule makes it necessary. Also, do not use commas to separate two items joined with a coordinating conjunction *(and, but, for, nor, or, yet,* and *so).*

No	The gymnasium was decorated with, **red, white, and blue** ribbons for the Fourth of July.
No	The gymnasium was decorated with **red, white, and blue,** ribbons for the Fourth of July.
Yes	The gymnasium was decorated with **red, white, and blue** ribbons for the Fourth of July.
No	**The moon, and the stars** were shining last night.
Yes	**The moon and the stars** were shining last night.

Section 24d discusses the correct use of commas with coordinate adjectives°. Do not put a comma after the final coordinate adjective and the noun it modifies. Also, do not use a comma between non-coordinate adjectives.

No	The **large, restless,** crowd waited.
Yes	The **large, restless** crowd waited.
No	The concert featured **several, new** bands.
Yes	The concert featured **several new** bands.

3 Avoiding misuse of commas with restrictive elements

Section 24e discusses the correct use of commas with restrictive (essential) and nonrestrictive (nonessential) elements. Do not use a comma to set off a restrictive (essential) element from the rest of a sentence.

No	Vegetables, **stir-fried in a wok,** are uniquely crisp and flavorful. [The information about being stir-fried in a wok is essential. It should not be set off with commas.]
Yes	Vegetables **stir-fried in a wok** are uniquely crisp and flavorful.

4   Avoiding misuse of commas with quotations

Section 24g discusses the correct use of commas with quoted material. Do not use a comma to set off an indirect quotation.

No	John Jones **said that, he likes stir-fried vegetables.**
Yes	John Jones **said that he likes stir-fried vegetables.**
Yes	John Jones **said, "I like stir-fried vegetables."**

5   Avoiding use of a comma to separate a subject from its verb, a verb from its object, a verb from its complement, and a preposition from its object

No	**Orville and Wilbur Wright, made** their first successful airplane flights on December 17, 1903. [As a rule, do not let a comma separate a subject from its verb.]
Yes	**Orville and Wilbur Wright made** their first successful airplane flights on December 17, 1903.
No	These inventors enthusiastically **tackled, the problems** of powered flight and aerodynamics. [As a rule, do not let a comma separate a verb from its object°.]
Yes	These inventors enthusiastically **tackled the problems** of powered flight and aerodynamics.
No	Flying has **become, both** an important industry and a popular hobby. [As a rule, do not let a comma separate a verb from its complement°.]
Yes	Flying has **become both** an important industry and a popular hobby.
No	Airplane hobbyists visit Kitty Hawk's flight museum **from, all over the world.** [As a rule, do not let a comma separate a preposition° from its object.]
Yes	Airplane hobbyists travel to Kitty Hawk's flight museum **from all over the world.**

Because the comma occurs so frequently, advice against overusing it sometimes clashes with a rule requiring it. In such cases, follow the rule that calls for the comma.

The town of Kitty Hawk, North Carolina, attracts thousands of tourists each year. [Although the comma after *North Carolina* separates the subject and verb, it is required because the state is set off from the city and from the rest of the sentence; see 24i.]

ANSWERS: EXERCISE 12 (starts next page)

1. Wilbur [*omit: coordinating conjunction joining two nouns*] and Orville Wright proved that people could fly in 1903.

2. U.S. engineers were building [*omit: do not separate verb from object*] rocket planes for research as early as 1943.

(continued next page)

ANSWERS: EXERCISE 12 *(continued)*

3. The planes were built to withstand the intense air pressure [*omit: clause is restrictive*] that is present at Mach 1.

4. Mach 1 [*omit: don't separate subject and verb*] is defined as the speed of sound, [*keep: opens nonrestrictive clause*] which is approximately 738 miles per hour [*omit: restrictive phrase*] at sea level.

5. Finally, [*optional keep: one-word transition*] the Bell X-1, [*keep: open nonrestrictive appositive*] the product of many engineering challenges, [*keep: close nonrestrictive appositive*] was perfected.

6. Air Force Captain [*omit: restrictive appositive*] Charles E. Yeager [*omit: restrictive appositive*] reached Mach 1 and broke the sound barrier [*omit: restrictive prepositional phrase*] in a Bell X-1 rocket plane in 1947.

7. This [*omit: do not separate subject and verb*] was the first supersonic flight [*omit: restrictive phrase*] in history.

8. At first, [*optional omit: the introductory phrase is short*] all supersonic jets were military, [*keep: coordinating conjunction joining two independent clauses*] but Russia initiated commercial supersonic transport (SST) [*omit: contextually restrictive*] in 1968.

9. England and France, [*keep: open parenthetical*] you may remember, [*keep: close parenthetical*] cooperated with each other to build an SST, [*keep: open appositive*] the Concorde.

10. Landings of the Concorde SST at American airports [*omit: do not separate subject and verb*] has been a topic [*omit: do not separate verb from object*] of much debate, [*keep: coordinating conjunction joining two independent clauses*] for many people worry [*omit: restrictive clause*] that such planes might inflict long-term damage on areas around the airports.

EXERCISE 12

Some commas have been deliberately misused in these sentences. Delete commas as needed.

EXAMPLE Airplanes started as little more than motorized, double-winged, gliders, and have advanced to supersonic transportation in less than a century.

Airplanes started as little more than motorized, double-winged gliders and have advanced to supersonic transportation in less than a century.

1. Wilbur, and Orville Wright proved that people could fly in 1903.

2. U.S. engineers were building, rocket planes for research as early as 1943.

3. The planes were built to withstand the intense air pressure, that is present at Mach 1.

4. Mach 1, is defined as the speed of sound, which is approximately 738 miles per hour, at sea level.

5. Finally, the Bell X-1, the product of many engineering challenges, was perfected.

6. Air Force Captain, Charles E. Yeager, reached Mach 1 and broke the sound barrier, in a Bell X-1 rocket plane in 1947.

7. This, was the first supersonic flight, in history.

8. At first, all supersonic jets were military, but Russia initiated commercial supersonic transport (SST), in 1968.

9. England and France, you may remember, cooperated with each other to build an SST, the Concorde.

10. Landings of the Concorde SST at American airports, has been a topic, of much debate, for many people worry, that such planes might inflict long-term damage on areas around the airports.

REVISING YOUR WRITING

If you make comma errors when you write, go back to your writing and locate the errors. Using this chapter as a resource, revise your writing to correct the errors. Use the chart on the first page of this chapter to help you locate each use of the comma.

CASE STUDY: REVISING FOR CORRECT USE OF COMMAS

Observation

A student wrote the following draft for a course called Introduction to Sociology. The assignment was to write about a person who organizes group efforts to improve society. This material is well organized and includes excellent specific details, but the draft's effectiveness is diminished by the presence of comma errors.

Read through the draft. The errors are highlighted and explained. Before you look at how the student revised to eliminate the comma errors, revise the material yourself. Then compare what you and the student did.

Millard Fuller, executive director of Habitat for Humanity, believes that all people have a right to decent housing. Habitat for Humanity an organization that depends on volunteer labor and donations of money and materials builds modest sturdy homes that are sold at cost to low-income families. Previously these families had rented substandard housing without plumbing or heat. The full cost of each Habitat home is approximately $28000. To buy a home each family has to make a small down payment and support a mortgage. The monthly mortgage

Commas missing to set off nonrestrictive phrase: 24e-1

Commas missing to set off nonrestrictive phrase: 24e-1

Comma missing between coordinate adjectives: 24d

Comma missing after introductory word: 24b-3

Comma missing after introductory phrase: 24b-2

Comma missing in a number of five digits: 24h

COVERAGE: PARTICIPATION ESSAY
(starts next page)

Consumers often feel that choosing a new car is a *difficult time-consuming* [24d: commas for coordinate adjectives] matter. Most automobile customers tend to concentrate on *the price, the special features the look and the reputation* [24c: commas in a series] of the car. Truly *experienced informed* [24d: commas for coordinate adjectives] car buyers *however* [24f: commas for transitional word in middle of a sentence] carefully investigate the car manufacturer's grievance procedures.

A common mistake that consumers make is to assume that the *helpful friendly* [24d: commas for coordinate adjectives] car salesperson will help resolve problems with the automobile after it is purchased. *In fact* [24b: comma after introductory words] the salesperson's job is essentially finished once the car is *sold so a consumer* [24a: comma before coordinating conjunction that joins two independent clauses] with a complaint will usually *hear "You'll* [24g: comma before quoted words] have to talk to the service department."

If a car salesperson offers little or no help [24b: comma after introductory clause] a consumer may feel cheated by the indifference. One reaction *one felt by many people who end up with a lemon of a car* [24e: commas for nonrestrictive appositive] is to write an angry letter to the chief executive officer of the automobile manufacturer. *Before writing* [24b: comma after introductory phrase; also 24i: comma needed for clarity] the consumer should realize that complaints to the manufacturer are referred back to the dealership. *After all* [24b: comma after introductory words; also 24i: comma needed for clarity] dealerships and manufacturers are not owned and managed by the same people.

In some cases [24b: comma after introductory words] consumers may benefit from legal advice. States have varying "lemon laws" to help consumers who purchase de-

---

payment is usually about $150 an amount less than the monthly rent that the family had been paying for their indecent housing. Nevertheless Habitat for Humanity is not a charitable organization. The families offered the homes must be able to take on the financial responsibility involved participate in the labor of building their house and donate time to help build other houses.

When Fuller asks people to help he says "It's not your blue blood your pedigree or your college degree. It's what you do with your life that counts." One famous volunteer recruited to take on a yearly assignment is Jimmy Carter former President of the United States. The concept of Habitat for Humanity is catching on for the number of new Habitat U.S. affiliates increased from 11 to 171 between 1980 and 1986. This seems like an excellent way to fight poverty housing doesn't it?

Comma missing after introductory word: 24b-3
Comma missing to set off nonrestrictive appositive: 24e-2
Commas missing between items in a series: 24c
Commas missing between items in a series: 24c
Comma missing after introductory clause: 24b-1
Comma missing before quoted words: 24g
Commas missing between items in a series: 24c
Comma missing to set off nonrestrictive appositive: 24e-2
Comma missing between independent clauses joined by for: 24a
Comma missing to set off tag question: 24f

Here is how the student revised to correct the comma errors. Compare it with your revision. Make sure that your revision has eliminated each of the errors highlighted in the draft.

Millard Fuller, executive director of Habitat for Humanity, believes that all people have a right to decent housing. Habitat for Humanity, an organization that depends on volunteer labor and donations of money and materials, builds modest, sturdy homes that are sold at cost to low-income families. Previously, these families had rented substandard housing without plumbing or heat. The full cost of each Habitat home is approximately $28,000. To buy a home, each family has to make a small down payment and support a mortgage. The monthly mortgage payment is usually about $150, an amount less than the monthly rent that the family had been paying for their indecent housing. Nevertheless, Habitat for Humanity is not a charitable organization. The families offered the homes must be able to take on the financial responsibility involved, participate in the labor of building their house, and donate time to help build other houses.

When Fuller asks people to help, he says, "It's not your blue blood, your pedigree, or your college degree. It's what you do with your life that counts." One famous volunteer recruited to take on a yearly assignment is Jimmy Carter, former President of the United States. The concept of Habitat for Humanity is catching on, for the number of new Habitat U.S. affiliates increased from 11 to 171 between 1980 and 1986. This seems like an excellent way to fight poverty housing, doesn't it?

Participation

A student wrote the following draft for a course called Introduction to Political Science. The assignment was to discuss an example of the power of consumers. The material is clear and logically presented, but the draft's effectiveness is diminished by comma errors.

Read through the draft. Then revise it to eliminate the errors. Also, make any additional revisions you think would improve the content, organization, and style of the material.

Consumers often feel that choosing a new car is a difficult time-consuming matter. Most automobile customers tend to concentrate on the price, the special features the look and the reputation of the car. Truly experienced informed car buyers however carefully investigate the car manufacturer's grievance procedures.

A common mistake that consumers make is to assume that the helpful friendly car salesperson will help resolve problems with the automobile after it is purchased. In fact the salesperson's job is essentially finished once the car is sold so a consumer with a complaint will usually hear "You'll have to talk to the service department."

If a car salesperson offers little or no help a consumer may feel cheated by the indifference. One reaction one felt by many people who end up with a lemon of a car is to write an angry letter to the chief executive officer of the automobile company. Before writing the consumer should realize that complaints to the manufacturer are referred back to the dealership. After all dealerships and manufacturer are not owned and managed by the same people.

In some cases consumers may benefit from legal advice. States

fective cars. In some states *for example* [24f: commas for transitional word in middle of a sentence] the existence of a problem, *that is unresolved,* [24e: drop commas with restrictive element] after six repair attempts by the dealership's service department can require a dealer to substitute a new vehicle. Chrysler Motors has the Customer Arbitration Board (CAB), which consists of a consumer advocate, a member of the general public, and an *independent, technical expert* [24d: drop comma with noncoordinate adjectives]. Any solution that the CAB proposes is binding on the dealer and Chrysler Motors.

It is comforting to know that a consumer, *who buys a lemon of a car,* [24e: drop commas with restrictive clause] is not always *helpless isn't it?* [24h: comma for tag question] Sometimes a lemon can be made into lemonade, right?

ANSWER: PARTICIPATION ESSAY

This version revises the comma errors. Answers will vary if students have revised content, organization, or style.

Consumers often feel that choosing a new car is a difficult, time-consuming matter. Most automobile customers tend to concentrate on the price, the special features, the look, and the reputation of the car. Truly experienced, informed car buyers, however, carefully investigate the car manufacturer's grievance procedures.

A common mistake that consumers make is to assume that the helpful, friendly car salesperson will help resolve problems with the automobile after it is purchased. In fact, the salesperson's job is essentially finished once the car is sold, so a consumer with a complaint will usually hear, "You'll have to talk to the service department."

If a car salesperson offers little or no help,

(continued next page)

ANSWER: PARTICIPATION ESSAY
(continued)

a consumer may feel cheated by the indifference. One reaction, one felt by many people who end up with a lemon of a car, is to write an angry letter to the chief executive officer of the automobile manufacturer. Before writing, the consumer should realize that complaints to the manufacturer are referred back to the dealership. After all, dealerships and manufacturers are not owned and managed by the same people.

In some cases, consumers may benefit from legal advice. States have varying "lemon laws" to help consumers who purchase defective cars. In some states, for example, the existence of a problem that is unresolved after six repair attempts by the dealership's service department can require a dealership to substitute a new vehicle. Chrysler Motors has the Customer Arbitration Board (CAB), which consists of a consumer advocate, a member of the general public, and an independent technical expert. Any solution that the CAB proposes is binding on the dealer and Chrysler Motors.

It is comforting to know that a consumer who buys a lemon of a car is not always helpless, isn't it? Sometimes a lemon can be made into lemonade, right?

have varying "lemon laws" to help consumers who purchase defective cars. In some states for example the existence of a problem, that is unresolved, after six repair attempts by the dealership's service department can require a dealer to substitute a new vehicle. Chrysler Motors has the Customer Arbitration Board (CAB), which consists of a consumer advocate, a member of the general public, and an independent, technical expert. Any solution that the CAB proposes is binding on the dealer and Chrysler Motors.

It is comforting to know that a consumer, who buys a lemon of a car, is not always helpless isn't it? Sometimes a lemon can be made into lemonade, right?

25 The Semicolon

The **semicolon** joins units that are separate but related in meaning. When you use a semicolon between independent clauses°, you are communicating greater separation than a comma provides but less than a period provides (25a, 25b, 25c). Also, a semicolon may be quite useful in organizing items in a series (25d).

25a Using a semicolon between closely related independent clauses

When independent clauses are related in meaning, you can separate them with a semicolon instead of a period.

> **SEMICOLON PATTERN I**
>
> Independent clause; independent clause.

The choice is yours in relation to the meaning you want your material to deliver. A period signals complete separation between independent clauses; a semicolon tells readers that the separation is softer.

> This is my husband's second marriage; it's the first for me.
> —Ruth Sidel, "Marion Deluca"

> Our Constitution is in actual operation; everything appears to promise that it will last; but in this world nothing is certain but death and taxes.
> —Benjamin Franklin

BACKGROUND

Beginning in the eighth century, the inverted semicolon served as a pause somewhere between a comma and a colon. After about 700 years of use, it was discarded. The semicolon as it is known today dates from the seventh century.

QUOTATION ABOUT WRITING

It is almost always a greater pleasure to come across a semicolon than a period. The period tells you that that is that; if you didn't get all the meaning you wanted or expected, anyway you got all the writer intended to parcel out and now you have to move along. But with a semicolon there, you get a pleasant little feeling of expectancy; there is more to come; read on; it will get clearer.

> —Lewis Thomas, "Notes on Punctuation"

QUOTATION ABOUT WRITING

From the reader's point of view, punctuation provides a map for one who must otherwise drive blindly past the by-ways, intersections, and detours of a writer's thought.

> —Mina Shaughnessy,
> *Errors and Expectations*

QUOTATION ABOUT WRITING

Punctuation contributes to art as well as to correctness, to style as well as to styling. Make it work for you, not just to develop prose that is "clear enough"—not just to prevent confusion—but to help you express yourself, or your characters express themselves. Don't lean on it; don't shy away from it; just *use* it—and in doing so, let it help you convey nuances too subtle for words alone to convey; let it help you evoke effects so delicate that talk would shatter them. And remember that if you frequently use more marks than usual—or fewer than usual—you will call attention to your craft, with the results possibly seeming artful rather than artistic, posturing rather than expressive. Nor do I for a moment suggest that punctuation can, or should, be charged with sole responsibility for effectiveness: descriptive detail, diction, sentence length, sentence rhythm, paragraph structure, timing—these and other elements of style can and must share the load.

—Robert M. Pierson, "Punctuation as Art"

ALTERNATE EXAMPLES

1. Each year people from all over the world visit the Tower of London; for centuries, it served as a prison for famous persons who were deemed to be enemies of the crown.

2. The Tower is located in the Borough of Stepney; it covers about eighteen acres.

3. The central portion, called the White Tower, was begun in 1078; it was modernized by Christopher Wren.

4. The Beauchamp Tower has 91 inscriptions of prisoners in it; the Bloody Tower served as the prison of Sir Walter Raleigh, who wrote an incomplete *History of the World* during his stay there in 1614.

5. The place of execution within the walls was Tower Green; there Anne Boleyn was beheaded in 1536.

One or more of the clauses joined by a semicolon may contain a comma.

> It is rare for us to leave wild animals alive; when we do, we often do not leave them wild.
>
> —Brigid Brophy, "The Rights of Animals"

❖ COMMA CAUTION: Do not use only a comma between independent clauses, or you will create the error called a comma splice (see Chapter 14). ❖

25b Using a semicolon before a coordinating conjunction joining independent clauses containing commas

You will usually use a comma to separate independent clauses linked by a coordinating conjunction *(and, but, or, nor, for, yet, so).* When one or more of the independent clauses contains a comma or commas, however, you can use a semicolon before the coordinating conjunction.

SEMICOLON PATTERN II

- Independent clause, one that contains commas; coordinating conjunction independent clause.

- Independent clause; coordinating conjunction independent clause, containing commas.

- Independent clause, one that contains commas; coordinating conjunction independent clause, one that contains commas.

> When the peacock has presented his back, the spectator will usually begin to walk around him to get a front view; but the peacock will continue to turn so that no front view is possible.
>
> —Flannery O'Connor, "The King of the Birds"

> For anything worth having, one must pay the price; and the price is always work, patience, love, self-sacrifice.
>
> —John Burroughs

25c Using a semicolon when conjunctive adverbs or other transitional expressions connect independent clauses

Use a semicolon between two independent clauses when the second clause begins with a conjunctive adverb (*therefore, however;* for a complete list, see page 186) or other transitional expression (*in fact, as a result;* for a complete list, see page 96). Your other option is to use a period, creating two sentences.

> **SEMICOLON PATTERN III**
>
> Independent clause; conjunctive adverb or other transitional expression, independent clause.

The average annual rainfall in Death Valley is about two inches; **nevertheless,** hundreds of plant and animal species survive and even thrive there.

Patient photographers have spent years recording desert life cycles; all of us, **as a result,** have watched barren sands flower after a spring storm.

 COMMA ALERTS: (1) Do not use only a comma between independent clauses connected by a conjunctive adverb or other words of transition, or you will create the error called a comma splice, as explained in Chapter 14. (2) Use a comma *after* a conjunctive adverb or a transitional expression that begins an independent clause. Some writers omit the comma after short words, such as *then, next, soon.* (3) When you position a conjunctive adverb or a transitional expression somewhere after the first word in an independent clause, set it off with commas. See the example with *as a result,* above. ♣

25d Using a semicolon between long or comma-containing items in a series

When a sentence contains series of words, phrases°, or clauses°, commas usually separate the items from each other. When the items are long and contain commas for other purposes, use semicolons

1. A newborn baby exhibits what we interpret to be fear at a sudden, loud, unexpected noise; the removal of parental, mechanical, or other physical support; and the appearance of strange, unexpected, unknown objects mixed with familiar ones.

2. A baby shows rage when its free, uninhibited movement is constrained; when its regular, nourishing feeding pattern is interrupted; or when its expected, traditional, physical comfort is disturbed.

3. Most practical jokes, such as unexpected, loud, exploding fireworks; collapsing, unstable seats; and mysterious, deceptive, disappearing objects are an exploitation of these situations.

4. Laughter can be explained in terms of feelings of malice or envy; awareness of contrast, incongruity, or ugliness; relief from this experience; or in terms of its more positive result, a feeling of sudden glory; a surge of vital feeling; or a sense of freedom.

ANSWERS: EXERCISE 1 (next page)

1. As early as colonial days, Brazilian officials had expressed a desire to move the capital inland; they hoped that this would encourage development.

2. Correct

3. In 1956 Juscelino Kubitschek was elected president of Brazil; one of his campaign promises was that a new capital would be built.

4. Kubitschek kept his promise; indeed, construction of the new capital began within a year.

5. Lucio Costa planned the city; Oscar Niemeyer designed the buildings.

6. Correct

7. The city officially became the capital in 1960; however, many governmental

instead of commas to separate items. The semicolons show exactly where one item ends and the next begins. This makes your message much easier for readers to understand.

SEMICOLON PATTERN IV

Independent clause that includes a series of items, one or all of which contain commas; another item in the series; another item in the series.

Functioning as assistant chefs, the students chopped onions, green peppers, and parsley; sliced chicken and duck meat into strips; started a delicious-smelling broth simmering; and filled a large, low, long-handled pan with oil before the head chef moved up to the stove.

25e Avoiding the misuse of the semicolon

1 Not using a semicolon between a dependent clause and an independent clause

No Although the new computers had arrived at the college; the computer lab was still being built.

Yes Although the new computers had arrived at the college, the computer lab was still being built.

2 Using a colon, not a semicolon, to introduce a list

No The newscast featured three major stories; the latest pictures of Uranus, a speech by the president, and a series of brush fires in Nevada.

Yes The newscast featured three major stories: the latest pictures of Uranus, a speech by the president, and a series of brush fires in Nevada.

EXERCISE 1

Insert semicolons where they are needed. If a sentence is correct, circle its number.

EXAMPLE   On April 20, 1960, the capital of Brazil was Rio de Janeiro, on April 21 of that year Brasilia became the new capital.

Until 1960 the capital of Brazil was Rio de Janeiro; on April 21 of that year Brasilia became the new capital.

1. As early as colonial days, Brazilian officials had expressed a desire to move the capital inland they hoped that this would encourage development.

2. When the Brazilian constitution was written in 1891, one clause stated that Rio de Janeiro should no longer be the capital.

3. In 1956 Juscelino Kubitschek was elected president of Brazil, one of his campaign promises was that a new capital would be built.

4. Kubitschek kept his promise, indeed, construction of the new capital began within a year.

5. Lucio Costa planned the layout of the streets, and Oscar Niemeyer designed the buildings.

6. When viewed from above, the city looks a little like a jet, with the suburban areas making up the wings and the government areas the fuselage.

7. The city officially became the capital in 1960, however, many governmental agencies remained in Rio de Janeiro for some time.

8. Many Brazilians argue that the capital should be returned to Rio de Janeiro, nevertheless, it appears that Brasilia will remain the seat of government.

9. The cost of the city was far too great to abandon it now, moreover, it has improved life in the interior regions.

10. Brasilia has helped the economy of the region, it has drawn people to the country's interior, especially Planalto, it continues to serve the country well as the center of government.

ANSWERS: EXERCISE 1 *(continued)*

agencies remained in Rio de Janeiro for some time.

8. Many Brazilians argue that the capital should be returned to Rio de Janeiro; nevertheless, it appears that Brasilia will remain the seat of government.

9. The cost of building the city was far too great to abandon it now; moreover, it has improved life in interior regions.

10. Brasilia has helped the economy of the region; it has drawn people to the country's interior, especially Planalto; it continues to serve the country well as the center of government.

COVERAGE: EXERCISE 1

(1) between two independent clauses, with one clause containing a comma; (2) correct; (3) between two independent clauses; (4) between two independent clauses, with the second starting with a transitional word; (5) between two independent clauses; (6) correct; (7), (8), and (9) between two independent clauses, with the second starting with a conjunctive adverb; (10) between independent clauses in a series

---

ANSWERS: EXERCISE 2 (next page)

1. The first roller coaster in the United States, installed in the late nineteenth century, was part of an amusement park in the Coney Island section of New York City; it was named the "Switchback Gravity Pleasure Railway."

2. The first roller coaster was extremely primitive; it was built of wood, had only two inclines, and reached a downhill speed of a mere six miles per hour.

3. Riders got on at the top of the first incline and climbed out when the train

(continued next page)

ANSWERS: EXERCISE 2 *(continued)*

reached the bottom; then the riders walked up the hill to the top of the second incline and climbed in for the ride to the bottom.

4. Soon a chain drive for roller coasters was developed to power the train on the uphill parts; therefore, higher inclines could be built to give riders a greater thrill.

5. Major breakthroughs in roller-coaster design occurred in the 1970s, when roller coaster designers drew on advanced knowledge from physics, mathematics, and human physiology; and the designers used computer simulations to check their work.

6. Extraordinarily sophisticated scientific applications to roller coasters began to appear in the 1980s; in fact, some high school physics teachers were so impressed that they began to use examples of modern roller-coaster design to illustrate principles in physics.

7. A 360-degree circle cannot be used for a roller coaster loop because speed reduction at the top of a 360-degree circle could pull riders from their seats; in contrast, the tear-shaped clothoid loop has been found to permit roller-coaster riders to speed along safely upside down at 70 miles per hour.

8. The Shock Wave, opened in the late 1980s at an Illinois amusement park, has a height of 17 stories; a short downhill run of 70 miles per hour; rapidly reversing directions, patterned after a twisted pretzel; and a sequence of corkscrew spirals.

9. A recent visitor to New York's Coney Island amusement park reported that the 61-year-old wooden Cyclone was half-empty; and the new Double Loop, designed with the latest advances in roller-coaster engineering, drew huge crowds.

10. Many roller-coaster enthusiasts drive long distances to try out a new roller coaster; however, many other people are repelled by the thought of riding a roller coaster.

EXERCISE 2

Combine each set of sentences into one sentence containing two independent clauses. Use a semicolon between the two clauses. You may add, omit, revise, and rearrange words. Try to use all the patterns in this chapter. More than one revision may be correct, so be ready to explain the reasoning behind your decisions.

EXAMPLE Roller coasters have been around for a long time. Today's roller coasters barely resemble their ancestors. Today's roller coasters are scientifically designed.

> *Roller coasters have been around for a long time; however, today's scientifically designed roller coasters barely resemble their ancestors.*

1. The first roller coaster in the United States was installed in the late nineteenth century. It was installed as part of an amusement park. The park was in the Coney Island section of New York City. It was named the "Switchback Gravity Pleasure Railway."

2. The first roller coaster was extremely primitive. It was built of wood. It had only two inclines. It reached a downhill speed of a mere six miles per hour.

3. Riders got on at the top of the first incline. Riders climbed out when the train reached the bottom. Then the riders walked up the hill to the top of the second incline. Once again they climbed in for the ride to the bottom.

4. Soon a chain drive for roller coasters was developed. The chain drive powered the train on the uphill parts. Higher inclines could be built. The higher inclines gave riders a greater thrill.

5. Major breakthroughs in roller-coaster design occurred in the 1970s. Roller coaster designers drew on advanced knowledge from physics, mathematics, and human physiology. The designers used computer simulations to check their work.

6. Extraordinarily sophisticated scientific applications to roller coasters began to appear in the 1980s. Some high school physics teachers were very impressed. The teachers began to use examples of modern roller-coaster design to illustrate principles in physics.

7. A 360-degree circle cannot be used for a roller coaster loop. Speed reduction at the top of a 360-degree circle could pull riders from their seats. The clothoid loop has been found to permit roller-coaster riders to speed along safely upside down at 70 miles per hour. A clothoid loop is tear shaped.

8. The Shock Wave opened in the late 1980s. It opened at an Illinois amusement park. It has a height of 17 stories. It has a short downhill

run of 70 miles per hour. It has rapidly reversing directions, patterned after a twisted pretzel. It has a sequence of corkscrew spirals.

9. A recent visitor to New York's Coney Island amusement park gave a report. The report was that the 61-year-old wooden Cyclone was half-empty. The new Double Loop drew huge crowds. The Double Loop was designed with the latest advances in roller-coaster engineering.

10. Many people are roller-coaster enthusiasts. They drive long distances to try out a new roller coaster. Many other people are repelled by the thought of riding a roller coaster.

EXERCISE 3

Insert needed semicolons in the following sentences, and delete unnecessary ones. If a sentence is correct, circle its number.

1. The sound of Muzak has invaded our banks, supermarkets, and elevators, furthermore, it often assaults our ears when we are placed on hold on a busy telephone line.

2. Muzak plays in government offices, in the White House, in the Pentagon, in Congress, it played during the Olympics, and it even played in the Apollo XI spaceship carrying Neil Armstrong to the moon.

3. The Muzak Corporation, now part of Westinghouse; estimates that its recordings are heard by 80 million people every day, and the company and its affiliates take in more than $150 million annually.

4. Not all listeners appreciate Muzak novelist Vladimir Nabokov, artist Ben Shahn, and composer Philip Glass have used adjectives such as "horrible," "abominable," "offensive," and "tormenting" to describe it.

5. The Muzak system was the creation of an unusual general, George Owen Squier; a West Pointer who devoted much of his army career to science.

6. During World War I, Squier invented a system for transmitting several messages simultaneously over electric power lines, in the era following the war, he took his ideas and patents to the North American Company, a utilities combine.

7. The company backed him in launching Wired Radio, Inc.; a kind of competitor to the booming fad for wireless radio.

8. The company wanted a catchy new name for this product; therefore, they combined the sound of the word "music" with the name of the manufacturer of popular cameras, Kodak.

9. The first customers for Muzak were residents of Cleveland however, a series of experiments in the late 1930s opened a much larger market.

COVERAGE: EXERCISE 2

1. ; it (25a)
2. ; it (25a)
3. ; then (25c)
4. ; therefore, (25c)
5. ; and (25b)
6. ; in fact, (25c)
7. ; in contrast (25c)
8. series of items, some containing commas (25d)
9. ; and (25b)
10. ; however, (25c)

ANSWERS: EXERCISE 3

1. The sound of Muzak has invaded our banks, supermarkets, and elevators; furthermore, it often assaults our ears when we are placed on hold on a busy telephone line.

2. Muzak plays in government offices, in the White House, in the Pentagon, in Congress; it played during the Olympics; and it even played in the Apollo XI spaceship carrying Neil Armstrong to the moon.

3. The Muzak Corporation, now part of Westinghouse, estimates that its recordings are heard by 80 million people every day; and the company and its affiliates take in more than $150 million annually.

4. Not all listeners appreciate Muzak; novelist Vladimir Nabokov, artist Ben Shahn, and composer Philip Glass have used adjectives such as "horrible," "abominable," "offensive," and "tormenting" to describe it.

5. The Muzak system was the creation of an unusual general, George Owen Squier, a West Pointer who devoted much of his army career to science.

6. During World War I, Squier invented a system for transmitting several messages simultaneously over electric power lines; in the era following the war, he took his ideas and patents to the North American Company, a utilities combine.

(continued next page)

ANSWERS: EXERCISE 3 (continued)

7. The company backed him in launching Wired Radio, Inc., a kind of competitor to the booming fad for wireless radio.

8. Correct

9. The first customers for Muzak were residents of Cleveland; however, a series of experiments in the late 1930s opened a much larger market.

10. These tests proved that Muzak could get more work out of people and animals; in factories, absenteeism was reduced, early departures were curbed, and morale was raised; on farms, cows gave more milk and chickens laid more eggs.

ANSWERS: EXERCISE 4

1. Our inner clocks help determine our times of elation and depression; they also regulate our times of patience, irritability, precision, and carelessness.

2. We need to understand how these clocks work and what they are; we need to know how they interact and how they can be thrown off schedule.

3. Understanding these principles can help us to organize our lives so that we will be able to maximize performance and pleasure; we will not waste energy fighting the body's natural inclinations.

4. Some valuable facts about the internal time clocks are already known; for example, people are least likely to be alert after they have eaten lunch, and calories consumed at breakfast are less likely to turn to body fat than those eaten at supper.

5. Many people find certain other facts useful; for instance, a high-protein breakfast enhances alertness while a high-carbohydrate supper helps induce sleep.

10. These tests proved that Muzak could get more work out of people and animals, in factories, absenteeism was reduced, early departures were curbed, and morale was raised, on farms, cows gave more milk and chickens laid more eggs.

EXERCISE 4

Combine each set of sentences into one sentence containing two independent clauses. Use a semicolon between the independent clauses. You may omit, add, revise, or rearrange words. More than one revision may be correct, so be ready to explain the reasoning behind your decisions.

EXAMPLE   Some people live by the clock on the wall. All of us are governed by internal clocks. These clocks regulate hundreds of biological functions.

Some people live by the clock on the wall; however, all of us are governed by internal clocks which regulate hundreds of biological functions.

1.   Our inner clocks help determine our times of elation and depression. They also regulate our times of patience and irritability. Our inner clocks also regulate our precision and carelessness.

2.   We need to understand how these clocks work. We need to know what they are. We need to know how they interact. We also need to know how they can be thrown off schedule.

3.   Understanding these principles can help us to organize our lives. We will be able to maximize performance and pleasure. We will not waste energy fighting the body's natural inclinations.

4.   Some valuable facts about the internal time clocks are already known. People are least likely to be alert, for example, after they have eaten lunch. In addition, calories consumed at breakfast are less likely to turn to body fat than those eaten at supper.

5.   Many people find certain other facts useful. A high-protein breakfast enhances alertness. A high-carbohydrate supper helps induce sleep.

26 The Colon

In sentence punctuation, the colon introduces what comes after it: a quotation, a summary or restatement, or a list. The colon has the effect of pointing a bit dramatically to what follows it. The colon has a few special separating functions as well.

26a Using a colon to introduce quotations, summaries, lists

Use a colon at the end of your words introducing a formal quotation. When you use a colon to introduce a quotation, the words before the colon should be an independent clause°. When your words introducing a quotation are not an independent clause, use a comma between the introductory words and the quotation (see 24g).

COLON PATTERN I

Independent clause containing words that introduce a quotation: "Quoted words."

E. B. White writes of his annual surge of interest in gardening: "We are hooked and are making an attempt to kick the habit."

—MARIE WINN, *The Plug-In Drug*

You can use a colon to introduce statements that summarize, restate, or explain what is said in an independent clause°. When you display a quotation, as shown in 28a-1, and the words that lead into the quotation are a complete sentence, end the sentence with a colon.

QUOTATION ABOUT WRITING

Remember that colons—perhaps the mark we exploit least—generally mean that what is to come will explain what has just gone by. They imply identity, whereas semicolons imply "separate but equal" status. "I have just learned three facts: that St. Paul is the capital of Minnesota; that Helena is the capital of Montana; and that Lincoln is the capital of Nebraska." Everything after the colon adds up to "three facts"—whereas the three statements of fact, though they have much in common, are not identical (there are three, not one). Colons can also save words and create special effects. Compare:

√ I admire her poetry. Its imagery is magnificent.

√ I admire her poetry for its magnificent imagery.

√ I admire her poetry: its imagery is magnificent.

All three versions are "correct." The first is emphatic and probably clear—or clear enough: *Probably* your reader will realize that the second sentence explains the first. The second version is clearer, and it flows along smoothly. The third is clearer than the first and just as clear as the second, and it gives us a unique kind of silence—not just a break (the period did *that*) but mild suspense. Your job is to decide which way of punctuating best expresses what *you* want to express.

—Robert M. Pierson, "Punctuation as Art"

QUOTATION ABOUT WRITING

When we are very young, we tend to regard the ability to use a colon much as a budding pianist regards the ability to play with crossed hands: many of us, when we are older, regard it as a proof of literary skill, maturity, even of sophistication: and many, whether young, not so young, or old, employ it gauchely, haphazardly, or at best inconsistently.

—Eric Partridge, *You Have a Point There*

COLON PATTERN II

Independent clause: summarizing or restating words.

Perhaps it is this specter that most haunts working men and women: the planned obsolescence of people that is of a piece with the planned obsolescence of the things they make.

—STUDS TERKEL, *Working*

Anthropology provides a scientific basis for dealing with the crucial dilemma of the world today: How can peoples of different appearance, mutually unintelligible languages, and dissimilar ways of life get along peaceably together?

—CLYDE KLUCKHOHN, *Mirror for Man*

You can use a colon to lead into an appositive—a word or group of words that renames or restates a noun or a pronoun.

The Metropolitan Museum in New York City now owns the best-known works of Louis Tiffany's studio: those wonderful stained-glass windows. [*Stained-glass windows* renames *best-known works*.]

Use a colon before a list or a series of items referred to in an independent clause°.

COLON PATTERN III

Independent clause: listed items.

If you really want to lose weight, you need give up only three things: breakfast, lunch, and dinner.

When you use phrases like *the following* or *as follows,* a colon is usually required. A colon is not called for with the words *such as* or *including* (see 26c).

The students' demands included the following: an expanded menu in the cafeteria, improved janitorial services, and more up-to-date textbooks.

❖ CAPITALIZATION ALERTS: (1) Either a capital letter or a lower-case letter is correct for the first word of an independent clause or a question following a colon. Whichever practice you choose, be consistent throughout a paper. (2) Use a lower-case letter following a colon for a list, an appositive, or any other set of words *not* an independent clause, unless the first word is a proper noun. ❖

26b Using a colon to separate standard material

TITLE AND SUBTITLE

A Brief History of Time: From the Big Bang to Black Holes
Charles Dickens: His Tragedy and Triumph

HOURS, MINUTES, AND SECONDS

The plane took off at 7:15 p.m.
The track star passed the halfway point at 1:23:02.

CHAPTERS AND VERSES OF THE BIBLE

Psalms 23:1–3
Luke 3:13

MEMO FORM

To: Dean Kristen Olivero
From: Professor Daniel Black
Re: Student Work-Study Program

SALUTATION OF FORMAL OR BUSINESS LETTER

Dear Ms. Beins:

MLA BIBLIOGRAPHIC FORMAT: CITY OF PUBLICATION AND PUBLISHER (BOOK)

Atwood, Margaret. *The Handmaid's Tale.* Boston: Houghton, 1986.

MLA BIBLIOGRAPHIC FORMAT: YEAR FROM PAGES (ARTICLE)

McGrath, Anne, "Books that Speak for Themselves." *U.S. News & World Report.* 14 July 1986: 49.

26c Avoiding misuse of the colon

A complete independent clause° must precede a colon except when the colon separates standard material (26b). Especially with listed items, take care that lead-in words make a grammatically complete statement. When they do not, do not use a colon.

ALTERNATE EXAMPLES

1. To introduce quotations, summaries, lists

   a. Alice Roosevelt Longworth's colorful reputation is exemplified by this remark: "I have a simple philosophy. Fill what's empty. Empty what's full. And scratch where it itches."

   b. Greek mythology comprises the description of the gods and the various stories told about them: it is a series of narratives depicting their personalities, functions, and relationships.

   c. Zeus, the supreme god of the Greeks, served in a number of capacities: as weather god, sender of rain and lightning, and ruler over the other gods.

2. To separate material

   a. Eric Partridge is the author of *You Have a Point There: A Guide to Punctuation and Its Allies* as well as *Usage and Abusage: A Guide to Good English.*

   b. I will cite the work in the bibliography as follows:

      O'Connor, Flannery. "The Life You Save May Be Your Own." *The Realm of Fiction: Seventy-Four Stories.* Ed. James B. Hall and Elizabeth Hall. 3rd ed. New York: McGraw, 1977. 479–88.

   c. To: Professor Dorothy Bankston
      From: Professor Sylvia Iskander
      Re: Selection of textbooks

QUOTATION ABOUT WRITING

For what is Punctuation, and what its aim? It is the art of dividing a literary composition into sentences, and parts of sentences, by means of points, for the purpose of exhibiting the various combinations, connections, and dependencies of words. And what is this process but a means of facilitating that analysis and combination which must be made, consciously or unconsciously, before we can penetrate to the very core of an author's thoughts, and appropriate them as food for the life and growth of our own minds?

—John Wilson, *A Treatise on English Punctuation,* 32nd ed., 1899

ALTERNATE EXERCISE

You may want to ask your students to rewrite the following sentences, omitting the colons. The students will probably have to divide each into several sentences.

1. The institution of marriage is generally divided by sociologists into four main types: monogamy, polygyny, polyandry, and group marriage.

2. An early reference to group marriage was made by Julius Caesar concerning the early Britons: "Ten and even twelve have wives common to them, and particularly brothers among brothers, and parents among their children."

3. Monogamy, the marriage of one man with one woman, is the most widely approved form in contemporary society: it is the basis of the modern family.

4. Polygyny is practiced by some religious sects: it is acceptable, for example, in some Arab countries.

5. Most American women do not generally favor such an arrangement: they have no desire to be one of several wives.

No	The shy boy bought: eggs, milk, cheese, and bread.
YES	The shy boy bought eggs, milk, cheese, and bread.

The words *such as, including, like,* and *consists of* can be tricky: Do not let them lure you into using a colon incorrectly.

No	The health board discussed a number of problems, such as: poor water quality, an inadequate sewage treatment system, and the lack of an alternate water supply.
YES	The health board discussed a number of problems, such as poor water quality, an inadequate sewage treatment system, and the lack of an alternate water supply.
YES	The health board discussed a number of problems: water quality, the inefficiency of the sewage treatment system, and the lack of an alternate water supply.
No	Five dates were chosen, including: April 3, June 11, and July 6.
YES	Five dates were chosen, including April 3, June 11, and July 6.
YES	Five dates were chosen, including the following: April 3, June 11, and July 6.

Do not use a colon to separate a dependent clause° from an independent clause°.

No	After the drought ended: the mayor appointed a commission to plan water-saving measures for the future.
YES	After the drought ended, the mayor appointed a commission to plan water-saving measures for the future.

EXERCISE 1

Insert colons where they are needed. If a sentence is correct, circle its number.

EXAMPLE   Most gamblers ignore how slim their chances are of hitting the jackpot in a slot machine, about one in 2,000.

Most gamblers ignore how slim their chances are of hitting a jackpot in a slot machine: about one in 2,000.

1. Researchers at Washington University have discovered a startling new fact, not only do you dream approximately every 90 minutes when you are asleep, but you daydream approximately every 90 minutes when you are awake.

2. Among the forgers who have committed these crimes for hundreds of years, three continue to interest experts, William Henry Ireland, who forged a series of letters he claimed were written by Shakespeare; Hans Van Meegeren, who produced amazingly accurate copies of Jan Vermeer's paintings; and Clifford Irving, who convinced a New York publisher that he had been hired to ghost-write Howard Hughes's autobiography.

3. Writing about the problems of leadership, the historian Barbara Tuchman reaches this conclusion "As witnesses of the twentieth century's record, comparable to the worst in history, we have little confidence in our species."

4. The worst insurance risks in the United States include astronauts, drivers of hydroplanes, race drivers in the Indianapolis 500, and drivers in Grand Prix auto races.

5. Many proper Victorians were shocked by Thomas Hardy's novel *Tess of the D'Urbervilles; A Virtuous Woman.*

6. Halley's comet made its predicted return in 1986, passing nearest to the sun on February 9, just before 1100 a.m. Greenwich time.

7. The text was based on Psalms 85,10, "Mercy and truth are met together: righteousness and peace have kissed each other."

8. Two characteristics aided Einstein in his work, his curiosity and his ability to concentrate.

9. Wills have been written on unusual surfaces, napkins, wallpaper, hospital charts, and even the side of a corncrib.

10. For those who think there must be a pleasant way to lose weight, consider the following fact, you have to kiss 389 times to lose one pound.

11. On April 8, 1974, Babe Ruth's home run record was finally broken. Henry Aaron became the new home run king.

12. In the past century, vaccines have been developed for five diseases, diphtheria, measles, polio, typhoid fever, and whooping cough.

13. To;   All Employees
    From; Management
    Re;   Vacation Schedules

14. In *Silent Spring,* the environmentalist Rachel Carson wrote these words about pollution, "The chemical barrage has been hurled against the fabric of life."

15. The city's budget crisis carries a message, How long can government continue to spend beyond its means?

ANSWERS: EXERCISE 1

1. fact: Not only
2. experts: William Henry
3. conclusion: "As witnesses
4. Correct
5. Tess of the D'Urbervilles: A Virtuous Woman
6. 11:00
7. 85:10
8. work: his
9. surfaces: napkins
10. fact: You
11. broken: Henry Aaron
12. diseases: diphtheria
13. To: All Employees
    From: Management
    Re: Vacation Schedules
14. pollution: "The chemical
15. message: How long

COVERAGE: EXERCISE 1

(1) summarizing; (2) listing; (3) quoting; (4) correct; (5) separating material in title; (6) separating material in time citation; (7) separating material in Bible citation; (8) summarizing; (9) listing; (10) summarizing; (11) summarizing; (12) listing; (13) separating material in memo; (14) quoting; (15) summarizing

QUOTATION ABOUT WRITING

An unnecessary mark is worse than useless. It is an interruption.

—George Summey, *American Punctuation*

27 The Apostrophe

BACKGROUND

The English apostrophe was adopted from French, which had taken it from Latin *apostrophus*. It had, not surprisingly, come to Latin from Greek, in which it referred to elision or omission.

The apostrophe plays three major roles: it helps to form the possessive of nouns and a few pronouns; it stands for one or more omitted letters; and it helps to form the plurals of letters and numerals. It does *not* help form plurals of nouns or the possessive case of personal pronouns.

 Using an apostrophe to form the possessive case of nouns and indefinite pronouns

The **possessive case** serves to communicate ownership or close relationship.

OWNERSHIP The writer's pen
CLOSE RELATIONSHIP The novel's plot

Possession in nouns and certain indefinite pronouns can be communicated by an apostrophe in combination with an *-s* (*the instructor's comments*) or by phrases beginning with *of the* (*the comments of the instructor*).

 Adding -'s to show possession when nouns and indefinite pronouns do not end in -s

The **dean's** duties included working closely with the resident assistants. [*dean* = singular noun not ending in -s]

In one more year I will receive my **bachelor's** degree. [*bachelor* = singular noun not ending in -s]

They care about their **children's** futures. [*children* = plural noun not ending in -s]

The accident was really **no one's** fault. [*no one* = indefinite pronoun not ending in -s]

2 **Adding -'s to show possession when singular nouns end in -s**

That **business's** system for handling complaints is inefficient.
Chris's ordeal ended.
Lee **Jones's** insurance is expensive.

When adding -'s could lead to tongue-twisting pronunciation, practice varies. All writers use the apostrophe. Some writers do not add the -s. Other writers prefer to use the full -'s for consistency with other cases; the result is pronounced as it sounds in its singular form. This handbook chooses consistency and writes -'s.

Charles **Dickens's** story "A Christmas Carol" is a classic tale. [*Dickens's* is pronounced *Dickens,* without any attempt at two *z* sounds in a row.]

3 **Using only an apostrophe to show possession when a plural noun ends in -s**

The **boys'** statements were recorded.
The newspapers have publicized several **medicines'** severe side effects recently.
Three **months'** maternity leave is in the **workers'** contract.

4 **Adding -'s to the last word in compound words and phrases**

His **mother-in-law's** corporation just bought out a competitor.
The **tennis player's** strategy was brilliant.
They wanted to hear **somebody else's** interpretation of the rule.
Helen of Troy's beauty was legendary.

5 **Adding -'s to each noun in individual possession**

Olga's and Joanne's books are valuable. [Olga and Joanne each own some of the valuable books; but they do not own the books together.]

After the fire, **the doctor's and the lawyer's** offices had to be rebuilt. [The doctor and the lawyer had separate offices.]

QUOTATION ABOUT WRITING

Punctuation marks are one means of helping us get our exact meaning on the page. They do more than mark such obvious facts of language as "This is a sentence," "This is a question." They help us separate words (and thoughts) and so present them distinctly to a reader; they help group and keep together related ideas; they set off certain words for emphasis. Their use affects the tempo of writing: Too many marks may slow the reader to the point of exasperation, and too few may make him go over a passage two or three times to get its probable meaning. The writer who wishes his work to appear to the best advantage will give close attention to its punctuation.

—Porter Perrin, *Writer's Guide and Index to English,* 1942

ALTERNATE EXERCISE

The questions that follow this brief paragraph are designed to point out how much information about the situation has been provided by the apostrophes. You may want to use the questions in a class discussion of apostrophe usage.

The jury's deliberations were over. Charles's lawsuit had at last come to an end. The defendants' lawyers seemed calm as they waited, but the prosecuting attorney's hands twitched with nervousness. Charles's and Robert's businesses would be either ruined or saved by the verdict of the court. Charles and his family's holdings would be seriously affected. The judge's face was impassive as he addressed the jury about its verdict. The jury foreman's voice trembled as he began to speak.

1. Does the writer think of the jury as a single body or as individuals?

2. Is there one defendant, or are there several?

3. Is there one prosecuting attorney, or are there several?

4. Do Charles and Robert own businesses together or separately?

5. Does Charles share in his family's holdings?

6. Why is there no apostrophe in *its verdict?*

7. Why do the words *jury's* (first sentence), *judge's* (next to last sentence), and *foreman's* (last sentence) end in *'s?*

ANSWERS: ALTERNATE EXERCISE

(1) a single body; (2) several; (3) one; (4) separately; (5) yes; (6) the personal pronoun is possessive without an apostrophe; (7) each word is a singular noun that does not end in *-s*

---

6 Adding *-'s* to only the last noun in joint or group possession

Olga and Joanne's books are valuable. [Olga and Joanne own the books together.]

Anne Smith and Glen Smith's article on solar heating interests me. [Anne Smith and Glen Smith wrote the article together.]

27b Not using an apostrophe with the possessive forms of personal pronouns

Some pronouns have specific possessive forms. Do not use an apostrophe with these forms.

PRONOUN	POSSESSIVE FORM(S)
he	his
she	her, hers
it	its
we	our, ours
you	your, yours
they	their, theirs
who	whose

Be especially alert to *it's* and *its,* as well as *who's* and *whose,* which are frequently confused. (*It's* stands for *it is; its* is a personal pronoun showing possession. *Who's* stands for *who is; whose* is a personal pronoun showing possession.)

| **No** | The government has to balance **it's** budget. |
| **YES** | The government has to balance **its** budget. |

| **No** | The professor **who's** class was canceled is at a convention. |
| **YES** | The professor **whose** class was canceled is at a convention. |

| **No** | This briefcase is mine and that one is **your's.** |
| **YES** | This briefcase is mine and that one is **yours.** |

❖ APOSTROPHE CAUTION: The following forms are nonstandard, so do not use them: *its', his', hers', yours', theirs', whos'.* ❖

27c Using an apostrophe to stand for omitted letters, numbers, or words in contractions

Contractions are words from which one or more letters have been intentionally omitted and in which apostrophes are inserted to signal the omission. Contractions are common in speaking and in informal writing, but many readers dislike them in formal writing. Always consider your proposed audience and the degree of formality you want to convey when you choose between a contraction and the full phrase.

COMMON CONTRACTIONS
I'm = I am
he's, she's, it's = he is, she is, it is
you're, we're, they're = you are, we are, they are
isn't = is not
aren't = are not
wasn't = was not
weren't = were not
he'll, she'll = he will, she will
you'll, we'll, they'll = you will, we will, they will
won't = will not
didn't = did not
I'd = I would
I've, we've = I have, we have
you've, they've = you have, they have
who's = who is
there's = there is
let's = let us
can't = cannot

TEACHING TIP

Some instructors despair of ever having students remember the differences between certain common contractions and their homonyms *(their, they're; its, it's).* You might find it helpful to let students know how experienced writers recognize the differences. Many writers pronounce the two-word form of each possibility. If the two-word form makes no sense in that context, then the other word (usually a possessive pronoun) is needed. If the two-word form makes sense, experienced writers ask themselves if the informal contraction is appropriate. Of course, experienced writers do this in a microsecond, but some of our students need to do it slowly, consciously, and methodically.

I need to know if *their/they're* home. [I need to know if *they are* home.]

I need to know if *their/they're* gas meter is working. [I need to know if *they are* gas meter is working = nonsense; therefore, *their* is correct]

Contractions can help to show informal speech or dialect, especially in dramatic or fictional writing.

Scout yonder's been **readin'** ever since she was born, and she **ain't** even started school yet. You look right puny for **goin'** on seven.

—HARPER LEE, *To Kill a Mockingbird*

Apostrophes also indicate the omission of the first two numerals in years. Use this contraction only in informal writing.

The class of '50 is having a reunion this year.
They moved to Florida after the blizzard of '78.

27d Using an apostrophe to form plurals of letters, numerals, symbols, and words used as terms

Billie always has trouble printing **W's.**
The address includes six **6's.**
The *for's* in the paper were all misspelled as *four's.*
When the keys jammed, a series of *&'s* showed on the computer screen.

❖ UNDERLINING ALERT: **Always underline letters as letters and words as words in typewritten or handwritten material. In printed material, they are set in italic type.** ❖

```
Most of the first-graders consistently had trouble
making 8's and trying to pronounce eight's phonetically.
```

For the plural form of years, two styles are acceptable: with an apostrophe (1980's) or without (1980s). Whichever form you prefer, use it consistently. This handbook uses the form without the apostrophe.

27e Avoiding misuse of the apostrophe

Do not overuse apostrophes by inserting them where they do not belong. The chart on the opposite page lists the major causes for apostrophe errors. If you are unsure about apostrophe use or if you tend to make apostrophe errors, use the chart to identify your weaknesses and then try to stay conscious of them as you revise and edit your writing.

,

27e

LEADING CAUSES OF APOSTROPHE ERRORS

1. Do not use an apostrophe with the present-tense verb form.

   No   Cholesterol **plays'** an important role in how long we live.

   Yes   Cholesterol **plays** an important role in how long we live.

2. Do not add an apostrophe at the end of a nonpossessive noun ending in *s*.

   No   Medical **studies'** reveal that cholesterol is the primary cause of coronary heart disease.

   Yes   Medical **studies** reveal that cholesterol is the primary cause of coronary heart disease.

3. Use an apostrophe after the *s* in the possessive plural of a noun.

   No   The medical community is seeking more information from **doctor's** investigations into heart disease.

   Yes   The medical community is seeking more information from **doctors'** investigations into heart disease.

4. Do not use an apostrophe to form a nonpossessive plural.

   No   **Team's** of doctors are trying to predict who might be most harmed by cholesterol.

   Yes   **Teams** of doctors are trying to predict who might be most harmed by cholesterol.

EXERCISE 1

Rewrite these sentences to insert 's or an apostrophe alone to make the words in parentheses show possession. Delete the parentheses.

1. At Pablo (Picasso) birth, two (midwives) errors nearly allowed him to be left for dead.

2. Luckily for Picasso, his cigar-smoking (uncle) quick act saved him.

3. The uncle filled his (nephew) lungs with a blast of much-needed, yet smoke-filled, air.

4. When (Paris) most celebrated beauty, Mme. Virginie Gautreau, was depicted by the painter John Singer Sargent as vain and immodest in a portrait entitled ''Madame X,'' those who knew her agreed with the portrayal.

ANSWERS: EXERCISE 1

1. Picasso's midwives'
2. uncle's
3. nephew's
4. Paris's
5. painting's, Madame Gautreau's
6. Max Jacob and Pablo Picasso's
7. Picasso's, experts', Jacob's, Picasso's
8. anyone's
9. children's, others'
10. contemporaries'

ANSWERS: EXERCISE 2 (next page)

1. Athletic competition is encouraged in accordance with the participants' age and ability.

2. These athletes' training takes place in schools and other institutions.

3. Participants' handicaps do not prevent them from competing in sports from basketball to gymnastics and ice skating to wheelchair exercise.

(continued next page)

ANSWERS: EXERCISE 2 (continued)

4. The program's sponsor is the Joseph P. Kennedy, Jr., Foundation, which first sponsored the event in 1968.

5. The foundation's true beneficiary is American society, for a democracy's aim is equal opportunity and participation for all its members.

COVERAGE: EXERCISE 2

(1) plural possessive noun; (2) plural possessive noun; (3) plural possessive noun; (4) singular possessive noun; (5) singular possessive noun; singular possessive noun

ANSWERS: EXERCISE 3

(1) One of Albert Einstein's biographers tells about the famous physicist's encounter with a little girl in his neighborhood. (2) The little girl stared at Einstein's soaking wet feet and said, "Mr. Einstein, you've come out without your boots again!" (3) Einstein laughed and, pulling up his trousers, replied, "Yes, and I've forgotten my socks, too." (4) Most people aren't as forgetful as Einstein, but sometimes our memories let all of us down. (5) We may not be able to remember if our first job started in '81 or '82; we may forget whether our employer's husband spells his name with two *t*'s or with one. (6) No one is absolutely sure how memory works. (7) Dr. Barbara Jones' study of memory suggests that personality styles affect memory. (8) People with rigid personalities whose livelihoods depend on facts tend to have good memories. (9) Mr. Harry Lorayne's and Dr. Laird Cermak's studies of memory each provide a different approach to improving that useful faculty. (10) Mr. Lorayne suggests relating what you want to remember to something verbal or visual. (11) For instance, if you want to remember that your sister-in-law's name is Rose, you would picture her wearing a rose corsage.

5. Nevertheless (the painting) notoriety and Madame (Gautreau) hysterics forced Sargent to leave for London.

6. (Max Jacob and Pablo Picasso) shared Paris apartment caused them some problems.

7. (Picasso) work habits included leaving paintings all over the floor, and many years later art (experts) skills were needed to remove (Jacob) footprints from (Picasso) valuable canvases.

8. The American painter Charles Willson Peale believed that (anyone) desire to paint could be fulfilled.

9. He acted on his belief and helped to develop his seventeen (children), and many (other), artistic talents.

10. His faith was rewarded: his sons Rembrandt and Raphaelle both earned their (contemporaries) praise.

EXERCISE 2

Rewrite these sentences so that each contains a possessive noun.

EXAMPLE   The Special Olympics is an international program promoting the physical fitness of mentally retarded children and adults.
The Special Olympics is an international program promoting mentally retarded children's and adults' physical fitness.

1. Athletic competition is encouraged in accordance with the age and ability of the participants.

2. The training of these mentally retarded athletes takes place in schools and other institutions.

3. Handicaps of the participants do not prevent them from competing in sports from basketball to gymnastics and ice skating to wheelchair exercise.

4. The sponsor of the program is the Joseph P. Kennedy, Jr. Foundation, which first sponsored the event in 1968.

5. The true beneficiary of the foundation is American society, for the aim of a democracy is equal opportunity and participation for all its members.

EXERCISE 3

Correct any errors in the use of apostrophes in the paragraph below.

(1) One of Albert Einsteins biographers tells about the famous physicists encounter with a little girl in his' neighborhood. (2) The little girl stared at Einstein's soaking wet feet and said, "Mr. Einstein, youve come out without you'r boots again!" (3) Einstein laughed and, pulling up his trousers, replied, "Yes, and Ive forgotten my socks, too." (4) Most peo-

ple arent as forgetful as Einstein, but sometimes our memories' let all of us down. (5) We may not be able to remember if our first job started in '81 or 82; we may forget whether our employers' husband spells his name with two *ts* or with one. (6) No one is absolutely sure how memory works. (7) Dr. Barbara Jones study of memory suggests that personality style's affect memory. (8) People with rigid personalities who's livelihoods depend on facts tend to have good memories. (9) Mr. Harry Lorayne and Dr. Laird Cermak's studies of memory each provide a different approach to improving that useful faculty. (10) Mr. Lorayne suggest's relating what you want to remember to something verbal or visual. (11) For instance, if you want to remember that your sister's-in-law's name is Rose, you would picture her wearing a rose corsage. (12) Dr. Cermaks suggestions include consideration of physiological factors. (13) He notes that doctors' are currently developing drugs that will prevent older people from losing the memories that are rightfully their's.

EXERCISE 4

Correct any errors in the use of apostrophes in the paragraph below.

(1) Every summer Twinsburg, Ohio, comes to life when over one thousand pair's of twins gather for the towns annual festival. (2) The conversation at the gathering usually involves twin's stories about tricking people by exchanging identities, about knowing each others thoughts, and about sharing secret's. (3) The stories' are entertaining, but many psychologists' find them informative as well. (4) Many studies' have involved identical twins' who were separated at birth. (5) Identical twins come from a single fertilized egg that split's soon after conception, resulting in two fetuses' with identical genes. (6) Some studies have revealed that twins sometimes feel each others pain, that they often share the same interests and fear's, and that they frequently give their children the same name's. (7) One researchers report cites the story of a pair of twins' who suffered from the same kind of headache at the same time, even though they lived far apart. (8) Its difficult to believe that the headaches were merely a coincidence. (9) We need not fear that our fates are sealed as soon as were conceived, however. (10) Regardless of the role played by genes, environment contribute's to personality as well. (11) Parent's influence on their children cannot be disputed. (12) Although identical twins may look like carbon copies of each other, theyre like snowflakes: no pair is exactly alike.

ANSWERS: EXERCISE 4

(1) Every summer Twinsburg, Ohio, comes to life when over one thousand pairs of twins gather for the town's annual festival. (2) The conversation at the gathering usually involves twins' stories about tricking people by exchanging identities, about knowing each other's thoughts, and about sharing secrets. (3) The stories are entertaining, but many psychologists find them informative as well. (4) Many studies have involved identical twins who were separated at birth. (5) Identical twins come from a single fertilized egg that splits soon after conception, resulting in two fetuses with identical genes. (6) Some studies have revealed that twins sometimes feel each other's pain, that they often share the same interests and fears, and that they frequently give their children the same names. (7) One researcher's report cites the story of a pair of twins who suffered from the same kind of headache at the same time, even though they lived far apart. (8) It's difficult to believe that the headaches were merely a coincidence. (9) We need not fear that our fates are sealed as soon as we're conceived, however. (10) Regardless of the role played by genes, environment contributes to personality as well. (11) Parents' influence on their children cannot be disputed. (12) Although identical twins may look like carbon copies of each other, they're like snowflakes: no pair is exactly alike.

28 Quotation Marks

Most commonly, quotation marks enclose **direct quotations**—spoken or written words from an outside source (28a). Quotation marks also set off some titles, and they can call attention to words used in special senses.

Always use quotation marks in pairs, and be especially careful not to omit the second (closing) quotation mark. **Double quotation marks** (" ") are standard. **Single quotation marks** (' ') are used only for quotation marks within quotation marks. In print, opening and closing quotation marks look slightly different from each other, but they look identical when made on a typewriter or computer printer. You will find examples of both print and typewritten quotation marks in this chapter.

For information about the functions in quotations of brackets, see 29c; of the ellipsis, see 29d; of the slash, see 29e. For information about capital letters with quotations, see 30c.

When you quote the words of others in your writing, be sure to remain alert to these important matters:

- Incorporate quotations correctly and smoothly into your writing: see 31e-4.
- Avoid plagiarism—the use of another person's words as if they were your own: see Chapter 31.
- Document direct quotations correctly: for the MLA parenthetical system, see 33b-1; for the APA parenthetical system, see 33b-2; for a footnote or endnote system, see 33e.

28a Using quotation marks to enclose direct quotations of not more than four lines

Direct quotations are exact words copied from a print source or transcribed from a nonprint source.

1 | Using double quotation marks to enclose short quotations

A quotation is considered "short" if it can be typed or hand-written to occupy no more than four lines on a page. Short quotations are enclosed in double quotation marks. Longer quotations are not enclosed in quotation marks—they are **displayed.** A displayed quotation starts on a new line, and all typewritten lines indent ten spaces. (In the examples, parenthetical documentation is used—see 33b.)

SHORT QUOTATIONS

```
Hall explains the practicality of close conversational

distances: "If you are interested in something, your

pupils dilate; if I say something you don't like, they

tend to contract" (47).


Personal space "moves with us, expanding and

contracting according to the situation in which we

find ourselves" (Fisher, Bell, and Baum 149).
```

LONG QUOTATION

```
Robert Sommer, an environmental psychologist, uses

literary and personal analogies to describe personal

space:

            Like the porcupines in Schopenhauer's fable,

            people like to be close enough to obtain

            warmth and comradeship but far enough away

            to avoid pricking one another.  Personal

            space . . . has been likened to a snail shell,

            a soap bubble, an aura, and "breathing

            room." (26)
```

For a complete discussion of displaying quotations, see Appendix B, Using Correct Manuscript Format.

2 | Using single quotation marks for quotations within quotations

When you want to quote four lines or less and the original words already contain quotation marks, use double quotation marks at the start and end of the directly quoted words. Then, substitute single quotation marks (' ') wherever there are double quotation marks in the original source.

TEACHING TIP

You might point out to your students that typewriter face is used in 28a-1 so that writers can see how such material should look on their typed papers. All material is double spaced. A short quotation is "run in" with the writer's prose; a long quotation is displayed. For additional examples in typewriter face, you might direct your students' attention to the student research paper in Chapter 34. In particular, you might point out that paragraphs are indented five spaces and displayed quotations are indented ten spaces for all lines.

TEACHING TIP

As the study summarized in the margins of Chapter 31 points out, many students think that they are not plagiarizing as long as they use quotation marks to indicate material taken from sources. These students do not realize that they must also document the source. Now that MLA recommends a system of parenthetical references, the direction to "use footnotes" no longer can help college instructors deal easily with documentation. You might find it useful, therefore, to take some time to explain the word *documentation,* which, in contrast to *footnotes,* is not widely known to students inexperienced in writing research papers. You might also explain that the placement of the parenthetical reference depends on the length of the quotation. If the quotation is "run in," the parenthetical reference comes before the period; if the quotation is displayed, the parenthetical reference comes after the period.

ORIGINAL SOURCE

Personal space . . . has been likened to a snail shell, a soap bubble, an aura, and "breathing room."

—ROBERT SOMMER, *Personal Space: The Behavioral Bases of Design,* page 26

SINGLE QUOTATION MARKS WITHIN DOUBLE QUOTATION MARKS

Robert Sommer, an environmental psychologist, compares personal space to "a snail shell, a soap bubble, an aura, and 'breathing room' " (26).

If there are quotation marks in a quotation of more than four lines, display it without enclosing it in quotation marks. But be sure to use any quotation marks that appear in the original source. See 28a and Appendix B, Using Correct Manuscript Format, for a complete discussion of displayed quotations.

3   Using quotation marks correctly for short quotations of poetry and for direct discourse

A quotation of poetry is "short" if it is no more than three lines of the poem. As with short prose quotations, use double quotation marks to enclose the material. If you quote more than one line of poetry, use a slash with one space on each side to show the line divisions (see 29e).

> As W. H. Auden wittily defined personal space, "some thirty inches from my nose / The frontier of my person goes. . . ."

For a complete discussion of displayed quotations of poetry, see Appendix B, Using Correct Manuscript Format.   ❖ CAPITALIZATION ALERT: When you quote lines of poetry, follow the capitalization of the version you are quoting. ❖

Quotation marks are also used to enclose speakers' words in **direct discourse.** Whether you are reporting the exact words of a real speaker or making up dialogue in, for example, a short story, quotation marks let your readers know which words belong to the speaker and which words do not. Use double quotation marks at the beginning and end of a speaker's words, and start a new paragraph each time the speaker changes.

> "I don't know how you can see to drive," she said.
> "Maybe you should put on your glasses."
> "Putting on my glasses would help you to see?"
> "Not me; you," Macon said. "You're focused on the windshield instead of the road."

—ANNE TYLER, *The Accidental Tourist*

Indirect discourse reports what a speaker said. In contrast, direct discourse presents a speaker's exact words. Do not enclose indirect discourse in quotation marks.

DIRECT DISCOURSE

The mayor said, "I cannot attend the conference."

INDIRECT DISCOURSE

The mayor said that he could not attend the conference.

See 15a-4 for advice on revising incorrect shifts between direct and indirect discourse.

EXERCISE 1

Correct the use of double and single quotation marks in the following sentences. If a sentence is correct, circle its number.

EXAMPLE   According to J. F. Perkins, "O. Henry "solves" most of his short story plots with surprise endings.

According to J. F. Perkins, "O. Henry 'solves' most of his short story plots with surprise endings."

1. Canfield and Lebson write, No one understands the sleeping habits of these sharks.

2. In the last two lines of the poem, Dickinson creates a powerful contrast: Parting is all we know of heaven, / And all we need of hell.

3. "One can put up with "Service with a Smile" if the smile is genuine and not mere compulsory toothbaring," wrote Cornelia Otis Skinner. She did not, on the other hand, advocate 'Service with a Snarl.'

4. "Promises," said Hannah Arendt, are the uniquely human way of ordering the future.

5. According to Henry James, "Nothing . . . will ever take the place of the good old fashion of "liking" a work of art or not liking it."

6. Pauline Kael, the movie critic, notes that "certain artists can, at moments in their lives, reach out and unify the audience" and in so doing give people the opportunity for "a shared response.

7. Don't let anyone convince you that you can't fulfill your ambitions, warned the speaker, or you surely won't.

8. Why have women passion, intellect, moral activity—these three—and a place in society where no one of the three can be exercised? asked Florence Nightingale in the 1850s.

9. "In seven cases, the report continued, outlets with the lowest prices had the highest percentages of defective merchandise.

10. Leslie Hanscom reports about the latest volume of the *Oxford English Dictionary,* Most of the new words are originating in the USA.

ANSWERS: EXERCISE 1

1. Canfield and Lebson write, "No one understands the sleeping habits of these sharks."

2. In the last two lines of the poem, Dickinson creates a powerful contrast: "Parting is all we know of heaven, / And all we need of hell."

3. "One can put up with 'Service with a Smile' if the smile is genuine and not mere compulsory toothbaring," wrote Cornelia Otis Skinner. She did not, on the other hand, advocate "Service with a Snarl."

4. "Promises," said Hannah Arendt, "are the uniquely human way of ordering the future."

5. According to Henry James, "Nothing . . . will ever take the place of the good old fashion of 'liking' a work of art or not liking it."

6. Pauline Kael, the movie critic, notes that "certain artists can, at moments in their lives, reach out and unify the audience" and in so doing give people the opportunity for "a shared response."

7. "Don't let anyone convince you that you can't fulfill your ambitions," warned the speaker, "or you surely won't."

8. "Why have women passion, intellect, moral activity—these three—and a place in society where no one of the three can be exercised?" asked Florence Nightingale in the 1850s.

9. "In seven cases," the report continued, "outlets with the lowest prices had the highest percentages of defective merchandise."

10. Leslie Hanscom reports about the latest volume of the *Oxford English Dictionary,* "Most of the new words are originating in the USA."

(Coverage: see next page)

COVERAGE: EXERCISE 1 (previous page)

(1) direct discourse; (2) short poetry quotation; (3) quotation within a quotation; short quotation; (4) direct discourse following an interruption; (5) quoted word within a quotation; (6) closing quotation marks needed; (7) interrupted direct discourse; (8) direct discourse; (9) interrupted short quotation; closing quotation marks needed; (10) short quotation

ANSWERS: EXERCISE 2

Answers may vary in the rewritten sentences. Here is one set of possibilities.

1. *Indirect discourse.* The auctioneer said, "My company does sell manuscripts, but only original ones by famous authors."

2. *Direct discourse.* The woman replied that the manuscript was original.

3. *Direct discourse.* She said that the author inscribed it with the words "A Christmas gift to a dear child" and that she was that child.

4. *Direct discourse.* Astonished, the auctioneer asked if the manuscript was what he thought it was.

5. *Indirect discourse.* The woman said, "Yes, it is the original Lewis Carroll manuscript of *Alice in Wonderland.*"

EXERCISE 2

Indicate whether each sentence is direct or indirect discourse. Then rewrite each sentence in the other form.

EXAMPLE   In 1928 an elderly woman contacted a London auctioneer and asked, "Would you be interested in selling this manuscript?
(Direct discourse)

In 1928 an elderly woman contacted a London auctioneer and asked if he would be interested in selling a manuscript.

1. The auctioneer said that his company did sell manuscripts, but only original ones by famous authors.
2. "This manuscript is original," the woman replied.
3. "The author inscribed it with these words—'A Christmas gift to a dear child'—and I was that child," she continued.
4. Astonished, the auctioneer said, "Is this manuscript what I think it is?"
5. The woman acknowledged that it was the original Lewis Carroll manuscript of *Alice in Wonderland.*

28b   Using quotation marks to enclose certain titles

When you refer to certain types of works by their titles, enclose the titles in quotation marks. Use quotation marks around the titles of short published works, like poems, short stories, essays, articles from periodicals, pamphlets, and brochures. Also use them around song titles and individual episodes of television or radio series.

> Discuss the rhyme scheme of Andrew Marvell's "Delight in Disorder." [poem]
>
> Have you read "Young Goodman Brown"? [short story]
>
> One of the best sources I have found is "The Myth of Political Consultants." [magazine article]
>
> "Shooting an Elephant" describes George Orwell's experience in Burma. [essay]

Underlining (for italics) is used for titles of many other types of works, such as books and plays. A few titles are neither underlined nor enclosed in quotation marks. You will find useful lists showing how to present titles in 30e and 30f.

Do not put the title of your own paper in quotation marks either on a title page or at the top of a page. (See 28d.)

EXERCISE 3

Make the use of quotation marks correct in the following sentences. If a sentence is correct, circle its number.

1. Almost everyone who has had to make a difficult choice in life can relate to Robert Frost's poem The Road Not Taken.
2. On a *Twilight Zone* episode called Healer, the main character steals a magic artifact.
3. In her essay titled "In Search of Our Mothers' Gardens, Alice Walker says that she found her own garden because she was guided by a "heritage of a love of beauty and a respect for strength.
4. Unable to get enough peace and quiet to write songs, such as his famous Over There and You're a Grand Old Flag, George M. Cohan would sometimes hire a Pullman car drawing room on a train going far enough away to allow him to finish his work.
5. A snake gives Sherlock Holmes the clue he needs to solve a puzzling murder in the mystery story The Speckled Band.

28c Using quotation marks for words used in special senses or for special purposes

Writers sometimes enclose in quotation marks words or phrases meant ironically or in some other nonliteral way.

> The proposed tax "reform" is actually a tax increase.
> The "wonderful companion for children" snarled menacingly.

Writers sometimes put technical terms in quotation marks and define them the first time they are used. No quotation marks are used once such terms have been introduced and defined.

> "Plagiarism"—the unacknowledged use of another person's words or ideas—can result in expulsion. Plagiarism is a serious offense.

The translation of a word or phrase can be enclosed in quotation marks. (Underline words or phrases that require translation.)

> My grandfather usually ended arguments with *de gustibus non disputandum est* ("there is no disputing about tastes").

Words being referred to as words can be either enclosed in quotation marks or underlined. Follow consistent practice throughout a paper. This handbook uses italics to indicate underlining.

> **YES**   Many people confuse "affect" and "effect."
> **YES**   Many people confuse *affect* and *effect.*

539

28d Avoiding the misuse of quotation marks

Writers sometimes enclose in quotation marks words they are uncomfortable about using, such as slang in formal writing or a cliché. Do not use quotation marks around language you sense is inappropriate to your audience or your purpose. Take the time to find accurate, appropriate, and fresh words instead.

No	They "eat like birds" in public, but they "stuff their faces" in private.
YES	They eat very little in public, but they consume enormous amounts of food in private.

Do not enclose a word in quotation marks merely to call attention to it.

No	"Plagiarism" can result in expulsion.
YES	Plagiarism can result in expulsion.

In papers, when you refer to published or performed works by title, you will often need quotation marks (28b) or underlining (30f) to set the title off. When you put the title of your paper at the top of a page or on a title page, however, do not enclose the title in quotation marks.

No	"The Elderly in Nursing Homes: A Case Study"
YES	The Elderly in Nursing Homes: A Case Study

The only exception is if the title of your paper refers to another title or a word that requires setting off.

No	Character Development in Shirley Jackson's story The Lottery
YES	Character Development in Shirley Jackson's story "The Lottery"

Do not put a nickname in quotation marks unless you are giving a nickname with a full name. When a person's nickname is widely known and used, you do not have to give both the nickname and the full name. For example, use *Senator Ted Kennedy* or *Senator Edward Kennedy,* whichever is appropriate to your audience and purpose. You do not have to write *Senator Edward "Ted" Kennedy.*

EXERCISE 4

Make the use of quotation marks correct in the following sentences. If a sentence is correct, circle its number.

EXAMPLE   Many people confuse the spellings of "there," *their,* and *they're.*

           Many people confuse the spellings of "there," "their," and "they're."

1. "Accept" and *except* sound enough alike to confuse many listeners.
2. "Mickey" Mantle, "Yogi" Berra, and Whitey Ford helped make the Yankees champions in the 1950s.
3. Although the district attorney thought it would be an "open and shut case," she found out that "life is full of surprises."
4. An "antigen" is any substance from outside the body that activates the body's immune system. Today scientists are focusing intensive research on "antigens."
5. *Valross,* whale-horse, is the Norwegian word from which we get *walrus.*

Following accepted practices for other punctuation with quotation marks

28e

1   **Placing commas and periods inside closing quotation marks**

Because the class enjoyed F. Scott Fitzgerald's "The Freshest Boy," they were looking forward to his longer works.
Ms. Rogers said, "Don't stand so close to me."
Edward T. Hall coined the word "proxemics."

2   **Placing colons and semicolons outside closing quotation marks**

We have to know "how close is close": we do not want to offend.
Some experts claim that the job market now offers "opportunities that never existed before"; others disagree.

3 Placing question marks, exclamation points, and dashes inside or outside closing quotation marks, according to the context

If a question mark, exclamation point, or dash belongs with the words enclosed in quotation marks, put that punctuation mark *inside* the closing quotation mark.

"Did I Hear You Call My Name?" was the winning song.

"I've won the lottery!" he shouted.

"Who's there? Why don't you ans—"

If a question mark, exclamation point, or dash belongs with words that are *not* included in quotation marks, put the punctuation *outside* the closing quotation mark.

Have you read Nikki Giovanni's poem "Knoxville, Tennessee"?

If only I could write a story like Erskine Caldwell's "The Rumor"!

Weak excuses—a classic is "I have to visit my grandparents"—change little from year to year.

EXERCISE 5

Make the use of quotation marks and other punctuation with quotation marks correct in the following sentences. If a sentence is correct, circle its number.

1. One of the most famous passages in Shakespeare's plays is Hamlet's soliloquy, which begins with the question "To be, or not to be"?

2. "Take this script", Rudyard Kipling said to the nurse who had cared for his first-born child", and someday if you are in need of money you may be able to sell it at a handsome price."

3. Ernest Hemingway claimed this was the source of his famous phrase "a lost generation:" in conversation with "Papa" Hemingway, a garage owner used the words to describe the young mechanics he employed.

4. After lulling the reader with a description of a beautiful dream palace in his poem Kubla Khan, Coleridge changes the mood abruptly: And 'mid this tumult Kubla heard from far / Ancestral voices prophesying war.

5. The words that Emma Lazarus wrote, "Give me your tired, your poor, your huddled masses yearning to breathe free", open the inscription on the Statue of Liberty.

ANSWERS: EXERCISE 5

1. One of the most famous passages in Shakespeare is Hamlet's soliloquy, which begins with the question "To be, or not to be?"

2. "Take this script," Rudyard Kipling said to the nurse who had cared for his first-born child, "and someday if you are in need of money you may be able to sell it at a handsome price."

3. Ernest Hemingway claimed this was the source of his famous phrase "a lost generation": in conversation with Papa Hemingway, a garage owner used the words to describe the young mechanics he employed.

4. After lulling the reader with a description of a beautiful dream palace in his poem "Kubla Khan," Coleridge changes the mood abruptly: "And 'mid this tumult Kubla heard from far / Ancestral voices prophesying war."

5. The words of Emma Lazarus, "Give me your tired, your poor, your huddled masses yearning to breathe free," open the inscription on the Statue of Liberty.

COVERAGE: EXERCISE 5

(1) quotation is a question; (2) commas always placed inside closing quotation marks; (3) colon always placed outside closing quotation marks; (4) title of poem; quotation from poem; (5) commas always placed inside closing quotation marks

29 Other Marks of Punctuation

This chapter explains the uses of the dash, parentheses, brackets, ellipsis, and slash.

THE DASH

29a Using the dash to emphasize interruptions in sentences

The dash, or a pair of dashes, lets you interrupt a sentence's structure to add information—an explanation, examples, a definition, even a personal comment or reaction. Dashes are like parentheses in this function of setting off "asides," or extra material (see 29b for parentheses). Such asides can come at the beginning, in the middle, or at the end of a sentence. Unlike parentheses, dashes emphasize the interruptions. Use dashes sparingly—if you do use them—so that their impact is not diluted by overexposure.

In typed papers, make a dash by hitting the hyphen key twice. Don't put a space before, between, or after the hyphens. In handwritten papers, make a dash slightly longer than a hyphen, using one unbroken line for each dash.

1 Using a dash or dashes to emphasize explanations, including appositives, examples, and definitions

APPOSITIVES°

On television, a cattle drive or a cavalry charge or a chase—the climax of so many a big movie—loses the dimensions of space and distance that made it exciting, that sometimes made it great.

—PAULINE KAEL, *Kiss Kiss Bang Bang*

ALTERNATE EXAMPLES: DASH

Appositive

Elizabeth Barrett Browning—the wife of Robert Browning—was probably a more popular poet than her husband in the nineteenth century.

Example

Many students—elementary school, high school, and college students—find themselves taking required courses that they could not choose for themselves.

Definition

A meaningful relationship—one that is satisfying to those involved and promises to last—is sought by most single people.

Futuristic novels with a bleak vision of the prospects for the free individual characteristically portray a society in which history—knowledge of the past—has been systematically eliminated.

—Diane Ravitch, "Decline and Fall of Teaching History"

Dinner at the Huntercombe's possessed only two dramatic features—the wine was a farce and the food a tragedy.

—Anthony Powell

QUOTATION ABOUT WRITING

The dash has been described as the interruption, the mark of abruptness, the sob, the stammer, and the mark of ignorance. The last name—which might be equally well applied to the comma as crude writers use it—records the fact that the uninformed mistake the dash for an all-purpose mark for every possible occasion.

—George Summey, *American Punctuation*

Two of the strongest animals in the jungle are vegetarians—the elephant and the gorilla.

—DICK GREGORY, *The Shadow that Scares Me*

EXAMPLES

The care-takers—those who are helpers, nurturers, teachers, mothers—are still systematically devalued.

—ELLEN GOODMAN, "Just Woman's Work?"

Two large plots of land have been appropriated for lucrative wildlife parks—Masai Mara in Western Masailand and, in the east, Amboseli National Park, at the foot of snow-capped Mt. Kilimanjaro.

—KATHLEEN HUNT, "Subduing the Lion Killers"

DEFINITIONS

Although the emphasis at the school was mainly language—speaking, reading, writing—the lessons always began with an exercise in politeness.

—ELIZABETH WONG, *Fifth Chinese Daughter*

Personal space—"elbow room"—is a vital commodity for the human animal, and one that cannot be ignored without risking serious trouble.

—DESMOND MORRIS, *Manwatching*

Be sure to place the words you set off in dashes next to or near to the words they explain. Otherwise, the interruption will distract or confuse your reader.

No   The current argument is—one that parents, faculty, students, and coaches all debate fiercely—whether athletes should have to meet minimum academic standards to play their sports.

YES   The current argument—one that parents, faculty, students, and coaches all debate fiercely—is whether athletes should have to meet minimum academic standards to play their sports.

2 Using a dash or dashes to emphasize a contrast

Tampering with time brought most of the house tumbling down, and it was this that made Einstein's work so important—and controversial.

—BANESH HOFFMANN, "My Friend, Albert Einstein"

Today a majority of men in this part of the country, especially in Texas, wear some type of "Western" hat—and so do a number of the women.

—ALISON LURIE, *The Language of Clothes*

3 | **Using a dash or dashes to emphasize an "aside"**

"Asides" are writers' comments, within the structure of a sentence or a paragraph, on something they have written. Especially in writing that is otherwise meant to seem objective, asides let writers introduce their personal views or convey their attitudes. Writers who want to emphasize asides set them off with dashes.

These five passages have not been picked out because they are especially bad—I could have quoted far worse if I had chosen—but because they illustrate various of the mental vices from which we now suffer.

—GEORGE ORWELL, "Politics and the English Language"

Television showed us the war. It showed us the war in a way that was—if you chose to watch television, at least—unavoidable.

—NORA EPHRON, *Scribble Scrabble*

If the words you put between a pair of dashes would take a question mark or an exclamation point written as a separate sentence, use that punctuation before the second dash.

A first date—do you remember?—stays in the memory forever.

Do not use commas, semicolons, or periods next to dashes. When such a possibility comes up, revise your sentence to avoid it.

No — We walked and talked for hours—the time sped by—, and after we each got home, we spoke on the phone for another hour.

YES — The time sped by as we walked and talked for hours, and after we each got home, we spoke on the phone for another hour.

4 | **Using a dash to show hesitating or broken-off speech**

"Naturally," said Mr. Lorry. "Yes—I—"

After a pause, he added, again settling the crisp flaxen wig at the ears, "It is very difficult to begin."

—CHARLES DICKENS, *A Tale of Two Cities*

ANSWERS: EXERCISE 1

1. The adult blue, or lycaenid, butterfly is tiny—about big enough to cover a 20 cent stamp.

2. This personality—so runs the erroneous belief—will be revealed in all its splendor if the individual just forgets about courtesy . . . .

3. We decide about our health habits—whether we exercise, what we eat, whether we smoke or drink.

4. Per capita, Japan has a twentieth of the lawyers—and crime—of America.

5. Different as they were—in background, in personality, in underlying aspiration—these two great soldiers had much in common.

COVERAGE: EXERCISE 1

(1) explanation; (2) aside, (3) appositive; (4) contrast; (5) explanation

BACKGROUND

Literally *parenthesis* indicates "an insertion beside" the basic meaning of the sentence because etymologically the Greek from which it comes (by way of Medieval Latin) is composed of *para,* beside, *en,* meaning in, and *thesis,* a placing, from *tithenai,* to place or put. Hence a parenthesis is a placing beside the principal meaning.

EXERCISE 1

Supply dashes in the following sentences.

EXAMPLE   In the Middle Ages nearly everyone believed as Aristotle had that the intellect was located in the heart.

In the Middle Ages nearly everyone believed—as Aristotle had—that the intellect was located in the heart.

1. The adult blue, or lycaenid, butterfly is tiny about big enough to cover a 20 cent stamp.

—Matthew Douglas, "The Butterfly Connection"

2. This personality so runs the erroneous belief will be revealed in all its splendor if the individual just forgets about courtesy. . . .

—Margaret Halsey, "What's Wrong with 'Me, Me, Me'?"

3. We decide about our health habits whether we exercise, what we eat, whether we smoke or drink.

—Joan Borysenko, *Minding the Body, Mending the Mind*

4. Per capita, Japan has a twentieth of the lawyers and crime of America.

—John Train, *Preserving Capital and Making It Grow*

5. Different as they were in background, in personality, in underlying aspiration these two great soldiers had much in common.

—Bruce Catton, "Grant and Lee: A Study in Contrasts"

PARENTHESES

29b Using parentheses to enclose interrupting material in sentences, as well as for a few special purposes

Parentheses let you interrupt a sentence's structure to add information of many kinds. Parentheses are like dashes in this function of setting off extra or interrupting words. Unlike dashes, which make interruptions stand out, parentheses deemphasize what they enclose.

Dashes	The books and journals—and tapes, filmstrips, even the people you want to interview—are all too often unavailable when you are ready.
Parentheses	The books and journals (and tapes, filmstrips, even the people you want to interview) are all too often unavailable when you are ready.

Do not use parentheses too frequently in any one piece of writing. They can be very distracting for readers.

1 Using parentheses to enclose interrupting words, including explanations, examples, and asides

EXPLANATIONS

After they've finished with the pantry, the medicine cabinet, and the attic, they will throw out the red geranium (too many leaves), sell the dog (too many fleas), and send the children off to boarding school (too many scuffmarks on the hardwood floors).

—SUZANNE BRITT, "Neat People vs. Sloppy People"

In *division* (also known as *partition*) a subject commonly thought of as a single unit is reduced to its separate parts.

—DAVID SKWIRE, *Writing with a Thesis*

EXAMPLES

Though other cities (Dresden, for instance) had been utterly destroyed in World War II, never before had a single weapon been responsible for such destruction.

—LAURENCE BEHRENS and LEONARD J. ROSEN,
Writing and Reading Across the Curriculum

ASIDES

The older girls (non-graduates, of course) were assigned the task of making refreshments for the night's festivities.

—MAYA ANGELOU, *I Know Why the Caged Bird Sings*

The sheer decibel level of the noise around us is not enough to make us cranky, irritable, or aggressive. (It can, however, affect our mental and physical health, which is another matter.)

—CAROL TAVRIS, *Anger: The Misunderstood Emotion*

2 Using parentheses for certain numbers and letters of listed items

When you number listed items within a sentence, enclose the numbers (or letters) in parentheses.

These four items are on the agenda for tonight's meeting: (1) current membership figures, (2) current treasury figures, (3) the budget for renovations, and (4) the campaign for soliciting additional public contributions.

 PUNCTUATION ALERT: Separate items of a run-in list (a list within the structure of a sentence) with commas or semicolons.

ALTERNATE EXAMPLES: PARENTHESES

Explanations

Most Americans try to be honest about filling their income tax returns (no matter how much it hurts to pay).

Examples

Many modern zoos (such as the Santa Barbara Zoo) try to present the animals so that young children can easily see them.

Asides

House plants are subject to bug infestations (at least mine are) which require special treatment if the attack is to be repelled.

QUOTATION ABOUT WRITING

Though parentheses seem to say "here it is if you wish it; it's only an aside," such an aside may be intended for special notice—like many a remark that begins with the disarming *by the way* or *incidentally.*

—George Summey, *American Punctuation*

ALTERNATE EXAMPLES: PARENTHESES

Numbers and letters

There are five basic ingredients in a good gumbo: (1) a roux, (2) chopped vegetables, (3) water, (4) seafood or chicken, and (5) seasonings.

Numerical repetition

A freshman is required to take twelve (12) hours of course work to be in regular status.

Expression of doubt

We have $900 (?) in the bank.

EXAMPLES OF PARENTHESES WITH OTHER PUNCTUATION

When eating at a formal restaurant (such as Chez Marcelle), a man is expected to wear a coat and tie.

Although the rain kept falling (and the river rising!), we decided to wait for the rescue boat instead of striking out on our own.

Casablanca has become a favorite film of many people too young to have seen it when it was originally released (or to have seen Bogart and Bergman in their other films).

 3 Using parentheses to enclose a numeral repeating a spelled-out number in business and legal writing

The monthly rent is three hundred sixty-five dollars ($365).
Your order of fifteen (15) gross was shipped today.

 4 Using a question mark enclosed in parentheses for a doubtful date or number

When information is unknown or doubtful despite your best attempts to determine it, you can use (?) after the number or fact. Using the word *about* is equally acceptable. (See 23d.)

YES   Sappho was born in 612 (?) B.C.

YES   Sappho was born about 612 B.C.

 5 Knowing how to use other punctuation with parentheses

Never put a comma before an opening parenthesis even if what comes before the parenthetical material requires a comma. Put the parenthetical material in, and then use the comma immediately after the closing parenthesis.

No   Although clearly different from my favorite film, *(The Wizard of Oz) Gone with the Wind* is an important film and one worth studying.

YES   Although clearly different from my favorite film *(The Wizard of Oz), Gone with the Wind* is an important film and one worth studying.

You can use a question mark or an exclamation point with parenthetical words that occur within the structure of a sentence.

Looking for clues (what did we expect to find?) wasted four days.

Use a period, however, only when you enclose a complete statement in parentheses outside the structure of another sentence. In this case, use a capital letter as well.

No   Looking for clues (now I wonder whether we really expected to find any.) wasted four entire days.

YES   Looking for clues wasted four entire days. (Now I wonder whether we really expected to find any.)

YES   Looking for clues (now I wonder whether we really expected to find any) wasted four entire days.

EXERCISE 2

Supply needed or useful parentheses.

EXAMPLE   We know that many imaginative people, artists and writers, for example, become so involved in their work that they forget to eat.

We know that many imaginative people *(artists and writers, for example)* become so involved in their work that they forget to eat.

1. Ann Landers and Dear Abby they are actually twin sisters are the most famous advice columnists in the country.
2. Nowadays you can order almost anything clothing, toys, greeting cards, and even meat through mail-order catalogs.
3. Some actors refuse to accept their Oscars, both George C. Scott and Marlon Brando, for example, refused their Best Actor awards even though the Academy Award is considered Hollywood's highest honor.
4. To be a President of the United States, a person must be 1 at least thirty-five years old and 2 a native-born American citizen.
5. Between 1970 and 1978, the price of gold on the free market went from under thirty-five dollars $35 to over two hundred forty dollars $240 an ounce.

BRACKETS

29c Using brackets to enclose insertions into quotations or into parentheses

1 Using brackets to enclose words you insert into quotations

When you work quoted words into your own sentences (see 31e), you may have to change a word or two to make the quoted words fit into the structure of your sentence. Enclose any changes you make in square brackets.

ORIGINAL SOURCE

Surprisingly, this trend is almost reversed in Italy, where males interact closer and display significantly more contact than do male/female dyads and female couples.

—ROBERT SHUTER, "A Field Study of Nonverbal Communication in Germany, Italy, and the United States," page 305

ANSWERS: EXERCISE 2

1. Ann Landers and Dear Abby (they are actually twin sisters) are the most famous advice columnists in the country.

2. Nowadays you can order almost anything (clothing, toys, greeting cards, and even meat) through mail-order catalogs.

3. Some actors refuse to acknowledge their Oscars. (Both George C. Scott and Marlon Brando, for example, refused their Best Actor awards even though the Academy Award is considered Hollywood's highest honor.)

4. To be a President of the United States, a person must be (1) at least thirty-five years old, and (2) a native-born American citizen.

5. Between 1970 and 1978, the price of gold on the free market went from under thirty-five dollars ($35) to over two hundred forty dollars ($240) an ounce.

COVERAGE: EXERCISE 2

(1) interruptive explanation; (2) interruptive examples; (3) examples added; (4) numbers of listed items; (5) repetition of a spelled-out number

ALTERNATE EXAMPLES: BRACKETS

Insertion of words

Describing the end of grief, Marjorie Waters wrote, "[it] was a homecoming, a returning to myself made sweeter by the long separation."

—Majorie Waters, "Coming Home"

To be reasonably comfortable for even short walks outdoors [in Moscow during the winter] it is necessary to wear coats of natural fur.

—Leona P. Schecter, "Moscow"

We hold these truths to be self-evident, that all men are created equal, that they are endowed by their Creator with certain unalienable [sic] Rights, that among these are Life, Liberty and the pursuit of Happiness.

—The Declaration of Independence

Brief parenthetical material

If you pick twenty adults at random [in contemporary American society], the odds are that fifteen of them drink moderately, two are problem drinkers and one is a desperate alcoholic.

—Joel Fort, "The Drug Explosion"

QUOTATION WITH BRACKETS

Although German and American men stand farthest apart and touch each other least, "[this phenomenon] is almost reversed in Italy, where males interact closer and display significantly more contact than do male/female dyads and female couples" (Shuter 305).

The same technique—enclosing your words in brackets—lets you add explanations and clarifications to quoted material.

ORIGINAL SOURCE

This sort of information seems trivial, but it does affect international understanding. Imagine, for example, a business conference between an American and an Arab.

—CHARLES G. MORRIS, *Psychology: An Introduction,* page 516

QUOTATION WITH BRACKETS

"This sort of information [about personal space] seems trivial, but it does affect international understanding" (Morris 516).

QUOTATION WITH BRACKETS

"This sort of information seems trivial, but it *does* affect international understanding [emphasis mine] (Morris 516)."

Now and then you may find that an author or a typesetter has made a mistake in something you want to quote—a wrong date, a misspelled word, an error of fact. You cannot change another writer's words, but you do not want readers to think you made the error. You can show that you know about the error by inserting the Latin word *sic* in brackets, next to the error. Meaning "so" or "thus," *sic* in brackets says to a reader, "it is thus in the original."

In the report, the construction supervisor points out one unintended consequence of doubling the amount of floor space: "With that much extra room per person, the tennants [sic] would sublet."

 2 **Using brackets to enclose very brief parenthetical material inside parentheses**

From that point on, Thomas Parker simply disappears. (His death [c. 1441] is unrecorded officially, but a gravestone marker is mentioned in a 1640 parish report.)

The abbreviation "c." means "about" when referring to time. (See 30i.)

THE ELLIPSIS

Using an ellipsis to signal omissions from quotations or to show hesitating or broken-off speech

An **ellipsis** is a set of three spaced dots (use the period key on a typewriter). Its most important function is to show that you have left out some of the original writer's words in material you are quoting. Ellipses can also show hesitant or broken-off speech, as does the dash (29a-4).

BACKGROUND

Ellipsis is the descendant of one of the classical rhetorician's schemes of omission, the deliberate dropping of a word or words that are readily implied by the context. Edward P. J. Corbett points out that ellipsis can be "an artful and arresting means of securing economy of expression. We must see to it, however, that the understood words are grammatically compatible."

—Edward Corbett, *Classical Rhetoric for the Modern Student*

 1 **Using an ellipsis to show that you have omitted words from material you are quoting**

ORIGINAL SOURCE

Personal space is not necessarily spherical in shape, nor does it extend equally in all directions. (People are able to tolerate closer presence of a stranger at their sides than directly in front.) It has been likened to a snail shell, a soap bubble, an aura, and "breathing room."

—ROBERT SOMMER, *Personal Space:
The Behavioral Bases of Design,* page 26

SOME MATERIAL USED IN A QUOTATION

Surprisingly, Sommer has been able to define its dimensions: "Personal space . . . not necessarily spherical in shape . . . has been likened to a snail shell, a soap bubble, an aura, and 'breathing room' " (26).

If an omission occurs at the beginning of your quoted words, you do not need to use an ellipsis to show the omission. Also you do not need to use an ellipsis at the end as long as you end with a complete sentence. (Otherwise, almost everything you quote would require an ellipsis.)

No   According to Sommer, it may not be ". . . spherical in shape, nor does it extend equally in all directions" (26).

No   According to Sommer, it may not be "spherical in shape, nor does it extend equally in all directions. . . ." (26).

ALTERNATE EXAMPLES: ELLIPSIS

Give me liberty or . . . death!

—Patrick Henry

As a recommendation for raising children in the future, Elizabeth Janeway urges "the establishment of enriching and exciting child-care facilities at industrial plants, commercial centers, educational establishments. . . ."

—"Raising Children in the Year 2000"

In a comment about Dashiell Hammett, Lillian Hellman says, "He had made up honor early in his life and stuck with his rules . . ." *(An Unfinished Woman 126),* and then she cites examples of that honor from his own acts.

QUOTATION ABOUT WRITING

Speech is highly elliptical. It would scarcely be endurable otherwise. Ellipsis is indispensable to the writer or speaker who wants to be brief and pithy, but it can easily cause confusion and obscurity and must be used with skill.

—Cornelia Evans and Bergen Evans,
*A Dictionary of Contemporary
American Usage*

If you select for quotation two or more sentences separated by material you do not want to quote, show the omission with (1) the period that ends the sentence before the omission and (2) the three spaced periods of an ellipsis. Use this procedure for sentences in the same paragraph or in sequential paragraphs.

> Sommer explains, "Personal space is not necessarily spherical in shape, nor does it extend equally in all directions. . . . It has been likened to a snail shell, a soap bubble, an aura, and 'breathing room' " (26).

If you stop quoting before the end of the sentence in the original and your own sentence continues, you may use an ellipsis to show that the quoted sentence continues.

> Personal space "has been likened to a snail shell, a soap bubble, . . ." (Sommer 26), but the shape varies among cultures.

When a quotation comes at the end of your sentence but the quoted words are *not* the end of a sentence in the original source, you must use an ellipsis. If the quotation is not followed by parenthetical documentation, use (1) a sentence period after the last quoted word, (2) three spaced dots for the ellipsis, and then (3) closing quotation marks.

ELLIPSIS AT END OF SENTENCE WITHOUT PARENTHETICAL DOCUMENTATION

> Still, on that same page, Sommer says people have described personal space as "a snail shell, a soap bubble, an aura. . . ."

But if the quotation is followed by parenthetical documentation, use (1) three spaced dots for the ellipsis, (2) closing quotation marks, (3) the parenthetical reference, and then (4) the sentence period.

ELLIPSIS AT END OF SENTENCE WITH PARENTHETICAL DOCUMENTATION

> Sommer says people have described personal space as "a snail shell, a soap bubble, an aura . . ." (26).

When you delete words immediately after an internal punctuation mark in the quotation, include that mark in your sentence and then add the three spaced dots for the ellipsis.

> Sommer says that it has been likened to a snail shell, . . . and "breathing room" (26).

2 | Using an ellipsis to show broken-off speech

Like the dash (29a-4), an ellipsis shows a speaker's broken-off or interrupted speech.

"And, anyway, what do you know of him?"
"Nothing. That is why I ask you . . ."
"I would prefer never to speak of him."

—UMBERTO ECO, *The Name of the Rose*

THE SLASH

29e Using the slash correctly for quoting poetry lines, for numerical fractions, and for *and/or*

1 Using the slash to separate up to three lines of quoted poetry

If you quote more than three lines of a poem in writing, set the poetry off with space and indentations as you would a prose quotation of more than four lines (see 28a and Appendix B). For three lines or less, quote poetry—enclosed in quotation marks—in sentence format, with a slash to divide one line from the next. Leave a space on each side of the slash.

> Consider the beginning of Anne Sexton's poem "Words": "Be careful of words, / even the miraculous ones."

Capitalize and punctuate each line as it is in the original, with this exception: End your sentence with a period, even if the quoted line of poetry does not have one.

2 Using the slash for numerical fractions in typed manuscripts

If you have to type numerical fractions, use the slash to separate numerator and denominator and a hyphen to tie a whole number to its fraction: *1/16, 1-2/3, 2/5, 3-7/8.* (See 30j for advice on using spelled-out and numerical forms of numbers.)

3 Using the slash for *and/or*

Try not to use word combinations like *and/or* for writing in the humanities. Where their use is acceptable, separate the words with a slash. Leave no space before or after the slash.

BIOGRAPHY

Anne Sexton (1928–1974) began writing poetry in her late twenties. She composed a large body of work, much of it focused on domestic and personal crises and on nature. Among her works are *To Bedlam and Part Way Back* (1960), *Live or Die* (1967), and *The Awful Rowing Towards God* (1975). In her poetry, Sexton struggled to overcome mental illness and suicidal urges—unfortunately, those urges were too strong and she died, a suicide, in 1974.

ANSWERS: EXERCISE 3

Answers may vary slightly. Here are some possibilities.

1. Albert Einstein's last words—they were spoken in his native German—will never be known because his attending nurse spoke only English. [parentheses also acceptable]

2. During one five-week span in 1841, three different men served as President of the United States: (1) Martin Van Buren finished his term on March 3; (2) William Henry Harrison—Van Buren's successor—was inaugurated on March 4; and (3) John Tyler assumed the Presidency when Harrison died on April 6 after only thirty-two days in office.

3. Gold is so malleable that a single ounce can be beaten out into a thin film (less than 1/282,000th of an inch) that would cover 100 square feet. [dashes also acceptable]

4. Correct

5. The American portrait artist Charles Willson Peale made George Washington an innovative set of dentures—elks' teeth set in lead.

6. Henri Matisse's painting *Le Bateau* once hung in New York's Museum of Modern Art for forty-seven days (not to mention being viewed by about 116,000 people) before someone noticed that it was hung upside down. [dashes also acceptable]

7. When Thomas Edison learned that one of the batteries his company manufactured was defective, he offered a refund to all buyers—a pledge made good by $1 million from his own pocket.

8. In 1816 a strange chain of events (beginning with a volcanic eruption in the Dutch East Indies [now Indonesia]) caused New England to experience snow in June and killing frosts through July and August.

9. Although the identity of the famous Jack the Ripper was never proven, when the con-

In the humanities, listing both alternatives in normal sentence structure is usually better than separating choices with a slash.

No	The best quality of reproduction comes from 35mm slides/direct positive films.
Yes	The best quality of reproduction comes from 35mm slides or direct positive films.

EXERCISE 3

Supply needed dashes, parentheses, brackets, ellipses, and slashes. If a sentence is correct as written, circle its number. In some sentences you can choose between dashes and parentheses; when you make your choice, be ready to explain it.

EXAMPLE Every year in the United States, four times the amount of money spent on baby food is spent on pet food $1.5 billion.

Every year in the United States, four times the amount of money spent on baby food is spent on pet food ($1.5 billion).

1. Albert Einstein's last words they were spoken in his native German will never be known because his attending nurse spoke only English.

2. During one five-week span in 1841, three different men served as President of the United States: 1 Martin Van Buren finished his term on March 3; 2 William Henry Harrison Van Buren's successor was inaugurated on March 4; and 3 John Tyler assumed the Presidency when Harrison died on April 6 after only thirty-two days in office.

3. Gold is so malleable that a single ounce can be beaten out into a thin film less than 1 282,000th of an inch that would cover 100 square feet.

4. To get at every ounce of gold, miners have dug as deep as 2-1/2 miles.

5. The American portrait artist Charles Willson Peale made George Washington an innovative set of dentures elks' teeth set in lead.

6. Henri Matisse's painting *Le Bateau* once hung in New York's Museum of Modern Art for forty-seven days not to mention being viewed by about 116,000 people before someone noticed that it was hung upside down.

7. When Thomas Edison learned that one of the batteries his company manufactured was defective, he offered a refund to all buyers a pledge made good by $1 million from his own pocket.

8. In 1816 a strange chain of events (beginning with a volcanic eruption in the Dutch East Indies (now Indonesia) caused New England to experience snow in June and killing frosts through July and August.

9. Although the identity of the famous Jack the Ripper was never proven, when the convicted murderer Dr. Thomas Cream was hanged his last words were the unfinished sentence, "I am Jack the."

10. Maxine Kumin the winner of the 1973 Pulitzer Prize for Poetry wrote these memorable lines about calves as they are being born: "They come forth with all four legs folded in / like a dime-store card table."

EXERCISE 4

Follow the directions for each item. Use dashes, parentheses, ellipses, and slashes as needed.

EXAMPLE   Write a sentence using dashes that exclaims about love.
          I am in love—again!

1. Write a sentence that quotes only three lines of Sonnet XLIII by Elizabeth Barrett Browning:

    How do I love thee? Let me count the ways.
    I love thee to the depth and breadth and height
    My soul can reach, when feeling out of sight
    For the ends of Being and ideal Grace.
    I love thee to the level of every day's
    Most quiet need, by sun and candlelight.
    I love thee freely, as men strive for Right;
    I love thee purely, as they turn from Praise.
    I love thee with the passion put to use
    In my old griefs, and with my childhood's faith.
    I love thee with a love I seemed to lose
    With my lost saints,—I love thee with the breath,
    Smiles, tears, of all my life!—and, if God choose,
    I shall but love thee better after death.

2. Write a sentence that includes a list of four numbered items.

3. Quote a few sentences from a source. Choose one from which you can omit a few words without losing meaning. Correctly indicate the omission. At the end, give the source of the quotation.

4. Write a sentence in which you use dashes to set off a definition.

5. Write a sentence in which you use parentheses to enclose a brief example.

victed murderer Dr. Thomas Cream was hanged his last words were the unfinished sentence, "I am Jack the—" [the . . ." also acceptable]

10. Maxine Kumin—the winner of the 1973 Pulitzer Prize for Poetry—wrote these memorable lines about calves as they are being born: "They come forth with all four legs folded in / like a dime-store card table." [parentheses also acceptable]

COVERAGE: EXERCISE 3

(1) dashes or parentheses for interruptive explanation; (2) parentheses for numbers of listed items, dash for explanatory material; (3) parentheses or dashes for definition; (4) correct; (5) dash for appositive; (6) parentheses or dashes for an aside; (7) dash for appositive; (8) brackets within parentheses for explanation within explanation; (9) dash for broken-off speech; (10) dashes or parentheses for appositive

ANSWERS: EXERCISE 4

Answers will vary greatly. When checking them, note whether the directions were followed.

1. only three lines of the sonnet, with slash marks between the first and second and between the second and third lines—quoted in a sentence.

2. parentheses to enclose the numbers 1–4 that label the list within a sentence

3. ellipsis to indicate an omission from a quotation, with the meaning of the whole still clear

4. dashes to set off a definition in a sentence

5. parentheses to enclose a brief example in a sentence

30 Capitals, Italics, Abbreviations, and Numbers

Capital letters, italics (shown as underlining in handwritten or typed material), abbreviations, and styles of writing numbers are sometimes referred to as **mechanics.** Knowing which forms to use and when to use them, however, is far from mechanical. Issues of mechanics involve making choices: Does a word start with a capital letter or a lower-case one? Does a group of words need to be underlined, put in quotation marks, or left alone? Is an abbreviation acceptable in a given case? When is a figure used rather than a number spelled out in words?

CAPITALS

The terms *uppercase* and *lowercase* originally referred to the drawers, or cases, that held the fonts in a print shop. Although the use of capital letters is still not entirely standardized, by the seventeenth century the spread of printing had made it regular practice to place capital letters at the beginning of sentences and of proper names and titles. Before the advent of printing, lowercase characters, a full set of which existed by the sixth century, were generally mixed with uppercase ones, and large letters, though not necessarily uppercase letters, were used to mark the beginning of a sentence.

30a Capitalizing the first word of a sentence

Always capitalize the first letter of the first word in a sentence, a question, or a command.

Records show that snow fell in Antarctica while the thermometer registered minus 65 degrees.
Does it ever get too cold to snow?
Verify that temperature immediately.

Practice varies for starting each question in a series of questions with a capital letter.

YES   What facial feature would most people change if they could? Their eyes? Their ears? Their mouths?

YES   What facial feature would most people change if they could? their eyes? their ears? their mouths?

556

Whichever practice you choose, be consistent throughout a piece of writing. Of course, if the questions are complete sentences, start each with a capital letter.

Practice also varies for using a capital letter for a complete sentence following a colon. Whichever practice you choose, be consistent throughout a piece of writing.

> **YES**   I need advice about what to do: The instructions give contradictory commands.
>
> **YES**   I need advice about what to do: the instructions give contradictory commands.

A complete sentence enclosed in parentheses may stand alone or may fall within the structure of another sentence. Those that stand alone start with a capital letter. Those that fall within the structure of another sentence do not start with a capital letter. ❖ PUNCTUATION ALERTS: (1) When a complete sentence within parentheses stands alone, always end it with a period, question mark, or exclamation point—as needed for meaning. (2) When a complete sentence within parentheses falls within the structure of another sentence, use only a question mark or an exclamation point at the end, as needed for meaning; if meaning calls for a period, omit it. ❖

> I didn't know till years later that they called it the Cuban Missile Crisis. But I remember Castro. (We called him Castor Oil and were awed by his beard—beards were rare in those days.) We might not have worried so much (what would the Communists want with our small New Hampshire town?) except that we lived 10 miles from an air base.
>
> —JOYCE MAYNARD, "An 18-Year-Old Looks Back on Life"

> The journey from the first clues to the final interpretation was a long one (it took six years), and the route was not straightforward.
>
> —EVELYN FOX KELLER, *A Feeling for the Organism*

When you quote lines of poetry, follow the practice of the version you quote from concerning capital letters at the beginning of lines and within lines. (See 28a-3 for advice on formats for quoted poetry.)

30b Capitalizing listed items correctly

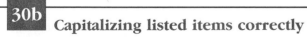

In a **run-in list,** the items are worked into the structure of a sentence or a paragraph rather than being set up vertically with each item on a new line. When the items in a run-in list are complete sentences, capitalize the first letter of each item.

We found three reasons for the delay: (1) Bad weather held up delivery of raw materials. (2) Poor scheduling created confusion and slowdowns. (3) Lack of proper machine maintenance caused an equipment failure.

When the items in a run-in list are not complete sentences, do not begin them with capital letters.

The reasons for the delay were (1) bad weather, (2) poor scheduling, and (3) equipment failure.

In a **displayed list,** the items are set up vertically, one below the other. Capitalize the first letter of all items in a displayed list if any item is a complete sentence. If the items are not sentences, you may either start all of them with capital letters or start all of them with lower-case letters. Whichever practice you choose, be consistent throughout a piece of writing. ✣ PARALLELISM ALERT: Make list items parallel in structure. If one item is a sentence, make all the items sentences (18e). ✣

YES	The reasons for the delay are as follows: 1. Bad weather 2. Poor scheduling 3. Equipment failure
YES	The reasons for the delay are as follows: 1. bad weather 2. poor scheduling 3. equipment failure

In a **formal outline,** each item must start with a capital letter (for more information, see 2e-5).

30c Capitalizing the first letter of an introduced quotation

If you have made quoted words part of the structure of your own sentence, do not capitalize the first quoted word.

Mrs. Saintonge says that when students visit a country whose language they are trying to learn, they "absorb a good accent with the food."

Doris Lessing believes that "the way to learn a language is to breathe it in."

If the words in your sentence serve only to introduce quoted words or if you are directly quoting speech, capitalize the first letter of the quoted words if it is capitalized in the original.

Mrs. Saintonge says, "Students should always visit a country when they want to learn its language. They'll absorb a good accent with the food."

According to Doris Lessing, "The way to learn a language is to breathe it in."

Do not capitalize a quotation you resume within a sentence, and do not capitalize a partial quotation.

"Persistence," says my supervisor, "is more important than quickness for this task."

Winking, she encouraged me to try "very speedy persistence."

See Chapter 28 for full coverage of quotation marks.

30d Capitalizing the interjection *O* and the pronoun *I*

I would drink from the river, which I would meet again and again.
—MAXINE HONG KINGSTON, *The Woman Warrior*

Temper, O fair Love, Love's impetuous rage.
—JOHN DONNE, "On His Mistress"

❖ CAPITALIZATION ALERT: Do not capitalize *oh* unless it starts a sentence or unless it is capitalized in what you are quoting. ❖

30e Capitalizing nouns and adjectives according to standard practice

Capitalize **proper nouns** (nouns that name specific people, places, or things) and **proper adjectives** (adjectives formed from proper nouns).

PROPER NOUNS	PROPER ADJECTIVES
Mexico	Mexican literature
Rome	the Roman legions
Shakespeare	a Shakespearean comedy

Notice that articles *(the, a, an)* in front of proper nouns or adjectives are not capitalized.

TEACHING TIP

You might find that students overcapitalize in their writing. Comparison can be a useful tool in getting them to distinguish between common and proper nouns. First, review the basic rule: proper (capitalized) nouns name specific people, places, or things; common (uncapitalized) nouns refer to nonspecific people, places, or things. Then give students pairs of noun phrases, one of which contains a proper noun and one a common noun. Omit all capitals. Ask students to identify and capitalize the proper noun: president Washington, the president of the country; hunter high school, the high school band; a new car, a lincoln continental; psychological testing, psychology 101. Augment this list with pairs representing your students' most common errors.

Your students will probably find this rather easy, because contrast highlights the specific nouns. The next step can be to make up or edit a paragraph to eliminate all capital letters except those that begin sentences. Ask students to capitalize the first letters of all proper nouns. Upon completion, you might have students exchange papers and discuss the correct answers. Then students can correct one another's exercises and you can collect the papers to review or record grades.

Do not capitalize common nouns (nouns that name general classes of people, places, or things) unless they start a sentence.

COMMON NOUNS

a state	team	tomatoes
the car	people	an exercise
a doctor	high school	whales
the holiday	professors	parents
the sea	a ship	the party

❖ CAPITALIZATION ALERT: A proper noun or adjective sometimes takes on a "common" meaning, losing its very specific "proper" word associations. When that happens, the word loses its capital letter as well. Examples include *arabic numeral, derringer, french fry, india ink, italics, oriental rug, panama hat, pasteurize.* ❖

Many common nouns are capitalized when names or titles are added to them. For example, *lake* is not ordinarily capitalized, but when a specific name is added, it is: *Lake Ontario.* Without the specific name, however, even if the specific name is implied, the common noun is not capitalized.

No Canada and the United States cleaned up Lake Ontario in the 1970s, for the **Lake** was near death from industrial pollution.

YES Canada and the United States cleaned up Lake Ontario in the 1970s, for the **lake** was near death from industrial pollution.

This chapter shows you capitalization guidelines for academic writing in the humanities. In your reading, you will sometimes see capitalized words you are told in this book not to capitalize. How writers capitalize has a good deal to do with audience and purpose. A corporation's annual report usually uses *the Board of Directors* and *the Company,* not *the board of directors* and *the company.* The administrators of your school might write *the Faculty* and *the College* or *the University,* words you would not capitalize in a paper. The conventions set out here—and in dictionaries—apply to writing for a general audience.

The Capitalization Guide starting on the next page can help you with capitalization questions. Although it cannot cover all possibilities, you can apply what you find in the list to similar items.

cap **30e**

CAPITALIZATION GUIDE

	CAPITALS	LOWER-CASE LETTERS
NAMES	Bob Ojeda	
	Mother Teresa	my mother (*relationship*)
	Doc Holliday	the doctor (*role*)
TITLES	Chief Justice Earl Warren	the chief justice
	President Truman	a president
	the President (*who is now in office*)	
	Democrat (*a party member*)	democrat (*a believer in democracy*)
	Representative Marge Roukema	the congressional representative
	Senator Dole	the senator
	Professor Roberts	the professor
	Pope John XXIII	the pope
	Rabbi Gale Weiss	the rabbi
	Queen Elizabeth II	the queen
GROUPS OF HUMANITY	Caucasian (*race*)	white (*also* White)
	Negro (*race*)	black (*also* Black)
	Oriental (*race*)	
	Muslim	
	Jewish	
ORGANIZATIONS	Congress	congressional
	the Ohio State Supreme Court	the state supreme court
	the Communist Party	the party
	Eastman Kodak Company	the company
PLACES	Los Angeles	
	India	
	the South (*a region*)	turn south (*a direction*)
	Main Street	the street
	Atlantic Ocean	the ocean
	the Atlantic	
	Orinoco River	the river

(continued on next page)

BACKGROUND

In the eighteenth century there was a movement to reduce the frequency with which capital letters were used. Nevertheless, the final text of the Declaration of Independence is liberally sprinkled throughout with capital letters. As evidence of how conventions regarding capitalization have changed, consider the following passage; you might rewrite it as a contemporary document.

> We hold these truths to be self-evident, that all men are created equal, that they are endowed by their Creator with certain unalienable Rights, that among these are Life, Liberty and the pursuit of Happiness. That to secure these rights, Governments are instituted among Men, deriving their just powers from the consent of the governed. That whenever any Form of Government becomes destructive of these ends, it is the Right of the People to alter or to abolish it and to institute new Government . . . as to them shall seem most likely to affect their Safety and Happiness.

ALTERNATE EXAMPLES

Can your students cite the rules governing the following uses of capital letters?

1. The Koran is the sacred book of the Moslems.

2. A generation ago all high school students read Charles Dickens' novel *A Tale of Two Cities.*

3. The price of an airline ticket will increase on Monday, April 16.

4. My sister had her baby at Women's and Children's Hospital.

5. Spanish is now the primary language of many people in the Southwest.

6. Next semester I want to take Humanities 101.

7. The job with General Motors will give me the opportunity to travel.

(continued next page)

ALTERNATE EXAMPLES *(continued)*

8. John Steinbeck's novel *The Grapes of Wrath* tells the story of the Joad family coping with the problems of the Great depression.

9. Earth-bound people have always wondered about the possibility of life on Mars or Venus.

10. A history class cannot cover all aspects of the Renaissance.

11. The letter announcing that the company was closing its doors and everyone was losing their jobs ended with the words "*Have* a happy day."

12. The book that has sold the most copies of any book throughout the world is the *Bible*.

13. I registered for *Biology* 101 and *History* 121, but the courses I wanted in psychology and in art were filled by the time I got to registration.

14. The *Capitol* building is located in the nation's capital.

15. The sun does not shine for 186 days at the *North Pole*.

ALTERNATE EXERCISE

To point out the importance of capitalization, you might want to give your students a paragraph that has been typed with only lowercase letters. Then ask them to sort out the sentences and meaning, placing capital letters where they are needed. Here is a paragraph you can use:

> drugs are one of the techniques of western therapy of which we are most proud. however, drugs are used by healers in other cultures as well. rauwulfia root, for example, which was introduced into western psychiatry in the 1950s as resperine, a major tranquilizer, has been used in india for centuries as a tranquilizer and has also been in wide use in west africa for many years. another example is shock therapy. when electric shock therapy was intro-

---

CAPITALIZATION GUIDE *(continued)*

	CAPITALS	LOWER-CASE LETTERS
BUILDINGS	the Capitol (in Washington, D.C.)	the state capitol
	Union High School	the high school
	China West Cafe	the restaurant
	Highland Hospital	the hospital
SCIENTIFIC TERMS	Earth (*the planet*)	the earth (*where we live*)
	the Milky Way	the galaxy
		the moon
		the sun
	Streptococcus aureus	a streptococcal infection
	Gresham's law	the theory of relativity
LANGUAGES, NATIONALITIES	Spanish	
	Chinese	
SCHOOL COURSES	Chemistry 342	a chemistry course
	my English class	
NAMES OF THINGS	the *St. Louis Post-Dispatch*	the newspaper
	Time	the magazine
	Purdue University	the university
	Campbell's vegetable soup	
	the Dodge Colt	
TIME NAMES	Friday	
	August	
SEASONS		spring, summer, fall, autumn, winter
HISTORICAL PERIODS	World War II	the war
		the cold war

(continued on next page)

CAPITALIZATION GUIDE *(continued)*

	CAPITALS	LOWER-CASE LETTERS
HISTORICAL PERIODS *(cont.)*	the Great Depression (*in the 1930s*) the Reformation	the depression (*any economic depression*) an era, an age the eighteenth century fifth-century manuscripts the civil rights movement
RELIGIOUS TERMS	God Buddhism the Torah the Koran the Bible	a god, a goddess
LETTER PARTS	Dear Ms. Tauber: Sincerely yours, Yours truly,	
TITLES OF WORKS	"The Lottery" *A History of the United States to 1877* *Catcher in the Rye*	[Capitalize the first word and all other words except articles°, short prepositions°, and short conjunctions°]
COMPOUND WORDS	un-American post-Victorian Mexican-American native American Indo-European	
ACRONYMS AND INITIALISMS	IRS FBI NATO UCLA AFL-CIO IBM NAACP CUNY	

duced by cerletti in the 1930s, he was not aware that it had been used in some cultures for up to 4,000 years. the technique of applying electrical eels to the head of a patient is referred to in the writings of aristotle, pliny, and plutarch. what kind of results do therapists in other cultures—witch doctors—achieve? a canadian psychiatrist, dr. raymond prince, spent 17 months studying 46 nigerian witch doctors and judged that the theraputic results were about equal to those obtained in north american clinics and hospitals.

—Edwin Fuller Torrey, *The Mind Game*

ANSWERS TO ALTERNATE EXERCISE

The words capitalized in the original paragraph, grouped by sentences, are: Drugs, Western; However; Rauwulfia, Western, India, West Africa; Another; When, Cerletti; The, Aristotle, Pliny, Plutarch; What; A, Canadian, Dr. Raymond Prince, Nigerian, North American.

ALTERNATE EXAMPLES

Can your students explain why certain words in the following sentences are capitalized and why the underlined ones are not?

1. I enjoy spending Sunday afternoon reading the New York Times.

2. Last week I read an article by Paul Goldberger about contemporary architecture in Paris, France.

3. In the article he discusses the new addition to the Louvre, the art museum located in the heart of the city.

4. The new addition is a glass pyramid designed by I. M. Pei.

5. New buildings in beautiful, historic cities often cause controversy.

6. In Paris, for example, the Pompidou Center has been described as "a high-tech toy."

7. Now ten years old, it has come to be considered a modernist monument.

8. The Eiffel Tower was initially thought to be an ugly embarrassment to the city.

ANSWERS: EXERCISE 1

A slash indicates no capital is needed. A capitalized italicized word indicates that a capital is needed.

1. President Abraham Lincoln's /secretary, whose name was Kennedy, and President John F. Kennedy's /secretary, whose name was Lincoln, advised these ill-fated presidents not to go out just before their assassinations.

2. The first child of *European* /parents to be born in *North America* was Snorro, whose /mother was the /widow of Leif Erickson's /brother.

3. The /ancient *Egyptians,* the first to embalm their /dead /citizens, also embalmed their /dead /crocodiles.

4. In 1659 *Massachusetts* outlawed *Christmas* and fined anyone celebrating the /holiday five /shillings.

5. Mark Twain, the author of *"The Celebrated Jumping Frog of Calaveras County,"* once refused to invest in a friend's invention, calling it a "/wildcat speculation." The invention was the telephone!

6. An artificial hand invented in 1551 by a *Frenchman* (his name was Ambroise Tare) had /fingers that moved by cogs and levers, thus enabling a handless member of the /cavalry to grasp the reins of his horse.

7. "Take care, *O* traitor," roared the hero, "/or your /villainy will do you in!"

8. Researchers at the *Institute* for *Policy Studies* of *Harvard University* discovered that the following jobs are considered most boring by those who hold them: (1) /assembly line worker, (2) elevator operator, (3) pool typist, (4) /bank /guard, (5) /housewife.

9. What is the most common item in a family medicine chest? Is it /aspirin? *Adhesive* bandages? *A* thermometer? *An* antibacterial agent? [lower case for *adhesive, a,* and *an* also acceptable]

10. "I don't care what you do, my dear," the /actress *Mrs.* Patrick Campbell is supposed to have said, "as long as you don't do it in the /street and frighten the horses!"

EXERCISE 1

Add capital letters as needed.

1. President Abraham Lincoln's secretary, whose name was Kennedy, and President John F. Kennedy's secretary, whose name was Lincoln, advised these ill-fated presidents not to go out just before their assassinations.

2. The first child of european parents to be born in north america was Snorro, whose mother was the widow of Leif Erickson's brother.

3. The ancient egyptians, the first to embalm their dead citizens, also embalmed their dead crocodiles.

4. In 1659 massachusetts outlawed christmas and fined anyone celebrating the holiday five shillings.

5. Mark Twain, the author of "the celebrated jumping frog of calaveras county," once refused to invest in a friend's invention, calling it a "wildcat speculation." The invention was the telephone!

6. An artificial hand invented in 1551 by a frenchman (his name was Ambroise Tare) had fingers that moved by cogs and levers, thus enabling a handless member of the cavalry to grasp the reins of his horse.

7. "Take care, o traitor," roared the hero, "Or your villainy will do you in!"

8. Researchers at the institute for policy studies of harvard university discovered that the following jobs are considered most boring by those who hold them: (1) assembly line worker, (2) elevator operator, (3) pool typist, (4) bank guard, (5) housewife.

9. What is the most common item in a family medicine chest? Is it aspirin? adhesive bandages? a thermometer? an antibacterial agent?

10. "I don't care what you do, my dear," the actress mrs. Patrick Campbell is supposed to have said, "as long as you don't do it in the street and frighten the horses!"

11. The letter announcing that the company was closing its doors and everyone was losing their jobs ended with the words "have a happy day."

12. The book that has sold the most copies of any book throughout the world is the bible.

13. I registered for biology 101 and history 121, but the courses I wanted in psychology and in art were filled by the time I got to registration.

14. The capitol building is located in the nation's capital.

15. The sun does not shine for 186 days at the north pole.

ITALICS (UNDERLINING)

In printed material, **roman type** is the standard; type that slants to the right is called **italic.** Words in italics contrast with standard roman type, so italics create an emphasis readers can see. In typewritten and handwritten manuscripts, underlining stands for italics.

HANDWRITTEN	*Catch 22*
TYPED	Catch 22
TYPESET	*Catch 22*

30f   Following standard practice for underlining titles and other words, letters, or numbers

Underlining is conventional for titles of long written works, names of ships and some aircraft, film titles, titles of television series, titles of works of graphic art and sculpture, and titles of long musical compositions, such as operas. Underlining also calls the reader's attention to words in languages other than English and to letters, numbers, and words that are mentioned as such. For example, refer to the Guide to Underlining, which starts below. The guide also points out which titles call for quotation marks. It gives standard treatments for titles in notes and bibliographies. For other treatments of titles in documentation, consult Chapters 32–34.

GUIDE TO UNDERLINING

TITLES	
UNDERLINE	**DO NOT UNDERLINE**
The Bell Jar [a novel]	
Death of a Salesman [a play]	
Collected Works of O. Henry [a book]	"The Last Leaf" [one story in the book]
Simon & Schuster Handbook for Writers [a book]	"Writing Argument" [one chapter in the book]
Contexts for Composition [a collection of essays]	"Science and Ethics" [one essay in the collection]
The Iliad [a long poem]	"Nothing Gold Can Stay" [a short poem]
The African Queen [a film]	*(continued on next page)*

11. The letter announcing that the company was closing its doors and everyone was losing their jobs ended with the words "*Have* a happy day."

12. The book that has sold the most copies of any book throughout the world is the *Bible.*

13. I registered for *Biology* 101 and *History* 121, but the courses I wanted in psychology and in art were filled by the time I got to registration.

14. The *Capitol* building is located in the nation's capital.

15. The sun does not shine for 186 days at the *North Pole.*

BACKGROUND

The three basic type forms are gothic, old-style roman, and modern roman. (There are many variations of these basic ones.) Italic type is a companion form of modern roman, one that is lighter and slopes to the right. The earliest type forms were based on contemporary manuscript hands, for the printer was replacing the scribe. The old-style roman form reached its zenith in the fifteenth century, and in 1501 Aldus Manutius of Venice produced and used the first italic form in the printing of a series of Latin texts, the first volume of which was called "Aldine Virgil." The "modern" roman form, the kind of type most used in Western publishing today, originated about 1693 with Philippe Grandjean. Benjamin Franklin was responsible for introducing a variety of roman type, designed by William Caslon, to the American colonies. The Declaration of Independence was printed using it. The early type founders were artists who were concerned about the esthetics of their type faces. In the nineteenth century, however, emphasis shifted from artistry to quantity, and attention to the beauty of printed letters suffered a decline.

ALTERNATE EXAMPLES

Can your students cite the rule governing the following italicized words?

1. *Hamlet* is still one of the world's most frequently produced plays.

2. Several magazines, such as *Life* and *The Saturday Evening Post,* have significantly changed their format in recent years.

3. Some people prefer to keep up with current events by watching *CBS Evening News* instead of reading *USA Today.*

4. The reruns of *Star Trek* continue to attract viewers.

5. The *Challenger* disaster will be long remembered.

6. Children should know their *abc*'s before starting first grade.

7. The literary works of the *fin de siècle* were shocking to many readers.

8. English has borrowed many words from other languages, such as *chauffeur, taco,* and *moccasin.*

9. *The Red Badge of Courage* is a modern epic.

10. The *Titanic* was thought to be invulnerable.

ALTERNATE EXERCISE

What is the difference in meaning suggested by the following changes in the italicized words?

1. a. *Six* different bodies compose the United Nations.
 b. Six different bodies compose the *United Nations.*

2. a. All members of the U.N. can send *five* representatives to the General Assembly.
 b. All members of the U.N. can send five representatives to the *General Assembly.*

3. a. The *primary* responsibility of the Security Council is to maintain international peace and security.
 b. The primary responsibility of the Security Council is to maintain *international* peace and security.

GUIDE TO UNDERLINING *(continued)*

UNDERLINE	DO NOT UNDERLINE
the <u>Los Angeles Times</u>	[a newspaper. Note: Even if *The* is part of the title printed on a newspaper, don't use a capital letter and don't underline it in your paper. In documentation°, omit the word *The*.]
<u>Scientific American</u> [a magazine]	"The Molecules of Life" [an article in a magazine]
<u>The Barber of Seville</u> [title of an opera]	Concerto in B-flat Minor Symphony No. 8 in F
<u>Symphonie Fantastique</u> [title of a long musical work]	[identification of a musical work by form, number, and key. Use neither quotation marks *nor* underlining.]
<u>Twilight Zone</u> [a television series]	"Terror at 30,000 Feet" [an episode of a television series]
<u>The Best of Bob Dylan</u> [a record album or a tape]	"Mr. Tambourine Man" [a song or a single selection on an album or a tape]

OTHER WORDS

UNDERLINE	DO NOT UNDERLINE
the <u>Intrepid</u> [a ship; don't underline preceding initials like U.S.S. or H.M.S.]	aircraft carrier [a general class of ship]
<u>Voyager 2</u> [names of specific aircraft, spacecraft, and satellites]	Boeing 747 [general names shared by classes of aircraft, spacecraft, and satellites]
<u>summa cum laude</u> [term in a language other than English]	burrito, chutzpah [widely used and commonly understood words from languages other than English]
What does <u>our</u> imply? [a word referred to as such]	
the <u>abc</u>'s; confusing <u>3</u>'s and <u>8</u>'s [letters and numbers referred to as themselves]	

30g **Underlining sparingly for special emphasis**

Professional writers sometimes use italics to clarify a meaning or stress a point.

Many people we *think* are powerful turn out on closer examination to be merely frightened and anxious.
—MICHAEL KORDA, *Power!*

Meanings can change when the emphasized word changes.

Isabella ordered Ferdinand to outfit the ships.
Isabella *ordered* Ferdinand to outfit the ships.
Isabella ordered *Ferdinand* to outfit the ships.

Instead of counting on underlining to deliver impact, try to make word choices and sentence structures convey emphasis. Excessive underlining makes writing seem immature.

No   One hundred and fifty years ago in England working men were <u>not</u> <u>allowed</u> to wear moustaches. The moustache was a privilege reserved <u>exclusively</u> for aristocrats. When some feisty tradesmen <u>defied</u> tradition by growing moustaches, members of the upper class were <u>furious</u>. They called the popularization of the moustache a <u>profound</u> <u>threat</u> to national institutions.

EXERCISE 2

Cross out unneeded underlining and quotation marks and add needed underlining. Correct capitalization if necessary.

1. The first rule in an old book about <u>Rules of Etiquette</u> reads, "Do not eat in mittens."
2. When he originated the role of <u>Fonzie</u> in the television series "Happy Days," Henry Winkler earned about $750 per episode.
3. The Monitor and the Merrimac were the first iron-hulled ships to engage in battle.
4. <u>Iowa's</u> name comes from the Indian word <u>ayuhwa</u>, which means "sleepy ones."
5. The New York Times does not carry comic strips.
6. Judy Garland was the second-lowest-paid star in the film classic The Wizard of Oz; only the dog who portrayed <u>Toto</u> was paid less.
7. For distinguished accomplishments of people over age 70, we should look to Goethe, who finished the poem "Faust" at age 80; Verdi, who wrote the song "Ave Maria" at age 85; and Tennyson, who wrote the short poem "Crossing the Bar" at age 80.
8. Handwriting experts say personality traits affect the way an individual dots an i and crosses a t.
9. The <u>Italian</u> word <u>ciao</u> is both a greeting and a farewell.
10. A sense of danger develops slowly in Shirley Jackson's short story <u>The Lottery</u>.

ANSWERS: EXERCISE 2

1. The first rule in an old book about rules of etiquette reads, "Do not eat in mittens."
2. When he originated the role of Fonzie in the television series <u>Happy Days</u>, Henry Winkler earned about $750 per episode.
3. The <u>Monitor</u> and the <u>Merrimac</u> were the first iron-hulled ships to engage in battle.
4. Iowa's name comes from the Indian word <u>ayuhwa</u>, which means "sleepy ones."
5. The <u>New York Times</u> does not carry comic strips.
6. Judy Garland was the second lowest paid star in the film classic <u>The Wizard of Oz</u>; only the dog who portrayed Toto was paid less.
7. For distinguished accomplishments of people over age 70, we should look to Goethe, who finished the poem "Faust" at age 80; Verdi, who wrote the song "Ave Maria" at age 85; and Tennyson, who wrote the short poem "Crossing the Bar" at age 80.
8. Handwriting experts say personality traits affect the way an individual dots an <u>i</u> and crosses a <u>t</u>.
9. The Italian word <u>ciao</u> is both a greeting and a farewell.
10. A sense of danger develops slowly in Shirley Jackson's short story "The Lottery."

COVERAGE: EXERCISE 2

(1) underlining not needed because title is not cited; (2) omit underlining with proper name; underline title of television show; (3) underline names of ships; (4) omit underlining with proper name; (5) underline title of a newspaper (does not include *the*); (6) underline movie title, underlining not needed for proper name; (7) do not underline title of short literary or musical works; (8) underline letters used as themselves; (9) omit underlining with proper name; underline foreign word; (1) use quotation marks for titles of short works

TEACHING TIP

The letters B.C. follow a date, while the letters A.D. precede a date. William Safire, essayist on language for the *New York Times,* reports in his column of June 22, 1986 that a plaque left on the moon by the first Americans reads: "July 1969, A.D." He further reports that at the time he was a speechwriter at the White House and he approved the wording. He writes:

> In a century or so, I hope some descendant of mine will take a sharp stylus on some weekend rocket to the moon and, while awaiting a transfer rocket to Mars, will draw a little circle around the *A.D.* and put an arrow placing it in front of the word *July.* This will show that human beings in the early days of space were grammatically fallible; that mankind (since changed to *humankind,* but you can leave it the old way on the plaque, Junior) is forever editing, and that a little precision is a dangerous thing.

BACKGROUND

During the administration of President Franklin D. Roosevelt, a number of new government agencies became known by their initials. The Tennessee Valley Authority, for example, was called TVA, and the National Industrial Recovery Act was the NIRA. World War II strengthened the policy of using initials without periods, and since that time it has been common practice to use an abbreviation without periods in place of some proper names, such as the UN (United Nations), USC (University of Southern California), the NYPD (New York Police Department), and DDT (dichlorodiphenyl-trichloroethane).

ABBREVIATIONS

30h Using abbreviations in the body of a paper according to standard practice

What you are writing and who will read that writing affect whether you should abbreviate or spell a word out. A few abbreviations are standard in any writing circumstances.

A.M. (OR a.m.) AND P.M. (OR p.m.) WITH SPECIFIC TIMES

7:15 A.M.   7:15 a.m.   3:47 P.M.   3:47 p.m.

Whether you use capital or lower-case letters for specific times, be consistent.

A.D. AND B.C. WITH SPECIFIC YEARS

A.D. 977 [A.D. precedes the year]

12 B.C. [B.C. follows the year]

TITLES OF ADDRESS BEFORE NAMES	ACADEMIC DEGREES AFTER NAMES
Dr. D. K. Gooden	D. K. Gooden, Ph.D.
Mr. Charles Piatagorski	Charles Piatagorski, J. D.
Ms. S. R. Odell	S. R. Odell, M.D.

❖ ABBREVIATION ALERT: Do not use a title of address before a name *and* an academic degree after the name. Use one or the other. ❖

No	Dr. Joyce A. Brown, M.D.
YES	Dr. Joyce A. Brown
YES	Joyce A. Brown, M.D.

If you use a long name or term frequently in a paper, you can abbreviate it. The first time you use it, give the full term, with the abbreviation in parentheses immediately after the spelled-out form. After that you can use the abbreviation alone.

> Spain voted to continue as a member of the North Atlantic Treaty Organization (NATO), to the surprise of other NATO members.

You can use *USSR* without giving the spelled-out form first. You can abbreviate *U.S.* as a modifier (the U.S. ski team, a U.S. government official); spell out *United States* when you use it as a noun, however.

No	Louisiana is one of the few places in the **U.S.** where rice can be grown.
YES	Louisiana is one of the few places in the **United States** where rice can be grown.

Other than these cases, you should seldom use abbreviations in the body of a paper you write for a course in the humanities.

No   Robt. Frost taught at Amherst Col. in Amherst, Mass., where Doctor Eliz. Adams (my lit. prof.) taped an interview with him in Sept. 1957.

Yes   Robert Frost taught at Amherst College in Amherst, Massachusetts, where Dr. Elizabeth Adams (my professor of literature) taped an interview with him in September 1957.

❖ ABBREVIATION ALERT: If you include a full address—street, city, and state—in the body of a paper, you can use the postal abbreviation for the state name (see 30i for a list), but spell out any other combination of a city and a state. ❖

No   The Center for Disease Control in **Atlanta, GA,** sometimes quarantines livestock.

Yes   The Center for Disease Control in **Atlanta, Georgia,** sometimes quarantines livestock.

Abbreviations in documentation° are common in the humanities; see 30i for a list. In the social and natural sciences, abbreviations are common in the body of a paper as well as in documentation; for guidance, see the latest editions of *Publication Manual of the American Psychological Association,* the *CBE Style Manual,* or similar guides.

Symbols are seldom used in the body of papers written for courses in the humanities. You can use a percent symbol (%) or a cent sign (¢), for example, in a table, graph, or other illustration, but in the body of the paper spell out *percent* and *cent.* You can, however, use a dollar sign with specific dollar amounts: $23 billion, $7.85. As with other decisions, let common sense and your readers' needs guide you. If you mention temperatures once or twice in a paper, spell them out: *ninety degrees, minus twenty-six degrees.* If you mention temperatures throughout a paper, use figures and symbols: 90°, − 26°.

30i Using abbreviations in documentation according to standard practice

Documentation styles are discussed in Chapter 33. The list of scholarly abbreviations on the following page gives forms you may find in the sources you consult as well as those you will need to document your own work.

SCHOLARLY ABBREVIATIONS

anon.	anonymous
b.	born
c. *or* ©	copyright
c. *or* ca.	about (with dates)
cf.	compare
col., cols.	column, columns
d.	died
ed.; eds.	editor, edited by; editors
e.g.	for example
esp.	especially
et al.	and others
f., ff.	and the following page, pages
i.e.	that is
ms., mss.	manuscript, manuscripts
n.b.	note carefully
n.d.	no date (of publication, for a book)
p., pp.	page, pages
pref.	preface
rept.	report, reported by
sec., secs.	section, sections
v. *or* vs.	versus (legal case)
vol., vols.	volume, volumes

Use month abbreviations and postal abbreviations as needed in your lists of works cited.

MONTH ABBREVIATIONS

Jan.	January	July	
Feb.	February	Aug.	August
Mar.	March	Sept.	September
Apr.	April	Oct.	October
May		Nov.	November
June		Dec.	December

ab **30i**

POSTAL ABBREVIATIONS

AL	Alabama	MT	Montana
AK	Alaska	NB	Nebraska
AZ	Arizona	NV	Nevada
AR	Arkansas	NH	New Hampshire
CA	California	NJ	New Jersey
CO	Colorado	NM	New Mexico
CT	Connecticut	NY	New York
DE	Delaware	NC	North Carolina
DC	District of Columbia	ND	North Dakota
FL	Florida	OH	Ohio
GA	Georgia	OK	Oklahoma
HI	Hawaii	OR	Oregon
ID	Idaho	PA	Pennsylvania
IL	Illinois	RI	Rhode Island
IN	Indiana	SC	South Carolina
IA	Iowa	SD	South Dakota
KS	Kansas	TN	Tennessee
KY	Kentucky	TX	Texas
LA	Louisiana	UT	Utah
ME	Maine	VT	Vermont
MD	Maryland	VA	Virginia
MA	Massachusetts	WA	Washington (state)
MI	Michigan	WV	West Virginia
MN	Minnesota	WI	Wisconsin
MS	Mississippi	WY	Wyoming
MO	Missouri		

EXERCISE 3

Make needed changes so that abbreviations are used correctly.

1. In 1665, Harvard U. graduated its first N. American Indian, Caleb Cheesheateaumuck.

2. The first swim across the Eng. Channel took twenty-one hrs., forty-five mins.

3. According to most drs., the best places in the U.S. for allergy sufferers to live in are the deserts of AZ.

4. When Sandra Day O'Connor was appt. to the Supreme Ct. by Pres. R. Reagan in 1981, she became the 1st woman Supreme Ct. justice in Amer. history.

ALTERNATE EXERCISE

You may want to organize your class into competing teams, giving each in turn a postal abbreviation to which a member is to respond by naming a city in that state. For example, an acceptable answer for a player who is given the abbreviation MN would be Minneapolis. When a player cannot answer, the abbreviation is given to a player on the other team.

ANSWERS: EXERCISE 3

1. In 1665, Harvard University graduated its first North American Indian, Caleb Cheeshateaumuck.

2. The first swim across the English Channel took twenty-one hours, forty-five minutes.

3. According to most doctors, the best places in the United States for allergy sufferers to live in are the deserts of Arizona.

4. When Sandra Day O'Connor was appointed to the Supreme Court by President Ronald Reagan in 1981, she became the first woman Supreme Court justice in American history.

5. Many college students today are required to take courses in literature, social science, and language.

6. The energy crisis of 1973 prompted enforcement of a national speed limit of 55 mph.

7. It seems ironic that the paintings of Vincent van Gogh, who died penniless, now sell for millions of dollars.

8. The route of the Boston Marathon, run every April, covers twenty-six miles between Hopkinton, Massachusetts, and Boston, Massachusetts.

9. At fifty minutes before the scheduled liftoff, the Saturday launch was postponed.

10. The United Nations building in New York City has been a popular tourist attraction for years.

5. Many coll. students today are required to take courses in lit., soc. sci., and lang.

6. The energy crisis of 1973 prompted enforcement of a natl. speed limit of 55 mph.

7. It seems ironic that the paintings of Vincent van Gogh, who died penniless, now sell for millions of $.

8. The route of the Boston Marathon, run every Apr., covers twenty-six mi. between Hopkinton, MA, and Boston, MA.

9. At fifty mins. before the liftoff, the Sat. launch was postponed.

10. The UN bldg. in NYC has been a popular tourist attraction for yrs.

NUMBERS

30j Using figures and spelled-out numbers according to standard practice

Depending on how often numbers occur in a paper and what they refer to, you will sometimes express the numbers in words and sometimes in figures. The guidelines here, like those in the *MLA Handbook for Writers of Research Papers,* 3rd edition, are suitable for writing in the humanities. For the guidelines other disciplines follow, ask your course instructors or consult other style manuals.

If conveying numerical exactness to your readers is not a prime purpose in your paper, and if you mention numbers only a few times, spell out numbers that can be expressed in one or two words: *Iceland's population increases by more than one percent a year, but that gain translates into fewer than three thousand individuals.*

✤ HYPHENATION ALERT: Use a hyphen between spelled-out two-word numbers from *twenty-one* through *ninety-nine.* ✤

If you use numbers fairly frequently in a paper, spell out numbers from *one* to *nine* and use figures for numbers *10* and above.

Never start a sentence with a figure. If a sentence starts with a number, spell it out.

> Three hundred seventy-five dollars per credit is the tuition rate for nonresidents.

> Nineteen twenty-nine saw the stock market crash, wiping out speculators and conservative investors alike.

In practice, you can usually revise a sentence so that the number does not come first.

> The tuition rate for nonresidents is $375 per credit.

> The stock market crashed in 1929, wiping out speculators and prudent investors alike.

Do not mix spelled-out numbers and figures in a paper when they both refer to the same thing. Use figures for all the numbers.

No　　In four days, our volunteers increased from five to eight to 17 to 233.

Yes　　In four days, our volunteers increased from 5 to 8 to 17 to 233. [All the numbers referring to volunteers are given in figures, but *four* is still spelled out because it refers to a different quantity—days.]

Give specific numbers—dates, addresses, measurements, identification numbers of many kinds—in figures.

GUIDE FOR USING SPECIFIC NUMBERS	
DATES	August 6, 1941 1732–1845 34 B.C. to A.D. 230
ADDRESSES	10 Downing Street 237 North 8th Street Export Falls, MN 92025
TIMES	8:09 a.m.;　3:30 [but *six o'clock,* not *6 o'clock*]
DECIMALS AND FRACTIONS	5.55;　98.6;　3.1416;　7/8;　12-1/4 [but *three quarters,* not *3 quarters*]
CHAPTERS AND PAGES	Chapter 27, page 245
SCORES AND STATISTICS	a 6-0 score;　a 5 to 3 ratio;　29 percent
IDENTIFICATION NUMBERS	94.4 on the FM dial;　call 1-212-555-0000
MEASUREMENTS	2 feet;　67.8 miles per hour;　1.5 gallons; 2 level teaspoons;　3 liters;　8-1/2″ × 11″ paper or 8-1/2 × 11-inch paper
ACT, SCENE, AND LINE NUMBERS	act II, scene 2, lines 75–79
TEMPERATURES	43° F;　4° Celsius
MONEY	$1.2 billion;　$3.41;　25 cents

TEACHING TIP

William Safire, essayist on language for the *New York Times,* pointed out in his column of April 23, 1986, that practice varies greatly on how to write *noon* or *midnight* when the number 12 is involved. Some people use 12:00 A.M. for midnight while others use 12:00 P.M. The same is true for noon. Safire suggests using *12 noon* and *12 midnight* for greater clarity.

TEACHING TIP

Some students may need a review of Roman numerals. The major ones are: I = 1; V = 5; X = 10; L = 50; C = 100; D = 500; M = 1,000.

In academic writing, Roman numerals have few uses. They designate the major divisions in outlines; sometimes they are used in lists. They are used as parts of names and titles: *Peter Brown III, Queen Elizabeth II, Rocky IV.* You might remind students that Roman numerals are not interchangeable with arabic (regular) numerals in addresses, dates, or measurements.

ANSWERS: EXERCISE 4

1. The film *Quo Vadis* used 30,000 extras and 63 lions. [*or* thirty thousand extras and sixty-three lions.]

2. The best time to use insecticides is 4:00 p.m. because that is when insects are most susceptible.

3. People in the United States spend $600 million a year on hot dogs. [Also correct are the spelled-out form, $600,000,000 and 600,000,000 dollars, but $600 million is most appropriate for academic writing.]

4. Four-fifths of everything alive on this earth is in the sea.

5. The earliest baseball game on record was played in 1846 on June 19 [*or* 19th] for a final score of 23 to 1 in four innings.

6. Aaron Montgomery Ward started the first mail order company in the United States in 1872 at 825 North Clark Street in Chicago.

7. The record for a human's broad jump is about 28 feet, one-quarter inch, and the record for a frog's broad jump is 13 feet, 5 inches.

8. Two hundred fifty words per minute is the reading speed of the typical reader. [*or:* The typical reader reads 250 words per minute.]

9. The yearly income of the average family in the United States in 1915 was $687. [Spelled-out form for money is also correct.]

10. Three out of four people who wear contact lenses are between 12 and 23 years of age.

COVERAGE: EXERCISE 4

(1) numbers over 10 expressed in words and figures; (2) time; (3) money; (4) fraction; (5) date, words and figures mixed in statistics; (6) address; (7) statistics expressed with mixed figures and words; (8) sentence opened with figures; (9) date and money; (10) sentence opened with figures

---

EXERCISE 4

Revise so that numbers are in correct form—spelled out or in figures.

1. The film *Quo Vadis* used thirty thousand extras and 63 lions.

2. The best time to use insecticides is four p.m. because that is when insects are most susceptible.

3. People in the United States spend six hundred million dollars a year on hot dogs.

4. 4/5 of everything alive on this earth is in the sea.

5. The earliest baseball game on record was played in 1846 on June nineteenth for a final score of 23 to one in 4 innings.

6. Aaron Montgomery Ward started the first mail order company in the United States in 1872 at eight hundred twenty-five North Clark Street in Chicago.

7. The record for a human's broad jump is about twenty-eight feet, one-quarter inch, and the record for a frog's broad jump is 13 feet, 5 inches.

8. 250 words per minute is the reading speed of the typical reader.

9. The yearly income of the average family in the United States in nineteen fifteen was six hundred and eighty-seven dollars.

10. 3 out of 4 people who wear contact lenses are between 12 and 23 years of age.

30

REVISING YOUR WRITING

If you make errors in using capitals, italics, abbreviations, or numbers, go back to your writing and locate the errors. Using this chapter as a resource, revise your writing to correct the problems.

CASE STUDY: REVISING FOR CORRECT CAPITALS, ITALICS, ABBREVIATIONS, AND NUMBERS

This case study lets you observe a student writer revising. It also gives you the opportunity to revise some student writing on your own.

Observation

A student wrote the following draft for a course called The United States in the Twentieth Century. The assignment was to discuss an important political moment that occurred between 1945 and the present. This material is well organized and includes many specific details, but the draft's effectiveness is diminished by the presence of errors in capitalization, italics (underlining), abbreviations, and numbers.

Read through the draft. The errors are highlighted and explained. Before you look at how the student revised to eliminate the errors, revise the material yourself. Then compare what you and the student did.

Capital needed for nationality: 30e ——

Quotation marks, not italics, needed for song title: 30f ——

Lower case needed: 30e

Many american people have forgotten some interesting details of the historic march on Washington, D.C., that took place in 1963. More than 200,000 people, black and white, linked arms and chanted the song We Shall Overcome. Crowds listened peacefully to the sounds of Folksingers Joan Baez and Peter, Paul and Mary. Radio and television audiences felt the passion and power in the words of

(continued on next page)

Period needed for abbreviation: 30h

Dr Martin Luther King, Jr., who delivered the speech that rang with the now-famous phrase "I have a dream."

Historians marvel at the coalition that came together to sponsor the march. Labor leaders,

Lower case needed: 30e

Church leaders, representatives of both pacifist and more militant civil rights organizations all joined together with a common goal—to make the country aware of the need for jobs and freedom for all people in the United States.

Capital needed for title: 30e

Although initially opposed to the march, president John F. Kennedy finally endorsed it and met with its leaders early in the day. he later watched the rally on television.

Capital needed for first word in sentence: 30a

Even more amazing was the orderliness of the demonstration.

Numerals needed: 30j

In anticipation of possible trouble, almost six thousand police had been called out, and the armed services had 4,000 people standing by. The worst problem that the

Lower case needed: 30e

Police had to deal with was traffic control. Even the sanitation department had little to do. After the march was over, the demonstrators cleaned up virtually all of the litter from the bag

Italics (underlining) not needed: 30g

Lower case needed: 30e

lunches most of them had brought. The city and Nation had never seen anything like this march.

Here is how the student revised the essay to correct errors in capitalization, italics (underlining), abbreviations, and numbers.

Many American people have forgotten some interesting details of the historic march on Washington, D.C., that took place in 1963. More than 200,000 people, black and white, linked arms and chanted the song "We Shall Overcome." Crowds listened peacefully to the sounds of folksingers Joan Baez and Peter, Paul and Mary. Radio and television audiences felt the passion and power in the words of Dr. Martin Luther King, Jr., who delivered the speech that rang with the now-famous phrase "I have a dream."

Historians marvel at the coalition that came together to sponsor the march. Labor leaders, church leaders, representatives of both pacifist and more militant civil rights organizations all joined together with a common goal—to make the country aware of the need for jobs and freedom for all people in the United States. Although initially opposed to the march, President John F. Kennedy finally endorsed it and met with its leaders early in the day. He later watched the rally on television.

Even more amazing was the orderliness of the demonstration. In anticipation of possible trouble, almost 6,000 police had been called out, and the armed services had 4,000 people standing by. The worst problem that the police had to deal with was traffic control. Even the sanitation department had little to do. After the march was over, the demonstrators cleaned up virtually all of the litter from the bag lunches most of them had brought. The city and nation had never seen anything like this march.

Participation

A student wrote the following draft for a course called Introduction to United States History. The assignment was to write about a leading figure around the time of the Revolutionary War. This material is well organized and uses specific examples well, but the draft's effectiveness is diminished by errors in capitalization, italics (underlining), abbreviations, and numbers.

Read through the draft. Then revise it to eliminate the errors. Also, make any additional revisions that you think would improve the content, organization, and style of the material.

Benjamin Franklin played a leading role in the drive for american independence from the rule of England. He also helped improve the quality of daily life in many other ways.

Franklin's devotion to social improvement showed itself in his efforts to improve the quality of daily life in Philadelphia, where he worked as a printer. He proposed a city-paid Police force and helped start up a volunteer fire department. He successfully campaigned for a library, and his writing about education led to the founding of the university of Pennsylvania. His first important contribution to politics was in organizing a militia to guard

COVERAGE: PARTICIPATION ESSAY

Benjamin Franklin played a leading role in the drive for *american* [capital needed for nationality: 30e] independence from the rule of England. He also helped improve the quality of daily life in many others ways.

Franklin's devotion to social improvement showed itself in his efforts to improve the quality of daily life in Philadelphia, where he worked as a printer. He proposed a city-paid *Police* [lower case needed: 30e] force and helped start up a volunteer fire department. He successfully campaigned for a library, and his writing about education led to the founding of the university of *Pennsylvania.* [capital needed for name: 30e] His first important contribution to politics was in organizing a militia to guard Philadelphia against raids threatened by French and Spanish ships.

Franklin gained prestige for his work with electricity. [underlining not needed; 30g] His flying a kite in a thunderstorm to learn more about lightning is a familiar image from colonial days. Beyond science, Franklin gained fame as a politician. *he* [capital needed for first word in sentence: 30a] served in London as spokesperson for the American colonies. When negotiations with England fell apart, he returned to the colonies, where he helped write the Declaration of Independence. When war between the colonies and England broke out, he traveled to France as an *Ambassador* [lower case needed: 30e] to secure military and economic aid for the colonies. Franklin persuaded France to send *twelve thousand* [numerals needed: 30j] soldiers and 32,000 sailors to *Gen* [period needed for abbreviation: 30h] George Washington. Franklin helped frame the treaty that finally gave the American colonies their independence, and he had a hand in writing the Constitution of the *U.S.* [United States needs to be spelled out as a noun: 30h].

Benjamin Franklin's legacy to our nation is his wisdom, energy, and rare and varied talents.

ANSWER: PARTICIPATION ESSAY

Benjamin Franklin played a leading role in the drive for American independence from the rule of England. He also helped improve the quality of daily life in many other ways.

Franklin's devotion to social improvement showed itself in his efforts to improve the quality of daily life in Philadelphia, where he worked as a printer. He proposed a city-paid police force and helped start up a volunteer fire department. He successfully campaigned for a library, and his writing about education led to the founding of the University of Pennsylvania. His first important contribution to politics was in organizing a militia to guard Philadelphia against raids threatened by French and Spanish ships.

Franklin gained prestige for his work with electricity. His flying a kite in a thunderstorm to learn more about lightning is a familiar image from colonial days. Beyond science, Franklin gained fame as a politician. He served in London as spokesperson for the American colonies. When negotiations with England fell apart, he returned to the colonies, where he helped write the Declaration of Independence. When war between the colonies and England broke out, he traveled to France as an ambassador to secure military and economic aid for the colonies. Franklin persuaded France to send 12,000 soldiers and 32,000 sailors to Gen. George Washington. Franklin helped frame the treaty that finally gave the American colonies their independence, and he had a hand in writing the Constitution of the United States.

Benjamin Franklin's legacy to our nation is his wisdom, energy, and rare and varied talents.

Philadelphia against raids threatened by French and Spanish ships.

Franklin gained prestige for his work with electricity. His flying a kite in a thunderstorm to learn more about lightning is a familiar image from colonial days. Beyond science, Franklin gained fame as a politician. he served in London as spokesperson for the American colonies. When negotiations with England fell apart, he returned to the colonies, where he helped write the Declaration of Independence. When war between the colonies and England broke out, he traveled to France as an Ambassador to secure military and economic aid for the colonies. Franklin persuaded France to send twelve thousand soldiers and 32,000 sailors to Gen George Washington. Franklin helped frame the treaty that finally gave the American colonies their independence, and he had a hand in writing the Constitution of the U.S.

Benjamin Franklin's legacy to our nation is his wisdom, energy, and rare and varied talents.

Seven

WRITING
RESEARCH

When you write research, you engage in two processes: doing research and writing a research paper. Part Seven explains how to find and write from sources, how to conduct research and write a paper based on your findings, and how to document your sources completely and accurately. As you use Chapters 31 through 34, be aware that the activities of research writing foster habits of mind that will serve you well throughout your life.

31 Paraphrasing, Summarizing, and Quoting Sources

The core of every writing project is its content. In many writing assignments, the source of that content is expected to be your own thinking. For many other assignments, however, you are expected to draw upon outside sources—such as books, articles, films, and interviews—to explain and support your ideas. **Paraphrasing** (31b), **summarizing** (31c), and **quoting** (31d) are three techniques you can use to incorporate information from sources. Along with these techniques you are always expected to document your sources (31b) and avoid plagiarism (31a).

GUIDELINES FOR USING OUTSIDE SOURCES IN YOUR WRITING

1. Avoid plagiarism by always attributing ideas and words that are not yours to their source.

2. Document sources accurately and completely.

3. Know how and when to use these techniques:

   - **Paraphrase:** a detailed restatement of someone else's statement expressed in your own words and your own sentence structure

   - **Summary:** a condensed statement of the main points of someone else's passage expressed in your own words and sentence structure

   - **Quotation:** the exact words of a source set off in quotation marks

31a Avoiding plagiarism

To **plagiarize** is to present another person's words or ideas as if they were your own. Plagiarism is like stealing. The word *plagiarize* comes from the Latin word for kidnapper and literary thief. Plagiarism is a serious offense that can be grounds for failure of a course or expulsion from a college. Plagiarism can be intentional, as when you deliberately incorporate the work of other people in your writing without mentioning and documenting the source. Plagiarism can also be unintentional—but no less serious an offense—if you are unaware of what must be acknowledged and how to go about documenting. All college students are expected to know what plagiarism is and how to avoid it. If you are not absolutely clear about what is involved, take time *now* to learn the "rules of the game" so that you never expose yourself to charges of plagiarism.

What should you document? Everything that you get from an outside source. If you use quotation (31e), document (31b). If you use paraphrase (31c) or summary (31d), document (31b). Writing the words of others in your own words does not release you from the obligation to document.

What do you *not* have to document? When you write a paper that draws on outside sources, you are not expected to document common knowledge (if there is any on your topic) or your own thinking.

Common knowledge

You do not have to document **common knowledge.** Common knowledge is information that most educated people know, although they might need to remind themselves of certain facts by looking up information in a reference book. For example, every educated person knows that the U.S. space program included moon landings. Some people might have to look in a reference book to remind themselves that Neil Armstrong, the first man to set foot on the moon, landed on July 20, 1969. That fact is common knowledge and does not have to be documented. You move into *the realm of research and the need to document* as soon as you get into less commonly known details about the moon landing: the duration of the stay on the moon, the size and capabilities of the spaceship, what the astronauts ate during their journey, and similar details. If you feel that you are walking a thin line between knowledge held in common and knowledge learned from research, be safe and document. Some-

TEACHING TIP: STOPPING PLAGIARISM BEFORE IT HAPPENS

All of us, unfortunately, have to deal with plagiarism from time to time. Techniques for plagiarism-proofing assignments are plentiful: requiring the submission in the student's own hand of working bibliographies, note cards, outlines, and rough drafts; assigning unusual topics and changing them every semester; replacing the semester-long research project with several shorter ones to prevent students from having time to contact research paper mills; limiting research to the use of a particular casebook. All of these work to some degree, but at the price of turning us into thought-police, ever on the alert for the student who might find a way around our system. We take on extra stress and extra paperwork—students continue to think of us as fussy creatures who demand they follow rituals peculiar to English classes. If we are not to continue to waste our energies tracking down plagiarized passages in the library stacks, we need to take steps to counter the mixed signals about plagiarism that our students have received over the years—and continue to receive.

Doris R. Dant, in "Plagiarism in High School: A Survey" (*English Journal,* Feb. 1986, pp. 81–84), makes several points about how students are taught to write reports in high school and the impact on plagiarism in college. In a survey of fourteen freshman composition classes at Brigham Young University (1984), she found that seventeen percent of the students reported being advised by their high school teachers to copy "the information word for word from other sources." Dant also found that there was a correlation between the number of teachers who taught when to document sources and the students' avoidance of plagiarism. Students who reported that all their teachers explained how to credit sources were far more likely to understand the con-

(continued next page)

times, of course, a research paper does not happen to contain common knowledge. For example, Amy Brown, whose research paper appears in Chapter 34, had no common knowledge about her topic of personal space. In fact, Brown wanted to write about something new to her. In such cases, the research paper consists of documented material from sources and the writer's own thinking.

Your own thinking

You do not have to document **your own thinking.** As you conduct your research, you learn new material by building on what you already know. You are expected to think about the new material, formulate a thesis about the information, and organize a paper. Here are illustrations of a student's own thinking, drawn from the research paper by Amy Brown in Chapter 34:

- the thesis statement° (see paragraph 1)
- most organizing sentences (for example, the opening sentences of many of the paragraphs after paragraph 1; also, see annotation G)
- comments (for example, the sentence in paragraph 1 after the anecdote and parenthetical reference; also, the sentence in paragraph 13 after the paraphrase of Morris and parenthetical reference)
- transitional sentences (for example, the sentence in paragraph 13 after the summary of information from Davis and Skupien and parenthetical reference)
- the "call to action" in paragraphs 13 and 14

Be particularly careful about plagiarism slipping into a thesis statement. A thesis statement must reflect your thinking. It is plagiarism to put a source's main idea into your words and pass that off as your thesis. Similarly, it is plagiarism to combine the main ideas of several sources, put them into your own words, and pass that off as your thesis.

To prevent plagiarism from slipping into your work, take careful notes as you conduct research using outside sources (see 32j-2). Here are practices that help researchers avoid plagiarism.

1. *Record complete documentation information.* Become entirely familiar with the documentation style you intend to use in your paper (31b). Make a master list of the documentation facts required for each source, and write down all the facts on a bibliography card (see 33a).

2. *Record documentation information as you go along.* Never forget to write down documentation facts as you take notes. Use very clear handwriting. Do not expect to retrace your steps and get documentation facts after you finish taking notes or writing your paper. **Your chances of unintentional plagiarism increase sharply if you have to recreate your research process. Do not expect to be able to relocate your sources or to reconstruct what came from the source and what was your own thinking.** In addition to increasing your risk of plagiarizing, retracing your steps wastes your time. You also risk not being able to find a source again because someone else might be using it.

3. *Use a consistent note-taking system.* Good notes give you more than a report of what you have read. **To avoid the risk of plagiarism, you must always be able to tell what in the notes is yours and what belongs to an outside source.** You must keep three things separate: (1) material you have paraphrased or summarized from a source; (2) quotations from a source; and (3) your own thoughts triggered by what you are reading. For quotations, always write clear, perhaps oversize quotation marks that you have no chance of missing later. To keep material separate, use color coding. Stores stock different colors of cards, inks, highlighter pens, and clips. A more cluttered but acceptable method is to underline one type of material, circle another, and leave the third unmarked.

Understanding the concept of documentation

Basic to paraphrasing, summarizing, and quoting is the concept and practice of **documentation**—acknowledging your sources by giving full and accurate information about the author, title and date of publication, and related facts. Whenever you paraphrase (31c), summarize (31d), or quote (31e), you must document your source according to correct documentation style.

Documentation styles vary among the disciplines. Some use a system of footnotes or endnotes, and others place reference information in parentheses within the text. Some styles abbreviate and capitalize differently than others. Each style sequences information and punctuates it a little differently. In courses for which you write

3. Levi Strauss, the inventor of blue jeans, came to the United States from Germany in 1848.

4. Coca-Cola is a popular soft drink all around the world.

5. According to Germaine Greer, the reason few women artists have achieved greatness is that they have historically internalized their oppression, thereby draining the energy required for creative work.

6. The United States is a substantially less secure society today than it was forty years ago.

7. The Olympic Games are held every four years.

8. The initials GNP stand for the term *gross national product.*

9. As a society we should read poetry because it makes us live more fully and live more deeply.

10. Henry David Thoreau lived at Walden Pond for two years.

ANSWERS: EXTRA EXERCISE A

1. No. Common knowledge.
2. Yes. Not common knowledge.
3. Yes. Not common knowledge.
4. No. Common knowledge.
5. Yes. Opinion of someone besides the writer.
6. No, if opinion of the writer. Yes, if opinion of someone besides the writer.
7. No. Common knowledge.
8. No. Common knowledge.
9. No, if opinion of the writer. Yes, if opinion of someone besides the writer.
10. No. Common knowledge.

TEACHING TIP

As Charles Bazerman (*The Informed Writer,* Boston: Houghton Mifflin, 1981, p. 14) says, "there are . . . ways . . . of appearing to read while not really reading": (1) We may open a book with the assumption that it is worthless—and spend our time and energy looking for errors. As no book can be all things to all people, finding an error or some sort is easy, and it is then even easier to dismiss the book. In doing so, unfortunately, we also dismiss whatever valuable insights there may be. (2) We may assume a book means what we wish it to mean. A few familiar phrases may encourage us to misinterpret an entire argument; we may go as far as not to see important words, *not, sometimes, rarely.* At the least, we may gloss over details that do not fit our notion of what the book ought to say. (3) We may misinterpret words, such as abstractions and jargon, or ignore the context of words—all in an effort to see what we want to see. (4) We may fail to see how pieces of the argument fit together, giving undue or insufficient weight to material in proportion to how it suits our ideas. Once students are aware of these pitfalls, they are more likely to avoid them.

using outside sources, find out what documentation style you are expected to use. Chapter 33 explains and illustrates documentation styles you may be required to use.

31c Paraphrasing accurately

When you **paraphrase,** you make a detailed restatement of someone else's words in your own. The word *paraphrase* combines the Greek word for "tell" with the Greek prefix *para-,* meaning "alongside." Thus, *paraphrase* describes a parallel text, one that goes alongside an original writing. When you paraphrase, you precisely restate in your own words a passage written by another author (or spoken by someone interviewed, or heard on a film). Your paraphrasings offer an account of what various authorities have to say, not in their words but in yours. (For advice about identifying authoritative sources in a subject, see 32d-2.) The ideas of authorities can give substance and credibility to your message, and they can offer support for your thesis°.

Equally important, the process of writing a paraphrase helps you untangle difficult passages and gain domination over a thought. Paraphrasing forces you to read closely and to extract precise meaning from complex passages.

GUIDELINES FOR WRITING A PARAPHRASE

1. Say what the source says, but no more.
2. Reproduce the source's order of ideas and emphases.
3. Use your own words, phrasing, and sentence structure to restate the message. If certain synonyms are awkward, quote the material—but resort to this very sparingly.
4. Read over your sentences to make sure that they make sense and do not distort the source's meaning.
5. Expect your material to be as long as, and possibly longer than, the original.
6. Avoid plagiarism.
7. Write down all documentation facts so that you can document your source when you use it in your writing. Even though a paraphrase is not a direct quotation, you must document the source (see 31b).

Select for paraphrase only the passages that carry ideas that you will need to reproduce in detail. Because paraphrase calls for very close approximation of a source, it is not practical to paraphrase whole chapters—or indeed much more than a page. Usually, two or three paragraphs in a chapter are the most you should attempt to translate in the detail required by paraphrase; use summary (31d) for the rest.

1 | Restating the material completely

When you paraphrase, you restate the material—and no more. You do not skip points, you do not guess at meaning, and above all, you do not insert your own opinions or interpretations. You may later select what parts you want to use in your writing, but do not make those decisions when you are taking the notes.

If the source's words trigger your own thinking, do not lose your thought or assume you will recall it later. *Be sure, however, to write down your thought so that it is physically separate from your paraphrase:* put it in the margin, use an alternate color of ink, or circle it clearly so that you will know it does not belong in the paraphrase.

2 | Using your own words, not the source's words

To paraphrase, translate the writer's or speaker's language into your own. If you do not use your own words, you will be quoting, not paraphrasing. Use words that come naturally to you. Use synonyms for the source's words wherever you can. Use your own sentence structures. Read over your sentences to be sure that your paraphrase makes sense and does not distort the meaning.

In paraphrasing, the farther you get from the original phrasing, the more likely you are to sound like yourself. Do not be surprised to find that when you change language and sentence structure you might also have to change punctuation, verb tense°, and voice°.

Sometimes, synonyms or substitute phrases are not advisable. For example, if you are dealing with a basic concept such as *people,* the phrase *homo sapiens* might make the material seem strained. Consider how each synonym fits into the flow of your sentence. Also, do not rename terms that the author identifies as coined; quote them. For example, in the student research paper in Chapter 34, Amy Brown does not need a synonym for Edward Hall's word "proxemics," because Hall originated it.

QUOTATION ABOUT WRITING

You could compile the worst book in the world entirely out of selected passages from the best writers in the world.

—G. K. Chesterton

QUOTATION ABOUT WRITING

He invades authors like a monarch, and what would be theft in other poets is only victory in him.

—John Dryden of Ben Jonson

TEACHING TIP

In the belief that most students who plagiarize from their sources do so because they don't know how to avoid the problem, Katheleen Mouton has devised a technique that can be demonstrated in class to help students avoid taking notes that are too close to the words of the source. She suggests that instructors ask students to read a short, informative passage of material, then put it away and make notes from memory. Students can check afterwards to make sure that facts (such as dates and names) are correct. With larger amounts of material, students can stop frequently to make their notes, still being careful not to look at the source while recording the note.

TEACHING TIP

Working in small groups or in pairs, students can learn good techniques of paraphrasing by trying to find acceptable synonyms for key words in a passage. The underlined words and phrases in the following excerpts can be used for the exercise.

(1) It is clear that between what a man calls "me" and what he simply calls "mine," the line is very difficult to draw. We feel and act about certain things that are ours very much as we feel and act about ourselves. . . . In its widest possible sense, a man's Self is the sum total of all that he can call his, not only his body and his psychic powers, but his clothes and his house, his wife and his children, his ancestors and his friends, his reputation and his works, his land and horses and yacht and bank account. If they wax and prosper, he feels triumphant, if they dwindle and die away, he feels cast down—not necessarily in the same degree for each thing, but in much the same way for all.

—William James, *Principles of Psychology*

(2) Subject to infinite variables of winds and currents, of supply and demand, of crops and markets, trade has a way of carving its own paths not always obedient to the mercantilist faith. The faith was embodied in Britain's Navigation Act, enacted under Oliver Cromwell in 1651 in the interests of the rising middle class and the industrial towns and major trading ports—the so-called Cinque Ports, so long influential in British history. Aimed specifically at the Dutch to protect British trade against its most dangerous rival, the Act raised a wall of customs duties, and permitted transshipment of goods only in British bottoms calling at British ports. The natural result had been maritime war with Holland and bitter resentment of customs duties in the Colo-

As you turn someone else's words into your own, you can expect your material to be as long as or longer than the source's. To paraphrase well, you must use as many words as you need to extract every drop of meaning. Conciseness is a virtue in writing (see Chapter 16), but it runs counter to the nature of paraphrase. Your paraphrase should be accurate and complete, not necessarily concise.

3 | Avoiding plagiarizing when you paraphrase

Be sure to reword your source material so that you are not plagiarizing. Compare these three passages: an original, a paraphrase that plagiarizes, and an acceptable paraphrase that uses many synonyms and alternate sentence structures.

SOURCE

Morris, Desmond. *Manwatching.* New York: Abrams, 1977: 131.*

ORIGINAL

Unfortunately, different countries have different ideas about exactly how close is close. It is easy enough to test your own "space reaction": when you are talking to someone in the street or in any open space, reach out with your arm and see where the nearest point on his body comes. If you hail from western Europe, you will find that he is at roughly fingertip distance from you. In other words, as you reach out, your fingertips will just about make contact with his shoulder. If you come from eastern Europe, you will find you are standing at "wrist distance." If you come from the Mediterranean region, you will find that you are much closer to your companion, at little more than "elbow distance."

UNACCEPTABLE PARAPHRASE (UNDERSCORED WORDS ARE PLAGIARIZED)

Regrettably, different nations think differently about exactly how close is close. Test yourself: when you are talking to someone in the street or in any open space, stretch your arm out to measure how close that person is to you. If you are from western Europe, you will find that your fingertips will just about make contact with the person's shoulder. If you are from eastern Europe, your wrist will reach the person's shoulder. If you are from the Mediterranean region, you will find that you are much closer to your companion, when your elbow will reach that person's shoulder (Morris 131).†

---

*Source information throughout this chapter is in MLA style (see Chapter 33).
†Parenthetical references are in MLA style (see Chapter 33).

ACCEPTABLE PARAPHRASE

People from different nations think that "close" means different things. You can easily see what your reaction is to how close to you people stand by reaching out the length of your arm to measure how close someone is as the two of you talk. When people from western Europe stand on the street and talk together, the space between them is the distance it would take one person's fingertips to reach to the other person's shoulder. People from eastern Europe converse at a wrist-to-shoulder distance. People from the Mediterranean, however, prefer an elbow-to-shoulder distance (Morris 131).

The first attempt to paraphrase fails because the writer has simply changed a few words here and there. What remains contains much plagiarized material because the passage keeps most of the original's language and sentence structure and no quotation marks are used.

The second paraphrase is acceptable. It captures the essence of the original in the student's own words, and it gives credit to the source and provides a page number.

Here is another example of an acceptable paraphrase. It was written by Amy Brown, the student whose research paper appears in Chapter 34.

SOURCE

Worchel, Stephen, and Joel Cooper. *Understanding Social Psychology* 3rd ed. Homewood, IL: Dorsey, 1983: 535. (The material from Worchel and Cooper shows the APA style of parenthetical documentation. APA style is described in Chapter 33.)

ORIGINAL

One of the more consistent findings in the personal-space literature is that females have smaller personal spaces than males (Willis, 1966; Aiello & Aiello, 1974; Edwards, 1972; Heckel & Hiers, 1977; Evans & Howard, 1973). Further, smaller personal space zones are found between male–female pairs than between same-sex pairs. We can speculate about the reasons for these differences. In Western cultures there are strong taboos against homosexuality, especially male homosexuality. Children are often punished by their parents for touching or caressing another child of the same sex. However, direct teaching and available models inform children that heterosexual behavior is accepted. Hence, children's spatial behavior may result in part as a response to norms about permitted sexual behavior. Children learn, however, that such behavior with members of the opposite sex is all right under some circumstances.

nies, feeding the spirit of rebellion which led to the American war. For Britain, the expense of fighting the Dutch and trying to suppress the American revolt was more costly than anything that could be gained by the trade laws, causing higher taxes at home and their natural consequence, a rise in domestic disaffection. That was not the least of Britain's afflictions in her embattled time.

—Barbara W. Tuchman, *The First Salute*

In light of this speculation, it is interesting to note that stable personal-space norms do develop around the time that the child reaches puberty. Investigations reveal that children do not begin to exhibit consistent spatial behavior before the age of four or five (Eberts & Lepper, 1975). After that age, the size of personal space increases until the age of 12 or 13 when it stabilizes (Aiello & Aiello, 1974; see Figure 13–2).

ACCEPTABLE PARAPHRASE

People do differ as to how much private space they need around them, depending on whether they are male or female and on how old they are. Many scientists have confirmed that men feel more comfortable with more space around them while women maintain less private space. It is also true that between any two people, a male and a female will approach each other more closely, each person maintaining less personal space, than a male will approach a male or a female, a female. Why do these differences exist? In the West, society clearly forbids homosexual behavior, among men in particular. Many parents punish their children if they catch them behaving in any intimate way with others of the same sex.

Until children reach the beginning of sexual maturity, they do not settle into consistent patterns with regard to how much private space they need and how far they should keep from males and females. Before they are four or five, children act in all sorts of different ways with regard to how near they come to people. After four or five, they gradually seem to expand their private space until they are twelve or thirteen. After that, their behavior changes very little (Worchel and Cooper 535).

EXERCISE 1

Read the original material and then the paraphrase that is unacceptable because it plagiarizes. Point out each example of plagiarism. Then write your own paraphrase. Be sure to end it with the parenthetical reference that is correct MLA style.

ORIGINAL MATERIAL

This paragraph is from *The Death and Life of Great American Cities* by Jane Jacobs, published by Random House in 1961, page 141.

A good street neighborhood achieves a marvel of balance between its people's determination to have essential privacy and their simultaneous wish for differing degrees of contact, enjoyment, or help from the people around. This balance is largely made up of small, sensibly managed details, practiced and accepted so casually that they normally seem taken for granted.

UNACCEPTABLE PARAPHRASE

A good neighborhood maintains an impressive balance between the people being determined to have privacy and wishing for varying degrees of contact, pleasure, or assistance from others nearby. People managed this with small details that are normally taken for granted (Jacobs 141).

EXERCISE 2

A. For a paper on economic conditions in third world countries, paraphrase this paragraph. End your paraphrase with this parenthetical reference; it conforms to MLA documentation style, explained in Chapter 33: (Ehrenreich and Fuentes 87)

For many Third World women, electronics is a prestige occupation, at least compared to other kinds of factory work. They are unlikely to know that in the United States the National Institute on Occupational Safety and Health (NIOSH) has placed electronics on its select list of high health-risk industries using the greatest number of toxic substances. If electronics assembly work is risky here, it is doubly so in countries where there is no equivalent of NIOSH to even issue warnings. In many plants toxic chemicals and solvents sit in open containers, filling the work area with fumes that can literally knock you out.

—Barbara Ehrenreich and Annette Fuentes, "Life on the Global Assembly Line"

B. Write a paraphrase of a paragraph of at least 150 words from one of the sources you are using for a paper assigned in one of your courses. If you have no such assignment, choose any material suitable for a college-level paper. Your instructor may request that you submit a photocopy of the original material to accompany your paraphrase.

31d Summarizing accurately

A **summary** reviews the main points of a passage and gets at the gist of what an author or speaker says. A summary condenses the essentials of someone else's thought in a few general statements.

Summaries and paraphrases both restate someone else's words using your own words and your own sentence structure, but they differ in one primary way. A paraphrase restates the original material completely; a summary is much shorter and provides only the main points of the original source. Paraphrases and summaries must be properly documented (see 31b). To understand the difference between paraphrase and summary, consider the following original material and a paraphrase and a summary of it.

ANSWERS: EXERCISE 1

Analysis: This paraphrase is unacceptable because it uses many words and phrases from the original. Also, the first sentence uses the same sentence structures. *Acceptable paraphrase* (answers will vary considerably): When people want to create a sense of neighborhood where they live, they need to balance their interest in privacy with their desire for knowing their neighbors. Practically without being conscious of it, people manage the details of their lives to achieve the balance they need (Jacobs 141).

ANSWERS: EXERCISE 2

A. Answers will vary, but here is one acceptable paraphrase:

Women who live in underdeveloped or emerging countries frequently regard working with electronics as giving them higher status than other assembly line work. Most of these women are unaware that the electronics occupation may pose significant threats to their physical well-being. They have no way of knowing that NIOSH (National Institute on Occupational Safety and Health) has identified electronics plants in the United States as employing the largest amount of poison materials that may have a negative effect on workers' health in any industry. Certainly the dangers here in the United States are twice as threatening when they exist in Third World nations, which have no organization like NIOSH to act as watchdogs. In underdeveloped countries, the air in factories is often polluted with toxic vapors that arise from poisonous materials that are stored in uncovered vessels. The gas created by these chemicals and other substances is strong enough to make a worker lose consciousness (Ehrenreich and Fuentes 87).

B. Answers will vary.

TEACHING TIP

Paraphrasing and summarizing are not only research tools. They are also effective study techniques that can be applied to any reading assignment. They are particularly helpful to students trying to identify the main points of a piece of writing and relate them to each other. Students often find it informative to compare their paraphrases and summaries, discussing why they made certain choices.

EXTRA EXERCISE B

Following the guidelines for writing a summary, summarize one of the following paragraphs.

1. The Elizabethan Age takes its name from the queen who reigned over England and Ireland from 1558 to 1603. She was an intelligent and gifted ruler, managing for decades to escape political disasters at home and abroad. Always an insightful judge of character, she achieved her success in large part because of her tendency to make use of the shrewdest people around her. However, her clear awareness of what she wanted and why she wanted it sometimes led her to go her own way, using a variety of means to reach the ends she desired. She was on occasion devious, even false, but she managed to outwit her opposition time after time. As a result, it was a glorious time in the history of Britain, for under her rule the nation rose from a relatively weak position among the nations of Europe to the highest rank. England's power and success grew rapidly in the sixteenth century, leaving it, at the death of Elizabeth I, a leader in navigation and exploration, in literary productivity—particularly in the drama—and in colonization of the New World.

2. When she died in 1986, Georgia O'Keeffe the person generated almost as much interest among the public as Georgia O'Keeffe the artist. Sometimes she was thought of as the wife and often-photographed model of

SOURCE

Raudsepp, Eugene. "Daydreaming," *Success Unlimited* Nov. 1975: 64.

ORIGINAL

During times of stress, daydreaming erects a temporary shield against reality, in much the same way that building a house protects our bodies from the elements. Both may be seen as forms of escapism, but no one wants to spend life in unrelieved battle for survival. We are entitled to occasional strategic withdrawals to regroup our forces.

PARAPHRASE

Just as we construct buildings to shield ourselves from extreme climate and weather conditions, our minds create daydreams as protection against difficult emotional situations (Raudsepp 64).

SUMMARY

Our minds create daydreams to protect us from pressure (Raudsepp 64).

Writing summaries is an excellent way to learn material because the process helps you lock information into your memory. Summarizing forces you to read closely and to comprehend clearly.

Writing summaries is probably the most frequently used technique for taking notes and for incorporating sources into your writing. To summarize a paragraph, a chapter, or a statement, isolate its separate points and, in your own words, write a statement that

---

GUIDELINES FOR WRITING A SUMMARY

1. Identify the main points.
2. Condense the main points without losing the essence of the material.
3. Use your own words to condense the message. If certain synonyms are awkward, quote the words.
4. Keep your summary short.
5. Avoid plagiarism.
6. Write down all documentation facts so that you can document your source when you use it in your writing. Even though a summary is not a direct quotation, you must document the source (see 31b).

digests the material. To do this, you must discover the material's main ideas and their relation to one another. The length of your summary should be in proportion to the length of the passage you are summarizing: a general guide is one sentence per paragraph, though sometimes more is needed when the material is particularly complex. Summaries must be documented, the same way that paraphrases are.

1   Isolating the main points

A summary must capture the entire sense of a paragraph in very little space, so you must read through all the content before you write. A good summary reports only the main points contained in a passage. Isolating the main points involves making decisions. These are the controlling questions: What is the subject? What is said about it? You have to take in the complete message, and then you must differentiate between main ideas and supporting facts, examples, or reasons. A summary excludes more than it includes, so you must make substantial deletions.

Sometimes, but not often, the points for your summary are available in topic sentences° in the source material. If so, you must rewrite the topic sentences in your own words, and you must make sure that the connections among the ideas are clear. If you find no topic sentences, your summary serves to supply their equivalent.

Condensing information into a table is another option you can use to summarize, particularly when you are summarizing numerical data. For an example, see paragraph 5 in Amy Brown's research paper in Chapter 34: Table 1 summarizes ten pages of a source.

2   Condensing without losing meaning

As you summarize, you will be tracing a line of thought. This involves deleting less central ideas and sometimes transposing certain points into an order more suited to summary. A summary is always significantly shorter than the original. In fact, it should reduce the original by at least half. The essential content should take no more than one or two sentences per paragraph. In summarizing a longer original—about ten pages or more—you may find it helpful to first divide the original into subsections. These subsections may fall under a main heading, or they may be a few pages of text that has no heading. Group your subsection summaries, and use them as the basis for further condensing the material into a final summary.

Alfred Stieglitz, but more often she was pictured as a romantic recluse who, when she grew older, moved increasingly away from the world of art critics and historians and closer to the rugged but exotic New Mexico countryside and culture. In the long run, however, it will be for her art that she will be best remembered. Some viewers admire her abstractions, others her figurative works. Even those who disagree about the relative quality of her paintings agree that her art is memorable, clear, and strong. She painted with a distinctive, powerful, personal vision, one that continues to speak strongly to viewers today. Her red poppies, purple hills, and bleached skulls fix themselves in the mind's eye not to be easily erased.

3. To the non-Scot, the tartan is perhaps the most picturesque and original costume in Europe. To a Scot, it is a costume of national distinction. Even without considering the causes for the veneration paid to it by the Highlanders, its merits are several. For one, it bears extraordinarily well the inclemency of weather. It also is economical, light, and unencumbering to the wearer, making it comfortable to wear in a variety of situations. In addition, the plaid of the tartan designates the clan, or family, of the wearer. In the mid-eighteenth century it came to be such a powerful symbol of Scottish culture that it was banned by the English in a law that was not repealed until 1782.

Sometimes students fall into the habit of using summaries to take notes, forgetting that they can also be used in developing the thesis of a paper. You may find it helpful to remind students that when they want to introduce ideas from sources but have no need to use direct quotation, summaries are a useful strategy to employ. In them the writer can provide unusual facts, background information, and even other points of view regarding the subject. When summaries are used in this way, however, it is important to make sure that they fit smoothly and easily into the text. A series of unconnected summaries will not make an effective piece of writing.

As you summarize, you may be tempted to interpret something the author says or make some judgment about the value of the argument. Your own opinions do not belong in a summary, but you do not have to lose a good thought. Jot down your ideas immediately, but *be sure to place them in your notes so that they are physically separate from your summary*—in the margin, in an alternate color of ink, or clearly circled so that they stand out.

Until you are experienced at writing summaries, you will likely have to revise them more than once. Always be firm in your resolve to see that any summary accurately reflects the source and its emphases.

3   Avoiding plagiarizing when you summarize

In summarizing, use your own language. If you have no alternative but to use a source's key terms because synonyms would not work, use quotation marks. When you copy exact words from a source, use clear, perhaps oversize, quotation marks. If you do not, you will surely forget whose words are whose when you incorporate your summary into your paper—and your summary will be plagiarizing (see 31a) words from the author.

Compare these three passages written by Amy Brown for her research paper shown in Chapter 34: an original, a summary that plagiarizes, and an acceptable summary.

SOURCE

Hall, Edward T. *The Hidden Dimension.* New York: Doubleday, 1966: 109.

ORIGINAL

The general failure to grasp the significance of the many elements that contribute to man's sense of space may be due to two mistaken notions: (1) that for every effect there is a single and identifiable cause; and (2) that man's boundary begins and ends with his skin. If we can rid ourselves of the need for a single explanation, and if we can think of man as surrounded by a series of expanding and contracting fields which provide information of many kinds, we shall begin to see him in an entirely different light. We can then begin to learn about human behavior, including personality types. . . . Concepts such as these are not always easy to grasp, because most of the distance-sensing process occurs outside the awareness. We sense other people as close or distant, but we cannot always put our finger on what it is that enables us to characterize them as such. So many different things are happening at once it is difficult to sort out the sources of information on which we base our reactions.

UNACCEPTABLE SUMMARY (ITALICIZED WORDS ARE PLAGIARIZED)

Concepts such as identifying causes and determining boundaries *are not always easy to grasp* (Hall 109).

ACCEPTABLE SUMMARY

Human beings make the mistake of thinking that an event has a "single and identifiable cause" and that people are limited by the boundaries of their bodies. Most people are unaware that they have a sense of interpersonal space, and they also do not know that the concept of interpersonal distance exists and contributes to their reactions to other people (Hall 109).

The unacceptable summary does isolate the main point, and it plagiarizes. The writer used almost all the language in the source.

The second summary is acceptable because it not only isolates the main idea but also recasts it in the student's words. One phrase—"single and identifiable cause"—is borrowed, but it is set off in quotation marks. No one would charge this student with plagiarism.

| 4 | **Turning long paraphrases into summaries to use in your writing** |

When a paraphrase is too long and involved to use in your paper, condense your paraphrase by summarizing it. Here is a summary written from the paraphrase of the Worchel and Cooper material in 31c-3.

> People have different needs for interpersonal space, depending on their sex and age (Worchel and Cooper 535).

EXERCISE 3

Read the original material and then the summary that is unacceptable because it plagiarizes. Point out each example of plagiarism. Then write your own summary. Be sure to end it with the parenthetical reference that is correct MLA style.

ORIGINAL MATERIAL

This is from *Overcoming the Fear of Success* by Martha Friedman, published by Seaview Books in 1980, page 69.

The manner in which we respond to negative criticism is a clue to the level of our self-esteem, which in turn is a good index to the degree of our fear of success. If we harbor a feeling of inadequacy, as many of us do, about something, no matter how slight, negative criticism can wipe us out. Many of us carry too many internalized low-esteem messages from the past, negative things our parents or siblings or teachers or schoolday peers said to us.

ANSWERS: EXERCISE 3

Analysis: This summary is unacceptable because it uses many words and phrases from the original. *Acceptable summary* (answers will vary considerably): When people respond badly to negative criticism, they are revealing poor self-esteem that usually results from childhood experience and that also indicates that they are afraid of success (Friedman 69).

ANSWERS: EXERCISE 4

A. Answers will vary, but here is one possible summary:

A cloud hangs over testing programs because of an increase in cheating, as when students in New York State sold the state Regents examination in advance. This led to warnings that educators should watch for student scores that appear in unusual patterns (Robbins 12).

B. Answers will vary, but here is one possible summary:

Many women in underdeveloped countries regard electronics as a desirable career, but they are usually unaware that this industry has been identified by experts in the United States as posing serious threats to the health of workers (Ehrenreich and Fuentes 87).

C. Answers will vary.

UNACCEPTABLE SUMMARY

Many people harbor feelings of low self-esteem as a result of internalized negative messages from the past, and if people respond badly to negative criticism, no matter how slight, it indicates a low level of self-esteem, which is also an excellent index of their fear of success (Friedman 69).

EXERCISE 4

A. For a paper explaining the problems of large-scale competency testing, summarize this material. End your summary with this parenthetical reference; it conforms to MLA documentation style, explained in Chapter 33: (Robbins 12).

More and more states are requiring students to pass competency tests in order to receive their high school diplomas. And many educators fear that an increase in the use of state exams will lead to a corresponding rise in cheating. They cite the case of students in New York State who faced criminal misdemeanor charges for possessing and selling advance copies of state Regents examinations. Approximately 600,000 students take the Regents exams. And it proved impossible to determine how many of them had seen the stolen tests. As a result, 1,200 principals received instructions from the State Education Commissioner to look for *unusual scoring patterns* that would show that students had the answers beforehand. This put a cloud over the test program.

                        —Stacia Robbins, "Honesty: Is It Going Out of Style?"

B. Write a summary of your paraphrase of the Ehrenreich and Fuentes material in Exercise 2. End it with the parenthetical reference given.

C. Write a summary of one or two paragraphs that total about 200 words. Take it from a source you are using for a paper assigned in one of your courses, or select material suitable for a college-level paper. Your instructor may request that you submit a photocopy of the original material to accompany your summary.

31e Using quotations effectively

Quotations are the exact words of a source—in written form set off in quotation marks. (See 28a for rules on using quotation marks.) Quotations lend special credibility and support to your statements. Whereas paraphrase (31c) and summary (31d) distance your reader one step from your source, quotations give your reader the chance to encounter directly the words of your source.

31e

Two conflicting demands confront you when you use quotations in your writing. Along with the effect and support of quotations, you also want your writing to be coherent and readable. You gain authority by quoting experts on the topic, but if you use too many quotations, you lose coherence, as well as control of your own paper. Rather than a single piece of carefully woven fabric, you get a patchwork quilt. As a general rule, if more than a quarter of your paper consists of quotations, you have written what some people call a "scotch tape special." Having too many quotations may give readers—including instructors—the impression that you have not developed your own thesis and that you are letting other people do your talking. Use quotations sparingly, therefore. When you want to draw on support from an authority, rely mostly on paraphrase and summary. (In contrast, a literary analysis that rests on examination of specific passages usually uses fairly extensive quotations; for an example, see the paper by Chris Johns in 36c.)

QUOTATION ABOUT WRITING

One has to secrete a jelly in which to slip quotations down people's throats and one always secretes too much jelly.

—Virginia Woolf

QUOTATION ABOUT WRITING

The wisdom of the wise and the experience of the ages are perpetuated by quotations.

—Benjamin Disraeli

QUOTATION ABOUT WRITING

I often quote myself. It adds spice to my conversation.

—George Bernard Shaw

QUOTATION ABOUT WRITING

Quotations are the wisdom of the wise and the experience of ages.

—Isaac D'Israeli

QUOTATION ABOUT WRITING

Originality consists in thinking for yourself, and not in thinking unlike other people.

—J. Fitzjames Stephen

QUOTATION ABOUT WRITING

Tout est dit et l'on vient trop tard depuis plus de sept mille ans qu'il y a des hommes et qui pensent.

Everything has been said and we come more than seven thousand years of human thought too late.

—Jean de la Bruyere

GUIDELINES FOR WORKING QUOTATIONS INTO YOUR WRITING

1. Set off quotations with quotation marks—otherwise you will be plagiarizing.
2. Do not use quotations in more than a third of your paper; rely mostly on paraphrase and summary to report information from sources.
3. Use quotations to *support* what you say, not to present your thesis and main points.
4. Choose a quotation if
   a. its language is appropriate or distinctive.
   b. its thought is particularly difficult to rephrase accurately.
   c. the authority of the source is especially important to support your thesis and main ideas.
   d. the source's words are open to interpretation.
5. Quote accurately.
6. Select quotations from authorities in your subject.
7. Select quotations that fit your message.
8. Keep long quotations to a minimum.
9. Work quotations smoothly into your writing.
10. Document your source.

Well-chosen quotations should support, not make, your points. Draw on authorities to confirm what you are saying, not to deliver the message of your thesis or main ideas. Use quotations only when (1) the language is especially striking; (2) the thought is particularly difficult to rephrase accurately; (3) the authority conveyed by the quotation is especially important for your thesis or main ideas; or (4) the source's words could be open to alternate interpretations, so your reader needs direct access to the words.

1 Quoting accurately

Be very careful not to misquote a source. Always check your quotations against the originals—and then recheck. It is very easy to make mistakes when you are copying from the source into your notes or from your notes into your paper. If you photocopy material, be sure to mark off on the copy the exact place that caught your attention, as possible material to quote in your paper; otherwise, you might forget your impressions and will have to spend time trying to reconstruct your thought processes.

If you have to add a word or two to a quotation so that it fits in with your prose, put those words in brackets (see 29c). Make sure that your additions do not distort the meaning of the quotation. The following quotation is taken from original *Manwatching* material, excerpted in 31c. The bracketed material replaces the word *he* in the original quote. The meaning of *he* was clear in context. When the student used this sentence, she realized that a reader would not know to whom *he* referred. Therefore she added the bracketed information. Without the bracketed information, a reader could not know to whom *he* referred.

> "If you hail from western Europe, you will find that [the person you are talking to] is at roughly fingertip distance from you" (Morris 131).

Similarly, if for the sake of conciseness and focus, you delete a portion of a quotation, indicate the omission with an ellipsis (see 29d). When using ellipses, make sure that the remaining words accurately reflect the source's meaning. Also, make sure that the sentence structure does not become awkward. Amy Brown, who wrote the sample research paper in Chapter 34, wanted to quote Robert Sommer, author of *Personal Space: The Behavioral Bases of Design*. But she wanted to use only some of his words, so she used an ellipsis to indicate an intentional omission.

ORIGINAL

Like the porcupines in Schopenhauer's fable, people like to be close enough to obtain warmth and comradeship but far enough away to avoid pricking one another. Personal space is not necessarily spherical in shape, nor does it extend equally in all directions. (People are able to tolerate closer presence of a stranger at their sides than directly in front of them.) It has been likened to a snail shell, a soap bubble, an aura, a "breathing room" (Sommer 26).

WITH ELLIPSIS

Like the porcupines in Schopenhauer's fable, people like to be close enough to obtain warmth and comradeship but far enough away to avoid pricking one another. Personal space . . . has been likened to a snail shell, a soap bubble, an aura, a "breathing room" (Sommer 26).

2 Selecting quotations that are from accepted authorities and that fit your meaning

Quotations enhance your message only when you use authorities who bring credibility to your discussion. For example, Amy Brown, author of the research paper in Chapter 34 about personal space, quoted from Edward T. Hall. Hall, who founded the field of "proxemics," which deals with personal space, is an accepted authority in that area. Conversely, your neighbors may work in a large building and may have strong opinions about crowding and personal space, but their angry letter to the superintendent of the building in which they work does not constitute an authoritative source. See Guidelines For Evaluating Sources in 32d-2.

Similarly, choose words to quote that fit your context. Never hunt for a quotation simply because you want to include a person's words. Do not resort to a quotation because you do not want to take the time to paraphrase or summarize. If you force a quotation to fit your material, most readers will quickly discern the manipulation.

3 Keeping long quotations to a minimum

When you use a quotation, your purpose is to supply evidence or support your assertion, not to reconstruct someone else's argument. Occasionally, however, you may need to present a complicated argument in detail and thus quote long passages. Make sure every word in the quotation counts. Edit out irrelevant parts (using an ellipsis to indicate deleted material) while maintaining proper

QUOTATION ABOUT WRITING

Stay at home in your mind. Don't recite other people's opinions. I hate quotations. Tell me what you know.

—Ralph Waldo Emerson

QUOTATION ABOUT WRITING

I quote others only the better to express myself.

—Montaigne

sentence structure. When you must use a long quotation, prepare your reader by explaining its importance. Otherwise, your reader might simply skip over it.

Quotations that run more than four typed lines are set off (see paragraphs 3, 4, and 13 in the sample research paper in Chapter 34). Quotations that need fewer than four typed lines are run in with your own writing (see paragraph 6 in the sample research paper in Chapter 34). For more explanation, see 28a.

4   Working quotations smoothly into your own prose

The greatest risk you take when you use quotations is that you will end up with choppy, incoherent sentences in which the quoted portions do not quite mesh with the style, grammar, or logic of your prose. Listen and try to hear whether the language flows smoothly and gracefully. Consider these examples using the original material shown on the previous page.

No   Sommer says personal space for people "like the porcupines in Schopenhauer's fable, people like to be close enough to obtain warmth and comradeship but far enough away to avoid pricking one another" (26). [problem with grammar]

Yes   Sommer says concerning personal space that "like the porcupines in Schopenhauer's fable, people like to be close enough to obtain warmth and comradeship but far enough away to avoid pricking one another" (26).

Equally important, avoid tossing disembodied quotations into your paper. Mention the author's name as you introduce a quotation. If the flow of language is not seriously interrupted, also give the title of the source you are quoting. Moreover, if the source is a noteworthy figure, you can give additional authority to your message by referring to his or her credentials as part of this introductory tag. Consider the treatments that follow this quotation, which Amy Brown uses in paragraph 13 in her research paper in Chapter 34. The sentence is from *The Hidden Dimension* by Edward T. Hall, published by Doubleday in 1966, page 171. The name of the work in shortened form is mentioned in the parenthetical reference because Brown uses two works by the same author.

Original Material

"Therefore, people from different cultures, when interpreting each other's behavior, often misinterpret the relationship, the activity, or the emotions."

AUTHOR'S NAME

Edward T. Hall claims that "people from different cultures, when interpreting each other's behavior, often misinterpret the relationship, the activity, or the emotions" (*Hidden* 171).

AUTHOR'S NAME AND SOURCE TITLE

Edward T. Hall claims in *The Hidden Dimension* that "people from different cultures, when interpreting each other's behavior, often misinterpret the relationship, the activity, or the emotions" (171).

AUTHOR'S NAME, CREDENTIALS, AND SOURCE TITLE

Edward T. Hall, an anthropologist who has studied personal space, claims in *The Hidden Dimension* that "people from different cultures, when interpreting each other's behavior, often misinterpret the relationship, the activity, or the emotions" (171).

Occasionally quotations speak for themselves, but at times they do not. Usually the words you are quoting are part of a larger piece, and you know the connection that the quotation has to the original material. Without the original material, however, your reader may puzzle over why you included the quotation or may need to have the quoted material fully identified. A brief introductory remark gives your reader the needed information.

AUTHOR'S NAME AND INTRODUCTORY ANALYSIS

Edward T. Hall believes that people from different societies perceive personal space in varying ways, claiming that "people from different cultures . . ." (*Hidden* 171).

Also, see paragraphs 3 and 4 in Amy Brown's research paper in Chapter 34.

In adding your own words to fit a quotation into your writing, you may interrupt the quotation.

"Therefore," claims Edward T. Hall, "people from different cultures . . ." (*Hidden* 171).

Many verbs can help you work paraphrases, summaries, and quotations into your writing smoothly. As you revise your writing, make sure that you have used these verbs without any strain of style. To see many of these verbs in use, read the research paper by Amy Brown in Chapter 34. Note especially annotation X, which goes with paragraph 10. As you use this list of verbs, note that some have rather specific meanings, while others are general enough to use in most situations. Choose them according to the meaning that you want your sentences to deliver.

TEACHING TIP

To give your students practice in note taking before they are assigned research paper topics, you might distribute copies of a newspaper or magazine article on a popular subject and ask your students to take notes in support of a particular thesis.

Once they (and you) are sure of their skills, the students can move on to more complex issues with confidence, but at first keeping to popular subjects will help interest students.

Encourage students to paraphrase, summarize, and quote as they feel necessary, and to take as many (or as few) notes as they feel would be useful in supporting a thesis. Then collect their notes and distribute copies of all or some sets of notes. As a class (or in groups), discuss the notes one set at a time.

1. Do all the notes support the thesis?
2. Are paraphrases accurate?
3. Are summaries accurate?
4. Are quotations appropriate and accurate?
5. Are quoted words within paraphrases and summaries placed in quotation marks?
6. Would any material be better presented in a different kind of note?

VERBS USEFUL FOR PARAPHRASE, SUMMARY, AND QUOTATION				
analyze	complain	find	offer	show
argue	concede	illustrate	point out	speculate
ask	conclude	insist	report	suggest
assert	consider	maintain	reveal	suppose
claim	describe	note	say	think
comment	explain	observe	see	write

ANSWERS: EXERCISE 5

A. *Analysis:* The quotation does not relate clearly to the sentence it follows. A transitional introduction to the quotation is needed. *Acceptable* (answers will vary): Many problems are caused when sensitive equipment overheats. Until now, researchers have failed to develop sensors that would warn of such overheating mainly because nearly all "microchips develop amnesia long before the temperature climbs to the boiling point of water" (Siwolop 111).

B. *Analysis:* The quotation omits several words but does not provide an ellipsis to indicate where material has been deleted. *Acceptable* (answers will vary): Many researchers believe that they would be able to "improve the efficiency of engines . . . if only they could supply them with electronic sensors" (Siwolop 111).

C. *Analysis:* The sentence is grammatically incorrect. The quotation does not fit with the rest of the sentence. Words need to be added so that the information flows smoothly. *Acceptable* (answers will vary): Several new developments have taken place at North Carolina State University in Raleigh where researchers "have successfully made microelectronic transistors that operate at temperatures of up to 1,200 F" (Siwolop 111).

EXERCISE 5

Read the original material, and evaluate the passages that follow it. Point out problems with the quotations, and suggest possible revisions. End your quotations with this parenthetical reference, which conforms to MLA documentation style, explained in Chapter 33: (Siwolop 111).

ORIGINAL MATERIAL

This is from "Helping Computer Chips to Keep Their Cool" by Sana Siwolop in *Business Week,* January 25, 1988.

> Engineers could improve the efficiency of engines, chemical reactors, furnaces, and other equipment if only they could supply them with electronic sensors. But computer chips can't take the heat. Most microchips develop amnesia long before the temperature climbs to the boiling point of water. But that may change. Researchers at North Carolina State University in Raleigh have successfully made microelectronic transistors that operate at temperatures of up to 1,200 F. The key: using silicon carbide, a material familiar to most people as the grit on sandpaper, instead of the crystalline silicon usually used for computer chips.

UNACCEPTABLE USE OF QUOTATIONS

A. Many problems are caused when sensitive equipment overheats. "Most microchips develop amnesia long before the temperature climbs to the boiling point of water" (Siwolop 111).

B. Many researchers believe that they would be able to "improve the efficiency of engines and other equipment if only they could supply them with electronic sensors" (Siwolop 111).

C. Several new developments have taken place at North Carolina State University in Raleigh "have successfully made microelectronic transistors that operate at temperatures of up to 1,200 F" (Siwolop 111).

D. In the past, there have been serious problems with sensors designed to detect heat. Until recently, "computer chips can't take the heat" (Siwolop 111), but now that problem may be solved.

E. One of the problems in designing a heat sensor is that many "microchips develop amnesia before the temperature climbs up to the boiling point of water" (Siwolop 111).

EXERCISE 6

A. For a paper describing how and why twins make important contributions to scientific research, write a three- to four-sentence passage that includes your own words and a quotation from this material. After the quoted words, use this parenthetical reference; it conforms to MLA documentation style, explained in Chapter 33: (Begley 84).

For over a century twins have been used to study how genes make people what they are. Because they share precisely the same genes but live in different surroundings under different influences, identical twins reared apart are helping science sort out which qualities of body and mind are shaped by our genes, and which by upbringing. Researchers needn't worry about running out of subjects: according to the Twins Foundation, there are approximately 4.5 million twin individuals in the United States alone, and about 70,000 more are born each year.

—Sharon Begley, "Twins"

B. For a paper arguing that it is difficult, if not impossible, to assure honesty in large-scale testing, quote from the Robbins material in Exercise 3. Be sure to include at least one numerical statistic in your quotation.

C. Write a three- to four-sentence passage that includes your own words and a quotation from a source you are using for a paper assigned in one of your courses. If you have no such assignment, choose any material suitable for a college-level paper. Your instructor might request a photocopy of the material you quote from.

D. *Analysis:* The tense of the verb in the quotation shifts from the tense of the verb in the previous sentence. Brackets can be used to change the tense of the verb in the quotation so that it agrees grammatically with the previous verb. *Acceptable* (answers will vary): In the past, there have been serious problems with sensors designed to detect heat. Until recently, "computer chips [couldn't] take the heat" (Siwolop 111) but now that problem may be solved.

E. *Analysis:* The quotation is inaccurate; the word "long" is omitted while "up" is added. *Acceptable* (answers may vary): One of the problems in designing a heat sensor is that many "microchips develop amnesia long before the temperature climbs to the boiling point of water" (Siwolop 111).

ANSWERS: EXERCISE 6

A. Answers will vary, but here is one possibility:

Because genetic research is becoming increasingly important, scientists are seeking twins who are willing to participate in experiments either for pay or as volunteers. The Twins Foundation is confident that researchers will find the subjects they need because "there are approximately 4.5 million twin individuals in the United States alone, and about 70,000 more are born each year" (Begley 84).

B. Answers will vary, but here is one possibility:

It is becoming increasingly difficult to assure that large-scale testing will be taken honestly. For example, in New York State students stole copies of the Regents exam, and because of their actions "1,200 principals received instructions from the State Education Commissioner to look for *unusual scoring patterns* that would show that students had the answers beforehand" (Robbins 12).

C. Answers will vary.

32 The Process of Research Writing

Conducting research for the purpose of writing helps you gain authority over knowledge and join yourself to groups of people recognized as experts. *Research* literally means repeated *(re-)* going over or looking through to find something *(search)*. Research is a process that seeks to answer a question—to move from the known to the unknown. Seeing research as a quest for an answer makes clear that you cannot know whether you have found something unless you know what it is you are looking for.

Not all research assignments in college are given in the form of questions, but all imply that you will need to search for answers. Research questions, explicit or implicit, and the processes needed to answer them vary widely. You might be asked to explain information: "How does penicillin destroy bacteria?" You might be asked to argue one side of an issue: "Is Congress more important than the Supreme Court in setting social policy?"

To attempt to answer such questions, you must conduct experiments or track down information from varied sources. *Attempt* is an important word in relation to research. Not all research questions lead to a final, definitive answer. The question about penicillin, for example, leads to a definitive answer—the antibiotic destroys the cell walls of some bacteria (though researchers did not learn this information until the electron microscope was invented). The question about social policy, on the other hand, does not lead to a definitive answer. It invites an informed opinion based on evidence gathered from research.

Some research assignments, like the one about penicillin, may require you to conduct experiments and make direct observations. Such activities are called *primary research.* The reports written from such research are one type of **primary source.** Primary sources include original works of an author—novels, poems, short stories, autobiographies, diaries, first-hand reports of observations and of research, and so on. When you use primary sources, no one comes between you and your direct exposure to the author's own words.

602

For many research assignments, primary sources provide invaluable information and offer excellent material for quotation, paraphrase, and summary (techniques explained in Chapter 31).

Secondary sources, also important for writing research, talk about someone else's original work. The information comes to you second-hand, influenced by the intermediary between you and the primary source. Secondary sources explain events, analyze information, and draw conclusions. The question about social policy, for example, calls for an informed opinion based on your reading of secondary sources. Consulting secondary sources gives you the opportunity to read closely—and listen closely, if you interview authorities—and thereby work to understand what scholars and other experts know about your subject. But some caution is needed also, for you want to avoid distorted reports and biased analyses.

Whether you use primary or secondary sources, or a combination, research is an engrossing and creative activity. By gathering information and composing a synthesis of it, you come to know your subject deeply. You make fresh connections and gain unexpected insights. Equally important, you sample the pleasures of being an independent learner. Little is more rewarding than the realization that you have the self-discipline and intellectual resources to locate and understand information on your own.

This chapter shows you methods for doing secondary research and writing research papers about it. To help you further, Chapter 33 explains and illustrates how to document sources, and Chapter 34 presents a student research paper with commentary on it and on the research that produced it.

Understanding what a research paper project involves

A "research paper," sometimes called a "library paper" or a "term paper," involves two processes. You conduct the research, and you write the paper based upon it. Both processes take time. If you are aware of the steps involved in a research paper project, you will be able to plan ahead and budget your time intelligently. Use or adapt the schedule in the chart on the next page.

The processes of researching and of writing are interwoven throughout a research-paper project. The **writing process** for a research paper is much like the writing process for all academic papers. As discussed in Chapter 1 of this book, you begin by thinking about your paper's purpose, audience, and sources. As discussed in Chapters 2 and 3, you plan, draft, revise, edit, and proofread. The

BACKGROUND

As we struggle to teach the Research Paper, we may sometimes wonder if we are struggling alone. According to James E. Ford and Dennis R. Perry ("Research Paper Instruction in the Undergraduate Writing Program," *College English,* Dec. 1982, 825–31), we are definitely not alone.

> Research paper instruction is currently being offered in 84.09% of freshman composition programs and in 40.03% of advanced composition programs. In general this high level of occurrence is fairly uniform in all types and sizes of institutions and in all regions of the country. There is, however, a slight tendency for research paper instruction to decrease as the size of the school increases (down to 71.06% in the large schools). Also, occurrence is highest in the Rocky Mountain region (91.66% and . . . lowest on the Pacific coast (72.40%). Instruction in the research paper is required in 78.11% of freshman composition programs offering it and 42.35% of advanced writing programs where it is offered. Although 4.16% of the schools not offering instruction in the research paper at the basic level indicated their reason for omitting it as "faculty think it unnecessary," the most common reason given for not offering it came under the "other" category, checked by 12.12%. About half of these (that is, about 6% of the total respondents) said the course was already too full to allow time for such instruction.
>
> . . . No institution surveyed had eliminated a research paper requirement during the past five years and only two now have plans to do away with it. (827)

Ford and Perry also say:

> Not surprisingly, research paper instruction is offered more in freshman programs (50.56%) during the second semester of the freshman year, but it also is included in a significant number of courses offered during the first semester (41.57%). It is a feature in both semesters at 15.17% of the

---

SAMPLE SCHEDULE FOR A RESEARCH PAPER PROJECT

Assignment received (date) _____   **FINISH BY**

1. Choose a suitable topic (32b).   _____
2. Determine purpose and audience (32c).   _____
3. Prepare to conduct research.
   a. Gather equipment (32d-1).   _____
   b. Know how to evaluate sources (32d-2).   _____
   c. Determine documentation style (32d-4).   _____
4. Use a search strategy (32e), keep a research log (32j), take notes (32j-2), and make bibliographic cards (33a). *Use whichever steps fit your situation.*
   a. Get a broad overview (32e-1).   _____
   b. Draft a preliminary thesis statement (32k).   _____
   c. Decide whether to interview experts (32e-2).   _____
   d. Decide whether to send for information (32e-3).   _____
   e. Use reference books (32f).   _____
   f. Use indexes to periodicals and read periodicals (32g).   _____
   g. Use the card catalog or microfiche and read books (32h).   _____
   h. Use computerized databases (32i).   _____
5. Compile a working list of sources to consult (33a).   _____
6. Finish note taking (32j-2).   _____
7. Draft and revise a final thesis statement (32k).   _____
8. Outline as required (32l).   _____
9. Draft paper (32m).   _____
10. Use parenthetical references (33b).   _____
11. Revise paper (32m).   _____

Assignment due (date) _____

---

research process is an added dimension to consider throughout. In planning, you choose a suitable topic, refine it into a research question, use a search strategy to find sources of information, evaluate those information sources, and take notes on useful sources. In drafting and revising, you integrate sources into the paper by paraphrasing, summarizing, and quoting. (These techniques are the subject of Chapter 31.) Also, during revising, you watch for sections that need additional support from sources.

Once you know what is involved, you can design your research-paper project according to the limits of time and information resources available. As soon as your instructor gives a research-paper assignment, work out a schedule for finishing each step. You might need one day for a number of steps and two weeks for another. The more you do research-paper projects, the more skilled you will become at mapping out the work and handling it efficiently. The schedule shown on the opposite page lists typical steps in a research-paper project (the parentheses give the section in which each step is discussed). The items in the schedule also provide an overview of this chapter. No two research-paper projects are alike. The steps do not proceed in a straight line, but often loop back or work in concert. This chapter covers all major steps, but you have to adapt them to your assignment and personal work style.

institutions. Such instruction on the advanced level most often comes during the sophomore year (63.83%), but it is common also during the junior year (46.81%). . . . Whenever it is offered, research paper instruction constitutes, on the average, a very considerable 34.66% of one basic course and 36.71% of an advanced course. (828)

32b Choosing and narrowing a topic suitable for a research paper project

In your college years, you will find that instructors assign topics for research papers in a variety of ways. Some assign the specific topic. Others assign a general subject area and require you to narrow it to a topic that can be researched within the constraints of time and length imposed by the assignment. Still other instructors expect you to choose a general subject area and then narrow it suitably.

Except when you are assigned the specific topic, your first step in the research writing process is to **choose your topic.** Here are guidelines to use (also, see 2c).

Communication was the general topic assigned to Amy Brown, the student who wrote the paper in Chapter 34. Her instructor required a paper of 1800 to 2000 words to be written in five weeks based on about twelve secondary sources. To get started, Brown borrowed two textbooks from a friend, one an introduction to psychology and the other an introduction to business communications. Browsing through the textbooks helped Brown make her first major choice. She decided to focus on *nonverbal communication.* To further narrow her focus, Brown read a book that a psychology professor recommended during an interview. She then began to concentrate on *personal space,* a topic that particularly caught her interest. She was fascinated to learn that cultures have unspoken standards for the accepted distances between people who are conversing and interacting. Brown also liked the topic of personal space because her

TEACHING TIP

All too often, the Research Paper looms over Freshman Composition like a thundercloud. It requires much time, students resent "doing" it, and the results are dismal. James Strickland ("The Research Sequence: What To Do Before the Term Paper," *College Composition and Communication,* May 1986, pages 233–36) offers a useful semester plan that incorporates the research project into the ongoing concerns of Freshman Composition.

The sequence begins with an opinion paper in the form of a letter to the editor. No research is required, and Strickland encourages students to submit the letters to local papers (with a publication rate of almost fifty percent and a concomitant increase in students' self-esteem).

Strickland next splits the class into groups of readers whose jobs are to go over one another's letters and indicate what points need support to be more convincing. Wanting to close the holes in their arguments, students are now ready to learn the research skills they need.

As periodicals are the most likely source for the information students need, Strickland begins with the use of periodical indexes. Students must locate and read several articles bearing on their subjects to see if their "original position was accurate and/or reasonable." Students at this stage learn to decipher periodical indexes, to make bibliography notecards, and to paraphrase and take notes.

Based on their research, students now write "documented essays" on the subjects of their original letters to the editor. They are asked to imagine that, on the basis of their letters, they have been asked to write 750-word essays for the Sunday newspaper's magazine section. These two- to three-page essays provide an opportunity to revise the thrust of the original letters, and to use quo-

GUIDELINES FOR CHOOSING A TOPIC FOR A RESEARCH PAPER

1. **Expect to think through various topics before making your final choice.** Avoid rushing; give yourself time to think. Keep your mind open to flashes of insight and to alternative ideas. Still, avoid allowing indecision to block you.

2. **Be practical.** Plan to do the work within the established time limit and word count. Also, remember that you, along with most college researchers, are limited to working with the resources available at your college and the libraries in your community. Be sure that sufficient resources on your topic are available and accessible so that you can carry out a productive search strategy (see 32e).

3. **Narrow the topic sufficiently.** Avoid topics that are too broad, such as *communication* or even *nonverbal communication*. At the same time, avoid topics that are so narrow for a general research paper that you cannot write a suitable mix of generalizations and specific details, such as *sighs used in public to communicate exhaustion.*

4. **Choose a topic worth researching.** Avoid trivial subjects, such as how close together a bridge and groom stood during a wedding ceremony you recently attended. Such a topic prevents you from doing what you as a student researcher are expected to do: show that you can investigate related ideas and think about them critically. You are expected to bring together complex and/or conflicting concepts.

5. **Try to select a topic that interests you.** Know that your topic will be a companion for quite a while, sometimes most of a semester. Select, when possible and practical, a topic that arouses your interest. Try to pick a topic that allows you to sample the pleasure of satisfying your intellectual curiosity as you gather information and write the research paper. If you cannot think of a topic, try browsing in the library to find books and articles that catch your attention. Also, use the techniques for gathering ideas for writing discussed in 2d.

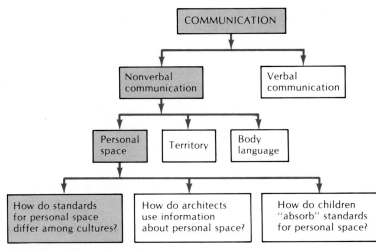

Flow Chart of Amy Brown's Narrowing Process

tation and paraphrase in support of a thesis. Several parenthetical references or endnotes and a bibliography are standard.

The next step is a "researched paper," using more thorough research and fuller documentation. This time students are asked to imagine that they have been invited to expand their Sunday newsmagazine piece into a full-size article (14–24 pages) for a major national magazine. Each student serves as "editor" to another student, in addition to writing his or her own article. The editor's job is to point out places in the essay where additional evidence is needed or where logic is unclear or faulty. The students explore a variety of heuristics as they seek to fill developmental gaps and correct logical flaws.

Overall, Strickland feels, the sequence has resulted in superior papers, exhibiting better documentation skills than papers written by students before he used this sequence. Student attitude has also changed in a positive way: students are more willing to go to the library, are more confident in their ability to do research, and complain less about assignments.

college had excellent sources to which she could refer. As she began to read closely on the topic, Brown evolved her research question: "How do standards for personal space differ among cultures?" The flow chart below illustrates Brown's process of narrowing the topic. Although this chart makes each decision look as if it flowed smoothly from the one before, the process looks clear-cut only after all the thinking, debating, and choosing is over. The process in action is rarely neat and tidy. As you think through your topic, do not be surprised if you have to back out of dead ends and make some sharp turns to new avenues. To help yourself define your choices and find a suitable path to a research question, try charting your decision process as you go along.

32c Determining your research paper's purpose and audience

Your research process involves making decisions about your paper's purpose and audience. The two major purposes for writing academic papers are *to inform* and *to persuade* (see 1b). The question that guides your research process helps determine your paper's purpose. If the question asks for facts or information, your purpose

Students might feel overwhelmed if they had to do a research paper on, say, the role of the media in shaping public attitude toward the Vietnam war or the impact of wheat sales to Russia on the American farmer. The problem has more to do with students' fears than the actual complexity of such assignments. Students' confidence can be built as research skills are developed if "accessible" topics are assigned—especially for preliminary exercises in library skills and note taking. Here are a few possible assignments:

1. Write a biography of someone you would like to know more about: a sports figure, a cartoonist, a movie director, a state legislator, a deposed dictator.

2. Write an essay recommending a particular type or model of some fairly expensive consumer item that you are interested in buying yourself, such as a car, a VCR, or a microwave oven.

3. Write an essay recommending and explaining an eating regimen that can help someone lose weight, train for a sport, or control a health problem (e.g., diabetes or high blood pressure).

4. Imagine you are a travel agent who has been asked to plan a tour of Asia or Africa. Money is no object. You have been told to arrange stops in all countries with which the United States has friendly relations. Advise your clients of (1) entry requirements such as a visa and limitations on what they may bring in to each country; (2) health precautions that they ought to take including innoculations; and (3) local laws or customs that they must not violate such as the non-use of alcohol or drugs.

is to inform. The question "How do standards for personal space differ among cultures?" requires an answer that calls for informative writing. On the other hand, if the question raised by a topic asks for an informed opinion supported with evidence, your purpose is to persuade. The question "Why should people be aware of intercultural differences in standards for personal space?" calls for persuasive writing. A paper's purpose may shift during the research process. Remain open-minded as you work. By the time you are writing your paper, however, be sure to have defined your purpose.

The audience for your college writing is primarily (but perhaps not exclusively) your instructor; see 1c. When you think of writing for your instructor, remember that he or she is both a member of the general reading public and a person responsible to see how well you have understood your material and the forms for presenting it. Sometimes the audience for a research paper includes other people—students in your class or perhaps specialists on your topic. Consider your reader's expertise on your topic when you make decisions about content, specific details in explanations, and word choice.

32d Preparing to conduct your research

Before you start your research, you need to prepare. You need equipment to facilitate your work. You need also to be familiar with how to evaluate sources, use headings or key words, and determine a documentation style.

1 Equipping yourself

Experienced researchers use equipment that helps them work efficiently. Gather the materials listed in the chart below. Keep them separate from your regular books and materials so that you can locate them easily.

Color coding is an option many researchers find helpful in establishing categories for information. For example, you might use one color of index cards or colored clips for notes and another for bibliographic information. You might use one color ink for summarized information, another for quotations taken from sources, and a third for your own comments on a source.

BASIC EQUIPMENT FOR CONDUCTING RESEARCH

1. A copy of your assignment.

2. A separate notebook to use for a research log. This important tool is explained in 32f.

3. Pens—several different colors—for taking notes. Writing in pencil tends to blur when notes are shuffled and handled often.

4. Index cards for two purposes. Cards that measure 4 × 6″ give you more room for notes. The 3 × 5″ size is fine for bibliographic data. If you prefer cards all one size, use different colors for notes and for bibliographic information. Use one index card per source to record bibliographic information (see Chapter 33). Also, use a separate index card for each idea you take down in notes. (See 32f about taking notes, and see Chapter 31 for avoiding plagiarism by learning to paraphrase, summarize, and quote sources.) Index cards give you the flexibility to move information around; pages in a notebook do not.

5. Dimes, quarters, or whatever coins you need for the library's copying machines. (See 32f about the uses and limitations of photocopying.)

6. Paper clips, a small stapler, or rubber bands to help you organize index cards and other papers.

7. A book bag if you intend to check out books from the library. Librarians joke about researchers with wheelbarrows. You might need a backpack.

---

2   Knowing how to evaluate sources

A **source** is any information-providing person, book, article, document, or other form of communication. But not all sources are equally valuable. Before you start to gather information from sources, learn how to evaluate them. Follow the guidelines in the chart below. If you are using a secondary source, use the Checklist for Evaluating a Secondary Source in 5c.

QUOTATION ABOUT RESEARCH

Research is a way of learning, important in formal study, which we can use for the rest of our lives: we can research the voting records of congressmen, recipes, genealogy, precedents in zoning for the neighborhood, or types of schooling for information of the PTA. Research is a method. The research paper is a particular embodiment of the general method.

—Donald Hall

GUIDELINES FOR EVALUATING SOURCES FOR RESEARCH

1. **Authoritative:** Check encyclopedias, textbooks, articles in academic journals, and bibliographies, and ask experts. If a particular name or a specific work in mentioned often, that source is probably recognized as an authoritative one on your topic. Also, to see whether the author of a source has a background that makes him or her an authority, consult one of the biographical references listed in 32f-1.

2. **Reliable:** Check different sources. If the same information appears, the material is likely to be reliable.

3. **Well supported:** Check that each source supports assertions or information with sufficient evidence. If the material expresses the source's point of view but offers little to back up that position, turn to another source.

4. **Balanced tone:** Read a source critically (see 5b through 5f). If the tone is unbiased and if the reasoning is logical, consider the source to be balanced.

5. **Current:** Check that the information is up-to-date. Sometimes long-accepted information is replaced or modified by new research. Check indexes to journals or computerized databases to see if anything newer has come along.

---

3 | **Starting to compile a list of headings or key words**

Researchers use headings and key words to look up information. **Headings** are subject categories in books and periodicals. **Key words**—sometimes called *descriptors* or *identifiers*—identify subject categories in periodicals and computerized databases.

Knowing how to locate headings and key words is central to the research process. The people who prepare reference books, catalog cards, and indexes to periodicals do not have the resources to maintain an infinite number of headings. Their job is to group information into categories and arrange efficient retrieval systems.

Your paper constructs its own category of information. You have to locate the headings and key words that lead you to books and articles on your topic. For example, the topic *nuclear energy* is identified with various headings or key words: *energy, nuclear;*

32e

atomic energy; energy, atomic; nuclear power; power, nuclear; and so on. You have to "break the code" to figure out what words identify the category you are seeking in each source. As you conduct your research, keep an ongoing list in your research log of headings and key words that relate to your topic. Then when you approach a new source, your search process will be more efficient.

TEACHING TIP

You may find it helpful to ask students to bring to class research assignments made in other classes. Working in groups, they can analyze the assignments in terms of audience, purpose, and scope of topic. Given sufficient time, they may be able to discuss a search strategy for carrying out the assignment that will be helpful to the student charged with doing the work.

4   Determining your documentation style

The term **documentation style** refers to various systems for providing information about the sources you have used in a research paper. Documentation styles vary among the disciplines. Some styles use footnotes or endnotes; others put reference information in parentheses within the text. Styles also differ in requirements for the complete list of sources at the end of a paper.

Before you start consulting sources, know what documentation style you will be using in your paper. If your assignment does not specify a documentation style, ask your instructor which to use. Be aware of what information the style calls for about each source. Then as you take notes on each source, keep a record of that information so that you can document your sources correctly and fully.

The **Modern Language Association (MLA)** has developed the documentation styles used most often in the humanities. MLA style is explained and illustrated in Chapter 33. The **American Psychological Association (APA)** has developed another documentation system commonly used for research papers, especially in the social sciences. APA style is explained and illustrated in 33b-2, 33c-2, and 33d. Documentation in the sciences is discussed in 33g.

32e   Using a search strategy to conduct your research

Inexperienced researchers can easily feel overwhelmed by a seemingly limitless choice of sources. Inexperience can tempt the student into mistaking activity for productivity. Going to the library to spend days at the card catalog to find everything even remotely related to a topic can be exhausting and fruitless when writing a general research paper.

Researchers can interview experts, send for information by mail, and—most of all—use the resources of a library. Experienced researchers use a **search strategy** for working systematically through these sources. A search strategy is an organized procedure

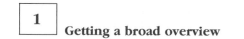

The Search Strategy

that leads step-by-step from general to specific sources. A structured approach helps you use time efficiently and cover the necessary territory. No two research processes are exactly alike, so the search strategy explained here should serve as a guide to your personally tailored strategy. A search strategy is rarely as tidy as it seems to be when described in a textbook. Expect to adapt the explanation here to your needs in each research project.

1 Getting a broad overview

If you have to choose a topic of your own or narrow a subject into a researchable topic, start by getting a broad overview. Use the suggestions in the chart on the opposite page.

SUGGESTIONS FOR GETTING A BROAD OVERVIEW

1. Confer briefly with a **professor** in your general field of interest (psychology, biology, literature, and so on). Ask for advice in narrowing your topic. Also inquire about the names of major books and authorities on your topic.

2. Browse through a **textbook** in your field of interest. Look for material that points toward ways to narrow your topic. Consult the table of contents and the major headings, usually shown in color or darker print, within each chapter. Also look for names of major books and authorities on your topic.

3. Read an **encyclopedia article** about your field of interest or subcategories of the field. Get basic information that might help you narrow your topic. Look for the names of major books and authorities. *Do not, however, stop with the encyclopedia.* College-level research demands a thorough search of a variety of sources.

| 2 | **Deciding whether to interview experts** |

As you pursue a broad overview, you might decide to interview experts on your subject, either in person or on the telephone. An expert can often offer valuable leads or advice. If your topic relates to an event that your family or friends lived through, they qualify as experts, and access to them will likely be easy.

The faculty at your college or nearby colleges have special expertise about many topics. Corporations and professional organizations can often suggest experts in many fields; a customer service department or public relations office is a good place to begin. Public officials are sometimes available for interviews. Many federal and state government offices have employees who specialize in providing information to the public.

If you want to interview other people, start early. It takes time to set up appointments and fit your research needs into other people's schedules. You may not always be granted the interviews you seek, but many people remember their own experiences doing academic research and try to help.

Prepare questions that use time efficiently. Know why you are interviewing the person and what you want to know. Ask questions that elicit information, not merely a "yes" or "no" answer. Be constructive; avoid language that shows bias or a hostile attitude. Experienced interviewers take notes or use a tape recorder so that they do not have to rely on their memories. Always ask permission of the person you are interviewing before you take notes or tape record. Some people routinely refuse to allow their comments to be taped, so be ready with a note-taking system as a backup. An efficient way to take notes is to put each question on an index card with space left for your notes during the interview.

Carefully evaluate any information you get from interviewing experts, using the guidelines in 32d-2. Even the information of experts may be slanted to suit special interests. Always follow up an interview, no matter how short, with a brief note of thanks. Aside from its being polite, this courtesy helps pave the way for the next student who might ask for an interview.

3 Deciding whether to send for information

As a result of getting a broad overview, you might decide to send for publications or other kinds of information available by mail. A month or more can go by before an inquiry is processed, so send early and leave time in your schedule to use the material. Never depend entirely on mail-order sources for your research. The material might not arrive in time or might turn out to be unsuitable. Also, remember that a well-handled research paper project draws on a variety of sources, including those found in a library.

When you write to businesses involved with matters related to your topic, target your request carefully to get the material you need. If you are unsure of what is available, call the company and talk with someone in its public relations office, customer service department, or the equivalent. Large libraries sometimes have corporate reports and specialized technical reports on file, so check with a reference librarian *before* you order through the mails. When you consult corporate materials, evaluate them carefully for bias and promotion of special interests. To be useful, corporate publications must go well beyond the kinds of information usually written for consumers.

United States government publications are available in an almost astounding variety. You can get information on population figures, weather patterns, agriculture, national parks, and much more. Large libraries often have many government documents on file, so ask a reference librarian before you order. To find out what publications are available and how to order them, consult one of these directories in the reference section of a large library.

The *Monthly Catalog of United States Government Publications* is an up-to-date listing of all offerings. Items are cataloged according to subject.

American Statistics Index (ASI) is published in two volumes. The *Index* catalogues all statistical documents produced by government departments. The *Abstracts* gives concise summaries of the documents' contents.

CIS, published by the Congressional Information Service, indexes all the papers produced by congressional panels and committees. These documents include the texts of hearings (for example, testimony about the plight of the homeless) and reports (for example, a comparative study of temporary shelters for the homeless).

4 | Being ready to use all the resources of the library

Using the library as a resource for a research-paper project takes time. In his work as associate director for public services of the New York Public Library, Rodney Phillips has become extremely familiar with the time needed to prepare a good undergraduate research paper. Division staff receives an average of 2,000 inquiries per day, and many of them are from students like you who want to know how to find information for their papers. To do a decent job, Mr. Phillips says, you will want to gather and look over at least 25 different items. Some you will need to skim, and some you will need to read slowly. You will need to take notes on many. "Plan to spend at least 15 hours in the library," Mr. Phillips says. "You will sometimes be frustrated to find that others have been there before you and taken books you want. Then you'll have to look further, just as they probably did. You will find that titles you thought were promising will not give you what you were after. Other sources might pay off enormously." Mr. Phillips says the typical undergraduate, new to research writing, expects to obtain a paper from one book and two or three other sources. These students, he states flatly, are not budgeting anywhere near the time they need to do a good job.

Librarians are information experts. They are highly skilled at searching for and finding information. Reference librarians seek to help people learn how to use library resources well. Nevertheless, the research task remains yours. Professor Mary Cope, chief of materials processing of the library at the City College of the City University of New York, says she holds "reference interviews" with

BACKGROUND

Some very famous people have been librarians. A few of them may even have helped students with term papers.

- German philosopher-mathematician and diplomat Gottfried von Leibniz (1646–1716) served two terms as a librarian.
- British philosopher, economist, and historian David Hume (1711–1776) spent five years as a librarian at the Library of the Faculty of the Advocates at Edinburgh while writing his *History of England.*
- The infamous Casanova (1725–1798) served as a private librarian to royalty for thirteen years at the end of his life.
- Pope Pius XI (1857–1939) spent nineteen years at the Ambrosian Library in Milan, and he was then appointed chief librarian. In 1911, he began reorganization and updating of the Vatican Library, and in 1915 was named prefect of the Vatican Library. He went on to become pope in 1922.
- Archibald MacLeish (1892–1982), poet, playwright, Assistant Secretary of State, and three-time Pulitzer Prize winner, served as Librarian of Congress under Franklin D. Roosevelt.
- Mao Tse-Tung (1893–1976) at one time was assistant to the chief librarian of the University of Peking.
- J. Edgar Hoover (1895–1964) was a messenger and cataloguer in the Library of Congress as a young man.

BACKGROUND

The Nuremberg Chronicle (1493) was the world's first encyclopedia. Its three volumes were written by one man, Hartmann Schedel, using his extensive personal library for most of his research. Schedel did overlook one event, though: Columbus's discovery of the New World one year earlier.

USING THE LIBRARY IN YOUR RESEARCH

Many colleges and large public libraries prepare written guides to their resources. Find out if your library has such a guide. With or without a guide, get to know your library well. Wander around and browse. Libraries differ from each other in physical layout and in the breadth and depth of resources. Consult the librarians. Even experienced researchers take advantage of librarians' knowledge of the library's resources and how best to use them.

---

students "to determine what they want to learn. We direct them, then, to the resources and tell them to return if they need more guidance." Professor Cope thinks that the best assistance she offers is to point out different aspects of subjects covered in reference sources. By doing so, she helps students narrow their topics.

32f Using reference books

1 Using general reference books

Reference books range from general sources to specialized ones. Reference books summarize or list much important information. You can choose from encyclopedias, yearbooks and almanacs, atlases, dictionaries, biographies, bibliographies, indexes, and other reference books. Some of these are general references; others focus on a particular subject.

The *Guide to Reference Books* is a valuable resource. It covers reference works in all fields, describing general ones first, and then specialized ones. This book, or another like it, is worth getting to know well.

Encyclopedias

Articles in general encyclopedias summarize information about a wide variety of subjects. The articles are most useful for a broad overview but not as major sources for college-level research. They are written by specialists for nonspecialist readers. Many articles end with a brief bibliography of major works on the subject. Because encyclopedias take long to write and publish, some kinds of information in them—about technology, for example—quickly becomes outdated. Look for up-to-date editions and annual supplements. To locate the information you want, start with the Index volume. If you cannot find what you are looking for, try alternate headings or key words (see 32d-3). General encyclopedias are not the place to look for reports on recent events or current research.

Collier's Encyclopedia, Encyclopaedia Britannica, and *Encyclopedia Americana* are among the respected multivolume general encyclopedias. They are all widely available.

One-volume general encyclopedias cover subjects very briefly. You may want to consult one, such as *The New Columbia Encyclopedia* or the *Random House Encyclopedia,* to see whether a general subject area interests you enough for further research. A one-volume encyclopedia may also be useful when something comes up in your research that you need not explore fully but do need to understand in a general way.

Specialized encyclopedias exist in many fields. See the list (pp. 619–620) of specialized reference works arranged by academic discipline.

Almanacs, Yearbooks, Fact Books

Almanacs—books such as *The World Almanac and Book of Facts*—briefly present a year's events and data in government, politics, sports, economics, demographics, and many other categories. *Facts on File* covers world events in a weekly digest and in an annual one-volume *Yearbook.*

Congressional Record and *Statistical Abstract* contain a wealth of data about the United States. *Demographic Yearbook* and *United Nations Statistical Yearbook* carry worldwide data. Other specialized yearbooks and handbooks are named in the list of reference works below, arranged by academic discipline.

Atlases

Atlases contain maps—and remember that seas and skies and even other planets have been mapped. You have probably looked up places in a geographical atlas, such as *National Geographic Atlas of the World.* These comprehensive books contain many kinds of geographic information: topography, climates, populations, migrations, natural resources, crops, and so on.

Dictionaries

Dictionaries define words and terms. The kinds of dictionaries described in 20a define words in the English language and give various other information about these words.

Specialized dictionaries exist in many fields, among them literature, music, folklore, economics, and the sciences. These dictionaries define the words and phrases specific to a field. See 32f-2 for a list of specialized reference books arranged by academic discipline.

Biographies

Biographical reference books give brief information about the major events in many famous people's lives. Various *Who's Who* series cover noteworthy people, male or female, living or dead. *Current Biography: Who's News and Why*—well-described by its title—is published monthly, with six-month and annual cumulative editions. *Dictionary of American Biography* and *Webster's Biographical Dictionary* are very widely available.

Specialized biographical reference books focus on artists, musicians, important people of various historical periods or nationalities, and so on. See the list below of specialized reference works arranged by academic discipline.

Bibliographies

Bibliographies list books. *Books in Print* lists all books available through their publishers and sometimes other sources in the United States. This multivolume work classifies its entries by author name, title, and general subject headings, but it does not describe a book's content in any way.

The *Book Review Digest* excerpts book reviews. If a book has been reviewed in major newspapers and magazines, you can use this source to find out what critics thought of it. These excerpts can help you evaluate a source (see also 32d-2). This digest is published every year. The reviews appear in the volume that corresponds to the year a book was published or the one immediately following. The *Book Review Index* and *Current Review Citations* list where reviews have appeared, but these volumes do not carry the actual reviews.

Consulting specialized bibliographies—ones that list many books on a particular subject—can be very helpful in your research process. Annotated or critical bibliographies describe and evaluate the works they list and so are especially useful. You will find some specialized bibliographies in the following list of reference works arranged by academic discipline. Most libraries have back issues on microfilm of the *New York Times;* many libraries have back issues of major journals. Each library has its own collection, so get to know your library's reference resources.

BACKGROUND

In *Form and Substance* (John Wiley, 1981) Richard Coe suggests that in establishing a broad overview of a subject, some sources are more helpful than others. He suggests using review articles that summarize major books and articles on a topic, a general textbook that includes the topic, a good encyclopedia, and the *Book Review Digest*. He points out that at this stage of the research process, it is not important to take notes. The writer should simply read quickly and broadly, getting a general background and watching for critical problems or researchable questions.

2 Using specialized reference books

As you work into a research topic, you need increasingly specific and focused information. First, get an overview from general reference works (32f-1), and then consult specialized ones. Here are some titles, grouped by general academic disciplines. This list only hints at the wide variety available at many libraries.

BUSINESS AND ECONOMICS

Accountant's Handbook
A Dictionary of Economics
Encyclopedia of Advertising
Encyclopedia of Banking and Finance
The Encyclopedia of Management
Handbook of Modern Marketing

FINE ARTS

Crowells' Handbook of World Opera
Harvard Dictionary of Music
International Cyclopedia of Music and Musicians
Oxford Companion to Art
Popular Music: An Annotated List of American Popular Songs

HISTORY AND POLITICAL SCIENCE

Dictionary of American Biography
Encyclopedia of American History
An Encyclopedia of World History
Foreign Affairs Bibliography
New Cambridge Modern History
Political Handbook and Atlas of the World
Political Science Bibliographies

LITERATURE

American Authors, 1600–1900
Cassell's Encyclopedia of World Literature
Contemporary Authors
Dictionary of Literary Biography
A Dictionary of Literary Terms
Funk & Wagnall's Guide to Modern World Literature
MLA International Bibliography of Books and Articles on the Modern Languages and Literature
The Oxford Companion to American Literature
The Oxford Companion to English Literature
The Oxford Companion to the Theatre

BACKGROUND

The Guinness Book of World Records was founded as a result of the curiosity of Sir Hugh Beaver, the managing director of Arthur Guinness, Son and Co., Ltd. One day in 1954, Sir Hugh went bird hunting. He shot at some plovers—and missed. He started wondering if plovers were the fastest game birds, and he tried to satisfy his curiosity in the encyclopedia. Neither it nor any other reference work had the answer.

As a result, Sir Hugh decided that people needed a book that would accurately list record sizes, speeds, and durations. His plan was to have a copy of the book in every pub that sold Guinness stout, as an aid in settling bets. He set about finding someone to author such a book, and one of his executives recommended the McWhirter brothers. Trivia history was made.

Norris and Ross McWhirter, identical twin sons of a newspaper writer, had grown up around newspapers, magazines, and reference books. Their childhood hobby had been to collect information of the very type Sir Hugh was seeking. They had frequently found contradictions in their sources, and so as adults they had founded a company to verify these statistics and to "supply facts and figures to newspapers, yearbooks, encyclopedias, and advertisers."

Four months after Sir Hugh had interviewed them, the McWhirters published the first book in the series. The 198 page bestseller became England's number one nonfiction best seller in only four months. Immediately, readers began submitting their own fantastic facts. The McWhirters collected and checked these submissions, and soon an updated volume was on the way. Norris and Ross McWhirter acted as co-editors until 1975.

BACKGROUND

Libraries are as old as recorded history. In fact, they were the repository of the records of past civilizations. In what was ancient Mesopotamia, for example, temples and princely houses have been excavated that held thousands of clay tablets inscribed with epic poems, liturgic and magic texts, and commercial records. The palace of Ashurbanipal, who reigned from 668–633 B.C. in Nineveh, has provided tablets bearing stamps of ownership, catchwords, and sometimes source and place indications, thereby testifying to the existence of a well-developed cataloging system. In Egypt every temple had its library and school. Although the Egyptian collections were made on papyrus (and thus have been found mostly in graves and tombs rather than in temples), the content was similar. Much has been lost, but records often remain. In the temple at Edfu, for instance, a full catalogue of all the hieratical works the library contained was incised on the walls, bearing witness to what was once there.

BACKGROUND

Before it was burnt down in the third century A.D., the famous library at Alexandria, Egypt contained as many as 700,000 scrolls. Under the Ptolemies (third century B.C. on) the library became a depository for copies of all important texts. Books were edited into a standard format, and systems of punctuation and accents were introduced. Textual scholarship, revisions of books to incorporate new knowledge, and the writing of new books went on constantly. Most of the books have been lost. Only those works which were widely copied and distributed have managed to survive. For example, evidence indicates that Aeschylus, Sophocles, Euripides, and Aristophanes wrote about 330 plays in total; only 43 remain.

MYTHOLOGY

Bulfinch's Mythology
Funk & Wagnall's Standard Dictionary of Folklore, Mythology, and Legend
Larousse World Mythology

PHILOSOPHY AND RELIGION

The Concise Encyclopedia of Western Philosophy and Philosophers
Dictionary of the Bible
Eastern Definitions: A Short Encyclopedia of Religions of the Orient
Encyclopedia of Philosophy
A Reader's Guide to the Great Religions

SCIENCE AND TECHNOLOGY

The Encyclopedia of the Biological Sciences
Encyclopedia of Chemistry
Encyclopedia of Computer Science and Technology
The Encyclopedia of Oceanography
Encyclopedia of Physics
Introduction to the History of Science
The Larousse Encyclopedia of Animal Life
The McGraw-Hill Encyclopedia of Science and Technology

SOCIAL SCIENCES

Dictionary of Anthropology
Dictionary of Education
Encyclopedia of Psychology
International Encyclopedia of the Social Sciences
Sources of Information in the Social Sciences

TELEVISION AND FILM

International Encyclopedia of Film
International Television Almanac
New York Times Film Reviews, 1913–1970
World Encyclopedia of the Film

32g Using periodicals

Periodicals are magazines and journals published at set periods during a year. **Indexes to periodicals** list articles written between the dates on the cover on each edition. Many indexes are kept up-to-date with supplements between editions. Some but not all indexes include abstracts—brief summaries—of each article. Classifi-

32g

cation systems vary among indexes, so take time to learn how to decipher the codes and abbreviations in the index you need. Most indexes include a guide for readers in the front or back of each volume and supplement. As you learn to use an index, update your list of headings and key words (32d-3) for future reference.

Indexes are packaged in a variety of ways. Some are in print, with yearly bound volumes and interim paperback updates. Some indexes are on microfilm or microfiche. Many indexes are also part of computerized databases (32i).

---

1 Using general indexes

General indexes list articles in magazines and newspapers. Headings and key words on the same subject vary among indexes, so think of every possible way to look up the information you seek. Large libraries have many general indexes. Almost all libraries have these two major indexes:

The *New York Times Index* catalogs all articles that have been printed in this encyclopedic newspaper since 1851. Supplements are published every two weeks in paperbound volumes. The supplements are organized into volumes (bound or on microfilm) periodically.

The *Readers' Guide to Periodical Literature* is the most widely used index to over 100 magazines and journals with general (rather than specialized) readers. Paperback supplements are published every

COMMUNICATION, Nonverbal ———————— Subject heading
Does your body *parle francais*? French body ——— Title of article
language; teaching methods of (L. Wylie) pors ——— Author
(Time) 113:107 + My 14 '79 ————————— Periodical title
Watching your every move: what you reveal
about yourself without saying a word. J.
Marks. Teen (23:36 + Jl '79) ————————— Vol. 23, p. 36 +, July 1979
When tensions talk—listen! Subtle motion tells
a story. E. Hamilton. (por) Sci Digest 85:30-2 + ——— Has portrait
Ap '79
Women smile less for success; study of job
success by Wendy McKenna and Florence
Denmark. M. B. Parlee. Psychol Today 12:16
Mr '79
  See also
Eye—Movements
Gesture ——————————————————— Related subject
Sign language   headings
Touch

Annotated Excerpt from *Readers' Guide to Periodical Literature*

BACKGROUND

During the Middle Ages, the libraries of Western Europe were affiliated with religious houses and cathedrals. The few private libraries belonged to bishops. The clergy were the only people who could read, and even if the level of literacy was sometimes low, the church maintained the tradition of schools and libraries. These religious libraries were quite small by twentieth-century standards. The largest (at Canterbury and Bury St. Edmunds) had 2,000 volumes each, but libraries of only a few hundred volumes were the rule. The libraries contained theological and biblical works, law books, classical texts, medical and historical works. Contemporary histories, written in monasteries, remain the best records of what happened during the period. In the thirteenth and fourteenth centuries, the rise of the new universities, the rediscovery of Aristotle (from Arabic), and the position of the friars as university teachers undermined the dominance of the monastic libraries. Although the university libraries were not open to undergraduates, the Franciscan friars opened their own libraries (some still survive in England), and they printed small, portable books which contrasted with the bulky illuminated manuscripts of the monasteries. The monastic libraries of England were destroyed in 1536–1540 (during Henry VIII's reign) and their books dispersed. In 1550, university libraries, schools, and churches were purged. Many treasures saved during the 1000 years of the Dark Ages were lost.

BACKGROUND

One of the most famous libraries of antiquity was the one at Alexandria, founded by Ptolemy I (c. 323–285 B.C.) and greatly augmented by his son Ptolemy II Philadelphus (c. 285–247 B.C.) and his grandson Ptolemy III Euergetes (c. 247–221 B.C.). Manuscripts were imported from all parts of Greece and Asia, resulting in holdings that are estimated to have been as high as 700,000 papyrus rolls during the time of Caesar. Because of its riches, leading scholars of the Hellenistic world were drawn to it, resulting in a flurry of scholarly activity. Books were edited into a standard format, and systems of punctuation and accents were introduced. Textual scholarship, revisions of books to incorporate new knowledge, and the writing of new books went on constantly. Most of the books have been lost. Only those works which were widely copied and distributed have managed to survive. As the political importance of Alexandria waned, the library suffered from neglect. Finally, in 270 A.D., much of it was razed to the ground, and a good part of the rest was destroyed by fire a little over a century later.

BACKGROUND

Benjamin Franklin organized the Library Company of Philadelphia in 1731. It was the first American subscription library. Its original purpose was to provide ready access to books for members of the Junto Club, a public service group to which Franklin belonged. Franklin himself said that he spent time at the library almost daily, learning foreign languages or reading for general knowledge.

two weeks. These supplements are organized into volumes (bound or on microfilm) periodically. This index does not include scholarly journals, so its uses are often limited for college-level research. It can be useful, however, for getting a broad overview and for ways to narrow a subject. Illustrated on the previous page is an entry from *Readers' Guide* showing listings for Communication, the subject of Amy Brown's research paper assignment.

2 Using specialized indexes

Specialized indexes list articles published in academic and professional periodicals. When researching a college-level paper, you will often find the material in specialized indexes more appropriate than that in general indexes. Many specialized indexes carry an abstract (a summary) of each listed article.

Depending on their resources, libraries stock many or few specialized indexes. Commonly available specialized indexes include *America: History and Life,* published every four months; *Applied Science and Technology Index,* published monthly; *Art Index,* published every three months; *Biological Abstracts,* published monthly; *Biological and Agricultural Index,* published monthly; *Business Periodicals Index,* published monthly; *Education Index,* published monthly; *General Science Index,* published monthly and cumulative editions published every three months; *Humanities Index,* published every three months. (Before 1974, it was part of the *Social Sciences and Humanities Index.* Before 1965, the *Social Sciences and Humanities Index* were combined and called the *International Index*); *MLA International Bibliography of Books and Articles in the Modern Languages and Literatures,* published annually; *Music Index,* published monthly; *Psychological Abstracts,* published monthly; *Social Science Index,* published quarterly.

Here is an entry from the *Humanities Index* that Amy Brown used in her research for the paper in Chapter 34. The abbreviations have the same meaning as those in the excerpt from the *Readers' Guide to Periodical Literature* shown on the previous page.

> Nonverbal communication
> *See also*
> Expression
> Gesture
> Background to kinesics. R. L. Birdwhistell. *Etc* 40:352-61
> Fall '83
> Mediated interpersonal communication: toward a new typology. R. Cathcart and G. Gumpert. *Q J Speech* 69:267-77 Ag '83

Excerpt from *Humanities Index*

32h Using the card catalog or microfiche catalog

Years ago, all libraries used a **card catalog** for their record of holdings. In recent years, many libraries have transferred their cards onto a **microfiche catalog.** Some libraries call their record of holdings a **library catalog,** which usually means that it uses either microfiche or a combination of microfiche and cards. The key word in these terms is *catalog.* A catalog in this sense is a detailed list of all books in the library. Some libraries also include periodicals (see 32g) and other holdings in the catalog.

Whether the catalog is on cards or microfiche, the same information is offered. You can locate information in a card catalog by going through drawers of cards by hand. You can locate information in a microfiche catalog by using a microfiche reader. Each microfiche is a thin film that contains miniature reproductions of many cards. A microfiche reader enlarges the material so that it can be read easily. Various companies manufacture microfiche readers, but they are basically quite similar. Get to know how to work the microfiche reader in your library. Many microfiche readers include an instruction diagram; if you need help, do not hesitate to ask a librarian. Once you become familiar with a few different microfiche readers, you will be comfortable with any of them.

Catalog information is organized alphabetically in three categories: authors' names, book titles, and subjects. In some libraries, authors and titles are in one file, subjects in another. In other libraries, the three types of information are filed together.

Each card in the card catalog or on microfiche contains much useful information. The **call number** is most important. Be sure to copy it down *exactly* as it appears, with all numbers, letters, and decimal points. The call number tells where the book is located in the stacks. If you are working in a library with open stacks (one where you can go into the book collection yourself), the call number leads you to the area in the library where all books on the same subject can be found. Being there is an excellent search strategy in itself, even though some books might have been checked out and other books might be at the reserve desk. The call number is also crucial in a library with closed stacks. In this case, to get a book, you must fill in a call slip, hand it in at the call desk, and wait for the book to arrive. If you have filled in the wrong number or an incomplete number, your wait will be in vain.

Some libraries carry two microfiche catalog files: a *base catalog,* which includes books through a given date, and an *update*

BACKGROUND

Melvil Dewey (1851–1931) is famous for the Dewey Decimal System of book classification (1876). He was also a founder and editor of the *Library Journal* and of the American Library Association. In 1883, he became librarian at Columbia University, New York City, and founded its school of library economy, the first program to train and certify librarians. Dewey and the school moved to Albany, New York, where it became the State Library school. Dewey served as director of the New York State library (1899–1906), secretary of the University of the State of New York (1899–1900), and state Director of Libraries (1904–1906). He remade the state library into one of the most efficient in the country, and he set up traveling libraries and picture collections. His innovations were widely copied in the United States and abroad.

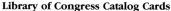

Library of Congress Catalog Cards

catalog, which starts where the base catalog stops and continues to the present. Often the microfiche for each catalog is color-coded to help people not mix up the two.

Libraries classify books according to one of two systems. You can tell what system a particular library uses from the call numbers on the catalog cards. Cards in the **Library of Congress system** have call numbers that start with a letter. Each letter indicates a major classification of information: *A* stands for general works, *B* for philosophy, *C* and *D* for history, and so on. Cards in the **Dewey Decimal system** have call numbers that start with numbers. Each number indicates a major classification of information: 0–99 signals general works, 100–199 philosophy, 200–299 religion, and so on. Find out what system your library uses, and ask for a complete list of the classifications.

Tracers are another important feature of cards in the card catalog. Tracers are words, numbered and in fine print below a book's publication data. Tracers give other headings used to classify information related to the subject of the card. They are valuable hints for

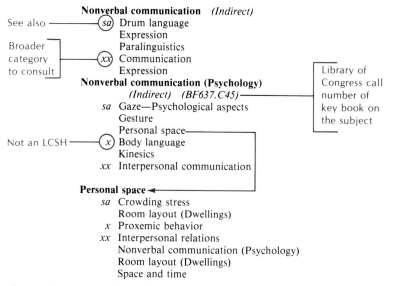

Nonverbal communication *(Indirect)*

See also ——— *sa* Drum language
                Expression

Broader
category ——— *xx* Paralinguistics
to consult   Communication
                Expression

Nonverbal communication (Psychology)
       (Indirect) *(BF637.C45)* ——— Library of Congress call number of key book on the subject

      sa Gaze—Psychological aspects
          Gesture
          Personal space

Not an LCSH ——— *x* Body language
          Kinesics
      xx Interpersonal communication

Personal space ◄

      sa Crowding stress
          Room layout (Dwellings)
       x Proxemic behavior
      xx Interpersonal relations
          Nonverbal communication (Psychology)
          Room layout (Dwellings)
          Space and time

Library of Congress Subject Headings

other topics to look up in the subject file of the card catalog when you want to find more about a subject. As you find tracers, be sure to add them to your list of headings and key words (see 32d-3).

At libraries that use the Library of Congress cataloging systems, the multi-volume *Library of Congress Subject Headings (LCSH)* is an excellent guide. Available in the reference or reserve section of a library, it is a catalog of the subject headings (not title or author) used in the card catalog.

This valuable resource helps you in three ways. First, you can look up your subject without having to go through the cards. Second, if the term you are using is not in the card catalog, it might be in the *LCSH* with a cross reference to the term used in the card catalog. The expense and time is enormous to change subject headings in the card catalog, so the terms are not always up-to-date. For example, until recently, sources related to "World War I" were filed in the card catalog under "The European War." People who consulted the *LCSH* easily found out that the old term for "World War I" was still in effect, and they could continue with their research. Third, at each subject heading, you can find a list of tracers—related headings that can lead you to additional sources. As a bonus, the *LCSH* also lists related terms (marked by *x*) that are *not* used to classify information in the system; knowing these terms will help you avoid unproductive searching. All the terms in the *LCSH* suggest alternate key words you

BACKGROUND

Until the founding of the Library Company of Philadelphia in 1731, there were few public libraries in the American colonies. The earliest one was the library of Harvard College, founded in 1638 with around 400 volumes bequeathed by John Harvard. Libraries were established at Yale and at William and Mary around 1700. In the Southern colonies the Reverend Thomas Bray (1656–1730), working by appointment of the Bishop of London as commissary of the Anglican Church, established parochial libraries. In 1876 a report on *Public Libraries in the United States* stated: "So far as is known, there were, in 1776, twenty-nine public libraries in the thirteen American colonies, and they numbered altogether 45,623 volumes; in the year 1800 the number of libraries had increased to forty-nine, and the number of volumes to about 80,000." The Library of Congress, which contains over 72 million pieces of material (among them 16.5 million books and 31 million manuscripts), was begun by Congress in 1800 with a budget of $5,000. Today it costs over $150 million per year to operate.

can use when searching through other sources. Amy Brown, whose research paper appears in Chapter 34, found this when she looked up "nonverbal communication" as well as "personal space," the two entries shown in the illustration.

Many libraries today have card catalogs "on-line." These computerized access systems often list millions of titles, some of which are in the library you are using. On-line systems vary, so if your library has one, learn how to use it to best benefit. (See also 32i.)

32i Using computerized databases

A **computerized database** is a bibliographic computer file of articles, reports, and—less often—books. Each item in a computerized database provides information about title, author, and publisher. If the database catalogs articles from scholarly journals, the entry might also provide a summary—called an *abstract*—of the material. Once you locate an entry that seems promising for your research, you must then locate the source itself. A computerized database entry is only the beginning.

The idea of letting a computer do the work is very attractive, but for a computerized database to be useful, you as a researcher have to lay much groundwork. To use a database, you must know how to search by consulting a list of key words (as explained in 32d-3). Cast a net too widely and you can get far too many entries; cast a net too narrowly and you can get too few. Some computerized databases may be complicated to use. Ask a reference librarian to guide you if you need help.

Most computerized databases are operated by commercial companies. Libraries pay a fee for computer time and for each entry. Often that charge is passed on to the user—you. Find out the arrangement at your library. The cost of locating entries can vary from nothing to over one dollar per entry, with a set minimum charge. The cost of a printout may be extra per entry.

Amy Brown, the student who wrote the research paper in Chapter 34, used the DIALOG Information System to search for sources. DIALOG contains over 100 million references—mostly journal articles and reports—combined from over 200 smaller databases in the humanities, the social sciences, business, the sciences and technology, medicine, economics, and current events. A librarian helped Brown choose key words. Brown's topic was *personal space,* an area of nonverbal communication. Brown started with *nonverbal communication,* but the librarian soon discovered that the term was too general. It would have yielded 1,486 citations. The expense of

Computer file access number ——— 61-13392 Vol No: 61 Abstract No: 13392

Title ——— Tactile relationships in the subway as affected by racial, sexual, and crowded seating situations.

Author ——— Maines, David R.

Author's affiliation ——— Yale U

Source ———
Environmental Psychology & Nonverbal Behavior 1977 Win Vol 2(2) 100-108
CODEN: EPNBDI   ISSN: 03613496
Language: ENGLISH   Document type: JOURNAL ARTICLE

Abstract (summary) ———
Observations of touching behavior were made on a New York City subway line to determine whether homogeneous behavioral patterns exist in the subway. Direct observations of race, sex, and crowding on subway car benches were made. These factors were coded as variables that might affect touching among strangers. Data indicate the presence of tactile avoidance behavior in crowded situations, but statistical significance was achieved only in the case of racial and sexual heterogeneous relationships. Data support M.G. Leichty's (1975) hypothesis concerning the existence and operation of universes of touch. The demonstration of patterned interaction challenges the view of subways as environments of heterogeneity. (20 ref)

Descriptors (database index words and phrases) ———
Descriptors: RACIAL DIFFERENCES .(42620), HUMAN SEX DIFFERENCES .(23510), CROWDING .(12610), PUBLIC TRANSPORTATION .(42250), TACTUAL STIMULATION .(51400), PERSONAL SPACE .(37680), INTERPERSONAL INTERACTION .(26250)
Identifiers: race & sex & crowding, touching among strangers on subway
Section Headings: 3020 .(GROUP & INTERPERSONAL PROCESSES)

A DIALOG Entry

BACKGROUND

Abdul Kassem Ismael (938–995), Grand Vizier of Persia, had a library of 117,000 volumes. When he traveled, he took his books along—all of them. He had 400 camels trained to walk in order; the books they carried remained in strict alphabetical sequence. His camel drivers doubled as librarians.

BACKGROUND

Swiss naturalist Konrad von Gesner (1516–1565) wrote the *Universal Library,* a summary of *all* books known in Hebrew, Greek, and Latin.

such a list, as well as its lack of focus, led Brown to limit her search to the journal *Psychological Abstracts* (called *PsycINFO* in the DIALOG system). To get the number of entries down to manageable size, Brown crossed *nonverbal communication* with other key words such as *conversation, personal space, social perception,* and *ethnic values.* One of those citations is illustrated here, with an explanation of its parts.

32j Keeping a research log and taking useful notes

Your research process includes taking notes as you consult sources and recording your ideas as you move through the process.

QUOTATION ABOUT RESEARCH

[Research] method is so central to the understanding and evaluation of the final written product that in many disciplines a writer is obliged to describe as part of the statement the method used to produce and analyze the data. In this way, many articles contain stories of how they were made.

—Charles Bazerman, *The Informed Writer*

QUOTATION ABOUT WRITING

It's not a bad idea to get in the habit of writing down one's thoughts. It saves one having to bother anyone else with them.

—Isabel Colegate

1 Keeping a research log

A **research log** is like a diary. Keep it in a notebook reserved exclusively for your research project. A thorough research log helps you think about your evolving material. Your log is a history of your search strategy and of ideas that occur to you during the research process. It keeps you from having to retrace your steps or reconstruct your thoughts unnecessarily. It is *not* for notes about the content of sources: put your notes on index cards, as explained in 32j-2. Rereading your log can help you make decisions about the next research step or about the content of your paper. Although much of your log will not find its way into your paper, its entries become valuable aids when you move from gathering material to organizing information to writing the paper. An excerpt of an entry from Amy Brown's log written for the research paper in Chapter 34 is shown below.

> Nov. 15: Found Sommer and made a biblio. card. Excellent source. He is an environmental psychologist. Tone is calm, seems to be unbiased. I now realize that I was overlapping two concepts: territory and personal space. Territory refers to the places we carve out as "our own" — a chair in a classroom, a room in a house. Personal space is the "bubble" of space we carry around with us. We don't like intrusions in our bubbles. Sommer's description on page 26 is the best I've seen. I photocopied the page and marked off the part I will probably quote in my paper.

Excerpt from Amy Brown's Research Log

2 | Taking useful notes

Taking good notes is the key to using sources well in your research paper. Together with your research log and bibliography cards, your notes give you a complete record of your research and the information you found.

Notetaking is a decision-making process. The first decision concerns whether a source related to your topic is worth taking notes on. To decide, evaluate it according to the guidelines in 32d-2. If it seems to be a good source, take notes. If it does not, record its title and location in your research log—along with a message to yourself about why you rejected it. What seems useless one day might have potential if you revise your focus or narrow your topic.

The second decision concerns what to put into your notes. Knowing how to select material for notes comes with experience. Dive in and get that experience. Use critical reading skills (see 5b) to sort major information from minor information as it relates to your topic. Do not get bogged down in unimportant details. At the same time, do not overlook important material. Try for a reasonable balance.

When you begin, if you have only a general sense of your topic, read and take notes widely. Stay alert for ways to narrow your topic. Use your research log to keep track of your thoughts—ideas tend to pop in and out of mind during a selection process. Topic narrowing takes time and patience (for advice, see 32b). Do not get discouraged. All researchers cast about at first. Once you have narrowed your subject, takes notes focused within the boundaries of your choice.

The third decision in the notetaking process concerns the form of your notes. **You must use procedures that prevent plagiarism.** This matter is so important that Chapter 31 is devoted to avoiding plagiarism and to the skills of paraphrasing, summarizing, and quoting. To plagiarize is to steal someone else's words and pass them off as your own. To avoid the risk of plagiarism, take notes in such a way that you will always be able to tell from your notes what is yours and what belongs to a source. You might want to use one color ink for your thoughts and ideas and another color ink for words that are paraphrases, summaries, or quotations.

To take notes, use index cards. You can write more on a 4 × 6″ than on a 3 × 5″ card. Cards, in contrast to pages in a notebook, provide flexibility for organizing information to write your paper.

EXTRA EXERCISE A

To practice methods of preventing unconscious plagiarism, paraphrase or summarize the following paragraphs.

(1) Jane Austen, an English novelist, was born in 1775 the daughter of the Reverend George Austen, rector of Steventon and Deane, and Cassandra Leigh Austen. She was the youngest of seven children. Her childhood at Steventon was quiet, domestic, and moderately studious. Much of her spare time was spent in writing, mostly for her own amusement. In 1801 the family moved to Bath. After the death of her father in 1805, she settled in Chawton, where she remained until shortly before her death.

(2) Jane Austen began writing stories at an early age, and by the time she was twenty-two had completed one of her best known novels, *Pride and Prejudice.* Other works for which she is remembered include *Sense and Sensibility* and *Northanger Abbey,* which was published by her family after her death. The novels were not especially popular in Jane Austen's lifetime, but today are regarded as among the best novels in the English language. Although her people are neither intellectual nor heroic, and her plots are not elaborate, her skill at storytelling and drawing characters continues to please her readers.

(3) On the map, Mexico resembles a great funnel, or rather, a cornucopia, with its widest part towards the north and its smallest end twisting to the south and east, meeting there the sudden expansion of the Maya area. There are few regions in the world with such a diverse geography as we find within this area—Mexico is not one, but many countries. All the climatic extremes of our globe are found, from arctic cold near the summits of the highest volcanoes to the

(continued next page)

Turkish-bath atmosphere of the coastal jungle. Merely to pass from one valley to another is to enter a markedly different ecological zone.

—Michael D. Coe, *Mexico,* p. 12

(4) In 1773 we know that [Francisco] Goya was in Madrid, where he married Josefa Bayeu, the sister of the painter who had introduced him into Madrid society. His first important chance was a commission for a series of cartoons for tapestries, which Mengs (possibly advised by Bayeu, who had acquired a certain reputation and had become part of a group of young academic painters, which included his brothers) commissioned for the Royal Tapestry Factory at Santa Barbara. It was an important opportunity because it meant that Goya was admitted to court circles; in addition this kind of work allowed him great freedom in his choice of subject matter and of technique. Perhaps most important of all, the sketchy nature of the cartoon medium spared Goya the necessity of "finishing" his work. His style was slow to mature; until now he had displayed a dextrous hand but had shown no signs of genius.

—Margherita Abbaruzzese, *Goya,* p. 5

One of the skills of research is knowing when you have enough information; in considering too many side issues or too many perspectives, you may lose the main thread of your subject.

—Charles Bazerman, *The Informed Writer*

A Note Card Summarizing a Source

Never put notes from more than one source on the same index card. If your notes on a source require more than one index card, number the cards sequentially. (For example, if you use the labels "1 of 2" and "2 of 2" for two cards, you will know each card's number and the total number of cards on that one source in your records.) If you take notes on more than one idea or topic from a particular source, start a new card for each new area of information. Head each index card with identifying information that clearly relates to one of your bibliographic cards. Include the source's title and the number of the page or pages from which you are taking notes. Also, clearly identify the *type* of note on the card: paraphrase, summary, or quotation. Think of note cards as one half of a set of cards—the second half is the bibliographic card (see 33a). Without bibliographic information you cannot write parenthetical references or a final bibliography. A note card written by Amy Brown, the student whose paper is in Chapter 34, is shown above.

Photocopying can save you time if you want a word-for-word record of a source. Photocopying, however, can be a seductive trap for researchers. It is a waste of time and money to photocopy everything you come across. Write your paraphrases and summaries as you go along. When you do photocopy, always mark the paper with (1) identifying information and (2) notations about what you consider important and why. Do not merely pile up stacks of photocopies without any record of your thought processes. A photocopy Amy Brown made and annotated is shown on the opposite page.

Sommer, p. 26

The best way to learn the location of invisible boundaries is to keep walking until somebody complains. Personal space refers to an area with invisible boundaries surrounding a person's body into which intruders may not come. [Like the porcupines in Schopenhauer's fable, people like to be close enough to obtain warmth and comradeship but far enough away to avoid pricking one another. Personal space ~~is not necessarily spherical in shape, nor does it extend equally in all directions. (People are able to tolerate closer presence of a stranger at their sides than directly in front.) It~~ has been likened to a snail shell, a soap bubble, an aura, and "breathing room."] There are major differences between cultures in the distances that people maintain—Englishmen keep further apart than Frenchmen or South Americans. Reports

I'll paraphrase this

I'll quote this with ellipses

Photocopy of Source, with Annotations

TEACHING TIP

Assigning a group a single topic for research using three or four specified sources can result in some interesting differences in the information that is selected for notes and the information that is rejected. You may want to ask students to bring their notes to class for comparison with those taken by their fellow students. The comparison will be even more interesting if the student-researchers keep a complete record of their research in their logs, recording the title and location of any book or article not used, with a note as to why it was rejected.

32k Drafting a thesis statement

Drafting a **thesis statement** for a research paper is the beginning of the transition between the research process and the writing process. A thesis statement in a research paper is like the thesis statement in any essay: it tells the central theme. (Thesis statements are discussed thoroughly in 2e; a chart listing the basic requirements for a thesis statement appears there.) Any paper must fulfill the promise of its thesis statement. Because readers expect unified material, the theme of the thesis must be sustained throughout a research paper.

Most researchers draft a **preliminary thesis statement** before or during their research process. They expect that they will revise the thesis somewhat after their research, because they know that the sources they will consult will enlarge their knowledge of a subject. Still, these researchers find that a preliminary version of a thesis statement serves as a helpful focus while they search for sources. Other researchers draft a thesis statement after the research process.

No matter at what point you draft your thesis statement, expect to write many alternatives. Your goal is to draft the thesis carefully so that it delivers the message you intend. In writing any **revised thesis statement,** take charge of your material. Reread your research log. Reread your notes. Look for categories of information. Rearrange your note cards into logical groupings. Begin to impose a structure on your material.

Amy Brown, whose research paper appears in Chapter 34, drafted two different preliminary thesis statements before she composed one that worked well with her material.

EXTRA EXERCISE B

For each of the following subjects devise a narrowed topic, then a research question, followed by a thesis statement, noting its purpose.

1. Fishing
2. Large families
3. Retirement communities
4. Competitive swimming
5. Study habits
6. Current styles
7. Contemporary American novels
8. Horse racing
9. Professional football
10. Diets

QUOTATION ABOUT RESEARCH

Research is the ability to investigate systematically and truly all that comes under your observation in life.

—Marcus Aurelius

QUOTATION ABOUT RESEARCH

. . . You should always collect more material than you will eventually use. Every article is strong in proportion to the surplus of details from which you can choose the few that will serve you best—if you don't go on gathering facts forever. At some point you must decide to stop researching and start writing.

—William Zinsser, *On Writing Well*

FIRST PRELIMINARY VERSION	Standards for personal space vary among cultures.
NEXT PRELIMINARY VERSION	These different norms can lead to intercultural misunderstandings when people from different countries come together unaware of how their expectations concerning interpersonal distances can affect their reactions to each other.
FINAL VERSION	Everyone has expectations concerning the use of personal space, but accepted distances for that space are determined by each person's culture.

Brown knew that the first version of her thesis statement was too broad. Still, she used it as she wrote the first draft of her paper because she knew she would revise it once she saw how the material from her research would come together in her paper. Brown wrote the second version of her thesis statement in the middle of her revising process, after she had written a few drafts of her paper. She immediately saw that her second version was wordy and complicated. She composed her final thesis statement after she put her drafts aside for a few days and got some distance from her material.

In addition to presenting the central theme of a paper, a thesis statement reflects a writing purpose—*to inform* or *to persuade* (see 32b). Also, a thesis statement implies the amount of expertise in the subject expected from an audience. For example, when writing for people who likely have little background about your topic, your thesis cannot be too technical. As you revise your thesis statement, go back to the research question that guided your research process. Your thesis statement should be one answer to the question. Here are examples of subjects narrowed to topics, then focused into research questions, and then cast as thesis statements. The thesis statements are written on the assumption of a nonspecialist audience.

SUBJECT	*Rain forests*
TOPIC	The importance of rain forests
RESEARCH QUESTION	What is the importance of rain forests?
THESIS STATEMENT (informative)	Rain forests provide the human race with many resources.
THESIS STATEMENT (persuasive)	Rain forests must be preserved because they offer the human race many irreplaceable resources.

SUBJECT	*Nonverbal communication*
TOPIC	Personal space
RESEARCH QUESTION	How do standards for personal space differ among cultures?
THESIS STATEMENT (informative)	Everyone has expectations concerning the use of personal space, but accepted distances for that space are determined by each person's culture.
THESIS STATEMENT (persuasive)	To prevent intercultural misunderstandings, people must be aware of cultural differences in standards for personal space.

SUBJECT	*Smoking*
TOPIC	Curing nicotine addiction
RESEARCH QUESTION	Are new approaches being used to cure nicotine addiction?
THESIS STATEMENT (informative)	Some approaches to curing nicotine addiction are themselves addictive.
THESIS STATEMENT (persuasive)	Because some methods of curing addiction are themselves addictive, doctors should prescribe them with caution.

SUBJECT	*College entrance requirements*
TOPIC	College Board examinations
RESEARCH QUESTION	What weight do college admissions officers place on College Board examinations?
THESIS STATEMENT (informative)	Many colleges no longer require students to submit College Board scores with their applications for admissions.
THESIS STATEMENT (persuasive)	Because College Board examination questions do not accurately predict the success or failure of many students, all colleges and universities should make submission of scores optional.

QUOTATION ABOUT RESEARCH

The process of doing research is not dissimilar from the process of writing anything else. It starts with a question, a problem, a topic which the writer examines, probes, and analyzes. The difference is that the writer is not alone in this game. When doing research, the writer participates with others who have also been taken with the subject.

—Ann Sullivan

QUOTATION ABOUT RESEARCH

Research means to give each and every element its final value by grouping it in the unity of an organized whole.

—Pierre T. DeChardin

As you draft a thesis statement, remember that one of your major responsibilities in a research paper is to support the thesis. Be sure that the material gathered during the research process offers effective support. If it does not, revise your thesis statement, or conduct further research, or both.

Composing a formal outline of an article read by the entire class can be either a small group activity or a whole class activity. It will not only provide practice for students in following formal outline form, but it will also help them, through discussion, to improve their ability to distinguish between major ideas, subordinate ideas, and supporting details.

321   Outlining a research paper

In thinking about outlining, you might want to review the discussion of outlining in 2e-5.

To organize your material, you can make an **informal outline.** Look over your note cards and group them into piles of related information. If the content of one note relates to more than one category, make a new card that contains the material so that each topic's pile of cards will be complete.

Make a list of the categories of information represented by the piles. Then look over the list to see if material needs to be regrouped. During this process, you might find that you lack sufficient material for some categories. If so, go back to your sources or research new sources to fill in what you need. Once you feel comfortable with your list, look within each pile for subcategories of information. Group the subcategories. List them and regroup as needed.

Your instructor may ask you to submit a **formal outline** with your research paper. Writing a formal outline before drafting helps some people plan. Writing a formal outline after drafting helps some people check a paper's organization. Do the main ideas clearly relate to each other? Do the subordinate ideas offer support clearly connected to their main ideas?

A formal outline is headed with the paper's thesis statement. It can be a **topic outline,** a format that requires words or phrases for each item. It can be a **sentence outline,** a format that requires full sentences for each item. It cannot be a mixture of the two types. See Chapter 34 for a sentence outline of Amy Brown's research paper on personal space. A sentence outline has the advantage of having complete thoughts in its items. A reader can tell not only what topics are covered but also what is said about those topics.

A formal outline uses rankings for levels of information. It goes into detail according to the material it covers. If you outline only main and subordinate ideas, your outline has entries for Roman numeral and capital letters. If you go into more detail, your outline includes lower-case letters. Follow one important principle: subdivide information only when you have at least two entries to make.

    I. Main idea
      A. Subordinate idea
      B. Subordinate idea
        1. Example of subordinate idea
        2. Example of subordinate idea
          a. Supporting detail
          b. Supporting detail
   II. Main idea

32m   Drafting and revising your research paper

Drafting and revising a research paper have much in common with the writing processes for writing any type of paper. (See Chapters 2 and 3.) But more is demanded. You must demonstrate that you have followed the research steps in this chapter. You must demonstrate an understanding of the information you have located. You must organize for effective presentation. You must integrate sources into your writing without plagiarizing, by properly using the techniques of paraphrase, summary, and quotation described in Chapter 31. And you must use parenthetical references (33b) to document your sources. These special demands take extra time for drafting, thinking, redrafting, and rethinking.

Expect to write a number of drafts of your research paper. Successive drafts help you to gain authority over the information you

---

SUGGESTIONS FOR DRAFTING A RESEARCH PAPER

1. Some researchers work with their notes in front of them. They use the organized piles made for drafting a thesis statement (32h) and for outlining (32i). They spread out each pile and work according to the categories of information that have emerged from their material. They proceed from one pile to the next. They expect this process to take time, but they are assured of a first draft that includes much of the results of their research.

2. Some researchers gather all their information and then set it aside to write a **partial first draft,** a quickly written first pass at getting the material under control. Writing this way helps researchers get a broad view of the material. The second step is to go back and write a **complete first draft** with research notes at hand. The researchers go over their partial draft slowly to correct information, add material left out, and—most important—insert parenthetical references (33b).

3. Some researchers write their first draft quickly to get words down on paper when they feel "stuck" about what to say next. When they have a clear idea of how to proceed, they slow down and use their notes. Also, the researchers draw on their experiences with gathering ideas (2d), shaping ideas (2e), getting started (3a), and drafting (3b).

TEACHING TIP

As the processes of drafting and revising vary from one writer to another, students may gain insight into their own processes by interviewing each other about how they approach these stages of writing a research paper. They can base their interviews on the following questions.

1. Do you organize your note cards in piles?

2. Do you work with your notes in front of you?

3. Do you write the first draft without referring to your note cards?

4. Is your first draft a complete draft?

5. When do you insert parenthetical references?

6. Is your first draft composed slowly and carefully? Or quickly and sketchily?

7. Do you proceed immediately to a second draft, or do you let some time elapse between drafting and revising?

8. Do you show your work to other people for responses and suggestions?

32m

QUOTATION ABOUT RESEARCH

A research paper is not a list of findings; it is the coherent communication of a meaningful pattern of information.

—Richard M. Coe, *Form and Substance*

learn from your research. The **first draft** is your initial attempt to structure your notes into a unified whole. It is also a chance to discover new insights and fresh connections. Only the act of writing makes such discovery possible. A first draft is a rough draft. It is a prelude to later work at revising and polishing. Here are some alternative ways to write the first draft of a research paper.

Your **second and subsequent drafts** are the results of reading your first draft critically and revising it. If at all possible, get some distance from your material by taking a break of a few days (or a few hours, if you are pressed for time). Then, reread your first draft and get a fresh look at it. Think how it can be improved. You also might ask friends or classmates to read it and react.

Some researchers photocopy their first drafts and cut up the paper to move paragraphs and sentences around. If a new order suggests itself, the researchers tape the paper together in its new form.

As you work, pay attention to any uneasy feelings you have that hint at the need to rethink or rework your material. Experienced writers expect to revise; they know that writing is really rewriting. Research papers are among the most demanding composing assignments, and most writers have to revise their drafts more than a few times. As you revise, consult the Revision Checklists in 3c to remind yourself of general principles of writing. Also, consult the special

TEACHING TIP

Using the Revision Checklists in 3c and their own previously written and marked papers, students can devise individualized checklists for themselves to serve as reminders of their own problem areas. If, for example, they consistently leave the *-s* off third person singular verbs, they should make that instance an item to be checked during the editing stage. Compiling such a checklist not only provides students with an efficient means of self-editing, it also makes them more conscious of where they need to exercise the greatest concern about mechanics.

REVISION CHECKLIST FOR A RESEARCH PAPER

1. Does the introductory paragraph lead effectively into the material (see 4e-1)?
2. Are you fulfilling the promise of the thesis statement?
3. Do the ideas follow from one another?
4. Do you stay on the topic?
5. Are important questions answered?
6. Do you avoid bogging down the paper with irrelevent or insignificant information?
7. Do you avoid leaving gaps in information?
8. Have you integrated source material without plagiarizing?
9. Have you used paraphrases, summaries, and quotations well?
10. Does the concluding paragraph end the material effectively (see 4e-2)?

revision checklist here for a research paper. If the answer to any question asked in the list is "no," revise your draft.

The **final draft** shows that you have revised well. It shows also that you have edited and proofread for correct grammar, spelling, and punctuation. No amount of careful research and good writing can make up for a sloppy manuscript. Strive to make the paper easy to read. If any page is messy with corrections, retype it. If your instructor accepts handwritten papers, use ruled white paper that has *not* been torn out of a spiral notebook. (If at all possible, however, type your work because it will present itself better.) Use black or blue ink and write very legibly.

For an example of the writing process in action for research writing, and for a sample research paper, see Chapter 34.

33 Documenting Sources for Research Writing

When you write a research paper, you always have to **document** your sources. This involves creating a working bibliography on cards (33a) so that you can keep careful track of all the sources you take notes on. In your research paper itself, you are expected to document your sources in two separate but equally important ways.

1. Within the body of the paper, use **parenthetical references** (33b). Some courses might require endnotes or footnotes instead of parenthetical references (33e).

2. At the end of the paper, provide a **list of sources** (33c and 33d).

Two documentation styles are featured in this chapter. The most frequently used style in the humanities was developed by the Modern Language Association (MLA). Another style used in some humanities and most social sciences was developed by the American Psychological Association (APA). The MLA style and APA style for parenthetical references are given in 33b. The MLA style and APA style for listing sources are given in 33c and 33d. Content notes are explained in 33e. Use *only* MLA style, *only* APA style, or *only* a different style required by your instructor. Never mix documentation styles.

If you are expected to use a note style (footnotes or endnotes) of documentation, consult 33f. If you are documenting a research paper in the natural or technological sciences, consult 33g. Always ask your instructor what documentation style you are expected to use in a research paper.

33a Creating a working bibliography

To create a working bibliography, write out a bibliographic card for every source you take notes on. (*Bibliography* literally means "description of books.") Include on each card all the bibliographic information you need to fulfill the requirements of the documentation style you are using. Also, for each card on a library source, write the call number in the upper lefthand corner, being careful to copy it exactly. When the time comes to compile a final list of sources for your research paper, you can easily arrange bibliographic cards in correct order. Two bibliographic cards are shown here, one for a book and one for an article. They are by Amy Brown, the student whose research paper appears in Chapter 34.

HM
285
H3

Hall, Edward J. *The Hidden Dimension.* New York: Doubleday, 1969.

Martin, Judith. "Here's Looking at You." *Newsday* 27 Jan. 1981, Section 2: 9–13.

WORD HISTORY

According to the *Oxford English Dictionary, bibliography* comes from the Greek word meaning *book writing.* In the sense that we use the word with undergraduate students (a list of the books of a particular author or publisher, or those in a particular subject), it is relatively new, going back just to 1869. However, the word earlier meant *the writing of books* (1678). In the early 19th century, *bibliography* was first used to refer to "the systematic description and history of books, their authorship, printing, publication, editions, etc." or a book about such matters.

BACKGROUND

Nicolás Antonio (1617–1684) is credited with the creation of modern bibliography and the shaping of literary history into a scholarly discipline. His *Bibliotheca Hispana* is an index in Latin of Old World and New World Spanish writers after 1500. It also contains a history of earlier Spanish literature.

BACKGROUND

The term *bibliography* is derived from two Greek roots. The first is *biblia,* the plural form of the word meaning book or papyrus, so named after the Phoenician city *Byblos* (now Jubayl) from which papyrus was exported. The second is *graphos,* meaning *to write.* Thus the word *bibliography* has come to mean a written description of books including details of authorship, editions, dates, perhaps even typography. More strictly, it refers to a list of the works of an author, or of the literature bearing on a particular subject. *Biblia* has been responsible for many words in the English language dealing with books. For example, a *biblioclast* is a destroyer of books, and *bibliognost* refers to one who is knowledgeable about books. A *bibliolater* is a lover of books. A *bibliopegist* is a bookbinder.

639

EXTRA EXERCISE A

Devise parenthetical references for the following paraphrase, summary, and quotation. The source is provided at the end of each selection.

1. "If indeed we note in his [Thomas Carlyle's] writings those passages in which the words and rhythms are most resonant, and the accent falls with the strongest emphasis, we shall find they are the expression of the cosmic wonder and terror which formed the darkly flaming background of all his thoughts." (Logan Pearsall Smith, "Thomas Carlyle: The Rembrandt of English Prose," *Reperusals and Re-Collections,* Harcourt, Brace and Company, Inc., 1936, p. 115.)

2. Ethologists study the traits that distinguish a group—a group of people or a group of animals. They try to discover how the group usually acts by observing its members in their natural surroundings, and to understand their behavior by testing it, when possible, in the laboratory. (Sally Carrighar, "Ethology," from *Wild Heritage,* Houghton Mifflin Company, 1965, pp. 174–175.)

3. May Sarton, who now lives in Maine, is the author of over forty books of poetry, fiction, journals, and memoirs. Since her first book of poetry appeared in 1937, and her first novel the year following, she has been known to the reading public as one who explores the solitary life and different forms of female creativity. She has been an influential figure in the Women's Movement. (Karen Saum, "May Sarton, *Writers at Work,* ed. George Plimpton, Viking Penguin Inc., p. 71.)

As you organize and write your paper, you may find that you have not drawn on certain sources at all, even though you took notes on them. In MLA documentation and in APA documentation, list only the sources you mention in your paper. In MLA style, the list is called Works Cited; in APA style, the list is called References. If you are *not* using either MLA or APA documentation, ask your instructor whether your source list should include all the sources you consult or only sources you refer to.

33b Documenting sources with parenthetical references

As you draft and revise your research paper, be sure to use **parenthetical references.** The purpose of parenthetical references is to lead your readers to the sources for your paraphrases (see 31c), summaries (see 31d), and quotations (see 31e). In the past, you may have used footnotes or endnotes to document your sources, but current practice in some of the humanities and most of the social sciences calls for parenthetical references. When you need to use footnotes or endnotes, refer to section 33f.

Make parenthetical references brief and accurate. When you are deciding what information to include in a reference, you need to consider what information about the source already appears in the sentence or the immediate context.

For illustrations and explanations of parenthetical references, consult section 33b-1 if you are using MLA style and section 33b-2 if you are using APA style.

FUNCTIONS OF PARENTHETICAL REFERENCES WITHIN A PAPER

1. They signal places in your paper where you have paraphrased, summarized, or quoted material from another source.
2. They say exactly where that material is located in the source.
3. They give information enabling a reader to find the source in the list of sources that appears at the end of your paper. (This list is called Works Cited in MLA documentation style and References in APA documentation style.)

1   Understanding the MLA system of parenthetical references

Paraphrased, summarized, and quoted material requires documentation in MLA style. MLA parenthetical references direct a reader to the full citation list on a separate page called Works Cited at the end of a paper.

In the first example below, the author's name and the page number appear in parentheses. The author's name, which a reader needs to find an entry for the Works Cited list, is presented in parentheses because it does not appear elsewhere in the sentence. No punctuation separates the author's name from the page number. In the second example, the author's name is mentioned in the sentence, so only the page number appears in parentheses. In the third example, the author's name and the title of the work appear in the sentence, so only the page number is given in parentheses.

PARAPHRASE

```
People from the Mediterranean prefer an elbow-to-shoulder
distance (Morris 131).
```

```
Desmond Morris notes that people from the Mediterranean prefer
an elbow-to-shoulder distance (131).
```

```
In Manwatching: A Field Guide to Human Behavior, Desmond
Morris notes that people from the Mediterranean prefer
an elbow-to-shoulder distance (131).
```

When you quote fewer than four handwritten or typewritten lines, you integrate the quoted material into your own sentence.

SHORT QUOTATIONS

```
Personal space "moves with us, expanding and contracting
according to the situation in which we find ourselves" (Fisher,
Bell, and Baum 149).
```

```
Hall explains the practicality of close conversational distance,
noting that "If you are interested in something, your pupils
dilate; if I say something you don't like, they tend to
contract" (47), an observation that explains why people of some
cultures speak standing so near to each other.
```

BACKGROUND

Copyright is the term used to refer to a group of exclusive rights given for limited times to the authors or owners of original literary, dramatic, artistic, or musical writings. It includes the exclusive right to copy an author's work and to prevent others from doing so without permission. It also allows the owner to translate a work, to dramatize or arrange it, and to change it into other versions.

To be granted a copyright, a work must be original, but merit and aesthetic quality are of no importance. The law specifies several classes of works that can receive copyright protection. They include books, periodicals, musical compositions, dramatic works, motion pictures, works prepared for oral delivery, maps and other scientific or technical works, photographs, works of art, works of the graphic arts, and commercial prints and labels. Words, names, titles, slogans, and catch phrases cannot be copyrighted.

QUOTATION ABOUT WRITING

l'écrivain original n'est pas celui qui n'imite personne, mais celui que personne ne peut imiter.

An original writer is not one who imitates no one, but one whom no one can imitate.

—François-René de Chateaubriand

Note that documentation for quotations is handled as it is for paraphrases and summaries. You must give your reader enough information to locate the full source from which you quote in your Works Cited list. The first example gives the authors' names and page number in parentheses, with no punctuation separating them. The second example gives only the page number in parentheses because the author's name is mentioned in the sentence. Placing the page reference immediately after the quotation signals that the rest of the sentence consists of the words and ideas of the writer of the research paper.

When you quote more than four handwritten or typewritten lines, you set the quoted material off from your own writing by indenting it ten spaces from the left margin. Do not put quotation marks around an indented quotation.

LONG QUOTATION

```
Robert Sommer, an environmental psychologist, uses literary and
personal analogies to describe personal space:
          Like the porcupines in Schopenhauer's fable, people
          like to be close enough to obtain warmth and
          comradeship but far enough away to avoid pricking one
          another.  Personal space . . . has been likened to a
          snail shell, a soap bubble, an aura, and "breathing
          room." (26)
```

The reference is in parentheses at the end of the quotation and *after* the final period. Because the author's name is in the sentence that introduces the quotation, only the page number is given in the parenthetical reference. (See 31e-4 for a discussion of how to work quotations smoothly into your own prose.)

Some references are not as straightforward as these examples, however. Here are some additional examples of parenthetical references in MLA style. To avoid lengthy parenthetical references, get in the habit of putting reference information into your sentence. Whether you put documentation information in a parenthetical reference or a sentence, remember that your reader must be able to find an entry in the Works Cited list for each reference to a source in your paper. The following cases discuss format and methods for handling parenthetical references within a paper.

Work by one author—MLA

The examples above illustrate parenthetical references to a work by one author.

Work by two or more authors—MLA

If you use a source written by more than one author, you have the option of providing the names and page number in the parenthetical reference—(Leghorn and Parker 115)—or providing the names in the sentence itself, followed by just the page number in parentheses. If a book is by two or three authors, you must give all the names. If a book is by more than three authors, you can use the first author's name plus *et al.* either in the parenthetical reference—(Moore et al. 275)—or in the sentence.

One author with two or more works—MLA

If you use two sources by the same author, when you refer to one of the sources, supply the author's last name, an abbreviated title of the work, and the relevant page numbers—(Morris, Manwatching 95). Notice that a comma separates the author and underlined title, but no punctuation separates the title and page number. To shorten the parenthetical reference, use the author's name and the title of the work in your sentence and give only the page number in parentheses.

Two or more authors with the same last name—MLA

If you use sources that include works by different authors with the same name, you must supply the author's first and last names—(Charles G. Morris 516). Notice that no comma separates the author from the page numbers. To shorten the parenthetical reference, you can include the author's complete name in your sentence and give only the page numbers in parentheses.

Corporate author—MLA

If the author of a source is the name of the corporation, a parenthetical reference might use the corporate author's name and relevant page number—(Boston Women's Health Collective 11). Whenever possible, incorporate long names in your sentence to avoid a long parenthetical reference. The parentheses would then contain only the page number.

Work cited by title—MLA

If you use a source with no author given, substitute the title or abbreviated title for the author's name in the parenthetical reference—(Chicago 305)—or in the text itself. Notice that the title is underlined. If you use a shortened version of the title, be sure it starts with the word by which you alphabetize the source in your Works Cited list.

TEACHING TIP

Because dealing with methods of documentation is tedious stuff for many students, working in groups can alleviate some of the frustration that they feel. Initially a class can work as a whole, with one or two people recording choices on the chalkboard. Later, small groups can work on documentation exercises in parenthetical documentation, footnoting, or preparation of lists of Works Cited or References.

BACKGROUND

Until the middle of the fifteenth century, the only books available to Europeans were handwritten manuscripts, which were costly and often inaccurate. The development of printing made books available to the common people for the first time.

The major breakthrough in the history of printing was the invention of movable type, the making of a stamp for each letter on a separate base so that the letters could be assembled to form a page. Although this system was already known in China and Korea (where it was little used because of the large number of Chinese characters and the lack of suitable ink), its discovery in Europe was made independently. Credit for the European development is given to Johann Gutenberg (c. 1400–1468). Although his "Gutenberg Bible," printed in 1455, was not his first printed work, it is his most famous one.

Today it is often remarked that the world is going through another printing revolution. With the availability of copying machines, memory typewriters, word processing computer programs, and a variety of desktop printers, methods of producing printed material have undergone another major shift. Whereas only a few years ago having a document printed meant handing it over to a professional printer, today it is likely to be produced on equipment readily available in most offices and many homes.

BACKGROUND

As commonly used, the term *bibliography* sometimes refers to a science, sometimes to an art, or sometimes to the product of the art. As a science, it is an organized body of knowledge dealing with all aspects of books, both as physical objects and as the expression of ideas. Bibliography as an art consists of the techniques for finding, organizing, and presenting information about books. The bibliography that is produced by that art is a systematic listing of books which share common characteristics.

Originally a Greek term, the word did not receive wide usage in Latin until the seventeenth century when it came to mean writing *about* books, as opposed to the writing *of* books, as the Greek usage had indicated. At that time it began to replace such words as *catalogus* and *bibliotheca* in the titles of bibliographies, the making of which became increasingly important as bibliographers struggled to devise some type of organization for keeping track of the flood of publications produced by the invention of printing. Nevertheless, the term *bibliography* was not included in Samuel Johnson's dictionary of 1755, and was not found in the *Encyclopaedia Britannica* until its third edition in 1797.

Today the objectives of bibliography may be analytical or systematic. Analytic bibliography tries to discover information about authorship, publication, and derivation of a text. Systematic bibliography, on the other hand, produces systematic lists of books. The result is many different kinds of bibliographies. For example, they may be critical (critically appraising the books they list), current or retrospective, comprehensive or selective, annotated or not, enumerative (presenting an inventory) or subject oriented (presenting content). In all their varied forms, they provide the modern researcher with invaluable assistance in finding out where to look to learn what is already known about a subject.

Multivolume work—MLA

Suppose you have used both volumes of a work by John Herman Randall, Jr. To cite a reference from one volume, indicate the volume number as well as the page number in the parenthetical reference—(Randall 1:64). Notice that a colon and a space separate the volume number and the page number. If the entry in the Works Cited list refers only to one volume of a multivolume work, give only the page number, not volume number too, in the parenthetical citation—(Ernest 130). If you include the author's name in your sentence, supply only the page number, or the volume and page number, in the parenthetical reference.

Literary work—MLA

If you use an edition of a classic novel, play, or poem, give more information than a page reference. (Readers might be using other editions.) For prose works, in addition to a page number to your edition, give additional information about parts, sections, or chapters—(3; pt. 1, ch. 1). Notice that a semicolon separates the page number from other information. Use standard abbreviations, such as *pt.* (part); *sec.* (section); and *ch.* (chapter). For classic verse, plays, and poems, the MLA recommends that you omit page references altogether and cite divisions (canto, book, part, act, or scene and line), using periods to separate the various numbers: (King Lear 4.1.5–6). This means act 4, scene 1, lines 5–6 of Shakespeare's *King Lear.* Some instructors still prefer roman numerals for citing acts and scenes—(King Lear IV.i).

One-page work—MLA

If you use a work that is only one page long, such as a short newspaper or magazine article, you can omit the page number in the parenthetical reference—("Hospitals"), though you must include the page number in the Works Cited list. The title is in quotation marks, not underlined, because it is a short work. If you include the work's author and title in your sentence, no parenthetical reference is needed.

Reference to more than one source—MLA

If more than one source has contributed to an idea or opinion in your paper, acknowledge multiple sources by putting all necessary information for each source in the parenthetical reference. Separate the sources with a semicolon—(Morris, Intimate 193; Mead 33).

Article in a book—MLA

If you use an article that appears in an edited book, give the name of the author of the article, not the editor of the book. If you were quoting from Ernesto Galarza's "The Roots of Migration," which appears in a book edited by Luis Valdez and Stan Steiner, you would use the following citation form: (Galarza 127).

An indirect source—MLA

If you are quoting an author who has been quoted by another author, indicate both names: (Cather qtd. in McClave). This form tells the reader that you are quoting the words of Willa Cather, that you found them in McClave's work, and that the Works Cited entry is in McClave's name.

2 | Understanding the APA system of parenthetical references

Paraphrased, summarized, and quoted material requires documentation in the APA style of documentation. APA parenthetical references direct a reader to the full citation, listed on a separate page called References at the end of a paper.

In the APA system, any quotation shorter than forty words is considered short, and any quotation forty words or longer is considered long. Integrate short quotations into your own material. (Section 31e-4 discusses how to work quotations smoothly into your own writing.) Long quotations are set off, indented five spaces from the left margin.

When you quote material, always include the page number with *p.* for one page or *pp.* for more than one page. Give the page number immediately after the end of the quotation, even in mid-sentence. If you do not mention the name of the author or the year in your sentence, include all three pieces of information in the parenthetical reference—(Morris, 1977, p. 131). Use a comma after the author and after the year. If your sentence includes the author's name, give the year of publication immediately after the name, even if the page number falls at a different place in the sentence—Morris (1977) found "elbow-to-shoulder distance" (p. 131) is preferred. If your sentence includes the author's name and the date of publication, then give only the page—(p. 131).

When you paraphrase or summarize material, APA practice is that the writer can decide whether or not to give a page number, depending on whether the reader is likely to want to know the specific location of information. As a student writer, you might be required to give the page number so that your instructor can verify your information. Check with your instructor to find out the requirements in any class that calls for APA documentation style.

If you refer to a work more than once in a paper, give the author and date the first time that you mention the work, and then give only the author in subsequent mentions.

Some references are not as straightforward as these examples, however. Here are some additional examples of parenthetical references in APA style. Whether you put documentation information in a parenthetical reference or a sentence, remember that your reader must be able to find an entry in the References list for each reference to a source in your paper.

Work by one author—APA

The examples above illustrate parenthetical references to a work by one author.

Work by two or more authors—APA

If you are citing a source that has two authors, always use both last names. If the authors' last names appear in your sentence, only the year appears in parentheses. If the authors' last names do not appear in your writing, the reference includes them and the year—(Worchel & Cooper, 1983). Note that APA style permits the use of the ampersand—&—to stand for the word *and*.

If a work has more than two authors but fewer than six authors, use all the authors' last names in the first reference, but use only the last name of the first author followed by et al. for subsequent references. In the actual reference, do not underline any item—(Peat et al., 1987).

If a work has six or more authors, use only the last name of the first author and et al. for each citation.

Author(s) with two or more works—APA

If you use more than one source written in the *same year* by the same author(s), alphabetize the works and assign letters (*a, b,* etc.) to them. Then, use the letters next to the year for works in the References list and in the parenthetical references—(Jones, 1989a).

Two or more authors with the same last name—APA

If you use sources that include works by different authors with the same last name, use first- and middle-name initials in all text citations—(A. J. Jones, 1988).

*Corporate author—*APA

If the author of a source is the name of a corporation, a parenthetical reference usually does not abbreviate the name. An abbreviation can be used, as long as a reader could easily identify the work in your References list—(National Aeronautics and Space Administration [NASA], 1990). Note that brackets enclose the abbreviation. Subsequent citations would have this form: (NASA, 1990).

*Work cited by title—*APA

If you use a source that gives no author, substitute the title or the first two or three words of the title and the year—(Chicago Manual, 1982). The title is underlined because the source is a book. An article title would appear in quotation marks.

*Reference to more than one source—*APA

If more than one source has contributed to an idea or opinion in your paper, cite the sources alphabetically in a single reference and separate them with a semicolon—(Morris, 1977; Worchel & Cooper, 1983).

33c Documenting sources with a list of sources

In MLA documentation style and APA documentation style, you must present a final list of sources. Use *only* MLA style or *only* APA style. Never mix them. In MLA style, the list is called Words Cited. In APA style, the list is called References. Whichever style you follow, the list contains all sources referred to in your paper. The list includes only the sources from which you paraphrase, summarize, or quote. It does not include sources that you consulted but do not refer to in the paper. The list begins on a new page that is numbered sequentially with the rest of your paper. Entries are arranged alphabetically by author name. If the author's name is unknown, the entry is alphabetized by the first significant word of the title (not by *A, An,* or *The*).

In citing books, you may find most of the information you need on the title page or the copyright page (the reverse of the title page). In citing articles, the information you need usually appears on the cover, title page, contents page, or sometimes on the first page of the article.

The MLA documentation style for Works Cited is illustrated and explained in section 33c-1. The APA documentation style for

BACKGROUND

The Bibliographical Society of America was organized at the American Library Association's St. Louis Conference in 1904. It succeeded the Bibliographical Society of Chicago, which had been in existence for the preceding five years. The object of the society is "to promote bibliographical research and to issue bibliographical publications." Its membership is made up of professors, librarians, instructors, rare book dealers, collectors, and other bibliophiles. It is responsible for many publications dealing with published American writing.

EXTRA EXERCISE B

Using the following information, compile a Works Cited list following MLA style.

1. *Abraham Lincoln: The Man Behind the Myths,* by Stephen B. Oates. Harper & Row, Publishers, New York, Cambridge, Philadelphia, San Francisco, London, Mexico City, Sao Paulo, and Sydney, 1984.

2. Barbara W. Tuchman. *Practicing History.* Alfred A. Knopf, Inc. Copyright 1936, 1959, 1966, 1974, 1981. Introduction copyright 1981. New York.

3. *Time's Arrow, Time's Cycle: Myth and Metaphor in the Discovery of Geological Time.* Stephen Jay Gould. Harvard University Press, Cambridge, Massachusetts. 1987.

4. T. C. Smout. *A Century of the Scottish People, 1830–1950.* New Haven and London. 1986, Yale University Press.

5. Thomas J. Peters and Robert H. Waterman, Jr. *In Search of Excellence.* Harper & Row, Publishers, New York, 1982.

6. *The Man Who Mistook His Wife for a Hat, and Other Clinical Tales.* Oliver Sacks. New York. Summit Books. "The Autist Artist." No year of publication listed.

7. *The Rise and Fall of the House of Medici.* 1974. Penguin Books. Christopher Hibbert.

8. *Capote: A Biography.* 1988. Simon & Schuster. Gerald Clarke.

References is illustrated and explained in section 33c-2. Then on the red-bordered pages of 33d is a directory of forms, followed by an example of each form in MLA style and in APA style.

The major differences between MLA style and APA style are summarized in the chart below.

MAJOR DIFFERENCES BETWEEN MLA STYLE AND APA STYLE

■ **FORMAT**

MLA indents the second and subsequent lines five spaces.
APA indents the second and subsequent lines three spaces.

■ **AUTHOR'S NAME**

MLA includes first name and any middle initials.
APA uses initials for first name and any middle initials.

■ **ORDER OF AUTHORS' NAMES FOR MORE THAN ONE AUTHOR**

MLA reverses the order (last name, first name) only for the first name and uses regular order (first name, last name) for all subsequent names.
APA reverses the order (last name, initials) for all names.

■ **THE WORD *and* FOR LISTING MORE THAN ONE AUTHOR**

MLA uses the word *and*.
APA uses the ampersand (&).

■ **YEAR OF PUBLICATION**

MLA gives the year toward the end of the citation.
APA gives the year in parentheses followed by a period immediately after the author name.

■ **CAPITALIZATION IN TITLES**

MLA capitalizes all major words in titles.
APA capitalizes only the first word, a word after a colon, and proper nouns in titles.

■ **QUOTATION MARKS FOR NAMES OF SHORTER WORKS**

MLA uses quotation marks for the names of shorter works.
APA omits quotation marks for names of shorter works.

(continued on next page)

<table>
<tr><td>

MAJOR DIFFERENCES BETWEEN MLA STYLE AND APA STYLE *(cont.)*

■ **CITING A SELECTION IN A LARGER WORK**

MLA gives the name of the selection followed by a period. Then it gives the name of the larger work followed by a period.

APA does the same but uses the word *In* to introduce the name of the larger work.

■ **PUBLISHER**

MLA uses short forms as long as they are clear: *Prentice* for *Prentice Hall.* Also, MLA uses *UP* for *University Press, U* for University, and *P* for *Press.*

APA uses the complete name except it drops words such as *Inc.* and *Publishers.*

■ **INCLUSIVE PAGE NUMBERS**

MLA uses the full second number through 99. Then it uses only the last two digits, unless confusion would result: 103–04 is clear, but the full numbers are needed for 567–602.

APA uses complete numbers.

■ **DISCONTINUOUS PAGES**

MLA uses the plus sign (+) after the first page number: 32 + .

APA lists all pages, with discontinuous numbers set off by commas: 32, 44–45, 47–49, 50.

</td></tr>
</table>

---

1 | **Using MLA documentation style: the Works Cited list**

*Citing books—*MLA

Citations for books have three main parts: author, title, and publication information (place of publication, publisher, and date of publication). Each part is followed by a period and two spaces.

NAME	TITLE	PUBLISHING INFORMATION
Didion, Joan.	Salvador.	New York: Simon, 1983.

Many sources need additional items of information included in the citation. Indent all lines after the first line five spaces.

```
Chester, Laura, and Sharon Barba, eds. Rising Tides:
     Twentieth Century American Women Poets. Intro.
     Anaïs Nin. New York: Simon, 1973.
```

In the title, capitalize all major words. If several cities are listed for the place of publication, give only the first. If a foreign city might be unfamiliar to a reader, add an abbreviation of the Canadian province or country. You can shorten the publisher's name as long as the shortened version is easily identifiable. *(Prentice Hall* can be *Prentice; Oxford University Press* can be *Oxford UP; Simon & Schuster* can be *Simon.)* Give the latest copyright date for the edition you are using. If the book has had several printings (rather than editions), use the original publication date. See 33d for a directory of forms followed by an example of each form in MLA style.

Citing articles—MLA

Citations for articles in periodicals (such as journals, magazines, and newspapers) contain three major parts: author, title of article, and publication information. The publication information usually includes the periodical title, volume number, year of publication, and inclusive page numbers.

Additional information may be required depending on the source. Indent all lines after the first line five spaces. In the citation for an article, each part is followed by a period and two spaces. Within each part, use one space between each word and after punctuation. In the title, capitalize all major words. ❖ NUMBER ALERT: In citing inclusive page numbers, give the second number in full for numbers through 99 (for example, 23–24). For numbers 100 and above, give only the last two digits unless this would create confusion (for example, 103–04 and 2234–67; however, 567–602.) ❖

See 33d for a directory of forms followed by an example of each form in MLA style. If you have further questions about citations using MLA style, consult Joseph Gibaldi and Walter S. Achtert, *MLA Handbook for Writers of Research Papers,* 3rd ed., New York: MLA, 1988.

 2   **Using APA documentation style: the References list**

Citing books—APA

Citations for books have four main parts: author, date, title, and publication information. Indent all lines after the first line three spaces.

NAME	DATE	TITLE	PUBLISHING INFORMATION

Didion, J. (1977). A book of common prayer. New York:

Simon & Schuster.

Give the last name first and then the initial of the first and, if any, middle name. In the title, capitalize only the first word and any word after a colon. If several cities are listed for place of publication, give only the first. If the city might be unfamiliar to a reader, add an abbreviation of the state (use U.S. Postal Service abbreviations), province, or country. Do not use a shortened form of the publisher's name, but you may omit terms such as *Publishers, Co.,* and *Inc.* Give the latest copyright date for the edition you are using.

Citing articles—APA

Citations for articles in periodicals (such as journals, magazines, and newspapers) contain four major parts: author, date, title of article, and publication information. For articles, the publication information usually includes the periodical title, volume number, and inclusive page numbers.

NAME	DATE	ARTICLE TITLE

Shuter, R. (1977). A field study of nonverbal

communication in Germany, Italy, and the United

	PERIODICAL TITLE	VOLUME NUMBER	PAGE NUMBERS

States.   Communication Monographs, 44, 298–305.

In the citation for an article, each part is followed by a period and two spaces. Within each part, use one space between words and after punctuation. In the title, capitalize only the first word and any word after a colon. Additional items of information may be required, depending on the source. ❖ NUMBER ALERT: Use complete inclusive page numbers (for example, 103–104, 344–347, 2334–2367). ❖

If you have further questions about citations using APA style, consult American Psychological Association, *Publication Manual of the American Psychological Association,* 3rd ed., Washington, D.C.: APA, 1984.

33d Using MLA forms or APA forms for list of sources

The following directory presents a numbered list of the forms shown in the examples in this section. The MLA style and the APA style appear together for each pattern so that you can compare them easily. Use *only* MLA style or *only* APA style. Never mix them.

Not every possible documentation model is given. You may find that you have to combine features of more than one model to document a particular source.

DIRECTORY

1. Book by one author
2. Book by two or three authors
3. Book by more than three authors
4. Two or more books by same author(s)
5. Book by group or corporate author
6. Book with no author named
7. Book with an author and an editor
8. Translation
9. Work in several volumes or parts
10. One selection from an anthology or an edited book
11. Two selections from one anthology or an edited book
12. Signed article in a reference book
13. Unsigned article in a reference book
14. Edition
15. Anthology or edited book
16. Introduction, preface, foreword, or afterword
17. Unpublished dissertations or essays

18. Reprint of an older book
19. Books in a series
20. Books with a title within a title
21. Government publication
22. Published proceedings of a conference
23. Article from a daily newspaper
24. Editorial, letter to the editor, review
25. Unsigned article from a daily newspaper
26. Article from a weekly or biweekly magazine or newspaper
27. Article in a monthly or bimonthly periodical
28. Unsigned article from a weekly or monthly periodical
29. Article from a collection of reprinted articles
30. Article in a journal with continuous pagination
31. Article in a journal that pages each issue separately
32. Interview
33. Published and unpublished letters
34. Lectures, speeches, and addresses
35. Films and videotapes
36. Recordings
37. Live performance
38. Works of art or musical composition
39. Radio and television programs
40. Computer software
41. Information services
42. Maps and charts

1. BOOK BY ONE AUTHOR

MLA   Welty, Eudora. <u>One Writer's Beginnings</u>. Cambridge:
Harvard UP, 1984.

APA   Welty, E. (1984). <u>One writer's beginnings</u>. Cambridge:
Harvard University Press.

2. BOOK BY TWO OR THREE AUTHORS

MLA   Leghorn, Lisa, and Katherine Parker. <u>Woman's Worth</u>.
Boston: Routledge, 1981.

MLA   Kelly, Alfred H., Winfred A. Harbison, and Herman Belz.
<u>The American Constitution: Its Origins and
Development</u>. New York: Norton, 1983.

Give only the first author's name in reversed order; give other authors' names in normal order. Use commas to separate authors' names, including a comma before the *and* preceding the last name in the series. Give the names in the order in which they appear on the title page of the book.

APA   Leghorn, L, & Parker, K. (1981). <u>Woman's worth</u>.
             Boston: Routledge & Kegan Paul.

APA   Kelly, A. H., Harbison, W. A., & Belz, H. (1983). <u>The</u>
             <u>American constitution: Its origins and development</u>.
             New York: Norton.

Give each author's name in reversed order. Use initials for first and middle names. Use commas to separate authors' names, including a comma before the ampersand (the symbol &) with more than two authors. Give the names in the order in which they appear on the title page of the book.

3. Book by More than Three Authors

MLA   Moore, Mark H., et al. <u>Dangerous Offenders: The Elusive</u>
             <u>Target of Justice</u>. Cambridge: Harvard UP, 1984.

Give only the first author's name, in reversed order; *et al.* ("and others") indicates that three or more authors wrote the work.

APA   Moore, M. H., Estrich, S., McGillis, D, & Spelman, W.
             (1984). <u>Dangerous offenders: The elusive target of</u>
             <u>justice</u>. Cambridge: Harvard University Press.

Give last names and initials, in reversed order, for all authors, no matter how many.

4. Two or More Books by Same Author(s)

MLA   Morris, Desmond. <u>Manwatching: A Field Guide to Human</u>
             <u>Behavior</u>. New York: Abrams, 1977.
             ---, ed. <u>Primate Ethology</u>. London: Wiedenfeld, 1967.

When citing two or more books by the same author(s), give the name(s) in the first entry only. In the second and subsequent entries, use three hyphens and a period to stand for exactly the same name(s). If the person served as editor or translator, put a comma and the appropriate abbreviation *(ed.* or *trans.)* following the three hyphens. Alphabetize the works listed according to book title, regardless of such labels as *ed.* or *trans.*, and regardless of the chronological order in which they were published.

APA   Morris, Desmond. (1977). <u>Manwatching: A field guide to</u>
            <u>human behavior</u>. New York: Henry N. Abrams.

APA   Morris, Desmond, ed. (1967). <u>Primate ethology</u>.
            London: Wiedenfeld.

Give the author's name in full in all entries.

5. BOOK BY GROUP OR CORPORATE AUTHOR

MLA   The Boston Women's Health Collective. <u>Our Bodies,</u>
            <u>Ourselves</u>. New York: Simon, 1986.

Cite the full name of the corporate author first.

APA   The Boston Women's Health Collective. (1986). <u>Our</u>
            <u>bodies, ourselves</u>. New York: Simon & Schuster.

Cite the full name of the corporate author first. If the author is also
the publisher, use the word *Author* as the name of the publisher.

6. BOOK WITH NO AUTHOR NAMED

MLA   <u>The Chicago Manual of Style</u>. 13th ed. Chicago: U of
            Chicago P, 1982.

If there is no author's name on the title page, begin the citation with
the title. Alphabetize the entry according to the first significant word
of the title (not *A, An,* or *The*).

APA   <u>The Chicago manual of style</u> (13th ed.). (1982).
            Chicago: University of Chicago Press.

If there is no author's name on the title page, begin the citation with
the title. Alphabetize the entry according to the first significant word
of the title (not *A, An,* or *The*).

7. BOOK WITH AN AUTHOR AND AN EDITOR

MLA   Brontë, Emily. <u>Wuthering Heights</u>. Ed. David Daiches.
            London: Penguin, 1985.

MLA   Daiches, David, ed. <u>Wuthering Heights</u>. By Emily
            Brontë. London: Penguin, 1985.

If what you refer to in your paper is the work of the book's author,
begin the citation with the author's name. If you refer instead to the
work of the editor, begin the citation with the editor's name.

APA   Brontë, E. (1985). <u>Wuthering heights</u> (D. Daiches,
            Ed.), London: Penguin.

8. TRANSLATION

> **MLA** Freire, Paulo. <u>Pedagogy of the Oppressed</u>. Trans. Myra
> Bergman Ramos. New York: Seabury, 1970.

> **APA** Freire, P. (1970). <u>Pedagogy of the oppressed</u> (M. B.
> Ramos, Trans.). New York: Seabury Press.

9. WORK IN SEVERAL VOLUMES OR PARTS

> **MLA** Jones, Ernest. <u>The Last Phase</u>. New York: Basic, 1957.
> Vol. 3 of <u>The Life and Work of Sigmund Freud</u>.
> 3 vols.

> **MLA** Randall, John Herman, Jr. <u>The Career of Philosophy</u>.
> 2 vols. New York: Columbia UP, 1962.

If you are citing only one volume of a multivolume work, place this information after the publication date. You may end the entry giving the total number of volumes. MLA recommends using arabic numerals, even if the source uses roman numerals *(Vol. 6* for *Vol. VI).*

  If you have drawn from two or more volumes of a multivolume work, give the total number of volumes.

> **APA** Randall, J. H., Jr. (1962). <u>The career of philosophy</u>
> (Vols. 1–2). New York: Columbia University Press.

10. ONE SELECTION FROM AN ANTHOLOGY OR AN EDITED BOOK

> **MLA** Galarza, Ernest. "The Roots of Migration." <u>Aztlan: An
> Anthology of Mexican American Literature</u>. Eds.
> Luis Valdez and Stan Steiner. New York: Knopf,
> 1972. 127–132.

Give the author and title of the selection first. Place titles of essays, short stories, or short poems in quotation marks. Underline the title of a book or a play. Then give the full title of the anthology. Follow it with the editor(s). Note that the editors' names are preceded by *Eds.* (use *Ed.* for only one editor) and are given with the first name before the last. End the citation with the inclusive page number of the selection; do not use the abbreviation *p.* or *pp.*

> **APA** Galarza, E. (1972). The roots of migration. In L.
> Valdez and S. Steiner (Eds.), <u>Aztlan: An anthology of
> Mexican American literature</u> (pp. 127–132). New York:
> Alfred A. Knopf.

The word *In* introduces the larger work from which the selection is taken.

11. Two Selections From One Anthology or an Edited Book

MLA   Gilbert, Sandra M., and Susan Gubar. <u>The Norton Anthology of Literature by Women</u>. New York: Norton, 1985.

MLA   Kingston, Maxine Hong. "No Name Woman." Gilbert and Gubar 2337-47.

If you cite more than one selection from the same anthology, list the anthology as a separate entry with all the publication information. Also list each selection from the anthology by author and title of the selection, but give only the names of the editor(s) of the anthology and the page number(s) of the selection.

APA   Gilbert, S., & Gubar, S. (1985). <u>The Norton anthology of literature by women</u>. New York: W. W. Norton.

APA   Kingston, M. H. (1985). No name woman. In Gilbert, S., & Gubar, S., <u>The Norton anthology of literature by women</u>. New York: W. W. Norton.

You must provide full reference information for each selection from an anthology (or collection) you cite. Use *In* to show the larger work from which the selection is taken.

12. Signed Article in a Reference Book

MLA   Holt, Robert R. "Freud, Sigmund." <u>International Encyclopedia of the Social Sciences</u>. Ed. David L. Sills. 18 vols. New York: Macmillan, 1968.

If articles are alphabetically arranged in the work, omit the volume and page numbers. If the reference book is frequently revised, give only the edition and year of publication.

APA   Holt, R. R. Freud, Sigmund. In D. L. Sills (Ed.), <u>International encyclopedia of the social sciences</u> (pp 1-11). New York: Macmillan.

The word *In* introduces the larger work from which the selection is taken.

13. Unsigned Article in a Reference Book

MLA   "Ireland." <u>Encyclopaedia Britannica</u>. 1974 ed.

APA   Ireland. (1974). In <u>Encyclopaedia Britannica</u>.

14. EDITION

> **MLA**   Mandell, Maurice I. <u>Advertising</u>. 4th ed. Englewood
> Cliffs: Prentice, 1984.

When a book is not the first edition, the edition number appears on the title page. Place this information between the title and the publication information.

> **APA**   Mandell, M. I. (1984). <u>Advertising</u> (4th ed.).
> Englewood Cliffs, NJ: Prentice Hall.

15. ANTHOLOGY OR EDITED BOOK

> **MLA**   Valdez, Luis, and Stan Steiner, eds. <u>Aztlan: An
> Anthology of Mexican American Literature</u>. New
> York: Knopf, 1972.

> **APA**   Valdez, L., & Steiner, S. (Eds.). (1972). <u>Aztlan: An
> anthology of Mexican American literature</u>. New York:
> Alfred A. Knopf.

16. INTRODUCTION, PREFACE, FOREWORD, OR AFTERWORD

> **MLA**   Boaz, Frank. Introduction. <u>Patterns of Culture</u>. By
> Ruth Benedict. 1934. Boston: Houghton, 1959.

If you are citing an introduction, preface, foreword, or afterword, give its author's name first and then the name of the part cited. Capitalize the first letter of the part cited, but neither underline it nor put it in quotation marks. If the writer of the introduction, preface, foreword, or afterword is different from the author of the book, give the word *By* and the author's full name after the title. Give the inclusive page numbers of the part you are citing after the publication information. Note that such page numbers from a preface or an introduction are in roman numerals, just as they appear in the work.

> **APA**   Boaz, F. (1959). Introduction. In <u>Patterns of culture</u>
> by R. Benedict. Boston: Houghton Mifflin. (Original
> work published 1934)

17. UNPUBLISHED DISSERTATIONS OR ESSAYS

> **MLA**   Geissinger, Shirley Burry. "Openness versus Secrecy in
> Adoptive Parenthood." Diss. U. of North Carolina
> at Greensboro, 1984.

To cite an unpublished dissertation or essay (your own or another person's), state the author's name first, then the title in quotation marks (not underlined), then a descriptive label (such as *Diss.* or

Unpublished essay), then the degree-granting institution (for dissertations), and finally the date.

APA   Geissinger, S. B. (1984) <u>Openness versus secrecy in adoptive parenthood</u>. Unpublished dissertation, University of North Carolina at Greensboro.

18. REPRINT OF AN OLDER BOOK

MLA   Hurston, Zora Neale. <u>Their Eyes Were Watching God</u>. 1937. Urbana: U of Illinois Press, 1978.

A republished book may be the paperback version of a book originally published as a hardbound, or it may be the reissue of a book. Republishing information can be found on the copyright page. Give the date of the original version before the publication information for the version you are citing.

APA   Hurston, Z. N. (1978). <u>Their eyes were watching god</u>. Urbana, IL: University of Illinois Press. (Original work published in 1937)

19. BOOK IN A SERIES

MLA   McClave, Heather. <u>Women Writers of the Short Story</u>. Twentieth Century Views Series. Englewood Cliffs: Prentice, 1980.

APA   McClave, H. (1980). <u>Women writers of the short story</u>. Englewood Cliffs, NJ: Prentice Hall.

20. BOOK WITH A TITLE WITHIN A TITLE

MLA   Lumiansky, Robert M., and Herschel Baker, eds. <u>Critical Approaches to Six Major English Works:</u> Beowulf <u>Through</u> Paradise Lost. Philadelphia: U of Pennsylvania P, 1968.

When a book title includes the title of another work that is usually underlined (such as a novel, play, or long poem), do *not* underline the incorporated title. If the incorporated title is usually enclosed in quotation marks (such as a short story or short poem), keep the quotation marks and underline the complete title of the book.

APA   Lumianksy, R. M., & Baker, H. (Eds.). (1968). <u>Critical approaches to six major English works:</u> Beowulf <u>through</u> Paradise Lost. Philadelphia: University of Pennsylvania Press.

21. GOVERNMENT PUBLICATION

> **MLA**   United States. Cong. House. Committee on the Judiciary.
>
> > Immigration and Nationality with Amendments and
> >
> > Notes on Related Laws. 7th ed. Washington: GPO,
> >
> > 1980.

If a government publication has no stated author, use the government, governmental body, and/or government agency as the author, with periods and two spaces separating the parts. *GPO* is the standard abbreviation for Government Printing Office.

> **APA**   United States Congressional House Committee on the
>
> > Judiciary. (1980). Immigration and nationality with
> >
> > amendments and notes on related laws (7th ed.).
> >
> > Washington, D.C.: U.S. Government Printing Office.

22. PUBLISHED PROCEEDINGS OF A CONFERENCE

> **MLA**   Harris, Diana, and Laurie Nelson-Heern, eds.
>
> > Proceedings of NECC 1981: National Educational
> >
> > Computing Conference. 17-19 June 1981. Iowa City:
> >
> > Weeg Computing Center, U of Iowa, 1981.

> **APA**   Harris, D., & Nelson-Heern, L. (Eds.). (1981).
>
> > Proceedings of NECC 1981: National education
> >
> > computing conference [17-19 June 1981]. Iowa City:
> >
> > Weeg Computing Center, University of Iowa.

23. ARTICLE FROM A DAILY NEWSPAPER

> **MLA**   Dullea, Georgia. "Literary Folk Look for Solid
>
> > Comfort." New York Times 16 April 1986: C14.

Cite the title of the newspaper exactly as it appears on the masthead, omitting any introductory *A* or *The.* If the city of publication is not in the title of the periodical, add it in square brackets after the title, not underlined: for example, Patriot Ledger [Quincy, MA]. Give the day, month, and year of the issue. Be sure to give the section letter as well as the page number, if appropriate: C14. If an article does not run on consecutive pages (if, for example, it starts on 23 and continues on 42), give the first page number and add a plus sign (23+).

> **APA**   Dullea, G. (1986, April 16). Literary folk look for
>
> > solid comfort. New York Times, p. C14.

24. Editorial, Letter to the Editor, Review

MLA   "Facing Space, After the Cold War." Editorial. New
          York Times 1 May 1989: A16.

MLA   Childress, Glenda Teal. Letter. Newsweek 9 June 1986:
          10.

MLA   Linebaugh, Peter. "In the Flight Path of Perry
          Anderson." Rev. of In the Tracks of Historical
          Materialism, by Perry Anderson. History Workshop
          21 (1986): 141–46.

APA   Facing space, after the cold war. (1989, May 1).
          [Editorial.] New York Times, p. A16.

APA   Childress, G. T. (1986, June 9). [Letter to the
          editor.] Newsweek, p. 10.

APA   Linebaugh, P. (1986). In the flight path of Perry
          Anderson [Review of In the tracks of historical
          materialism]. History Workshop, 21, pp. 141–146.

25. Unsigned Article from a Daily Newspaper

MLA   "Hospitals, Competing for Scarce Patients, Turn to
          Advertising." New York Times 20 April 1986: 47.

Alphabetize in Works Cited by first word of title.

APA   Hospitals, competing for scarce patients, turn to
          advertising. (1986, April 20). New York Times, p.
          47.

Alphabetize in References by first word of title.

26. Article from a Weekly or Biweekly Magazine or Newspaper

MLA   Toufexis, Anastasia. "Dining with Invisible Danger."
          Time 27 March 1989: 28.

If a periodical is published every week or every two weeks, give the
complete date. First cite the day, then the month (abbreviated if necessary), and finally the year. Drop any introductory *A, An,* or *The*
from the title of a periodical.

APA   Toufexis, A. (1989, March 27). Dining with invisible
          danger. Time, p. 28.

33d

27. ARTICLE IN A MONTHLY OR BIMONTHLY PERIODICAL

MLA   Roosevelt, Anna. "Lost Civilizations of the Lower
Amazon." Natural History Feb. 1989: 74–83.

If a periodical is published monthly or every two months, give the month(s) and year.

APA   Roosevelt, A. (1989, February). Lost civilizations of
the lower Amazon. Natural History, pp. 74–83.

28. UNSIGNED ARTICLE FROM A WEEKLY OR MONTHLY PERIODICAL

MLA   "A Salute to Everyday Heroes." Time 10 July 1989: 46+.

APA   A salute to everyday heroes. (1989, July 10). Time,
pp. 46–51, 54–56, 58–60, 63–64, 66.

29. ARTICLE FROM A COLLECTION OF REPRINTED ARTICLES

MLA   Ryan, Bill. "Nuclear Waste Crisis—Don't Dump on Us."
In Social Issues Resources Series. Pollution.
Vol. 3 Article 14. Boca Raton: Social Issues
Resources Series, 1984.

APA   Ryan, B. (1984). Nuclear waste crisis—don't dump on
us. In Social issues resources series. Pollution
(Vol. 3 Article 14). Boca Raton: Social Issues
Resources.

30. ARTICLE IN A JOURNAL WITH CONTINUOUS PAGINATION

MLA   Cochran, D. D., W. Daniel Hale, and Christine P. Hissam.
"Personal Space Requirements in Indoor versus
Outdoor Locations." Journal of Psychology 117
(1984): 132–33.

If a journal pages its issues continuously through an annual volume, give only the volume number before the year. (*National Geographic* is such a journal. If the first issue of a volume ends on page 224, for example, the second issue starts on page 225.) Notice that all numbers, even the volume, are arabic numerals.

APA   Cochran, D. D., Hale, W. D., & Hissam, C. P. (1984).
Personal space requirements in indoor versus outdoor
locations. Journal of Psychology, 117, 132–133.

The volume number is underlined.

31. ARTICLE IN A JOURNAL THAT PAGES EACH ISSUE SEPARATELY

MLA   Hashimoto, Irvin. "Pain and Suffering: Apostrophes and Academic Life." <u>Journal of Basic Writing</u> 7.2 (1988): 91–98.

Some journals page each issue of an annual volume separately. (Each issue begins with page 1.) To cite articles from such journals, give both the volume number and the issue number (7.2 because 7 is the volume and 2 is the issue).

APA   Hashimoto, I. (1988). Pain and suffering: Apostrophes and academic life. <u>Journal of Basic Writing</u>. <u>7</u>(2), 91–98.

The volume number is underlined, and the issue number appears immediately after it, within parentheses.

32. INTERVIEW

MLA   Friedman, Randi. Telephone interview. 30 June 1989.

In APA style, a personal interview is considered personal correspondence and is not included in the References list. Cite the interview parenthetically in the text: Randi Friedman (personal communication, June 30, 1989).

    Personal communications do not provide recoverable data, and so in the APA system, do not include personal communications in the References list. Personal communications can be cited only in the text of a paper.

33. PUBLISHED AND UNPUBLISHED LETTERS

MLA   Lapidus, Jackie. Letter to her mother. 12 Nov. 1975. <u>Between Ourselves: Letters Between Mothers & Daughters</u>. Ed. Karen Payne. Boston: Houghton, 1983. 323–26.

MLA   Brown, Theodore. Letter to the author. 13 June 1988.

APA   Lapidus, J. (1983). Letter to her mother. In K. Payne (Ed.), <u>Between ourselves: Letters between mothers & daughters</u> (pp. 323–326). Boston: Houghton Mifflin.

    In the APA system, unpublished letters are considered personal communication and so do not appear in the References list. Personal communications can be cited only in the text of a paper.

34. LECTURES, SPEECHES, AND ADDRESSES

MLA   Kennedy, John Fitzgerald. Address. Greater Houston Ministerial Association. Houston, Sept. 12, 1960.

APA   Kennedy, J. F. (1960, September 12). Address. Speech presented to the Greater Houston Ministerial Association, Houston.

35. FILMS AND VIDEOTAPES

MLA   Erendira. Writ. Gabriel Garcia Marquez. Dir. Ruy Guerra. With Irene Pappas. Miramax, 1984.

APA   Marquez, G. G. (Writer), & Guerra, R. (Director). (1984). Erendira [Film]. New York: Miramax.

36. RECORDINGS

MLA   Smetana, Bedřich. My Country. Cond. Karel Anserl. Czech Philharmonic Orch. Vanguard, SV-9/10, 1975.

MLA   Turner, Tina. "Show Some Respect." Private Dancer. Capitol, ST-12330, 1983.

Begin the citation of a recording with either the composer, conductor, or performer, depending on whom or what you are emphasizing in your paper. Then give the information shown in the examples. The abbreviation stands for "no date" available.

APA   Smetana, B. (Composer). (1975). My country. Anserl (Conductor). Czech Philharmonic Orch. (Recording No. Sv-9/10).

APA   Turner, T. (Performer). (1983). Show some respect. On Private dancer [Album].

The word On is used to show where the selection came from.

37. LIVE PERFORMANCE

MLA   The Real Thing. By Tom Stoppard. Dir. Mike Nichols. With Jeremy Irons and Glenn Close. Plymouth Theatre, New York. 3 June 1984.

Begin with the title or a particular individual (for example, writer, conductor, or director) if that is the emphasis in your paper.

APA   Stoppard, T. (Author), Nichols, M. (Director), Irons, J. (Performer), & Close, G. (Performer). (1984, June 3). The Real Thing [Live performance]. New York: Plymouth Theatre.

38. WORKS OF ART OR MUSICAL COMPOSITIONS

MLA   Cassatt, Mary. La Toilette. Art Institute of Chicago, Chicago.

MLA   Handel, George Frideric, Water Music.

Underline an opera, a ballet, or named instrumental music. Do not underline or put in quotation marks a composition identified only by form, number, and key.

APA   Cassatt, M. La toilette [Art work]. Chicago: Art Institute of Chicago.

APA   Handel, G. F. Water music [Musical composition].

39. RADIO AND TELEVISION PROGRAMS

MLA   The Little Sister. Writ. and dir. Jan Egleson. With Tracy Pollan and John Savage. Prod. Rebecca Eaton. American Playhouse. PBS. WGBH, Boston. 7 April 1986.

To cite radio or television programs, include all information shown in the example: the title of the program (underlined); the network; the local station and its city; and the date of the broadcast. For a series also supply the title of the specific episode (in quotation marks) before the title of the program and the title of the series (neither underlined nor in quotation marks).

APA   Egleson, J. (Writer and Director), Pollan, T. (Performer), Savage, J. (Performer), & Eaton, R. (Producer). (1986, April 7). The little sister [Television program]. Boston: WGBH, PBS American Playhouse.

40. COMPUTER SOFTWARE

MLA   Microsoft Word. Vers. 5.0. Computer software. Microsoft, 1989. MS-DOS 2.0 or higher or OS/2 1.0 512K, disk.

To cite computer software, give the writer of the program (if known), the title (underlined), a descriptive label, the distributor, and the year of publication. Add any other important information, such as the computer on which the program can be used, number of kilobytes or units of memory, the operating system, and the form of the program (cartridge, cassette, or disk).

APA   Microsoft word. Vers. 5.0 [Computer software]. (1989). Microsoft. MS-DOS 2.0 or higher or OS/2 1.0. 512K, disk.

41. INFORMATION SERVICES

> **MLA**   Breland, Hunter. <u>Assessing Writing Skill</u>. ERIC ED 286
>   920.
>
> **If the material in ERIC (Educational Resources Information Center) or any other information service was previously published, give the publishing information before the ERIC number.**

APA   Breland, H. <u>Assessing writing skill.</u> (ERIC Document
                Reproduction Service No. ED 286 920).

If the material in ERIC (Educational Resources Information Center) or any other information service was previously published, give the publishing information before the ERIC number.

42. MAPS AND CHARTS

> **MLA**   <u>The Caribbean & South America</u>. Map. Falls Church: AAA,
>   1982.

APA   <u>The Caribbean and South America</u> [Map]. (1982). Falls
                Church, VA: American Automobile Association.

33e Using content endnotes or footnotes

When you want to add observations to your paper that do not fit into your text, use endnotes or footnotes. The chart on the next page presents guidelines used in both the MLA and APA systems. In the MLA system, the page is headed *Notes;* in the APA system, the page is headed *Footnotes.*

The MLA system of endnotes and footnotes

Note style, either as endnotes or footnotes, was used by the MLA for citing all sources until 1984. This format has been replaced by the Works Cited method, although note style for citing sources is still used in some humanities courses. In MLA's current system, footnotes or endnotes serve two specific purposes. You can use them for commentary that does not fit into your paper but is still worth relating.

TEXT OF PAPER

> Eudora Welty's literary biography, <u>One Writer's</u>
> <u>Beginnings</u>, shows us how both the inner world of self
> and the outer world of family and place form a writer's
> imagination.[1]

33e

GUIDELINES FOR NOTE NUMBERS IN A PAPER

1. Put the number as near as possible to whatever you are referring to: at the end of a quotation, either direct or indirect, but after any punctuation that goes with whatever you are quoting.
2. Raise the number a little above the line of words; leave no extra space before the number.
3. Leave one space after the number except at the end of a sentence. Leave two spaces after the number before starting a new sentence.

EXAMPLE

We cannot know exactly why the Greeks included the myth of Icarus in their mythology or why Ovid wrote the myth down and included it in the <u>Metamorphoses</u>.[1] However, the importance of

---

ENDNOTE WITH COMMENTARY

[1] Welty, who values her privacy, has resisted investigation of her life. However, at the age of 74, she chose to present her own autobiographical reflections in a series of lectures at Harvard University.

You can also put into notes extensive lists of bibliographic information supporting points you make in a paper. Otherwise, such information interrupts the flow of your paper.

TEXT OF PAPER

Barbara Randolph believes that enthusiasm is contagious (65).[2] Many psychologists have found that panic, fear, and rage spread more quickly in crowds than positive emotions do, however.

ENDNOTE WITH ADDITIONAL SOURCES

[2] Others agree with Randolph. See Thurman 21, 84, 155; Kelley 421–25; and Brookes 65–76.

EXTRA EXERCISE D

Using the Directory for MLA and APA forms, give the number of the correct documentation models for the following works.

A. "Kids as Capital." Written by Jonathan Rauch. Published in *The Atlantic* in August 1989, pp. 56–61.

B. *The Nine Nations of North America.* Written by Joel Garreau. Published in Boston by Houghton Mifflin Company in 1981.

C. "Joe's Place." Written by Babette Fraser. Collected in *Her Work: Stories by Texas Women.* Edited by Lou Halsell Rodenberger. Published by Shearer Publishing in Bryan, Texas, in 1982.

D. "Looking for Luck in Bangkok." Poem written by Maxine Kumin. Published in *The New Yorker,* June 12, 1989, p. 42.

E. "Rhetorical Implications of School Discourse for Writing Placement." Written by Kathryn R. Fitzgerald. Published in *Journal of Basic Writing.* Spring 1988, Volume 7, No. 1, pp. 61–72.

F. "The Whitney Interprets Museums' Dreams." Written by Roberta Smith. Published in *The New York Times* on July 23, 1989, pp. 31 and 33.

G. *Her Work: Stories by Texas Women.* Edited and with an Introduction by Lou Halsell Rodenberger. Published by Shearer Publishing in Bryan, Texas, in 1982.

H. "The Priciest Pyre." No author given. Published in *Time,* July 31, 1989, p. 30.

I. *The Floating Opera.* Written by John Barth. Published in New York by Appleton-Century-Crofts in 1956.

J. *Literary San Francisco: A Pictorial History from Its Beginnings to the Present Day.* Written by Lawrence Ferlinghetti and Nancy J. Peters. Published by City Lights Books and Harper & Row, Publishers in San Francisco in 1980.

(answers on next page)

33f Documenting sources with endnotes or footnotes in MLA style

Put documentation information in notes either at the bottom
of pages (footnotes) or on a separate page or pages following the
end of your paper (endnotes). The content is the same, whether you
use footnotes or endnotes. Unless your instructor requires footnotes,
use endnotes because they are easier to manage when you are typing
a paper.

GUIDELINES FOR FORMATTING ENDNOTES IN MLA STYLE

1. Center the word *Notes* two inches from the top of a separate page at the end of the paper. Do not put *Notes* in quotation marks or underline it.
2. Skip four lines before starting the first note.
3. Indent the first line of each note five character spaces. Start other lines at the left margin.
4. Raise each note number a little above the words. Do not put a period after the number.
5. Leave one space between the note number and the first word.
6. Double space within *and* between endnotes.

EXAMPLE

Notes

[1] Publius Ovidius Naso, "Icarus and Daedalus," in
Metamorphoses (Amsterdam: Wetstein and Smith, 1932), I, 257–260.

[2] Pieter Brueghel, Landscape with the Fall of Icarus, Musée
des Beaux Arts, Brussels, Belgium.

If your paper refers to only one or two primary sources, you
may be permitted to use simplified documentation. (Such papers typ-
ically are about one or two works of literature, like the essay by
Chris Johns in 36c-3.) A single note tells where quotations come
from. For example, this note tells that the entire primary source is
given in the paper's appendix:

> [1] All quotations are from Tennyson's poem "Break, Break, Break." The full text appears in the appendix at the end of this paper.

When the primary source is not given in the paper's appendix, give full publication information:

> [1] All quotations are from Alfred Lord Tennyson, "Break, Break, Break," <u>Literature: An Introduction to Reading and Writing</u>, Edgar V. Roberts and Henry E. Jacobs. Prentice, 1986: p. 629.

First-reference note form in MLA style

In a note system of documentation, the first time you refer to a source in your writing, the note gives complete bibliographic facts as well as the specific place you are referring to or quoting from in that source. Here are first-reference note forms for common sources.

BOOK WITH ONE AUTHOR—MLA NOTE FORM

> [1] Joan Didion, <u>Salvador</u> (New York: Simon, 1983) 64.

BOOK WITH TWO OR THREE AUTHORS—MLA NOTE FORM

> [2] Irving Wallace, David Wallechinsky, and Amy Wallace, <u>Significa</u> (New York: Dutton, 1983) 177.

BOOK WITH A CORPORATE AUTHOR—MLA NOTE FORM

> [3] Music Educators' National Conference, <u>Music in the Senior High School</u> (Washington: Music Educators' National Conference, 1959) 42.

WORK IN SEVERAL VOLUMES OR PARTS—MLA NOTE FORM

> [4] Robert Kelley, <u>The Shaping of the American Past</u>, vol. 2 (Englewood Cliffs, NJ: Prentice, 1975), 724–25.

WORK IN AN ANTHOLOGY OR A COLLECTION—MLA NOTE FORM

> [5] Wayne Tosh, "Computer Linguistics," <u>Linguistics Today</u>, ed. Archibald A. Hill (New York: Basic, 1969) 200.

ARTICLE IN A REFERENCE WORK—MLA NOTE FORM

> [6] "Fraudulence in the Arts," <u>The New Encyclopaedia Britannica</u>, 1979 ed.

ARTICLE FROM A JOURNAL WITH CONTINUOUS PAGINATION—MLA NOTE FORM

[7] William A. Madden, "Wuthering Heights: The Binding Passion," Nineteenth-Century Fiction 27 (1972): 151.

ARTICLE FROM A JOURNAL THAT PAGES EACH ISSUE SEPARATELY—MLA NOTE FORM

[8] Michael C. T. Brookes, "A Dean's Dilemmas," Journal of Basic Writing 5. 1 (1986): 65.

ARTICLE FROM A WEEKLY OR BIWEEKLY MAGAZINE OR NEWSPAPER—MLA NOTE FORM

[9] Barbara Randolph, "Hailing the Eureka Factor," Time 21 April 1986: 65.

ARTICLE FROM A MONTHLY PERIODICAL—MLA NOTE FORM

[10] Patti Hogan, "Setting the Pace," Ms. Aug. 1985: 20.

ARTICLE FROM A DAILY NEWSPAPER—MLA NOTE FORM

[11] Georgia Dullea, "Literary Folk Look for Solid Comfort," New York Times 16 April 1986: C14.

FILM—MLA NOTE FORM

[12] Last Tango in Paris, dir. Bernardo Bertolucci, with Marlon Brando, United Artists, 1972.

INTERVIEW—MLA NOTE FORM

[13] Shirley Stearns, personal interview, 17 July 1985.

WORK REPRINTED IN ANOTHER WORK—MLA NOTE FORM

[14] W. H. Auden, "Prologue: The Birth of Architecture," About the House (New York: Random; London: Faber and Faber), 1965; rpt. in Understanding Social Psychology, 3rd ed., Stephen Worchel and Joel Cooper (Homewood, IL: Dorsey, 1983) 539.

Note forms for second and subsequent references in MLA style

After the first note for a source, you should shorten all further references to the source. If you are citing only one work by the author, the author's last name and the page references are enough:

[15] Hogan, 31.

If you are citing more than one work by the same author, you must include a shortened form of the title of the particular book—along with the author's last name and the page reference.

[16] Didion, <u>Salvador</u> 45.

[17] Didion, <u>Common</u> <u>Prayer</u> 92–94.

List of sources when note is used in MLA style

When you use MLA note style, you have two options for listing your sources at the end of a paper. You can list all sources consulted, not only the sources referred to or quoted from. If you do this, call the list Bibliography. Alternatively, you can list only the sources referred to or quoted from. If you do this, call the list Works Cited. Whether you use a Bibliography or a Works Cited list, the MLA system of documentation calls for the *format* for Works Cited (see 33c and 33d). Because first-reference notes give full bibliographic data for each source, your instructor may not require you to submit a separate list of sources. If your instructor requires a list of sources, ask whether you should include in it all sources consulted or only those cited.

33g Using other styles to document sources

The documentation styles of the various fields within the natural and technological sciences may vary slightly from one another. Many fields have manuals (see the list following) that explain the documentation style common to their professional journals. If you are writing in a field that does not have a style manual, refer to a journal in the field and imitate its documentation style.

In each course, ask your instructor what documentation style is required. If the choice is yours, use the style of your major field so that you can practice it, or follow the style of the subject of your course. Here is a list of some style manuals in the sciences.

BACKGROUND

Additional professional style manuals include the following:

Geology: Suggestions to Authors of the Reports of the United States Geological Survey, 6th ed., Government Printing Office, 1978.

Law: A Uniform System of Citation, 14th ed., Harvard Law Review Association, 1986.

Medicine: International Steering Committee of Medical Editors, "Uniform Requirements for Manuscripts Submitted to Biomedical Journals," *Annals of Internal Medicine* 90 (Jan. 1979), 95–99.

Petroleum Geology: Bulletin of the American Association of Petroleum Geologists, AAPG, Tulsa, OK.

BIOLOGY

Council of Biology Editors Style Manual Committee. *CBE Style Manual.* 5th ed. Bethesda, MD: Council of Biology, 1983.

CHEMISTRY

American Chemical Society. *Handbook for Authors of Papers in American Chemical Society Publications.* Washington, DC: American Chemical Society, 1978.

MATHEMATICS

American Mathematical Society. *A Manual for Authors of Mathematical Papers.* 8th ed. Providence, RI: American Mathematical Society, 1984.

PHYSICS

American Institute of Physics. *Style Manual for Guidance in Preparation of Papers.* 3rd ed. New York: American Institute of Physics, 1978.

34 Case Study: A Student Writing Research

This chapter presents a case study of a student, Amy Brown, going through the processes of conducting research and writing a paper based on her findings. Section 34a narrates the processes. It includes her personal feelings as she moved along. Section 34b shows Brown's final draft of her paper, along with annotations that draw attention to the paper's key elements. The annotations include Process Notes that explain many of Brown's decisions during her writing process. Section 34c discusses the research paper of another student, Jill Max, who wrote on the same subject as Brown but with a persuasive instead of informative purpose.

Amy Brown was given this assignment for a research paper:
Write a research paper on the general subject of "communication." The paper should run 1800 to 2000 words and should be based on a variety of sources. The final paper is due in five weeks. Interim deadlines for parts of the work will be announced. To complete this assignment, you need to engage in two interrelated processes: conducting research and writing a paper based on the research. For the steps in these processes, consult the *Simon & Schuster Handbook for Writers, Second Edition,* especially Chapter 32.

As you conduct your research, expect to establish a work schedule (32a), narrow the subject to a suitable topic (32b), determine your purpose and audience (32c), use a search strategy (32e), and keep a research log and take useful notes (32j). As you take notes, make sure that you record your information so that you can document your sources (Chapter 33) and avoid plagiarism (31a). As you write your paper based on your research, expect to engage in the writing process (32k through 32m, as well as all chapters in Part One).

34a ## Observing the process

Brown made many decisions as she worked on her assignment. Some of the decisions did not come easily, especially in the early stages of the research process. Brown expected that the process would lead to a few puzzles and frustrations, and she resolved to remain patient with herself and the project.

Narrowing the subject of communication to a more **suitable topic** proved the most difficult challenge. Because the idea of unspoken messages among people interested her, Brown decided to concentrate on nonverbal communication. She started her research by compiling a list of **headings and key words** (32d-3) that she found by looking up "nonverbal communication" in periodical indexes (32g) and the library catalog (32h) in her college library. She located many terms: *eye movements, gesture, sign language, body language, touch, expression, space perception, space and time,* and *territory.* Such a varied list confirmed what Brown had suspected: nonverbal communication was too broad a subject for her paper. She thought she might write about expressions on people's faces when they use public transportation, but she found that that topic was too narrow when she found almost no resources on it in the library. At this point, Brown was getting a little discouraged and was tempted to switch to an entirely different aspect of communication, but she did not want to give up too soon. Brown wrote in her **research log** to help herself think on paper and discover ideas. Also, her log gave her a record of her thought processes in case something came up later that tied into her earlier thinking.

Deciding that more information would help her think of a suitable topic, Brown browsed through a psychology textbook and interviewed a psychology professor. One book that the professor recommended was especially interesting to Brown: *The Hidden Dimension,* by Edward T. Hall. Hall talks about personal space as a major factor in nonverbal communication. Personal space concerns the amount of physical distance people expect to maintain between themselves and other people during social interaction. When Brown read Hall, she recalled an experience she had had when a cousin had come for a weekend and had stayed three weeks while looking for a job. Brown's family lives in a small apartment, and although Brown likes her cousin, she felt that she had lost her "space" and she became cranky with her cousin. Brown knew that the crowding she had felt during her cousin's visit was not directly related to Hall's concept of personal space, but the idea of space as a part of communication intrigued her. She decided to see what she could find in her college's library.

Hall calls the study of personal space *proxemics.* Brown assumed it was a key word and went to the library to look for books and articles. She drew several blanks. Nowhere could she find the term *proxemics*—not in the *Readers' Guide to Periodical Literature,* not in any encyclopedia, not in the library catalog. She then looked the word up in a dictionary, and the closest she could get was the word *proximity.* She looked up *proximity* and found nothing in indexes or the library catalog. She began to suspect that Hall had coined *proxemics.* Brown felt she was running out of time, and she considered switching to a different topic. But then she had a breakthrough. She tried a specialized index (see 32g-2), and the *Social Science Index* listed *proxemics* with the cross-reference "See personal space." She checked and found numerous articles exploring aspects of personal space. Brown had "broken the code" and felt very good. She recorded in her research log all the information about her find so that she could come back to it easily when it was time to take notes.

The key term *personal space* produced an important title in the library catalog of her college: *Personal Space,* by Robert Sommer. She also looked under *body language,* a term she had seen in the titles of a few articles listed in the *Social Science Index.* She found the book *Body Language,* by Julius Fast. At the back of Fast's book is a bibliography of key references. Brown was delighted to find Hall's book and Sommer's book listed. The listings helped her confirm that Hall and Sommer were **authoritative, reliable sources,** two among a number of criteria used to evaluate sources (see 5c and 32d-2). Brown now knew that the books and articles she had found offered her a sufficient number of sources for her research.

Next, Brown wanted to formulate a **research question,** which would further narrow her topic. Brown had become most interested in Hall's discussion of differing standards for personal space in different cultures. Some research questions Brown thought of did not work. The question "What is personal space?" was too broad and lacked focus. The question "How do standards for personal space differ between North Americans and Arabs?" was too narrow for the resources in her college library. Then Brown settled on this research question: "How do standards for personal space differ among cultures?" (For a flow chart that shows Brown's narrowing process, see 32b.)

Now Brown was ready to think about her purpose and audience (1c and 32c). For an audience, she chose a **general reader**—rather than a specialized reader—because she wanted to assume that the audience would know little about the topic of personal space. Deciding on a purpose proved more complicated. Brown started by wanting to write with a persuasive purpose, but she soon switched to an informative purpose (for a discussion of purposes in academic writing, see 1b). At first, she wanted to argue that people from different countries will have serious trouble with cross-cultural communication unless they are aware of varying expectations concerning personal space. While reading and taking notes to answer her research question, however, Brown realized that she could not explain basic cross-cultural concepts *and* argue a position within the time and length limits of the assignment. She settled on an informative purpose. (For an example of how another student wrote on the same topic but with a persuasive purpose, see 34c.)

Brown's research process now shifted to finding additional sources and taking notes. Earlier Brown had used a search strategy (32e) to help her think of a suitable topic. Now she used the search strategy again, this time to take notes on the sources she had found before and to find additional sources that would permit her to give a full picture in her paper.

Now Brown had a working bibliography. Using MLA documentation style (see 33b through 33d) she had made bibliography cards (see 33a) on three key books, fifteen articles, and two textbooks. It was time to read closely and take notes. Brown carefully headed each index card with the author of the source. Making sure to avoid plagiarism, she paraphrased, summarized, and copied quotations according to the techniques described in Chapter 31 of this handbook. Whenever she used an author's exact words, Brown wrote oversized quotation marks so that she would be sure to see them when using her notes.

While taking notes, Brown realized that some of the articles she had found were not as useful as she had thought. She rejected a few sources that were duplications of what she already had. Later, as she was writing her paper, she dropped a few sources that were related to personal space but not to her paper (for example, the duration of eye contact in different cultures). She ended up using fourteen references.

In organizing her paper, Brown looked through her notes and saw that they fell into two piles: standards for personal space in North America and standards in other countries. She tried to outline the material and quickly realized that she had to start with a definition of personal space. Going back through her cards, she created a third pile for definitions.

Composing her thesis statement was next. Brown knew that her thesis statement would be the last sentence of her introductory paragraph. She drafted a preliminary thesis statement to use as she wrote the first full draft of her paper. Later she revised the thesis statement (for a description of the evolution of her final thesis statement, see 32k). Here is an early draft of Brown's introductory paragraph; the last sentence contains the preliminary thesis statement.

> People know unconsciously what close is when they stand near other people during conversations. This relates to the concept of personal space--the amount of physical distance people expect during social interaction. Standards for personal space vary among cultures.

Brown knew that the paragraph was flawed. It lacked interest, the word "this" was a vague pronoun reference, and the thesis statement did not give a full picture of the paper. She showed her draft to three friends and asked them to react. One friend who was majoring in psychology had a newspaper clipping in his files that Brown thought would be a good source to draw on for introducing her essay. Then, as Brown worked on drafts of her paper, she refined her thesis statement, a process shown in 32k. For the result, see page 1 of Brown's paper in 34b.

In writing her paper, Brown composed three drafts. In addition to rewriting her opening paragraph, Brown made other improvements as she revised. Her first draft lacked clear signals to readers about the material's organization. In her second draft, Brown used topic sentences to start many of her paragraphs. The topic sentences helped her readers follow the sequence of presentation that she used. Her first draft relied too much on quotation. In her second draft, Brown used paraphrase (31c) and summary (31d). She also used quotations (31e), but only when an author's language carried some special significance (see, for example, her third and fourth paragraphs) or helped establish the credibility of the information. In her third draft, Brown polished her word choice, corrected her grammar and spelling, and reworked her conclusion. Brown decided that the conclusion should be a "call to action," urging people to become sensitive to the concept of personal space and thereby avoid intercultural misunderstandings. Brown's first draft of a concluding paragraph was only one sentence long. She consulted section 4e for an idea for a device that would provide an effective close to her material.

Brown's final draft appears in this chapter. Each page of the paper is accompanied by annotations that explain elements of the paper. The annotations include Process Notes that explain Brown's thinking and writing process.

34b

QUOTATION ABOUT WRITING

A title page is like a tray of hors d'oeuvres; it suggests what is to come.

—Susie R. Rambo

BACKGROUND

A direct title tells exactly what the essay will be about. An indirect title hints at the essay's topic. In either case, it stands alone, not as part of the body of the essay. (See 3c-2.)

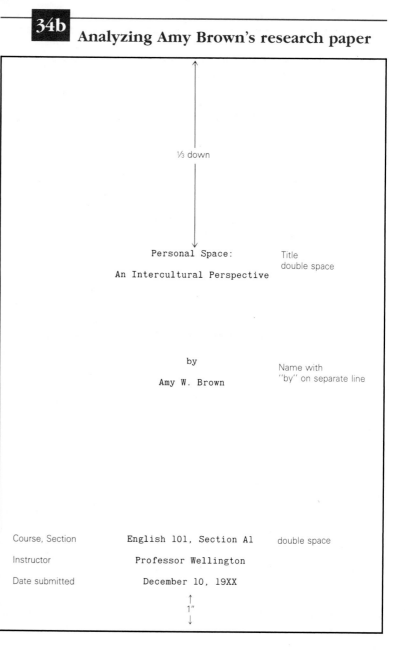

⅓ down

Personal Space:

Title
double space

An Intercultural Perspective

by

Name with
"by" on separate line

Amy W. Brown

Course, Section   English 101, Section A1   double space

Instructor   Professor Wellington

Date submitted   December 10, 19XX

1"

Cover page. If your instructor requires a cover page, use the format and types of information shown on the opposite page. Then on page 1 of your paper, repeat only the paper's title. A cover page is needed when an outline is included with the paper, as is the case with Amy Brown's paper. The outline appears on the next two pages.

First page. If your instructor does not require a cover page, follow the style shown below for heading your first page (which shows MLA format). If you do use a cover page, use the format on the first page of Amy Brown's paper.

HEADING FOR FIRST PAGE WITHOUT COVER PAGE   1

Amy W. Brown   Name

Professor Wellington   Instructor

English 101, Section A1   Course, Section

10 December 19XX   Date submitted
                                                double space
                    Personal Space:

            An Intercultural Perspective
                                              quadruple
                                              space

        When she returned home after a year in South

America, Judith Martin, a North American writer, began

to have a problem. People kept interpreting her

behavior as flirtatious, but she was not flirting.

Fairly soon she figured out what was happening. When

most South Americans talk to each other face-to-face,

they stand closer together than do North Americans.

Martin had not readjusted to North American distances (9).

Apparently, she had forgotten about the phenomenon known

as personal space--the amount of physical distance

people expect during social interaction. Everyone has

expectations concerning the use of personal space, but

Outline

Thesis statement: Everyone has expectations concerning
the use of personal space, but accepted distances for
that space are determined by each person's culture.

I. Observations about personal space began about
   twenty years ago.

   A. Most people are unaware that interpersonal
      distances exist.

   B. Personal space depends on invisible boundaries.

   C. Personal space moves with people as they
      interact.

   D. People do not like anyone to trespass on their
      personal space.

II. Research reveals North Americans' expectations
    for personal space.

    A. Hall identifies four zones for personal
       space.

    B. Subcultures help determine expectations for
       personal space.

    C. Age affects how people use personal space.

    D. Gender influences people's use of personal
       space.

III. Research reveals standards for personal space in
     countries other than the United States.

     A. Conversational distances vary in different
        cultures.

Brown ii

1   Western Europeans use fingertip-to-shoulder
       distance.

2. Eastern Europeans use wrist-to-shoulder
       distance.

3. Mediterraneans use elbow-to-shoulder
       distances.

B. Amounts of touching vary in different cultures.

C. Arabs prefer close interpersonal distances.

D. Japanese do not prefer close interpersonal
       distances.

Outline. Brown's instructor required that a formal outline be submitted with the final draft of each student's research paper. To format her outline, Brown referred to sections 2e-5 and 32l in this handbook. She numbered the pages with lower-case roman numerals, with her name placed before the numeral to indicate that the outline comes before page 1 of the actual paper. She placed the name/page information in the upper right corner, one-half inch from the top edge of the page. She then centered the word "Outline," using a capital letter to start it, one inch from the top of the page. She then double spaced before the start of the thesis statement. She underlined the words "thesis statement" and placed them at the left margin. Brown's thesis statement matches the last sentence of the first paragraph of her paper. Brown wrote the outline as a **sentence outline,** not a topic outline (see 2e-5). To reflect the organization of her paper, she divided the material in the outline into three major parts numbered I, II, and III. Each item within those three major parts is numbered A, B, etc. Because Part III.A needs more detail, items in that part are added and are numbered 1, 2, and 3. Each item in the outline is in parallel form; each item starts with a subject and is followed with a verb in the present tense.

BACKGROUND

A formal outline (see 2e-5) follows conventions concerning content and format that ensure that relationships among ideas are clear and that the content is orderly. If it is a topic outline, each item in it is only a word or a phrase. If it is a sentence outline, each item is a complete sentence.

1   **A**

B

Personal Space:

An Intercultural Perspective

1   When she returned home after a year in South   **C**
America, Judith Martin, a North American writer, began
to have a problem. People kept interpreting her
behavior as flirtatious, but she was not flirting.
Fairly soon, she figured out what was happening. When
most South Americans talk to each other face-to-face,
they stand closer together than do North Americans.
Martin had not readjusted to North American distances (9).
Apparently, she had forgotten about the phenomenon known
as personal space--the amount of physical distance
people expect during social interaction. Everyone has   **D**
expectations concerning the use of personal space, but
accepted distances for that space are determined by each
person's culture.

2   Observations about personal space began about
twenty years ago. Anthropologist Edward T. Hall was a   **E**
pioneer in the field. He became very interested in how
interpersonal distances affected communication between
people. In his aptly titled book The Hidden Dimension,
Hall coined the word "proxemics" to describe people's
use of space as a means of communication (1). As Hall's
book title indicates, most people are unaware that
interpersonal distances exist and contribute to people's **F**
reactions to one another (109).

General Note: Amy Brown uses MLA Style for format (see Appendix B: Manuscript Format), parenthetical references (33b) and Works Cited (33c).

A. **Page number.** Because Brown used a cover page, she typed the number 1 in the upper right-hand corner, placed a half inch from the top edge. On continuation pages, she typed the page number preceded by her last name.

B. **Title.** Brown's title prepares readers for her paper in two important ways. It gives the paper's major term (personal space) and the focus of the paper's discussion (more than one culture). ❖ PROCESS NOTE: In an earlier draft, Brown's title was "Proxemics: An Intercultural Perspective on the Need for Space." She rejected it because "space" was too general and "proxemics" was too technical. She then tried "Being Close: An Intercultural Perspective." Brown liked the second half because it was an accurate description of her focus, but the first half had multiple meanings. ❖

C. **Introductory device.** Brown uses an anecdote. (Introductory devices are discussed in 4e.) She felt the anecdote served four functions: to make the abstract concept of personal space concrete and familiar; to tie into the paper's title; to lead into the thesis statement; and to capture readers' interest. ❖ PROCESS NOTE: For an early draft of Brown's introductory paragraph, see 34a. ❖

D. **Thesis statement.** The last sentence of Brown's introductory paragraph is the paper's thesis statement. The thesis presents the central idea of the paper. Emerging from the paper's title and opening anecdote, the thesis prepares readers for what to expect. ❖ PROCESS NOTE: To see the evolution of Brown's thesis statement, see 32k. ❖

E. **Evaluation of source.** Brown establishes Hall as an expert by identifying him as an anthropologist and as a pioneer on the subject of personal space. ❖ PROCESS NOTE: To see how Brown was able to confirm that Hall was an authoritative, reliable source, read 34a. ❖

F. **Parenthetical reference to author and book named in the text.** Brown uses two sources by Edward T. Hall (see "Works Cited" on Brown's page 10). She has to be sure to keep them separate. In this paragraph, therefore, she mentions Hall's name and the title of the work she is referring to, and her two parenthetical references include only the page numbers. The references are inserted before the periods that end the sentences. Brown uses quotation marks to set off the coined word "proxemics." (The other work by Hall is cited in paragraph 11.)

3   Personal space depends on invisible boundaries.
Those boundaries move with people as they interact.
Personal space gets larger or smaller depending on the
circumstances of the social interaction at any moment
(Fisher, Bell, and Baum 149). Robert Sommer, an
environmental psychologist, uses literary and visual
analogies to describe personal space:

> Like the porcupines in Schopenhauer's fable,
> people like to be close enough to obtain warmth
> and comradeship but far enough away to avoid
> pricking one another. Personal space . . . has
> been likened to a snail shell, a soap bubble,
> an aura, a "breathing room." (26)

4   People do not like anyone to trespass on their
personal space. As Worchel and Cooper explain, invasions
of personal space elicit negative reactions that range
from mild discomfort to retaliation to walking out on the
situation (539-40). The poet W. H. Auden threatens a
uniquely negative reaction to intrusions in his space.

> Some thirty inches from my nose
> The frontier of my person goes
> And all the untilled air between
> Is private pagus or demesne
> Stranger, unless with bedroom eyes
> I beckon you to fraternize
> Beware of rudely crossing it
> I have no gun but I can spit.
>
>   (qtd. in Worchel and Cooper 539)

G

H

I

J

K

L

BACKGROUND

An ellipsis is a set of three spaced dots used to show that some of the original writer's words have been left out of a quotation. If an omission occurs at the beginning of a quotation, an ellipsis is not needed to show the omission. Also, an ellipsis is not necessary at the end of a quotation as long as it ends in a complete sentence. (See 29d.)

TEACHING TIP

Students sometimes think they are the only readers who skip over long quotations. You may want to assure them that they are not alone. The implication for the students as writers, of course, is that when they feel they must include a lengthy quotation, in order to present a complicated idea in detail, for example, it is helpful to prepare the reader by explaining its importance. To make it as brief as possible, all irrelevant material should be deleted so that every word counts.

G. **Topic sentence.**   Brown uses a topic sentence (see 4a) to start many of her paragraphs. ❖ PROCESS NOTE: Brown did not want to engage in plagiarism, so she thought carefully about what she could say in her paper without citing a source. She realized that she had read a great deal and had categorized her notes into logical units for presentation in the paper. She therefore decided that her topic sentences—which she usually put at the beginning of her paragraphs—were her own and did not need a citation. The topic sentences are organizing sentences that allow Brown to present information from her sources. ❖

H. **Paraphrase of original source.** ❖ PROCESS NOTE: This is a paraphrase of the source. In an earlier draft, Brown quoted the material and worked it into her prose. In her final draft, she uses a paraphrase because she does not want too many quotations. ❖

I. **Parenthetical reference to author not named in the text.** The source (author and page) is added in parentheses.

J. **A long quotation.**   A quotation of more than four typewritten lines is set off from the rest of the text. Brown introduces it with a colon because she has written a complete sentence (compare with paragraph 13). She indents the material 10 spaces and does not paragraph indent the first line. In the fourth line Brown uses a three-dot ellipsis to indicate the place where she omitted words (the full original source is shown in 32j-2). The page reference for the quotation is given in parentheses after the punctuation that ends the quotation. The words "breathing room" are in quotation marks because they appear this way in the original source.

K. **Use of an unexpected source.** ❖ PROCESS NOTE: Brown realized that W. H. Auden is not a likely expert on personal space. She uses his poem nonetheless because (a) she discovered it reprinted in a discussion of personal space by social psychologists, so she decided its content had credibility for her paper, and (b) she decided that it would suit her audience well, given the paper was for her freshman English class. ❖

L. **Parenthetical reference for an indirect source.**   Brown did not find the poem in its original source. After she found it, she tried to locate the book in which the poem was first published, but her library did not have a copy. So she relied on the indirect source. In her parenthetical reference, she used *qtd. in,* the abbreviation for "quoted in." ❖ PROCESS NOTE: Brown quotes the poem because she feels that the message of the poem has more impact in its original than in any paraphrase or summary she could write. ❖

5   Research provides information about the distances that North Americans prefer when interacting. The pioneering work was done by Hall. He observed the behavior of a group of middle-class adults in business and professions in the northeastern United States. He saw four zones of personal space; they are summarized and explained in Table 1.

Table 1

Hall's "Distance Zones"[a]

	Intimate	Personal	Social	Public
Close	0 to 6"	1½' to 2½'	4' to 7'	12' to 25'
Far	6" to 1½'	2½' to 4'	7' to 12'	25' +

Source: Discussion in Hall, <u>Hidden</u> 110–20; also Henley 32–33; Fisher, Bell, and Baum 153.

[a] Selected illustrations of each zone are: <u>Close</u> <u>Intimate</u>: lovers, children with parents; <u>Far</u> <u>Intimate</u>: strangers in crowds; <u>Close</u> <u>Personal</u>: husband and wife talking on the street; <u>Far</u> <u>Personal</u>: friends talking on the street; <u>Close</u> <u>Social</u>: boss and subordinate at a meeting; <u>Far</u> <u>Social</u>: receptionist and people in a waiting room; <u>Close</u> <u>Public</u>: teacher and students in a classroom; <u>Far</u> <u>Public</u>: actors or public speakers with audiences.

M

N

O

P

TEACHING TIP

You may want to point out to students that symbols, such as # % ə + and =, should not be used in the body of a paper although they often appear in graphs and tables. The dollar sign can be used anywhere when accompanied by figures.

M. **Word choice.** ✤ PROCESS NOTE: Before starting to conduct research for her paper, Brown always assumed that "American" meant someone from the United States. She discovered, however, that many people from South America consider themselves Americans (as well as being from a particular country in South America). Brown therefore began to use the term "North American" to refer to people in the United States. Brown uses this term in her introductory paragraph and continues it here and throughout her paper. ✤

N. **Table.** A table is an excellent way to summarize complex information that involves numbers and/or repeated categories. A table should be placed as close as possible to the paragraph in which it is first mentioned. If a table cannot fit in the space remaining on the page, it can be placed on the following page after the end of the first paragraph on that page. Some instructors permit students to put tables on a separate page at the end of the paper, before "Notes," if any, or before "Works Cited." Brown uses the format described in the *MLA Handbook:* the table number and title at the left margin, a lettered—not numbered—footnote, and source information immediately below the data, before the footnote. In MLA style, footnotes in tables are signaled with lower-case letters, and endnotes or footnotes are signaled by number's (see paragraphs 11 and 13). ✤ PROCESS NOTE: In an early draft, Brown wrote sentences to present the information now in a table. She did not think of using a table until she showed her early draft to a friend who said that the material was somewhat hard to follow and boring in prose form. She then tried to condense the material, and as she was writing she thought a table would be a concise, clear way to present numerical information. ✤

O. **Source identification.** Because Brown uses two works by Hall, she includes a shortened title *(Hidden)* here so that readers will know which Hall work she is referring to. She uses semicolons to separate each item in a series of multiple references. The other Hall work is cited in paragraph 11.

P. **Choice of examples.** ✤ PROCESS NOTE: In writing the footnote to the table, Brown had many choices of illustrations for each zone. She chose the ones that seemed to her to be good examples. ✤

Brown 4

6   Researchers working with Hall's data found that accepted interpersonal distances in the United States also depend on other factors. For example, subcultures help determine expectations concerning personal space. Fisher, Bell, and Baum report that groups of Hispanic–Americans generally interact more closely within their subculture than Anglo–Americans do within theirs. They further explain that in general "subcultural groups tend to interact at closer distances with members of their own subculture than with nonmembers" (158). **Q**

R

7   Age also affects how people use personal space. Worchel and Cooper report that North American children seem unaware of boundaries for personal space until the age of four or five. As the children get older they become more aware of standards for personal space. By the time they reach puberty, they have completely adapted to their culture's standards for interpersonal distances (535–37). **R**

8   Gender also influences people's use of personal space. For example, North American males' most negative reaction is reserved for anyone who enters their personal space directly in front of them. Females, on the other hand, feel most negative about approaches from the side. Also, females have smaller interpersonal distances than do males, although pairs of the same sex communicate across larger spaces than do pairs of males **S**

T

Q. **Quotation within sentence.** Brown fits a quotation into her prose. She uses quotation marks to avoid plagiarism. ❖ PRO-CESS NOTE: Brown worked a quotation into paragraph 6 because she felt that the material comparing one subgroup with another might be sensitive. She wanted her readers to have particular confidence in her presentation of the information. This is Brown's third quotation in her paper; the other two (paragraphs 3 and 4) are long quotations, which are displayed. This is a short run-in quotation, which Brown felt would demonstrate her skill at using both types of presentations for quotations. ❖

R. **Placement of parenthetical references.** Parenthetical references go immediately after a quotation or after a block of information from a source, as long as the block of information has not been interrupted by comments made by the writer of the research paper.

S. **Word choice.** Brown uses "gender," not "sex" here.❖ PROCESS NOTE: In an early draft, Brown used "sex," not "gender." As she was reading journal articles, she saw that "gender" is used in discussions of comparisons between men and women. The psychology professor she had interviewed also used "gender." Before she changed to "gender," she looked it up in her *New World Dictionary* and found it was labeled as a colloquial word for a person's sex. She was therefore uncertain about whether to use the word until she checked Charles G. Morris's *Psychology: An Introduction,* a source she cites later in this paper. When she looked up "sex" in the index to that book, she found "Sex differences. See Gender differences." She decided to use "gender," here and in her topic sentence in paragraph 8. ❖

T. **Paraphrase of an original source.** Brown uses a paraphrase here. ❖ PROCESS NOTE: The original source contains all the information here, but as she paraphrased she reordered its sequence slightly to fit the logic of her paper. She knew that reordering of sequence of material is permitted as long as the rearrangement does not distort the meaning of the original. Here is the original, from Worchel and Cooper, page 535 (the elipsis indicates intervening material): "One of the most consistent findings in the personal space literature is that females have smaller personal spaces than males. . . . Further, smaller personal-space zones are found between male-female pairs than between same-sex pairs. . . . Males responded most negatively to frontal invasions of their space, whereas females reacted most negatively to invasions from the side." ❖

Brown 5

and females (Worchel and Cooper 535). The gender factor

shifts, however, in high density situations such as

crowded subways or elevators in the United States. As

Maines observes, when people have some choice about

where they stand or sit in crowded settings, they

gravitate to people of the same sex (100).

9   Expectations concerning personal space exist in all

cultures, but such expectations vary greatly from

culture to culture (Fast 29). Research reveals

standards for personal space in countries other than the

United States. For example, conversational distances

vary between people from different countries, according

to Desmond Morris, a British zoologist. He notes that

when people from Western Europe stand on the street and

talk, the space between them is the distance it would take

one person's fingertip to reach the other's shoulder.

People from Eastern Europe converse at a wrist-to-shoulder

distance. People from the Mediterranean, however,

prefer elbow-to-shoulder distance (131).

10   Permitted amounts of touching also illustrate

intercultural differences in standards for personal

space. Touching while conversing differs in Germany,

Italy, and the United States, reports Robert Shuter, a

communications specialist. His research shows that

Germans and North Americans behave alike in that males

stand farther apart and touch less when talking than do

male-female pairs or female pairs. The opposite is

U

V

W

U. **Use of sources.** ❧ PROCESS NOTE: Brown wondered where to put her parenthetical reference when she was using three pieces of related information from one source. She thought that she might have to use the parenthetical reference three times (after the second, third, and fourth sentences in paragraph 8). She asked her instructor, who explained that she need put the parenthetical reference only after the full set of information, as long as the information does not spill over to another paragraph and the material is not interrupted by information from another source or by a comment of the writer. The instructor noted that Brown should not use too much information from one source, but was pleased when Brown showed that the paragraph also included information from a second source. ❧

V. **Summary of original source.** Brown uses a summary to condense the source. ❧ PROCESS NOTE: Brown liked the informal tone of Morris's material, but she did not quote it so that she could avoid too many quotations. ❧ Here is the original, which uses British, not American, rules for quotation marks.

> Unfortunately, different countries have different ideas about exactly how close is close. It is easy enough to test your own 'space reaction': when you are talking to someone in the street or in any open space, reach out with your arm and see where the nearest point on his body comes. If you hail from western Europe, you will find that he is at roughly fingertip distance from you. In other words, as you reach out, your fingertips will just about make contact with his shoulder. If you come from eastern Europe you will find you are standing at 'wrist distance'. If you come from the Mediterranean region you will find that you are much closer to your companion, at little more than 'elbow distance'.

W. **Transferring information from note to paper.** In paragraph 10, Brown uses the summary from her note card.

> *Shuter, p. 305*
> Intercultural differences
> Summary:
> Germans and N. Americans behave alike in that males stand farther apart and touch less while talking than do male-female pairs. The opposite is true in Italy, where males interact more closely and touch more during conversations than do male-female pairs or female pairs. Thus, Italian males expect to use personal space as females do in Germany and the United States.

691

Brown 6

true in Italy, where males interact more closely and touch more during conversations than do male—female pairs or female pairs. Shuter concludes that Italian males expect to use personal space as females do in Germany and the United States (305). In another experiment, adults were asked to put dolls in position for what was called "comfortable interaction." People from Italy and Greece placed the dolls closer together than did people from Sweden, Scotland, or the United States. Also, in doctors' waiting rooms, Australians were less likely to start conversations with strangers that were Indonesians (Worchel and Cooper 536).

X

11   Arabs prefer close interpersonal distances. Polhemus explains that Arab students move close together more often, confront each other directly, and touch each other more frequently when talking than do American students (21). In an interview called "Learning the Arabs' Silent Language," Hall notes that Arabs know the practicality of close conversational distances: "If you are interested in something, your pupils dilate; if I say something you don't like, they tend to contract" (47).[1] Conversational distances of two feet—that preferred by many Arabs—permits people to see each other's pupils better than does the typical North American distance of five feet (48).

Y

Z

34b

X. **Word choice.** ❖ PROCESS NOTE: In an early draft, Brown used the word "explains" in most places where she presented information from a source. When she revised, Brown wanted to vary her word choice. She looked at the chart in 31e to get ideas for different words. In her final draft Brown uses forms of these words: "explain," "note," "report," "conclude," and "observe." ❖

Y. **Quotation from an interview.** Brown quotes what Hall said at an interview. She can be sure of the exact wording because the interview is reported in a respected magazine. In general, professional writers check the wording of a quotation before they use it in print. When material is even slightly controversial, professional writers usually also reconfirm all paraphrases and summaries with the source. Some of the most highly respected publications have a staff whose sole job is to verify information and reconfirm quoted material. Some instructors require students to follow these practices. Also, some instructors prefer that material from an interview be paraphrased or summarized, unless a student has tape-recorded an interview. ❖ PROCESS NOTE: While reading her sources, Brown repeatedly was impressed with the language of Edward T. Hall. She kept feeling that her paraphrases and summaries could not possibly do justice to Hall. But she resisted the temptation to quote him extensively. She was aware that a student research paper, in one sense, is an exercise in which a student is expected to demonstrate the ability to conduct research and write a paper based on it. She knew that she would be judged, in part, by her ability to paraphrase and summarize well. She decided to quote Hall here and in paragraph 13 because she considered him a major reference for her paper, and she felt that this material was particularly effective for establishing the credibility of her information. ❖

Z. **Comment in an endnote.** Brown uses an endnote to comment on her information. The number for the endnote is raised slightly above the line after the period ending the sentence. The endnote appears on Brown's page 9. ❖ PROCESS NOTE: Brown uses notes when she has information that she considers particularly interesting but that does not fit neatly into the logic of her paragraphs. She does not want to digress, so she puts the information in notes (when they are placed at the end of a paper, on a separate sheet of paper, they are often referred to as "endnotes"). ❖

Brown 7

12   Japanese do not prefer close interpersonal
distances. Because the island of Japan is quite small
for its population of about 120 million, public places
are often very crowded. To cope, the people remain
formal and aloof even when in very close proximity to
one another (Fast 38).

13   People can easily be misunderstood if they are   **AA**
insensitive to how people from another culture use
personal space. Clearly, what is considered obnoxious
in one culture might be considered polite in another
(Fisher, Bell, and Baum 167). As Hall says, virtually
everything people are and do

> is associated with the experience of   **BB**
>
> space. . . . Therefore, people from different
>
> cultures, when interpreting each other's
>
> behavior, often misinterpret the relationship,
>
> the activity, or the emotions. This leads to
>
> alienation in encounters or distorted
>
> communications. (<u>Hidden</u> 171)

In the next few years, more studies will be undertaken
to uncover information about cultural differences
in matters such as personal space (Davis and Skupien,
xix). The information will be important. International
understanding cannot thrive unless people recognize
and accept such disparities. Charles G. Morris,
a professor of psychology, explains that this   **CC**
information is important because without it people from
different countries might misunderstand each other. He

AA. **Concluding device.** In paragraphs 13 and 14, Brown concludes her paper with a call for action (concluding devices are discussed in 4e). ❖ PROCESS NOTE: In her first and second drafts, Brown's concluding paragraph was quite long. In her final draft, Brown divided it into two and added a relevant quotation. ❖

BB. **Combined quotation from two paragraphs in original source.** Brown combines into one quotation material from two paragraphs in Hall. See the Process Note in annotation Y that explains Brown's decision to quote Hill. She uses no punctuation to lead into the quotation (compare to colon used before next quotation). She does this because her lead-in is an incomplete sentence that is completed by the quotation. Brown uses a four-dot ellipsis to show that the quotation is taken from two paragraphs. Here is the original source (Hall, *Hidden* 171):

> This book emphasizes that virtually everything that man is and does is associated with the experience of space. Man's sense of space is a synthesis of many sensory inputs: visual, auditory, kinesthetic, olfactory, and thermal. Not only does each of these constitute a complex system—as, for example, the dozen different ways of experiencing depth visually—but each is molded and patterned by culture. Hence, there is no alternative to accepting the fact that people reared in different cultures live in different sensory worlds.
>
> We learn from the study of culture that the patterning of perceptual worlds is a function not only of culture but of *relationship, activity,* and *emotion.* Therefore, people from different cultures, when interpreting each other's behavior, often misinterpret the relationship, the activity, or the emotions. This leads to alienation in encounters or distorted communications.

CC. **Paraphrase of original source and using same last names.** ❖ PROCESS NOTE: In an early draft, Brown used a displayed quotation from Morris. When she revised, she decided to paraphrase so that she would not have too many quotations in her paper. She also had to wrestle with two alike names: Desmond Morris, author of *Manwatching,* and Charles G. Morris, author of *Psychology: An Introduction.* She differentiated by identifying the profession of each (Desmond Morris is identified in paragraph 9) and by avoiding the use of the last name alone. ❖

Brown 8

imagines what might happen at a business meeting between
North Americans and Arabs. The North American is most
comfortable at a business conference when interpersonal
distances are about three or four feet. In contrast,
the Arab prefers less distance.[2] If the American backs
away from the Arab, the American is considered cold and
the Arab is considered pushy (516). All that is really
going on is that each person is behaving according to
cultural customs.

14

DD

     As international travel and commerce increase,
intercultural contact is becoming commonplace. Soon,
perhaps, cultural variations in expectations for
personal space will be as familiar to everyone as are
cultural variations in food and dress. Until then,
people need to make a special effort to learn one
another's expectations concerning personal space. Once
people are sensitive to such matters, they can stop
themselves from taking the wrong step—either away from
or toward a person from another culture.

DD. **Revising.** ✤ PROCESS NOTE: Brown rewrote paragraph 14 almost as many times as she did her introductory paragraph. She wanted to get some punch into the ending. After many revisions, she felt her last sentence delivered the impact she was searching for. She also consulted the chart in 4e that explains what to avoid in conclusions, and she decided to get rid of the phrase "of the sort discussed in this paper." The idea of using steps as a metaphor came to her nearly at the last minute, and she quickly worked it into her final draft. Here is a very early draft of paragraph 14. ✤

> Contact between cultures is happening more
> frequently. After all, international travel and
> commerce increase daily. It is urgent, therefore, that
> everyone knows that there are lots of variations among
> cultures in personal space. That means there are more
> differences than those in food and dress. Researchers'
> observations of the sort discussed in this paper help
> people understand more about the wide variety of
> expectations concerning proper amounts of interpersonal
> closeness and distance.

34b

TEACHING TIP

So that students realize that not all research papers include endnotes, you may want to point out to them that endnotes are a convenient way to include information that makes an interesting addition to the discussion but is not essential to it. They may provide more detail than the average reader is interested in learning, or they may explain background information that enhances the subject but does not bear directly on it.

1″   ½″   Brown 9

Notes   **EE**

[1] This explains why some Arab leaders wear sunglasses indoors.

[2] Both Charles G. Morris and Edward T. Hall agree   **FF**
that North Americans prefer larger conversational distances than do Arabs. They do not, however, seem to agree on the precise distances. Morris says the distance is three to four feet. Hall says five feet. These differences do not detract, however, from the central point concerning the contrasts in cultural preferences.

EE. **Endnotes.** On a separate numbered page headed "Notes," Brown provides commentary that does not fit into the text of her paper. Notes in MLA style comment upon, explain, or clarify material written in the text. Each note starts with a number raised a half line and indented five spaces, paragraph style. Double spacing is used within and between all notes. The format of the page is the same as for other pages: the name/page line is one-half inch from the top edge of the page, in the right-hand corner. The word "Notes," with the first letter capitalized, is centered one inch from the top edge of the paper.

FF. **Comment in an endnote.**   ❖ PROCESS NOTE: In this endnote, Brown uses the full names of the two people she mentions because she wants to differentiate between the two sources that have Morris as a last name. She uses the full name of Charles G. Morris, and to maintain parallelism she uses Hall's first name and middle initial. ❖   Brown used notes to include this material. She felt that it was interesting information, but she knew that it did not fit into the paper itself. In her first note, Brown draws on her knowledge of newspaper photographs of some Arab leaders. Brown uses the second note to present a discrepancy in the information she found during her research process. She wanted to be sure not to gloss over this information, but she could not fit it into the body of her paper.

TEACHING TIP

Even when a writer is very experienced in using a particular documentation system, it is helpful to have a handbook nearby for ready reference. For novice writers it is even more important not to work entirely from memory when it comes to making a Works Cited (MLA style) or References (APA style) list. Unusual citations will always appear, making it necessary to find a rarely used form, and because each period, comma, and space is stipulated, even common citations need scrupulous checking. You may want to suggest to students that when they think they have finished their lists, they should make a final comparison of their forms and those found in this handbook (section 33d) to discover discrepancies that might otherwise be missed. That way students can be sure that they are adhering precisely to the mandates of the selected system of documentation.

Brown 10

Works Cited

Davis, Martha, and Janet Skupien, eds. <u>Body Movement and Nonverbal Communication: An Annotated Bibliography 1971–1981</u>. Bloomington: Indiana UP, 1982. **GG**

Fast, Julius. <u>Body Language</u>. New York: Evans, 1970. **HH**

Fisher, Jeffrey D., Paul A. Bell, and Andrew Baum. <u>Environmental Psychology</u>. 2nd ed. New York: Holt, 1984. **II**

Hall, Edward T. <u>The Hidden Dimension</u>. New York: Doubleday, 1966.

---. Interview. "Learning the Arabs' Silent Language." With Kenneth Friedman. <u>Psychology Today</u> Aug. 1979: 44–54. **JJ** **KK**

Henley, Nancy M. <u>Body Politics: Power, Sex, and Nonverbal Communication</u>. Englewood Cliffs: Prentice, 1977.

Maines, David R. "Tactile Relationship in the Subway as Affected by Racial, Sexual, and Crowded Seating Situations." <u>Environmental Psychology and Nonverbal Behavior</u> 2 (1977): 100–108. **LL**

Martin, Judith. "Here's Looking at You." <u>Newsday</u> 27 Jan. 1981, sec. 2: 9+. **MM**

Morris, Charles G. <u>Psychology: An Introduction</u>. 4th ed. Chapter 16. Englewood Cliffs: Prentice, 1982. **NN**

Morris, Desmond. <u>Manwatching: A Field Guide to Human Behavior</u>. New York: Abrams, 1977.

34b

General Format. A bibliography, called "Works Cited," is used in MLA documentation style (see 33c-1 and 33d). Entries are in alphabetical order by author's last name, with a 5-space indention after the first line of each entry. Punctuation and spacing between words and lines are as shown. Double spacing is used within and between entries. Two spaces occur after each period in an entry.

GG. **Entry for edited book.** Inverted order for name of first editor (last name, first name), but regular order for second name. *University Press* abbreviated *UP*.

HH. **Entry for book by a single author.**

II. **Entry for book by three authors.** Inverted order (last name, first name) for name of first author, but regular order for others. *Second edition* abbreviated to *2nd ed.* Publisher abbreviated from *Holt, Rinehart and Winston* to *Holt.* (*Note:* In a work with three or fewer authors, all names are listed; in a work by four authors or more, the first author is named and then *et al.* is used.)

JJ. **Second work by same author.** Three hyphens and a period stand for the repetition of the preceding author's name. (*Note:* In such instances, works by the same author are listed alphabetically by title, not chronologically according to date of publication.)

KK. **Entry for an interview published in a magazine.** Entry listed by person interviewed, not by the person doing the interviewing. The page numbers are not preceded by *pp.*

LL. **Entry for an article in a journal with continuous pagination.** Article title in quotation marks. Journal title underlined. Then volume number, year (in parentheses), and page numbers without *pp.*

MM. **Entry for article in a daily newspaper.** Title of article in quotation marks. Name of newspaper underlined. Date of newspaper in this order: day, month (abbreviation permitted), year. Then newspaper section, columns, and page numbers without *pp.* The + symbol is used *only* for newspaper articles when material continues on another page.

NN. Publisher abbreviated from *Prentice Hall* to *Prentice.*

Brown 11

Polhemus, Ted. "Social Bodies." The Body as a Medium

of Expression. Ed. Jonathan Benthall and Ted

Polhemus. New York: Dutton, 1975. 13-35.

Shuter, Robert. "A Field Study of Nonverbal

Communication in Germany, Italy, and the United

States." Communication Monographs 44 (1977): 298-

305.

Sommer, Robert. Personal Space: The Behavioral Bases of

Design. Englewood Cliffs: Prentice, 1969.

Worchel, Stephen, and Joel Cooper. Understanding Social

Psychology. 3rd ed. Homewood, IL: Dorsey, 1983.

OO

PP

OO. **Entry for article in a book.** Author of article heads the entry. Editors of book, with names in regular order, follow book title. Title of article in quotation marks. Title of book underlined. Pages numbers—without *pp.*—after city of publication and publisher.

PP. **Entry for book by two authors.** Inverted order (last name, first name) for name of first author, but regular order for second name. Place of publication includes city *and* two-letter postal abbreviation for state because many readers might not know that Homewood is in Illinois.

34c Observing features of another research paper

Another student, Jill Max, was given the same assignment as Amy Brown, the student whose paper is discussed in 34a and presented in 34b. (The assignment is shown at the opening of this chapter.) Max narrowed the general topic of the assignment, *communication,* in much the same way as Brown did (see flow chart in 32b), but she asked a different research question. It reflected her interest in majoring in political science with a minor in foreign languages. Max's research question was: Why should diplomats understand the concept of personal space?

In conducting her research, Max located many of the same sources as Brown did. Max found, as had Brown, that Edward T. Hall was a key authority on the subject, and his book *The Hidden Dimension* was a major resource. Max, however, concentrated more than Brown did on Hall's discussion of his experiences years ago when he had visited various countries and had discovered practices that differed greatly from what is done in the United States. As a result of reading Hall and other authorities, Max decided that the purpose of her research paper would be persuasive. She wanted to argue that members of the diplomatic service should be trained to understand the concept of personal space in different countries. Here is her introductory paragraph. Her thesis statement is the last sentence.

> Most people who aspire to careers in diplomatic
> service plan to study political science. Many also
> learn one or more foreign languages. Some take classes
> in psychology. Few, however, have heard the term
> "proxemics," a word coined by anthropologist Edward T.
> Hall to describe people's use of space as a means of
> communication (Hidden 1). Hall's studies, and the work
> of those who have followed him, suggest that
> understanding differences in the way various cultures
> perceive personal space could lead to an innovative and
> more effective approach to international politics.
> People who plan to be diplomats should study proxemics
> as part of their career preparation.

To develop her argument, Max selected information from her sources that focused on possible misunderstandings between people of different cultures who were unaware of widely varying intercultural standards for personal space. She also used sources that Amy Brown did not. Max found sources to support her argument that the current training of diplomats does not include training in proxemics. She drew on that information to explain why the training of diplomats should be changed. In addition, she made inferences from her information on proxemics in various cultures to suggest specific ways that international diplomacy might be improved. Throughout her discussion, Max avoided making only generalizations. She was careful to describe the details of situations that call for an understanding of proxemics, and she used concrete illustrations to explain the potential value of her suggestions.

To conclude her research paper, Jill Max summarized her material and stressed the persuasive purpose of her work. Here is her concluding paragraph.

> Nearly everything people do, as Hall explains, "is associated with the experience of space . . ." (Hidden, 171). International understanding cannot thrive unless people recognize and accept differences in personal space. Our American diplomats cannot communicate effectively if they do not understand how the people they are dealing with use personal space. Diplomats could unintentionally alienate those they are seeking to make allies. The United States government should require all members of the diplomatic corps to learn the theory developed by Edward T. Hall and to understand the cross-cultural applications of proxemics in the nations to which the diplomats are assigned.

Eight

WRITING ACROSS THE CURRICULUM

When you write for the different disciplines that you encounter during your college years, you become familiar with the perspectives and assumptions that underlie each discipline. Part Eight compares and contrasts the various disciplines so that you can respond effectively to the major types of writing assignments in each discipline. As you use Chapters 35 through 40, be aware that the information in this handbook serves as a resource for your entire college career and beyond.

35 Comparing The Different Disciplines

Because people learn when they write about a subject, writing is a key to acquiring an education. As a student, you have the chance to study and write in each of the academic disciplines and thereby to become familiar with alternative ways of thinking. As you come to know the habits of mind that characterize each discipline, and as you develop various specialized vocabularies that allow you to participate in the conversations of each discipline, your perspectives are broadened. You gain lifelong access to the pleasures of informed insight, which is one of the major purposes of a college education.

In most areas of the curriculum in college, you will encounter writing assignments. A literature instructor may require you to write an analysis of a poem or a research paper on literary critics' reactions to a novel. A psychology instructor may require you to write a case study based on your observations of a person or write a research report that synthesizes experts' observations about the causes of divorce or the problems of the homeless. A biology instructor may require you to write a laboratory report or a formal scientific paper.

When college instructors give writing assignments, they assume that you have the requisite reading and writing skills to complete college-level assignments. Instructors also expect your writing to conform to standards for content, style, and format common to each separate discipline.

35a Recognizing similarities and differences among the disciplines

The humanities, the social sciences, and the natural and technological sciences each has its own perspectives on the world and its own philosophies about academic thought and research. To understand some of the differences among the disciplines, consider these three quite different paragraphs about a mountain.

708

HUMANITIES

The mountain stands above all that surrounds it. Giant timbers—part of a collage of evergreen and deciduous trees—conceal the expansive mountain's slope, where cattle once grazed. At the base of the mountain, a cool stream flows over rocks of all sizes, colors, and shapes. Next to the outer bank of the stream stands a shingled farmhouse, desolate, yet suggesting its active past. Unfortunately, the peaceful scene is interrupted by billboards and chairlifts, landmarks of a modern, fast-paced life.

SOCIAL SCIENCES

Among the favorite pastimes of American city dwellers is the "return to nature." Many outdoor enthusiasts hope to enjoy a scenic trip to the mountains, only to be disappointed. They know they have arrived at the mountain that they have traveled hundreds of miles to see because huge billboards are directing them to its base. As they look up the mountain, dozens of people are riding over the treetops in a chairlift, littering the slope with paper cups and food wrappers. At the base of the mountain stands the inevitable refreshment stand, found at virtually all American tourist attractions. Land developers consider such commercialization a way to preserve and utilize natural resources, but environmentalists are appalled.

SCIENCES

The mountain is approximately 5,600 feet in height. The underlying rock is igneous, of volcanic origin, composed primarily of granites and feldspars. Three distinct biological communities are present on the mountain. The community at the top of the mountain is alpine in nature, dominated by very short grasses and forbs. At middle altitudes, a typical northern boreal coniferous forest community is present, and at the base and lower altitudes, deciduous forest is the dominant community. This community has, however, been highly affected by agricultural development along the river at its base and, more recently, by recreational development.

Though such examples cannot demonstrate all differences among the disciplines, they do illustrate that each discipline has its writing traditions and preferences. The paragraph written for the humanities describes the mountain from the individual perspective of the writer—a perspective both personal and yet representative of a general human response. The paragraph written for the social sciences focuses on the behavior of people as a group. The paragraph written for the sciences reports observations of natural phenomena.

No matter what differences exist among the disciplines, all subject areas interconnect and overlap. When you study biology in your

QUOTATION ABOUT WRITING

But liberal learning does not permit us to hold on to any single answer for too long. As soon as you find one answer, you discover that that answer leads to other questions. Liberal learning can be unsettling. People like certainty, the right answer, the only way. Because of this desire for certainty and security, people can find themselves living with answers that other people have imposed upon them. In a free society, people learn to cultivate inquiring minds. They see that in broad areas of life there are no single right answers, that knowledge has a peculiar way of generating more questions, and that the world is more ambiguous than it appears. Liberal learning frees the mind to experience a sense of wonder at this ambiguous and fascinating world. F. Scott Fitzgerald writes, "The test of a first-rate intelligence is the ability to hold two opposed ideas in the mind at the same time, and still retain the ability to function." A liberally educated person learns to use this first-rate intelligence to function—even to prevail—in the midst of ambiguity.

Elaine P. Maimon, et al.,
Writing in the Arts and Sciences

QUOTATION ABOUT WRITING

The main assumption behind Writing Across the Curriculum seems to embody a resurrected sense of the responsibility of entire faculties and administrative bodies for the literary competence of the graduate. . . . Literacy is the concern of all faculty members since it is the cornerstone of education. Another assumption is that some rhetorical principles—careful description, explanation and proof, problems of definition and classification, and consideration of style and audience—transcend departments. Everyone can teach writing in a way. All faculty members can learn some general writing-teaching skills.

—James Kinneavy, interview, December 1984

SIMILARITIES AND DIFFERENCES IN WRITING FOR VARIOUS DISCIPLINES

SIMILARITIES

1.	Consider your purpose and audience.	Chapters 1–2
2.	Use the writing process to plan, shape, draft, revise, edit, and proofread.	Chapters 2–3
3.	Develop a thesis.	Chapters 2–3
4.	Arrange and organize your ideas.	Chapter 2
5.	Use supporting evidence.	Chapters 2–4
6.	Develop paragraphs thoroughly.	Chapter 4
7.	Read and think critically, and use correct reasoning and logic.	Chapter 5
8.	Argue well.	Chapter 6
9.	Write effective sentences.	Chapters 16–19
10.	Choose words well.	Chapters 20–21
11.	Use correct grammar.	Chapters 7–15
12.	Spell correctly.	Chapter 22
13.	Use correct punctuation and mechanics.	Chapters 23–30

DIFFERENCES

1. Conduct research and select sources according to the discipline.
2. Select a style of documentation appropriate to the discipline.
3. Follow special format requirements, if any, in each discipline.
4. Use specialized language, when needed, in each discipline.

---

biology class, literature in your literature class, and psychology in your psychology class, you will likely notice that distinctions among fields of study are not absolutely rigid. For example, in a humanities class you might read *Lives of a Cell,* a collection of essays about science and nature, by Lewis Thomas, both a noted physician and prize-winning author, but you will also be thinking deeply about biology and other sciences. Similarly, if you write a research paper on senility for your psychology class, you might refer to medical texts and scientific journals for some information.

35a

1 | Conducting research and selecting sources according to the discipline

Primary sources offer you first-hand exposure to information. No one comes between you and the exciting experience of discovering and confronting material on your own. Research methods differ among the disciplines when primary sources are used. In the humanities, existing documents are primary sources; the task of the researcher is to analyze and interpret these primary sources. Typical primary-source material for research could be a poem by Dylan Thomas, the floor plans of Egyptian pyramids, or early drafts of music manuscripts. In the social and natural sciences, primary research involves the design and undertaking of experiments involving direct observation. The task of the researcher in the social and natural sciences is to conduct the experiments or to read the first-hand reports of experiments and studies written by people who conducted them.

Secondary sources—articles and books about a primary source—are also important in all disciplines. In the humanities, you can learn much from the examples of others who have analyzed and interpreted primary sources. In the social sciences, secondary sources can usefully synthesize findings in many areas and draw parallels that offer new insights. In the natural sciences, if some primary sources are outdated by the time they are published, review articles and monographs can be useful for making connections among studies and bringing major questions into focus.

Because a secondary source puts one step or more between you and the primary source, many instructors prefer that whenever possible you work with primary sources for certain assignments. At other times, instructors assign secondary sources so that you can get a more comprehensive perspective.

2 | Selecting a style of documentation appropriate to the discipline

Writers use **documentation** to give credit to the sources they have used. A writer who does not credit a source is guilty of **plagiarizing**—a serious academic offense. Avoiding plagiarism is discussed at length in 31a. Styles of documentation differ among the disciplines.

In the humanities, many fields use the documentation style of the Modern Language Association (MLA). MLA documentation style is explained and illustrated in 33b through 33e. The paper by Amy Brown in Chapter 34 and the paper by Sandra Jane Reardon in Chapter 36 use MLA documentation style. In the social sciences, most fields use the documentation style of the American Psychological Association (APA). APA documentation style is explained and illustrated in Chapter 33. The paper by Douglas Franklin in Chapter 38 uses APA documentation style. In the natural and technological sciences, documentation style varies. An explanation of the major styles appears in 33g. The paper by Shannon Wagner in Chapter 37 uses the documentation style of the American Chemistry Society.

3 **Following special format requirements, if any, in each discipline**

Because of the differences among disciplines, different formats are expected in each for presentation of material. These special formats have evolved to communicate a writer's purpose, to emphasize content by eliminating distracting variations in format, and to make the reader's work easier. Writing in the humanities (Chapter 36) is less often subject to set formats, although writing is expected to be well organized and accepted documentation formats are expected. Writing in the social sciences (Chapter 37) and natural and technological sciences (Chapter 38) often calls for using fixed special formats for specific types of writing.

4 **Using specialized language, when needed, in each discipline.**

Specialized language is often referred to as **jargon.** Jargon is useful when it helps people who are specialists communicate easily with each other in a kind of "verbal shorthand." When specialized material is communicated to the general reading public, however, any jargon has to be defined so that everyone can understand the message. Jargon is not useful when it is unnecessarily obscure and overblown (see 21e-2).

All disciplines use specialized language to some extent. The specialized terms in the natural and social sciences are generally more technical and less accessible to nonspecialists than are those in the humanities. The more important observable or theoretical exactness is to a discipline, the more likely there will be many words with very special meanings. For example, consider the word *niche.* It has two generally known meanings: "a place particularly suitable to the person or thing in it," and "a hollowed space in a wall for a statue or vase." *Niche* in the natural sciences, however, has a very specialized meaning: "the set of environmental conditions—climate, food sources, water supply, enemies—that permit an organism or species to survive." The extent to which you define the specialized language in your writing depends on your readers' level of expertise (see 8m-8n).

The acceptability of the active voice or passive voice in writing varies with the disciplines. Writers in the humanities generally prefer the active voice: *John Priestly discovered oxygen in 1774.* Writers in the social and natural sciences often use the passive voice: *Oxygen was discovered in 1774.* The use of the passive voice in the sciences occurs when a writer wishes to emphasize the observation rather than the observer: "The gorillas were observed in their natural setting" focuses on the gorillas, not on the person observing the gorillas. In science writing when the focus can be on the observer, however, the writer uses the active voice: "Susan Kohn Green observed Lulu and Patty Cake, mother and daughter gorillas in New York City's Central Park Zoo, for one and a half years."

35b Using collaborative writing in various disciplines

In some areas of the curriculum, you might be called upon to engage in **collaborative writing.** This means that you will be expected to work with others in your class in undertaking a project. The collaborative writing group might consist of only two people or of many more, according to the instructor's directions. (Be aware that in many classes your instructor might prefer that you work alone on projects. To avoid any risk of charges of cheating or plagiarism, be sure to get permission from your instructor if you want to work collaboratively with other students.)

In many job settings, people are expected to write with others. Many professions at some point require people to serve on committees, to reach general agreement, and to write reports of their deliberations and recommendations. Many businesses and academic fields require people to work together on reports or papers that draw upon the different skills and information each person in the group can contribute. Some college courses incorporate into the curriculum the experience of writing collaboratively. For example, in a marketing course, the class might be divided into groups of three or four to develop a new product, conduct research for marketing the product, and write a paper explaining their plan and its outcome. Similarly, in a science course, a collaborative project might involve jointly conducting an experiment, assessing its results, and writing a report.

Collaborative writing gives you the advantage of being able to share your knowledge and hear what others know. "Two heads are better than one" often proves true. Still, working with others on writing projects demands patience and graciousness. You have to work along with the pace of the group, listen carefully as you consider closely what others are saying, and contribute your part to the endeavor. Here are guidelines to help you function productively when writing collaboratively.

GUIDELINES FOR COLLABORATIVE WRITING

GETTING UNDERWAY

1. Get to know each other's names. Consider exchanging phone numbers so that you can be in touch outside of class.

2. Participate in the group process. Neither dominate nor retreat. Help set a tone that encourages everyone to participate, including people who do not like to interrupt a discussion, or who want time to think before they talk, or who are shy. If you are not used to contributing in a group setting, try to take a more active role. Let your opinion be heard.

3. Facilitate the collaboration. Assign work to be done between meetings, and distribute the responsibilities as fairly as possible over the length of the project. Choose a discussion leader, or decide to rotate the leadership each meeting.

PLANNING THE WRITING

4. After discussing the project, brainstorm (see 2d-3) for ideas for the group's paper. As needed, use other planning techniques to think of ideas (see 2d and 2e).

5. As a group, choose the ideas that seem best. Incubate (see 2d-7), if time permits. Then discuss again the choice of ideas.

6. Divide the project into parts, and make assignments.

7. As you work on your part of the project, take notes that you can photocopy and distribute to the group. Be ready to report on your work.

8. Sketch out an overview (if you like, outline—see 2e-5) of the paper so that the group has a preliminary idea of how best to use the material gathered by individuals.

(continued on next page)

GUIDELINES FOR COLLABORATIVE WRITING *(continued)*

DRAFTING THE WRITING

9. Draft a first paragraph or two. This material sets the direction for the rest of the paper. Each member of the group can draft a version. Agree on the draft for these paragraphs before getting too far into the rest of the draft. Your group might rewrite the beginning later on, once the whole paper has been drafted, but a preliminary beginning helps to focus everyone.

10. Work on the rest of the paper. Decide whether each member of the group should write a complete draft or a different part of the whole. Photocopy the drafts for each member of the group so that they can be discussed easily when you meet together.

REVISING THE WRITING

11. Read over the drafts. Check that everything useful from the research, interviewing, and/or experimenting has been incorporated into the draft. Check that all parts of the overview of the paper (item 8 above) have been covered.

12. Use the Revision Checklists in 3c of this handbook to decide on revisions. Work on the revisions as a group, or assign them to subgroups. Use photocopies to share work.

13. Agree on a final version. Assign someone to prepare it in final form and make photocopies.

EDITING THE WRITING

14. Meet as a group to review the photocopies of the final version. Do not leave the last stages to a subgroup. Everyone's knowledge of grammar, spelling, and punctuation has to be drawn upon. And everyone's eyes are needed to proofread.

15. Use the Editing Checklist in 3d of this handbook to make sure that the paper has no errors. If necessary, retype the paper. No matter how well the group has worked collaboratively, or how well the group has planned and written the paper, a sloppy final version will reflect poorly on the group.

36 Writing About Literature And Other Humanities

QUOTATION ABOUT WRITING

Writing in the humanities involves an act of judgment or interpretation based on values. Humanists are especially concerned with skillful judgment—understanding and valuing ideas and creations. They encourage unique insight into past thought and action, asking of readers a similar interpretive skill—the ability to see new significance, impose a new structure, redefine meaning, or unveil assumptions. While interpretations may often conflict, making us question their reliability or validity, the goal is not reliability. Rather, the goal is to model reality in a way that helps us understand and appreciate it.

—Diane B. Durkin

QUOTATION ABOUT THE HUMANITIES

Human affairs are not serious, but they have to be taken seriously.

—Iris Murdoch

QUOTATION ABOUT THE HUMANITIES

Man is the only animal that laughs and weeps; for he is the only animal that is struck with the difference between what things are and what they might have been.

—William Hazlitt

Disciplines in the **humanities** include literature, language, philosophy, religion, and other subject areas. Some colleges consider history to be part of the humanities, while other colleges consider it part of the social sciences. Similarly, art and music are sometimes included in the humanities and sometimes not.

36a Understanding methods of inquiry in all the humanities

The humanities are concerned with questions that focus on human values. Reading, writing, and discussing—sometimes referred to as *discourse*—are key activities in the pursuit of answers to questions in the humanities. The humanities operate from the perspective that the well-reasoned thoughts of one person are typical of a general human response. The humanities draw on individual engagement and personal point of view. In so doing, inquiry in the humanities seeks to locate "truth" based on values, ideas, and interpretations that relate to the human condition. Such inquiry must avoid emotionalism in favor of balanced, unbiased exploration.

Some questions in the humanities ask you to deal with material in its literal level. You might be asked to explain what a literary passage says, or you might need to describe the major tenets of a particular religion or philosophy. Other questions in the humanities call for inferential and evaluative thinking—looking "between the lines" and "beyond the lines" (see 5b). You might be asked to discuss the relative merits of abstract and representational art or your personal interpretation of Jean-Paul Sartre's statement "life is absurd." Your answers must be thorough, well-reasoned, and informed by knowledge of the material and the major questions it raises.

716

36b Understanding writing purposes and practices in all the humanities

The major purposes of writing in the humanities are to inform and to persuade (see 1b). **Informative writing** includes explaining what a passage means or what constitutes the key features of a philosophy. **Persuasive writing** includes arguing the merits of an opinion or interpretation. To those ends, writers synthesize, analyze, interpret, and evaluate (see the opening section of Chapter 5).

In the humanities, some instructors ask students to use the first person *(I, we, our)* to write about points of view or personal evaluations, and the third person *(he, she, it, they)* for all other assignments. Other instructors prefer students to write always in the third person. Be sure to inquire about and adapt to your instructor's requirements. In research papers for the humanities, the first person is generally acceptable only when you present your personal experience, your own conclusions, or your personal views contrasted with those of the sources you consult and document.

Some assignments in the humanities call only for your own ideas about the subject of your essay. Other assignments ask you to support your analysis with **secondary sources.** Secondary sources include books and articles in which an expert discusses the subject of your essay. You can locate secondary sources by using the research process discussed in Chapter 32.

Whenever you use secondary sources, **avoid plagiarism** (31a). So that no reader thinks that the ideas of another person are yours, always document your sources (see 31b and Chapter 33). Also, to work material from secondary sources into your writing, use the techniques of paraphrase (31c), summary (31d), and quotation (31e). For information about what documentation style to choose when writing in the humanities, see 36d.

36c Writing different types of papers in all the humanities

The types of papers in the humanities described in this section focus on literary works, but you can adapt the principles to works of art, music, and other humanities. Before you write a paper in which you refer or react to a literary work, be sure to read the work closely. To read well, use your understanding of the reading process (5a) and critical reading skills (5b).

QUOTATION ABOUT LITERATURE

Great writers leave us not just their works, but a way of looking at things.

—Elizabeth Janeway

QUOTATION ABOUT LANGUAGE

Language is a uniquely human characteristic. Each person has programmed into his genes a faculty called universal grammar.

—Noam Chomsky

QUOTATION ABOUT RELIGION

Nobody can deny but religion is a comfort to the distressed, a cordial to the sick, and sometimes a restraint on the wicked; therefore, whoever would laugh or argue it out of the world, without giving some equivalent for it, ought to be treated as a common enemy.

—Lady Mary Wortley Montagu

1 **Writing reaction papers**

A reaction paper presents the writer's thoughts, reactions, and feelings about a work of literature, or about an idea or an interpretation related to a work (or group of works). In a reaction paper, you might ask and try to answer a central question that the work made you think about, criticize a point of view in the work, or present a problem that you see in the work. For example, if you are asked to respond to a play, you might write about why you did or did not enjoy reading the play, how the play does or does not relate to your personal experience or to your view of life, what the play made you think about and try to puzzle through. You can focus on the entire play or on a particular scene, character, or set of lines.

2 **Writing interpretations**

An interpretation discusses either what the author means by the work or what the work means personally to the reader. When you are writing an interpretation paper, always consider the questions in the chart below.

QUESTIONS FOR AN INTERPRETATION PAPER

1. What is the theme of the work?
2. How are particular parts of the work related to the theme?
3. If patterns exist in various elements of the work, what do they mean?
4. What message does the author convey through the work's setting, characters, narrator, etc.?
5. What symbols are used, and what do they mean?
6. Why is the ending what it is?

---

3 **Writing analyses and reviews**

Analysis is the examination of the relationship of a whole to its parts. It is a common method of development in writing about literature (as well as films, works of art, architecture, and music). In a **literary analysis,** you discuss your well-reasoned ideas about a work of fiction, poetry, or drama. To get to know the work well and to gather ideas for your analysis, you read thoroughly, again and again. Stay on the lookout for patterns in all the aspects of literary analysis listed on the chart below. Look up or consult with other people about any word, reference, allusion, or idea you do not understand. Keep notes as you go along so that you have a record of two important resources for your writing: the patterns you find in the material, and your reactions to the patterns and the whole work.

This list is an introductory guide to what to look for, think about, and seek to understand in a literary work.

BACKGROUND

In *Writing Themes About Literature* (5th ed., Prentice Hall, 1986) Edgar V. Roberts considers the objection that too much literary analysis "spoils" appreciation of a work. Pointing out that the purpose is not "to cut up literature like a frog and leave it in pieces," he explains that literary analysis should make it possible to see more in a work, to find greater appreciation of its literary excellence. To that end, he suggests four broad areas that literary analysis explores: (1) meaning, (2) structure, (3) style, and (4) background and influences.

MAJOR ASPECTS OF LITERARY WORKS TO ANALYZE	
PLOT	The story and its emphases
THEME	Central idea or message
STRUCTURE	Organization and relationship of parts to each other and to the whole
CHARACTER(S)	Traits, thoughts, and actions of the person(s)
SETTING	Time and place of the action
POINT OF VIEW	Perspective or position from which the material is presented—sometimes by a narrator or a main character
STYLE	How words and sentence structures present the material
IMAGERY	The pictures created by the words (similes, metaphors, figurative language)
TONE	The attitudes expressed through the choice of words and the imagery
SYMBOLISM	The meaning beneath the surface of the words and images
RHYTHM AND RHYME	Beat, meter, repetition of sounds, etc.

36c

WRITING ABOUT LITERATURE AND OTHER HUMANITIES

TEACHING TIP

Students who enjoy Tennyson's poem "Break, Break, Break" may want to try their hand at an analysis of another one of his poems that uses strong imagery to suggest a state of mind. Because "The Eagle" is brief but powerful, it yields itself readily to analysis.

The Eagle: A Fragment

He clasps the crag with crooked hands;
Close to the sun in lonely lands,
Ringed with the azure world, he stands.

The wrinkled sea beneath him crawls;
He watches from his mountain walls,
And like a thunderbolt he falls.

This chapter includes two sample student essays of literary analysis. The essay written by Chris Johns did not call for secondary sources. In his essay, Johns analyzes the imagery and style of the following poem.

Alfred Lord Tennyson

Break, Break, Break

Break, break, break,
  On thy cold gray stones, O Sea!
And I would that my tongue could utter
  The thoughts that arise in me.

O well for the fisherman's boy
  That he shouts with his sister at play!
O well for the sailor lad,
  That he sings in his boat on the bay!

And the stately ships go on
  To their haven under the hill;
But O for the touch of a vanished hand,
  And the sound of a voice that is still!

Break, break, break,
  At the foot of thy crags, O Sea!
But the tender grace of a day that is dead
  Will never come back to me.

SAMPLE LITERARY ANALYSIS (No Secondary Sources)

Chris Johns

Professor Perkins

English 105

April 22, 19XX

Emotion in Alfred Lord Tennyson's
"Break, Break, Break"

1 In the poem "Break, Break, Break," Alfred Lord Tennyson avoids direct description of his feelings of grief. Instead he alludes to and only suggests his essential emotion. Tennyson uses two vehicles to convey his feelings: personal musings and sea

720

imagery. The personal musings are not descriptions of what Tennyson is feeling, but rather are statements of what he is thinking: "But the tender grace of a day that is dead / Will never come back to me."[1] From the knowledge of these thoughts the reader can infer the content and intensity of Tennyson's feelings.

/ indicates break between two lines of poetry

2

The imagery also suggests the poet's feelings. This is conveyed by the line structure of the poem and from the intensity of the image. In the first, third, and fourth stanzas the imagery is presented in the first two lines, and Tennyson's thoughts are given in the second two lines (which are also the last lines, because each verse contains four lines). In the second stanza the relationship between the imagery and Tennyson's thoughts is closest, in that all four lines are devoted to his reaction to an image.

3

Each element in the poem is designed to define and modify Tennyson's grief. The images are controlled, simple, and always clear. Tennyson deals with each image separately; there is no pictorial confusion. In the first and last verses the image is clearly of breaking waves:

> Break, break, break,
>
> On thy cold gray stones, O Sea!

Indicates skipped lines

> . . . .
>
> Break, break, break
>
> At the foot of thy crags, O Sea!

The third verse's image is equally specific: "And the stately ships go on / To their haven under the hill; . . ."

Indicates the sentence continues

[1] All quotations are from Alfred Lord Tennyson, "Break, Break, Break," <u>Literature: An Introduction to Reading and Writing</u>, Edgar V. Roberts and Henry E. Jacobs. Prentice, 1986: 629.

BIOGRAPHY

Alfred, Lord Tennyson was, by the end of his life, almost a symbol of his age. His poetry was so popular with readers in England and the United States that he was looked to by many as a spokesperson for Victorianism.

He was born in 1809, the fourth son in a family of twelve children. Although he began writing as a young man, it was at Cambridge that he decided to devote his life to poetry. He associated himself there with a group of young men called the "Apostles," one of whom, Arthur Hallam, became his closest friend. Hallam's sudden, early death was the source of many of Tennyson's poems, most notably the long elegy *In Memoriam.*

His early years of writing were full of struggle, but with his appointment as poet laureate, his life became considerably more comfortable. Having at last the means to support a wife, he married Emily Sellwood after fifteen years of courtship and moved to a house in the country, where they lived quietly. When he died in 1892, he was buried in Westminster Abbey. He is still read with pleasure for his ability to link scenery to states of mind and for the musical quality of his language.

4   Images rather than direct statement of feeling are Tennyson's resource. As the waves beat against the rocks, so does Tennyson's grief beat against his heart; as the rocks can find no refuge, so Tennyson's tongue cannot release the feelings from his heart. The reader can sense the intensity of Tennyson's grief and can then imagine his pain and what lies behind it.

The following essay by Sandra Jane Reardon asked for secondary sources. She used MLA documentation style (see Chapter 33) for parenthetical references and the list of Works Cited.

BIOGRAPHY

Arthur Miller is best known for his plays about the American family. His first Broadway success, *All My Sons,* is the portrayal of a family divided because of the father's insistence on business as usual during World War II. His best-known work, *Death of a Salesman,* which was produced in 1949, won the Pulitzer Prize. Disturbed by the environment of McCarthyism in the 1950s, he wrote *The Crucible,* a story of a man who allows himself to be executed in the Salem witch trials of this country's early history, a parallel, in Miller's eyes, to the search for Communists in cold-war America. For five years he was married to the movie star Marilyn Monroe, writing a film in which she starred in 1961, *The Misfits.* In the 1980s he traveled to China to help direct a new production of *Death of a Salesman.*

LITERARY ANALYSIS (With Secondary Sources)

Sandra Jane Reardon

Professor Estes

English 102

May 1, 19XX

The Deterioration of Willy Loman

1   Arthur Miller, a playwright and author, has written several outstanding plays, and Death of a Salesman is usually considered to be the best of them. Miller received the New York Drama Critics' Circle Award and the Pulitzer Prize for this excellent work. Although the play was released in 1949, it is still relevant in today's world. Miller reviews the tragic life of a middle-class traveling salesman, Willy Loman, who is a victim of his own false values and those of the modern world.

2   When the play begins, Willy returns home unexpectedly to tell Linda, his wife, that he was too unstable to drive up to New England to make his calls. He learns that his sons, Biff and Happy, are upstairs in their old room. Biff had gone west to try to make a fresh start after repeated failures. Now he is back and broke. As for Happy, he has

a secure job, an apartment and a car of his own, and he seems to have a more stable life than his father or older brother has. We soon learn that Willy, now in his sixties, is an exhausted and disturbed man. He is a salesman who no longer sells, and a father who has a poor relationship with his sons. Willy is a failure because of the pressure of the competitive system, his inability to tell the truth, and his emotional, illogical thinking.

3   In the first instance, Willy is a failure because of the pressure of the competitive system. He is no longer able to meet the demands of the competitive system at work. Howard Wagner, his boss, is not satisfied with his performance. He keeps Willy on a commission-only basis because he feels sorry for Willy. However, despite Willy's long service and ties with the company, he is no longer a salaried employee. He has become nonproductive and is an embarrassment to the company, a reminder of the past. Willy is shocked when Howard refuses to give him a New York assignment, and after a painful scene, Howard goes on to say, "I don't want you to represent us. I've been meaning to tell you for a long time now" (907). Jeffrey Helterman of the University of South Carolina points out the irony of the tape-recorded voice of Howard's son naming the capitals of all the states, as it "is the prelude to Willy's being fired" (93). Willy does not belong in the mechanical world of tape recorders.

4   As a result of Willy's not being able to meet the demands of the competitive system at work, he is unable to meet the demands of the competitive system at home. He is not up-to-date in paying his bills and cannot afford the bare necessities. Linda has to struggle to "make ends meet." She darns her stockings and worries about the repair bills. Willy rants and raves about the various appliances and things that need to be fixed. He is contradictory about both the refrigerator and the car, one minute condemning the item because he is frustrated at not being able to afford the repair bill, and the next minute

QUOTATION ABOUT WRITING

Writing is the yeast of the learning process, not merely the frosting.

—Barbara E. Fassler Walvoord

commending it as he has a pride in his possessions.

In order to pay his bills, Willy borrows money every week from Charley, his only real friend besides Linda. He does not want Linda to know that he did not earn anything as he obviously does not want her to worry. When she asks him how much he made on his trip, he lies and says he made "two hundred gross on the whole trip" (884). Of more significance, though, is the fact that he does not want to face the realities of his situation.

In the second instance, Willy is a failure because of his inability to tell the truth and his emotional, illogical thinking. His lies make him a failure because everyone knows that he is a fraud. An example is his lying to Bernard, Charley's son, about Biff's success. He finds out that Bernard has a promising career as a lawyer and is going to Washington to appear before the Supreme Court. He tries to give Bernard the impression that Biff is also successful but realizes that Bernard only pretends to believe him.

On the other hand, Biff is not so sympathetic. He tells his father in no uncertain terms that his father is a fraud and a fake. When Biff finds a woman in Willy's hotel room, he says to Willy, "You fake! You phony little fake! You fake!" (962). Biff realizes what Willy fails to realize—Willy's life is a lie. Willy has not had the good sense or the character to recognize the impact of his lies and deceptions. Unaware of the answers, he subjects himself and his loved ones to immeasurable suffering. His deception of Linda when he has an affair with a woman in a Boston hotel room is the cause of the breakdown of Biff and Willy's relationship, but Willy does not realize this. Biff is shocked and embittered by what he views as a betrayal. In his book <u>Arthur Miller</u>, Ronald Hayman says that Willy's adultery "is judged mainly in terms of the effect that it has on Biff" (52).

8   Besides his lies and deceptions, Willy is a failure because his emotional, illogical thinking dominates his actions. Gerin Bliquez writing in the journal <u>Modern Drama</u> states that "Willy is a dreamer. What joys he has are always projections into a friendly heaven that is ignorant of a hostile earth" (383). He teaches his sons to be dishonest because he is governed by his emotions instead of his mind. An example of this nature appears when Willy tells Bernard to give Biff the answers to the Regents' examination. Willy wants Biff to do well, but he disregards the fact that Biff will have to cheat. In another incident when the boys steal sand and have already stolen lumber, Willy admires what he considers "bold initiative" (881).

9   Finally, Willy can no longer bear to live, and he commits suicide just after he learns how much Biff really loves him. This realization, together with imagined advice from his brother Ben, lends in his view even greater importance to providing for the financing of Biff's future. Willy's manner of death, however, denies his family the insurance money. Willy had hoped that this money would also guarantee him Biff's gratitude. Willy also uses Linda as justification for his suicide because "the woman has suffered" (933). As Irving Jacobson of the State University of New York explains, "What Linda has suffered is a failure, and the failure is Willy himself. He knows this instinctively and it only heightens his anxiety and his helplessness" (385). Only Linda, the sons, and Charley and Bernard attend Willy's funeral. His death attracts virtually no attention.

10   After Willy's death, Charley insists that no one blame Willy. Willy has, in a way, been destroyed by his environment. On the other hand, though, Willy cannot be forgiven completely for the shambles of his life and death. He must assume at least some responsibility for

725

his self-deception, his duplicity with Linda and the boys, and his deteriorated career. As a human being, Willy is not alone in his inability to cope with business life. He therefore deserves sympathy and understanding to a certain extent.

11   In Richard Evans's discussion with Arthur Miller, Miller asserts that Willy's guilt is resolved by his suicide, which reflects a growth in his character (76). The play, therefore, does not end on a completely pessimistic note. Hayman views Death of a Salesman as "probably the only successful twentieth-century tragedy with an unheroic hero" (37). Biff explains the reasons for Willy's deterioration very well with the statements, "He had the wrong dreams" and "He never knew who he was" (934).

Works Cited

Bliquez, Gerin. "Linda's Role in Death of a Salesman." Modern Drama 10.4 (1968): 383-86.

Evans, Richard. Psychology and Arthur Miller. New York: Praeger, 1981.

Hayman, Ronald. Arthur Miller. World Dramatists Series. New York: Ungar, 1972.

Helterman, Jeffrey. "Arthur Miller." Dictionary of Literary Biography. Ed. John MacNicholas. Detroit: Bruccoli Clark, 1981. 7: 86-111.

Jacobson, Irving. "Family Dreams in Death of a Salesman." American Literature 47 (1975): 245-58.

Miller, Arthur. Death of a Salesman. Literature and the Writing Process. Ed. Elizabeth McMahan, Susan Day, and Robert Day. New York: Macmillan, 1986. 871-935.

4   Writing research papers in the humanities

A research paper in the humanities has either an informative purpose or a persuasive purpose (see 1b). It draws on secondary sources to support its thesis. For an example of a research paper in literary analysis, see the essay by Sandra Jane Reardon in this chapter. Reardon uses MLA-style parenthetical references and Works Cited (see Chapter 33).

Research papers in the humanities often draw connections between more than one work. Theresa A. Shannon's paper below is an example of such a paper. It makes a connection between a poem and a painting. Shannon's assignment called for documentation according to MLA style for endnotes (see 33f) and for Works Cited. If Shannon had included sources that she had not referred to or quoted from, she would have had to call the list Bibliography. This option is not available to users of the MLA parenthetical system of documentation, which calls only for a Works Cited list.

SAMPLE HUMANITIES RESEARCH PAPER

Theresa A. Shannon
Professor Anderson
Humanities 32
March 10, 19XX

The Influence of the Myth of Icarus

1   We cannot know exactly why the Greeks included the myth of Icarus in their mythology or why Ovid wrote the myth down and included it in the <u>Metamorphoses</u>.[1] However, the importance of the myth is evident by its obvious influence on other works of art and literature. These influences can be seen in Brueghel's painting <u>Landscape with the Fall of Icarus</u>[2] and in Stephen Spender's poem "Icarus."[3] Even psychologists have named a personality that exhibits a particular pattern of behavior the Icarus complex.[4] The fact that the Icarus myth has generated so many other works indicates that it is more than an interesting story.

2   According to the myth, Daedalus, Icarus' father, designs wings of wax and feathers for himself and his son

BIOGRAPHY

Pieter Brueghel the Elder was a Flemish painter of the sixteenth century. His work is generally seen as a reflection and criticism of life. While his contemporaries were executing elegant figures based on antique monuments recently exhumed at Rome, Brueghel was traveling through the countryside to see the peasants enjoying fairs and weddings. He captured their exuberance, picturing them as they danced, drank, and laughed, sometimes criticizing them in his paintings for their foolishness and their self-indulgence. A series of five paintings executed for Niclaes Johnghelinck of Antwerp depicts the months of the year, each depicting the different activities of peasants. Brueghel never painted a portrait, and the faces of his figures are often hidden beneath broad-brimmed hats or scarves, emphasizing his intent—not to depict individuals, but to capture the spirit of humanity. His well-known *Fall of Icarus* hangs today at the Musees Royaux des Beaux Arts in Brussels. His son, Pieter Brueghel the Younger, also painted genre and rural subjects, as well as fantastic scenes of hell which earned him the nickname Hell Brueghel.

BIOGRAPHY

Stephen Spender achieved his greatest reputation as a poet of English during the economic depression of the 1930s. He has also published a number of prose works, including his autobiography, *World Within World,* published in 1951. He often lectures at American universities.

BIOGRAPHY

W. H. Auden was born and educated in England, but in 1939 immigrated to the United States, where he became a citizen in 1946. By that time he had already achieved critical notice as a member of an active group of young poets, including Stephen Spender, who were trying to bring new techniques and attitudes to English poetry. Disturbed by the economic depression of the 1930s, and impressed by Freud and Marx, Auden depicted the English, in his early poetry, as victims of an antiquated economic system. Later he developed a more religious view of personal responsibility, although toward the end of his life he was skeptical of the possibility of ever curing modern ills. He returned to England to live in Oxford the last year of his life, where he could be among friends. He died there in 1973.

so that they may fly to freedom. Daedalus warns Icarus to fly directly between the sun and the ocean to prevent damage to the wings from either of these elements. Icarus ignores his father's warning and flies too close to the sun, causing the wax to melt. Icarus then plunges into the ocean and drowns. After Icarus' death, Daedalus offers a sacrifice of appeasement to the sun god, Apollo.

3

Pieter Brueghel's painting <u>Landscape</u> with <u>the</u> <u>Fall</u> of <u>Icarus</u> is not merely a representation of Icarus' death. Brueghel shows Icarus falling from the sky on a typical day near an average village. A ploughman either does not notice Icarus falling or chooses to ignore the event. A nearby sailing ship continues on its route. The poet W. H. Auden interpreted the painting as a representation of human suffering. In "Musée des Beaux Arts," a poem about Brueghel's painting of Icarus, Auden writes about suffering: "they were never wrong, / The Old Masters: how well they understood / Its human position."[5] He continues to describe the ploughman's reaction to Icarus' fall: "But for him it was not an important failure;" and observes how the ship "Had somewhere to go and sailed calmly on."[6]

4

Stephen Spender's poem, on the other hand, focuses on Icarus instead of on those who observed his death. He presents Icarus as a bold and arrogant boy who "almost had won War on the sun." He writes:

> This aristocrat, superb of all instinct,
> With death close linked
> Had paced the enormous cloud, almost had won
> War on the sun.[7]

5

Although these are not the only allusions in art and literature to the myth of Icarus, they are representative of the importance of the myth as an influence on artists. The myth of the fall of Icarus, like any other myth, serves to educate us, not just to entertain us. Artists will undoubtedly continue to interpret the myth according to their own insights, perhaps viewing it from a perspective that only the future can offer.

Start new page
for endnotes   Notes

[1] Publius Ovidius Naso, "Icarus and Daedalus,"
Metamorphoses, vol. 1 (Amsterdam: Wetstein and Smith,
1932) 257–260.

[2] Pieter Brueghel, Landscape with the Fall of Icarus,
Musée des Beaux Arts, Brussels, Belgium.

[3] Stephen Spender, "Icarus," The Norton Anthology of
Poetry, eds. Richard Ellman and Robert O'Clair (New York:
Norton, 1973) 790.

[4] Daniel Ogilvie, "The Icarus Complex," Psychology
Today 20. 6 (1976): 31–4.

[5] W. H. Auden, "Musée des Beaux Arts," The Norton
Anthology of English Literature, eds. M. H. Abrams et al.
(New York: Norton, 1979). 2396.

[6] Auden 2397.

[7] Spender 790.

Start new page
for Works
Cited   Works Cited

Auden, W. H. "Musée des Beaux Arts." The Norton Anthology
     of English Literature. Eds. M. H. Abrams et al. New
     York: Norton, 1979. 2396–2397.
Brueghel, Pieter. Landscape with the Fall of Icarus. Musée
     des Beaux Arts, Brussels, Belgium.
Ogilvie, Daniel. "The Icarus Complex." Psychology Today.
     20. 6 (1976): 31–4, 67.
Ovidius Naso, Publius. "Icarus and Daedalus."
     Metamorphoses. Amsterdam: Wetstein and Smith, 1932.
     257–260.
Spender, Stephen. "Icarus." The Norton Anthology of
     Poetry. Eds. Richard Ellman and Robert O'Clair. New
     York: Norton, 1973. 790.

BACKGROUND

Artists other than those mentioned in Theresa Shannon's paper who have also treated the myth of Icarus include Lucian of Samosata (A.D. 120), who saw in Daedalus a great master of astrology who taught the science to his son. Like Samosata, André Gide's *Thésée* also treats Icarus as a metaphysician, a victim of soaring too close to Platonic truths. Breughel's work seems based on Ovid's account of the flight in the eighth book of the *Metamorphoses,* where he describes the amazement of a fisherman, a shepherd, and a plowman when they saw Daedalus and Icarus flying through the sky, an event they interpreted as an epiphany of the gods. James Joyce took the legend of Daedalus and Icarus as his own, identifying himself as the master-craftsman and innovator, the rebel and artist by taking the name of Stephen Daedalus as the hero of his largely autobiographical novels. In 1947 the artist Henri Matisse created the lithograph *Falling Icarus* as part of his Jazz series. It now hangs in the Museum of Modern Art in New York.

36d Using documentation style in the humanities

The Modern Language Association (MLA), an organization of scholars and teachers in language and literature, has long been a leading developer of documentation style. Before 1984, MLA recommended endnotes or footnotes for presenting documentation information within the text of a paper and a Bibliography listing all the sources used.

MLA updated its documentation system in 1984. The newer MLA style calls for parenthetical references within the text of a paper and a list of bibliographic references called Works Cited at the end of a paper. Works Cited includes only sources referred to or quoted from in the paper; it does not include sources consulted but not referred to or quoted from in the paper. This newer MLA system is sometimes called "1984–MLA Style." The essay by Sandra Jane Reardon in this chapter uses the new MLA style.

For people who prefer footnotes or endnotes for documenting sources, MLA suggests an updated format for the Notes. For the bibliography, MLA suggests the same Works Cited format as it developed for its parenthetical system. If sources other than those cited in the paper are included, MLA says that the list should be called Bibliography. The essay by Theresa Shannon in this chapter uses the MLA endnote system.

MLA style is explained and illustrated in Chapter 33. Note that Section 33d contains a directory, examples, and explanations of MLA style and APA style. You can locate 33d quickly in this book because it has a red border so that its pages stand out from other pages when you look at the closed book.

Some humanities instructors require the documentation style developed by the American Psychological Association (APA). The essay by Douglas Franklin in Chapter 37 uses APA documentation style. APA style is explained and illustrated in Chapter 33.

37 Writing in The Social Sciences

Disciplines in the social sciences include subject areas such as economics, education, geography, political science, psychology, and sociology.

 Understanding methods of inquiry in the social sciences

The social sciences ask questions that focus on the behavior of people as individuals and in groups. As researchers and writers, social scientists want to know what people do and why. To find out, they usually follow a procedure that involves observation, investigation, and collection of data.

Observation is a common method for research in the social sciences (as well as the natural sciences). If you are asked to make observations, take along whatever tools or equipment you might need in order to work: writing or sketching materials, and perhaps recording or photographic equipment. As you make your observations, take very accurate and complete notes about what you see. If you use your own system of abbreviations to speed your note taking, make sure you can go back to your notes and understand them when the time comes to write up your observations. In your report, be sure to say what tools or equipment you used—because your method might have influenced what you saw (for example, taking photographs may make people too self-conscious to act as they usually do).

Interviewing is another common technique that social scientists use for collecting information. Interviews are useful for gathering people's opinions and impressions of events. Remember, however, that interviews are not always a reliable way to gather factual information because people's memories are not precise. If your only

QUOTATION ABOUT POLITICAL
SCIENCE

Politics is not an exact science.

—Prince Otto von Bismarck

QUOTATION ABOUT POLITICAL
SCIENCE

Politics is the science of how who gets what,
when and why.

—Sidney Hillman

QUOTATION ABOUT PSYCHOLOGY

Gossip: sociologists on a mean and petty
scale.

—Woodrow Wilson

QUOTATION ABOUT GEOGRAPHY

Anybody who believes that the way to a
man's heart is through his stomach flunked
geography.

—Robert Byrne

QUOTATION ABOUT GEOGRAPHY

To travel is to discover that everyone is
wrong about other countries.

—Aldous Huxley

source for facts is interviews, be sure to interview as many people as possible so that you can cross-check the information. As with observation, be prepared with whatever note-taking tools you might need. Practice with those tools so they do not intrude on the interview process (see also 32e-3).

Questionnaires are often useful for gathering information in the social sciences. If you are asked to write questions for a questionnaire, you need to make sure that the questions will elicit the information that you are looking for. The way that you phrase the questions will determine if your data are a true reflection of what people are thinking.

GUIDELINES FOR WRITING QUESTIONS FOR A QUESTIONNAIRE

1. Know clearly what you want to find out.
2. Write questions that are easy to understand.
3. Make the questions fair—do not use language that is slanted (see 21a-4) or that implies what *you* want to hear.
4. Test your questions on a small group of people before you use the questions for gathering data. If any question turns out to be hard to understand, or if it can be interpreted in more than one way, revise and retest it.
5. Use a sufficient number of people when you administer the final form of the questionnaire. You cannot generalize from small samples.

37b Understanding writing purposes and practices in the social sciences

Social scientists write to inform and to persuade. They achieve these purposes by classifying, analyzing, or explaining a human problem or condition. They most often use rhetorical strategies such as definition, analogy, and analysis of a problem and its solution.

Definition is extremely important when ambiguous social issues and terms are discussed. For example, if you are writing a paper on substance abuse in the medical profession, you first have to define

37c

substance and *medical profession.* By *substance* do you mean alcohol and drugs or only drugs? When you refer to the medical profession, are you including nurses and lab technicians or only doctors? Without defining these terms, you can confuse your readers or lead them to the wrong conclusions.

Analogy helps social scientists make unfamiliar ideas clear. When an unfamiliar idea is compared with one that is more familiar, the unfamiliar idea becomes easier to understand. For example, sociologists may talk of the "culture shock" that some people feel when they enter a very new society. The sociologists might compare this "shock" to the reaction that someone living today might have when moving suddenly hundreds of years into the future or the past.

Analysis helps social scientists write about problems and their solutions. For example, an economist writing about a major automobile company in financial difficulties might break the situation into parts, analyzing employee salaries and benefits, the selling price of cars, and the costs of doing business. Next, the economist can show how these parts relate to the financial status of the whole company. Then the economist might speculate about how specific changes would help to solve the company's financial problems.

In college courses in the social sciences, some instructors ask students to write their personal reactions to information or experiences, in which case the first person *(I, we, our)* is acceptable. In most writing for the social sciences, however, writers use the third person *(he, she, it, they).* Also, because the emphasis is on people or groups being observed rather than on the person doing the observing, the passive voice (see 8m-8n) is a frequent characteristic of such writing. An economist is likely to write, "The audits of The Frazzle Company were studied for indications of mismanagement" instead of "I studied the audits of The Frazzle Company for indications of mismanagement." Nevertheless, some material can be written about in the more engaging active voice (see 8n): "The Frazzle Company seems eager to improve its methods of operation" and "The audits reveal that The Frazzle Company needs major overhauling."

QUOTATION ABOUT EDUCATION

What sculpture is to a block of marble, education is to the soul.

—Joseph Addison

QUOTATION ABOUT EDUCATION

Education is an admirable thing, but it is well to remember from time to time that nothing that is worth knowing can be taught.

—Oscar Wilde

QUOTATION ABOUT EDUCATION

The primary purpose of a liberal education is to make one's mind a pleasant place in which to spend one's time.

—Sydney J. Harris

 37c **Writing different types of papers in the social sciences**

Two major types of papers in the social sciences are case studies and research papers.

37c

BACKGROUND

In addition to case studies and research papers, students in social science classes are sometimes asked to write analyses of standard texts in a field of study and reports of personal investigation into a specific question. They may find it helpful to know that a textual analysis begins with clear identification of the articles to be reviewed by citation of titles, authors, and publication data. It should include an introduction to the topic under examination, a review of the major views of the subject, and an evaluation of the sources surveyed. The thesis of the paper should indicate that the student has formulated certain concepts about the subject and is able to support them with arguments. It should end with a list of references. The research report on an investigated question should state the purpose of the research, name the processes by which it was carried out, specify what equipment was used, explain the results, and conclude with generalizations about the subject. It should also include citation of any outside sources that were used. In the case of original research, the report should include a survey of related theories in the field, as well as an explanation of the importance of the study and the significance of the findings.

1 Writing case studies in the social sciences

A **case study** is an intensive study of one group or individual. It is usually presented in a relatively fixed format, but the specific parts and order of case study formats vary. Most case studies contain the following components: (1) basic identifying information about the individual or group; (2) a history of the individual or group; (3) observations of the individual's or group's behavior; and (4) conclusions and perhaps recommendations as a result of the observations.

In writing a case study, be sure to differentiate between fact and opinion (see 5b-3). Describe situations; do not interpret them. For example, you may observe nursing-home patients lying in bed facing the door. Describe exactly what you see; do not interpret it as, say, patients watching for visitors. Perhaps medicines are injected in the right hip, and the patients are more comfortable lying on their left hip, and so face the door.

SAMPLE CASE STUDY (Excerpts)

Case Study: Child Observation

Theresa L. Cox

Basic Information

Name: Molly

Setting: Early Education Center

Age: 3 years

Sex: Female

Time: 10:30 to 11:00 A.M.

Date: 6-30-89

Activity: Painting and play

Observations

Molly stretched her arms out and said, "Me," as the teacher was giving another child a paint pencil. She watched as the other child began painting, reached for this child's paint pencil, and then turned to the teacher and said, "Me want some." Molly painted with a paint pencil, squeezed the paint pencil, and periodically

---

touched the paint with her finger. She observed the other
children frequently. Molly made marks on another girl's
paper, and after being reprimanded, she returned to her
paper. Molly marked another girl's arm and smiled
broadly, until she was reprimanded. Molly then marked on
the same child's arm a second time and was placed in
"time-out." She crossed her arms, looked down, frowned,
and muttered, "I'm mad."

[A section on background continues here]

Conclusion

Molly expressed her independence and demonstrated a self-
centered attitude in practically everything she did. She
often returned to activities for which she had earlier
been reprimanded, thus nonverbally (and sometimes
verbally) objecting to what she was told. Cognitively,
Molly is progressing from the sensorimotor stage to the
stage of symbolic thought. She frequently observed her
environment, was very expressive and imitative, and showed
imagination in her play. Molly's actions primarily met
her needs, but she did alter her behavior at times to
avoid punishment. Overall, Molly exemplifies the behavior
of one type of typical toddler.

---

2 Writing research papers in the social sciences

Research papers are common in the social sciences. In some
social science courses you may conduct an experiment or do other
primary research that offers you first-hand exposure to information. Papers that report primary research often have fixed formats,
depending on the subject area; be sure to ask your instructor if a
specific format is required.

You may be assigned a research paper for which you must consult outside sources. These sources are usually articles and books
that report, summarize, and otherwise discuss the findings of other
people's primary research. Following are excerpts from a research
paper for a sociology course, in APA style (see Chapter 33).

BACKGROUND

Some social scientists divide research papers into two categories: the qualitative and the quantitative. Qualitative research, as the name implies, investigates human values, patterns, or other characteristics that cannot be described numerically. It usually includes the personal involvement of the researcher with the subject being studied through interviews, observation, and, in some cases, participation. Throughout the study, the researcher is looking for meaning and patterns, moving progressively towards formulation of a hypothesis, and ultimately, a theory. A major problem for students who attempt to do qualitative research is time. Because the researcher must suit his or her schedule to the availability of the subject, sometimes the semester (or quarter) is not long enough to compile sufficient data to formulate significant conclusions. Also, the student may on occasion find it impossible to be present when important events occur. The quantitative research paper, on the other hand, follows a more structured (and predictable) process. Dealing with subjects that can be tested and expressed numerically, it is appropriate for comparing situations or examining frequency of occurrence. In many cases the researcher begins with a hypothesis, designs a means of testing it, then goes on to prove or disprove it. It requires some skill and knowledge on the part of the researcher in the use of graphs, statistics, and other techniques of quantitative expression.

SAMPLE SOCIAL SCIENCE RESEARCH PAPER (Excerpt)

Douglas Franklin
Professor Rubens
Sociology 101
February 21, 19XX

America's Street People

The number of homeless people in the cities of the United States is a social problem that has grown larger over the last few years. Estimates range from 250,000 (Huntley and Thorton, 1985) to 2-3 million (Bassuk, 1984; Fustero, 1984) people living in the streets of the United States. One fact experts agree on. The stereotypical "skid-row bum" is being replaced by a large assortment of people (Bassuk). As Fustero (1984) reports, the homeless now include "runaway children, immigrants, bag ladies, displaced families, a growing number of unemployed, alcoholics and drug abusers, and the mentally ill" p. 58).

[Paragraphs discussing each group given here]

These changes in the size and nature of the homeless population have many causes. Two stand out. First, the deinstitutionalization of the mentally ill (Bassuk; Fustero) led to a huge outpouring of people unable to take care of themselves. This trend of releasing people from mental institutions "followed the widespread introduction in the 1950s of psychoactive drugs, which seemed to offer the possibility of rehabilitating psychotic people within a community setting" (Bassuk, p. 41). Second, availability of low-cost housing in the cities has dropped sharply since single-room occupancy and other modest facilities have given way to urban development projects (Fustero).

[Paragraphs discussing each cause given here]

[Concluding paragraph with a call to action here]

37d

References

Bassuk, E. L. (1984, July). The homelessness problem.
   Scientific American, pp. 40–45.

Fustero, S. (1984, February). Home on the street.
   Psychology Today, pp. 56–63.

Huntley, S., & Thorton, J. (1985, December 9). Shielding
   the homeless from a deadly winter. U.S. News and World
   Report, p. 79.

37d Using documentation in the social
sciences

In the social sciences, the American Psychological Association
(APA) style is a common method of documentation. It is explained
and illustrated in Chapter 33.

38 Writing in the Natural and Technological Sciences

Disciplines in the **natural and technological sciences** include astronomy, biology, chemistry, engineering, geology, physics, computer science, health sciences, and electrical and mechanical technology, among others.

38a Understanding methods of inquiry in the sciences

The natural and technological sciences ask questions about natural phenomena. The sciences adhere to key principles of research: observation, collection, and organization of physical and factual material. The purpose of scientific investigation is discovery. Scientists observe and attempt to explain natural phenomena. To do this, scientists formulate and test hypotheses in order to explain cause and effect (see 5d) systematically and objectively.

The **scientific method,** commonly used in the sciences to make discoveries, is a procedure for gathering information related to a specific hypothesis. The scientific method is the cornerstone of all inquiry in the sciences. Guidelines for using the scientific method are shown in the chart on the opposite page. A hypothesis is a tentative explanation for an observed phenomenon. The information gathered by observing natural events is known as **empirical evidence.** Scientists need empirical evidence to decide whether a particular hypothesis is true or false. Ideas or opinions, even those stated by experts, do not provide empirical support for a scientific report.

GUIDELINES FOR USING THE SCIENTIFIC METHOD

1. Formulate a hypothesis. Be as specific as possible.
2. Collect previously published information related to the hypothesis.
3. Plan a method of investigation to uncover the information needed to test your hypothesis.
4. Experiment, exactly following the investigative procedures you have outlined. Observe carefully.
5. Analyze the results of the investigation. If the results prove the hypothesis to be false, rework it and begin again. If the results prove the hypothesis to be true, state that, and to finish off your work, suggest additional hypotheses that might be investigated.

38b Understanding writing purposes and practices in the sciences

Scientists usually write to inform their audiences about some piece of research or to relate factual information about some topic. For example, a chemist describes an experiment in detail so that others may evaluate the scientific procedure or may duplicate the experiment to compare results.

Exactness is extremely important in scientific writing. Readers expect precise descriptions of procedures and findings, free of personal biases. Scientists expect to be able to *replicate*—repeat step-by-step—the experiment or other process and get the same outcome as the writer.

Completeness is another essential characteristic of scientific writing. Unless complete information is available, the researcher and the readers can come to wrong conclusions. For example, a researcher may investigate how different types of soil affect plant growth. The researcher should report not only the make-up of each soil type, but also the amount of daylight each plant receives, the moisture content of the soil, the amount and type of fertilizer used,

BACKGROUND

In his discussion of scientific discourse, James Kinneavy, in *A Theory of Discourse* (W. W. Norton, 1971) asserts that it "consists in a consideration of one facet of an object and the making of certain kinds of assertions about this facet." Because its primary concern is with subject matter, all descriptive, narrative, classificatory, and evaluative statements are about the reality under consideration. In short, science is "thing" oriented, not person-oriented. Thus, the assertions must concern the subject of the research, exclude the feelings and emotions of the writer, and only indirectly involve the reader as an object of persuasion. The writing avoids literary effects, for it does not seek to call attention to itself as an object of pleasure . . . The encoder and decoder are less evident in scientific writing than in informative or exploratory discourse. A newspaper or the Platonic dialogues, for example, reflect the writer or speaker much more strongly than does a scientific report. A second difference is probability. Exploratory discourse, says Kinneavy, asks a question; informative discourse answers it; and scientific discourse proves it. "The presence in the discourse of proof, is, therefore, one distinguishing attribute of scientific discourse."

and all other related facts. Having all this information may lead the researcher to unexpected insights. For instance, plant growth may be less dependent on soil type than on a combination of soil type, fertilizer, and watering. This observation could not be reached unless the researcher had the necessary data.

The sciences generally focus on the experiment rather than the experimenter, and on objective observation rather than subjective interpretation. Writing in the sciences is often written in a style that distances a subject from both writer and reader. As a result, the passive voice (see 8m–8n) is common in scientific and technical writing because the observer of the action is either unimportant or understood to be present. Therefore, do not refer to *the experimenter* or *the technician* unless that person is the focus of the discussion. For example, readers expect to see "The plants were observed over a 3-month period" rather than "I observed the plants over a 3-month period." Unless you are writing a personal-reaction paper, generally avoid the first person *(I, we, our)* in writing science papers.

When writing for the sciences, often you are expected to follow fixed formats, which are designed to summarize a project and its results efficiently. Within each section you must organize the presentation of information to achieve clarity and precision. Writers in the sciences often use charts, graphs, tables, diagrams, and other illustrations to present material. In fact, illustrations sometimes explain complex material more clearly than words can.

38c Writing different types of papers in the sciences

Two major types of papers in the sciences are reports and reviews.

1 Writing science reports

Science reports tell about observations and experiments. Such reports may also be called "laboratory reports" when they describe laboratory experiments. Formal reports include the seven sections (plus the title) described in the chart that follows. Less formal reports, as are sometimes assigned in introductory college courses, might not include an abstract or a review of the literature (which would appear in the introduction section). Ask your instructor which sections to include in your report.

38c

PARTS OF THE SCIENCE REPORT

1. **Title.** Be precise; get the point of your paper across clearly.
2. **Abstract.** This is a short overview of the report.
2. **Introduction.** This section states the purpose behind your research and presents the hypothesis. Any needed background information and a review of the literature appear here.
4. **Methods and material.** This section describes the equipment, material, and procedures used.
5. **Results.** This section provides the information obtained from your efforts. Charts, graphs, and photographs help present the data.
6. **Discussion.** You interpret and evaluate the results. Did your efforts support your hypothesis? If not, can you suggest why not? Use concrete evidence in discussing your results.
6. **Conclusion.** This section lists conclusions about the hypothesis and the outcomes of your efforts, with particular attention to any theoretical implications that can be drawn from your work. Be specific in suggesting further research.
8. **References cited.** This list presents references cited in the review of the literature, if any. Its format conforms to the requirements of the documentation style in the particular discipline (see 33g).

QUOTATION ABOUT SCIENCE

Creativity in science could be described as the act of putting two and two together to make five.

—Arthur Koestler

QUOTATION ABOUT SCIENCE

The great tragedy of science—the slaying of a beautiful theory by an ugly fact.

—T. H. Huxley

QUOTATION ABOUT SCIENCE

The world, which took but six days to make, is like to take us six thousand years to make out.

—Sir Thomas Browne

QUOTATION ABOUT SCIENCE

The most incomprehensible thing about the world is that it is comprehensible.

—Albert Einstein

SAMPLE SCIENCE REPORT (Excerpts)

Avery Bird

Biology 101, Professor Ryan

March 3, 19XX

An Experiment to Predict Vestigial Wings
in an F_2 <u>Drosophila</u> Population

INTRODUCTION

The purpose of this experiment was to observe second filial generation (F_2) wing structures in <u>Drosophila</u>. The hypothesis was that abnormalities in vestigial wing structures would follow predicted genetic patterns.

QUOTATION ABOUT WRITING

The ability to translate data and scientific terms into clear, readable, interesting prose is the most important criterion for judging the success of an essay in a science course.
—Linda Simon

METHODS AND MATERIALS

On February 7, four <u>Drosophila</u> (P_1) were observed. Observation was made possible by etherizing the parents (after separating them from their larvae), placing them on a white card, and observing them under a dissecting microscope. The observations were recorded on a chart.

On February 14, the larvae taken from the parents on February 7 had developed to adults (F_1), and they were observed using the same methods as on February 7. The observations were recorded on the chart.

On February 19, the second filial generation (F_2) was supposed to be observed. This was impossible because they did not hatch. The record chart had to be discontinued.

RESULTS

No observations of F_2 were possible. For the F_1 population, according to the prediction, no members should have had vestigial wings. According to the observations, however, some members of F_1 did have vestigial wings.

[Discussion section omitted]

CONCLUSIONS

Two explanations are possible to explain vestigial wings in the F_1 population. Perhaps members from F_2 were present from the F_1 generation. This is doubtful since the incubation period is 10 days, and the time between observations was only 8 days. A second possible explanation is that the genotype of the male P_1 was not WW (indicating that both genes were for normal wings) but rather heterozygous (Ww). If this were true the following would be the first filial products in a 1:1 ratio:

$$P_1 \quad Ww \times ww$$
$$F_1 \quad Ww \ ww$$

Thus, the possibility for vestigial wings would exist. The problem remains, however, that the ratio was not 1:1 2:1 (i.e., 24 normal to 12 abnormal). One explanation could be that the total number was not large enough to extract an average.

The hypothesis concerning predicted genetic patterns in F_2 could not be confirmed because the F_2 generation did not hatch. This experiment should be repeated to get F_2 data. A larger F_1 sample should be used to see if the F_1 findings reported here are repeated.

2   Writing science reviews

A science review is a paper about published information on a scientific topic or issue. The purpose of the review is to inform readers about the current knowledge about the topic or issue. Sometimes the purpose of a science review is to suggest a new interpretation of the old material. Any reinterpretation is based on a synthesis of old information with new, more complete information. In such reviews, the writer must marshal evidence to persuade readers that the new interpretation is valid.

If you are assigned a review, do this: (1) choose a very limited scientific issue currently being researched; (2) use information that is current—the more recently published the articles, books, and journals you consult, the better; (3) accurately summarize and paraphrase material—as explained in Chapter 31; and (4) document your sources (see 33g). You can use headings to help your reader understand your paper's organization and progression of ideas. Here is an example of a science review.

SAMPLE SCIENCE REVIEW PAPER (Excerpt)

Shannon Wagner

Professor Lewis

Chemistry 101

November 12, 19XX

      Applications of the Molecular Beam Mass Spectrometer

               System to Flame Analysis

Flame combustion has long been the means for converting chemical energy into work. Industrial applications began in the sixteenth century with coal

processing to supplement wood charcoal in making iron in
blast furnaces. In the eighteenth century, carbonization
of coal was used to produce industrial gas and coke. The
study of flame has been extremely limited, however, even
with its long history. This is due not to a lack of
interest, but rather to the complexity of flames.
Analyzing the simplest flame requires the principles of
thermodynamics, fluid mechanics, transport phenomena, and
reaction kinetics.

In the 1970s, limited oil supplies forced the United
States to investigate alternative energy sources.
Consequently, research in coal combustion increased
considerably. Improving power-plant efficiency and
lessening pollutant emission into the environment also
have become major concerns. Therefore, a quantitative
description of flame combustion is needed that encompasses
the effects of burner design, fuel, and operating
conditions of the combustion unit. Extensive studies
conducted at the University of California at Los Angeles
(UCLA) examined the effect of fuel composition on
pollutant emissions. To specify concentrations of
contaminants released during combustion, it is necessary
to determine the reactions occurring in the flame. The
molecular beam mass spectrometer (MBMS) sampling system is
best suited for investigating reaction kinetics in flames.

Oxides of nitrogen and sulfur are two major
pollutants emitted into the environment during industrial
combustion processes. Studies of flame kinetics are
conducted to learn how these compounds are formed and to
find ways to control the emissions. The mechanisms of
sulfur and nitrogen oxide formation have been researched
in depth at UCLA (1-4).

[Discussion of chemical reactions and details of the MBMS continues]

Knuth (3) suggests the ideal instrument for flame
studies satisfy the following requirements: monitor all

chemical species, including intermediate species; monitor and transport the sample without disturbing the (nonequilibrium) thermodynamic state of the system; and function in the temperature, pressure, and composition ranges typical of flames. The MBMS system meets these requirements with the best balance.

The MBMS system is extremely versatile in measuring species concentrations. It can monitor several species simultaneously, a given species continuously, and low-concentration species accurately. The concentrations of stable and unstable species are traced as a function of distance from the burner surface. Reacting species exhibit initially high concentrations which then decline. At the same time, product concentrations increase with distance.

In obtaining accurate results, the sampled gas must be transported to the detector with minimum change in composition. The sudden pressure and temperature drop upon beam formation prevents further chemical change in the gas. In addition, the detector analyzes only the core of the beam. Therefore, the results are representative of the actual flame composition.

Flame combustion is usually conducted at high temperatures, moderate pressures, and with fuels of varying composition. Gorji and Saremi (2, 4) have shown the MBMS system to meet the requirements for high-temperature sampling. The system reports accurate results when operating at pressures ranging from 50 torr to high pressures (5). In addition, effective studies have been performed with both fuel-rich (low-oxygen content) and fuel-lean (high-oxygen content) flames (4).

[Conclusion that summarizes and makes a prediction about future research results given here]

1. Gargurevich, I. A. Masters Thesis, University of California at Los Angeles, 1980.

2. Gorji, K. M. Masters Thesis, University of California at Lost Angeles, 1974.

3. Knuth, E. L. In _Engine Pollutant Emission Formation and Measurement_; Springer, G. S., Patterson, D. J., Eds.; Plenum: New York: 1973; pp. 319–363.

4. Saremi, S. Masters Thesis, University of California at Los Angeles, 1979.

5. Stevenson, J. S. Masters Thesis, University of California at Los Angeles, 1980.

38d Using documentation in the sciences

The documentation styles in the various natural and technological sciences differ slightly from each other. Consult the manual of the discipline in which you are writing. See 33g for a list of manuals and related information about documentation in the sciences.

39 Business Writing

Business writing requires of you what other kinds of writing call for: understanding your audience and your purpose. This chapter explains how to write business letters (39a), job application letters (39b), résumés (39c), and memos (39d). As you write for business, use the guidelines listed in the chart below.

GUIDELINES FOR BUSINESS WRITING
■ Consider your audience's needs and expectations.
■ Show that you understand the purpose for a business communication and the context in which it takes place.
■ Put essential information first.
■ Make your points clearly and directly.
■ Use conventional formats.

39a Writing and formatting a business letter

Business letters are clear, usually short communications written to give information, to build good will, or to establish a foundation for discussions or transactions. Experts in business and government agree that the letters likely to get results are short, simple, direct, and human. Malcolm Forbes, editor in chief of *Forbes,* a popular business magazine, gives this advice: (1) call the person by name; (2) tell what your letter is about in the first paragraph; (3) be honest; (4) be clear and specific; (5) use accurate English; (6) be positive and natural; (7) edit ruthlessly.

Some students expect business writing to involve rules about margins, indentations, and abbreviations. While such concerns do matter, they should take only a small part of your time. Format can be taught in just a few lessons; the emphasis in business writing is on audience, tone, and organization.

Audience: Business writers need to keep acutely aware of their audiences. As business correspondence is aimed at a particular individual or limited group of individuals, rather than the general audience of essays, in certain aspects business writing differs markedly from essay writing. The most obvious difference is that the use of *you* and *I/we* is preferable to the third person often used in essays.

Tone: The tone of business correspondence needs to be adjusted to suit the actual relationship between author and audience. It is perfectly conceivable that a business person might write a very formal memo to the staff of one department about lax security and a minute later write a relatively friendly memo to another department congratulating it for exceeding production goals. The key word in deciding on the appropriate tone is *relationship.* Your students can judge the nature of the relationship by asking themselves a few questions as they prepare to write: Who is this person? How long and under what circumstances have we known one another? What do I want him or her to do? No matter what the relationship, correspondence should be written in standard, clear, and honest English. See Chapter 21 for discussions of levels of formality and artificial language.

For business letters and envelopes, use the guidelines given in the chart below, and use the standard formats that appear on the next two pages. Also, to avoid sexist language in the salutation of the letter, use the guidelines on page 750.

GUIDELINES FOR BUSINESS LETTER AND ENVELOPE	
LETTERHEAD	If printed stationery is not available, type the company name and address centered at top of white paper, 8½ × 11".
DATE	Place the date at left margin under letterhead, when typing in block form as shown in the example. If using paragraph indentations, type date to end at right margin.
INSIDE ADDRESS	Direct the letter to a specific person. Be accurate in spelling the name and in the address. If unsure of your information, call the company and ask questions.
SUBJECT LINE	Type at left margin. Be concise; in a few words inform your reader of the subject.
SALUTATION	Use a first name only if you know the person. Otherwise, use *Mr.* or *Ms.* or whatever title is applicable. Avoid sexist language.
CLOSING	*Sincerely* is generally appropriate unless you know the person very well and wish to use *Cordially.* Leave about four lines for your signature.
NAME LINES	Type your name and title. The title can be on the same line as your name or on the next line.
ENVELOPE	Use block form. If a printed envelope is not available, type the company name and return address in the upper left corner of a 9½ × 4" envelope. In the center of envelope, type the name and address of the person to receive your letter.

39a

```
                    BUSINESS LETTER FORMAT


              AlphaOmega Industries, Inc.         Letterhead
                   123456 Motor Parkway
                   Fresh Hills, CA 55555



    December 28, 19xx                             Date

    Ron R. London, Sales Director                Inside
    Seasonal Products Corp.                       address
    5000 Seasonal Place
    Wiscasset, ME 00012


    Subject: Spring Promotional Effort           Subject line


    Dear Ron:                                    Salutation

    Since we talked last week, I have completed plans
    for the Spring promotion of the products that we
    market jointly.  AlphaOmega and Seasonal Products
    should begin a direct mailing of the enclosed
    brochure on January 28th.

    I have secured several mailing lists that contain
    the names of people who have a positive economic
    profile for our products.  The profile and the
    outline of the lists are attached.            Message

    Do you have additional approaches for the
    promotion?  I would like to meet with you on
    January 6 to discuss them, and to work out the
    details of the project.

    Please call me and let me know if a meeting next
    week at your office accommodates your schedule.

    Sincerely,                                   Closing
```

Alan Stone   Signature

```
    Alan Stone, Director of Special Promotions   Name, Title

    AS/kw                                         Initials of
                                                  writer/
                                                  of typist
    cc:  Ken Lane, Vice President of Marketing

    Enc.: Brochure; Mailing Lists;               Other
          Customer Profile                        notations
```

TEACHING TIP

Some people are fascinated by those initials and abbreviations they see in letters, at the left margin a few lines below the signature. Few of our students have any need to use these on a regular basis, but in case you are asked about these symbols, here's a quick review.

AS/kw The writer's initials followed by the typist's initials (known as reference initials). Practice varies in the use of capital and lowercase letters. Sometimes a colon is used: *AS:kw.*

Enclosures: Typed below the reference initials, a numeric notation alerts the opener of the mail to the presence of additional material: brochures, résumés, photographs. A multi-page enclosure counts as one. Sometimes the notation is written out as "Enc.: résumé and letter of reference."

cc: Ken Lane Typed below the reference initials, the abbreviation *cc* indicates that a carbon copy has been sent. Carbon paper is passé, but the abbreviation lingers. The notation is followed by a name or initials.

P.S. A postscript may be added after everything else to highlight a point made within the letter or to add a brief personal message. Do not use a postscript to add important information that you forgot to include in the letter; rewrite the letter. Strings of postscripts (P.P.S., etc.) are definitely not suitable for business writing.

TEACHING TIP: SALUTATIONS

The salutation is the first thing a reader sees, so it must be suitable if the letter is to be taken seriously. In most situations the salutation presents no problem, but sometimes the writer has to make a difficult decision. Here are some guidelines:

1. When the recipient's name is known: *Dear Mr. ____; Dear Ms. ____; Dear Mrs. ____; Dear Miss ____.*

2. When the writer normally calls the recipient by his or her first name and when the letter is relatively informal: *Dear Heidi; Dear Elliot.*

3. When the letter is going to a position within an organization and the writer has not been able to get an individual's name: *Manager, Customer Service Department; Dear Manager.*

4. When the writer does not know the sex of the recipient: *Dear Mr. or Ms. Gery; Dear Director; Dear Mr. or Ms. Director.*

5. When the recipient is a group: *Dear Members of ____; Dear Committee Members.*

6. When there will be many anonymous recipients; *Dear Homeowners; Dear Student; Dear Customer.*

GUIDELINES FOR WRITING A NONSEXIST SALUTATION

You may want to send a business letter when you do not have a specific person to whom to address your letter. Use the following steps to prepare a nonsexist salutation.

1. Telephone the company to which you are sending the letter. State your reason for sending the letter, and ask for the name of the person who should receive it.

2. If you do not have and cannot find out the name of the person who should read your letter, use a general title in your salutation.

   YES   Dear Personnel Officer

   Dear Credit Card Manager

   Dear Sales Office Director

   No   Dear Sir [obviously sexist]

   Dear Madam/Sir or Dear Sir/Madam [few women want to be addressed as "Madam"]

The best-written letter means nothing if it does not reach its destination. For letters in the United States, use at least the zip code, which is five digits long. Some addresses include the zip code followed by a dash and an additional four digits. Use this nine-number code when available. For letters to other countries, use as complete an address as you have available, including the postal code when you know it.

```
                    BUSINESS ENVELOPE FORMAT
AlphaOmega Industries, Inc.
123456 Motor Parkway
Fresh Hills, CA 55555



                    Ron R. London, Sales Director
                    Seasonal Products Corp.
                    5000 Seasonal Place
                    Wiscasset, ME 00012
```

39b Writing and formatting a job application letter

One important type of business letter is the job application letter. A sample job application letter appears on the next page. Here are guidelines for a job application letter.

GUIDELINES FOR JOB APPLICATION LETTERS	
YOUR ADDRESS	To the right, type your address as you would on an envelope. Be sure to give as your address a place where you can be reached **by letter.** Include the zip code.
DATE	Put the date below your address.
INSIDE ADDRESS	Direct your letter to a specific person. You can phone a company to find out the name of the personnel director or department head to whom you are writing. Be accurate. A misspelled name can offend the receiver. A wrong address will likely result in a lost letter.
SALUTATION	Be accurate. No one likes to see his or her name misspelled. If you are replying to an ad that gives only a post-office box number, omit the salutation and start your opening paragraph directly below the inside address. To avoid sexist language, use the chart on the opposite page.
INTRODUCTORY PARAGRAPH	State your purpose for writing and the source of your information about the job.
BODY PARAGRAPH(S)	Interest the reader in the skills and talents you offer by mentioning whatever experience you have *that relates to the specific job*. Mention your enclosed résumé, but do *not* summarize it.
CLOSING PARAGRAPH	Suggest an interview, stating that you will call to make arrangements.
CLOSING	*Sincerely* is generally appropriate.
NAME LINES	Type your full name below your signature. Leave about four lines for your signature.
NOTATION	If you are enclosing any material with your letter, type *Enc.:* and briefly list what you are enclosing.

TEACHING TIP

Few letters are as difficult for students to write as those they send in hopes of getting a job interview. The following suggestions can be adapted to any job-seeking situation.

Before writing a letter of application, the student should already have prepared a stock résumé, one that can be used for any job in the student's area of interest. A properly written résumé will be good for six months to a year or more. As it lists the basics of a career to date, it should not have to be redone for each job sought.

In the cover letter, students should tell a prospective employer what they can bring to the job, why they feel they are qualified—not why they want the job. This is the place to expand upon the information listed in the résumé. Do not, however, summarize or repeat large parts of the résumé.

In paragraph 1, students should tell how they found out about the job (ad, friend with the company). In paragraphs 2 to 4, students should pick three skills or personal qualities that they know are needed for the job. These may include, but are not limited to, using office machines, driving a delivery truck, preparing a payroll, speaking a second language, being available for night shifts or out-of-town travel.

In the next paragraph, students should discuss their specific qualifications. They can draw upon work experience, education, volunteer work, family responsibilities, and hobbies. In the final paragraph, students should thank the reader for taking the time to consider the application. They should also express a wish for an interview at the employer's convenience and include a phone number and address.

JOB APPLICATION LETTER

422 Broward
University of Texas at Arlington
Arlington, Texas 75016
May 15, 19XX

Rae Clemens, Director of Human Resources
Taleno, Ward Marketing, Inc.
1471 Summit Boulevard
Houston, Texas 78211

Dear Ms. Clemens:

I am answering the advertisement for a marketing trainee
that Taleno, Ward placed in today's <u>Houston</u> <u>Chronicle</u>.

Marketing has been one of the emphases of my course work
here at the University of Texas, Arlington, as you will
see on my enclosed résumé. This past year, I gained
some practical experience as well, when I developed
marketing techniques that helped to turn my typing
service into a busy and profitable small business.

Successfully marketing the typing service (with flyers,
advertisements in college publications, and even a two-
for-one promotion) makes me a very enthusiastic novice.
I can think of no better way to become a professional
than working for Taleno, Ward.

I will be here at the Arlington campus through August 1.
You can reach me by phone at 555-1976. Unless I hear
from you before, I'll call on May 25 about setting up an
interview.

Sincerely,

Lee Franco

Lee Franco

Enc.: Résumé

39c Writing and formatting a résumé

A **résumé** is an easy-to-read, factual document that presents your qualifications for employment. The résumé that appears on the next page was enclosed with Lee Franco's job application letter. All résumés cover certain standard items: name, address, phone number; education; past experience; skills and talents; publications, awards, honors, membership in professional organizations; list of references or a statement that they are "available upon request."

A résumé gives you an opportunity to present a positive picture of yourself to a prospective employer. You are expected to give information about your skills, your experience, and your education. Employers understand that college students may have limited experience in the business world. Think of headings that allow you to emphasize your strengths. For example, if you have never done paid work, do not use *Business Experience.* You can use *Work Experience* if you have done volunteer or other unpaid work. If the experience you offer an employer is that you have run school or social events, you might use *Organizational Experience.* If your greatest strength is your academic record, put your educational attainments first.

You may choose to arrange your résumé in emphatic order with the most important information first and the least important last. Lee Franco's résumé on the next page uses emphatic order. Or you may choose to arrange information in chronological (time) order, a sequence that is good for showing a steady work history or solid progress in a particular field. Stephen Schmit's résumé uses chronological order; it is shown opposite Lee Franco's résumé on page 755.

39d Writing and formatting a memo

A **memo** can serve many purposes. It can call for action or document action. It can provide a written record of a conversation. It can make a brief informal report. A sample memo, its parts labeled, is shown on the last page of this chapter. It is in block style. Note that paragraphs are not indented, so double spaces are used between paragraphs. When you are writing a memo, determine who should receive the information by deciding on the audience and the purpose for the memo. At the **"to" line,** list the person or people who need to act on the information in the memo. List for **distribution** anyone else you think should be informed. The notation for distribution can be "Dist:" or "cc:".

EMPHATIC RÉSUMÉ

MARKETING TRAINEE

Lee Franco
422 Broward
University of Texas at Arlington
Arlington, Texas 75016

713-555-1976

The experience I acquired marketing my typing service
provided me with a good practical background for a
position as a marketing trainee.

MARKETING EXPERIENCE (program for campus typing service)

Evaluated typing-service capabilities; analyzed market
for service; drew up and implemented marketing plan;
produced 2-color flyer, designed print ads and wrote
copy, developed and ran special promotion. August
19XX to February 19XX

BUSINESS EXPERIENCE

Type-Right Typing Service: Ran campus typing service
for two years. Duties included word processing
(Wordstar, Displaywrite, SuperCalc), proofreading,
billing and other financial record-keeping, and
customer contact. August 19XX to present

Archer & Archer Advertising: Worked as general
assistant in the copy department under direct
supervision of John Allen, Director. Duties included
proofreading, filing, direct client contact. June
19XX to August 19XX

ADDITIONAL EXPERIENCE

Coordinated student-employment service at Hawthorne
High School, Baton Rouge, Louisiana. Duties included
contacting students to fill jobs with local employers,
arranging interviews, and writing follow-up reports on
placements.

EDUCATION

University of Texas, Arlington
B.A. May 19XX, Psychology, Marketing

EXTRACURRICULAR

Marketing Club, Computer Graphics Society

References available upon request.

CHRONOLOGICAL RÉSUMÉ

STEPHEN L. SCHMIT
5230 ST. STEPHENS STREET
BOSTON, MASSACHUSETTS 02188
617—555—8165

CAREER QUALIFICATIONS
Technical writer trained in preparation of technical
definitions and descriptions, manuals, catalogues, part
lists, and instructional materials. Experienced in
evaluating and editing computer documentation containing
syntax formats.

WORK EXPERIENCE
Northeastern University, Boston, Massachusetts
Reading and Writing Specialist, English Language Center.
March—July 1989, January—March 1990

Created individual lesson plans for each student
assigned to the Reading and Writing Laboratory. Designed
materials for use in the Laboratory. Ran the Laboratory
for approximately one hundred students for twenty hours
each week, maintained records of students' work, and
prepared written and oral reports on student progress
and the operation of the Laboratory.

Tutor of Foreign Students, September 1987—Present

Integrated foreign students into a large urban school
and community while being a positive role model
educationally and socially.

William M. Mercer, Incorporated, Boston, Massachusetts,
September—December 1986

Data Processing and general office duties. Initiated
and implemented a CRT search system for office
personnel.

American Architect Magazine, New York, N.Y., 1983—1986
Student intern.

SPECIAL SKILLS
BASIC programming. PASCAL, Edition and Graphics courses to
be completed June 1990.

EDUCATION
Northeastern University, Boston, Massachusetts
Bachelor of Arts, June 1988

Concentration: English with minors in Technical
Communications and Economics.
Activities: Selected to serve on the Residence Judicial
Board, an impartial group of faculty, staff and students
who adjudicate discipline problems; Northeastern News;
Northeastern Yearbook staff.

Use the **subject line** to define the memo's contents. A subject line is like an essay title.

In the **message,** give the most important information first. Give additional information or secondary points in decreasing order of importance, but include them only if they are essential to the picture. Be concise (see Chapter 16). When possible, set off listed items for ease of reference. If you expect action of some kind from the memo, end the memo with a clear statement of your expectations—about the action and about the time the action should take place.

MEMO FORMAT

Date	12 March 19XX
"To" Line	To: Len DeBeers
Sender	From: Ann Soukolov
Subject Line	Subject: Annual Meeting Publications Support

Message	For the annual meeting of our stockholders on 3 April we need the active participation of the following people:
	          —speech writer
	          —graphic artist
	          —graphics production specialist
	          —one copy editor
	          —typists and proofreaders

	We will use the office space on the second floor of the office building next to the auditorium. Word processing equipment should be in place by Monday. Six phones were installed today.
	Art Smith, the meeting manager, will be here on Monday for a kick-off meeting at 10:00 a.m.
	Please prepare a detailed list of critical items for that meeting.
Initials of writer/of typist	AS/ls

Distribution	Dist: A. Adams
	       R. Traub
	       T. Ziff-Smith

---

40 Writing Essay Tests

Writing answers for essay tests is one of the most important writing tasks in college. Essay tests give you the chance to synthesize and apply your knowledge, thereby helping your instructor determine what you have learned.

Common in the social sciences and humanities, essay tests are becoming increasingly common in the natural sciences as well. Essay tests demand that you recall information and also put assorted pieces of that information into contexts that lead to generalizations you can support. For example, from your reading and lecture notes, you may know many facts about the battles in the Korean War, but the facts become significant when you use them to show one side's superior military strength, or a general's brilliant tactics, or a pattern of defeats from seemingly inconsequential misjudgments.

40a Understanding cue words and key words

Most essay questions contain what is sometimes called a **cue word,** a word of direction that tells what the content of your answer is expected to emphasize. Knowing the major cue words and their meanings can increase your ability to plan efficiently and to write effectively. Be guided by the following list of cue words and sample essay-test questions.

Each essay question also has one or more **key words** that tell you the information, topics, and ideas you are to write about. For example, in the question "Criticize the architectural function of the modern football stadium," the key words are "architectural function" and "football stadium." To answer the question successfully, you must define "architectural function," then describe the typical modern football stadium (mentioning major variations when important), and then you must discuss how well the typical football stadium

BACKGROUND

Diane Durkin (*Writing in the Disciplines,* Random House, 1987) warns that students often go wrong in writing papers or answers to essay questions on tests because they spend too little time analyzing the task they are given. She suggests several steps that can help students understand assignments more clearly and thoroughly. She advises them to do the following:

1. Find the key verb in the assignment. Does it ask you to analyze? explain? define? summarize? If the verb is vague—e.g., *consider*—you must substitute another verb that is indicated by the question as a whole.

2. Determine the subject of the writing task. What is the topic?

3. Rewrite the assignment in a form that tells you precisely what you are to do.

CUE WORDS FOUND IN QUESTIONS FOR ESSAY TESTS

Analyze means to separate something into parts and discuss the parts.

Analyze Socrates's discussion of "good life" and "good death."

Clarify means to make clear.

Clarify T. S. Eliot's idea of tradition.

Classify means to arrange into groups on the basis of shared characteristics.

Classify the different types of antipredator adaptations.

Compare and contrast means to show similarities and differences.

Compare and contrast the reproductive cycles of a moss and a flowering plant.

Criticize means to give your opinion concerning the good points and bad points of something.

Criticize the architectural function of the modern football stadium.

Define means to give the definition of something and in so doing to separate it from similar things.

Define the term "yellow press."

Describe means to explain features to make clear an object, procedure, or event.

Describe the chain of events that constitutes the movement of a sensory impulse along a nerve fiber.

Discuss means to consider and evaluate as many details as possible concerning an issue or event.

Discuss the effects of television viewing on modern attitudes toward violence.

Evaluate means to give your opinion about the value of something.

Evaluate Margaret Mead's contribution to the field of anthropology.

CUE WORDS FOUND IN QUESTIONS FOR ESSAY TESTS *(continued)*

Explain means to give reasons for something.

> Explain how the amount of carbon dioxide in the blood regulates rates of heartbeat and breathing.

Illustrate means to give examples of something.

> Illustrate the use of symbolism in Richard Wright's novel *Native Son*.

Interpret means to explain the meaning of something.

> Give your interpretation of Robert Frost's poem "Fire and Ice."

Justify means to show or prove that something is valid or correct.

> Justify the existence of labor unions in today's economy.

Prove means to present evidence that cannot be refuted logically or with other evidence.

> Prove that smoking is a major cause of lung cancer.

Relate means to show the connections between two or more things.

> Relate increases in specific crimes in 1932–33 to the prevailing economic conditions.

Review means to reexamine, summarize, or reprise something.

> Review the structural arrangements in proteins to explain the meaning of the term *polypeptide*.

Show means to point out or demonstrate something.

> Show what effects pesticides have on the production of wheat.

Summarize means to repeat briefly the major points of something.

> Summarize the major benefits of compulsory education.

Support means to argue in favor of something.

> Support the position that passage of the equal rights amendment must occur at the national rather than the state level.

TEACHING TIP

Any instructor with more than a few weeks of classroom experience knows that making good essay questions for an examination is not a simple matter. Considerations regarding adequate coverage of material, clarity of instructions, and availability of time must play a part in what is asked and how it is asked as well. As a way to understand the students' task, and how one can reasonably expect it to be carried out, an instructor can always write the answers to the questions he or she poses. The results are often gratifying, but sometimes they reveal gaps in what is being tested, ambiguous directions, or unreasonable length. The teacher who recognizes these shortcomings before giving a test is more likely to have students who perform well than the teacher who finds out afterwards from the students themselves that there was not enough time to finish or that they were not sure what they were being asked to do.

meets the principles you named in your definition of "architectural function." Similarly, in the question, "Classify the different types of antipredator adaptations" you need to define "antipredator adaptations" by dividing them into groups that are based on their shared characteristics.

BACKGROUND

The first use of the word *essay* to refer to a literary form was made by Montaigne in 1580 for his informal written reflections about himself and mankind in general. Resigning from a judicial post in 1570, he devoted himself to writing his *Essays,* an edition of Books I and II appearing in 1580 and the final emended edition of books I, II and III in 1595. Close to the same time (1597) in England, Francis Bacon's *Essays* were written as "counsels for the successful conduct of life and the management of men." Since the seventeenth century, essayists in England and America have found an omnivorous audience for their work. The names of Addison, Steele, Lamb, Hazlitt, and Chesterton in England, Mencken, E. B. White, Lincoln Steffens and others in this country have proved as memorable as their counterparts in poetry and fiction and drama.

40b Writing effective responses to essay-test questions

An effective response to an essay-test question is complete and logically organized. Here are two answers to the question, "Classify the different types of antipredator adaptations." The first one is successful; the second is not. The sentences are numbered for your reference, and they are explained on the next page.

ANSWER 1

(1) Although many antipredator adaptations have evolved in the animal kingdom, they all can be classified into four major categories according to the prey's response to the predator. (2) The first category is hiding techniques. (3) These techniques include cryptic coloration and behavior in which the prey assumes characteristics of an inanimate object or part of a plant. (4) The second category is early enemy detection. (5) The prey responds to alarm signals from like prey or other kinds of prey before the enemy can get too close. (6) Evasion of the pursuing predator is the third category. (7) Prey that move erratically or in a compact group are displaying this technique. (8) The fourth category is active repulsion of the predator. (9) The prey kills, injures, or sickens the predator, establishing that it represents danger to the predator.

ANSWER 2

(1) Antipredator adaptations are the development of the capabilities to reduce the risk of attack from a predator without too much change in the life-supporting activities of the prey. (2) There are many different types of antipredator adaptations. (3) One type is camouflage, hiding from the predator by cryptic coloration or imitation of plant parts. (4) An example of this type of antipredator adaptation is the praying mantis. (5) A second type is the defense used by monarch butterflies, a chemical protection that makes some birds ill after eating the butterfly. (6) This protection may injure the bird by causing it to vomit, and it can educate the bird against eating other butterflies. (7) Detection and evasion are also antipredator adaptations.

Here is an explanation of what happens, sentence by sentence, in the two responses.

	ANSWER 1	ANSWER 2
Sentence 1	Sets up classification system and gives number of categories based on key word	Defines key word
Sentence 2	Names first category	Throwaway sentence—accomplishes nothing
Sentence 3	Defines first category	Names and defines first category
Sentence 4	Names second category	Gives an example for first category
Sentence 5	Defines second category	Gives an example for second (unnamed) category
Sentence 6	Names third category	Continues to explain example
Sentence 7	Defines third category	Names two categories
Sentence 8	Names fourth category	
Sentence 9	Defines fourth category	

Answer 1 sets about immediately answering the question by introducing a classification system as called for by the cue word, *classify.* Answer 2, on the other hand, defines the key word, a waste of time on a test that will be read by an audience of specialists. Answer 1 is tightly organized, easy to follow, and to-the-point, whereas answer 2 rambles, never manages to name the four categories, and says more around the subject than on it.

40c Developing strategies for writing essay tests

If you develop strategies for writing essay tests, you will be more comfortable as you take essay tests and your writing will likely become more effective. Remember that your purpose in answering

TEACHING TIP

In *Helping Students Write Well* (MLA 1982) Barbara E. Walvoord lists six guidelines for students taking essay exams. Pointing out that "the race goes not to the swiftest writers but to those who best organize and present what they know," she suggests that the student taking an essay test follow these general procedures.

1. Organize around a clear focus, one that is limited enough to cover in the time allotted and that allows inclusion of all the material the teacher will expect to find. This focus should be expressed in a thesis sentence.

2. Outline the answer. Know the three or four points to be covered to be sure that they all develop, explain, or prove the thesis sentence.

3. Come to the point quickly, perhaps even beginning with the thesis sentence.

4. Stick to the subject. Telling everything isn't expected. The test is to select, organize, and analyze major points.

5. Be thorough. Do not leave out anything important to the defense of the thesis sentence.

6. Support generalities with specific and relevant evidence.

40c

Some students have a harder time than others writing under a time limit. For those who have serious difficulty in pacing themselves, and thus suffer greater anxiety about the process, a few suggestions may help. Making an outline at the outset, or at least jotting down the major points to be covered, can save the student time by charting the direction of the answer. Leaving a few minutes at the end for quick editing will produce more polished copy. Some students leave blank space at the beginning of an answer so that an accurate introduction can be inserted after the answer is written. The student who has problems working efficiently under a time limit can improve his or her performance with practice. Before an examination, such a student should compose several questions an instructor is likely to ask, then, with a timer running, practice writing answers to them. A familiar process is always less threatening than an unfamiliar one.

essay exam questions is to show your instructor what you know in a clear, direct, and well-organized way. Most essay tests have a time limit, so test-taking strategies will help you work efficiently.

STRATEGIES FOR WRITING ESSAY TESTS

1. Do not start writing immediately.
2. If the test has more than one question, read them all at the start. If you know from the beginning what you will have to answer, you will know what to expect and you will have a better sense of how to budget your time by either dividing it equally or allotting more for some questions. If you have a choice, select questions about which you know the most—and the ones whose cue words you can work with best.
3. Reread each question you are going to answer and then underline the cue and key words to determine exactly what the question asks for.
4. Use the writing process as much as possible within the constraints of the time limit. Try always to find time to plan and revise. For a one-hour test of one question, take about 10 minutes to jot down preliminary ideas about content and organization, and save at least 10 minutes to reread your answer and to revise and edit it. For a one-hour test with more than one question, divide your time for planning, drafting, and revising accordingly. If you suddenly become pressed for time— but try to avoid this—consider skipping a question you cannot answer well or a question that counts less on your total score.
5. Organize and develop your answer to provide what a question's cue and key words (see 40a) ask for.

The more you use these strategies, the better you will be able to use them to your advantage. Try to practice them, making up questions that might be on your test and timing yourself as you write the answers. Doing this offers you another benefit: if you study by anticipating possible questions and writing out the answers, you will be very well prepared if one or two of them show up on the test. As you use these strategies, adapt them to your personal needs.

Appendix A: Writing with a Computer

Some people write with a pen, some with a typewriter, and some—an increasing number—with a computer. Unlike other writing tools, computers make relatively painless the activities of planning, shaping, drafting, revising, and editing (see Chapters 2 and 3). If you do not have a computer and word-processing program at your disposal, worry not. The usual methods of writing will continue to serve you well. If you can use a word processor, you will likely agree with most writers who rejoice over a new-found flexibility.

As much as possible, tailor your use of a computer to your personal needs. Some experienced writers prefer to use a computer only for preparing the final copy. Others like to plan and shape (see Chapter 2) by hand and to write all drafts on a computer. Still other writers feel more comfortable writing out drafts by hand and then revising with a computer. Yet others like to use a computer throughout the writing process. See what works best for you in each writing situation.

A1   Basic operations in word processing

You can write with any computer equipped with any word-processing software and printer. You need to type, but you do not have to be an expert typist. You need also to know how to make your particular equipment perform the operations you want. To use a computer to greatest benefit, expect to take the time to learn its various operations. Once you can handle word processing with ease you will not have to interrupt your writing process to figure out how to do something mechanical. Each program is a little different, and many call their functions by different names. Become familiar with your word processor's jargon so that you can learn from a manual or discuss the program's functions with other people.

Here are more or less generic terms you will likely encounter in word processing.

The Language of Word Processing

ADD = insert material

BLOCK = mark off a specific section of material on the screen

COPY = reproduce material in an additional location

CURSOR = the highlighted (sometimes pulsing) spot on the screen that signals where material can be typed in or operations begun

DELETE (CUT) = erase

FILE = a document identified by a name you create

INSERT = add material to what is already on screen

MOVE (PASTE) = transfer material from one place to another

PRINT = have the printer produce a "hard" (paper) copy

RETRIEVE (GET) = bring to the screen

SAVE = record on disk

SCROLL = look up and down the material on screen

SEARCH = locate a specific word or group of words on a page or in an entire document

TEXT = the typed material appearing on screen

Do not assume that your work is safe simply because it is on a computer disk. Disks are highly vulnerable, especially to magnetism. Place a disk too close to a magnetic source and, quick as a cursor's flash, your hours of work can be irretrievably garbled. In general, floppy disks do not survive well when they have to coexist with dust, cigarette ashes, food, or high humidity. Do not touch or bend your disks. Save your work frequently. Make a rule for yourself to save your work, say, every two pages or every ten to fifteen minutes. Some writers print out regularly. Having a printout, also called hard copy, means you have a record of your work, even if your disk incurs problems.

Relieved of the sometimes tedious work of copying and recopying material, many writers feel more creative when they use a computer. Their ideas seem to flow more freely when each new thought does not lead to a recopying job. Nevertheless, some writers find that recopying by hand helps them think of new ideas. Be careful, therefore, not to ignore what has always served you well when you wrote by hand. Also, do not let yourself be seduced by the wonders of a computer. It is only a machine.

A2 Using the computer for gathering ideas

At a computer terminal, you can record your thoughts as they occur to you. Try freewriting (2d-2) or brainstorming (2d-3). Consider using **invisible writing** by turning off your monitor so that you cannot see what you are writing. This helps you avoid the temptation of editing while you are getting ideas "on paper." After a while, turn your monitor back on to see what you wrote.

As you use idea-gathering techniques, resist the temptation to delete material. Disks hold a great deal. You never know what you might want later. A computer can save everything together for you legibly—without arrows, paper clips, or Scotch tape—then retrieve it when you are ready to decide which material you might use and in what order. If you are writing a research paper (see Chapter 32), be careful to keep full documentation of your sources also on disk.

A3 Using the computer for organization

You can shape, or outline, your essay (see 2e) at a computer. Read what you have written, and put a symbol near what seems most important. Now look over the marked parts, and copy them to the bottom of your text so that you can look at them grouped together. Shuffle them into several different orders. Does it matter which part comes first, second, and so on? Are the parts equally important, or do some seem subordinate to others? Try indenting the subordinate parts to make a rough outline (see 2e-5). Although what you have written may be so full of typos that only you can decipher it, it will still be more legible than its hand-written equivalent.

A4 Using the computer for drafting and development

Whether you are working with freewriting, invention notes, an outline, or all three, at some point you must create a "real draft." Try to write a whole draft at one session, second-guessing and rewriting as little as possible. If you have questions, or think you may want to elaborate on something but cannot think how at the moment, insert a symbol that will alert you to "talk to yourself" later. When you finish the draft and begin revising, your symbols will help you focus on areas that need reworking.

If your planning techniques result in clusters of ideas or freewriting, try picking any item (probably the one you know the most about) and adding details. Finish that item, whether it takes one or several paragraphs, and then move to another item and do the same thing. If you outlined, flesh out each section as you get to it. The computer automatically will move the remaining sections down to make room for what you add.

Be aware that even a handwritten draft may seem complete—simply because it has a beginning and end, with paragraphs in between. Many writers feel the urge to consider a rough draft the final version, and they type it up. Understandably, this urge is even stronger with computer drafts, which appear finished because they are already typed. Resist the urge to think neatness means completion. Rough drafts are excellent as springboards to revising. You can use them to ask a peer critic (see 3c-5) to react. Keep telling yourself not to confuse a draft with a final version.

A5 Using the computer for revision

Revision—addition to, deletion from, substitution for, and rearrangement of material—is a many-faceted activity (see 3c). You think through your ideas, and you change sentences and words. Because the computer can neither read nor think, you must decide what needs to be done.

As you read through your draft, word by word, use symbols and notes to yourself in brackets to alert you to what you want to revise. Remember, the computer screen does not become illegible from too many notations, as a written or typed draft can. Alternatively, some writers prefer to make changes on hard copy and enter those changes on disk.

If you think of something to add—for instance, something an expert said on your subject—move the cursor to the place in the draft that might be improved by the detail and type the detail in. You can add anything from a word to a many-paragraph segment. If you are unsure about the best place for an addition, type it at the end of the draft, then move the addition into more than one place. See where it helps most, then delete the extras.

Delete with caution. Move material you think you want to drop to the end of your document. Later you may find you want to return the deletion to your draft, so save it where you can find it. This method works for the deletion of a single word or of many pages.

Sometimes you may want to rearrange material. The computer makes rearranging relatively painless. You may make endless versions of your draft until you are satisfied with the order. Try reordering your body paragraphs, splitting or joining some existing paragraphs, and moving your last paragraph to the first position. You may be surprised. Save the most promising versions. Try printing several versions and asking your peers to react to them.

A6 Using the computer for editing and proofreading

Editing takes place throughout your writing. Proofreading takes place after the last draft has been written. Read your printed copy aloud, or listen to someone else read it. Note items that need to be corrected. Also, you can use the screen to help you proofread and edit. Use the block command to highlight a five- or six-line section, and read each section slowly and carefully. This strategy allows you to work in small segments, and thus you can reduce the tendency to read too quickly and thereby fail to detect errors.

You might try making your own "spell-and-style checker" by keeping a file of the mistakes that you have made in the past. For example, if the difference between *its* and *it's* always escapes you or if you know that you tend to misuse the colon, call up your mistake file, and search your draft for those items. Each time the search stops, check the item against the rules in this handbook.

After you have edited and proofread and you are ready to print out your final version, make sure that your hard copy conforms to manuscript format requirements from your instructor, or use Appendix B.

A7 Using writer's aid programs

A growing number of special programs—some of them built into word processors—are designed specifically to help writers.

Most *prewriting programs* ask you questions to help you generate ideas on a topic. You will quickly learn the questions, but having "someone to talk to" can help get you started. These programs do not give you ideas, but they do help you find ideas within yourself.

Outline programs can help you set up an outline fast, automatically realigning and renumbering to accommodate changes you make.

Spell-checking programs call attention to any of your words that they cannot match to their own dictionaries. The programs are a big help for spotting typos. These programs, however, have limits. Suppose you intended to type "west" but instead typed "rest." Because "rest" appears as a correctly spelled word in the program's dictionary, the program will not call "west" to your attention. You must read your work carefully yourself.

Thesaurus programs are no different from printed thesauruses. You must evaluate each suggested substitution for sense within the context of what you are writing.

Style-checking programs examine your file against grammar, usage, and punctuation rules, alerting you to what they do not find in their programs. Fixing what mistakes they find is still your job. You should use a style-check program with caution. For example, if you are told some of your sentences are in the passive voice, change them to the active voice only when you think the change is needed (see 8m and 8n for a discussion of occasional cases when the passive voice is needed). Bring the same level of critical thinking to other information that the program might provide.

Tutorials like **Blue Pencil,** available with the *Simon & Schuster Handbook,* offer you sets of exercises for you to work at your own pace. It closely resembles the editing process. It scores your answers, and, if you have entered an incorrect answer, the program explains what is wrong and how to fix it. **Blue Pencil** also refers you to the appropriate section in this handbook.

APPENDIX B:
USING CORRECT
MANUSCRIPT FORMAT

B1 **Following standard practices for typing
or handwriting marks of punctuation**

After each heading in this section, you will find typewritten and handwritten examples of each mark of punctuation.

PERIOD, QUESTION MARK, EXCLAMATION POINT ' . ? ! . ? !

Do not space before these marks. Space twice after each mark when it ends a sentence.

```
I do.  Do you?  You do!  I know you do.
```

In typing initials used in personal names, leave one space after each period.

```
B. A. Jones
W. E. B. Du Bois
```

In other abbreviations, practice varies both for the use of periods and for spacing after periods. An up-to-date dictionary can guide you.

COMMA, SEMICOLON, COLON , ; : , ; :

Do not space before these marks. Space once after them in sentences. (See 26b for cases where the colon separates numbers with no space before or after.)

```
Usually, I call first; nevertheless, I did not today.
My reason is this: I saw you walking out of your house.
```

APOSTROPHE ' '

Do not space before or after an apostrophe within a word.

```
Isn't that Ken's car?
```

Space once after a final apostrophe followed by another word.

```
He must be using the Clarks' garage.
```

When an apostrophe ends the word that ends a sentence, do not leave a space between the apostrophe and the final period, question mark, or exclamation point. Put the apostrophe before the final mark of punctuation.

```
Those cars in the driveway are the Clarks'.
```

QUOTATION MARKS " " ' ' " " ' '

Do not space between quotation marks and whatever they enclose. Do not space between double and single quotation marks.

```
I said, "'Here Comes the Sun' makes me smile whenever I
hear it."
```

Space once after a closing quotation mark unless it ends a sentence. In that case, space twice.

```
He said "plaster."  I heard "blister," but I guess I was
wrong.
```

HYPHEN – –

Do not space before or after a hyphen except to use one space after a "suspended" hyphen—that is, a hyphen showing that two prefixes or suffixes refer to one root word.

```
Many athletes trade the agony of defeat for pre- and post-game
shows.
```

When a hyphen occurs at the end of a line, always make it the last mark on the line. Do not carry the hyphen over to start a new line.

DASH — — —

In typed manuscripts, make a dash by striking the hyphen key twice, with no space between. In handwritten manuscripts, make a dash with a single line a little longer than a hyphen. Do not space before or after a dash.

Ap B

```
All of us--all of us!--think sentimentally about

adolescence.
```

SLASH / /

Do not space before or after a slash except when you use the slash to separate no more than three lines of quoted poetry.

```
and/or    1/16
```

When separating lines of poetry, space once before and once after the slash.

```
Consider these lines from Shakespeare's "Sonnet 30": "When to

the sessions of sweet silent thought  /  I summon up

remembrance of things past."
```

BRACKETS, PARENTHESES [ ] ( ) [ ] ( )

Do not space between brackets or parentheses and whatever they enclose.

```
The letter continued, "Parrish was borne [sic] June 30,

1830. At least that's what Ada Jencks (my great

grandmother) wrote."
```

ELLIPSES . . .   . . .

Use three evenly spaced dots for an ellipsis. Use one space before, between, and after the dots.

```
"Turning away . . . they began to laugh."
```

Use four evenly spaced dots to indicate the omission of one or more sentences. Because the first dot serves as the period at the end of the sentence, leave no space before it. After the first dot, use three evenly spaced dots. (See 29d about using other punctuation with ellipses.)

```
"The shopper felt crowded. . . . Moving away was natural."
```

UNDERLINING (ITALICS)

When you underline more than one word, you may use either style shown here—with or without breaks between words. Whichever style you choose, use it consistently throughout a paper.

```
Zen and the Art of Motorcycle Maintenance
Zen and the Art of Motorcycle Maintenance
```

B2 Following standard practices when preparing the final copy of a paper

The appearance of a paper sends important messages to your instructor. Although no paper will earn an *A* only because it looks exceptionally neat and shows your attention to the conventions of manuscript format, a first-rate appearance suggests to the instructor that you took the assignment seriously and that you value what you have written.

APPEARANCE

Paper: For typed papers, use 8½ × 11-inch white, standard typing paper. Do not use onionskin or erasable paper: onionskin is for copies only, and erasable paper smudges easily and resists handwritten corrections. Double space between lines. Type on only one side of each sheet of paper.

If your instructor accepts handwritten papers, use ruled 8½ × 11-inch standard white, lined paper. Do not use colored paper or paper torn from a spiral-bound notebook. Write on only one side of each sheet of paper. Some of your instructors might require that you write on every other line, to provide space for you to make neat corrections and for them to write comments. If you are unsure of your instructor's requirements, ask. Make your handwriting as clear as you can. If your handwriting is not easily readable, slow down and work to improve it. Be consistent in your presentation; letters and spacing should be uniform.

Ink: Use a black typewriter ribbon, and keep the typewriter keys clean so that the letters will be clear, not blurred.

For handwritten papers, use dark blue or black ink, not red, green, brown, or other colors. Do not use pencil.

Computer printouts: If a printer has both capital and lower-case letters and produces an easy-to-read type, most instructors accept papers prepared on word processors. Ask first, however. When you submit the paper, be sure to tear off the hole-punched edges and separate the pages.

FORMATS

First page: At the end of this appendix is a sample of a first page when a cover page is not used. It shows where to place name, date, course, and other information that your instructor might specify. The format conforms to the recommendations of the Modern Language Association (MLA). A sample cover page, along with a first page when a cover page is used, in MLA style appears at the beginning of Amy Brown's research paper in Chapter 34.

Page from the body of a paper: At the end of this appendix is a sample page from the body of a paper. It shows the measurements for layout and the entry for writer's name and page number. It also illustrates how a displayed quotation is indented.

Works Cited page: At the end of this appendix is a sample first page of a Works Cited list. It shows the measurements for layout and the style of indentation for each entry on the list according to MLA style. A detailed discussion of the features of a Works Cited list appears at the end of Amy Brown's research paper in Chapter 34.

Displaying quotations: When a prose quotation runs more than four typed lines or four handwritten lines, it is displayed. It starts on a new line, and all lines are indented ten spaces. The first line of a paragraph within the displayed quotation is indented an additional three spaces. See examples in 28a and in Amy Brown's research paper in Chapter 34.

When you quote more than three lines of poetry, set the quotation off from your own words. Start a new line and lay the quoted poetry out so that it looks as much as possible like the printed version you are quoting from. If indenting ten spaces from the left causes you to have to break lines, you can indent less than ten spaces or not at all.

```
O Captain! my Captain! our fearful trip is done,

The ship has weather'd every rack, the prize we sought is won,

The port is near, the bells I hear, the people all exulting,

While follow eyes the steady keel, the vessel grim and daring;

    But O heart! heart! heart!

        O the bleeding drops of red,

            Where on the deck my Captain lies,

                Fallen cold and dead.
```

Punctuation leading into a displayed quotation: When the words that lead into a displayed quotation are a complete sentence, end the sentence with a colon (for an example, see 28a-1). When the words are not a complete sentence and flow directly into the wording of the displayed quotation, use no punctuation (for an example, see the sample page from the body of a paper shown at the end of this appendix). ❖ PUNCTUATION ALERT: In MLA documentation style (explained in Chapter 33), the source of a displayed quotation is given in parentheses two spaces after the end punctuation of the quotation. ❖ You will find other examples in Chapter 34 (Amy Brown's research paper, page 2) and Chapter 36 (Theresa Shannon's paper). Chapter 33 presents MLA and APA documentation systems and references for other documentation systems. Check with your instructor for which system to use.

B3 | **Making careful handwritten corrections and insertions in typed papers**

If your typewriter lacks any special characters that you need, such as accent marks, you can handwrite them. You can also make a few handwritten corrections in a paper that you intend to hand in. Use the standard correction marks shown below. Note, however, that if you have more than three handwritten corrections on a page, you should retype the page.

Draw one line through words you want to take out.

These ~~extra words~~ are deleted.

To insert words, make a caret (∧) where the missing words should be, and then write them in above the caret.

A caret shows *where words* should be inserted.
∧

To transpose letters, use a mark like this:

squigg➎l

You can transpose words in a similar way:

Transpose ⌐in the⌐ words⌐ wrong order.

You can indicate the start of a new paragraph like this:

Molly's actions primarily met her needs. ¶ Overall, Molly exemplifies the behavior of one type of typical toddler.

You can close up space between letters this way:

Avoid in‿correct spacing.

You can open space between letters this way:

Leave one space between words in‖a sentence.

You can drop a letter and close up the remaining letters this way:

Some spellers have trouble with doub⫝le letters.

Ap B

FIRST PAGE WITHOUT COVER PAGE

Amy W. Brown   Name

Professor Wellington   Instructor

English 101, Section A1   Course, Section

10 December 19xx   Date submitted

                Personal Space: } Double space

           An Intercultural Perspective   } Double space

                                  } Quadruple space

    When she returned home after a year in South America,

Judith Martin, a North American writer, began to have a

problem. People kept interpreting her behavior as flirta-

tious, but she was not flirting. Fairly soon she figured

PAGE FROM THE BODY OF A PAPER,
WITH DISPLAYED QUOTE

1″ Brown 7   ½″

personal space. Clearly, what is considered obnoxious in

one culture might be considered polite in another (Fisher,

Bell, and Baum 167). As Hall explains, virtually every-

thing people are and do

> is associated with the experience of space. . . .
>
> Therefore, people from different cultures,
>
> when interpreting each other's behavior, often
>
> misinterpret the relationship, the activity, or
>
> the emotions. This leads to alienation in
>
> encounters or distorted communications.
>
> (Hidden 171)

10 space indent for displayed quotation

In the next few years, more studies will be undertaken to

uncover information about cultural differences in matters

½"

Brown 10

1"

Indent 5 spaces after
first line of entry

Double space throughout

Works Cited

Davis, Martha, and Janet Skupien, eds. Body Movement and
Nonverbal Communication: An Annotated Bibliography
1971–1981. Bloomington, IN: Indiana UP, 1982.

Fast, Julius. Body Language. New York: Evans, 1970.

Fisher, Jeffrey D., Paul A. Bell, and Andrew Baum.
Environmental Psychology. 2nd ed. New York:
Holt, 1984.

Hall, Edward T. The Hidden Dimension. New York:
Doubleday, 1966.

---. Interview. "Learning the Arabs' Silent Language."
With Kenneth Friedman. Psychology Today Aug. 1979:
44–54.

Henley, Nancy M. Body Politics: Power, Sex, and Nonverbal
Communication. Englewood Cliffs: Prentice, 1977.

Maines, David R. "Tactile Relationship in the Subway as
Affected by Racial, Sexual, and Crowded Seating
Situations." Environmental Psychology and Nonverbal
Behavior 2 (1977): 100–108.

Martin, Judith. "Here's Looking at You." Newsday 27 Jan.
1981, sec. 2: 9+.

Morris, Charles G. Psychology: An Introduction. 4th ed.
Englewood Cliffs: Prentice, 1982.

Morris, Desmond. Manwatching: A Field Guide to Human
Behavior. New York: Abrams, 1977.

Polhemus, Ted. "Social Bodies." The Body as a Medium of
Expression. Ed. Jonathan Benthall and Ted Polhemus.
New York: Dutton, 1975. 13–35.

Usage Glossary

A **glossary** is a list of words or phrases singled out for special attention. This glossary relates to **usage,** the customary manner of using particular words or phrases.

The term "customary manner" refers to usage by educated people, as demonstrated especially in books, newspapers, and speeches. "Customary manner," however, is not as firm in practice as the term implies. Indeed, little demonstrates as dramatically as does a usage glossary that standards for language use change. Some words slip away from usage: for example, *thee* and *thou* are no longer used in everyday life. Some constructions considered nonstandard a decade ago are accepted as standard today; for example, *shall* used to be required for the first-person future (*I shall finish the work tomorrow*), but today most dictionaries and usage surveys report that *shall* and *will* can be used interchangeably in such constructions.

This Usage Glossary, which contains over 200 entries in alphabetical order, reflects customary practice for academic writing—as of the date this handbook was published. If you think that any information reported here might have changed, consult one of the dictionaries discussed in Chapter 20 with a publication (or revision) date later than this handbook's. The entries in this Usage Glossary cover matters of usage as well as many frequently confused homonyms and commonly confused words. Additional homonyms and commonly confused words appear in Chapter 22.

You will find this glossary easier to use if you understand two terms used frequently in the discussion: *Informal* indicates that the word or phrase occurs commonly in speech but should be avoided in academic writing. *Nonstandard* indicates that the word or phrase is unacceptable for standard spoken English and for writing.

This glossary can help you in at least two ways: (1) You can browse through it to become familiar with the words and phrases that are subject to usage constraints in academic writing. (2) You can consult it as a reference when you are editing your writing to make sure that you are using the words or phrases correctly.

As in the rest of this book, words marked here with a degree symbol (°) are defined in the Glossary of Grammatical and Selected Composition Terms in this handbook.

a, an Use *a* before words beginning with consonant sounds: ***a*** *dog,* ***a*** *grade,* ***a*** *hole.* Also, use *a* before words beginning with vowels that sound like consonants: ***a*** *unit,* ***a*** *one-page paper,* ***a*** *European.* Use *an* before words beginning with vowel sounds or a silent *h*: ***an*** *apple,* ***an*** *onion,* ***an*** *hour.* (7a)

accept, except To *accept* means "to agree to" or "to receive." To *except* (verb°) means "to exclude or leave out"; *except* (preposition°) means "leaving out." (22c-1)

> **Except** [preposition] for one or two details, the striking workers were ready to **accept** [verb] management's offer. The workers wanted the no-smoking rule **excepted** [verb] from the contract.

advice, advise *Advice* (noun°) means "recommendation"; to *advise* (verb°) means "to give a recommendation." (22c-1)

> I **advise** you to follow your doctor's **advice.**

affect, effect To *affect* means "to influence" or "to arouse the emotions"; to *effect* means "to bring about"; *effect* (noun°) means "result or conclusion." (22c-1)

> One **effect** [noun] of the weather is that it **affects** [verb°] some people's moods. We **effected** [verb] some changes in our system for weather forecasting.

aggravate, irritate *Aggravate* is used colloquially to mean *irritate.* Each word has a precise meaning, however: to *aggravate* means "to intensify or make worse"; to *irritate* means "to annoy or make impatient."

> The executive was **irritated** by her assistant's carelessness, for it further **aggravated** the company's financial problems.

ain't is a nonstandard contraction for *am not, is not, are not, has not,* and *have not.*

all ready, already *Already* means "before or by this time"; *all ready* means "completely prepared." (22c-1, 22c-3)

> The new players were **all ready**; the warmup had **already** begun.

all right is two words, never one (not *alright*). (22c-3)

all together, altogether *All together* means "in a group, in unison"; *altogether* means "entirely or thoroughly." (22c-3)

> The sopranos, altos, and tenors were supposed to sing **all together**, but their first attempt was not **altogether** successful.

allude, elude To *allude* means "to refer to indirectly or casually"; to *elude* means "to escape notice of." (22c-1)

> The researchers **alluded** to budget cuts when they discussed why the identification of the virus had **eluded** them.

allusion, illusion An *allusion* is a reference to something; an *illusion* is a false impression or idea. (22c-1)

> The candidate wanted to create the **illusion** that he was sympathetic to the poor, so he made a snide **allusion** to his rival's wealth.

a lot (two words, not *alot*) is informal for *a great deal* or *a great many* and should be avoided in academic writing.

a.m., p.m. (or **A.M., P.M.**) are used only with numbers, not as substitutes for the words *morning, afternoon,* or *evening.* (30h)

> Our class, which usually meets early in the **morning** [not *a.m.*], will meet at 7:10 **p.m.** tomorrow.

among, between Use *among* for three or more people or things; use *between* for two people or things.

> The problem was discussed **among** the three students. They had to choose **between** staying in school and getting full-time jobs.

amount, number Use *amount* for concepts or things that are collective rather than separate (wealth, work, happiness); use *number* for anything that can be counted (coins, jobs, joys).

> A large **number** of people had to do a great **amount** of work.

an, and *An* is an article° (see *a, an*) and should not be confused with *and,* which is a conjunction°. (7h)

> They saw **an** eagle **and** its chicks in the nest.

and/or occurs in business or legal writing when either one or both of the items it connects can apply.

> The office needs a modem **and/or** fax machine to transmit data.

In the humanities and most other disciplines, alternatives are usually expressed in words (*The office needs a modem, a fax machine, or both to transmit data.*) (29e-3)

anybody, any body *Anybody* is any person not specified; *any body* is a specific person, object, or group. (22c-3)

> The purity of **any body** of water can be tested by **anybody** with the correct materials.

anyone, any one See *anybody, any body.*

anyplace is informal for *any place* or *anywhere.* Avoid it in academic writing.

anyways, anywheres are nonstandard for *anyway, anywhere.*

apt, likely, liable *Apt* and *likely* are loosely interchangeable. Strictly, however, *apt* is used to indicate a tendency or inclination; *likely* is used to indicate a reasonable expectation that something will happen. *Liable* means "having undesirable consequences."

> Although the roads are **apt** to be icy, you **likely** will arrive on time. However, you are **liable** to have an accident if you speed on icy roads.

as, like, as if

1. Use *like,* not *as,* in a comparison when resemblance but not equivalence is suggested.

> Mexico, **like** [not *as*] Argentina, is a Spanish-speaking country.

779

2. Use *as*, not *like*, in a comparison when equivalence is suggested—that is, when the subject equals the description.

> John served **as** [not *like*] moderator of the debate. [John = moderator]

3. *As* functions as a subordinating conjunction° or a preposition°, depending on the meaning of the sentence. *Like* functions only as a preposition. To start a clause°, *as* is required.

> That hamburger tastes good, **as** [not *like*] a hamburger should. [subordinating conjunction]
> That hamburger tastes **like** chopped leather. [preposition]

4. Use *as if*, not *like*, with the subjunctive mood°. (8l)

> This hamburger tastes **as if** [not *like*] it has been grilled for an hour.

assure, ensure, insure To *assure* means "to promise or convince"; to *ensure* or to *insure* means "to make certain." *Insure* is reserved for financial or legal certainty, especially related to insurance.

> The insurance agent **assured** me that I could **insure** my life, but he explained that no one could **ensure** that I would have a long life.

as to should be avoided as a substitute for *about*.

> The pilot was unsure **about** [not *as to*] the airplane's safety.

awful, awfully *Awful* (adjective°) means "causing fear"; it should not be used as a substitute for intensifiers such as *very* or *extremely*. *Awfully* (adverb°) is informal for *very* or *extremely* and should be avoided in academic writing.

> The cyclone was an **awful** phenomenon to watch. It caused **serious** [not *awful*] damage. It came **very** [not *awfully*] close to our house.

a while, awhile *A while* is an article° and a noun°; it functions as a subject° or object°. *Awhile* is an adverb°; it modifies verbs°. (22c-3) In a prepositional phrase°, the correct form is *a while: for* **a while**, *in* **a while**, *after* **a while**.

> We waited **awhile** for our friends to arrive, but after **a while** we had to leave.

bad, badly *Bad* is an adjective° (*bad* feelings); it is used after linking verbs° such as *feel* or *felt* (*He felt* **bad**). *Badly* is an adverb° and is nonstandard after linking verbs. For more information, see 12c.

> The farmers felt **bad** [not *badly*]. [*Felt* in this example is a linking verb.]
> The **bad** drought had **badly** damaged the crops.

been, being *Been* is the past participle° of *to be*; *being* is the progressive form° of *to be*.

> Alcohol abuse has **been** [not *being*] on the rise recently. We see lives **being** [not *been*] ruined by drinking.

being as, being that are nonstandard for *because* or *since*.

> **Because** [not *being as* or *being that*] the catcher injured his arm, he had to leave the game.

beside, besides *Beside* (preposition°) means "next to or by the side of"; *besides* (when functioning as a preposition) means "other than or in addition to"; *besides* (when functioning as an adverb°) means "also or moreover."

U GL

With keys in her hand, she stood **beside** the new car. No one **besides** her had a driver's license. **Besides,** she owned the car.

better, had better Used in place of *had better, better* is informal. Avoid it in academic writing.

We **had better** [not *we better*] be careful.

between, among See *among, between.*

breath, breathe *Breath* is a noun°; *breathe* is a verb°.

The jogger had to rest and **breathe** rapidly before he could catch his **breath.**

bring, take Use *bring* for movement from a distant place to a near place; use *take* for any other movement.

The coach will **bring** her team to our college, and then she will **take** the team on a tour of the campus.

broke is nonstandard for past participle° *broken.* Avoid it in academic writing, except as the past tense°. (8c-2)

The jogger's ankle was **broken** [not *broke*]. He **broke** it yesterday.

burst, bust To *burst* means "to break apart suddenly and violently"; its principal parts are *burst, burst, burst* (not *bursted*). To *bust* is slang for to *burst* and should be avoided in academic writing. (8c-2)

The bubble **burst** [not *busted* or *bursted.*]

but, however, yet Use *but, however,* and *yet* alone, not in combination with each other. (7h)

The economy is strong, **but** [not *but yet* or *but however*] unemployment is still high.

but that, but what are nonstandard for *that.* Avoid them in academic writing.

The supervisor does not doubt **that** [not *but that* or *but what*] the job can be done.

calculate, figure, reckon are informal for *imagine* or *expect.* Avoid such informal uses in academic writing.

The farmers **expect** [not *figure* or *reckon*] that they will have a good crop.

can, may *Can* indicates ability or capacity; *may* requests or grants permission. In the negative, however, *can* is acceptable in place of *may.*

May I leave the room so that I **can** have a cigarette?
Why **can't** I?

can't hardly, can't scarcely are double negatives and are nonstandard; use *hardly* and *scarcely* only. For more information, see 12b.

They can **hardly** [not *can't hardly* or *can't scarcely*] see through the fog.

censor, censure To *censor* means "to judge" or "to delete objectionable material"; to *censure* means "to condemn or officially reprimand."

The town council **censured** the mayor for permitting a citizen's committee to **censor** books in the public library.

chairman, chairperson, chair Usage is changing concerning *chairman,* which has a masculine implication. The gender-free terms *chairperson* and *chair* often are preferred, although *chair* seems to be more widely used at this time. (21b)

choose, chose *Choose* is the simple form of *to choose*; *chose* is the past tense of *to choose*. (8c-2)

> Today I will **choose** the college I will attend. Yesterday she **chose** the college she will attend.

cloth, clothe *Cloth* (noun°) means "fabric"; to *clothe* (verb°) means "to dress" or "to cover with garments."

> The king wanted to **clothe** himself with garments made of fine **cloth.**

complement, compliment To *complement* means "to complete" or "to supplement"; to *compliment* means "to express praise or flattery."

> The instructor **complimented** the student for her research project, saying that it **complemented** work done twenty years before.

conscience, conscious *Conscience* (noun°) means "a sense of right or wrong"; *conscious* (adjective°) means "being aware or awake."

> The thief was **conscious** that his **conscience** was bothering him.

consensus of opinion is a redundant phrase. Use *consensus* only.

continual, continuous *Continual* is occurring repeatedly; *continuous* is going on without interruption in space or time.

> Although all essential systems of the spacecraft were expected to operate **continuously,** the astronauts **continually** checked their instrument panels. The washing machine **continually** breaks down, and then it makes a **continuous** humming sound.

couple, couple of are nonstandard for *a few* or *several.*

> You should rest for **a few** [not *a couple* or *a couple of*] minutes before you begin again.

data is the plural of *datum,* a rarely used word. Informal usage now treats *data* as singular, but it should be treated as plural in academic writing.

> **These** [not *this*] **data show** [not *shows*] that the virus is spreading.

different from, different than *From* is the preferred preposition after *different,* although *than* is commonly used in speech.

> Football is **different from** [not *different than*] soccer.

disinterested, uninterested *Disinterested* means "impartial"; *uninterested* means "indifferent or not concerned with."

> They were **uninterested** in hearing my side of the story, so we agreed to ask a **disinterested** person to settle our dispute.

done is a past participle°; it cannot substitute for the past tense *did.* (8c-2)

> The farmers raised [not *done* raised] a fine crop. They **did** [not *done*] a good job.

don't is a contraction for *do not,* not for *does not (doesn't).*

> She **doesn't** [not *don't*] like loud music.

due to Many people object to *due to* as a preposition° meaning "because of." As an adjective°, *due to* following a form of the verb *to be* is acceptable.

He was late **because of** [not *due to* as a preposition] an accident.
His being late was **due to** [an adjective following a form of *to be*] an accident.

emigrate from, immigrate to To *immigrate to* means "to enter a new country to live there." To *emigrate from* means "to leave one country to live in another."

> After the ballet star **emigrated from** Russia, he **immigrated to** the United States to start a new life.

ensure, assure, insure See *assure, ensure, insure.*

enthused as an adjective° is nonstandard for *enthusiastic.*

> The student was **enthusiastic** [not *enthused*] about going to college.

especially, specially *Especially* and *specially* are not interchangeable. *Especially* means "mainly or particularly"; *specially* is for a special purpose.

> Because the quarterback was **especially** tired, he could not attend the **specially** organized party celebrating his team's victory.

etc. is the abbreviation for the Latin *et cetera,* meaning *and the rest.* Do not use it in academic writing; acceptable substitutes are *and the like, and so on,* or *and so forth.*

> The Greenlawn Resort offers water sports such as snorkeling, scuba diving, windsurfing, **and the like** [not *etc.*].

everyday, every day *Everyday* is an adjective°; it means "daily" and modifies nouns. *Every day* is an adjective-noun combination that functions as a subject° or object°. (22c-3)

> I missed the bus **every day** last week. Arriving at work late has become an **everyday** occurrence.

everywheres is nonstandard for *everywhere.*

except, accept See *accept, except.*

explicit, implicit *Explicit* means "directly stated or expressed"; *implicit* means "implied or suggested."

> The warning on cigarette packs is **explicit:** Smoking may be dangerous to your health. The warning's **implicit** message is that people should not smoke.

farther, further are used interchangeably, although many writers prefer to use *farther* for geographical distances and *further* for all other cases.

fewer, less Use *fewer* for anything that can be counted (***fewer** dollars,* ***fewer** jobs,* ***fewer** joys*); use *less* for concepts or things thought of collectively, not separately (***less** money,* ***less** work,* ***less** happiness*). (12d)

figure, calculate, reckon See *calculate, figure, reckon.*

fine, find *Fine* is an adjective° *(She bought a **fine** electric drill)*; it is nonstandard for *well* or any other adverb° (not *The new electric drill worked **fine**). Find* is the simple form of the verb *to find (We **find** the defendant "not guilty").*

former, latter When two ideas or things are referred to, *former* refers to the first of the two, and *latter* refers to the second of the two. When more than two ideas or things are referred to, do not use these words.

> Brazil and Ecuador are two Latin American countries. The **former** is Portuguese-speaking, the **latter** Spanish-speaking.

gender, sex *Gender* is attributed to words, *sex* to people and animals. (21b)

> My instructor uses **gender-free** [not *sex-free*] language, like *police officer* instead of *policeman.*
> What **sex** [not *gender*] is the guard dog?

given, giving *Given* is the past participle° of *to give; giving* is the progressive° form.

> A reward was **given** to a citizen for **giving** the police valuable help in preventing a robbery.

goes, says *Goes* is nonstandard for *says.*

> He **says** [not *goes*] we will have a test tomorrow.

gone, went *Gone* is the past participle° of *to go; went* is the past tense° of *to go.* (8c-2)

> *They* **went** [not *gone*] to the concert after their friends **had gone** [not *had went*] home.

good and is nonstandard for *very.*

> *He was* **very** [not *good and*] *sorry.*

good, well *Good* is an adjective° (***good idea***); it is nonstandard as an adverb; *well* is an adverb° (***run well***). (12c)

> The **good** writer spoke **well.**

got, have *Got* is the past tense° of *to get (He* **got** *an A)* and is also one of the past participles° of *to get (She has* **got**—or ***gotten***—*excellent grades). Got* is nonstandard in place of *have; got to* is nonstandard as a substitute for an intensifier such as *must.* (8d)

> What do we **have** [not *got*] for dinner?
> You **must** [not *got to*] help me.

great is an informal adjective meaning "good," "wonderful," "skillful," or "clever." Reserve it for its precise meaning: "a high degree of," "eminent," "large," "grand."

> **No**   She has a **great** personality.
> **Yes**   Einstein was a **great** scientist.
> **Yes**   Her work gave her **great** satisfaction.

had best, had better are nonstandard for *ought* or *should.*

> She **ought** to [not *had best* or *had better*] call home.

had ought, hadn't ought are nonstandard for *ought* and *ought not.*

> He **ought** [not *had ought*] to call home.

hanged, hung Use *hanged* only to refer to executions *(The prisoner was* ***hanged*** *this morning).* Use *hung* for all other meanings *(They* ***hung*** *her portrait in the living room).* (8b)

have, got See *got, have.*

have, of *Have,* not *of,* should be used after such verbs as *could, may, might, must, should.*

> They *could* **have** [not *of*] telephoned. They *may* **have** [not *of*] tried to call.

he, she, he or she Using *he* to refer to both males and females is avoided by people who want to avoid using sexist language°. Many writers use *he or she* or *he/she.* If at all possible they switch to plural nouns and pronouns. (21b, 11n-2)

> If **they** want [not *he* wants] to avoid accidents, **drivers** [not *a driver*] should drive defensively.

himself, herself See *myself, yourself, himself, herself.*

hisself is nonstandard for *himself.*

hopefully is an adverb° that means "with hope," "in a hopeful manner," or "it is hoped that." It can modify a verb°, an adjective°, or another adverb. Some people use it as a sentence modifier° meaning "I hope," but this usage is not appropriate in academic writing. Always say in your sentence who is doing the hoping.

> **No** **Hopefully,** the plane will land safely.
> **Yes** They waited **hopefully** for the plane to land safely.
> **Yes** They **hoped** that the plane would land safely.

however, yet, but See *but, however, yet.*

hung, hanged See *hanged, hung.*

if, whether *If* is a subordinating conjunction°. *Whether* occurs in three situations: (1) in an indirect question *(She asked **whether** I had heard from the hikers),* (2) to express doubt *(She was not sure **whether** they would be safe in the storm),* and (3) to express alternatives with or without *or not (I did not know **whether** [or whether or not] to search for them).*

illusion, allusion See *allusion, illusion.*

immigrate to, emigrate from See *emigrate from, immigrate to.*

implicit, explicit See *explicit, implicit.*

imply, infer To *imply* means "to hint or suggest without stating outright"; to *infer* means "to draw a conclusion from what has been written or said." Speakers and writers *imply;* listeners and readers *infer.*

> The governor **implied** that she might not seek reelection, and the reporters **inferred** that she had decided to run for president.

incredible, incredulous *Incredible* means "extraordinary" or "not believable"; *incredulous* means "unable or unwilling to believe." A person would be *incredulous* in response to something that is *incredible.*

> Their families were **incredulous** as the freed hostages told of the **incredible** cruelty they had suffered while captives.

illusion See *allusion, illusion.*

individual, person, party are not interchangeable in academic writing. Use *individual* to emphasize the uniqueness of a single human being; otherwise use *person*. Use *party* only for a group of people.

> The Constitution guarantees every **individual** certain rights.
> Each **person** received a written invitation.
> The governor and his **party** entered the room together.

infer, imply See *imply, infer*.

inside of, outside   are nonstandard when used with *of (She waited* ***outside*** [not *outside of*] *the dormitory)*. Also, *inside of* is nonstandard when referring to time *(She waited* ***about*** [not *inside of*] *five minutes)*.

insure, assure, ensure See *assure, ensure, insure*.

irregardless is nonstandard for *regardless*.

irritate, aggravate See *aggravate, irritate*.

is when, is where In giving definitions, *is* should not be followed by *when* or *where*.

> Defensive driving means that [not *is when*] drivers stay on the defense against accidents that might be caused by other drivers.

its, it's *Its* is a personal pronoun in the possessive case *(The dog lost* ***its*** *bone). It's* is a contraction of *it is* or *it has* ***(It's*** *a warm day;* ***It's*** *been a hot day.)* (22c-1, 22c-3)

-ize is a suffix used to change a noun° or adjective° to a verb° *(hospital + ize = hospitalize, brutal + ize = brutalize)*. Be careful not to attach *-ize* indiscriminately to create new words rather than using good words that already exist. When in doubt, check your dictionary to see if a word ending in *-ize* is acceptable.

kind, sort are singular words and should therefore be paired with *this*, not *these. These* can be paired with *kinds* or *sorts*.

kind of (a), sort of (a) *Kind of* and *sort of* are nonstandard if used as adverbs° meaning "in a way" or "somewhat." Also, the *a* with these phrases is nonstandard.

> The hikers were **somewhat** [not *kind of*] tired when they got home.
> That **kind of** [not *kind of an*] exercise is healthy.

later, latter *Later* means "after some time" or "subsequently"; *latter* refers to the second of a pair of ideas or things. (22c-1)

> That restaurant opens **later** than we had thought. It serves lunch and dinner, the **latter** starting at 7 p.m.

latter, former See *former, latter*.

lay, lie *Lay* (principal parts: *laying, laid*) is always followed by a direct object°. As a substitute for *lie* (principal parts: *lying, lay, lain), lay* is nonstandard. (8c-2)

> **Lay** the blanket on the beach so you can **lie** [not *lay*] down and rest.

learn, teach *Learn* is nonstandard for *teach*. Students *learn;* teachers *teach*.

> *The instructor will* **teach** us [not *learn* us] chemistry.

leave, let To *leave* means "to depart"; to *let* means "to permit." *Leave* is nonstandard for *let* unless *leave* is followed by *alone.*

> I had to **leave** the classroom early because I was ill. My instructor will **let** [not *leave*] me take a retest tomorrow. She will have to find a proctor, because she cannot **leave** a student alone during an exam.

likely, apt, liable See *apt, likely, liable.*

loose, lose, loss *Loose* means "not tight"; to *lose* means "to be unable to find"; *loss* means "that which cannot be found or retrieved."

> Before I **lose** this **loose** belt, I had better tighten it.
> The **loss** from the fire included most of his clothing.

lots, lots of, a lot of are informal for *many, much, a great deal of.*

> **Many** [not *a lot of*] bees were in the hive.

may, can See *can, may.*

may be, maybe *May be* is a verb phrase°; *maybe* is an adverb°. (22c-3)

> Our team **may be** out of practice, but **maybe** we will win anyway.

media is the plural of *medium* and therefore requires a plural verb.

> The **media** *cover* [not *covers*] the elections, but the **medium** that reaches most people is television.

mighty is a nonstandard substitute for *extremely* or *very.*

mind, mine *Mind* is a noun° *(She had a good **mind**); mine* is a personal pronoun° *(That key is **mine**).*

morale, moral *Morale* (noun°) means "a mental state relating to courage, confidence, or enthusiasm." *Moral* (noun) means "the conclusion of, or lesson from, a story"; *moral* (adjective°) means "right in conduct or character." (22c-1)

> The president's good **moral** character boosted the country's **morale.**
> The **moral** of that story is that people should be kind to animals.

most is nonstandard for *almost* (**Almost** all [not *most*] of the people agree). It is correct as an adjective° (**most** people agree) and in superlative forms of adjectives and adverbs° (the **most** important fact; the **most** lively debate). (12d)

Ms. is the title free of reference to marital status for women; it is equivalent to the male title *Mr.* Unless a woman specifically requests *Miss* or *Mrs.*, use *Ms.*

myself, yourself, himself, herself are reflexive pronouns° *(I told **myself** to stay home)* and intensive pronouns° *(I **myself** will volunteer).* They are nonstandard when used as a subject° or an object in a prepositional phrase°.

> The dean and **I** [not *myself*] will explain the facts to the president.
> First, however, the class has to explain them to the dean and **me** [not *myself*].

nothing like, nowhere near are nonstandard for *not nearly.*

> Last month's rain was **not nearly** [not *nowhere near*] enough.

nowheres is nonstandard for *nowhere.*

number, amount See *amount, number.*

of, have See *have, of.*

off of is nonstandard for *off.*

> He fell **off** [not *off of*] the chair.

OK, O.K., okay are acceptable, but avoid them in academic writing in favor of a word more specific to the meaning of the sentence.

> The weather was **satisfactory** [not *okay*] for the race. Course officials gave the **approval** [not *okay*] for the final lap.

on account of is wordy for *because, because of.*

> **Because of** [not *on account of*] the rainy weather, we stayed home.

outside of, inside of See *inside of, outside of.*

party, individual, person See *individual, person, party.*

per The Latin word *per* is acceptable in technical and commercial contexts (*miles **per** hour, **per** capita income*). For writing in the humanities and some other academic areas, *per* is not preferred.

> A mine shaft collapsed **as reported in** [not *per*] this morning's newspaper.

percent, percentage *Percent* is used with specific numbers (*two percent, 95 percent*). *Percentage* is used with descriptive words or phrases (a *small percentage*), but only for amounts that have been expressed as percentages. Do not use it as a synonym for *part, portion, number, amount,* or other words denoting quantity.

> **Several people** in my class are bilingual [not *A percentage* of my class is bilingual].
> A large **percentage** of the voters watch the presidential debates on television.

person, individual, party See *individual, person, party.*

photocopy, Xerox® To *photocopy* (verb°) means "to make a copy on a copier machine"; *photocopy* (noun°) is the copy. *Xerox®* is a registered trademark, not a synonym for either the noun or the verb *photocopy.*

plenty is nonstandard for words such as *quite* and *very* (*She was **very*** (not *plenty*) *tired from the workout*). When used as a noun meaning *a large amount, plenty* must be followed by *of* (*They must have **plenty of** food for the winter*).

plus is acceptable as a preposition° meaning "in addition to." *Plus,* however, should not be used (1) as a substitute for *and* between independent clauses° and (2) as a transitional word° such as *besides, moreover, in addition.*

> **YES** She had talent **plus** good work habits.
> **No** He studied hard **plus** he played hard.
> **No** **Plus,** he had a long commute between his home and campus.

p.m., a.m. See *a.m., p.m.*

practical, practicable *Practical* means "useful or sensible"; *practicable* means "capable of being put into practice."

> The mayor wanted a **practical** evacuation plan, but none of the proposals was **practicable** for a large city.

precede, proceed To *precede* means "to come before"; to *proceed* means "to continue." (22c-1)

> The attorney **preceded** her client to court and then **proceeded** to unpack her briefcase.

pretty is informal for words such as *rather, quite, very,* and *somewhat.* Avoid such use in academic writing.

> The flu epidemic was **quite** [not *pretty*] severe.

principal, principle *Principle* means "a basic truth or rule." *Principal* (noun°) means "chief person" or "main or original amount"; *principal* (adjective°) means "most important." (22c-1)

> The school **principal** paid interest on the **principal** of her bank loan.
> One of the **principal** values in the United States is the **principle** of free speech.

raise, rise *Raise* (principal parts: *raised, raising*) needs a direct object° *(Please **raise** your hand);* rise (principal parts: *rose, risen, rising*) does not take a direct object *(The sun will **rise**).* Using these verbs interchangeably is nonstandard. (8e)

> The governor will **rise** [not *raise*] to speak after we **raise** [not *rise*] the flag.

rarely ever is an informal expression for *rarely* or *hardly ever;* avoid it in academic writing.

> He **rarely** [not *rarely ever*] came to class, so I **hardly ever** [not *rarely ever*] saw him.

real is nonstandard for intensifiers such as *really* (informal) or *very.*

really is informal for intensifiers such as *very* and *extremely.*

reason is should not be used in combination with *because.* (15d-2)

> The **reason is** [not *the reason is because*] we want to lower taxes.

reason why is redundant; drop *why.*

> The **reason** [not *reason why*] they left home is a mystery.

reckon, calculate, figure See *calculate, figure, reckon.*

regarding, in regard to, with regard to are used in some legal and technical writing but are too stiff for most academic writing. Useful substitutes are words such as *about* and *concerning.*

> The committee members asked **about** [not *regarding, in regard to,* or *with regard to*] the plan for a new park.

respectful, respectfully; respective, respectively *Respectful* and *respectfully* relate to showing respect; *respective* and *respectively* refers to items that are in the given sequence.

> The staff **respectfully** requested that the dean hear their complaints.
> He suggested that the typist and telephone operators go back to their desk and switchboards, **respectively.** They then returned to their **respective** jobs.

right is nonstandard for intensifiers such as *very* or *extremely.*

> The workers were **very** [not *right*] pleased to hear that the factory will reopen.

says, goes See *goes, says.*

seen nonstandard substitute for *saw*. *Seen* is the past participle° of *to see* and must be used with an auxiliary verb° such as *have*, *has*, or *had*. (8c-2)

> *They* **saw** [not *seen*] the film. I **had seen** [not *I seen*] it last week.

set, sit *Set* (principal parts: *set*, *setting*) is nonstandard as a substitute for *to sit* (principal parts: *sat*, *sitting*). *Set* means "to place" and is followed by a direct object°. *Sit* means "to be seated." (8d)

> After you carefully **set** [not *sit*] the rare Chinese vase on the table, please **sit** [not *set*] down.

sex, gender See *gender, sex*.

shall, will Use *shall* for questions in the first person (***Shall** I leave?*) or in very formal settings (*The judge **shall** render her verdict after hearing the testimony*). In all other cases, *will* is now accepted for the future tense in first, second, and third persons.

should, would Use *should* to express obligation (*They **should** practice what they preach*) or condition (*If you **should** need advice, call me*). Use *would* to express a wish (*I wish my family **would** buy a VCR*) or habitual action (*I **would** tape all the comedy specials*).

sit, set See *set, sit*.

so is colloquial as an intensifier like *very* and *extremely*.

some is both nonstandard and vague as a substitute for modifiers such as *somewhat*, *a little*, and *remarkable*.

> That was **a remarkable** [not *some*] performance.

somebody, some body See *anybody, any body*.

someone, some one See *anybody, any body*.

sometime, sometimes, some time *Sometime* means "at an unspecified future time"; *sometimes* means "now and then"; *some time* is a span of time. (22c-3)

> **Sometime** next semester we have to take qualifying exams.
> **Sometimes** I worry about the tests. I need **some time** to get used to the pressure.

sort, kind See *kind, sort*.

sort of (a), kind of (a) See *kind of (a), sort of (a)*.

specially, especially See *especially, specially*.

stationary, stationery are not interchangeable. *Stationary* means "standing still"; *stationery* refers to paper and related products. (22c-1)

such is informal and overused as an intensifier such as *very* or *extremely*. Avoid it in academic writing, unless it is part of a comparison including *that*.

> **No** It was **such** a poorly written play.
> **Yes** It was a **very** poorly written play.
> **Yes** It was **such** a poorly written play **that** no one went to see it.

U GL

supposed to, used to The final *d* is essential in both expressions. (8c-1)

> The weather is **supposed to** [not *suppose to*] improve. It **used to** [not *use to*] be sunny this time of year.

sure is nonstandard when used as an adverb° meaning *surely* or *certainly*.

> I **surely** [not *sure*] hope to go to college.

take, bring See *bring, take*.

teach, learn See *learn, teach*.

than, then *Than* indicates comparison *(One is smaller **than** two)*. *Then* relates to time *(He tripped and **then** fell)*.

that there, them there, this here, these here are nonstandard for *that, those, this*, and *these*, respectively.

that, which Use *that* with restrictive (essential) clauses°; *which* can be used today for both restrictive and nonrestrictive (nonessential) clauses°, but most writers prefer to use it only with nonrestrictive (nonessential) clauses. (10f)

> We visited the house **that** Jack built. Jack built the house, **which** is on Beanstalk Street, for his large plant collection.

their, there, they're *Their* is possessive; *there* means "in that place" or serves as an expletive°; *they're* is a contraction of *they are*. (22c-1)

> The students attended **their** classes in the lecture hall, which is over **there**. At this college, **there** are many courses to take, but **they're** all scheduled in the morning.

theirself, theirselves, themself are nonstandard for *themselves*.

them is nonstandard when used for *these* or *those*.

> Let's buy **those** [not *them*] strawberries.

then, than See *than, then*.

thusly is nonstandard for *thus*. Because *thus* is already an adverb°, the *-ly* ending is not needed.

till, until are both acceptable, although most writers prefer *until* in academic writing. Avoid the contraction *'til* in academic writing.

to, too, two *To* is a preposition°; *too* is an adverb°; *two* is the number. (22c-1)

> They went **to** the game. They ate at a restaurant, **too**. The check was not **too** expensive for the **two** of them.

toward, towards are both acceptable, although some writers prefer *toward*.

try and, sure and are nonstandard for *try to* and *sure to*.

> She wanted to **try to** [not *try and*] get a part-time job. Therefore, she had to be **sure to** [not *sure and*] prepare a résumé.

type is nonstandard for *type of*.

uninterested, disinterested See *disinterested, uninterested*.

unique is an absolute word and therefore cannot be modified by intensifiers such as *very* or *most.*

> Her talent was **unique** [not *very unique* or *most unique*].

used to, supposed to See *supposed to, used to.*

wait on is informal when used instead of *wait for.* It is correct when used in the context of waiting on tables.

ways is colloquial for *way.*

> California is a long **way** [not *ways*] from New York.

well, good See *good, well.*

went, gone See *gone, went.*

what is nonstandard when used for *that* or *who.* (10f)

> The house **that** [not *what*] Jack built contains a beanstalk.

where is nonstandard when used for *that.*

> I read in the newspaper **that** [not *where*] tuition will be increased.

where . . . at is redundant; drop *at.*

> is the house [not *house at*]?

whether, if See *if, whether.*

which, that See *that, which.*

which, who Use *which* to refer to things or ideas; use *who* to refer to people.

who, whom Use *who* for the subjective case° (*The person **who** can type has an easier time in school*). Use *whom* for the objective case° (*I asked to **whom** my professor was speaking*). (9d)

who's, whose *Who's* is the contraction of *who is; whose* is possessive.

> **Who's** going to run for mayor?
> **Whose** campaign is well organized?

will, shall See *shall, will.*

-wise The suffix *-wise* means "in a manner, in a direction, or in a position" (*clockwise, otherwise*). Be careful not to attach *-wise* indiscriminately to create new words rather than using good words that already exist. When in doubt, check your dictionary to see if a word ending in *-wise* is acceptable.

> The **weather** [not *Weatherwise, the*] outlook is excellent.

would, should See *should, would.*

Xerox®, photocopy See *photocopy, Xerox®*

Xmas is an abbreviation for *Christmas;* avoid using it in academic writing.

yet, however, but See *but, however, yet.*

your, you're *Your* is possessive; *you're* is the contraction of *you are.* (22c-1)

> generous to share **your** food with us.

yourself See *myself, yourself, himself, herself.*

GLOSSARY OF GRAMMATICAL AND SELECTED COMPOSITION TERMS

The first time that a term is used in this handbook, it is defined. After that, the term is marked with a degree symbol (°) to signal that it is defined in this glossary. Also, when a definition in this glossary uses terms that are themselves defined here, the terms are marked with a degree symbol. Each definition here concludes with a reference, in parentheses, to the handbook section(s) or chapters where the term is most fully discussed.

abstract noun A noun° that names things not knowable through the five senses: *idea, guilt.* (7a)

absolute phrase A phrase containing a subject° and a participle° and modifying an entire sentence: ***Summer being over,*** *we left the seashore.* (7m)

acronym A word made up of the first letters of other words that acts as an abbreviation for those words: *NASA.* (30h)

active voice The form of a verb° in which the subject° performs the action named by the verb. This voice° emphasizes the doer of the action, in contrast to the passive voice°, which emphasizes the action. (8m and 8n)

adjective A word that describes or limits (modifies) a noun° or pronoun° or word group functioning as a noun: *silly, three.* (7e, 12)

adjective clause A dependent clause° that usually begins with a relative pronoun° and that modifies nouns° or pronouns°. (7n-2)

adverb A word that describes or limits (modifies) verbs°, adjectives°, other adverbs, or whole sentences: *wearily, very.* (7f, 12)

adverb clause A dependent clause° that begins with a subordinating conjunction° and that modifies verbs°, adjectives°, adverbs°, or whole sentences. (7n-2)

agreement The match in expressing number° and person° required between a subject° and its verb° or a pronoun° and its antecedent°. For pronouns and antecedents, expressions of gender° must match as well. (11)

analogy An explanation of the unfamiliar in terms of the familiar, analogy compares objects or ideas from different classes, things not normally associated with each other. Analogy is also a method of developing one or more paragraphs. (4d, 21c, 37b)

analysis A thinking process, analysis divides something into its component parts to make clear the relationship between the whole and the parts. Sometimes called *division,* analysis is also a method of developing one or more paragraphs. (4d, opening section Chapter 5)

antecedent The noun° or pronoun° to which a pronoun refers. (10, 11l–11o)

antonym A word opposite in meaning to another word. (20a)

APA style See *documentation style.*

appositive A word or group of words that renames a noun° or a noun group preceding it: *my favorite month,* **October.** (7l-3)

argument A written argument seeks to convince a reader to agree with the writer concerning a topic open to debate. (1b, 6)

articles The words *a, an,* and *the.* Also called *limiting adjectives, noun markers* or *noun determiners.* (7a)

assertion A statement that gives a position about a debatable topic and that can be supported by evidence, reasons, and examples (including facts, statistics, names, experiences, and experts). (6b)

audience The readers to whom a piece of writing is directed. Knowing the characteristics of the audience can help the writer shape the message so that it will effectively inform or persuade readers. (1c, 6d)

auxiliary verb Also known as a *helping verb,* an auxiliary verb is a form of *be, do, have, can, may, will,* and others that combine with main verbs° to make verb phrases°. Auxiliary verbs help main verbs to express tense°, mood°, and voice°. (7c, 8a, 8d)

balanced sentence A sentence that uses parallelism° to enhance the message of similar or dissimilar ideas. (18b-3)

base form See *simple form.*

bibliography A list of sources used in a paper. In MLA style°, it is called Works Cited°, and in APA style°, it is called References°. (33a, 33c)

brainstorming An invention technique° that calls for listing all the ideas that come to mind in connection with a topic and then grouping the ideas according to patterns that emerge. (2d-3)

bureaucratic language Stuffy, overblown language that is marked by jargon°, euphemism°, and unnecessary complexity. (21e-5)

case The way a noun° or pronoun° changes form to show whether it is functioning as a subject°, an object°, or a possessor: *she, her, hers.* (9)

cause-and-effect analysis Examination of the relationship between outcomes (effects) and the reasons for them (causes). Cause-and-effect analysis can be used to develop one or more paragraphs°. (4d, 5d)

chronological order An arrangement of ideas according to a time sequence. Paragraphs°, essays, and larger works may be in chronological order. (2e-2, 4c)

clarifying sentence See *limiting sentence.*

classical pattern of argument A structure developed by the ancient Greeks and Romans that is used in writing argument. (6c)

classification A method of developing a paragraph° or a larger piece of writing in which separate categories that share some characteristics are grouped together. Classification is often used along with analysis°. (4d)

clause A group of words containing a subject° and a predicate°. A clause that delivers full meaning is called an *independent clause*° (or main clause). A clause that needs another sentence structure to deliver full meaning is called a *dependent clause*° (or subordinate clause). (7n)

cliché An overused, worn-out phrase that has lost its capacity to communicate effectively: *smooth as silk, ripe old age.* (21d)

climactic order An arrangement of ideas in a paragraph° or larger piece of writing from least important to most important. Climactic order is sometimes called *emphatic order.* (2e-2, 4c)

climactic sentence See *periodic sentence.*

clustering See *mapping.*

coherence The clear progression from one idea to another in a piece of writing. Transitional expressions°, pronouns°, selective repetition, and parallelism° enhance coherence. A piece of writing is coherent when its parts relate to one another not only in content but also in grammatical structures and choice of words. (4b)

collective noun A noun° that names a group of people or things: *family, team.* (7a, 11g, 11o)

colloquial language Language characteristic of conversation and informal writing. (21a-3)

comma fault See *comma splice.*

comma splice The error that occurs when only a comma connects two independent clauses°. (14)

common noun A noun° that names general groups, places, people, or things: *dog, house.* (7a)

comparative The form of an adjective° or adverb° that reflects a different degree of intensity between two: *blue, **bluer**; easy, **more easily**.* See also *positive* and *superlative.* (12d-1)

comparison and contrast A pattern for developing a paragraph° or whole essay in which the similarities (comparison) and differences (contrast) of subjects are discussed. (4d)

complement A word or group of words in the predicate° of a sentence that renames or describes a subject° or object° in that sentence. (7l-1)

complete predicate See *predicate.*

complete subject See *subject.*

complex sentence A sentence containing one independent clause° and one or more dependent clauses°. (7o-3)

compound-complex sentence A sentence containing at least two independent clauses° and one or more dependent clauses°. (7f-4)

compound predicate See *predicate.*

compound sentence A sentence containing two or more independent clauses° joined by a coordinating conjunction. (7o-2)

compound subject See *subject.*

concrete noun A noun° that names things that can be seen, touched, heard, smelled, or tasted: *smoke, sand.* (7a)

conjunction A word that connects words, phrases°, or clauses°, including coordinating conjunctions°, correlative conjunctions°, and subordinating conjunctions°. (7h)

conjunctive adverb A kind of adverb° that creates logical connections between independent clauses°: *therefore, however.* (7f)

connotation The emotional associations suggested by a word that, along with its denotation°, make up its complete meaning. (20b-1)

coordinate adjectives Two or more adjectives that equally modify a noun° or pronoun°. They are separated by a comma: ***heavy, round*** *paperweight.* (24d)

coordinating conjunction A conjunction that joins two or more grammatically equivalent structures. The seven coordinating conjunctions are *and, or, for, nor, but, so,* and *yet.* (7h)

coordination The technique of using grammatically equivalent forms to show a balance or sequence of ideas. (17a-17c)

correlative conjunction A pair of words that joins equivalent grammatical structures, including *both . . . and, not only . . . but also, either . . . or, neither . . . nor,* and *whether . . . or.* (7h)

cumulative sentence A sentence that begins with the subject° and verb° and then adds modifiers°—the most common kind of sentence. Also known as a *loose sentence.* (19d-2)

dangling modifier A modifier° that describes something implied but not stated: ***Walking down the street,*** *the Sears Tower came into view.* (15c)

796

deadwood Empty, unneeded words and phrases that increase the word count but do not add to the meaning. Also called *padding*. (16b)

declarative sentence A sentence that makes a statement: *I walked home.* (opening section "Structures of the Sentence," Chapter 7)

deduction The process of reasoning from general claims to a specific instance. (5e-2)

demonstrative pronoun A pronoun° that points out the antecedent°. The demonstrative pronouns are *this, these, that,* and *those.* (7b)

denotation The dictionary definition of a word. (20b-2)

dependent clause A clause° that cannot stand alone as an independent grammatical unit, usually preceded by a relative pronoun° or subordinating conjunction°. (7n-2)

descriptive adjective An adjective° that describes the condition or properties of the noun° it modifies and has comparative° and superlative° forms: *round, rounder, roundest.* (7e)

descriptive adverb An adverb° that describes the qualities of the verb° and has comparative° and superlative° forms: *happily, more happily, most happily.* (7f)

diction Word choice. (20a, 20b)

dictionary form See *simple form.*

direct address Words of direct address indicate the person or group spoken to and are set off by commas: *The answer, **Phil,** may be found at the end of the chapter.* (24f)

direct discourse In writing, words that repeat speech or conversation exactly, requiring the use of quotation marks. (15a-4, 24g, 28a-3)

direct object A noun° or pronoun° or group of words functioning as a noun that receives the action—that is, completes the meaning—of a transitive verb°. (7k-1, 8d)

direct question A sentence that asks a question and ends with a question mark: *Are you going?* (23c)

direct quotation The exact words spoken or written by someone other than the writer of the paper; such words must be enclosed in quotation marks. (24g, 28a, 31e)

division See *analysis.*

documentation Acknowledging the sources used in any piece of writing, by giving full and accurate information about the source's author and the work's title, date of publication, and related facts. (31-b, 32d-4, Chapter 33)

documentation style Any of various systems for providing information about the sources other than oneself used in writing others read. Most cite information in parenthetical references at appropriate places within the text;

others use footnotes or endnotes. The form of the bibliography also varies among styles. Two of the most widely used styles are those of the Modern Language Association (MLA) and the American Psychological Association (APA). (31b, 32d-4, Chapter 33)

doublespeak Evasive language intentionally used to hide the truth. (21e-4)

double negative A nonstandard statement that contains two negative modifiers°, the second of which repeats the message of the first. (12d)

drafting A part of the writing process° in which writers compose ideas in sentences and paragraphs. (2a, 3b)

edited American English Also called *standard English,* the language that conforms to established rules of grammar, sentence structure, punctuation, and spelling. (21a-2)

editing A part of the writing process° in which writers check the technical correctness of their grammar, spelling, punctuation, and mechanics°. (2a, 3d)

elliptical clause See *elliptical construction.*

elliptical construction A sentence structure, such as a clause° or phrase°, that deliberately omits words that have already appeared in the sentence and can be inferred from the context. (7n-2, 15e-1)

etymology The study of a word's origins and historical development, including its changes in form and meaning. (opening section Chapter 20; 20a)

euphemism Language that attempts to avoid the harsh reality of some truths by using more pleasant-sounding, overly "tactful" words. (21e-3)

evaluative reading A part of the reading process in which the reader determines the author's tone, differentiates between fact and opinion, and assesses the author's reasoning. (5b-3)

evidence Facts, statistical information, examples, and opinions of others used by a writer to support assertions and conclusions. (5c)

exclamatory sentence A sentence that expresses strong emotion by making an exclamation: *That's ridiculous!* (opening section "Structures of the Sentence" Chapter 7, 19b)

expletive A term that describes the function of *there* and *it* when they combine with a form of the verb *to be* to postpone the subject of the sentence: ***It is*** *Mars that we want to reach.* (11e)

expository writing See *informative writing.*

extended definition A definition that includes in addition to the denotation° of a word or phrase, its connotations° as well as concrete details to clarify abstract terms. An extended definition may require an entire paragraph° or more. (4d, 6e)

faulty predication An error that occurs when a subject° and its predicate° do not make sense together. (15d-2)

finite verb A verb° form that shows tense°, mood°, voice°, person°, and number° while expressing an action, occurrence, or state of being. (8a-2)

first person See *person*.

freewriting Writing nonstop for a specified time in order to generate ideas by free association of thoughts. Freewriting that starts with a set topic or that builds on one sentence taken from an earlier piece of freewriting is called "focused freewriting." (2d-2)

fused sentence The error of running independent clauses° together without a semicolon or a comma and a coordinate conjunction° between them. Also called a *run-on* or *run-together sentence*. (14)

future perfect progressive tense The form of the future perfect tense° that describes an action or condition ongoing until some specific future time: *they will have been talking.* (8f, 8i)

future perfect tense The tense° indicating that an action will have been completed or a condition will have ended by a specified point in the future: *they will have talked.* (8f, 8h)

future progressive tense The form of the future tense° showing that a future action will continue for some time: *they will be talking.* (8f, 8i)

future tense The form of a verb, made with the simple form° and either *shall* or *will*, expressing an action yet to be taken or a condition not yet experienced: *they will talk.* (8d, 8f)

gender Concerning languages, the labeling of nouns° and pronouns° as masculine, feminine, or neutral. This division occurs in English only in third person singular personal pronouns *(he, she, it)* and in a few nouns *(prince, princess).* (34b)

gerund A verbal°, the present participle° functioning as a noun°: ***Walking** is good exercise.* (7d)

helping verb See *auxiliary verb*.

highly formal level of language A level of language characterized by multisyllabic Latinate words and stylistic flourishes. (21a-1)

homonyms Words spelled differently that sound alike: *to, too, two.* (22c)

illogical predication See *faulty predication*.

imperative mood The mood° that expresses commands and direct requests: *Go.* It uses the simple form° of the verb. (8j-2)

imperative sentence A sentence that gives a command: *Go home now.* (opening section "Structures of the Sentence" Chapter 7)

incubation The time you give your ideas to grow and develop. (2d-7)

indefinite pronoun A pronoun° that refers to nonspecific persons or things but that takes on meaning in context: *any, few.* (7b, 11f)

independent clause A clause° that can stand alone as an independent grammatical unit. (7n-1)

indicative mood The mood° of verbs° used for statements about real things, or highly likely ones, and questions about fact: *I think Grace will be there.* (8k)

indirect discourse Discourse that reports speech or conversation and is not enclosed in quotation marks because it does not give the speaker's exact words. (15a-4, 24g, 28a-3)

indirect object A noun° or pronoun° or group of words functioning as a noun that tells *to whom* or *for whom* the action expressed by a transitive verb° was done. (7k-2)

indirect question A sentence that reports a question and ends with a period: *I wonder whether you are going.* It contrasts with a direct question°. (23c)

induction The process of arriving at general principles from particular facts or instances. (5e-1)

inferential meaning A part of the reading process that calls for the reader to read "between the lines" and thereby understand what is implied but unstated. (5b-2)

infinitive A verbal° made of the simple form° of a verb and usually, but not always, *to.* It functions as a noun°, adjective°, or adverb°. (7d, 8a-2, 9g)

infinitive phrase An infinitive° and its modifiers°. It functions as a noun°, adjective°, or adverb°. (7m)

informal language Word choice that creates a tone° appropriate for casual writing or speaking. The words may be slang°, colloquial language°, or regional language°. (21a-1)

informative writing Also known as *expository writing,* informative writing gives information and, when necessary, explains it. In contrast to persuasive writing°, informative writing focuses on the subject being discussed rather than the reader's reaction to the information. (1b-1)

intensive pronoun A *-self* form of a pronoun°, which intensifies the antecedent. (7b, 9h)

interjection A word (or words) conveying surprise or another strong emotion. (7i)

interrogative pronoun A pronoun° that asks a question, such as *whose* or *what.* (7b)

interrogative sentence A sentence that asks a question: *Did you see that hat?* (opening section of "Structures of the Sentence" Chapter 7)

intransitive verb A verb that does not take a direct object° and is not a linking verb°. (8e)

invention techniques Ways writers gather ideas. Some techniques are keeping an idea book or journal, freewriting°, brainstorming°, using the journalist's questions, mapping°, reading, and incubating. (2d)

T GL

irony Suggesting the opposite of the usual sense of the words. (21c)

irregular verb A verb that forms the past tense and past participle° in some way other than by adding *-ed* or *-d: see, saw, seen.* (8c)

jargon Specialized vocabulary of a particular field or group that a general reader might not understand. The unnecessary use of jargon creates pretentious language°. (21e-2)

limiting adjective An adjective° that limits the noun° it modifies by pointing out, questioning, enumerating, showing possession, or showing its relation to other words in the sentence. (7a, 7e)

limiting sentence A sentence that follows the topic sentence in a paragraph and narrows the focus of the paragraph; sometimes called *clarifying sentence.* (4a-1)

linking verb A main verb° that connects a subject° with a subject complement°. Linking verbs indicate a state of being, relate to the senses, or indicate a condition. (7c, 11h, 12c)

literal meaning A part of the reading process that calls for the reader to read "on the line" and thereby get information about major and minor points that are explicitly stated. (5b-1)

logical appeal The use of logical, sound reasoning in a written argument. Also called *logos.* (6f)

logical fallacies Flaws in reasoning that lead to illogical statements. Common fallacies are hasty generalization, false analogy, circular reasoning, *non sequitur, post hoc,* self-contradiction, red herring, *ad hominem,* bandwagon, appeal to false authority, special pleading, the either-or fallacy, taking something out of context, appeal to ignorance, and ambiguity and equivocation. (5f)

loose sentence See *cumulative sentence.*

main clause See *independent clause.*

main verb A verb that expresses action, occurrence, or state of being. It shows mood°, tense°, voice°, number°, and person°. (7c, 8a)

mapping An invention technique° for generating ideas. This process is also called *webbing* and *clustering.* (2d-5)

mass noun A noun° that names "uncountable" things: *furniture, weather.* (7a)

mechanics Conventions regarding the use of capital letters, italics, abbreviations, and numbers. (30)

medium level of formality A level of language that is neither too scholarly nor too casual. This level, which uses standard vocabulary, conventional sentence structure, and few or no contractions, is acceptable for academic writing. (21a-1)

801

metaphor A comparison between otherwise dissimilar things. It does not use a word like *like* or *as* to form the comparison, as a simile° does, but directly equates the things being compared. (21c)

misplaced modifier A modifier° that is incorrectly positioned in a sentence, and thus distorts meaning. (15b)

mixed construction A sentence that begins by setting up one grammatical form but switches unintentionally to another, thus garbling the meaning of the sentence. (15d-1)

mixed metaphors Incongruously combined images. (21c)

MLA style See *documentation style.*

modal auxiliary verbs Auxiliary verbs° that have only one form: *can, could, may, might, should, would, must,* and *ought.* They add a sense of needing, wanting, or having to do something, a sense of possibility, likelihood, obligation, permission, or ability. (8d)

modifier A word or group of words that describes or limits other words, phrases°, or clauses°. The most common modifiers are adjectives° and adverbs°. (7l-2)

mood The ability of verbs° to convey the attitude that the writer or speaker is expressing toward the action. English has three moods: indicative°, imperative°, and subjunctive°. (8k)

nonessential element See *nonrestrictive element.*

nonfinite verb A participle° or infinitive° functioning as a noun° or modifier°. Also known as a *verbal*°. (8a-2)

nonrestrictive element A limiting or descriptive word, phrase°, or dependent clause° that provides information not essential to understanding the element it modifies. A nonrestrictive element, sometimes called a *nonessential element,* is set off by commas. (24-e)

nonsexist language See *sexist language.*

nonstandard Generally taken to mean language not written in edited American English°. (opening section Usage Glossary)

noun The name of a person, place, thing, or idea. Nouns can be classified as proper°, common°, concrete°, abstract°, collective°, or mass°. Nouns function as subjects°, objects°, and complements°. (7a)

noun clause A dependent clause° that functions as a subject°, object°, or complement°. (7n-2)

noun phrase A noun° and its modifiers° functioning as a subject°, object°, or complement°. (7m)

number Relates to how many subjects act or experience an action, one (singular) or more than one (plural). (opening section Chapter 8; opening section "Subject-verb agreement" Chapter 11)

object complement A noun° or adjective° that immediately follows a direct object° and either describes or renames it. (7l-1)

objective case The case° of the pronoun° functioning as direct object°, indirect object°, object of a preposition°, or object of a verbal°. (9)

object A noun° or pronoun° or group of words functioning as a noun or pronoun that receives the action of a verb° (direct object°), tells to whom or for whom something is done (indirect object°), or completes the meaning of a preposition° (object of a preposition°). (7k)

padding See *deadwood.*

paragraph A group of sentences that work together to develop a unit of thought. Introductory paragraphs prepare the reader for what will follow in a piece of writing. Concluding paragraphs bring a sense of completion to a piece of writing. Transitional paragraphs link major sections within a piece of writing. Most paragraphs are topical paragraphs°, stating a main idea and offering specific, logical support of that idea. (4)

paragraph development Specific, concrete details (RENNS) to support a generalization. Arrangement and organizational patterns include general to specific, specific to general, climactic order°, problem to solution, spatial order°, chronological order°, narration, description, process, example, definition, analysis°, classification°, comparison and contrast°, analogy°, and cause-and-effect analysis°. (4)

parallelism The use of equivalent grammatical forms or matching sentence structures to express equivalent ideas. (18)

paraphrase A restatement of someone else's ideas in language and sentence structure different from those of the source. (31c)

parenthetical documentation Information enabling a reader to identify the source of ideas or of direct quotations°. This information is placed in parentheses immediately after the quotation or information. (33b)

parenthetical reference See *parenthetical documentation.*

participial phrase A phrase containing a present participle° or past participle°, and any modifiers, that functions as an adjective°. (7m)

passive construction See *passive voice.*

passive voice The form of a verb° in which the subject° is acted upon. If the subject is mentioned in the sentence, it usually appears as the object of the preposition° *by.* This voice° emphasizes the action, in contrast to the *active voice*°, which emphasizes the doer of the action. (8m, 8n)

past participle The third principal part° of the verb°. In regular verbs°, it adds *-d* or *-ed* to the simple form° and is identical to the past tense°. In irregular verbs°, it often differs from the simple form and the past tense. To function as a verb, it must have an auxiliary verb°. Used alone, it functions as an adjective°. (7d, 8a-1, 8b)

past perfect progressive tense The past perfect tense° form that describes an ongoing condition in the past that has been ended by something stated in the sentence: *I **had been talking.*** (8i)

803

past perfect tense The tense° that describes a condition or action that started in the past, continued for a while, and then ended in the past: *I **had talked.*** (8h)

past progressive tense The past tense form° that shows the continuing nature of a past action: *I **was talking.*** (8i)

past tense form The second principal part of the verb°. It shows an action or occurrence or state of being completed in the past. The past tense of regular verbs° add -*ed* or -*d* to the simple form°: *watched.* The past tense of irregular verbs° changes in spelling or uses a different word than the simple form°: *wrote.* (8a-1, 8b)

perfect tenses The three tenses—the present perfect°, the past perfect°, and the future perfect°—that show complex time relationships in the present, past, and future. (8h)

periodic sentence A sentence that begins with modifiers° and ends with the independent clause°, thus saving the main idea—and the emphasis—for the end of the sentence. Also called *climactic sentence.* (19d-2)

person Who or what acts or experiences an action. First person is the one speaking *(I, we);* second person is the one being spoken to *(you, you);* and third person is the person or thing spoken about *(he, she, it; they).* (opening section Chapter 11)

personal pronoun A pronoun° that refers to people or things, such as *I, you, them, hers,* and *it.* (7b, 9)

personification A type of figurative language that gives human traits to nonhuman things: *Mother earth.* (21c)

persuasive writing Persuasive writing seeks to convince the reader about a matter of opinion. It focuses on the reader, whom the writer wants to influence. (1b-2, 6)

phrase A group of related words that does not contain a subject° and predicate°. It cannot stand alone as an independent grammatical unit. A phrase functions as a noun°, verb°, or modifier°. (7m)

plagiarism Plagiarism occurs when a writer presents another person's words or ideas without giving credit to that person. Writers must use documentation° to give proper credit to their sources. Plagiarism is a serious offense, like stealing. It is a form of intellectual dishonesty that can lead to course failure or expulsion. (31a)

planning An early part of the writing process° in which writers gather ideas, often using invention strategies°. Along with shaping°, planning is sometimes called *prewriting°.* (2a-2d)

plural See *number.*

positive The form of an adjective° or adverb° when it is not being compared. Also see *comparative, superlative.* (12d-1)

possessive case The case° of a noun° or pronoun° that shows ownership or possession. (9)

predicate The part of the sentence that contains the verb° and tells what the subject° is doing or experiencing or what is being done to the subject. A *simple predicate* contains only the main verb° and auxiliary verb°, if any. A *complete predicate* contains the verb and all its modifiers°, objects°, and other related words. A *compound predicate* contains two or more verbs and their objects and modifiers. (7j-2)

predicate adjective An adjective° used as a subject complement°. (7l-1)

predicate nominative See *subject complement.*

prefix One or more syllables in front of a root word° that modify its meaning. (20c, 22d-3)

premise In the syllogism of a deductive argument, the first premise is an assumption and the second premise is either a fact or another assumption based on evidence. These two premises are followed by a conclusion. (5e-2)

preposition A word that shows a relationship between a noun° or pronoun° and other words in the sentence. A preposition is followed by a noun or pronoun object°. (7g)

prepositional phrase A preposition° and its object° and any modifiers° of its object. A prepositional phrase often shows a relationship in time or space. Prepositional phrases function as adjectives° or adverbs°. (7g, 7m)

present participle Used with one or more auxiliary verbs° in a main verb phrase°, shows action, occurrence, or state of being: *I am **running.*** As a verbal°, the *-ing* form of the verb° functioning as an adjective° *(**running** water)* or a noun° (***running** pleases me*). (6d, 8a-1)

present perfect progressive tense The present perfect tense form° that describes something ongoing in the past that is likely to continue into the future. *I **have been talking.*** (8i)

present perfect tense The tense° indicating that an action or its effects continue into the present though begun or perhaps completed in the past: *I **had talked.*** (8h)

present progressive tense The present tense° form of the verb° that indicates something taking place at the time it is written or spoken about: *I **am talking.*** (8i)

present tense The tense that describes what is happening, what is true at the moment, and what is consistently true. It uses the simple form° *(I **talk**)* and in the third person singular, it uses the *-s* form° *(she **talks**).* (8a-1, 8f, 8g)

pretentious language Showy, overblown writing that calls attention to itself with complex sentences and long words for their own sakes. (21e-1)

prewriting A term for all activities in the writing process before drafting°. See *planning* and *shaping.*

primary evidence First-hand evidence from direct observation by the writer or an authoritative reporter. (5c)

primary source An original work of an author—novels, poems, short stories, autobiographies, diaries—and first-hand reports of observations and of research. (opening section Chapter 32)

progressive forms Verb forms made in all tenses° with the present participle° and forms of *to be*. These forms show that an action is ongoing. (8i)

pronoun A word that takes the place of a noun°. Types of pronouns are personal°, relative°, interrogative°, demonstrative°, reflexive°, intensive°, reciprocal°, and indefinite°. Pronouns function in the same ways that nouns° do. (7b)

pronoun-antecedent agreement The match in expressing number°, person°, and gender° required between a pronoun° and its antecedent°. (11l-11o)

pronoun case The way a pronoun changes in form to reflect its use as the agent of action (subject case°), the thing being acted upon (objective case°), or the thing showing ownership (possessive case°). (9)

pronoun reference The relationship between a pronoun° and its antecedent°. (10)

proofreading The final step in the writing process°, proofreading calls for the writer to read the final copy of a piece of writing to find and correct typing errors or handwriting illegibility. (2a, 3e)

proper adjective An adjective° formed from a proper noun°: *Victorian, American*. (7e, 30e)

proper noun A noun° that names a specific person, place, or thing: *St. Louis, Toni Morrison, Corvette*. (7a, 30e)

purpose The goal or aim of a piece of writing: to express oneself, to provide information, to persuade, or to create a literary work. (1b)

quotation Words another person has spoken or written. Direct quotation° repeats the words of the source exactly and encloses them in quotation marks. Indirect quotation° reports what the source said, without the requirement for using quotation marks unless some of the source's words are repeated as well. Quotation requires documentation° of the source. (24g, 31e)

reciprocal pronoun A pronoun° that refers to individual parts of a plural antecedent°: *each other, one another*. (7b)

References In the APA style° of documentation, the list of sources cited in a research paper. (33c-2, 33d)

reflexive pronoun A *-self* form of the pronoun° that reflects the antecedent°. A reflexive pronoun cannot substitute for subjects° or objects°. (9h)

regional language Language specific to a geographic area. (21a-3)

regular verb A verb° that forms its past tense° and past participle° by adding *-ed* or *-d* to the simple form°. Most English verbs are regular. (8c)

relative clause See *adjective clause*. (7e-2)

relative pronoun A pronoun° that introduces certain noun clauses° and adjective clauses°, for example, *who, which, that, what,* and *whomever.* A relative pronoun is a subordinating word°. (7b, 7n-2)

restrictive appositive An appositive° renaming a noun° or pronoun° by giving information that is essential to distinguish it from other things in its class: *the college instructor **Pat Murphy.***

restrictive clause A dependent clause° that limits a noun° or pronoun° by giving information necessary to distinguish it from others in its class. In contrast to a nonrestrictive clause°, this kind of dependent clause is never set off with commas. (24e)

restrictive element A word, phrase°, or dependent clause° that provides information essential to the understanding of the element it modifies. In contrast to a nonrestrictive element, a restrictive element is never set off with commas. (24e)

revision A part of the writing process° in which writers evaluate their rough drafts and, based on their decisions, rewrite by adding, cutting, replacing, moving, and often totally recasting material. (2a, 3c, 6h, 32m)

rhetoric The area of discourse that focuses on arrangement of ideas and choice of words as a reflection of the writer's purpose° and sense of audience°. (1)

Rogerian argument An argument form adapted from the principles of communication developed by psychologist Carl Rogers. (6d)

root word The central part of a word to which a prefix° and/or suffix° is added. (20c-2)

run-on (run-together) sentence See *fused sentence.*

second person See *person.*

secondary evidence Evidence° from experts, reliable sources in their fields. Reliable secondary evidence appears in respected publications, is current, and is stated in relatively objective language. (5c, 32d-2)

secondary source A source that talks about someone else's original work. It explains events, analyzes information, and draws conclusions. (5c, opening section Chapter 32, 36b, 36c)

sentence See *simple sentence, compound sentence, complex sentence, compound-complex sentence.*

sentence fragment A portion of a sentence that is punctuated as though it were a complete sentence. (13)

sexist language Language that unfairly assigns roles or characteristics to people on the basis of sex. Language that avoids stereotyping according to sex is called *nonsexist language.* (21b)

shaping An early part of the writing process° in which writers consider ways to organize their material. Along with planning°, shaping is sometimes called prewriting°. (2e)

807

simile A comparison, using *like, as,* or *as if,* between otherwise dissimilar things. (21c)

simple form The form of the verb° that shows action (or occurrence or state of being) taking place in the present. It is used in the singular° for first and second person° and in the plural° for first, second, and third person°. It is also the first principal part° of a verb. The simple form is also known as the *dictionary form* or *base form.* (8a-1)

simple predicate See *predicate.*

simple sentence A single independent clause° with no dependent clauses°. The subject° or predicate° or both may be compound. (7o-1)

simple subject See *subject.*

simple tenses The present°, past°, and future tenses°, which divide time into present, past, and future. (8f)

singular See *number.*

slang Coined words and new or extended meanings for established words, which quickly pass in and out of use. Inappropriate for any but the most informal communications. (21a-3)

slanted language Biased or emotionally loaded language. (21a-4)

source A book, article, document, other work, or person providing information. (32d-2)

spatial order A description of objects according to their physical relationship to one another, often in terms of a central reference point. Spatial order is a pattern that may be used to organize a paragraph°. (2e-2, 4c)

speaker tag Explanatory words that identify the speaker of directly quoted words: *"Stay,"* **said the dog trainer.** (24g)

standard English See *edited American English.*

subject The word or group of words in a sentence that acts, is acted upon, or is described by the verb°. A *simple subject* includes only the noun° or pronoun°. A *complete subject* includes the noun or pronoun and all its modifiers°. A *compound subject* includes two or more nouns or pronouns or their modifiers. (7j-1)

subject complement Also called a *predicate nominative,* a noun° or adjective° that follows a linking verb° and describes or renames the subject° of the sentence. (7l-1, 8d)

subject-verb agreement The match of the subject° and verb° in expressing number° and person° required between a subject° and its verb°. (11a-11k)

subjective case The case° of the pronoun° functioning as subject°. (9)

subjunctive mood The verb mood° that expresses wishes, recommendations, indirect requests, and speculations: *I wish I* **were going.** (8l)

subordinate clause See *dependent clause.*

subordinating conjunction A conjunction that introduces an adverbial clause°, showing its relationship to the independent clause°. (7h, 7n-2)

subordination The technique of using grammatical structures to reflect the relative importance of ideas. A sentence with subordinated information contains an independent clause° to express important ideas in the sentence, and it contains dependent clauses° or phrases° to express ideas of lesser importance. (17d-17g)

suffix A syllable or syllables added to the end of a root word° that modify its meaning. (20c-2, 22d-1)

summary A condensed version of the essentials of ideas originally expressed in a longer version. (31d)

superlative The form of the adjective° or adverb° when three or more things are being compared: *green, greener,* **greenest***; quickly, more quickly,* **most quickly***.* (12d-1)

syllogism The structure of an argument reflecting deduction°. It has two premises°, the first one an assumption and the second a fact or an assumption based on evidence°. The conclusion, which is about a specific instance, follows logically from the premises. (5e-2)

synonym A word that is close in meaning to another word. (20a)

synthesis A component of critical thinking in which one makes connections among ideas. (opening section Chapter 4)

tag question A question that consists of a helping verb, a pronoun, and often the word *not,* generally contracted. A tag question is set off by commas: *The temperature was too hot,* **wasn't it?** (24f)

tense The time at which the action of the verb° occurs—in the past, present, or future. (8j)

tense sequence The accurate matching of verbs° to reflect the logical time relationships in sentences that have more than one verb. (8j)

thesis statement A statement of the central theme of an essay that makes clear the main idea of the essay, the writer's purpose, and the focus of the topic. It may also suggest the organizational pattern of the essay. (2e-4, 3c-2, 6b)

third person See *person.*

tone The writer's attitude towards his or her material and reader, especially as reflected in the writer's choice of words. (1c-1, 2e-3, 5b-3, 21a)

topic The subject of a piece of writing. (2c)

topical paragraph See *paragraph.*

topic sentence The sentence in a paragraph° that contains the main idea of the paragraph. (4a-1)

transition The logical connection of one idea to another in a piece of writing. Transition is achieved through the use of transitional expressions°, pronouns°, parallelism°, and the repetition of key words and phrases. (4b)

transitional expressions Words and phrases that signal connections among ideas and create coherence. A transitional expression lets the reader know how one idea connects to the next. (4b-1)

transitive verb A verb° that takes a direct object. (8e)

transitional words See *transitional expressions.*

understatement Deliberate restraint for emphasis. (21c)

unity The clear and logical relationship between the main idea of a paragraph° and the supporting evidence for that main idea. (4a)

usage The customary manner of using particular words or phrases. (20a; opening section Usage Glossary)

valid A term applied to an argument based on deduction° when the conclusion logically follows from the premises°. Validity has to do with the structure of the argument, not the truth of the premises. An argument based on untrue premises is valid if the conclusion follows from those premises. (5e-2)

verb The part of the predicate° in a sentence that acts or describes a state of being. Verbs change form to show time (tense°), attitude (mood°), and role of the subject (voice°). Verbs can be main verbs° or auxiliary verbs°, and they appear in verb phrases°. Verbs can be described as transitive° or intransitive° depending on whether they take a direct object°. (7m, 8)

verb phrase A verb° and its modifiers°. A verb phrase functions as a verb in the sentence. (7d)

verbal phrase A group of words that contains a verbal°—an infinitive°, participle°, or gerund°—and its modifiers°. Verbals function as nouns° or modifiers° rather than as verbs°. (7m)

verbals Verb parts functioning as nouns°, adjectives°, or adverbs°. Verbals include infinitives°, present participles°, past participles°, and gerunds°. (7c)

voice An attribute of a verb° showing whether the subject° acts (active voice°) or is acted upon (passive voice°). (8m)

webbing See *mapping.*

Works Cited In the MLA style° of documentation, the list of sources cited in a research paper. (33c-1, 33d)

writing process Stages of writing in which a writer gathers and shapes ideas, organizes material, expresses those ideas in a rough draft, evaluates the draft and revises it, edits the writing for technical errors, and proofreads it for typographical mistakes or illegibility. The stages often overlap and do not always proceed in a linear progression: that is, the writing process is recursive. See planning°, shaping°, drafting°, revising°, editing°, and proofreading°. (2, 3)

INDEX

A degree symbol (°) after an index entry signals that the term is defined in the Glossary of Grammatical and Selected Composition Terms. An entry in boldface italics (***advice, advise***, for example) is discussed in the Usage Glossary. Section numbers are in boldface type and page numbers in regular type. The listing **6a**: 160 thus refers you to page 160, which is in section 6a.

ABOUT THE AUTHOR

Lynn Quitman Troyka earned her Ph.D. at New York University. She started teaching in 1960, and in 1967 she joined the faculty of Queensborough Community College of the City University of New York (CUNY), where she later became a professor with a specialty in writing. At CUNY she has also taught at the Center for Advanced Studies in Education at the Graduate School and in the graduate program in Language and Literacy at City College. She is now Senior Research Associate in the Instructional Resource Center of the CUNY Office of Academic Affairs.

Editor of the *Journal of Basic Writing* 1985–88, Dr. Troyka now serves as editorial board member and/or reviewer for a number of journals in composition. Her articles have appeared in journals such as *College Composition and Communication*, *College English*, and *Writing Program Administration* and in books from Southern Illinois Press and Boynton/Cook.

Dr. Troyka is author of *Structured Reading*, Third Edition, Prentice Hall, 1989. She is co-author (with Richard Lloyd-Jones, John Gerber, et al.) of *A Checklist and Guide for Reviewing Departments of English*, Associated Departments of English of the Modern Language Association, 1985; of *Steps in Composition*, Fifth Edition (with Jerrold Nudelman), Prentice Hall, 1990; of the *Simon & Schuster Workbook for Writers*, Second Edition (with Emily R. Gordon), Prentice Hall, 1990; and of *Taking Action* (with Jerrold Nudelman), Prentice Hall, 1975, a book based on the research in her doctoral dissertation.

Dr. Troyka has been a consultant to numerous federal and state agencies, including the National Endowment for the Humanities, and to various testing agencies, including the National Assessment for Educational Progress. She has been a consultant and/or guest lecturer at dozens of colleges and universities. She has been a featured speaker at local, national, and international meetings. She is a past chair of the Conference on College Composition (1981), of the College Section of the National Council of Teachers of English (1985–1987), and of the Writing Division of the Modern Language Association (1987).

CHARTS IN TINTED BOXES *(continued)*

CHARTS IN TINTED BOXES

(continued on inside leaf)